HANDBOOK
of
SPORTS STUDIES

Edited by
JAY COAKLEY AND ERIC DUNNING

SAGE Publications
London • Thousand Oaks • New Delhi

Editorial arrangement and Editors'
Introductions © Eric Dunning
 and Jay Coakley 2000
Chapter 1 © John W. Loy
 and Douglas Booth 2000
Chapter 2 © Bero Rigauer 2000
Chapter 3 © Jennifer Hargreaves
 and Ian McDonald 2000
Chapter 4 © Susan Birrell 2000
Chapter 5 © Peter Donnelly 2000
Chapter 6 © Patrick Murphy,
 Ken Sheard and Ivan Waddington 2000
Chapter 7 © David L. Andrews 2000
Chapter 8 © Kendall Blanchard 2000
Chapter 9 © Marc Lavoie 2000
Chapter 10 © John Bale 2000
Chapter 11 © Nancy Struna 2000
Chapter 12 © William J. Morgan 2000
Chapter 13 © Barry Houlihan 2000
Chapter 14 © Diane L. Gill 2000
Chapter 15 © Allen Guttmann 2000
Chapter 16 © George Sage 2000
Chapter 17 © C. Roger Rees
 and Andrew W. Miracle, Jr. 2000
Chapter 18 © Garry Whannel 2000
Chapter 19 © John Sugden
 and Alan Tomlinson 2000
Chapter 20 © Nancy Theberge 2000
Chapter 21 © Grant Jarvie 2000
Chapter 22 © Lincoln Allison 2000
Chapter 23 © Joseph Maguire 2000
Chapter 24 © D. Stanley Eitzen 2000
Chapter 25 © Kevin Young 2000
Chapter 26 © Ivan Waddington 2000
Chapter 27 © Howard L. Nixon II 2000
Chapter 28 © Cheryl Cole 2000
Chapter 29 © Günther Lüschen 2000
Chapter 30 © Mary Duquin 2000
Chapter 31 © Ian Henry
 and Eleni Theodoraki 2000
Chapter 32 © Robert Rinehart 2000
Chapter 33 © Denver J. Hendricks 2000
Chapter 34 © Chris Collins 2000
Chapter 35 © Gyöngyi S. Földesi 2000
Chapter 36 © Jacques DeFrance 2000
Chapter 37 © Klaus Heinemann 2000
Chapter 38 © Ian McDonald 2000
Chapter 39 © Koichi Kiku 2000
Chapter 40 © Burn-Jang Lim 2000
Chapter 41 © Joseph L. Arbena 2000
Chapter 42 © Kari Fasting
 and Mari-Kristin Sisjord 2000
Chapter 43 © Salomé Marivoet
 and Claudia Pinheiro 2000
Chapter 44 © Núria Puig 2000

First published in hardback 2000
First published in paperback 2002
Reprinted 2004.

Paul Chapman Publishing Ltd
A SAGE Publications Company
1 Oliver's Yard
55 City Road
London EC1Y 1SP

SAGE Publications Inc
2455 Teller Road
Thousand Oaks, California 91320

SAGE Publications India Pvt Ltd
B-42 Panchsheel Enclave
Post Box 4109
New Delhi 100 017'

**British Library Cataloguing in Publication
data**

A catalogue record for this book is available
from the British Library

 ISBN 0 8039 7552 X
 ISBN 0 7619 4949 6 (pbk)

Library of Congress Control Number: 2002104181

Typeset by SIVA Math Setters, Chennai, India
Printed in Great Britain by The Cromwell Press
Ltd, Trowbridge, Wiltshire

CONTENTS

CONTRIBUTORS

Lincoln Allison is Reader in Politics and International Studies and Director of the Warwick Centre for the Study of Sport in Society at the University of Warwick. He was educated at Oxford University. He edited *The Politics of Sport* (1986), *The Changing Politics of Sport* (1993) and *Taking Sport Seriously* (1998), and is the author of other books and articles. His singly authored book *Amateurism in Sport* has gone to press with the publisher Frank Cass.

David L. Andrews is an assistant professor of sport and leisure studies at the University of Memphis, and a senior visiting research fellow at De Montfort University. He received a PhD in Kinesiology from the University of Illinois at Urbana–Champaign. He is an assistant editor of the *Journal of Sport and Social Issues*, as well as being a member of the editorial board of the *Sociology of Sport Journal*, *International Sports Studies* and *Football Studies*.

Joseph L. Arbena is a Professor of History at Clemson University, where he has taught since 1965. He holds degrees in Latin American history and culture from the George Washington University (1961) and the University of Virginia (1970). He has compiled two annotated bibliographies of sports in Latin America (Greenwood Press, 1989 and 1999), edited a collection of essays on Latin American sports, and published some thirty articles on sports topics. He also served as editor of the *Journal of Sport History* (1993–6). Currently his research focuses on sport and national identity in Latin America.

John Bale is Professor of Sports Geography at Keele University, UK. He received his degrees from the University of London. During the past two decades he has pioneered the geographical study of sports and has lectured in universities in North America, Australia and Europe. His books include *Sport, Space and the City* (1993), *Landscapes of Modern Sport* (1994), and *Kenyan Running: Movement Culture, Geography and Global Change* (1996, co-authored with Joe Sang).

Susan Birrell is Chair of the Department of Health, Leisure, and Sport Studies at the University of Iowa and is affiliated with both the American Studies Program and the Women's Studies Program. She is also co-editor, with Cheryl Cole, of *Women, Sport and Culture* (1994). Her latest book, *Reading Sport: Critical Essays on Power and Representation*, co-edited with Mary McDonald, is to be published by Northeastern University Press (2000). Her current research focuses on the cultural meanings of Mt Everest.

Kendall Blanchard is President and Professor of Anthropology at Fort Lewis College in Colorado. He received a PhD in anthropology from Southern Methodist University in 1971. He is a past president of the Association for the

Study of Play. He has co-authored (with Alyce Cheska) *The Anthropology of Sport: An Introduction* (1984). He wrote a single-author version of that book that was published in 1995. Other books that have sport and play themes include *The Serious Side of Leisure: The Mississippi Choctaws at Play* (1981), and *The Many Faces of Play* (1986).

Douglas Booth teaches courses in sports history and sports policy at the University of Otago, New Zealand. He is the author of *The Race Game: Sport and Politics in South Africa* (1998) and serves on the editorial boards of several journals, including *Sporting Traditions and the Journal of Sport History*.

Jay Coakley is a Professor of Sociology at the University of Colorado in Colorado Springs. He received his PhD in Sociology from the University of Notre Dame in 1972. He served as editor of the *Sociology of Sport Journal* (1984–9) and as President of the North American Society for the Sociology of Sport (1992) and the Sport Sociology Academy of the American Alliance for Health, Physical Education, Recreation and Dance (1983–4). He is author of *Sport in Society: Issues and Controversies* (2001, 7th edition) and co-editor (with P. Donnelly) of *Inside Sports* (1999).

Cheryl Cole is an Associate Professor of Kinesiology, Sociology and Women's Studies at the University of Illinois, Urbana-Champaign. She holds PhD degrees in Sport Studies from USC and in the Sociology of Culture/Women's Studies from the University of Iowa. Her research focuses on the relations among sport, the visualization of deviant bodies and national identity in post-war America. She co-edited *Women, Sport and Culture* with S. Birrell (1994), is co-editor of the State University of New York book series 'Sport, Culture, and Social Relations' and is editor of the *Journal of Sport and Social Issues*.

Chris Collins is a Senior Fellow at Massey University, New Zealand, and undertook his undergraduate and postgraduate studies at Otago and Victoria Universities in New Zealand. At the time of writing he was Director of Sport and Recreation at Massey University and headed the university's academic programme in Sport Management and Coaching, delivered from the Department of Management Systems. His teaching responsibilites lie primarily in the area of sport in society and, to a lesser extent, sport management. His research interests are related to sport and religion, sport and politics and sport and social mobility. He is co-editor of *Sport Management in New Zealand* (1994), and *Sport Business Management in New Zealand* (1999) and is editor of *Sport in New Zealand Society* (2000). He has recently moved into a senior management role in the University.

Jacques DeFrance was born in Paris in 1948 and prepared his 'Doctorat' (PhD) on 'The Genesis of Modern Physical Education in France (1770–1914)' under the supervision of Pierre Bourdieu at the Ecole Pratique des Hautes Etudes, Paris. He has studied alcohol and drug use, environmental conflicts and comparative water policies in England, France and Germany. He is currently Professeur des Universités at the University of Paris X-Nanterre in the Department of Sports Sciences and director of the Laboratory on Sport and Culture. He has published on the social history of gymnastics and sports, the divisions among organizations in athletics in the 1980s, the role of the state in sports since the 1930s (with Jean Harvey and Rob Beamish), and on the use of the sociologies of Pierre Bourdieu and Norbert Elias in sports studies.

Peter Donnelly is a Professor in the Faculty of Physical Education and Health at the University of Toronto. He received his PhD in Sport Studies from the University of Massachusetts in 1980. He has served in various offices for professional organizations in the sociology of sport, and is currently Director of the Centre for Sport Policy Studies at the University of Toronto. He edited the *Sociology of Sport Journal* from 1990 to 1994, is co-editor (with N. Theberge) of *Sport and the Sociological Imagination*, editor of *Taking Sport Seriously*, and co-editor (with J. Coakley) of *Inside Sports*.

Eric Dunning is Emeritus Professor of Sociology at the University of Leicester and Visiting Professor of Sociology at University College Dublin. He studied sociology under Norbert Elias as an undergraduate and as a postgraduate student, later coming to write two books and several articles with him. His main research interest is in sport and violence, and his latest book, *Sport Matters: Sociological Studies of Sport, Violence and Civilization*, was published by Routledge (1999).

Mary Duquin is an Associate Professor at the University of Pittsburgh. She received a PhD in Education from Stanford University in 1975. She has served as Chair of the Sport Sociology Academy and as President of the North American Society for the Sociology of Sport. Her research interests include the psychosocial and philosophical aspects of sport, health and the body in culture. She has written numerous articles on the importance of implementing an ethic of care in sport.

D. Stanley Eitzen is Professor Emeritus of Sociology at Colorado State University. He has an AB from Bethel College, an MS in social science from Emporia State University, and an MA and PhD in sociology from the University of Kansas. He is the author or editor of 16 books, including three on sport: *Sociology of North American Sport* (6th edition) with G. H. Sage, *Sport in Contemporary Society* (5th edition), and *Fair and Foul: Beyond the Myths and Paradoxes of Sport*. He is a former president of the North American Society for the Sociology of Sport, former editor of the *Social Science Journal*, and was recipient of the John N. Stern Distinguished Professorship at Colorado State University.

Kari Fasting is a professor at the Department of Social Science of the Norwegian University of Sport and Physical Education in Oslo, Norway. She lectures in sociology of sport, feminist theory of science and research methods. Her area of research is sociological and social psychological aspects of gender and sport. She has held many administrative positions, nationally and internationally. She was the first rector (president/vice-chancellor) of her university from 1989 to 1992, the first president of the Norwegian Society for Sport Research (1983–9), president of the International Sociology of Sport Association (1992–5), and is currently the vice-president of the executive board of WomenSport International.

Gyöngyi S. Földesi is Professor of Sociology at the Hungarian University of Physical Education in Budapest. She received her PhD in Sociology from the University of Physical Education in Warsaw in 1982 and in Physical Education from the University of Physical Education in Budapest in 1983. She served as Vice President of the International Committee for Sociology of Sport (now ISSA) from 1984 to 1992 and as Associate Editor of the *International Review for the Sociology of Sport* from 1988 to 1996. She has held various offices in Sport Science bodies, and she is the author of five books (1983, 1983, 1984, 1994, 1999) and the editor of three others (1985, 1994, 1996).

Diane L. Gill is a professor and head of the Department of Exercise and Sport Science at the University of North Carolina at Greensboro. She received her PhD from the University of Illinois in 1976 and was on the faculty at the Universities of Waterloo and Iowa before moving to UNCG in 1987. She is a past-president of the North American Society for the Psychology of Sport and Physical Activity, and has served as president of Division 47 (Exercise and Sport Psychology) of the American Psychological Association. She is a past-editor of the *Journal of Sport & Exercise Psychology*, author of several research articles and chapters, and is preparing a revised book, *Psychological Dynamics of Sport and Exercise*.

Allen Guttmann teaches at Amherst College and is President-Elect of the North American Society for Sport History. Of the dozen books he has written or translated on the history of sports, the best known are *From Ritual to Record* (1978) and *Women's Sports* (1991). The most recent titles are *Games and Empires* (1994) and *The Erotic in Sports* (1996). He is working on a history of Japanese sports and on a forthcoming International Encyclopedia of Women's Sports.

Jennifer Hargreaves is Professor of Sport Sociology at Brunel University. She edited *Sport, Culture and Ideology* (1982), and is the author of *Sporting Females: Critical Issues in the History and Sociology of Women's Sports* (1994) and *Heroines of Sport: The Politics of Differance and Identity* (2000). She has worked as a guest professor in Germany and Hong Kong and is on the editorial boards of four international journals.

Klaus Heinemann is Professor of Sociology at the University of Hamburg, having previously taught at the University of Trier. Besides having published, among other things, studies of youth unemployment, he has researched and written extensively on sports organizations and he is one of the pioneers of the study of the economics of sport. He was Editor-in-Chief of the *International Review for the Sociology of Sport* from 1988 to 1997 and is a leading figure in the comparative study of sport in Western Europe.

Denver J. Hendricks was born in Cape Town, South Africa and completed most of his schooling in the Port Elizabeth area of the Eastern Cape Province. He obtained a BA(Honours) degree in Physical Education from Rhodes University, majoring in the Sociology of Sport. He was awarded a Fulbright Scholarship and proceeded to the University of California at Berkeley. He obtained a Masters Degree from Berkeley, focusing on the sociology of sport and issues of race and sport in particular. Upon returning to South Africa, he took up a teaching position at the University of the Western Cape, eventually becoming Professor and Head of the Department of Human Movement Studies there. He was subsequently appointed Deputy Dean in the Faculty of Arts at the University of the Western Cape and later as Dean of Students at the University of Port Elizabeth.

Ian Henry is Professor of Recreation Management and Director of the Institute of Sport and Leisure Policy at Loughborough University. His research interests focus on the analysis of leisure policy at the urban, national and transnational levels. His publications include *The Politics of Leisure Policy* (Macmillan) and a series of co-edited books on European Leisure Studies and Policy (Routledge and CAB International) including *Leisure Policies in Europe* and *Leisure Research in Europe: Methods and Traditions.*

Barrie Houlihan is Professor of Sport Policy at Loughborough University. He received his PhD from the University of Salford in 1984. He has written widely on aspects of sport policy and politics and is the author of *Sport and International Politics* (1994), *Sport, Policy and Politics: a Comparative Analysis* (1997) and *Dying to Win: Doping in Sport and the Development of Anti-Doping Policy* (1999). His recent research interests concern sports development activity and the development of policy to counteract doping in sport.

Grant Jarvie is Professor of Sports Studies at the University of Stirling in Scotland. He received his PhD in Sociology from the University of Leicester in 1988. He is past convenor of the British Sociological Association's Sport Study Group and has served as President of the British Society of Sports History. He is author of *Highland Games: the Making of the Myth* (1991); co-author (with J. Maguire) of *Sport and Leisure in Social Thought* (1994); and editor of *Scottish Sport in the Making of a Nation* (1994), *Sport in the Making of Celtic Cultures* (1999) and *Sport, Scotland and the Scots* (2000).

Koichi Kiku is Associate Professor of Sport Sociology and Sport Pedagogy at the Nara Women's University, Japan. He received his PhD in Pedagogy from the Tsukuba University in 1988. He was Director of the Japanese Society of Sport Sociology from 1995 to 1998. He is the author of *The Historical Sociology of Professional Sport in Modern Japan* (1993), and the co-author of *The Sociology of Life-Long Sport* (1997) and *Changing Contemporary Society and Sport* (1998).

Marc Lavoie is Professor of Economics at the University of Ottawa. He received his PhD from the University of Paris-1 (Panthéon-Sorbonne) in 1979. A specialist of growth theory and monetary theory, he has published articles on discrimination and salary determination in sport and two books on ice hockey, *Avantage numérique: l'argent et la Ligue Nationale de Hockey* (1997) and *Désavantage numérique: les francophones dans la LNH* (1998).

Burn-Jang Lim is Professor of Sport Sociology at the Department of Physical Education, College of Education, Seoul National University, Korea. He received a PhD in Educational Sociology from Hanyang University in 1986. He has served as an Executive Board member of the International Sociology of Sport Association

(1992–5), President of the Korean Society for Sociology of Sport (1985–96), President of the Korean Alliance for Health, Physical Education, Recreation and Dance (1997–8), Executive Board member of the Korean Olympic Committee (1990–4), and a Board member of the Korean Sport Council (1997–9). He has edited the *Bulletin of ISSA* (1992–9), is the author of *Sociology of Sport* (1994), *Swimming* (1979), *Advanced Swimming* (1982), *Gymnastics* (1982), and is co-author of *Hockey* (1982) and *Skiing* (1998).

John Loy is Professor of Sport and Leisure Studies at the University of Otago, New Zealand. He is past president of the North American Society for the Sociology of Sport and past vice president of the International Sociology of Sport Association. He is the co-author of 10 books, and has published more than 100 papers, including articles in the *American Sociological Review*, the *British Journal of Sociology, Sociology of Work and Occupations, Urban Life, Quest, Research Quarterly for Exercise and Sport,* and *Sport Science Review*.

Günther Lüschen, PhD, HonD, is Professor of Sociology, University of Alabama at Birmingham. He is also Professor Emeritus of the Universities of Düsseldorf and Illinois. In 1981 he edited (with George Sage) the *Handbook of Social Science of Sport*. His most recent publications include *Das Moralische in der Soziologie* (1998), *Sport and Public Health in America and Europe* (1998), *Sportpolitik* (1996 with A. Rütten) and *Health Systems in the European Union* (1995).

Joseph Maguire is Professor of the Sociology of Sport at Loughborough University, England. He received a BEd (Hons) from the University of London (1979) and a PhD in Sociology from Leicester University in 1985. He has served on the editorial boards of the *Sociology of Sport Journal* and the *International Review for the Sociology of Sport*, and is co-editor and author of several books including *Sport and Leisure in Social Thought* (1994, with G. Jarvie) and *Global Sport: Identities, Societies and Civilizations* (1999). He is currently President of the International Sociology of Sport Association.

Salomé Marivoet is a Lecturer at the Technical University of Lisbon where she teaches the Sociology of Sport. She graduated in 1985, earned a Masters Degree in Sociology in 1994 at the Technical University of Lisbon and she is currently working on her PhD on 'Sports Ethics: A Sociological Analysis of Value-Orientations Towards Action in Portugal (1974–2000)' under the supervision of Eric Dunning. Her research has been on violence, performance and sports habits. In addition to journal articles and reviews, she has published *Aspectos Sociológicos do Desporto* (1998; *Sociological Aspects of Sport*).

Ian McDonald is based in the Chelsea School at the University of Brighton, where he lectures and researches in sport and policy. He is co-author of *Anyone for Cricket? Equal Opportunities and Changing Cricket Cultures in Essex and East London* (1998), co-editor of *The Production and Consumption of Sport Cultures* (1999) and *Sport, Race and British Society* (2000). He also studies the politics of sporting nationalism in South Asia with particular reference to Hindu nationalism in India.

Andrew Miracle is professor and chair of the Department of Health Sciences at Cleveland State University. He received a PhD in Anthropology from the University of Florida in 1976. He has served as president of the Association for the Study of Play and of the Southern Anthropological Society. He has published eight books, including *Lessons of the Locker Room: the Myth of School Sport* (1994, with C. Roger Rees).

William Morgan is a professor of cultural studies at the University of Tennessee. He received his PhD from the University of Minnesota in 1976. He has been editor of the *Journal of the Philosophy of Sport* since 1994, and is a long-standing member of its editorial board. He is the author of *Leftist Theories of Sport: a Critique and Reconstruction* (1994), and co-editor, with Klaus Meier, of *Philosophic Inquiry in Sport* (1988). He has authored numerous articles in the philosophy and social theory of sport.

Patrick Murphy graduated from the University of Leicester in 1972. He is currently a Senior Lecturer in Sociology at Leicester and a Director of the University's Centre for Research into Sport and Society. His main research interests are football hooliganism, the management and administration of association football, and sports policy in general. He is co-author of *The Roots of Football Hooliganism, Hooligans Abroad* and *Football on Trial*. He is also the editor of the *Singer and Friedlander Review*.

Howard L. Nixon II is Professor of Sociology and Chair of the Department of Sociology, Anthropology and Criminal Justice at Towson University. He received his PhD in Sociology from the University of Pittsburgh in 1971. He is the author of a number of articles and three books related to sport: *Sport and Social Organization* (1976), *Sport and the American Dream* (1984), and (with James Frey) *A Sociology of Sport* (1996). He has also taught courses and published in other areas of sociology, including organizations, organizational deviance, small groups, the family, disability and society, and structural analysis.

Claudia Pinheiro is a Lecturer in the Faculty of Sports Sciences and Physical Education, University of Coimbra where she teaches the Sociology of Sport. She graduated in 1990 from the Faculty of Sports Sciences and Physical Education, University of Porto, earned an MA in the Sociology of Sport at the University of Leicester in 1993, and she is currently working on her PhD. Her main academic interests are in women's sports and gender relations.

Núria Puig is Professor of the Sociology of Sport at the Institut Nacional d'Educació Fisica de Catalunya (INEF-Catalunya), of the Universitat de Barcelona, in Spain. She earned her degree in Modern History at the Universitat de Barcelona in 1973, her PhD in Sociology at the Université de Paris VII in 1980 and her PhD in the Philosophy and Science of Education at the Universitat de Barcelona in 1993. Her main research areas related to sports are socialization, sports policy, sport organizations and urban problems. Her last two books are *Joves i Esport* (*Youth and Sport*; Barcelona, 1996) and *Sociología del Deporte* (*Sociology of Sport*, Madrid, 1998; co-edited with M.G. Ferrando and F. Lagardera).

C. Roger Rees is a professor in the Department of Health Studies, Physical Education and Human Performance Science at Adelphi University on Long Island, NY. He received his PhD in the sociology of sport and physical education from the University of Maryland in 1978. He has published several books including (with A. Miracle) *Sport and Social Theory* (1986), and *Lessons of the Locker Room: the Myth of School Sports* (1994), and numerous articles in sociology, sport and physical education journals.

Bero Rigauer studied Sociology at the Main Institute for Social Research in Frankfurt, Germany, and Sociology and Physical Education at the University of Frankfurt. He is a Professor in the Department of Sportwissenschaft (Sports Sciences) at the University of Oldenburg, Germany, where he teaches courses in the Sociology of Sport, the Social and Cultural History of Sport, the General Theory of Sport, and the Methodology of the Sciences. He is an 'elder sportsman' who enjoys skiing, basketball, volleyball and Chinese *pa tuan chin*.

Robert Rinehart is with California State University, San Bernardino. He earned his PhD in sport sociology from the University of Illinois. His major research interests are in qualitative methods of enquiry, alternative sport forms and sport as performance. He is the author of the book *Players All: Performances in Contemporary Sport* (1998), and he has published articles in sport-related journals in history, sociology, philosophy, and cultural studies. His most recent project is as co-editor (with Synthia Sydnor) of *To the Extreme: Alternative Sport, Inside and Out* (State University of New York Press).

George Sage is a professor emeritus of Sociology and Kinesiology at the University of Northern Colorado. He received BA and MA degrees from the University of Northern Colorado, and an EdD from UCLA. He has served as President of the North American Society for the Sociology of Sport and Vice President of the Executive Board of the International Sociology of Sport Association. He edited three editions of *Sport and American Society*, authored two editions of *Power and Ideology in American Sport: a Critical Perspective*, and co-authored (with D.S. Eitzen) six editions of *Sociology of North American Sport*.

Ken Sheard obtained his BA and MPhil degrees from the University of Leicester and his PhD from the Council for National Academic Awards. Having taught at the University of Evansville (English campus) and Anglia Polytechnic University, he is now Lecturer in Sociology at the University of Leicester and a Director of the University's Centre for Research into Sport and Society. His main research areas have been the development of rugby, the development of boxing and the emergence of bird-watching as a sport-like activity.

Mari-Kristin Sisjord holds a PhD in Sport Sociology from the Norwegian University of Sport and Physical Education. The title of her thesis was 'Sport and Youth Culture'. She is currently an Associate Professor in Sport Sociology at the same university and a Member of the Executive Board of the International Sociology of Sport Association. Her main research fields are youth sports and gender.

Nancy Struna is a professor of American Studies at the University of Maryland, College Park. She has published widely on the social history of sport and leisure in early America, including *People of Prowess: Sport, Leisure and Labor in Early Anglo-America* (1996). Dr Struna is currently doing research on the social history of taverns and tavern life and on the transformation of ordinary life in the United States during the late eighteenth and nineteenth centuries. She is also a past-president of the North American Society for Sport History.

John Sugden is Professor of the Sociology of Sport, Chelsea School Research Centre, University of Brighton, England. He studied politics and sociology for his BA and took MA and PhD degrees in the Sociology of Sport at the University of Connecticut. He has written on sport politics and comparative aspects of sport cultures. His most recent books, both co-authored with A. Tomlinson, are *FIFA and the Contest for World Football – Who Rules the Peoples' Game* (1998) and *Great Balls of Fire – How Big Money is Hijacking World Football* (1999). He also wrote *Boxing and Society* (1996) and, with Alan Bairner, *Sport, Sectarianism and Society in a Divided Ireland* (1993).

Nancy Theberge is a professor at the University of Waterloo in Canada, where she holds a joint appointment in the Departments of Kinesiology and Sociology. She received a PhD in Sociology from the University of Massachusetts at Amherst in 1977. She has served on the editorial board of the *Sociology of Sport Journal* and has published articles in a variety of journals, including the *Sociology of Sport Journal*, *Gender and Society* and *Social Problems*. She is co-editor (with Peter Donnelly) of *Sport and the Sociological Imagination* and author of *Higher Goals: Women's Ice Hockey and the Politics of Gender*.

Eleni Theodoraki is Lecturer in Sport Management and a member of the Institute of Sport and Leisure Policy at Loughborough University, England. Her publications include chapters on organizational analysis of sport-governing bodies in edited books by K. Heinemann and A. Rütten, and the Greek Association of Sport Managers. Her current research interests focus on managerial rationality and the decision-making process.

Alan Tomlinson is Professor of Sport and Leisure Studies, Chelsea School Research Centre, University of Brighton, England. He studied Humanities and Sociology for his BA at the University of Kent, and took Masters and Doctoral degrees in Sociological Studies at the University of Sussex. He has written on the social history and sociology of sport, leisure and consumption. His most recent books include (both co-authored with J. Sugden) *FIFA and the Contest for World Football – Who Rules the Peoples' Game* (1998) and *Great Balls of Fire – How Big Money is Hijacking World Football* (1999). He wrote *The Game's Up – Essays in the Cultural Analysis of Sport, Leisure and Popular Culture* (1999) and *Sport and Leisure Cultures – Local and Global Dimensions* is due to appear in 2001. He is Editor of the *International Review for the Sociology of Sport*.

Ivan Waddington is a Senior Lecturer in Sociology at the University of Leicester and a Director of the University's Centre for Research into Sport and Society. His major research interests concern the relationships between sport and health, and he authored *Sport, Health and Drugs* (2000). He has also studied the roles of club doctor and club physiotherapist in English professional football (soccer) for the Professional Footballers Association.

Garry Whannel is Professor of Television Cultures at the University of Luton and was a Co-Director of the Centre for Sport Development Research. He has a BA in Media Studies and a PhD in Cultural Studies. He serves on the editorial boards of *Leisure Studies* and *The Journal of Sport and Social Issues*. He is the author of *Fields in Vision: Television Sport and Cultural Transformation* (1992), *Blowing the Whistle: the Politics of Sport* (1983) and co-author (with J. Horne and A. Tomlinson) of *Understanding Sport* (1999).

Kevin Young is Senior Research Fellow in the Department of Physical Education, Sport Science and Recreation Management at Loughborough University, UK. Kevin has published on a variety of sports-related issues and is the co-editor (with Philip White) of *Sport and Gender in Canada* (1999). He has served terms on the editorial boards of the *Sociology of Sport Journal* and *Avante*, and on the Executive Board of the North American Society for the Sociology of Sport. He is currently Vice President of the International Sociology of Sport Association.

PREFACE

We intend this Handbook to be a 'user-friendly' collection that will meet the interests of a diverse set of readers from many countries. We expect that most readers will have a background in sociology but others will have backgrounds primarily in psychology, social and economic history, politics, philosophy, or the geography of sport. The content of the chapters has been aimed at undergraduate and postgraduate students as well as their teachers. We asked the authors to define fully and clearly technical and philosophical terms so as to make their meanings accessible to a diverse readership.

Although the content of many chapters draws heavily on research done in Western Europe and North America, the authors were careful to avoid ethnocentrism in their chapters, and they made concerted attempts, when possible, to draw on materials from non-North American and non-West European parts of the world.

We have divided the book into four parts:

1 Major perspectives in the sociology of sport
2 Cross-disciplinary differences and connections
3 Key topics
4 Sport and society research around the globe.

The chapters in the first section outline key features of seven major theoretical perspectives used in the sociology of sport. The authors pay special attention to the emergence and development of the perspectives, especially in terms of how they have been used in sociological analyses of sport. The authors also include comprehensive bibliographies of general sources and relevant work that provide insights into the perspectives and examples of how they have been used in the sociology of sport.

The chapters in Part Two provide state-of-the-art summaries of the disciplines in which analyses of sport are most closely related to work in the sociology of sport. The authors outline the major claims about the special value of their fields and then show how their disciplines have linked with, or failed to link with, other disciplines in connection with work on sport and society. The bibliographies presented in the chapters are designed to enable readers to have immediate access to key work in the seven disciplines.

Part Three contains discussions of theory and research on 18 key topics in the sociology of sport. We selected topics on the basis of three criteria: first, the amount of interest and attention received since the publication of the last (1981) Handbook; secondly, the centrality of the topic in the sociology of sport; and thirdly, our sense that the topic will become increasingly important in future work in the field. Authors outline the major issues and controversies related to the topics, and then provide bibliographies that enable readers to identify the range of research that deals with the topics.

Finally, the 12 chapters in Part Four provide brief summaries of sport and society research in those countries or regions of the world where sociological work is being done. These chapters are intended as overviews rather than detailed accounts of the history, focus and current status of the field. They are meant to provide a general sense of the global scope of the sociology of sport and the range of scholars, programmes and research that is included in the field. It is also our hope that they may play a small part in reducing the North American and Western European dominance that has characterized sport and society research and writing up to now.

The overall goal of the Handbook is to enable new as well as experienced scholars to grasp the scope and importance of theory and research on sport and society.

ACKNOWLEDGEMENTS

We thank each of the contributors to this volume. We asked for, received and appreciated their patience as we pulled together this collection of 44 chapters. We also thank the Sociology Department at the University of Colorado at Colorado Springs and the Centre for Research into Sport and Society at the University of Leicester, especially Sue Smith and Lisa Heggs, for their support as we called, faxed, mailed and e-mailed back and forth between Colorado Springs and Leicester. Dominic Malcolm of the CRSS was also very helpful regarding biblio-graphic matters and even more so in helping Eric Dunning begin to come to grips with computers and information technology.

Finally, we note that, where possible, our names appear side-by-side to denote equal roles and effort in editing this volume. Although Eric Dunning and Chris Rojek originally conceived and proposed the idea of the Handbook, both editors shaped its table of contents, recruited authors, edited chapter manuscripts, wrote introductions, checked the page proofs word by word, and handled all the other administrative chores associated with such an undertaking. Therefore, we have chosen to have our names appear in alphabetical order to emphasize our shared effort.

J.C.   E.D.

GENERAL INTRODUCTION

At the beginning of the twenty-first century, the study of sport and society in various forms and from various perspectives has become a rapidly expanding field of scholarly endeavour across the world. Our aim in editing this *Handbook of Sports Studies* is to mark and celebrate that fact. We have done so at this historical moment, the dawning of the third Christian millennium, because we think that the challenge of living in a new time frame creates an apposite moment for taking stock.

There is, we think, also a need at this moment for a comprehensive, up-to-date and authoritative reference book for scholars working in the broad field of 'sport and society' studies. We include under this rubric all those who study sports as social phenomena, namely anthropologists, economists, geographers, historians, philosophers, psychologists, political scientists as well as sociologists. However, because the sociology of sport is the largest and best established of the subdisciplines in this area and because it is the field that we as sociologists know best, the majority of our contributors are sociologists or have written from one or more of the sociological perspectives that are currently on offer. To have attempted at the present juncture to secure greater equality in the representation of the different subdisciplines of sport and society studies would, we feel, have resulted in a distorted representation of the current state of the literature.

As a stocktaking exercise, it is our hope that this handbook will:

1 Mark any advances of knowledge that have been made in the field during the second half of the twentieth century.
2 Provide a guide to the principal conflicts and difficulties that have arisen in this connection.
3 Alert readers to some of the mistakes that have been made and some of the strategies that have been advocated for avoiding them.
4 Recruit new scholars to the field by providing an accessible and comprehensive text

that can be used readily as a teaching and research resource.
5 Serve as a guide for teachers who wish to establish new curricula and develop courses and programmes in the area of sport and society studies.

A brief overview of the history and development of the field will help us to assess the advances that have been made in our understanding of sport and society.

Among the subdisciplines concerned with the study of sport as a social phenomenon, the sociology of sport was the first to emerge in an institutionalized form. For example, it was the first to be named as such, to have a named professional body (The International Committee for Sport Sociology – ICSS) and its own 'house' journal (*The International Review of Sport Sociology – IRSS*), and to be researched and taught in universities and other centres of higher education in specifically named and dedicated courses. The ICSS, recently renamed the International Sociology of Sport Association (ISSA), was and remains dedicated to organizing conferences and promoting the field. At the same time, the IRSS has continuously published research and a range of conceptual and theoretical discussions.

This process of institutionalization began in the mid-1960s, largely in conjunction with five main interrelated and interacting developments. The *first* was a dawning recognition among university teachers of physical education that sport and physical education are social practices and that they are culturally and historically relative. This, in turn, led them to see traditional teacher training curricula – emphasizing sports, athletics and gymnastics practice, together with biomechanics and exercise physiology – as unnecessarily restrictive and lacking the benefits associated with locating and looking at a subject sociologically.

The *second* development was that a few university teachers of sociology (including Theodor Adorno, Norbert Elias, Max Horkheimer, Charles H. Page and Gregory P.

Stone) realized that sport was an increasingly visible and important social practice, and that a sociology in which this was not clearly recognized would represent and foster an impoverished, perhaps distorted, view of the social world.

The *third* development was the general process of university expansion that took place in the 1960s. This expansion was accompanied by increased competition both within and between disciplines, and it both intensified the pressure on university teachers to publish and expanded the need for publication outlets. *The International Review of Sport Sociology* was one of the new journals that met this need. At the same time, it encouraged the formulation of research and theory related to sport and society.

The *fourth* development associated with the institutionalization of the sociology of sport was the advent of what might be called the 'permissive revolution'. This has been described by Norbert Elias (1996) and others (Wouters, 1986) as a process of 'informalization', the origins of which were grounded in significant equalizing shifts in the balance of class, racial/ethnic, gender and intergenerational power largely in favour of hitherto subordinate groups. Permissiveness/informalization was conducive to the expansion of sociology and the spread of sociological ways of thinking, especially left-orientated, 'radical' forms of thinking, into areas such as the study of science, religion, law, the arts, medicine, education and sport. In its turn, the expansion of left-orientated, 'radical' forms of sociology reciprocally fuelled the process of informalization and the associated 'permissive' ways of behaving which gathered momentum through the 1960s and early 1970s.

The *fifth* development was the East–West struggle or 'Cold War' which started in the 1940s and lasted through the 1980s. This global polarization and nuclear stand-off between the 'first' or 'capitalist' and the 'second' or 'communist' worlds created a context in which there was a perceived need to increase understanding of global power relations and the prominent and complex part that came to be played by sport in those relations.

However, the institutionalization of the sociology of sport during the 1960s is perhaps best understood as one of the key moments in a long-term ongoing process, the roots of which can be traced back as far as the eighteenth and nineteenth centuries and the initial emergence of modern sport. In Britain, for example, works such as Peter Beckford's *Thoughts on Hare and Foxhunting* (1796), Pierce Egan's *Boxiana* (1812)

and Montague Shearman's (1887, 1889) studies of the history and development of soccer, rugby and athletics – although they were not produced in academic institutions or intended for the instruction of students – marked the inception of the *serious* study of sport in that nation. Later, these works became rich research resources for twentieth-century scholars. Then, at the end of the nineteenth century, Thorstein Veblen wrote about American college sports in his *Theory of the Leisure Class* (1899). Shortly thereafter, Max Weber, widely identified as one of the 'founders' of sociology (see Giddens, 1971), discussed the opposition of the English Puritans to sport in his famous book *The Protestant Ethic and the Spirit of Capitalism* (Weber, 1958). His analyses were published in two parts in 1904 and 1905 respectively, and made available in English translation in 1930.[1] In 1906 William Graham Sumner devoted part of a chapter to 'popular sports' in his *Folkways*, and somewhat later, Willard Waller wrote about the integrating functions of sport in US high schools in *The Sociology of Teaching* (1932). However, despite their historical significance in sociology, none of these texts was devoted to the sociological study of sport *per se*. Rather, sport was discussed in them in the context of a sociological analysis of some wider issue. Accordingly, they can be regarded as containing, at best, proto-sociological studies of sport.

To our knowledge, the sociology of sport first emerged as a named endeavour and the subject of a book-length study in 1921, when Heinz Risse, a student of Theodor Adorno, published his *Soziologie des Sports*. Along with Max Horkheimer, Adorno founded the Frankfurter Institut für Sozialforschung (the Frankfurt Institute of Social Research) which was the location of the earliest productions in 'critical theory' of the so-called 'Frankfurt School'.[2] However, after 1921 Risse seems to have disappeared from the academic scene and the sociological study of sport did not become firmly established in that context. This is not surprising given what happened in Germany between the 1920s and the 1940s when a majority of sociologists were forced into silence, conformity with Nazi dogma, or exile. In fact, Adorno, Elias and Horkheimer were among those forced into exile. At any rate, it was not until 1969, at the height of the worldwide student protest movement, that the second piece of 'critical theory' dealing with sport, Bero Rigauer's *Sport und Arbeit* (Sport and Work), was published. By that time, the sociology of sport was well on the way towards becoming a recognized and institutionalized, if not a high status, area of academic endeavour.

We have already noted how the early institutionalization of the sociology of sport as a university subject took place as part of the expansion of higher education that occurred in most Western countries during the 1950s and 1960s. Sociology was one of the subjects that expanded most rapidly in that context, and public awareness of its existence spread – although this awareness did not always take the form of accurate knowledge of the ways in which specialists defined and understood sociology. It was during this time that the insightful and original essay 'American Sports: Play and Display' was published by the University of Chicago-educated, symbolic interactionist Gregory P. Stone (1955). If we are right, this was the first sustained and unambiguously sociological piece of work on sport to appear after Risse's text was published in 1921. Then, in Britain in 1961, Anthony Giddens at the London School of Economics, and Eric Dunning at the University of Leicester, successfully defended sociological Masters theses on sport-related topics (Dunning, 1961; Giddens, 1961). Their theses drew on the 'proto-sociological' work on sport done by physical education scholars such as Peter McIntosh, A.D. Munro, Bill Slater and Barbara Knapp of Birmingham University.[3] Perhaps not surprisingly, one of the central concerns of these physical education scholars during that period was to combat what they saw as the deleterious effects of the professionalization and commercialization of sports. In some ways, the work they did anticipated the later Marxist critiques of the commercialization and commodification of sports but they did so in a context of research which was empiricist and lacking in the rigour and penetration characteristic of Marxist studies at their best.

It was not until 1965, however, when the ICSS was formed and the IRSS was first published, that the sociology of sport 'came of age'. Centrally involved in this formalization and institutionalization of the subject were German (later substantially American-based) scholar Günther Lüschen, the First General Secretary of the ICSS, and Andrzej Wohl from Poland, the first ICSS President and first Editor of the IRSS, together with Peter McIntosh and Gregory P. Stone. It was Günther Lüschen who, in 1966, organized the first ICSS Symposium. Its theme was small groups in sport and it was convened in Cologne.[4] Subsequent ICSS Symposia were held in Champaign–Urbana (1967), Leicester (1968), and Magglingen/Macolin (1969).[5] In addition to the ICSS officials listed above, other participants in these early meetings included Rolf Albonico (Switzerland); Michel Bouet (France); Norbert Elias, Eric Dunning and Barbara Knapp (UK); Kalevi Heinila (Finland); Gerald S. Kenyon (Canada); John W. Loy, John C. Phillips and Walter Schafer (USA); and Brian Sutton-Smith (New Zealand/USA). It was characteristic both of the early development of the field and of sport *per se* that, at that stage, all but one of the participants were male and, with the exception of a few Japanese scholars such as Takaaki Niwa of Nara Women's University, all were white.

A further mark of the early institutionalization of the sociology of sport as a subject researched and taught in universities was the appearance in the 1960s and early 1970s of the first textbooks. With the exception of George Magnane's *Sociologie du sport*, published in 1964 (little known in the English-speaking world),[6] edited collections or 'readers' were the first to appear. Loy and Kenyon's *Sport, Culture and Society* (1969) was the first major collection to be published, followed by Dunning's *The Sociology of Sport: a Selection of Readings* (1971). German 'readers', *Texte zur Soziologie des Sports* edited by Kurt Hammerich and Klaus Heinemann and *Die Soziologie des Sports* edited by Günther Lüschen and Kurt Weis, followed in 1975 and 1976 respectively.

Other signs that the field was beginning to mature appeared around the same time. For example, in the United States Harry Edwards's text, *The Sociology of Sport*, was published in 1973, and three additional texts were published in 1978 – *Sport in Society: Issues and Controversies* by Jay Coakley; *Sociology of American Sport* by D. Stanley Eitzen and George Sage; and *Social Aspects of Sport* by Eldon Snyder and Elmer Spreitzer. Since that time, confining the discussion for present purposes to the English-speaking world, many introductory-type 'readers' and textbooks have been published in Australia, Canada and the United Kingdom as well as the USA.[7]

Beginning in the 1970s and 1980s publication outlets continued to expand with the publication of new journals devoted to social analyses of sports. These journals represented many disciplines in addition to sociology (see Table I). Furthermore, many mainstream journals in both sociology and physical education began to accept and publish research using sociological perspectives to study sports. Further growth in the field was fuelled as national and regional professional associations in both sociology and physical education in many countries began to sponsor regular sessions in the sociology of sport at annual conferences. Such conferences have also been sponsored regularly by national and regional sociology of

Table 1   *Some major English-language sport and society journals*

Subject	Journal title	First published
Anthropology	*Play and Culture*	1988
Economics	*Journal of Sports Economics*	2000
Geography	*Sport and Place*	1987
History	*British Journal of Sport History*	1984
	Canadian Journal of the History of Sport	1980[1]
	Journal of Sport History	1974
	International Journal of Sport History	1984
	Soccer and Society	1999
	Sporting Traditions	1985
	The European Sports History Review	1999
	The Sports Historian	1981
Philosophy	*Journal of the Philosophy of Sport*	1974
Political science	no journal	
Psychology	*International Journal of Sport Psychology*	1970
	Journal of Applied Sport Psychology	1989
	Journal of Sport and Exercise Psychology	1979
	The Sport Psychologist	1988
Sociology	*International Review for the Sociology of Sport*	1966
	Journal of Sport and Social Issues	1976
	Leisure Studies	1982
	Society and Leisure	1968
	Sport, Culture, Society	1998
	Sociology of Sport Journal	1986
Interdisciplinary	*Journal of Sport Behavior*	1978

[1] Founded in 1970 as *The Canadian Journal of the History of Sport and Physical Education*.

sport associations around the world, including those in Japan, Korea and Brazil, as well as the countries of North America and Europe. Attendance at most of these conferences has been consistent, and the quality of conference programmes generally has been impressive.

An indication of the growing public awareness of the value of research on sport and society is provided by the fact that scholars who use sociology and other related disciplinary perspectives to study sports have become recognized widely as 'public intellectuals' by journalists and reporters associated with the media. Quotes from and references to the research of these scholars appear increasingly in the popular print and electronic media. Another indicator of widespread interest in sports as social phenomena is the fact that 'Amazon.com', the major Internet bookseller in the world, listed over 490 books in its 'Sociology of Sport' reference category as of June 2000. Additionally, according to an organization that tracks the number of students taking various courses in the United States, there were nearly 30,000 students around the world expected to take 'sport in society' courses during the 1998–9 academic year (CMG College Mailing List). This organization also reported that in the United States

alone there were about 580 instructors in all disciplines who taught such courses.

The existence of organizational endorsement and support along with the continued growth in the pervasiveness, visibility and significance of sports in society supports our thesis that the study of sport and society is a growing field. But at the same time, even in countries where scholars have been using sociology to research sports, mainstream sociology has been slow at the institutional level to acknowledge the growing social and cultural significance of sports and sports participation. The tendency among most sociologists to give priority to studies of work and other 'serious' subjects (politics, for example) over studies of play, sports, or leisure has accounted for much of this inertia in the parent discipline. Many sociologists around the world have seen sports as trivial, non-productive dimensions of society and culture that do not merit scholarly attention relative to more 'serious' issues and concerns. Furthermore, they have not identified sports as sites for the existence of the issues and problems deemed by many as important in the field. Consequently, the sociology of sport has continued to exist on the fringe of sociology as a whole, and studying sports has not contributed generally to scholars' career enhancement in many sociology departments. For example, data from the American Sociological Association (ASA) indicate that during 1999 only 149 (1.3 per cent) of 11,247 members declared 'Leisure/Sport/Recreation' as one of their three major areas of interest, and over half of those scholars focused primarily on leisure rather than sports. Only 37 ASA members, 0.3 per cent of the Association's total membership, identified 'Leisure/Sports/Recreation' as their primary research and/or teaching topic, and according to the *1999 Guide to Graduate Departments of Sociology*, only two Canadian and two US sociology departments offered a graduate emphasis in the sociology of sport. Furthermore, at the 1998 annual ASA meeting there were approximately 3,800 presenters and co-presenters, and just 20 dealt with sport-related topics in their presentations; two of the 525 sessions were devoted to the sociology of sport. Patterns in the late 1990s were similar in Canada, Britain and Australia (Rowe et al., 1997). The number of scholars doing research and teaching in the sociology of sport in each of these countries has increased. However, they do not constitute a critical mass large enough to present themselves as formal subsections in the major professional sociology associations in their countries.

Patterns have been slightly different in physical education where professional associations have incorporated the sociology of sport in a formal manner and often designated an organizational subsection to represent those doing research and teaching related to sport and society. This is not to say that these subsections assume prominent positions within the organizations, but they do exist and they do provide institutional support for the field in ways that have not been characteristic in professional sociology associations. In large part this is because those who have figured prominently in the institutionalization of the field have backgrounds in departments of physical education or departments that have grown out of the field of physical education. The development of the field and the backgrounds of those who claim a professional attachment to the sociology of sport reflect this history.

In addition to an expansion of the field during the last half of the twentieth century, there have also been significant changes in the study of sport and society. There are many ways to highlight this but we will identify some of these changes by comparing the contents of the present volume with the contents of the 1981 *Handbook of Social Science of Sport* edited by Günther Lüschen and George Sage.[8] The most obvious contrasts between the two

can be inferred through an analysis of the respective tables of contents (see Figure I for the Table of Contents of the 1981 volume, and Table II for a comparison of chapter titles in the 1981 volume with titles of Chapters in the Key Topics Section of this volume). With the exception of two chapters dedicated to anthropological and social psychological analyses, the contents of the 1981 *Handbook* focused almost exclusively on the sociology of sport – a fact implied by their title. The table of contents in the present volume is considerably broader in scope because, as editors, we have been able to draw on expanding contributions from scholars in the disciplines of economics, geography, history, philosophy and political science as well as sociology. The expansion of the study of sport and society is also seen in the fact that the 1981 *Handbook* contained 24 chapters, while the present volume contains 44. Of course, it is important to note that the 1981 volume devoted over 200 pages, nearly 30 per cent of its content, to an international bibliography and cross-listed index of sport and society publications.

Contributors to the 1981 volume represented five countries, while contributors for this volume represent 13. Table III shows that 16 of 26 contributors to the 1981 *Handbook* were born in the United States and an additional five lived in the USA for some time. Only two of the contributors, one from England and one from Germany, lived entirely outside the United States. The fact that the majority of contributors to the present volume come from the United Kingdom and that contributors represent 13 countries in total provides a measure of the increasingly international scope of the sociology of sport and the global reach of research on sport and society. This trend is further documented by the membership of the International Sociology of Sport Association (the former ICSS) which, in the year 2000, included 170 paid-up members representing 34 countries.

In saying this, we do not wish to exaggerate the degree to which sport and society studies, and particularly the sociology of sport, have spread internationally. The continuing predominance in this volume of contributions from scholars living in the UK and the USA inevitably reflects our own national backgrounds and professional networks as editors. However, it also reflects, we think, the tradition that the field is more clearly identified and developed through research and academic curricula in the English-speaking countries than it is elsewhere, at least in terms of the number of scholars and students. The exceptions to this would be Germany and France, where Bero

Figure 1   Contents and contributors to the Handbook of Social Science of Sport, *editors G. Lüschen and G. H. Sage, Stipes Publishing Co., 1981*

Table II　Handbook *content comparison*

The 24 chapter titles from the 1981 *Handbook* are listed below. On the right, we have listed the 18 chapter titles from the Key Topics section in the present *Handbook*; in parentheses are listed disciplinary chapters that parallel titles from the 1981 *Handbook*. When there is at least partial overlap in content we have matched the titles from the two Handbooks. The purpose of this comparison is to illustrate differences and similarities in focus and content as a means of indicating changes and developments in the sports studies field.

Lüschen and Sage (1981)	Coakley and Dunning (2000)
• The sociology of sport in the ancient world	• The development of modern sports
• Games of the native North Americans	• (Anthropology)
• Life and games of the traditional Canadian Eskimo	• (Anthropology)
• Olympic success: a cross-cultural perspective	
• Sport, education & the schools	• Sport and education
• Sport and religion	
• Sport and the mass media	• Sport and the media
• Leisure and sport	• Alternatives to formal sports
• The system of sport: problems of methodology, conflict and social stratification	• Theorizing sport, social place & status
• Sport as a community representation	• Sport and nationalism
• Socialization into and through sport	• Social control and sport
• Femininity and athleticism	• Gender and sport
• Group performance, interaction and leadership	• (Psychology)
• The analysis of sport organizations	• Management, organizations and theory in the governance of sport
• Alternatives in American sports policy	• (Politics and sports)
• Fandom & functions of spectator sports	
• Sport, achievement and social criticism	• (Philosophy)
• Authority, power and intergroup stratification by race and sex in American sport and society	• Sport, racism and ethnicity
• Sport and deviance	• Doping in sport as deviant behavior and its social control
• Riotous outbursts in sport events	• Sport and violence
• Play and seriousness	
• The social psychology and anthropology of play and games	• (Psychology & Anthropology)
• Motivational theories of play: definitions and explanations	• Emotions and sports
• Sport personology	• (Psychology)
	• Political economy and sport
	• Sport and globalization
	• Sport and health: a sociological perspective
	• Sport and disability
	• Body studies in the sociology of sport

Rigauer, Klaus Heinemann, Pierre Bourdieu and their colleagues have made important contributions to the field. And we should add that notable developments and contributions from various regions and countries around the globe are summarized in the 12 short chapters that make up Part Four of this volume. Part of our intent in including this section is to stimulate further research in the countries represented by the chapters and in other countries and regions where the study of sport and society is just now being initiated. The ultimate goal is to promote greater global representation in this regard.

The proportions of male and female contributors in each of the volumes highlights one of the most significant changes in the field in the two decades separating the two publications. Men constituted 21 of 26 contributors to the earlier volume, a male–female ratio of roughly 4:1. Men constitute 37 of 51 contributors to the present volume, a male–female ratio of around 2.5:1. We believe that the 1981 ratio was a reflection primarily of patriarchal structures and values in the world at large and in the social sciences at that time. That these structures and values persist both in the sociology

Table III   *Countries of birth of contributors to Lüschen and Sage (1981) and Coakley and Dunning (2000)*

Lüschen and Sage (1981)		Coakley and Dunning (2000)	
Country	Number	Country	Number
Canada	2	Canada	3
Finland	1	France	2
Germany	4[1]	Germany	3
New Zealand	1[1]	Hungary	1
United Kingdom	2[1]	Japan	1
United States	16	Norway	2
		New Zealand	3
		Portugal	2
		South Africa	1
		South Korea	1
		United Kingdom	16
		United States	14

[1]The New Zealand contributor, one of the UK contributors and three of the contributors who were German-born, were US residents at the time of writing.

of sport and the wider social world is indicated by the continuing, although lesser, predominance of male contributors in this present volume. However, it is important to stress that the greater number of female contributors to this handbook also represents a clear increase in the number of women scholars who have made contributions to sport and society studies. It also reflects the impact of feminism on the field and the associated – and at least embryonic – transformations in taken-for-granted patriarchal assumptions that have traditionally influenced research as well as relationships between colleagues.

Sociological contributions predominate in this volume as they also did in the 1981 *Handbook*. However, apart from Gregory Stone's symbolic interactionist discussion of 'Sport as a Community Representation', a majority of contributions in the earlier volume were implicitly and in some cases explicitly grounded in empiricist (that is, data-based analyses that lacked an explicit theoretical focus) and structural-functionalist assumptions. This emphasis did not represent the Marxist, critical and figurational theoretical perspectives which were emerging at the time. But it did highlight the extent to which early work on sport and society was grounded in and influenced by the notion that societies are most accurately conceptualized as 'social systems' possessing 'needs' and 'goals' and delimited by clear-cut, impermeable and easily determinable boundaries. Of course, these assumptions have been criticized to the point that structural functionalism has been used less and less often to guide research and analysis in sport and society studies since the early

1970s. However, that structural-functionalist assumptions continue to be implicit even in the work of its critics is demonstrated by Loy and Booth in their chapter (Chapter 1).

At the beginning of the twenty-first century scholars in the field are more likely to take the following positions:

1 Societies are fluid and interpenetrating products of human interaction and interdependence which change and develop over time.
2 Sports and societies are most accurately conceptualized as the unplanned products of the interaction over time of pluralities of conscious, interdependent, differentially powerful, emotional as well as rational 'embodied' human beings who make choices.
3 Social life is more open-ended and less determined than previously assumed by structural functionalists and some kinds of Marxists (although to say this is not to claim that it is chaotic, contingent and entirely undetermined).
4 Social processes are best understood in connection with various forms of power relations that are inter-societal as well as intra-societal.
5 The balance and tension that exists between continuity and change in social life has been shifting in favour of change at an accelerating rate at least since the seventeenth and eighteenth centuries.

Overall, it has been widely recognized that there are serious difficulties associated with attempts to understand social life within a framework of essentially static, process-reducing assumptions such as those underlying the Parsonian version of structural functionalism.

Despite the priority given to structural functionalism in the 1981 *Handbook*, there was, beginning in the 1960s, considerable conflict over theoretical paradigms.[9] This conflict heated up during the late 1970s and early 1980s when Marxist/neo-Marxist, feminist and Marxist–feminist scholars became increasingly vocal and powerful, if not hegemonic, figures in the sociology of sport. As they grew more influential there was an associated change in the dominant professional self-image among sociologists of sport. Rather than seeing themselves as technocratic servants of sport-forms which they uncritically accepted as 'good', many began to see themselves as critics whose principal goal was to use research and action to 'purify' the 'pathological' sport-forms produced under capitalism. The ultimate goal was to secure more egalitarian articulations of sports into more egalitarian social frameworks. Sociologists of sport today continue to have variants of both these self-images but, if we are right, the 'critics' have come to outnumber the 'technocrats'.

We suggest that the paradigm conflicts that intensified during the 1960s and 1970s in sociology remain today. These conflicts raise complex issues that are perhaps best addressed in this context by means of an historical detour. The first thing worthy of note is that sociology was named as a subject in a conflict-situation, more particularly when Auguste Comte reacted critically to a book published in 1835 by Belgian statistician Adolphe Quetelet. The subtitle of Quetelet's book was *An Essay on Social Physics* and, although Comte himself had used the term 'social physics' up until that time, he ceased from then on to use it. He did so for two main reasons: first, he objected to Quetelet's vision of 'social physics' as a primarily statistical subject; and secondly, he objected to what he regarded as Quetelet's scientifically unwarranted egalitarianism. Comte's alternative term was 'sociology' (Coser, 1971).

Another term coined by Comte was 'positivism', and the chief positive method that he recommended for use in sociology was the method of historical comparison. In a word, even though the meaning of 'positivism' has been changed so that it now refers to the inappropriate advocacy and use of natural science methods in studies of the social field, a struggle between sociologists who advocate comparative-historical methods and those who advocate statistics has been built into our subject since its early days. In the 1960s, this struggle surfaced in the sociology of sport in the different paradigms advocated by Kenyon (1969), Loy (1968), and Lüschen (1967) on the one hand, and by Elias (Elias and Dunning, 1986) and Dunning (1971) on the other. Paraphrasing Ralf Dahrendorf's description (1959) of the new middle class in capitalist societies, sociology and the sociology of sport can be said, like the new middle class, to have been 'born decomposed', that is, with differences, conflicts and tensions built into their very core.[10]

Other early conflicts in sociology were also noteworthy as we try to put current conflicts in perspective. In late nineteenth-early twentieth-century France there were heated differences between 'realist', Emile Durkheim and 'nominalist', Gabriel Tarde. Around the same time in Germany there took place what they called the *Methodenstreit*, the not dissimilar 'fight over method', between the 'positivists' (in Comte's sense, they were wrongly named)[11] and the 'historicists'. Max Weber sought to resolve this conflict through the suggestion that sociologists should seek explanations that are both 'causally adequate' and 'adequate at the level of meaning'. Interestingly, Weber advocated the establishment of causal relations, not by means of statistical analyses, but by means of counterfactual reasoning.

These early sociological conflicts were fiercely fought. However, the conflicts between proponents of opposing paradigms that began in the 1960s and continue through today are more intense than past conflicts. For 20 or so years following the end of the Second World War, advocates of functionalist and non-Comtean (that is, ahistorical and even anti-historical) 'positivist' sociology, most of them from the United States, reigned supreme. Then, for various sociological and extra-sociological reasons, the functionalist-empiricist hegemony collapsed and the subject, which had been 'born decomposed', became multiply fractured. The sociological reasons for this process of decomposition included, among other things, the difficulties encountered by Parsonian functionalism in dealing with issues such as conflict, power and change.[12] The extra-sociological reasons included the effects on a younger generation of sociologists whose subject-identities and identifications were being forged in a context that was influenced by powerful events and forces which included: (a) the Vietnam war and the protest against it, (b) the civil rights struggle, (c) the rise of second-wave feminism, (d) the campus rebellions which broke out in North America and many countries in Western

Europe, (e) the growth of 'permissiveness'/ 'informalization' and (f) the power shift towards the younger generation. The latter centrally underlay and was reciprocally fuelled by many of these other changes.

If we are right, the fact that Canadian scholars and others who had not been born in the United States were centrally involved in the left-radicalization of the sociology of sport which took place during the 1970s and 1980s correlatively with these powerful events and forces was no accident. Processes of radicalization are more likely to occur in dependencies than in centres of imperial power such as the USA. But more to the point for present purposes, it seems that sociologists of sport who received their sociological training in the 1960s and early 1970s differed from their predecessors. The former worried less about the dangers of the 'Cold War' and focused more on struggling against capitalism which, for most Marxists or near-Marxists, was seen as the principal cause of inequities and global conflict. Perhaps because fewer of them had directly experienced the Second World War, they were more inclined to take peace for granted? Be that as it may, what is certain is the fact that it was precisely when the conflict over paradigms was especially intense that the sociology of sport began to come of age. Like the parent discipline, having been 'born decomposed' it, too, became multiply fractured.[13]

Since the 1960s, there have been on offer in sociology and the sociology of sport a variety of named paradigms. They include various forms of functionalism (for example, 'soft' and 'hard'), Marxism (for example, 'humanist' and 'structuralist') and feminism (for example, 'liberal', 'socialist', 'Marxist' and 'cultural'), together with conflict theory, Weberian theory, rational choice theory, action theory, symbolic interactionism, exchange theory, ethnomethodology, structuralism, post-structuralism, postmodernism, structuration theory and figurational sociology. Among other things, these paradigms differ regarding the positions taken by their advocates in relation to epistemological/methodological issues and ontological/factual issues. Among the epistemological/methodological issues are the following:

1   Where they see sociology located on the continuum between the humanities and the sciences.
2   *If* they see sociology as a science, whether they see it as a science in a 'soft', for example, comparative-historical or participant observational orientated, sense or in a 'hard', that is, non-Comtean 'positivist'

sense based on statistics and equivalents to experimentation.
3   Whether they see the purpose of sociological knowledge as an 'end in itself' (that is, as something that is interesting and valuable for its own sake), as a tool for improving human performance (in our case in the field of sport), or as a means to identify and achieve political goals.

Among the ontological/factual issues are where their advocates stand in relation to such dualisms as 'materialism' versus 'idealism', 'agency' versus 'structure', 'social statics' versus 'social dynamics', and 'synchronic' studies versus 'diachronic' studies (that is, whether they see sociology as concerned solely with the present day or whether they see it as an historical subject).

Approached in these terms, the abundance of paradigms listed above can be categorized into five basic types: functionalist paradigms, conflict paradigms, action paradigms, feminist paradigms and attempted syntheses, such as structuration theory and figurational sociology. Mention of these last two suggests another source of basic differences: the way that advocates of each sociological paradigm deal with the sociology–philosophy relationship. Thus while Anthony Giddens, the primary architect of structuration theory, advocates a heavy dependency of sociology on philosophy, Elias, the principal originator of figurational sociology, urged sociologists to maximize their autonomy in this and other regards. In a word, while Giddens recommends the continuing relevance for sociology of philosophy, a subject based on metaphysical, armchair speculation and reading other people's books, Elias advocated the constant cross-fertilization of theory and research as the only secure means of advancing knowledge.[14] Of course, he stressed comparative-historical research on balance in this connection, rather than research of a statistical kind. Most of the paradigms discussed above are now well represented in the sociology of sport and, up to a point, the conflict and competition between their proponents could be said to provide empirical confirmation of Marx's dictum 'without conflict, no progress'. That is, the conflict and competition have contributed to the advancement of knowledge in the field. For example, much of the work of 'male feminists' owes its insights and acceptance to the sustained and highly effective feminist critique of the hitherto hegemonic status of patriarchal assumptions in the sociology of sport (Klein, 1993; Messner, 1992; Messner and Sabo, 1990, 1994). Seen solely from a present-centred perspective, these advances may not appear particularly great, but seen from the standpoint of those who knew what the sociology of sport was like in the 1960s and 1970s, they are substantial. As another example, there has been a definitive shift from a 'sociology of women' to a 'sociology of gender relations' perspective as represented in a wide range of 'female feminist' work (Birrell and Cole, 1994; Hall, 1996; Hargreaves, 1994; see Chapters 4 and 20 by Birrell and Theberge respectively in this volume). The clash over interpretations of the globalization of sport has also given rise to fruitful and creative analyses. Interpretations informed by Marxism have consistently emphasized that strong elements of 'Americanization' have been involved in the worldwide spread of sports (Donnelly, 1996; Kidd, 1991), while interpretations guided by figurational theory have shown, equally persuasively, that globalization is best understood as a trend or social process that is both homogenizing and heterogenizing (Maguire, 1994, 1999).

In fact, we would suggest that, with the possible exception of the sociology of education which is in certain respects structurally similar, the sociology of sport has been one of the liveliest and most fruitful of the parent subject's subdisciplines since the late 1970s. We realize that such a judgement may reflect our greater familiarity with our own subdiscipline and our relative ignorance of others. Nevertheless, it seems to us – and we hasten to add that this has not yet been established empirically – that recent output in the sociology of sport has outstripped output in the sociology of law, the sociology of medicine, the sociology of science and probably the sociology of religion. This is almost certainly the case in terms of quantity and probably in terms of quality as well.

Assuming the validity of this judgement, we hypothesize that the putative fruitfulness of our field relative to others can, in part, be explained structurally. That is, the power and status gap between sociologists and physical educators, like the gap between sociologists and school teachers, is considerably more narrow than it is in the relations between sociologists and lawyers, sociologists and doctors, sociologists and natural scientists, and even sociologists and the clergy. This relative equality has been centrally involved in constituting sociologists of sport as a figuration and the sociology of sport as a social field both of which are characterized by a tension-balance between the polarities of consensus and dissensus, cooperation and rivalry. This tension-balance has fostered creativity in the subdiscipline and this creativity has defused the centrifugal potential that is inherent in the paradigmatic fragmentation of post-1960s sociology. That is to say, in highly differentiated and individualized societies such as the 'advanced' or 'complex' societies of today, tension in the relations between people who pursue different specializations within a common field is less likely to produce hostility and a spirit of perversity when relationships are relatively equal than when the power and status gap is wide. Relative equality is also more likely to foster greater mutual recognition of what such groups can offer each other. That is to say, lawyers, doctors, and natural scientists are more likely than physical educators to ignore or deny the possibility that sociological investigation can be valuable and add to understanding in their fields of endeavour.

In a related sense, the relative fruitfulness and high creativity of the sociology of sport may also be fostered by the relative equality between the people in the field employed in sociology departments and physical education departments. This equality within the context of universities has enabled an open dialogue to be maintained between scholars whose principal aim in their work is the advancement of knowledge and scholars whose principal aim is securing socio-political or 'practical' sport-related goals. An effective balance has been struck, in other words, between socio-political and 'practical' detachment and socio-political and 'practical' involvement. On no side have people allowed the search for 'pure' knowledge, for 'practical interventions' or for idealized political goals to become paramount and exclusive. As a result, the search for knowledge has been aimed at the *real* world of sports and games, and at increasing our ability to make practical interventions in that world. Finally, the bonds between different specialists in the sociology of sport are further consolidated through a widely shared fondness for sports and a common belief in the value of sociology as a means of enhancing our understanding of sports and society and as a means of informing our involvement in related practical and political issues.

This discussion of fruitfulness and creativity in the sociology of sport is not meant to imply that we think there are no challenges or problems facing the field as we begin the new millennium. In fact, we are facing a series of serious interrelated challenges that seem to us to revolve around the following.

1 Dealing with the Consequences of Paradigmatic Fragmentation in Sociology as a Whole This fragmentation has negatively affected our subdiscipline in at least two ways. First, it has on more than one occasion been accompanied by potentially dangerous caricatures of the work of others. When these caricatures become deeply embedded in segments of disciplinary discourse, they are not only difficult to dislodge, but they become subversive of the mutual respect that is required for relationships in the field that are simultaneously critical *and* supportive. Secondly, fragmentation has weakened sociologists relative to specialists in other subjects, thus making it difficult collectively to resist the intrusion into the field of the representatives of higher status subjects such as philosophy. The prestige that has been or is recurrently heaped on abstract theorizers such as Parsons and Giddens, who are nominally sociologists but really types of philosophers, is one example. Another example is the overly positive reaction of some scholars in our field to 'postmodernist' philosophers, primarily those from France, who advocate approaches to the social world parts of which verge on solipsism. Although it is crucial for us to interrogate what is knowable about the social world, the existence of that world, although it may be complex, is a precondition for sociology itself. The challenge for sociology and the sociology of sport is to utilize that which is of value in what the postmodernists have said and continue to say and to abandon the rest. The high status of philosophy should not allow what philosophers argue to go unchallenged.

2 Maintaining a Balance between Understanding and Action in the Sociology of Sport When scholars in our field place the need for action above the need for understanding, there is a possibility that 'truth claims' will come to rest primarily on normative commitments rather than theory-guided empirical research. Although it is important for scholars in any of the social sciences or humanities to discuss *what ought to be* in a critically reflective and morally reasoned manner, it should not supplant systematic and replicable attempts to understand *what is and how it has come to be.* This means that while we recognize that sociologists are not morally or culturally neutral analysts who stand apart from the societies in which we participate and, indeed that our socio-political involvements are a source of motivation and knowledge, the viability of our field depends on our ability to develop collective agreement about rules for making 'truth claims' or, perhaps better, claims about the 'reality-congruence' of our propositions and findings. In the absence of such an agreement, we cannot share and criticize each other's ideas and research in a manner that produces general understanding as well as a foundation of knowledge that can be used to inform intervention and transformational efforts.

We would argue that there are indeed circumstances when the need to take assertive action must take precedence over the need for understanding, but we would also argue that the identification of such circumstances requires a thorough and thoughtful assessment. We remember Karl Marx's observation that 'philosophers have interpreted the world in various ways; the point, however, is to *change it*'. But we also remember that he devoted his life to laying the foundations for a 'scientific socialism' through a detailed, empirically based understanding of social relationships and social dynamics. In fact, if he were alive today, he might even look back at history and say that 'Marxists have tried to change the world in various ways, the point, however, is to *understand* it'. At any rate, it is important to balance understanding and action.

3 Engaging in Critical Self-reflection as a Field This challenge should be self-evident in any academic discipline or subdiscipline. However, it is important for scholars to engage in constructively critical self-reflection while avoiding forms of self-deconstruction and deconstruction of the work of others that can jeopardize the political and intellectual foundations of the field. For example, while it is extremely important for the sociology of sport to serve as a site for integrating a range of dissenting voices concerned with sport and society, without a basis for identifying a unity of focus and for making 'truth claims' that will be respected and seen as legitimate by others it is possible that the field will lack the status required to elicit and maintain funding within the institutional structure of contemporary universities.

It is also important for scholars in sociology and the sociology of sport to interrogate the assumptions of cultural neutrality that have traditionally informed theory and research, the organization of the field including professional networks and relationships, the evaluation of colleagues, and the identity development of scholars themselves. Although sociologists in the past have dealt with this challenge from a distance through the sociologies of knowledge and sociology, the growth of various forms of feminist theory, especially cultural feminism (Tong, 1998), has presented this challenge to us in a close-up, face-to-face manner. This has caused considerable discomfort among some men in the field, a few of whom have made considerable contributions to sociology and/or the sociology of sport. During their professional socialization these men learned and accepted at least to some degree that being a good sociologist called for and valorized objectivity in research, and for competition and individualism in their professional relationships. Then certain feminist theorists made a convincing case that this way of being a sociologist was part of a gendered system through which the values and experiences of men were used as the basis for making 'truth claims', assessing the quality of research, evaluating colleagues and defining oneself as a scientist. Joining the feminist theories were racial theories and queer theories that critically interrogated 'whiteness' and heterosexuality in the same way that feminists had interrogated masculinity in connection with the field. As a result, some white, male, heterosexual sociologists with records of achievement and participation in the parent discipline and our subdiscipline were faced with the accusation that all their 'truth claims' were contentious, and that their theories and research were tainted by various combinations of sexism and patriarchy, racism and colonial privilege, and/or heterosexism and homophobia. In the same context there was and continues to be a tendency among some younger scholars to reject previously identified classical scholars and theories as a matter of course. Thus, we are faced with a two-sided challenge. One side involves acknowledging and dealing with the pervasive consequences of longstanding systems of privilege within sociology in general and the sociology of sport in particular. The other side involves coming to terms with the value of past theory and research in the field as a form of data and with the value of those who have done this work as colleagues (Loy and Booth, in press). An inability to face and deal with this dual challenge could leave the field hopelessly decomposed (see Risman and Tomaskovic-Devey, 1999). It is our suspicion as sociologists who no longer consider themselves to be young that forms of 'ageism' on the part of both older and younger generations of scholars – a mutual inability or unwillingness to recognize common problems of humanity, for example, the old forgetting they were once young and the young being unwilling to entertain the fact that they will age – may be among the contributories to this problem.

4   Maintaining Professional Commitment in the Clash over 'Modernism' and 'Postmodernism'   One of the central struggles in sociology and related disciplines today is over what one might call the validity and value of the promise of 'modernism' and whether we have entered or are currently entering a 'postmodern' era. Centrally at issue in this connection is the belief that the success of sociology rests in the promise of its theories and methods in delivering the tools necessary for contributing to the creation of a future that will be better than the past and present. In short, what is at issue is whether sociology can make a contribution to human 'progress'. The seeds of such a belief can be traced, for example, to Condorcet and Turgot in the eighteenth century. However, it first began to be given an explicitly sociological form by thinkers such as August Comte and Herbert Spencer in the nineteenth century. Although he considered himself to be a 'political economist', it has come to be customary to include Karl Marx among the earliest contributors to this sociological way of thinking. Despite the often considerable political and scientific differences between them, all these thinkers were united in their belief that history and social development equal 'progress', and that social scientific research and theory can be of help in bringing this 'better future' into being.[15]

Turn-of-the-century sociologists such as Durkheim and Weber were among the first to be involved in the institutionalization of sociology as a university subject and they were also among the first to entertain doubts about the 'inevitability of progress'. Durkheim, for example, claimed to have demonstrated that nineteenth-century social developments in Europe were leading to increasing rates of suicide, social disintegration and anomie, while Weber hypothesized that the processes of rationalization, which he showed were occurring correlatively with the development of capitalism, were likely in the future to lead to growing 'disenchantment' with and of the world (*Entzaüberung*) and an increase in irrational behaviour.[16] There was an attack on 'progress theories' in anthropology, too, for example, by Franz Boas and his students,[17] and, whilst at the end of his career he became involved in a revival of 'evolutionary' sociology, Talcott Parsons began his elaboration of what he called 'the theory of social action' with an attack on the 'evolutionary individualism' of Herbert Spencer (see Parsons, 1937). Nevertheless, whether he was writing in his earlier ahistorical and static mode or in his latter mode which was diachronic and evolutionary, Talcott Parsons can be said to have played a central role after the Second World War in spreading and consolidating the idea that the promise of 'modernism' and 'modernity' has to be grounded in an understanding of the properties of social systems (see Parsons, 1951). Such an idea grew during the 1960s and 1970s as a number of more 'radical' sociologies, including most importantly varieties of Marxism, were fuelled by the belief that the promise of 'modernism' could only be fulfilled through various revolutionary movements and transformations. However, a majority of the proponents of these more radical sociologies continued alongside their more 'liberal' (for example, Parsonian) colleagues to stress that more adequate sociological knowledge is a necessary prerequisite for effective social revolution and reform.

What might be called 'mainstream sociology' as we enter the third Christian millennium continues to be organized by and large around the pursuit of social possibilities grounded in the 'modernist' notion that it is possible to discover a body of sociological theory which will enable us 'scientifically' to establish a 'normative centre' or 'consensus', that is, a set of normative propositions or principles around which work for a better future might be organized. At least since the writings of the German philosophers, Nietzsche and Heidegger and more recently of French philosophers such as Foucault and Baudrillard who were more or less heavily influenced by their reading of their German predecessors,[18] there has been a growing number of social observers and analysts, many with a literary rather than social scientific background, who have concluded in various and what are widely regarded as 'compelling' ways that the social world is comprised of unstructured and unstructurable differences (Lemert, 1995: 209–11). The goal of their social and cultural analyses has been and continues to be that of understanding that world in as many of its particular and differential details as possible (Rail, 1998). Apparently forgetting or being unaware of earlier sociologists who attacked 'grand theories' (such as C. Wright Mills, Norbert Elias, Robert K. Merton, Barney Glaser and Anselm Strauss[19]), such 'postmodernist' writers also proclaim the 'impossibility' of 'grand narratives' or 'universal theories' (itself a kind of 'grand narrative' or universal law-like statement, it seems to us!). However, be that as it may, their work has served to disrupt the mainstream search for 'the normal'. These individuals are describing what they regard as a variety of social worlds in ways that give rise

to what they think of as critical analyses of the dynamics of power, denial, marginalization and exclusion that have been at the core of the self-same economic, political, academic and scientific structures in and through which the 'promise of modernism' was first formulated and through which it has subsequently been sustained (cf. Lemert, 1995).

As one might expect, heated debates occur when mainstream sociologists encounter these analysts and their analyses that are not premised on the modernist quest for a normatively 'centred' social world. We have seen this in the sociology of sport as well as in sociology as a whole. The futures of the organized discipline of sociology and subdisciplines such as the sociology of sport, rest in the extent to which these debates foster a culture of critical self-reflection and mutual tolerance and respect among dissenting sociological voices and a recognition that the vitality of sociology should not be measured simply by the standards of modern progress. The purpose of these debates should not be to dismiss what 'classical' and 'mainstream' sociology have to offer in our attempts to understand the social world and the many varieties of lived experiences that constitute that world. Nor should the purpose be to arrive at a single, general explanation of the world and how we might use that explanation to make the world unified through a particular normative consensus. Instead, the purpose, if we wish to continue coming together in formal gatherings to share our experiences and understandings, should be to give voice to a range of experience-based descriptions and explanations of the world. If these descriptions and explanations contain the necessary particular details, we should be able to use them to acknowledge and come to terms with our own differences and then deal with the dilemmas associated with social factors and forces that constrain people's lives, including our own. If we can manage this, sociology can become a means for a critically informed body of knowledge that can serve as a basis for engaging an ever-changing collection of social relationships and the unanticipated problems and issues often associated with them.

CONCLUDING COMMENT

Our sense is that in practical terms the sociology of sport consists of a collection of scholars most of whom claim to do 'science', agree on the rules we use to make 'truth claims', and then share our claims and how we have arrived at them through publications and discussions. If our 'truth claims' are based on empirical data, if there is general agreement on what constitutes data, and if we are committed to a rigorous pursuit of understanding, the diversity and dynamism of the field will enrich our awareness of sport and society and enhance our potential to transform both. The chapters in this handbook represent a version of the 'state of our understanding' of sport and society at this point in time – along with where we have been and where we might go in the immediate future.

As we anticipate that future from our perspective as editors of this volume, we wonder about the connection between this present *Handbook of Sports Studies* and the next similar volume that might be published (probably electronically) in 2020. If the editors of the 2020 volume are a Latin American woman and a black man from postcolonial Africa, how might they select authors and chapter topics? Might they look back at this volume and wonder about our naivety as editors and ask why we did not select other authors or foresee issues related to sport and the law, sport and the environment, sport and postcolonial development, and other topics that should have been discussed at the turn of the millennium? We expect so. And for the sake of the vitality of our field, we hope so.

NOTES

1 As Loy and Kenyon (1969) note, Weber also discussed the knightly games of feudal Europe.

2 The Frankfurt Institut für Sozialforschung was founded in 1923 at the University of Frankfurt by Felix Weil, the son of a rich businessman. Its first Director was Max Horkheimer and among its prominent early members were Theodor Adorno, Walter Benjamin and Erich Fromm. More recently, its members have included Herbert Marcuse and Jürgen Habermas. The Frankfurt School (or 'critical theorists' as they are also called) are Marxists but it is characteristic of their approach that they concentrate in their work on elements of 'the superstructure', that is, on aspects of 'culture'.

3 Together with their colleagues M. Baument, M.A. Madders and Beryl Sanders, these four scholars were the authors of an influential pamphlet, *Britain*

in the World of Sport: An Examination of the Factors Involved in Participation in Competitive International Sport (University of Birmingham, 1956). Perhaps the best-known member of the Birmingham group, and certainly the one most influential in the sociology of sport, was Peter McIntosh. See, above all, his *Sport in Society* (1960).

4 The proceedings were published by Günther Lüschen (1966).

5 See Lüschen (1970) for the proceedings of the Champaign–Urbana Conference, and Albonico and Pfister-Binz (1972) for the proceedings of the Magglingen Conference (the French-Swiss name for Magglingen is Macolin).

6 Rather surprisingly, M. Magnane never took part in the affairs of the ICSS.

7 A sample of these includes the following: Bryant and McElroy, 1997; Cashmore, 1996; Coakley, 1998; Coakley and Donnelly, 1999; Donnelly, 1997; Eitzen, 1996; Eitzen and Sage, 1997; Figler and Whitaker, 1991; Hall et al., 1991; Hart and Birrell, 1981; Harvey and Cantelon, 1988; Horne et al., 1987; Horne et al., 1999; Lawrence and Rowe, 1986; Leonard, 1998; McPherson et al., 1989; Nixon and Frey, 1996; Phillips, 1993; Sage, 1980; Vogler and Schwartz, 1993; Yiannakis et al., 1993.

8 It is difficult to compare the 1981 *Handbook* with the present volume because each was edited under different circumstances. The 1981 volume was originally conceived as part of a larger project that was to take the form of an Encyclopaedia of Physical Education. The Lüschen and Sage contribution was to be one volume in the series that would make up the encyclopaedia. This is partly why over 200 pages of the 1981 volume consisted of a detailed bibliography and cross-listed index of sources that could be considered a foundation for the field at that time. Also, contributors to the volume were chosen in part because of their connection with physical education as it had developed primarily in the United States. In fact, the series editor was an exercise physiologist who had reservations about the critical nature of some of the work done in the sociology of sport during the 1970s.

9 Related to this observation on our part, it should be noted that a handbook, or any similar volume, is often a more or less conservative representation of a field or body of literature. Authors are selected on the basis of their past work and the extent to which it has been accepted by established

publication outlets and incorporated into the mainstream literature of the discipline or subdiscipline. Although we, too, may be guilty of this charge, we have tried in this volume, within the limits of our own professional experiences, to stretch the understanding of what the sociology of sport comprises by including new ideas and perspectives along with those that are widely recognized and discussed.

10   Dahrendorf's (1959) point was that the new middle class of the twentieth century had consisted of white-collar workers and bureaucrats, differentiated groups with few, if any, common interests.

11   Towards the end of the nineteenth century, German academics became sharply divided over the status of the 'human' or 'social sciences'. The 'positivists' in this debate (for example, the psychologist Wundt) argued that the social sciences can use the same methods as the natural sciences, whilst the 'historicists' (for example, the philosophers Dilthey, Rickert and Windelband) argued that the human 'mind' or *Geist* (spirit) constitutes an autonomous sphere of reality which is not subject to law-like regularities similar to those which are studied by the natural sciences. It is reasonable to hypothesize that, like Weber, Comte would not have identified with either side in this dispute but would have sought a higher level resolution. What is certain, though, is that the main 'positive' method recommended for sociology by Comte was the method of historical comparison (see Andreski, 1974: 192ff).

12   It is clear that Mertonian functionalism did not encounter these difficulties to the same extent, except perhaps in relation to power.

13   This fact is not apparent in the volume edited by Lüschen and Sage.

14   According to Anthony Giddens, 'the social sciences are lost if they are not directly related to philosophical problems by those who practise them' (1984: xvii). For Elias, by contrast, Western philosophy has been locked at least since Descartes and Kant in what he (Elias) called *homo clausus* modes of thinking which are not conducive to the advancement of knowledge about human beings and human societies. For a discussion of this complex issue, see Elias (1978).

15   The Reverend Thomas Malthus's *Essay on Population* (1798), in which he pessimistically argued that population growth will always outstrip food supply, constituted an exception in this context.

16   See Durkheim (1952) for his arguments, and see Gerth and Mills (1946, especially p. 139ff) for a discussion of Weber's theory of 'disenchantment'. Weber took this term from poet and playwright Friedrich Schiller.

17   German-born Franz Boas (1858–1942) was Professor of Anthropology at Columbia University, New York, from 1899 to 1936. Probably the most famous of his students were Margaret Mead and Ruth Benedict. Whilst accepting the reality of biological evolution, Boas and his followers denied the reality of its socio-cultural equivalents, that is, social or cultural 'evolution' or 'development'.

18   For a clear and insightful sociological diagnosis of the relationships between sociology and philosophy, see Kilminster (1998).

19   Already in the 1950s, C. Wright Mills (1959) developed a sharp critique of what he called 'grand theory'. Around the same time, R.K. Merton (1957) argued for 'theories of the middle range'. Somewhat later, Barney Glaser and Anselm Strauss in lectures and private discussions suggested that sociology needed 'grounded theories'. Norbert Elias's favoured term in this connection was 'central theory' of which he considered his own theory of civilizing processes to be an exemplar.

REFERENCES

Albonico, R. and Pfister-Binz, K. (eds) (1972) *Sociology of Sport: Theoretical Foundations and Research Methods [Soziologie des Sports: Theoretische und Methodologische Grundlagen].* Basle: Magglinger Symposium.

Andreski, S. (ed.) (1974) *The Essential Comte.* London: Croom Helm.

Beckford, P. (1796) *Thoughts on Hare and Foxhunting.* London.

Birrell, S. and Cole, C. (eds) (1994) *Women, Sport, and Culture.* Champaign, IL: Human Kinetics.

Bryant, J. and McElroy, M. (1997) *Sociological Dynamics of Sport and Exercise.* Englewood, CO: Morton.

Cashmore, E. (1996) *Making Sense of Sport,* 2nd edn. London: Routledge.

Coakley, J. (1978) *Sport in Society: Issues and Controversies.* St Louis, MO: CV Mosby.

Coakley, J. (1998) *Sport in Society: Issues and Controversies,* 6th edn. New York: McGraw–Hill.

Coakley, J. and Donnelly, P. (eds) (1999) *Inside Sports*. London: Routledge.

Coser, L. (1971) *Masters of Sociological Thought*. New York: Harcourt, Brace, Jovanovich.

Dahrendorf, R. (1959) *Class and Class Conflict in Industrial Society*. Palo Alto, CA: Stanford University Press.

Donnelly, P. (1996) 'The local and the global: globalization in the sociology of sport', *Journal of Sport and Social Issues*, 20 (3): 239–57.

Donnelly, P. (ed.) (1997) *Taking Sport Seriously*. Toronto, ON: Thompson Educational.

Dunning, E. (1961) 'Early stages in the development of football as an organized game: an account of some of the sociological problems in the development of a game'. MA thesis, University of Leicester.

Dunning, E. (1971) *The Sociology of Sport: a Selection of Readings*. London: Cass.

Durkheim, E. (1952) *Suicide: a Problem in Sociology*. London: Routledge & Kegan Paul.

Edwards, H. (1973) *The Sociology of Sport*. Homewood, IL: Dorsey Press.

Egan, P. (1812) *Boxiana*. London: Sherwood.

Eitzen, D.S. (ed.) (1996) *Sport in Contemporary Society*, 5th edn. New York: St Martin's Press.

Eitzen, D.S. and Sage, G.H. (1978) *Sociology of American Sport*. Dubuque, IA: Wm. C. Brown.

Eitzen, D.S. and Sage, G.H. (1997) *Sociology of North American Sport*. Madison, WI: Brown & Benchmark.

Elias, N. (1978) *What is Sociology?* London: Hutchinson.

Elias, N. (1996) *The Germans: Power Struggles and the Development of Habitus in the Nineteenth and Twentieth Centuries* (edited by Michael Schröter & translated from the German by Eric Dunning and Stephen Mennell). Cambridge: Polity Press.

Elias, N. and Dunning, E. (1986) *Quest for Excitement: Sport and Leisure in the Civilizing Process*. Oxford: Basil Blackwell.

Figler, S.K. and Whitaker, G. (1991) *Sport and Play in American Life*, 2nd edn. Dubuque, IA: Wm. C. Brown.

Gerth, H. and Mills, C.W. (eds) (1946) *From Max Weber*. New York: Oxford University Press.

Giddens, A. (1961) 'Sport and society in contemporary England', MA thesis, London School Economics.

Giddens, A. (1971) *Capitalism and Modern Social Theory*. Cambridge: Cambridge University Press.

Giddens, A. (1984) *The Constitution of Society: Outline of the Theory of Structuration*. Cambridge: Polity Press.

Glaser, B. and Strauss, A. (1967) *Grounded Theory: Strategies for Qualitative research*. Chicago, IL: Aldine.

Guttmann, A. (1978) *From Ritual to Record*. New York: Columbia University Press.

Hall, M.A. (1996) *Feminism and Sporting Bodies: Essays on Theory and Practice*. Champaign, IL: Human Kinetics.

Hall, M.A., Slack, T., Smith, G. and Whitson, D. (1991) *Sport in Canadian Society*. Toronto, ON: McClelland & Stewart.

Hammerich, K. and Heinemann, K. (eds) (1975) *Texte zur Soziologie des Sports*. Schorndorf: Hoffman.

Hargreaves, J. (1994) *Sporting Females: Critical Issues in the History and Sociology of Women's Sports*. London: Routledge.

Hart, M. and Birrell, S. (eds) (1981) *Sport in the Sociocultural Process*, 3rd edn. Dubuque, IA: Wm. C. Brown.

Harvey, J. and Cantelon, H. (eds) (1988) *Not Just a Game: Essays in Canadian Sport Sociology*. Ottawa, ON: University of Ottawa Press.

Horne, J., Jary, D. and Tomlinson, A. (eds) (1987) *Sport, Leisure and Social Relations*. London: Routledge & Kegan Paul (Sociological Review Monograph 33).

Horne, J., Tomlinson, A. and Whannel, G. (1999) *Understanding Sport: an Introduction to the Sociological and Cultural Analysis of Sport*. London: E&FN Spon.

Ingham, A. and Donnelly, P. (1997) 'A sociology of North American sport: disunity in unity, 1965–1996', *Sociology of Sport Journal*, 14 (4): 362–418.

Kenyon, G. (ed.) (1969) *Aspects of Contemporary Sport Sociology*. North Palm Beach, FL: The Athletic Institute.

Kidd, B. (1991) 'How do we find our voices in the "new world order"'? A commentary on Americanization. *Sociology of Sport Journal*, 8 (2): 178–84.

Kilminster, R. (1998) *The Sociological Revolution*. London: Routledge.

Klein, A. (1993) *Little Big Man: Bodybuilding Subculture and Gender Construction*. Albany, NY: State University of New York Press.

Lawrence, G. and Rowe, D. (eds) (1986) *Power Play: Essays in the Sociology of Australian Sport*. Sydney: Hale & Iremonger.

Lemert, C. (1995) *Sociology after the Crisis*. Boulder, CO: Westview Press.

Leonard, W.M. II (1998) *A Sociological Perspective of Sport*, 5th edn. Boston, MA: Allyn and Bacon.

Loy, J. (1968) 'The nature of sport: a definitional effort', *Quest* 10 (May): 1–15.

Loy, J. and Booth, D. (in press) 'Emile Durkheim', in J. Maguire and K. Young (eds), *Research in the Sociology of Sport (Vol. 1): Perspectives in the Sociology of Sport*. London: JAI Press and Ablex Publishing Ltd.

Loy, J.W. and Kenyon, G.S. (eds) (1969) *Sport, Culture and Society*. New York, NY: Macmillan.

Lüschen, G. (1966) *Kleingruppenforschung und Gruppe im Sport*. Cologne: Westdeutscher Verlag.

Lüschen, G. (1967) 'The interdependence of sport and culture', *International Review of Sport Sociology*, 2: 127–39.

Lüschen, G. (ed.) (1970) *The Cross-Cultural Analysis of Sport and Games*. Champaign, IL: Stipes.

Lüschen, G. and Sage, G. (eds) (1981) *Handbook of Social Science of Sport*. Champaign, IL: Stipes.

Lüschen, G. and Weis, K. (eds) (1976) *Die Soziologie des Sports*. Darmstadt: Luchterhand.

Magnane, G. (1964) *Sociologie du Sport*. Paris: Gallimard.

Maguire, J. (1994) 'Sport, identity politics, and globalization: diminishing contrasts and increasing varieties', *Sociology of Sport Journal*, 11 (4): 398–427.

Maguire, J. (1999) *Global Sport: Identities, Societies, Civilizations*. Cambridge: Polity Press.

McIntosh, P. (1960) *Sport in Society*. London: Watts.

McPherson, B.D., Curtis, J.E. and Loy, J.W. (1989) *The Social Significance of Sport: an Introduction to the Sociology of Sport*. Champaign, IL: Human Kinetics.

Merton, R.K. (1957) *Social Theory and Social Structure*. New York: The Free Press.

Messner, M.A. (1992) *Power at Play: Sports and the Problem of Masculinity*. Boston, MA: Beacon Press.

Messner, M.A. and Sabo, D.F. (eds) (1990) *Sport, Men, and the Gender Order: Critical Feminist Perspectives*. Champaign, IL: Human Kinetics.

Messner, M.A. and Sabo, D.F. (eds) (1994) *Sex, Violence and Power in Sports: Rethinking Masculinity*. Freedom, CA: The Crossing Press.

Mills, C. Wright (1959) *The Sociological Imagination*. New York: Oxford University Press.

Nixon, H.L. II and Frey, J.H. (1996) *A Sociology of Sport*. Belmont, CA: Wadsworth Publishing Company.

Parsons, T. (1937) *The Structure of Social Action*. New York: The Free Press.

Parsons, T. (1951) *The Social System*. Glencoe, IL: The Free Press.

Phillips, J.C. (1993) *Sociology of Sport*. Boston, MA: Allyn and Bacon.

Rail, G. (ed.) (1998) *Sport and Postmodern Times*. Albany, NY: State University Press of New York.

Rigauer, B. (1969) *Sport und Arbeit*. Frankfurt: Suhrkamp Verlag (trans. A. Guttmann (1981) *Sport and Work*). New York: Columbia University Press).

Risman, B. and Tomaskovic-Devey, D. (eds) (1999) 'Symposia – Values, politics, and science: the influence of social movements on sociology', *Contemporary Sociology: a Journal of Reviews*, 28 (3): 255–88.

Risse, H. (1921) *Soziologie des Sports*. Berlin: Reher.

Rowe, D., McKay, J. and Lawrence, G. (1997) 'Out of the shadows: the critical sociology of sport in Australia, 1986–1996', *Sociology of Sport Journal*, 14 (4): 340–61.

Sage, G.H. (ed.) (1980) *Sport and American Society: Selected Readings*, 3rd edn. Reading, MA: Addison-Wesley Publishing Company.

Shearman, M. (1887) *Football: Its History for Five Centuries*. London: Longmans.

Shearman, M. (1889) *Athletics and Football*. London: Longmans.

Snyder, E.E. and Spreitzer, E. (1978) *Social Aspects of Sport*. Englewood Cliffs, NJ: Prentice-Hall.

Stone, G. (1955) 'American sports – play and display', *Chicago Review* 9 (Fall): 83–100.

Sumner, W.G. (1906) *Folkways: a Study of the Sociological Importance of Usages, Manners, Customs, Mores, and Morals*. Boston, MA: Ginn.

Tong, R. (1998) *Feminist Thought: a More Comprehensive Introduction*, 2nd edn. Boulder, CO: Westview Press.

Veblen, T. (1899) *The Theory of the Leisure Class*. New York, NY: Macmillan.

Vogler, C.C. and Schwartz, S.E. (1993) *The Sociology of Sport: an Introduction*. Englewood Cliffs, NJ: Prentice-Hall.

Waller, W. (1932) *The Sociology of Teaching*. New York: John Wiley & Sons.

Weber, M. (1958) *The Protestant Ethic and the Spirit of Capitalism* (translated by Talcott Parsons). New York: Charles Scribners.

Wouters, C. (1986) 'Formalization and informalization: changing tension-balances in civilizing processes', *Theory, Culture and Society*, 3 (2): 1–18.

Yiannakis, A., McIntyre, T. and Melnick, M. (eds) (1993) *Sport Sociology: Contemporary Themes*, 4th edn. Dubuque, IA: Kendall/Hunt.

PART ONE

MAJOR PERSPECTIVES IN THE SOCIOLOGY OF SPORT

EDITORS' INTRODUCTION

In the General Introduction, we introduced the reader to the currently divided and multi-paradigmatic character of sociology in general and the sociology of sport in particular. This in many ways fruitful but not in all respects satisfactory state of affairs is illustrated in the present section by means of a series of 'state-of-the-art' summaries by leading scholars of:

1 what seven of these competing paradigms/perspectives entail;
2 how the different paradigms have been used sociologically to illuminate aspects of sport;
3 how their advocates view and characterize work in paradigms other than their own and which they often perceive, or at least publicly represent, as inferior rivals.

The seven paradigms, some of them overlapping to a certain degree, are: functionalism, Marxism, cultural studies, feminism, interpretive sociology, figurational sociology and post-structuralism.

CHAPTER OVERVIEWS

Part one opens with 'Functionalism, Sport and Society' by John W. Loy and Douglas Booth, both from the University of Otago, New Zealand. Functionalist theories, they suggest, are holistic, that is, concerned with societies as 'systems' or 'wholes'. They have their roots in the use of organic analogies by pioneering sociologists such as Comte, Spencer and Durkheim. However, Loy and Booth note that functionalist theories do not constitute a single, undifferentiated category. That is, there are *different types* of functionalism, and in order to make sense of them, Loy and Booth opt for Abrahamson's (1978) distinction between 'individualistic', 'interpersonal' and 'societal'

types: the first involves explanation by reference to the socio-cultural satisfaction of individual needs, the second by reference to recurring relationships, and the third by reference to the meeting of 'system needs'.[1] Towards the end of their chapter, Loy and Booth discuss the emergence of a fourth type, 'neofunctionalism', a type which emerged in the 1980s and 1990s as part of what has sometimes been referred to as 'the functionalist revival'.

Taking care to provide judicious illustrations from the sociology of sport, Loy and Booth undertake an original, insightful, thorough and scholarly survey of their field. Functionalism, they suggest, gave the early sociologists of sport 'a powerful weapon' to counter charges that they were engaging in a 'trivial scholarly pursuit'. More particularly, functional theories guided them towards the investigation of the relationships between sport and institutions of acknowledged importance such as the economy, the polity and education, in that way helping to confer legitimacy and a degree of prestige on the fledgling field. Loy and Booth go on to suggest that early North American work in the sociology of sport was characterized by 'instrumental positivism', that is, it involved an emphasis on 'value-freedom, objective measurement and statistical data'. However, they are not so sure whether instrumental positivism was as closely connected with structural-functionalism as has sometimes been alleged, and they plausibly – and provocatively! – identify functionalist elements even in the writings of anti-functionalist sociologists such as Elias and Dunning. (On this, see also Chapter 6 by Murphy et al.) This is an argument which points to elements of common ground and possible synthesis between paradigms which their advocates see as contradictory. As such, it deserves to be taken seriously.[2]

The second chapter is on 'Marxist Theories' and is written by German sociologist Bero Rigauer. Rigauer was a student of Theodor Adorno at the University of Frankfurt, and his early work was in the tradition of 'critical theory', that is, the philosophical Marxism of the 'Frankfurt School'. More recently, Rigauer has been trying to synthesize aspects of critical theory and figurational sociology. (It is perhaps worth noting parenthetically that the roots of the latter lay partly in the Sociology Department at the University of Frankfurt where Norbert Elias was Assistant to Karl Mannheim, the founder of the sociology of knowledge. Although they shared the same building – often referred to as the *'Marxburg'* – the Sociology Department was separate from the Institute for Social Research.)

'Marxism', suggests Rigauer, is a complex, differentiated and multidisciplinary approach to human societies which incorporates philosophical, anthropological, historical and economic as well as sociological elements. It is also susceptible to a variety of interpretations, some more scientific, others more ideological. It is Rigauer's contention that a distinction has to be drawn between Marx's own work, which Rigauer calls 'Marxian', and the use and interpretation of Marx's theories by others which he labels 'Marxism'. Further to this it is necessary, Rigauer suggests, to distinguish between Marxism as a 'distinctive political ideology' and academic/scientific interpretations of Marx.

Rigauer shows how, as Marx himself intended, the political/ideological use and interpretation of his theory preceded its academic/scientific use. More particularly it was used before the First World War by members of left-wing/working-class political parties. Political/ideological elements continue to colour even the academic/scientific interpretations of Marx and Marxism but they were at their strongest and most dogmatic, Rigauer notes, in the former Soviet Union and its 'satellites' where Marxism, or more correctly 'Marxism–Leninism', became a kind of secular religion which was propagated by the state as a body of supposedly proven knowledge. This had deleterious consequences for the development of sociology in those countries, including for the sociology of sport. It implied, for example, the state diktat that sport could only be used for the pursuit of such collective goals as the socialization of people into a 'socialist personality'. A critical attitude

towards 'bourgeois' sport-forms was also demanded but, given the dominance of the latter in the world at large, this was necessarily ambivalent and many aspects of these 'bourgeois' forms were adopted in order to facilitate effective competition with the countries of the 'decadent' West.

Rigauer ends by discussing academic/scientific (and mainly Western) interpretations of Marx and Marxism under the headings of 'reproduction theory', 'critical theory' and 'hegemony theory' (that is, work based on Antonio Gramsci's interpretation – revision? – of Marx).[3] He concludes that hegemony theory has been the most fruitful of these approaches but suggests that there is considerable scope for further development within the Marxist sociology of sport more generally. This will be most effectively realized, Rigauer suggests, through the adoption by Marxist sociologists of an open-minded and non-dogmatic attitude towards other paradigms. If such an attitude is reciprocated by the advocates of non-Marxist approaches, a sociological synthesis will be more quickly arrived at.

The third chapter in this section – 'Cultural Studies and the Sociology of Sport' by Jennifer Hargreaves and Ian McDonald – is also concerned with a perspective influenced by Marxism, in this case the hegemony theory of Antonio Gramsci. Cultural studies, Hargreaves and McDonald maintain, is difficult to anchor within the corpus of sociological traditions because 'it is cross-disciplinary in nature, drawing on such diverse academic discourses as communication studies, film theory, history, literacy criticism, philosophy, politics and semiology, as well as sociology'. It originated, they note, in England, especially at the Centre for Contemporary Cultural Studies (CCCS), which was founded at the University of Birmingham in 1964. Besides Gramsci, it includes among its founding figures Richard Hoggart, Raymond Williams, E.P. Thompson and later, Stuart Hall. According to Hargreaves and McDonald, up until the intervention of these scholars, the term 'culture' had been predominantly understood as synonymous with 'high' culture, a definition which contributed to making the study of sport a low-status academic endeavour.[4] From a cultural studies standpoint, however, 'culture' came to mean all the ways in which people think, feel and act, in that way legitimizing sport as 'culture' and the academic study of it. As Hargreaves and McDonald tell us, these scholars also 'pointed towards a form of intellectual engagement that was openly interventionist'.

It was Gramsci, however, who was the main source of inspiration for 'cultural studies'. As Hargreaves and McDonald express it, he rejected Marxist 'economism' and the crude positing by 'economistic' Marxists of culture 'as a mere reflection of the economic base'. Such an approach, they imply, is too deterministic, so Gramsci opted instead for a view of history as actively produced by individuals and groups yet under determinate conditions. His key concept was that of 'hegemony', that is, the establishment of political and cultural leadership by a dominant group or class. According to Hargreaves and McDonald, hegemony is 'a tool for explaining how ideas and practices which seem against the interests of subordinate groups are believed in and carried out by them so as to become "commonsense"'. As Gramsci conceived it, the achievement of hegemony is an unstable process in which control is not simply imposed but based on 'the winning of consent from subordinate groups'. A dialectical understanding of the relationship between individuals and societies is involved which, as Hargreaves and McDonald put it, 'allows for cultural experiences such as sports to be understood as both exploitative and worthwhile'. Through this perspective, sport is perceived as 'an aspect of culture embodying struggle and contestation' and the focus is on 'the processes through which cultural practices and the ideologies and beliefs underlying those practices are created, reproduced, and changed through human agency and interaction'.

Hargreaves and McDonald provide lucid summaries of the major work on sport carried out from a cultural studies perspective in Britain and the United States. They show how, in the 1980s and 1990s, this work was subjected to a searching feminist critique, an intervention which, as Hargreaves and McDonald express it, 're-enlivened the politicization of theory' and played an important part in leading increasing attention to be paid to such categories as race, age, disability and sexuality as well as class and gender in cultural studies research on sport. Nevertheless, Hargreaves and McDonald contend, an unreflecting male dominance continues to characterize the field, and women's contributions are neither adequately recognized nor adequately integrated into the field overall. Hargreaves and McDonald conclude their chapter by discussing what they call the 'paradigm wars'. In that context, they respond to criticisms of cultural studies work on sport offered by writers such as Rojek, Dunning, MacAloon, Jarvie and Maguire, and Loy and Andrews.

Hargreaves and McDonald's provocative chapter is followed by 'Feminist Theories for Sport', a scholarly yet engaged account by Susan Birrell of the University of Iowa of sociological work on sport and gender. Birrell starts by stating that the main purpose behind feminist theories in the sociology of sport is to 'theorize about gender relations within our patriarchal society as they are evidenced by, played out in, and reproduced through sport and other body practices'. According to Birrell, all feminists share the assumption that human societies are 'patriarchal', that is, ruled by men, and that women are oppressed in patriarchal contexts. Feminist theory, Birrell suggests, is a 'self-reflexive theoretical practice' and, accordingly, open to criticism from outsiders as well as insiders. Birrell begins by discussing 'the view from outside'.

It is Birrell's contention that 'outsider' criticisms of feminist theories tend to be conservative and founded in a belief that the differences between men and women are either 'divinely ordained' or 'genetically determined'. The protagonists of such beliefs tend to view sport as a 'masculine activity' which is 'not meant for women'. As an example, Birrell cites a 1986 essay by Australian John Carroll in which it is asserted that 'women spoil sport' and 'sport spoils women'. Other critics have labelled feminist theories as 'pseudo-science' and Birrell notes that it has even been argued that the balance of power between the sexes has recently shifted so much in favour of women that it is now men who are the oppressed and exploited sex!

As far as feminist theories of sport *per se* are concerned, Birrell shows how these have developed through three broad but overlapping stages: a stage involving an atheoretical focus on 'women in sport'; a stage involving a self-conscious search for theoretical homes; and finally a stage influenced by postmodernist conceptions.

The first, atheoretical stage lasted from the mid-1960s to the late 1970s and, in it, research was dominated by a focus on psychological topics. Sociologically, most attention was devoted to sex role socialization in and through sport. Above all, as Birrell succinctly puts it, at this stage gender was 'conceived of as a variable or distributive category rather than as a set of relations sustained through human agency and cultural practice'.

The second stage identified by Birrell took place primarily in the 1980s and principally involved theorizing in terms of what she calls the *ur* or 'originating categories' (*ur* is a

German prefix meaning 'age-old', 'primitive' or 'originating'), namely 'liberal feminism' and 'radical feminism'. 'Liberal feminism' is a humanist perspective which involves a stress on securing equality for women within the context of an overall social structure and structure of sporting organization which remain unchanged. 'Radical feminism' is revolutionary and based on the idea that, in order to secure a more equitable integration of females into sport and society at large, patriarchal structures will have to be dismantled.

Birrell goes on to show how liberal and radical feminist theories stressed gender to the exclusion of other categories of differentiation such as class, age, race and sexual orientation. It was in an attempt to develop more all-inclusive theories, she suggests, that the synthesizing theories of 'Marxist feminism' and 'socialist feminism' were constructed. The former saw class as the primary category of social differentiation, exclusion and oppression; the latter was more open-ended and involved a focus on the 'interacting impacts of gender, class and race'.

According to Birrell, the third stage in the development of feminist theories of sport took place in the 1990s. It depended, as she puts it, on the 'emergence of cultural studies as the dominant paradigm for feminist analysis in the 80s' (see Chapter 3 by Hargreaves and McDonald). More particularly, cultural studies served, says Birrell, as a bridge to 'more inter-disciplinary, postmodern sensibilities'; that is, it took sociology and the sociology of sport 'beyond the boundaries of social science into the relatively unbounded territory occupied by Lacan, Derrida, Foucault and Gramsci where the languages spoken include discourse analysis, hegemony theory, post-structuralism, deconstruction and postmodernism' (see the chapter by David Andrews). Finally, Susan Birrell examines 'queer theory' and what she calls the 'transgender challenge', paying attention to their implications for the sociological theorization of sport.

In his erudite chapter on the use of 'interpretive sociology' in the sociology of sport, Canada-based, British-born sociologist Peter Donnelly of the University of Toronto begins by noting that his chapter title refers to 'a particular group of sociologies which have as their basis the interpretation and understanding of human meaning and action'. Included under this rubric are: Weberian sociology, symbolic interactionism, dramaturgical sociology, phenomenological sociology, ethnomethodology and existential sociology. These are all approaches to the subject, Donnelly tells us, which use methods akin to those of anthropology, namely ethnography and in-depth interviewing. In sum, whatever differences there may be between them, these approaches all share in common a concern with 'the way in which the social world is not just something to be confronted by individuals, but is continually constructed and reinvented by the participants'.

Donnelly then goes on to note that the forms of interpretive sociology that have been most prominently used in the sociology of sport are symbolic interactionism and dramaturgical sociology,[5] approaches that grew partly out of the Chicago School of urban sociology that flourished between the two World Wars, and partly out of the influence on Chicago sociology in that period of philosopher George Herbert Mead. However, it is only fairly recently that these approaches have begun to have a major impact on the sociology of sport and Donnelly singles out for special mention in this connection the work of Charles Page, Gregory Stone, John Loy and Donald Ball. According to Donnelly, other influences on interpretive studies work in the sociology of sport include Birmingham University's CCCS (see Chapter 3 by Hargreaves and McDonald), anthropologist Clifford Geertz and French sociologist Pierre Bourdieu and his students.

Donnelly next proceeds to examine the major criticisms that have been levelled at the interpretive sociologies, for example, the alleged tendency towards extreme relativism in the work of their advocates, the subjectivity/lack of objectivity of the latter, their tendency 'to go native', that is, to over-identify with their subjects, and the 'journalistic' character of much of their work. After that, in his balanced account Donnelly examines the responses of interpretivists and their defenders, for example, Manford Kuhn of the University of Iowa's quantification of symbolic interactionism and Anthony Giddens's elaboration of the key differences between 'natural facts' and 'social facts', for example, that, 'whilst atoms cannot get to know what scientists say about them, human beings can and do, thus implying that the relations between sociologists and their subjects are necessarily different from those between natural scientists and theirs'.

After reviewing interpretive work dealing with the analysis of media texts, Donnelly turns to research into the related issues of sport subcultures and socialization into sports and through them. As far as the study of sport subcultures is concerned, he shows how changes occurred in the 1980s as a result, first, of the application of Geertz's method of 'thick description' and, secondly, of the influence of British subculture theory which became more radical and critical in that decade. Donnelly goes on to note that, although a concern with sport and socialization has been a focus since the early days of the sociology of sport, the initial work tended to be quantitative in character and that it is only since those involved in the interpretive sociology of sport have turned their attention to socialization that a number of rich insights have been made into the process'. As Donnelly graphically and perceptively expresses it, 'perhaps the major impact of interpretive sociology has been the way in which it hangs flesh on the skeletons of survey data'.

The sixth chapter in this 'Major Perspectives' section is 'Figurational Sociology and its Application to Sport' by British sociologists Patrick Murphy, Ken Sheard and Ivan Waddington of the University of Leicester. They begin by noting that 'figurational' or 'process sociology' has grown out of the foundational work of Norbert Elias and that its key concept is that of 'figurations', that is, structures or networks of 'mutually oriented and dependent people'. Elias adapted the term, they tell us, on account of its dynamic and relational properties, and they go on to add that a central aspect of any figuration according to Elias is power, 'conceptualized not as a substance or property possessed by particular individuals and groups but as a characteristic of all human relationships'. According to Elias, in other words, power is a question of relative and relatively fluid balances or 'power-ratios'. Further to this, Murphy, Sheard and Waddington note that Elias was critical of many standard conceptual distinctions, such as those between 'truth' and 'falsehood', 'subjectivity' and 'objectivity', 'bias' and 'value-freedom/value-neutrality', suggesting that they are better formulated not as dichotomies, but in terms of continua, balances and degrees. It follows from this that, according to Elias, the task of sociology (as of any science) should be, not to search for '*the* truth' but to add to the existing 'social fund of knowledge' understandings and explanations which are *more* 'object-adequate' or *more* 'reality-congruent' than those which were previously available.

Murphy, Sheard and Waddington next provide a lucid and succinct exposition of Elias's now increasingly well-known theory of 'civilizing processes', pointing out how Elias uses this term in a technical, non-evaluative way. They note in this connection how a process that is of central relevance for understanding the development of specifically modern forms of sport has been a change in the societies of Western Europe since their Middle Ages in the direction of a 'taming of peoples' conscious desire and capacity for obtaining pleasure from attacking others'. Murphy, Sheard and Waddington go on to describe Elias's hypothesis that modern sport-forms first began to emerge in England in the eighteenth century on account of the correlative occurrence of what he called 'the parliamentarization of political conflict' and 'the sportization of pastimes', a 'civilizing spurt' in the habitus of England's ruling groups which was manifested in both their political and their leisure lives.

The 'Leicester trio' next go on to discuss Elias and Dunning's early work on the development of football and Dunning and Sheard's work on the development of rugby. After that, they provide an account of 'the Leicester School's' work on football hooliganism, going on to discuss the contributions of Jarvie and Maguire to the figurational 'oeuvre', paying special attention in this connection to Maguire's ground-breaking work on sport and globalization (see Chapter 23). Murphy, Sheard and Waddington conclude their chapter by summarizing the responses to the major criticisms of figurational sociology which have so far been advanced.

The final chapter in this section is 'Posting up: French Post-structuralism and the Critical Analysis of Contemporary Sporting Culture' by American-based British scholar David Andrews of the University of Memphis. Post-structuralism, Andrews informs us – it is a term that he prefers to the more trendy 'postmodernism' – 'emerged as a loosely aligned series of philosophical, political and theoretical rejoinders to the unrest and turbulence that engulfed modernizing France during the late 1960s and early 1970s'. It has since become, he argues, 'a constituent feature of contemporary intellectual life'. Despite this, according to Andrews, until relatively recently it 'has been received with a perplexing mixture of defensive dismissal and haughty disdain by large sections of the sociology of sport community'. Andrew's lucid account will hopefully help members of this 'community' to decide for themselves whether there is much of enduring value in the works of the post-structuralists.

Borrowing from Featherstone (1985), Andrews tells us that 'post-structuralism ... allows us to expose *the dark side* of sporting modernity by challenging the ethos of rational human progress embodied by – and within – modern sport culture'. According to Andrews, it (post-structuralism) is the third in a sequence of philosophies – the first two were existentialism and structuralism – which emerged in France after the Second World War as 'important epistemological and ontological challenges to the modern hegemony of the liberal humanist subject which uncritically placed "man [sic] at the centre of history" and made "him the privileged creator of meaning"'. More particularly, structuralism emerged as a reaction to existentialism's unscientific subjectivism, that is, its value-laden stress on individual freedom, and both it and post-structuralism made heavy use of the structural linguistics of the Swiss semiologist of the turn of the last century, Ferdinand de Saussure. It is this which has led some commentators to depict structuralism and post-structuralism as having emerged as part of a 'linguistic turn'. It is generally agreed, though, that post-structuralism emerged at a specific historical conjuncture, more particularly in May 1968 when there took place in France a revolt against the regime of President de Gaulle which was perceived as repressive and bureaucratic. It started in the universities and spread on to the streets of Paris before being defeated. It was in that context that it became clear to thinkers on the left that the socialist future they believed in was not going to arrive automatically and that the denial of individual agency in the writings of structuralist authors such as the anthropologist Lévi-Strauss, and the structural Marxist Althusser, had gone too far. As Andrews puts it, 'the events of May 1968 demonstrated the contingent and constructed nature of knowledge and its manifestations within institutions and expressions of power'. It was in that highly politicized climate, Andrews notes, that structuralism came to be viewed on the left as involving 'virtual intellectual capitulation' to the prevailing order. From that point on, the term 'post-structuralism' began increasingly to be applied to the work of a loose collection of left-intellectuals who strove, as they saw it, to generate 'politically subversive knowledge' centred on 'identifying and nurturing difference, disunity and disorder within the oppressive formations of [French] modernity'.

In his chapter, David Andrews concentrates on the work of Derrida, Foucault and Baudrillard as examples of the post-structuralist *genre*. More particularly, he seeks, as he puts it, to demonstrate the relevance of 'Derrida's grammatology for deconstructing the philosophical foundations of sporting modernity; Foucault's genealogy for excavating sport's status and influence as a modern disciplinary institution; and Baudrillard's hyperreal cosmology for mapping sport's immersion within new regimes of representation'. Although, like those of Derrida, Foucault and Baudrillard, the language and concepts that David Andrews employs are often abstract, obtuse and not always adequately explained to the reader, it is our view that his lively, scholarly and original chapter will repay close and careful study.

NOTES

1   It is also common practice to distinguish between 'normative functionalism' and 'general functionalism'. The former term applies to the functional theory of Talcott Parsons, with its stress on social integration *via* value-consensus. The latter applies to the functional theory of Robert Merton which involves no such mono-causal stress.

2   Loy and Booth are mistaken in identifying Comte as a positivist in the modern sense. As we noted in the General Introduction, Comte coined the term 'sociology' in opposition to the statistical 'social physics' of Quetelet, and suggested that the historical comparative method is the one best suited to the study of human societies, the most complex and rapidly changing of all humanly known phenomena.

3   John Hargreaves also distinguishes between three Marxist approaches to the sociological study of sport, namely 'correspondence theory', 'representation theory' and 'hegemony theory' (John Hargreaves (1982) 'Sport and hegemony: some theoretical problems', in Hart Cantelon and Richard Gruneau (eds), *Sport, Culture and the Modern State*, Toronto, University of Toronto Press). From Hargreaves's standpoint, it seems that Rigauer conflates the 'correspondence theory' and 'reproduction theory' categories, though Rigauer's classification is arguably superior because it is difficult to see where 'critical theory' fits into Hargreaves's scheme.

4   Jennifer Hargreaves and Ian McDonald do not explain that the term 'culture' was used in a general and non-evaluative sense by American anthropologists long before its usage in that way by the authors whom they cite. Interestingly, one of those authors – Raymond Williams – had a sophisticated awareness of the term's history. See his *Keywords* (1988), London, Fontana, pp. 87–93.

5 The distinction between 'symbolic interactionism' and 'dramaturgical sociology' is not one that is always drawn. That is to say, the dramaturgical approach that Erving Goffman first introduced in *The Presentation of Self in Everyday Life* (Reading, Mass: Cox and Wyman, 1959) is often included under the rubric of symbolic interactionism and not as a separate sociological approach.

1

FUNCTIONALISM, SPORT AND SOCIETY

John W. Loy and Douglas Booth

One of the oldest theoretical traditions in anthropology and sociology is functionalism, also called 'functional analysis', 'the functional approach', 'functional orientation', 'functional theory', and 'structural-functionalism' (Zeitlin, 1973: 3). The functionalist paradigm once dominated general sociology; however, we reject the view that functionalism – while influential – ever achieved the status of a dominant paradigm in sport sociology.

The roots of functionalism in modern sociology can be traced back to the nineteenth-century work of Auguste Comte, the founding father of, and the first to use the term, sociology. Functionalism reached its zenith in general sociology shortly after the Second World War. But, as Ritzer (1988: 58) notes, 'the 1940s and 1950s were paradoxically the years of greatest dominance and the beginnings of decline of structural-functionalism.' Just 'as it was gaining theoretical hegemony, structural-functionalism came under attack, and the attacks mounted until they reached a crescendo in the 1960s and 1970s' (p. 59). Ironically, structural-functionalism gained its strongest foothold within the sociology of sport when it was under its heaviest attack within the ranks of general sociology. For example, Jarvie and Maguire (1994: 5) contend that 'during the late 1960s and early 1970s it played a key part in the early development of the sociology of sport in North America and on both sides of what was then the European "iron curtain".'

The criticisms of structural-functionalism were so many, so prolonged and so devastating that many sport sociologists, like many sociologists in general, tend 'to believe that everything worth saying about functionalism has already been said, and to express that view in a way that implies that functionalism is as dead as a dodo' (Barnes, 1995: 37). On the other hand, there are good reasons for reconsidering functionalism. Barnes (1995: 37) makes the case:

> whatever is worth saying about functionalism bears repeating, for it is the most misunderstood and misused of social theories. And it remains in any case clearly alive; in the work, for example, of Luhmann and Habermas. Moreover, functionalist forms of thought have penetrated so deeply into the culture of the social sciences that they are often employed without being explicitly recognized as such, so that an understanding of their strength and weaknesses remains necessary even if they are no longer as widely advocated and defended as once they were.

Certainly it is worth while re-examining the functionalist perspective within the sociology of sport, as its principles and assumptions continually reappear. This is especially true of studies that focus on sport as a means of social integration or as a site of social conflict. And like mainstream sociology, these functionalist tenets found within sport sociology are rarely spelled out.

Accordingly, we offer a re-examination of functionalism. We first outline the central assumptions, main forms and major formalizations of functionalism. Secondly, we review functionalism's key contributions to the sociology of sport. We then discuss the chief criticisms of functionalism and highlight the major controversies surrounding functionalism in the sociology of sport. We conclude with an overview of new forms of functionalism and their implications for the sociology of sport.

THE FUNCTIONALIST PERSPECTIVE

Functionalism represents a holistic approach to the study of society in particular, and social systems in general. Specifically, 'from a functionalist perspective, the key feature of "society" considered as a unified system is its orderliness and relative stability in the context of a changing environment' (Barnes, 1995: 37).

Although holistic approaches to the study of society date from the ancient Greeks, the early exemplars of modern versions of functionalism in anthropology and sociology appear in the works of Herbert Spencer and Emile Durkheim. Following the lead of Auguste Comte, they espoused organic models of society and analysed the structure and functioning of societies in a manner analogous to the study of the structure and functioning of biological organisms. Spencer, for example, drew the following parallels between society and organisms:

1   Both society and organisms can be distinguished from inorganic matter, for both grow and develop.
2   In both society and organisms an increase in size means an increase in complexity and differentiation.
3   In both, a progressive differentiation in structure is accompanied by a differentiation in function.
4   In both, parts of the whole are interdependent with a change in one part affecting other parts.
5   In both, each part of the whole is also a micro society or organism in and of itself.
6   And in both organisms and societies, the life of the whole can be destroyed but the parts will live on for a while. (Turner, 1974: 16–17)

While critical of much of Spencer's sociological thought, Durkheim nevertheless utilized several of Spencer's ideas in formulating his own notions of functionalism. Turner and Maryanski (1979: 96–7) cite Durkheim as 'the first to advocate an explicitly functional set of assumptions'. These were:

1   A social system must reveal some degree of internal integration among it constituent parts.
2   The important theoretical task is to determine the consequences, or functions, of a constituent part for the integration of the systemic whole.
3   The 'causes' of a part must be analysed separately from its 'functions' for social integration.

4   The need for social integration operates as a selective mechanism for the persistence of those parts that promote integration of the social whole.

Functionalist assumptions underpin Durkheim's four classic sociological works: *The Division of Labor in Society* ([1893] 1938), *The Rules of Sociological Method* ([1895] 1938), *Suicide* ([1897] 1952) and *Elementary Forms of the Religious Life* ([1912] 1954). His functional analysis of religion greatly influenced the development of anthropological functionalism under A.R. Radcliffe-Brown (1952) and Bronislaw Malinowski (1945). Their work in turn greatly influenced the sociological functionalism of Talcott Parsons and Robert K. Merton.[1]

In sum, functionalism has a long history and takes many forms. Space limits detailed discussions of its many varieties, but we outline the main forms of functionalism below.

Forms of Functionalism

A number of typologies of the forms of functionalism, ranging from the simple to the complex, are found in the sociological literature. Spiro (1953) provides the most elaborate typology, identifying 12 varieties of functionalism. However, for present purposes Abrahamson's (1978) three-fold typology, of individualistic, interpersonal and societal forms, serves to illustrate both classic and contemporary forms of functionalism.[2]

Individualistic Functionalism This particular perspective is most closely associated with the anthropological writings of Bronislaw Malinowski. He argued that social institutions and cultural values are functional responses to the needs of individuals whether those be psychological (love, identity) or biological (hunger, sex). Every society, he contended, must cater for individuals' needs, although he acknowledged that culture also determined how individuals expressed their needs.

Interpersonal Functionalism Expounded by A.R. Radcliffe-Brown, this framework emphasizes interpersonal interactions. He identified a host of interpersonal practices, such as joking, gift-giving and avoidance, as 'strain accommodating mechanisms'. These mechanisms, later called 'functional equivalents', were viewed as solutions for minimizing inherent social strains and functioned to connect individuals into an integrated whole.

Societal Functionalism Durkheim was the first proponent of this perspective. He used the term function to refer to practices that satisfy the needs of the social system. And he indicated that 'causes' and 'effects' of a function interact and reciprocate. For example, most social systems punish crimes because collective sentiments 'cause' the system to act this way. But collective sentiments are also an effect of punishment; that is, punishment is functional to the maintenance of anti-crime sentiments.

Structural-functionalism   To varying degrees, all three forms of functionalism described by Abrahamson are incorporated into contemporary sociological functionalism generally called 'structural-functionalism' (hereafter S-F). With reference to S-F, Demerath (1967: 506) suggests that:

> On the one hand, it is possible to concentrate on the 'part', using the 'whole' as a kind of backboard off which to bounce effects and consequences. On the other hand, one can concentrate on the whole itself. Here the various parts are constituent elements and only really interesting as they contribute to the entirety.

He proposes terming the first option 'structuralism' and the second option 'functionalism', 'thus giving new life to a once moribund hyphen' (p. 506).

Following Demerath's distinction, the work of Robert K. Merton (1957) best highlights 'structuralism', whereas the work of Talcott Parsons (cf. for example, 1966, 1971) best exemplifies 'functionalism' (cf., for example, Turner, 1974). We emphasize the key features of these two branches of S-F in our description of selected theories and typologies of functionalism below.

Formalizations of Functionalism

As there is little consensus within the social sciences as to what precisely constitutes a model, paradigm, or theory, it is not surprising that different sociologists have attached each of these labels to S-F. For example, Burrell and Morgan (1979: 25) regard S-F as the paradigm that 'has provided the dominant framework for the conduct of academic sociology and the study of organizations'; Ritzer (1975: 48) views S-F as one of two dominant theories within the 'social facts' paradigm; while Sztompka (1974) conceptualizes S-F as a systemic model that provides a formal framework for constructing a theory of society. Here we simply note that S-F is a broad and diverse theoretical perspective containing several explicit models, theories and typologies. By way of highlighting the particular viewpoints of

notable proponents of S-F, and in order to lay the groundwork for discussing the substantive applications of S-F to sport sociology, we summarize selected formalizations of Parsons, Merton, Durkheim, and Davis and Moore, respectively.[3]

Parsons's AGIL Model of Functional Imperatives   One of Talcott Parsons's most notable contributions to S-F is his 'general theory of action'. According to Parsons (1966: 5), 'action consists of the structures and processes by which human beings form meaningful intentions and, more or less successfully, implement them in concrete situations.' Parsons (1966) conceptualized all general human action systems as being comprised of four primary subsystems of action, namely: the behavioral organism, personality, social system and culture. Moreover, Parsons (1966) theorized that all action systems must deal with four functional problems which he labelled adaptation, goal-attainment, integration and latency (alias pattern-maintenance and tension-management). Denoted by the acronym AGIL, these problems are referred to as the 'functional prerequisites' of systems of action, or more commonly the 'functional imperatives' of action systems.

Craib (1984: 43) describes Parsons's functional imperatives as follows:

1   Each system must adapt to its environment *(adaptation)*.
2   Each system must have a means of mobilizing its resources in order to achieve its goals and obtain gratification *(goal attainment)*.
3   Each system must maintain the internal co-ordination of its parts and develop ways of dealing with deviance – in other words, it must keep itself together *(integration)*.
4   Each system must maintain itself as nearly as possible in a state of equilibrium ... *(pattern maintenance)*.

Parsons (1966: 7) theorized that 'within action systems, cultural systems are specialized around the function of pattern-maintenance, social systems around the integration of acting units ..., personality systems around goal-attainment, and the behavioral organism around adaptation.' He further theorized that every subsystem of action can be analysed in terms of the four functions of A, G, I and L. For example, in the case of the social system, specific institutional spheres serve particular functions: the economy is primarily related to adaptation, the polity to goal-attainment, socializing institutions to integration and the community to pattern-maintenance.

Finally, we note that Parsons theorized that his general system of action constituted a cybernetic hierarchy wherein interaction among the four primary subsystems of action relies on the constant exchange of energy and information (Craib, 1984: 46–7; Rocher, 1974: 50–1; Skidmore, 1979: 157–60; Turner, 1974: 40–2). 'At the base of the hierarchy are the parts highest in energy, acting as *factors conditioning action*; the high information units are at the top of the hierarchy, as *factors controlling action*' (Rocher, 1974: 51; original emphasis). Thus, in terms of energy, 'the organism provides the energy necessary for the personality system, the personality system provides the energic conditions for the social system, and the organization of personality systems into a social system provides the conditions necessary for a cultural system' (Turner, 1974: 41–2). Conversely, the cultural system informationally controls the social system, the social system informationally regulates the personality system, and the personality system informationally governs the behavioural organism.

Parsons's AGIL scheme appears in Heinila's (1969: 14) description of football as a 'social system' wherein the rules of the game 'fit Parsons's functional imperatives surprisingly neatly'. The technical rules of football, Heinila claimed, promote goal-attainment; training rules serve an adaptive function; rules of competition and eligibility maintain value patterns; and refereeing rules assist integration.

More formally, Günther Lüschen (1969: 57–66) provides a Parsonian model of the sport group as a social system and examines the relationships between structural levels of a sport group and its functional problems (see Table 1.1). Responding to Lüschen's model, John Loy (1969a: 67–75) offers an alternative Parsonian model of sport teams viewed as social systems (see Table 1.2). Drawing upon the small group research of Robert Bales (Parsons's colleague and co-author at Harvard University), Loy's model focuses on leadership roles in team sports and emphasizes the external versus internal, and instrumental versus expressive, dimensions of sport teams.

Merton's Theory of Anomie   Using a functionalist framework, Merton identifies two key elements of social and cultural structures. 'The first consists of culturally defined goals, purposes and interests, held out as legitimate objectives for all', irrespective of their social status (Merton, 1957: 132). 'A second element of the cultural structure defines, regulates and controls the acceptable modes of reaching out for these goals' (Merton, 1957: 133). By focusing on institutionalized goals and means, Merton in effect views society as a social system that varies in its degree of integration. A social system reaches equilibrium when there is a satisfactory balance between institutionalized goals and means. However, structural imbalances result in a poorly integrated social system wherein individuals adopt different modes of adaptation to institutionalized goals and means. In short, 'the social structure ... produces a strain toward anomie and deviant behavior' (Merton, 1957: 157).

Merton offers a five-fold typology of the ways that individuals can respond to institutionalized goals and means:

1 *conformity* – where an individual accepts both the cultural goals and the institutionalized means for achieving them;
2 *innovation* – where an individual subscribes to the cultural goals, but does not accept the preferred or legitimate means for reaching them;
3 *ritualism* – where an individual limits his or her horizons and instead of aspiring to lofty goals, such as those held out in the American Dream, compulsively abides by institutionalized norms like those associated with the Protestant work ethic;
4 *retreatism* – where an individual rejects both cultural goals and institutionalized means;
5 *rebellion* – where an individual feels alienated from current cultural values and normative means and considers them purely arbitrary.

Merton uses his typology to answer the sociological question, 'what ... are the consequences for the behavior of people variously situated in a social structure or a culture in which the emphasis on dominant success-goals has become increasingly separated from an equivalent emphasis on institutionalized procedures for seeking these goals?' (Merton, 1957: 139).

Loy (1969b) addressed Merton's question in a theoretical essay about the possible relationships between social structure, game forms and anomie. More specifically, he juxtaposed Merton's typology of modes of individual adaptation with Caillois's (1961) four-fold typology of game forms (that is, *agon, alea, ilinx, mimicry*) and hypothesized that certain game forms would be more prominent among certain social classes. For example, he linked *agon* (competition) to 'conformity' among the upper-middle classes; *alea* (chance) to 'innovation' among the lower class; and solitary variants of Caillois' four game forms to 'retreatism' among individuals in the lowest societal positions. To illustrate the latter, Loy

Table 1.1   *The sport group as a social system*

Structural levels	Functional problems
Values (achievement, fair play)	Pattern maintenance
Norms (defining amateur, foul; rules of a game; defining 'good' team member)	Integration
Subcollectivities (offence or defence; 'braintrusts' of a team; cliques, friendships)	Goal attainment
Roles (unique clusters of recognized formal or informal rights and obligations of individual members; specific quarterback, peacemaker, scapegoat on a team)	Adaptation

Source: adapted from Lüschen, 1969: 61.

Table 1.2   *Relationships between leadership roles and functional imperatives in sport groups as social systems*

	External dimension (Cultural)	Internal dimension (Social structural)
Instrumental dimension	Adaptive problem – winning games from other teams	Decision-making problem – relating of team members to each other to reach and carry out group decisions
(members as means)	Leader role – coach as technical expert and executive leader	Leader role – team member as task leader
Expressive dimension	Pattern maintenance and member recruitment and retention problem – acquisition, training and control of group members	Integrative problems – relating members to each other to 'get along' with each other
(members as ends)	Leader role – coach as educator and morale leader	Leader role – team member as socio-emotional leader

Source: adapted from Loy, 1969a: 69.

referred to Olmsted's (1962: 63) analysis of the solitary race track gambler:

> Horse racing also appeals to the social isolate, since to play the horses 'seriously' requires many hours of solitary paper work – very congenial to such a person – and a minimum of contact with others. The horse player, even more than most gamblers, lives in a dream world of his own, far removed from everyday life.

Durkheim's Theory of Suicide   Although Durkheim acknowledged that suicides are the consequence of individual actions, he argued that suicide is best explained as a social phenomenon. He was particularly interested in explaining a number of empirical generalizations about suicide, such as his finding that in a variety of populations Catholics have lower suicide rates than Protestants. His theoretical analysis of suicide is quite complex (cf. Jones, 1986: 82–114) and only implicitly formalized. However, Merton (1957: 97) has formally

summarized Durkheim's theoretical assumptions as follows:

1 Social cohesion provides psychic support to group members subjected to acute stresses and anxieties.
2 Suicide rates are functions of *unrelieved* anxieties and stresses to which persons are subjected.
3 Catholics have greater social cohesion than Protestants.
4 Therefore, lower suicide rates should be anticipated among Catholics than among Protestants.

While much of functional thought is highly abstract and complex, Durkheim shows that it is possible to apply formal functionalist theories to social phenomena.

Drawing upon Durkheim's work on suicide and religious life and Merton's theoretic formulation above, Karnilowicz (1982: 6) developed the following propositions:

1 Suicides result, in part, from unrelieved anxieties and stresses of individuals in society.
2 Social integration provides emotional and psychic support to individuals subjected to acute anxieties and stresses.
3 Ceremonial occasions serve to increase social integration among individuals in society.
4 *Therefore*, frequency of suicides is anticipated to be lower on and around ceremonial occasions than on and around comparable non-ceremonial days.

He specifically hypothesized that the frequency of suicide is lower on, and around, national religious and civil holidays and major sporting events than on, and around, comparable non-ceremonial days. Karnilowicz chose Easter Sunday and Christmas Day as national religious holidays, 4th July and Thanksgiving as national civil holidays, and Super Bowl Sunday (that is, the national championship game of American professional football) and the last game of the World Series (of North American professional baseball) as major sporting events to test this hypothesis. In collaboration with Curtis and Loy, and using nationwide suicide data published by the US Public Health Service for 1972–8, Karnilowicz found empirical support for the Durkheimian notion that public ceremonial occasions simultaneously increase social integration and lessen the incidence of suicides (Curtis et al., 1986: 11).

The Davis–Moore Theory of Social Stratification Perhaps the most cited, and certainly the most controversial, formal theory found within the S-F paradigm is the functional theory of social stratification formulated by Kingsley Davis and Wilbert Moore. They published various statements of their theory over a 20-year period (cf. Davis, 1942, 1948, 1953, 1959a; Davis and Moore, 1945; Moore, 1953, 1963a, 1963b) and, not surprisingly, a number of different interpretations of their theory exist. Huaco (1963) discusses four versions of the Davis–Moore theory: the causal, unqualified and minimal assumption; the 'consequential'; the qualified; and the maximal assumption. For present purposes, we outline Huaco's (1963: 802) interpretation of the causal, unqualified and minimal assumption version of the Davis–Moore theory as follows:

(A) All societies have unequal rewards attached to different positions (this empirical generalization is the dependent variable).
(B) The state of affairs described in (A) is determined by two factors (which constitute the independent variables):

(1) Different positions have unique importance for the preservation or survival of the society.
(2) Adequate performance in different positions requires incumbents equipped with different (and socially scarce) amounts of talent or training.
(C) The independent variables determine the dependent variables in the following manner: incumbents with greater talent or training are induced to occupy the functionally more important positions by attaching greater rewards to these positions.
(D) It follows from (A), (B) and (C) that in all societies those positions which receive the greater rewards will be the ones which are functionally most important and will be the ones occupied by the most talented or qualified incumbents.

Another assumption should be added to the preceding formulation: rewards attached to any particular position may be either material (for example, income) or symbolic (for example, prestige). Thus a functionalist might argue that within professional American football the position of quarterback requires the most talent and training, and, as there is a scarcity of well-trained, talented quarterbacks, they accordingly receive the highest salaries and the greatest prestige for their leadership and athletic prowess on the field.

To the best of our knowledge no effort has been made to test the Davis–Moore theory of social stratification at the macro-level in the sociology of sport. However, Loy, Knoop and Theberge (1979) made an exploratory test of the Davis–Moore theory using data from North American baseball organizations. They based their study on both objective and subjective measures of the four key variables underlying the Davis–Moore theory, namely, functional importance, prestige, skill and rewards, and they focused largely on the 'imputed' functional importance of particular playing positions in baseball. Their study suggests that 'macro-theories of social stratification are ... of heuristic use in explaining patterns of differential distributions of rewards within sport organizations' (p. 123).

CONTRIBUTIONS OF FUNCTIONALISM TO SPORT SOCIOLOGY

There is a longstanding belief in sport sociology that functionalism was the initial, and dominant, paradigm. For example, in an influential 'state of the art review' two decades ago, Merrill Melnick (1975: 46) warned that 'there is an uneasy feeling which suggests that the sociology of sport has become "locked into" a single paradigm that may eventually inhibit its future growth and development, its general acceptance by the public, and ultimately its value to man [sic] and society.' Yet, a decade later, Gerald Kenyon (1986) conducted an extensive review of the sport sociology literature and concluded that 'serious contributions based on an explicit functionalist approach have been rare' (p. 11). Thus, the assumed predominance of functionalism in sport sociology is a subject of debate.[4]

The Myth of Functionalism as the Dominant Paradigm in Sport Sociology

We agree with Kenyon that few substantive applications of functionalism can be found in the sociology of sport literature. At best we can identify only three or four self-professed functionalist sport sociologists, another three or four influential sport sociologists who implicitly employed a functionalist framework, and a half-dozen sport sociologists who made functional analyses of selected problems.[5]

Moreover, functionalist-orientated sport sociologists never ruled the editorial boards of the *International Review of Sport Sociology* (*IRSS*, first published in 1966) or the *Sociology of Sport Journal* (*SSJ*, first published in 1984). Indeed, the editors of both journals fostered a multi-paradigm approach to sport sociology. Andrzej Wohl, the first Editor-in-Chief of the *IRSS*, stated in the first volume of the journal that 'not one of the methods used by the various sociological schools nor any of the spheres of research proposed by these schools, could, in isolation from other spheres and methods, be of any use to present an as complete as possible reflection of the many-sided nature of sports' (1966: 10). Similarly, the statement of editorial policy of the first issue of *SSJ* announced that 'all types of scientific research methodologies' are appropriate as are 'theoretical perspectives' from a range of disciplines including social psychology, sociology, and anthropology. Finally, we point out that sport sociologists with functionalist leanings, unlike their colleagues in general sociology, never sponsored graduate students who entered the field as dedicated disciples of an S-F perspective.

On the other hand, one can readily identify several first-generation and many second-generation sport sociologists who espoused alternative paradigms. For example, noted early proponents of symbolic interactionism within North American sport sociology included Gregory P. Stone, Donald W. Ball, Norman Denzin, Robert Faulkner and Edmund Vaz (see Chapter 5). And in England Norbert Elias and Eric Dunning simultaneously condemned the faults of functionalism and commended the merits of figurational sociology (see Chapter 6).

In making the preceding points we do not wish to imply that S-F was absent from early sport sociology. Rather, we stress that sport sociology has always embraced a diversity of paradigms, of which S-F was one. The remainder of this section highlights the substantive contributions made by functionalism to the sociology of sport at both the macro and micro levels of analysis.

Macro-Functionalism: Sport in Society

Functionalism's holistic approach helped direct early sport sociologists to consider sport as a social institution and to look more closely at sport as a reflection of the total society and its complex relationships with other institutions. Thus functionalism gave sport sociologists a powerful weapon to counter charges that they were engaging in a 'trivial scholarly pursuit'. While second-generation sport sociologists abandoned the 'sport as a mirror of society thesis',[6] the significance of sport as an institutional sphere of daily life remains an ongoing concern.

The most explicit functionalist analyses of sport in society are found in the writings of Harry Edwards, Kalevi Heinila, Gunther Lüschen, Christopher Stevenson and Hideo Tatano.[7] Among these sport sociologists, Lüschen, a German sociologist and long-time American resident, has been most instrumental in fostering the functionalist framework in sport sociology. His first major paper presenting a Parsonian perspective of sport in society, 'The Interdependence of Sport and Culture', appeared in the *IRSS* in 1967. In this paper Lüschen examined sport from an action system frame of reference, discussed the functions and dysfunctions of sport within culture and society, and speculated about sport and cultural evolution. According to Lüschen, in preliterate cultures 'sport's function is universal, often religious, collectivity orientated, and in the training of skills representative and related to adult and warfare skills, while modern sport's function may be called specific for pattern maintenance and integration' (Lüschen, 1967: 139).

Fifteen years later Lüschen (1981b) made another structural analysis of sport which focused on the internal and external systems of sport. He asserted that structural analysis 'conceptualizes the system of sport (notably in the sport contest and its system of rank) as a fundamental structural pattern of human and social existence'. This, he said, 'provides as much for sociology and sport science in terms of scientific insight as for the individual athlete, who experiences in and through sport borderline situations of human existence' (Lüschen, 1981b: 209). More recently, Lüschen has argued the case for 'new structuralism' as a programme to analyse sport in society (1988, 1990). We discuss his recent work in the last section of this chapter.

Christopher Stevenson and his mentor John Nixon (Stevenson and Nixon, 1972; Stevenson, 1974) also made early contributions to functional analyses of sport in society. They identified five basic functions of sport at the societal level:

1 socio-emotional function, wherein sport contributes to the maintenance of socio-psychological stability;
2 socialization, wherein sport contributes to the inculcation of cultural beliefs and mores;
3 integrative function, wherein sport contributes to the harmonious integration of disparate individuals and diverse groups;
4 political function, wherein sport is used for ideological purposes;
5 social mobility function, wherein sport serves as a source of upward mobility.

Harry Edwards also espoused a functionalist view of sport in society. Because his political activism and critical social commentary on racism in American society contradict the notion of conservatism held to be an inherent aspect of S-F, Edwards has seldom been identified as a functionalist. However, Edwards is a direct academic descendant of the father of American functionalism, Talcott Parsons, in that Edwards studied with Robin M. Williams, Jr for his doctorate at Cornell University and Williams was a doctoral student of Parsons at Harvard University.

Edwards's text *Sociology of Sport* (1973), the first North American textbook in sport sociology, reflects a strong emphasis on what might best be termed 'conflict functionalism'. Drawing upon his mentor's functional analysis of American society (Williams, 1968), Edwards devotes a chapter of his text to describing the functions of sport as a social institution and he offers an original functional explanation for fan enthusiasm:

> As an institution having primarily socialization and value maintenance functions, sport affords the fan an opportunity to *reaffirm the established values and beliefs defining acceptable means and solutions to central problems in the secular realm of everyday societal life.* But this fact does not stand alone; particular patterns of values are expressed through certain intrinsic features of sports activities; in combination, the two aspects explain not only fan enthusiasm but sport's predominantly male following. (Edwards, 1973: 243; original emphasis)

The functionalist perspectives of Heinila and Tatano are less well known to English-speaking sport sociologists as most of their publications appear in their respective native languages of Finnish and Japanese. A flavour of Heinila's mode of functional analysis can be gleaned from a paper in the first volume of the *IRSS* entitled 'Notes on the Inter-Group Conflicts in International Sport'. In this article Heinila (1966) examined the significance of 'the goodwill function in sport ideology.'

Tatano's most formal functional analysis of sport in English is a 1981 article in the *IRSS* entitled 'A Model-Construction of Sport as Culture: A Working Paper Toward a Systematic Analysis of Sport'. Here Tatano emphasizes the importance of sport symbols. Following Parsons, he provides a three-fold classification in terms of their primacy of orientation: '1) cognitive or instrumental sport symbol, 2) cathectic or expressive sport symbol, 3) evaluative or integrative sport symbol' (Tatano, 1981: 15). He relates sport symbols to the sport system and applies his framework to both the macro and micro analyses of sport phenomena. Tatano concludes his theoretical analysis with the observation that 'even if the sport system is not a closed or separate system, we can systematically analyse empirical and complex sport phenomena, because we can analyse the mechanism of structural-functional interrelations between the sport system and other systems' (1981: 24).

Given the fact that there are few overall functional analyses of sport in society, it is not surprising that there are only a small number of substantive macro-level applications of S-F. We previously mentioned Loy's (1969b) merger of Merton's typology of modes of individual adaptation with Caillois's (1961) classification of games, and Curtis, Loy and Karnilowicz's (1986) test of an aspect of Durkheim's theory of suicide. In addition to these two substantive contributions we are only aware of Milton's (1972) unpublished Master's thesis on 'sport as a functional equivalent of religion'. However, more examples of substantive applications of S-F within the sociology of sport are found at the micro level of analysis.

Micro-Functionalism: Sport Groups as Social Systems[8]

As previously discussed, both Lüschen (1969) and Loy (1969a) provide functionalist models for the analysis of group dynamics among sport teams (see also Lüschen, 1986). Their models largely reflect the collaboration of Parsons, Bales and Shils (1953). Lüschen's model emphasizes the analysis of sport groups in terms of structural levels, functional problems and subsystems of action; whereas, Loy's model emphasizes the analysis of leadership role differentiation in terms of expressive and instrumental team leaders.

Roger Rees and Mary Segal (1984) provide one of the few empirical investigations of leadership role differentiation within sport teams. Examining two American university football teams, they analysed the structures and processes that produce task and socio-emotional team leaders. They defined task leaders as the best players on the team, and socio-emotional leaders as those team members identified by their peers as contributing most to group harmony. Their major findings were that skill and ability are the most important qualifications for selection as a task leader, while years of experience is most important in deciding a socio-emotional team leader.

In addition to leadership behaviour, functional analyses have been made of group competition and group conflict in sport situations. The classic functional analysis of social conflict is Lewis Coser's *The Functions of Social Conflict* (1956). He examines the significance of social conflict in terms of 16 theoretical propositions largely derived from the work of Georg Simmel (1955). Four of the 16 functions analysed by Coser seem especially relevant to the study of conflict in sport situations:

1 the function of group binding;
2 the safety-valve function of releasing hostility;
3 the scapegoat function of searching for enemies;
4 the function of acquiring alliances (see Loy et al., 1978: 110–12).

The most detailed theoretical analyses of conflict and tension in sport are provided by

Norbert Elias and Eric Dunning (1986). Although they consider themselves figurational sociologists rather than functionalist sociologists, functionalist overtones appear in their writings about group sports. For example, Dunning (1973) examines the social development of sport in a paper entitled 'Structural-Functional Properties of Folk-Games and Modern Sports: A Sociological Analysis'. In a collaborative effort, Elias and Dunning (1966) look at the 'dynamics of sport groups with special reference to football'. Here they focus on 'a complex of interdependent polarities' that 'contribute towards maintaining the "tone", the tension-balance of the games', including: '(1) the overall polarity between two opposing teams; (2) the polarity between attack and defence; (3) the polarity between co-operation and tension of the two teams; (4) the polarity between co-operation and competition within each team' (see pp. 398–400). In sum, their essay is suggestive of a S-F analysis of the structures and processes maintaining an equilibrium of tension-balances for players and spectators alike.

Also at the micro level of analysis, Loy, McPherson and Kenyon (1978: 185–6) point out that occupational, avocational and deviant sport subcultures confront functional problems, including:

(1) *pattern-maintenance*, such as the recruitment and socialization of new members, the retention of members through rewards and inducements, retirement and desocialization from the scene, and the maintenance of cultural elements (for example, norms, values, beliefs, symbols, language, dress, legends, traditions, technology); (2) *integration*, such as the learning of job-related skills and moral attributes, the functional specialization of tasks, the social status and mobility paths (career benchmarks) within the structure, the rites of passage, and the establishment of reciprocal collegial relationships; (3) *goal-attainment*, such as information control and the acquisition and demonstration of cognitive and motor skills unique to the subculture; and (4) *adaptation*, such as differential relations with the dominant culture and with 'outsiders'.

Interestingly, most functional analyses of sport subcultures have focused on aspects of deviance. For example, Lüschen has made functional analyses of delinquency (1971), cheating (1976) and drug abuse and doping (1984) as examples of deviant behaviour in sport. In the case of drug abuse and doping, he applies Merton's (1957) theory of anomie and Parsons's pattern-variables in comparing the drug abuser in sport with the regular drug abuser (see Chapter 15).

One of the most in-depth functional analyses of sport subcultures is Pooley's (1976) study of structural assimilation among members of ethnic soccer clubs in Milwaukee. His investigation addressed two basic questions. First, 'to what degree does participation in ethnic soccer influence assimilation' (both positively and negatively)? Secondly, 'what forces within ethnic soccer explain this influence' (both structural and functional factors)? Pooley's major finding was that 'club policies of ethnic soccer clubs inhibit the structural assimilation of members' (1976: 491).

Finally, we note that several studies by Emil Bend and Christopher Stevenson provide S-F analyses of the functions and dysfunctions of socialization (Bend, 1970, 1971; Stevenson, 1975, 1976a, 1976b), and the antecedents and consequences of social mobility (Bend, 1974; Bend and Petrie, 1977; Stevenson, 1974), in and through sport.

CRITICISMS AND CONTROVERSIES

Between the late 1930s and the early 1960s S-F 'was virtually unchallenged as the dominant sociological theory in the United States' (Ritzer, 1988: 101). But during the 1960s critics launched blistering attacks, citing dozens of different weaknesses and flaws in the paradigm (Abrahamson, 1978; Cohen, 1968; Craib, 1984; Gouldner, 1971; Mills, 1959; Skidmore, 1979; Turner and Maryanski, 1979; Zeitlin, 1973). By the end of that decade S-F's credibility lay in tatters. In this section we analyse these criticisms under three headings: theoretical and substantive, methodological and logical, and ideological and political. We also elaborate on the controversies precipitated by these criticisms.

Theoretical and Substantive Issues

The theoretical and substantive criticisms of S-F reflect two principal charges: *a contemporary bias* and a *consensus bias*.

Contemporary Bias The main criticism associated with what we call the contemporary bias is that S-F is ahistorical or non-historical and that it 'fails to account for social change' (Zeitlin, 1973: 15): 'Is it not the height of naiveté,' Zeitlin (1973: 14) asks, 'to suppose that one can explain the present exclusively by means of the present – to suppose that the chain of events leading from the past has no effect on the present?'

On the other hand, while Turner and Maryanski (1979: 110) agree that functionalism is not historiography, they also note that 'Durkheim's functional approach was decidedly historical' (p. 109), that Parsons's 'concern with social evolution among Western societies … reveal[s] a concern with historical events' (p. 111), and that 'Merton's "net balance of functions" approach does not preclude historical accounts' (p. 111). Moreover, Durkheim, Merton, Parsons and Davis and Moore have, 'in a wide variety of contexts, performed important historical analyses – probably among the very best in the social sciences' (p. 112).

Certainly, early sport sociologists who adopted functionalist theories embraced history. In a study of soccer, Heinila (1969), for example, applied Parsons's AGIL model to describe the different norms and rules in the transition from amateurism to professionalism.

Consensus Bias The specific criticisms related to the consensus bias are that functionalism 'overemphasizes the normative element' (Cohen, 1968: 56), that it 'exaggerates the unity, stability, and harmony of social systems' (Zeitlin, 1973: 15), and that, therefore, it 'minimizes the importance of social conflict' (Cohen, 1968: 56). But, charges of a consensus bias beg an important question about the 'function' of conflict. We demonstrate this by briefly examining a major sociological debate in the late 1960s and early 1970s.

Consensus versus Conflict Debate Charges that functionalism contains a consensus bias initially emanated from critics who subscribed to conflict perspectives. In contrast to consensus approaches, which see 'shared norms and values as fundamental to society, focus on social order based on tacit agreements, and view social change as occurring in a slow and orderly fashion' (Ritzer, 1988: 78), conflict theories 'emphasize the dominance of some social groups by others, see social order as based on manipulation and control by dominant groups, and view social change as occurring rapidly and in a disorderly fashion as subordinate groups overthrow dominant groups' (Ritzer, 1988: 78).

However, Pierre Van den Berghe (1963) was among the first to recognize that conflict and consensus theories share important similarities. Both take a holistic view of society and are concerned with the way component parts interrelate; both assume an evolutionary approach to Western social development; both theories recognize social equilibrium, with conflict theories assuming that conflict has a long-term equilibrating effect. Indeed, such are the similarities between these theories that Ritzer (1988: 392) includes both in the social facts paradigm. It is rather ironic that the self-professed functionalists in sport sociology adopted perspectives which focused on conflict, deviance and social change.

The consensus versus conflict debate became a major controversy in sociology (cf. Bernard, 1983; Horton, 1966), which also spilled over into sport sociology. Here we compare Michael Novak's *The Joy of Sports* (1976) and Jean-Marie Brohm's *Sport: a Prison of Measured Time* (1978) to illustrate the functionalist assumptions which underpin *both* consensus and conflict theories.

Novak believes that 'sports … serve a religious function' (1976: 20), and he contends that the 'central rituals' of religion reveal 'the unconscious needs of the civilization' (p. 29). According to Novak (1976), American sports illustrate the unconscious qualities of the modern nation. For example, baseball reflects 'rural culture' in which the 'fundamental unit is the individual' who encourages and assists his team mates and who is determined not to let his team down (p. 69); football represents 'daily reality' – 'the obstructions, fierce denials and violence the immigrants have faced, and still face at every step in our society' (p. 77); and basketball signifies black urban style – 'sophisticated, cool, deceptive, swift, spectacular, flashy, smooth' (p. 105).

Contrary to Novak, Brohm (1978) argues that sport serves political, ideological, repressive and mystifying functions. For example, sport meets the ideological functional requirements of the capitalist mode of production by strengthening bourgeois rule. Sport, *inter alia*, mystifies class conflict, justifies and stabilizes the established order, depoliticizes social life, prepares youth for labour, helps to militarize and regiment youth, and commodifies humans (1978: 175–82).

Both Novak and Brohm recommend political intervention to 'save' sport. Novak (1976) advocates reformation. Sport, he says, has been corrupted by social institutions associated with entertainment (p. 252) and professionalism (p. 302). Brohm, however, believes that 'revolutionary action' (p. 64), to forge 'alternative, non-alienating and non-repressive forms' of sport (p. 78), is the only viable course.

Methodological and Logical Issues

Paradoxically, the methodological and logical criticisms of S-F rest on the claims that the paradigm is, on the one hand, *non-scientific*, and, on the other hand, that it is *too scientific*.

Non-scientific Bias Many critics challenge the perceived non-scientific character of S-F. Common claims are that the concept of functionalism is ambiguous, that its statements are tautological, that its explanations are teleological, and that its hypotheses are untestable. Moreover, some critics contend that S-F reflects 'a level of scientific inquiry that doesn't exist' and that it 'inhibits comparison' (Cohen, 1968: 47–56).

Ambiguity has been a longstanding problem in functionalism: 'The term function is ambiguous,' writes Abrahamson (1978: 38), 'because it is used inconsistently and without clearly identified referents.' Other terms face the same problems: 'What exactly is a structure?' or 'a social system?' asks Ritzer (1988: 103). Similarly, tautologies pervade functional analysis where 'variables are defined in terms of each other, thus making causes and effects obscure and difficult to assess' (Turner and Maryanski, 1979: 124).

Functionalism is adversely teleological to the extent that it 'presume[s] that social processes and structures come into existence and operate to meet end states or goals, *without* being able to document the causal sequences whereby end states create and regulate these structures and processes involved in their attainment' (Turner and Maryanski, 1979: 119). Durkheim, Parsons, Merton and other functionalist theorists were aware of the problem and tried to avoid the teleological trap by stressing human action and organization. However, as Turner and Maryanski (1979: 124) point out, the problem remains because of 'implicit organicism'. While biologists can assess life and death, and operationalize pathological states within living organisms, sociologists face a virtually insurmountable task when they attempt to do the same for societies.

According to Abrahamson (1978: 40), the consequences of ambiguity, teleology and tautology are that many of the assumptions of functionalism 'violate logic and defy empirical assessment'. In short, functionalism is seen by some sociologists as a non-scientific paradigm.

Hyper-scientific Bias Given the above observations, it is ironic that other sociologists attack functionalism on the grounds that it pretends to be too scientific by attempting to fully adopt the models and methods of the natural sciences. For example, Burrell and Morgan (1979: 26) argue that functionalists subscribe to an objectivist philosophy that is realist, positivist, determinist and nomothetic. Debates about these philosophical tenets characterize bipolar perspectives on the nature of social science which Burrell and Morgan (1979) call objectivism and subjectivism (see Figure 1.1). Their subjective–objective dimensional analysis is outlined below.

First, *nominalism versus realism* constitutes an **ontological** debate about the nature of reality. Nominalists believe that social reality is based on the actions, cognitions and perceptions of individual agents and that culture, social structures and social systems are simply labels and nothing more than names. In contradistinction, realists believe that wholes are greater than the sum of their individual parts, and that cultures, social structures and social systems are immutable realities and not mere names.

Secondly, *anti-positivism versus positivism* represents an **epistemological** debate. Positivists believe that science is objective and value-free, that hypotheses can be empirically tested and that law-like generalizations about human behaviour can be discovered; anti-positivists believe that social research is subjective, that all knowledge is relative and that the social world is best understood from the viewpoints of participants rather than observers.

Thirdly, *voluntarism versus determinism* revolves around the **human nature** debate. The former view holds that human actions are autonomous and free-willed, whereas the latter view holds that genetic and environmental factors and/or socio-cultural forces determine human behaviours.

Fourthly, *ideographic versus nomothetic* represents a **methodological** debate about searching for generalizations in social science. Those holding to a nomothetic viewpoint believe that systematic research produces empirical and theoretical generalizations about patterns of human behaviour. Those who ascribe to an ideographic viewpoint contend that social laws do not exist, that generalizations are meaningless, and that the only worthy knowledge is 'local knowledge' based on detailed anthropological, clinical, historical or sociological case studies.

Philosophical debates between the subjectivist and objectivist perspectives about the nature of social science underpin most of the fundamental differences between neo-positivists and new humanists in sport sociology.

Neo-positivism and New Humanism Debate Auguste Comte, the founding father of sociology, laid the foundations of positivism in sociology. Thus sociology began as a positivistic discipline. Positivism reached its peak in sociology in the late 1920s and early 1930s under the influence of George A. Lundberg (1939, 1941–42). He emphasized the importance of deductive theory, quantitative measurement and 'operationalism'. The latter was an extreme form of neo-positivism made famous by Percy Bridgeman (1928), a professor of physics at Harvard University in the 1920s. Sjoberg (1959) gives a good overview of the use of operationalism in sociology in particular and social research in general.

In present-day sociology, forms of neo-positivism appear in the writings of formalized and mathematically orientated sociologists, as well as in the theoretical agendas of sociologists who continue to endorse the application of natural science models to the study of social behaviour (see, for example, Blalock, 1969; Gibbs, 1972; Turner, 1984; Wallace, 1971, 1983). Of course, other leading figures in sociology have rejected positivism in both its classical and contemporary forms.

Warshay (1975) labels the contemporary critics of neo-positivism 'the new humanists'. He cites Peter Berger (1963) and Irving Louis Horowitz (1964) as leading figures among the new humanists. Although the new humanists comprised a mixed group of sociologists, Warshay (1975: 88) argues that in general they viewed 'sociology as a scholarly and humane discipline that must (1) utilize the work of the older masters without being limited by their vision, (2) create further theory without being bound by the necessity of formalizing or "verifying" it, and (3) make use of a great variety of methods for defining,

The **Subjectivist** approach to social science	Philosophical issues	The **Objectivist** approach to social science
Nominalism	**Ontology**	Realism
Anti-positivism	**Epistemology**	Positivism
Voluntarism	**Human nature**	Determinism
Ideographic	**Methodology**	Nomothetic

Figure 1.1 *A scheme for analysing assumptions about the nature of social science (adopted from Burrell and Morgan, 1979: 3)*

gathering, measuring, interpreting, and presenting data'.

The new humanist movement in sociology arose between the mid-1960s and early 1970s during the height of social protests about civil rights, student rights, women's rights and the Vietnam War. As this period corresponded with the initial development of sport sociology, it is not surprising that the philosophical orientations of new humanists in general sociology appealed to younger sport sociologists. For example, Melnick (1975) concludes his critical look at the sociology of sport by arguing for a 'humanistic-existential sociology of sport'.

Under different guises, neo-positivists and new humanists continue their debates in sport sociology. Susan Hekman (1983: 5) observes that 'although philosophers of social science may regard positivism as a dead issue, it continues to guide most research activities undertaken by social scientists'. She also notes, 'positivism remains the dominant standpoint because none of the alternative standpoints has managed to assume the prominence enjoyed by positivism' (p. 5).

Spatial limitations preclude any lengthy analysis of the issues surrounding antipositivism/positivism, but we wish to make two concluding points. On the one hand, we have little doubt, especially in the North American context, that there was an orthodoxy of method in the formative years of sport sociology that can best be labelled 'instrumental positivism' (cf. Bryant, 1985). It overemphasized value-free enquiry, empirical data, objective measurement and statistical analysis. On the other hand, we are not convinced that there was a close connection between this instrumental positivism and structural-functionalism. For example, the leading functionalists in sport sociology such as Harry Edwards, Kalevi Heinila, Günther Lüschen or Christopher Stevenson seldom, if ever, used quantitative methods in conjunction with their functional analyses. Moreover, some functionalist orientated sport sociologists were outspoken critics of neo-positivists. For example, Hideo Tatano charged that 'in the extreme case, their factual research suffers the fallacies of false empiricism and hyper-factualism' (1981: 5). In sum, we believe that several critics of S-F in sport sociology have conflated positivism and functionalism.

Ideological and Political Issues

Conservative Bias The major ideological and political criticism of S-F is that it contains a *conservative bias*. Ritzer (1988: 102) attributes S-F's conservative orientation to three qualities. First, it tends to ignore change, history and conflict. Secondly, it is 'orientated to the analysis of how elements contribute to the perpetuation of a system'. Thirdly, it implies that human actors are passive participants following the dictates of social structures.

Structure versus Agency Debate Allegations of a conservative bias, especially the notion of human beings as passive actors, serve to introduce a third controversy in sociology: the 'agency/structure' debate. Social theorists have long grappled with the question, what determines social outcomes? Indeed, Keat and Urry (1975: 229) assert that 'the key problem for contemporary social theory … is to develop a theory that satisfactorily synthesizes the structural analysis of social formations and the explanations of human action in terms of subjective states and meanings' (cited in Hekman, 1983: 9–10). In their discussion of this problem, Ingham and Loy (1973: 17) observe that the 'structural components' of sport may 'appear immutable', that is, force individuals 'to accommodate their "selves" to pre-established forms and pre-established roles'. However, they insist that individuals are knowledgeable and reflective and that they retain 'the ability to step outside of taken-for-granted routines of society'.[9]

A number of contemporary social theorists have attempted to reconcile the structure/agency debate by proposing different syntheses, including Berger and Luckman (1966), Keat and Urry (1975), Fay and Moon (1977), Bourdieu (1977), and Giddens (1977). Both Bourdieu and Giddens have been particularly influential in sport sociology (cf., for example, Gruneau, 1983; Ingham and Hardy, 1984; Jarvie and Maguire, 1994). Discussions of the structure/agency debate are found in some form in all chapters of Part One of this present book.

Summary To conclude this section on controversies and criticisms, we make five points. First, two decades ago Abrahamson (1978: 37) observed that attacks on functionalism have been 'frequent and extensive' while 'defense and counterattack have been surprisingly sparing'. Defences have been made, however. For example, Kincaid (1996: 141), in a more recent text on the philosophical foundations of the social sciences, asserts that 'functional explanations can be perfectly legitimate causal explanations, they are amenable to ordinary causal evidence, and they rest on no untoward analogies to biological evolution'.[10] 'Moreover,' Kincaid states, 'good work is not only possible but actual.' Yet, notwithstanding defences of functionalism in sociology at large, it is interesting that, to the best of our knowledge, not one functionalist-orientated sport sociologist has ever formally defended the paradigm.

Secondly, 'much of the criticism is largely beside the point, since the chief weaknesses of functionalism were often recognized by those who formulated the doctrine' (Cohen, 1968: 47). For example, Merton (1957) provided an early critique of the prevailing postulates of functional analysis, discussed functional analysis as ideology, and offered a protocol for pursuing functional analyses. In the case of sport sociology, Frey (1986) clearly outlines the shortcomings of the functional paradigm in a functional analysis of college athletics.

Thirdly, it is ironic that many critics of functionalism adopted perspectives that were implicitly functionalist in varying degrees. For example, Norbert Elias in a paper published near the end of his career describes four 'universal elementary survival functions which one encounters in every human group' (Elias, 1987: 231). Specifically, he refers to the 'economic function', the 'conflict management function', the 'knowledge acquisition and transmission function', and the 'self-restraint function' (or civilizing process). Elias's universal elementary survival functions seem similar to Parsons's four functional imperatives and some of the functional prerequisites of a society given by Aberle and others (1950). In any event, like Parsons, Elias links elementary functions to institutional spheres. For instance, in respect of the 'self-restraint function' he comments that 'one of the social institutions that performs this function can be found in the initiation rites of less complex human groups' (Elias, 1987: 231).

Our fourth point is that some of the charges against functionalism were simply false. We agree, for example, with Merton (1957), who denies that the paradigm is intrinsically conservative. Indeed, as discussed above, several sport sociologists adopted radical forms of functionalism and advocated revolutionary changes to the structure and practice of sport. A chief example is Harry Edwards, who helped establish the Olympic Project for Human Rights which instigated the 'revolt' by African American athletes at the 1968 Olympic Games in Mexico City (Edwards, 1969).

And fifth, and lastly, since the mid-1980s a number of German and American sociologists have made concerted efforts to overcome the early criticisms and revive S-F (Ritzer, 1988: 71). Indeed, Marco Orr describes 'the revival of Parsonian thought' as 'one of the distinguishing features of 1980s sociology' (Alexander and Colomy, 1990: 34). Revived forms of S-F have been coined neofunctionalism.

NEW FORMS OF FUNCTIONALISM IN SPORT SOCIOLOGY

In concluding this chapter, we note the recent emergence of neofunctionalism and discuss its potential contributions to sport sociology.

Development of Neofunctionalism

Alexander and Colomy (1990: 36) identify three phases of postwar sociology. The first phase, which lasted until the 1960s, was dominated by Parsonian and Mertonian S-F. In the second phase, from the 1960s until the 1980s, sociology assumed a multiparadigmatic character, as warring schools, some of which 'aligned' themselves to revolutionary social movements, sought hegemony. (Our discussion of the controversies and debates precipitated by S-F in the preceding section refers to these warring schools.) The third phase began in the mid-1980s. One of its distinguishing features is the 'movement back to synthesis' as 'the old lines of confrontation are being discredited'.

Alexander (1985) recognizes neofunctionalism as one of several attempts to develop a new synthesis.[11] Neofunctionalist research programmes have emerged in a host of areas, including sport sociology, notwithstanding Jarvie and Maguire's (1994: 25) claims to the contrary and Charles Page's (1985) warning to younger scholars about the dangers of reviving functionalism.

Although not a neofunctionalist *per se*, Mouzelis (1995: 7) is 'very sympathetic to the type of neofunctionalist analysis that J. Alexander, P. Colomy or N. Smelser are producing in an effort to retrieve the useful features of Parsonian functionalism and evolutionism'. However, he believes that these neofunctionalists have not gone far enough, and has, accordingly, provided the most in-depth sociological reconsideration of functionalism to date. In brief, Mouzelis: (a) argues that the agency/structure distinction must be retained in social theory; (b) recognizes that Parsonian functionalism 'overemphasized the systemic/ functionalist dimensions of social systems at the expense of agency' (p. 4); and (c) suggests how the major limitations of Parsonian functionalism can be remedied by incorporating key concepts from the works of Elias, Marx, Bourdieu and Giddens. In sum, Mouzelis (p. 8) attempts to 'formulate a set of conceptual tools which try both to solve certain puzzles related to functionalist theorizing and to help the empirically-orientated sociologist to move from micro to meso and macro levels of analysis – while avoiding both the reductive and reificatory treatment of social phenomena'.

Neofunctionalism and Sport Sociology

Although they might deny the neofunctionalist label, we believe that 'the action-theoretical perspective' of Nitsch (1985) and 'the new structuralism' of Lüschen (1988, 1990) contain functionalist overtones. For example, Lüschen cites Nitsch and points out 'that it is Parsons (1951) in particular who provides some interesting leads for such action system and theory' (Lüschen, 1990: 53).

Specifically, Lüschen refers to Parsons's conception of four primary subsystems of action and their interrelationships through the cybernetic hierarchy of control and conditioning. Lüschen suggests that 'sport as an action system could thus be integrated by building its theory from the partial insights of such fields like sport physiology, biomechanics, sport psychology, sport sociology, sport philosophy or whatever other subdiscipline might provide information' (Lüschen, 1990: 53). In short, Lüschen seeks to formulate a theoretical perspective that would result in a unified sport science as well as a more mature sociology of sport.

Postscript

In conclusion, we make a few brief observations about functionalist theory and method and close our chapter with a short summary of what we consider to be the most substantive functionalist contribution to the sociology of sport literature.

Theory   Nearly 40 years ago, in his presidential address at the annual meeting of the American Sociological Association, Kingsley Davis pointed out that 'historically the rise of functionalism represented a revolt against reductionist theories, anti-theoretical empiricism, and moralistic or ideological views under the name of sociology or social anthropology' (1959b: 757, see abstract). 'The early rise of functionalism,' he added, had

> helped to make a place in sociology and anthropology for those wishing to explain social phenomena in terms of social systems, as against those

who wished to make no explanation at all, to explain things in terms of some *other* system, or plead a cause. Now, however, the movement that was once an asset has turned into a liability. (1959b: 771)

Kingsley Davis concluded his presidential address with the pronouncement that: 'The designation of a school called functionalism will doubtless die out in time' (p. 772).

But four decades later, Kincaid (1996: 101) contends that functionalism is still alive and well.

> Nearly every tradition in the social sciences, from ecological anthropology to stratification theory to neo-classical economics, employs functional explanations. Moreover, such explanations are unlikely to go away. Much in the social world is the result of individuals pursuing their own interests, often while proclaiming some more selfless motivation. Much in the social world is the result of competition, both between individuals and between social institutions and practices. Much in the social world seems to have a life of its own; in short, to persist for reasons not obvious to common sense. Explaining such social phenomena leads quite naturally to invoking functions – to explaining the existence of social practices by the functions, explicit or hidden, that they serve.

Similarly, but perhaps more trenchantly, Mouzelis (1995: 7) asserts that in their haste and determination to 'reject ... all forms of functionalist theorizing', influential contemporary theorists such as Anthony Giddens, Norbert Elias and Pierre Bourdieu have 'failed to transcend functionalism in general, and Parsonian functionalism in particular'. Rather 'they have simply avoided ... unfashionable functionalist vocabulary ... while retaining its fundamental logic – with the result that crypto-functionalist elements and related distinctions are clandestinely reintroduced into their writings.' One cannot, Mouzelis (1995: 159) concludes, 'eliminate functionalist logic without paying an unacceptably high price.'

Method   Broadly speaking sociological functionalism has emphasized theoretical issues, while anthropological functionalism has focused on methodological issues, especially gathering data through ethnographic research. Turner and Maryanski (1979: 132–40) urge sociologists to employ what they call 'comparative requisite analysis' and 'holistic requisite analysis' in their empirical inquiries about social life. Whether sport sociologists should adopt these methods of analysis is a moot point, but certainly different forms of ethnography have much to offer.[12]

An early exemplar of anthropological functionalism based on ethnography is found in
Ronald Frankenberg's (1957) book *Village on the
Border: A Social Study of Religion, Politics and
Football in a North Wales Community*. It is unfortunate that Frankenberg's seminal study was
largely overlooked by early sport sociologists.[13]

Application Frankenberg produced a study
that not only contained most attributes of
good sociological methodology but in many
ways he pre-empted the current agenda of
neofunctionalists.

1 It is historical. Frankenberg took care to
   learn the history of the Welsh community in
   which he lived for a year as a participant
   observer.
2 It focuses on social change. Frankenberg
   'tells the story of a struggle to survive as a
   community against the pressure of the outside world' (Gluckman, 1957: 7).
3 It is concerned with social structure. On the
   one hand, it discusses the way class, gender, nationality and religion intersect, relate
   and cut across village life. On the other
   hand, it describes how local institutions
   such as the football club, brass band, choir,
   annual carnival, dramatic society and community council simultaneously 'serve' and
   'determine' village life.
4 It is non-reductionist in that no one social
   force or social structure assumes overarching determinacy.
5 It is political in the sense that it shows how
   villagers confront and deal with their problems, especially conflicts between different
   cliques, sects and occupational groups, and
   how different groups secure resources and
   convert them into commodities and facilities, and distribute them. Frankenberg provides particularly good insights into the
   way 'conflicts are carried over from one
   form of recreational activity to another, as
   from football to carnival', and how 'new
   conflicts engendered in disputes over football and carnivals may extend back into
   everyday life and cause further divisions
   within the village' (1957: 154).
6 It examines both the internal system and
   the external system. Frankenberg shows
   that 'geographically, economically and historically, the village is part of a larger
   whole' (1957: 9).
7 It is comparative. As noted by his mentor
   Max Gluckman, Frankenberg's study is of
   interest from the viewpoint of social anthropology for 'its application of ideas developed in the study of tribal society to a
   community in Britain' (1957: 7).

NOTES

We wish to thank our colleague Rex
Thomson for reviewing an early draft of this
chapter and note in passing that he unwittingly expressed functionalist leanings in an
early analysis of 'sport and ideology in contemporary society' (Thomson, 1978).

1 For excellent overviews of Parsons's work
   we refer the reader to Black (1961),
   Bourricaud (1981) and Rocher (1974);
   Merton's most famous work is *Social
   Theory and Social Structure* (1957) and
   Crothers (1987) provides a good synopsis
   of Merton's life and sociological writings.
2 The most recent and very different three-
   fold typology of functionalism is that of
   Habermas (1988: 74–88).
3 Robert Merton, Kingsley Davis and Wilbert
   Moore all studied as doctoral students with
   Talcott Parsons at Harvard University.
4 The assumed predominance of S-F was not
   restricted to North America or Europe. For
   example, Lawrence and Rowe (1986) contend that S-F hindered the development of
   sport sociology in Australia in the 1970s.
5 The second author places himself in this
   category, having been influenced early in
   his career by the dictums of Stinchcombe
   (1968) to the effect that 'theory ought to create the *capacity to invent explanations*' (p. 3;
   original emphasis); and 'the crucial question to ask of a strategy is not whether it
   is true, but whether it is sometimes useful'
   (p. 4).
6 This thesis was abandoned on two
   accounts: first, there was the belief that it
   reified the concept of society; secondly, it
   was passive in nature and did not consider
   sport as an active agent in the reproduction
   of systemic societal relations.
7 For greater insights about these sport sociologists we refer the reader to Edwards's
   autobiography (1980), the Festschrift in
   honour of Kalevi Heinila (Olin, 1984), and
   the Festschrift in honour of Günther
   Lüschen (Bette and Rütten, 1995). Sadly,
   Hideo Tatano died at the age of 50, immediately after hosting the sociology of sport
   session of the sport science conference held
   in conjunction with the 18th Universiade
   1995 Fukuoka. Christopher Stevenson
   moved from a functionalist orientation to a
   symbolic interaction orientation later in his
   career. Finally, we note that the irony of an
   African American (Edwards), a Jew (Bend),
   a Canadian (Stevenson), a Finn (Heinila), a
   German (Lüschen) and a Japanese (Tatano)

as the pillars of functionalism in sport sociology will not be lost on postmodernists.

8   Martindale (1960: 501–22) gives a brief history of micro-functionalism and group dynamics.

9   Interestingly, notwithstanding his political activism, Edwards (1973: 356–7) disagrees. He privileges structure over agency and warns African Americans that sporting structures will always restrain change.

10 For early logical analyses and defences of functionalism we refer the reader to Hempel (1959), Nagel (1961) and Stinchcombe (1968).

11 The leading figures are Jeffrey Alexander, Paul Colomy and Richard Munch in North America and Jürgen Habermas in Germany. Alexander and Colomy (1990: 56) describe Habermas's *Theory of Communicative Action* (1987) as 'a neo-Marxist revision of Parsonian concepts'.

12 For a critical account of ethnography in contemporary social research, see Hammersley (1992).

13 An even earlier but unpublished field study of sport and the community was by Frolich (1952).

REFERENCES

Aberle, D.F., Cohen, A.K., Davis, A.K., Levy, M.J. and Sutton, F.X. (1950) 'The functional prerequisites of society', *Ethics*, 100–11.

Abrahamson, M. (1978) *Functionalism*. Englewood Cliffs, NJ: Prentice-Hall.

Alexander, J. (1985). 'The "individualist dilemma" in phenomenology and interactionism', in S.N. Eisenstadt and H.J. Helle (eds), *Macrosociological theory*. London: Sage. pp. 25–57.

Alexander, J. and Colomy, P. (1990) 'Neofunctionalism today: reconstructing a theoretical tradition', in G. Ritzer (ed.), *Frontiers of Social Theory: the New Synthesis*. New York: Columbia University Press. pp. 33–67.

Barnes, B. (1995) *The Elements of Social Theory*. London: UCL Press.

Bend, E. (1970) 'Some functions of competitive team sports in American society', PhD thesis, University of Pittsburgh. Ann Arbor, MI: University Microfilms.

Bend, E. (1971) 'Some potential dysfunctional effects of sports upon socialization'. Paper presented at the Third International Symposium on the Sociology of Sport, University of Waterloo, Waterloo, Ontario, Canada.

Bend, E. (1974) 'A paradigm for analysing some relationships between sport and social mobility'.

Paper presented at the Eighth World Congress of Sociology, Toronto, Canada.

Bend, E. and Petrie, B.M. (1977) 'Sport participation, scholastic success, and social mobility', *Exercise and Sports Science Reviews*, 5: 1–44.

Berger, P. (1963) *Invitation to Sociology: a Humanistic Perspective*. New York: Anchor Books.

Berger, P. and Luckman, T. (1966) *The Social Construction of Reality*. New York: Anchor Books.

Bernard, T.J. (1983) *The Consensus–Conflict Debate: Form and Content in Social Theories*. New York: Columbia University Press.

Bette, K.H. and Rütten, A. (eds) (1995) *International Sociology of Sport: Contemporary Issues. Festschrift in Honor of Günther Lüschen*. Stuttgart: Naglschmid.

Black, M. (ed.) (1961) *The Social Theories of Talcott Parsons: a Critical Examination*. Englewood Cliffs, NJ: Prentice-Hall.

Blalock, H.M. (1969) *Theory Construction: From Verbal to Mathematical Constructions*. Englewood Cliffs, NJ: Prentice-Hall.

Bourdieu, P. (1977) *Outline of a Theory of Practice*. Cambridge: Cambridge University Press.

Bourricaud, F. (1981) *The Sociology of Talcott Parsons*. Chicago: University of Chicago Press.

Bridgeman, P.W. (1928) *The Logic of Modern Physics*. New York: Macmillan.

Brohm, J.M. (1978) *Sport: a Prison of Measured Time*. London: Ink Links.

Bryant, C. (1985) *Positivism in Social Theory and Research*. Houndmills: Macmillan.

Burrell, G. and Morgan, G. (1979) *Sociological Paradigms and Organizational Analysis*. Portsmouth, NH: Heinemann.

Caillois, R. (1961) *Man, Play, and Games*. New York: Free Press.

Cohen, P. (1968) *Modern Social Theory*. New York: Basic Books.

Coser, L.A. (1956) *The Functions of Social Conflict*. Glencoe, IL: Free Press.

Craib, I. (1984) *Modern Social Theory: From Parsons to Habermas*. New York: St Martin's Press.

Crothers, C. (1987) *Robert K. Merton*. London: Tavistock.

Curtis, J.E., Loy, J.W. and Karnilowicz, W. (1986) 'A comparison of suicide-dip effects of major sport events and civil holidays', *Sociology of Sport Journal*, 3: 1–14.

Davis, K.A. (1942) 'A conceptual analysis of stratification', *American Sociological Review*, 3: 309–21.

Davis, K.A. (1948) *Human Society*. New York: Macmillan.

Davis, K.A. (1953) 'Reply to Tumin', *American Sociological Review*, 13: 394–7.

Davis, K.A. (1959a) 'The abominable heresy: a reply to Dr. Buckly', *American Sociological Review*, 24: 82–3.

Davis, K.A. (1959b) 'The myth of functional analysis as a special method in sociology and anthropology', *American Sociological Review*, 24: 757–72.

Davis, K.A. and Moore, W.E. (1945) 'Some principles of stratification', *American Sociological Review*, 10: 243–7.

Demerath, N.J. (1967) 'Synecdoche and structural-functionalism', in N.J. Demerath and R.A. Peterson (eds), *System Change and Conflict*. New York: Free Press. pp. 501–20.

Dunning, E. (1973) 'The structural-functional properties of folk-games and modern sports: a sociological analysis', *Sportwissenschaft*, 3: 215–37.

Durkheim, E. ([1893] 1938) *The Division of Labor in Society*. Glencoe, IL: Free Press.

Durkheim, E. ([1895] 1938) *The Rules of Sociological Method*. Glencoe, IL: Free Press.

Durkheim, E. ([1897] 1952) *Suicide*. London: Routledge & Kegan Paul.

Durkheim, E. ([1912] 1954) *Elementary Forms of the Religious Life*. London: Allen & Unwin.

Edwards, H. (1969) *The Revolt of the Black Athlete*. New York: Free Press.

Edwards, H. (1973) *Sociology of Sport*. Homewood, IL: Dorsey Press.

Edwards, H. (1980) *The Struggle that Must Be: an Autobiography*. New York: Macmillan.

Elias, N. (1987) 'The retreat of sociologists into the present', *Theory, Culture and Society*, 4: 223–47.

Elias, N. and Dunning, E. (1966) 'Dynamics of sport groups with special reference to football', *British Journal of Sociology*, 17: 388–401.

Elias, N. and Dunning, E. (1986) *Quest for Excitement: Sport and Leisure in the Civilizing Process*. Oxford: Basil Blackwell.

Fay, B. and Moon, J.D. (1977) 'What would an adequate philosophy of social science look like?', *Philosophy of Social Science*, 7: 209–27.

Frankenberg, R. (1957) *Village on the Border: A Social Study of Religion, Politics and Football in a North Wales Community*. London: Cohen & West.

Frey, J.H. (1986) 'College athletics: problems of a functional analysis', in C.R. Rees and A.W. Miracle (eds), *Sport and Social Theory*. Champaign, IL: Human Kinetics. pp. 199–210.

Frolich, P.E. (1952) 'Sport and community: A study of social change in Athens, Ohio', unpublished PhD dissertation, University of Wisconsin, Madison, WI.

Gibbs, J. (1972) *Sociological Theory Construction*. Hinsdale, IL: Dryden Press.

Giddens, A. (1977) *Studies in Social and Political Theory*. New York: Basic Books.

Gluckman, M. (1957) 'Introduction', in R. Frankenberg, *Village on the Border. A Social Study of Religion, Politics and Football in a North Wales Community*. London: Cohen & West. pp. 1–8.

Gouldner, A. (1971) *The Coming Crisis of Western Sociology*. New York: Basic Books.

Gruneau, R. (1983) *Class, Sports, and Social Development*. Amherst, MA: University of Massachusetts Press.

Habermas, J. (1987) *The Theory of Communicative Action*, Volume 2: *Lifeworld and System: a Critique of Functionalist Reason*. Boston, MA: Beacon Press.

Habermas, J. (1988) *On the Logic of the Social Sciences*. Cambridge, MA: MIT Press.

Hammersley, M. (1992). *What's Wrong with Ethnography?* London: Routledge.

Heinila, K. (1966) 'Notes on the inter-group conflicts in international sport', *International Review of Sport Sociology*, 1: 31–40.

Heinila, K. (1969) 'Football at the crossroads', *International Review of Sport Sociology*, 4: 5–30.

Hekman, S. (1983) *Weber, the Ideal Type, and Contemporary Social Theory*. Notre Dame, IN: University of Notre Dame Press.

Hempel, G.C. (1959) 'The logic of functional analysis', in L. Gross (ed.), *Symposium on Sociological Theory*. New York: Harper & Row. pp. 271–307.

Horowitz, I.L. (ed.) (1964) *The New Sociology: Essays in Social Science and Social Theory in Honour of C. Wright Mills*. New York: Oxford University Press.

Horton, J. (1966) 'Order and conflict theories of social problems as competing ideologies', *American Journal of Sociology*, 71: 701–13.

Huaco, G.A. (1963) 'A logical analysis of the Davis–Moore theory', *American Sociological Review*, 28: 801–4.

Ingham, A. and Hardy, S. (1984) 'Sport: structuration, subjugation, and hegemony', *Theory, Culture and Society*, 2: 85–103.

Ingham, A. and Loy, J.W. (1973) 'The social system of sport; a humanistic perspective', *Quest*, 19: 3–23.

Jarvie, G. and Maguire, J. (1994) *Sport and Leisure in Social Thought*. London: Routledge.

Jones, R. (1986) *Emile Durkheim: an Introduction to Four Major Works*. London: Sage.

Karnilowicz, W. (1982) 'An analysis of the effects of ceremonial occasions on frequency of suicides in the United States, 1972–1978'. Unpublished Masters thesis, University of Illinois, Urbana, IL.

Keat, R. and Urry, J. (1975) *Social Theory as Science*. London: Routledge & Kegan Paul.

Kenyon, G. (1986) 'The significance of social theory in the development of sport sociology', in C.R. Rees and A.W. Miracle (eds), *Sport and Social Theory*. Champaign, IL: Human Kinetics. pp. 3–22.

Kincaid, H. (1996) *Philosophical Foundations of the Social Sciences: Analysing Controversies in Social Research*. Cambridge: Cambridge University Press.

Lawrence, G. and Rowe, D. (1986) 'Introduction: towards a Sociology of Sport in Australia', in G. Lawrence and D. Rowe (eds), *Power Play: The Commercialisation of Australian Sport*. Sydney: Hale & Iremonger. pp. 13–45.

Loy, J.W. (1969a) 'Small group research and the group in sport: a reaction to Günther Lüschen', in G.S. Kenyon (ed.), *Aspects of Contemporary Sport Sociology*. Chicago: The Athletic Institute. pp. 67–8.

Loy, J.W. (1969b) 'Game forms, social structure, and anomie', in R. Brown and B. Cratty (eds), *New Perspectives of Man in Action.* Englewood Cliffs, NJ: Prentice-Hall. pp. 181–99.

Loy, J.W., Knoop, J. and Theberge, N. (1979) 'Implications of the Davis–Moore theory of social stratification for the study of social differentiation within sport organizations', in M.L. Krotee (ed.), *The Dimensions of Sport Sociology.* West Point, NY: Leisure Press. pp. 106–26.

Loy, J.W., McPherson, B. and Kenyon, G.S. (1978) *Sport and Social Systems.* Reading, MA: Addison-Wesley.

Lundberg, G. (1939) *Foundations of Sociology.* New York: Macmillan.

Lundberg, G. (1941–42) 'Operational definitions in the social sciences', *American Journal of Sociology,* 47: 739.

Lüschen, G. (1967) 'The interdependence of sport and culture', *International Review of Sport Sociology,* 2: 127–42.

Lüschen, G. (1969) 'Small group research and the group in sport', in G.S. Kenyon (ed.), *Aspects of Contemporary Sport Sociology.* Chicago: The Athletic Institute. pp. 57–66.

Lüschen, G. (1971) 'Delinquency', in L.A. Larson and D.E. Hermann (eds), *Encyclopedia of Sport Sciences and Medicine.* New York: Macmillan. pp. 1391–3.

Lüschen, G. (1976) 'Cheating in sport', in D. Landers (ed.), *Social Problems in Athletics: Essays in the Sociology of Sport.* Urbana, IL: University of Illinois Press. pp. 67–77.

Lüschen, G. (1981a) 'The analysis of sport organizations', in G. Lüschen and G. Sage (eds), *Handbook of Social Science of Sport.* Champaign, IL: Stipes. pp. 316–29.

Lüschen, G. (1981b) 'The system of sport – problems of methodology, conflict and social stratification', in G. Lüschen and G. Sage (eds), *Handbook of Social Science of Sport.* Champaign, IL: Stipes. pp. 197–213.

Lüschen, G. (1984) 'Before and after Caracas: drug abuse and doping as deviant behaviour in sport', in K. Olin (ed.), *Contribution of Sociology to the Study of Sport.* Jyvaskyla: University of Jyvaskyla. pp. 51–68.

Lüschen, G. (1986) 'On small groups in sport: methodological reflections with reference to structural-functional approaches', in C.R. Rees and A.W. Miracle (eds), *Sport and Social Theory.* Champaign, IL: Human Kinetics. pp. 149–58.

Lüschen, G. (1988) 'Towards a new structural analysis – the present state and the prospectives of the international sociology of sport', *International Review for the Sociology of Sport,* 24: 269–85.

Lüschen, G. (1990) 'On theory of science for the sociology of sport: new structuralism, action, intention and practical meaning', *International Review for the Sociology of Sport,* 25: 69–83.

Malinowski, B. (1945) *The Dynamics of Cultural Change.* New Haven, CT: Yale University Press.

Martindale, D. (1960) *The Nature and Types of Sociological Theory.* Boston, MA: Houghton Mifflin.

Melnick, M. (1975) 'A critical look at sociology of sport', *Quest,* 24: 34–47.

Merton, R.K. (1957) *Social Theory and Social Structure.* Glencoe, IL: Free Press.

Mills, C.W. (1959) *The Sociological Imagination.* Harmondsworth: Penguin.

Milton, B. (1972) 'Sports as a functional equivalent of religion'. Unpublished Masters thesis, University of Wisconsin, Madison, WI.

Moore, W.E. (1953) 'Comment', *American Sociological Review,* 18: 397.

Moore, W.E. (1963a) 'But some are more equal than others', *American Sociological Review,* 28: 13–18.

Moore, W.E. (1963b) 'Rejoinder', *American Sociological Review,* 28: 27.

Mouzelis, N. (1995) *Sociological Theory: What Went Wrong?* London: Routledge.

Nagel, E. (1961) *The Structure of Science: Problems in the Logic of Scientific Explanation.* New York: Harcourt, Brace & World.

Nitsch, J.R. (1985) 'The action-theoretical perspective', *International Review for the Sociology of Sport,* 20: 263–82.

Novak, M. (1976) *The Joy of Sports.* New York: Basic Books.

Olin, K. (1984) *Contribution of Sociology to the Study of Sport: In Honor of Kalevi Heinila.* Jyvaskyla: University of Jyvaskyla.

Olmsted, C. (1962) *Heads I Win, Tails You Lose.* New York: Macmillan.

Page, C. (1985) 'On neofunctionalism', *Footnotes,* 13: 10.

Parsons, T. (1951) *The Social System.* Glencoe, IL: Free Press.

Parsons, T. (1966) *Societies: Evolutionary and Comparative Perspectives.* Englewood Cliffs, NJ: Prentice-Hall.

Parsons T. (1971) *The System of Modern Societies.* Englewood Cliffs, NJ: Prentice-Hall.

Parsons, T., Bales, R.F. and Shils, E.A. (1953) *Working Papers in the Theory of Action.* New York: Free Press.

Pooley, J. (1976) 'Ethnic soccer clubs in Milwaukee: a study in assimilation', in M. Hart (ed.), *Sport in the Sociocultural Process.* Dubuque, IA: Wm C. Brown. pp. 475–92.

Radcliffe-Brown, A.R. (1952) *Structure and Function in Primitive Society.* Glencoe, IL: Free Press.

Rees, C.R. and Segal, M.W. (1984) 'Role differentiation in groups: the relationship between instrumental and expressive leadership', *Small Group Behavior,* 15: 109–23.

Ritzer, G. (1975) *Sociology: a Multiple Paradigm Science.* Boston, MA: Allyn and Bacon.

Ritzer, G. (1988) *Contemporary Sociological Theory*. New York: Alfred Knopf.

Rocher, G. (1974) *Talcott Parsons and American Sociology*. London: Thomas Nelson.

Simmel, G. (1955) *Conflict* (translated by K.H. Wolff). Glencoe, IL: Free Press.

Sjoberg, G. (1959) 'Operationalism and social research', in L. Gross (ed.), *Symposium on Sociological Theory*. New York: Harper & Row. pp. 603–28.

Skidmore, W. (1979) *Theoretical Thinking in Sociology*, 2nd edn. Cambridge: Cambridge University Press.

Spiro, M.E. (1953) 'A typology of functional analysis', *Explorations*, 1.

Stevenson, C. (1974) 'Sport as a contemporary social phenomenon: a functional explanation', *International Journal of Physical Education*, 11: 8–14.

Stevenson, C. (1975) 'Socialization effects of participation in sport: a critical review of the research', *Research Quarterly*, 46: 287–301.

Stevenson, C. (1976a) 'Institutional socialization and college sport', *Research Quarterly*, 47: 1–8.

Stevenson, C. (1976b) 'Alternative theoretical approach to sport socialization: a concept of institutionalized socialization', *International Review of Sport Sociology*, 11: 65–76.

Stevenson, C. and Nixon, J.E. (1972) 'A conceptual scheme of the social functions of sport', *Sportwissenschaft*, 2: 119–32.

Stinchcombe, A. (1968) *Constructing Social Theories*. New York: Harcourt, Brace & World.

Sztompka, P. (1974) *System and Function: Toward a Theory of Society*. New York: Academic Press.

Tatano, H. (1981) 'A model-construction of sport as a culture: a working paper toward a systematic analysis of sport', *International Review of Sport Sociology*, 16: 5–28.

Thomson, R. (1978) 'Sport and ideology in contemporary society', *International Review of Sport Sociology*, 13: 81–94.

Turner, J.H. (1974) *The Structure of Sociological Theory*. Homewood, IL: Dorsey Press.

Turner, J.H. (1984) *Social Stratification: a Theoretical Analysis*. New York: Columbia University Press.

Turner, J. and Maryanski, A. (1979) *Functionalism*. Menlo Park, CA: Benjamin Cummings.

Van den Berghe, P. (1963) 'Dialectic and functionalism: toward reconciliation', *American Sociological Review*, 28: 695–705.

Wallace, W.L. (1971) *The Logic of Science in Sociology*. Chicago: Aldine Atherton.

Wallace, W.L. (1983) *Principles of Scientific Sociology*. New York: Aldine.

Warshay, L.H. (1975) *The Current State of Sociological Theory: a Critical Interpretation*. New York: David McKay.

Williams, R.M. (1968) *American Society: a Sociological Interpretation*. New York: Alfred Knopf.

Wohl, A. (1966) 'Conception and range of sport sociology', *International Review of Sport Sociology*, 1: 5–17.

Zeitlin, I.M. (1973) *Rethinking Sociology: a Critique of Contemporary Theory*. New York: Appleton-Century-Crofts.

2

MARXIST THEORIES

Bero Rigauer

In 1977, the City Council of Frankfurt am Main and the University of Frankfurt awarded the first 'Theodor W. Adorno Prize' to Norbert Elias, who outlined in his acceptance speech the close links that exist between his own sociological research and theory and the work of Adorno and Marx. Elias particularly emphasized their 'critical humanism' in his lecture, repeatedly referring to Marx as a key influence on his own thinking.

> Marx was undoubtedly the first person who succeeded in creating a comprehensive and coherent theoretical model of human society and its development based on the perspective of the less powerful and poorer groups of people. One cannot understand the extraordinary and far-reaching impact of his work in the present age of diminishing, even though in some respects not completely disappearing power imbalances, unless one comprehends this characteristic of Marx's social synthesis. (Elias, 1977: 45)

According to Elias, although he based his intellectual work on a 'critique of political economy', Marx must be understood as a sociologist, The development of Marx's theory by himself and others – often labelled under the heading 'Marxism' – is complex. First, this theory takes a multidisciplinary approach and integrates philosophical, anthropological, historical and economic studies. Secondly, there is Marx's own theoretical writing which I will refer to as 'Marxian'. Thirdly, we have to distinguish between several directions and stages of theoretical and practical development: the Marxian theory itself and its orthodox interpretations; the ongoing discussions of and enquiries into the Marxian theory by scholars adhering to various Marxist paradigms (see

Bottomore, 1979); Marxism as a political ideology applied to the interpretation of different societal configurations and social processes, for example, political parties, cultural institutions, state formation, the development of sports; attempts at synthesising Marxian and Marxist ideas with other scientific theories and political ideologies (see Bottomore, 1979). These short introductory comments already clearly show the need to distinguish between Marxian and Marxist theories, between orthodox and advanced concepts, between aspects of the Marxian and Marxist theories integrated into other academic theories and subjects, and the theory and practice of Marxism as a distinctive political ideology.

In relation to the historical and sociological development from Marxian to Marxist theory and Marxism, the following four aspects have to be taken into consideration.

1   The focus of Karl Marx's (1818–1883) intellectual and analytical work on socio-economic developments in capitalist societies clearly reflects the subjective experiences of his own biography: political and economic conflicts and revolutions interwoven with the increasingly capitalist industrialization of Western societies (especially England, France and Germany – but also the USA), in conjunction with emerging and intensifying class conflicts interrelated with dramatic political changes and subsequent power imbalances between the aristocracy, the newly emerging bourgeoisie and the working class. Marx himself was directly affected by some of these societal struggles, for example, he experienced persecution, exile, antisemitism and financial difficulties. As Marx obviously became a victim

of some of these processes, it is understandable that he took a stand for the poor and oppressed. Despite some critical detachment as an academic, it was impossible for Marx to remain unaffected by and uninvolved as a citizen in the political and economic crisis of industrial capitalism during the nineteenth century which was the central subject of his research. According to Blumenberg, Marx's theoretical and practical efforts were deeply affected by his biographical and social experiences and sufferings (1962: 105–18).

2   During his lifespan Marx worked as journalist, editor (for example, of the *Rheinische Zeitung*), political activist (for example, member and associated founder of the 'Kommunistenbund' [Communist Association]), author (for example, of the *Communist Manifesto*) and as an independent scholar. Therefore it is hardly a surprise that his ideas initially received appreciation from a wider public, particularly those contemporaries who were interested in politics, before his writings were appreciated for their analytical and academic qualities. Eventually, his theory became what he 'intended, in some sense ... the pre-eminent theory or doctrine of the working-class movement. It established itself most strongly in this form in the German Social Democratic Party, whose leaders, as a result of the rapid growth of the socialist movement, and also through their close association with Engels, became the principal intellectual and political heirs of Marx and largely dominated the international labour movement up until 1914' (Bottomore, 1979: 126).

After Marx's death in 1883, Marxism as a political ideology developed into many competing paradigms. They were heavily influenced and modified by various groups, political parties and working-class movements in Europe and all over the world. An endless number of debates emerged focusing on traditional and modern concepts of Marxist theory, driven by the activities and interests of socialist and communist groups, associations or parties in Europe, particularly during the 1880s and 1890s and the first three decades of the twentieth century. Labels such as 'orthodox', 'revisionist', 'Austro-Marxist' emerged during that period (cf. Bottomore, 1979: 126–30). The Russian Revolution in 1917 led to the foundation of the USSR. Lenin, Trotsky and other revolutionaries developed a new model of Marxism, referred to as 'Marxism–Leninism' which subsequently competed with 'Trotskyism'. Both ideologies and their institutional implementation during the formation process of the Soviet state were rejected and

radically reformed by Stalin who introduced a dictatorial Soviet system in the late 1920s based on his own dogma, 'Stalinism' (cf. Bottomore, 1979: 130–2). After the Second World War this form of totalitarian Marxism was widely adopted in Eastern Europe (the 'Eastern bloc' or 'Warsaw Pact' countries) and by the political elite of the USSR. Despite this harmonization, there were also a number of variations, for example, that of Mao Zedong in China (1949; Maoism) or of Castro in Cuba (1959; Fidelism). The ideological influence of Marxism rapidly decreased with the disintegration and subsequent democratization process of the former communist Eastern bloc (including Russia) during the 1990s. Only a few communist states using Marxism as their ideological basis still exist, for example, China, Cuba, North Korea and Vietnam. These examples clearly show the political instrumentalization of Marxism through communist power elites who contributed significantly to the gradual destruction of Marx's idea of critical humanism. Two further examples will demonstrate this point:

> Lenin did not set out to re-examine in any systematic way the Marxist theoretical system, but instead adopted a conception of Marxism as 'the theory of the proletarian revolution' and devoted his efforts to working out, and embodying in an effective organization, its implications for political strategy. (Bottomore, 1979: 130)

Furthermore Stalin 'put an end to ... theoretical debates and the possibility of any serious advances in Marxist social science. Thereafter, Soviet Marxism became an increasingly rigid and dogmatic ideology', functionalized as an instrument of a state-centralized and rigorous process of industrialization and collectivization (Bottomore, 1979: 131). This development is responsible for a number of major problems Marxism has encountered, including the academic treatment of the sociological theory.

3   Academic discussions of Marxist theory began in the late 1880s after Marx's death, particularly in philosophy, sociology and economics (for example, by Toennies, Grünberg, Labriola, Durkheim, Böhm-Bawerk, Hilferding and Masaryk). During the twentieth century these debates were widely influenced by a number of different contextual factors: political (the two World Wars; socialist/communist revolutions and associated processes of state formation; fascisticization, etc.), economic (for example, capitalist/socialist industrialization; the 'world economic crisis' of 1929/30), cultural (concerning the arts, literature, the mass media of communication, etc.), and the development

of the social sciences (societal impact of the humanities, the social and natural sciences). Some of the academic controversies (for example, Seligman, Simmel, M. Weber) about Marxism show parallels with the debates about Marxism and political and social practice – as outlined before. The social-scientific elaboration of Marxist theory and research in the past has almost always been dogmatic and is even nowadays often very orthodox. This can only be explained adequately if we separate out the development of a Marxist theory which on the one hand became increasingly an ideologized general theory used by socialist/communist states and their educational institutions (schools, colleges, universities) – the so-called 'scientific socialism' grounded in 'Marxism–Leninism' and its variations (for example, Maoism) – while on the other hand, a number of critical and progressive scholars and schools of Marxist theory developed advanced theories and linked these with non-Marxist paradigms and methods, for example, 'structuralist Marxism', 'critical theory', 'hegemony theory', 'critical philosophy', feminist criticisms of Marxist theory, Marxist theories of 'underdeveloped' societies (cf. Bottomore, 1979: 125–43). In a nutshell, the academic development of Marxist theory has always been overshadowed by controversies about Marxism as an ideology.

4   This conflict between ideology and academia emerged from a fundamental objective of Marxism, namely the utopian idea of a future communist society. All historical attempts to put socialism and communism into practice had to face the dilemma that Marx did not develop any practical models of communist society. In addition, the socio-economic conditions under which communist revolutions occurred never fulfilled the fundamental conditions Marx had identified. Some of the revolutionary movements did not have widespread support from the people, others took place before the predicted self-destructing crisis of industrial capitalism had set in. Consequently, the leaders of communist revolutions remained elitist minorities introducing and establishing totalitarian forms of state socialism (see point 3 above) which they justified with a modified ideology of Marxism, such as 'democratic centralism' (Lenin). They believed that they had created social realities according to Marxist ideas. However, they simply reversed ideology and reality. A corresponding transposition became more and more a central epistemological problem of academic Marxist theory and research: the results and interpretations of Marxist sociological enquiries were often

determined by a theory referring either to the development of capitalism during the nineteenth and early twentieth centuries or to paradigms that ideologized capitalist societies as regressive and destructive, and socialist/communist societies as progressive and constructive. In this connection, academic Marxist theories came increasingly to involve a contradiction between dogmatic and open thinking about social development and research into this field.

The main political and scientific problem of Marxism is based on the dogmatic treatment of historical and societal processes. Epistemological difficulties emerge from an attitude of abstract realism, which is methodologically connected with the suggestion of Marxism being 'the only valid theory'. Nevertheless – and there are other theories which lay claim to sole validity – as mentioned above, Marxist theory contains ideas of substance, together with theoretical and empirical characteristics which are sufficiently methodologically important to be applied and advanced in sociological research into sport.

MARXIST THEORY AND SOCIOLOGY

Marx's Theory of Society

Marx developed a theory of social development which is based on research into socio-economic and political relations, interdependencies and power imbalances. 'Society does not consist of individuals but expresses the sum of relations and conditions in which these individuals stand by one another.' Marx also suggests that 'being a slave and [or: B.R.] a citizen, is grounded on social relations, relations of human beings A and B. The human being A is as such not a slave. He is slave within and through society' (Marx, 1939/41: 176). Subsequently, Marx also argues that all historical societies – especially the 'bourgeois system' (capitalism) – are characterized by increasing efforts to establish totalitarian forms ('totalities') of social differentiation and integration (see Marx, 1939/41: 189).

The Base–Superstructure Distinction The advanced Marxian theory focuses upon economic activities and relations, the 'base', and their impact on other social institutions, such as politics and culture, the 'superstructure'. Marxist theorists assume and stress that societal developments are initiated through economic processes, in particular by any change in the mode of production, that is, the structured relationship between the means of production and the way humans are involved in this process. The economic conditions of capitalism automatically generate a socio-economic conflict between the 'masters of production' (capitalists; owners of the means of production) and the 'direct producers' (workers; owners of labour power). Both societal groups are best understood in terms of classes competing for power ('class struggle') as the owners of the means of production exploit the direct producers financially (wages less than the economic values produced) and suppress them politically (socio-political dependencies). This power imbalance is also characterized by the increasing impoverishment and alienation of the workers and phases of high unemployment (caused by overproduction, the declining rate of profit, etc.). As an inevitable result, class struggles turn into revolutions driven by the working class with the aim of establishing socialist or communist societies. In a nutshell, the history of humankind is a history of class conflict. Marx and Marxist theorists claim that such class conflict is leading to the emergence of communist societies and that these must be seen as the highest level of human cultural development.

Equally important in the range of Marxist concepts is that of the superstructure, a term which refers to all social and cultural forms other than the economy. That is because the superstructure is of fundamental significance for societal developments. From a Marxist perspective, it is the economy which has determining effects on the superstructure. One key function of the superstructure is to act as a framework for ideologies that justify and stabilize the modes of production and consumption under capitalism. Due to the dependence of the superstructure on the base there will, eventually, be a relationship of total correspondence between them. Consequently, the superstructure reproduces the key ideologies of the capitalist system and reinforces the social realization of the latter. As part of this arrangement, cultural practices, processes and relations are fully integrated and merged in the superstructure and yet are distinguishable from each other, for example, education, leisure time, mass media, the arts, religion, sciences, politics, state, the legal system, etc. Participation in these practices and processes requires structured forms of socialization whose aims and objectives are based on the key ideologies of the capitalist economy. Although the Marxist concept of the relationship between the base and the superstructure is perceived as highly deterministic, it also

recognizes the relative autonomy of cultural processes. However, this autonomy occurs relatively rarely, for example, during historical periods of economic development which take place without social and political conflicts.

Marxist Methodology According to Marx, Marxist theorists refuse any epistemologically founded idealist methodology (such as Hegel's philosophical method). For Marx, historical developments and social processes emerge from concrete realities (realism), which can only be investigated with the help of a materialist approach. Materialism, for Marx, relates methodologically to empirical phenomena. Furthermore, he suggests that 'materialism' should be conceptualized as the attempt to develop a theory of society which focuses upon the interdependencies between the economic relations of the base and the cultural processes and practices of the superstructure. Based on these premises about the nature of research, Marx and Marxist theorists integrate two distinctive methodological concepts.

Historical Materialism Historical changes in societal processes and arrangements are always caused by concrete and organized human activities. Although human beings are actively involved in creating their social environment, they also enter already existing forms of production and interdependency which determine their social life. The need for research into those social relations which are determined by economic activities (modes of production, including distribution, consumption and reproduction), whilst using abstract categories and concepts (for example, philosophical, economic and political terms) arises from applying the method of historical materialism. This is what Marxists consider to be the scientific method of descending from an abstract totality (such as the class structure) to the concrete realities of social life (for example, the social relations that are determined by class structures; see Marx, 1939/41: 21–9).

Dialectical Materialism The concept of dialectical materialism is methodologically interwoven with the concept of historical materialism and forms the basis of a 'scientific philosophy'. It was Engels who developed this dialectical method. It draws on the results of his research into the history of nature (evolution) and of human society and thought (revolution). He discovered three fundamental 'laws' of development which all involve dialectical relationships: 'the law of change from quantity into quality and *vice versa*; … the penetration of contradictions; … the negation of negations' (Engels, 1973: 51). In this epistemological context, Marx also referred to Hegel's formalized model of dialectical developments: thesis, antithesis and synthesis. These three cornerstones symbolize concrete stages of developing societal configurations. The historical subjects (classes) produce changes (revolutions) due to increasing conflicts (class struggles). The outcome also contains social innovations through advanced modes of economic production and cultural reproduction.

Marx, Engels and some of their successors combined and used both methodological concepts, historical and dialectical materialism, as a central method for their multidisciplinary research into societal development and change.

It is important to recognize when summarizing the Marxist theory of society that its 'distinctiveness … consists of … emphasizing the importance of labour in the economic sense (the developing interchange between man and nature) as the foundation of all social life' and progress (Bottomore, 1979: 119). In this respect, the main problem of capitalism is caused by the 'alienation of labour' (see Marx, 1970: 149–66). Alienated labour is based upon the established socio-economic relation between the 'masters of production' and the 'direct producers'. Individual members of the working class are increasingly dependent on their employers, that is, the industrialist class within a capitalist society which exploits the workers' production by appropriating its economic results. Estranged labour power also becomes a commodity on the labour market and denies workers the chance of developing their human potential and creativity. Therefore, a class structure based on economic and political power imbalances dehumanizes social relations. As long as production affects societal developments functionally, however, the future of social progress will depend on a nonalienating organization and practice of human labour. Marx's and the Marxist conception of 'alienated labour' is epistemologically and methodologically a constitutive element of Marxist sociology.

Marxist Sociology

Marxist Sociology – a Contradiction in Terms? Marxist and non-Marxist scholars agree that there are scientific and ideological problems which make it difficult (and perhaps impossible) to establish Marxism as a sociological approach. If 'one believes Marxists like Karl Korsch, sociology was never anything but a bourgeois invention to counteract the critical impact of Marxism on the dominant self-descriptions of capitalist societies. The influence of Marx's thought in sociology should therefore be ubiquitous' (Ganssmann, 1994: 81). Korsch, Lukács and other Marxists rejected 'the idea of Marxism as a positive science of society – as sociology …; instead, it was conceived as a "critical philosophy" which expressed the world view of the revolutionary proletariat just as, according to Korsch, German idealist philosophy had been the theoretical expression of the revolutionary bourgeoisie' (Bottomore, 1979: 132). In addition, there are other reasons that question attempts to conceptualize Marxism as sociology: Marxist theory is based upon political preferences, interdisciplinary research, a philosophical methodology (dialectical materialism) and the paradigm of economic determinism. With regard to these epistemological positions, Marxist theory cannot be reduced to an academic subject such as sociology. However, the so-called bourgeois scholars also rejected the idea and possibility of establishing a Marxist sociology as they believed it would be politically and ideologically connected with the revolutionary interests of the working class and the deterministic concept of Marxism (see, for example, Popper, 1968: 336–46). Despite all these arguments and points of resistance, Marxist sociology has become firmly based within the general framework of sociological theories and methods.

Western Marxist Sociology The academic development of Marxist sociology was initiated and occurred predominantly in Western Europe. During the 1920s and 1930s members of the 'Frankfurt School of Critical Theory' founded a neo-Marxist social-philosophical and sociological theory based on the assumption that an analysis of long-term societal and capitalistic processes makes it necessary to conceptualize distinct theoretical and methodological preconditions: (1) to do interdisciplinary research; (2) to connect social philosophical and empirical research; and (3) to undertake materialistically founded social research. In 1931, Horkheimer proclaimed in a public lecture that: 'The present stage of scientific knowledge makes a continuous synthesis between philosophy and the sciences necessary. There is a central philosophical and sociological question that has to be investigated. What are the relations between social life, the psychological development of individuals, and cultural changes?' (Rigauer, 1995: 2; see also Bottomore, 1979: 132–3). Until the 1970s the Frankfurt School continued to develop a concept of Marxist sociology and to integrate it into the social-philosophical framework of 'critical theory' (for example, Habermas, 1967, 1973). This penetration of Marxist sociology with epistememological concerns characterized its foundation. All 'Western' theorists who have suggested the outline designs of a Marxist sociology, such as structuralist (Althusser et al.), cultural (Gramsci et al.), historical (Croce et al.), developmental (Frank et al.), were deeply interwoven with Marxism – a critical philosophy of society (see Bottomore, 1979: 136–42). As a result, a coherent sociological concept of a 'Marxist sociology' focusing on the previously outlined key methodological positions was never established. This epistemological stage can be described as involving a tentative progress towards sociological standards of research: 'The development of Marxism as a theory is now accorded a greater independence from direct political concerns and is more clearly located in the context of a general development of sociological theory' (Bottomore, 1979: 142).

Marxist–Leninist Sociology Another interesting development of Marxist sociology that has to be taken into consideration took place in the Eastern bloc whilst it was dominated and heavily influenced by the communist regime of the Soviet Union. In that part of the world, due to the ideological pressure of communist governments after the Second World War, sociological thinking and methods only emerged reluctantly. Establishing sociology formally as an academic subject in the postwar era was a very difficult enterprise as sociology struggled to distance itself from the official 'Marxist–Leninist' sociology of the communist states. Theoretically and methodologically, it remained as a dogmatic, ideological academic subject justifying and stabilizing existing political structures without any critical sensitivity (see Bottomore, 1979: 130–5). However, there were some groups of scholars who developed and conceptualized advanced and critical paradigms (theories, methods) of Marxist sociology (see Kiss, 1971). Comparing 'Eastern' and 'Western' Marxist sociology, the already mentioned epistemological problem of philosophical involvement is certainly substantial and hampered the necessary elaboration of sociological theory and methods. During the past ten years or so, the traditional Marxist–Leninist sociology has been undergoing a gradual process of transformation. The result will certainly be closer to mainstream 'Western' concepts of sociology. In particular, in Germany

since the 'reunification', the critical concepts of Marxist sociology are neither recognized nor appreciated; mostly they are rejected and certainly not employed for sociological analyses (cf. Kreckel, 1994: 240–51).

Epistemological Basis of Marxist Sociology Despite the obvious variations within Marxist sociology mentioned above, the following summary will focus on key theoretical and methodological aspects and neglect the previously mentioned differences. The epistemological basis of Marxist sociology is the materialist method, which combines historical and dialectical materialism. In terms of the methods used this means: observing, documenting, reconstructing and analysing short- or long-term societal processes with particular reference to unilinear developments and conflict, whilst focusing upon economic relations and interdependencies with particular reference to the politics of power. Proceeding in this manner means that empirical sociological research is theory-led. In addition, a constant exchange between theory and empirical methods is happening within a particular framework of paradigms, subjects and aims:

1 Applying Marxist paradigms linked with sociological methods to investigate the relationship between base and superstructure, emerging and developing economic and cultural interdependencies (assuming the predominance of economic influences); theory–practice relations being implicated in a unification of sociological research and politically transformed sociological knowledge (science as a force of societal reproduction, innovation and change); developing and applying general laws of societal progress from lower to higher stages of social, economic, political and cultural organization (towards socialist/communist forms of society).

2 Sociological enquiry into processes which are emerging from (i) economic and political relations; (ii) cultural differentiations evolving between autonomy and economic/political functionalization; (iii) class structures and their inherent societal functions and revolutionary potential; (iv) the ideological manipulation of human thinking, knowledge and socialization processes against the background of the economic, political and cultural functions of social development.

3 The main purpose of Marxist sociology is guided by sociological criticism of societal and scientific processes, including ideological ones. The methodological term 'criticism'

refers to the tradition of political and philosophical enlightenment (central interest of sociological knowledge).

The flow diagram opposite (Figure 2.1) summarizes and highlights the conceptualizing process of Marxist sociology.

MARXIST SOCIOLOGY OF SPORT

Introduction

The Emerging Interest in Sociological Research into Sport Like sociology itself, modern sport emerged in the context of the civilizing processes that occurred within European societies during the eighteenth and nineteenth centuries. The development of modern sport is closely linked with processes of increasing democratization, industrialization, rationalization, rising standards of social control, emancipation and freedom. The emergence of modern sport involved formal and informal forms of participation of athletes and supporters in social activities emphasizing special motor skills, competition and leisure. When sport became a widespread and visible cultural phenomenon, it started socially to differentiate, expand and create nexuses with other areas of society. Currently, sport is a global phenomenon whose development is interwoven with the cultural, political and economic phases of societal development being experienced worldwide. Therefore, it is no surprise that sport has attracted the interest of sociological investigators. Already at the end of the nineteenth and the beginning of the twentieth centuries, sociologists started to observe, describe and analyse the social functions, structures and innovations of the ongoing sportization process. However, it took until the 1960s for sociological research to focus systematically on the social aspects of sport. Despite this progress, one has to take note of the fact that the study of sport continues to be a low-status activity within the profession of sociology more generally (see Elias and Dunning, 1993: 1–6). There is no doubt that sport is an interesting sociological subject that provides an exciting challenge for sociological enquiries. It can also help to advance debates about the relationship between empirical and theoretical enquiries. This also applies to Marxist sociology in general and Marxist research into sport in particular.

The Development of Marxist Analyses of Sport Prior to the emergence of interest in sport among Marxist scholars, members of the socialist and communist movements in continental Europe had developed a keen interest in sport as early as the second half of the nineteenth and beginning of the twentieth century. They considered sport to be a social practice of great political significance. In addition, they were critical of the ideological content of sport.

A Marxist theory of 'physical culture' and sport (combined with sociological research) was founded during the second half of the twentieth century by Marxist scholars who were in various ways supported by socialist and communist organizations and governments (for example, the Soviet Union; and after the Second World War, the 'Eastern bloc'). Their research is based on the assumption that sport is a social and historical phenomenon. The increasing influence of science on 'physical culture' and sport happened after the first steps had been taken to realize these activities in practice. This more or less intended process, or one may say method, is part of a functionally conceptualized relation and interdependency between theory and practice, allocating priority to the latter within socialist/communist policy and Marxist science (see Figure 2.1).

What were these early processes of socialist/communist physical culture including sport which increasingly acquired an empirical foundation in Marxist theory, and later on, in the Marxist sociology of sport?

The following four examples will demonstrate more clearly what this means. All four case studies focus on the development of working-class sport between 1850 and 1930 and must be seen against the background of a fairly coherent set of dominant ideologies:

1   There is general agreement that the interest and participation in (informal and organized) sport of members of the working class grew during this period in Britain. On the one hand, workers' sports participation was seen as a type of amusement and uncritical consumption, but at the same time also as a valuable form of physical recreation connected with the increasing importance of competitive team sports (football, for example). Therefore what people perceived to be 'working-class sport' became more and more part of the so-called middle class or bourgeois sport culture. On the other hand, this development was criticized by a small group of educated middle-class socialists who had their own dreams of creating a more elevated 'high' culture of the masses, including sport (Holt, 1992: 145). They 'refused to accept commercial sport as an authentic element in working-class

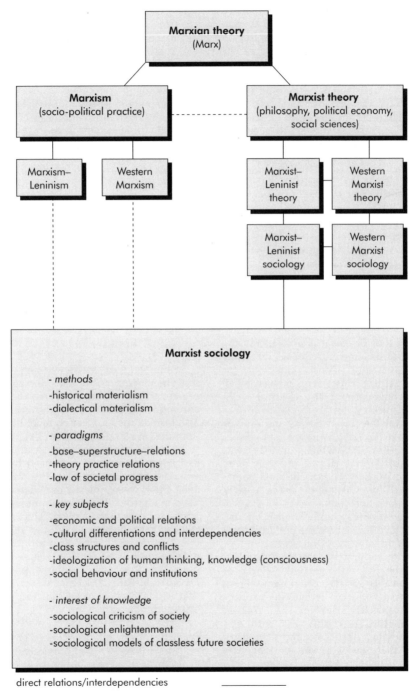

Figure 2.1 *Flow diagram - Marxist sociology*

culture', because it would create political passivity. They suggested that sport was 'demoralised and damned by capitalism' (Holt 1992: 146; see also Hargreaves, 1995: 80–2). Consequently, ambivalent attitudes towards sport in general and differing interpretations of its social and political qualities and functions emerged. 'The absence of a socialist alternative, the lack of imagination, was due at least in part to the low priority that leaders of the working-class movement gave to cultural matters in the broad sense' (Hargreaves, 1995: 81). Therefore sport in Britain never became an ideological tool of the socialist movement and remained marginal in the field of socialist activities. The organization of sports participation was considered to be fairly apolitical, occurring within people's leisure time and involving the simultaneous rejection of and adaptation to capitalist civilization and culture (see Holt, 1992: 146–8). The working-class movement did 'not seem to have taken ... sports as a whole very seriously. In fact, ... the British working-class movement and the Left as a whole continued to ignore the growing significance of sport in working-class people's lives, tacitly allowing this terrain to be hegemonized by forces unsympathetic to the Left', that is, by middle-class and bourgeois aims, purposes, and organizations (Hargreaves, 1995: 92–3).

2   From the 1850s onwards in Germany, the working-class movement organized what one might call 'proto-sports clubs' (*Turnvereine*), for example, in Leipzig. This movement resisted all political counter-currents (by the monarchy and the aristocracy, for example) and was responsible for the foundation of the *Arbeiter Turner Bund* (ATB) – the Workers' Gymnastics Association – in 1893 which, in 1919, was changed into *Arbeiter Turn- und Sportbund* (ATSB) – the Workers' Gymnastics and Sports Association. This change of name clearly reflects the open and fundamental ideological conflict between *Turnen* and 'English Sports'. Until the turn of the century, the politically and ideologically orientated working-class gymnastics and sports movement was strongly influenced by the SPD (the Socialist Party of Germany) and its socialist programme. From the beginning of the twentieth century onwards, especially during the Weimar Republic (1919–33), communist influence had an increasing impact on the movement and caused the division of the working-class sports movement (*Arbeiter Sportbewegung*) into Socialist Party (SPD) and Communist Party (KPD) sections. This ideological conflict endured until the elimination of the working-class sports movement and its organizations by the National Socialists in 1933. Between 1850 and 1933, the following features of the working-class gymnastics and sports movement are worth being singled out for sociological mention:

(a)   the existence of a close political, ideological and organizational connection with the SPD and the KPD and their aims;

(b)   a critical approach to the bourgeois ideal that was said to be part of capitalistic sport (a critique of sport meant a critique of capitalism);

(c)   attempts to justify and develop socialist/communist aims and forms of sportspractice (integration of sports-political and socio-political agitation [cf. Wagner, 1973/1931]);

(d)   growing ideological conflicts between proponents of the socialist (SPD) and the communist (KPD) concepts of sport;

(e)   growing ideological adaptation to the bourgeois concept of competitive sport (such as the Olympic movement, high performance and competitive sports). In this context, the bourgeois-orientated German tradition of *Kultur* (*Turnen*) was more and more taken over as the guiding ideology of sport whereas the modern conception of civilization (democratic industrial society) was rather neglected (see Dwertmann, 1997).

To sum up: the German working-class sports movement was politically, ideologically and organizationally integrated into the socialist/communist working-class movement which also formed the basis for its revolutionary programme (working-class sport as class struggle).

3   In the USSR, the first socialist/communist sports movement organized by the state emerged immediately after the revolution in 1917. Sport was primarily organized and practised to improve the nation's fitness during the period of 'war communism' which refers to the Civil War between 1917 and 1920. During the 'Decade of Physical Culture', three different strands of sport emerged. These were influenced by the 'new economic policies' and favoured by three different communist groups, that is, by teachers, scientists and politicians. These strands were:

(a)   The 'Concept of Proletarian Culture' (prioritized by the Proletkultists): in addition to the contribution of sport to important political events, the 'Concept of Production-Gymnastics' was introduced into the world of work to raise the productivity of the workforce.

(b)   The 'Concept of Hygiene' (favoured by the Hygienists): sport was regarded as a vital part of health education and particular sports, like boxing, Association football, gymnastics and weight-lifting, were rejected as being conducive to injuries, disadvantageous to health and too competitive.

(c) The 'Concept of Spartacism' ('Spartak'; reference to Spartacus who led a slave rebellion in the Roman Empire 74–71 BC): unspecialized and unprofessional practising of high performance and competitive sport.

These three different approaches to physical culture and sport had a number of factors in common. First, they were critical of and rejected the bourgeois-capitalist concept of competitive sport, especially high performance sport. Secondly, they preferred the area of physical culture to be developed and organized by communist intellectuals rather than by the members of Russian society as a whole (given the then-contemporary level of development of the USSR). Thirdly, they considered sport to be a means to an end and intended to use it in order to solve social problems, for example, alcoholism and illness. Fourthly, sport was expected to support women's emancipation. Fifthly, all three approaches supported the development, practice and renewal of the concept of 'physical culture' (including physical education, games, leisure activities and sport) and the political and ideological functionalization of sport by the Communist Party of the Soviet Union (CPSU) were influenced by its aims and ideas. Finally, there was also a consensus that Soviet sport should be centrally organized by the Communist Party in conjunction with the government and the state. This represents the first attempt to apply and institutionalize Marxist ideas and concepts to and in the world of sport (see Riordan, 1980a, 1980b, 21–5; Ruffmann, 1980: 37–55, 134ff).

4   After the First World War, European working-class sportsmen and women started to organize themselves nationally and internationally: in 1920 they founded the 'Lucerne Social Democratic Sports International' (LSDSI). One year later the Communist 'Red Sports International' (RSI) came into existence. In Frankfurt am Main (1925), Vienna (1931) and Antwerp (1937) 'Workers' Olympics' were organized by the International Socialist Working Class Movement in an attempt to stress their political resistance. Due to the different Democratic-Socialist and Marxist–Leninist concepts of sport, ideological conflicts between the LSDSI and the RSI arose.

The following aspects drawn from the four above-mentioned examples will highlight the historical and empirical base of the Marxist

theory of sport which will be dealt with subsequently. This theoretical approach can be understood adequately only against this social and political background. The following developmental aspects of socialist/communist sport in the second half of the nineteenth century and the first three decades of the twentieth century are of crucial importance for understanding the Marxist sociology of sport.

- The working class (proletariat) is of central significance.
- Whilst on the one hand, sport has a marginal role for the working-class movement, on the other hand sport also provides the possibility to develop an autonomous, anti-bourgeois concept of sport as part of proletarian culture.
- The working-class sports movement runs the risk of going through a bourgeoisification process and thus of adapting itself to bourgeois norms and values.
- As an integral part of the revolutionary class struggle, the working-class sports movement will become politically emancipated.
- Proletarian sport is partial and biased. It is associated with socialist/communist politics.
- The working-class sports movement has an international orientation. Therefore it exerts international solidarity and participates in the international class struggle.
- The Soviet model of sport performs the following socialist/communist functions: physical and cultural education; health care; increase of human working and productive power; paramilitary training; emphasis on top-level competitive sport; recreational activities; solving social problems; emancipation of women; political and ideological socialization.
- The (inter)national working-class sports movement reflects the different political programmes of Democratic Socialism and Marxist–Leninist centralism.

Most of these social and political elements can be observed in the developing Marxist theories of sport in the 1920s and 1930s. References to: the proletarian masses; the marginality as well as the centrality of sport's functions; problems of bourgeoisification; concepts based on ideologies and class struggle; internationalism; use of the organizational structuring of Soviet sport as a role model; controversies between dogmatic and undogmatic programmes of socialism/communism. Almost all the above-mentioned dimensions of socialist/communist sport form the historical and empirical base for Marxist theories of sport. Due to the increasing differentiation of sport in both capitalist and communist societies, especially after the Second World War, academics started to investigate sport systematically. This development commenced primarily in the USSR and other societies with well-developed Marxist academic traditions, for example, in Great Britain, France, Italy and Germany.

Marxist–Leninist Theories of the Relationship between Sport and Society

The Institutional Monopolization of Science In the USSR, the institutional foundations for the development of a Marxist–Leninist 'theory of physical culture' were laid in the 1920s and 1930s. During this period a number of academic institutions were founded which were operated by the state and/or the Communist Party (CPSU): for example, the 'State Institute for Physical Culture' (1920, Moscow) and the 'Central Institute for Research into Physical Culture' (1933, Moscow; see Riordan, 1980b). After the Second World War, the entire structure of institutions became more and more differentiated. This pattern of organizational structuring was copied by European 'People's Republics', such as Albania, Bulgaria, Czechoslovakia, East Germany, Poland and Romania (see Riordan, 1981) as well as by non-European states under the influence of the Soviet Union such as China and Cuba (see Riordan, 1981). All these states have in common the fact that their academic research into sport was based on the Marxist–Leninist ideology. In them, Marxism–Leninism was defined as the only acceptable political paradigm and this led to a dogmatic influence on academic research and theoretical debates.

The Marxist–Leninist 'Theory of Physical Culture and Sport' The Marxist (and also Maoist) 'Theory of Physical Culture and Sport' emerged on the basis of the above-mentioned socio-historical and ideological developments. The term 'Socialist Physical Culture' was at the centre of each concept (see Ruffmann, 1980). The forms and contents of human movement were divided into different physical and cultural aspects and primarily linked with political functions (see discussion of Marxist analyses of sport above, especially point 4 and summary). All aims, tasks and contents (aspects of theory and research) were integrated into the ideology of Marxism–Leninism and led to the following conceptualization:

- The paradigm and methodology of the 'Theory of Physical Culture and Sport' were integrated into historical and dialectical materialism (see discussion of Marx's theory of society above).
- Research issues were linked to specific functions of the socialist/communist practice of physical culture and sports: human productivity (industrial, agricultural and other work); health (in particular prevention, improvement and rehabilitation); education into the 'socialist personality' (collectivism); games, sport and leisure time; high performance and competitive sport; paramilitary training.
- With reference to the academic treatment of sport and physical culture, the following aspects were taken into consideration: the foundations of Marxism–Leninism, the history of physical culture and sport, the foundations of pedagogy, medicine, psychology, sociology and the theory of training and coaching (see Schafrik, 1972).

Looking back to that earlier discussion of Marx's theory of society, the dilemma of all theories relating to physical culture and sport becomes obvious: The historical and contemporary developments of physical culture and sport depend on the social and material conditions of human life as reflected in the base–superstructure distinction. Founded on science, they can be politically planned and realized through 'scientific socialism and central planning'. Not the individual but the collectivity, whose social function consists of the differentiation of socialist/communist forms of society and the integration of physical culture and sports practice, stands at the centre of all revolutionary tasks. To achieve this objective, the following preconditions have to be fulfilled:

- Marxist–Leninist research into physical culture and sport must be conducted on the basis of interdisciplinary cooperation.
- A Marxist–Leninist ideology of physical culture and sport must have a rationale.
- A critique of the bourgeois-capitalist development of international sport (ideological criticism) must be undertaken.

Overall, the Marxist–Leninist 'Theory of Physical Culture and Sport' was characterized by scientism, economic determinism and dogmatism. How can we evaluate the academic achievements of the people who worked within this framework? Against the background of the ideological influences they were subject to we can distinguish two academic strands.

On the one hand, there were the less ideologically biased natural and technical sciences, such as sports medicine, biomechanics, the theory of training and coaching as well as the manufacture of sports equipment which achieved an outstanding international reputation for their quality research. On the other hand, there were the ideologically biased humanities and social sciences, such as philosophy, pedagogy, psychology, sociology and history which, due to their dogmatism, never managed to achieve high international standards. In general, whilst the social-scientific treatment of sport by dogmatic Marxists bolstered the *status quo*, in the natural-scientific and technological spheres analysis and application developed very well. Nevertheless, the academic openness of Marx's social theory was partly discontinued.

Marxist–Leninist Contributions to the Sociology of Sport The Marxist–Leninist theory of physical culture claimed meta-theoretical leadership in the scientific analysis of sport. All the other sport sciences were expected to accept a subordinate role. A differentiation into specific subdisciplines was only allowed in a very restricted range of subjects such as history, pedagogy, medicine and the theory of training but entirely rejected for psychology and, in particular, for sociology since the latter was perceived as a 'bourgeois academic discipline'. Sociological research as part of the sport sciences only emerged in the 1960s. In the German Democratic Republic (GDR), for example, sociology did not gain the status of an independent academic subject and was defined as an integral part of the Marxist–Leninist theory of society until the 1960s. The same applies to the sociology of sport in the GDR. Sociology in general and the sociology of sport in particular, were only introduced because of the international competition of scientists in which the GDR wanted to participate. Therefore, in 1961 the first research centre for the sociology of sport was established at the 'Deutsche Hochschule für Körperkultur' (DHfK – German University for Physical Culture) in Leipzig which initiated and influenced the further development of the Marxist–Leninist sociology of sport theoretically (see Erbach, 1966; Gras and Reinhardt, 1987) and empirically (see Gras, 1982; Hinsching, 1981). However, the empirical project could not be continued in terms of the established standards of sociological methodology. Subsequently, a kind of sociological empiricism based on Marxism–Leninism and what they called bourgeois forms of empirical

research was created (see Friedrich, 1970). However, in the area of sociological theory, the Marxist–Leninist paradigm continued to be the most significant influence and due to its dogmatism hampered the development of sociology. As a result, only those theoretical and empirical results of sociological research into sport were officially accepted and published that fitted the dominant socialist/communist doctrine of the state and the party. Nearly all sociological theories based on empirical studies were expected to conform to the 'socialist reality' of sport and society (see Voigt, 1975). Nevertheless, despite rigorous censorship by the state not all sociological research could be manipulated ideologically.

According to Gras and Reinhardt (1987: 42–6), the foci of empirical research and theory construction in the sociology of sport in the former Eastern bloc can be put into the following areas:

• The objects, objectives and functions of the Marxist–Leninist sociology of sport.
• Sociological research into societal living conditions and their influences on active sports participation within organized and unorganized areas (everyday physical culture and sport for all).
• Sociological research to improve the development of high performance sport.
• Sociological research to differentiate sports organizations, management and planning.
• Sociological insights into sport as a basis for a differentiated sports information system.
• Sociological research into other relevant areas that have an impact on sport (for example, sociological enquiries into youth cultures, investigation of socialization processes).
• Critical evaluation of selected concepts and theories of the 'bourgeois' sociology of sport.
• In addition, other relevant areas, such as, group dynamics in sport, voluntary work in sport, sports development connected with social, ideological, economic and cultural factors in general.

In a nutshell, sociological research and theories of sport in the former German Democratic Republic focused on the following key issues:

• The development of a Marxist–Leninist sociology of sport, including a critical ideological analysis of the so-called bourgeois sociology of sport (with particular reference to West Germany).
• Empirical research into sports development in the GDR, with particular emphasis on

both general sociological issues such as social activities, motivation, socialization, ideology, achievement, health, professionalization, age, gender and very specific questions, such as the organizational structuring of sport, management and planning (see Gras and Reinhardt, 1987).

• Interdisciplinary research exploring pedagogical, biological, medical, anthropological, psychological and sociological issues (see Erbach, 1966; Gras and Reinhardt, 1987).

The development of the sociology of sport in the former GDR between 1945 and 1989 can be regarded as typical and representative of the influence on the development of the sciences in the Eastern bloc of the USSR. The following aspects constituted three key foci in this connection:

1 Focusing on societal developments, sports and their social functions were integrated conceptually into a model of base–superstructure relations as part of socialist physical culture.
2 As an element of base–superstructure relations, sports were said to contribute to the social, that is, the physical and psychological, reproduction of society.
3 On the assumption that, in socialist societies, class conflicts had ceased to occur, sport was expected to contribute to the political socialization of people into socialist values and norms and, thus, to the development of a socialist personality. This function was centrally organized and supported by the state and the Communist Party and involved scientific planning.

In this context, the scientific and political function of the sociology of sport was to establish and promote the development of sport through a theoretical underpinning (socialist physical culture) and empirical research (sports development under socialism). Accordingly, it appears logical to argue that the Marxist–Leninist sociology of sport introduced and differentiated structural-functionalist and empiricist elements within the epistemological framework of a dogmatic paradigm (Marxism–Leninism; see as an example Pietsch and Gras, 1986). As a consequence, a paradoxical admixture between Marxism and 'bourgeois' functionalism emerged.

Summary The Marxist–Leninist sociology of sport is an integral part of the Marxist academic tradition. Its theoretical and empirical reference to historical and societal developments provides a number of interesting areas for research. Through an interdisciplinary approach these

areas can be expanded and integrated into the theory of physical culture (see above). However, due to the dogmatic nature of Marxism–Leninism and its claim to be an exclusive meta-theory within the socialist development of the sciences from 1917 until 1990, all epistemological aspects were politically functionalized and censored by the state (see Lutz, 1988; Voigt, 1975). As a result, the sociological potential of Marxian theory and Marxism more generally could not be fully exploited and developed.

The Neo-Marxist Sociology of Sport

The development of Marxist sociology in Western capitalist-industrial societies was orientated towards a Marxian and Marxist (–Leninist) sociology. However, its protagonists also developed the Marxist paradigm in conjunction with other academic traditions, such as structuralism, functionalism, systems theory, existentialism and psychoanalysis. A complex and contested set of concepts with various differentiations emerged. So-called 'neo-Marxism' was applied both to sociology and to its subdisciplines, for example, the sociology of sport. The following strands of the neo-Marxist sociology of sport will now be discussed: reproduction theory, critical theory and hegemony theory.

Reproduction Theory Reproduction theory is based on a Marxist theory of labour in which societal functions are integrated: the simple and the complex reproduction of labour power. In the case of simple reproduction, sport as a social form ensures the physical preservation and reproduction of labour power (the recreation function). In the case of complex reproduction, sport has additional functions. Labour power with its purely economic function of reproduction increasingly involves qualifications and knowledge as bases for sports activities (the qualification function). As we can see, the relationship between sport, work and reproduction has two levels. The following Marxist assumptions underlie these relations:

1 Work and reproduction are mutually involved in a historical, dynamic interdependence.
2 Sport in this connection has to be considered as an element of the extended reproduction functions of labour power.
3 Of central significance in democratic societies are those functions that contribute

to the acquisition of qualifications (Güldenpfennig, 1974: 15).

Consequently, the sociology of sport, its empirical research and theoretical underpinning, have to focus on societal correlations between sport and the development of work within historical, economic, political and social processes. Seen from the point of view of reproduction theory, the relationship between sport and work within capitalist and socialist industrial societies needs to be conceptualized as follows:

- Under capitalism, sport, like other societal fields, reproduces the capitalist system under economic and political conditions of class conflict but without revolution (simple reproduction).
- Under socialism, sport, like other societal fields, reproduces the socialist system with the aim of improving the individual and social aspects of human behaviour.

The ideological underpinning of these two statements makes them empirically unacceptable as they do not comply with standards of sociological research and theory construction. Therefore this paradigm employed by neo-Marxist sociologists of sport is of interest only as a theoretical framework. However, sociological research into sport does need to be orientated towards the sport–work relationship (reproduction, socialization, ideology).

Critical Theory A confluence of academic and scientific interests, biographical and personal concerns, and societal developments in the Weimar Republic (1918–33), particularly the emergence of fascist totalitarianism in the context of three interwoven social, political and economic processes – nationalism, racism and capitalism – created a distinctive social reality and *Zeitgeist*, within which the members of the 'Institute for Social Research' (IFSR) founded in 1922 in Frankfurt am Main (some of its outstanding members were Horkheimer, Adorno, Marcuse, Fromm, Benjamin and, after 1950, Habermas and Friedeburg) created their theoretical and methodological concept of the 'Critical Theory (of Society)', often also referred to as the 'Frankfurt School (of Sociology)'. Members of the Frankfurt School founded and developed an expanded dialectical model of 'base and superstructure'. They rejected any form of economic determinism and assumed dynamic relations and interdependencies between the economy and the culture of a society. Due to a lack of Marxist research into cultural and ideological superstructures, they placed special emphasis on research into this field. The growth of fascism reinforced their theoretical assumptions. For these reasons, they grounded their research programme in social philosophical, sociological, historical and social psychological (based on Freud's psychoanalysis) research into superstructural fields, but they also undertook research into economic issues and tried to connect 'base and superstructure' in their studies. Basically, the scientific approach of 'critical theory' can be described as an attempt to integrate Marxist and Freudian methodology.

Members of the IFSR did not explicitly elaborate and conceptualize empirical methods, but they did implicitly develop techniques during the research process itself. The focus of their work was 'a debate over an appropriate non-positivistic epistemology for the social sciences' (Jary and Jary, 1995: 243). The application of empirical methods should always be related to a theoretical framework of social research. Not the quantitative, but the qualitative properties of empirical data are the most relevant. This methodological approach implied the need to find ways to connect data, and how to interpret their social relations, meanings and process characteristics (see Rigauer, 1995).

Unlike many members of the Frankfurt School such as Adorno, Horkheimer and Habermas, who only marginally touched on social developments in sport, some of their successors critically engaged with its social and political aspects. While doing so, they were influenced by the 1960s students' rebellion in the Federal Republic of Germany (FRG). In that context they developed the sociological foundations for a 'critical theory of sport'.

Rigauer (1969, English translation 1981; 1979) investigated the relationship between sport and work with particular reference to the organizational structuring, practices and functions of work and their effects on socio-cultural, socio-political and socio-economic developments in sport in capitalist societies. According to his central sociological thesis, under conditions of industrial capitalism sport as an integral part of the superstructure (culture, ideology) reproduces features of social behaviour that are functionally and normatively ingrained in capitalistically organized processes of working, marketing, rationalization, scientification, communication and socialization. All these social processes are reduced in sport to the quantitative principle of 'ideal' and 'material surplus value' (reification, alienation). On the one hand, the central ideological function of sport consists of transposing its base-related (economic) superstructural relation and interdependence into societal practice. On the other hand, it also has to blur this very structural correspondence ideologically in a way that allows the idea of sport as a socially autonomous area to be maintained. The main purpose of a Marxist sociological theory of sport should be to explain the real societal functions of sport with the help of critical analyses focused on culture and ideology. In addition, a Marxist sociology has to generate concepts that relate sport to the aim of political emancipation, thus contributing to the defeat of capitalism.

Vinnai (1970) researched the system of social correspondences between capitalist forms of production, consumption and forms of social behaviour in sport. He takes the example of soccer and identifies individual and social patterns of adaptation using the Marxist model of 'commodity structure': the reduction of human behaviour in sport to market exchanges. As an element of capitalist mass culture, sport takes over socialization functions that lead to the adaptation of human behaviour to authoritarian patterns (connected with narcissistic, masochistic and aggressive personality characteristics). In this process the personal and social autonomy of individuals becomes increasingly restricted and can lead to complete alienation. Integrated with these sociological and socio-psychological concepts, Vinnai (1970: esp. 9–104) allocates ideological functions to sport: 'Sport, like other manifestations of the culture industry that have been structured and planned, brings out the identification of people with already established norms. The system of sport is one in which conformism is hammered into everybody's emotions and prohibits behaviour that is not adapted to social norms' (Vinnai, 1970: 104). Consequently, sport develops cultural-industrial forms of behaviour concerned with creating an ideological consciousness within capitalism which fosters economic growth, profits and exploitation materially, socially and psychologically.

An investigation conducted by Prokop in 1971 concludes the sociological contributions to a 'critical theory of sport' of the Frankfurt Institute of Social Research. Prokop's sociological analysis of sport concentrates on the historical and societal genesis of the modern Olympic movement, starting from its founder, Coubertin, who initiated the first Olympic Games of modern times in Athens in 1896. She investigated technocratic system structures and structures of behaviour within the stage of social differentiation reached in industrial capitalism at the turn of the century. She shows how ideological relations under capitalism are conducive to positivist scientific developments and uses this framework in order to analyse typical forms of consciousness and behaviour. Sport, she suggests, stabilizes the power structures of capitalist societies whilst reproducing technocratic practices: it produces technical and disciplined behaviour and a corresponding positivist ideology which leads to patterns of objectification, quantification and reductionism. Furthermore, sport legitimates these technocratic capitalist practices and uses them as a repressive method of general socialization: 'Sport is a capitalistically modified form of game!' (Prokop, 1971: 21).

The main difference between reproduction theory (see above) and critical theory is that the latter integrates and critically evaluates the development of sport in both capitalist and socialist societies. Critical theorists uncovered the ways in which sportspersons in the former Soviet bloc were subjected to a repressive instrumentalization of their consciousness and behaviour through the socialist ideology of the state (see Prokop, 1971: 121–3). The critical theory of sport was influential in the development of sociological theories in the former German Federal Republic and internationally until the 1980s. Rütten (1988) applied the cultural and ideological processes emphasized sociologically by Adorno (including their aesthetic basis) to the internal world of sport. He also stressed the potential of sport for social emancipation. Rütten (1988) was able to conceptualize a sociological approach to the social dialectics of sport that, on the one hand, supports the development of social behaviour and on the other hand restricts the same. Morgan (1994) reconstructs neo-Marxist approaches to the sociology of sport in an international comparison drawing on critical theory. He develops a convincing concept in order to pursue the sociological establishment of a critical theory of sport. His 'intent in doing so is to break the impasse that has thus far stymied the Left's efforts to come to grips adequately with contemporary sport. The revamped critical theory of sport I offer to accomplish this aim, to get the critical process going again, takes its point of departure from sport conceived as a social practice, and from a critically extended use of the liberal device of walling off social spheres to protect them from unsavoury outside influences' (Morgan, 1994: 179).

Hegemony Theory Hegemony theory is based on the thinking and writing of the Italian Marxist Antonio Gramsci (1891–1937). He rejected the deterministic character of the traditional 'base–superstructure' distinction and integrated philosophical and sociological aspects into his analysis in order to develop it further. He also rejected the straightforward matter–consciousness relationship and the corresponding ideological processes, and replaced it on the theoretical level with a group- and class-related model of power and conflict. According to Gramsci, neither the economic base of capitalism nor the material circumstances of human existence determine people's social, political and cultural forms of behaviour and the underlying ideologies. On the contrary, there are dominant social groups whose intellectual members – both in the ruling and subject classes – develop, define and negotiate values, norms and class fractions. They build social hegemonies on the basis of language, knowledge, common thinking and everyday practice in religion, art, literature, etc. that concur with each other. However, people are also exposed to permanent innovation, the results of which are handed down from one generation to the next. Hegemonic, class-bound groups differentiate, transform and convey material (base) and imaginary (superstructure) values, norms and functions within these processes. Within the scope of such ideological and political interchanging and enforced processes, open class struggles for power between competing groups emerge. The upper and middle classes have material, cultural and political advantages (for example, wealth, knowledge and the capacity to define values, norms, rules, etc.) over the working class in the course of social production and reproduction processes. However, the lower classes are able to translate their material and ideological aims and values into action with the help of their own organizations (for example, parties, trade unions). In capitalist societies, hegemonic processes of differentiation and development take the course of ideological and institutional mediation between base and superstructure. The superstructure influences the material base just as the base influences the ideological superstructure (see Gramsci, 1987: 56–103).

Employing hegemony theory, Gruneau (1983, 1993) and Hargreaves (1995) investigate social developments in sport under capitalism and make useful contributions to a critical sociology of sport (see Morgan, 1994: 60–127). They see social classes as defining, delivering, improving and enforcing sport-related norms, values and functions within hegemonic processes on the basis of their ideological and political power positions, including the economically, culturally and socially reproduced base–superstructure/superstructure–base relations of capitalist societies. Yet, it is not determinism that results from this process but the contrary: 'Hegemony is never guaranteed: it must be worked for continually and renewed by the hegemonic class or class fraction' (Hargreaves, 1995: 220). One can find this phenomenon repeated in every era of the capitalist development of sport. All groups involved in sport, that is, dominant as well as subordinate groups, compete with each other and struggle for the sports-practical realization of their aims, cultural values, social functions, organizational and material framework. Gruneau (1983, 1993) and Hargreaves (1995) show how these class-specific cultural and political struggles within sport emerged and how they continue to occur. These processes can be revealed as hegemonial social conflicts in which base and superstructure ideologies that are economically, politically and culturally founded take over central functions. They refer to 'residual' (ideologically lasting) and current sports processes. Key themes in these hegemonic discourses are the following:

- Amateurism, fair play, rational recreation.
- Athletics, competition; leisure (sport for all).
- Professionalization, commercialization, mass mediatization.
- Sports consumption.
- Physical education (socialization).
- Gender relations, politicization of the body and racism; within social contexts of alienation, emancipation, relative autonomy.
- Organization, bureaucratization, institutionalization.
- National identifications, nationalism, racism.
- Globalization.

This list demonstrates the research interests of Gruneau (1983, 1993) and Hargreaves (1995). The empirical foci of sociological theory are the cultural, economic and political developments of sport as they have been initiated and pushed ahead on the basis of hegemonic conflicts and struggles. Similar to Hargreaves (1995), Gruneau (1983, 1993) supports the thesis 'that certain class, gender, and Western cultural and bodily practices continue to be represented in modern sport as if they were universal and natural, thereby marginalizing many alternative conceptions of sport and the body'. But none 'of this should be taken to suggest that sport today is any more stable or less contradictory than in the past. No hegemonic settlement of forces and interests is forever …. Indeed, there is a notable tension between all totalizing visions of "modern" life and the sweeping forces of social and cultural differentiation characteristic of contemporary … consumer societies' (Gruneau, 1993: 98). With these assertions the author provides additional support for a Marxist-orientated sociological analysis of sport in the same way as Hargreaves (1995) does when he objects that 'Policy cannot automatically be deduced from analysis: its formation is a creative process requiring imaginative leaps, and above all, a genuine interaction between policy-makers and subjects' (Hargreaves, 1995: 223).

Conclusion At the heart of the neo-Marxian sociology of sport are investigations into the social processes of reproduction that take place as part of capitalist base–superstructure relations. They assume that the developments of sport that take place within capitalist societies are structurally determined by the principle of simple reproduction. Therefore, sports are held to perform social functions of adaptation. Supporters of critical theory, however, investigate the social structures and functions of the reproduction of sport within the context of capitalist labour, marketing and rationalization processes, and examine the political, cultural and ideological effects of these processes on various modern sport developments. The authors of hegemony theory emphasize the effects of the social reproduction processes of sport within capitalism on the intermediate, social, political and cultural levels of hegemonic class conflicts. Their main thesis claims that the agents of politically competing power elites generate and institutionalize socially differentiated values, norms and functions in the world of sport against the background of interdependent material and ideological base–superstructure relations.

All these constructs have in common the fact that their authors attempt to separate the sociological paradigm of reproduction from the Marxist base–superstructure dogma and its inherent economic determinism in order to research capitalistically influenced social processes of sports development on a more open, scientific basis. It has to be concluded that this approach is used most consistently by the advocates of the hegemony theory.

Summary: the Marxist Sociology of Sport

Based on the key concepts outlined in the second and third sections of this chapter, I suggest the following thesis: the development of a Marxist sociology of sport is founded on both the theory and practice of Marxism. The real political and societal manifestations of the Marxist dogma (political parties, trade unions and people's republics) can be found in the organizations of working-class sport. Using the experience of working-class sport, Marxist theories of physical culture and sport argue that the nature of sport is closely linked to societal and state institutions (capitalism; socialism/communism). As a consequence of the academic analysis of the bourgeois development of sport under capitalism, Marxist concepts of the sociology of sport emerged. The flow diagram opposite (Figure 2.2) summarizes and highlights the conceptualizing process of the Marxist sociology of sport.

TOWARDS AN ADVANCED NEO-MARXIST SOCIOLOGY OF SPORT: CONCEPTUAL PERSPECTIVES

Currently, the majority of social developments at a national and international level are ideologically influenced by production, reproduction and consumption processes based on the principles of capitalism. Social agents link the '*Homo socialis*' with the '*Homo oeconomicus*'. This observation also applies to the national and international spheres of sport. Sport operates in a global market and is a global industry (see Maguire, 1993; Rigauer, 1992). Consequently, sociological research into the relationships between sport and capitalism is becoming more urgently needed than ever as the findings will certainly contribute to a better understanding and explanation of current and future social developments of sport within the context of specific economic frameworks. Therefore, it is necessary to continue further sociological enquiries on the basis of a Marxist paradigm which has to integrate the historical and dialectical materialist theory of society and at the same time avoid deterministic concepts (see Morgan, 1994: 179–203). The intellectual problem of the Marxist sociology of sport is well known and was the main topic of this chapter. Here and now, it is worth summing up the problem from a figurational sociological point of view: Marxist sociology involves socio-economic determinism, a nomothetic

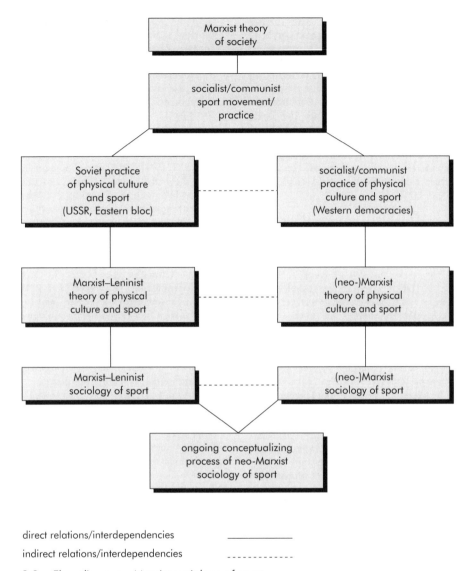

direct relations/interdependencies _____

indirect relations/interdependencies - - - - - - - - - - -

Figure 2.2   *Flow diagram - Marxist sociology of sport*

model of social development and what one might call 'utopian determinism' (see Dunning, 1992: 226–35). Such epistemological fixations hinder and prevent the development of a sophisticated Marxist sociology of sport. The key question now is, what theoretical and methodological conditions have to be fulfilled to open and widen the Marxist sociology of sport paradigm? The following list contains a set of preliminary and incomplete suggestions:

1   Emphasis should be on an open and critical 'sociological realism'.
2   The individual–society dualism or structure–agency dilemma needs to be overcome.

3   Constructive debates are needed with other sociological paradigms and other methodological approaches.
4   The different forms of empirical (including historical) research consistent with a Marxist framework need to be specified.
5   Sociological fragmentation needs to be combated.

With such a programme, the Marxist sociology of sport will not have to abandon its specific scientific concepts. On the contrary, it might develop them further within the permanent stream of sociological debates and critical evaluations (see Morgan, 1994: 204–51). The same applies to all other sociological theories used for the analysis of sport. The further development of these theories depends on how far academics are able to elaborate competing sociological theories (preserving sociological differences) whilst at the same time recognizing paradigmatic commonalities. Such a process of communication and cooperation will prevent unnecessary tensions and provide the basis for a productive future for the entire field of sociology. The claim for dominance of one theory would necessarily lead to a dogmatic reductionism of the sociology of sport and all scientific development would come to a standstill.

REFERENCES AND FURTHER READING

Blumenberg, W. (1962) *Karl Marx in Selbstzeugnissen und Bilddokumenten*. Reinbek: Rowohlt.

Bottomore, T. (1979) 'Marxism and sociology', in T. Bottomore and R. Nisbet, *A History of Sociological Analysis*. London: Heinemann. pp. 118–48.

Dunning, E. (1992) 'Figurational sociology and the sociology of sport: some concluding remarks', in E. Dunning and C. Rojek (eds) (1992) *Sport and Leisure in the Civilizing Process*. London: Macmillan. pp. 221–84.

Dunning, E., Maguire, J. and Pearton, R. (eds) (1993) *The Sports Process: a Comparative and Developmental Approach*. Champaign, IL: Human Kinetics.

Dwertmann, H. (1997) *Zwischen deutscher Kulturtradition und zivilgesellschaftlichem Aufbruch. Eine entwicklungssoziologische Studie zur Arbeiter-Turn- und Sportbewegung in Hannover*. Münster: Lit Verlag.

Elias, N. (1977) 'Adorno – Rede. Respekt und Kritik', in N. Elias and W. Lepenies, *Zwei Reden anläßlich der Verleihung des Theodor W. Adorno-Preises*. Frankfurt am Main: Suhrkamp. pp. 37–68.

Elias, N. and Dunning, E. (1993) *Quest for Excitement. Sport and Leisure in the Civilizing Process*. Oxford/ Cambridge, MA: Blackwell.

Engels, F. (1973) *Dialektik der Natur* (1873–1883, 1925). Berlin: Dietz.

Erbach, G. (1966) 'The science of sport and sports sociology – questions related to development – problems of structure', *International Review of Sport Sociology*, 1: 59–73.

Friedrich, W. (ed.) (1970) *Methoden der marxistisch-leninistischen Sozialforschung*. Berlin: Deutscher Verlag der Wissenschaften.

Ganssmann, H. (1994) 'Karl Marx', in B. Schäfers, (ed.), *Sociology in Germany*. Opladen: Leske and Budrich. pp. 81–94.

Gramsci, A. (1987) *Marxismus und Kultur. Ideologie, Alltag, Literatur*. Hamburg: VSA Verlag.

Gras, F. (1982) 'Theoretical and methodological questions of the development of needs and motives in sports as a presupposition for a higher level of sporting activity', *International Review of Sport Sociology*, 17: 91–8.

Gras, F. and Reinhardt, B. (1987) 'The situation and developmental tendencies of Marxist–Leninist sport sociology in the German Democratic Republic (GDR)', *International Review of Sport Sociology*, 22: 39–49.

Gruneau, R. (1983) *Class, Sports, and Social Development*. Amherst, MA: The University of Massachusetts Press.

Gruneau, R. (1993) 'The critique of sport in modernity: theorising power, culture, and the politics of the body', in E. Dunning, J. Maguire and R. Pearton (eds), *The Sports Process: a Comparative and Developmental Approach*. Champaign, IL: Human Kinetics. pp. 85–109.

Güldenpfennig, S. (1974) 'Erweiterte Reproduktion der Arbeitskraft: Ein Ansatz zur Bestimmung des Verhältnisses von Sport und Arbeit', in S. Güldenpfennig, W. Volpert and P. Weinberg (eds), *Sensumotorisches Lernen und Sport als Reproduktion der Arbeitskraft*. Cologne: Pahl-Rugenstein. pp. 11–59.

Habermas, J. (1967) *Zur Logik der Sozialwissenschaften*. Tübingen: Mohr and Siebeck.

Habermas, J. (1973) *Legitimationsprobleme im Spätkapitalismus*. Frankfurt: Suhrkamp.

Hargreaves, J. (1995) *Sport, Power and Culture*. Cambridge: Polity Press.

Hinsching, J. (1981) 'Sport as a leisure pursuit of older school youth', in *International Review of Sport Sociology*, 16: 97–103.

Holt, R. (1992) *Sport and the British. A Modern History*. Oxford: Clarendon Press.

Jary, D. and Jary, J. (eds) (1995) *Collins Dictionary of Sociology*. Glasgow: Collins.

Kiss, G. (1971) *Marxismus als Soziologie. Theorie und Empirie in den Sozialwissenschaften der DDR, UdSSR, Polens, der CSSR, Ungarns, Bulgariens und Rumäniens*. Reinbek: Rowohlt.

Kreckel, R. (1994) 'Sociology in East German universities: decomposition and reconstruction', in B. Schäfers (ed.), *Sociology in Germany*. Opladen: Leske and Budrich. pp. 240–51.

Lutz, W. (1988) *Ideologie und Wissenschaft in der Sportsoziologie der DDR*. Bochum: Brockmeyer.

Maguire, J. (1993) 'American football, British society, and global sport development', in E. Dunning, J. Maguire and R. Pearton, *The Sports Process: a Comparative and Developmental Approach*. Champaign, IL. pp. 207–29.

Marx, K. (1970) *Ökonomisch-philosophische Manuskripte* (1844). Leipzig: Reclam.

Marx, K. (1939/41) *Grundrisse der Kritik der politischen Ökonomie* (1857–59). Moscow: Europäische Verlagsanstalt.

Morgan, W.J. (1994) *Leftist Theories of Sport*. Urbana, IL and Chicago: University of Illinois Press.

Pietsch, K. and Gras, F. (1986) 'Athletic activities in the life of students and graduates in the German Democratic Republic', in *International Review for the Sociology of Sport*, 21: 323–37.

Popper, K.R. (1968) *Conjectures and Refutations: the Growth of Scientific Knowledge*. New York and Evanston: Harper and Row.

Prokop, U. (1971) *Soziologie der Olympischen Spiele. Sport und Kapitalismus*. Munich: Hanser.

Rigauer, B. (1969) *Sport und Arbeit. Soziologische Zusammenhänge und ideologische Implikationen*. Frankfurt am Main: Suhrkamp (*Sport and Work*, trans. by A. Guttmann, New York, 1981, Columbia University Press).

Rigauer, B. (1979) *Warenstrukturelle Bedingungen leistungssportlichen Handelns*. Lollar: Achenbach.

Rigauer, B. (1992) 'Sportindustrie. Soziologische Betrachtungen über das Verschwinden des Sports in der Markt- und Warenwelt', in R. Horak and O. Penz (eds), *Sport. Kult und Kommerz*. Vienna: Verlag für Gesellschaftskritik. pp. 185–201.

Rigauer, B. (1995) 'The Frankfurt School of Critical Theory: philosophy or sociology? A developmental and methodological study'. Unpublished paper, University of Leicester.

Riordan, J. (1980a) *Sport in Soviet Society. Development of Sport and Physical Education in Russia and the USSR*. Cambridge: Cambridge University Press.

Riordan, J. (1980b) *Sportmacht Sowjetunion*. Bensheim: päd.extra.

Riordan, J. (ed.) (1981) *Sport under Communism: the USSR, Czechoslovakia, the GDR, China, Cuba*. London: Hurt.

Ruffmann, K.-H. (1980) *Sport und Körperkultur in der Sowjetunion*. Munich: dtv.

Rütten, A. (1988) *Sport – Ideologie – Kritische Theorie*. Frankfurt am Main: Lang.

Schafrik, J. (ed.) (1972) 'Ergebnisse der sportwissenschaftlichen Forschung und Entwicklung in der Deutschen Demokratischen Republik', in *Theorie und Praxis der Körperkultur*, Volume 3. Sportverlag.

Trogsch, F. (1966) 'The state and development of sport sociology research in the German Democratic Republic (review and bibliography)', in *International Review of Sport Sociology*, 1: 218–26.

Vinnai, G. (1970) *Fußballsport als Ideologie*. Frankfurt am Main: Europäische Verlagsanstalt.

Voigt, D. (1975) *Soziologie in der DDR*. Cologne: Verlag Wissenschaft und Politik.

Wagner, H. (1973) *Sport und Arbeitersport* (1931). Cologne: Pahl-Rugenstein.

3

CULTURAL STUDIES
AND THE SOCIOLOGY OF SPORT

Jennifer Hargreaves and Ian McDonald

Put in simple terms, cultural studies is concerned with the social significance and systematic analysis of cultural practices, experiences and institutions. Its particular characteristic is to direct attention to, and analyse critically, 'the everyday world of lived reality' (Blundell et al., 1993: 2–3) – activities that people take part in, feelings engendered by them, and meanings associated with them. Since sport touches the lives of millions and millions of people across the world, the cultural studies perspective provides an important method of understanding its social importance. But other perspectives in the sociology of sport also make this claim,[1] to the extent that the field has become highly contested. Nevertheless, it is widely recognized that cultural studies is one of the key players (Horne, 1996; Ingham and Loy, 1993; Morgan, 1994).

In this chapter we outline the origins and characteristics of cultural studies, assess the distinctive ways in which it has been applied to analyses of sport, and reflect on criticisms of its analytical value. Because we are sympathetic to the cultural studies tradition, we point to what we argue are the flawed arguments and theoretical misrepresentations of some of its critics.

THE ORIGIN AND CHARACTERISTICS OF CULTURAL STUDIES

An immediate difficulty in anchoring cultural studies within a particular sociological tradition is that it is cross-disciplinary in nature,

drawing on such diverse academic discourses as communication studies, film theory, history, literary criticism, philosophy, politics and semiology, as well as sociology. It has been characterized 'not so much as a "discipline", but an area where different disciplines intersect in the study of the cultural aspects of society' (Hall et al., 1980: 7). Unlike functionalism (with Durkheim and Parsons), Marxism (with Marx and Engels) and figurationalism (with Elias), cultural studies is without an obvious canonical figurehead, although it is generally acknowledged that the work of the Italian Marxist Antonio Gramsci has been pivotal.

The authors of a growing number of histories of cultural studies (for example, Blundell et al., 1993; Brantlinger, 1990; Grossberg et al., 1992; Turner, 1990) agree that its origin was located in England, and, more specifically, was linked to three major publications: Richard Hoggart's *The Uses of Literacy* (1957); Raymond Williams's *Culture and Society* (1958); and E.P. Thompson's *The Making of the English Working Class* (1963). Collectively, these books established a radically different conception of culture from the one that was previously dominant in both academic and popular discourses (culture understood as synonymous with 'high' culture, embracing literary texts and artefacts), and they provided the inspiration for further analyses of the complexities of cultural formations, in particular social, political and historical conditions.

Williams's *Culture and Society* is cited by both Brantlinger (1990: 38) and Turner (1990: 52) as the key text. Williams challenged the predominant conception of culture as high art and as the product of 'creative geniuses'. He took issue with literary thinkers like Matthew Arnold (1869: 6), who described culture as 'the best that has been thought and said in the world'. Williams (1958: 310) also protested against the reduction of culture to a set of arte-facts, insisting that 'a culture is not only a body of intellectual and imaginative work: it is also and essentially a whole way of life'.

Williams had moved away from an elitist, narrow definition of culture to a more general-ized, anthropological definition that empha-sized social practices – the gamut of ways in which people think, feel and act. Activities from football to brass bands were thus legit-imized as culture every bit as much as opera and poetry. But, although Williams (1965: 364) eulogized football as 'a wonderful game' and argued that 'the need for sport and entertain-ment is as real as the need for art', he did so only in passing and failed to explore the links between sport and popular consciousness.

Hoggart (1957: 91) was the same. He also understood the seductive appeal of sport when he wrote '[a]t work, sport vies with sex as the staple conversation. The popular Sunday newspapers are read as much for their full sports reports as for their accounts of the week's crimes', but chose to concentrate on other cultural practices in his work. He embraced a similar understanding of culture to Williams, by insisting upon creative, authentic features of working-class life that could not easily be dismissed as vacuous and insignifi-cant. He did so by providing a rich ethno-graphic account of an urban 'culture of the people', although he deplored the growing commercial penetration of culture which was affecting the communities, families, language and sensibilities of working-class people.[2] E.P. Thompson (1963) also opposed elitist con-ceptions of culture by showing how human experience arises from the connection between material circumstances and different, but historically specific forms of consciousness, linked to class identity. He captured the role of conflict and struggle as the crucial ingredient in the making of working-class cultures.

Although these three authors worked independently of each other, and had different political orientations, together their texts have been characterized as foundational, not only because they paved the way for the acceptance and systematic sociological study of working-class and popular culture, but also because they pointed towards a form of intellectual engage-ment that was openly interventionist. In their account of the genesis and development of cultural studies, Barker and Beezer (1992: 5–6) argue that:

> always implicit in early analyses was the question: what can be done about the oppressive relations we are revealing? What forces are there, even if only potentially, that could lead to liberation? What strategies suggest themselves for supporting emancipatory forces? And in consequence, what will count as liberation and emancipation?

THE INFLUENCE OF GRAMSCI

It was the writings of the Italian Marxist Antonio Gramsci – especially the *Prison Notebooks,* where the centrality of culture within relations of power was articulated – that provided a way of answering these ques-tions. Gramsci showed that in Western soci-eties the power of the dominant class rests mainly not on physical force and coercion through military-police apparatuses (as in totalitarian regimes), but on ideological leader-ship exercised through a network of voluntary institutions that pervade everyday life ('civil society') – for example, political parties, trade unions, the mass media, the family, schools, churches and all cultural processes (which would include sport, although it had far less cultural importance during the interwar period, when Gramsci was writing, than it has today).

Gramsci's theoretical ideas were tied to his political position. His vision was to under-stand the complex ways in which culture was related to political domination and to work out strategies for a change towards socialism. Gramsci argued that control of culture was a prerequisite for social change. But he rejected Marxist economism with its crude base–superstructure metaphor which posits culture as a mere reflection of the economic base. He favoured a position that, as Grossberg (1993: 29–30) points out, 'sees history as actively produced by individuals and social groups as they struggle to make the best they can out of their lives under determinate conditions'.

Gramsci used the concept of hegemony to explain how a dominant group or class estab-lishes political and cultural leadership and control throughout civil society and the state, and how a whole complex series of cultural, political and ideological practices work to 'cement' a society into a relative – though never complete – unity (Bennett et al., 1979: 192). According to Stuart Hall (1980: 36), Gramsci's use of the concept of hegemony was 'always made specific to a particular historical phase in specific national societies', and, further, was 'elaborated specifically in relation to those advanced capitalist societies in which the institutions of state and civil society have reached a stage of great complexity'. Hegemony is a tool for explaining how ideas and practices which seem against the interests of subordinate groups are believed in and carried out by them so as to become 'commonsense'. Commonsense was understood by Gramsci to be the unconscious and unquestioning way in which the social world is understood and hence organized and lived day-by-day – a 'cultural battle' for the legitimation of ideas and practices so that they become 'universal' (1971: 348). Hegemony, then, is a process of experience, negotiation and struggle by individuals in real-life situations, rather than one in which subordinate groups are simply duped by dominant ideologies. In Gramsci's formulation, it is not simply a matter of class control, but an unstable process which requires the winning of consent from subordinate groups. It is, then, never 'complete' or fixed, but rather diverse and always changing.

The concept of hegemony raises questions about the relationship between cultural, political and economic processes – Gramsci avoided the view of culture as distinctly separate from politics and economics, but saw it as reciprocally related to them. Although he did not look at sport, specifically, Pivato's (1990) analysis of the bicycle as a political symbol in Gramsci's Italy suggests that, in their struggle for power, both the nationalists and socialists used sport to mobilize different fractions of the Italian working class (Jarvie and Maguire 1994: 117–19). It could be argued that this was made possible, in line with Gramsci's ideas, because, although at one level culture is an individual phenomenon, it is also an experience shared with other people. As he put it:

> Culture, at its various levels, unifies in a series of strata, to the extent that they come into contact with each other, a greater or lesser number of individuals who understand each other's mode of expression in differing degrees, etc. (Gramsci, 1971: 349)

Gramsci's analysis of culture, embodying the concept of hegemony and a rejection of reductionism, in particular of economism, recognizes the importance of praxis – a term describing human activity, energy, expression, agency – a process through which people are involved in the making of history. It is understood to be the result of people's positive reactions to values and beliefs, which in specific social and historical situations, support established social relations and structures of power (Anderson, 1976; Gramsci, 1971; Williams, 1977). This is very different from straightforward indoctrination or a strict system of ideological control. In summary, hegemony resists the idea that people are passive recipients of culture and keeps intact what is arguably the inherent humanism of Marxism. The concept of hegemony proposes a dialectical relationship between individuals and society, accounting for ways in which individuals are both determined and determining, and it allows for cultural experiences such as sports to be understood as both exploitative and worth while.

INSTITUTIONALIZING CULTURAL STUDIES

Gramsci's ideas became a seminal influence in analyses of British culture following the translation of the *Prison Notebooks* into English in 1971. This became possible because cultural studies had already become institutionalized with the formation of the Centre for Contemporary Cultural Studies (CCCS) at the University of Birmingham in 1964. Under the intellectual leadership of Stuart Hall, who succeeded Richard Hoggart as Director in 1968, a distinctive critical approach to the study of contemporary forms of culture was developed.

At the beginning, the work of the Centre was predominantly concerned with the culture of the English working classes. Ethnography was a favoured approach to research because the endeavour was to understand how individuals made sense of their social worlds. Resistance to a sense of subordination along the lines of class and age, through the display of 'spectacular' styles and behaviour of young working-class English men, was a focus of the 1970s (Clarke et al., 1975; Cohen 1980; Hall and Jefferson 1976). In the later part of the decade, a Women's Studies Group was set up which moved attention to gendered relations of power – a shift that was described by Stuart Hall (1992, cited in M.A. Hall 1996: 35) as a 'specific, decisive and ruptural' feminist intervention. Later, other structures of domination entered the cultural studies agenda, including analyses of the subcultures of adolescent girls, ethnic minorities, peoples in the Third World, and gays and lesbians. Cultural studies lost its initial 'Englishness' as it spread abroad and was institutionalized through research (mostly on aboriginal people) in university departments in North America and Australia. To a large extent, attempts to understand marginalized groups replaced class-dominated research.

However, Blundell et al. have argued that there has always been an intrinsic contradiction to the general theme of understanding subordination and the struggle for hegemony. From the early years of the CCCS, many of the academics carrying out the research were from different class and ethnic groups than the subjects under investigation. They were also predominantly male and the few female researchers were, almost without exception, the only ones who looked at female cultures. Blundell and her co-writers (1993: 6–7) claim that the situation has not changed radically, even with the expansion and diffusion of cultural studies:

This contradiction, embedded deep in the history and practice of cultural studies, raises the question of who cultural studies is for. Is it for those about whom cultural studies writes? Is it relevant to their lives? Can it make a difference? Or is it for cultural studies practitioners? Does it achieve little but advance the academic careers of those who engage in it? Does it always provide an 'authentic' critique as distinct from a voyeuristic celebration of all that is generated at the level of popular culture? And, at worst, does it function primarily to assuage the political conscience of those (predominantly white, bourgeois and male) who are conscious of difference and differences in power?

Problems for cultural studies were also created by new 'critical dialogues' and problematics arising from changes in political and economic structures (Morley and Kuan-Hsing Chen, 1996). The 'culturalist tradition' (favouring agency and experience) was challenged during the 1970s by the emergence of structuralist theories of linguistics and ideology[3] (stressing determination and control). Stuart Hall argued that although the two paradigms appeared as incompatible, it was possible to achieve a synthesis through Gramsci's concept of hegemony (1980: 286), which, though by no means universally used, became one of the organizing ideas at the CCCS. Hegemony theory provided the potential for understanding both the liberative and controlling features of culture. Feminists who at this time were involved in the debate around agency and structure introduced a new dimension, pointing to the inadequacies of theories which left out or marginalized patriarchal structures of power.[4] In more recent years, the character of cultural studies has changed further with the

development of global politics and economics, and with postcolonial questions of nationhood, identity and power. The continued topicality of these issues is reflected in the publication, in 1998, of a new Sage journal, entitled *International Journal of Cultural Studies*.

The latest shift in focus has resulted from debates over the fragmentation of culture in postmodernist societies and through engagements with post-structural theories. The term 'postmodern cultural studies' has been used by Lawrence Grossberg (1993: 58) to describe the increasingly transnational context of difference within which subjectivity and identity are constituted. He argues that:

Postmodern cultural studies returns to the questions that animated the original passion of cultural studies: what is the 'modern' world? How do we locate ourselves as subjects within that world? How do our investments in that world provide the possibilities for regaining some sense of its possible futures? (p. 64)

THE APPLICATION OF CULTURAL STUDIES TO SPORT

Although sport did not receive sustained treatment in the development of cultural studies at the CCCS, in the 1970s and 1980s the Centre supported a number of research projects into sport and leisure which were published in the Working Papers in Cultural Studies or the Stencilled Occasional Papers series. The focus was predominantly on working-class male subjectivities through such subcultural forms as football hooliganism or through the broader theme of sport and the media (Clarke 1973; Critcher 1971; Peters 1976; Watson 1973), but they also included research on marginal and innovative activities, such as kung-fu, pool, skateboarding and squash (Critcher et al., 1979). In 1974, following a symposium on Women in Sport, organized by the Physical Education Department at the University of Birmingham the previous year, the CCCS published two papers given at that conference – by Chas Critcher and Paul Willis. A CCCS 1982 publication on 'Sporting Fictions' (Jenkins and Green, 1982) was also the product of a conference with the same title.

The CCCS publications on sport, although spasmodic, were original, varied and well theorized and opened the doors for a specific cultural studies of sport which became institutionalized mostly in university departments of physical education, sport studies and leisure studies.[5] Starting from the basic premise that sport and leisure are important for an understanding of power relations throughout society, the development of a cultural studies perspective in the sociology of sport has followed along similar lines and embodied similar problematics to those of cultural studies in general.

The publication in 1982 of Jennifer Hargreaves's edited collection, *Sport, Culture and Ideology* marked a watershed in the development of sports sociology. Many of the authors adopted a cultural studies perspective and collectively produced the first sport sociology book with this orientation. It was very much a reaction to the orthodox Marxist tendency in sport sociology to reduce sports to a mirror of capitalist society, thoroughly infiltrated by commercialization, and acting as an efficient repository for dominant ideology (see Brohm, 1978; Hoch, 1972; Vinnai, 1973). It was argued that the concept of hegemony would avoid this reductionism and encourage questions about the specific nature of dominance and subordination in sport:

> If cuts in welfare services close a community swimming pool, for example, or a notice is erected outside council flats where families are housed, 'NO BALL GAMES ON THE GRASS', such questions as 'Who made the decision?' and 'In whose interests?' direct attention to the relationship between power in society and the lived experiences of ordinary people. (J.A. Hargreaves, 1982: 15)

The key problematic of the book was the complex relationship between sport, ideology and the wielding of power. As well as theoretical explorations, it included chapters on a range of issues relevant to sport at the time: for example, the significance of the media treatment of sport in the hegemonic process; the patriarchal character of sport and the importance of sport as a site for feminist intervention; the relatively autonomous and oppositional nature of specific youth sports cultures and the interpenetration of class with other factors such as race, sex and deviance; football hooliganism as an aspect of the historically specific totality of social relations which have generated it and particularly relating to the crisis of the British state at that time; the highly specific forms of state involvement in cultural hegemony in the USSR and South Africa, respectively. It was claimed that:

> This collection as a whole has identified the way in which sport is 'constitutive and constituting',

recognizable only in a dialectical relationship to political, economic, ideological and other cultural forms. Sport exists as a paradox – it has been shown here how its manipulative manifestations need to be counterposed to its liberative tendencies. (1982: 22–3)

In this perspective of cultural studies, sport is perceived to be an aspect of culture embodying struggle and contestation, and the concern is with the processes through which cultural practices and the ideologies and beliefs underlying those practices are created, reproduced and changed through human agency and interaction.

Following the parent tradition, the use and interrogation of the concept of hegemony has been pivotal in both the British and North American variants of sport cultural studies. Hegemony has been applied specifically to the classic sociological agency-structure problematic which Gruneau refers to as the 'paradox of sports' (1983: 147–53).

For example, in *The Devil Makes Work* (which includes numerous references to sport), John Clarke and Chas Critcher (1985: 225) set out to apply to the analysis of leisure an approach derived from cultural studies. They selected this approach because it embodies a double sense of culture – 'culture as a whole, connected to economic, political and social arrangements' and the sense of culture 'as subsets of meaning actively created by individuals and groups' (p. 227). From this perspective, sport and leisure are understood as neither wholly determined nor completely autonomous, but areas of life that can be sites of contestation between dominant and subordinate groups. Furthermore, hegemony is a concept that Clarke and Critcher find useful in explaining: (a) the effectiveness of leadership by persuasion – in particular through everyday events in our lives, and (b) the incompleteness of, and tensions intrinsic to, cultural conflict. They argue that, 'leisure has been, and remains, integral to the struggle for hegemony in British society', manifest through cultural conflict over meanings and through the control of free time in people's lives (p. 228).

Richard Gruneau also explores the double sense of culture in several of his publications, including *Class, Sports, and Social Development* (1983), and *Popular Cultures and Political Practices* (1988). He utilizes the concept of hegemony to explain how sport is a contested zone and to illuminate fundamental differences in the ways 'modern' sports have developed their unique forms of institutional and cultural expression in Canada, Britain and the United States. Simply, he shows how the regulation of cultural life is central to class relations. By examining the development of Canadian sport from colonial times until the 1980s, and relating it to the wider class structure, the state, political life, militarism and religion, Gruneau is able to tease out the dynamic behind the commercial and 'rational-bureacratic' forms of organization predominant in Canadian sport. He demonstrates how some cultural forms and practices are 'driven out of the centre of popular life, actively marginalized, so that something else can take their place', and that in sport 'the focus of these struggles has been the monopolistic capacity to define the dominant forms and meanings of sport practices and the "legitimate" uses of time and the body' (Gruneau 1988b: 20).

In *Sport, Power and Culture* (1986), John Hargreaves also uses hegemony as his central conceptual tool, to argue that sport was integral to the class and cultural struggles of the nineteenth century. His central thesis is that 'sport was significantly implicated in the process whereby the growing economic and political power of the bourgeoisie in nineteenth-century Britain was eventually transformed into that class's hegemony in the latter part of the century' (1986: 6–7).

Arguing that sport must be understood historically, he points to its centrality in the culture of twentieth-century capitalism and to the ways in which it can be penetrated by ideology as well as autonomous from it. As Charles Critcher (1986: 339) points out, both Gruneau and Hargreaves view hegemony as a process and sport 'as part of the contestation of meanings that arise in class societies' (p. 336). Using historically specific and culturally specific examples, they demonstrate the dialectical and changing relationships between human agency and social and political structures.

Reflecting on these (and other) studies, Holt (1993: 365) notes that:

> The 'cultural' approach fits well into the established pattern of British social history which has taken the relationship between classes and levels of class-consciousness as a central issue for discussion.

The identification with popular subjectivities flows from a political commitment to the struggles of subordinate groups and oppressed classes. For example, Garry Whannel's socialist analysis of sport, *Blowing the Whistle* (1983), puts the case for more progressive forms of sport, rooted in social ownership and democratic control. Class is also central in Stephen

Jones's *Workers at Play* (1986), a detailed account of the ways in which working-class sport and leisure practices were part of the various political struggles of the interwar period (1918–1939). Jones examines these practices as cases of counter-hegemonic struggle which (at least implicitly) challenged the values and organization of bourgeois sport.

As a result of advances in media technology and communications, and because of the exceptional popularity of sport, the question of media-based representations has been a key issue in the work of cultural studies writers. One of the first media-sport-based interventions was made by Alan and John Clarke in 1982 when they demonstrated how sport is 'enmeshed in the media's reproduction and transmission of ideological themes and values which are dominant in our society' in ways that are contested and contradictory (p. 68). Ten years later, in *Fields in Vision* (1992), Garry Whannel examines the cultural and economic relations between television and sport, and highlights the ways in which television and sponsorship have reshaped sport in the context of the enterprise culture. But he is aware that this process is not a cohesive one and he highlights the changing and ambivalent characteristics of representations of sport. For example, in a discussion about race and Britishness, Whannel shows how representations of black athletes can appear as radical and transformative views of blackness at the same time as they reflect commonsense racist views based on the myth of 'natural ability'. He argues that:

> As with gender, there is a degree of ambivalence around images of race in sport on television. While sport offers a fund of positive images of talented black athletes succeeding, it does also serve to reproduce elements of stereotypical attitudes. (p. 129)

Whannel uses empirical material to show how 'blackness, Britishness, physicality and femininity are not unchanging terms, but are subject to negotiation'. He conceptualizes popular culture as 'neither imposed from above nor generated spontaneously from below' (1992: 9). In common with other cultural studies writers, his central concern is with power and, specifically, with the complexities of the media–sport–power axis. In a more general account of power in sport, Gruneau (1988a) identifies three key dimensions: (a) the capacity to structure sport in preferred ways; (b) the capacity to select sports traditions; and (c) the capacity to define the range of 'legitimate' practices and meanings associated with dominant sports practices.

The concepts and issues outlined above that have informed the development of the cultural studies of sport remain topical today. In 1993 Ingham and Loy edited a collection of papers in a publication entitled, *Sport in Social Development: Traditions, Transitions and Transformations* that are anchored around Raymond Williams's (1977) theme of 'dominant-residual-emergent', chosen, the editors explain, because 'it highlights the compexity of social development and provides insights into the currently fashionable theory of hegemony' (p. 1). Although some of the authors are English, or originated in England, the book was produced specifically as a challenge to what the editors describe as 'the conventional, statistical, neo-positivistic paradigm that has been dominant within North American sport studies' (p. vii). The anti-positivist stance in North American sociology of sport literature has followed the British anti-positivist/reductionist trend. However, unlike Ingham and Loy's (1993) collection, the work of some writers does not fit so obviously into a cultural studies perspective and the umbrella description, 'critical' paradigm, has been used as a replacement. For example, in *Sport in Society: Issues and Controversies,* Jay Coakley (1990) suggests three major theoretical frameworks for studying the relationship between sport and society, namely, 'structural functionalism', 'conflict theory' (by which he means Marxism) and 'critical theory' (which subsumes cultural studies along with other approaches, such as variants of Marxist, socialist and feminist approaches). However, although Coakley emphasizes the importance of changing social relations, there is no explicit discussion of the concept of hegemony in his 'inclusive' procedure, so that he runs the risk of losing the specific character and meaning of the cultural studies project. But in other US publications, such as Sage's (1990) methodical analysis of *Power and Ideology in American Sport,* the application of cultural studies has not been diluted. Sage explains that the 'critical' in critical theory has two meanings:

> First, it is critical of the ideas that form the conventional wisdom about sport in American society. In the realm of sport, as in many others, dominant groups use political, economic, and cultural resources to define societal norms and values to sustain their influence. Their interests are legitimized by compatible ideologies disseminated by schools, mass media, and various agencies of social control, and the processes they use to suppress alternative versions. Second, ... critical

> through my use of the orientation of hegemony, which is directly linked to social criticism of modern capitalist society. (p. 3)

Although the original impetus for a cultural studies of sport sprang from Britain, a wealth of research in the field has followed in other Western countries – notably, Canada and the United States, and also Australia (Rowe, 1995; Rowe and Lawrence, 1986). In spite of culturally specific differences, Jarvie and Maguire (1994: 124) summarize some general aims of the cultural studies of sport tradition: (i) to consider the relationship between power and culture; (ii) to demonstrate how a particular form of sport or leisure has been consolidated, contested, maintained or reproduced within the context of society as a whole; and (iii) to highlight the role of sport and leisure as a site of popular struggle.

THE FEMINIST CRITIQUE

A major criticism of the sport cultural studies trajectory is its failure to grasp the relevance of sport to sexual politics. It has been argued by sport and leisure feminists, who themselves work in a cultural studies perspective, that there has been a huge gender imbalance of focus (Deem, 1988; Hall, 1996; J.A. Hargreaves, 1994). Rosemary Deem (1988: 347) is extremely critical of John Hargreaves's (1986) failure to acknowledge or engage with research carried out by feminists about gender, leisure and sport,[6] and his failure to carry out research in the field. She points to the way in which, in common with Clarke and Critcher (1985), he alludes to gender as if it is an 'extra' which must not move attention too far away from the priority of class. Most cultural theorists of sport are male and, without exception, though in different ways, they marginalize gender relations of cultural power and by doing so reproduce one feature of the cultural dominance that they set out to critique. Although references are made to the relationship between class and gender, and even to the way that class and gender divisions are constructed together, there have been no attempts to explore this relationship rigorously nor to look at the specific complexities of male hegemony. In so far as they fail to do so, they can be accused of perpetuating sexist sociology (see Critcher, 1986: 338–9).

In *Sporting Females* (1994), Jennifer Hargreaves has attempted to address this deficiency by applying the concept of hegemony specifically to male leadership and domination of sports. In a critical account of the development of female sports from the nineteenth century to the present day, she looks at both the lived experiences of women in sports and the structural forces influencing participation in order to reveal the complex and paradoxical character of female sports. By applying the concept of male hegemony specifically to male leadership and domination of sports, she argues that it is possible to recognize the advantages experienced by men, in general, in relation to women, but also the inability of men to gain total control. She goes on:

> Some men and some women support, accommodate, or collude in existing patterns of discrimination in sports that are specific to capitalism and to male domination, while other men and women oppose them and struggle for change. Male hegemony is not a simple male vs female opposition, which is how it is often presented, but complex and changing. (1994: 23)

Ann Hall (1996: 29–48) argues for a specifically feminist cultural studies applied to sport. She states that, 'Increasingly, and primarily in the United States, it is suggested that the theoretical underpinnings of a truly radical, gendered (and non-racialized) theory of sport lie in the combination of feminism and cultural studies' (p. 34). For Ann Hall, such a project would include: more historically grounded research; a sensitivity to difference; studies of men, sport and masculinity; acknowledgement of the significance of the body; and work that relates feminist cultural politics to sport.

The feminist cultural studies initiative has re-enlivened the politicization of theory. Feminist researchers of sport have systematically related their work to practice. They are not merely researchers who describe what women do; they also set out to transform the structures that oppress women in sport and to create liberating changes (Hall, 1996: 29). By focusing on gender and its relationship to other structures of power, their work has also drawn attention to the diversity of women and to other subordinated groups. Their work also makes clear that hegemony is by no means restricted to class and gender divisions alone. Indeed, the essential usefulness of the concept is its sensitivity to questions of domination and subordination as expressions of the totality of social relations.

Feminist interventions have had a lot to do with the fact that such categories as race, age, disability and sexuality, as well as class and gender, have become important considerations in cultural studies research. And it is not only women who have characterized themselves as sports feminists, but men as well. Arguing that sports feminism is a necessary way forward, Michael Messner and Donald Sabo (1990), editors of *Sport, Men and the Gender Order: Critical Feminist Perspectives*, are examples of the growing number of men who adopt a feminist stance and who concern themselves with multiple structures of power and their interrelationships. They propose a liaison between critical sport sociology and feminism and the formulation of a 'non-hierarchical theory' which 'allows us to conceptualize varied and shifting forms of domination in such a way that we do not privilege one at the expense of distorting or ignoring the others' (p. 10). This is why sports feminists point out that they were articulating the need to take account of difference and diversity before the postmodern claim of authorship (Scraton, 1994). But in spite of the fundamental contribution that feminist scholars have made to advances in sport cultural studies, most debates about the field generalize from male examples and fail adequately to recognize or integrate women's contributions.

PARADIGM WARS

The development of the cultural studies of sport has not been without opposition. Some of the most vociferous criticisms have come from proponents of figurational sociology. Chris Rojek (1992: 26) considers the possibility of transference between the two perspectives, arguing that both would view sport as historically constructed and would agree that there is no single culture (p. 27). More importantly, however, he also points to a range of discrepancies between them, some of which are foundational and clearly irreconcilable. Citing Clarke and Critcher (1985) as key cultural studies theorists, Rojek argues that the concept of hegemony hardly constitutes a theory and that Clarke and Critcher's work is really 'nothing more than the recording of history' (p. 8); that the authors have a 'Little Englander mentality' by focusing on home territory and omitting the global dimension (p. 10); and that they tend to 'conflate every aspect of social practice into culture' (p. 27). The more serious denunciation of cultural studies is the claim that it fails to escape from class reductionism (p. 9). Eric Dunning and his co-writers (1988: 218) berate cultural studies proponents for reifying social life through their insistence that, in the last instance, the economic base is the key to identity, practice and association. Rojek (1992: 26) concurs, by arguing that:

> cultural studies writers insulate themselves from the criticism that class relations in the post-war period have become less important in explaining sport and leisure relations and that lifestyle has become more important, by dismissing lifestyle as an epiphenomenon of class.

Finally, Rojek points out that, 'On the question of social and political involvement, figurational sociologists and cultural studies proponents, really are poles apart.' With reference to the figurationists' support of methodological detachment (Elias and Dunning, 1986: 3–5), he goes on, 'Figurational sociologists ... regard 'praxis' ... as the betrayal of science because it continuously involves political values muddying the quest for objectivity' (p. 28). The debates between the two positions are complex and cannot be dealt with fully here. In defence of cultural studies we would argue that in their critiques of it, opponents, and especially Dunning (see, for example, his entries in Dunning and Rojek 1992), have returned to selected extracts from the original texts of Marx and Lenin, have ignored 'cultural' Marxist interpretations, and have chosen not to engage with the complexities of the concept of hegemony as explicated in Gramsci's original writings (1971). The irony is that the cultural studies approach was developed precisely to avoid the reductionism and economism that it is purported to embody. Gramsci understood the power and complexities of culture in non-totalitarian, fast-developing capitalist societies, but explicitly refused the idea that it was a mere reflection of the economic base. In figurational sociology, because class is seen as one form, rather than the fundamental form of power, it has not featured as a determining structure of social relations, and has tended therefore to be used as a descriptive category of difference. In the cultural studies tradition there is no inevitability about social and cultural developments, and writers in the field have used a wealth of empirical examples to explain the complexities of culture as everyday, commonsense experiences in specific historical and cultural contexts. Referring to the work of cultural studies, John Horne and David Jary (1987) argue that:

> theoretical analysis and empirical research on relations between cultural forms and state, class and economy are handled – actually or potentially – more fully than Figurational Sociology, reflecting

what, following Gramsci, ... researchers recognize as the need to capture the 'current moment' of hegemony. (p. 107)

Much of the figurational critique of cultural studies does not address the large range of research that has been carried out, but engages only with limited examples and huge generalizations. For example, the work of feminist cultural writers, and their critiques of power and male domination have not been integrated into the main debates, and in their specific engagements with sports feminism, they do not engage adequately with the bulk of the literature in the field (Hargreaves, 1994: 12–16). The figurational critique of praxis is also rejected by cultural theorists, who argue that it is possible to carry out worthwhile and 'scientifically' sound research without the spurious pretence of objectivity (Hargreaves, 1994; Horne and Jary, 1987). Although figurationalists deny the possibility of 'objective' or 'value-neutral' research, their methodological adherence to a balance between 'involvement' and 'detachment' has in practice distanced researchers from struggles over power, an action, many cultural studies writers would argue, that can implicitly support those who dominate.

A related methodological critique has come from John MacAloon (1992), who claims that cultural analysts of sport have failed to carry out ethnographic research and depend on 'large processes and structures' (he cites late capitalism, dependency, and commodification as examples) (p. 112), derived from predetermined historical accounts and theoretical ideas, so that 'all comparisons are automatically controlled comparisons' (p. 113). He argues that 'identification and depiction of large historical structures and social logics, if such things exist at all, can never initiate any interesting or truly comparative analysis because methodologically manipulable differences are suppressed in absentia' (p. 112). MacAloon seems to forget that the traditional methodologies of cultural analysts were ethnographic, used specifically in order to understand the everyday experiences and feelings of individuals and sub-groups – and that current researchers continue to use this method. But MacAloon also objects to the social contexting of cultural events, which, he says, should itself be investigated. MacAloon is arguing that a tendency has developed among analysts of sport not to engage in sufficient investigative research and to work within a pre-ordained frame of analysis. It is ironical that Joseph Maguire is one of the theorists criticized by MacAloon (for using the concept of 'Americanization' uncritically as an over-riding structure of power) because he is usually identified as a figurational sociologist, and because, in his joint publication with Grant Jarvie (1996: 54), he supports MacAloon's assertion that hegemony theorists have tended to overuse the concept at the expense of providing sufficient substantive evidence to support their arguments. Jarvie and Maguire (1994: 112) claim that:

> To some extent, a violence of abstraction has occurred in the sense that some writers have been quick to highlight the importance of hegemony at the expense of other aspects of Gramsci's thinking or worse an abstraction of hegemony has been exercised at the expense of concrete modalities of historical and cultural situations ... The gulf between theory and evidence has still to be closed.

MacAloon urges change, because, he says:

> the exploration of cultural conceptions underlying one context of practice will reveal connections to other institutions and contexts that may be quite surprising or unexpected, that is, concealed or suppressed by cultural commonsense, everyday speech, disciplinary or professional boundaries. In this way inquiry into sport can broaden toward the very general social morphologies that cultural studies researchers are most interested in, not by a theoretical reductio but by demonstrated relationships among widening circles of actors and contexts. (p. 117)

Hargreaves and Tomlinson (1992) disagree with MacAloon's argument and defend the methodology under attack. In particular, Hargreaves (1992: 132) claims that cultural researchers link sociology with history in fundamental ways and 'in the sense that both disciplines attempt to produce theoretically informed, testable propositions about social events, relations, and processes, there is no real difference between them'. He points out that historical research precludes participant observation and interview techniques and that although primary sources are important, the use of existing historical evidence 'constitutes some of the most important work in the social sciences'. He emphasizes the role of theory – that is, the use of analytical processes in order to make sense of the social world of sport.

David Andrews and John Loy (1993: 270) recognize that cultural studies 'is a continuously evolving, materialist, anti-essentialist, and anti-reductionist strategy for analyzing conjuncturally specific relationships between culture and power'. However, they also criticize most of the writers in the field because, they claim, they have failed to ground their ideological analyses 'in the realm of corporeality' (p. 270). Whilst in some instances this may be the case, there is a growing attention to the body in recent literature, and, in particular, on representations of masculinity, femininity and sexuality in sport.

Of course, among the researchers from every tradition, it is possible to identify weaknesses in procedures and in the application of theoretical ideas, but by association they do not render the whole field as weak. The extensive work that has emanated from the cultural studies tradition has been produced, in the main, by researchers who skilfully combine empirical material with theoretical concepts and who do not have predetermined ideas about their findings. Together, they have produced an extensive and insightful analysis of sport in culture.

CONCLUSION

There is no question that in spite of the uneven development of and critical comments on the cultural studies paradigm, it has made a major contribution to our understanding of the complex relationships between culture (sport) and power, and about the activeness of culture. Indicative of the important influence of cultural studies to the development of the sociology of sport is the fact that most of the authors of the Key Topics section of this book are either from, or have directly engaged with, the cultural studies perspective.

Nevertheless, there have been contestations within the field itself and it has never produced a static set of ideas, but, rather, has adapted to developments in (mainstream) social theory, and, in turn, has spearheaded new approaches in the sociology of sport. Radical work is currently being produced by cultural theorists who are engaging in debates with postmodernism and with the work of post-structural theorists, with the literature on globalization and postcolonialism, and with developments related to the body and identity.

The challenge facing cultural studies within the sociology of sport is to continue the engagement with other and new paradigms, whilst maintaining its distinctiveness. This requires an understanding of what we have characterized as 'good' cultural studies research, which, we argue, has three critical attributes. First, it is receptive to, and engages with, different theoretical traditions. Secondly, unlike much of contemporary social theory within the academy, its starting point has been the real world, linking theory to empirical investigations and producing theoretically grounded research. And, thirdly, it has taken sides politically – by developing a form of intellectual engagement that is interventionist. Cultural studies exposes power relationships where none have been assumed, and respects the contribution and creative potential of marginalized, oppressed and exploited groups.

One of the best examples of good cultural studies writing on sport is also one of the oldest – *Beyond a Boundary*, written by C.L.R. James in 1963. Quite properly, it is still considered a classic account of sport as a social and cultural form, and should provide both a benchmark and an inspiration for good cultural studies research.[7] Intertwining autobiography, political prose and penetrating portraits of the greats of West Indian cricket, James presents cricket in the West Indies as simultaneously a form of art, politics and philosophy, thus challenging the aestheticians who have 'scorned to take notice of popular sports and games' (1963: 195). It is an account which enables James to identify and agitate around cricket as a privileged site in the struggle for West Indian independence against colonial rule. By raising questions about the role of sport in emergent constructions of postcolonial national identities, and exploring the complex relationship between sport and resistance to racial oppression, *Beyond a Boundary* transcends the specifics of its own socio-historic moment. Above all, it demonstrates that the question posed by James in his preface in 1963, 'What do they know of cricket who only cricket know?', is one that still needs to be asked about all sports 25 years later.

NOTES

We would like to thank our colleague, Garry Whannel, for his painstaking reading of the first draft of this chapter and for his helpful comments.
1 Functionalist, Marxist and figurational sports sociologists, for example, all claim to understand the nature of sport in society and to provide the best theoretical and analytical potential.
2 For critics' accounts of the 'levelling down' of culture as a result of mass production and standardization (e.g. T.S. Eliot and

F.R. Leavis), see, for example, Chapter 1 in J.A. Hargreaves (1982).
3 The work of Louis Althusser and his account of ideological state apparatuses was particularly influential.
4 The first major feminist intervention was made by Angela McRobbie in 1980.
5 For information about the early development of a cultural studies perspective in the sociology of sport, see Jennifer Hargreaves's (1982) introductory chapter in her edited book *Sport, Culture and Ideology*.
6 See, for example, R. Deem (1986) *All Work and No Play? The Sociology of Women and Leisure*, Milton Keynes, Open University Press; E. Green, S. Hebron and D. Woodward (1987) *Leisure and Gender: A Study of Sheffield Woman's Leisure Experiences*, London, ESCR/Sports Council; C. Griffin, D. Hobson, S. MacIntoch and T. McCabe (1982) 'Women and Leisure', in J.A. Hargreaves (ed), *Sport, Culture and Ideology*, London, Routledge & Kegan Paul, pp. 88–116; M. Talbot and E. Wimbush (1986) *Women, Leisure and Well-Being*, Edinburgh, Centre for Leisure Resarch, Dunfermline College.
7 We are aware that C.L.R. James omitted to mention gender and, as with all authors, there are other analytical weaknesses in his work. Nevertheless, we argue that the strengths of his arguments provide an excellent guide for others entering the field.

REFERENCES AND FURTHER READING

Althusser, L. (1971) 'Ideology and ideological state apparatuses', in *Lenin and Philosophy*. London: New Left Books.
Anderson, P. (1976) 'The antimonies of Antonio Gramsci', *New Left Review*, No. 100.
Andrews, D. and Loy, J. (1993) 'British cultural studies and sport: past encounters and future possibilities', *Quest*, 45: 255–76.
Arnold, Matthew (1869) *Culture and Anarchy*. London: Smith, Elder.
Barker, M. and Beezer, A. (eds) (1992) *Reading into Cultural Studies*. London: Routledge.
Bennett, T., Martin, G., Mercer, C. and Woollacott, J. (eds) (1979) *Culture, Ideology and Social Process*. Milton Keynes: Open University Press.
Blundell, V., Shepherd, J. and Taylor, I. (eds) (1993) *Relocating Cultural Studies: Developments in Theory and Research*. London: Routledge.

Brantlinger, P. (1990) *Crusoe's Footprints: Cultural Studies in Britain and America*. London: Routledge.

Brohm, J.-M. (1978) *Sport: a Prison of Measured Time*. London: Ink Links.

Clarke, A. and Clarke, J. (1982) 'Highlights and action replays – ideology, sport and the media', in J.A. Hargreaves (ed.), *Sport, Culture and Ideology*. London: Routledge & Kegan Paul. pp. 62–87.

Clarke, J. (1973) 'Football hooliganism and the skinheads', *CCCS Stencilled Occasional Paper Series* No. 42. Birmingham: CCCS.

Clarke, J. and Critcher, C. (1985) *The Devil Makes Work: Leisure in Capitalist Britain*. Houndsmills: Macmillan Press. esp. pp. 225–30, 'Leisure culture and hegemony'.

Clarke, J., Hall, S., Jefferson, T. and Roberts, B. (1975) 'Subcultures, culture and class: a theoretical overview', *Working Papers in Cultural Studies*, 7 (8): 9–74.

Coakley, J. (1990) *Sport in Society: Issues and Controversies*, 4th edn. St Louis: Times Mirror.

Cohen, P. (1980) 'Subcultural conflict and working class community', in S. Hall et al. (eds), *Culture, Media, Language*. London: Hutchinson. pp. 78–87.

Critcher, C. (1971) 'Football and cultural values', *Working Papers in Cultural Studies*, 1 (Spring): 103–19 (Birmingham: CCCS).

Critcher, C. (1974) 'Women in sport', *Working Papers in Cultural Studies*, 5 (Spring): 3–20 (Birmingham: CCCS).

Critcher, C. (1986) 'Radical theorists of sport: the state of play', *Sociology of Sport Journal*, 3: 333–43.

Critcher, C. et al. (1979) 'Fads and fashions', *CCCS Stencilled Occasional Paper Series* No. 63. London: Sports Council/CCCS.

Davies, I. (1995) *Cultural Studies and Beyond: Fragments of Empire*. London: Routledge.

Deem, R. (1988) '"Together we stand, divided we fall": social criticism and the sociology of sport and leisure', *Sociology of Sport Journal*, 5: 341–54.

Dunning, E. and Rojek, C. (eds) (1992) *Sport and Leisure in the Civilising Process: Critique and Counter-Critique*. Basingstoke: Macmillan.

Dunning, E., Murphy, P. and Williams, J. (1988) *The Roots of Football Hooliganism: an Historical and Sociological Study*. London: Routledge.

Elias, N. and Dunning, E. (1986) *Quest for Excitement: Sport and Leisure in the Civilizing Process*. Oxford: Basil Blackwell.

Gramsci, A. (1971) *Selections from the Prison Notebooks* (eds Q. Hoare and P. Nowell Smith). London: Lawrence & Wishart.

Grossberg, L. (1993) 'The formations of cultural studies', in V. Blundell, J. Shepherd and I. Taylor (eds), *Relocating Cultural Studies: Developments in Theory and Research*. London: Routledge. pp. 21–66.

Grossberg, L., Nelson, C. and Jones, P. (eds) (1992) *Cultural Studies*. London: Routledge.

Gruneau, R. (1983) *Class, Sports, and Social Development*. Amherst, MA: University of Massachusetts Press.

Gruneau, R. (1988a) (ed.) *Popular Cultures and Political Practices*. Toronto: Garamond Press.

Gruneau, R. (1988b) 'Modernization or hegemony: two views on sport and social development', in J. Harvey and H. Cantelon (eds), *Not Just a Game: Essays in Canadian Sport Sociology*. Ottawa: University of Ottawa Press. pp. 9–32.

Hall, M. Ann (1996) 'The potential of feminist cultural studies', in M. Ann Hall, *Feminism and Sporting Bodies*. Champaign, IL: Human Kinetics. pp. 29–48.

Hall, S. (1980) 'Cultural studies and the centre: some problematics and problems', in S. Hall et al. (eds), *Culture, Media, Language*. London: Hutchinson. pp. 15–47.

Hall, S. (1992) 'Cultural studies and its theoretical legacies', in L. Grossberg, C. Nelson and P. Jones (eds), *Cultural Studies*. London: Routledge. pp. 277–86.

Hall, S. and Jefferson, T. (eds) (1976) *Resistance through Rituals: Youth Subcultures in Post War Britain*. London: Hutchinson.

Hall, S., Hobson, D., Lowe, A. and Willis, P. (1980) *Culture, Media, Language*. London: Hutchinson.

Hargreaves, J.A. (1982) 'Theorising sport: an introduction', in J.A. Hargreaves (ed.), *Sport, Culture and Ideology*. London: Routledge & Kegan Paul. pp. 1–29.

Hargreaves, J.A. (1994) *Sporting Females: Critical Issues in the History and Sociology of Women's Sports*. London: Routledge. esp. pp. 21–4, 'Cultural Marxism: hegemony theory'.

Hargreaves, J.E. (1982) 'Sport, culture and ideology', in J.A. Hargreaves (ed.), *Sport, Culture and Ideology*. London: Routledge & Kegan Paul. pp. 30–61.

Hargreaves, J.E. (1986) *Sport, Power and Culture*. Cambridge: Polity Press.

Hargreaves, J.E. (1992) 'Sport and socialism in Britain', *Sociology of Sport Journal*, 9 (2): 131–53.

Hargreaves, J.E. and Tomlinson, A. (1992) 'Getting there: cultural theory and the sociological analysis of sport in Britain', *Sociology of Sport Journal*, 9 (2): 207–19.

Hoch, P. (1972) *Rip Off the Big Game*. New York: Doubleday.

Hoggart, R. (1957) *The Uses of Literacy*. Harmondsworth: Penguin.

Holt, R. (1993) *Sport and the British*. Oxford: Clarendon Press.

Horne, J. (1996) 'British cultural studies and the study of sport and leisure', in G. Jarvie, L. Jackson, J. Lyle and K. Robinson (eds), *Scottish Centre Research Papers in Sport, Leisure and Society*, Vol. 1, Moray House Institute of Education, Heriot-Watt University, Edinburgh. pp. 103–22.

Horne, J. and Jary, D. (1987) 'The figurational sociology of sport of Elias and Dunning: and exposition and critique', *Sport, Leisure and Social Relations*. London: Routledge & Kegan Paul. pp. 86–112.

Ingham, A. and Loy, J. (eds) (1993) *Sport in Social Development: Traditions, Transitions and Transformations*. Champaign, IL, Human Kinetics. esp. pp. 1–21, 'Introduction: sport studies through the lens of Raymond Williams' (A. Ingham and S. Hardy).

James, C.L.R. (1963/1987) *Beyond a Boundary*. London: Serpent's Tail.

Jarvie, G. and Maguire, J. (1994) *Sport and Leisure in Social Thought*. London: Routledge. esp. pp. 108–29, 'Culture as a war of position and a way of life'.

Jarvie, G. and Maguire, J. (1996) 'Sport and historical sociology: some observations', in G. Jarvie, L. Jackson, J. Lyle and K. Robinson (eds), *Scottish Centre Research Papers in Sport, Leisure and Society*, Volume 1, Moray House Institute of Education, Heriot-Watt University, Edinburgh. pp. 38–73.

Jenkins, C. and Green, M. (1982) *Sporting Fictions*. Birmingham: Birmingham University PE Department/CCCS.

Jones, S. (1986) *Workers at Play: a Social and Economic History of Leisure 1918–1939*. London: Routledge & Kegan Paul.

MacAloon, J. (1992) 'The ethnographic imperative in comparative Olympic research', *Sociology of Sport Journal*, 9 (2): 104–30.

McRobbie, A. (1980) 'Settling accounts with subcultures: a feminist critique', *Screen Education*, No. 34: 37–49.

Messner, M. and Sabo, D. (eds) (1990) *Sport, Men and the Gender Order: Critical Feminist Perspectives*. Champaign, IL: Human Kinetics.

Morgan, W. (1994) *Leftist Theories of Sport*. Urbana and Chicago, IL: University of Illinois Press. esp. pp. 60–128, 'Hegemony theory of sport'.

Morley, D. and Chen, Kuan-Hsing (eds) (1996) *Stuart Hall: Critical Dialogues in Cultural Studies*. London: Routledge.

Peters, R. (1976) 'Television coverage of sport', *CCCS Stencilled Occasional Paper Series* No. 48. Birmingham: CCCS.

Pivato, S. (1990) 'The bicycle as a political symbol: Italy 1885–1995', *International Journal of the History of Sport*, 7 (2): 173–87.

Rojek, C. (1992) 'The field of play in sport and leisure studies', in E. Dunning and C. Rojek (eds), *Sport and Leisure in the Civilizing Process*. London: Macmillan.

Rojek, C. (1995) 'Cultural studies', in C. Rojek, *Decentring Leisure: Rethinking Leisure Theory*. London: Sage. pp. 20–5.

Rowe, D. (1995) *Popular Cultures: Rock Music, Sport and the Politics of Pleasure*. London: Sage.

Rowe, D. and Lawrence, G. (eds) (1986) *Power Play: Essays in the Sociology of Australian Sport*. Sydney: Hale and Ironmonger.

Sage, G. (1990) *Power and Ideology in American Sport: a Critical Perspective*. Champaign, IL: Human Kinetics.

Scraton, S. (1994) 'The changing world of women and leisure: feminism, post-feminism and leisure', *Leisure Studies*, 13 (4): 249–61.

Thompson, E.P. (1963) *The Making of the English Working Class*. Harmondsworth: Penguin.

Turner, G. (1990) *British Cultural Studies: an Introduction*. Boston, MA: Unwin Hyman.

Vinnai, G. (1973) *Football Mania*. London: Ocean Books.

Watson, R. (1973) 'The public announcement of fatality', *Working Papers in Cultural Studies*, 4 (Spring): 5–20. (Birmingham: CCCS).

Whannel, G. (1983) *Blowing the Whistle: the Politics of Sport*. London: Pluto.

Whannel, G. (1992) *Fields in Vision: Television Sport and Cultural Formation*. London: Routledge.

Williams, R. (1958) *Culture and Society, 1780–1950*. London: Chatto and Windus.

Williams, R. (1965) *The Long Revolution*. Harmondsworth: Penguin.

Williams, R. (1977) *Marxism and Literature*. Oxford: Oxford University Press.

Willis, P. (1974) 'Women in sport', *Working Papers in Cultural Studies*, 5 (Spring): 21–36. (Birmingham: CCCS).

4

FEMINIST THEORIES FOR SPORT

Susan Birrell

Feminist theory is a dynamic, continually evolving complex of theories or theoretical traditions that take as their point of departure the analysis of gender as a category of experience in society. In the past it seemed to make sense to distinguish among varieties of feminist theories (liberal feminism, radical feminism, Marxist feminism, etc.); today it is more useful to conceive of feminist theor*ies* in the plural, as a series of theoretical approaches marked by rapid development and comprised of an intermix of voices and responses to earlier theoretical traditions. Whatever the sources, whatever the mix of voices privileged by a particular scholar, feminist theory within the sociology of sport has as its main purpose to theorize about gender relations within our patriarchal society as they are evidenced by, played out in, and reproduced through sport and other body practices.

Sport is clearly a gendered activity, that is, an activity that not only welcomes boys and men more enthusiastically than girls and women but that also serves as a site for celebrating skills and values clearly marked as 'masculine' (see, for example, Bryson, 1983). This is what we mean when we refer to sport as a 'male preserve' (Dunning, 1986; Sheard and Dunning, 1973; Theberge, 1985). Thus it is not surprising that feminist scholars find sport to be a logical site for analysis of relationships of gender.

When one talks about 'feminist theory and sport' what is generally meant is not just that one is studying gender in sport but *how* one is studying it: to claim that one is doing feminist analysis is to make a commitment to an explicitly theoretical approach to the interpretation of sport as a gendered activity. Feminist theory

is not to be confused with a focus on 'women in sport', which was an early subject of study; rather, it is a framework for understanding women in sport that draws on and contributes to the development of feminist theories outside the field.

Just as all research on girls and women in sport is not necessarily feminist, not all feminist work focuses on girls and women. A growing area of interest, fostered by the growth of the men's studies movement, is on men in sport, on the ways that sport serves to consolidate male privilege, and on the often deleterious impact that masculine ideologies played out in sport have on many boys and men (Kidd, 1990; Messner and Sabo, 1990, 1994; Curry, 1991). As our theoretical understandings have become more sophisticated, the subject of our theorizing has expanded to include more critical analyses focused on the reproduction of gender relations and male privilege through sport, sport as a patriarchial practice, and sport as a site for masculinist hegemony. Each reconceptualization of the subject reflects and requires a shift in theoretical thinking, and these shifts are evident in the feminist theories we draw on for our analyses in sport. In the final analysis, however, gender relations must always be a key feature: a theory that does not take gender seriously as a category of experience cannot be considered a feminist theory.

One of the most salient features of feminist theorizing is that it is a dynamic process. While it may appear to produce particular frameworks which can be differentiated from one another, at least for heuristic purposes (and that will be one focus reviewed in the next few pages), in reality it is the provisionary status of feminist theory which is its hallmark. Feminist theory is not neat: as hard as we scholars might work to simplify it, it refuses to be disciplined into discrete categories. This is both the strength and the frustration of feminist theories and a testimony to their resilience as useful frameworks for understanding. Feminist theory is unsettled – and thus unsettling to those of us trying to use it appropriately. But it is precisely because we live in a world of increasing complexity, confusion and contradiction that our theories must meet the social world on these terms.

Finally, feminist theory is an openly political or critical practice committed not just to analyzing gender in sport but to changing those dynamics. As the grounding of a plan of action for social action or praxis, feminist theory has clear implications for social change in sport.

FEMINISM AS A THEORY

Like other sociological theories, feminist theory offers an explanation of our lives within culture by attempting to abstract from concrete individual lives a general pattern of experience. Thus a theory is a framework for understanding, but it always develops within a particular cultural context and it is always provisional. Theory is never perfect, never complete, never proven. Instead, theory provides us with a starting point for our understanding but it begs to be expanded, contradicted, refined, replaced.

Theories often begin as critiques of current or dominant theories or ways of thinking, and feminist theories began as critiques of the limitations of the dominant theories in the disciplines that did not include women or did not take women's issues and insights seriously. The particular focus of feminist theories is to provide new ways to understand ourselves as gendered beings, that is, as women and men, and new ways to see the connections between our individual lives and the lives of other women and men. All feminist theories privilege gender as the central category of analysis because they are founded on the belief that human experiences are gendered.

Feminist theory is grounded in an analysis of personal experience – it bears, in fact, strong resemblance to the process of consciousness-raising central to many critical theories (see MacKinnon, 1989) – but the crucial step in this analysis is to overcome one's focus on the purely personal so that one is able to understand one's personal bad luck or misfortune as a small incident in a greater pattern of oppression experienced to some extent by all those who share the same life situation. Thus we learn to see beyond our own personal condition to the broader social conditions that surround us.

All feminists share an assumption that women are oppressed within patriarchy and a commitment to change those conditions. But not all feminists agree on how those oppressive relations are produced and reproduced, and not all feminists share the same vision for the future or the same agenda for change. In our application of feminist theories to sport, then, it makes sense to speak of the threads of feminist theories that spin together to produce a myriad of patterns useful in extending our understanding of the meaning of sport as a gendered practice.

The point of this chapter (as with feminist theory in general) is not to condense the complexities of feminist thought into one unifying theory but to reflect the multivocality of current thinking within the theoretical range that can be generally referred to as feminist theory. In what follows, I will review some basic tenets of feminist theorizing, discuss critiques of feminist theory by non-feminists, and introduce three stages through which feminist theorizing about sport appears to have traveled. Within those stages, theoretical threads of importance to contemporary feminist theory will be delineated and discussed. This will include a discussion of liberal and radical feminism as the founding categories of feminist thought about sport; attempts to theorize difference more profoundly by turning (in the 1980s) toward synthetic and critical theories such as Marxist feminism, socialist feminism, racial relations theories and cultural studies; and the status of feminist theories in a postmodern world, as we move toward more truly interdisciplinary theoretical frameworks, borrowing insights from Foucault, discourse analysis, Gramscian hegemony theory and poststructuralism.

Before we begin, however, a brief discussion of the resistance to feminist theories seems appropriate. Feminist theory is a self-reflexive theoretical practice that changes because those who produce and use the insights the theories offer are constantly unsatisfied with their scope, their focus or their limitations. Thus some of the harshest critics of feminist theory are feminists themselves, that is, those who make 'inside the paradigm' critiques. But feminists are not the only ones engaged in analyzing feminist theory.

Criticisms from 'outside the paradigm' must also be taken seriously. Because these critiques are aimed at the entire enterprise of feminist theorizing and not the particularities of specific feminist theories, it makes sense to discuss them at this point. The more specific critiques generated by feminists as they work to broaden and improve theory will be integrated into the text in an appropriate place, partly to demonstrate concretely the self-reflexive nature of feminist theorizing.

RESISTING FEMINIST THEORY

The View from Outside

While feminist self-criticism, or 'inside the paradigm' critiques, generally take a dialectical form as scholars work to address shortcomings and produce more useful theories, criticisms of feminist theories which originate 'outside the paradigm' generally discredit the practice of feminist theory altogether. Most criticisms from outside are conservative in nature. Often they are founded on a belief that women and men are different by design (that is, genetically, biologically, divinely) and were thus ordained to live different lives, lives that surely were not meant to include such a masculine activity as sport. Such critics see no need to analyze or advocate change for women.

Not surprisingly, one early and particularly effective form of critique has been apathy: the wholesale ignoring of women's interests in sport or the dismissal of women-centered critiques of dominant forms of sport. A more active critique dismisses feminist theory by discrediting women as unsuitable athletes and/or unworthy topics for scholarship. John Carroll's (1986) essay, 'Sport: virtue and grace', in which he argues that women spoil sport as sport spoils women, stands out as the most explicit example of this sort of critique (see also J.A. Hargreaves, 1986, for a direct rebuttal).

Another main line of criticism attacks feminist theory (and other critical theories as well) for not adhering to the mainstream notions of social science they believe should characterize the field. John Phillips (1993), for example, labels critical feminist analyses 'pseudoscience', complaining that they lack objectivity and are value-laden and politically motivated. Feminists respond that feminist theory is a critical theory *intended* to be coupled with social action. Likewise, critical feminists see no inherent value in objectivity (even if that elusive

goal could ever be achieved). They are convinced that a range of methodological and theoretical approaches, which could include but would not privilege social science traditions, is more appropriate for the study of gender, sport, power and culture.

A final criticism of feminist theories could be referred to as the backlash or reverse discrimination position. This criticism is that as the result of affirmative action and such scholarly developments as women's studies and feminist theory, the scales of gender inequity have tipped and women now have an unfair advantage over men both theoretically and socially. This critique is sadly out of touch with the real world, where inequities of gender, race and class continue to flourish.

FEMINIST THEORIES FOR SPORT: THREE STAGES[1]

For the purposes of this review, I discuss the relationship between feminist theories and sport as occurring in three general stages. First was an early atheoretical stage, focused on developing a research area focused on 'women in sport'. Next, came a self-conscious search for theoretical homes within feminism, which began roughly in 1978 (see Birrell, 1988). Finally, our current stage emerged in the late 1980s, strongly influenced by postmodern sensibilities, during which we are moving, often reluctantly, beyond modernist conceptions of theory and toward less unified, less linear analyses. My review focuses largely on the latter two stages, which cover the past two decades, as the dialogue between feminist theories and sport developed.

Early Atheoretical Attention to Women in Sport

Although important critical analyses of the dominance of masculine values in sport existed in England (Sheard and Dunning, 1973; Willis, 1974), analyses of the place of girls and women in sport undertaken in North America and Europe in the 1970s contented themselves with documenting inequalities and arguing for the expansion of opportunities for women. With notable US exceptions (Felshin, 1975; Hart, 1972), they did not do so within an explicit theoretical frame. Research at the time was dominated by psychological topics focused on sex or gender roles, traits and motives, and role conflict. Sociological attention was primarily paid to socialization (see, for example, Greendorfer, 1978). Gender was conceived of as a variable or distributive category rather than a set of relations sustained through human agency and cultural practice (see Birrell, 1988, and Hall, 1988, 1996, for a more extensive discussion of this history).

In 1978, two books appeared in North America which marked a significant turn toward feminist theory: Carole Oglesby's edited book *Women in Sport: From Myth to Reality* (1978), and Ann Hall's monograph *Sport and Gender: a Feminist Perspective on the Sociology of Sport* (1978). Two years later, at the first NASSS conference in Denver, the influence of feminist theory on sport was clearly evident in papers presented by Ann Hall (1980), Nancy Theberge (1980), and Mary Boutilier and Cindy SanGiovanni (1980). Even more importantly, the conference provided a site for feminist scholars from several countries to meet one another for the first time, to create a feminist network and to develop a sense that a critical mass of scholars did exist to further this interest. Boutilier and SanGiovanni gave a particularly important paper which introduced one important typology of the current state of feminist theories outside of sport. Relying on Alison Jaggar and Paula Struhl (Rothenberg)'s (1978) classifications of feminist frameworks, Boutilier and SanGiovanni identified and discussed liberal feminism, radical feminism, Marxist feminism and socialist feminism. These paradigms, particularly liberal feminism, informed much of the feminist research on sport in the decade of the 1980s, though by the end of the decade increasingly critical and synthetic theoretical efforts were shifting the focus.

Moving Toward Theory: The Modernist Project

The decade of the 1980s was one of exciting change in the study of gender and sport. This second stage was characterized by self-conscious critiques of the atheoretical beginnings of the field from feminist scholars such as Susan Birrell (1984) in the United States, Ann Hall (1981, 1984) and Nancy Theberge (1984) in Canada, and Lois Bryson (1983) in Australia. As our understanding grew of feminist theories developing outside the field, we used those insights to inform our own analyses. But while some feminists urged the field toward more

sophisticated theoretical models, most of the research in the field was influenced by a liberal feminist approach. By the end of the decade, however, the turn to critical theories that explicitly theorized relations of power, and more inclusive theories which explicitly theorized difference in terms of relations of class and race as well as gender, moved us toward a critical feminist cultural studies approach and again changed the direction of the field.

The Ur Categories of Feminist Theory: Liberal and Radical Feminism Liberal feminism and radical or cultural feminism are to a great extent the grandmother categories that created and nurtured all the rest. Because they seem to dominate popular understandings of feminist thought (that is, most people who are at all familiar with feminism can recognize these two strands but not others), they can be seen as the *Ur*, or originating categories. Despite much movement away from these generative categories, they remain so central that they might also be considered residual categories of feminist theory.

Liberal feminism is the dominant form of feminist thought and action in North America, Great Britain and Europe. Liberal feminism is based on the humanist ontological position that men and women are more alike than different. Despite their inherent similarities, however, women and men come to live different lives, with different experiences, different opportunities and different expectations, because society erects barriers that restrict their equal participation in society. Extending the rights that women naturally deserve requires removing these artifically constructed barriers (such as the right of college men to receive athletic scholarships while college women had virtually no opportunities to participate at all). Liberal feminists advocate equal access, equal opportunity, equal reward structures, equal pay for equal work, comparable worth and similar equal rights for women.

In terms of sport, liberal feminists work to remove the barriers to girls' and women's participation in sport through legislation such as Title IX and the Equal Rights Amendment in the United States. The limit of liberal feminist thought is that it entails no fundamental critique of the structures themselves, advocating instead that women merely be allowed to take their equal place alongside men in them. To the extent that it focuses on structural limitations, liberal feminism focuses little attention on ideology, or the dominant way of seeing the world that works to keep social structures in place.

Radical or cultural feminism responds to the liberal agenda for change by arguing that it does not go far enough. Men and women, they argue, are essentially different. The patriarchal system men have established (and which continues to benefit all men, even those pro-feminist men who would like to see the system changed) has failed dramatically; what is needed is another vision of the world emanating from the insights of women. Radical change entails a fundamental societal transformation, not just equal access to the system that already exists. Rather than agitating to get women involved in the male-dominated athletic system that already exists, for example, radicals argue that the entire system must be dismantled and reconstructed from the standpoint of women. The way to accomplish this is not through legislation but through revolution. Another radical solution is for women to establish their own separate spaces and practices outside the purview of patriarchy. Lesbian separatism is a particularly strong voice in this movement.

Beginning in the early 1980s, research and analysis was explicitly framed by or read through particular theoretical traditions. Liberal feminism which advocates the inclusion of women and girls within the structure of opportunity and privilege enjoyed by men and boys clearly underlies the bulk of research documenting inequalities of opportunity, advocating Title IX and documenting the precipitous decline in coaching and administration positions for women within women's sport (Acosta and Carpenter, 1994).

Critiques of the conservative limitations of such a feminist approach generally advocate that radical feminist theory should replace liberal feminism theory as the grounding for analysis and, more importantly, social change. The main focus of radical feminism is that sport as we know it must be entirely dismantled so that a feminist alternative might be constructed. But some writers have looked to organized athletics for such situations. Slatton (1982) makes the case for the Association of Intercollegiate Athletics for Women (AIAW) in the United States, Grant (1984) makes the case for international women's field hockey, and McKay (1997) explores the effect of affirmative action initiatives in sport in Canada, Australia and New Zealand. Other feminist alternatives are built outside institutionalized sport, in softball (Birrell and Richter, 1987; Lenskyj, 1994), rugby (Wheatley, 1994), body building (Miller and Penz, 1991), and aerobics (Haravon, 1995).

The Move Toward Synthesis

Theorizing Difference: Gender, Race, Class, Sexuality Liberal and radical feminism can be seen, and criticized, as 'pure' categories of feminist theory. That is, they focus on gender as the primary category of oppression to the exclusion of other categories such as class, race, sexuality, age, nationality, religion. This is a serious problem for those engaged in critical analyses of sport because gender is only one part of an interconnected matrix of relations of power which also include relations of class, race, sexuality, religion, age, etc. Neatly separating gender out of this matrix can happen only theoretically, and, through ignorance and neglect, this strategy does violence to those in other oppressive relationships, such as race and class. If the proper subject of feminist theory is women in all our diversity, then the proper project of feminist theory is theorizing that diversity. The subject of feminist theory must shift from wom*a*n to wom*e*n to reflect the vast experiential diversity of women's lives. A central part of the contemporary feminist project is to discover and theorize links to the lived experiences of other oppressive relationships.

The move is not without its problems, however, particularly issues of 'primacy' (Harding, 1993) or arguments over whether race or class or gender is the primary and most oppressive category of experience. While such commitments to one group isolated from others may serve an important purpose in the development of particular theoretical positions, and more importantly, strategies for social action (and this is the strength of identity politics espoused by the Combahee River Collective, 1984), they offer incomplete grounds for analysis in a world which we increasingly understand as structured by the complex interactions of all these relationships. This realization paved the way for the first synthetic theories, that is, theories that try to combine the insights from two or more theoretical traditions.

The first attempts at synthesis were between radical feminist theories and Marxism – the theoretical approach called Marxist feminism. But Marxist feminism is generally agreed to privilege the primacy of class over gender, a situation not acceptable to many feminists (the classic statement here is Hartman, 1981). Marxist feminism is grounded in the assumptions of Marxism: that the basic oppression is economic and that class is the most important category of experience and analysis. Gender oppression, the Marxist would argue, is derivative of class oppression; rid the world of economic exploitation and gender inequities would also disappear. Contemporary Marxist feminist analyses focus on women's oppression through labor. Women are kept outside the system of waged labor, are systematically located in poorer-paid segments of the workforce, engage in labor which does not count as work within the dominant notions of waged labor, and in contrast to men who are characterized as being engaged in production, women are engaged in reproduction: not only the biological reproduction of children (the next generation of workers) but reproduction of the necessities of domestic life needed to refresh the (male) worker. All of these insights can be applied to the situation of women in sport in capitalist countries. Although not often couched within the language of Marxist feminism, analyses of woman athletes, coaches and administrators as laborers could be enhanced in this way.

This first-order synthetic theory reflected in Marxist feminism was quickly reformulated in the more equitable socialist feminist theory. Socialist feminist theory privileges neither capitalism nor feminism but acknowledges class and gender as mutually supporting systems of oppression: capitalist patriarchy is the proper subject for analysis and social action. In sport, this move began with calls to join feminist interests to the Marxist theoretical project (Beamish, 1984) or to develop a socialist feminism for sport (Bray, 1983; Hall, 1985; Theberge, 1984). Although explicit attention to this paradigm appears to have decreased, feminist analysis continues to take account of the material relations of women in sport in more subtle ways. For example, in a particularly interesting study that takes gender, class, race and nationalism into account, Thompson (1988) discusses Australian women's refusal to support their men through reproductive labor as a means of protesting against the Australian rugby team's involvement with the white South African team.

Socialist feminism was quickly recognized as the appropriate site for second-order synthesis theories or the matrix model which works to focus on interacting impacts of gender, class and race. Even with the acknowledgement of the equal importance of gender and class, theorizing difference along lines of race and ethnicity remains an underdeveloped focus in sport studies. Early efforts (Birrell 1989, 1990) had to depend on theoretical work outside the field for guidance.

Women of color – African American, Latina, Asian American, Native American – have never been absent from feminist movements, but they have often not been recognized or honored in feminist theories in any meaningful way. This is despite the fact that the Combahee River Collective's (1984) early essay on identity politics was a major theoretical contribution to feminist theorizing. Moreover, one early and unsatisfactory solution to the absence of women of color from feminist theories was to include 'women of color' into already existing feminist theories. At least two problems immediately surface. First, such an approach clearly diminishes the experiences of women of color because it assumes that they can be contained in existing theories, grounded in the experiences of white, middle-class women. Secondly, this strategy assumed that 'women of color' was a unified category of experience not differentiated by the variety of experiences that mark the life course of women from different cultures. As a result of such egregious shortcomings, many women of color developed a deep distrust of feminist theories, seeing the act of theorizing as an act of colonization (Christian, 1987).

Another suggestion from women of color was to build feminist theory around the experiences of the most oppressed and marginalized group: to build feminist theory from margin to center (hooks, 1984) or to produce Afrocentric feminist thought (Collins, 1991). The solution generally accepted today fits within the notion of producing synthetic theories by theorizing a 'matrix of domination' (Collins, 1991). Early examples of the successful application of such a theory can be found in Angela Davis's (1983) analysis of slavery as a product of race, class and gender, and the collaborative work of Bulkin, Pratt, and Smith (1984), which argued that oppression is understood as situational, that is, as the product of particular times and places. Solutions to oppression, then, must also be situational. They argue for forming strategic alliances across identities, around the oppressive relationships most dramatically in need of redress at particular times.

In recent years, we have begun to investigate the relationships between gender and race as they are played out in sport. For example, Stan Eitzen and David Furst (1989) brought women into the time-honored tradition of stacking with their focus on volleyball. Brenda Bredemeier (1992) clearly refigured the research program on morality and sport from a multicultural perspective. Mike Messner's feminist essay 'White men misbehaving' (1992b) serves as an important reminder that women are not the only humans who are gendered, and blacks are not the only humans who are raced. Indeed, a good deal of work on the intersection of race and gender takes as its subject the analysis of black masculinity (Andrews, 1996b; Awkward, 1995; Baker and Boyd, 1997; Cole, 1996; McDonald, 1996a, 1996b). Still, Yvonne Smith (1992) reminds us of the need for further work on women of color. Especially needed is research that extends our understanding of race beyond African Americans (Birrell, 1989, 1990).

The relationship between gender and sexuality receives increasing attention within feminist theories. The clear attempts of sport to enforce gender difference through the heterosexualization of women athletes is one aspect of this (Birrell and Theberge, 1994a; Davis, 1997; Duncan, 1990, 1993). Early radical feminist theories often theorized sexuality, more specifically lesbianism, as an integral part of the separatist move (Bunch, 1975; Rich, 1980). They found the relationship to be clear: feminism is the theory and lesbianism is the practice.

Women in sport have long dealt with the assumption that any woman strange enough to want to tread in male territory to play sport is probably not just a tomboy but a lesbian. When we turned our attention to this in the 1980s, the topics of most concern were bringing lesbian existence within the scope of feminist attention and producing an analysis of the ideology of homophobia, which as many feminists pointed out, kept both lesbians and heterosexual women out of sport. In North America, Pat Griffin (1992, 1993), Helen Lenskyj (1986) and Dorothy Kidd (1983) did groundbreaking work in this area. In the 1990s, Susan Cahn's (1994) book furnished one of the more comprehensive discussions of the history of homophobia in sport and physical education; and Pat Griffin (1998) and Mariah Burton Nelson (1991, 1994) brought these issues before the general population. While work on sexuality in the 1980s focused on lesbian identity, even more complicated theoretical models for understanding sexuality, and its relationship to sport, emerged in the next decade.

The Critical Agenda and Feminist Cultural Studies

As the 1980s progressed, more and more feminist energy was directed toward the critical agenda in sport. Critical approaches are explicitly about power and how gender relations are reproduced by, resisted in, and transformed through sport. Cultural studies, or more properly, feminist cultural studies (Cole and Birrell, 1986), was the logical product of the moves to theorize difference through synthesis. Cultural studies was initially developed in England, and it has had significant influence on the study of sport in North America as well. Cultural studies is based on the assumption that power is distributed inequitably throughout society, often along lines of gender, class and race. These relations of power are not fixed but contested. Although the inertia of power generally rests with those already in power, in fact power is constantly contested. It is that struggle that interests critical scholars. Moreover, power is usually not maintained by force or coercion but through more subtle forms of ideological dominance. Ideology is the set of ideas that serve the interests of dominant groups but are taken up as the societal common sense even by those who are disempowered by them (Theberge and Birrell, 1994a). Sport is a particularly public site for such ideological struggle: 'what is being contested … is the construction and meaning of gender relations' (Birrell and Theberge, 1994a: 344). The usefulness of the theoretical vocabulary of cultural studies to explore the intersections of gender, race and class in sport has been clearly recognized.

In 1988, Birrell identified four themes central to the critical feminist cultural studies project:

1 The production of an ideology of masculinity and male power through sport.
2 The media practices through which dominant notions of women are reproduced.
3 Physicality, sexuality, the body as sites for defining gender relations.
4 The resistance of women to dominant sport practices.

Ten years later, these themes still receive significant attention. Based on the work of Eric Dunning (Dunning, 1986; Sheard and Dunning, 1973), the first theme functions today as the primary assumption of the field. Mike Messner's (1988) essay 'Sports and male domination: the female athlete as contested ideological terrain' is a cornerstone of this tradition (see also Birrell and Theberge, 1994a, 1994b, and Theberge and Birrell, 1994a, for an extensive discussion and application of this paradigm). Increasingly this area is theoretically informed by Gramscian hegemony theory: 'Hegemony is a fairly complete system of ideological dominance that works through the apparent complicity of those disenfranchised by it' (Theberge and Birrell, 1994a: 327). One particularly active site for the construction of masculinist hegemony around sport is through media practices.

As feminists expand our notions of what the proper subject of feminist theorizing is, increasing attention is being paid to the place of men within the patriarchal structures of sport. This is a far cry from earlier focuses on men in sport; these analyses are informed by the realization that, although all men benefit from life within a patriarchal culture, some men find their own gendered roles as hypermasculine jocks difficult to fulfill. Most of this pro-feminist work is conducted by men, most notably Mike Messner (1990b, 1996), who has theorized the process as well as applying the new men's studies to his own work (1990a, 1992a). Don Sabo has also been an ally in providing feminist analyses of men's experiences in sport (1990) and editing two anthologies that bring that perspective to sport (Sabo and Runfola, 1980; Messner and Sabo, 1990). Tim Curry's (1991) account of what takes place in male locker rooms gave a rare insider's view of a central site for the reproduction of masculine hegemony. In Canada, Bruce Kidd (1990) offers an insightful view of the 'dynamic of women's oppression/men's repression' through the structures of sport. In addition, a number of these articles single out male violence through or surrounding sport as a mainstay in the production of male privilege (Curry, 1991; Disch and Kane, 1996; Kane and Disch, 1993; Messner, 1990a, 1992a; Theberge, 1989; see also the *IRSS* issue on 'the macho world of sport', Klein, 1990).

Much of the provocative critical work on the ways that the media produce images of women in sport has been conducted by Margaret Duncan. She has studied photographic images of women in the Olympic games (1990), the presentation of women in *Shape* magazine (1994) and, with Cindy Hasbrook (1988), televised images of women's sports. All of her essays provide thoughtful analyses of the dynamics of representation and the struggle for agency in that representation (1993, 1994). In their review of the ideological control of women through media images, Birrell and Theberge (1994a) discuss several themes: the underrepresentation of women athletes in the media; the trivialization and marginalization of their accomplishments; the sexualization, or more properly, heterosexualization of women athletes; the hidden discourse on homophobia; the depiction of women's involvement in sport as tragic; and

the construction of women as unnatural athletes and of female athletes as unnatural women. In the most extensive study of a particular site in this process, Laurel Davis (1997) explores the production, textual features and reception of the *Sports Illustrated* swimsuit issue.

The tradition of documenting resistance to dominant sport practices remains a vital one in the field, no doubt influenced by the work of John Fiske (1989a, 1989b). In the 1990s, Bryson (1990) and Birrell and Theberge (1994b) explored several channels of resistance for women in sport, and Helen Lenskyj (1994) explored feminist softball, Libby Wheatley (1994) reported on songs sung by feminist rugby players, Miller and Penz (1991) watched female bodybuilders 'colonize a male preserve'; and Haravon (1995) suggested ways to make the aerobics gym a resistant space for feminists.

Of the four themes identified by Birrell in 1988, however, by far the most attention has been paid to issues of physicality and the body, and for that we give credit to the turn toward Foucault and postmodernism.

FEMINIST THEORIES FOR A POSTMODERN AGE

The term 'postmodernism' is best applied to the conditions of contemporary life rather than assigned to a particular theory, although some theories, such as post-structuralism, discussed below, are better adapted than others to express the confusions and contradictions of life in a postmodern era. Life in postmodern times has exploded a number of modernist (mis)conceptions about the world, and many of them have deep effects on feminist theory. Postmodernism deconstructs modernist fallacies about unity. The authenticity of the self, a central notion in many theoretical schemes, including the focus on identity politics which underlies radical feminism, is replaced with notions of subjectivity, that is, our self as subject is always contexted within dominant discourses. Postmodernism also disrupts our belief in an essential relationship between language and reality. In a way, reality eludes language. Far from being a tool for our self-expression, language is reconceived as the primary means through which our consciousness is structured. This way of thinking also decenters the notion of truth; there is no truth, there are, at best, provisional truths. Finally, postmodernism challenges the notion of totalizing theories – theories that aim to understand the world within one cohesive explanatory structure – such as those fashioned by modern sociological theories.

The emergence of cultural studies as the dominant paradigm for feminist analysis in the 1980s served as a bridge to the more interdisciplinary, postmodern sensibilities. Another round of stocktaking essays appeared at the end of the 1980s (Birrell, 1988; Deem, 1988; Hall, 1988; J.A. Hargreaves, 1990; Talbot, 1988), attempting to trace a direct line from the relatively organized feminist frameworks of the past to the sorts of intellectual forces that would guide the future. Cultural studies was taking us beyond the boundaries of social science into the relatively unbounded territory inhabited by Lacan, Derrida, Foucault and Gramsci where the languages spoken include discourse analysis, hegemony theory, post-structuralism, deconstruction and postmodernism. Jennifer Hargreaves (1986, 1990) and Talbot (1988) were clearly anticipating the entrance of Foucault, and in 1993, with the publication of her important essay, Cheryl Cole was identified as a major visionary for the post-structuralist feminist studies move in sport.

Michel Foucault and post-structuralism are at the center of these shifts in several ways. Post-structuralism focuses on the 'analysis of social organization, social meanings, power, and individual consciousness' (Weedon, 1987: 21) constructed through language or other forms of representation. The theoretical and methodological strategies of analysis influenced by post-structuralist thought require us to focus our attention on the construction of narratives and the contesting of meanings. The narratives that surround sport and the body furnish obvious sites for this analysis because sport figures so prominently in the production of 'celebrity bodies'. Discourse analyses that attend to the construction of gender relations through sport narratives include focuses on Renee Richards (Birrell and Cole, 1990), Magic Johnson (Cole and Denny, 1995; King, 1993), Lisa Olson (Disch and Kane, 1996; Kane and Disch, 1993), Mike Tyson (Birrell and McDonald, 1993; Awkward, 1995) and Michael Jordan (see the essays in Andrews, 1996b).

The Foucauldian concept of the production of power through surveillance and discipline provides provocative new points of departure for the study of the athletic body. As a wide range of scholars have demonstrated, sport and other body practices are a central site for training the docile body. One needs merely to think back on one's experiences in physical education, with its emphasis on 'schooling the body' (J.E. Hargreaves, 1986), to see why this is so. Most of the work which follows this lead is discussed by David Andrews in his chapter in this volume, but the work of Mary Duquin (1994a, 1994b), Margaret Duncan (1994), Susan Bordo (1989), Laurie Schultz (1990), Brian Pronger (1995, 1990), Genevieve Rail and Jean Harvey (1995), Cheryl Cole and Harry Denny (1995), Cole and Amy Hribar (1999), Sindy Sidnor (Slowikowski, 1993), Dave Andrews (1993), Elizabeth Grosz (1994) and Pierkko Markula (1995) all deserve special mention here as well.

Queer Theory and the Transgender Challenge

One important reconceptualization in our theories of gender was Judith Butler's (1990) identification of the heterosexual matrix: the interrelationships among sex, gender and sexuality (or desire). Since the 1970s, it has been customary to use the term 'sex' to refer to one's biological and genetic category: one is embodied either male or female. 'Gender' was used to refer to the cultural scripts and behaviors that those born male or female were expected to fulfill: one acts masculine or feminine. 'Sexuality' refers to one's choice of sexual partner. The three, sex/gender/sexuality, are not causally related, but our cultural assumptions lead us to believe they are. We assume the three naturally come in a complete package: female, feminine, heterosexual. We assume we can read one category from information we have about another. And finally, we assume that each category belongs in a binary.

The first of these terms to be questionned was gender, and it was soon recognized that masculine and feminine roles were not the only choices, even in a sexist society. Both scholars and the general population were drawn to the notion of 'androgyny' or the combination within one person of traits characteristic of both genders. Gender was the easiest term to deconstruct because it was increasingly apparent that gender was culturally constructed. In the past few years, however, our notion of sex as a binary and our notion of sexuality as a binary have both been seriously challenged, with far more dramatic results.

To argue that there may be more than two mutually exclusive sexes is to challenge the notion of difference itself, for metaphors of difference often rely on the male/female binary for their meaning. Nevertheless, research in sport has provided a particularly compelling site for examining this logic, for sport remains one of the few cultural activities still felt to be logically arranged by sex. Susan Birrell and Cheryl Cole's (1990) analysis of the cultural meaning of Renee Richards, the male-to-constructed-female transsexual who fought a legal battle to be allowed to play tennis on the women's tour, offered one opportunity to recognize that sex categories are cultural constructions that require enormous cultural work to maintain. John Hood-Williams (1995) performs the same deconstruction of sex testing for athletics, and Laurel Davis and Linda Delano (1992) read the subtext of an anti-drug campaign to find fears of transgendered bodies lurking beneath.

The third concept, sexuality, has also been dislodged from its binary assumptions. Other possibilities for sexual choices, such as bisexual and more recently transgender, work not only to disrupt the binary but to dislodge sexuality from its position as an identity. Instead, it is argued that actions or particular choices may have a sexuality, but individuals do not have a permanent sexual identity. Thus the phrase 'I am a lesbian' (a statement of identity) is replaced by 'I am in a lesbian relationship' (a situated choice). Sykes (1996) explores the implications of this in her post-structuralist critique of lesbian identities.

A transsexual, like Renee Richards, is someone who believes he or she was born into the wrong body. The transsexual undergoes considerable anguish and work in order to have the sex signifiers of one gender exchanged surgically with those of the other. Dramatic as the plight of the transsexual is, 'transgender' is a more radical concept. A transgendered person believes that sex, gender and sexuality do/should not exist as permanent conditions, nor do they have any necessary connection to one another. The transgendered person wants to live in a body (and, more radically, a society) where sexed bodies do not matter.

The deconstruction of the heterosexual matrix disrupts some aspects of the feminist project. If sex and gender do not exist as real, enduring categories, what happens to our central category, woman? What is the subject of feminist theory? In this sense we can say that the transgender movement has queered the categories of our analysis. This fascinating development is a clear challenge for our future.

FEMINIST THEORY, SPORT AND CULTURAL PRACTICE

Theorizing is a challenging and rewarding activity in its own right, but as a critical theory, feminist theory is committed to producing frameworks of understanding that can serve as the basis for thoughtful and profound social change. The connection of feminist theories to sporting practice can best be characterized as providing the theoretical underpinnings for the arguments made by advocacy groups as they work to redress the inequities and increase the opportunities for girls and women in sport. Some are involved in particular research projects with a conscious concern for identifying barriers to girls' and women's participation and helping girls discover and enjoy sport. The research traditions of socialization, role models and coaching burn-out are examples of this impulse. Other feminist work assesses and documents inequities and injustices in sport, at both the practical and the ideological level.

Feminist practitioners in sport work to fulfill that promise so that social action in sport can take place within a comprehensive plan. Unlike their counterparts in men's athletics, women collegiate athletic administrators in North America pay attention to the more accessible writings of liberal feminist theorists, sometimes working together at conferences or in workshops to build bridges between theory and practice. The New Agenda conferences sponsored by the Women's Sport Foundation in the US in 1983 and 1984 are good examples of this collaborative process. While the practitioner and the theorist may not always be the same person, their commitment to each other's work and to the same feminist end strengthens their respective work.

Among those concerned with day-to-day gains for women in sport there is an acknowledgement that theory helps to arrange our ideas and to see the bigger picture, the broader context. And while theory is not always explicitly invoked in the work they do – the memos they produce, the expert court testimony they provide, the speeches they give to booster clubs, parents and young athletes – it often underlies and strengthens their messages.

As evidence of these connections, I mention four arenas in which theory and practice exist together in sport. First, in terms of advocacy, many who speak on behalf of the interests of girls and women in sport – by supporting legislation such as the Civil Rights Restoration

Act in the US, by bringing Justine Blainey's case to play ice hockey before the Canadian Supreme Court, by providing expert testimony in court cases such as *Bell* v. *Grove City* and *Cohen* v. *Brown* in the US – rely on research informed by feminist theory to frame their arguments.

Secondly, organizations that advocate for women in sport have been founded all over the world. In Canada, the Canadian Association for the Advancement of Women and Sport and Physical Activity (CAAWS/ACAFS) has been in existence since 1981; they have held several national conferences and publish a newsletter. In the US, the Women's Sports Foundation (WSF) takes a leadership role in disseminating information, supporting legislative initiatives, and sponsoring research studies and national conferences, such as the New Agenda conferences in 1983 and 1984 which focused on turning research into action. The Women's Sports Foundation in the United Kingdom, Women-Sport International (WSI), WomenSport Australia and the International Working Group (IWG) all work to bridge common interests. In general, these groups follow a liberal agenda for change.

Thirdly, several publications draw on the resources of those involved at all levels of analysis and theory. CAAWS publishes a newsletter, *Action* (formerly *The Starting Line*), and the Citizens for Sports Equity publish *Full Court Press*. In a more radical vein, *Girl Jock* and other clearly feminist 'zines focused on sport and the body, such as *Fat! So?* and *Fat Girl*, work to provide spaces for all women to enjoy sport and their bodies on their own terms. Unfortunately, no mainstream magazine in the US, even those that appear to focus on women and sport, offers the full encouragement toward empowerment that a feminist grounded publication would. The mainstream magazine with the most disappointing history, from this perspective, is the magazine most recently sold as *Women's Sports and Fitness*. Founded as *Womensport* in 1984 by Billie Jean King as a means to provide support for girls and women interested in and involved in sport, the magazine has gone through several reorganizations, generally shifting its focus away from competitive sport and toward appearance-driven fitness activities (Endel, 1991). Most recently, the magazine has been bought out by Conde Nast and consolidated with their new publication *Conde Nast Sports for Women*. Time Inc. have apparently abandoned their attempt to capture the emerging women's market, stopping production of their occasional *Sports Illustrated Womensport* after three numbers.

Fourth, homepages for CAAWS (*www. caaws.ca*) and the Women's Sport Foundation (*www.womenssportsfoundation.org*) facilitate connection to those important organizations. In addition, the Feminist Majority maintains a site (*www.feminist.org/sports*) where one can find links to a variety of sport topics, including Title IX, gender equity, Olympic sport, NCAA and WNBA basketball, the martial arts, and much more. Information specific to Title IX in the US is maintained at bailiwick.lib.uiowa.edu/ge. Finally, some measure of success can be gleaned from the fact that mainstream media, such as *USA Today* (no doubt facilitated by the NASSS 'expert' file) regularly seek out feminist or 'alternative' approaches to issues of women in sport.

THE FUTURE OF FEMINIST THEORIES FOR SPORT

As a dynamic and evolving theoretical practice, feminist theories will continue to change and develop as scholars struggle towards more complete understandings of the complex dynamics of power relations of which gender relations are a fundamental part. At the present, that course seems to be dominated by two important trends. One trend is the move towards synthetic theories that use the insights of feminist theories as one thread to weave into more complex theories of power and the inter-relationships of gender, race and class. The second is the move across the disciplinary boundaries of sociology towards the powerful insights offered through post-structuralist approaches. In the future, new cultural conditions that we cannot yet even envision will challenge us to provide new forms of understanding. That mandate is the most exciting prospect in the process of theory.

Whatever the challenges are, feminist theory will surely be an important part of the theoretical process. For that reason, references to a postfeminist era are both wrong-headed and politically dangerous. To assert that we are in a postfeminist world is to assert that feminism is no longer necessary. This goal – the dissolution of feminism – can be sought from two very different political positions: working towards the end of gender or working towards the end of feminism. The first scenario would envision a world in which the gendered nature of social life has been eradicated so that gender is no longer an index of the provision of privilege or a key point around which power revolves. Although such a state of affairs is not likely to happen in our lifetime, that condition would be greeted with different responses by feminists located within different theoretical groups. Some feminist theories see the end of gender as the goal of feminist theory, feminist thought and feminist action; interestingly, the end of gender would eradicate the need for feminist theory as the primary tool both to explain and protest those conditions. More nefarious, however, are calls for the end of feminism before gender privileges are deconstructed. This second scenario, which implies that feminism and feminist theory are *passé*, is a counter-revolutionary move that must be resisted.

As long as a culture is characterized by gender privilege and as long as sport remains a preferred site for the reproduction of that privilege – and there is no prospect of those fundamental relationships changing in the foreseeable future – feminist theories will continue to make a fundamental contribution to our understandings of the meanings of sport in culture.

NOTES

I am grateful to Mary McDonald and Nancy Theberge for their thoughtful feedback on earlier drafts of this chapter.
1 In the discussion that follows, my focus will be on the generation of theory concurrent with the second wave of feminism, particularly in the second half of the twentieth century, and I will draw upon several different schemes for understanding the overlaps and distinctions among feminist theories. Tour guides for this excursion include Jaggar and (Struhl) Rothenberg (1978, 1993), Tong (1989), Donovan (1985) and Collins (1991), and in sport, Boutilier and SanGiovanni (1983), Hargreaves (1994), Birrell (1988) and Hall (1996). Among the labels these scholars apply to various strands of feminist thought are liberal feminism, radical or cultural feminism, Marxist feminism, socialist feminism and postmodern feminism. I will discuss each of these to the extent that they are vital frameworks within the sociology of sport, and I will introduce several other frameworks which are clearly significant in our current studies of sport and gender

relations but which often rest uneasily within the overarching label of 'feminist' theory.

With some important exceptions, most of the excitement within feminist theory and sport appears to be taking place within North America, England and Australia. Articles published in the *IRSS*, for example, our premier international journal, primarily feature articles on participation figures and structural analyses from other countries.

REFERENCES AND FURTHER READING

Acosta, V. and Carpenter, L. (1994) 'The status of women in intercollegiate athletics', in S. Birrell and C. Cole (eds), *Women, Sport and Culture*. Champaign, IL: Human Kinetics. pp. 111–18.

Andrews, D. (1993) 'Desperately seeking Michel: Foucault's geneology, the body and critical sport sociology', *Sociology of Sport Journal*, 10 (2): 148–67.

Andrews, D. (1996a) 'Deconstructing Michael Jordan: reconstructing postindustrial America', *Sociology of Sport Journal* (Special Issue), 15 (4): 315–18.

Andrews, D. (ed.) (1996b) Special Issue: Deconstructing Michael Jordan: Reconstructing Post-industrial America. *Sociology of Sport Journal*, Volume 15.

Awkward, M. (1995) 'Representing rape: on Spike, Iron Mike, and the "desire dynamic"', in *Negotiating Difference: Race, Gender and the Politics of Positionality*. Chicago, IL: Chicago Press. pp. 93–135.

Baker, A. and Boyd, T. (eds) (1997) *Out of Bounds: Sports, Media, and the Politics of Identity*. Bloomington, IN: Indiana University Press.

Beamish, R. (1984) 'Materialism and the comprehension of gender related issues in sport', in N. Theberge and P. Donnelly (eds), *Sport and the Sociological Imagination*. Fort Worth, TX: Texas Christian University Press. pp. 60–81.

Birrell, S. (1984) 'Separatism as an issue in women's sport', *Arena Review*, 8: 49–61.

Birrell, S. (1988) 'Discourses on the gender/sport relationship: from women in sport to gender relations', *Exercise and Sport Science Reviews*, 16: 459–502.

Birrell, S. (1989) 'Racial relations theories and sport: suggestions for a more critical analysis', *Sociology of Sport Journal*, 6: 212–27.

Birrell, S. (1990) 'Women of color, critical autobiography, and sport', in M.A. Messner and D.F. Sabo (eds), *Sport, Men, and the Gender Order: Critical Feminist Perspectives*. Champaign, IL: Human Kinetics. pp. 185–99.

Birrell, S. and Cole, C. (1990) 'Double fault: Renee Richards and the construction and naturalization of difference', *Sociology of Sport Journal*, 7: 1–21.

Birrell, S. and Cole, C.L. (eds) (1994) *Women, Sport, and Culture.* Champaign, IL: Human Kinetics.

Birrell, S. and McDonald, M. (1993) 'Privileged assault: representations of violence and the inadequacy of segmented category analysis'. Invited paper presented at the National Girls and Women in Sport Symposium, Slippery Rock University, February.

Birrell, S. and Richter, D. (1987) 'Is a diamond forever? Feminist transformation of sport', *Women's Studies International Forum*, 10: 395–409.

Birrell, S. and Theberge, N. (1994a) 'Ideological control of women in sport', in D.M. Costa and S.R. Guthrie (eds), *Women and Sport: Interdisciplinary Perspectives.* Champaign, IL: Human Kinetics. pp. 361–76.

Birrell, S. and Theberge, N. (1994b) 'Feminist resistance and transformation in sport', in D.M. Costa and S.R. Guthrie (eds), *Women and Sport: Interdisciplinary Perspectives.* Champaign, IL: Human Kinetics. pp. 361–76.

Bordo, S. (1989) *Gender/Body/Knowledge: Feminist Reconstructions of Being and Knowing.* New Brunswick, NJ: Rutgers University Press.

Boutilier, M. and SanGiovanni, L. (1980) 'Women, sport and public policy'. Paper presented at NASSS conference, Denver.

Boutilier, M. and SanGiovanni, L. (1983) *The Sporting Woman.* Champaign, IL: Human Kinetics.

Bray, C. (1983) 'Sport, capitalism and patriarchy', *Canadian Women's Studies*, 4: 11–13.

Bray, C. (1984) 'Gender and the political economy of Canadian sport', in N. Theberge and P. Donnelly (eds), *Sport and the Sociological Imagination.* Fort Worth, TX: Texas Christian University Press. pp. 104–24.

Bredemeier, B. (1992) '"And ain't I a woman?": Toward a multicultural approach to gender and morality', *Quest*, 14 (2): 179–209.

Bryson, L. (1983) 'Sport and the oppression of women', *Australian and New Zealand Journal of Sociology*, 19 (3): 413–26.

Bryson, L. (1990) 'Challenges to male hegemony in sport', in M.A. Messner and D.F. Sabo (eds), *Sport, Men, and the Gender Order: Critical Feminist Perspectives.* Champaign, IL: Human Kinetics. pp. 173–84.

Bulkin, E., Pratt, M.B. and Smith, B. (1984) *Yours in Struggle: Three Feminist Perspectives on Anti-Semitism and Racism.* Brooklyn, NY: Long Haul Press.

Bunch, C. (1975) 'Lesbians in revolt', in *Lesbianism and the Women's Movement.* Oakland, CA: Diana Press. pp. 29–37.

Butler, J. (1990) *Gender Trouble: Feminism and the Subversion of Identity.* New York and London: Routledge.

Cahn, S.K. (1994) *Coming on Strong: Gender and Sexuality in Twentieth-century Women's Sport.* New York: Free Press.

Carroll, J. (1986) 'Sport: virtue and grace', *Theory, Culture, and Society*, 3: 91–8.

Christian, B. (1987) 'The race for theory', *Cultural Critique*, 6: 51–63.

Cole, C. (1993) 'Resisting the canon: feminist cultural studies, sport, and technologies of the body', *Journal of Sport and Social Issues*, 17: 77–97.

Cole, C. (1996) 'P.L.A.Y., Nike, and Michael Jordan: national fantasy and the racialization of crime and punishment', *Working Papers in Sport and Leisure Commerce*, 1 (1). University of Memphis.

Cole, C. and Birrell, S. (1986) 'Resisting the canon: feminist cultural studies'. Paper presented at NASSS meetings, Las Vegas, October.

Cole, C. and Denny, H. (1995) 'Visualizing deviance in post-Reagan America: Magic Johnson, AIDS, and the promiscuous world of professional sport', *Critical Sociology*, 20: 123–47.

Cole, C. and Hribar, A. (1999) 'Celebrity feminism Nike style: Post-Fordism, transcendence and consumer power', *Sociology of Sport Journal*, 12: 347–69.

Collins, P.H. (1991) *Black Feminist Thought: Knowledge Consciousness, and the Politics of Empowerment.* New York: Routledge.

Combahee River Collective (1984) 'A black feminist statement', in A.M. Jaggar and P.S. Rothenberg (eds), *Feminist Frameworks*, 2nd edn. New York: McGraw Hill. pp. 202–9.

Curry, T.J. (1991) 'Fraternal bonding in the locker room: a profeminist analysis of talk about competition and women', *Sociology of Sport Journal*, 8: 119–35.

Davis, A. (1983) *Women, Race, and Class.* New York: Vintage.

Davis, L. (1997) *The Swimsuit Issue and Sport: Hegemonic Masculinity in* Sports Illustrated. Albany, NY: SUNY Press.

Davis, L. and Delano, L. (1992) 'Fixing the boundaries of physical gender: side effects of anti-drug campaigns in athletics', *Sociology of Sport Journal*, 9 (1): 1–19.

Deem, R. (1988) '"Together we stand, divided we fall": social criticism and the sociology of sport and leisure', *Sociology of Sport Journal*, 5: 341–54.

Disch, L. and Kane, M.J. (1996) 'When a looker is really a bitch: Lisa Olson, sport, and the heterosexual matrix', *Signs*, 21: 278–308.

Donovan, J. (1985) *Feminist Theory.* New York: Frederich Ungar.

Duncan, M.C. (1990) 'Sport photographs and sexual difference: images of women and men in the 1984 and 1988 Olympic Games', *Sociology of Sport Journal*, 7: 22–40.

Duncan, M.C. (1993) 'Beyond analyses of sport media texts: an argument for formal analyses of institutional structures', *Sociology of Sport Journal*, 10: 353–72.

Duncan, M.C. (1994) 'Politics of women's body images and practices: Foucault, the panopticon and *Shape* magazine', *Journal of Sport and Social Issues*, 18: 48–65.

Duncan, M.C. and Hasbrook, C. (1988) 'Denial of power in televised women's sport', *Sociology of Sport Journal*, 5: 1–21.

Dunning, E. (1986) 'Sport as a male preserve: notes on the social sources of masculinity and its transformations', *Theory, Culture and Society*, 3: 79–90.

Duquin, M.E. (1994a) '"She flies through the air with the greatest of ease": the contributions of feminist psychology', in D.M. Costa and S.R. Guthrie (eds), *Women and Sport*, Champaign, IL: Human Kinetics. pp. 285–306.

Duquin, M.E. (1994b) 'The body snatchers and Dr Frankenstein revisited: social construction and deconstruction of bodies and sport', *Journal of Sport and Social Issues*, 18: 268–81.

Eitzen, S. and Furst, D. (1989) 'Racial bias in women's collegiate volleyball', *Journal of Sport and Social Issues*, 13: 46–51.

Endel, B. (1991) 'Working out: the dialectics of strength and sexuality', *Women's Sports & Fitness* magazine. PhD dissertation, The University of Iowa.

Felshin, J. (1975) 'The triple option … for women *in* women's sport', *Quest*, 21: 36–40.

Fiske, J. (1989a) *Reading the Popular*. Boston, MA: Unwin Hyman.

Fiske, J. (1989b) *Understanding Popular Culture*. Boston, MA: Unwin Hyman.

Grant, C. (1984) 'The gender gap in sport: from Olympic to intercollegiate level', *Arena Review*, 8 (2): 31–47.

Greendorfer, S. (1978) 'Socialization into sport', in C. Oglesby (ed.), *Women and Sport: From Myth to Reality*. Philadephia: Lea & Febiger. pp. 15–140.

Griffin, P. (1992) 'Changing the game: homophobia, sexism, and lesbians in sport', *Quest*, 44: 251–65.

Griffin, P. (1993) 'Homophobia in women's sports: the fear that divides us', in G.L. Cohen (ed.), *Women in Sport: Issues and Controversies*. Newbury Park, CA: Sage. pp. 193–203.

Griffin, P. (1998) *Strong Women, Deep Closets: Lesbians in Sport*. Champaign, IL: Human Kinetics.

Grosz, E. (1994) *Volatile Bodies: Toward a Corporeal Feminism*. Bloomington, IN: Indiana University Press.

Hall, M.A. (1978) *Sport and Gender: a Feminist Perspective on the Sociology of Sport*. CAHPER Sociology of Sport Monograph Series. Ottawa: Canadian Association for Health, Physical Education, and Recreation.

Hall, M.A. (1980) 'Sport and gender: a feminist perspective on the sociology of sport'. Keynote address, NASSS meetings, Denver, CO, October.

Hall, M.A. (1981) *Sport, Sex Roles, and Sex Identity*. The CRIAW Papers. Ottawa, ON: Canadian Research Institute for the Advancement of Women.

Hall, M.A. (1984) 'Feminist prospects for sociology of sport', *Arena Review*, 8: 1–10.

Hall, M.A. (1985) 'How should we theorize sport in a capitalist patriarchy?', *International Review for the Sociology of Sport*, 20: 109–15.

Hall, M.A. (1988) 'The discourse of gender and sport: from femininity to feminism', *Sociology of Sport Journal*, 5: 330–40.

Hall, M.A. (1996) *Feminism and Sporting Bodies: Essays in Theory and Practice*. Champaign, IL: Human Kinetics.

Haravon, L. (1995) 'Exercise in empowerment: toward a feminist aerobic pedagogy', *Women in Sport and Physical Activity*, 4 (2): 23–44.

Harding, S. (1993) 'After the science question in feminism', in L. Richardson and V. Taylor (eds), *Feminist Frontiers III*. New York: McGraw-Hill. pp. 12–20.

Hargreaves, J.E. (1986) 'Schooling the body', in J.E. Hargreaves, *Sport, Power and Culture*. New York: St Martin's Press. pp. 161–81.

Hargreaves, J.A. (1986) 'Where's the virtue? Where's the grace? A discussion of the social production of gender relations through sport', *Theory, Culture and Society*, 3: 109–21.

Hargreaves, J.A. (1990) 'Gender on the sports agenda', *Internation Review for the Sociology of Sport*, 25: 287–308.

Hargreaves, J.A. (1994) *Sporting Females: Critical Issues in the History and Sociology of Women's Sports*. London and New York: Routledge.

Hart, M. (1972) 'On being female in sport', in M. Hart (ed.), *Sports in the Sociocultural Process*. Dubuque, IA: William C. Brown. pp. 291–301.

Hartman, H. (1981) 'The unhappy marriage of Marxism and feminism', in L. Sargent (ed.), *Women and Revolution*. Boston, MA: South End Press. pp. 1–41.

Hood-Williams, J. (1995) 'Sexing the athletes', *Sociology of Sport Journal*, 12 (3): 290–305.

hooks, B. (1984) *Feminist Theory: From Margin to Center*. Boston, MA: South End Press.

Jaggar, A.M. and Rothenberg, P.S. (eds) (1993) *Feminist Frameworks: Alternative Theoretical Accounts of the Relations between Women and Men*, 3rd edn. New York: McGraw Hill.

Jaggar, A.M. and Struhl (Rothenberg), P.S. (eds) (1978) *Feminist Frameworks: Alternative Theoretical Accounts of the Relations between Women and Men*. New York: McGraw Hill.

Kane, M.J. and Disch, L. (1993) 'Sexual violence and the reproduction of male violence in the locker room: the Lisa Olson incident', *Sociology of Sport Journal*, 10 (4): 331–52.

Kidd, B. (1990) 'The men's cultural centre: sports and the dynamic of women's oppression/men's repression', in M. Messner and D. Sabo (eds), *Sport, Men and the Gender Order*. Champaign, IL: Human Kinetics. pp. 31–43.

Kidd, D. (1983) 'Getting physical: compulsory heterosexuality and sport', *Canadian Women's Studies Journal*, 4: 62–5.

King, S. (1993) 'Politics of the body and the body politic: Magic Johnson and the ideology of AIDS', *Sociology of Sport Journal*, 10: 270–85.

Klein, M. (ed.) (1990) Special Topical Issue on the Macho World of Sport. *International Review for the Sociology of Sport*, 25 (3).

Lenskyj, H. (1986) *Out of Bounds: Women, Sport and Sexuality*. Toronto: Women's Press.

Lenskyj, H. (1994) 'Girl-friendly sport and female values', *Women in Sport and Physical Activity Journal*, 3 (1): 35–45.

Lopiano, D. (1984) 'A political analysis of the possibility of impact alternatives for the accomplishment of feminist objectives within American intercollegiate sport', *Arena Review*, 8 (2): 49–61.

Loy, J. and Harris, J. (1991) Special issue on Body Culture. *Quest*, 43 (2).

MacKinnon, C. (1989) *Toward a Feminist Theory of the State*. Cambridge, MA: Harvard University Press.

Markula, P. (1995) 'Firm but shapely, fit but sexy, strong but thin: the postmodern aerobicizing female bodies', *Sociology of Sport Journal*, 12 (4): 424–53.

McDonald, M. (1996a) 'Michael Jordan's family values: marketing, meaning, and post-Reagan America', *Sociology of Sport Journal*, 15 (4): 344–65.

McDonald, M. (1996b) 'Horatio Alger with a jump shot: Michael Jordan and the American dream', *Iowa Journal of Cultural Studies*, 15: 33–47.

McDonald, M. and Birrell, S. (1998) 'Reading sport critically'. Paper presented at the International Sociology of Sport Association, Montreal, July.

McKay, J. (1997) *Managing Gender: Affirmative Action and Organization Power in Australia, Canada and New Zealand Sport*. Albany, NY: State University of New York Press.

Messner, M. (1988) 'Sports and male domination: the female athlete as contested ideological terrain', *Sociology of Sport Journal*, 5: 197–211.

Messner, M. (1990a) 'When bodies are weapons: masculinity and violence in sport', *International Review for the Sociology of Sport*, 25: 203–20.

Messner, M. (1990b) 'Men studying masculinity: some epistemological issues in sport sociology', *Sociology of Sport Journal*, 7: 136–53.

Messner, M. (1992a) *Power at Play: Sports and the Problem of Masculinity*. Boston, MA: Beacon Press.

Messner, M. (1992b) 'White men misbehaving: feminism, Afrocentrism and the promise of a critical standpoint', *Journal of Sport and Social Issues*, 16 (2): 136–43.

Messner, M. (1996) 'Studying up on sex', *Sociology of Sport Journal*, 13 (3): 221–37.

Messner, M. and Sabo, D. (eds) (1990) *Men, Sport, and the Gender Order*. Champaign, IL: Human Kinetics.

Messner, M. and Sabo, D. (1994) *Sex, Violence and Power in Sport*. Freedom, CA: Crossing Press.

Messner, M. and Solomon, W. (1993) 'Outside the frame: newspaper coverage of the Sugar Ray Leonard wife abuse story', *Sociology of Sport Journal*, 10 (2): 119–34.

Miller, L. and Penz, O. (1991) 'Talking bodies: female bodybuilders colonize a male preserve', *Quest*, 43 (2): 148–63.

Nelson, M.B. (1991) *Are We Winning Yet?* New York: Random House.

Nelson, M.B. (1994) *The Stronger Women Get, the More Men Love Football: Sexism and the American Culture of Sports*. New York: Harcourt Brace.

Oglesby, C.A. (ed.) (1978) *Women and Sport: From Myth to Reality*. Philadelphia: Lea and Febiger.

Phillips, J. (1993) *Sociology of Sport*. Boston, MA: Allyn and Bacon.

Pronger, B. (1990) *Arena of Masculinity: Sports, Homosexuality and the Meaning of Sex*. New York: St Martin's Press.

Pronger, B. (1995) 'Rendering the body: the implicit lesson of gross anatomy', *Quest*, 47: 427–46.

Rail, G. and Harvey, J. (1995) 'Body at work: Michel Foucault and the sociology of sport', *Sociology of Sport Journal*, 12: 164–79.

Rich, A. (1980) 'Compulsory heterosexuality and lesbian existence', *Signs*, 5 (4): 647–50.

Sabo, D. and Panepinto, J. (1990) 'Football ritual and the social reproduction of masculinity', in M. Messner and D. Sabo (eds), *Sport, Men, and the Gender Order*. Champaign, IL: Human Kinetics Press.

Sabo, D.F. and Runfola, R. (eds) (1980) *Jock: Sports and Male Identity*. Englewood Cliffs, NJ: Prentice-Hall.

Schultz, L. (1990) 'On the muscle', in J. Gaines and C. Herzog (eds), *Fabrications: Costume and the Female Body*. New York: Routledge. pp. 59–78.

Sheard, K. and Dunning, E. (1973) 'The rugby football club as a type of male preserve: some sociological notes', *International Review of Sport Sociology*, 5: 5–24.

Slatton, Y. (1982) 'AIAW: the greening of American athletics', in J. Frey (ed.), *Governance of Intercollegiate Athletics*. West Point: Leisure Press. pp. 144–54.

Slowikowski, S. (1993) 'Cultural performance and sport mascots', *Journal of Sport and Social Issues*, 17 (1): 23–33.

Smith, Y. (1992) 'Women of color in society and sport', *Quest*, 44 (2): 228–50.

Sykes, H. (1996) 'Constr(i)(u)cting lesbian identities in physical education: feminist and poststructural approaches to researching sexuality', *Quest*, 48: 459–69.

Talbot, M. (1988) 'Understanding the relationship between women and sport: the contributions of British feminist approaches in leisure and cultural studies', *International Review for the Sociology of Sport*, 23 (1): 31–42.

Theberge, N. (1980) 'The convergence between radical and feminist critiques of sport'. Paper presented at the NASSS meetings, Denver, CO, October.

Theberge, N. (1984) 'Joining social theory to social action: some Marxist principles', *Arena Review*, 8: 21–30.

Theberge, N. (1985) 'Toward a feminist alternative to sport as a male preserve', *Quest*, 10: 193–202.

Theberge, N. (1989) 'Women's athletics and the myth of female frailty', in J. Freeman (ed.), *Women: a Feminist Perspective*, 4th edn. Mountain View, CA: Mayfield. pp. 507–22.

Theberge, N. and Birrell, S. (1994a) 'The sociological study of women and sport', in D. Costa and S. Guthrie (eds), *Women and Sport: Interdisciplinary Perspectives*. Champaign, IL: Human Kinetics. pp. 323–30.

Theberge, N. and Birrell, S. (1994b) 'Structural constraints facing women in sport', in D. Costa and S. Guthrie (eds), *Women and Sport: Interdisciplinary Perspectives*. Champaign, IL: Human Kinetics. pp. 331–40.

Thompson, Shona (1988) 'Challenging the hegemony: New Zealand women's opposition to rugby and the reproduction of a capitalist patriarchy', *International Review for the Sociology of Sport*, 23 (3): 205–12.

Tong, R. (1989) *Feminist Thought: a Comprehensive Introduction*. Boulder, CO: Westview Press.

Weedon, C. (1987) *Feminist Practice and Poststructuralist Theory*. New York: Basil Blackwell.

Wheatley, E. (1994) 'Subcultural subversions: comparing discourses on sexuality in men's and women's rugby songs', in S. Birrell and C. Cole (eds), *Women, Sport, and Culture*. Champaign, IL: Human Kinetics. pp. 193–212.

Willis, P. (1974) 'Performance and meaning: a sociological view of women in sport'. Unpublished paper, Birmingham, CCCS.

Willis, P. (1982) 'Women in sport in ideology', in J.A. Hargreaves (ed.), *Sport, Culture and Ideology*. London: Routledge. pp. 117–35.

5

INTERPRETIVE APPROACHES TO THE SOCIOLOGY OF SPORT

Peter Donnelly

Interpretation is the basis of all sociology, and all science. If I observe a recurring event, or discover a relationship between two variables, a statistical tendency, or empirical evidence of causality, such discoveries require interpretation. However, within the field of sociology, the term *interpretive* is used more narrowly to refer to a particular group of sociologies which have as their basis the interpretation and understanding of human meaning and action. Johnson notes that:

> a sociological understanding of behaviour must include the meaning that social actors give to what they and others do. When people interact, they interpret what is going on from the meaning of symbols to the attribution of motives to others. (1995: 146)

Interpretive sociology represents, in large part, one of 'the two sociologies' (Dawe, 1970). In their task of exploring the relationship between the individual and society sociologists have divided, since the earliest days of sociology, between the 'system' approach and the 'action' approach. This division is captured well in Thompson and Tunstall's question: 'Do the two approaches of social systems and social action theory simply correspond to our own ambivalent experience of society as something that constrains us and yet also something that we ourselves construct?' (1975: 476). Interpretive sociology fits clearly into the social action side of the divide, a position that is both its strength and its weakness.

Included in interpretive sociology are Weberian sociology, the 'sociologies of everyday life' (symbolic interactionism, Goffman's

dramaturgical sociology, labelling theory, phenomenological sociology, ethnomethodology, and existential sociology) (Douglas et al., 1980), and hermeneutics.[1] Marshall (1994) notes that these sociologies differ in two ways. First, in the extent to which they view interpretation as problematic (p. 255) – Weberian sociology and symbolic interactionism take a relatively unproblematic (commonsense) approach to interpretation; phenomenology, ethnomethodology and hermeneutics developed more refined approaches. Second, in the degree to which they go beyond the actor's own understanding of what he or she is doing (p. 255). As Jary and Jary note:

> all social reality is 'pre-interpreted' in that it only has form as (and is constituted by) the outcome of social actors' beliefs and interpretations. Thus it is, or ought to be, a truism that no form of sociology can proceed without at least a preliminary grasp of actors' meanings. (1995: 336)

Thus, while Weberian sociology takes *Verstehen* (understanding) as its basis, and distinguishes between 'descriptive' and 'explanatory' understanding; and Alfred Schutz (phenomenological sociology) developed Weber's work to distinguish between 'because' motives and 'in order to' motives; other interpretive sociologies (for example, existential sociology) assume that the actor's own meanings are the basis for analysis, while the remainder (such as ethnomethodology, Goffman's dramaturgy) focus more on discovery of the rules of social action and interaction.

Just as interpretive sociology is related to the social systems/social action debate in sociology, it is also connected with, but not congruent to, two other sociological debates – that between macro- and micro-sociology (with the sociologies of everyday life usually being equated with micro-sociology); and that between the so-called quantitative and qualitative methodologies. Since methodology is a key feature of the practice, and the critique, of interpretive sociology, it is important to address it here. Although 'understanding' is the key to Weber's methodology (Weber, 1904–17, 1922), the actual methods of the sociologies of everyday life often approximate those of anthropology – primarily ethnography and in-depth interviewing. Hermeneutic methods are now likely to be termed 'textual analysis', and overlap with ethnographic and interview work at the level of 'discourse analysis'. The quantitative–qualitative debate has been largely resolved now by interpretive sociologists who are likely to turn to, or collect appropriate forms of quantitative data (cf. Denzin's (1970) strategy of 'triangulation'; or Willis's (1978) use of a cluster of methods – both qualitative and quantitative).

In sum, interpretive sociology may be defined by its opposite in that it 'differs from the view that social life is governed by objective cultural and structural characteristics of social systems (external to individuals, and relatively independent of them); and from the view that it is possible to construct rigid scientific laws to explain patterns of social behaviour' (Johnson, 1995: 146). Thus, interpretive sociology is concerned with the way in which the social world is not just something to be confronted by individuals, but is continually constructed and reinvented by the participants. The following sections deal with the emergence of this perspective in sociology and in the sociology of sport; with criticisms of the perspective and the responses of interpretive sociologists; with examples of sport-related research; and with an examination of the way in which that research has developed our knowledge of the social world in and beyond sport.

EMERGENCE AND DEVELOPMENT OF INTERPRETIVE SOCIOLOGY

Modern sociology is grounded in classical philosophical ideas about the individual versus society. Douglas et al. summarized the key concepts of sociology in two interrelated questions:

First, can human actions be explained in terms of concrete individual factors (such as individual

will, choice, or the concrete situations individuals face) or in terms of something outside of the individual (such as culture or social structure) that determines or causes what they will do? Second, are we to determine the answers to our first question by observing individuals in concrete situations of everyday life, or by observing something (such as a social structure), supposedly outside of the individuals, by experimentally controlled methods? (1980: 183)

Douglas suggests that psychology chose the individual perspective and the social sciences generally opted for a more collectivist perspective; but both preferred abstracted empirical methodology. However, interpretive sociology, which is sometimes referred to as 'social psychology' or 'sociological social psychology', certainly opted for the observation of individuals in everyday situations and for individual free will and choice. The interpretive sociologies differ in the extent to which they deal with the way that individuals produce culture and social structure, and in the extent to which they also regard individual action as constrained by the structures it produces.[2]

Among the various interpretive sociologies, hermeneutics has the oldest provenance. The term, derived from Hermes (the messenger), originally referred to biblical studies as practised by individuals attempting to divine the 'true' meaning of biblical texts. In its modern incarnation, hermeneutics is closely connected to critical media studies, and it is in that context that it is evident in the sociology of sport. Hermeneutics involves the methodology and 'the theory or philosophy of the interpretation of meaning' (Bleicher, 1980: 1). Rather than the 'factual particulars' of written or visual texts, researchers 'deconstruct' texts by 'look[ing] for recurring themes and messages. Are some issues being given more attention than others? Are certain ideological perspectives being emphasized?' (Kane and Disch, 1993: 339; see also Duncan, 1986).

A great deal has been written about Max Weber and Weberian sociology (for example, Bendix, 1960; and Gerth and Mills (1946) for a collection of his work). Along with Durkheim and Marx, Weber is considered to be one of the classic founders of sociology. Unlike Marx's historical materialism, and Durkheim's attempt to found a positivist science of sociology, Weber's contribution is rooted in the German philosophical thought of Kant and Rickert, and led him to draw a sharp distinction between the natural and social sciences. 'For Weber, the aim of sociology was to achieve an *interpretative understanding* of subjectively meaningful human action which exposed the actors' motives, at one level "the causes" of actions, to view' (Jary and Jary, 1995: 726; original emphasis). Weber argued that, 'action is social insofar as by virtue of the subjective meaning attached to it by the acting individual or individuals, it takes account of the behaviour of others and is thereby oriented in its course' (1947: 88). Weber's work has been enormously influential in the development of sociology, but somewhat less so in the sociology of sport.

The most prominent of the interpretive sociologies in the sociology of sport are the sociologies of everyday life, particularly symbolic interactionism and dramaturgical sociology. These forms of interpretive sociology are primarily American in origin, and the Chicago School of urban sociology that flourished between the First and Second World Wars is often cited as the source. Perhaps the most important contributions of the Chicago School were the development of urban ethnographic fieldwork as a methodology, and W.I. Thomas's fundamental dictum of interpretive sociology – 'if men define situations as real, they are real in their consequences' (1923). Thus, in seventeenth-century Salem, certain women were defined as witches; while we recognize that such definitions had no basis in reality, they had real consequences for the women who were imprisoned and executed.

Interpretive thinking in American sociology progressed through C. Everett Hughes, George Herbert Mead and Alfred Schutz (who arrived from Austria in 1935), but remained marginal to the main trends in sociology which, in an attempt to establish scientific credibility in the academy, were being modelled on the positivist and empiricist natural sciences. It was not until the late 1960s and 1970s that, in a backlash against the natural science model, interpretive sociologies began to flourish in North American Sociology Departments. Blumer's collection of essays was published as *Symbolic Interactionism* (1969); Goffman's work was beginning to be taught widely; and Garfinkel's ethnomethodology was beginning to gain recognition. Berger and Luckmann's *The Social Construction of Reality* (1967) took the definition of the situation a step further to describe how individuals construct and reconstruct their social worlds. Interpretive sociology has continued to develop and adapt, most recently in its attempts to deal with social structure and attempts to find common ground with cultural studies (for example, Becker and McCall, 1990; Denzin, 1992).

Although the emergence of a distinct sociology of sport was coincident with the 1970s growth of interpretive sociology, interpretive sociology has not, until recently, had a major impact on the development of the sociology of sport. While the influence of Weber has been evident and implicit in the sociology of sport, very little of the work in the sociology of sport has been explicitly Weberian. Only Guttmann's much praised, and much criticized *From Ritual to Record* (1978), and the earlier work of Alan Ingham (1975, 1978, 1979), were clearly Weberian. Hermeneutic analyses are coincident with the recent interest in sport media studies, and have been carried out in the sociology of sport for the past ten years or so. Some examples of these are given subsequently.

As noted previously, the sociologies of everyday life have been the most evident form of interpretive sociology in the sociology of sport.[3] These began both independently of the sociology of sport as a part of the countercultural growth of interpretive sociology in mainstream sociology (for example, Scott's (1968) work on horse racing, and Polsky's (1969) work on pool hustling), and in the sociology of sport itself. Greg Stone, who is recognized as one of the major early contributors to the sociology of sport, was alone among the original group in his involvement in interpretive sociology (for example, Stone, 1955, 1957). Interpretive sociology of sport began to develop at the University of Massachusetts in the 1970s. Friendships between Charles Page and Greg Stone, and John Loy and Donald Ball (see, for example, Ball, 1976), led Page and Loy to encourage several graduate students (Susan Birrell, Peter Donnelly, Alan Ingham and Nancy Theberge) to engage in subcultural studies. Rob Faulkner's (1974a, 1974b, 1975) presence in the Sociology Department, especially his course on Qualitative Methods, provided additional encouragement.[4]

During this time, there was a great deal of 'muckraking sports journalism', some of the 'new journalism' began to deal with sport, and several athletes' biographies exposed inside information and corrupt practices in sport. While these were not so sociological, they certainly provided rich 'insider' information for sociologists of sport interested in the experience and meaning of being an athlete.

The final step in the development of an interpretive sociology of sport began in the 1980s as sport sociologists began to be exposed to the work of the Centre for Contemporary Cultural Studies at Birmingham University in England. For several sociologists of sport this work led them from a rather descriptive and relatively atheoretical form of participant observation, to a much more critical ethnographic approach to interpretive sociology. However, even those who did not shift to critical cultural studies were affected by the anthropologist Clifford Geertz's (1973) notion of 'thick description', and have generally begun to provide a much more richly textured level of description as a result of their fieldwork. Independent of these North American trends, Pierre Bourdieu and his students in France began to develop an extremely sophisticated interpretive sociology based on fieldwork, and they considered sport to be a part of their mandate from the very beginning. North American sport sociologists began to become aware of Bourdieu's work in the 1980s and, in combination with the cultural studies approach, interpretive sociology of sport has now become a central aspect of the field of study, making important contributions to our understanding of sport in society.

CRITIQUES AND RESPONSES

Critiques of interpretive sociology take issue with both the theoretical and methodological aspects of the approach. The most obvious theoretical critiques are from the forms of sociology that take a social systems approach, or maintain a view that some aspects of social reality are unproblematic in terms of meaning, and may be understood directly (Marshall, 1994), or believe that it is possible to discover standard laws that govern human behaviour. While these critiques only amount to differences in approach to the study of sociology, others zero in on specific aspects of the theoretical approach such as the overemphasis on agency, or cultural relativism.

For example, phenomenology and ethnomethodology emphasize the capacity of individuals ('agents') to construct and reconstruct their worlds, which can then only be understood in the agents' terms (Jary and Jary, 1995). While the approach is obviously criticized by those approaches that emphasize social structure (for example, functionalism, and some forms of Marxism), it is also criticized by those approaches seeking to incorporate both processes (for example, cultural studies) in an attempt to show that there are some structural constraints on freedom to act. With regard to relativism, Jary and Jary note that a distinguishing characteristic of interpretive sociology is 'the recognition that any

statement about the social world is necessarily relative to any other' (1995: 336).

In an approach that is based on the social construction of reality, there is an obvious concern about what constitutes 'reality'. Shotter notes that:

> ... there is currently something of a 'flight' into realism. For one of the major objections to the whole social constructionist movement is as follows. It claims that there is no independent reality to which claims to truth may be compared or referred – for all human 'realities' (*Umwelten*) are only known *from within*, so to speak – means that there are no independent standards to which to appeal in their adjudication; thus 'anything goes!', and we slide into relativistic nihilism. (1993: 89)

At the cultural level, a relative approach permits sociologists to understand and interpret cultures on their own terms, but when taken to extremes it may find slavery, torture and female circumcision to be 'justifiable'. While the evidence for the social construction of characteristics such as gender, and behaviour such as participating in sport, is overwhelming, sociologists continue to struggle with the issues of human values and relativity.

Methodological critiques, which to a great extent overlap with theoretical issues, usually concern the quality of the data produced by fieldwork and in-depth interviewing. Bottomore has captured the methodological dilemma:

> The exclusive insistence, in much recent sociology, upon a rigorous 'scientific method', has tended to create an unusually conservative outlook; the existing framework of society is accepted as given, because it is too complex for scientific study, and all the resources of a truly 'scientific' sociology are then marshalled for the investigation of small-scale problems carefully isolated from the wider social structure. It is desirable, therefore, to emphasize once more as the distinctive feature of sociological thought that it attempts to grasp every specific problem in its whole social context ... (1979: 323)

Insistence on 'scientific method' led to much of the criticism of hermeneutics and the sociologies of everyday life. Researchers were accused of subjectivity, of 'going native', and of producing unreplicable results.

Subjectivity is anathema to the 'scientific method' where the researcher is considered to be a dispassionate and objective observer and/or manipulator of events. Given systematic observations of human behaviour, particularly if the observer is also a participant; and given in-depth interviews with subjects, advocates of the 'scientific method' questioned why the sociologist's interpretations were any more valid than any other person's interpretations. The *Rashomon* phenomenon was invoked (from the Japanese film in which the stories of three participants in an event – a robbery – are quite different), and researchers were also accused of 'going native' (that is, losing objectivity by empathizing with their subjects). And, given that it was usually only one researcher engaged in the work, and that studies were rarely repeated (the replicability of results being a benchmark of reliability in the 'scientific method', although one that is not always used), the work was considered to be unreliable.

An initial response to such criticism was the attempt to become more 'scientific'. Hermeneutic analysis became a more strictly quantitative 'content analysis'; Manford Kuhn developed a more quantitative approach to symbolic interactionism that came to be known as 'the Iowa School'; and methodological texts warned researchers against 'going native'. However, more recently there has been a recognition that, in sociology, both the researcher and the focus of research are subjects; thus sociology must be thought of as a subjective or better still, a reflexive science.[5] As Giddens notes:

> 1) We *cannot* approach society, or 'social facts', as we do objects or events in the natural world, because societies only exist in so far as they are created and re-created in our own actions as human beings ...
>
> 2) ... Atoms cannot get to know what scientists say about them, or change their behaviour in the light of that knowledge. Human beings can do so. Thus the relation between sociology and its 'subject-matter' is necessarily different from that involved in the natural sciences. (1982: 13–15)

Just as some natural scientists are now beginning to recognize the element of subjectivity present in the type of research questions asked and assumptions made, 'there is now a tendency among field workers to recognize and reveal, rather than deny and conceal, the part that personal interests, preferences and experiences play in the formulation of field-work plans' (Georges and Jones, 1983: 233). Recognition of this 'cultural baggage' now easily extends to open acknowledgement of 'going native' and conducting research that is designed to affect social policy and social change.[6]

Willis has suggested that, 'We are still in need of a method which respects evidence, seeks corroboration and minimizes distortion, *but which is without rationalist natural-science-like pretence*' (1980: 91; original emphasis), and has gone a long way towards developing that method (for example, Willis, 1978). Researchers using hermeneutic and ethnographic methods now regularly deal with the methodological issues in an open and reflexive manner. For example, with regard to hermeneutics:

> At issue in this methodology is the role of the reader. How do we know that readers will interpret the features of photographs in the ways that the researcher uncovers? ... A number of authors have argued that texts of all kinds – written and visual – embody multiple realities and suggest multiple meanings. The researcher can never be certain of how a particular individual may perceive a given text because meaning is created in the interaction between the text and the reader ... The reader brings his/her personal set of experiences, history, and social and cultural contexts to the text, and all of these influences shape the reader's interpretation of that text. Although texts may strongly suggest a particular reading ... there is always the possibility of oppositional readings ...
>
> Responsible textual studies do not assert with absolute certainty how particular texts are interpreted. But they suggest the kinds of interpretations that may take place, based on the available evidence, and *likely* interpretations of a particular text. Ultimately these interpretations must be judged on the basis of the persuasiveness and logic of the researcher's discussion. (Duncan, 1990: 27)

Methodological concerns overlap with theoretical concerns precisely in the issues of theoretical assumptions and *interpretation*. Because of the critical nature of much recent hermeneutic work, an assumption is made that media messages are designed to maintain an unequal status quo in society – hermeneutic analysis attempts to deconstruct those messages. However, a more recent assumption also allows that any 'reader' potentially has the power to reject those in-built messages and make an oppositional or alternative reading.

A final critique of research in interpretive sociology concerns the 'journalistic' nature of research reports. Critics announce that they find no difference between sociology and journalism in this area. Of course, there are important differences in terms of explicit methodological and theoretical assumptions and techniques, and in terms of the academic review processes and academic responsibility, but there are also important similarities – especially in the 'new journalism' (cf. Tomlinson, 1984). There is even an important symbiosis here because journalists are sometimes able to achieve access to areas out of bounds to sociologists, and provide important data and insights useful to sociological research. Donnelly has advocated that, when studying sport subcultures, all sources of data are appropriate and may be useful:

> … the researcher should go beyond … traditional forms of data to see what members of the subculture write about themselves for other members (every sport and many leisure subcultures publish at least one newsletter or magazine) or for the general public in biographies, introductory or how-to books, and general books and magazine articles; and what is written about the subculture by journalists and freelance writers …
>
> Nor should the researcher be constrained by nonfiction since many other forms of writing and artistic work are frequently available and offer points of view that are often unique and frequently enlightening. [These include novels] poetry and songs (both of which may supplement the narrative folklore of the subculture), painting and sculpture, cartoons and films … (1985: 568–9)

In the final analysis though, it is not surprising if good journalistic accounts are somewhat like sociological accounts. As Giddens (cited previously) noted, human beings can get to know what scientists say about them, and sociological knowledge is widely reported in the media, and widely available in bookstores and libraries, as well as being taught in university courses. It would be more surprising if good insider journalistic accounts were not similar to good ethnographic research.

INTERPRETIVE STUDIES IN THE SOCIOLOGY OF SPORT

As noted previously, although Weber is frequently included under the umbrella of interpretive sociology, and although his influence on the development of sociology, and to some extent the sociology of sport, is widespread, very few works in the sociology of sport can be considered as explicitly Weberian. Only Guttmann (1978) and Ingham (1975, 1978, 1979) adopt an explicitly Weberian perspective in major works in the sociology of sport. Seppanen (1981) and Stone (1981) employ Weberian concepts in their respective analyses of Olympic success and sport and community.

Also, as noted, hermeneutic analyses of sport have most frequently taken the form of critical analyses of print and television media (see Kinkema and Harris (1992) for a recent review essay on sport and the mass media). The overwhelming majority of such studies have been concerned with the representation of gender in the media, with violence/masculinity a distant, though related, second. Among the more significant analyses of the representation of women are Duncan (1990) on sports photographs, Duncan and Hasbrook (1988) and Duncan, Messner, Williams and Jensen (1990) on televised sports, and MacNeill (1988) on television coverage of women's bodybuilding and an exercise programme. Trujillo (1995) on televised coverage of (American) football violence, and White and Gillett's (1994) analysis of print advertisements[7] for bodybuilding products, are examples of work addressing issues of masculinity.

Some of the best work in hermeneutics focuses on specific incidents in sport, but again these are primarily concerned with gender issues. For example, Birrell and Cole (1990) examined the reaction to Renee Richards (formerly Richard Raskind), a 'constructed-female transexual' when she/he began to play on the women's tennis tour; Kane and Disch (1993) examined media accounts of the sexual harrassment of Lisa Olson, a female sports reporter, in a men's (American football) locker room; King (1993) and Cole and Denny (1995) explored the public announcement that 'Magic' Johnson was HIV positive; McKay and Smith (1995) reviewed media coverage of the O.J. Simpson case; Messner and Solomon (1993) analysed the media coverage of Sugar Ray Leonard's wife beating incident;[8,9] Young (1986) examined media responses to the Heysel Stadium incident in which 39 soccer fans died; and Theberge (1989) reviewed newspaper responses to a major incident of sports violence at the World Junior Hockey Championships.

Although there are now many studies of the actual content of media texts, Kinkema and Harris (1992) and others have noted the absence of studies dealing with the production of those texts, and studies dealing with the way in which audiences (rather than researchers) interpret the texts. Hermeneutic analyses and ethnographic analyses combine around these types of studies. Hesling (1986) reviewed the development of sportscasting codes; while Gruneau (1989) and MacNeill (1996) conducted production ethnographies on a World Cup skiing event and Olympic ice hockey coverage respectively; and Theberge and Cronk (1986) examined the production of newspaper sports news. Duncan and Brummett (1993) and Eastman and Riggs (1994) have conducted 'living room' ethnographies of television sports spectators in order to explore both oppositional readings and rituals. A great deal more work needs to be done in these areas.

There are distinct overlaps in all of the sociologies of everyday life, in both methodology and theoretical assumptions. With few exceptions, most of the studies in the sociology of sport employing an interpretive approach do not identify a specific sociological theory, and most of those published between the 1960s and 1980s fall into the general category of symbolic interactionism and Goffman's dramaturgical approach (since that time there has been a clear shift toward a cultural studies approach to ethnographic research). The exceptions include: Howe (1991) and Whitson's (1976) calls for the use of phenomenology in the sociology of sport, and Pronger (1990) and Rail's (1992) actual uses of phenomenology in their studies of gay male athletes and female basketball players respectively; and Kew's series of studies (1986, 1987, 1990, 1992) of the development of rules in sport, employing an ethnomethodological perspective.

There are two distinct, but overlapping themes of studies employing the remaining sociologies of everyday life (primarily symbolic interactionism and Goffman's dramaturgy;[10] but since the 1980s, an increasingly cultural studies approach): (a) descriptions and analyses of sport subcultures (including the themes of careers and cultural production); (b) the process of socialization (which overlaps to a great extent with the theme of career).

Sport Subcultures[11] Subcultures are 'any system[s] of beliefs, values and norms ... shared and actively participated in by an appreciable minority of people within a particular culture' (Jary and Jary, 1995: 665), and the study of subcultures is an important aspect of interpretive sociology. Subcultural studies in the United States developed from Chicago School interest in youth, delinquents and deviance, and posited that the formation of subcultures was either a result of 'differential interaction' or an 'environmental response'. Cohen (1955) combined these views into a powerful explanation of subcultural formation, and it was a short step from examining deviant 'careers' to the study of non-deviant careers, eventually including sports careers.[12]

Although Weinberg and Arond's (1952) study of boxers was the first of many studies of sport subcultures as 'careers', the majority of such studies were not carried out until after the full recognition of a sociology of sport (Loy and Kenyon, 1965). Stone's studies of wrestlers (Stone, 1972; Stone and Oldenberg, 1967) were followed by Scott's (1968) work on horse racing, Polsky's (1969) study of pool hustlers, and Faulkner's (1974a, 1974b) study of hockey players. This early work came to fruition in 1975 in four major chapters in Ball and Loy's *Sport and Social Order*. Ingham (1975) began to develop his theoretical work on occupational subcultures in sport; Haerle (1975) raised the issue of career patterns and career contingencies (for baseball players); while Faulkner (1975) and Rosenberg and Turowetz (1975) carried out comparative work – hockey players and Hollywood musicians in the former, professional wrestlers and physicians in the latter. The use of 'career' as a defining concept carried on for some time after 1975 – for example, Theberge (1977) on women professional golfers, and Birrell and Turowetz (1979) in another Goffman-inspired comparative study (professional wrestlers and female university gymnasts) – but by the time Prus (1984) summarized the notion of career contingencies the concept of 'career' and work on subcultures had both changed.

Careers were being thought of as any time spent progressing in a sport – a competitive swimmer who began at age 6, retired[13] at age 14 and never earned any money, could now be considered to have had a 'career' in swimming. And the cultural characteristics of subcultures were now being studied without resort to the concept of 'career'. Vaz (1972) anticipated this with his work on young hockey players, and was followed by Thomson (1977) on rugby players, Pearson (1979) on surfers, Donnelly (1980) and Vanreusel and Renson (1982) on rock climbers and other high-risk sport participants, and Albert's series of studies on racing cyclists (1984, 1990, 1991).

However, during the 1980s, there was a further change in the study of sport subcultures resulting from two sources. First, Geertz's (1973) methodological refinement of 'thick description' – '[i]ntensive, small scale, dense descriptions of social life from observation, through which broader cultural interpretations and generalizations can be made' (Marshall, 1994: 533) – led to much richer and textured descriptions of social contexts. Secondly, British subculture theory took a radical theoretical/political turn in the direction of critical sociology (for example, Hall and Jefferson, 1976; Hebdige, 1979). As a result, the sociology of subcultures not only shows how sports and other leisure practices are socially constructed and defined activities, meaningful only to the extent that meaning is attached to them by the participants, but also how 'subcultures, with their various "establishment" and "countercultural" emphases, have been constitutively inserted into the struggles, the forms of compliance and opposition, social reproduction and transformation, associated with changing patterns of social development' (Gruneau, 1981: 10).[14] These changes have had a powerful impact on subcultural studies of sport.

The changes noted above have produced an extremely rich crop of studies, and the following examples have been influenced by one or both of the changes: Williams's (Williams et al., 1989) and Giulianotti's (1995a, 1995b) studies of British soccer hooligans; Klein's observations of bodybuilders (1993) and baseball players in the Dominican Republic (1991); Foley's (1990) study of the American high school football subculture; the Adlers' (1991) work on university basketball players; Crosset's (1995) study of women professional golfers; Sugden's (1987) study of boxing; Tomlinson's (1992) study of a British folk game (knur and spell); Curry's (1991) study of the male locker room subculture; Birrell and Richter's (1987) study of transformations in women's softball; Theberge's (1995) study of women's ice hockey; Beal's (1995) study of skateboarding; and Markula's (1995) work on women aerobics participants.

Most of these studies have been carried out by researchers from the United States, Canada and Britain. However, there is also a French school of subcultural research rooted in the sociology of Pierre Bourdieu and mostly carried out by his students.[15] For example, Wacquant's series of studies on boxing (1989, 1992, 1995a, 1995b), Clément's (1984, 1985) studies on the martial arts, Bruant's (1992) ethnography of running, Pociello's (1983) work on rugby, Suaud's (1989) study of tennis clubs, and Midol's studies (1993; Midol and Broyer, 1995) of extreme ('whiz') sports.

Socialization and Sport[16]   Research on who becomes involved in sport, how they become involved and the effect that sport has on them, has been important since the beginning of the sociology of sport. However, the early research was based on survey methods, and it is only since those involved in the interpretive

sociology of sport have turned their attention to socialization that a number of rich insights have been made into the process.

> Socialization is an active process of learning and social development that occurs as people interact with each other and become acquainted with the social world in which they live, and as they form ideas about who they are, and make decisions about their goals and behaviours. Human beings are not simply passive learners in the socialization process. Instead, they actively participate: they influence those who influence them, they make their own interpretations of what they see and hear, and they accept, revise, or reject the messages they receive about who they are, what the world is all about, and what they should do as they make their way in the world. (Coakley, 1998: 88)

The processes of becoming an athlete and becoming an adult person, and the way these two interact, were addressed to a certain extent in some of the 'career' subculture studies noted above. However, primary recognition of the socialization process seems to have occurred as a consequence of the 1980s changes in subcultural studies of sport.

Early involvement in sport and physical activity has been studied by Hasbrook (1993, 1995) in school playgrounds, Fine (1987) in little league baseball and Ingham and Dewar (1989) in PeeWee hockey. But these studies go well beyond the actual processes of involvement to show how sport and physical activity are major sites for the production and reproduction of traditional and stereotypical notions of gender. Grey (1992) has shown how new immigrants fail to become socialized into high school sport; and Chafetz and Kotarba (1995) remind us that socialization is a two-way process when they show how little league baseball affects the players' mothers.

Once involved in sport, the socialization process continues. Donnelly and Young (1988) examined the way in which rookie athletes constructed appropriate subcultural identities for themselves, to be confirmed (or rejected) by established athletes in the subculture; Coakley and White (1992) showed how English teenagers made the decision to continue, or not continue, sport participation; Stevenson (1990) demonstrated how international athletes began to focus on their particular sport; and Messner (1992) explored the meaning of success and relationships in the lives of elite male athletes. The process continues to be two-way, and Thompson (1992) showed the way in which the involvement of husbands and children in tennis had an impact on the lives of wives/mothers. Many of the subcultural studies noted above also deal with the continuing process of socialization.

Career interruptions and endings (retirements, sometimes referred to as desocialization) form the final phase of sport socialization. Coakley (1992) has studied burnout among adolescent athletes as a problem of social development, and Swain (1991) and Messner (1992) have taken different approaches to the problem in their analyses of the retirement of elite athletes. Young (Young, White and McTeer, 1994; Young and White, 1995) has provided the most focused view of the way that male and female athletes view and deal with injuries. Of course, except in the case of traumatic injury, such retirements rarely signal a complete end to sport involvement – rather, they indicate a change in the way a person participates.

Finally, several new approaches to interpretive sociology should be noted. While sport sociologists have often accepted athletes' biographies as reasonable sources of data, more recent sophisticated methodologies (including case studies, life histories and narrative sociology) have brought biography and autobiography to the fore in the interpretive sociologist's repertoire of techniques. Henning Eichberg's special issue of the *International Review for the Sociology of Sport* (29 (1), 1994) on 'Narrative Sociology' provides a number of examples of this type of work by scholars from Finland and Denmark; while in North America, Tim Curry (1993, 1996; Curry and Strauss, 1994) has been an exponent of the case study/life history technique.[17] Interpretive sociologists have also begun to explore innovative ways of reporting research – see, for example, Curry and Strauss's (1994) photo-essay; and Wacquant's (1989) split-page technique. Finally, Cole (1991) and Foley (1992) have reminded interpretive sociologists of sport of the politics of interpretation, perhaps ensuring that reflexivity is maintained in the use of these techniques.

THE IMPACT OF INTERPRETIVE SOCIOLOGY ON THE SOCIOLOGY OF SPORT

Studies using an interpretive sociology approach, particularly ethnographic studies, are extremely time-consuming. They usually require enormous commitment on the part of the researcher, but that commitment has paid off in the sociology of sport with a number of rich and rewarding studies. With the refinements in theory (a critical cultural studies approach is now widely used) and methodologies (reflexivity, 'thick description', ethnography), interpretive sociology has recently come to be what many consider the predominant approach in the sociology of sport. The recent publication dates of the majority of studies noted above attest to the growth of interest in interpretive sociology in the sociology of sport and, as an example of this recent prominence, all of the Presidential Addresses given at the North American Society for the Sociology of Sport annual conferences in the 1990s have taken an interpretive sociology approach.

Weberian sociology has given us important insights into the emergence and development of modern sport; and hermeneutics has shown us the ideological underpinnings and dynamics of the sport–media complex, particularly in terms of gender relations. But perhaps the major impact of interpretive sociology has been the way in which it hangs flesh on the skeletons of survey data. For example, surveys have continually shown that boys and men are more involved in sport and physical activity than girls and women, but researchers were obliged to speculate about the reasons for this difference. Recent observations and in-depth interviews have shown the dynamics of gender relations in sport – how sport is a gendering practice, and how males and females make decisions about participation – thus giving a much clearer explanation for the participation differences. Interpretive sociology has also given us a much richer notion of careers, subcultures and group dynamics in sport, and a great many insights into how we become involved in sport, live our lives as athletes and retire from intense participation. In the final analysis, though, interpretive sociology is about meaning, and in the sociology of sport we are beginning to attain a powerful sense of what sport means, and how sport means, in the lives of human beings.

NOTES

I should like to thank John Loy for his careful reading of an earlier version of this chapter.

1   While I have included Weberian sociology in this list because of his typology of 'action', his emphasis on subjective meanings, and so on, it is clear that Weber was much more than an interpretive sociologist

(for example, his comparative historical sociology focusing on culture and social structure), and that his work is quite distinct from the sociologies of everyday life. Also, some commentators (for example, Marshall, 1994) suggest that structuralism, post-structuralism and Giddens's theory of structuration might also be included as interpretive sociologies.

2   This is often referred to as the 'structure–agency' debate. Some modern approaches to sociology (for example, cultural studies) follow a Marxian compromise between these two positions – 'Men make their own history, but they do not make it just as they please; they do not make it under circumstances chosen by themselves, but under circumstances directly encountered, given and transmitted from the past' (Marx, 1852/1991: 15).

3   Parts of this section are adapted from Ingham and Donnelly (1997).

4   Jack Hewitt also taught a graduate course on symbolic interactionism in the same department at that time, and provided further encouragement (see Hewitt, 1976).

5   Some of the following is adapted from Donnelly (1985).

6   Elias (1956, 1987) attempted to deal with the sociological problems of 'involvement' and 'detachment' some time ago.

7   Renson and Careel (1986) also examine print advertising in Belgium to explore notions of social status.

8   McKay and Smith and Messner and Solomon employ the notion of 'frame analysis'. This is derived from Goffman's later work, and connects Goffman with hermeneutic analysis (1974, 1979, 1981). Schmitt (1991, 1993) has used frame analysis more directly to examine media coverage of a strike by professional athletes.

9   Several of these studies also explore issues of race. However, the issue of representation by race and ethnicity is examined more directly by Sabo, Curry Jansen, Tate, Duncan and Leggett (1995).

10 Note should be made of Birrell's (1981) derivation of the 'rules' of everyday life from Goffman, and their application to the study of sport.

11 For an earlier definition of sport subcultures, see Donnelly (1981); for a more in-depth review of the literature on sport subcultures to the mid-1980s, see Donnelly (1985).

12 Becker (1963) made the bridge with his analysis of marijuana use as a 'career'.

13 The issue of retirement is considered subsequently as a part of 'socialization'.

14 See Donnelly (1993) for a more recent theoretical analysis of sport subcultures.

15 For more on the anthropological sociology of Bourdieu, and his contributions to the sociology of sport, see Clément (1995) and Defrance (1995).

16 See Coakley (1993, 1996, 1998) for reviews of research on socialization; and Coakley and Donnelly (1999) for a series of studies on the theme of socialization into sport.

17 Curry (1986) and Snyder (1990) have also used photo-elicitation interview techniques, which are part of the new visual sociology.

REFERENCES

Adler, P. and Adler, P. (1991) *Backboards and Blackboards: College Athletes and Role Engulfment.* New York: Columbia University Press.

Albert, E. (1984) 'Equipment as a feature of social control in the sport of bicycle racing', in N. Theberge and P. Donnelly (eds), *Sport and the Sociological Imagination.* Fort Worth, TX: Texas Christian University Press. pp. 318–33.

Albert, E. (1990) 'Constructing the order of finish in the sport of bicycle racing', *Journal of Popular Culture*, 23: 145–54.

Albert, E. (1991) 'Riding a line: competition and cooperation in the sport of bicycle racing', *Sociology of Sport Journal*, 8: 341–61.

Ball, D. (1976) 'Failure in sport', *American Sociological Review*, 41: 726–39.

Ball, D.W. and Loy, J.W. (eds) (1975) *Sport and Social Order: Contributions to the Sociology of Sport.* Reading, MA: Addison-Wesley.

Beal, B. (1995) 'Disqualifying the official: an exploration of social resistance through the subculture of skateboarding', *Sociology of Sport Journal*, 12: 252–67.

Becker, H. (1963) *Outsiders: Studies in the Sociology of Deviance.* New York: Free Press.

Becker, H. and McCall, M. (eds) (1990) *Symbolic Interaction and Cultural Studies.* Chicago: University of Chicago Press.

Bendix, R. (1960) *Max Weber: an Intellectual Portrait.* London: Heinemann.

Berger, P. and Luckmann, T. (1967) *The Social Construction of Reality.* London: Allen Lane.

Birrell, S. (1981) 'Sport as ritual: Interpretation from Durkheim to Goffman', *Social Forces*, 60: 354–76.

Birrell, S. and Richter, D. (1987) 'Is a diamond forever?: feminist transformation of sport', *Women's Studies International Forum*, 10: 395–409.

Birrell, S. and Cole, C. (1990) 'Double fault: Renee Richards and the construction and naturalization of difference', *Sociology of Sport Journal*, 7: 1–21.

Birrell, S. and Turowetz, A. (1979) 'Character work-up and display: collegiate gymnastics and professional wrestling', *Urban Life*, 8: 219–46.

Bleicher, J. (1980) *Contemporary Hermeneutics: Hermeneutics as Method, Philosophy and Critique*. London: Routledge & Kegan Paul.

Blumer, H. (1969) *Symbolic Interactionism: Perspective and Method*. Englewood Cliffs, NJ: Prentice–Hall.

Bottomore, T. (1979) *Sociology: A Guide to Problems and Literature*. London: George Allen & Unwin.

Bruant, G. (1992) *Anthropologie du geste sportif: la construction sociale de la course à pied*. Paris: Presses Universitaires de France.

Chafetz, J. and Kotarba, J. (1995) 'Son worshippers: the role of little league mothers in recreating gender', *Studies in Symbolic Interaction*, 18: 219–43.

Clément, J.-P. (1984) 'La pratique de l'aiki-do en France: "Contre-culture" ou "avant-garde"', in *Sports et sociétés contemporaines*. Paris: Société Française de Sociologie du Sport. pp. 375–80.

Clément, J.-P. (1985) 'Etude comparative de trois disciplines de combat et leurs usages sociaux'. Thèse de 3e cycle en sociologie, Université de Paris V.

Clément, J.-P. (1995) 'Contributions of the sociology of Pierre Bourdieu to the sociology of sport', *Sociology of Sport Journal*, 12: 147–57.

Coakley, J. (1992) 'Burnout among adolescent athletes: a personal failure or social problem', *Sociology of Sport Journal*, 9: 271–85.

Coakley, J. (1993) 'Sport and socialization', in J. Holloszy (ed.), *Exercise and Sport Sciences Reviews*, vol. 21. Baltimore, MD: Williams & Wilkins. pp. 169–200.

Coakley, J. (1996) 'Socialization through sports', in O. Bar-Or (ed.), *The Child and Adolescent Athlete* (Volume 6 of the *Encyclopaedia of Sports Medicine*). Oxford: Blackwell Scientific. pp. 353–63.

Coakley, J. (1998) 'Sports and socialization', in *Sport in Society: Issues and Controversies*, 6th edn. St Louis: Times Mirror/Mosby. ch. 4.

Coakley, J. and Donnelly, P. (eds) (1999) *Inside Sports*. London: Routledge.

Coakley, J. and White, A. (1992) 'Making decisions: gender and sport participation among British adolescents', *Sociology of Sport Journal*, 9: 20–35.

Cohen, A. (1955) *Delinquent Boys*. Chicago: Free Press.

Cole, C. (1991) 'The politics of cultural representation: visions of fields/fields of vision', *International Review for the Sociology of Sport*, 26: 37–49.

Cole, C. and Denny, H. (1995) 'Visualizing deviance in post-Reagan America: Magic Johnson, AIDS, and the promiscuous world of professional sport', *Critical Sociology*, 20 (3): 123–47.

Crosset, T. (1995) *Outsiders in the Clubhouse: the World of Women's Professional Golf*. Albany, NY: State University of New York Press.

Curry, T. (1986) 'A visual method of studying sports: the photo-elicitation interview', *Sociology of Sport Journal*, 3: 204–16.

Curry, T. (1991) 'Fraternal bonding in the locker room: a profeminist analysis of talk about competition and women', *Sociology of Sport Journal*, 8: 119–35.

Curry, T. (1993) 'A little pain never hurt anyone: athletic career socialization and the normalization of sports injury', *Symbolic Interaction*, 16: 273–90.

Curry, T. (1996) 'Beyond the locker room: sexual assault and the college athlete'. Presidential address presented at the North American Society for the Sociology of Sport Annual Meeting, Birmingham, AB.

Curry, T. and Strauss, R. (1994) 'A little pain never hurt anybody: a photo-essay on the normalization of sport injuries', *Sociology of Sport Journal*, 11: 195–208.

Dawe, A. (1970) 'The two sociologies', *British Journal of Sociology*, 21: 207–18.

Defrance, J. (1995) 'The anthropological sociology of Pierre Bourdieu: genesis, concepts, relevance', *Sociology of Sport Journal*, 12: 121–31.

Denzin, N. (ed.) (1970) *Sociological Methods: A Source Book*. Chicago: Aldine.

Denzin, N. (1992) *Symbolic Interactionism and Cultural Studies*. Oxford: Basil Blackwell.

Donnelly, P. (1980) 'The subculture and public image of climbers'. Unpublished doctoral dissertation, University of Massachusetts, Amherst, MA.

Donnelly, P. (1981) 'Toward a definition of sport subcultures', in M. Hart and S. Birrell (eds), *Sport in the Sociocultural Process*, 3rd edn. Dubuque, IA: William C. Brown. pp. 565–87.

Donnelly, P. (1985) 'Sport subcultures', in R. Terjung (ed.), *Exercise and Sport Sciences Reviews*, Volume 13. New York: Macmillan. pp. 539–78.

Donnelly, P. (1993) 'Subcultures in sport: resilience and transformation', in A. Ingham and J. Loy (eds), *Sport in Social Development: Traditions, Transitions, and Transformations*. Champaign, IL: Human Kinetics. pp. 119–45.

Donnelly, P. and Young, K. (1988) 'The construction and confirmation of identity in sport subcultures', *Sociology of Sport Journal*, 5: 223–40.

Douglas, J., Adler, P.A., Adler, P., Fontana, A., Freeman, C.R. and Kotarba, J.A. (1980) *Introduction to the Sociologies of Everyday Life*. Boston: Allyn and Bacon.

Duncan, M.C. (1986) 'A hermeneutic of spectator sport: the 1976 and 1984 Olympic Games', *Quest*, 38: 50–77.

Duncan, M.C. (1990) 'Sports photographs and sexual difference: images of women and men in the 1984 and 1988 Olympic Games', *Sociology of Sport Journal*, 7 (1): 22–43.

Duncan, M.C. and Brummett, B. (1993) 'Liberal and radical sources of female empowerment in sport media', *Sociology of Sport Journal*, 10: 57–72.

Duncan, M.C. and Hasbrook, C. (1988) 'Denial of power in televised women's sports', *Sociology of Sport Journal*, 5: 1–21.

Duncan, M.C., Messner, M., Williams, L. and Jensen, K. (Wilson, W., ed.) (1990) *Gender Stereotyping in Televised Sports*. Los Angeles: The Amateur Athletic Foundation.

Eastman, S.T. and Riggs, K. (1994) 'Televised sports and ritual: fan experiences', *Sociology of Sport Journal*, 11: 249–74.

Elias, N. (1956) 'Problems of involvement and detachment', *British Journal of Sociology*, 8: 226–52.

Elias, N. (1987) *Involvement and Detachment*. Oxford: Basil Blackwell.

Faulkner, R. (1974a) 'Coming of age in organizations: a comparative study of career contingencies and adult socialization', *Sociology of Work and Occupations*, 1: 131–73.

Faulkner, R. (1974b) 'Making violence by doing work: selves, situations, and the world of professional hockey', *Sociology of Work and Occupations*, 1: 288–312.

Faulkner, R. (1975) 'Coming of age in organizations: a comparative study of the career contingencies of musicians and hockey players', in D. Ball and J. Loy (eds), *Sport and Social Order*. Reading, MA: Addison-Wesley. pp. 521–58.

Fine, G.A. (1987) *With the Boys: Little League Baseball and Preadolescent Culture*. Chicago: University of Chicago Press.

Foley, D. (1990) 'The great American football ritual: reproducing race, class, and gender inequality', *Sociology of Sport Journal*, 7: 111–35.

Foley, D. (1992) 'Making the familiar strange: writing critical sports narratives', *Sociology of Sport Journal*, 9: 36–47.

Geertz, C. (1973) *The Interpretation of Culture*. New York: Basic Books.

Georges, R. and Jones, M. (1983) 'Review of: *People Studying People: The Human Element in Fieldwork* (J. Nash)', *Urban Life*, 12 (2): 233–5.

Gerth, H. and C.W. Mills (eds) (1946) *From Max Weber: Essays in Sociology*. New York: Oxford University Press.

Giddens, A. (1982) *Sociology: A Brief but Critical Introduction*. London: Macmillan.

Giulianotti, R. (1995a) 'Football and the politics of carnival: an ethnographic study of Scottish fans in Sweden', *International Review for the Sociology of Sport*, 30: 191–224.

Giulianotti, R. (1995b) 'Participant observation and research into football hooliganism: reflections on the problems of entrée and everyday risks', *Sociology of Sport Journal*, 12: 1–20.

Goffman, E. (1974) *Frame Analysis*. New York: Harper Colophon.

Goffman, E. (1979) *Gender Advertisements*. London: Macmillan.

Goffman, E. (1981) *Forms of Talk*. Philadelphia: University of Pennsylvania Press.

Grey, M. (1992) 'Sports and immigrant, minority and Anglo relations in Garden City (Kansas) High School', *Sociology of Sport Journal*, 9: 255–70.

Gruneau, R. (1981) 'Review of "Surfing Subcultures of Australia and New Zealand"', *ICSS Bulletin*, 21: 8–10.

Gruneau, R. (1989) 'Making spectacle: a case study in television sports production', in L. Wenner (ed.), *Media, Sports, and Society*. Newbury Park, CA: Sage. pp. 134–54.

Guttmann, A. (1978) *From Ritual to Record: the Nature of Modern Sports*. New York: Columbia University Press.

Haerle, R. (1975) 'Career patterns and career contingencies of professional baseball players: an occupational analysis', in D. Ball and J. Loy (eds), *Sport and Social Order*. Reading. MA: Addison-Wesley., pp. 457–519.

Hall, S. and Jefferson, T. (1976) *Resistance Through Rituals: Youth Subcultures in Post-War Britain*. London: Hutchinson.

Hasbrook, C. (1993) 'Gendering practices and first graders' bodies: physicality, sexuality, and body adornment in a minority inner-city school'. Paper presented at the North American Society for the Sociology of Sport Annual Conference, Ottawa, Canada.

Hasbrook, C. (1995) 'Physicality, boyhood and diverse masculinities'. Paper presented at the North American Society for the Sociology of Sport Annual Conference, Sacramento, CA.

Hebdige, D. (1979) *Subculture: the Meaning of Style*. London: Methuen.

Hesling, W. (1986) 'The pictorial representation of sports on television', *International Review for the Sociology of Sport*, 21: 173–91.

Hewitt, J. (1976) *Self and Society: a Symbolic Interactionist Social Psychology*. Boston: Allyn and Bacon.

Howe, C. (1991) 'Considerations when using phenomenology in leisure inquiry: beliefs, methods and analysis in naturalistic research', *Leisure Studies*, 10: 49–62.

Ingham, A. (1975) 'Occupational subcultures in the work world of sport', in D. Ball and J. Loy (eds), *Sport and Social Order*. Reading, MA: Addison-Wesley. pp. 333–89.

Ingham, A. (1978) 'American sport in transition: the maturation of industrial capitalism and its impact upon sport'. Unpublished doctoral dissertation, University of Massachusetts, Amherst, MA.

Ingham, A. (1979) 'Methodology in the sociology of sport: from symptoms of malaise to Weber for a cure', *Quest*, 31 (2): 187–215.

Ingham, A. and Dewar, A. (1989) 'Through the eyes of youth: "Deep play" in PeeWee ice hockey'. Paper presented at the North American Society for the Sociology of Sport Annual Conference, Washington, DC.

Ingham, A. and Donnelly, P. (1997) 'A sociology of North American sociology of sport: disunity in unity, 1965–1996'. *Sociology of Sport Journal*, 14 (4): 362–418.

Jary, D. and Jary, J. (1995) *Collins Dictionary of Sociology*, 2nd edn. Glasgow: HarperCollins.

Johnson, A. (1995) *The Blackwell Dictionary of Sociology*. Cambridge, MA: Blackwell.

Kane, M.J. and Disch, L. (1993) 'Sexual violence and the reproduction of male power in the locker room: the "Lisa Olson incident"', *Sociology of Sport Journal*, 10 (4): 331–52.

Kew, F. (1986) 'Playing the game: an ethnomethodological perspective', *International Review for the Sociology of Sport*, 21 (4): 305–22.

Kew, F. (1987) 'Contested rules: an explanation of how games change', *International Review for the Sociology of Sport*, 22 (2): 125–35.

Kew, F. (1990) 'The development of games: an endogenous explanation', *International Review for the Sociology of Sport*, 25 (4): 251–67.

Kew, F. (1992) 'Game rules and social theory', *International Review for the Sociology of Sport*, 27: 293–308.

King, S. (1993) 'The politics of the body and the body politic: Magic Johnson and the ideology of AIDS', *Sociology of Sport Journal*, 10 (3): 270–85.

Kinkema, K. and Harris, J. (1992) 'Sport and the mass media', in J. Holloszy (ed.), *Exercise and Sport Sciences Reviews*, Volume 20. Baltimore, MD: Williams & Wilkins. pp. 127–59.

Klein, A. (1991) *Sugarball: the American Game, the Dominican Dream*. New Haven, CT: Yale University Press.

Klein, A. (1993) *Little Big Men: Bodybuilding Subculture and Gender Construction*. Albany, NY: State University of New York Press.

Loy, J. and Kenyon, G. (1965) 'Towards a sociology of sport', *Journal of Health, Physical Education and Recreation*, 36 (5): 24–5, 68–9.

McKay, J. and Smith, P. (1995) 'Frames and narratives in media coverage of the O.J. Simpson story', *Media Information Australia*, 75: 57–66.

MacNeill, M. (1988) 'Active women, media representations, and ideology', in J. Harvey and H. Cantelon (eds), *Not Just a Game: Essays in Canadian Sport Sociology*. Ottawa: University of Ottawa Press. pp. 195–211.

MacNeill, M. (1996) 'Networks: producing Olympic ice hockey for a national television audience', *Sociology of Sport Journal*, 13: 103–24.

Markula, P. (1995) 'Firm but shapely, fit but sexy, strong but thin: the postmodern aerobicizing female bodies', *Sociology of Sport Journal*, 12: 424–53.

Marshall, G. (1994) *The Concise Oxford Dictionary of Sociology*. Oxford: Oxford University Press.

Marx, K. (1852/1991) *The Eighteenth Brumaire of Louis Bonaparte*. New York: International Publishers.

Messner, M. (1992) *Power at Play: Sport and the Problem of Masculinity*. Boston, MA: Beacon Press.

Messner, M. and Solomon, W. (1993) 'Outside the frame: media coverage of the Sugar Ray Leonard wife abuse story', *Sociology of Sport Journal*, 10 (2): 119–34.

Midol, N. (1993) 'Cultural dissents and technical innovations in the 'whiz' sports', *International Review for the Sociology of Sport*, 28: 23–32.

Midol, N. and Broyer, G. (1995) 'Toward an anthropological analysis of new sport cultures: the case of whiz sports in France', *Sociology of Sport Journal*, 12: 204–12.

Pociello, C. (1983) *Le rugby ou la guerre des styles*. Paris: Métailié.

Polsky, N. (1969) *Hustlers, Beats and Others*. New York: Anchor.

Pearson, K. (1979) *The Surfing Subcultures of Australia and New Zealand*. St Lucia: University of Queensland Press.

Pronger, B. (1990) 'Gay jocks: a phenomenology of gay men in athletics', in M. Messner and D. Sabo (eds), *Sport, Men, and the Gender Order*. Champaign, IL: Human Kinetics. pp. 141–52.

Prus, R. (1984) 'Career contingencies: examining patterns of involvement', in N. Theberge and P. Donnelly (eds), *Sport and the Sociological Imagination*. Fort Worth, TX: Texas Christian University Press. pp. 297–317.

Rail, G. (1992) 'Physical contact and women's basketball: a phenomenological construction and contextualization', *International Review for the Sociology of Sport*, 27 (1): 1–25.

Renson, R. and Careel, C. (1986) 'Sporticuous consumption: an analysis of social status symbolism in sport ads', *International Review for the Sociology of Sport*, 21: 53–171.

Rosenberg, M. and Turowetz, A. (1975) 'The wrestler and the physician: identity work-up and organizational arrangements', in D. Ball and J. Loy (eds), *Sport and Social Order*. Reading, MA: Addison-Wesley. pp. 559–74.

Sabo, D., Curry, T., Jansen, S., Tate, D., Duncan, M.C. and Leggett, S. (Wilson, W., ed.) (1995) *The Portrayal of Race, Ethnicity and Nationality in Televised International Athletic Events*. Los Angeles: The Amateur Athletic Foundation.

Schmitt, R. (1991) 'Strikes, frames, and touchdowns: the institutional struggle for meaning in the 1987 National Football League season', *Symbolic Interaction*, 14: 237–59.

Schmitt, R. (1993) 'Enhancing frame analysis: five laminating functions of language in the 1987 NFL strike', *Sociology of Sport Journal*, 10: 135–47.

Scott, M. (1968) *The Racing Game*. Chicago: Aldine.

Seppanen: (1981) 'Olympic success: a cross-national perspective', in G. Lüschen and G. Sage (eds), *Handbook of Social Science of Sport*. Champaign, IL: Stipes. pp. 93–116.

Shotter, J. (1993) *Cultural Politics and Everyday Life*. Toronto: University of Toronto Press.

Snyder, E. (1990) 'Emotion and sport: a case study of collegiate women gymnasts', *Sociology of Sport Journal*, 7: 254–70.

Stevenson, C. (1990) 'The early careers of international athletes', *Sociology of Sport Journal*, 7: 238–53.

Stone, G. (1955) 'American sports: play and display', *Chicago Review*, 9 (3): 83–100.

Stone, G. (1957) 'Some meanings of American sport', *Proceedings of the National College Physical Education Association for Men*. Washington, DC: 6–29.

Stone, G. (1972) 'Wrestling: the great American passion play', in E. Dunning (ed.), *Sport: Readings from a Sociological Perspective*. Toronto: University of Toronto Press. pp. 301–35.

Stone, G. (1981) 'Sport as a community representation', in G. Lüschen and G. Sage (eds), *Handbook of Social Science of Sport*. Champaign, IL: Stipes. pp. 214–45.

Stone, G. and Oldenberg, R. (1967) 'Wrestling', in R. Slovenko and J. Knight (eds), *Motivations in Play, Games and Sports*. Springfield, IL: Charles C. Thomas. pp. 503–32.

Suaud, C. (1989) 'La diffusion du tennis: démocratisation ou différenciation? Le système des clubs de tennis dans l'agglomération nantaise'. Lersco-CNRS, Université de Nantes.

Sugden, J. (1987) 'The exploitation of disadvantage: the occupational sub-culture of the boxer', in J. Horne, D. Jary and A Tomlinson (eds), *Sport, Leisure, and Social Relations*. London: Routledge & Kegan Paul. pp. 187–209.

Swain, D. (1991) 'Withdrawal from sport and Schlossberg's model of transitions', *Sociology of Sport Journal*, 8: 152–60.

Theberge, N. (1977) 'An occupational analysis of women's professional golf'. Unpublished doctoral thesis, University of Massachusetts, Amherst, MA.

Theberge, N. (1989) 'A feminist analysis of responses to sports violence: media coverage of the 1987 World Junior Hockey Championship', *Sociology of Sport Journal*, 6: 247–56.

Theberge, N. (1995) 'Gender, sport, and the construction of community: a case study from women's ice hockey', *Sociology of Sport Journal*, 12: 389–402.

Theberge, N. and Cronk, A. (1986) 'Work routines in newspaper sports departments and the coverage

of women's sports', *Sociology of Sport Journal*, 3: 195–203.

Thomas, W.I. (1923) *The Unadjusted Girl*. Boston, MA: Little Brown.

Thompson, K. and Tunstall, J. (eds) (1975) *Sociological Perspectives*. Harmondsworth: Penguin.

Thompson, S. (1992) 'Sport for others, work for women, quality of life for whom?'. Paper presented at the Olympic Scientific Congress, Malaga, Spain.

Thomson, R. (1977) 'Sport and deviance: a subcultural analysis'. Unpublished doctoral dissertation, University of Alberta.

Tomlinson, A. (1984) 'The sociological imagination, the new journalism and sport', in N. Theberge and P. Donnelly (eds), *Sport and the Sociological Imagination*. Fort Worth, TX: Texas Christian University Press. pp. 21–39.

Tomlinson, A. (1992) 'Shifting patterns of working class leisure: the case of knur-and-spell', *Sociology of Sport Journal*, 9: 192–206.

Trujillo, N. (1995) 'Machines, missiles and men: images of the male body on ABC's "Monday Night Football"', *Sociology of Sport Journal*, 12 (4): 403–23.

Vanreusel, B. and Renson, R. (1982) 'The social stigma of high risk sport subcultures', in A. Dunleavy, A. Miracle and R. Rees (eds), *Studies in the Sociology of Sport*. Fort Worth, TX: Texas Christian University Press. pp. 183–202.

Vaz, E. (1972) 'The culture of young hockey players: some initial observations', in A.W. Taylor (ed.), *Training: Scientific Basis and Application*. Springfield, IL: Charles C. Thomas. pp. 222–34.

Wacquant, L. (1989) 'Corps et âme: notes ethnographiques d'un apprenti-boxeur', *Actes de la recherche en sciences sociales*, 80: 33–67.

Wacquant, L. (1992) 'The social logic of boxing in black Chicago: toward a sociology of pugilism', *Sociology of Sport Journal*, 9: 221–54.

Wacquant, L. (1995a) 'Pugs at work: body capital and bodily labour among professional boxers', *Body and Society*, 1: 65–93.

Wacquant, L. (1995b) 'Protection, discipline et honneur: une salle de boxe dans le ghetto américain', *Sociologie et Sociétés*, 27: 75–90.

Weber, M. (1904, 1905, 1917/1949) *The Methodology of the Social Sciences* (trans. by E. Shils and H. Finch) Glencoe, IL: Free Press.

Weber, M. (1922/1968) *Economy and Society: An Outline of Interpretive Sociology* (trans. G. Roth and G. Wittich). New York: Bedminster Press.

Weber, M. (1947) *The Theory of Social and Economic Organization*. New York: The Free Press.

Weinberg, S. and Arond, H. (1952) 'The occupational culture of the boxer', *American Journal of Sociology*, 57: 460–9.

White, P. and Gillett, J. (1994) 'Reading the muscular body: a critical decoding of advertisements in *Flex* magazine', *Sociology of Sport Journal*, 11: 18–39.

Whitson, D. (1976) 'Method in sport sociology: the potential of a phenomenological contribution', *International Review for the Sociology of Sport*, 11: 53–66.

Williams, J., Dunning, E. and Murphy, P. (1989) *Hooligans Abroad: the Behaviour and Control of English Fans in Continental Europe*, 2nd edn. London: Routledge.

Willis, P. (1978) *Profane Culture*. London: Routledge & Kegan Paul.

Willis, P. (1980) 'Notes on method', in S. Hall, D. Hobson, A. Lowe and P. Willis (eds), *Culture, Media, Language*. London: Hutchinson. pp. 88–95.

Young, K. (1986) '"The killing field": themes in mass media responses to the Heysel Stadium riot', *International Review for the Sociology of Sport*, 21 (2/3): 253–66.

Young, K. and White, P. (1995) 'Sport, physical danger, and injury: the experiences of elite women athletes', *Journal of Sport and Social Issues*, 19: 45–61.

Young, K., White, P. and McTeer, W. (1994) 'Body talk: male athletes reflect on sport, injury, and pain', *Sociology of Sport Journal*, 11: 175–94.

6

FIGURATIONAL SOCIOLOGY AND ITS APPLICATION TO SPORT

Patrick Murphy, Ken Sheard and Ivan Waddington

Figurational sociology or, as it is sometimes called, process sociology, has grown out of the work of Norbert Elias (1897–1990).[1] The central organizing concept of figurational sociology is, unsurprisingly, the concept of 'figuration' itself. Elias described a figuration as 'a structure of mutually oriented and dependent people' (1978a: 261). He developed the concept as a means of trying to overcome some of the difficulties associated with more conventional sociological terms and theories. In particular, he was critical of what he regarded as misleading and unhelpful dualisms and dichotomies, such as that between the individual and society, and also of the tendency towards what he called process reduction, in which everything that is experienced and observed as dynamic and interdependent is represented in static, isolated categories. Elias explicitly conceptualized figurations as historically produced and reproduced networks of interdependence.

In criticizing what he termed the *Homo clausus* model of human beings – that is the view of individuals as self-contained and separate from other people – Elias argued that it is not fruitful to view 'the individual' and 'society' as two independently existing objects (1978b: 119). For Elias, these two concepts refer to inseparable levels of the same human world. The concept of figurations was developed to convey the idea that sociology is concerned not with *Homo clausus*, but with *Homines aperti*, with people bonded together in dynamic constellations. As he put it:

> The image of man [sic] as a 'closed personality' is ... replaced by the image of man as an 'open personality' who possesses a greater or lesser

degree of relative (but never absolute and total) autonomy *vis-à-vis* other people and who is, in fact, fundamentally oriented toward and dependent on other people throughout his life. The network of interdependencies among human beings is what binds them together. Such interdependencies are the nexus of ... the figuration, a structure of mutually oriented and dependent people. Since people are more or less dependent on each other first by nature and then through social learning, through education, socialization, and socially generated reciprocal needs, they exist, one might venture to say, only as pluralities, only in figurations. (Elias, 1978a: 261)

Elias argued that in order to understand what sociology is about, one must be aware of oneself as a human being among other human beings, and that one has to recognize that what are often conceptualized as reified 'social forces' are in fact nothing other than constraints exerted by people over one another and over themselves. It is mistaken to see 'social structures' as existing apart from ourselves or from human beings in general. Moreover, the peculiar constraint which is exerted by 'social structures' (figurations) over those who form them – and the fact that social processes, though produced by the interweaving of pluralities of individual acts, are *relatively autonomous* of particular individual intentions – should not lead us to ascribe to these processes an existence, an objective reality, over and above the groups of people whose actions constitute those processes. However, it is the case that the very complexity and dynamic character of the interweaving of the actions of large numbers of people continuously give rise to outcomes that no one has chosen and no one has designed; unintended and unplanned outcomes of this kind, which Elias stressed were usual aspects of social life, he called 'blind' social processes (1987a: 99).

One of the main objectives of figurational sociology as Elias saw it was to encourage sociologists to 'think processually' by always studying social relations as emerging and contingent processes. To him it was axiomatic that figurations should be studied as interdependent relations which are continually in flux and that shifts and transformations in patterns of social bonding can be identified in all patterns of development. Moreover, he believed it was possible to discern such shifts because interdependence is neither arbitrary nor random. On the contrary, the individuals and groups that make up a specific figuration are interconnected by a multiplicity of dynamic bonds. Whereas Marxists, for example, have tended to stress the importance of economic relations in social bonding, figurationalists suggest that the importance of economic relations is likely to vary from one situation to another and that in some situations political and emotional (affective) bonds may be equally or more significant. The concept of the social bond is intended to reinforce the two-edged character of figurations which may be both enabling and constraining (Rojek, 1985: 160).

A central dimension of figurations or dynamic interdependency ties is power, conceptualized not as a substance or property possessed by particular individuals and groups but as a characteristic of all human relationships (Elias, 1978b: 74). Power is always a question of relative balances, never of absolute possession or absolute deprivation, for no one is ever absolutely powerful or absolutely powerless. Neither is the balance of power between groups in a society permanent, for power balances are dynamic and continuously in flux.

THE CIVILIZING PROCESS

The work for which Elias is most famous is undoubtedly *The Civilizing Process* (Volume 1, 1978a, Volume 2, 1982, single volume, 1994). It is important to emphasize that Elias does not use the concept of a civilizing process in an evaluative way, for he does not suggest that people whose behaviour may be considered more 'civilized' are in any way morally superior to those whose behaviour is less 'civilized'. The theory of civilizing processes is based on the examination of empirical data which indicate that, in the societies of Western Europe between the Middle Ages and the early years of the twentieth century, a long-term process took place generally involving the refinement of manners and social standards and an increase in the social pressure on people to exercise stricter, more continuous and more even self-control over their feelings and behaviour. As part of this unplanned process, there occurred a shift in the balance between external constraints and self-constraints in favour of the latter, and at the level of personality, an increase in the importance of 'conscience' as a regulator of behaviour. That is, social standards came to be internalized more deeply and to operate, not only consciously, but also beneath the level of rationality and conscious control, for example by means of the arousal of feelings of shame, guilt and anxiety.

One aspect of this process which is of central relevance to the study of the development of sport has been the increasing social control of violence and aggression, together with a long-term decline in most people's propensity for obtaining pleasure from directly taking part in and/or witnessing seriously violent acts. Elias refers in this connection to a 'dampening of *Angriffslust*', literally to a dampening down or curbing of the lust for attacking, that is, a taming of people's conscious desire and capacity for obtaining pleasure from attacking others. This has entailed at least two things: first, a lowering of what Elias called the 'threshold of repugnance' regarding bloodshed and other direct and symbolic manifestations of physical violence. As a result, according to Elias, most people nowadays tend to recoil more readily in the presence of such manifestations than tended to be the case with people in the Middle Ages. Secondly, it has entailed the internalization of a stricter taboo on violence. A consequence of this is that guilt feelings and anxieties are liable to be aroused whenever this taboo is violated. At the same time, said Elias, there has occurred a tendency to push violence behind the scenes and, as part of this, to describe people who openly derive pleasure from violence in terms of the language of psychopathology, with such people being treated and/or punished by means of stigmatization, hospitalization, imprisonment or a combination of these (Dunning, 1990a).

In popular understanding, the terms 'violence' and 'civilization' are usually taken as antitheses, but the civilizing process in Western Europe may be seen as an unplanned outcome of violent 'hegemonial' or 'elimination' struggles among monarchs and other feudal lords. These struggles were associated with the development of emergent European nation-states, each of which was characterized by the increasingly stable and effective monopolization of the twin, mutually supportive means of ruling: the use of force and of the imposition of taxes. In other words, far from being simple antitheses, violence and 'civilization' are characterized by specific forms of interdependence. More particularly, civilizing processes are related to the establishment of increasingly effective control over the use of violence and an increasingly effective monopoly over taxation, both of which facilitate internal pacification and economic growth. Civilizing processes are also held to be associated with the lengthening of interdependency chains (in more conventional sociological language, the growth in the division of labour); the growing monetization of social relationships; functional democratization (the gradual historical tendency towards more equal – though not wholly equal – power balances between different groups and subgroups in society); and lastly, the decreasing privatization of the force and tax monopolies and their increasing public control.

As we shall see, the theory of civilizing processes has been widely used in the study of modern sports, especially with reference to issues concerning violence in sport.

INVOLVEMENT AND DETACHMENT

Another distinctive characteristic of Elias's approach is his position on the relationship between human understanding and values, an issue which has usually been discussed in abstract, static, ahistorical and dichotomic terms in which protagonists have argued either for 'objectivity' or 'subjectivity', for 'value freedom' or the 'inevitability of bias'. In contrast, for Elias a balance of emotional involvement and detachment is present in virtually all human behaviour. Similarly, it is not possible to identify an historical moment when wholly 'objective' scientific knowledge suddenly emerged, fully formed, out of what had formerly been wholly subjective forms of knowledge. These insights point up the shortcomings of approaching the problem of the growth of human knowledge and its relationship to changing values in terms of dichotomous either/or categories.

Elias (1987a) offers a properly sociological approach to the problem of knowledge. He conceptualizes the problem in terms of *degrees* of involvement and detachment. This is held to be more adequate than conventional arguments because, first, it does not involve a radical dichotomy between categories such as 'objective' and 'subjective', as though these were mutually exclusive categories; and, secondly, it is relational and processual and, as such, provides us with a framework with which we can examine the development, over time, of more object-adequate from less object-adequate knowledge.

One important implication of Elias's approach is that researchers can realistically only aspire to develop explanations that have a greater degree of adequacy than preceding explanations. Notions such as 'ultimate truth' and 'complete detachment' have no place in his approach. Yet, strangely, some critics of figurational sociology (such as Hargreaves, 1992; Horne and Jary, 1987) have still concluded that its adherents claim to provide 'objective' analyses from a value-neutral stance. It cannot be stressed too strongly that this was not his view and that Elias did not use such terms, preferring to speak in terms of degrees of object-adequacy, or, more latterly, of reality-congruence.

Elias noted that sociologists, like everyone else, are members of many social groups outside of their academic communities and they cannot cease to take part in, or to be affected by, the affairs of these groups. In this sense, they cannot be wholly detached. However, Elias notes that there is at least one sense in which it would not be desirable, in terms of the development of sociology, for them to be wholly detached, even if this were possible. Thus, while one need not know, in order to understand the structure of a molecule, what it 'feels like' to be one of its atoms, in order to understand the way in which human groups work one needs to know from 'inside', as it were, how human beings experience their own and other groups, and one cannot know this without active involvement. The problem for sociologists, then, is not how to be completely detached, for that is impossible, but rather how to maintain an appropriate balance between being an everyday participant and a scientific enquirer and, as a professional group, to establish in their work the undisputed dominance of the latter.

While the foregoing explication cannot do justice to the subtlety and complexity of Elias's general position, we hope that it will serve as an introduction to some of the central aspects of figurational or process-sociology. In the next section, we consider some of the ways in which the figurational perspective has been used in the sociology of sport.

FIGURATIONAL SOCIOLOGY AND SPORT

As we have seen, the basic principles of figurational sociology are potentially applicable to a range of social phenomena, but it is the ways in which they have been applied in the sociology of sport with which we are concerned here. At the risk of considerable over-simplification it might be suggested that this work falls into four main categories: early sportization processes and the control of violence; increasing seriousness of involvement and the growth of 'professional' sport; football hooliganism; and the relationship between globalization processes and sport. Of course, these categories are essentially artificial given the stress figurational sociologists place on networks of interdependency.

It is now generally accepted that the word 'sport' acquired its modern meaning, and the activities to which it is applied first developed, in eighteenth-century England. Elias attempted to explain why (Elias, 1971: 88–115). An important part of his explanation lay in attempting to demonstrate how what he called the 'sportization' process was linked with the process of 'the parliamentarization of political conflict'.

Elias used the term 'sportization' to refer to a process in the course of which the framework of rules applying to sport became stricter, including those rules attempting to provide for fairness and equal chances for all to win. The rules governing sport became more precise, more explicit, written down and more differentiated and supervision of rule-observance became more efficient. Moreover, in the course of the same process, self-control and self-discipline increased, while in the game-contests which became known as sports a balance was established between the possibility of attaining a high level of combat-tension and what was then seen as reasonable protection against injury (Elias and Dunning, 1986: 21–2).

Elias's explanation as to why the sportization process occurred first in England centres around differences in state formation processes between various European societies and the related differences in balances of power between ruling groups in those societies (1986: 26–40). For example, Germany and Italy remained relatively disunited until well into the nineteenth century, while France and

England were both relatively united nationally as early as the seventeenth and eighteenth centuries. France, though, had become highly centralized and its people subject to a form of 'absolute' rule, one aspect of which was that the right of subjects 'to form associations of their own choosing was usually restricted ... if not abolished' (1986: 38).

In England movement towards a highly centralized state and 'absolutism' had been more or less destroyed in the seventeenth century by the Civil War, one consequence of which was the restrictions placed on the powers of the monarch. Moreover, the reliance placed by the English on naval force meant that the large centralized bureaucracy required to coordinate a huge land army did not develop. A variety of processes, then, contributed to the landed ruling classes not only retaining a high degree of autonomy relative to the monarchical state but, *via* parliament, sharing with the monarch in the tasks of ruling (Dunning, 1992a: 7–18).

Elias argued that there occurred simultaneously with this 'parliamentarization of political conflict', the 'sportization' of pastimes. The more civilized habits developed by the aristocracy and gentry for governing also found expression in their organization of less violent, more civilized ways of enjoying themselves. These incipiently modern forms of sport developed through the type of voluntary associations known as 'clubs' (Dunning, 1992a: 13; Elias and Dunning, 1986: 38–9).

Figurational sociologists argue that this initial sportization of pastimes occurred in two main waves: an eighteenth-century wave in which the principal pastimes that began to emerge as modern sports were cricket, fox hunting, horse racing and boxing; and a second, nineteenth-century wave in which soccer, rugby, tennis and athletics began to take on modern forms (Dunning, 1992a; Elias and Dunning, 1986). Elias himself contributed to the study of fox hunting and boxing (1971, 1986) while Brookes produced a figurational analysis of the development of cricket[2] (Brookes, 1974, 1978).

In the mid-1960s Elias and Dunning undertook comparative and developmental investigations into early Greek and Roman sports, such as boxing and wrestling, and medieval folk-games, such as 'football' (Dunning, 1971). These studies were designed to probe just how different were the sport-like activities of people at relatively early stages in civilizing processes and nation-state formation processes, by comparison with the sports of the modern period. Elias (1971) stressed that Greek combat 'sports', for example, which were often a direct training for warfare, involved much higher levels of violence and open emotionality than those permitted today, and were less highly regulated. This is what Elias's theory of civilizing processes would lead one to expect. Compared with relatively developed nation-states, levels of physical insecurity in Greek city-states were high and conscience-formation was much less developed than is the case in the West today.[3] Elias suggested that internalized inhibitions against physical violence were also lower and the associated feelings of guilt and shame correspondingly much weaker.

Elias and Dunning's (1986) work on the folk football 'games' of medieval and early modern Britain extended this analysis and demonstrated just how different such activities were from modern football. Such games were less highly regulated than their modern counterparts and were governed primarily by local oral custom. They differed from town to town and region to region and were 'played' over open country or through the streets of towns by an indeterminate number of participants. They involved elements of what nowadays we would probably consider different games and, above all, they involved a much higher level of open violence than would be contemplated or permitted today. These activities, although 'mock-fights', bore a greater resemblance to real fighting than their modern-day equivalents.

Dunning and Sheard's *Barbarians, Gentlemen and Players* (1979), a sociological study of the development of rugby football, took Elias and Dunning's earlier work on the development of football much further and provided the template for much of the work of what later became known as the 'Leicester school' of figurational sociologists. The book addressed three themes: the development of more 'civilized' team games; the growth of increasingly serious, competitive, professionalized games; and the phenomenon of 'football hooliganism'. The first two themes were examined in considerable detail while the third, football hooliganism, was merely touched upon. However, it was the work on football hooliganism which was to earn the Leicester school an international reputation in the years that followed (Williams et al., 1984; Dunning et al., 1988; Murphy et al., 1990).

Barbarians, Gentlemen and Players emphasized just how central the English public schools were in the second, nineteenth-century, wave of sportization. These schools operated, in characteristically English fashion, with a high degree of independence from the state. Dunning and Sheard show how this degree of relative autonomy facilitated competition among and innovation within the public schools which was one of the preconditions for the sportization of football and the emergence of soccer and rugby as modern sports. They also show how a civilizing process was involved in this process as the violence of the games was gradually brought under greater control.

Barbarians, Gentlemen and Players also offered a figurational explanation of the trends towards more intense competition, professionalization, greater achievement-orientation, greater rewards and growing seriousness of involvement observed in many, if not most, modern sports. The argument was a complex one but basically involved the suggestion that an increase in seriousness could be attributed in part to what Elias termed 'functional democratization' in the modern world. Elias argued that in the course of nation-state formation processes in the West many power balances have become relatively more equal. These processes are interconnected with the lengthening chains of interdependence that increasingly tie people together, both within state societies and throughout the modern world. The reciprocal pressures and controls to which people are subject and which they are able to exert on others within industrial societies inevitably make their presence felt in their sporting activities. Top-level sportspeople in modern, urban-industrial societies, Dunning and Sheard suggested, are not independent and hence are not able to play solely for 'fun'. The sheer numbers of people involved in modern sport mean that a well-developed desire to achieve is necessary if one is to stand a realistic chance of getting to the top. If one wants to be recognized as a 'success' at sport, one has to play seriously. Moreover, top-level sportspeople can no longer play just for themselves but are representatives of wider communities such as cities, counties and nations. They are, therefore, increasingly constrained to provide the sorts of satisfactions demanded by their supporters; for example, they are expected to provide them with a certain measure of excitement and the satisfaction which comes from supporting a successful team. They have, that is, to validate in competition the community with which the supporters identify (Dunning and Sheard, 1976, 1979; Elias and Dunning, 1986).

Under such circumstances, Dunning and Sheard suggest, it is not surprising that players on occasions resort to the calculated use of illegitimate violence in order to try to achieve victory (1979: 272–89). This would, at first sight, seem to be a contradiction of Elias's theory of civilizing processes in which he argued that there has been a long-term decline in people's propensity for obtaining pleasure from directly engaging in and witnessing violent acts, and that the threshold of repugnance regarding violent acts has become lower, with people increasingly feeling guilty when such taboos are broken. However, Dunning has argued that in the course of civilizing processes there occurs in conjunction with an increase in socially generated competitive pressures, an increase in people's tendency and ability to plan, to use foresight and to use longer-term, more rational means for achieving their goals (Dunning, 1986a: 237). In this context, the deliberate use of violence to achieve advantage or victory in a game is, argues Dunning, consistent with the personality and habitus of people who consider themselves to be highly civilized because it involves a high level of control, relatively little pleasure from directly inflicting pain, and is utilized to achieve specific ends. Dunning, in fact, suggests that in the course of civilizing processes there occurs a change in the balance between 'expressive' and 'instrumental' violence, in favour of the latter (1986a: 227). He suggests that this distinction, although not one made by Elias, helps make sense of what appears to be an increase in violence on the field of play as sports have become more professionalized, 'spectacularized' and internationalized in recent decades.

It was also in *Barbarians, Gentlemen and Players* that the germ of an explanation for football hooliganism – and the relevance of 'segmental bonding' in that explanation – was outlined (Dunning and Sheard, 1979: 282–5). However, it was in *The Roots of Football Hooliganism* (Dunning et al., 1988), that the Leicester group brought together in one volume the fruits of their own and other people's work on this contemporary social problem. Before the publication of this study, and the earlier work upon which it was based, it was much less commonly accepted than it is today that violent disorder at football matches has deep historical roots. It tended to be assumed that 'hooliganism' was a relatively new phenomenon, a product, among other things, of the 'permissive' 1960s. The Leicester sociologists, after tracing the historical flows of the 'hooligan' phenomenon and linking it with the civilizing changes in British society over at least a century, attempted to explain why football hooligan gangs, and the rougher sections of society from which they were predominantly drawn, should have remained relatively unincorporated into the more 'civilized' society of the late twentieth century. They also addressed some of the implications of this fact. Briefly, the argument advanced was that the

'rougher' working-class neighbourhoods from which football hooligans are mainly drawn are characterized more by 'segmental' and less by 'functional' bonding – that is by bonds of similitude rather than difference – than most other groups in contemporary British society. We have been familiarized with the social attributes of such neighbourhoods through a plethora of sociological studies (Cloward and Ohlin, 1960; Cohen, 1955; Miller, 1958; Suttles, 1968). The main point for present purposes is that their characteristic patterns – including relative poverty, unemployment, mother-centred families, male-dominance, etc. – mutually reinforce each other to produce, *inter alia*, norms of aggressive masculinity and intense feelings of attachment to narrowly defined 'we-groups' and correspondingly intense feelings of hostility towards 'outsider' or 'they-groups'. Such groups, of what the Leicester group call 'segmentally bonded' young males, tend to find their opponents locally from amongst groups who resemble themselves in many ways. However, just like the segmentary lineages described by Evans-Pritchard (1940) in simpler societies, these 'segments' may combine to fight an external enemy, that is, fans from other towns or cities. Not only do these groups find in football an attractive locale for the expression of their rivalries, but the development of transport systems, internationalization and other processes, means that formerly internecine rivalry and conflict become transposed to the national and international levels. Such a pattern of intra-working-class conflict is not easily explained by a Marxist, dichotomous model of class conflict in which the 'enemy' is hypothesized as 'the bourgeoisie' or the 'representatives of the state'.

Figurational sociologists have recently turned their attention to the diffusion of modern sporting forms on a global scale, linking this to broader globalization processes. Maguire has attempted to clarify some of the conceptual confusions surrounding the term 'globalization', while extending and refining aspects of the figurational approach, especially as it applies to an understanding of global sport development and the role of the 'media–sport production complex' in those developments. He has also attempted to bring out the interconnections between globalization and national identity (Jarvie and Maguire, 1994; Maguire, 1991, 1993a, 1993b, 1994).

The 'conceptual snares' which Maguire (1994: 399) believes characterize work on globalization include dichotomous thinking, the use of monocausal explanation and the tendency to view globalization processes as governed by *either* the intended *or* the unintended consequences of the actions of groups of people: 'Globalization processes involve a blend between intended and unintended practices' (Jarvie and Maguire, 1994: 147). Maguire also distances himself from the implication that 'globalization' implies homogenization (1994: 400). However, on the negative side, Jarvie and Maguire sometimes display a tendency to reify which figurational sociologists would normally try to avoid.[4]

All writers agree that globalization involves processes that transcend the boundaries of nation-states, and that such processes are uneven, long-term and historically rooted. Most also recognize the difficulty of understanding local or national experiences without reference to global developments or what Maguire calls 'flows' (1993a). Jarvie and Maguire (1994: 231) also suggest that globalization may be leading 'to a form of time–space compression'[5] in which people experience spatial and temporal dimensions differently. There is, they suggest 'a speeding up of time and a "shrinking" of space. Modern technologies enable people, images, ideas and money to criss-cross the globe with great rapidity. This leads … to a greater degree of interdependence, but also to an increased awareness of the world as a whole.' At the same time, however, these processes may also be associated with a concomitant resurgence – as the two sides of the same coin – of local/national identifications.

Other ideas developed by figurational sociologists might also be applied to understanding relations between Western and non-Western societies, particularly relating to the development and spread of sport. Attention is directed towards four key insights: the concept of diminishing contrasts and increasing varieties, the idea of the commingling of Western and non-Western cultures, the subsequent emergence of a new amalgam and the ongoing attempts by established groups to integrate outsider people(s) as workers and/or consumers (Jarvie and Maguire, 1994: 151; Maguire, 1994: 404).

According to Maguire (1993a), aspects of globalization are 'powered' by specifically Western notions of 'civilization' with various commercial and industrial interest groups active in spreading the cult of consumerism and a staple diet of Western products. This has been associated with diminishing contrasts between nations, as members of the 'media–sport production complex' have achieved success in marketing virtually identical sport-

forms, products and images. However, the people involved in global marketing also attempt to celebrate difference, with new varieties of ethnic wares sought and targeted at specific market niches leading, sometimes, to the strengthening of 'local' ethnic identities. An example of this would be the spread to Britain of Japanese martial arts (Jarvie and Maguire, 1994: 151; Maguire, 1994: 409). The development of sport, then, is seen as being contoured by the interlocking processes of diminishing contrasts and increasing varieties.

Involvement in sports may also provide people with 'anchors of meaning' as national cultures and identities are affected by global 'time–space compression' (Bale and Maguire, 1994; Jarvie and Maguire, 1994). The development of the British Empire resulted in a diverse commingling of 'British' national culture and identity with that of other cultures. It involved the spread of British 'civilization' and sport-forms, and hence the diminishing of contrasts, but other sports, such as polo, diffused westwards from the East. The process of cultural interchange, though unequal, is not all one-way. Maguire (1994: 408) suggests that this process continues, with revamped versions of British sport-forms – for example, American football and Australian Rules – re-emerging in the mother country.

Moreover, Jarvie and Maguire argue that the effects of the spread of sport from the British to their colonial subjects have been double-edged. Although originally an indication of the success of British colonizers in spreading their sport-forms to other parts of the world, most former colonial peoples now regularly beat the British at 'their own games', boosting their sense of nationhood and difference in the process. Jarvie and Maguire suggest that, in the context of the loss of the former colonies, British/English sporting success may help restore, however superficially, a symbolic sense of stability, but that losing to former colonies may compound the general sense of dislocation (1994: 152).

The association of particular sports with specific places and seasons, it is suggested, can provide a sense of permanence and belonging – however illusory – which helps counteract the breakdown of identity often thought to accompany globalization processes. Jarvie and Maguire argue, however, that the development of the media–sport production complex may also serve to erode this sense of stability. Satellite broadcasting means that 'consumers' of sport can 'be at' any sport venue across the globe, while the introduction of novel varieties of sports subcultures to existing national cultures facilitates the forging of new sport and leisure identities. Although they argue that involvement in sport has reinforced and reflected a diminishing of contrasts between nations, they are also aware that the close association of sport with national cultures and identities may mean the undermining of the integration of regions at a political level and conclude, despite recognizing the tentative emergence of a *European* sports identity, that: 'As with European integration more generally, the sports process occupies contested terrain in which the defensive response of strengthened ethnic identities may yet win out over broader pluralizing global flows' (1994: 153).

CRITICAL EVALUATION AND OVERVIEW

In this section, we outline and comment on some of the major criticisms of the figurational perspective. For didactic purposes it may be useful to comment on these criticisms under the following headings:

1 General criticisms of figurational sociology.
2 Criticisms specifically of the theory of civilizing processes.
3 Criticisms of the figurational approach to the sociology of sport.

At the outset, we should note that several critics of figurational sociology have acknowledged the substantial contribution which figurational sociologists have made, both to sociology in general and to the sociology of sport in particular. Curtis (1986: 58), for example, though criticizing Elias's work on civilizing processes, nevertheless states that *The Civilizing Process* is 'macro sociology and social history par excellence ... there has been nothing written which even begins to approximate the sweep of history ... and the painstaking detail' of Elias's work. Horne and Jary, while criticizing figurational sociology mainly from a Gramscian Marxist perspective, nevertheless acknowledge that:

If the objective of a sociology of sport is now widely recognized as the provision of a theoretically adequate and historically grounded analysis of changing patterns of sport, then Figurational Sociology has contributed strongly to this recognition. The study of sport's role in the long-term transformation of culture and manners, and of the changes in class and power associated with this

'civilizing process' marked a major step forward in the sociological analysis of sport and leisure. (Horne and Jary, 1987: 86–7)

Notwithstanding comments such as these, however, it is the case that the debate between figurational sociologists and their critics has not always been as constructive as we would like. Figurational sociologists and their critics have, on occasions, accused each other of caricaturing the others' work (Dunning, 1992b: 256; Horne and Jary, 1987: 99) and, within the context of what Dunning (1992b: 257) has called 'a failure of communication of massive proportions', Bauman (1979: 125) has expressed the fear that figurational sociology may develop 'into one more sect on the already sectarian sociological scene'. Such a development would be unhelpful both to figurational sociology and to sociology more generally and we want to encourage a more constructive dialogue between figurational sociologists and their critics. One step towards *rapprochement* involves recognizing the substantial amount of common ground between these groups.

General Criticisms of Figurational Sociology

Perhaps the two most general criticisms of figurational sociology are, first, that whatever its contribution to date, it does not represent a distinctive perspective within sociology as claimed by its advocates and, secondly, that figurational sociology is, in effect, a form of functionalism.

The first point has been forcefully argued by Curtis, who, writing of Elias's *What is Sociology?* (1978b), states:

I doubt that many sociologists will find this approach and subject matter to be very new or absent from their own thoughts on society. Elias does, however, suggest some new terms for social phenomena and sets of phenomena known previously under other labels. For example, what are *figurations* except people in structures (or networks or systems) with these structures limited to interdependent relationships? *What is Sociology?* is often old wine in a new bottle ... Much of it is fairly standard fare in sociology ... (Curtis, 1986: 59)

Horne and Jary (1987: 87) similarly argue that the contribution which figurational sociologists have made to the sociology of sport has not resulted from any distinctive perspective but 'simply from the raising of classical sociological questions and from recourse to conventional sociological "best practice" in an area where these had hitherto been conspicuously absent'. They argue that 'any thesis of the distinctiveness or the indispensability of the concept of figuration in making Figurational Sociology's contribution possible must be challenged' and they assert that there is little difference between the concept of figuration and the more traditional sociological concepts of 'pattern' and 'situation'.

In order to evaluate this criticism, it is necessary to understand why Elias rejected these more conventional sociological concepts. As we saw earlier, a central aspect of Elias's sociology involved the attempt to conceptualize social processes in a way that did not perpetuate traditional and unhelpful dichotomies such as those between the individual and society, or structure and change. In relation to the latter, Rojek (1992: 15) suggests that the concepts of pattern and situation both have rather static connotations and that neither of them conveys 'the mobile, unfinished qualities of human relations as unequivocally as the concept of figuration'. Bauman (1979: 119) similarly concludes:

> The 'figuration' approach could – and should – incorporate change, open-endedness, multiplicity of chances, essential unpredictability of outcome, fluidity of any current pattern of interdependencies, into the very description of all historically generated social totalities. Figuration cannot help but being at the same time stable ... and dynamic ...; figurations, as a matter of fact, negate and transcend the very opposition between stability and change.

The concept of figuration also helps us, in similar fashion, to move away from the individual/society dichotomy. Thus, Bauman (1979: 118–19) has pointed out that the concept of figuration is a 'two-edged sword', with one edge aimed effectively against individualistic explanations of social processes, and the other edge aimed at reifying concepts such as 'social system'. Turner (1985: 159–60) makes a similar point, noting that the concept of figuration is a means of avoiding both 'methodological individualism and the reification of sociological categories by concentrating on the webs of interdependence ("figurations") between people and the power balances which characterise these webs'.

That Elias did offer a more useful conceptualization of the individual–society relationship is suggested by some of the responses to *The Civilizing Process*. Abrams (1982: 231–2), for example, has written that:

> The civilizing process ... was ... simultaneously and symbiotically a way of life for individuals, a

distinctive 'structure of affects' ... and a social system; it was a unified working-out of meaning-*and*-structure. [Elias] shows, in a set of very detailed studies ... just how impossible it is to split or disentangle the meaning-and-structure pair if one seriously wishes to understand either.

Bauman (1979: 121) similarly argued that, in *The Civilizing Process*, Elias demonstrated:

> with merciless logic and overwhelming empirical evidence, that long term changes in what is normally classified as 'personality structure' and in what is normally considered under a separate heading of 'socio-political structure' were aspects of the same historical process; not only intertwined, but mutually instrumental in each other's occurrence.

A second general criticism of the figurational approach relates to its alleged 'functionalism'. For example, Horne and Jary (1987: 88–9) suggest that the concept of figurations refers to 'chains of functions' and argue that figurational sociology 'retains roots in functionalist sociology, particularly the functionalism of Durkheim'. Later they argue that figurational sociology is premised on an explicit or implicit reference to 'societal needs' and 'functional requirements', and further suggest that some observers have wanted to locate figurational sociology clearly in the ranks of the 'social order' and 'social control' sociologies, since leisure is seen as performing 'compensatory' functions (1987: 100).

How valid are these criticisms? Elias certainly uses the term 'function' in his work, though this hardly indicates that his work is functionalist, for the concept of function has – unfortunately in the view of the present writers – been incorporated into mainstream sociology and is now widely used by sociologists representing a variety of perspectives. We might note here that Horne and Jary themselves called for study of the 'contested functions of sport' (1987: 100), though it would be foolish to suggest that they are therefore functionalists. More specifically, in relation to their suggestion that figurational sociology should be located in the ranks of functionalist 'social order' and 'social control' sociologies, it should be noted that Elias himself criticized precisely this aspect of structural-functionalism. He argued:

> the concept of 'function' as it has been used ... especially by 'structural-functionalist' theorists, is not only based on an inadequate analysis of the subject matter to which it relates, but also contains an inappropriate value judgement which,

moreover, is made explicit in neither interpretation nor use. The inappropriateness of the evaluation is due to the fact that they tend – unintentionally – to use the terms for those tasks performed by one part of the society which are 'good' for the 'whole', because they contribute to the preservation and integrity of the existing social system. Human activities which either fail or appear to fail to do that are therefore branded as 'dysfunctional'. It is plain that at this point social beliefs have become mixed up in scientific theory. (1978b: 77)

Rojek points out that figurational sociologists do not, as Horne and Jary suggest, 'see compensatory functions in sport and leisure everywhere', and neither do they, like many functionalists, 'resolutely ignore conflict and contradiction'; indeed, he suggests that the work of Dunning et al. on football hooliganism in Britain 'can hardly be taken as a paean to the power of sport to enhance harmony or stability in society' (Rojek, 1992: 23).

In conclusion, the critics have not effectively sustained their argument that figurational sociology is functionalist, though we might note that the influence of the then popular non-Parsonian functionalism was certainly evident in some very early work by Dunning (for example, Dunning, 1967), though it is much less evident in his later work.

Criticisms of the Theory of Civilizing Processes

The most frequently made criticism of Elias's *The Civilizing Process* is that it is a form of 'latent evolutionism' (Horne and Jary, 1987: 101). Curtis, for example, writes of Elias's 'assumption of more or less unilinear evolution' and he continues:

> Does not the record of aggression and violence in this century put the lie to this linear view, at least with respect to the increased internalization of controls on violence? While reading *The Civilizing Process*, I could not help thinking of all the contrary evidence ... from the past few years: the slaughter of Jews in Nazi Germany; the devastation laid on people in Dresden; the annihilation provided the people of Hiroshima; ... to name but a very few. How do we reconcile these events with a notion that people are moving toward a pinnacle in self-restraint of aggression? (Curtis, 1986: 59–60)

Newman (1986: 322) has similarly referred to what he calls 'Elias's notion of the ever-civilizing trend of social life' whilst Taylor (1987: 176) writes of 'the evolutionary and idealist social theory of Norbert Elias'.

All these criticisms have in common the idea that Elias's theory of civilizing processes is a theory of a continuous and 'progressive' trend towards ever-more civilized standards of conduct in relation to the control of aggression. It is, however, difficult to sustain this criticism by reference to Elias's work, for Elias indicated many times that European societies have experienced decivilizing phases of varying intensity and varying duration. For example, he wrote (1982: 251) that the civilizing process 'moves along in a long sequence of spurts and counter spurts' and pointed out that:

> this movement of society and civilization certainly does not follow a straight line. Within the overall movement there are repeatedly greater or lesser counter-movements in which the contrasts in society and the fluctuations in the behaviour of individuals, their affective outbreaks, increase again. (1982: 253)

As Rojek (1992: 21) has noted, one can hardly take statements of this kind 'as a sign of enthusiasm for evolutionary doctrine'.

Moreover, Elias has written at length on the de-civilizing processes associated with the rise of Nazism in Germany. Elias made a contribution to understanding this phenomenon in his paper 'Civilization and violence' (1982/3) and, at considerably greater length, in his *Studien über die Deutschen* (1989), now made available in English as *The Germans* (1996). Elias, whose mother died in Auschwitz, says that the book 'originated in the attempt to make understandable, to myself and anyone who is prepared to listen, how the rise of National Socialism came about, and thus also the war, concentration camps and the breaking apart of the earlier Germany into two states'. The core of the book was 'an attempt to tease out developments in the German national habitus which made possible the de-civilizing spurt of the Hitler epoch' (Elias, 1996: 1). It is all but impossible to imagine how anyone could interpret such a statement as being indicative of a commitment to a theory of unilinear 'progress'. We concur with Rojek's conclusion that, 'having considered the evidence, the criticism of evolutionism ... is not warranted. Demonstrably, the theory of the civilizing process allows for counter-civilizing as well as civilizing movements' (Rojek, 1992: 22).

Criticisms of the Figurational Sociology of Sport

Writing from a position which is broadly sympathetic to figurational sociology, Stokvis (1992) has offered one specific and one general criticism of the work of Elias and Dunning. The specific criticism relates to Elias's work on the development of fox hunting in England, while the more general criticism concerns what Stokvis argues is too narrow a concentration on matters of violence and its control in the work of figurational sociologists.

Elias (1986) discussed the development of fox hunting in England in terms of the theory of civilizing processes. He noted that, characteristic of the form of fox hunting that developed from the eighteenth century onwards was a restriction on the use of violence. For example, the hunters were unarmed and were required from the eighteenth century onwards to kill foxes not directly, but 'by proxy', that is, through the hounds. Elias argued that the development of these less violent forms of hunting took place in conjunction with the 'parliamentarization of political conflict', for, as the cycle of violence which had characterized English society in the seventeenth century began to wane, a more civilized ruling class began to emerge which developed less violent ways of behaving in both the political and the leisure spheres. The leisure side of this process, like the political side, involved what Elias called a 'civilizing spurt', one aspect of which involved the development of less violent ways of hunting.

However, Stokvis argues that the more civilized traits in fox hunting to which Elias refers developed first in France during the rise of the absolute monarchy, independently of any form of parliamentarization. He notes that the *'chasse par force'* which developed in France during the sixteenth century involved a move away from the earlier crude slaughtering of the quarry and that the violence involved in the killing 'was reduced to a minimum' (Stokvis, 1992: 123). Stokvis notes that this French style of hunting was diffused to England during the reign of James I (1603–25), this diffusion taking place in much the same way as English sports were diffused to other countries some centuries later. Thus, in the seventeenth century, France became the dominant power in Europe and the manners of the French elite became a prestigious model to be followed by the elites of neighbouring countries.

The interest of the English gentry and aristocracy in the French way of hunting during the reign of James I demonstrates, suggests Stokvis, 'that they had already acquired a taste for pastimes in which the level of violence was relatively restrained before parliament acquired its leading role in politics', and he argues that 'there is no indication that the experience of non-violent competition between opposing parties in Parliament had anything to do with the development of the typically English way of fox hunting' (1992: 124–5). He suggests that Elias's misconception about the origins of English fox hunting arose, in part, from his reliance on a limited number of contemporary sources. Elias certainly bases his study on limited sources and Stokvis offers a clear, cogent and telling critique of Elias's work.

More generally, Stokvis argues that what he sees as figurational sociologists' over-concentration on violence and its control has led to the neglect of what he considers to be more important areas for research such as the formal organization and standardization of sport, its diffusion in national societies and throughout the world and its professionalization and commercialization. He suggests that figurational sociologists have focused narrowly on the restriction of the level of tolerated violence with the result that 'what is only one aspect in the development of some modern sports is considered the defining characteristic of modern sports in general' (Stokvis, 1992: 131). He adds: 'the basic distinguishing characteristic of modern sports is their international organization and standardization and not, as Elias suggests, the relatively low level of tolerated violence' (1992: 134). Stokvis suggests that while one must take account of changes in the levels of socially permitted violence within sport, 'the rise of modern sports should, however, primarily be interpreted as another manifestation of the increase in the scale and complexity of social life' (1992: 127).

Stokvis's criticism implies, quite wrongly in our view, that figurational sociologists have explained changes in socially permitted levels of violence without reference to other aspects of the development of modern sport. For example, in their analysis of the structural properties of folk games and modern sports, Dunning and Sheard (1979: 33–4) list 15 characteristics in terms of which one can differentiate between folk games and modern sports, only one of which relates specifically to levels of socially tolerated violence, with the other characteristics including reference to many aspects of the informal and formal organization of folk games and modern sports. They point out, for example, that folk games were characterized by a diffuse, informal organization which was largely implicit in the local social structure, whereas modern sports are characterized by highly specific, formal organizations which are institutionally differentiated at the local, regional, national and international levels. They also point out that folk games involved regional variations in the rules whereas modern sports are characterized by national and international standardization of rules. If we locate Dunning and Sheard's analysis of differences in socially tolerated levels of violence within the context of their much broader analysis of modern sports we see that they do indeed address many of the very issues which Stokvis identifies as 'more important areas' for research.

The final criticism – that figurational sociologists have neglected gender issues – has been forcefully made by Jennifer Hargreaves (1992). Hargreaves (1992: 163) writes of Elias and Dunning's *Quest for Excitement*:

> with the exception of a section about fox hunting, in which a limited number of upper-class women would have actively participated, the book is exclusively about *male* sports and shared traditions. The cover signals its contents: it shows a boxing match with one man knocking another out of the ring, a male referee and an all-male audience. Turn inside and there is an all-male crowd celebrating a football triumph … Elias ignores the traditions of women in sport and also the ways in which women, however unobviously, were integral to dominantly male cultures.

This neglect of gender issues, she argues, is not accidental but grows out of the methodology of figurational sociology. Figurational sociologists' stress on the need to study phenomena in a relatively detached manner results, she suggests, not in 'objective' knowledge, but in an uncritical acceptance of gender inequalities in sport:

> it is not an accident that all figurational sports sociology has been written by men about male sports and, in contradiction to Dunning's claim, such a position represents an alignment with the 'dominant values and modes of thinking of Western societies'. Because it claims to be objective and uncritical, in a subtle but fundamental manner it is supporting the popular idea that sport is more suited to men than to women and represents a celebration of male bonding and male sport. (Hargreaves, 1992: 165)

Hargreaves's charge is thus not merely that figurational sociologists have neglected gender issues, but that their emphasis on detachment leads them to accept prevailing male-dominated ideologies about sport. To what extent are these charges valid?

It is certainly the case that figurational sociologists have, for the most part, neglected gender issues, though they have not ignored them altogether. Elias wrote a book-length manuscript on gender relations which was accidentally destroyed and all that remains is a reconstructed journal article (Elias, 1987b). Other figurational sociologists have also written on aspects of gender relationships within sport (Dunning, 1986b, 1990b; Sheard and Dunning, 1973; Waddington et al., 1998). There have also been two recent and interesting attempts to examine the relationship between figurational sociology and feminist approaches with a view to possible synthesis (Colwell, 1999; Maguire and Mansfield, 1998). Notwithstanding these recent developments, however, there has been a relative neglect of such issues, and to this degree the charge is substantiated; indeed, Dunning has accepted that 'we have in the past been too silent on questions of gender' (1992b: 255).

However, we believe that Hargreaves has misunderstood what is involved in the concepts of involvement and detachment, and that there is nothing in the methodology of figurational sociology which militates against the systematic study of gender. The emphasis in figurational sociology on studying phenomena in a relatively detached way does not involve, either explicitly or implicitly, a celebration of male sport but neither does it imply that, *as sociologists*, we should celebrate female sport; rather, it involves the idea that our primary task is to develop sociologically more adequate explanations of the structure of sport. Figurational sociologists simply claim that, in so far as we are able to examine social processes in a relatively detached way, we are likely to generate more adequate explanations than are those who, for one reason or another, are unable to develop such a degree of detachment. We believe this is a reasonable claim that most sociologists would share. We also believe that relatively adequate explanations of this kind will provide a more secure basis for action designed to overcome existing gender inequalities.

NOTES

1   For a detailed biography and analysis of Elias's work, see S. Mennell (1989).
2   Although Brookes chose to exclude all direct references to sociological theory in his book, his PhD thesis, from which the book was taken, drew explicitly on Eliasian theory.
3   When studying the Greek city-states one is dealing with a vast period of human history. We would tentatively suggest that there is some evidence which points to the existence of a civilizing process in this era.

The principal indication of the presence of this process is the growing power of political groupings over the military. We are, of course, not proposing that such a process – were it to be shown to have occurred – would have been unilinear in character. Like Western European civilizing processes, we would anticipate that it is likely to have been uneven and prone to reversals.

4   For example: 'Western societies were acting, as it were, as a form of upper class or established group on a world level' (Jarvie and Maguire, 1994: 149). The reification here consists in the treatment of the collective plural noun 'Western societies' as an entity that could act. The point that Jarvie and Maguire are making is, of course, taken from Elias. However, his formulation avoids reification. It is: 'From Western society — as a kind of upper class — Western "civilized" patterns of conduct are today spreading over wide areas outside the West, …' (Elias, 1982: 253).

5   The concept of 'time–space compression', it might be noted, is not specifically Eliasian and in some respects is misleading. It is not that time 'speeds up' or that space 'shrinks', but that people are able to travel and communicate faster and over greater distances than used to be the case. For a figurational approach to the significance of time, see Elias (1992) and Dunning (1994, 1999).

REFERENCES

Abrams, P. (1982) *Historical Sociology.* Shepton Mallet: Open Books.

Bale, J. and Maguire, J. (eds) (1994) *The Global Sports Arena: Athletic Talent Migration in an Interdependent World.* London: Frank Cass.

Bauman, Z. (1979) 'The phenomenon of Norbert Elias', *Sociology,* 13: 117–25.

Brookes, C.C.C.P. (1974) 'Cricket as a vocation: a study of the development and contemporary structure of the occupation and career patterns of the cricketer'. PhD dissertation, University of Leicester.

Brookes, C.C.C.P. (1978) *English Cricket: the Game and Its Players through the Ages.* London: Weidenfeld & Nicolson.

Cloward, R. and Ohlin, L. (1960) *Delinquency and Opportunity.* New York: Free Press.

Cohen, A. (1955) *Delinquent Boys.* New York: Free Press.

Colwell, S. (1999) 'Feminisms and figurational sociology: contributions to understandings of sports, physical education and sex/gender', *European Physical Education Review,* 5 (3): 219–40.

Curtis, J. (1986) 'Isn't it difficult to support some of the notions of "The Civilizing Process"? A response to Dunning', in C.R. Rees and A.W. Miracle (eds), *Sport and Social Theory.* Champaign, IL: Human Kinetics. pp. 57–65.

Dunning, E. (1967) 'Notes on some conceptual and theoretical problems in the sociology of sport', *International Review of Sport Sociology,* 2: 143–53.

Dunning, E. (1971) *The Sociology of Sport.* London: Frank Cass.

Dunning, E. (1986a) 'Social bonding and violence in sport', in N. Elias and E. Dunning, *Quest for Excitement: Sport and Leisure in the Civilizing Process.* Oxford: Basil Blackwell. pp. 224–44.

Dunning, E. (1986b) 'Sport as a male preserve: notes on the social sources of masculine identity and its transformations', in N. Elias and E. Dunning, *Quest for Excitement: Sport and Leisure in the Civilizing Process.* Oxford: Basil Blackwell. pp. 267–83.

Dunning, E. (1990a) 'Sociological reflections on sport, violence and civilization', *International Review for the Sociology of Sport,* 25 (1): 65–82.

Dunning, E. (1990b) 'Sport and gender in a patriarchal society'. Paper delivered at the World Congress of Sociology, Madrid.

Dunning, E. (1992a) '"Culture", "Civilization" and the Sociology of Sport', *Innovation,* 5 (4): 7–18.

Dunning, E. (1992b) 'Figurational sociology and the sociology of sport: some concluding remarks', in E. Dunning and C. Rojek (eds), *Sport and Leisure in the Civilizing Process: Critique and Counter-Critique.* Basingstoke: Macmillan. pp. 221–84.

Dunning, E. (1994) 'Sport in space and time: "civilizing processes", trajectories of state-formation and the development of modern sport', *International Review for the Sociology of Sport,* 29 (4): 331–47.

Dunning, E. (1999) *Sport Matters: Sociological Studies of Sport, Violence and Civilization.* London: Routledge.

Dunning, E. and Rojek, C. (eds) (1992) *Sport and Leisure in the Civilizing Process: Critique and Counter-Critique.* Basingstoke: Macmillan.

Dunning, E. and Sheard, K. (1976) 'The bifurcation of Rugby Union and Rugby League: a case study of organizational conflict and change', *International Review of Sport Sociology,* 2 (11): 31–72.

Dunning, E. and Sheard, K. (1979) *Barbarians, Gentlemen and Players: a Sociological Study of the Development of Rugby Football.* Oxford: Martin Robertson.

Dunning, E., Murphy, P. and Williams, J. (1988) *The Roots of Football Hooliganism: an Historical and Sociological Study.* London and New York: Routledge & Kegan Paul.

Elias, N. (1971) 'The genesis of sport as a sociological problem', in E. Dunning (ed.), *The Sociology of Sport.* London: Frank Cass. pp. 88–115.

Elias, N. ([1939] 1978a) *The Civilizing Process,* Volume 1: *The History of Manners* (trans. E. Jephcott). Oxford: Basil Blackwell.

Elias, N. (1978b) *What is Sociology?* London: Hutchinson.

Elias, N. (1982) *The Civilizing Process, Volume 2: State Formation and Civilization.* Oxford: Basil Blackwell.

Elias, N. (1982/83) 'Civilization and violence: on the state monopoly of physical violence and its infringements', *Telos,* 54: 134–54.

Elias, N. (1986) 'An essay on sport and violence', in N. Elias and E. Dunning, *Quest for Excitement: Sport and Leisure in the Civilizing Process.* Oxford: Basil Blackwell. pp. 150–74.

Elias, N. (1987a) *Involvement and Detachment.* Oxford: Basil Blackwell.

Elias, N. (1987b) 'The changing balance of power between the sexes – a process-sociological study: the example of the Ancient Roman state', *Theory, Culture and Society,* 4 (2/3): 287–317.

Elias, N. (1989) *Studien über die Deutschen.* Frankfurt am Main: Suhrkamp Verlag.

Elias, N. (1992) *Time: an Essay.* Oxford: Basil Blackwell.

Elias, N. (1994) *The Civilizing Process* (single volume edition). Oxford: Basil Blackwell.

Elias, N. (1996) *The Germans* (trans. Eric Dunning and Stephen Mennell). Cambridge: Polity Press.

Elias, N. and Dunning, E. (1986) 'Folk football in medieval and early modern Britain', in N. Elias and E. Dunning, *Quest for Excitement: Sport and Leisure in the Civilizing Process.* Oxford: Basil Blackwell. pp. 175–90.

Evans-Pritchard, E.E. (1940) *The Nuer.* Oxford: Oxford University Press.

Hargreaves, J. (1992) 'Sex, gender and the body in sport and leisure: has there been a civilizing process?', in E. Dunning and C. Rojek (eds), *Sport and Leisure in the Civilizing Process.* Basingstoke: Macmillan. pp. 161–82.

Horne, J. and Jary, D. (1987) 'The figurational sociology of sport and leisure of Elias and Dunning: an exposition and critique', in J. Horne, D. Jary and A. Tomlinson (eds), *Sport, Leisure and Social Relations* (Sociological Review Monograph 33). London and New York: Routledge & Kegan Paul. pp. 86–112.

Jarvie, G. and Maguire, J. (1994) *Sport and Leisure in Social Thought.* London and New York: Routledge.

Maguire, J. (1991) 'The media–sport production complex: the emergence of American sports in European culture', *European Journal of Communication,* No. 6: 315–36.

Maguire, J. (1993a) 'Globalization, sport development and the media–sport production complex', *Sport Sciences Review,* No. 2: 29–47.

Maguire, J. (1993b) 'Globalization, sport and national identities: the empires strike back?', *Leisure and Society,* 16 (2): 293–322.

Maguire, J. (1994) 'Sport, identity politics, and globalization: diminishing contrasts and increasing varieties', *Sociology of Sport Journal,* 11 (4): 398–427.

Maguire, J. and Mansfield, L. (1998) 'No-body's perfect: women, aerobics and the body beautiful', *Sociology of Sport Journal,* 15: 109–37.

Mennell, S. (1989) *Norbert Elias: Civilization and the Human Self-Image.* Oxford and New York: Basil Blackwell.

Miller, W. (1958) 'Lower class culture as a generating milieu of gang delinquency', *Journal of Social Issues,* 14: 5–9.

Murphy, P., Williams, J. and Dunning, E. (1990) *Football On Trial: Spectator Violence and Development in the Football World.* London and New York: Routledge.

Newman, O. (1986) 'Review of Chris Rojek, *Capitalism and Leisure Theory*', *Sociology,* 20 (2): 322.

Rojek, C. (1985) *Capitalism and Leisure Theory.* London and New York: Routledge.

Rojek, C. (1992) 'The field of play in sport and leisure studies', in E. Dunning and C. Rojek (eds), *Sport and Leisure in the Civilizing Process.* Basingstoke: Macmillan. pp. 1–35.

Sheard, K. and Dunning, E. (1973) 'The rugby football club as a type of "Male Preserve"': some sociological notes', *International Review of Sport Sociology,* 3–4 (8): 5–24.

Stokvis, R. (1992) 'Sport and civilization: is violence the central problem?', in E. Dunning and C. Rojek (eds), *Sport and Leisure in the Civilizing Process.* Basingstoke: Macmillan. pp. 121–36.

Suttles, G. (1968) *The Social Order of the Slum.* Chicago: University of Chicago Press.

Taylor, I. (1987) 'Putting the boot into working-class sport: British soccer after Bradford and Brussels', *Sociology of Sport Journal,* 4: 171–91.

Turner, B. (1985) 'Review Article', *Theory, Culture and Society,* 2 (3): 158–61.

Waddington, I., Malcolm, D. and Cobb, J. (1998) 'Gender stereotyping and physical education', *European Physical Education Review,* 4 (1): 34–46.

Williams, J., Dunning, E. and Murphy, P. (1984) *Hooligans Abroad.* London: Routledge & Kegan Paul.

7

POSTING UP: FRENCH POST-STRUCTURALISM AND THE CRITICAL ANALYSIS OF CONTEMPORARY SPORTING CULTURE

David L. Andrews

> In varying ways, then, the post-structuralists show the tensions within seeming truths, the difficulties involved even in seemingly ordinary understandings, the constant effort of construction involved in accepted truths, as well as the constant tendency of those truths to break down and reveal their internal inconsistencies and aporias.
> (Calhoun, 1995: 113–14)

The *Zeitgeist* of the modern era was based on the Enlightenment assumption of the inevitable progress and advancement of individuals, and hence society, resulting from the circulation of rational scientifically based knowledges, technologies and institutions. To many these foundations of modernity have conclusively failed to live up to their advanced billing. According to Stuart Hall, 'The troubled thought surfaces that modernity's triumphs and successes are rooted, not simply in progress and enlightenment, but also in violence, oppression and exclusion, in the archaic, the violent, the untransformed, the repressed aspects of social life' (Hall, 1992a: 16). Rather than alleviating the social divisions of the pre-Enlightenment, premodern age, the production, circulation and institutionalization of modern knowledges has merely exacerbated the separation between the informed and the ill-informed, the empowered and the disempowered, the exploiter and the exploited, the haves and the have-nots. Given the incestuous relationship between conventional social theorizing and the project of modernity – most deleteriously manifest in the modern search for objective and scientific analyses of human existence that would contribute to the

'rational organization of everyday social life' (Habermas, 1981: 9) – post-structuralism emerged as a loosely aligned series of philosophical, political and theoretical rejoinders to the unrest and turbulence that engulfed modernizing France during the late 1960s and early 1970s. Thus, from its roots within the popular responses to the perverse flowering of the Enlightenment project in postwar France, through its appropriation within North American, British, Japanese and Australasian intellectual cultures, the unifying element of post-structuralism's varied strands has been the generation of the type of knowledge that would ameliorate the deindividualizing rationalities, and violent subject hierarchies, that have come to characterize the dystopian conditions of late modernity.

French post-structuralism's extraordinary global diffusion is matched by its expansive migration across intellectual domains. Originally the preserve of literary studies and criticism, over the past 15 years post-structuralism has made its presence felt throughout the (sub)disciplinary structure of the fragmenting social sciences and humanities. Indeed, as evidenced by its appearance in areas as diverse as African studies (Pouwels, 1992), education (Usher, 1989), family studies (Fish, 1993), geography (Lawson, 1995), health (Lupton, 1993), Italian studies (Smith, 1994), rural studies (Martin, 1995) and social history (Steinberg, 1996), it is evident that post-structuralism has become a constituent feature of contemporary intellectual life. Despite such academic ubiquity, post-structuralism is only now beginning to make its presence felt within the sociology of sport. Indeed, until relatively recently post-structuralist-orientated research has been received with a perplexing mixture of defensive dismissal and haughty disdain by large sections of the sociology of sport community. While such sentiments persist among certain circles within the internecine conflicts that mark the sociology of sport's intellectual maturation, there are significant rumblings which would suggest that post-structuralist texts are being read, and imaginatively appropriated, by a small group of scholars seeking to critically theorize the interplay between contemporary sporting formations, language, power and subjectivity.

As has long been established by advocates of contrasting theoretical frameworks (Brohm, 1978; Dunning and Sheard, 1979; Gruneau, 1988; Guttmann, 1978; Hargreaves, 1986; Ingham, 1978), the appearance of contemporary sport formations was inextricably bound to the careering institutional and ideological 'juggernaut' (Giddens, 1990) of modernity:

> Sport, as we experience it, developed in response to and as part of the dynamics and practices associated with modernity. … Sport is celebrated for its diversity, individuality, discipline, order, and solidarity: as a mythic practice, sport is understood as a democratic and meritocratic site in which individuals compete. (Cole, 1995: 228)

Taking into consideration its preoccupation with the constitution and crisis of modernity, post-structuralism represents a legitimate alternative to the more established theoretical schools within the sociology of sport (see Jarvie and Maguire, 1994) for those seeking to examine the nature and influence of modern sport discourses, practices and institutions. As well as expressing modernity's individualistic, rational and instrumental impulses, the formations and discourses of modern sport simultaneously embody the de-individualizing rationalities, and violent subject hierarchies, that characterize the unravelling modern condition. Paraphrasing Featherstone (1985), post-structuralism thus allows us to expose the *dark side* of *sporting* modernity by challenging the ethos of rational human progress embodied by – and within – modern sport culture.

This chapter is intended to provide an overview of the growing body of post-structuralist informed scholarship within the sociology of sport. Following a broad-based genealogy of the post-structuralist project, focused on its roots within French intellectual culture, this discussion concentrates on the work of three pivotal French post-structuralist theorists, namely, Jacques Derrida, Michel Foucault and Jean Baudrillard. This list is necessarily short since the work of other post-structuralists (such as Georges Bataille, Gilles Deleuze, Emmanuel Levinas, Jean-François Lyotard) appears so infrequently, if at all, within the sociology of sport literature. In addition, while it is tempting to include the work of Pierre Bourdieu – who is of the same generation of French intellectuals, and has done important work on cultural (re)production, much of which discusses sport (see Bourdieu, 1978, 1984, 1988) – his work will not be discussed within this chapter. It is felt Bourdieu's project exhibits significantly different intellectual antecedents and sensibilities to those displayed by the post-structuralists identified herein. As Bourdieu himself stated:

> If I had to characterize my work in a couple of words, that is, as is often done these days, to apply a label to it, I would talk of *constructivist structuralism* or of *structuralist constructivism*, taking the word structuralist in a sense very different from that given to it by the Saussurean or Lévi-Straussian tradition. (Bourdieu, 1990: 123)

Returning to what is discussed in this chapter, the overviews of Derridean, Foucauldian and Baudrillardian theorizing will provide a necessarily brief summary of their respective post-structuralist approaches, and highlight the noteworthy studies which – to varying degrees – have appropriated these theories as a means of, and framework for, interrogating particular aspects of contemporary sport culture. The chapter concludes by offering some future directions for the burgeoning relationship between post-structuralist theory and the sociology of sport.

Far from being a definitive statement – something hardly appropriate in any post-structuralist orientated discussion – this chapter is intended to stimulate the all-important, and as of yet not fully realized, goal of critically engaging and evaluating the philosophical, epistemological and ontological significance of post-structuralism for the sociology of sport. In reference to the uncritical adoption of contemporary French social and cultural philosophy by North American intellectuals within an array of academic fields, Gottdiener has opined that such intellectual trends occurred without rigorous discussion 'as if they [North American scholars] had sprung, like Athena, full-blown from some Gallic source of intrinsic truth' (1995: 156). In order for the *global* sociology of sport community to avoid falling foul of such accusations, we are compelled to initiate an exacting debate pertaining to the merits, or otherwise, of post-structuralist theorizing as contributions to our body of knowledge. More than a decade ago, Kurzweil (1986: 113) announced that Derrida 'is no longer discussed in Paris', and since there has long been talk of a *post-post-structuralism* (Brantlinger, 1992; Johnson, 1987), to many this call to evaluate post-structuralism would seem a *passé* project in the extreme. Nevertheless, we cannot, and indeed should not, feel any guilt or embarrassment for not having fully worked through this task. At the present time, what we should be conscious of is recognizing the need to rigorously engage post-structuralist thought before we either blithely relegate it to some intellectual waste-land, or blindly appropriate it as the next theoretical *nirvana* for the sociology of sport.

A GENEALOGY OF THE DISCURSIVE POST-STRUCTURALIST SUBJECT

Overwhelmingly, the direction of post-structuralist thought has been to emphasize the 'constituted' nature of the subject – not merely aspects of the subject … but the very constitution of subjectivity *per se*. In locating this process of constitution at the level of language structure and acquisition, post-structuralist theory indicates both the inevitability of experiencing 'subject-ness' and also its unavoidable emptiness. (Macdonald, 1991: 49)

Before delving any further into the post-structuralist morass it should be noted that some commentators use 'post-structuralism' and 'postmodernism' interchangeably. Others acknowledge their interchangeable nature, yet choose to use derivatives of the more seductive term postmodern as an umbrella term for both (see Firat and Venkatesh, 1995; Grenz, 1996; Rosenau, 1992). This chapter studiously counters this trend. It is my contention that post-structuralism's distinct intellectual lineage, and focus, render it too important to be subsumed under the broad and ambiguous banner of postmodernism. Although postmodern to the extent that they uniformly repudiate modern notions of the centred subject, and related claims to the existence of universal objective truths (Ashley, 1994), post-structuralists clearly differ in the extent to which they engage – or even acknowledge the existence of – the well-rehearsed manifestations of the postmodern condition (see Connor, 1989; Featherstone, 1991; McRobbie, 1994). Post-structuralists are linked by their mutual concern with radically problematizing modernity, utilizing their own

interpretation of post-Saussurean theory, but they also differ markedly with respect to their particular engagements with the modern project: whereas Derrida deconstructed the philosophical foundations of modernity, Foucault excavated modern disciplinary knowledges and institutions, and Baudrillard effectively announced the end of modernity. In this manner, post-structuralism incorporates theorizing that respectively asserts that the modern project either should be in, is presently in, or has been deposed by, a state of terminal crisis. The focus of post-structuralism would thus appear to oscillate between modern, late modern and indeed postmodern conjunctures. Any uncritical conflation of post-structuralism and postmodernism would therefore appear to be misleading, inaccurate and thereby ill-advised.

It is a well-rehearsed dictum that French post-structuralism sprang forth during the late 1960s and early 1970s as both a political response to particular historical circumstances, and as a counter to the interpretive inadequacies of prevailing social doctrines. Regardless of the veracity of this assertion, if we are to truly engage both the complexities and vagaries of post-structuralism, we are implored – albeit briefly – to revisit the context of modernizing France, which spawned this 'post-Marxian, postcommunist Left standpoint' (Seidman, 1994: 201). Failing to do so would make us liable to the charges of indiscriminate theoretical pillaging (Bannet, 1989) that, within wider academic circles, has characterized much research aligned under the post-structuralist banner. This dubious practice is especially troublesome when researchers appropriate particular theoretical discourses and concepts without fully acknowledging, or perhaps even recognizing, the social, political, economic, technological and philosophical contexts which fashioned them, and which are necessarily implicated in their use. In mitigating against such a potentially debilitating tendency within the sociology of sport, this section contextualizes the post-structuralist project, and provides the foundation for the more detailed discussions of the work of Derrida, Foucault and Baudrillard which follows. More simply expressed, as one commentator noted, it is important not to overlook the 'Frenchness of French philosophy' (Matthews, 1996: 1–13).

As with the Enlightenment movement in eighteenth-century Europe – vanguarded as it was by French *philosophes* such as Voltaire, Diderot and Rousseau – the vibrancy and dynamism of French intellectual culture in the post-Second World War era played a significant role in the advancement of post-Enlightenment social philosophies. The attendant social, political, economic and technological modernization that followed France's liberation from Nazi occupation wrought profound changes in the constitution and experience of everyday French life (Rigby, 1991). In order to account for these radical transformations which neutered the relevance of existing social philosophies, 'New social theories emerged to articulate the sense of dynamic change experienced by many in post-war France, analysing the new forms of mass culture, the consumer society, technology, and modernized urbanization' (Best and Kellner, 1991: 17). These social philosophies, emanating from the intense ferment of postwar French intellectual culture, could be collectively labelled postempiricist to the extent that they countered the dominant positivist empiricism, which asserted that knowledge can only be gleaned from that which can be experienced, and thereby verified, through sensory perception (Hamilton, 1992). It should be stressed, however, that 'The unity defined by the very term *postempiricist* is defined by a shared opposition to positivism, rather than a settled agreement about the alternative' (Morrow, 1994: 75).

The Enlightenment rational humanism that underpinned the mastery of the human sciences in the eighteenth and nineteenth centuries provided the dominant stratagem for interpreting the structure and experience of modernity during the early and middle twentieth century. Nevertheless, existentialism in the 1940s, structuralism in the 1960s, and post-structuralism in the 1970s, sequentially developed as competing, and oftentimes contradictory, postempiricist responses to what Halton (1995) described as the 'unbearable enlightenment of [modern] being'. Although in very differing ways, existentialism, structuralism and post-structuralism all represent important epistemological and ontological challenges to the modern hegemony of the liberal humanist subject, which uncritically placed 'man [sic] at the centre of history' and made 'him the privileged creator of meaning' (Kearney, 1987: 119). Hence, from one vantage point, this section is centrally concerned with highlighting the changing understandings of the human subject and subjectivity in postwar French social thought, each of which offered contrasting explanations for the derivation of 'the conscious and unconscious thoughts and emotions of the individual, her [sic] sense of herself and her ways of understanding the world' (Weedon, 1997: 32).

Existentialism

In order to chart – in a genealogical fashion – the trajectories of postempiricist social theorizing, one is implored to briefly return to the rise of French existentialism within the late 1940s and early 1950s. The flowering of existentialism has been linked to the heroism of the French resistance movement which dominated the national popular imagination in the immediate postwar era. French public culture enthusiastically embraced the heroes and heroines of the resistance as selfless individuals who successfully challenged the violence and oppression imposed by the fascist totalitarianism of the occupying Nazis. These underground volunteers, willing to sacrifice their lives in the cause of French freedom, became an important source of postwar collective pride and identity. French intellectual culture could hardly be divorced from the 'heroic ethos of the war resistance' (Seidman, 1994: 199). Thus, within this context, existentialism's celebration of the autonomous subject came to the fore as a critical response to the de-individualizing tendencies of both logical positivism, and Cartesian speculative philosophy:

> In philosophy, especially since the end of the war, we have witnessed a general reaction against the systematizing mind, and perhaps even against science itself. It is probably because the passion for final and totalitarian truths has become so pervasive that the individual, threatened by the generality and abstraction which are shutting him in, is fighting a fight of the last hour against his imminent drowning in universal laws. (Campbell, 1968: 137)

Descombes described postwar French existentialists such as Jean-Paul Sartre, Simone de Beauvoir and Maurice Merleau-Ponty, as the generation 'of the three H's' (1980: 2), because both the phenomenological and Marxist strands of existentialism were profoundly informed by varied appropriations of Hegelian dialectics, Husserlian phenomenology and Heideggerian hermeneutics (Descombes, 1980: 9–74; Morrow, 1994: 121–3). Although far from a unified philosophical doctrine – indeed, Macquarrie preferred to view existentialism as a philosophical *style* – there do exist some identifying tenets of existential philosophy which Macquarrie characterized as 'family resemblances' (1972: 18). Uppermost amongst these unifying traits stands the existential notion of the human subject as agent, which clearly counters the domineering presence of the Cartesian self as a thinking subject within Western philosophy (Macmurray, 1957). Existential ontology argues that human existence cannot be reduced to Descartes's *cogito ergo sum*, rather it is prefigured on the understanding of a potentially absurd universe, populated by isolated individuals who are solely responsible for the creation of their own conscience, consciousness, actions and thereby existence. According to Sartre:

> We mean that man first of all exists, encounters himself, surges up in the world – and defines himself afterwards. If man, as the existentialist sees him, is not definable, it is because to begin with he is nothing. He will not be anything until later, and then he will be what he makes of himself. (1956: 290)

In a political sense, this condition of radical voluntarism necessitates that individuals become responsible for their involvement in, and the stance they take toward, the world in which they exist (Cooper, 1990: viii).

Without question existentialism reached deep into the recesses of postwar popular existence. Primarily through the work of Jack Kerouac, existentialism was vaunted as a *de rigueur* intellectual accessory for the near-mythic Beat generation, and the sizeable cohort of predominantly young and middle-class, angst-ridden, black-enrobed disciples on both sides of the Atlantic (for a lighthearted synopsis of the relationship between existentialism and popular culture see Thorne, 1993: 220–1, 73–4). However, as with any popular movement, existentialism's ascendance within the academy proved to be considerably less enduring. As befits the irrational process of epistemic evolution (Kuhn, 1970), in true adversarial fashion, structuralism surfaced as an attempt to wrestle the 'role of the subject in social thought' away from existentialism's unscientific subjectivism (Poster, 1975: 306).

Structuralism

Once again, it is important to broadly 'recontextualize' (Bannet, 1989) the epistemological and ontological shift from existentialism to structuralism in relation to the broader changes experienced within postwar France. While it continued to resonate with the French psyche, as the 1950s drew on, the cultural centrality of the resistance movement became subsumed under the weight of more immediate concerns. Similarly, the radical voluntarist subjectivity vaunted by existentialism became less germane to the changing experiences of the French populace. The French leader, General de Gaulle, had initiated an aggressive process of postwar modernization – based on the rapid industrialization, urbanization, commercialization and centralized bureaucratization of French society – with the goal of engineering France's belated re-emergence as a global power to rival the United States and the Soviet Union. Although failing to reassert the world significance France had enjoyed during much of the nineteenth century, by the end of the 1950s, de Gaulle's policies had wrought substantial changes in the experience of everyday French life (Rigby, 1991). As Ardagh recorded:

> France went through a spectacular renewal. A stagnant economy turned into one of the world's most dynamic and successful, as material modernization moved along at a hectic pace and an agriculture-based society became mainly an urban and industrial one. Prosperity soared, bringing with it changes in lifestyles, and throwing up some strange conflicts between rooted French habits and new modes. (Ardagh, 1982: 13)

It is perhaps too simplistic to attribute the ascent of structuralism solely to the birth of a French technocratic and neocapitalist state (Bannet, 1989). Nevertheless it would be foolish to think there were no connection whatsoever. Certainly, there would appear to exist a homologous relationship between de Gaulle's modern French technocracy, and structuralism's highly rationalized and scientific goal of constructing predictive models pertaining to the order and coherence of human existence (Seidman, 1994).

The man widely thought responsible for bringing 'structuralism from the quiet halls of linguistic faculties to the cacophony of the philosophical marketplace was the anthropologist Claude Lévi-Strauss' (Poster, 1975: 307). Formed within his earlier works (Lévi-Strauss, 1961, 1967, 1969), the publication of Lévi-Strauss's *The Savage Mind* (1966b) in 1962 marked the beginning of the era in which structuralism dominated the French intellectual scene (Poster, 1975). Within the final chapter of *The Savage Mind* (1966b), Lévi-Strauss engaged in a rambling critique of Sartre's brand of existentialism, and explicated the ontological and epistemological foundations of a structuralism defined in explicit opposition to existentialism. Existentialism posited a voluntarist ontology based upon the centrality of human agency, which Lévi-Strauss renounced for contributing nothing to the understanding of the nature of Being:

> As for the trend of thought which was to find fulfillment in existentialism, it seemed to me to be the exact opposite of true thought, by reason of

its indulgent attitude toward the illusions of subjectivity. To promote private preoccupations to the rank of philosophical problems is dangerous and may end in a kind of shop-girl's philosophy ... [which disrupts the mission of philosophy as being] ... to understand Being in relation to itself, and not in relation to oneself. (Lévi-Strauss, 1961: 62)

In shifting the nexus of ontological understanding from subject to structure, Lévi-Strauss favored a radical antihumanism that dissolved or – to engage what became a (post)structuralist leitmotif – *decentered* the human subject through the assertion of objective, universal structures as the principal definers of human existence. Lévi-Strauss honed this structuralist understanding under the tutelage of the renowned phonologist Roman Jakobson, whom he encountered at the New School in New York during his enforced exile from the antisemitism which accompanied the Nazi occupation of France. Jakobson drew Lévi-Strauss's attention to the structural linguistics of the turn-of-the-century Swiss semiologist Ferdinand de Saussure, whose posthumously assembled *Course in General Linguistics* (Saussure, 1959) laid the groundwork for the *linguistic turn* that spawned structuralism and post-structuralism.

Saussure's most important bequest to his theoretical heirs can be found in his repudiation of the rationalist view of language as a natural mechanism of naming, based on the existence of intrinsic and immutable links between words and material or imaginary objects. Instead of slavishly reflecting reality, Saussure argued that language actively shaped human consciousness, and thereby informed the understanding, and experience, of material and imaginary worlds. In conceptualizing language as a social – rather than natural – phenomenon, Saussure stressed the difference between *la langue* (the rules and depth structure of the language system) and *la parole* (the spoken product of individuals' engagement with the language system). Or, as Sturrock put it, 'If *langue* is a structure then *parole* is an event' (1986: 9). Saussure asserted that language had to be analysed synchronically, with particular regard to what were identified as constant structural elements, as opposed to adopting a diachronic focus on the historical shifts in linguistic expression. This ahistoric synchronic approach to understanding the structure of language revolved around the identification of the bifurcated constitution of the sign as the primary mechanism of meaning construction, or signification. Saussure

described the difference and interrelationship between the two intimately united elements of the linguistic sign – the signifier (the visual mark, acoustic expression, or sound-image of the sign) and the signified (the concept or mental image associated with the sign) – as an 'opposition that separates them from each other and for the whole which they are parts' (Saussure, 1959: 67).

Perhaps Saussure's most profound statement, regarding furthering the understanding of language as a system of meaning, can be gleaned from his assertion of the differential relation between signs through which meaning is created, 'Everything that has been said up to this point boils down to this: in language there are only differences ... The idea or phonic substance that a sign contains is of less importance than the other signs which surround it' (Saussure, 1959: 120). Leading on from this insight, Saussure stressed the importance of binary oppositions (his example being father and mother), in as much as the 'entire mechanism of language ... is based on oppositions of this kind and on the phonic and conceptual differences that they imply' (Saussure, 1959: 121). Another of Saussure's important dictates related to his understanding of linguistics centered on his assertion of the arbitrary nature of the sign. The sign can be considered arbitrary, because in almost all cases, there is no fixed or natural unity between the signified and the signifier. The arbitrary linkage between the two elements of the sign is based not on some necessary and immutable connection, but rather 'every means of expression used in a society is based, in principle, on a collective norm – in other words, on convention' (Saussure, 1959: 68). As Saussure pointed out, there is no preordained link between the letter 't' and the sound with which it has come to be associated (Saussure, 1959: 119). Moreover, the sound-image, or word, 'tree' (to cite another of Saussure's examples) is associated with the concept *tree* only because of the contingent conventions of the linguistic community in which the process of signification takes place.

In conjunction with selective readings of Mauss, Durkheim and Jakobson, Saussure's ground-breaking insights provided the basis for Lévi-Strauss's structural anthropology (1967), which revolved around the 'systematic search for unconscious universal mental structures' (Kurzweil, 1986: 113). This ahistoric project involved applying Saussurean linguistics to the analysis of the myths, totems, kinship patterns and exchange rituals of numerous *primitive* societies (see Lévi-Strauss, 1961, 1966b, 1967):

He transposed the structuralist conceptions to the study of anthropological data, relying on the sign as a central term. It was not simply an analysis of the transmission of signs which functions within sociality, but also a matter of envisaging structures as symbolic systems, that is, the structural arrangement as productive of meaning. (Coward and Ellis, 1981: 155)

From the findings of his own field research, and from that of others, Lévi-Strauss asserted that the structure of the human mind is directly related to that of the linguistic and material expressions that frame social existence: all are based on a set of universal binary oppositions, including those of nature/culture, life/death, sacred/profane, light/darkness, raw/cooked, male/female. Confounding the patronizing Eurocentrism of traditional anthropology, Lévi-Strauss declared his findings were equally applicable to *modern* societies. In other words, according to Lévi-Strauss, there did exist a truly universal logic, and the varied linguistic and material articulations of particular cultural formations are simply the shifting permutations and coalitions of the omnipresent binary code.

Lévi-Strauss's assertion that 'everything in culture, in society and in the mind is governed by the same universal and unconscious structures' (Bannet, 1989: 259) advanced structuralism as a legitimate *scientific* practice, involving the objective, rational and rigorous search for predictive universal knowledge of the human condition. As Harland noted, 'The Structuralists, in general, are concerned to *know* the [human] world – to uncover it through detailed observational analysis and to map it out under extended explicatory grids' (Harland, 1987: 2). Structuralism decreed that human existence could only be understood by identifying the universal logics within the cultural systems of (language, ritual, myth) that gave expression to human experience, instead of by dissecting the individual articulations of such cultural systems. In this way, Lévi-Strauss advanced the radical notion that 'the ultimate goal of the human sciences [is] not to constitute, but to dissolve man [sic]' (1966a: 247). Ironically, given its avowed 'scientific pretensions' (Best and Kellner, 1991: 20), structuralism displayed less congruence with other edicts of Enlightenment thought; most notably those linked to the nature of the human subject.

As Grenz noted in relation to Lévi-Strauss's structuralism, 'it is not just the idea of the self that he rejects: he also rejects subjectivity' (1996: 119). Lévi-Strauss clearly countered the European humanism that undergirded understandings of the modern subject as the fully centered and unified subject, innately endowed with the capacity for reasoned thought and action. In asserting that the structuralist subject is only constituted in, and through, its relationship with language, Lévi-Strauss, through Saussure – and in sharp contrast to the overt humanism of Sartre's radical voluntarism – decentered the modern subject by refuting any notion of agency in regard to individuals' ability to create their own meanings of self and surroundings. According to Saussure, since linguistic convention only exists 'by virtue of a sort of contract signed by the members of the community', the creation of meaning becomes a 'largely unconscious' act (1959: 14, 72) in which the individual plays little more than a reproductive role. So, as Coward and Ellis so succinctly expressed it, 'Lévi-Strauss's structuralism shows us that the human subject is not homogenous and in control of himself, he is constructed by a structure whose very existence escapes his gaze' (1981: 160).

Post-Structuralism

The events of May 1968 represent an important watershed in the political, economic, cultural, and intellectual history of postwar France. Fermenting student dissatisfaction with the systemic inequities that dominated de Gaulle's repressive bureaucratic regime erupted from the universities, and spread on to the streets of Paris. The center of Paris thus became the site of mass demonstrations, and numerous violent clashes between students and the police. As the popular agitation escalated, the student movement found willing allies among, and forged strategic alliances with, both the trade unions and teachers' organizations. This broad-based anti-establishment coalition called a general strike on 13 May, which within days was heeded by a sizeable proportion of France's working population. The nation was thus brought to a complete standstill. Significantly, many of France's professional élite – among them many actors, journalists, lawyers, physicians and musicians – also became actively involved in this popular unrest, by assisting in seizing control of the cultural institutions – including television, radio, newspapers – through which knowledge of current events was produced and circulated. Hence, 'What began as incidents of student unrest escalated into a broad-based revolt against French capitalism, Catholicism, and consumerism' (Seidman, 1994: 200).

Within weeks, de Gaulle's government engineered the collapse of the mass insurrection. Nevertheless, as well as creating a climate of instability within the nation in general, the whole demonstration of dissent stirred a sentiment that had been brewing for some time amongst certain factions of the French cultural intelligentsia; namely, that structuralism's rigid and ahistorical scientism was an inadequate theoretical framework for critically deciphering the complexities, contradictions and dynamism of life within modernizing France. Moreover, the events of May 1968 demonstrated the contingent and constructed nature of knowledge, and its manifestations within institutions and expressions of power. Within this highly politicized climate, structuralism's focus on establishing universal rules of linguistic and social order was viewed as virtual intellectual capitulation to, and thereby reproduction of, the contemporary French power structure. Structuralism's newly found untenability thus provided the impetus for the loose aggregation of a number of philosophically and theoretically aligned French intellectuals under the 'amorphous' (Denzin, 1991: 2) banner of post-structuralism, whose unifying feature was the generation of politically subversive knowledge concerned with identifying and nurturing difference, disunity and disorder within the oppressive formations of (French) modernity.

The intellectual journey of noted French semiologist Roland Barthes, from his enthusiastic appropriation of Saussurean linguistics in the classic *Mythologies* (1972) to his later focus on the fragmented and subjective aspects of reading in works such as *The Pleasure of the Text* (Barthes, 1975), provides a neat summation of the shift from structuralism to post-structuralism. Barthes is also an interesting figure for sport sociologists since, as evidenced by his analyses of wrestling (1972: 15–25) and the Tour de France (1979: 79–90), he was the only French (post-)structuralist to discuss sport in any sort of depth. Yet, in order to better fathom structuralism's metamorphosis into post-structuralism, at this juncture it would be more instructive to turn to the profoundly influential figure of Jacques Derrida. According to Docker (1994), post-structuralism's 'formative text' can be charted to a paper given in 1966 by Derrida entitled 'Structure, sign and play in the discourse of the human sciences' (Derrida, 1970). Within this noted 'and by now fetishized' (Radhakrishnan, 1990: 145) presentation, Derrida was expected to introduce structuralism to the American academy. In the event, he used influences from Heidegger,

Nietzsche and Freud, to weave a systematic and scathing critique of Lévi-Strauss's work in particular, which identified the need to go beyond, or *post*, structuralism.

Before taking this discussion any further, it should be noted that the prefix 'post', and particularly its usage within the term post-structuralism, should not be interpreted as a comprehensive and conclusive repudiation of structuralism. Rather, post-structuralism is 'not "post" in the sense of having killed structuralism off, it is "post" only in the sense of coming after and of seeking to extend structuralism in its rightful direction' (Sturrock, 1986: 137). Refining this point, it is evident that post-structuralism builds upon structuralism's Saussurean understanding and focus on the constitution of meaning, reality and subjectivity within language. For this reason, Weedon makes the crucial point that in 'this sense all poststructuralism is post-Saussurean' (1997: 22). Instead of delving into the intricacies of particular post-structuralist theories (which after all is the focus of the subsequent section), this discussion will concern itself with providing a broad outline of the post-Saussurean, and for that matter post-Lévi-Straussian, nature of the post-structuralist project.

Evidently, Derrida's post-structuralist proclamation, 'There is nothing outside of the text [there is no outside text; *il n'y a pas d' hors texte*]' (Derrida, 1976: 158), is derived from Saussure's recognition of the importance of discourse – in the Foucauldian (Foucault, 1974) sense of the term, subjectifying symbolic systems or productions of truth – in establishing the meanings that individuals attribute to themselves, others and their social surroundings. Harking back to the Saussurean roots of post-structuralism, Brown noted:

> Language, according to this perspective, does not *reflect* reality but actively *constitutes* it. The world, in other words, is not composed of meaningful entities to which language attaches names in a neutral and mimetic fashion. Language, rather, is involved in the construction of reality, the understandings that are derived from it, the sense that is made of it. (1995: 291)

Some critiques have misconstrued post-structuralism's linguistic focus as a denial of material existence itself. However, Derrida in particular, and post-structuralists in general, are not advocates of a transcendental solipsism laboring under the 'absurd delusion' that nothing *exists* 'outside the play of textual inscription' (Norris, 1987: 148–9). Since the meaning of the world is constituted through language, it is not that there is *nothing* outside of the text, rather post-structuralism is based on the assumption that there is nothing *meaningful* outside of the text. This is a crucial, if sometimes conveniently overlooked, distinction.

Despite evident influences, post-structuralists differ from Saussure in that they deny the existence of any stable relationship between the signifier and the signified. According to Saussure, although it is purely arbitrary, the connection between signifiers and signifieds' once established by the relatively inert conventions of the linguistic community, becomes virtually immediate, unitary and stable (Coward and Ellis, 1981): 'the statement that everything in language is negative is true only if the signified and the signifer are considered separately; when we consider the sign in its totality, we have something that is positive in its own class' (Saussure, 1959: 14, 120). Post-structuralist thought asserts the impossibility of a fixed and stable relationship between signifier and signified, and hence points to the necessary instability of the process of signification. Once again, this refinement was prompted by Derrida's seminal work. Foremost amongst post-structuralists, it was Derrida who demonstrated Saussure's failure to comprehend, or indeed develop, the full significance of his linguistic theorizing (Sturrock, 1986).

Derrida highlighted the incomplete nature of Saussure's understanding of difference through his invention of the term *différance*. Whilst 'neither a word nor a concept', Derrida's *différance* cleverly conflated the two meanings associated with the Latin verb *differre* (Derrida, 1982a: 7). It incorporated both the notion of to differ, 'to be not identical, to be other, discernible, etc.', and the concept of to defer, 'to temporize, to take recourse … a detour that suspends the accomplishment' (Derrida, 1982a: 8). Evidently, Saussure's notion of deriving meaning from phonic and conceptual difference leads Derrida to proclaim the necessary emptiness of language (the sign). Denying the existence of a fixed, immutable unity between signifiers and signifieds, Derrida viewed the meaning of the signified as deriving from the infinite 'play of differences which are generated by signifiers which are themselves the product of those differences' (Sarup, 1993: 44). The dynamism of the sign arises because 'The play of differences supposes, in effect, syntheses and referrals which forbid at any moment, or in any sense, that a simple element be *present* in and of itself, referring only to itself' (Derrida, 1981: 26). Turning to Eagleton in order to clarify and underline this pivotal aspect of post-structuralist thought:

Another way of putting what we have just said is that meaning is not immediately present in the sign. Since the meaning of a sign is a matter of what the sign is not, its meaning is always in some sense absent from it too. Meaning, if you like, is scattered or dispersed along the whole chain of signifiers; it cannot be easily nailed down, it is never fully present in any sign alone, but is rather a kind of constant flickering presence and absence together. Reading a text is more like tracing this process of constant flickering than it is like counting the beads on a necklace. (Eagleton, 1983: 128)

Within any sign there is the '"trace" of a now-absent reality or a trace of its former connections to other elements' (Grenz, 1996: 145). Thus, it is the interplay between presence and absence invoked by the notion of the 'trace' (Derrida, 1981) which explains how the signified is implicated in a never-ending chain of self-referential signifiers which leads to the perpetual deferral of meaning: the 'indefinite referral of signifier to signifier … gives the signified meaning no respite … it always signifies again' (Derrida, 1978: 25). In order to demonstrate the always inadequate, incomplete nature of the signified, Derrida (1976) utilized the Heideggerian strategy of putting a cross through words, thereby indicating that their meaning is always *sous rature* (under erasure).

The very impossibility of the 'transcendental signified' – a single, stable and universal meaning of a sign outside of language – 'extends the domain and the play of significations infinitely' (Derrida, 1978: 146). And yet, without wishing to detract from Derrida's assertions pointing to the emptiness and incompleteness of language, communication only works when the meaning of a sign is at least temporarily fixed, and furnished with a fleeting aura of permanence. This points to post-structuralism's concern with the necessarily political nature of language, meaning and knowledge. According to Seidman, 'whenever a linguistic and social order is said to be fixed or meanings are assumed to be unambiguous and stable, this should be understood as less a disclosure of truth than as an act of power' (1994: 202). While structuralism's scientism initiated a search for rational, objectively researched and universal linguistic knowledge, post-structuralism's scepticism sought to unearth its irrational, subjectively constructed and localized character. Thus, post-structuralism focused on illuminating:

the tensions within seeming truths, the difficulties involved even in seemingly ordinary understandings, the constant effort of construction involved in accepted truths, as well as the constant tendency of those truths to break down and reveal their internal inconsistencies and aporias. (Calhoun, 1995: 113–14)

Recognizing the constructed and contingent nature of discursive formations (in simple terms, what Bannet (1989) described as systems or regimes of interpretation) has had important ramifications for the post-structuralist understanding of the human subject. According to post-structuralists, the human subject is far from being stable, unified and whole. Rather, like the language through which it is constituted, the subject is necessarily unstable, disunited and fragmented (Hall, 1992b).

While decentering the sovereign individual (Locke, 1967) from its status as a 'bounded entity pristine and separate unto itself' (Kondo, 1995: 96), structuralism's universalism inadvertently replicated the 'humanist notion of an unchanging human nature' (Best and Kellner, 1991: 20). Post-structuralism 'radically problematized' (Grossberg and Nelson, 1988: 7) structuralism's implicit humanism, by advancing an understanding of the human subject as a dynamic and multi-accentual entity constituted 'within, not outside, discourse ... produced in specific historical and institutional sites within specific discursive formations and practices, by specific enunciative strategies' (Hall, 1996a: 4). As much as people are invested in being seen to uphold the modern myth of the essential, originary, fixed and guaranteed identity, the subject can more accurately be described as a strategic and unstable point of identification, or suture, to the conjuncturally specific forms of subjectivity, or subject positions, constructed for us within particular discursive contexts (Cole, 1993; Hall, 1990, 1995, 1996a; Kondo, 1995). As Hall eloquently described, the process of identification through which the subject is constructed is a strategic '"production", which is never complete, always in process, and always constituted within, not outside, representation' (Hall, 1990: 222).

Invoking Althusserian conceptualizing (1971) (admittedly more structural Marxist than post-structuralist, but a figure whose theorizing ably complements post-structuralism's focus on language and subjectivity), post-structuralism notoriously decentered the originary, unified and essential post-Cartesian subject (Hall and Gay, 1996). This was achieved by indicating how, instead of being the point of origin, the subject is in fact interpellated, or hailed, by the subject positions imbued within particular discursive formations. Despite the power of

discursive structures to define subjectivity and experience, post-structuralism does involve a sense of human agency, however overdetermined (Cole, 1994). Such is the 'psychological and emotional force' (Weedon, 1997: 31) of the subject positions embedded within popular discourse, that individuals routinely, and mistakenly, credit themselves as the authors of their discursively constructed subjectivities. Thus, the individual unconsciously assumes itself to be the source of the subjective meanings, and identities, of which it is merely an effect (Heath, 1981). Further emphasizing the contradictory nature of existence, the individual is the *subject* of the multitudinous discursive formations within late modernity, and *subjected* to these discursive regimes. For in shaping (or constituting) the individual's view of itself and the social world in which it is located, language provides the interpretive framework for both enabling and constraining the individual's experience of that world. Hence, by dint of its perpetual reconstitution in, and through, late modernity's shifting and multiple discursive formations, post-structuralism pointedly proclaims the precarious, constructed, contextual and processual nature of the subject (Hall, 1990, 1996a; Weedon, 1997).

POST-SPORT: RECONFIGURING THE FOCUS OF THE SOCIOLOGY OF SPORT

Post-structuralists offer new and challenging perspectives on the history of Western societies. Departing from liberal and Marxist social ideas which draw our attention to the economy, the state, organizational dynamics, and cultural values, they center social analysis on processes relating to the body, sexuality, identity, consumerism, medical-scientific discourses, the social role of the human sciences, and disciplinary technologies of control. (Seidman, 1994: 229)

It is interesting to note that of the post-structuralist concerns highlighted in the above quote, all have been addressed to varying degrees within the small body of post-structuralist orientated literature emanating from the sociology of sport. For instance, the body (Gruneau, 1991), sexuality (Miller, 1995), identity (Sykes, 1996), consumerism (Van Wynsberghe and Ritchie, 1998), medical-scientific discourses (Harvey and Sparks, 1991), human sciences (Whitson and MacIntosh, 1990), and disciplinary technologies (Cole and Denny, 1995), have all been addressed in sporting contexts by researchers with at least a passing affinity with, and interest in, the post-structuralist project. This sporting replication of research interests is by no means surprising, as post-structuralism's focus on the discourses, processes and institutions that shaped modernity, strongly encourages researchers into particular avenues of enquiry related to the relationship between modern knowledge, power and the constitution of subjectivity. Since sport is dialectically implicated in the discourses (progress, rationality, individualism) and processes (industrialization, urbanization, globalization) of modernity, it could be considered an explicitly modern institution. It would thus seem wholly appropriate for the sociology of sport to use post-structuralist thought as a vehicle for excavating the discursive formations, and allied subjectivities, of contemporary sport culture.

While by no means voluminous, both individually and collectively, the growing body of post-structuralist orientated literature within the sociology of sport interrogates the structure and experience of modern sport formations. Paraphrasing Judith Butler's (1993b) understanding of post-structuralism's implicit critique of modernity, these studies identify that the uncritical belief in the possibility of progress as expressed through the sporting modern simply cannot be upheld with the plausibility or conviction it once possessed. These critical works make 'accessible to sight' the 'not seen' (Derrida, 1976: 163) aspects of contemporary sport culture, and thereby illuminate the contradictions, corruptions and coercions that fester beneath the common-sense fetishizing of sport within the late modern era. In this respect, it could be argued that the focus and goal of a post-structuralist sociology of sport is, and indeed should be, *post-sport*. Not that the terrain of sport should be deserted altogether. Rather, post-structuralism compels researchers to problematize sport's implicit relation to the modern project; a brief which involves developing politically subversive readings of sport which seek to take it beyond – or post – the oppressive, symbolically violent and exclusionary vices of its modern incarnations.

Since time and space constraints prohibit a fully in-depth overview of Derrida's, Foucault's and Baudrillard's complex, extensive, yet frequently shifting bodies of work, I am forced to concentrate on highlighting the aspects of each theorist's work that are most pertinent to furthering contemporary sport criticism. With specific reference to sociology of sport studies that have appropriated, either singly or in combination, the work of these noted post-structuralists, I intend to demonstrate the relevance of: Derrida's grammatology for deconstructing the philosophical foundations of sporting modernity; Foucault's genealogy for excavating sport's status and influence as a modern disciplinary institution; and, Baudrillard's hyperreal cosmology for mapping sport's immersion within new regimes of representation. Each of these theorists provides important and provocative insights into developing understandings of sport as a contingent, contested and coercive discursive formation, whose popular presence significantly contributes to the constitution of the late modern subject. Thus, each of them has the potential to make important contributions to the advancement of the post-sport criticism to which I briefly alluded.

Jacques Derrida: the Discursive Logic of Modern Sport

Due to its evident complexity, it would seem an absurd task to even attempt to capture Derrida's work within the space of a few paragraphs. Nevertheless, even such a cursory discussion is long overdue. Since Derrida's ground-breaking works were published over 30 years ago, and since the wider reception of his writing has been through at least three distinct phases – those marked by enthusiasm and indifference, consolidation and adjustment, and finally productive yet critical engagement (Woods, 1992) – Derrida's writing unquestionably warrants a more considered airing within the sociology of sport community. Despite arguably being the leading instigator of the post-structuralist movement, Jacques Derrida's challenging work has been virtually ignored by sociology of sport researchers. Indeed, up to this point there have been less than a handful of sport-related studies which have utilized Derrida's important theoretical and methodological insights in any degree of depth. Such intellectual neglect has contributed to what is perhaps the most glaring theoretical absence within the sociology of sport. More important a motivation than even overcoming the intellectual lag that, for some reason, seems to haunt the sociology of sport, Derrida's deconstructive project continues to be of explicit relevance to the project of articulating modern sport's relation to the stultifying discourses of modernity. This is because, as well as being Derrida's main focus, the 'monological statements of truth' (Calhoun, 1995: 113) structuring Western philosophy, and indeed modern society, are graphically embodied and suggestively vindicated within the discursive economy of modern sport.

While Roland Barthes announced the 'death of the author' (Barthes, 1977) and, with equal deference to post-structuralist sensibilities related to textual instability, Foucault asked the pointed question 'What difference does it make who is speaking?' (Foucault, 1979: 160), embellishing discussions of theory with even the briefest biographical information would still seem an appealing – if perhaps inconsequential – exercise. To this end, Derrida was born in El Biar, Algiers, in 1930 (at the time Algeria was still a French *département*), into a lower middle-class Sephardic Jewish family. Having attained his baccalaureate in Algeria, Derrida subsequently moved to Paris to further his education. From 1952 to 1956 he studied philosophy at the École Normale Supérieure, where he became particularly interested in the work of Hegel, Heidegger and Husserl, and came into contact with the renowned Hegel scholar Jean Hippolite. Derrida subsequently taught philosophy at the Sorbonne from 1960 to 1964, followed by a more extended tenure at the École Normale Supérieure from 1964 to 1984, during which time he completed what are arguably his most significant works (see Derrida, 1973, 1976, 1978). As a result of his controversial and extensive scholarly output, Derrida became an important figure within French intellectual culture, and in 1984 was appointed to the prestigious position of Director of Studies at the École des Hautes Études en Science Sociales. Since the early 1970s Derrida also made regular teaching and lecturing trips to North America, especially to Yale University, the Johns Hopkins University and the University of California at Irvine. These trips inspired the 'Yale deconstruction' movement (headed by the controversial figure of the late Paul de Man) and secured for Derrida an important place within the American academy, such that Matthews commented 'his fame is even greater in the United States than in his own country' (1996: 166).

In other academic circles, the reception for Derrida's radical philosophy has been less welcoming. Nowhere is this better exemplified than in the much publicized 'Derrida affair' (*The Times*, 13 May 1992) that engulfed the normally sedate halls of Cambridge University in 1992. In March of that year, senior Cambridge faculty held their annual meeting in which they decide upon the recipients for that year's honorary degrees. Derrida's name had been put forward for this honor yet, breaking three decades of unopposed nominations, four professors objected so virulently that they forced a university ballot over his candidacy. The whole issue thus became the forum for a public debate over Derrida's work, and indeed post-structuralism in general. Probably the most aggressive indictment of Derrida came within a letter written to *The Times* by 19 members of the *Internationale Akademie für Philosophie*:

> M. Derrida's work does not meet accepted standards of clarity and rigour … M. Derrida's voluminous writings in our view stretch the normal forms of academic scholarship beyond recognition … Academic status based on what seems to be little more than semi-intelligible attacks upon the values of reason, truth and scholarship is not, we submit, sufficient grounds for the awarding of an honorary degree in a distinguished university. (Barry Smith et al., Letter to the Editor, *The Times*, 9 May 1992)

On 16 May the result of the university ballot supported Derrida's nomination for the honorary degree. Nevertheless, the anti-post-structuralist sentiments expressed throughout the 'Derrida affair', and illustrated in the above letter, would appear to have found support within many academic disciplines, including the sociology of sport. Derrida incites such defensiveness from many mainstream academics largely because his radical deconstructive project undermines the claims to foundational knowledge espoused by mainstream philosophy, and assumed as the epistemological and ontological basis of traditional academic disciplines. Turning Barry Smith et al.'s critique back on itself, Derrida's project blatantly delights in *stretching* the normal forms of *academic scholarship* beyond recognition, by *disrupting* the values of *reason* and *truth* championed by traditional scholars.

Within his '*general strategy of deconstruction*' (Derrida, 1981: 41), Derrida championed a 'vigilant scepticism' (Norris, 1987: 20) toward the binarism underpinning the Western tradition of rational thought (Boyne, 1990). As Brown neatly surmised, although it has emerged within 'popular parlance as a chic synonym for "criticism", "investigation" or "analysis", deconstruction is a procedure for interrogating texts, which, by means of careful and detailed reading, seeks to expose their inconsistencies, contradictions, unrecognized assumptions and implicit conceptual hierarchies' (Brown, 1994: 36–7). Deconstruction represents 'guerrilla warfare against the Enlightenment heritage' (Boyne, 1990: 90), because, influenced by Heidegger's reading of

Nietzsche, Derrida is centrally concerned with the politics and practice of subverting language, knowledge and truth. Nevertheless, Derrida affirmed the need to do more than invert binary hierarchies by substituting one pole of the binary for the other. Doing so would mean 'simply *residing* within the closed field of these oppositions, thereby confirming it' (Derrida, 1981: 41). According to Derrida:

> Deconstruction cannot limit itself or proceed immediately to a neutralization; it must, by means of a double gesture, a double writing, practice an *overturning* of the classical opposition *and* a general displacement of the system. It is only on this condition that deconstruction will provide itself the means with which to *intervene* in the field of oppositions that it criticizes. (Derrida, 1982b: 329; emphasis in original)

Derrida thus incorporates a new form of *parasitic* writing, requiring a *host* text which the *deconstructive* text inhabits and disrupts, leading to the explication of the contingent, unstable, dispersed and absent nature of any meaning (Brown, 1994). As an intellectual practice, deconstruction seeks to inhabit, resist and disorganize philosophical oppositions, by challenging them from the inside (Boyne, 1990; Derrida, 1981). For Derrida, the ultimate goal of deconstruction's textual interventions is to demonstrate 'the ultimate *undecidability*' and impossibility of the 'deep-laid conceptual oppositions' (Norris, 1987: 82) which constitute the basis of Western thought. To this end, he encouraged the following points of textual inhabitation and engagement.

Derrida identified that the Western philosophic tradition is based upon the logic of logocentrism, which asserted that objective, centered and universal knowledge (logos) pertaining to the empirical world exists prior to – yet can be identified and potentially expressed through – language. As Cobley put it, traditional thought has 'unwittingly reconstructed referential modes in which the signifier operates, but it does so purely for the purposes of referring to a self-contained preexisting "concept" which exists independently of signification' (1996: 206). The dominant strands of Western philosophy were prefigured on a binary opposition between reality and myth, which posited language's ability to articulate, against its potential for distorting, the objective reality which was thought to exist outside consciousness: philosophy being the faithful representation of this reality, mythology being its deceptive corruption. Derrida attacked this logocentrism by denying the possibility of some '"word" presence, essence,

truth, or reality' serving as the authentic foundation for 'thought, language, and experience' (Grenz, 1996: 141–2). In other words, Derrida asserted the impossibility of any foundational, originary or essential 'transcendental signifieds' (Derrida, 1978) as the basis of Western rational thought.

Closely allied to logocentrism, which Grossberg cited as being 'constitutive of modernity' (1996: 94), is the phonocentric prejudice within modern Western philosophy. Phonocentrism refers to the privileging of the phonic (the temporal substance of speech) over the graphic (the spatial substance of writing), as the medium of true expression. Phonemes, or spoken phrases, are viewed as being pure representations of thought and consciousness, whereas graphemes, or written phrases, are less immediate, derivations and corrupted forms of speech. According to thinkers ranging from Aristotle, through Rousseau, to Saussure, speech is closer to psychic interiority, as it is a more direct, natural, sincere form of articulation, and thus a transparent expression of inner truth (Sarup, 1993). Phonocentrism is a foundation of modern notions of the fully centered, authorial human subject, for it reaffirms the 'metaphysics of presence' (Derrida, 1976), which asserts that individual consciousness is immediately and faithfully present in speech:

> The perfection of such a language would be marked by its utter transparency. It would in no way obscure or distort the world which it represented. The dream, then, is one of language and one world perfectly attuned. The world represented by the language, unobscured by the language, would be perfectly *present* to the observing subject, who could then *speak* of what was seen. (Boyne, 1990: 91)

Phonocentrism is thus an ally of Western philosophy's logocentrism, for it is through speech that the 'self-presence of full self-consciousness' (Sarup, 1993: 36) articulates the logos of universal and foundational knowledge.

Derrida undermined the phonocentric privileging of speech, by highlighting the 'strange economy of the supplement' (Derrida, 1976: 154) at work within binary oppositions such as that of speech and writing. According to Derrida, the word supplement refers to acts of addition and replacement. In Rousseau's terms, writing is a 'dangerous supplement' (Derrida, 1976: 144) to speech, because it is both an addition to, and replacement for, the originary consciousness expressed within speech. Hence, the speech/writing binary is hierarchically ordered between the natural presence of the phoneme, and the artificial presence of the grapheme. Confounding Rousseau, Derrida argues that 'the infinite process of supplementarity has always already *infiltrated* presence, always already inscribed there the space of repetition and the splitting of the self' (Derrida, 1976: 163). Far from speech being originary, and writing derivative, both are supplements: traces of each inhabit the other, which is 'ultimately dependent on the absent other for its own presence and meaning' (Storey, 1993: 87).

As with the speech/writing binary, the other oppositions which structure Western thought (such as reality/myth, presence/absence, nature/culture, good/evil, sacred/profane, masculine/feminine) are based on a 'violent hierarchy' (Derrida, 1981: 41) in which the first term is privileged, and the second term is subordinate and therefore inferior to it. Derrida demonstrates how binary structures rely on supplementarity for their very existence, thus forbidding the possibility that any element is a unitary presence which refers to itself alone (Derrida, 1981). No element of a binary opposition is ever fully present or absent, they are both present and absent at one and the same time. This point prompted Derrida's commentary on Rousseau, 'who *declares* what he *wishes to say*' while he simultaneously *'describes* that which he *does not wish to say*' (Derrida, 1976: 229, emphasis in original). Rather than exhibiting the universal truth of foundational knowledge, the hierarchically ordered binary oppositions, underpinning Western thought, science and culture, strategically naturalize modern power relations, by including, valuing and avowing certain terms and positions, while simultaneously excluding, devaluing and disavowing others (Best and Kellner, 1991; Docker, 1994). As Hollinger concluded, 'what is privileged, what is present, depends on the absent other that it seeks to dominate and erase' (1994: 110).

Turning to Derrida's negligible *presence* within the sociology of sport. Although a self-confessed 'card carrying Foucauldian' (Cole, 1997), within her recent work Cheryl Cole has engaged Derrida's oeuvre in a uniquely informed and informative manner. While Cole's (1998) broad-ranging discussion of deviance and the (re)territorialization of exercising/sporting bodies, incorporates an invigorating theoretical synthesis of Derrida, Michel Foucault and Eve Sedgwick, her appropriation of Derridean deconstruction proves to be of most relevance to this discussion. Rigorously contextualizing the discussion within contemporary American popular cultural politics, Cole unearthed the 'naturalistic metaphysics'

(p. 272) present within the discursive logics of exercise and sport. In true deconstructionist fashion and 'in order to unravel it or to show how it unravels itself from within', Cole inhabited, resisted and disorganized, the *new* deviant subject position of the exercise addict (p. 266). On a superficial level, the 'discourse of addiction is one that continually reasserts and reinvents the natural', by policing the boundary between the natural and the un-natural, between the pure and the corrupt, and most crucially, between free will and compulsion (p. 268). However, Cole identified the impossibility of the exercise addict being an originary or essential entity, by indicating how this subject position inhabits, and is constituted by, both poles of the aforementioned binaries, the insides of which are always already 'contaminated by their outside' (p. 272). Moreover, the subject addicted to exercise displays a complex and seemingly contradictory relation to the free will/compulsion binary. For, the exercise addict 'is addicted to the idea of free subjectivity, addicted to the repeated act of freely choosing health – that act which is supposed to be anti-addiction' (p. 271). Cole's deconstruction of the exercise addict thus pointed to the supplementary, unstable and contradictory disposition – in other words the failure – of modern rational subjectivities and thought.

Cole also pointed to sport's status as a context for amplifying 'the crisis of the natural', particularly as it equates to 'the presumed naturalness of the body (the persistent elision of the technological condition)' (1998: 271). Derrida confounded the opposition between natural and un-natural bodily states, engaged within debates surrounding the artificial enhancement of bodies through prosthetic devices. According to Derrida (1993: 17), these challenges to common understandings of the body emerge in 'discourses on the subject of, for instance, artificial insemination, sperm banks, the market for surrogate mothers, organ transplants, euthanasia, sex changes, the use of drugs in sport, and especially, especially on the subject of AIDS' (quoted in Cole, 1998: 265). Derrida indicates how the rhetorical strategy involved within these emotive discourses presumes the existence of a natural, originary, organic body, which is somehow corrupted by prosthetic engineering. Using Derrida's insights as a starting point, Cole questions the taken-for-granted assumption of sport's status as a natural 'zone of authentic work', and an appropriate vehicle for the organic and pure body (p. 271). By being articulated as 'the anti-drug', *pure* sport is positioned in opposition to sporting practices and bodies *artificially* enhanced by 'chemical prosthetics' (pp. 271, 270). The use of drugs in sport is criminalized, because it threatens the assumed '"natural" normality of the body, of the body politic and the body of the individual member' (Derrida, 1993: 14, quoted in Cole, 1998: 269). However, in seeking to 'discern, render visible, and measure the natural and the foreign, the pure and the impure', drug-testing regimes that classify what is – and what is not – a drug, continually destabilize and reinvent understandings of nature and the natural (Cole, 1998: 272). Consequently, as Cole indicates, any conceptualizing of the natural body is hopelessly outmoded, for, as well as notions of the natural always being contaminated by those of the un-natural, the natural/un-natural binary is in a perpetual state of flux. Instead of pointing toward the corruption of the natural sporting body, the 'scopic regime of drug-testing' which 'attempts to discern, render visible, and measure the natural and the foreign, the pure and the impure' is founded on, and advances, a 'politics of and nostalgia for an organic corporeality and the moral valuations inscribed through its diagnostics' (pp. 272, 273).

Within her intriguingly titled chapter 'Viktor Petrenko's mother-in-law', and framed by Derrida's reflection on 'What is a pair?' (1987: 259), Marjorie Garber offered an interesting stratagem for deconstructing the sexual and gender politics at play within ice skating. Whilst Derrida's question was prompted by a pair of shoes represented in a series of Van Gogh paintings, Garber's (1995) focus is answering the question 'What is a pair?' in relation to the highly mediated world of figure skating. Different-sex ice skating couples advance an assumed complementarity between, and correspondence of, the oppositional elements (male/female) which comprise the pairing. They are 'pairs' which '[complete] the set' and reassuringly, if presumptuously, leave 'no excess, no supplement, no fetish' with regard to the sexual orientation of the respective elements of the pairing (1995: 100). Predictably, therefore, the narration of conventional pairs figure skating has become 'the cultural story of the heterosexual romance' (Garber, 1995: 98). Conversely, same-sex ice skating couples represent a 'double which does not make a pair' (Garber, 1995: 100). The perceived similarity, and lack of symbolic correspondence, between their two parts (male/male, or female/female), precludes such couples from acting 'as one' (Garber, 1995: 101). Same-sex couples are thus unable to provide the 'reassurance' of a privileged heterosexuality, and seemingly point to the

'"problem" of homosexuality' (Garber, 1995: 100, 98). In inventive fashion, Garber identifies 'Nancy and Tonya' as a same-sex skating dyad, thrown together by the crass machinations of the popular press. In contrast with other examples, however, this same-sex couplet was based upon regressive intra-gender differences, as opposed to threatening sexual similarities. Hence, the Nancy and Tonya pairings were differentiated by oppositions (nasty/nice, sweetheart/bitch, virgin/whore, daughter/loner, butch/femme) which graphically dichotomized women, with the intent of keeping them 'in their place'. In this respect, they *were* a pair, after all, to everyone but each other' (Garber, 1995: 102).

Lastly, and albeit to a lesser extent, Derrida has also informed research related to the dynamic representation of race and racial difference within popular sport culture. Cheryl Cole and David Andrews (1996) invoked Derrida when illustrating how the boundaries between binary terms are constantly transgressed, and thus require constant policing if they are to be maintained:

> Because deconstructionists emphasize the transgression always taking place at the border, deconstruction examines the force relations between the terms: the constant exertion of pressures at their boundaries, the policing required to maintain those boundaries, the incompleteness of the category of the will and the violence that it does. (Cole and Andrews, 1996: 152)

Focusing on two prominent African American NBA basketball players, Magic Johnson and Michael Jordan, Cole and Andrews indicated how their mediated identities became sites for the reinvention of the '*what* and *who* categories which organize the racial imagination' (Cole and Andrews, 1996: 154). As carefully constructed African American superstars, Johnson and Jordan occupied discursive spaces which distanced themselves from – and in doing so reinforced – the stereotypical images and embodiments of a threatening black masculinity which inhabit the American imaginary. Evidencing the Derridean notion of supplementarity, their (Johnson and Jordan) identities were 'never simply self-identical or self-contained' but were dependent upon the absent other that they sought to dominate and erase (Cole and Andrews, 1996: 152). Cole and Andrews explicated how both Johnson and Jordan subsequently transgressed the racial boundaries which their previously virtuous images had helped to maintain. The disclosure of Johnson's HIV-positive status made acutely evident his sexuality, whilst coverage of

Jordan's gambling exploits revealed an apparently compulsive persona, both of which rendered visible that from which they were previously distanced – the pathologized and demonized bodies of African American racial others. Furthering one aspect of this analysis, Andrews (1996) flirted with Derridean theorizing whilst problematizing the very notion of Michael Jordan's blackness. Andrews identified Jordan as a *floating* and unstable racial signifier that, within its various manifestions, seductively reproduced the violent racial hierarchy of the evolving American cultural formation.

Michel Foucault: the Disciplinary Formation of Modern Sport

Michel Foucault was once described as 'the single most famous intellectual in the world' (Miller, 1993: 13). Certainly, of all French poststructuralists, Foucault's is the theorizing most evident within sociology of sport research. Indeed, at the time of writing, the poststructuralist presence within the sociology of sport could be described as being *primarily Foucauldian*. In contrast to the apparent disregard for things Derridean, and the widespread disdain for things Baudrillardian, the work of Foucault has been widely and enthusiastically embraced by numerous researchers interested in examining varied aspects of the modern sport problematic. While Derrida's discomforting absence is somewhat perplexing, Foucault's healthy presence is more easily attributable. Since the body constitutes the material core and most redolent expression of sporting activity (Hargreaves, 1987), and since much of Foucault's research keyed on explicating how the growth of systematic modern knowledges coincided with the expansion of power relations into the realm of controlling bodily practices and existence (Turner, 1982), it is clear to see how Foucault's understanding of 'the discourses of discipline and pleasure that surround the body in modern societies has much to offer students of sport' (Whitson, 1989: 62). Indeed, the noted French Marxist Jean-Marie Brohm, even designated sport as 'perhaps the social practice which best exemplifies the "disciplinary society", analysed by M. Foucault' (1978: 18). Rather than addressing Foucault's scholarly output in its expansive entirety, and following Whitson and Brohm's implied directives, this discussion is limited to the aspects most germane to the study of modern sport culture: namely, Foucault's later genealogical approach to modern disciplinary knowledge, subjectivity and society developed within his 'masterpiece' (Sarup, 1993: 67) *Discipline and Punish: the Birth of the Prison* (1977a) and furthered within the *History of Sexuality* trilogy (1988a, 1988b, 1988c).

Paul-Michel Foucault (he dropped the Paul in later years) was born in Poitiers in 1926. His father and both his grandfathers had been surgeons in the French provincial city. Although disappointing his father by not following in the family's professional footsteps, and while enduring periods of academic failure, the young Paul-Michel ultimately excelled at school by coming fourth in the nationwide university entrance exam for the prestigious École Normale Supérieure in Paris. Once at university Foucault suffered bouts of severe depression, allegedly linked to his homosexuality, which prompted his father to arrange for him to visit a psychiatrist. As a result of these visits, Foucault became highly skeptical of the role and influence of psychiatrists, and equally motivated to study psychology himself. To this end, he received his Licence de Philosophie and Licence de Psychologie from the Sorbonne in 1948 and 1950 respectively. In 1952 he was awarded his Diplôme de Psycho-Pathologie from the Université de Paris. Between 1951 and 1955 Foucault lectured at the École Normale Supérieure, until taking up a brief appointment lecturing French at the University of Uppsala in Sweden. While at Uppsala, Foucault took advantage of the university's extensive medical history library, where he carried out much of the research for his first two major works, an examination of madness (Foucault, 1973a) and an examination of the clinic (Foucault, 1975).

After a five-year stint living and teaching in Sweden, Poland, and Germany, in 1960 Foucault returned to France to take up the position of director of the Institut de Philosophie at the Faculté des Lettres in Clermont Ferrand. In this position, Foucault finalized his archaeological approach (Foucault, 1973b, 1974) to the history of ideas which 'attempts to identify the conditions of possibility of knowledge, the determining rules of formation of discursive rationality that operate beneath the level of intention or thematic content' (Best and Kellner, 1991: 40). From this juncture, Foucault embarked on an inexorable rise to academic superstardom, which was confirmed by his election to the chair of 'History of Systems of Thought' at the Collège de France in 1970. The original publication of *Discipline and Punish* in 1975 marked Foucault's shift from an archaeological to a more conjuncturally based genealogical approach focused on 'the mutual relations between systems of truth and modalities of power, the way in which there is a "political regime" of the production of truth' (Davidson, 1986: 224). The final phase of Foucault's intellectual project was envisioned as a six-volume genealogy of modern sexuality, focusing on the politics of pleasure and the self. This grand design was brought to a halt by Foucault's untimely death from AIDS in 1984, by which time only the first of the volumes had been published (Foucault, 1988a) leaving two others to be posthumously released (Foucault, 1988b, 1988c).

Despite sharing Derrida's neo-Nietzschean interest in the relationship between language, knowledge and truth, Foucault offers a markedly different approach toward deciphering this fundamental post-structuralist problematic. Derrida even took Foucault to task for the way in which the rhetorical structure of his *Madness and Civilization* (Foucault, 1973a) reinforced the violence of the reason/madness binary: 'How could Foucault capture the spirit of madness when he was so obviously writing from the viewpoint of reason' (Derrida, 1978: 34). Although failing to openly acknowledge this critique, following it, there was a noticeable shift in Foucault's work to 'an engagement with the thickness and duplicity of this world, an engagement which is less obviously tainted by the search for an origin' (Boyne, 1990: 108). Foucault subsequently became a '"specific intellectual" as opposed to the "universal" intellectual' (Foucault, 1977b: 12), evermore motivated by a desire 'not to formulate the global systematic theory which holds everything in place, but to analyse the specificity of mechanisms of power, to locate the connections and extensions, to build little by little a strategic knowledge' (Foucault, 1980c: 83).

For his own part, Foucault criticized Derrida's abstracted philosophical reflections in favour of an approach that 'reasserts the primacy of the social real' (Boyne, 1990: 108). As 'first and foremost, an analyst of modernity, indeed early modernity' (Calhoun, 1995: 107), Foucault's critical historical analyses concretized, or empirically substantiated, the ways in which modern discursive formations act to both enable and constrain the everyday lives of human subjects. Not that Foucault furthered the teleological and rationalist idealism of Enlightenment history, rather his approach was focused on identifying historical ruptures and discontinuities (Young, 1990). Perhaps the most significant historical fissure identified by Foucault was that between the highly visible *externalized* practice of pre-modern power, and the anonymous *internalized* practice of modern

power which ultimately replaced it. Foucault (1977a) famously expressed this discontinuity as a contrast between the public displays of authority embroiled within the practice of pre-modern ritualized execution, and the discrete individualizing mechanisms of control associated with modern disciplinary institutions. As Boyne succinctly noted, 'discipline is the precise reverse of the spectacle' (1990: 114).

Although focused on the 'birth of the prison', *Discipline and Punish* (Foucault, 1977a) represents an important Foucauldian introduction to the 'political anatomy' (Smart, 1985: 90) of modern society. Concretizing his earlier archaeological design (Foucault, 1973b, 1974), *Discipline and Punish* demonstrated that the historical analysis of modern existence should not revolve around an understanding of the knowing subject, but should rather center on an historically grounded theory of discursive practice. Foucault's aim was to thematize the operations of the bio-power which, in discursively dissecting the body, rendered the modern individual both the object and subject of disciplinary knowledge. In broad terms, this genealogical approach illustrated how scientific, rational and implicitly modern discourses of the human body (for example, criminology, penology, psychology, psychiatry, economics and demography) emerged from within, and provided the philosophical and organizational bases for the carceral network of modern disciplinary institutions (for example, prisons, factories, schools and hospitals) which expedited the rise of industrial capitalism. Foucault's concern with the repressive character of modernity involved disentangling the 'arbitrary construction of the subject as a disciplinary ploy, and the inescapable mutual imbrication of power and knowledge' (Calhoun, 1995: 107).

In order to explicate how individual subjects became constituted as correlative elements of bio-power and knowledge, Foucault famously turned his attention to Jeremy Bentham's 1791 design for the modern prison, known as the Panopticon. Indeed, for Foucault, such was the exemplary nature of the Panopticon that he characterized modern society as 'an indefinitely generalizable mechanism of "panopticism"' (Foucault, 1977a: 216). Derived from the Greek *pan* (all) and *optos* (visible), the word Panopticon ably described the form and function of a structure designed for the normalization, through surveillance, of its incarcerated populace. Disciplinary institutions, such as the Panopticon, were centered around regimes of measured, corrective and continuous corporal training, designed to facilitate the controlled manufacturing of suitably docile bodies. Less a mechanism of overt repression, modern disciplinary power was primarily a force of normalization (McNay, 1994). More than merely training the human body, modern bio-power was prefigured on 'a design of subtle coercion' over the human soul (Foucault, 1977a: 209). The medical-scientific technologies of the body, formulated, circulated and instantiated through the corrective regimes of disciplinary institutions, generated normative models of human behaviour and identity. With the spread of these discursive fields of comparison (Foucault, 1977a), individuals were objectified in such a way that they became conscious of themselves, and were thus in a position to constitute themselves as social subjects, only in relation to this *'new and mythical presence of the norm'* (Boyne, 1990: 113; emphasis in original).

While its discursively based disciplinary regimen sought to compare, differentiate and hierarchically order penal subjects, the effective operation of the Panopticon's normalizing technology depended upon its revolutionary structural design. Bentham's model consisted of a central observation tower, replete with Venetian blinds on the windows, and surrounded by a circle of inward facing and perpetually observable cells. The architecture of the Panopticon ensured that power and authority were visible (prisoners could not avoid the imposing presence of the observation tower) yet unverifiable (prisoners could never be sure that they were *not* being observed). The omnipresent, yet anonymous, gaze of the Panopticon's hierarchical observer manufactured a state of constant anxiety amongst prisoners, who were psychologically coerced by the ever-present threat of normalizing judgement, assessment and/or examination. Since it demanded an unquestioned obedience to the corporal norms of the prison's meticulously rehearsed daily regimen, the experience of constant surveillance proved an effective 'guarantee of order' (Foucault, 1977a: 200):

> He who is subjected to a field of visibility, and who knows it, assumes responsibility for the constraints of power; he makes them play spontaneously upon himself; he inscribes in himself the power relation in which he simultaneously plays both roles: he becomes the principle of his own subjection. (Foucault, 1977a: 202–3)

Illustrating the internalized 'penality of the norm' (Foucault, 1977a: 183), the incarcerated subjects of surveillance were the principal regulators of their own existence, and prompted Foucault's famous aphorism that 'discipline "makes" individuals; it is the specific technique of power that regards individuals as objects and instruments of its exercise' (1977a: 170).

Foucault's dissection of the Panopticon is important since it illustrated the apparatus and arrangements of disciplinary power at work within various modern institutional spaces, 'penitentiaries, certainly, but also schools, hospitals, military centres, psychiatric institutions, administrative apparatuses, bureaucratic agencies, police forces, and so on' (McHoul and Grace, 1995: 66). However, Foucault's critique of modern power relations was considerably more broad-ranging, since the practice of normalizing corporal existence through the Panoptic gaze soon spread into 'non-institutional spaces and populations' (Smart, 1985: 89). The spread of bio-scientific discourses within the wider society has contributed to a situation wherein the human subject has become constituted, and controlled, by a normalizing 'conscience of self-knowledge' relating to every facet of individual existence (Foucault, 1982: 212). Illustrating this discursive understanding of the process of subjectification, Foucault's extended genealogy of sexuality (Foucault, 1988a, 1988b, 1988c) demonstrated how the spread of bio-power in the modern era was responsible for creating, and policing the boundaries between, what became considered as normal and abnormal sexual identities, practices and desires. As Foucault concluded, the swarming of modern disciplinary mechanisms and practices of surveillance 'from the closed fortresses in which they once functioned', to their circulation 'in a "free" state', has led to the emergence of 'panopticisms of every day' (Foucault, 1977a: 211, 223).

Despite at one time being castigated for its relative absence within the field (Andrews, 1993), in recent times Foucauldian-influenced sport research has become somewhat of a growth area. There have been two overviews of Foucault's oeuvre and its applicability for researchers within the sociology of sport (Andrews, 1993; Rail and Harvey, 1995), both of which provide more detailed explications of Foucault's theorizing than is possible within the constraints of the present project. Rail and Harvey's (1995) article is additionally important in two ways. First, it brings to the fore numerous Foucauldian studies of sport by Francophone scholars, many of which have been virtually disregarded due to the Anglocentric nature of the wider sociology of sport community. Secondly, it represents the most comprehensive presentation of works that have applied Foucault's theoretical framework to the analysis of either sport or physical education. Rail and Harvey's discussion is also useful since it grouped sociology of sport research directly influenced by Foucauldian theory into four substantive clusters: studies that made appeals to the sociology of sport community to engage Foucault's work (for example, Cole, 1993; Theberge, 1991; Whitson, 1989); studies that engaged Foucault's early archaeological approach to epistemic understanding (for example, Clément, 1993; Defrance, 1987; Loudcher, 1994); studies that embraced aspects of Foucault's Panoptic model of modern disciplinary society (for example, Cole and Denny, 1995; King, 1993; Vigarello, 1978); and, studies more directly influenced by Foucault's later work on the technologies of the self (for example, Boudreau et al., 1992; Heikkala, 1993).

Rather than merely summarizing their findings, this discussion concentrates on reviewing a selection of the most significant Foucauldian studies published since – or in one case (Duncan, 1994) not included within – Rail and Harvey's informative piece. Cole and Orlie (1995) provide a brief, yet illuminating, Foucauldian epistemic diagnosis of sport as a prominent modern technology. According to their analysis, sport is imagined as a site at which particular modern bio-knowledges and practices

> converge in, produce, and regulate so-called athletic bodies. The athletic body is a body through which particular claims are made: it is a body whose symbolic purchase accrues most obviously around the categories health, discipline, and productivity. Sport, then, can be more usefully understood as the site where apparatuses produce, control, and regulate bodies under the guise of protecting a space that displays the pure body and the proficiencies of its will. (Cole and Orlie, 1995: 229)

Sport is thus implicated as an optic of modern disciplinary power: a mechanism of surveillance which renders visible and intelligible the normal body, and the abnormal body against which the norm is constituted. Influenced by Foucault's notion of 'substantive geographies' (Philo, 1992), John Bale's (1992, 1993, 1994) ground-breaking work in the area of sports geography examined the relationship between sport, space and power. Bale (1994) drew attention to the similarity between the modern evolution of sport and punishment, both of which were relocated from corporal/public to carceral/private spaces. As Bale noted, 'The sports place, therefore, has changed from being one of open, public space to one of segmented and panopticised confinement' (1994: 84). The

panopticism of the modern sport space is succinctly captured within Robert Rinehart's (1998) engaging description of the swimming pool as a mechanism of surveillance, focused on the bodies of the swimmers who execute their repetitious training regimen within it. As Rinehart noted, the individuating and normalizing horizontal panopticism of the swimming pool turned it into a site of 'hundreds of tiny theatres of punishment' (Foucault, 1977a: 113, quoted in Rinehart, 1998: 42).

The opening section of Toby Miller's intriguingly titled article 'A short history of the penis' (1995: 2–8) also represents a useful Foucauldian precis of modern sport as a derivative of institutional and discursive power, particularly as it relates to the formulation and circulation of gendered public knowledges and truths. Miller broadly anchors the institutionalization of physical education, exercise, health and contemporary sport forms within the context of industrial and social modernity. According to Miller, these varied manifestations of modern physical culture were linked by a common political objective regarding the governance of the male sporting body, 'rendering it efficient, aesthetic, and self-monitoring' and the 'standard currency of sporting discourse' (Miller, 1995: 3, 2). Ably complementing Miller's article, Brian Pronger (1995) draws heavily from Foucault's work in his explication of the way 'gross anatomy' courses contribute to the discursive and politically charged technologization of the human body as a productive machine of late modern consumer capitalism. Pronger graphically demonstrates how scientific-medical knowledges of the body informed the production, and ultimately the practice, of physical education, sport, exercise and health professionals. The bio-discursive objectification of the human form rendered the *normal* (that is, productive) sporting, exercising, or healthy body an oppressive yet seductive 'instrument in the project of technological modernity' (Pronger, 1995: 435). Shifting to a more culturally grounded focus, Susan Brownell (1995) fashioned an imaginative synthesis of Foucauldian and Eliasian theorizing, during the course of her analysis of the power relations linking sport to national, class and gender formations within modernizing China. Within the popular discourses of the body promulgated by the state institutions of the People's Republic – of which sport was perhaps the most redolent expression – Brownell discerned a complex and dynamic fusion of the Chinese versions of discipline (*jilü*) and civilization (*wenming*). As a consequence, Brownell argued that Foucault's understanding of discipline and Elias's concept of the civilizing process 'complement each other and offer comparative insights into the nature of Chinese state power' (Brownell, 1995: 26), and its influence upon shaping popular discourse through sport.

Although Foucault has been roundly criticized for disregarding the oppressed and subordinated experiences and conditions of women (cf. Hartsock, 1993; Ramazanoglu, 1993; Sawicki, 1991), his critical appropriation by post-structuralist feminists has generated some of the most vibrant and incisive work related to the cultural politics of gender and sex (cf. Bordo, 1989, 1993a, 1993b; Butler, 1989, 1990, 1993a). This trend is equally evident within the sociology of sport, where Foucauldian theoretical imperatives have been extensively appropriated as a means of critically dissecting the sporting body as an important locus of control in the discursive constitution of gendered and sexed norms, practices and identities (Theberge, 1991). Margaret Duncan (1994) analysed the politics of women's body images within two issues of *Shape* magazine (a fitness-oriented magazine targeted at the female market). In pinpointing explicitly gendered bio-discourses that unproblematically reified individual will and responsibility, and implicitly valorized the aesthetic – as opposed to health-deriving – benefits of exercise, Duncan graphically portrayed how *Shape* acted as a panoptic mechanism in the true Foucauldian meaning of the concept. Duncan demonstrated how the circulation of public discourses pertaining to the *preferred* shape of the female body, became complicit in *shaping* private experiences of female subordination. In a comparable panoptic vein, MacNeill (1998: 170) cast the iconic celebrity bodies, which front celebrity fitness videos, as 'an economically and politically useful site for exerting power and for the embodiment of the "scientific" knowledges s/he espouses'. Similarly, Cole and Hribar's (1995) broadranging disassemblage of Nike's calculated mobilization of the postfeminist body within the promotional culture of late modern America, faithfully invoked Foucault's understanding of the normalizing epistemic regimes that pervade modern society.

Moving from the media spectacles to the material experience of female sport culture, Markula's (1995) engaging ethnography grounded Foucauldian theorizing within the experiences of female aerobicizers. Acknowledging the panoptic power arrangements at work within the cultural space of aerobics, Markula asserted the ambivalence of women who, while wishing to conform to the idealized female body shape, perceived its actualization to be a wholly 'ridiculous' proposition (1995: 450). In this way, Markula asserted that the pervasiveness of power within disciplinary society does 'not mean one is trapped and condemned to defeat no matter what' (Foucault, 1980b: 141–2). Instead, Markula's skeptical aerobicizers vindicated Foucault's notion of discursive power as an inalienable *producer* of resistance, since the very constitution of normalizing bio-power provides the means whereby it may be resisted (Dumm, 1996). Synthesizing Foucauldian theorizing and feminist cultural studies, Gwen E. Chapman (1997) studied the practice of 'making weight' amongst a women's lightweight rowing team. Her analysis illustrated how extreme regimes of physical activity, coupled with stringent controls of food intake, acted as a disciplinary mechanism for mobilizing broader technologies of femininity within the context of women's rowing. Chapman also used the experience of female rowers to invoke the later Foucault's (1988d, 1996) understanding of the contradictory relations between freedom and constraint, involved in the active experience of constituting the self. For, as Chapman concluded, 'At the same time that sport offers women discursive tools to oppose oppressive power relations, it also further enmeshes them in normalizing discourses that limit their vision of who and what they can be' (1997: 221). Through reference to Foucault's (1980a) narration of the tragic experience of Herculine Barbin, a mid-nineteenth-century hermaphrodite, Hood-Williams vilified the sex testing procedures of the International Olympic Committee (IOC) for habitually trying 'to distinguish, to differentiate, to discover the true sex' (1995: 297). According to Hood-Williams, the IOC's dogmatic adherence to a dimorphic model of sex-typing is founded in the populist desire to corroborate traditional and natural gender divisions and identities, and obscures the fact that far from being fixed, natural and biologically based, 'sex is no less a discursive construct than gender' (1995: 291).

Strangely, in recent times Foucault has been largely neglected by the growing band of productive scholars interested in examining the relationship between sport and the male/masculine form. This oversight would appear destined to be rectified, as Foucauldian theorizing offers blatantly fruitful strategies for challenging the blithe, uncritical celebration of sport's status as a *natural* male domain, by problematizing the mutually constitutive discursive linkage between sport and masculinity.

Foucault has influenced research focused on
the intersections between race and masculinity
within contemporary sport culture. John M.
Sloop's dissection of the dominant cultural discourses which enveloped Mike Tyson's trial for
the rape of Desiree Washington, brazenly
emerged 'in the interstices of Foucault's
archaeological and genealogical methods'
(Sloop, 1997: 105). Following Foucault, Sloop
sought to decipher the discursive rules,
regimes of truth and social conventions
through which Tyson was 'positioned rhetori-
cally' in relation to the customarily pejorative
signifiers 'boxer' and 'African American'
(Sloop, 1997: 107). Regardless of his innocence
or guilt (which obviously had not been ascertained during the build-up to, or the unfolding
of, the trial), Tyson's discursively demonized
subject position cast him as representing the
type of person whose guilt would be viewed as
being 'highly feasible, indeed probable' by the
majority of the American viewing public. As
well as being influenced by the sedimented
manifestations of cultural meaning, the mediated dialogue surrounding the Tyson trial has
clearly come to influence the way we 'frame
our cultural understanding of future actors
walking onto the stage' (Sloop, 1997: 119).
Lastly, within her cogent interrogation of
Michael Jordan's position within the contemporary American imaginary, Cheryl Cole
(1996) blended a Foucauldian approach to
modern disciplinary power, identity and the
body with a Derridean comprehension of sov-
ereignty and presence. Cole (1996) demonstrated how the commercially crafted
'American Jordan' was both a product, and
producer, of the discursive knowledges that
governed the popular American imagination.
Jordan's iconic status as part of the American
national fantasy (Berlant, 1991) was produced
and stabilized in opposition to the 'location,
containment and visualization of the deviant'
(Cole, 1996: 373) urban African American
youth. Jordan's venerated mediated identity
was thus complicit in criminalizing the African
American youth populace, in a manner that
conveniently diverted popular attention – and
thereby party political obligation – away from
addressing the profound socially deleterious
effects of anti-welfarist politics and transnational economics (Cole, 1996).

Jean Baudrillard: the Hyperreality of Postmodern Sport

Jean Baudrillard has been described as the
'high priest' (Willis, 1990: 152), 'guru' (Best and

Kellner, 1991: 111), 'Jimi Hendrix' (Levin, 1996)
and even the 'drag queen' (Ashley, 1997: 49) of
the postmodern Left. The elevation of
Baudrillard to the status of a postmodern intellectual icon has been attributed to the hasty
conclusions circulated by the first generation
of North American readers of his work
(Genesko, 1994). While it is true Baudrillard's
idiosyncratic attention has long been drawn to
the much-vaunted postmodern 'civilization of
the image' (Kearney, 1989: 1), it is important
not to overlook his post-structuralist lineage.
According to Christopher Norris, 'Baudrillard
was waiting at the end of the road that structuralism and post-structuralism had been travelling for the past three decades and more'
(Norris, 1992: 25). Not that Baudrillard has
been an apologist for post-structuralism. As
indicated by his pointedly titled manuscript
Forget Foucault (1987), Baudrillard has been
highly critical of his post-structuralist contemporaries. Nevertheless, in terms of his critical
engagement with the work of Ferdinand de
Saussure, Georges Bataille, Henri Lefebvre,
Roland Barthes and Guy Debord (cf. Genesko,
1994; Gottdiener, 1995; Kellner, 1989), and
in radically problematizing the very nature
of modernity and modern subjectivity,
Baudrillard is every bit as much a representative of French post-structuralist thought as
Derrida and Foucault. Albeit taking it in an
ever-more radical direction, Baudrillard has
certainly made an important contribution to
the post-structuralist debate. For, while
Derrida deconstructed the epistemological and
ontological foundations of modernity, and
Foucault excavated modern disciplinary
knowledges and institutions, Baudrillard her-
alded the 'end of modernity and the transition
to a new stage of society and history beyond
modernity' (Kellner, 1989: 94).

Like that of Derrida and Foucault,
Baudrillard's work has produced extreme reactions amongst the global academic community,
as evidenced by both the enthusiasm of his
numerous advocates, and the vociferousness of
his many detractors. During the course of his
intellectual development, Baudrillard's writing
has evolved from relatively conventional academic discussions of his innovative synthesis of
Marxist political economy and semiology,
to a kind of science-fiction-like cosmology,
projecting visions of futuristic worlds which
expose, through ironic exaggeration, the
technologically driven nature of everyday
culture (Hebdige, 1988). In a 1983 interview,
Baudrillard forthrightly admitted 'My work
has never been academic, nor is it getting
more literary. It's evolving, it's getting less

theoretical, without feeling the need to furnish proof or rely on references' (Baudrillard, 1993a: 43). In adopting this radical approach, Baudrillard's work has veered toward an undertheorized abstraction, shallow provocation and apolitical nihilism, which has exasperated and infuriated his many critics (cf. Callinicos, 1990; Kellner, 1989; Norris, 1992; Rojek and Turner, 1993). Nevertheless, while Baudrillard's later work continues to be critiqued, often to the point of ridicule (cf. Sturrock, 1990; Woods, 1992), there remains a sentiment amongst some cultural commentators that it would be disadvantageous to categorically abandon it. Certainly, Baudrillard's relevance to the analysis of contemporary sport culture should not be underestimated. As Charles P. Pierce commented, the American – and increasingly the global – sports industry is dominated by 'media-driven celebrity entertainment' which means in the future 'for most people, sports will be even more exclusively a television phenomenon than it is today' (1995: 185, 187). This rapid and global growth of postmodern sport culture represents a particularly important point of engagement for Baudrillard's ontological, epistemological and political provocations.

Jean Baudrillard was born in the French cathedral town of Reims in 1929. Although his grandparents were peasants, his immediate family experienced a significant measure of upward social mobility resulting from his parents' forging careers in the French civil service (Levin, 1996). After a period of teaching in secondary schools, it was following his move to Paris in 1966 that Baudrillard's intellectual career took off. Having defended his thesis in sociology, entitled *Le système des objets*, at the Université de Nanterre (Paris X) in March 1966, he accepted a position as an assistant lecturer in sociology at Nanterre beginning in October of the same year. Apart from a number of periods of visiting lectureships – most notably perhaps, his sojourns to the United States – Baudrillard spent the entirety of his formal academic career at the Université de Nanterre. Indeed, he remained on the faculty there until his retirement from the position of junior lecturer in the Faculté des Lettres et Sciences Humaines in 1987. As Baudrillard noted in a 1991 interview, as far 'as the normal stages of a career are concerned, I've always missed them, including the fact that I was never a professor' (Baudrillard, 1993a: 19). In following a more circuitous route to intellectual notoriety, and while never attaining the same degree of formal academic recognition or status as Foucault or Derrida, Baudrillard still

became an influential and well-connected figure within Parisian intellectual circles. Between 1967 and 1970 he was closely involved in the sociology of urbanism group, and their journal *Utopie*. In 1975, and along with such other intellectual luminaries as Michel de Certeau and Paul Virilio, he became a member of the founding editorial board of the Centre Georges Pompidou's cultural theory journal, *Traverses*. From 1969 to 1973 Baudrillard was also affiliated with the Centre d'Études des Communications de Mass at the Ecole Pratique des Hautes Études (Genesko, 1994). Following his retirement in 1987, Baudrillard embraced a new intellectual mode, for which he had seemingly been preparing himself since the mid-1970s. Now liberated from the responsibilities of a formal academic post, Baudrillard assumed the mantle of a full-time roving intellectual, prodigiously documenting his global observations and experiences in a series of fragmented postmodern travelogues.

While Baudrillard's primary institutional affiliation remained unusually constant during his academic career, the evolution of his intellectual work has been marked by a series of significant transformations. As with any attempt to periodize a shifting intellectual project, there is a tendency to create artificial boundaries between works that often correspond considerably more than they differ. This is perhaps expressly true of Baudrillard, whose often impressionistic, idealized and ungrounded later narratives continue to incorporate important aspects of the more concretized theorizing which characterized many of his earlier exertions (Gottdiener, 1995). With this proviso in mind, it is nevertheless possible to dissect Baudrillard's project into at least five necessarily related phases. In examining the nature of modern consumer society, and specifically the regulating commodification of everyday life (1968, 1970), Baudrillard's earliest studies supplemented the classical Marxist critique of political economy with a semiological theorizing of the sign (Kellner, 1994). Baudrillard's innovative conflation of materiality and ideology within *The System of Objects* (1996c) (original 1968) even prompted Gottdiener to cite it as 'one of the most important books of post-structuralist cultural criticism' (1995: 35). Within his next major study, *For a Critique of the Political Economy of the Sign* (1981) (original 1972), Baudrillard first began to question the value of Marxist political economy as a tool for interpreting modern culture. In many ways, this work proved to be an intermediary point between Baudrillard's neo-Marxist and post-Marxist incarnations. The publication of *The Mirror of Production* (1975) (original 1973) represented a public condemnation of Marxist political economy for being a 'repressive simulation' of that which it seeks to overthrow, namely capitalism (Baudrillard, 1975: 48). Within *Symbolic Exchange and Death* (1993b) (original 1976) Baudrillard turned to a post-Marxist and post-Saussurian radical semiurgy. This approach to understanding a society dominated by the digital and cybernetic logic of the televisual code, was elaborated within subsequent works that keyed on Baudrillard's 'Holy Trinity' (Best and Kellner, 1991: 118) of simulation, implosion and hyperreality (see below for relevant works). Lastly, *Fatal Strategies* (1990b) (original 1983) has been cited as Baudrillard's last piece of serious intellectual work since, over the past decade, its model of provocative and nihilist pataphysics has been almost playfully 'replayed and recycled' (Kellner, 1989) within Baudrillard's numerous commentaries on the fin-de-millennium scene (cf. Baudrillard, 1988a, 1988b, 1988c, 1990a, 1990b, 1993c, 1994a, 1995, 1996a, 1996b).

Of central importance to Baudrillard's post-Marxist, post-Saussurian, radical semiurgic approach to the complexities of contemporary culture (cf. Baudrillard, 1980, 1981, 1982, 1983b, 1985, 1990c, 1993b), was his conceptualizing of the four orders of simulacra, each of which equated to the relation between appearance and representation within a given socio-historical epoch, and thus informed how reality is constituted and experienced within that context. Baudrillard identified four loosely historical orders of simulacra, based on natural, commercial, structural and fractal laws of value, which corresponded to four regimes of representation based on the processes of counterfeit, production, simulation and proliferation. This discussion focuses on Baudrillard's understanding of the society of simulation (his third order of simulacra), which incorporated some of his most fruitful ideas and among his most promising research directives for the sociology of sport.

Baudrillard's third order of simulacra can be characterized as one in which the simulated codes and models of media, computer and information systems have replaced material production as the organizing principle of social existence (Best, 1989; Best and Kellner, 1991; Bogard, 1996). The passage from a metallurgic to a semiurgic society (Baudrillard, 1981) has been expedited through advances made in communications and information technology, and has advanced a 'new reality logic' (Luke, 1991: 349) centered around

mediated simulations. Since any information which 'reflects or diffuses an event is already a degraded form of that event' (Baudrillard, 1980: 141), information communicated by the televisual media is necessarily an imploded, reformulated and bastardized interpretation of the real. Hence, the order of appearance within this semiurgic society 'is no longer that of a territory, a referential being or a substance. It is the generation by models of a real situation without origin or reality' (Baudrillard, 1983b: 2). The advent of an 'implosive socius of signs' (Best, 1989: 33), has resulted in the obliteration of the opposition between the medium and the real. Baudrillard's semiurgic culture is thus infused with simulated codes and models that actually produce the reality which they purport to represent (Seidman, 1994). Or, as Baudrillard famously put it, the 'real is not only what can be reproduced, but that which is already reproduced. The hyperreal' (Baudrillard, 1983b: 146–7).

According to Baudrillard, the 'endless reduplication of signs, images and simulations' (Featherstone, 1991: 15) has spawned a cybernetic culture: a closed systemic structure prompted by the reigning televisual code:

> Every image, every media message and also every surrounding functional object is a test. That is to say, in all the rigour of the term, it triggers response mechanisms in accordance with stereotypes or analytical models … Both object and information already result from a selection, an edited sequence of camera angles, they have already tested 'reality' and have only asked questions to which it has responded … Thus tested, reality tests you in return according to the same score-card, and you decode it following the same code, inscribed in its every message and object like a miniature genetic code. (Baudrillard, 1993b: 63)

In effect, the popular media test the mainstream cultural mores of consuming subjects: which are themselves a priori verifications of the same televisual code. It is in this sense that Baudrillard (1994b) asserted, 'There is no longer a medium in the literal sense: it is now intangible, diffused, and diffracted in the real, and one can no longer even say that the medium is altered by it' (Baudrillard, 1994b: 30).

Within Baudrillard's implosive postmodern mediascape, individuals lose their ability to differentiate between the medium and the real; between their active and passive responses to mediated codes; and between themselves as subjects or objects of the mode of information (Poster, 1990). Betraying his post-structuralist affiliation, and in familiar pataphysical tone, Baudrillard thus announced the death of the modern subject, through its absorption into the black hole of the imploding hyper-media (Baudrillard, 1983a), and its subsequent metamorphosis into the masses 'that space of ever greater density into which everything societal is imploded and ground up in an uninterrupted process of simulation' (Baudrillard, 1982: 8–9). Hence, according to Baudrillard, the triumph of the televisual code signals that the human subject has entered into a state of absolute manipulation, and has become 'a pure absorption and resorption of the influence networks' (Baudrillard, 1988b: 27). Baudrillard also declared the end of modern representative power, and its replacement with circulating simulations or illusions of power: '"power" (under erasure) is at once everywhere, in every code and simulation, and nowhere, in no particular centralized locus' (Kellner, 1989: 140). Given the indeterminate nature of postmodern power, Baudrillard argued that modern political struggles against supposedly identifiable sites of authority were completely futile. Instead, and to the disbelief of adherents to more conventional strategies of oppositional politics (cf. Harris, 1996; Jarvie and Maguire, 1994; Kellner, 1989) Baudrillard encouraged the practice of hyperconformity, or deliberate passivity, as an act of 'strategic resistance' against the domineering televisual code (Baudrillard, 1983a: 108).

Sara Schoonmaker (1994: 186) has justifiably critiqued Baudrillard's third-order simulacrum for its 'technological determinism, formalism, and epistemological confusion'. Added to his political nihilism, it is clear to see why many cultural commentators have renounced Baudrillard's work *in toto*. Nevertheless, and as one of his sternest detractors even acknowledged, there is an important reason for 'not ignoring Baudrillard' (Norris, 1992: 25). According to Christopher Norris, despite its flaws, Baudrillard's work is replete with 'canny diagnostic observations' pertaining to the influence of the mass media in shaping contemporary existence (1992: 25). For this reason, Douglas Kellner implored readers to adopt a critical stance in order that they may distinguish the 'valuable from the foolish, the important from the unimportant elements of Baudrillard's work' (1994: 20). So, while it may be foolhardy to take Baudrillard's exaggerated postmodern musings too literally, not taking them literally enough would seem to deny the sociology of sport community an important source of theoretical insights into a postmodern sport culture, dominated by a proliferating economy of mass-mediated sporting commodities, celebrities and spectacles.

Baudrillard's periodic commentaries on aspects of contemporary sporting culture vindicated his implosive postmodernism (Chen, 1987), and attested to the structure and influence of postmodern sport. To this end, Baudrillard drew attention to the French public's transfixation with the televisual drama of a qualifying game for the 1978 World Cup, and apathetic indifference toward the extradition of the German lawyer Klaus Croissant on the same evening: 'A few hundred people demonstrated in front of the Santé prison, there was some furious nocturnal activity on the part of a few lawyers, while twenty million people spent the evening in front of their TV screens' (Baudrillard, 1980: 143). Baudrillard argued that the French masses should not be castigated for privileging a football match over a politico-legal occurrence, since the depthless and aestheticized hyperreality of the third order of simulacra (Featherstone, 1991) has seduced the masses into resisting the imperatives of rational communication, in favour of the affective return of a 'dramatic sequence' (Baudrillard, 1980: 143). Baudrillard also passed comment on the tragic events at the Heysel Stadium, Brussels, in 1985, which resulted in the death of 39 Juventus supporters. Attacking the parasitic barbarism of the global televisual media, he controversially condemned 'not the violence *per se* but the way in which this violence was given worldwide currency by television, and in the process turned into a travesty of itself' (Baudrillard, 1990b: 75). Although openly condemning such displays of violence, the media also cynically celebrated such acts through the instantaneous global dissemination of video footage which augmented the dramatic content of the 'worldwide spectacle of sport', and thereby acted as global 'fodder for TV audiences' (Baudrillard, 1990b: 77). Lastly, Baudrillard spoke to the future of the sporting event through reference to a European Cup match played in Madrid, Spain, between Real Madrid and Naples in September 1987. Due to the unruly behavior of Madrid supporters in a previous game, the football authorities ordered this match to be played in a stadium devoid of spectators, but relayed to the adoring masses on television. Thus, this 'phantom football match' took place, and surgically prefigured the future of postmodern sport: where no one will directly experience events, 'but everyone will have received an image of them' … in this setting, sport becomes a 'pure event … devoid of any reference in nature, and readily susceptible to replacement by synthetic images' (Baudrillard, 1990b: 80, 79).

In denouncing his proclivity for 'calculated exaggeration', Chris Rojek (1990) likened Baudrillard's entry into the field of leisure studies to that of a garish postmodernist gate-crasher barging into a modernist party. This sentiment is equally applicable to Baudrillard's intrusion into the sociology of sport, which has been marked by expressions of dismissive disregard from those researchers more firmly anchored in modern epistemic, political and sporting logics. Although not explicitly discussing Baudrillard's work, within his lengthy expression of incredulity toward the apparent postmodern 'drift' within critical sport studies, Morgan (1995) best captured the general disdain that lies in wait for those seeking to appropriate elements of Baudrillard's project when examining contemporary sport culture. His use of terms such as 'facile', 'abnormal', 'sophomoric', 'relativist' and, most revealingly, 'trendy' as descriptors of the 'postmodernist drift' within the sociology of sport, is indeed damning. Yet, Morgan is circumspect enough to concede that there needs to be further enquiry into these 'strange new theories' (1995: 41), and would no doubt be encouraged by the small but growing number of studies which have appropriated, in deliberate fashion, Baudrillard's oeuvre as a tool for theorizing the complexities of postmodern sport. While disparately focused, these studies vindicate Mike Gane's guarded affirmation of Baudrillard's work as something worth pursuing with care and trepidation, since although 'vulnerable to the most harsh judgements … the overall impression we are left with is of a consistency and persistence of critical imagination which produces, sometimes, remarkable insights' (Gane, 1991: 157).

Up to this point in time, Geneviève Rail has formulated the most informed and instructive Baudrillardian understanding of postmodern sport 'as producer and reproducer of the culture present in postmodern society, and as privileged object of over-consumption' (Rail, 1998: 156). In charting the implosion of sport and aesthetic, corporal and media realms, Rail developed a suggestive theoretical synthesis of the early (1970, 1975, 1981), middle (1980) and later (1988a) phases of Baudrillard's writing. Rail's discussion is particularly imaginative and enlightening when substantiating the anti-mediatory, aesthetic populist, fragmented, depthless and history-effacing nature of the 'model used to mediate sport' (Rail, 1998: 154). Complementing Rail's work, John Bale (1994) mobilized numerous Baudrillardian concepts in depicting the future of sport as a world of material and televisual simulations, many of which can be found within North America, 'the engine which drives most parts of the machine of global popular culture' (Bale, 1994: 169).

Moving from the general to the particular, Steve Redhead (1994, 1998) appraised the relevance of Baudrillard's postmodern musings as a tool for realizing a popular cultural studies critique of the 1994 World Cup tournament held in the United States. Despite his acknowledgement that Baudrillardian theorizing should be taken 'seriously but with a good deal of caution, too' (1994: 302), Redhead concluded that Baudrillard's postmodern travelogue *America* (1988a), in tandem with elements of his dissection of the Gulf War simulacra (1995), provided a suggestive basis for interpreting USA '94 as a global media event: a simulated and hyperreal spectacle devoid of a 'real referent' (Redhead, 1994: 298). Influenced by similar Baudrillardian sources, David Andrews (1998) identified how NBC's coverage of the 1996 Summer Olympic Games in Atlanta manufactured a simulated model of Olympic reality, that was explicitly designed to constitute, and thereby seduce, the female viewing subject. Lawrence Wenner (1998) has furnished perhaps the most innovative engagement with Baudrillard's theorizing in his spatial-geography of the hypermediated, hypercommodified, hyperreal postmodern sports bar. As Wenner noted, this 'new genre is a high concept theme park … a cultural bin of simulations, a bunch of "important real things" that are put together for us to deconstruct by a helpful corporate sponsor' (Wenner, 1998: 323–4).

The centrality of symbolic value within Baudrillard's thought has also attracted scholars interested in the complex commodity-sign economy of contemporary sport. Rob Van Wynsberghe and Ian Ritchie (1998: 377) provided a compact, yet highly instructive, discussion of Baudrillard's research as a grounding to their postmodern semiotic analysis of the Olympic Games' five ring logo. The authors then graphically demonstrated how, within a postmodern culture dominated by the semiotic detritus of the media, advertising and marketing industries, the Olympic logo has been severed from the pseudo-sacred ideals that defined its modern signification. Within the postmodern mediascape, the Olympic logo has become a polysemic hypercommercial signifier: 'used to represent virtually any product, advertisers could construct any story they wanted around such a symbol, while at the same time it would mean something different for diverse groups of people' (Van Wynsberghe and Ritchie, 1998: 377). Lastly, in her broad-ranging discussion of sport mascots, Synthia Slowikowski (1993) referred to Native American mascots (such as 'Chief Illiniwek' at the University of Illinois at Urbana–Champaign) as nostalgically framed hyperreal simulations. These commodified 'Native American simulacra' evoked the dominant, and habitually subjugating, signifiers of Native American peoples drawn from the popular American imagination. In a Baudrillardian sense, they were thus hyperreal fabrications of 'the absolute fake' of postmodern American culture (Slowikowski, 1993: 28).

CONCLUSION: TOWARD A POST-STRUCTURALIST SOCIOLOGY OF SPORT

Finally, post-structuralist approaches lead us to recognize that no theoretical paradigm is flawless, and no theoretical paradigm is forever. But post-structuralisms that remain attentive to history and power relations allow us to understand and, perhaps, to transform our worlds. Provisionally, they are the best we have ... at least for now. (Kondo, 1995: 99)

Although merely scratching the surface of this vast topic, hopefully this discussion will have demonstrated the strength of the growing body of post-structuralist informed scholarship within the sociology of sport. More than anything, post-structuralist influenced analyses have demonstrated that sport's language, practice and structure 'can no longer be considered ideologically, educationally, socially or politically "neutral" and "innocent"' (Bannet, 1989: 264). Post-structuralism's overriding concern with subversion, dissent and the 'destabilising of certainty' (Docker, 1994: 142) confounds critics who have vilified it as a 'dead end for progressive thought' (Epstein, 1995; cf. Callinicos, 1990; Dews, 1987; Habermas, 1987; May, 1989). Nowhere is this more ably evidenced than in the way post-structuralist theory has been used to critically explicate sport's embroilment in contemporary formations of language, power and subjectivity. Clearly, the variants of post-structuralism offer important interpretative vehicles for disrupting the stifling and oppressive formations of sporting (post)modernity, by developing alternative modes of thought, more progressive vehicles of expression and, ultimately, more potentially enabling experiences of the (post)modern sporting self.

While the post-structuralist project has much to offer the sociology of sport, it would be remiss not to point out the dangers of post-structuralist theory being taken up in the sociology of sport in potentially unproductive ways. Many fields of enquiry have been swamped by vapid and superficial engagements with the variants of post-structuralism, something that Stuart Hall characterized as 'the endless, trendy recycling of one fashionable theorist after another, as if you can wear new theories like T-shirts' (1996b: 149). It is perhaps more productive to view post-structuralism less in terms of becoming an exclusively Derridean, Foucauldian, or Baudrillardian scholar, and more in terms of adhering to post-structuralism's particular type of politically informed intellectual practice. In this sense, I believe the practice of post-structuralist intellectualizing is closely allied to that of cultural studies (which itself has increasingly been informed by post-structuralist theorizing). Therefore, brief consideration of Lawrence Grossberg's (1997) six-pronged characterization of cultural studies would appear to be a profitable way of delineating the post-structuralist project for future research. For as with post-structuralism, the 'more people jump onto the cultural studies bandwagon' the more 'it needs to protect some sense of its own specificity as a way into the field of culture and power' (Grossberg, 1997: 7).

In short, Grossberg (1997) believed cultural studies – and by implication, a post-structuralist sociology of sport – should be: *disciplined* (far from wallowing in relativism, it constantly seeks new forms of intellectual authority); *interdisciplinary* (its focus demands the straddling of traditional disciplinary boundaries); *self-reflective* (never complacent in its intellectual authority, it realizes the inadequacies and potential contradictions of the knowledge it produces); *political* (fundamentally concerned with understanding, with a view to transforming, people's lived realities); *theoretical* (while not dogmatically adhering to one theoretical position, it stresses the necessity of theory); and *radically contextual* (the object, method, theory and politics of critical enquiry are inextricably tied to the context within which it is embroiled). By following these directives, a post-structuralist sociology of sport would confound Camille Paglia's sardonic indictment of 'Post-structuralism, that stale teething biscuit of the nattering nerds of trendy academe ... [which] ... cannot rival the dazzling analytic complexity of football' (Paglia, 1997: 22), by demonstrating its vitality as a tool for critically analysing the dazzling complexity of sport in general.

REFERENCES

Althusser, L. (1971) *Lenin and Philosophy and Other Essays*. London: New Left Books.

Andrews, D.L. (1993) 'Desperately seeking Michel: Foucault's genealogy, the body, and critical sport sociology', *Sociology of Sport Journal*, 10 (2): 148–67.

Andrews, D.L. (1996) 'The fact(s) of Michael Jordan's blackness: excavating a floating racial signifier', *Sociology of Sport Journal*, 13 (2): 125–58.

Andrews, D.L. (1998) 'Feminizing Olympic reality: preliminary dispatches from Baudrillard's Atlanta', *International Review for the Sociology of Sport*, 33 (1): 5–18.

Ardagh, J. (1982) *France in the 1980s*. Harmondsworth: Penguin.

Ashley, D. (1994) 'Postmodernism and antifoundationalism', in D.R. Dickens and A. Fontana (eds), *Postmodernism and Social Inquiry*. New York: Guilford Press. pp. 53–75.

Ashley, D. (1997) *History without a Subject: the Postmodern Condition*. Boulder, CO: Westview Press.

Bale, J. (1992) *Sport, Space and the City*. London: Routledge.

Bale, J. (1993) 'The spatial development of the modern stadium', *International Review for the Sociology of Sport*, 28 (2/3): 122–33.

Bale, J. (1994) *Landscapes of Modern Sport*. London: Leicester University Press.

Bannet, E.T. (1989) *Structuralism and the Logic of Dissent: Barthes, Derrida, Foucault, Lacan*. Urbana, IL: University of Illinois Press.

Barthes, R. (1972) *Mythologies*. New York: Hill and Wang.

Barthes, R. (1975) *The Pleasure of the Text*. New York: Hill and Wang.

Barthes, R. (1977) *Images, Music, Text*. New York: Hill and Wang.

Barthes, R. (1979) *The Eiffel Tower and Other Mythologies*. New York: Hill and Wang.

Baudrillard, J. (1968) *Le Système des Objets*. Paris: Denoel-Gonthier.

Baudrillard, J. (1970) *La Société de Consommation*. Paris: Gallimard.

Baudrillard, J. (1975) *The Mirror of Production*. St Louis: Telos.

Baudrillard, J. (1980) 'The implosion of meaning in the media and the implosion of the social in the masses', in K. Woodward (ed.), *The Myths of Information: Technology and Postindustrial Society*. Madison, WI: Coda Press. pp. 137–48.

Baudrillard, J. (1981) *For a Critique of the Political Economy of the Sign*. St Louis: Telos.

Baudrillard, J. (1982) 'The Beaubourg-effect: implosion and deterrence', *October*, 20: 3–13.

Baudrillard, J. (1983a) *In the Shadow of the Silent Majorities*. New York: Semiotext(e).

Baudrillard, J. (1983b) *Simulations*. New York: Semiotext(e).

Baudrillard, J. (1985) 'The masses: the implosion of the social in the media', *New Literary History*, 16 (3): 577–89.

Baudrillard, J. (1987) *Forget Foucault*. New York: Semiotext(e).

Baudrillard, J. (1988a) *America*. London: Verso.

Baudrillard, J. (1988b) *The Ecstasy of Communication*. New York: Semiotext(e).

Baudrillard, J. (1988c) *The Evil Demon of Images*. Sydney: Power Institute of Fine Arts.

Baudrillard, J. (1990a) *Cool Memories, 1980–1985*. London: Verso.

Baudrillard, J. (1990b) *Fatal Strategies*. New York: Semiotext(e).

Baudrillard, J. (1990c) *Seduction*. New York: St Martin's Press.

Baudrillard, J. (1993a) *Baudrillard Live: Selected Interviews* (ed. M. Gane). London: Routledge.

Baudrillard, J. (1993b) *Symbolic Exchange and Death*. London: Sage.

Baudrillard, J. (1993c) *The Transparency of Evil: Essays on Extreme Phenomena*. London: Verso.

Baudrillard, J. (1994a) *The Illusion of the End*. Cambridge: Polity Press.

Baudrillard, J. (1994b) *Simulacra and Simulation*. Ann Arbor, MI: University of Michigan Press.

Baudrillard, J. (1995) *The Gulf War Did Not Take Place*. Bloomington, IN: Indiana University Press.

Baudrillard, J. (1996a) *Cool Memories II, 1987–1990*. Durham, NC: Duke University Press.

Baudrillard, J. (1996b) *The Perfect Crime*. London: Verso.

Baudrillard, J. (1996c) *The System of Objects*. London: Verso.

Berlant, L. (1991) *The Anatomy of National Fantasy: Hawthorne, Utopia, and Everyday Life*. Chicago: University of Chicago Press.

Best, S. (1989) 'The commodification of reality and the reality of commodification: Jean Baudrillard and postmodernism', *Current Perspectives in Social Theory*, 9: 23–51.

Best, S. and Kellner, D. (1991) *Postmodern Theory: Critical Interrogations*. New York: Guilford Press.

Bogard, W. (1996) *The Simulation of Surveillance: Hypercontrol in Telematic Societies*. Cambridge: Cambridge University Press.

Bordo, S. (1989) 'The body and the reproduction of femininity: a feminist appropriation of Foucault', in A. Jagger and S. Bordo (eds), *Gender/Body/Knowledge: Feminist Reconstructions of Being and Knowing*. New Brunswick, NJ: Rutgers University Press. pp. 13–33.

Bordo, S. (1993a) 'Feminism, Foucault and the politics of the body', in C. Ramazanoglu (ed.), *Up against Foucault: Explorations of Some Tensions between Foucault and Feminism*. London: Routledge. pp. 179–202.

Bordo, S. (1993b) *Unbearable Weight: Feminism, Western Culture, and the Body*. Berkeley, CA: University of California Press.

Boudreau, F., Folman, R. and Konzak, B. (1992) 'Les techniques martiales orientales comme technologies du soi: une réponse à Michel Foucault', *Sociologie et Société*, 24 (1): 141–56.

Bourdieu, P. (1978) 'Sport and social class', *Social Science Information*, 17 (6): 819–40.

Bourdieu, P. (1984) *Distinction: a Social Critique of the Judgement of Taste*. Cambridge, MA: Harvard University Press.

Bourdieu, P. (1988) 'Program for a sociology of sport', *Sociology of Sport Journal*, 5 (2): 153–61.

Bourdieu, P. (1990) *In Other Words: Essays toward a Reflexive Sociology*. Stanford, CA: Stanford University Press.

Boyne, R. (1990) *Foucault and Derrida: the Other Side of Reason*. London: Routledge.

Brantlinger, P. (1992) 'Post-poststructuralist or prelapsarian? Cultural studies and the new historicism'. Paper presented at the Rethinking Culture conference, University of Montreal, Canada.

Brohm, J.M. (1978) *Sport – a Prison of Measured Time*. London: Pluto Press.

Brown, S. (1994) 'Marketing as multiplex: screening postmodernism', *European Journal of Marketing*, 28 (8/9): 27–51.

Brown, S. (1995) 'Postmodern marketing research: no representation without taxation', *Journal of the Market Research Society*, 37 (3): 287–310.

Brownell, S. (1995) *Training the Body for China: Sports in the the Moral Order of the People's Republic*. Chicago: University of Chicago Press.

Butler, J. (1989) 'Foucault and the paradox of bodily inscriptions', *Journal of Philosophy*, LXXXVI (11): 601–7.

Butler, J. (1990) *Gender Trouble: Feminism and the Subversion of Identity*. New York: Routledge.

Butler, J. (1993a) *Bodies that Matter: On the Discursive Limits of 'Sex'*. New York: Routledge.

Butler, J. (1993b) 'Poststructuralism and postmarxism', *Diacritics*, 223 (4): 3–11.

Calhoun, C. (1995) *Critical Social Theory: Culture, History, and the Challenge of Difference*. Oxford: Basil Blackwell.

Callinicos, A. (1990) *Against Postmodernism: a Marxist Critique*. London: St Martin's Press.

Campbell, R. (1968) 'Existentialism in France since the liberation', in M. Farber (ed.), *Philosophic Thought in France and the United States: Essays in Representing Major Trends in Contemporary French and American Philosophy*. Albany, NY: State University of New York Press. pp. 137–50.

Chapman, G.E. (1997) 'Making weight: lightweight rowing, technologies of power, and technologies of the self', *Sociology of Sport Journal*, 14 (3): 205–23.

Chen, K.H. (1987) 'The masses and the media: Baudrillard's implosive postmodernism', *Theory, Culture and Society*, 4 (1): 71–88.

Clément, J.P. (1993) 'L'enjeu identitaire', in J.P. Clément and M. Herr (eds), *L'Identité de l'Éducation Physique Scolaire au XXeme Siècle*. Clermont-Ferrand: Éditions A.F.R.A.P.S. pp. 13–25.

Cobley, P. (1996) 'The play of *différance*', in P. Cobley (ed.), *The Communication Theory Reader*. London: Routledge. pp. 26–208.

Cole, C.L. (1993) 'Resisting the canon: feminist cultural studies, sport, and technologies of the self', *Journal of Sport and Social Issues*, 17 (2): 77–97.

Cole, C.L. (1994) 'Resisting the canon: feminist cultural studies, sport, and technologies of the body', in S. Birrell and C.L. Cole (eds), *Women, Sport, and Culture*, Champaign, IL: Human Kinetics. pp. 5–29.

Cole, C.L. (1995) 'Hybrid athletes, monstrous addicts, and cyborg natures', *Journal of Sport History*.

Cole, C.L. (1996) 'American Jordan: P.L.A.Y., consensus, and punishment', *Sociology of Sport Journal*, 13 (4): 366–97.

Cole, C.L. (1997) Personal communication.

Cole, C.L. (1998) 'Addiction, exercise, and cyborgs: technologies of deviant bodies', in G. Rail (ed.), *Sport and Postmodern Times*. New York: State University of New York Press. pp. 261–76.

Cole, C.L. and Andrews, D.L. (1996) '"Look – Its NBA *ShowTime*!": visions of race in the popular imaginary', in N.K. Denzin (ed.), *Cultural Studies: a Research Volume*, Volume 1. pp. 141–81.

Cole, C.L. and Denny, H. (1995) 'Visualizing deviance in post-Reagan America: Magic Johnson, AIDS, and the promiscuous world of professional sport', *Critical Sociology*, 20 (3): 123–47.

Cole, C.L. and Hribar, A.S. (1995) 'Celebrity feminism: *Nike style* – post-fordism, transcendence, and consumer power', *Sociology of Sport Journal*, 12 (4): 347–69.

Cole, C.L. and Orlie, M. (1995) 'Hybrid athletes, monstrous addicts, and cyborg natures. *Journal of Sport History*, 22 (3): 228–39.

Connor, S. (1989) *Postmodernist Culture: an Introduction to Theories of the Contemporary*. Oxford: Basil Blackwell.

Cooper, D.E. (1990) *Existentialism*. Oxford: Basil Blackwell.

Coward, R. and Ellis, J. (1981) 'Structuralism and the subject: a critique', in T. Bennett, G. Martin, C. Mercer and J. Woollacott (eds), *Culture, Ideology and Social Process*. Milton Keynes: Open University Press. pp. 153–64.

Davidson, A.I. (1986) 'Archaeology, genealogy, ethics', in D.C. Hoy (ed.), *Foucault: a Critical Reader*. Oxford: Basil Blackwell. pp. 221–33.

Defrance, J. (1987) *L'Excellence corporelle*. Rennes: Presses Universitaires de France.

Denzin, N.K. (1991) *Images of Postmodern Society: Social Theory and Contemporary Cinema*. London: Sage.

Derrida, J. (1970) 'Structure, sign, and play in the discourse of the human sciences', in R. Macksey and E. Donato (eds), *The Languages of Criticism and the Sciences of Man*. Baltimore, MD: Johns Hopkins University Press. pp. 247–72.

Derrida, J. (1973) *'Speech and Phenomena' and Other Essays on Husserl's Theory of Signs*. Evanston, IL: Northwestern University Press.

Derrida, J. (1976) *Of Grammatology* (trans. G.C. Spivak). Baltimore, MD: Johns Hopkins University Press.

Derrida, J. (1978) *Writing and Difference* (ed. A. Bass). Chicago: University of Chicago Press.

Derrida, J. (1981) *Positions* (trans. A. Bass). Chicago: University of Chicago Press.

Derrida, J. (1982a) *'Différance', in Margins of Philosophy* (trans. A. Bass). Chicago: University of Chicago Press. pp. 1–27.

Derrida, J. (1982b) *Margins of Philosophy* (trans. A. Bass). Chicago: University of Chicago Press.

Derrida, J. (1987) *The Truth in Painting*. Chicago: University of Chicago Press.

Derrida, J. with Autrement (1993) 'The rhetoric of drugs: an interview' (trans. M. Israel) *Differences*, 5: 1–25.

Descombes, V. (1980) *Modern French Philosophy*. Cambridge: Cambridge University Press.

Dews, P. (1987) *Logics of Disintegration*. London: Verso.

Docker, J. (1994) *Postmodernism and Popular Culture: a Cultural History*. Cambridge: Cambridge University Press.

Dumm, T.L. (1996) *Michel Foucault and the Politics of Freedom*. Thousand Oaks, CA: Sage.

Duncan, M.C. (1994) 'The politics of women's body images and practices: Foucault, the panopticon, and *Shape* magazine', *Journal of Sport and Social Issues*, 18 (1): 48–65.

Dunning, E. and Sheard, K. (1979) *Barbarians, Gentlemen and Players: a Sociological Study of the Development of Rugby Football*. New York: New York University Press.

Eagleton, T. (1983) *Literary Theory: an Introduction*. Oxford: Basil Blackwell.

Epstein, B. (1995) 'Why poststructuralism is a dead end for progressive thought', *Socialist Review*, 25 (2): 83–119.

Featherstone, M. (1985) 'The fate of modernity: an introduction', *Theory, Culture and Society*, 2 (3): 1–5.

Featherstone, M. (1991) *Consumer Culture and Postmodernism*. London: Sage.

Firat, A.F. and Venkatesh, A. (1995) 'Liberatory postmodernism and the reenchantment of consumption', *Journal of Consumer Research*, 22 (December): 239–67.

Fish, V. (1993) 'Poststructuralism in family therapy: interrogating the narrative/conversational mode', *Journal of Marital and Family Therapy*, 19 (3): 223–4.

Foucault, M. (1973a) *Madness and Civilization: a History of Insanity in the Age of Reason*. New York: Vintage Books.

Foucault, M. (1973b) *The Order of Things: an Archaeology of the Human Sciences*. New York: Vintage Books.

Foucault, M. (1974) *The Archaeology of Knowledge*. London: Tavistock.

Foucault, M. (1975) *The Birth of the Clinic: an Archaeology of Medical Perception*. New York: Vintage Books.

Foucault, M. (1977a) *Discipline and Punish: the Birth of the Prison*. New York: Pantheon Books.

Foucault, M. (1977b) 'The political function of the intellectual', *Radical Philosophy*, 17: 12–14.

Foucault, M. (1979) 'What is an author?', in J. Harari (ed.), *Textual Strategies*. Ithaca, NY: Cornell University Press. pp. 141–60.

Foucault, M. (1980a) *Herculine Barbin*. London: Pantheon.

Foucault, M. (1980b) *Power/Knowledge: Selected Interviews and Other Writings, 1972–1977* (ed. C. Gordon). New York: Pantheon Books.

Foucault, M. (1980c) 'Two lectures', in C. Gordon (ed.), *Power/Knowledge: Selected Interviews and Other Writings, 1972–1977*. New York: Pantheon Books. pp. 92–108.

Foucault, M. (1982) 'The subject and power', in H.L. Dreyfus and P. Rabinow (eds), *Michel Foucault: Beyond Structuralism and Hermeneutics*. Brighton: Harvester Press. pp. 208–26.

Foucault, M. (1988a) *The History of Sexuality*, Volume 1: *an Introduction*. New York: Vintage Books.

Foucault, M. (1988b) *The History of Sexuality*, Volume 2: *The Use of Pleasure*. New York: Vintage Books.

Foucault, M. (1988c) *The History of Sexuality*, Volume 3: *The Care of the Self*. New York: Vintage Books.

Foucault, M. (1988d) 'Technologies of the self', in L.H. Martin, H. Gutman and P.H. Hutton (eds), *Technologies of the Self: a Seminar with Michel Foucault*. Amherst, MA: University of Massachusetts Press. pp. 16–49.

Foucault, M. (1996) 'The ethics of the concern for the self as a practice of freedom', in S. Lotringer (ed.), *Foucault Live: Interviews, 1961–1984*. New York: Semiotext(e). pp. 432–49.

Gane, M. (1991) *Baudrillard's Bestiary: Baudrillard and Culture*. London: Routledge.

Garber, M. (1995) 'Viktor Petrenko's mother-in-law', in C. Baughman (ed.), *Women on Ice: Feminist Essays on the Tonya Harding/Nancy Kerrigan Spectacle*. New York: Routledge. pp. 93–102.

Genesko, G. (1994) *Baudrillard and Signs: Signification Ablaze*. London: Routledge.

Giddens, A. (1990) *The Consequences of Modernity*. Stanford, CA: Stanford University Press.

Gottdiener, M. (1995) *Postmodern Semiotics: Material Culture and the Forms of Postmodern Life*. Oxford: Basil Blackwell.

Grenz, S.J. (1996) *A Primer on Postmodernism*. Grand Rapids, MI: W.B. Eeerdmans.

Grossberg, L. (1996) 'Identity and cultural studies: is that all there is?', in S. Hall and P. de Gay (eds), *Questions of Cultural Identity*. London: Sage. pp. 87–107.

Grossberg, L. (1997) 'Cultural studies, modern logics, and theories of globalisation', in A. McRobbie (ed.), *Back to Reality? Social Experience and Cultural Studies*. Manchester: Manchester University Press. pp. 7–35.

Grossberg, L. and Nelson, C. (1988) 'Introduction: the territory of Marxism', in C. Nelson and L. Grossberg (eds), *Marxism and the Interpretation of Culture*. London: Macmillan. pp. 1–13.

Gruneau, R.S. (1988) 'Modernization or hegemony: two views on sport and social development', in J. Harvey and H. Cantelon (eds), *Not Just a Game: Essays in Canadian Sport Sociology*. Ottawa: University of Ottawa Press. pp. 9–32.

Gruneau, R.S. (1991) 'Sport and "esprit de corps": Notes on power, culture and the politics of the body', in F. Landry, M. Landry and M. Yerles (eds), *Sport … The Third Millennium*. Les Sainte-Foy: Presses de L'Université Laval. pp. 169–85.

Guttmann, A. (1978) *From Ritual to Record: the Nature of Modern Sports*. New York: Columbia University Press.

Habermas, J. (1981) 'Modernity versus postmodernity', *New German Critique*, 22: 9.

Habermas, J. (1987) *The Philosophical Discourse of Modernity*. Cambridge: Polity Press.

Hall, S. (1990) 'Cultural identity and diaspora', in J. Rutherford (ed.), *Identity: Community, Culture, Difference*. London: Lawrence and Wishart. pp. 222–37.

Hall, S. (1992a) 'Introduction', in S. Hall and B. Gieben (eds), *Formations of Modernity*. Cambridge: Polity Press. pp. 1–16.

Hall, S. (1992b) 'The question of cultural identity', in S. Hall, D. Held and A. McGrew (eds), *Modernity and Its Futures*. Cambridge: Polity Press. pp. 273–325.

Hall, S. (1995) 'The whites of their eyes: racist ideologies and the media', in G. Dines and J.M. Humez (eds), *Gender, Race, and Class in the Media: a Text-reader*. Thousand Oaks, CA: Sage. pp. 18–22.

Hall, S. (1996a) 'Introduction: who needs "identity"?', in S. Hall and P. de Gay (eds), *Questions of Cultural Identity*. London: Sage. pp. 1–17.

Hall, S. (1996b) 'On postmodernism and articulation: an interview with Stuart Hall (ed. Lawrence Grossberg)', in D. Morley and K.H. Chen (eds), *Stuart Hall: Critical Dialogues in Cultural Studies*. London: Routledge. pp. 131–50.

Hall, S. and Gay, P. de (eds) (1996) *Questions of Cultural Identity*. London: Sage.

Halton, E. (1995) 'The modern error: Or, the unbearable enlightenment of being', in M. Featherstone, S. Lash and R. Robertson (eds), *Global Modernities*. London: Sage. pp. 260–77.

Hamilton, P. (1992) 'The enlightenment and the birth of social science', in S. Hall and B. Gieben (eds), *Formations of Modernity*. Cambridge: Polity Press. pp. 17–58.

Hargreaves, J. (1986) *Sport, Power and Culture*. New York: St Martin's Press.

Hargreaves, J. (1987) 'The body, sport and power relations', in J. Horne, D. Jary and A. Tomlinson (eds), *Sport, Leisure and Social Relations*. London: Routledge & Kegan Paul. pp. 139–59.

Harland, R. (1987) *Superstructuralism: the Philosophy of Structuralism and Post-structuralism*. London: Routledge.

Harris, D. (1996) *A Society of Signs?* London: Routledge.

Hartsock, N. (1993) 'Foucault on power: a theory for women?', in C. Lemert (ed.), *Social Theory: the Multicultural and Classic Readings*. Boulder, CO: Westview Press. pp. 545–54.

Harvey, J. and Sparks, R. (1991) 'The politics of the body in the context of modernity', *Quest*, 43: 164–89.

Heath, S. (1981) *Questions of Cinema*. Basingstoke: Macmillan.

Hebdige, D. (1988) *Hiding in the Light: On Images and Things*. London: Comedia.

Heikkala, J. (1993) 'Discipline and excel: techniques of the self and body and the logic of competing', *Sociology of Sport Journal*, 10 (4): 397–412.

Hollinger, R. (1994) *Postmodernism and the Social Sciences: a Thematic Approach*. Thousand Oaks, CA: Sage.

Hood-Williams, J. (1995) 'Sexing the athletes', *Sociology of Sport Journal*, 12 (3): 290–305.

Ingham, A.G. (1978) 'American sport in transition: the maturation of industrial capitalism and its impact upon sport'. Unpublished doctoral dissertation. Amherst: University of Massachusetts.

Jarvie, G. and Maguire, J. (1994) *Sport and Leisure in Social Thought*. London: Routledge.

Johnson, R. (1987) 'What is cultural studies anyway?', *Social Texts*, 6 (1): 38–79.

Kearney, R. (1987) 'The crisis of the postmodern image', in A.P. Griffiths (ed.), *Contemporary French Philosophy*. Cambridge: Cambridge University Press. pp. 113–22.

Kearney, R. (1989) *The Wake of the Imagination: Toward a Postmodern Culture*. Minneapolis, MN: University of Minnesota Press.

Kellner, D. (1989) *Jean Baudrillard: From Marxism to Postmodernism and Beyond*. Stanford, CA: Stanford University Press.

Kellner, D. (1994) 'Introduction: Jean Baudrillard and the fin-de-millennium', in D. Kellner (ed.), *Baudrillard: a Critical Reader*. Cambridge, MA: Basil Blackwell. pp. 1–24.

King, S. (1993) 'The politics of the body and the body politic: Magic Johnson and the ideology of AIDS', *Sociology of Sport Journal*, 10 (3): 270–85.

Kondo, D. (1995) 'Poststructuralist theory as political necessity', *Amerasia Journal*, 21 (1 & 2): 95–100.

Kuhn, T. (1970) *The Structure of Scientific Revolutions*. Chicago: University of Chicago Press.

Kurzweil, E. (1986) 'The fate of structuralism', *Theory, Culture and Society*, 3 (3): 113–24.

Lawson, V. (1995) 'The politics of difference: examining the quantitative/qualitative dualism in post-structuralist feminist research', *The Professional Geographer*, 47 (4): 449–57.

Lévi-Strauss, C. (1961) *Tristes Tropiques* (trans. J. Russell). New York: Criterion Books.

Lévi-Strauss, C. (1966a) 'History and dialectic', in *The Savage Mind*. Chicago: University of Chicago Press. pp. 245–69.

Lévi-Strauss, C. (1966b) *The Savage Mind*. Chicago: University of Chicago Press.

Lévi-Strauss, C. (1967) *Structural Anthropology*. New York: Anchor Books.

Lévi-Strauss, C. (1969) *The Elementary Structures of Kinship*. Boston, MA: Beacon Press.

Levin, C. (1996) *Jean Baudrillard: a Study in Cultural Metaphysics*. London: Prentice-Hall.

Locke, J. (1967) *An Essay Concerning Human Understanding*. London: Fontana.

Loudcher, J.F. (1994) 'Du duel à l'épée au duel à main nues: émergence d'une pratique physique, la savate', *Sciences et Motricité*, 21: 12–21.

Luke, T.W. (1991) 'Power and politics in hyperreality: the critical project of Jean Baudrillard', *Social Science Journal*, 28 (3): 347–67.

Lupton, D. (1993) 'Is there life after Foucault? Post-structuralism and the health social sciences', *Australian Journal of Public Health*, 17 (4): 298–9.

Macdonald, E. (1991) 'The trouble with subjects: feminism, Marxism and the questions of post-structuralism', *Studies in Political Economy*, 35 (Summer): 43–71.

Macmurray, J. (1957) *The Self as Agent*. London: Faber.

MacNeill, M. (1998) 'Sex, lies and videotape: the political and cultural economies of celebrity fitness videos', in G. Rail (ed.), *Sport and Postmodern Times*. New York: State University of New York Press. pp. 163–84.

Macquarrie, J. (1972) *Existentialism*. Harmondsworth: Penguin.

Markula, P. (1995) 'Firm but shapely, fit but sexy, strong but thin: the postmodern aerobicizing female bodies', *Sociology of Sport Journal*, 12 (4): 424–53.

Martin, P. (1995) 'The constitution of power in landcare: a post-structuralist perspective with modernist undertones', *Rural Society*, 5 (2/3): 30–37.

Matthews, E. (1996) *Twentieth-century French Philosophy*. Oxford: Oxford University Press.

May, T. (1989) 'Is post-structuralist political theory anarchist?', *Philosophy and Social Criticism*, 15 (2): 167–82.

McHoul, A. and Grace, W. (1995) *A Foucault Primer: Discourse, Power and the Subject*. London: University College London Press.

McNay, L. (1994) *Foucault: a Critical Introduction*. Cambridge: Polity Press.

McRobbie, A. (1994) *Postmodernism and Popular Culture*. London: Routledge.

Miller, J. (1993) *The Passion of Michel Foucault*. New York: Simon & Schuster.

Miller, T. (1995) 'A short history of the penis', *Social Text*, (43): 1–26.

Morgan, W.J. (1995) '"Incredulity toward metanarratives" and normative suicide: a critique of post-modernist drift in critical sport theory', *International Review for the Sociology of Sport*, 30 (1): 25–45.

Morrow, R.A. (1994) *Critical Theory and Methodology*. Thousand Oaks, CA: Sage.

Norris, C. (1987) *Derrida*. London: Fontana.

Norris, C. (1992) *Uncritical Theory: Postmodernism, Intellectuals, and the Gulf War*. Amherst, MA: University of Massachusetts Press.

Paglia, C. (1997) 'Gridiron feminism', *The Wall Street Journal*, 12 September, p. 22.

Philo, C. (1992) 'Foucault's geography', *Society and Space*, 10: 137–61.

Pierce, C.P. (1995) 'Master of the universe', *GQ*, April: 180–7.

Poster, M. (1975) *Existential Marxism in Postwar France*. Princeton, NJ: Princeton University Press.

Poster, M. (1990) *The Mode of Information: Post-structuralism and Social Context*. Chicago: University of Chicago Press.

Pouwels, R.L. (1992) 'Swahili literature and history in the post-structuralist era', *International Journal of African Historical Studies*, 25 (2): 261–84.

Pronger, B. (1995) 'Rendering the body: the implicit lessons of gross anatomy', *Quest*, 47: 427–46.

Radhakrishnan, R. (1990) 'The changing subject and the politics of theory', *Differences: a Journal of Feminist Cultural Studies*, 2 (2): 126–52.

Rail, G. (1991) 'Postmodernity and mediated sport: the medium is the model (author's translation of *Technologie postmoderne et culture: un regard sur le sport mediatisé*), in F. Landry, M. Landry and M. Yerles (eds), *Sport ... the Third Millennium*. Les Sainte-Foy: Presses de L'Université Laval. pp. 731–39.

Rail, G. (1998) 'Seismography of the postmodern condition: three theses on the implosion of sport', in G. Rail (ed.), *Sport and Postmodern Times*. New York: State University of New York Press. pp. 143–62.

Rail, G. and Harvey, J. (1995) 'Body at work: Michel Foucault and the sociology of sport', *Sociology of Sport Journal*, 12 (2): 164–79.

Ramazanoglu, C. (1993) *Up against Foucault: Explorations of Some Tensions between Foucault and Feminism*. London: Routledge.

Redhead, S. (1994) 'Media culture and the World Cup: the last World Cup?', in J. Sugden and A. Tomlinson (eds), *Hosts and Champions: Soccer Cultures, National Identities and the USA World Cup*. Aldershot: Arena. pp. 291–309.

Redhead, S. (1998) 'Baudrillard, "Amérique" and the hyperreal World Cup', in G. Rail (ed.), *Sport and Postmodern Times*. New York: State University of New York Press. pp. 221–38.

Rigby, B. (1991) *Popular Culture in Modern France: a Study of Cultural Discourse*. London: Routledge.

Rinehart, R. (1998) 'Born-again sport: ethics in biographical research', in G. Rail (ed.), *Sport and Postmodern Times*. New York: State University of New York Press. pp. 33–48.

Rojek, C. (1990) 'Baudrillard and leisure', *Leisure Studies*, 9: 1–20.

Rojek, C. and Turner, B.S. (1993) *Forget Baudrillard?* London: Routledge.

Rosenau, P.M. (1992) *Postmodernism and the Social Sciences: Insights, Inroads, and Intrusions*. Princeton, NJ: Princeton University Press.

Sartre, J.-P. (1956) 'Existentialism is a humanism', in W. Kaufmann (ed.), *Existentialism from Dostoevsky to Sartre*. New York: Meridian Books. p. 29.

Sarup, M. (1993) *An Introductory Guide to Poststructuralism and Postmodernism*. London: Harvester Wheatsheaf.

Saussure, F. de (1959) *Course in General Linguistics* (trans. W. Baskin). New York: Philosophical Library.

Sawicki, J. (1991) *Disciplining Foucault: Feminism, Power, and the Body*. New York: Routledge.

Schoonmaker, S. (1994) 'Capitalism and the code: a critique of Baudrillard's third order simulacrum', in D. Kellner (ed.), *Baudrillard: a Critical Reader*. Cambridge, MA: Basil Blackwell. pp. 168–88.

Seidman, S. (1994) *Contested Knowledge: Social Theory in the Postmodern Era*. Cambridge, MA: Basil Blackwell.

Sloop, J.M. (1997) 'Mike Tyson and the perils of discursive constraints: boxing, race, and the assumption of guilt', in A. Baker and T. Boyd (eds), *Out of Bounds: Sports, Media, and the Politics of Identity*. Bloomington, IN: Indiana University Press.

Slowikowski, S.S. (1993) 'Cultural performance and sport mascots', *Journal of Sport and Social Issues*, 17 (1): 23–33.

Smart, B. (1985) *Michel Foucault*. London: Routledge.

Smith, J. (1994) 'Realism and poststructuralism: Foucault, Bakhtin, de Marchi', *Italian Studies*, 49: 70–90.

Steinberg, M.W. (1996) 'Culturally speaking: finding a commons between poststructuralism and the

Thompsonian perspective', *Social History*, 21 (2): 193–214.

Storey, J. (1993) *An Introductory Guide to Cultural Theory and Popular Culture*. London: Harvester Wheatsheaf.

Sturrock, J. (1986) *Structuralism*. London: Fontana.

Sturrock, J. (1990) 'Global village idiocies', *The Independent on Sunday (Review Section)*, 8 August, p. 28.

Sykes, H. (1996) 'Constr(i)(u)cting lesbian identities in physical education: 'feminist and poststructural approaches to researching sexuality', *Quest*, 48: 459–69.

Theberge, N. (1991) 'Reflections on the body in the sociology of sport', *Quest*, 43: 123–34.

Thorne, T. (1993) *Fads, Fashions and Cults: From Acid House to Zoot Suit – via Existentialism and Political Correctness – the Definitive Guide to (Post-)Modern Culture*. London: Bloomsbury.

Turner, B.S. (1982) 'The discourse of diet', *Theory, Culture and Society*, 1 (1): 23–32.

Usher, R. (1989) 'Locating experience in language: toward a poststructuralist theory of experience', *Adult Education Quarterly*, 40 (1): 23–32.

Van Wynsberghe, R. and Ritchie, I. (1998) '(Ir)relevant ring: the symbolic consumption of the Olympic logo in postmodern media culture', in G. Rail (ed.), *Sport and Postmodern Times*. New York: State University of New York Press. pp. 367–84.

Vigarello, G. (1978) *Le Corps Redressé*. Paris: Éditions Universitaires.

Weedon, C. (1997) *Feminist Practice and Poststructuralist theory*, 2nd edn. Oxford: Blackwell.

Wenner, L.A. (1998) 'In search of the sports bar: masculinity, alcohol, sports and the mediation of public space', in G. Rail (ed.), *Sport and Postmodern Times*. New York: State University of New York Press. pp. 301–32.

Whitson, D. (1989) 'Discourses of critique in sport sociology: a response to Deem and Sparks', *Sociology of Sport Journal*, 6 (1): 60–5.

Whitson, D. and MacIntosh, D. (1990) 'The scientization of physical education: discourses of performance', *Quest*, 42 (1): 40–51.

Willis, P. (1990) '*Common Culture: Symbolic Work at Play in the Everyday Cultures of the Young*. Milton Keynes: Open University Press.

Woods, J. (1992) 'Lost in the wilder shores of reality', *Guardian*, 27 February, p. 23.

Young, R. (1990) *White Mythologies: Writing History and the West*. London: Routledge.

PART TWO

CROSS-DISCIPLINARY DIFFERENCES AND CONNECTIONS

EDITORS' INTRODUCTION

Scholars in the sociology of sport have been trained and work primarily in sociology and physical education departments. But they also come from anthropology, sports studies and cultural studies departments and programmes. This mix of backgrounds among scholars has created openness to using work on sport and society from a range of social science disciplines. Furthermore, most scholars in the field have realized that multiple disciplinary perspectives are required if they wish to understand more fully the complexities of sport as a social and cultural phenomenon. When scholars focus on a particular issue, problem, or sphere of life there is a tendency to seek information from all relevant disciplines. In the case of sport, scholars travel on a regular basis across disciplinary lines. This crossing of disciplinary lines has been institutionalized in connection with sports studies programmes where colleagues in the social and behavioural sciences are supportive of one another and collaborate on certain projects. It is important, though, to add that attempts are also made to synthesize different perspectives and, in that way, making sports research a simpler and more coherent task. Structuration theory and figurational sociology are recent attempts at synthesis. It must be recognized, though, that agreement on their value is far from universal.

It should be noted that four of the disciplines highlighted in the chapters below have one or more professional associations that reflect discipline-based scholarly interests in sport, and most of these professional associations sponsor regular conferences for members. The disciplines with professional associations are anthropology, history, philosophy and psychology. All these except anthropology

currently have one or more journals devoted to sport-related research and enquiry. Economics, geography and political science, each for different reasons, lack professional organizations representing scholars with interests in sport, and of these, only economics has a journal devoted exclusively to research on sport or sport-related topics. Table I (p. xxiv) lists the journals associated with the sociology of sport and each of the disciplines included in this section.

The chapters in Part Two provide explanations of the theory and research in seven disciplines. As you read them, you will notice differences manifested in terms of vocabulary, concepts, issues addressed, approaches used and literature cited. We believe strongly that each of these disciplines has generated important research and analyses of sport and society that are related substantively and significantly to the sociology of sport. These chapters illustrate collectively the richness, diversity and breadth of scholarly enquiry on sport and society. They also illustrate the complementarity and interconnections that exist between the interests of scholars who do research and develop theory related to sport and society. Because there was no way to order these chapters in terms of substantive criteria, we have presented them alphabetically by discipline.

CHAPTER OVERVIEWS

Kendall Blanchard's chapter on 'The Anthropology of Sport' provides a description of the breadth and diversity of anthropological enquiry. In his overview of research, Blanchard notes that games in traditional cultures have attracted the attention of some anthropologists over the past century. More recently, attention has been given also to play and sport. Blanchard explains that anthropologists have dealt with sport most often as a cultural institution and studied sports in comparative or cross-cultural perspective. Full-length ethnographies of sport as well as journal articles have become increasingly common since the early 1980s. Anthropologists interested in the study of sports have come together in The Association for the Study of Play, and also in organizations based in Europe and Asia. Recent research on sports has involved a wide range of topics. There have been cultural descriptions and analyses of sports in pre-literate, tribal cultures. There have been studies of the relationships between sport and play and sport and ritual. The definition of sport has been discussed in cross-cultural and comparative terms. Applied anthropology has focused on problems associated with sports in a range of cultural and international contexts. Archaeological evidence has been used in descriptions of sport in prehistory and early history. Human performance has been studied in terms of anatomy, physiology and genetics. And there is currently an emphasis on theory-based explanatory and interpretative research. Blanchard concludes by listing topics deserving research attention in the future. He calls for ethnographies documenting the diversity of sport forms around the world, for theoretically informed research on the meaning and role of sports in societies, for the use of new archaeological data in cultural research, and for studies of the relationships between sports and violence and sports and international relations.

In the chapter on 'Economics and Sport', Marc Lavoie provides an overview and summary of research on issues related to labour economics and the economics of the firm (that is, leagues/fixtures, franchises and teams). He notes that two traditions have emerged in this work. One is a North American, or more widely Anglo-Saxon, tradition with a micro-economic focus that centres on the individual and the firm and utilizes concepts of supply and demand to construct and test models of behaviour for individuals in sports, especially professional sports. The other is a Continental European tradition that relies on descriptive statistics rather than econometrics, and focuses on presenting descriptive tables and ratios on the economics of amateur and recreational sports more than on professional sports. Lavoie emphasizes studies done in the former

tradition, partly because the research is more accessible in English and partly because the analyses they present often require explanation. In his overview of labour economics, Lavoie synthesizes and summarizes research on salary determination, salary discrimination and the distribution of earnings. Most of this literature focuses on professional sports in North America because precise quantitative measures of individual output and productivity are available for these sports. The availability of salary data for individual athletes, more characteristic in North America than in Europe, also permits complex analyses of labour economics. Sociologists have frequently used economic studies of salary discrimination in their discussions of race and ethnic relations in sports. Lavoie also synthesizes and summarizes research on the economics of the firm. He highlights studies of profit maximization (as opposed to maximizing winning), event attendance, restrictions on players' mobility, revenue-sharing schemes and salary caps, and the financial impact of professional sport franchises on host communities. He concludes by noting that most economics research focuses on professional and other elite-level sports, and it revolves around the use of econometric methods and the construction of economic models. He predicts that future research will most likely continue along these lines.

In his chapter on 'Human Geography and the Study of Sport', John Bale begins by noting that sports studies involve at least some forms of disciplinary synthesis. This is especially evident in connection with research on the relationship between space and place and sport. Bale focuses his chapter on 'achievement sport' rather than on recreation and leisure. He outlines the basis for geographical concerns with sports, and notes that, despite the centrality of space and place issues related to and inherent in sports, the geography of sport remains on the margins of geography as a whole. He explains that geographical research on sports has focused generally on four major topics. First, there have been efforts to map variations in the production and distribution of athletic talent and to identify actual and ideal locations of facilities, clubs and franchises. Secondly, there has been research on the spatial dynamics of sports. This work has focused on the diffusion of sports and sports innovations, the migratory flow of sports participants, and the re-location of clubs and franchises. A third collection of studies has sought to identify the environmental and spatial impact of sports. This research overlaps with economics research and is often informed by social and cultural theories used in the sociology of sport. Fourthly, there has been a growth recently in research on sport and landscapes. This research moves beyond cartographic concerns. It is theoretically informed and utilizes cultural studies approaches. It focuses on issues related to territoriality and power, place and social control, place and meaning and pleasure, and the symbolic character of landscapes. Bale closes by noting that the future of the geography of sport depends on geographers becoming increasingly aware that sport is a significant part of culture and that the spatial dynamics and environmental issues associated with sports are worthy of serious attention.

Nancy Struna's chapter entitled 'Social History and Sport' illustrates clearly the close connection between social historians and sociologists. Struna explains that social historians view sports as practices, formations and texts that are constitutive features of societies at specific points in time. Recent work in social history is heavily informed and guided by the same social theories used by sociologists. Struna notes that historical research done prior to the 1980s tended to be descriptive and empiricist rather than analytical, critical and theoretically grounded. Despite this weakness, it still provides detailed and usable empirical 'maps' of some people and some sports around the world. Since 1980 historians have been more likely to produce three complementary but different genres of studies. First, there have been studies of the deep, internal history of sports. These studies focus on sporting experiences as identifiably distinct social experiences related to larger social movements and issues. Secondly, there have been studies of sports *and* society in which the histories of sports are told in connection with the web of social activities and processes characteristic in a society at particular points in time. Thirdly, there have been studies of sports as forms of popular culture or leisure through which are revealed various ideological interests, social relations and structural conditions. Struna then presents a review of recent historiography research. She notes that social historians have focused on issues of cultural production and reproduction as well as issues of agency and power relations in much of their recent work. She highlights sources that have focused on conflict and struggle around issues of class relations, gender relations, the body, racial and ethnic relations, and ideology. Finally, she suggests four lines of enquiry that address previously understudied topics in social history. These are:

1 Studies of ordinary life and society among people in Latin America, Africa, most of southern and central Europe, and Asia;
2 Comparative, cross-cultural studies of social relations, structural conditions and social meanings associated with sports;
3 Studies of sports as cultural practices associated with broader systems of behaviour and meanings;
4 Studies of the dynamics of persistence, change and transformation of sports over long periods of time.

Struna's bibliography highlights key sources published recently, especially since 1990.

In his chapter on 'The Philosophy of Sport' William Morgan notes that philosophers, like scholars in the social sciences, began to give concerted attention to sport-related enquiry in the 1960s. As physical education began to give way to sport studies, space in the form of academic appointments was opened for philosophers of sport. Although the analytical and positivist approaches that have been dominant in philosophy have discouraged enquiry into sport, some philosophers in the 1960s and 1970s gave attention to play, games and sports. Morgan presents a conceptual overview of the philosophy of sport in terms of the major questions addressed by philosophers. He explains that philosophers deal with ontological issues as they probe the question 'What is reality?'. They deal with epistemological issues as they probe the question 'What is knowledge?' And they deal with axiological issues of ethics and aesthetics as they probe the question 'What is value?' In connection with the first of these questions, philosophers of sport probe the metaphysics of sport and debate issues related to the nature and characteristics of sport and relationships between sports and games. In connection with epistemological questions, they probe the origin and organization of knowledge about sport. In connection with axiological questions, they consider issues related to ethics and aesthetics. Enquiries into ethics focus on sportsmanship, the competitive character of sport and cheating, gender identity and equity, the moral standing of animals in sports, and the use and detection of performance-enhancing substances in sports. Enquiries into aesthetics focus primarily on whether sports are best understood in artistic terms and as art forms. Morgan explains that axiological enquiry has attracted the bulk of attention among sport philosophers in recent years. He concludes on an optimistic note by suggesting that the philosophy of sport will continue to grow because of a recent revival of pragmatism in philosophy and an upsurge of moral studies in society and academia as a whole. Furthermore, as scholarly attention turns more to a consideration of cultural practices, philosophy provides useful tools of reform and renovation.

Barrie Houlihan's chapter on 'Politics and Sport' begins with examples of the diverse ways that politics and sports have intersected. These include everything from protest and terrorism to government policy and power relations in sport organizations. Houlihan distinguishes between politics *and* sport and politics *in* sport and then discusses research and analysis related to each of these two topics. He notes that the bulk of past research has focused on the former topic, especially on the role of the state in sport. Research has highlighted at least six domestic and foreign policy motives associated with government intervention in sport. For example, intervention may be designed to control (outlaw or regulate) particular sports or to facilitate military preparedness. It may be motivated by a desire to promote social integration or national identity, especially in nation-states where ethnic identities challenge the priority given to national identity, where shifting political boundaries have accentuated diversity rather than unity, or where there is a need to project a national identity on an international stage for purposes of internal or external reaffirmation. In more recent years it may be motivated by concerns with economic development as it occurs in connection with tourism and boosterism. And finally, it may occur in connection with international diplomatic efforts intended to build relations between enemies, maintain good relations with allies, register disapproval of policies enacted by other states, signal readmission into the international community, or promote national self-interest. Houlihan notes that research by political scientists and others has examined the efficacy of such policy interventions. Research on politics *in* sport has become more common in recent years. It focuses on the political goals of sport organizations such as the IOC and international and national federations. It explores issues of access to participation, especially as they are related to gender and ethnic relations and forms of discrimination in society. It has also begun to focus on issues related to sharing revenues generated by sports and to the complex relationships and dynamics associated with commercialization and new forms of funding and sponsorship. Houlihan closes with a discussion of future

themes that will appear in the politics and sports literature. He foresees analysis of policy issues related to equity of participation opportunities and to the political environment of sport itself, especially related to doping and doping control. There will also be research on context issues including the future roles of government, major international sport bodies and commercial interests in sports that are becoming increasingly global in scope and impact. He emphasizes that this research and the theory that guides it will bring scholars together from multiple disciplines including political science, sociology, economics, geography, history and philosophy.

Diane Gill's chapter on 'Psychology and the Study of Sport' highlights the development, growth and organization of the discipline more than its literature. Gill notes that the psychology and sociology of sport have overlapped frequently in terms of substantive content and issues. However, psychology's focus is clearly on individuals and the psychology of sport has given priority to application. Furthermore, of all the social and behavioural sciences, psychology is most closely aligned with the so-called 'hard sciences', a fact reflected in the continuing commitment among many scholars in the psychology of sport to emphasize experimental research. Gill explains that the discipline of sport psychology has grown primarily in the context of exercise and sport science rather than in the context of psychology. Although traditional psychology theories have been used widely, sport psychologists have developed their own sport-specific theoretical models and methods. Gill identifies the international, European and North American origins of sport psychology and notes that the field has traditionally encompassed motor learning and motor control as well as sport psychology. She outlines the history of the field beginning with efforts to build the knowledge base through research, forming professional organizations, publishing journals and establishing graduate programmes to train future generations of sport psychologists. Since the 1970s the field has given less emphasis to motor development and more to applied issues related to sport performance, health and the enhancement of experiences in physical activities. Since the late 1980s when the field research and the applied emphasis of many sport psychologists captured the interest of the public as well as many students, there has been increased interest in sports as settings for clinical and counselling work. Applied interests gave rise also to the increased use and legitimacy of idiographic, introspective and interpretive research methodologies. Specialization among scholars has led to the formation of different organizations and journals. Gill notes that sport psychologists have become formally recognized within the organization of the American Psychological Association, although few psychology departments in the United States or other countries offer undergraduate or graduate courses in the psychology of sport. In closing, Gill explains that sport psychology is clearly a global discipline characterized by a high degree of diversity in research and purpose, but that there has been a gradual trend towards the merger of research and practice in the field.

8

THE ANTHROPOLOGY OF SPORT

Kendall Blanchard

Anthropology is the most comprehensive of the social sciences. Its focus spans the entire range of human behavior, from the biological to the cultural and from the past to the future. Physical anthropologists study human anatomy and physiology, genetics, non-human primate biology and behavior, the fossil record, and evolution in all of its many manifestations. Archaeologists in most cases are anthropologists who study prehistory, the many centuries of human life that predate the advent of writing systems and the emergence of history. Anthropological archaeology relies on a variety of skills, methodologies and supporting sciences (such as paleontology, geology, paleobotany, paleozoology). Linguistic anthropologists study human language as a process and specialize in describing unwritten languages and reconstructing those languages no longer spoken or those not recorded in written history. Cultural anthropologists, also known as social anthropologists, ethnologists, or ethnographers, study human behavior from the perspective of culture and social structure. In short, every facet of human life and history is a legitimate subject for anthropology. Its theories and methodologies have roots that extend across the entire academic community. Thus it is not surprising that the discipline has been called 'the most humanistic of the sciences' and 'the most scientific of the humanities' (Wolf, 1964).

Anthropology in general is characterized by the following reasonably consistent themes that give the discipline a distinctive flair.

1   A tendency to give primary attention to people who live in small-scale societies (for example, tribal, folk, traditional, band and pre-state societies). For this reason, British social anthropologists have sometimes referred to their discipline as the branch of sociology that studies primitive people (Evans-Pritchard, 1962).

2   A primary focus on process as opposed to results. For example, physical anthropologists are more likely to highlight the process of evolution than a particular moment in evolutionary time. Likewise, cultural anthropologists are more likely to emphasize the importance of the culture change process than a specific time or event in cultural history.

3   The frequent use of cross-cultural comparison as a methodology. The comparison of two or more cultures, particularly along the lines of a single institution (such as marriage), is a way of better understanding culture and validating or discrediting generalizations about human behavior.

4   The use of fieldwork as the most common methodology for basic data collection. For the cultural anthropologist this involves living and working among the people being studied and assuming the role as 'participant observer'. In other words, it means becoming a part of the group yet at the same time maintaining a scientific objectivity.

5   A tendency to identify with the concerns and causes of its research subject, frequently minority or disadvantaged peoples in the developing areas of the world.

ANTHROPOLOGY OF SPORT

The anthropology of sport is the application of the perspectives, theories and methodologies of the discipline to the study of sport. By implication, sport is viewed as a distinctive component of culture, not unlike marriage, religion, or music. It is treated as a separate institution, but, like all cultural institutions, it is thoroughly integrated with the other institutions that characterize any given culture. Sport in this context is analyzed from a cross-cultural or comparative perspective. Particular attention is paid to the description and interpretation of sport in small-scale, traditional or tribal societies.

By implication, the anthropology of sport is an academic enterprise engaged in only by anthropologists. However, in reality, the anthropology of sport is more of a perspective or an approach than a subdiscipline of anthropology. Scholars of various academic backgrounds from countries around the world are bringing to the analysis of sport an anthropological perspective and in this sense doing the anthropology of sport. These scholars include historians, kinesiologists, psychologists, geographers, sociologists and political scientists. To call their work 'anthropology of sport' is not simply to co-opt these efforts, but rather to recognize the importance of their contributions, even though the authors themselves might not think of themselves as doing anthropology or of their writings as anthropological in nature.

Historical Background

The anthropology of sport has it roots in the work of early European anthropologists. For example, Sir Edward Burnett Tylor (1832–1917), a British scholar sometimes referred to as the father of anthropology, published an article entitled 'The history of games' (1879) in which he described several simple, natural sports (for example, wrestling, ball tossing) and argued that these had been invented independently in many different geographical settings. However, he viewed other more complicated games, like the forerunners of modern-day football (soccer), as not so easily invented. These he saw as evidence of prehistoric diffusion and contact among the major cultural centers of the world.

Although sport was not a central concern among nineteenth-century anthropologists, it did receive occasional attention from anthropologists other than Tylor. For example, James Mooney, an anthropologist and head of the Bureau of American Ethnology, published in 1890 a detailed description of the Cherokee ball game. The Cherokees, a Native American tribe located in the southeastern United States,

traditionally played a racket game sometimes referred to as the parent game of lacrosse. The racket game was widely known and played among Native American tribes during the eighteenth and nineteenth centuries. The Cherokee version of the game was similar to that of other tribes. Each player was equipped with two ball sticks, hickory staffs with pouches of twisted bear sinew at the end. The ball, less than two inches in diameter, was made of tightly packed deer hair and covered with deer hide. Two teams of players competed in the attempt to throw or carry the ball up and down a lengthy field and strike the opponent's goal and thus score points. The first team to reach an agreed-upon total was the winner. Rules for the sport were minimal. The most important and most frequently enforced rule was one which prohibited a player from touching the ball with his hand. The racket game among the Cherokees, as among other tribes, was an important community event with cultural implications that went well beyond the sport itself. Traditionally, it involved elaborate preparation by the entire community, fasting, religious ceremonies and celebrations, incantations and magical manipulations, and heavy wagering on the outcome of the game. Mooney's contribution was important in that it documented first-hand the game and its cultural context. In addition, and perhaps more importantly, it analyzed the integral relationship between the sport and its social setting, recognizing that sport is not played in a cultural vacuum.

The early twentieth century witnessed an increased interest in games and sports among anthropologists and other students of culture. One of the most important figures of this era was Stewart Culin (1859–1929). Culin, a business person, developed an interest in archaeology early in his career. This led eventually to a position as a museum curator. He was particularly interested in games and as curator of ethnology at the Brooklyn Museum he collected many sport and game artifacts from around the world and brought together volumes of information about those artifacts. Out of these efforts came several important books on games, perhaps his most significant being *Games of the North American Indians* (1907). Referred to by one biographer as the 'major game scholar of the past 100 years ... in the field of anthropology' (Avedon and Sutton-Smith, 1971), Culin, like Mooney before him, took the study and description of sport beyond that institution itself to elaborate on its full meaning for human society and culture. As one writer has noted:

Mr. Culin's studies ... not only afford an understanding of the technology of the games and their distribution, as well as their bearing on history ... but they contribute in a remarkable manner to an appreciation of native modes of thought and of the motives and impulses that underlie the conduct of primitive peoples generally. [Culin] ... creates the science of games and for the first time gives this branch its proper place in the science of man. (Holmes, 1907: xl)

European anthropologists were also taking an interest in sport during the early decades of this century. For example, German ethnographer Von Karl Weule wrote a lengthy article on sport that appeared in a volume on sport history that was published in 1925. In this article, entitled 'Ethnologie des Sportes' (Ethnology of sport), Weule wrote from the perspective of the culture-history school popular in Germany at that time to argue that the primary focus of an ethnology of sport should be two-fold. On the one hand, it should trace culture, and sport as an aspect of culture, back to its beginning. On the other, it should put sport into its proper theoretical perspective. Treating sport as an element of culture that had developed and evolved conjunctively with that culture, Weule argued that there were real differences between the sports of so-called primitive and modern peoples. Early humans, he claimed, the peoples of the pre-state world, used sport as a means for coping with the immediate problems of adaptation, survival and defense. Modern peoples, on the other hand, use sport for purposes of perfecting the human body, competing and pleasure. The ritual and practical aims of sport in a preliterate society have been supplanted by a new set of objectives endemic to life in industrial society. Although his work was notable for its excellent description, Weule remained largely dependent on secondary sources and maintained an implicitly racist view of what he called primitive society.

Also indicative of the interest in sport among anthropologists during this era is the work of scholars such as Elsdon Best, Raymond Firth and Alexander Lesser. Best was relatively generous in the attention he gave to sports in his ethnographic description. His 1924 two-volume work on the Maori is replete with details regarding the sport and play activities of this group of native New Zealanders. Firth (1930/31) likewise gave full attention to sport and games. In 1931, he published a lengthy article in the journal *Oceania* entitled 'A dart match in Tikopia: a study in the sociology of primitive sport'. This article, a detailed

description of the Polynesian dart match, has become a classic, in part because of the way in which Firth documented the important role of sport and its many functions in small-scale society.

Lesser's major contribution to the anthropology of sport was his *The Pawnee Ghost Dance Hand Game: a Study of Cultural Change* (1933). The Ghost Dance was a nativistic movement that originated among the Paiute Indians of the American Great Basin in the 1880s. It was based on the premise that if American Indians engaged in this ritual, the Ghost Dance, their ancestors would return from their graves and help them recapture their lands from the white man and reestablish their dominance across the North American continent. One of the groups that became a part of the Ghost Dance movement was the Pawnee Indians, who played a distinctive hand game, a guessing game in which players hid special bones or dice in their hands. In a short period of time after the introduction of the Ghost Dance into Pawnee society, the hand game became highly stylized and ritualized and in many ways a part of the Ghost Dance ceremony itself. According to Lesser, what was originally a game became under these circumstances a ritual. Lesser used the Pawnee case to argue against an earlier assertion of Culin (1907) that the games of North American Indians were either rituals themselves or games that had evolved from rituals. Lesser demonstrated that the reverse could be the case.

During the 1940s and 1950s there were other contributions to the literature on sport and culture by anthropologists (for example, Opler, 1944, 1945) and scholars from other areas (for example, Brewster, 1956; Frederickson, 1960; Stumpf and Cozens, 1947). Perhaps the most critically important publication of this era was an article entitled 'Games in culture' which appeared in a 1959 issue of the journal *American Anthropologist* (Roberts, Arth and Bush). This article was the first effort by anthropologists to deal with the issue of games from a strictly theoretical perspective. In this article the authors defined a game as 'a recreational activity characterized by (1) organized play, (2) competition, (3) two or more sides, (4) criteria for determining the winner, and (5) agreed upon rules' (1959: 597). They also classified games in three categories: those of (1) physical skill, (2) strategy and (3) chance. From here, the authors went to the Human Relations Area Files (HRAF), a systematic collection of basic ethnographic data from hundreds of groups from around the world (Murdock et al., 1961). Selecting 50 of these, they attempted to correlate the nature of games with other aspects of culture. As a result of this analysis, it was suggested that there is a significant relationship between games of strategy and social complexity; in other words, the more complex a society, the more likely the group to engage in games of strategy (chess, for example). They also found that games of chance appear to be associated with religious activities and that environmental conditions may affect the type and number of physical skill games engaged in by any particular group. Perhaps the most important contribution of 'Games in culture' is the fact that it brought attention to games and sports as important cultural phenomena and as legitimate subjects for anthropologists.

The 1960s witnessed the publication by anthropologists of various articles that had sport themes. One of the best known from that period is Robin Fox's essay on 'Pueblo baseball: a new use for old witchcraft' (1961). This piece is a description of how baseball was introduced among the Cochiti Pueblo of New Mexico and how it provided for a new form of expression for old forms of witchcraft. Of equal importance was Leslie White's 1964 presidential address to the American Anthropological Association. One of the most highly respected anthropologists of his time, White gave added credibility to the study of sport by suggesting that anthropology was an appropriate theoretical model for the analysis of professional sports, in particular baseball, which he saw as a microcosm of the larger American cultural system.

During the 1970s and 1980s the study of sport from a cross-cultural perspective and an interest in folk or traditional sport became increasingly popular among scholars in Europe and North America. In particular, American anthropologists developed a greater appreciation for the phenomenon. One of the most important publications of this period was Clifford Geertz's (1972) essay on the Balinese cockfight ('Deep play: notes on the Balinese cockfight'). In this article, Geertz described the cockfight and the betting and other intrigue that surrounds it. Painting a detailed picture of the event, he analyzed the nature of the wagering behavior that, though illegal, is an important part of the event. He then argued that what may appear to the outside observer to be irrational economic behavior is actually behavior driven by moral imperative more than by greed. In other words, it is as though there is a deep-seated moral compunction that drives participants to take great risks even though such risks may not be justified by the

potential economic reward. Ultimately, the real value of the article is the way in which it illustrates the complexity, depth and broad meaning of sport in human society.

Among the works written by non-anthropologists during the 1970s that address sports anthropology themes, perhaps the most widely read is Allen Guttmann's *From Ritual to Record: The Nature of Modern Sports* (1978). Guttmann, an historian, argued that so-called primitive sports are not sports in the strictest sense. These activities were more than ritual or pure religious expression. However, modern sports are different in that they are invariably quantified and involve the pursuit of a record. In his words,

> When we can no longer distinguish the sacred from the profane or even the good from the bad, we content ourselves with minute discriminations between the batting average of the .308 hitter and the .307 hitter. Once the gods have vanished from Mount Olympus or from Dante's paradise, we can no longer run to appease them or save our souls, but we can set a new record. It is a uniquely modern form of immortality. (Guttmann, 1978)

Throughout the course of anthropology's history, writers have frequently given some attention to sport within the context of monographs devoted to the description of particular cultures (for example, Boas, 1888; Hoffman, 1896; Howitt, 1904; Perry, 1923; Spencer and Gillen, 1927). Few dealt with sport as their primary focus, although there were some (for example, Stern, 1949). However, it was not until the 1980s that full-length works devoted to the ethnographic description and analysis of sport became common. Some of these were written by anthropologists, for example, Azoy's *Buzkashi: Game and Power in Afghanistan* (1982); Blanchard's *The Mississippi Choctaws at Play: the Serious Side of Leisure* (1981); Lawrence's *Rodeo: an Anthropologist Looks at the Wild and Tame* (1982); and MacAloon's *This Great Symbol* (1981). Some of these were written by scholars from other disciplines, for example, James's *Beyond a Boundary* (1984); Lever's *Soccer Madness* (1983); Mandle and Mandle's *Grass Roots Commitment: Basketball and Society in Trinidad and Tobago* (1988); Oxendine's *American Indian Sports Heritage* (1988); Poliakoff's *Combat Sports in the Ancient World* (1987); and Sansone's *Greek Athletics and the Genesis of Sport* (1988).

This trend continued into the 1990s. From this decade, work of particular importance to social scientists who study sport are Klein's *Sugarball: the American Game, the Dominican Dream* (1991); Lewis's *Ring of Liberation: a*

Deceptive Discourse in Brazilian Capoeria (1992); Guttmann's *Games and Empires: Modern Sports and Cultural Imperialism* (1994); and Vennum's *American Indian Lacrosse* (1994).

The growing popularity and importance of sport themes in cross-cultural studies among anthropologists and others is reflected not only in the volume of publications but also in the number of persons involved internationally in organizations and special events that highlight the study of sports culture and folk or traditional sports. In the 1970s, the Association for the Anthropological Study of Play (TAASP) was organized by a group of scholars, largely American and Canadian, and included many persons whose primary interest was sport. In recent years this organization has changed its name to the Association for the Study of Play (TASP), its membership has broadened to include scholars from around the world, and it has begun holding some of its annual meetings in Europe as well as in Canada and the United States.

In Asia, under the leadership of the Japanese Office of Foreign Ministry and members of the academic community, a new traditional sports movement has begun (Ogura, 1992). It is a movement whose goal is to describe, analyze and preserve traditional sports (that is, those sports that have not as yet been tainted by commercialism and that are tied to traditional cultures in areas around the world). It is also a movement designed to use sport as a mechanism for enhancing international communication. In many ways, it can be viewed as an effort to rediscover the original spirit of the Olympics. The Japanese government and Japanese scholars have sponsored a variety of special programs and exhibitions in recent years, such as the International Conference on the Preservation and Advancement of Traditional Sport, held in Tokyo in 1993. Likewise, in China, meetings devoted to the study of traditional ethnic sports are now held annually (see *Beijing Review*, 1995a, b, c).

The Europeans have also developed a new enthusiasm for the study and preservation of traditional sports and games. Members of the academic community, professionals who are part of private or public sports organizations, and amateur sports enthusiasts are working together to give new prominence and exposure to the folk sports of Europe. A committee for the Development of Sport (CCDS) has hosted a variety of seminars on the topic in recent years. Also, there have been many special exhibitions featuring traditional sport. One of the most important of these was the First International Festival of Traditional Sports, held in Bonn, Germany, in 1992, an innovation that has continued.

THE MAJOR ISSUES

The major issues addressed within the framework of the anthropological approach to the study of sport that has emerged over the past few decades include the following.

The Study and Description of Sports Activities in Preliterate, Tribal, Non-Western, or Developing Societies Consistent with anthropological tradition, the anthropology of sport tends to target the activities of simple or small-scale society. As indicated earlier, folk or traditional sport has been of particular interest to scholars in Europe and Asia in the past decade. The literature that has been amassed over the past several decades is a treasure trove of ethnographic descriptions of both sports behavior and its cultural context as these are part of traditional societies from around the world. Almost every area of the world is represented in this literature: *Afghanistan* (Azoy, 1982; Balikci, 1978); *Africa* (Baker and Mangan, 1987; Gini, 1939; Raum, 1953; Scotch, 1961; Stevens, 1973, 1975; van der Merwe and Salter, 1990); *Australia* (Harney, 1952; Howell and Howell, 1987; Moncrieff, 1966; Taylor and Toohey, 1995; Roth, 1902); *Caribbean* (Klein, 1991; Mandle and Mandle, 1988; Manning, 1981); *China* (Giles, 1906; Kanin, 1978; Knuttgen et al., 1990; Kolatch, 1972; Sasajima, 1973; Tien and Matthews, 1977); *Traditional Europe* (Renson, 1981; Renson et al., 1991; Renson and Smulders, 1978); *Japan* (Bull, 1996; Sogawa, 1991); *Latin America* (Arbena, 1988, 1989; Humphrey, 1981; Miracle, 1977; Pina Chan, 1968; Stern, 1949); *Micronesia* (Royce and Murray, 1971); *Native North America* (Blanchard, 1981; Cheska, 1981; Culin, 1903, 1907; Danielson, 1971; Eisen and Wiggins, 1995; Fox, 1961; Mathys, 1976; Vennum, 1994); *New Guinea* (Leach, 1976); *New Zealand* (Melnick and Thomson, 1996; Stumpf and Cozens, 1947; Sutton-Smith, 1959); *Polynesia* (Dunlap, 1951; Firth, 1930/31; Johnson and Johnson, 1955); and *Turkey* (Frogner, 1985).

The Relationship Between Sport and Play Sports studies have evolved in tandem with the study of play. The reasons for this relationship are obvious. However, definitions and theoretical clarity as they relate to the concepts of sport and play are not so obvious. Anthropologists have generally dismissed the idea that work and play are antonyms or points at opposite ends of a work–play continuum (for example, Blanchard, 1995; Stevens, 1980). Work is viewed as goal-driven activity and is generally viewed as the opposite of leisure behavior, activity in which the goal of the activity is the activity itself. Anthropologists are not so consistent in their efforts to define 'play'. The effort to understand the nature and meaning of human play has been well served by the work of comparative primatologists and their studies of monkeys and apes (for example, Bekoff, 1972; Carpenter, 1964; Fagen, 1981; Lawick-Goodall, 1971; Manson and Wrangham, 1991; Miller, 1973; Oakley, 1976). In fact, it was the observation of monkey play that led Gregory Bateson (1972) to a theory of play that many anthropologists find convenient. Observing monkeys playing at the Fleishhacker Zoo in San Francisco, he observed

> a phenomenon well known to everybody … young monkeys playing, that is, engaged in an interactive sequence of which the unit actions or signals were similar to but not the same as those of combat. It was evident, even to the human observer, that the sequence as a whole was not combat, and evident to the human observer that to the participant monkeys this was 'not combat'.

Bateson then suggested that play was paradox: what the monkeys appeared to be saying was they were not doing what they in fact seemed to be doing, fighting. This is the message of play, what Bateson (1972) calls 'metacommunication', communication about communication.

Play defined as paradox is a state that can in some cases characterize sport. Certainly, one can play at sport. However, one can also engage in sport in ways that cannot be viewed as playful. For that reason, it has been suggested that sport, depending on the context and the state of mind of the participants, can be characterized as play, not-play, work or leisure (Blanchard, 1995). However, sport is not play nor is it a form of play. It is simply an activity that can be play-like.

The Relationship Between Sport and Ritual
Anthropologists have debated over the meaning of this relationship for several decades. Sport is treated by some as secular ritual (for example, Lawrence, 1982; Miracle and Southard, 1993). On the other hand, it has also been argued that the idea of secular ritual is of little practical value and that rather than being ritual, sport is an independent institution that is ritual-like with a penchant for attracting a variety of ritual activities (for example, magic, fetishes, etc.; Blanchard, 1988). Sport is viewed by some as an activity that has evolved out of ritual (for example, Culin, 1907) and by others as a stand-alone phenomenon that has in some cases evolved into ritual (for example, Lesser, 1933).

Ritual can be defined as culturally patterned behavior, 'the symbolic dimension of social activities that are not specifically technical in nature' (Blanchard, 1995). 'Technique has economic consequences which are measurable and predictable; ritual on the other hand is a symbolic statement which says something about the individuals involved in the action' (Leach, 1954). In this sense ritual can be either sacred or profane. Like language, ritual serves to transmit culture and exercises a 'constraining effect on social behavior' (Douglas, 1973). For this reason, it is easy to see why anthropologist William Arens would call American football a ritual:

> … football, although only a game, tells us much about who and what we Americans are as a people, and if an anthropologist from another planet visited here, he would be struck by the American fixation on this game and would report on it with the glee and romantic intoxication anthropologists normally reserve for the exotic rituals of a newly discovered tribe. This assertion is based on the theory that certain significant symbols are the key to understanding a culture; football is such a symbol. (Arens, 1975)

Nevertheless, it is not generally agreed that simply because behavior is repetitive and symbolizes the basic values of a particular society that it is ritual. Clearly, though, sport has certain characteristics of ritual and because of its risks and uncertainties invites various types of ritual, such as magic (Gmelch, 1972; Stevens, 1988).

Perhaps more useful than the assertion that sport is ritual, is the observation that like ritual, sport is a window on culture. Sport becomes a vehicle for the manifestations of those norms and values fundamental to the culture of the society within which it is performed. Thus it is when the Trobriand Islanders of New Guinea play cricket, a game they learned from the British in the early part of this century, they play it in such a way that it becomes a Trobriand sport (Leach, 1976). What one observes during Trobriand cricket matches is a slice of Trobriand life. The same thing can be said about the baseball played by the Japanese (Kusaka, 1987; Whiting, 1982), the basketball played the Navajo Indians of the American Southwest (Blanchard, 1974), and the soccer played by the Zulu of South Africa (Scotch, 1961). In this regard, one might argue that sport is more perspective than ritual.

The Definition and Description of Sport from a Cross-Cultural Perspective A one-size-fits-all definition of sport, one that works in any cultural setting, has proven as illusive as a single definition for an institution like religion. The subtleties and nuances of sport behavior in any given cultural setting are difficult to encompass in a transcultural definition of 'sport'. Likewise, the diversity of theoretical orientations that social scientists bring to the study of sport make it difficult for any one definition to find widespread acceptance. Nevertheless, some definitions, such as the following, are cited more frequently than others:

> [Sport is] ... a physically exertive activity that is aggressively competitive within constraints imposed by definitions and rules. A component of culture, it is ritually patterned, gamelike and of varying amounts of play, work and leisure. (Blanchard and Cheska, 1985: 60)

The Application of Sports Study Results to the Solution of Real Problems The applied anthropology of sport frequently grapples with problems of *social and cultural change* (for example, Allison and Lüschen, 1979; Glassford, 1976; Tindall, 1975a); *education* (for example, Glamser, 1988; Miracle and Rees, 1994; Tindall, 1975b); *physical education, recreation, and health* (for example, Blanchard, 1977; Cheska, 1978; Cozens and Stumpf, 1951; Johnson, 1980); *violence* (for example, Collings and Condon, 1996; Sipes, 1973; Zoni and Kirchler, 1991); *gender issues* (for example, Howell, 1982); the analysis of *popular culture* (for example, Chandler, 1978, 1988); *international relations* (for example, Heinila, 1985); *immigration and adaptation* (Allison, 1979; Blanchard, 1991; Frogner, 1985; Robinson, 1978); the *Olympics* (for example, MacAloon, 1981; Wright, 1977); and the anthropology of *sport in the college classroom* (for example, Miracle and Blanchard, 1990).

The Description and Analysis of Sport in Prehistory and Early History Unfortunately, the anthropology of sport has been better at asking than answering the questions attendant to the origins and prehistoric development of sport (Fox, 1977). The archaeological evidence remains scanty, and, with some exceptions, much of the discussion about origins depends on early historical references and is sometimes speculative (for example, Guttmann, 1978; Palmer and Howell, 1973). One sport that archaeologists and prehistorians have studied extensively is the Mesoamerican ballgame. Among all the sports known from human prehistory, the rubber ballgame of the Olmecs,

Toltecs, Maya (*pok-ta-pok*) and Aztecs (*tlachtli*) is perhaps the best documented (for example, Blom, 1932; Coe, 1966; Ekholm, 1961; Humphrey, 1981; Schroeder, 1955; Stern, 1949). Much attention has also been given to the early history of sport as the institution first emerged and developed among such groups as the Egyptians, Etruscans, Greeks and Romans (for example, Gardiner, 1930; Harris, 1972; Howell and Sawula, 1973; Ioannides, 1976; Miller, 1991; Mutimer, 1970; Poliakoff, 1987; Sansone, 1988; Sasajima, 1973; Sweet, 1987).

The Analysis of Human Performance from the Perspective of Anatomy, Physiology and Genetics Physical anthropologists have studied body types, morphology and function for decades. Some of this work has been done with particular reference to sport and sports performance (for example, Adrian and Cooper, 1989; Carrier, 1984; Kukushkin, 1964; Malina, 1972; Malina and Bouchard, 1986).

The Application of Theory to the Analysis of Sports Behavior The anthropology of sport is not done in a theoretical vacuum. As is true of all the social sciences, it works from within paradigms, models and theories to attempt to understand better its primary subjects, in this case, sport. The wide range of theoretical models employed by social scientists as well as others are contexts within which those studying sport from an anthropological perspective frame their fundamental questions. Such models can be either explanatory or interpretive. In other words, they can suggest cause-and-effect relationships or simply expand the subject and provide alternative ways of understanding.

The anthropology of sport literature is shaped in many ways by the nature of the theoretical arguments that underlie the description and analysis. Questions about the nature and meaning of sport are addressed from these perspectives and debates over the meaning of sport, particularly sport in small-scale, Third World, or developing societies, are waged along theoretical lines and in many cases these debates become a battle among theories. As examples of the way in which sport is analysed with an aim toward explanation, there is the evolutionary perspective (for example, Guttmann, 1978), the functionalist perspective (for example, Gmelch, 1972), the structural-functionalist perspective (for example, Fox, 1961), the cultural materialist perspective (for example, Blanchard, 1979) and the conflict perspective (for example, Klein, 1991). Sport is also studied with an eye toward interpretation from such perspectives as symbolic anthropology (for example, Manning, 1981), ethnoscience (Kew, 1986) and postmodernism (Lewis, 1992). Sport, looked at from an anthropological point of view, remains a fertile ground for the application of theory.

CONCLUSION

The anthropology of sport is the application of the methods and perspectives of anthropology to the study of sport. It is grounded in the basic tenets, distinctive methodologies and theoretical assumptions of anthropology. It is also tied to the idea that sport is an institution and a component of culture.

The anthropological study of sport is becoming increasingly popular worldwide. The literature on sports culture, sport in small-scale society, sport in early history and prehistory, traditional sport, ethnic sport and folk sport is expanding rapidly (as the references and further reading to this chapter indicate). Nevertheless, the opportunities for additional research remain virtually unlimited. The issues falling under the anthropology of sport umbrella that deserve the most attention include the following:

1 The description and preservation of traditional, folk, ethnic, or aboriginal sport and sports culture. There is still a real need for good ethnographies so that the record of sporting diversity around the world will not be lost as a result of the homogenizing influence of globalism.

2 The continued debate over theoretical issues, particularly the meaning of sport, its relationship to other activities (for example, work, ritual and play), and its role in human society.

3 The continued collection and analysis of archaeological data. As the techniques of archaeological science become more sophisticated, it should become increasingly possible to retrieve and interpret the artifacts of sport culture and reconstruct the process by which human sport originated and evolved.

4 The relationship between sport and violence. There is much to be learned about this critical area from the cross-cultural analysis of sports behavior.

5 Sport as a model for international relations. The dream of world peace is well served by efforts to understand sporting diversity, encourage international and interdisciplinary cooperation, and revisit the original spirit of the Olympics.

REFERENCES AND FURTHER READING

Adrian, M.J. and Cooper, J.M. (1989) *The Biomechanics of Human Movement*. Indianapolis: Benchmark Press.

Allison, M.T. (1979) 'On the ethnicity of ethnic minorities in sport', *International Review for the Sociology of Sport*, 14: 89–96.

Allison, M.T. and Lüschen, G. (1979) 'A comparative analysis of Navajo Indian and Anglo basketball sports systems', *International Review of Sports Sociology*, 14: 75–86.

Arbena, J. (ed.) (1988) *Sport and Society in Latin America: Diffusion, Dependency and the Rise of Mass Culture*. Westport, CT: Greenwood Press.

Arbena, J. (1989) *Annotated Bibliography of Latin American Sport: Pre-conquest to the Present*. Westport, CT: Greenwood Press.

Arens, W. (1975) 'The great American football ritual', *Natural History*, 84: 72–81.

Avedon, E.M. and Sutton-Smith, B. (1971) *The Study of Games*. New York: John Wiley.

Azoy, G.W. (1982) *Buzkashi: Game and Power in Afghanistan*. Philadelphia: University of Pennsylvania.

Baker, W.J. and Mangan, J.A. (eds) (1987) *Sport in Africa: Essays in Social History*. New York: Africana Publishing.

Balikci, A. (1978) 'Buzkashi', *Natural History*, 87 (February): 54–63.

Bateson, G. (1972) 'A theory of play and fantasy', in G. Bateson (ed.), *Steps to an Ecology of Mind*. New York: Random House. pp. 177–93.

Beijing Review (1995a) 'Fifth traditional ethnic sports meeting held', *Bejing Review (Pei-ching chou pao)*, 38 (46): 24.

Beijing Review (1995b) 'Traditional minority sports in Yunnan', *Beijing Review (Pei-ching chou pao)*, 38 (46): 25.

Beijing Review (1995c) 'Lancang River Dai dragon boat races', *Beijing Review (Pei-ching chou pao)*, 38 (46): 26.

Bekoff, M. (1972) 'The development of social interaction, play, and metacommunication in mammals: an ethological perspective', *Quarterly Review of Biology*, 47: 412–34.

Best, E. (1924) *The Maori: Memoirs of the Polynesian Society*. Vol. 2. Wellington: Tombs.

Blanchard, K. (1974) 'Basketball and the culture-change process: the Rimrock Navajo case', *Council on Anthropology and Education Quarterly*, 5 (4): 8–13.

Blanchard, K. (1977) 'The cultural component in physical fitness', in P. Stevens, Jr (ed.), *Studies in the Anthropology of Play*. West Point, NY: Leisure Press. pp. 42–8.

Blanchard, K. (1979) 'Stickball and the American southeast', in E. Norbeck and C. Farrer (eds), *Forms of Play of Native Americans*. St Paul, MN: West Publishing. pp. 189–208.

Blanchard, K. (1981) *The Mississippi Choctaws at Play: the Serious Side of Leisure*. Urbana, IL: University of Illinois Press.

Blanchard, K. (1984) *Play and Adaptation: Sport and Games in Native America*. Oklahoma City: Oklahoma University Papers in Anthropology. pp. 173–95.

Blanchard, K. (1988) 'Sport and ritual: a conceptual dilemma', *Journal of Physical Education, Recreation, and Dance*, (November–December): 48–52.

Blanchard, K. (1991) 'Sport, leisure, and identity: reinventing Lao culture in Middle Tennessee', *Play and Culture*, 4 (2): 169–84.

Blanchard, K. (1995) *Anthropology of Sport*. New York: Greenwood (2nd edn. of Blanchard and Cheska, 1985).

Blanchard, K. and Cheska, A.T. (1985) *Anthropology of Sport*. South Hadley, MA: Bergin and Garvey.

Blom, F. (1932) *The Maya Ballgame Pok-ta-pok*. Middle American Research Series 4, No. 13. New Orleans, LA: Tulane University Press.

Boas, F. (1888) 'The Central Eskimo', in *Sixth Annual Report of the Bureau of American Ethnology*, 1964 edn. Lincoln, NB: University of Nebraska Press.

Brewster, P.G. (1956) 'The importance of the collecting and study of games', *Eastern Anthropologist*, 10 (1): 5–12.

Bull, D. (1996) 'Karuta: sport or culture?', *Japan Quarterly*, 43 (1): 67–77.

Carpenter, C.R. (1964) *Naturalistic Behavior of Nonhuman Primates*. University Park: Pennsylvania State University Press.

Carrier, D.R. (1984) 'The energetic paradox of human running and hominid evolution', *Current Anthropology*, 29 (5): 483–95.

Chandler, J. (1978) 'American pro football in Britain?', *Journal of Popular Culture*, 12 (1): 146–55.

Chandler, J. (1988) *Television and National Sport: the United States and Britain*. Urbana, IL: University of Illinois Press.

Chepyator-Thomson, J.R. (1993) 'Kenya: culture, history, and formal education as determinants in the personal and social development of Kalenjin women in modern sports', *Social Development Issues*, 15: 30–44.

Cheska, A.T. (1978) 'Navajo youth health, physical education, and recreation program evaluation'. Unpublished report, Navajo Tribal Council and BIA, Gallup, N.M.

Cheska, A.T. (1981) 'Games of the Native North Americans', in R.F.G. Lüschen and G.H. Sage (eds), *Handbook of Social Science of Sport*. Champaign, IL: Stipes. pp. 49–77.

Churchill, L.P. (1899) 'Sports of the Samoans', *Outing*, 33: 562–8.

Coe, M.D. (1966) *The Maya*. New York: Frederick A. Praeger.

Collings, P. and Condon, R.G. (1996) 'Blood on the ice: status, self-esteem, and ritual injury among Inuit hockey players', *Human Organization*, 55 (3): 253–62.

Cozens, F.W. and Stumpf, F. (1951) *Implications of Cultural Anthropology for Physical Education*. American Academy of Physical Education. Professional Contributions No. 1. Washington, DC. pp. 67–72.

Culin, S. (1903) 'American Indian games', *American Anthropologist*, 5 (1): 58–64.

Culin, S. (1907) 'Games of the North American Indians', in *Twenty-fourth Annual Report of the Bureau of American Ethnology*. Washington, DC: Government Printing Office.

Damm, H. (1970) 'The so-called sport activities of primitive people: a contribution toward a genesis of sport', in G. Lüschen (ed.), *The Cross-Cultural Analysis of Sport and Games*. Champaign, IL: Stipes.

Danielson, K. (1971) 'Development in Eskimo play'. Unpublished Master's thesis, University of Alberta.

Davidson, D.S. (1936) 'The Pacific and circum-Pacific appearances of the dart games', *Journal of the Polynesian Society*, 45 (3; 4): 99–114; 119–26.

De Vroede, E. and Renson, R. (eds) (1991) *Proceedings of the Second European Seminar on Traditional Games*. Leuven: Vlaamse Volkssport Centrale.

Diem, C. (1971) *Weltgeschichte des Sports*, 3rd edn, Volume I. Frankfurt: Cotta.

Douglas, M. (1973) *Natural Symbols*. New York: Vintage Press.

Dunlap, H.L. (1951) 'Games, sports, dancing, and other vigorous activities and their function in Samoan culture', *The Research Quarterly*, 22 (3): 298–311.

Durerger, C. (1978) *L'Esprit du jeu chez les Aztèques*. Paris: Mouton.

Eisen, G. and Wiggins, D.K. (eds) (1995) *Ethnicity and Sport in North American History and Culture*. Westport, CT: Praeger.

Ekholm, G.F. (1961) 'Puerto Rican stone "collars" as ball-game belts', in S.K. Lothrop et al. (eds), *Essays in pre-Columbian Art and Archaeology*. Cambridge, MA: Harvard University Press. pp. 356–71.

Evans-Pritchard, E.E. (1962) *Social Anthropology and Other Essays*. New York: Free Press.

Fagen, R.M. (1981) *Animal Play and Behavior*. New York: Oxford University Press.

Firth, R. (1930/31) 'A dart match in Tikopia: a study in the sociology of primitive sport', *Oceania*, 1: 64–97.

Fogelson, R. (1962) 'The Cherokee ball game: a study in southeastern ethnology'. Unpublished PhD dissertation, University of Pennsylvania, Philadelphia.

Fox, J.R. (1961) 'Pueblo baseball: a new use for old witchcraft', *Journal of American Folklore*, 74: 9–16.

Fox, S.J. (1977) 'A paleoanthropological approach to recreation and sporting behaviors', in P. Stevens (ed.), *Studies in the Anthropology of Play*. West Point, NY: Leisure Press. pp. 65–70.

Frederickson, F.S. (1960) 'Sports in the cultures of man', in W.R. Johnson (ed.), *Science and Medicine in Exercise and Sports*. New York: Harper and Row. pp. 633–8.

Frogner, E. (1985) 'On ethnic sport among Turkish migrants in the Federal Republic of Germany', *International Review for the Sociology of Sport*, 20: 75–86.

Gallmeier, Charles P. (1989) 'Towards an emergent ethnography of sport', *ARENA Review*, 13 (1): 1–8.

Gardiner, E. Norman (1930) *Athletics of the Ancient World*. Oxford: Clarendon Press.

Geertz, C. (1972) 'Deep play: notes on the Balinese cockfight', in C. Geertz (ed.), *The Interpretation of Cultures*. New York: Basic Books. pp. 412–53.

Giles, H.A. (1906) 'Football and polo in China', *The Nineteenth Century and After*, 59: 508–13.

Gini, C. (1939) 'Rural ritual games in Libya (Berber baseball and shinny)', *Rural Sociology*, 4: 282–98.

Giulianotti, R. (1996) 'Back to the future: an ethnography of Ireland's football fans at the 1994 World Cup finals in the USA', *International Review for the Sociology of Sport*, 31 (3): 323–48.

Glamser, F. (1988) 'School sport in England: a comparative view', *Journal of Sport Behavior*, 11: 193–203.

Glassford, R.G. (1976) *Application of a Theory of Games to the Transitional Eskimo Culture*. New York: Arno Press.

Gmelch, G. (1972) 'Magic in professional baseball', in G.P. Stone (ed.), *Games, Sports and Power*. New Brunswick, NJ: Dutton. pp. 128–37.

Guttmann, A. (1978) *From Ritual to Record: the Nature of Modern Sports*. New York: Columbia University Press.

Guttmann, A. (1994) *Games and Empires: Modern Sports and Cultural Imperialism*. New York: Columbia University Press.

Harney, W.E. (1952) 'Sport and play amidst the Aborigines of the northern territory', *Mankind*, 4 (9): 377–9.

Harris, H.A. (1972) *Sport in Greece and Rome*. Ithaca, NY: Cornell University Press.

Harris, J.C. and Park, R.J. (eds) (1983) *Play, Games and Sports in Cultural Contexts*. Champaign, IL: Human Kinetics.

Heinila, K. (1985) 'Sport and international understanding – a contradiction in terms?', *Sociology of Sport Journal*, 2 (3): 240–8.

Henderson, R.W. (1947) *Ball, Bat and Bishop: the Origin of Ball Games*. New York: Rockport Press. (Reprint: Gale Research Company, Book Tower, Detroit, 1974.)

Higgs, R.J. (1982) *Sports: a Reference Guide*. Westport, CT: Greenwood Press.

Hoffman, W.J. (1896) 'The Menomini Indians', in *Fourteenth Annual Report of the Bureau of American Ethnology*. Washington, DC: Government Printing Office.

Holmes, W.H. (1907) 'Introduction', in *Twenty-fourth Annual Report of the Bureau of American Ethnology*. Washington, DC: Government Printing Office. pp. ix–xl.

Howell, M.L. and Sawula, L.W. (1973) 'Sports and games among the Etruscans', in E.F. Zeigler (ed.), *A History of Sport and Physical Education*. Champaign, IL: Stipes. pp. 79–91.

Howell, R. (ed.) (1982) *Her Story in Sport: a Historical Anthology of Women in Sports*. West Point, NY: Leisure Press.

Howell, R. and Howell, M. (1987) *History of Australian Sport*. Birkenhead Point, Australia: Shakespeare Head Press.

Howitt, A.W. (1904) *The Native Tribes of South East Australia*. London: Macmillan.

Humphrey, R.L. (1981) 'Play as life: suggestions for a cognitive study of the Mesoamerican ball game', in A.T. Cheska (ed.), *Play as Context*. West Point, NY: Leisure Press. pp. 134–49.

Ioannides, I.P. (1976) 'Physical culture of the Greek antiquity', in R. Renson, P.P. deNayer and M. Ostyn (eds), *The History, Evolution and Diffusion of Sports and Games in Different Cultures*. Leuven, Belgium: BLOSO. pp. 105–15.

James, C.L.R. (1984) *Beyond a Boundary*. New York: Pantheon.

Jarvie, G. (ed.) (1991) *Sport, Racism and Ethnicity*. London: Falmer Press.

Johnson, I. and Johnson, E. (1955) 'South seas' incredible land divers', *National Geographic*, 107 (1): 77–92.

Johnson, W. (ed.) (1980) *Sport and Physical Education around the World*. Champaign, IL: Stipes.

Jokl, E. (ed.) (1964) *Medical Sociology and Cultural Anthropology of Sport*. Springfield, IL: Charles C. Thomas.

Jones, R.W. (1959) 'Sport and international understanding'. *Report of the UNESCO Congress 'Sport–Work–Culture'*. Helsinki, Finland. pp. 159–70.

Kanin, D.B. (1978) 'Ideology and diplomacy: the dimensions of Chinese political sport', in B. Lowe, D.B. Kanin and A. Strenk (eds), *Sport and International Relations*. Champaign, IL: Stipes. pp. 263–78.

Kauffman, H.E. (1941) 'Die Spiele der Thadou Kuki in Assam', *Zeitschrift für Ethnologie*, 73: 40–71.

Kew, F. (1986) 'Playing the game: an ethnomethodological perspective', *International Review for the Sociology of Sport*, 21 (4): 339–51.

Klein, A.M. (1991) *Sugarball: the American Game, the Dominican Dream*. New Haven, CT: Yale.

Knuttgen, H.G., Qiwei, M. and Zhongyvan, W. (eds) (1990) *Sport in China*. Champaign, IL: Human Kinetics.

Kolatch, J. (1972) *Sport, Politics and Ideology in China*. Middle Village, NY: Jonathan David.

Kukushkin, G.I. (1964) 'Growth, physique, and performance', in E. Jokl and E. Simon (eds), *International Research in Sport and Physical Education*. Springfield, IL: Charles C. Thomas. pp. 254–61.

Kusaka, Y. (1987) 'The development of baseball organization in Japan', *International Review for the Sociology of Sport*, 22 (4): 263–80.

Lawick-Goodall, J. (1971) *In the Shadow of Man*. New York: Houghton-Mifflin.

Lawrence, E.A. (1982) *Rodeo: an Anthropologist Looks at the Wild and Tame*. Knoxville, TN: University of Tennessee.

Leach, E. (1954) *Political Systems of Highland Burma*. Boston: Beacon Press.

Leach, J.W. (1976) 'Structure and message in Trobriand cricket', Unpublished paper written to accompany the movie *Trobriand Cricket*. Berkeley, CA: University of California Extension Media Center.

Lesser, A. (1933) *The Pawnee Ghost Dance Hand Game: a Study of Cultural Change*. (Columbia University Contributions to Anthropology 16.) New York: Columbia University Press.

Lever, J. (1983) *Soccer Madness*. Chicago: University of Chicago Press.

Lewis, J.L. (1992) *Ring of Liberation: a Deceptive Discourse in Brazilian Capoeria*. Chicago: University of Chicago.

Lüschen, G. (ed.) (1970) *The Cross-Cultural Analysis of Sport and Games*. Champaign, IL: Stipes.

MacAloon, J.J. (1981) *This Great Symbol*. Chicago: University of Chicago Press.

Malina, R. (1972) 'Anthropology, growth, and physical education', in Robert N. Singer (ed.), *Physical Education: an Interdisciplinary Approach*. New York: Macmillan. pp. 239–309.

Malina, R.M. and Bouchard, C. (1986) *Sport and Human Genetics*. Champaign, IL: Human Kinetics.

Mandle, J. and Mandle, J. (1988) *Grass Roots Commitment: Basketball and Society in Trinidad and Tobago*. Parkersburg, IA: Caribbean Books.

Manning, F. (1981) 'Celebrating cricket: the symbolic construction of Caribbean politics', *American Ethnologist*, 8 (3): 616–32.

Manson, J.H. and Wrangham, R.W. (1991) 'Intergroup aggression in chimpanzees and humans', *Current Anthropology*, 32 (4): 369–90.

Massingham, H.J. (1929) 'Origins of ball games', in *The Heritage of Man*. London: J. Cape Publishers. pp. 208–27.

Mathias, E. (1981) 'Italian-American culture and games: the Minnesota iron range and south Philadelphia', in A. Cheska (ed.), *Play as Context*. West Point, NY: Leisure Press. pp. 73–92.

Mathys, F.K. (1976) *Spiel und Sport der Indianer in Nordamerika*. Basle: Schweizerisches Turn- und Sport Museum.

Melnick, M.J. and Thomson, R.W. (1996) 'The Maori people and positional segregation in New Zealand rugby football', *International Review for the Sociology of Sport*, 31 (2): 139–54.

Miller, J. (1983) 'Description of games and sports in Tonga'. Paper presented at the annual meetings of the Association for the Anthropological Study of Play, Baton Rouge, Louisiana.

Miller, M.D. (1983) 'Changes in the games and pastimes of Australian aborigines'. Unpublished Master's thesis, University of California at Santa Barbara.

Miller, S. (1973) 'Ends, means and galumphing: some leitmotifs of play', *American Anthropologist*, 75 (1): 87–98.

Miller, S.G. (1991) *Arete: Greek Sports from Ancient Sources*. Berkeley, CA: University of California.

Miracle, A.W. (1977) 'Some functions of Aymara games and play', in P. Stevens Jr (ed.), *Studies in the Anthropology of Play: Papers in Memory of B. Allan Tindall*. West Point, NY: Leisure Press. pp. 98–105.

Miracle, A.W. and Blanchard, K. (1990) 'Buzkashi, toli, and football: teaching an anthropology course on sports', in David L. Vanderwerken (ed.), *Sport in the Classroom*. Rutherford, NJ: Fairleigh Dickinson University. pp. 153–70.

Miracle, A.W. and Rees, C.R. (1994) *Lessons of the Locker Room: the Myth of School Sports*. Buffalo, NY: Prometheus Books.

Miracle, A.W. and Southard, D. (1993) 'The athlete and ritual timing: an experimental study', *Journal of Ritual Studies*, 7 (1): 125–38.

Moncrieff, J. (1966) 'Physical games and amusements of the Australian Aboriginal', *The Australian Journal of Physical Education*, 36: 5–11.

Mooney, J. (1890) 'The Cherokee ball play', *American Anthropologist*, 3 (2): 105–32.

Murdock, G.P., Ford, C.S. and Hudson, A.E. (1961) *Outline of Cultural Materials*. New Haven, CT: Human Relations Area Files (HRAF).

Mutimer, B.T.P. (1970) 'Play forms of the ancient Egyptians', in *Proceedings, 1st Canadian Symposium on the History of Sport and Physical Education*. Ottawa, Canada: Department of National Health and Welfare. pp. 569–78.

Nabokov, P. (1981) *Indian Running*. Santa Barbara, CA: Capra Press.

Norman, J. (1976) 'The Tarahumaras: Mexico's long distance runners', *National Geographic*, 149 (5): 702–18.

Oakley, F.B. (1976) 'Methodological considerations for studies of play in primates', in D. Lancy and A. Tindall (eds), *The Anthropological Study of Play: Problems and Perspectives*. Cornwall, NY: Leisure Press. pp. 173–8.

Ogura, K. (1992) 'A new look at traditional sports', in *Enriching Traditional Sports*. Tokyo: Japan Folklore Association. pp. 3–4.

Olivova, V. (1985) *Sport and Spiele im Altertum*. Munich: Verlag Aschendorff.

Opler, M.E. (1944) 'The Jicarilla Apache ceremonial relay race', *American Anthropologist*, 46 (1): 75–97.

Opler, M.K. (1945) 'A sumo tournament at Tule Lake Center', *American Anthropologist*, 41 (l): 134–9.

Oxendine, J.B. (1988) *American Indian Sports Heritage*. Champaign, IL: Human Kinetics.

Palmer, D. and Howell, M.L. (1973) 'Archaeological evidence of sports and games in ancient Crete', in E.F. Zeigler (ed.), *A History of Sport and Physical Education*. Champaign, IL: Stipes. pp. 67–78.

Perry, W.J. (1923) *The Children of the Sun*. London: Methuen.

Pina Chan, R. (1968) *Spiele und Sport im Alten Mexico*. Leipzig: Edition Leipzig.

Poliakoff, M. (1987) *Combat Sports in the Ancient World: Competition, Violence, and Culture*. New Haven, CT: Yale University Press.

Pooley, J. (1981) 'Ethnic soccer clubs in Milwaukee: a study of assimilation', in M. Hart and S. Birrell (eds), *Sport in the Sociocultural Process*. Dubuque, IA: William C. Brown. pp. 430–47.

Rajagopalan, K. (1973) 'Early Indian physical education', in E.F. Zeigler (ed.), *A History of Sport and Physical Education*. Champaign, IL: Stipes. pp. 45–55.

Raum, O.F. (1953) 'The rolling target (hoop-and-pole) game in Africa', *African Studies*, 12: 104–21.

Reagan, A.B. (1932) 'Navajo sports', *Primitive Man*, 5: 68–71.

Rees, C.R. (1991) 'Beyond contact: sport as a site for ethnic and racial cooperation', in E.H. Katzenellenbogen and J.R. Potgieter (eds), *Sociological Perspectives of Movement Activity*. Stellenbosch, South Africa: Institute for Sport and Movement Studies. pp. 24–33.

Rees, C.R. and Miracle, A.W. (1984) 'Conflict resolution in games and sports', *International Review of Sport Sociology*, 19 (2): 145–56.

Reigelhaupt, J.A. (1973) 'Review (Three volumes on sport)', *American Anthropologist*, 75: 378–81.

Renson, R. (1981) 'Folk football: sport and/or as ritual?', *The Association for the Anthropological Study of Play Newsletter*, 8 (1): 2–8.

Renson, R., Manson, M. and De Vroede, E. (1991) 'Typology for the classification of traditional games in Europe', in E. De Vroede and R. Renson (eds), *Proceedings of the Second European Seminar on Traditional Games*. Leuven: Vlaamse Volkssport Centrale. pp. 69–81.

Renson, R. and Smulders, H. (1978) 'Situatieschets van de volkssporten in Vlaanderen', *Sport* (Brussels), 21: 167–76.

Renson, R. and Smulders, H. (1981) 'Research methods and the development of the Flemish Folk Games File', *International Review of Sport Sociology*, 16: 97–107.

Roberts, J. and Sutton-Smith, B. (1962) 'Child training and game involvement', *Ethnology*, 1 (2): 166–85.

Roberts, J.M., Arth, M.J. and Bush, R.R. (1959) 'Games in culture', *American Anthropologist*, 61: 597–605.

Robinson, C.E. (1978) 'The uses of order and disorder in play: an analysis of Vietnamese refugee children's play', in M. Salter (ed.), *Play: Anthropological Perspectives*. West Point, NY: Leisure Press. pp. 137–45.

Roth, W.E. (1902) *Games, Sports and Amusements*. North Queensland Ethnography, Bulletin No. 4. Brisbane: George Arthur Baughan, Government Printer.

Royce, J. and Murray, T. (1971) 'Work and play in Kapingamarangi, past and present', *Micronesia*, 7 (1–2): 1–17.

Salter, M.A. (1974) 'Play: a medium of cultural stability', in H. Groll (ed.), *Beiträge zur Geschichte der Leibeserziehung und des Sports*. Vienna: University of Vienna Press. pp. 1–22.

Sansone, D. (1988) *Greek Athletics and the Genesis of Sport*. Berkeley, CA: University of California.

Sasajima, K. (1973) 'Early Chinese physical education and sport', in E.F. Zeigler (ed.), *A History of Sport and Physical Education*. Champaign, IL: Stipes. pp. 35–44.

Schroeder, A.H. (1955) 'Ball courts and ball games in Middle America and Arizona', *Archaeology*, 8 (3): 156–61.

Scotch, N.A. (1961) Magic, sorcery, and football among urban Zulu: a case of reinterpretation under acculturation', *Conflict Resolution*, 5 (1): 70–4.

Sipes, R. (1973) 'War, sports, and aggression: an empirical test of two rival theories', *American Anthropologist*, 75 (1): 64–86.

Smith, J.C. (1972) 'The Native American ball games', in M.M. Hart (ed.), *Sport in the Sociocultural Process*. Dubuque, IA: William C. Brown. pp. 350–8.

Smulders, H. (1982) *'Typologie en spreidingspatronen van volkssporten in Vlaanderen'*. Unpublished doctoral dissertation, Katholieke Universiteit Leuven.

Sogawa, T. (1991) *Illustrated Sports History*. Tokyo: Asakura Shoten.

Sohi, A.S. and Yusuff, K.B. (1987) 'The socioeconomic status of elite Nigerian athletes in perspective of social stratification and mobility', *International Review for the Sociology of Sport*, 22 (4): 295–304.

Spears, B. (1984) 'A perspective of the history of women's sport in ancient Greece', *Journal of Sport History*, 11 (2): 32–47.

Spencer, B. and Gillen, F.J. (1927) *The Arunta: a Study of a Stone Age People* (1966 edn, Volume I). Oosterhout, Netherlands: Anthropologia Publications.

Stern, T. (1949) *The Rubber Ball Games of the Americas*. American Ethnological Society Monograph No. 17. Seattle, WA: University of Washington Press.

Stevens, P., Jr (1973) 'The Bachama and their neighbors: non-kin joking relationships in

Adamawa, northeastern Nigeria'. Unpublished PhD dissertation, Northwestern University, Evanston, IL.

Stevens, P., Jr (1975) 'Social and cosmological dimensions of Bachama wrestling'. Unpublished paper presented at the annual meetings of the American Anthropological Association, San Francisco.

Stevens, P., Jr (1980) 'Play and work: a false dichotomy?', in H.B. Schwartzman (ed.), *Play and Culture*. West Point, NY: Leisure Press. pp. 316–23.

Stevens, P., Jr (1988) 'Table tennis and sorcery in West Africa', *Play and Culture*, 1 (2): 138–45.

Strutt, J. (1876) *The Sports and Pastimes of the People of England from the Earliest Period to the Present Time*. London: Chatto and Windus (originally published in 1801).

Stumpf, F. and Cozens, F.W. (1947) 'Some aspects of the role of games, sports, and recreational activities in the culture of modern primitive peoples: the New Zealand Maori', *Research Quarterly*, 18: 198–218.

Suomi, S.J. and Harlow, H.F. (1971) 'Monkeys at play', *Natural History Special Supplement* (December), pp. 72–5.

Sutton-Smith, B. (1959) *Games of New Zealand Children*. Berkeley, CA: University of California Press.

Sutton-Smith, B. and Roberts, J.M. (1981) 'Play, games, and sports', in H.C. Triandis and A. Heron (eds), Volume 4. *Developmental Psychology. Handbook of Cross-Cultural Psychology*, New York: Allyn and Bacon. pp. 425–71.

Sutton-Smith, B. and Rosenberg, C.G. (1961) 'Sixty years of historical change in the game preference of American children', *Journal of American Folklore*, 74: 17–46.

Sweet, W.E. (1987) *Sport and Recreation in Ancient Greece: a Source Book with Translations*. New York: Oxford.

Taylor, T. and Toohey, K. (1995) 'Ethnic barriers to sports participation', *Australian Parks and Recreation*, 31 (2): 32–6.

Tien, H.Y. and Matthews, J.A. (1977) 'Transforming society through sports: the games that the Chinese people play'. Unpublished paper, Social Science Research Council, University of Chicago.

Tindall, B.A. (1975a) 'The cultural transmissive function of physical education', *Council on Anthropology and Education Quarterly*, 6 (2): 10–12.

Tindall, B.A. (1975b) 'Ethnography and the hidden curriculum in sport', *Behavioral Social Science Teacher*, 2 (2).

Tylor, E.B. (1879) 'The history of games', *The Fortnightly Review*. London: Chapman and Hall, 25, n.s. (January 1–June 1): 735–47. (Also in *The Study of Games*. Avedon & Sutton-Smith, 1971, pp. 62–76.)

van der Merwe, F.J.G. and Salter, M.A. (1990) *Possible Changes in the Play Patterns of the Qgu Bushmen of South West Africa/Namibia*. Human Sciences Research Council Project no. 15/1/3/3/912 (July): 46–9.

Vennum, T., Jr (1994) *American Indian Lacrosse: Little Brother of War*. Washington, DC: Smithsonian Institution.

Weule, V.K. (1925) 'Ethnologie des Sportes', in G.A.E. Boegeng (ed.), *Geschichte des Sportes aller Völker und Zeiten*. Leipzig.

White, L. (1965) 'Anthropology 1964: retrospect and prospect', *American Anthropologist*, 67: 629–37.

Whiting, R. (1982) 'Japan's passionate affair with baseball', *Asia*, 5 (1): 10–15.

Wilcox, D.R. (1991) 'The Mesoamerican ballgame in the American southwest', in V.L. Scarborough and D.R. Wilcox (eds), *The Mesoamerican Ballgame*. Tucson: University of Arizona. pp. 105–36.

Wolf, E. (1964) *Anthropology*. Englewood Cliffs, NJ: Prentice-Hall.

Wright, S. (1977) 'Are the Olympics games? The relationship of politics and sport', *Millennium*, 6: 30–44.

Zoni, B. and Kirchler, E. (1991) 'When violence overshadows the spirit of sporting competition: Italian football fans and their clubs', *Journal of Community and Applied Social Psychology*, 1 (1): 5–21.

9

ECONOMICS AND SPORT

Marc Lavoie

The economics of sport were given their first credentials when, 40 years ago, S. Rottenberg (1956) published his 'trailblazing' article on the economics of the baseball labor market, in a leading journal of economics, the *Journal of Political Economy*, edited by members of the Department of Economics at the University of Chicago. The department is well known for believing that the (neoclassical) principles of economics can be applied to all subjects and that free markets have the ability to achieve desirable outcomes, a somewhat ironic belief given the geographical location of the university, surrounded by run-down residential black ghettos. At the time Rottenberg first tackled the economics of professional baseball, the future Nobel Prize recipient, Gary Becker, was dealing with the economics of discrimination, the economics of marriage and the economics of the household.

From an historical viewpoint, one could thus see the development of the economics of sport as part of the growing imperialism of economics over other social sciences. This has been accompanied by the ever-increasing media attention over financial issues involving professional sport teams or athletic stars, their profits or their earnings, both in North America and in Europe. The players' strike in baseball and owners' lock-out in hockey also hyped up the media's attention towards the economics of sport.

An attempt to give a broad picture of the economics of sport quickly forces one to realize that two traditions have emerged in the field. One may say that there is a North American, or Anglo-Saxon tradition, and a Continental European tradition.[1] The Anglo-Saxon tradition generally has a micro-economic

focus, centering on the individual and the firm, applying the standard supply and demand tools of micro-economics in an attempt to formally model the behavior of the various participants in the world of sport. North Americans, and their Anglo-Saxon colleagues from Britain and Australia, usually focus their attention on professional sport, more specifically men's team sports. They use, whenever they can, the theories of statistics applied to economics, that is, econometrics and regression analysis. On the other hand, economists from Continental Europe make little use of econometrics, relying rather on descriptive statistics, with tables of numbers and the computation of various ratios. Their work is usually more of an institutionalist sort, that is, more descriptive, sometimes relying on more unorthodox economic theories. Although they are also concerned with the implications of professional teams, Continental Europeans are much concerned with the economics of amateur and recreational sport, and with the economics of the sports industry.

The present chapter will attempt to cover both of these traditions, but due to the sheer number of publications within the North American approach, a disproportionate amount of space is devoted to the Anglo-Saxon tradition. This chapter will be divided into two broad sections, both mainly devoted to professional team sports. We shall first deal with labor economics, while in the second section we shall deal with the professional club seen as a firm. The latter section will end with a theme covered by both traditions in the economics of sport: the development impact of major sporting events on a city or a region. We shall conclude with a brief assessment of the future outlook of the discipline.

LABOR ECONOMICS

Salary Determination

Many, if not most, economists attracted to the economics of sport are labor economists. The main fascination with the sports industry is that there are reliable measures of output and productivity *per individual*, something which is usually lacking in other industries. Although it is possible to obtain huge data matrices about the characteristics of individual employees, it is usually very difficult to have adequate and direct measures of their productivity. In sport, the reliable measures of individual output are, of course, the individual performance statistics, about which sports fans are so fascinated. There used to be one drawback, however: whereas in other industries it was often possible to have the salaries of individual employees, in sport it was very difficult to obtain a sufficiently large set of salary data, and their reliability could always be questioned. The situation has changed considerably since about 1980. First, due to legal court actions, salary data were collected and made available (Fort 1992); secondly, players' associations have gradually come to realize that salary secrecy was only to the advantage of the employer, and this has led to the media gaining access – officially or unofficially – to the salaries of all players on major league teams, with entire lists of them being published at once. In fact this explains why very little empirical work on this topic – in contrast to attendance determination – has been performed in Europe: besides stars, the salaries of professional or semi-professional players there, whatever the sport, are highly confidential.

There have been two approaches to the issue of salary determination in professional team sports.[2] The first approach, closer to micro-economic theory *per se*, attempts to verify whether players are exploited by their employers, or it attempts to estimate which sort of player is being most exploited – star players or journeymen, those with or without bargaining power. This normative approach is based on the neoclassical concept of the marginal revenue product. The idea is that a worker should be paid according to the additional revenue that his work generates. The degree of exploitation is then defined as the ratio of the actual salary of the player to his marginal revenue product. This approach was first put into operation by Scully (1974a) for baseball. Three steps are involved. One must first estimate by how much an additional win increases team revenues, having taken into account other factors such as metropolitan population. Then one must estimate how improved athletic performance – in baseball, better pitching and better batting – increases the likelihood of a win. From the individual performance statistics, one can then proceed to the third step, estimating the marginal revenue products of each individual player and comparing them with the actual salaries. With this first approach, a very restrictive set of performance variables is usually chosen, often one per sort of player.

Things are different with the second approach, more positive than normative, which purports to explain how salaries are actually determined. In this second approach, salaries are explained by the location characteristics of the team, the characteristics of players and their performance of the previous year. The set of variables considered as determinants of salaries is then enlarged, despite the problems this might create because of collinearity, that is, because a performance measure may be highly correlated with another, thus making it impossible to properly identify the contribution of each. In a brilliant article, Pascal and Rapping (1972) were the first to proceed with this approach, again applied to baseball. As is to be expected, it was shown that salaries depend on various measures of performance and on experience. Despite some claims to the contrary, the more recent studies on salary determination have shown only marginal additional ingenuity, repeatedly coming down to similar findings.[3] The real improvement is in the extent and reliability of the salary data set. Most measures of performance in these salary regressions rely on offensive statistics, such as slugging or on-base average for baseball, or points per game in basketball and in hockey. American football, where individual prowess is more elusive, has been less subjected to salary analysis (but see Ahlburg and Dworkin, 1991 and Kahn, 1992). There has been some reluctance to use and also some difficulty in finding statistically significant defensive statistics, but some regressions do find a role for these lesser-known performance measures: in basketball (Koch and Vander Hill, 1988) and in hockey (Lavoie and Grenier, 1992), the former with blocks and saves, and the latter with an indicator of short-handed play, and even in baseball, when considering golden gloves recipients of awards for defensive play (Johnson, 1992).

Coming back to the approach based upon marginal revenue product, it should be pointed out that salary regressions based on this approach have been used in the arbitration hearings between the Major League Baseball Players Association and the Major Leagues, when the union filed a grievance against the owners, accusing them of collusion in refusing to compete for the hiring of free agents in the mid-1980s (Zimbalist, 1992: 110). Scully (1989: 169) reports that in 1986 and 1987 'the free agents' salary is a much smaller fraction of their contribution to team revenues than is the case of the non-free agents', thus giving statistical support to those claiming the existence of owner collusion. MacDonald and Reynolds (1994) reach the same conclusions, showing that players who were forced or chose to take the arbitration route wound up with significantly higher salaries than those who declared themselves free agents. These results are not robust, however. Zimbalist (1992) and Oorlog (1995) come to opposite conclusions, by using procedures that are broadly similar, but with different variables or hypotheses. Their regressions show that the degree of exploitation is smallest for free agents, intermediate for those who could go to arbitration, and highest for those without any salary arbitration rights, a ranking that one would tend to expect.[4] This only shows that there are limits to what econometrics can prove. Whereas straightforward salary regressions tend to be robust – the significance and sign of most performance or experience variables will be consistent – this is not so when more complex theoretical and empirical constructions are being put to task. At least in baseball, it is relatively simple to relate individual performance to winning; in other team sports, it is not so.[5]

Salary Discrimination

Whereas measures of exploitation appear to be fragile, measures of salary discrimination have turned out to be highly resilient. The issue of salary discrimination is clearly a matter where the interests of sociologists and economists of sport have overlapped. Again, sport provides an extraordinary laboratory to identify and measure discrimination against minority groups, because sport provides direct or quasi-direct measures of individual labor productivity, something that cannot really be obtained in studies of discrimination pertaining to other industries, where evidence can only be indirect.

Once again there are two procedures that can be followed to estimate whether or not there is salary discrimination. In one procedure, first applied to sports by Scully (1974b), salary regressions are run separately for the majority and the minority groups (say whites and blacks), and the estimated parameters of the variables for the two regressions are compared. If, for instance, the salary increase for a one per cent increase in batting average is lower for a black baseball player than for a white one, we may conclude, as did Scully, that there is evidence of salary discrimination against blacks. But what if an extra year of experience is more highly rewarded for black than for white players, as Scully also found? Is there still salary discrimination?

Because its results avoid this sort of ambiguity, the most popular procedure is the one followed by Pascal and Rapping (1972). A single salary regression is run for all players, with a dummy variable identifying the players from the minority group. If the parameter of this variable is negative and statistically different from zero, then there is straightforward evidence of salary discrimination. Pascal and Rapping found no evidence of salary discrimination in baseball. This finding has been repeatedly rediscovered by others, in baseball (Kahn 1991: 400) and in football (Kahn, 1992). The case of basketball is more complex. The current view is that there is no evidence of widespread salary discrimination in basketball (Jenkins 1996; Hamilton 1997). However past studies, based on data of the early and mid-1980s, as reported by Kahn (1991), had shown significant salary discrepancies in favor of white athletes, for given levels of performance. This was rather surprising in a game now dominated by black athletes. But this domination is precisely the explanation that has been advanced: white spectators want to see at least some white players. It has been shown repeatedly that attendance rises when the proportion of whites on the team increases (Kahn 1991: 410; Hamilton 1997: 289). More precisely, still in basketball, Burdekin and Idson (1991: 185) note that there is a tight link between attendance and the racial composition of the team. Also, the greater the racial match between the team and its metropolitan population, the larger is average attendance.

This explanation, based on customer discrimination, is reinforced by several other pieces of evidence. Although there is no evidence of salary discrimination in baseball and football, it has been shown that in baseball the salaries of white players are positively linked to the proportion of black players on the team, whereas the salaries of black players are negatively linked to their representation on the team (Johnson, 1992: 200). For football, Kahn (1992: 307) finds that players make more money the greater the proportion of their race in the local population. Fans in the 1980s were not color-blind! Furthermore, evidence collected from the trading of the baseball cards of past players shows that fans in general – and not only those who go to watch the games – prefer to purchase cards of white rather than black players, for given performance achievements (Nardinelli and Simon, 1990; Andersen and La Croix, 1991). However, the market prices of baseball cards picturing current players show no such customer discrimination (Gabriel et al., 1995). Younger fans may be color-blind after all!

Salary discrimination is not necessarily limited to race. Language may also be an issue. While Latin baseball players have been subjected to some scrutiny, but with little result. There have been studies of salary determination in ice hockey which have shown that French-speaking Canadian players are sometimes significantly underpaid, compared to their English Canadian or American counterparts (Lavoie and Grenier, 1992). More recent evidence, based on the use of crossed variables, shows that such salary discrimination, when it occurs, arises from teams located in English Canada, and not from teams located in the United States (Longley, 1995). This seems to indicate that the observed differentials are due to discriminatory behavior rather than the linguistic costs imputed to French-speaking players.

The Distribution of Earnings

While salary discrimination can certainly modify the distribution of labor earnings between various groups of players, the overall question of the distribution of earnings generated increased attention in the 1990s than before. Before we leave the topic of discrimination, it should be pointed out that *entry* and *exit* discrimination are important means of modifying the structure of income. Although they have written several pages on the topics, economists have given less attention than sociologists have to entry discrimination and the phenomenon of stacking. Once again, the classic references are the papers by Pascal and Rapping (1972) and Scully (1974b), and Kahn's (1991) survey article. By denying access to the major leagues, where salaries are so much higher than in the minor leagues, entry discrimination has substantial repercussions on income distribution.

Two other issues around the distribution of earnings have attracted some interest. With greater access to salary data it has been possible to compute reliable Gini coefficients, that is, measures of inequality in the distribution of earnings among professional athletes. This Gini coefficient must stand between zero and one. A perfectly equal income distribution would bring down the Gini coefficient to zero; and the higher the Gini coefficient, the more unequal the income distribution. As background information, the Gini coefficient for family income in most industrialized countries is in the 0.300 to 0.350 range, while in the United States it exceeds 0.380. While the focus of attention has been again professional team sports, Scully (1995: 74) has shown that earnings in golf were much more unequally distributed than in team sports, the Gini coefficients both for the men's and the ladies' tours being around 0.630. However, if one takes only the best 150 players, which one may liken to the athletes playing in the major leagues in contrast to the minor leagues, then the Gini coefficients of individual sports are in the range of those of team sports. As one would expect, the earnings of the top 150 female athletes in tennis and golf are much more skewed than those of the top male athletes in those two sports.

In team sports, baseball has the most unequal distribution (with a Gini of 0.510), followed by basketball (0.420), hockey (0.400) and football (0.370). Where comparisons are possible, namely in baseball, basketball and hockey, the inequality of earnings has risen considerably since the mid-1970s. An obvious cause of the above is the advent of free agency, that is, the *possibility* for star players to offer their talent to any team. This is particularly so in baseball, where there has been hardly any expansion in the number of major league franchises. By contrast, in basketball and hockey, there has been a two-fold and a four-fold increase respectively in the number of major league teams. As a consequence, talent has been diluted and the dispersion in the number of points scored per player has increased considerably since the mid-1970s, both in basketball and in hockey. The increase in the Gini coefficient of salary earnings is thus to some extent a reflection of the increase in the Gini coefficient pertaining to performance and talent.[6]

While players' earnings from professional sports teams have become more unequal, this does not mean that the economic situation of the benchwarmer or that of the journeyman has deteriorated. Although mean salaries are biased upward because of salaries from star players, the evolution of these salaries shows that there has been a tremendous increase in the standard of living of the average major league athlete. In baseball for instance, salaries in the second half of the 1950s were around $US 14,000, in current dollars (Quirk and Fort, 1992: 211). This represents approximately $US 82,950 (in 1999 dollars). In 1999, baseball average salaries were $US 1,700,000, more than 20 times the salaries of the 1950s. Similarly, in hockey, salaries were around $US 8,000 in the late 1950s, or about $US 47,500 in 1999 dollars. Mean salaries for the 1999/2000 season were $US 1,350,000, nearly 30 times the salaries of the 1950s. These multi-fold increases in purchasing power can be contrasted to the small increases in the real earnings of the average American. Consider for instance the production worker or non-supervisory employee in manufacturing. Average annual earnings were about $US 4,300 in 1957, in current dollars. This represents approximately $US 25,500 in 1999 dollars. The annual mean earnings of the same kind of worker in 1999 are only $US 30,160 (in 1999 dollars).[7] Whereas in 1957 the ratio between the earnings of the average major league player and the average blue-collar manufacturing worker was somewhere between 2:1 and 4:1, this ratio is now 55:1 for baseball and 45:1 for ice hockey. In basketball, where the average salary is reported to exceed two and a half million dollars per year, this ratio is now over 80:1. No wonder sport(s) fans often think athletes are overpaid crybabies when they go on strike or threaten to go on strike!

Although the representative athlete from all major league sports has seen his earnings dramatically increase, it should be pointed out that these increases have not been simultaneous. The average earnings in some sports, relative to those of others, sometimes take off, only to be caught back later. What are the factors that explain these wide discrepancies? Undoubtedly, the popularity of the sport, that is, the demand for the sport – as reflected in the ticket prices that spectators are willing to disburse and in the fees that the television networks and the advertisers are willing to expend – explains the increase in sports salaries (Quirk and Fort, 1992: 219). There are, however, other important factors, such as the presence or the threat of a rival league (Ahlburg and Dworkin, 1991: 62; Lavoie and Grenier, 1992: 166), the availability of neutral salary arbitrators (MacDonald and Reynolds, 1994: 444), and the lack of constraints on the mobility of players. We shall deal with the latter factor in the next section, when we analyse the sports team as a firm.

ECONOMICS OF THE FIRM

Profit Maximization

An obvious characteristic of sporting leagues is their cartel nature. This brings us immediately to the issue of profit maximization by the firm versus profit maximization by the cartel as a whole, where the latter may constrain individual firms 'in the best interests of the league'. While this distinction carries interesting issues, some of which are to be examined later, the crucial issue to be discussed here is whether profit maximization by the firm constitutes an appropriate assumption for sporting firms. Profit maximization is the standard assumption in mainstream neoclassical economics. There are, however, famous models of the firm where sales rather than profits are assumed to be the maxim, on the grounds that high sales may bring more satisfaction to the managerial staff than high profits. In dynamic terms, the question is whether firms try to maximize their rate of profit or their rate of sales growth. With respect to sporting firms, the issue is whether professional clubs try to maximize profits or winning, that is, whether profits or victories bring more satisfaction to club owners.[8]

At first sight, this seems a moot point. One would expect winning teams to induce more spectators, and hence more revenues and more profits. Although it might be so, economists do not expect such a simple relationship to hold on. Two broad reasons can be advanced, one related to the demand side and the other to the supply side. First, after some point, an extra win may not generate many additional spectators or revenues; the revenue elasticity of winning may become weak. Secondly, it may become very costly to generate additional victories; the cost elasticity of winning may exceed unity. When a team is already loaded with all-star players, hiring an extra superstar may barely increase the probability of winning. This is an instance of the well-known law of diminishing returns. Thus, beyond some point, profits start to decrease although revenues still increase. This point is the point of profit maximization. Until this point is reached, the additional revenue (marginal revenue) generated by an extra win exceeds the additional cost (marginal cost) required to engineer this extra win.

Profit maximizers and winning maximizers behave differently on many fronts, as recalled by Cairns, Jennet and Sloane (1986: 7) in their exhaustive survey of the economics of professional team sports. While the latter will strive to win 'at all costs', or as long as they do not suffer heavy financial losses, the former will be content to remain in contention. Profit maximizers will have self-imposed limits on team strength, while winning maximizers will try to dominate the league standings and reduce the uncertainty of outcome. Profit maximizers will sell or trade away good players, merely to unload heavy salaries and increase their profits, whereas winning maximizers will trade players in an attempt to improve the team. It is highly important to know what are the true objectives of sporting firms – profit or winning maximization – for all or most models evaluating the economic and competitive impact of diverse institutional rules and features of sporting leagues assume that owners attempt to maximize profits. Whether firms maximize profits or winning is thus crucial when discussing the effects of reserve clauses, free agency, rookie drafts, revenue-sharing arrangements or salary caps.

Unfortunately, it is very difficult to distinguish empirically between winning and profit-maximizing behavior. As Cairns et al. (1986: 9) recall, various authors have claimed that the predictions of their theoretical or statistical models have given support to the standard neoclassical profit-maximizing assumption. A careful examination of their claims usually shows that either alternative behaviors have not been considered, or that their results are not inconsistent with winning maximization. An attempt at empirically settling this issue showed that owners in baseball have responded more to profit than to winning incentives (Porter 1992). There have also been interviews of club officials, where their goals were being ascertained. Generally speaking, it would seem that profit-seeking behavior – perhaps in contrast to profit-maximizing as such – is a feature of North American teams, whereas winning would be a more dominant objective in European and Australian professional sport. For instance, some rich European soccer teams, such as Real Madrid, pay talented players huge sums to sit on the bench, to prevent poorer rival teams from dressing them up, thus preventing their rivals from challenging their dominance over the national championship (Bourg, 1989: 160).

Attendance

Micro-economists show that for the marginal revenue of a firm to be above zero, the price elasticity of demand must be above one. At a unitary price elasticity, revenues – but not profits – are maximized. Since the additional costs related to additional sales are necessarily non-negative, profit-seeking behavior requires minimally that the price elasticity be equal to or above one. It turns out that most studies on team attendance show price elasticities below unity, and even near zero (Cairns, 1990: 9). An increase in the price of tickets would generate more revenues and hence more profits, for lower costs would be associated with the smaller number of spectators. This price inelasticity of attendance thus yields little evidence of genuine profit-maximizing behavior. There are, however, some authors who find price elasticities near unity, thus claiming the presence of profit-maximizing behavior on the grounds that there are hardly any additional costs associated with more spectators, for a given winning percentage, and hence that profit maximization coincides with revenue maximization (Ferguson et al., 1991).

The statistical analysis of attendance also yields some interesting insights *vis-à-vis* the interests of the cartel versus those of the team. In the previous subsection, it was mentioned that the league may want to impose restrictions on its team members, in particular to preserve a viable level of competition and to prevent the wealthier teams from dominating the league. Many different variables have been introduced to meter outcome uncertainty, but to no avail (Borland and Lye, 1992: 1058; Cairns, 1990). If competitive balance is not a determinant of attendance, then league officials running the sporting cartel have no economic grounds to impose restrictions such as reserve clauses upon teams and their players, since the financial viability of the cartel as a whole does not depend upon it.

Of course, this does not mean that the quality of the home team has no impact on attendance. All studies have shown, as one would expect, that a better home team attracts more spectators, but it should also be pointed out that good visiting teams also generally attract more spectators. Hence winning draws additional revenues, even when visiting, if there is gate-sharing. In addition, being in contention for a playoff spot draws more spectators.

One peculiar set of studies on attendance is the one done for ice hockey, linking attendance to violence. This is certainly a theme that is of interest to sociologists, and it may give some ammunition to those who argue that violence in European soccer is condoned or mandated by team owners because it is profitable (Brohm, 1993). Jones (1984) has shown that when a team with a fighting reputation is playing, it draws some 1,500 to 2,500 additional spectators. When acting on the quality side, to draw as many additional spectators the home team needs to improve its standing in the league by approximately *ten* positions. A team may thus wish to pursue two strategies to increase revenues: a winning strategy or a strategy of violence. The winning strategy is a risky one: chosen players may not perform up to expectations, while if they do, their salary cost may skyrocket. The fighting strategy, by contrast, is less risky: goons fight when they are asked to, and they are much less expensive than talented stars. In addition, from the point of view of the cartel, the fighting strategy would seem to be the optimal one. Winning is a zero-sum game: all teams cannot have winning records, whereas all teams can encourage fights. There is thus some economic incentive for league officials not to ban fighting in professional hockey, despite moral pressures to do so, because fighting and violence are profitable.[9]

Restrictions on Players' Mobility

No subject has generated more controversy than the restrictions that sporting leagues impose on the mobility of players. Among these restrictions, the better known are: the draft of junior, college or amateur players, where the negotiating rights of a young player are assigned to one team only; the reserve clause, where a player may play with only one team, unless that team decides to trade the player; free agency with compensation, where a player may decide on his own to switch teams, but where the new host team must compensate the previous team by trading away some equivalent talent or future rookie draft picks. All leagues, whether in North America or in Western Europe, now have free agency for veteran players. What differentiates one league from another is the accessibility to salary arbitration – when free agency status is yet to be achieved – and the definition of veteran: one may become a free agent once the first professional contract has expired, that is, after say three, five or six years; or the player may need to reach a certain age, say 32 years old, as in ice hockey. In Europe in particular, a cash transfer fee may also be required.

As is well known, team owners defend the rookie draft and the reserve clause on the grounds that unrestricted player mobility would destroy competitive balance: wealthy clubs, located in areas with large populations, would attract star players with lucrative salaries and endorsement opportunities, and would thus purchase championships. The

league would lose credibility, players would be perceived as mercenaries, poorer clubs in less populous areas would become consistent losers, their attendances would drop, and the league might be forced to fold or to reduce its operations. Many sport analysts and a handful of economists (such as Daly, 1992) support this appraisal.

Since Rottenberg's (1956) ground-breaking article, economists have systematically objected to the reserve clause or other similar restrictions on players' mobility. Rottenberg's claim is that profit-maximizing club owners will behave in such a way that the distribution of talent will remain the same, whether restrictions are kept in place or removed. Thus, whether there are restrictions or not, big-city franchises should have winning teams while small-city franchises should have losing teams. The competitive imbalance is invariant to the restrictions designed to alter it. However, because of the constraints already noted in the section dealing with the objective of profit maximization, the differences in the revenue-generating capacity of franchises should still yield a sufficient degree of sporting competitiveness. The only real effect of restrictions on players' mobility is to reduce the share of revenues going to these players, while increasing the share going to club owners. When there are restrictions, the player can negotiate a salary that is somewhere between his reservation wage – the salary that would induce him to abandon professional sport – and his marginal revenue product to the team that owns his rights. Under total free agency, the player can negotiate a salary which is in between the highest and the second highest marginal revenue products attributed to him by any team in the league (Quirk and Fort, 1992: ch. 6). The issue is one of income distribution: who gets the rent (the extra profits) generated by extraordinary athletic ability: club owners or athletes?[10] This is most obvious in European soccer, where huge cash transfer payments are pocketed by the club when it still owns the rights of the player, whereas they are pocketed by the player, as a signing bonus, when the contract has expired.

While the statements in the above paragraph constitute the representative opinion of economists, there has always been a minority current of contrary opinion on some of these statements. Furthermore, the arguments related to small franchises versus big franchises have been refined. First it should be pointed out, as did, along with many others before them, Cairns et al. (1986: 33) and Quirk and Fort (1992: 279), that Rottenberg's claim assumes a profit-maximizing behavior. If owners do try to maximize profits, small-franchise owners who have drafted players who turn out to be highly productive superstars will have an incentive to unload them to richer franchises, because the owners of these richer franchises will offer huge cash amounts, knowing that these superstars can generate large increases in revenues, as a result of the potentially larger attendance. If club owners maximize winning – and this may be not at all irrational in a league where there are playoffs or additional revenue-generating games as in European soccer cups – or if the league forbids the sale of players and unfair trades, Rottenberg's claim does not hold anymore: restrictions will make the league more balanced.[11]

However, even with free agency, large market teams may not necessarily dominate small market ones. This is the new view of economists on the topic, a view which has been put forth by Porter (1992) and Vrooman (1995). Again there are two sides to this claim. First, it may be that the salaries needed to be paid by teams located in big cities are much higher than those necessary to induce players to migrate to small-city franchises. The revenue advantage of large market teams may thus be wiped out by a cost disadvantage. There is as yet no empirical evidence of this supply-side effect however.[12] By contrast, there is empirical evidence that the fans of various franchises react differently to the performance of their team. If attendance is winning-elastic, that is, 'if fans demand a winner and express their distaste for losing by staying away from the game' (Porter, 1992: 75), additional revenues generated by extra wins will be high, and this will induce profit-maximizing owners to search for more talented players. On the other hand, if attendance is winning-inelastic, that is, if fans are loyal, there will be little incentive for club owners to improve the team. Small market team owners with winning-thirsty fans may thus be forced to be competitive with large market teams with loyal fans.

This encouraging result for small market team fans has, however, some drawbacks. First, it should again be pointed out that if club owners do not maximize profits, these results do not hold. If club owners of large market teams maximize winning, they will deplete the ranks of small market teams, especially those that have recently achieved success with bright rising stars. Secondly, a small market team needs a core of loyal fans, otherwise there will be an incentive for the owners to move the franchise to some other, more complacent city.[13] This brings in the issue of whether or not

efforts should be made by local public officials to keep the franchise in town, an issue that will be discussed later in the chapter.

Revenue-sharing Schemes and Salary Caps

Although the problems of small market teams seem to have been exacerbated recently, the issue is not a new one and it has generated some responses. Two broad answers to the problem have been or can be provided. The first possibility is to provide a revenue-sharing scheme that will allow small market teams to have access to the financial benefits inherent in markets with large metropolitan populations. Gate-sharing, where attendance revenues are split between the host and the visiting team, and sharing in national broadcast revenues are such revenue-sharing schemes. The second possibility is to devise some formula that will directly restrict the amounts spent on salaries. Salary caps are such a measure, but proposals for taxes on salary expenditures – positive taxes for teams with large payrolls and negative taxes for teams with small payrolls – were also proposed during the baseball 1994 strike and the ice hockey lockout of 1994–5. While, indeed, all of these schemes should improve the financial situation of small market teams, the issue is whether they would help to establish more balanced competition in the league.

On intuitive grounds, one would be tempted to answer 'yes' right away, and indeed Scully (1989: 80) does so. Surely, if all teams have more equal revenues, their capacity to hire good players should be equalized, and this ought to be a good thing for the sport. In fact, this is the standard argument made by league officials who have endorsed these schemes. The standard opinion of economists, however, is full of qualifications. Economists claim that under some circumstances the revenue-sharing schemes will not help to achieve a more competitive balance, and furthermore, that these schemes modify income distribution in favour of club owners, at the expense of players.

Take the gate-sharing scheme. Let us assume, as is standard, that team owners maximize profits. Their decisions to hire talented players will be based on the marginal revenue procured by the additional wins generated by the supplementary performance of these players. If the revenues from attendance are shared, however, the large market team will only get a portion of the increase in gate revenues at home, and marginal revenues when visiting will decrease whenever it wins away. Because winning is a zero-sum game within the league, the implications of gate-sharing will be identical for the small market team (Fort and Quirk, 1996). This is the revenue-sharing paradox. As long as all teams are subject to the same sharing formula, and as long as the shared revenue responds to win–loss records, revenue-sharing has no effect on competitive balance (Vrooman, 1995: 978). In other words, revenue-sharing is useless to equalize the field as long as the shared revenues are winning-elastic.

In addition, gate-sharing has unexpected negative consequences for players. Because it is winning-elastic and diminishes the marginal revenue product of each player for each team, gate-sharing induces profit-maximizing teams to reduce their salary offers to players. As a consequence, the share of revenues going to players should be reduced. Owners would pocket a larger fraction of the rent generated by the talent of athletes.

On the other hand, it can be surmised that national media revenues are revenue-inelastic from the point of view of each individual team. The distribution of lump sums from national media revenue-sharing should thus promote competitive balance and should have none of the above negative consequences on the share of income distribution of players. There is a conflict, however, with the interests of the cartel: one would presume that national media would be tempted to funnel more funds into contracts with professional leagues when these leagues are dominated by large market teams. A greater number of spectators would be happy to watch the network and its advertisers when their favourite large market team triumphs.[14]

There is still some controversy about the impact of a salary cap. Quirk and Fort (1992: 291) argue that the salary cap helps to equalize competition, as long as the cap is enforced. They also show that the overall revenues of the league would be reduced, since large market teams, with high marginal revenues due to their large potential audience, would win less often than without the cap, thus generating less winning-elastic revenues. On the other hand, Vrooman (1995: 980) believes that salary caps and a payroll surtax allow the league to act as a cartel. This helps the league to keep down salary costs and increase the degree of exploitation of the players. In addition, the salary cap would *increase*, rather than decrease, the competitive inequality between teams. Some authors have noted that competition in baseball

has been much more balanced between small market and large market teams than it has been in basketball, despite the salary caps of the latter (Gramlich, 1994). These opposite opinions no doubt explain that both the salary cap and the payroll surtax were highly contentious items during the labour stoppages in baseball and ice hockey in the mid-1990s. What kind of world is it, where capitalist owners want to impose rules and restrictions upon themselves whereas employed players want free markets to prevail?

The Impact of a Franchise in Professional Sport

With the advent of free agency, and with the increase in popularity of professional team sport, the salaries of professional athletes have skyrocketed. As a result, the future of several small market franchises has been questioned. Besides the league-wide schemes presented in the preceding section, this has induced the owners of these teams to pressure local public authorities, in the hope of getting public subsidies or other financial benefits.

The retention of major league teams has not been the only source of controversy between club owners, sports fans, city officials and economists. As A.T. Johnson (1993: 1) notes, the acquisition of sport franchises, be they at the minor or major league levels, has become the objective of sports entrepreneurs and local politicians in communities of all sizes. In North America, cities try to attract franchises from as high a league level as they can. In Europe, where teams are promoted and relegated according to their standings, city officials decide whether or not they will offer large subsidies that will allow their local team to purchase better players and help them to be promoted to an upper-grade league. In both continents, the renovation, construction, siting and use of public sports stadiums or arenas quickly become an issue on the political agenda.

Arguments of five sorts are usually advanced to justify the use of public money for what is basically a private endeavour. First, it is claimed that the presence of the sports franchise will directly create additional (low-paid) jobs: the ushers, the clerks at the sales booths, the parking attendants, etc. When a stadium is built or renovated, there will be a temporary increase in employment and tax revenues. Secondly, there will be indirect benefits, those that can be linked to the famous income multiplier. The public expenditures on the stadium will be injections in the economy, that will induce further spending by those who work on the construction site, or by those who provide goods and materials. These will produce further tax revenues to cover the granted subsidies. Thirdly, the franchise will be a business attraction, enticing visitors from outside, who will spend money inside the community, thus helping local business to be more profitable. Fourthly, the presence of a sports franchise will bring regional, national or international media attention and recognition to the city. This should help local firms to export their products and services, and more specifically it should help the tourist industry. Sport is thus seen as a strategic ploy for regional economic development. Finally, even if all these benefits are dubious when netted out against the costs of servicing a newer or bigger stadium or arena, there remains for the citizen the positive psychic and sociological benefits of being associated with a sports franchise and possibly a winning team. With this last claim, professional sport is said to be a public good, akin to good health.

While economist consultants hired to assess the economic impact of sports teams and their stadiums on host communities systematically find a positive impact, this is not so with academic economists. The latter are usually highly sceptical of the economic benefits associated with a new franchise, and a new or renovated stadium. The consensus among academic economists is that most of the benefits, if they exist, are intangible, and related to civic pride (Johnson, 1993: 4). The better known studies have been done by Baade and Dye (1988, 1990). Looking at major leagues with the help of regression analysis, they show that a new franchise, a new stadium or a renovated stadium, have no impact on the level of metropolitan income or retail sales. The only possible exception is that of baseball.[15] The opinion that major league sports have little, if any, impact on local economic activity has been reinforced by a study that has shown that the baseball strike of August and September 1994 had no negative economic impact on cities with baseball franchises (Zipp, 1996).

An interesting case study is that of Gouguet and Nys (1993: 230–9). They look at two widely different cases: the city of Limoges, which has a basketball team that is highly successful at the European level; and the city of Rennes, which has a soccer team usually ranked in the bottom half of the top French soccer league, always on the verge of being relegated down to the second division. In both cases, it turns out that the sums of money injected in the local

economy by each of these two professional teams were largely overturned by the sums of money leaking out of the local economy because of these professional sporting clubs. These leaks were due in large part to the players spending only a portion of their salaries within the local community. Most of these salaries, which constitute a large chunk of the clubs' expenses, were either taxed by the French government or saved by the players. The little that was spent was either spent in Paris, for the soccer players, or in the States, for the American stars of the Limoges basketball team. There was no room for any positive multiplier effect, for the multiplicand was negative![16]

There are obvious lessons to be drawn for North American cities desperately seeking to obtain a franchise in major league sports. There are also obvious lessons to be drawn for cities wishing to organize major sporting events such as the Olympic Games, the Pan-American Games, or the Commonwealth Games, as Gouguet and Nys (1993) show. Indeed, tourism may even drop during such games, as tourists fear being crowded out.

In general one must beware of economic consultants shuffling multiplier effects and complex input–output models. Whatever their degree of sophistication, by their very method, these studies of economic impact cannot but predict substantial financial benefits to the organization of large sporting events or to the arrival of major league franchises. But similar results would be obtained whenever any project with similar additional expenditures is being proposed. Studies of economic impact only demonstrate that a reduction in unemployment is a profitable venture. If such is the goal being pursued, then one must decide what sort of public expenditure is more desirable. Building a new stadium with a large number of private luxury boxes, filled with corporate executives and paid for by the consumers of the products that these corporations produce, may not be the most appropriate choice.

CONCLUSION

Despite the extraordinary development of the economics of sport, it is clear that much of its focus has been on the economics of professional team sports. There are basically three reasons for this: the topic offers many instances of micro-economic conundrums that can be solved; economists thrive on numbers, which professional sport generates; the topic is popular whereas amateur sports are not (in North America). Of course, many other topics which have attracted the attention of economists could have been covered. On the micro-economic front there have been studies on the cost of practising sport (Michon and Ohl, 1989), the logic of which has inspired the so-called 'economic hypothesis' purporting to explain positional segregation in team sports, that is, stacking (Medoff, 1977, 1986). Others have also tried to predict the demographics of professional tennis, giving economic explanations as to why young players would dominate the sport, or as to why older players would remain longer on the tour (Galenson, 1993, 1995). A problem with these hypotheses is that they can predict just about anything. On the macro-economic front, there have been qualitative and quantitative studies on the increasing globalization of sport, both for athletes and for the sporting goods being produced and exported (Andreff, 1989; Harvey and Saint-Germain, 1995).

What is the future of the discipline? On the pedagogical front, the discipline has now reached the point where it is possible to have whole courses devoted to the economics of sport. Bruggink (1993) shows how one could build a first-year introduction course on the principles of micro-economics, with illustrations taken entirely from the economics of baseball.[17] Obviously, a special topics course on the economics of baseball, or the economics and business of any other professional team sport, could also easily be constructed. Estenson (1994) describes how students were asked to maximize profits while pretending to be baseball team owners in search of free agents.

What about the academic front? As reported by Johnson (1995: 505), in 1991 the keynote speaker at a conference on the economics of baseball 'declared that everything important and interesting about the economics of professional sports had already been said, and no further work was necessary'. Since then dozens of books and articles on the economics of baseball and the economics of sport have been published. It is true that many of the more recent articles deal with arcane or trifling issues, or rely on highly dubious hypotheses to arrive at some practical result. There is no lack of ingenuity, however, in some of the newer articles. Just as one would think that an old model cannot be improved any more, someone comes along with an innovation that gives more insights or that makes the model more robust.[18] Where objections have been raised about previous interpretations of the data, new

means to test these interpretations have been found.[19]

What are future poles of research? There is still a great deal of uncertainty about the true impact of salary caps for competitive balance and the welfare of players regulated by such caps. There is also a great deal of uncertainty about the future of small market teams, and how their financial situation can be improved without damaging that of the players. The reverse-order rookie drafts have only been given scant attention, but they may be the only restriction still promoting competitive balance: should they be partially removed, like the reserve clause, limiting the draft to only the best prospects?[20] Finally, leaving theory for practice, one may predict that if professional athletes dared to go on strike in various countries to increase their share of the revenues generated by professional sport, the day cannot be too far off when the so-called amateur athletes will threaten to go on strike in order to get their share of the huge revenues generated by worldwide mega-events such as the Olympic Games.

NOTES

1 For a similar opinion, see Heinemann (1991). For examples of the Continental tradition, see Malenfant (1982), Andreff and Nys (1986) and the articles in Andreff (1989).

2 See Quirk and Fort (1992: 369–71) for a simple 'how to' presentation of salary regressions, in particular the meaning of semi-log regressions.

3 There are always some minor improvements to be made. For instance, when dealing with pitchers in baseball, Lavoie and Leonard (1990) and Fort (1992) take into account the fact that the productivity of starting pitchers and relief pitchers is not judged on identical criteria.

4 See also Gustafson and Hadley (1995).

5 For instance there are estimates of marginal revenue product in hockey that show that no such exploitation existed when the rival World Hockey Association was confronting the dominant National Hockey League, and that indeed journeymen were being overpaid (Jones and Walsh, 1987). With new estimates based on a new approach and data from the 1990s, Richardson (1997) concludes that the players in the first and the fifth salary quintiles are underpaid, while all the others are overpaid. As in baseball, these estimates may not be robust.

6   See Quirk and Fort (1992: 238) and Scully (1995: 79). Data on hockey also provided by Richardson (1997) and the author.

7   Historical data on consumer price indices and wages taken from the web site of the Bureau of Labour Statistics, www.bls.gov

8   Sporting clubs may also try to maximize winning on the field because the visibility due to winning championships allows the owners to maximize profits in their business of origin, for instance the beer industry. See Porter (1992: 70).

9   Gruneau and Whitson (1993: 186) argue that this is a misleading strategy, for if hockey would stop celebrating violence, a new wave of spectators would flow into the arenas, along with lucrative American TV network deals. Jones gives another look at this issue in Jones, Stewart and Sunderman (1996), trying to put the blame on violence-prone American fans.

10 The same occurs in team sports at the college or amateur level, especially in basketball and mostly in football. Collegiate rules forbid the jeopardizing of the amateur status of the student athlete, but the main objective of these rules is to allow universities to collect the rent associated with the talent of their best performing athletes. Brown (1993) estimates that the best college football players can generate as much as half a million dollars.

11 This is Daly's (1992: 26–7) main argument against the dismantling of the rookie draft and the limited reserve clause. In American football, for instance, there is an informal agreement since 1977 not to sell players for cash (Quirk and Fort, 1992: 283). American football is thought to have the most balanced competition.

12 Indeed, contrary evidence might prevail, because of the higher opportunities in big cities for endorsements and retirement employment (Krautman and Oppenheimer, 1994: 463; Gramlich, 1994: 127).

13 A typical example, so it seems, is the sale in ice hockey of the Quebec Nordiques, who became the Colorado Avalanche in 1995. The mayor of Quebec City refused to cave in to the demands of Marcel Aubut, the main owner of the Nordiques, and refused to build a new arena. Aubut, tired of the winning-thirsty Nordiques fans, sold the team to Denver businessmen.

14 Incidentally, from a purely economic welfare point of view, large market teams ought to win because they procure psychic satisfaction for a greater number of citizens.

15 See also Baade (1996), Baim (1994), Euchner (1993), Rosentraub (1997), and Noll and Zimbalist (1997).

16 See also the study of Colclough, Daellenbach and Sherony (1994). With a similar methodology, they show that the benefits of a new minor league baseball franchise, although positive, were greatly exaggerated by the promoters of the franchise.

17 There is a textbook by Cooke (1994), apparently designed to teach the principles of economics to students of sport and leisure, but while its level of difficulty is well targeted, the book contains few concrete examples.

18 I have two examples in mind: the Scully (1974a) model of the marginal revenue product and the Quirk and El Hodiri (1974) model of competitive balance, highly improved recently by Oorlog (1995) and Vrooman (1995) respectively.

19 See, for instance, Longley (1995) and Richardson (1997) in hockey, but there are many more in all sports.

20 See Grier and Tollison (1994).

REFERENCES AND FURTHER READING

Ahlburg, D.A. and Dworkin, J.B. (1991) 'Player compensation in the National Football League', in P.D. Staudohar and J.A. Mangan (eds), *The Business of Professional Sports.* Urbana, IL: University of Illinois Press. pp. 61–70.

Andersen, T. and La Croix, S.J. (1991) 'Customer racial discrimination in Major League baseball', *Economic Inquiry,* 29 (4): 66–7.

Andreff, W. (ed.) (1989) *Économie politique du sport.* Paris: Dalloz.

Andreff, W. and Nys, J.F. (1986) *Économie du sport.* Paris: Presses Universitaires de France.

Baade, R.A. (1996) 'Professional sports as catalysts for metropolitan economic development', *Journal of Urban Affairs,* 18 (1): 1–17.

Baade, R.A. and Dye, R.F. (1988) 'An analysis of the economic rationale for public subsidization of sports stadiums', *Annals of Regional Science,* 22 (2): 37–47.

Baade, R.A. and Dye, R.F. (1990) 'The impact of stadiums and professional sports on metropolitan area development', *Growth and Change: a Journal of Urban and Regional Policy,* 21 (2): 1–14.

Baim, D. (1994) *The Sports Stadium as a Municipal Investment.* Westport, CT: Greenwood Press.

Borland, J. and Lye, J. (1992) 'Attendance at Australian Rules football: A Panel Study', *Applied Economics,* 24 (9): 1053–8.

Bourg, J.F. (1989) 'Le marché du travail sportif', in W. Andreff (ed.), *Économie politique du sport*. Paris: Dalloz. pp. 145–69.

Brohm, J.M. (1993) *Les meutes sportives: critique de la domination*. Paris: L'Harmattan.

Brown, R.W. (1993) 'An estimate of the rent generated by a premium college football player', *Economic Inquiry*, 31 (4): 671–84.

Bruggink, T.H. (1993) 'National pastime to dismal science: using baseball to illustrate economic principles', *Eastern Economic Journal*, 19 (3): 275–94.

Burdekin, R.C.K. and Idson, T.J. (1991) 'Customer preferences, attendance and the racial structure of professional basketball teams', *Applied Economics*, 23: 179–86.

Cairns, J. (1990) 'The demand for professional team sports', *British Review of Economic Issues*, 12 (28): 1–20.

Cairns, J., Jennet, N. and Sloane, P.J. (1986) 'The economics of professional team sports: a survey of theory and evidence', *Journal of Economic Issues*, 13 (1): 3–8.

Colclough, W.G., Daellenbach, L.A. and Sherony, K.R. (1994) 'Estimating the economic impact of a Minor League baseball stadium', *Managerial and Decision Economics*, 15 (5): 497–502.

Cooke, A. (1994) *The Economics of Leisure and Sport*. London: Routledge.

Daly, G.G. (1992) 'The baseball player's labor market revisited', in P.M. Sommers (ed.), *Diamonds are Forever: the Business of Baseball*. Washington, DC: Brookings Institution. pp. 11–28.

Estenson, P.S. (1994) 'Salary determination in Major League baseball: a classroom exercise', *Managerial and Decision Economics*, 15 (5): 537–41.

Euchner, C.C. (1993) *Playing the Field: Why Sports Teams Move and Cities Fight to Keep Them*. Baltimore, MD: Johns Hopkins University Press.

Ferguson, D., Stewart, K.G., Jones, J.C.H. and LaDressay, A. (1991) 'The pricing of sporting events: do teams maximise profits', *Journal of Industrial Economics*, 39: 297–310.

Fort, R.D. (1992) 'Pay and performance: is the Field of Dreams barren?', in P.M. Sommers (ed.), *Diamonds are Forever: the Business of Baseball*. Washington, DC: Brookings Institution. pp. 134–60.

Fort, R.D. and Quirk, J. (1996) 'Cross-subsidization, incentives, and outcomes in professional team sports leagues', *Journal of Economic Literature*, 33 (3): 1265–99.

Gabriel, P.E., Johnson, C. and Stanton, T.J. (1995) 'An examination of customer racial discrimination in the market for baseball memorabilia', *Journal of Business*, 68 (2): 215–30.

Galenson, D.W. (1993) 'The impact of economic and technological change on the careers of American men tennis players, 1960–1991', *Journal of Sport History*, 20 (3): 127–50.

Galenson, D.W. (1995) 'Does youth rule? Trends in the ages of American tennis players', *Journal of Sport History*, 22 (1): 46–59.

Gouguet, J.J. and Nys, J.F. (1993) *Sport et développement économique régional*. Paris: Dalloz.

Gramlich, E.M. (1994) 'A natural experiment in styles of capitalism: professional sports', *Quarterly Review of Economics and Finance*, 34 (2): 121–30.

Grier, K.B. and Tollison, R.D. (1994) 'The rookie draft and competitive balance: the case of professional football', *Journal of Economic Behaviour and Organization*, 25 (2): 293–8.

Gruneau, R. and Whitson, D. (1993) *Hockey Night in Canada: Sport, Identities, and Cultural Politics*. Toronto: Garamond Press.

Gustafson, E. and Hadley, L. (1995) 'Arbitration and salary gaps in Major League baseball', *Quarterly Journal of Business and Economics*, 34 (3): 32–46.

Hamilton, B.H. (1997) 'Racial discrimination and professional salaries in the 1990s', *Applied Economics*, 29 (3): 287–96.

Harvey, J. and Saint-Germain, M. (1995) 'L'industrie et la politique canadienne du sport en contexte de mondialisation', *Sociologie et Sociétés*, 27 (1): 33–52.

Heinemann, K. (1991) 'The economics of sport: the institution of modern sport as an area of economic competition', in F. Landry, M. Landry and M. Yerlès (eds), *Sport … Le troisième millénaire*. Ste-Foy, Quebec: Presses de l'Université Laval. pp. 311–19.

Jenkins, J.A. (1996) 'A reexamination of salary discrimination in professional basketball', *Social Science Quarterly*, 77 (3): 594–608.

Jennings, K.M. (1990) *Balls and Strikes: the Money Game in Professional Baseball*. New York: Praeger.

Johnson, A.T. (1993) *Minor League Baseball and Local Economic Development*. Urbana, IL: University of Illinois Press.

Johnson, B.K. (1992) 'Team racial composition and players' salaries', in P.M. Sommers (ed.), *Diamonds are Forever: the Business of Baseball*. Washington, DC: Brookings Institution. pp. 189–202.

Johnson, B.K. (1995) 'Book review of *The Market Structure of Sports*, by Gerard W. Scully', *Southern Economic Journal*, 62 (2): 505–7.

Jones, J.C.H. (1984) 'Winners, losers and hosers: demand and survival in the National Hockey League', *Atlantic Economic Journal*, 12 (3): 54–63.

Jones, J.C.H., Stewart, K.G. and Sunderman, R. (1996) 'From the arena into the streets: hockey violence, economic incentives and public policy', *American Journal of Economics and Sociology*, 55 (2): 231–41.

Jones, J.C.H. and Walsh, W.D. (1987) 'The World Hockey League and player exploitation in the National Hockey League', *Quarterly Review of Economics and Business*, 27 (2): 87–101.

Kahn, L.M. (1991) 'Discrimination in professional sports: a survey of the evidence', *Industrial and Labor Relations Review*, 44 (3): 395–418.

Kahn, L.M. (1992) 'The effects of race on professional football players' compensation', *Industrial and Labor Relations Review*, 45 (2): 295–310.

Klamer, A. and Colander, D. (1990) *The Making of an Economist*. Boulder, CO: Westview Press.

Koch, J.V. and Vander Hill, C.W. (1988) 'Is there discrimination in the "black man's game"?', *Social Science Quarterly*, 69 (1): 83–94.

Krautman, A.C. and Oppenheimer, M. (1994) 'Free agency and the allocation of labor in Major League baseball', *Managerial and Decision Economics*, 15 (5): 459–69.

Lavoie, M. and Grenier, G. (1992) 'Discrimination and salary determination in the National Hockey League', in G.W. Scully (ed.), *Advances in the Economics of Sport*. Greenwich, CT: JAI Press. pp. 151–75.

Lavoie, M. and Leonard, W.M. (1990) 'Salaries, race/ethnicity, and pitchers in Major League baseball: a correction and comment', *Sociology of Sport Journal*, 7 (4): 394–8.

Longley, N. (1995) 'Salary discrimination in the National Hockey League: the effects of team location', *Canadian Public Policy*, 21 (4): 413–22.

MacDonald, D.N. and Reynolds, M.O. (1994) 'Are baseball players paid their marginal products?', *Managerial and Decision Economics*, 15 (5): 443–57.

Malenfant, C. (1982) 'The economics of sport in France', *International Social Science Journal*, 34 (2): 233–46.

Medoff, M.M. (1977) 'Positional segregation and professional baseball', *International Review of Sport Sociology*, 5: 5–23.

Medoff, M.H. (1986) 'Positional segregation and the economic hypothesis', *Sociology of Sport Journal*, 3 (4): 297–304.

Michon, B. and Ohl, F. (1989) 'Aspects socio-économiques du prix de la pratique sportive', in W. Andreff (ed.), *Économie politique du sport*. Paris: Dalloz. pp. 34–77.

Nardinelli, C. and Simon, C. (1990) 'Customer racial discrimination in the market for memorabilia: the case of baseball', *Quarterly Journal of Economics*, 105 (3): 575–95.

Noll, R.G. and Zimbalist, A. (eds) (1997) *Sports, Jobs and Taxes: The Economic Impact of Sports Teams and Stadiums*. Washington, DC: Brookings Institute.

Oorlog, D.R. (1995) 'Marginal revenue and labor strife in Major League baseball', *Journal of Labor Research*, 16 (1): 25–42.

Pascal, A.H. and Rapping, L.A. (1972) 'The economics of racial discrimination in organized baseball', in A.H. Pascal (ed.), *Racial Discrimination in Economic Life*, Lexington, MA: Lexington Books. pp. 119–56.

Porter, P.K. (1992) 'The role of the fan in professional baseball', in P.M. Sommers (ed.), *Diamonds are Forever: the Business of Baseball*. Washington, DC: Brookings Institution. pp. 63–76.

Quirk, J. and El–Hodiri, M. (1974) 'The economic theory of a professional league', in R.G. Noll (ed.), *Government and the Sports Business*. Washington, DC: Brookings Institution.

Quirk, J. and Fort, R.D. (1992) *Pay Dirt: The Business of Professional Team Sports*. Princeton, NJ: Princeton University Press.

Richardson, D.H. (1997) 'Pay, performance, and competitive balance in the National Hockey League'. Working Paper, University of St Lawrence, Canton, NY.

Rosentraub, M. (1997) *Major League Losers*. New York: Basic Books.

Rottenberg, S. (1956) 'The baseball player's labour market', *Journal of Political Economy*, 64 (3): 242–58.

Scully, G.W. (1974a) 'Pay and performance in Major League baseball', *American Economic Review*, 64 (6): 915–30.

Scully, G.W. (1974b) 'Discrimination: the case of baseball', in R.G. Noll (ed.), *Government and the Sports Business*. Washington, DC: Brookings Institution. pp. 221–70.

Scully, G.W. (1989) *The Business of Major League Baseball*. Chicago: University of Chicago Press.

Scully, G.W. (ed.) (1992) *Advances in the Economics of Sport*. Greenwich, CT: JAI Press.

Scully, G.W. (1995) *The Market Structure of Sport*. Chicago: University of Chicago Press.

Vrooman, J. (1995) 'A general theory of professional sports leagues', *Southern Economic Journal*, 61 (4): 971–90.

Zimbalist, A. (1992) 'Salaries and performance: beyond the Scully model', in P.M. Sommers (ed.), *Diamonds are Forever: the Business of Baseball*. Washington, DC: Brookings Institution. pp. 109–33.

Zipp, J.F. (1996) 'The economic impact of the baseball strike of 1994', *Urban Affairs Review*, 32 (2): 157–85.

10

HUMAN GEOGRAPHY AND THE STUDY OF SPORT

John Bale

A number of academic disciplines, for example sociology, philosophy, psychology and history, each have their sport-related subdiscipline with its academic journals, regular conferences and academic associations. The same cannot be said of geography.[1] Yet it would be difficult to deny that a geography of sport exists and that it constitutes a corpus of scholarship that focuses, in particular, on regional, spatial and landscape aspects of sports. Inevitably there is an overlap between the work of geographers *qua* geographers and those undertaking work of a geographical nature in cognate disciplines; and as disciplinary boundaries begin to collapse, this tendency is likely to continue. This chapter will concentrate mainly – but not entirely – on the work of professional geographers and their approaches to the study of achievement sport. The considerable geographical coverage afforded recreation and leisure cannot be included in the space available here, even if it is accepted that the distinction between sport and recreation is, at times, somewhat blurred. (Patmore, 1970, 1983)

The contributions made by geographers to interdisciplinary studies of sport during the past several decades are relatively easy to see. For example, in the United States Rooney (1975) contributed to the collection of essays in Ball and Loy's sociological overview of sports; Bale (1991a, 1991b, 1992a, 1993a, 1998) has contributed to various collections of essays on European soccer; in France Matthieu (1991), Praicheux (1991) and Augustin (1995) have vigorously supported various interdisciplinary initiatives; and in Sweden Moen (1993) and Aldskogius (1993a) have ensured the inclusion of sport in the *Swedish National Atlas*. These writers are but the tip of a large pyramid of geographers involved in contributing to sports studies. In addition, it is worth noting that scholars in sports history and sports sociology have been discovering space and place at the same time as geographers have been discovering sports. In the 1990s collections edited by scholars outside geography were published on *Sport in Space and Time* (Weiss and Schultz, 1995) and *Sport and Space* (Riiskjær, 1993); a special issue of the *International Review for the Sociology of Sport* covered the same subject (Púig and Ingham, 1993). From the contents of these publications it is often unclear to which academic 'disciplines' the various contributors are nominally attached. The same is true of other edited collections to which geographers have contributed, on such diverse subjects as the global migration of sports talent (Bale and Maguire, 1994) and the significance of the stadium to the modern city (Bale and Moen, 1995). Indeed, these kinds of projects seem to reflect the sort of 'disciplinary' synthesis between the history, geography and sociology of sport for which Maguire (1995) has called.

This review[2] is structured around five themes. First, I outline the emergence and context of a geography of sport, including a brief consideration of the rationale of a geographical approach. The second section of the chapter describes the dominant paradigm in sports-geographic writing, that of geographical variations in sporting attributes. This is followed by a section on the spatial dynamics of sports. A fourth area focuses on the spatial-economic and environmental impact of sports, examining the nature of the impacts and their spatial dimensions. The final section explores the landscape of sports. These are not discrete entities and obviously considerable overlap exists. They do, nevertheless, serve as a useful organizing framework.

RATIONALE AND DEBATES

The basic rationale for a geography of sport is that sports exist in time *and space*. While historical studies of sports have been relatively well developed, they have often been insensitive to the geographical dimensions of the historical trajectories which they describe (though see, for example, Metcalfe, 1990). The same might be said of sociological and anthropological studies of sport where, until recently, the spatial (geographical) dimension has been muted. It is also clear, however, that sports and geography share some conceptual bases. In sports two fundamental geographical concepts, space and place, are central essences. Sports are struggles over *space*; indeed, in most other areas of our lives space limitations are rather opaque, while in sports they are made thematic and integral; spatial rules govern us in more arbitrary ways in sport than in everyday life (Hyland, 1990). And sports teams almost always represent a *place*; people identify with a place through sport, arguably more so than through any other form of culture; we talk of 'representational' sports. The centrality of space and place in sports suggests that there is potential for a geographical theory of sports, but little has been done to probe further in this direction.

There is a general feeling within geography that the geography of sport is a marginal subdiscipline. It was only in the third edition of *The Dictionary of Human Geography* (Johnston et al., 1994) that it earned a modest, but unsatisfactory, entry. Nevertheless, some debates on the subdiscipline have occurred and these raise interesting questions and provide important insights about sport – and the nature of scientific enquiry. The widely perceived marginality of a geography of sport formed the subject of a minor debate around Dear's (1988: 271) view that a 'geography of sport is not central to the structure and explanation of geographical knowledge'. Dear prioritized fields such as political, social and economic geography – ignoring the fact that sport is political, social and economic and therefore part of each of these geographies. Scott and Simpson-Housley (1989) challenged Dear's view by observing

that 'the conditions predominating in any given field of study dictate which subdiscipline is more or less fruitful'. They added, as an example, that 'the geography of the sport of soccer governs key aspects of political, social and economic conditions of Rio de Janeiro, rather than *vice versa*'. It has also been argued, in relation to Dear's comments, that insights about the workings of human society can often be found from the most marginal of sources. Hence, a case can readily be made for studying (what many regard as the 'marginal' phenomenon of) sport, which may be

exceedingly helpful as we try to unravel the mysteries bound up in how geographical knowledge is constructed outside of the academy, and in how the everyday senses that people possess of themselves, their societies and their worlds have rolled into them sensations of bodies in movement through immediate surroundings as well as feelings of commonality sedimented in collective events, games, rituals and spectacles which so often embrace a sports component. (Philo, 1994)

What should be added, however, is that sports are not only significant as 'representations' of places and as 'rituals and spectacles' but also as examples of 'disciplinary mechanisms'.

The ways in which geographers have treated the study of sports cannot be understood outside the changes that have occurred in geography itself. An early paper in *The National Geographic Magazine* (Hildebrand, 1919) explained the games and sports which people played as being related to the physical environment in which they lived. Such an approach was understandable, given the prevailing geographical paradigm of environmental determinism. In academic writing this organizing framework continued to link sport and geography as late as the 1950s (Richards, 1953) and still lingers on in popular writing. From the late 1960s onwards, however, geography has been subjected to a number of philosophical shifts (Johnston, 1991), illustrated by the large number of 'adjectival geographies' and 'specialty groups' which have sprung up to accommodate the geography of almost anything.

An early attempt to provide an organizing schema for sports-geographic study was Rooney's (1975) 'conceptual framework for the geographical analysis of sport'. This was not a geographical model or theory of sport but a framework for its exploration. He suggested three possible approaches. These were:

1 a topical approach which starts with a sport (or sport *per se*) and identifies the location

of its prototypes and points of origin, its spatial diffusion, spatial organization and regionalization;

2   a regional approach which, having drawn up an inventory of an area's sports, analyses their spatial organization, the spatial variation and regionalization of involvement and interest, the internal and external spatial interaction associated with sport, an assessment of sports' impacts on the landscape, and prescriptions for spatial reorganization;

3   an approach focusing specifically on the changing landscape of sport through time and the impact of changes in sport technology.

Although undoubtedly helpful in assisting with many sports-geographic studies, there is little in this framework that draws specifically on the inherently geographical nature of sport itself. It could be used for the analysis of virtually any terrestrial phenomenon. It does not seek to construct a theory out of the geographical concepts which are intrinsic to modern sports – those of space and place. Nor does it draw on two of the norms of sport which have clear geographical manifestations – fair play and achievement-orientation. This is a theme to which I will return in the final section of the chapter.

A FETISH OF CARTOGRAPHY?

Despite the eclecticism of geographical enquiry, it is clear that since the late 1960s the major focus for sports-geographic writing has been one which explores regional variations in sports attributes. This approach marries geography's regional framework (that is, a concern with regional variability) with a positivist philosophy which seeks to find general patterns of spatial distribution. Hence, Rooney – unquestionably the father of modern sports geography (Louder, 1991) – and a large number of his followers, have tended to identify a geography of sport with the search for 'sports regions', using the map as the principal tool of analysis. Rooney's (1969) seminal study of the geographical implications of football in the United States illustrates such an approach. Although Rooney's general approach had been anticipated by a sociological study of the geographical origins of professional baseball players (Lehman, 1940) and a medical anthropologist's 'geographical' analysis of the 1952 Olympics (Jokl, 1965), he was the first to publish his findings in a mainstream academic

geographical journal and to apply widely the geographer's tool of the map in describing his findings. His work also inspired a long line of studies that imitated his approach. Rooney's basic research problem, replicated in his book on the geography of American sport (Rooney, 1974), was to identify geographical variations in the 'production' of élite sports participants. He did this by establishing the number of high-school athletes per state who were recruited by NCAA Division 1 colleges and universities in each of the major sports. He adjusted each state's absolute 'output' by taking into account the state population and represented variations from the national average with a per capita index of state production. He applied the same technique to the county scale. A typical map which represents this genre is shown in Figure 10.1.

A wide variety of sports have been analysed through the use of the 'per capita' or 'regional' approach. From examples taken almost at random, these range from the spatial analysis of rugby players in South Africa (Marais, 1979) to that of the world production of tennis players (Dumolard and Robert, 1989) and from the geographic origins of footballers at Pennsylvanian colleges (Schnell, 1990) to the spatial pattern of production of race horses in Ireland (Lewis and McCarthy, 1977).

An advantage of the data used in studies such as those outlined above is that they allow comparisons of geographic variations in player production (and, for example, facility provision) over time. This has enabled Rooney's 1960s analyses to be regularly updated with geographic shifts in the centres of production for each sport being monitored (Rooney and Pillsbury, 1992). Other such studies have included the changing geographical origins of British soccer players, which showed that although in 1950 and 1980 most players per capita came from the North (per capita indices of 2.45 and 2.05 respectively), by 1980 the polarization of production between North and the South had been reduced (the respective indices for the South East being 0.39 and 0.69). Indeed, in absolute terms, Greater London had become the major producer, with 13.4 per cent of professional footballers coming from the metropolis compared with only 6.2 per cent in 1950 (Bale, 1989). A similar approach has been used in analysing the geography of professional footballers in France (Matthieu, 1991) and, taking a much longer time period, the changing pattern of birthplaces of major league baseball players from 1875 to 1988 (Ojala and Gadwood, 1989). The number of such studies is potentially endless.

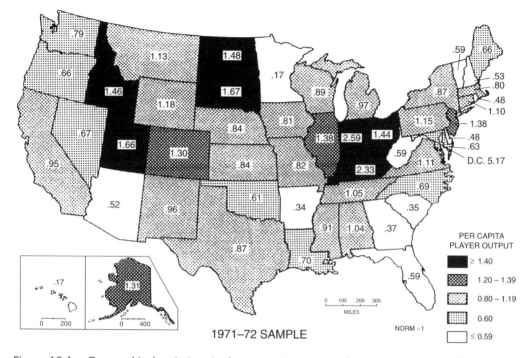

Figure 10.1   *Geographical variations in the per capita origins of major college football players: a traditional sports-geographic approach (Rooney, 1975)*

It is not only the analysis of where players come from that has attracted geographical interest. Variations in the distribution of facilities are also worthy of analysis. Whereas knowing where players grew up assists in their recruitment, knowing where facilities are found alerts planners or developers to gaps in the market. Multi-factor regionalization provides evidence of 'sports regions' which are of use in marketing. The geographical variations that exist in the provision of sports facilities such as sports halls, running tracks or golf courses traditionally attracted the interest of geographers whose primary interest was in recreation and leisure (for example, Patmore, 1970, 1983). Among geographers of sports, Rooney (1993; Adams and Rooney, 1989; Rooney and Higley, 1992) has been particularly active in analysing the changing geographical patterns of golf provision in the United States. An allied group of studies have been concerned with the location of sports clubs and franchises. These have adopted a similar approach to that outlined above (for example, Bale, 1982a; Matthieu, 1991; Matthieu and Praicheux, 1989; Moen, 1993). They basically describe where things are.

The cartographic approach logically lends itself to a particular genre of publication, a number of which have emerged in recent years. These are national atlases of sport. As might be expected, that for the United States (Rooney and Pillsbury, 1992) is the largest and most ambitious. It contains the work of a number of Rooney's former students and covers a very wide variety of American sports. It represents the pinnacle of sports-geographic research from this particular perspective. More modest sports atlases have been produced in France (Matthieu and Praicheux, 1987) and Canada (Dudycha et al., 1983). In Sweden, sections on various aspects of sports are found in the volume of the national atlas dealing with cultural life, recreation and tourism (Aldskogius, 1993a).

A somewhat different approach attempts to predict where sports franchises or clubs *ought to be* according to certain norms. In the United States, such an approach has been developed most elegantly by McConnell and McCulloch (1992), who produced a model of a 'geographically rational' National Football League in the United States. They drew attention to the geographical irrationality of the NFL, pointing out, for example, that only eight of the League's 28 teams were located in the same geographical division (that is, 'regional' organization) as their nearest neighbours. In order to minimize the distances between nearest neighbours, various scenarios were drawn up which served to minimize aggregate travel distance per season and produce compact divisions within conferences. In the constitution of sports leagues such modelling is valuable in suggesting more economically appropriate locations. Another study utilized one of geography's most well-known theories to investigate the premise that the Canadian city of Saskatoon had the potential to support a National Hockey League franchise despite the fact that central place theory predicted that its fixed 'threshold population' was too small (Geddart and Semple, 1987). It was argued that, despite a small metropolitan population, fan interest levels were very high, that there was a tradition of long-distance travel to Saskatoon by an affluent hinterland population, and that the competition from alternative entertainment options was minimal. Similar studies have been undertaken by scholars in cognate disciplines, such as one which sought to identify the optimal location of new entrants to the English Football League (Rivett, 1975).

THE SPATIAL DYNAMICS OF SPORTS

The static patterns described in the maps such as Figure 10.1 are complemented in a number of other studies that explore the time–space dynamism of the world of sports. Such studies focus on a number of themes, for example, the diffusion of sports and of sports innovations, migratory flows of sports participants from one region to another and the re-location of sports clubs. They can be dealt with here under each of those sub-headings.

Geographical Diffusion and Sport

Social scientists have shown a long-standing interest in the geographical diffusion of sports and games (Tylor 1880) but only a small number of studies have applied explicitly geographical approaches to this subject. The most well-known model of geographical diffusion is that formulated by Torsten Hägerstrand (1968). Essentially, the model predicts an 'adoption surface' upon which the contours marking the time–space extent of different 'waves' of innovation diffusion can be mapped. It is basically argued that an innovation is adopted in relation to both hierarchical and distance-based factors. In other words, the unit of adoption (for example, a city or nation) will adopt an innovation depending on its position both

on an economic hierarchy (for example, town size) and its distance from the initial adopter of the innovation. This model has been used in two contexts by Bale (1978, 1982b). The first explored the spatial diffusion of professionalism in English soccer. The twin hierarchical and distance-based model was found to fit the pattern of diffusion of the innovation as it spread away from the 'culture hearth' of professionalism in Lancashire. At the regional – if not the national – level, town size was also of importance. The second study took different sports (soccer, athletics and gymnastics) as innovations and explored their spatial diffusion in Europe. Again, hierarchical and distance-based components were observed (Bale, 1982b). A similar study, which took religious orientation as the dependent variable, was undertaken by Hurtebize (1991). The problem with these kinds of studies is that of operationalizing the notion of 'adoption'. Taking the date of foundation of a national governing bureaucracy for a sport as a surrogate for its adoption can produce spurious evidence of spatial regularity in the 'diffusion process'. *De facto* adoption could have occurred much earlier than the date indicated by the formal bureaucratization.

A somewhat different approach to geographical diffusion has been adopted by the Australian geographer Clive Forster (1986, 1988). He focuses on the development of a spatial pattern of country cricket in South Australia from the 1830s to the 1910s and finds that the changing character of clubs' fixtures – 'the problem of applied geography in organizing a cricket season' – reflected changes in population density, transport provision and economic prosperity. More recently, it has been recognized that such approaches are better replaced by those that are much more sensitive to the role of carriers of the innovation (Mangan, 1986) and the social processes through which information flows are differentially constituted (Bale and Sang, 1996).

Sports Talent Migration

A logical outcome of the kinds of studies pioneered by Rooney has been the analysis of the migration of sports talent. From Rooney's maps (for example, Figure 10.1) it is obvious that some regions produce more (say) footballers than their in-state universities can consume while others do not produce enough for their in-state needs. Using this notion of surplus and deficit regions, Rooney was able to map the inter-regional flows of sports talent between states. Through this approach he also addressed the problem of the abuses which exist in the USA in the recruiting of high-school sports talent to the nation's universities (Rooney, 1987). Sports sociologists Sage and Loy (1978), inspired by Rooney's approach, applied his general ideas, with considerable sociological embellishment, to the study of the geographical mobility patterns of US college sports coaches.

A more technical approach to sports talent migration was adopted by McConnell (1983, 1984) who, in a study of the migration of collegiate footballers from Florida, attempted to predict such migration patterns by use of the 'gravity model' which was used to test the hypothesis that the number of Floridians varied directly with gravitational attraction (that is, distance from Florida and size of state). The model was generally successful, gravitational attraction 'explaining' about 57 per cent of the variation in the number of players from Florida.

A somewhat different approach to migration involved the question of whether the escalation in player earnings, following the adoption of 'free agency' in US baseball, had led to a change in the migratory behaviour of baseball professionals. It was hypothesized that the attachment between players and the cities they 'represented' through their teams had weakened following the successful challenge to the 'reserve clause'. It was found that with increased wealth the players no longer felt committed to the city in which their team played and would reside elsewhere during the off-season. They did not have to change their residential location, as had occurred in the days of the reserve clause and the geographical linkage between player residence and the team he played for had weakened (Shelley and Shelley, 1993).

Talent migration in sport is not restricted to the national scale. Ojala and Gadwood (1989) noted that during a 112-year period, Puerto Rico, Cuba and the Dominican Republic had each supplied more baseball players to the US Major Leagues than many of the states in the USA itself. Such international migration of sports talent has attracted considerable research in recent years among geographers and others (Bale and Maguire, 1994; see Chapter 23 by Maguire in this book). For example, Klein (1991) has researched the impact on the Dominican Republic of the long-standing migration of the nation's baseball players to the US. He recognizes such migration as a form of 'underdevelopment'. Maguire (1994a) has examined the flow of Americans into English

basketball, basing his approach on figurational sociology. Among geographers, Bale (1991c) explored the recruitment of foreign students by US colleges and universities; Genest (1991, 1994) has examined the global migration of Canadian ice hockey players; and Bale and Sang (1996) have seen Kenyan track and field athletics as the outcome of a wide variety of long- and short-term global flows, both in and out of the country. A set of interdisciplinary essays on this subject tend to differ from the more traditional geographical approach in that 'patterns on the map' are not seen as unproblematic (Bale and Maguire, 1994).

The Re-location of Sports Clubs and Franchises

The re-location of sports clubs and franchises is a topical subject in many countries of the Western world. As a result of a variety of pressures resulting from planning and economic considerations, professional sports clubs are increasingly seeking to relocate at both urban and national scales. International relocation already exists in North America and has been mooted in Europe.

Relatively little work has been undertaken by geographers into this phenomenon, despite the fact that locational change takes place at a variety of scales. At the intra-urban scale Moen (1990) undertook an exhaustive analysis of the changing intra-urban pattern of sports sites in the Swedish cities of Borås and Uppsala. He observed a twin process of suburbanization and increased clustering of sports facilities at this level of scale. At the state level, Leib (1990) showed the instability of the geographical distribution of Minor League baseball club locations in Pennsylvania from 1902 to 1989 but it has been left to sociologists and economists to explore in a more interpretive way the locational dynamics of sports teams and franchises at the continental level. For example, Euchner (1993) has carefully charted the rationale for team relocation and new stadium developments in the United States. The most detailed analysis of the urban-political structures and agencies involved in locational change in franchises is probably that of Schimmel (1995), whose detailed study of the move of the Baltimore Colts football outfit to Indianapolis not only includes the geographical details of the move but also the urban-political machinations and an excellent review of urban economics and political economy (see also Ingham et al., 1987). The situation for the US is summed up as follows:

Overwhelming evidence shows that sports franchises and facilities do little to revive a local economy, but states and cities continue to spend hundreds of millions of dollars to get teams. Boosters promise the revival of neighborhoods, higher tax revenues, the attraction of new firms to the city, and even the amelioration of racial and ethnic strife. Ignoring the evidence, cities accept the grandiose claims. (Euchner, 1993: 185)

In Britain, the recommendations of the Taylor Report (1990) into the football (soccer) industry have led to scenarios for stadium relocation coming into conflict with planning policy and practice (Black and Lloyd, 1992, 1994). The way in which the notion of 'community' is invoked by both the relocating club and those opposing its relocation on the grounds that it constitutes a 'noxious facility' is explored in a study of the relocation plans of Portsmouth FC in England (Burnett, 1994).

In addition to the physical relocation of clubs it is also possible to observe the relocation of success. Using various geo-statistical analyses, Waylen and Snook (1990) noted that while the composition of the League had been more or less constant from 1920 to 1987, there had been a marked southward shift in the location of the more successful teams. A similar analysis of shifts in regional soccer success has been undertaken in The Netherlands (Volkers and Van Dam, 1992).

The above analyses form a group of geographical studies which often go under the collective term of 'spatial analysis'. This can be reduced to a series of patterns made up alternatively of points, lines, flows, movements and surfaces which provide some of the basic concepts of a 'spatial' approach to geography. A detailed analysis by Loïc Ravenel (1997) integrates these spatial analytic concepts and applies a variety of spatio-statistical techniques as part of a monumental study of top-class football in France (see also Ravenel, 1998).

There is another form of such spatial analytic studies which geographers have addressed, but at a rather different level of geographic scale – that of the field of play. One of the premier geographers in the United States, Peter Gould (Gould and Gattrell, 1979; Gould and Greenwalt, 1981) has researched such studies, which focus on the micro-spatial interaction of players themselves. In doing so, he used a statistical technique called multidimensional scaling which sought to explore the asymmetries in team interaction and, hence, 'the structure of a game'.

The spatial analytic studies outlined above follow positivist scientific philosophies.

These have been the most typical kinds of geographical studies of achievement-sport. Such work has not gone unrecognized. Rooney's (1969) seminal paper was warmly applauded by none other than the writer James Michener (1976: 303–6), who found it the most interesting of all the books he consulted for his mammoth *Sports in America*. However, while undoubtedly interesting and painstakingly researched, such studies have not been without criticism from geographers and others who have sought to locate a geography of sport within the broader academic arena of social and cultural studies. For example, Ley (1985) observed that

> While the maps are of great interest and their compilation is no small task, they exemplify a research style where description takes precedence over interpretation. Maps of the spatial origins of professional sports players, to take one theme, invite interpretive accounts of the places and practices which produced such 'social facts'. (p. 417)

He then noted that such a research agenda could be found by referring to work in the sociology of sport. Badenhorst (1988) critiqued the geography of sport for exploring diffusion patterns to the exclusion of processes and noted the relative isolation of scholars in the subdiscipline of sports geography from the broader field of cultural geography. Likewise, the sports sociologists Jarvie and Maguire (1994) pointed to the reification of space in such studies. Nevertheless, more interpretive accounts which draw on social and cultural theory (Springwood, 1996), as well as the 'new' cultural geography (Philo, 1991) will be found in studies described in later sections of this chapter.

SPORT AND SPILLOVERS

A group of studies somewhat different from those noted above seek to identify the spatial and environmental impact of sports events. The place of sport in regional economic development has been most comprehensively reviewed, citing mainly French evidence, by Goiugnet and Nys (1993), and only a few examples of the kind of geographical work in this area can be noted here. They draw their inspiration, not only from regional and welfare economics but also from more humanistic sources.

By far the largest number of 'spillover studies' of sports have addressed what are termed 'hallmark events'. These are global or continental sporting spectacles where the preparation for the event, as much as the effects of them at the time they are held, can induce considerable landscape change. A lengthy book of essays on *The Planning and Evaluation of Hallmark Events* (Symes et al., 1989) includes contributions on the economic and environmental impact of events such as the America's Cup on Freemantle, the Adelaide motor cycling Grand Prix, and the Calgary Winter Olympics. The latter study argued that the impact of the 1988 Winter Games went well beyond the construction of new facilities and the events themselves (Hiller, 1989). Because of the limitations on spectators and the limited duration of the event, the media became the key in redefining and projecting to the world the image of the city of Calgary as one which had come of age through recent economic development.

Studies of the spatial impact of, say, an annual ice hockey tournament (Marsh, 1984) utilize ideas such as the regional multiplier to arrive at the wealth generated in a region as a result of the event. What such a study is basically doing is to establish the economic spillover effects of a sporting event on the local area in which it takes place. Likewise, studies of the construction of new facilities for a 'hallmark' event can indicate the job-creation effects of the construction of facilities (Foley, 1991). The tacit objective of such studies is to explore the *positive* economic spillovers, that is, income or jobs generated within the region as a direct or indirect result of the event. It is widely regarded that the impact of stadium development, in particular, is much less than is widely perceived. Studies into such impacts have been relatively widespread in the United States though they have been undertaken mainly by scholars from economics (Baade, 1995; Baade and Dye, 1990) rather than geography. A Swedish study by Aldskogius (1993b, 1994, 1995) best illustrates the geographical approach. The small town of Leksand is well known in Sweden because of the disproportionate significance of its ice hockey team. Aldskogius (1993b, 1994) was able to show that the impact of Leksand was felt well beyond the town itself, supporter club affiliations extending, for example, from the north to the south of the country. It was indeed the case of a great club in a small town.

These positivistic studies have been complemented by more humanistic explorations which have sought to explore non-financial benefits of the presence of sports clubs on local fans and residents. Basing his ideas mainly on the work of the Chinese-American geographer

Yi-Fu Tuan (1974), Bale (1991b, 1993b) used Tuan's notion of 'topophilia' (a love of place) to describe the love and affection fans have for 'their stadium'. He used 'softer' indicators than those used by economists, taking, for example, the words of fans from football programmes and fanzines. A strong attachment to these places gives them 'meaning'; they become places to be defended against destruction and the sense of place they engender is close to being in love with a place, with a strength of attachment often underestimated by planners. A particularly dramatic case in Britain was that of the popular activism of fans of Charlton Athletic to return the club to its 'home' at The Valley in the face of pressures for the club to ground-share in another part of London (Everitt, 1991).

Such expressions of localism reflect the strength of the sport–place bond. The success – even the existence – of a local 'representative' in the form of a sports team may create a sense of place and provide 'psychic' income. The feel-good factor as generated by sports success has been explored in the context of Sunderland's surprise FA Cup Final victory in 1973 (Derrick and McRory, 1973). It was found that the improved fortunes of the local football team had been associated with a decrease in vandalism in the town, better behaviour of football crowds, a boost to the city's image and increased output in local factories. A more sensitive and in-depth ethnographic analysis by Bromberger (1995) into the partisan passion for football in Marseilles, Naples and Turin provides a model for such studies, while Hague and Mercer (1998) recognize that through the modest Scottish football club of Raith Rovers, the town of Kirkcaldy is mediated through texts of 'geographical memory'. At the global scale, sport is often thought to serve a similar function in bonding diffuse groups and forging 'national identity' (Maguire, 1994b).

Ideas borrowed from welfare economics, applied during the 1970s in the subfield of welfare geography (Smith, 1977), have attracted considerable interest from geographers who have applied them in studies of the *negative* effects of sports events. This interest was influenced, to a large degree, by the crisis in the British football industry during the 1980s. Such studies have explored the negative externalities of football stadiums, as perceived by local residents, and sought to identify which spillovers were perceived as being the most serious. In addition they identified the distances from stadiums that various nuisances were recognized (for example, Figure 10.2). Based on an examination of the

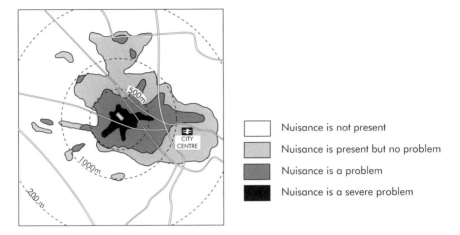

Figure 10.2   *The spatial extent of nuisances generated by football around Portman Road ground, Ipswich (after Chase and Healey, 1995)*

football-induced nuisances consumed by local residents living near 37 League football grounds, Bale (1990) concluded that football nuisances, as perceived by those who unwillingly consumed them, were less serious than expected by a sample of the general public. In addition, the main nuisances were car parking and traffic congestion. Hooliganism was rarely seen as the major nuisance, a finding confirmed by a number of other studies (for example, Humphrys et al., 1983). Studies reflecting 'rational' solutions to the football stadium 'problem' are illustrated by a comparison of the nuisances generated by a traditional, inner-city ground with that of a new suburban stadium. Mason and Moncrieff (1993) found that relocation at the urban edge in the case of St Johnstone FC in Perth, Scotland, had not eliminated the football-generated nuisance effects, though because about three-quarters of the new stadium's externality field was made up of non-residential areas, the number of people experiencing football-generated nuisances was less than that at the club's former inner-city location. In addition to suburbanization, a 'solution' to English football's economic 'crisis' was to increase the number of days per year when the stadium was in use. This initiative, undertaken at Luton Town FC's ground, led Mason and Robins (1991) to compare the negative externality fields of football and non-football uses. They found that non-football activities had less intense and more spatially restricted 'nuisance fields' than those generated by football matches. Another study, specifically comparing rock concerts with football, showed that despite the greater noise levels generated

by rock concerts, football-induced nuisances were perceived to be a greater problem overall (Chase and Healey, 1995).

The impacts of the kinds described above have a spatial and environmental dimension. The latter provides a point of contact between human and physical geography. Sport as a form of pollution is a problem addressed by observers of events such as the Winter Olympics and golf course development (McCormack, 1991). Eichberg (1988) sees achievement-sport as inherently anti-nature, a view supported by 'deep' ecologists such as Galtung (1984). The impact of sport has certainly led to replacement of natural or semi-natural landscapes by those of concrete, steel and plastic. Such a dystopian view of the impact of sport is not shared by everybody, however, as the next section shows.

SPORT AND LANDSCAPE

The shift in sport-geographic studies from the 'cartographic fetish' to a more sensitive landscape approach can be summarized by noting two papers by Richard Pillsbury. An early essay on stock car racing in the American 'South' focused on the geographic origins of stock car racing drivers. His maps revealed a concentration of such 'good ol' boys' in the cultural heartland of the sport in the Carolinas and Georgia (Pillsbury, 1972). Over 20 years later, Pillsbury (1995) was still writing about the same subject but his maps had been replaced by photographs while his text sensitively and evocatively sought to compare the old, unique, southern dirt tracks, with the more 'efficient' and rational arenas of the modern era.[3]

It is in such studies of the 'ordinary' landscapes of sports that the most interpretive of sports-geographic studies have been undertaken and it is arguably the area which has borrowed most vigorously from cultural and social theory. The sports landscape is viewed broadly. It is basically interpreted as everything that is sensed at a sports event. Although the geographer Jay Appleton (1975) suggested, through fleeting allusions, a landscape focus for sports-geographic studies, the first to seriously address the landscape of sport was the American cultural geographer Philip Wagner (1981), who seemed to view sport as a combination of culture and geography. He described sports places as eminently spatial phenomena, struggles over space possessing 'elaborate spatial strictures' where 'the infractions and the measurement of spatial progress in play are of great importance'. He added that sports were 'dramas acted out within minutely prescribed spatial frames', requiring 'exactly specified and formalized environments, for in most cases the contest explicitly concerns dominance of territory or mastery of distance' (Wagner, 1981: 92). This does not go quite so far as the neo-Marxist view that 'the reduction of space to geometry, the abstraction of what is concrete, real and tangible in nature, is carried to the ultimate in sport' (Brohm, 1974), but it is along the same lines.

These observations imply that the landscape of sport is a world of modernity – straight lines, measurement, rationality and performance. Following Le Corbusier, the sports landscape can be seen as a 'machine' for sport. Most sports places also show a tendency towards confinement, segmentation and artifice. Hence, a second 'reading' of the sports landscape might see a gradual tendency towards its spatial confinement, individualization and surveillance. One has only to look at the sports stadium to see the transition from games played in an open space with limited, if any, separation between players and spectators, through the process of separation of players from spectators, the enclosure of the field of play, the segregation of spectators, their confinement in individualized seats, and their surveillance by video camera (Bale, 1993b). The relevance of the work of Michel Foucault (1977) is difficult to ignore. So too is the imaginative scholarship of the eclectic 'cultural sociologist' Henning Eichberg (1986, 1989, 1990; Bale and Philo, 1998), whose studies of the spatiality of sport have been inspirational for some geographers (Philo, 1994). Geographical readings of the sports stadium as a 'Foucauldian landscape' have been undertaken by Bale (1993b) and Tomkins (1995), though the former's inspiration comes primarily from the work of Robert Sack (1986) and his view of territoriality as a form of power.

A less pessimistic view of the landscape of sport is outlined by the American geographer Karl Raitz (1987a, 1987b, 1995). Influenced by Edward Relph (1976), who used the term 'placelessness' to describe many of the landscapes of modernity, Raitz observed that there is more to a sports event than simply watching the game. He suggested that the sports landscape is made up of a 'landscape ensemble'. The field of play is a relatively constant milieu, verging on predictability and placelessness, but around it are a wide variety of elements which bring distinctiveness and uniqueness to particular sporting locations. Raitz suggested that the greater the variety within the ensemble, the greater the spectators' (and possibly players') gratification from the sport experience. Raitz's emphasis on the 'place-making' qualities of many sports venues provides a starting point for an interpretation of sport via the landscape perspective.

The trajectory of modern sport may, however, be seen differently from both Raitz's notion of the sports landscape as a source of (mainly) visual pleasures and the suggestion that sports landscapes possess prison-like qualities. Drawing on further ideas from Tuan (1984), Bale (1994) has applied the metaphors of the garden and pet to the stadium and athlete respectively. Stadiums and athletes – like gardens and pets – are uneasy mixes of nature and culture. They are, in Tuan's terms, examples of dominance and affection with neither being taken to an extreme. Sports places are examples of a blending of architecture and horticulture, of dominance with a human face. Much of this interpretation comes close to that of Giamatti (1989), who sees the baseball park as a modern, adult version of the *kindergarten*. However, the multifaceted character of modern sports landscapes is one of ambiguity (Kayser Nielsen, 1995) in which boundaries and borders are often liminal in character (Shore, 1995). The ambiguity of the modern sports landscape is addressed by Allen Pred (1995) in a fascinating analysis of the Stockholm 'Globe' ('a spectacular space for commodified entertainment spectacle, for the consumption of commodified bodies'). Pred sees this late modern structure as a source of (hyper)modernity – an ambiguous landscape that accommodates local pride and globalized sport, 'where the spectacle is made available as an everyday item of consumption'.

The sports landscape can also be seen as symbolic in character. Sport-landscape symbols are projected in such media as paintings, cartoons, poetry and other literary texts as well as in soil, timber and concrete. Baseball and cricket connote images of the rural – even if the reality is essentially urban (Bale, 1994). Drawing on the work of a number of geographers, the cultural anthropologist Charles Springwood (1996) sees place, space and landscape as central to his exploration of the cultural environments of the two mythical baseball-centred sites/sights of Cooperstown, New York and Dyersville, Iowa. In what is arguably the best piece of sport-geographic writing yet produced, Springwood's 'dual ethnography' of these two places teases out their 'meaning', mysteries and conservative ideologies. Symbolic landscapes can also be applied to the forging of national identity, the exposure of class tensions and the identifications of 'landscapes of hate'. This is exemplified by an examination of the campus of Liberty University, a fundamentalist Christian institution founded by the televangelist Jerry Falwell. Gallaher (1997) reads this as a training ground for the normalization, maintenance and reinforcement of a fundamentalist identity. Liberty appropriates sports symbols to normalize its identity position while, at the same time, enforcing difference. It can succeed in NCAA basketball competitions but at the same time exclude alcohol consumption. The campus landscapes of sports are identified as sources of a masculinist form of solidarity building and the creation of a group and institutional memory which seems to reinforce fundamentalist identity. In a somewhat different vein, a splendid essay by Bowden (1994) reads the landscape and place imagery in two sports movies (*The Loneliness of the Long Distance Runner* and *Chariots of Fire*) as metaphors for the deeply embedded British class system.

Finally, it can be suggested that landscapes of sport illustrate a tension between space and place. This tension may, in a sense, form the basis for a geographical theory of sport (Bale, 1998). It can be argued that the two norms of sport, that is, fair play and achievement-orientation, predict that sports should theoretically take place in 'pure space' or 'non-places' (Augé, 1995). This is because, logically, 'fair play' can only be achieved if extraneous factors such as the vagaries of the physical environment, on the one hand, and of spectators on the other, are isolated from the sports event. Individual players and teams should not be favoured by an idiosyncratic 'home field', for example. Likewise, 'achievement-orientation' or at least 'record seeking' also requires such a placeless landscape. All sites should be identical. If sports sites differ, they may provide favourable or unfavourable environments for records. It is not difficult to see the tendency towards placelessness in sports space, and scenarios for such dystopian futures have been presented in the writings of Baudrillard (1993) and Virilio (1991). Yet the question remains about how far fans can continue to be active participants in appropriating and resisting such cultural changes.

FUTURE DIRECTIONS?

A geography of sport has made a modest mark in both sports studies and cultural geography. However, given the current geographical interest in such themes as the spectacle, sites of resistance and globalization (Cosgrove and Rogers, 1992), and the recognition that the 'ordinary' landscapes of sports have great symbolic significance (Cosgrove, 1989), every likelihood exists that sports-geographic studies will increase in number and achieve greater visibility than hitherto. Given the mania for 'stadiumisation' and sports-complex gigantism, spatial and environmental impact studies will continue to develop. Geographers are certainly responding to the challenge of sports and globalization in various ways (for example, Bale and Sang, 1996; Donaghu and Barff, 1990) and an incipient interest exists in forging links between sport, geography and post-colonial studies (Bale, 1996) and geography and the sportized body (Johnston, 1998). But the future lies in the recognition by geographers that sport is a significant part of culture and that in it they may find many exemplars of their contemporary concerns.

NOTES

1   A sports-geographical journal, *Sport Place*, was published from 1987 through 1996, in which time 18 issues appeared. At the time of writing it is unclear whether the journal will continue to be published.

2   Several other reviews of the geography of sport have been authored (Augustin, 1995; Bale, 1988, 1989, 1992b; Buursink, 1993; Rösch, 1986; Volkers and Van Dam, 1992). The references included therein may be used to complement those in the present, more extensive and up-dated, review.

3   Pillsbury's two views of southern stock car racing and Rooney's (1993) golf paper, are reprinted in Carney (1995).

REFERENCES AND FURTHER READING

Adams, R. and Rooney, J. (1985) 'The evolution of American golf facilities', *The Geographical Review*, 75 (4): 419–38.

Adams, R. and Rooney, J. (1989) 'American golf courses: a regional analysis of demand', *Sport Place*, 3 (1/2): 2–17.

Aldskogius, H. (ed.) (1993a) *Cultural Life, Recreation and Tourism*. Stockholm: Swedish National Atlas.

Aldskogius, H. (1993b) *Leksand, Leksand, Leksand!* Hedemora: Gidlunds Bokförlag.

Aldskogius, H. (1994) 'Ice hockey and place: a great club in a small town', in J. Bale (ed.), *Community, Landscape and Identity: Horizons in a Geography of Sport*. Department of Geography, Keele University, Occasional Paper 20. pp. 33–53.

Aldskogius, H. (1995) 'Where sports and money meet: the economic geography of an ice hockey stadium', in J. Bale and O. Moen (eds), *The Stadium and the City*. Keele: Keele University Press. pp. 255–75.

Appleton, J. (1975) *The Experience of Landscape*. Chichester: Wiley.

Augé, M. (1995) *Non-Places: Introduction to an Anthropology of Supermodernity*. London: Verso.

Augustin, J-P. (1995) *Sport, Géographie et Aménagement*. Paris: Éditions Nathan.

Baade, R. (1995) 'Stadiums, professional sports and city economies: an analysis of the United States experience', in J. Bale and O. Moen (eds), *The Stadium and the City*. Keele: Keele University Press. pp. 277–94.

Baade, R. and Dye, R. (1988) 'An analysis of the economic rationale for public stadium subsidization of sports stadiums', *Annals of Regional Science*, 22 (2): 37–47.

Badenhorst, C.M. (1988) 'The geography of sport as a cultural process: a case study of lacrosse'. Unpublished MA thesis, University of British Columbia.

Bale, J. (1978) 'Geographical diffusion and the adoption of professionalism in football in England and Wales', *Geography*, 63: 181–97.

Bale, J. (1982a) *Sport and Place: a Geography of Sport in England, Scotland and Wales*. London: Hurst.

Bale, J. (1982b) 'Sports history as innovation diffusion', *Canadian Journal of the History of Sport*, 15: 38–63.

Bale, J. (1988) 'The place of "place" in cultural studies of sport', *Progress in Human Geography*, 12 (4): 507–24.

Bale, J. (1989) *Sports Geography*. London: E&FN Spon.

Bale, J. (1990) 'In the shadow of the stadium: football grounds as urban nuisances', *Geography*, 75: 325–44.

Bale, J. (1991a) 'Angstzone Fussball?', in R. Horak and W. Reiter (eds), *Die Kanten des Runden Leders*. Vienna: Promedia. pp. 62–70.

Bale, J. (1991b) 'Playing at home: British football and a sense of place', in J. Williams and S. Wagg (eds), *British Football and Social Change*. Leicester: Leicester University Press. pp. 130–44.

Bale, J. (1991c) *The Brawn Drain: Foreign Student-Athletes in American Universities*. Champaign, IL: University of Illinois Press.

Bale, J. (1992a) 'Il calcio come fonte di topofilia; il publico e lo stadio', in P. Lanfranchi (ed.), *Il Calcio e il Pubblico*. Naples: Edizioni Scientifiche Italiane. pp. 221–40.

Bale, J. (1992b) 'Cartographic fetishism to geographical humanism: some central features of a geography of sport', *Innovation in Social Sciences Research*. 5 (4): 71–88.

Bale, J. (1993a) 'Futbol stadi korku bölgesi mi?', in R. Horak, W. Reiter and T. Bora (eds), *Futbol ve Kültürü*. Ankara: Iletism. pp. 83–94.

Bale, J. (1993b) *Sport, Space and the City*. London: Routledge.

Bale, J. (1994) *Landscapes of Modern Sport*. London: Leicester University Press.

Bale, J. (1996) 'Rhetorical modes, imaginative geographies and body culture in early twentieth century Rwanda', *Area*, 28 (3): 289–97.

Bale, J. (1998) 'Virtual fandoms: futurescapes of football', in A. Brown, *Fanatics! Power, Identity and Fandom in Football*. London: Routledge. pp. 265–77.

Bale, J. and Maguire, J. (eds) (1994) *The Global Sports Arena: Athletic Talent Migration in an Interdependent World*. London: Cass.

Bale, J. and Moen, O. (eds) (1995) *The Stadium and the City*. Keele: Keele University Press.

Bale, J. and Philo, C. (eds) (1998) *Body Cultures: Essays by Henning Eichberg*. London: Routledge.

Bale, J. and Sang, J. (1996) *Kenyan Running: Movement Culture, Geography and Global Change*. London: Cass.

Baudrillard, J. (1993) *The Transparency of Evil*. London: Verso.

Black, J. and Lloyd, M. (1992) 'Home or away? Stadia redevelopment and relocation in Scotland', *Scottish Geographical Magazine*, 108 (1): 45–9.

Black, J. and Lloyd, M. (1994) 'Football stadia redevelopments: land-use policy and planning controls', *Town Planning Review*, 65 (1): 1–19.

Bowden, M. (1994) 'Jerusalem, Dover Beach and King's Cross: imagined places as metaphors of the British class struggle in *Chariots of Fire* and *The Loneliness of the Long Distance Runner*', in S. Aitken and L. Zonn (eds), *Place, Power, Situation and Spectacle: a Geography of Film*. Lanham: Rowman and Littlefield. pp. 69–100.

Brohm, J-M. (1974) *Sport: a Prison of Measured Time*. London: Ink Links.

Bromberger, C. (1995) *Le Match de Football*. Paris: Éditions de la Maison des Sciences de l'Homme.

Burnett, A. (1994) 'Community, local politics and football', in J. Bale (ed.), *Community, Landscape and Identity: Horizons in a Geography of Sport*. Department of Geography, Keele University, Occasional Paper 20. pp. 19–32.

Buursink, J. (1993) 'Geografie en sport: de Motite waard?', in J.J.M. van Steen (ed.), *Geografie in Beweging*. Groningen: Rijksuniversiteit. pp. 183–97.

Carney, G. (ed.) (1995) *Fast Food, Stock Cars and Rock 'n' Roll*. Lanham: Rowman and Littlefield.

Chase, J. and Healey, M. (1995) 'The spatial externality effects of football matches and rock concerts: the case of Portman Road Stadium, Ipswich', *Applied Geography*, 15 (1): 18–34.

Cosgrove, D. (1989) 'Geography is everywhere: culture and symbolism in the human landscape', in D. Gregory and R. Walford (eds), *Horizons in Human Geography*. London: Macmillan. pp. 118–35.

Cosgrove, D. and Rogers, A. (1992) 'Territory, locality and place', in C. Philo (compiler), *New Words, New Worlds*. Department of Geography, St David's University College, Lampeter. pp. 36–8.

Dear, M. (1988) 'The postmodern challenge: reconstructing human geography', *Transactions of the Institute of British Geographers*, n.s. 13: 262–74.

Derrick, E. and McRory, J. (1973) 'Cup in hand: Sunderland's self-image after the cup', Working Paper No. 8, Centre for Cultural Studies, University of Birmingham.

Donaghu, M. and Barff, R. (1990) 'Nike just did it: international subcontracting and flexibility in athletic footwear production', *Regional Studies*, 24 (6): 537–52.

Dudycha, D., Smith, S., Stewart, T. and McPherson, B. (1983) *The Canadian Atlas of Recreation and Exercise*. Department of Geography Publication Series No. 21, University of Waterloo.

Dumolard, P. and Robert, A. (1989) 'Le tennis dans le monde: état et prospective', *Mappemonde*, 89 (2): 32–5.

Eichberg, H. (1986) 'The enclosure of the body: on the historical relativity of "health", "nature" and the environment of sport', *Journal of Contemporary History*, 21: 99–121.

Eichberg, H. (1988) *Leistungsräume: Sport als Umweltproblem*. Münster: Lit Verlag.

Eichberg, H. (1989) 'Body culture as paradigm: the Danish sociology of sport', *International Review for the Sociology of Sport*, 19 (1): 43–63.

Eichberg, H. (1990) 'Race-track and labyrinth: the space of physical culture in Berlin', *Journal of Sport History*, 17 (2): 245–60.

Euchner, C. (1993) *Playing the Field: Why Sports Teams Move and Why Cities Fight to Keep Them*. Baltimore, MD: Johns Hopkins University Press.

Everitt, R. (1991) *Battle for the Valley*. London: Voice of the Valley.

Foley, P. (1991) 'The impact of the World Student Games on Sheffield', *Environment and Planning C: Government and Policy*, 9: 65–78.

Forster, C. (1986) 'Sport, society and space: the changing geography of country cricket in South Australia 1836–1914', *Sporting Traditions*, 2 (2): 23–47.

Forster, C. (1988) 'Cricket and community', in R.L. Heathcote (ed.), *The Australian Experience*. Longman: Melbourne. pp. 191–208.

Foucault, M. (1977) *Discipline and Punish*. Harmondsworth: Penguin.

Gallaher, C. (1997) 'Identity politics and the religious right: hiding hate in the landscape', *Antipode*, 29 (3): 256–77.

Galtung, J. (1984) 'Sport and international understanding: sport as a carrier of deep culture and structure', in I. Ilmarinen (ed.), *Sport and International Understanding*. Berlin: Springer-Verlag.

Geddart, R. and Semple, R.K. (1987) 'A National Hockey League franchise: the modified central place theory', *Leisure Sciences*, 9: 1–13.

Genest, S. (1991) 'Etude géographique du processus de diffusion du hockey sur glace dans le monde'. Unpublished MA thesis, Laval University.

Genest, S. (1994) 'Skating on thin ice? The international migration of Canadian ice hockey players', in J. Bale and J. Maguire (eds), *The Global Sports Arena: Athletic Talent Migration in an Interdependent World*. London: Cass. pp. 112–26.

Giamatti, B. (1989) *Take Time for Paradise: Americans and their Games*. New York: Summit Books.

Goiugnet, J-J. and Nys, J-F. (1993) *Sport et développement économique régional*. Paris: Dalloz.

Gould, P. and Gattrell, A. (1979) 'A micro-geography of team games: graphical explanations of social relations', *Area*, 11: 275–8.

Gould, P. and Greenwalt, N. (1981) 'Some methodological perspectives on the analysis of team games', *Journal of Sports Psychology*, 4: 283–304.

Hägerstrand, T. (1968) *Innovation Diffusion as a Spatial Process*. Chicago: Chicago University Press.

Hague, E. and Mercer, J. (1998) 'Geographical memory and urban identity in Scotland: Raith Rovers FC and Kirkcaldy', *Geography*, 83: 105–16.

Hildebrand, J.R. (1919) 'The geography of games', *The National Geographic Magazine*, 34 (2): 98–143.

Hiller, H. (1989) 'Impact and image: the convergence of urban factors in preparing for the 1988 Calgary Winter Olympics', in G. Symes et al., *The Planning and Evaluation of Hallmark Events*. Aldershot: Avebury. pp. 119–31.

Humphrys, D., Mason, C. and Pinch, S. (1983) 'The externality fields of football grounds: a case study of The Dell, Southampton', *Geoforum*, 14: 401–11.

Hurtebize, C. (1991) 'Géopolitique de la genè, de la diffusion et des interactions culturelles dans la culture corporelle et le sport', in *Géopolitique du Sport* (Proceedings of a colloquium held at Besançon, March 1990). Department of Human Geography, Université de Franche-Comté. pp. 87–114.

Hyland, D. (1990) *Philosophy of Sport*. New York: Paragon House.

Ingham, A., Hardy, S. and Schilperoort, T. (1987) 'Professional sport and community: an exegesis', *Sport Sciences Reviews*, 15: 427–65.

Jarvie, G. and Maguire, J. (1994) *Sport and Leisure in Social Thought*. London: Routledge.

Johnston, L. (1998) 'Reading the sexed bodies and spaces of gyms', in H. Nast and N. Thrift (eds), *Places through the Body*. London: Routledge. pp. 244–62.

Johnston, R. (1991) *Geography and Geographers: Anglo-American Human Geography since 1945*. London: Arnold.

Johnston, R.J., Gregory, D. and Smith, D. (eds) (1994) *The Dictionary of Human Geography*, 3rd edn. Oxford: Basil Blackwell. pp. 585–6.

Jokl, E. (1965) *Medical Sociology and Cultural Anthropology of Sport and Physical Education*. Springfield, IL: Charles C. Thomas.

Kayser Nielsen, N. (1995) 'The stadium in the city: a modern story', in J. Bale and O. Moen (eds), *The Stadium and the City*. Keele: Keele University Press. pp. 21–57.

Klein, A. (1991) *Sugarball: the American Game, the Dominican Dream*. New Haven, CT: Yale University Press.

Lehman, H. (1940) 'The geographic origin of professional baseball players', *Journal of Educational Research*, 34: 130–8.

Leib, J. (1990) 'The historical geography of minor league baseball in Pennsylvania: 1920–1989', *Pennsylvania Geographer*, 28 (1): 3–14.

Lewis, C. and McCarthy, M. (1977) 'The horse breeding industry in Ireland', *Irish Geography*, 10: 72–89.

Ley, D. (1985) 'Cultural/humanistic geography', *Progress in Human Geography*, 9: 415–23.

Louder, D. (1991) 'Etude géographique du sport en Amérique du Nord: survol et critique', in *Géopolitique du Sport* (Proceedings of a colloquium held at Besançon, March 1990). Department of Human Geography, Université de Franche-Comté. pp. 179–87.

Maguire, J. (1994a) 'American labour migrants, globalization and the making of English basketball', in J. Bale and J. Maguire (eds), *The Global Sports Arena: Athletic Talent Migration in an Interdependent World*. London: Cass. pp. 226–55.

Maguire, J. (1994b) 'Sport, national identities and globalization', in J. Bale (ed.), *Community, Landscape and Identity: Horizons in a Geography of Sport*. Department of Geography, Keele University, Occasional Paper 20. pp. 71–93.

Maguire, J. (1995) 'Common ground? Links between sports history, sports geography and the sociology of sport', *Sporting Traditions*, 12 (1): 3–25.

Mangan, J.A. (1986) *The Games Ethic and Imperialism*. London: Viking.

Marais, H. (1979) 'Heekomspatrone van Stellenbosch se Toprugbyspelers', *Geo-Stel*, 3: 45–53.

Marsh, J. (1984) 'The economic impact of a small city annual sporting event; an initial case study of the Perborough Church League Atom Hockey Tournament', *Recreational Research Review*, 11: 48–55.

Mason, C. and Moncrieff, A. (1993) 'The effects of relocation on the externality fields of football stadia: the case of St Johnstone Football Club', *Scottish Geographical Magazine*, 109: 96–105.

Mason, C. and Robins, R. (1991) 'The spatial externality fields of football stadiums; the effect of football and non-football uses at Kenilworth Road, Luton', *Applied Geography*, 11: 251–66.

Matthieu, D. (1991) 'Les productivités différentielles des espaces du football professionel en France', in *Géopolitique du Sport* (Proceedings of a colloquium held at Besançon, March 1990). Department of Human Geography, Université de Franche-Comté. pp. 51–60.

Matthieu, D. and Praicheux, J. (1987) *Sports en France*. Paris: Fayard/Reclus.

Matthieu, D. and Praicheux, J. (1989) 'Le football: essai d'explication d'un espace sportif', in *Geographes et le tiers temps*. Geography Department, University of Besançon. pp. 209–25.

McConnell, H. (1983) 'Floridians in major college football, 1981', *Florida Geographer*, 12: 17–31.

McConnell, H. (1984) 'Recruiting patterns in Midwestern major college football', *Geographical Perspectives*, 53: 27–43.

McConnell, H. and McCulloch, D. (1992) 'Phoenix is east of Atlanta: toward a geographically rational National Football League', *Sport Place*, 6 (1): 3–13.

McCormack, G. (1991) 'The price of affluence: the political economy of Japanese leisure', *New Left Review*, 188: 121–34.

Metcalfe, A. (1990) 'Sport and space: a case study of the growth of recreational facilities in east Northumberland, 1850–1914', *International Journal of the History of Sport*, 7 (3): 348–64.

Michener, J. (1976) *Sports in America*. New York: Random House.

Moen, O. (1990) *Idrottsanlaggningar och Idrottens Rumsliga Utveckling I Svenskt Stadbyggande under 1900-talet*. Occasional Paper 4, Gothenburg University, Institute of Cultural Geography.

Moen, O. (1993) 'Facilities for sports and physical training', in H. Aldskogius (ed.), *Cultural Life, Recreation and Tourism*. Stockholm: National Atlas of Sweden. pp. 48–53.

Ojala, C. and Gadwood, M. (1989) 'The geography of Major League baseball player production, 1876–1988', *Sport Place*, 3 (3): 24–35.

Patmore, J.A. (1970) *Land and Leisure*. Newton Abbott: David and Charles.

Patmore, J.A. (1983) *Recreation and Resources: Leisure Patterns and Leisure Places*. Oxford: Basil Blackwell.

Philo, C. (compiler) (1991) *New Words, New Worlds*. Department of Geography, St David's University College, Lampeter.

Philo, C. (1994) 'In the same ballpark? Looking in on the new sports geography', in J. Bale (ed.), *Community, Landscape and Identity: Horizons in a Geography of Sport*. Department of Geography, Keele University, Occasional Paper 20. pp. 1–18.

Pillsbury, R. (1972) 'Carolina thunder: a geography of southern stock car racing', *Journal of Geography*, 22: 39–46.

Pillsbury, R. (1995) 'Stock car racing', in K. Raitz (ed.), *The Theater of Sport*. Baltimore, MD: Johns Hopkins University Press. pp. 270–95.

Praicheux, J. (1991) 'Pour une lecture géopolitique de la performance olympique', in *Géopolitique du Sport* (Proceedings of a colloquium held at Besançon, March 1990). Department of Human Geography, Université de Franche-Comté. pp. 197–208.

Pred, A. (1995) *Recognizing European Modernities*. London: Routledge.

Púig, N. and Ingham, A. (eds) (1993) *International Review for the Sociology of Sport*, Special Issue on 'Sport and Space', 28 (2/3).

Raitz, K. (1987a) 'Perception of sports landscapes and gratification in the sport experience', *Sport Place*, 1: 49–62.

Raitz, K. (1987b) 'Places, spaces and environment in America's leisure landscapes', *Journal of Cultural Geography*, 8 (1): 49–62.

Raitz, K. (ed.) (1995) *The Theater of Sports*. Baltimore, MD: Johns Hopkins University Press.

Ravenel, L. (1997) 'Le Football de Haut Niveau en France: Espaces et Territoires'. Unpublished doctoral thesis, Université d'Avignon et des Pays de Vaucluse, Avignon.

Ravenel, L. (1998) *La Géographie du Football en France*. Paris: Presses Universitaires de France.

Relph, E. (1976) *Place and Placelessness*. London: Pion.

Richards, D. (1953) 'Athletic records and achievements in relation to climatic, social and environmental factors'. Unpublished Master's thesis, University of Wales.

Riiskjær, S. (ed.) (1993) *Sport and Space*. Copenhagen: Council of Europe.

Rivett, P. (1975) 'The structure of league football', *Operational Research Quarterly*, 26: 801–12.

Rooney, J. (1969) 'Up from the mines and out from the prairies; some geographical implications of football in the United States', *Geographical Review*, 59 (4): 471–92.

Rooney, J. (1974) *A Geography of American Sport: from Cabin Creek to Anaheim*. Reading, MA: Addison-Wesley.

Rooney, J. (1975) 'Sport from a geographic perspective', in D. Ball and J. Loy (eds), *Sport and Social Order: Contributions to the Sociology of Sport*. Reading, MA: Addison-Wesley. pp. 51–115.

Rooney, J. (1987) *The Recruiting Game: Toward a New System of Intercollegiate Sport* (first edition 1980). Lincoln, NB: University of Nebraska Press.

Rooney, J. (1993) 'The golf construction boom, 1987–1993', *Sport Place*, 7 (1): 15–22.

Rooney, J. and Higley, S. (1992) 'From Johns Island to Palm Springs: an analysis of the golf–real estate connection', *Sport Place*, 5 (2): 3–19.

Rooney, J. and Pillsbury, R. (1992) *Atlas of Amercian Sport*. New York: Macmillan.

Rösch, H.-E. (1986) 'Sport und Geographie', *Düsseldorfer Sportwissenschaftliche Studien*, 1. Düsseldorf University.

Sack, R. (1986) *Human Territoriality*. Cambridge: Cambridge University Press.

Sage, G. and Loy, J. (1978) 'Geographical mobility patterns of college coaches', *Urban Life*, 7 (2): 253–77.

Schimmel, K. (1995) 'Growth politics, urban development, and sports stadium construction in the United States: a case study', in J. Bale and O. Moen (eds), *The Stadium and the City*. Keele: Keele University Press. pp.111–56.

Schnell, G. (1990), 'Geographic origins of football players at Pennsylvania's colleges', *The Pennsylvania Geographer*, 28 (1): 15–29.

Scott, J. and Simpson-Housley, P. (1989) 'Relativising the relativisers: on the postmodern challenge to human geography', *Transactions of the Institute of British Geographers*, n.s. 14 (2): 231–6.

Shelley, A. and Shelley, F. (1993) 'Changing migration patterns of major league baseball players', *Sport Place*, 7 (1): 23–35.

Shore, B. (1995) 'Marginal play: sport at the borderlands of time and space', in O. Weiss and W. Schultz (eds), *Sport in Space and Time*. Vienna: University of Vienna Press. pp. 111–25.

Smith, D. (1977) *Human Geography: a Welfare Approach*. London: Arnold.

Springwood, C. (1996) *Cooperstown to Dyersville: a Geography of Baseball Nostalgia*. Boulder, CO: Westview Press.

Symes, G., Shaw, B., Fenton, D. and Mueller, W. (1989) *The Planning and Evaluation of Hallmark Events*. Aldershot: Avebury.

Taylor, Lord Justice (1990) *The Hillsborough Disaster: Final Report*. London: HMSO.

Tomkins, J. (1995) 'Football gazes and spaces: a Foucauldian history of the present'. Unpublished PhD thesis, University of Brighton.

Tuan, Y-F. (1974) *Topophilia*. Englewood Cliffs, NJ: Prentice-Hall.

Tuan, Y-F. (1984) *Dominance and Affection: the Making of Pets*. New Haven, CT: Yale University Press.

Tylor, E. (1880) 'Remarks on the geographical distribution of games', *Journal of the Anthropological Society of Great Britain and Ireland*, 9: 23–30.

Virilio, P. (1991) *The Lost Dimension*. New York: Semiotext(e).

Volkers, K. and Van Dam, F. (1992) 'Een sport-geografie beschouwing zu de Goffert', *Geografie*, 1: 16–21.

Wagner, P. (1981) 'Sport: culture and geography', in A. Pred (ed.), *Space and Time in Geography*. Lund: Gleerup. pp. 85–108.

Waylen, P. and Snook, A. (1990) 'Patterns of regional success in the Football League, 1921–1988', *Area*, 22 (4): 353–67.

Weiss, O. and Schultz, W. (eds) (1995) *Sport in Space and Time*. Vienna: University of Vienna Press.

11

SOCIAL HISTORY AND SPORT

Nancy L. Struna

The history of sport history stretches far back in time. Cave dwellers placed pictographs of their sporting pursuits on the walls of caves and shared their stories orally. Subsequently, in societies such as ancient Crete, Greece, Egypt, China and Rome, people recorded their experiences via symbols, hieroglyphics and other forms of writing. Centuries later in the West, late medieval and early modern chroniclers – Richard Carew and Joseph Strutt in Britain and the Flemish artist Jan Bruegel, for example – maintained the tradition of constructing scenes of popular sports. Many of us have used the records left by these people; they have become historians' evidence. We should not forget, however, that before these pictographs, hieroglyphics, sagas and paintings were forms of historical evidence, they were histories. Moreover, to their makers they were social histories. They were stories people told of themselves in their times and places.

These 'stories' of peoples' experiences located and understood in the context of their times and places are a part of the domain of contemporary social historians. Of course, we also construct larger stories from these particular stories, stories about patterns of change and persistence over time, stories that are critical to our understanding of social production and reproduction. A more succinct definition of the field comes from the British scholar Harold Perkin: 'Social history is … all history from the social point of view' (Perkin, 1973: 433). It is so, explained Eric Hobsbawm, because 'the societal aspects of man's [*sic*] being cannot be separated from other aspects of his being' (Hobsbawm, 1974: 5).[1]

Such positions will undoubtedly discomfort some sport historians; they see social and sport histories as distinguishable ventures, albeit ones with some common interests. As Larry Gerlach has suggested in a review of baseball history – and thus he was not addressing social history directly – such distinctions are deceptive, however. Any good history of a sport, of the economic dimensions of sports, or of ideas about health, the body, or sport, 'is necessarily about more' than a sport, economics, or ideas (Gerlach, 1994: 135). Such a history will also discuss the broader social setting, if not fully situate a practice in its complex social context, and it will identify social issues and trends even if it does not draw out the multiple levels of interaction between and among sporting performances, agents, structures and processes and the other dimensions of human social existence.

Precisely what do social historians of sport think and do? They examine sports as social practices, as social formations, or as social texts for the purpose of understanding both the sports and the society. Social historians ask and answer questions about the nature and 'fit' of sports in given times among given peoples, about how and why people constructed particular forms of sport, about the meanings that human agents assigned to sports, about conflicts and social contests evident or played out in sports, about patterns of continuity and change in sporting experiences and structures, and about the social significance of sporting practices in the context of other practices, processes and dynamics. We assume that sports are constitutive features of societies and, if a truth be told, we also assume that any given society would be quite different without its sports from what it was or is.

What follows in this chapter is a three-part essay about the social history of sport that draws on many historians' studies, whether or not they were consciously written as social histories. It attempts, first, to discuss some of historiographical trends evident in the literature, both past and present. Secondly, it reviews some of the recent research in sport as this bears on social history.[2] Finally, it suggests lines of inquiry for the future, most of which cross traditional disciplinary boundaries. Throughout, the chapter reflects this author's own boundaries, especially in terms of languages; the histories consulted are English-language publications that concentrate on Western experiences.[3] This chapter also relies on books and some of the journal literature. Thus the story constructed in the following pages is by no means a complete story; it is not even a comprehensive review of the field of sport history.

HISTORIOGRAPHICAL TRENDS

Before the 1980s one approach dominated Western sport historiography.[4] Historians often intended to reconstruct the past, and they focused on particular events such as the Olympics, the origins and developments of particular sports (especially modern ones), individuals and organizations, and occasionally the social bases for and attitudes that supported sports. The resultant histories tended to be descriptive rather than analytic; they told who did what at what point in time. They were also largely uncritical, in all senses of the word, owing in part to the dominant empiricist framework.[5] Researchers assumed that historical evidence existed independently of the historian, that the past as it had occurred could be reconstructed from that evidence, and that change over time was both inevitable and progressive. What interpretations emerged drew both from biology, especially biological evolution, and structural-functional sociology. The broader society appeared in references to milieu, the backdrop, rather than by way of context, or the ensemble of behaviors, meanings and events in which something occurred and must be examined and understood (Thompson, 1972).

The picture that resulted from these descriptive histories had a distinctive beginning in ancient societies and, if not quite an end, certainly a climax in modern, industrial societies. Participation in recognizable sports was clearly evident in places such as Sumer, Egypt, Greece and China. Some forms – archery and chariot races, for example – developed out of martial

practices. Other sports evolved from necessary endeavors; hunting and horse racing are classic examples. Still other forms emerged as individuals contested for place in a society, or, as did ball games, in the course of religious rituals and festivals. Indeed, given the significance of religions in these early societies, many sports occurred in the context of festivals that honored the gods and became ritualized themselves.[6]

Not surprisingly perhaps, the Middle Ages, which stretched for nearly a millennium between c. 500 and 1500 CE, constituted a second stage in the evolution of sports, according to this approach. During these centuries as societies multiplied and became more complex, not only did the evolution of ancient sports continue but newer ones also emerged. Given their persisting belief in evolution, historians continued to find the roots of more recently organized sports in ordinary tasks and religious festivals. Northern people added sports like skiing and skating, both derived from modes of transportation, to the record. Villagers in many places developed locally popular versions of football and many gambling games that pitted one's luck or skill against the fates. Elites continued to transform their martial practices into sports; examples include jousting and tilting in England. Animal sports such as cock fighting also emerged as ritual battles tied to conflicts among ethnic groups.

The Middle Ages came to a close as a series of processes – expanding trade, communication, exploration, education, nation-building, religious 'reformation', and inventiveness – moved human society into a third and climactic period in human history, at least in the West: the modern era. This period, especially the century and a half after 1800, witnessed the development of industrial capitalism, large urban areas, and complex, highly organized sports. Outside of Europe, where earlier periods retained their significance to sport scholars, historians have concentrated on sports in modern societies. Not surprisingly perhaps, it is precisely this historical type of sport, 'modern' sport, that has served for years as the classic, even paradigmatic definition of sport.[7]

Historians operating in this empiricist, descriptive approach examined three major questions about modern sports. First, where, when, by whom and in what steps were modern sports developed? Second, how and where did the organization, commercialization and institutionalization of sports proceed? Finally, how did major public sports in various countries reflect and express national interests and characteristics? What resulted were articles and, to a lesser extent, books that described particular sports, the lives of significant individuals, and broader movements that supported, opposed, or even impeded developments in sports. In many countries as well, historians uncovered sport clubs, chronicled the workings of sport federations and detailed the ideological underpinnings of sports in schools and religious and military organizations. Still others probed the role of the media in shaping and promoting sports, the development of transportation and communication infrastructures that permitted the geographic spread and cultural power of sports, the beliefs that institutional agents held about sports and the ways in which institutions embraced and promoted sports.

In Britain, Europe and North America especially, these descriptive works reached their apogee in the late 1970s, and they resulted in a fairly detailed map of some people and some sports. It was also a map with clear limits, not the least of which were meaningful explanations and generalizations. However, some historians had already begun to reconcile the field's traditional interest in the particular with the need to generalize, both across time and across societies and social groups. They had also begun to draw on social theories that helped in the search for explanations and encouraged a conscious reframing of questions, of evidence, and of historians' relationships to the data.

During the past 15-plus years, much of the published historical research about sport has been theoretically grounded, even if it has not aimed at grand theorizing and prediction *à la* sociology.[8] Some scholars have drawn on varieties of historical materialism to ask questions about social relations, processes, structures and significations. Gramscian historical blocs and hegemony, Giddens's structuration, the French Annales school and the approaches of E.P. Thompson and Raymond Williams and, in central Europe, Louis Althusser, are influential. Other historians have turned to a number of feminist perspectives and to post-structuralist theorists such as Lacan and Foucault; both perspectives are particularly apparent in the research on women, gender and the body. Still others have employed concepts and methods from cultural anthropology, especially its symbolic structures frameworks. From French social history Pierre Bourdieu'ş social fields and his earlier system of schemes, which theorizes how people dealt with contingencies in the past, have become influential. Finally, the positivist modernization theory has retained

some adherents, particularly in the United States.

What has also become clear in recent years is that historians employ these theoretical frameworks in distinct genres of social-historical analyses. The most common form is the deep, internal history of sport. Commonly such works hold that sporting experiences were distinctive and separable sets of social experiences that bore on the making of society, even as they were affected by and exemplified larger social movements and issues. In effect, scholars maintain, sports had particular internal histories that warrant telling, and in fact, the history of a society is incomplete until its sport history is understood. No subject thus is too small for social historical analysis: particular games or other contests, organizations, movements (including those related to health and the body), ideologies and sets of attitudes. Such studies also often address the interests and experiences of dominant and/or subordinate groups in sport contexts, as well as issues such as control and power, in comparatively short time frames.

This genre owes much to British historians, especially James Walvin and Tony Mason, who recognized quite early in the modern history of social history the importance of particular sports in the experiences of ordinary people. Their respective works on soccer, *The People's Game* (Walvin, 1975) and *Association Football and English Society, 1863–1915* (Mason, 1980), set a standard for impeccable scholarship and secured a place for sports in social history, especially insofar as it was history 'from the bottom up'. Wray Vamplew's *Pay Up and Play the Game* (1988), which explored the class and commercial bases underlying the development of professional sport, and *Sport in Britain* (Mason, 1989), an anthology whose contributors identified the social bases for and the patterns of many sports, extended our understanding of both the place and the significance of sport in British life.

Scholars have also analysed the development of modern sports as an historically specific social formation in the context of a nation's history; the internal history thus is a story of a movement rather than a sport. A number of fine books explore how and why modern sports were shaped, commercialized, institutionalized, promoted and politicized, as well as how this historically specific type and style of sport affected the larger society. Richard Cashman, for example, explored all these processes in Australia in his *Paradise of Sport* (1995), while many of the articles in *Sport and Society in Latin America* (Arbena, 1988) focused on the introduction, spread and impacts of modern sports in South and Central America. Alan Metcalfe's *Canada Learns to Play* (1987) remains the classic work on the social patterns and dynamics and the process by which modern sports became the dominant forms in capitalist, industrializing Canada through 1914. Bruce Kidd's *The Struggle for Canadian Sport* (1996) explored the Canadian story after the First World War and attributes the making of the country's major sports and its sport system, which are integral dimensions of Canadian life and society today, to four major organizations. In the United States, urban rather than national social histories represent this genre.[9] Melvin Adelman's *A Sporting Time* (1986) and Steven Riess's *City Games* (1989) both explicated how and why modern sports emerged in urban areas and how facilities, teams, entrepreneurs and popular interests shaped the city and urban living. A similar urban focus emerged in Robert Edelman's *Serious Fun: a History of Spectator Sports in the USSR* (1993).[10]

The second genre is more akin to classic Western social histories. Such works address sports *and* society, with the conjunction signifying equal attention, in contrast to the interior histories' sports *in* society perspective. One of the goals of this kind of social history is the telling of a 'large' story about the nature, fit and meanings of sporting practices as these were embedded in society; hence, the common focus on the making of sporting life as an inextricably linked dimension of the making of a nation, a people, or a sub-period. These works also often draw upon other social histories to compare and contrast sporting forms, relations and structures with other social practices. In effect, such histories describe and analyse sporting life, or at least some episodes, in the context of a web of social activities and processes, an effort that facilitates the historian's quest to assess sport's historical social significance.

In writing these histories of sport and society, British historians again defined the genre and set the standards. One of the earliest and most important books was Robert Malcolmson's *Popular Recreations in English Society, 1700–1850* (1973). Malcolmson simultaneously challenged conceptions of linear change and demonstrated the social power of sports in local experiences and social relations and on institutions and individuals. Subsequently, Peter Bailey (1978) and Hugh Cunningham (1980) produced fine books that explored sporting movements as dimensions of leisure patterns, which they situated within the social, ideological and industrial transformations of England during the nineteenth and early twentieth centuries. More recently, in *Sport and the British* (1989a) Richard Holt examined patterns of persistence and change in popular sporting experiences and accounted for critical nineteenth- and twentieth-century transformations in the context of larger structural and ideological processes occurring in Britain. Outside of the British sphere, in *Judas at the Jockey Club* (1987) William Beezley explored the social locus and base for and tensions evident in sporting contexts during a dynamic period in Mexican history, a period marked by conflicting traditional and emergent modern patterns and interests. My own *People of Prowess: Sport, Leisure, and Labor in Early Anglo-America* (Struna, 1996a) examined the making of sports and the dynamics of sporting practices as contested domains in the context of transformations in labor and leisure practices and relationships in the Anglo-American colonies of the early modern period.

The third genre frames sport within the study of popular culture or leisure. These kinds of works are first and foremost histories of popular culture or leisure. An insightful work in this vein is Phyllis Martin's *Leisure and Society in Colonial Brazzaville* (1995), which explored the interplay of indigenous and imperial interests and patterns of leisure and sport. Other authors frame popular sports as a set of instances or practices of leisure or popular culture, and they intend to explore a range of experiences in which a people engaged in order to understand the ideological interests, social relations and structural conditions in a locale. Such is the case with Donald Wetherell's and Irene Kmet's *Useful Pleasures: The Shaping of Leisure in Alberta, 1896–1945* (1990), *Workers' Culture in Imperial Germany: Leisure and Recreation in the Rhineland and Westphalia* by Lynn Abrams (1991), and Richard Waterhouse's *Private Pleasures, Public Leisure: A History of Australian Popular Culture* (1995). Anthologies in this genre also permit a thematic approach to popular experiences and thus describe experiences that actively link sports and other forms of leisure. *Workers' Worlds: Cultures and Communities in Manchester and Salford, 1880–1939* (Davies and Fielding, 1992), for instance, located and analysed organized betting in the context of street life. It thus tantalized a reader with clues about how sports might be connected within the web of social practices, as well as about how popular interests and traditions might have shaped sporting practices.

I have emphasized the differences among these kinds of social-historical studies because I believe that they are real and substantial. At the very least, the genres represent different ways of framing both sports and the relationships among sports, other social practices and formations, and societies. Beyond the pale of difference, however, we should also realize that these genres are actually complementary, rather than antagonistic. Indeed, considered as a body of literature, these works have produced considerable knowledge about the particulars of sports and for generalizations about the processes of social production and reproduction across sports and across countries. It is to these particulars and processes, via a topical discussion, that this chapter now turns.

RECENT HISTORIOGRAPHY

The recent literature in sport history can be read as a primer on social history writ large. Physical spaces and places, traditions, demography, community building, the construction of social categories and discourses, social structures and structuring and more, constitute research interests that cross scholars' national and political interests. Further, as the discussion of genres suggests, the broader realms of work and leisure, popular culture, national ideologies and movements such as industrialization and globalization have also received the attention of historians.

These social-historical interests cut across periods, as some of the recent research on sports in ancient and medieval societies makes clear. Drawing on both new and traditional sources of evidence, ancient historians have attempted to locate sporting practices in the contexts of the social experiences and systems of their subjects rather than to find the 'roots' of modern sports in such places or to produce ahistoric idealizations. Informed by poststructuralist and critical theories, historians of ancient Greece, for example, have offered new interpretations of class relations (Kyle, 1993; Miller, 1991), events as texts (Kyle, 1995), state support for athletes (Crowther, 1996; Young, 1985), and the social and cultural bases for and significance of violence (Poliakoff, 1987). This latter theme, along with that of the political signification of events in arenas, is also evident in new works on Roman sports (Auguet, 1994; Plass, 1995; Wiedemann, 1992). Theoretically less telling but containing valuable information about the social bases of sporting practices are books about understudied societies in

Egypt (Decker, 1992) and China (*Sports and Games*, 1986; Xihuan, 1991).

For medieval sports, the recent literature is more limited, both in terms of numbers and geographies. As a body, the research focuses on European societies and primarily therein on feudal structures and relations (for example, Carter, 1984). A significant book by Thomas Henricks (1991) employed symbolic analysis and presents sports as identity ceremonies, or display vehicles. The traits various generations displayed were primarily the products of larger political, economic and social movements, he argues. More descriptive and less well contexted are three works on various dimensions of medieval sporting experiences, formalized English tournaments (Young, 1987), the violence of low and high culture sports in England (Carter, 1992), and the impact of the code of chivalry (Ziegler, 1993). Finally, and perhaps most compelling, are Compton Reeves's (1995) broadly framed examination of English popular culture practices, including sports, and Joachim Ruhl's (1990) investigation of German tournament regulations in the fifteenth century.[11] The latter in particular is an artful exploration of an historically specific process of sport-making that augments our understanding of how a people constructed a sport from what had become a residual military skill.

Ruhl's work hints at the potential for exploring processes of social production and reproduction that scholars may find in prior centuries. Certainly this is the case in the early modern period in the West (that is, the sixteenth through the eighteenth centuries). For Britain, Europe and North America especially, these centuries witnessed important transformations in demography, economic action and relations, political structures, ideological systems (including religion), popular culture and ordinary life, even as some traditional patterns persisted. Two British historians, Dennis Brailsford (1969, 1991, 1992) and Robert Malcolmson (1973), recognized the significance of this period quite early; their books examined how and why customary sports persisted, the ways in which sports figured in broader social and political contexts, and the social and economic bases for emergent patterns of sports. Recent studies have augmented our understanding of this dynamic period by exploring such topics as emergent professional practices that were tied to changes occurring in theaters (McElroy and Cartwright, 1986), the social locus and meanings of multiple persisting practices (Holt, 1989a; Möller, 1984), the impact of cultural collisions and acculturation

(Salter, 1995), and changes in economic production and popular consumption that underlay the standardization and popularizing of particular forms of sport (McKendrick et al., 1982). In the context of Anglo-American colonial experiences, *People of Prowess* (Struna, 1996a) explored the determining impact of the rhythms and relations of ordinary life on sports, how and why some traditional sports either persisted or were adapted over time, and how the construction of labor and leisure as separable realms of experience affected sporting practices and the social relations forged in sporting contexts.

As has the research on ancient and medieval sport, so too have studies of the early modern period contributed to our understanding of the social history of sport and social processes over the long *dureé* in several important ways. First, they have provided some detail about the ways in which ordinary people constructed social categories – rank, race and gender – in sporting performances and in physical culture more generally. Secondly, they have heightened the significance of the locale as a major site for social production and as a major source of variations in social life. Particular practices, modes of organization and social relations, in other words, were rooted in the affairs and rhythms of ordinary life, modes and relations of production, traditions, physical environment and *mentalité* of the people(s) in an area. Even in the modern period when particular sports have emerged as international social practices, local variations – in styles of play, meanings, symbols and attendant celebrations – are still evident. Finally, the early modern studies have suggested that some social and economic processes and conditions – capitalization and emergent capitalism, boundary-making, standardization and codification of behaviors, and specialization, for example – once associated only or primarily with modern sports had begun long before modern sports were fully constructed. Some modern historians, especially in Britain, Europe and Australia, also realize that some of the traditions invented by early modern people persisted over time and remained meaningful as dimensions of the stories that later generations told about themselves.

Indeed, many historians of sports in the modern period, including some historians of modern sport, have attended to both persistence in time and continuity over time.[12] This trend is most noticeable in the research on the nineteenth and early twentieth centuries, where historians have examined the persistence of traditional sporting styles, as well as the tensions that emerged when traditional

ways and expectations collided with emergent ones. Such studies have at once deepened our understanding of the making of particular modern sports and made clear that earlier interpretations about the social functions of sport in the making of modern society, such as that of social control, are simplistic at best. In industrial, capitalist and urban societies, traditional practices were immensely powerful, and the construction of modern forms did not occur overnight or without contesting and negotiations.

Some of the most telling research on persisting traditional experiences focuses on men who were members of the working classes in many countries. In the United States Elliott Gorn (1986) explored the experiences of mostly unskilled laborers in New York City as it was undergoing profound economic and demographic changes in the mid-nineteenth century. Gorn suggested that traditional forms of bare-knuckle prize fighting expressed the values and relations of these men (as opposed to those of the dominant culture) and was one of the few venues in which they could exert their agency. In a similar vein, Alan Metcalfe (1982, 1988, 1990a) examined the persistence of traditional sports, including potshare bowling, among miners in the north of England, and N.L. Tranter (1990a) explored quoits play among miners, industrial laborers and craftsmen in central Scotland. Both sets of work revealed the traditional interests of the workers in displays of physical prowess, which were partly about achieving honor within the community, and the ongoing importance of the pub as a sporting site in which publicans were sports promoters.

Many other studies of male working-class patterns have been completed in recent years, and as a group they confirm and extend the conclusions drawn by Gorn, Metcalfe and Tranter.[13] Especially in the nineteenth century, working men in many countries had distinctive sporting styles that drew from particular interests, traditions and labor–leisure rhythms and relations. Their styles in turn often incorporated traditional sports that remained meaningful and were not residual in the sense of being mere residues of past formations; they were also at odds with those of the dominant middle and upper classes. Importantly, these studies elevate the agency of members of the working class in the context of modern sports, and, in so doing, they reinterpret class relations and challenge older notions of the 'trickle down' transmission of modern sports. Resistance and negotiations were complex processes engineered by the working classes as they retained traditional practices and became involved in emergent ones. On this latter point, several studies suggest that members of various working classes were agents in the construction of some modern team sports, especially baseball, rugby and soccer (Goldstein, 1989; Hargreaves, 1986; Holt, 1990; Jones, 1986, 1988; Vamplew and Stoddart, 1994). In so doing they confirmed earlier arguments that working-class men negotiated with middle- and upper-class organizers, promoters and entrepreneurs for membership of teams and about ways of playing. Research also suggests that professional sports, especially, depended on working-class producers and consumers and that workers' sport movements were far more complex and conflict-ridden than we have assumed in the past (for example, Holt, 1990; Krüger and Riordan, 1996).

Another research focus that has altered our view of sport and society in the nineteenth and early twentieth centuries involves women. Much of this work has moved beyond the earlier practice of identifying particular women as sport heroines or as victims of patriarchy; it focuses instead on women's agency in the production and consumption of sports.[14] Two important books, *Women First* by Sheila Fletcher (1984) and *Able-bodied Womanhood* by Martha Verbrugge (1988), are particularly telling about the agency of middle-class, educated women as revealed in their fashioning of professional physical education in the nineteenth century on both sides of the Atlantic Ocean. Kathleen McCrone added depth to Fletcher's picture in *Playing the Game* (1988), in which she examined women's efforts to liberate themselves as they shaped a distinctive set of sporting experiences in English schools. Not all women, however, realized the social emancipation they sought through physical education and sport, as Fan Hong and James A. Mangan (1995) made clear in their study of women in early twentieth-century China. Catriona Parrat (1994) also made the case for the constraining impact of persisting structural boundaries on the aspirations and experiences of working-class women in England, even as she documented changes resulting from women's agency.

Other recent works have addressed the shaping of distinctive sporting experiences by and for women in narrower but national contexts. Several chapters in *Sport in Australia* (Vamplew and Stoddart, 1994) trace the experiences and roles of women in the making of sports ranging from lawn bowls to Australian Rules football, while John Nauright and Jayne Broomhall (1994) examine women's agency in the construction and popularizing of netball in New Zealand. In Germany Gertrud Pfister (1990) has explored dimensions of the physical culture and sport contexts and experiences among women, as have scholars of women in Scandinavia, Finland, Russia and North America (Hult and Trekell, 1991; Laine, 1993; LeCompte, 1993; Riordan, 1991b). In time, perhaps, these and the studies yet to come may also affect historians' constructions of sport in the past.

One important effect of the research on women is already clear: gender has become an important analytic concept. Even historians who persist in treating sport as a predominantly male domain no longer wince at the possibility that it was and is a gendered domain, nor do historians of women as commonly interpret gender to mean women's experiences as they once did. Owing in part to the early work of Helen Lenskjy (1986), historians began to explore the once taboo subjects of sex and sexualization. Richard Cashman and Amanda Weaver (1991) and Marion Stell (1991), for example, examined in Australian contexts the ways in which the media sexualized sport and marginalized women. More recently, Susan Cahn (1994) has explored the making and impacts of sexual orientations, gendered expectations and power relations even more fully in her study of American women in sport (1994). The research of three sociologists, Jennifer A. Hargreaves (1986, 1994), Ann Hall (1993, 1996) and Nancy Theberge (1987, 1994), has also encouraged historical questions about the gendering of sports and the social construction of gender. Perhaps the most influential research in history and on historians, however, has been that of Patricia Vertinsky (for example, 1990, 1994b). In her *The Eternally Wounded Woman* (1990), Vertinsky explored how the body was socially constructed at given points in time, as well as how important particular constructions were to women's experiences and to the control over their bodies on which personal freedom hinged. Roberta Park (for example, 1987, 1991) also published a number of historical works that focused on the body, which is central to modern conceptions of sport, and to the gendering of sport and the construction of gendered relations in sport. On this latter theme, her 'Sport, gender, and the body in a transatlantic Victorian perspective' (Park, 1985) was particularly important.[15] It also heightened interests in historical examinations of the ways in which conceptions of and concerns for manliness, if not quite the process of masculinization, were expressed and figured in the making of modern sport (Krüger, 1991; Maguire, 1986; Mangan and Walvin, 1987; Riess, 1991).

A third group of studies that have sharpened our understanding of the multiple frames and framing of sport in the past is the recent research on racial groups. Some of these studies rely on ethnographic or ethnohistoriographic methods to acquire data about the past experiences of indigenous peoples, some of whom became minorities only recently in their histories. As do many of the studies of the working classes, the research on racial groups provides us with a more deeply textured picture of the rootedness of traditional sports in ordinary life. Studies of patterns among Africans before colonization, for example, suggest that many sports were deeply embedded in the life schemes and customary rituals of ordinary people (for example, Baker and Mangan, 1987). Moreover, although the physical movements and other practices such as gambling resembled those incorporated in modern sports, traditional practices often differed in terms of both form and structure. Recent scholarship on colonial Zaire (Martin, 1995), South Africa (Bose, 1994; Jarvie, 1992), Spain (Mitchell, 1991) and Australia (Daly, 1994; Paraschak, 1992; Taz, 1995) also suggests that such patterns persist even in the face of modern sport and that customary sports are critical tradition-maintaining practices. Among native Canadians Vicky Paraschak (1990, 1995) has documented similar patterns, but she has also explored some of the strategies native peoples have recently employed as they attempt to come to grips with modern sport.

In the Americas as well, people of African descent have received increased attention from historians over the past decade and a half. Building on the now classic essay by C.L.R. James (1963), Michael Manley (1988), Brian Stoddart (1987) and the contributors to *Liberation Cricket* (Beckles and Stoddart, 1995) explored the history, including the social base and structures, and meanings of sport in the Caribbean and the complex social relationships negotiated in sporting practices such as cricket. Richard Burton (1985) also clarified the impacts of the larger affairs and traditions of carnival in the construction of a style of cricket distinctive to the West Indies.

To the north, in the United States, studies of the experiences of African Americans have also become more common and more telling. Much of this research focuses on specific sports, such as boxing, baseball, or track and field, and it illuminates not only the interests and agency of African-descended people but also the conflicts and struggles they faced as they sought

to realize their interests in these sports (for example, Captain, 1991; Gissendanner, 1993; Roberts, 1983; Sammons, 1988; Tygiel, 1983; Wiggins, 1977, 1979, 1983, 1986). A few studies have also investigated the making of sports in African American communities (Coates, 1991; Ruck, 1987), and as does some of the research on women's and working-class experiences, these argue against over-generalizations, against universal race-based experiences and even against race as a universal construct.[16]

Important, too, is a smaller body of research on the experiences of modern ethnic groups. Much of the work on previously unexamined groups – Tartars, Ogu Bushmen, Samis, and Zhuang and Miao, for example – appears in two books that resulted from a conference on 'Sport and Minorities', sponsored by the Finnish Society for Research in Sport and Physical Education and the International Society for the History of Physical Education and Sport in 1992 (Laine, 1991, 1993). Not unexpectedly, much of this work is descriptive, but some articles also analyse some traditional practices and the experiences of ethnic groups with majority populations. Other works have explored expressions and impacts of ethnic and religious prejudices in and on sporting rivalries, as the basis for typecasting and denying opportunities, and in the construction of separate programmes (Eisen and Wiggins, 1994; Finn, 1991; O'Farrell, 1987; O'Hara, 1994; Whimpress, 1992). The most compelling examination of the experiences of an ethnic group in modern sport may be Peter Levine's *Ellis Island to Ebbet's Field* (1992), which focused on Jewish immigrants to the United States in the early twentieth century. Among these people, Levine argued, participation in sports popular within the dominant society encouraged assimilation without threatening many Jewish traditions; hence their embrace of modern sports helped to make Jewish Americans.

All of this recent research on the experiences of members of working classes, women, and racial and ethnic groups has contributed to a deeper understanding of the complexities of sport and society-making in the modern period. Few historians today suggest that women, workers and other segments of a population simply adopted some other group's sports. Rather, as agents in their own right, they engaged in a range of actions, including maintaining traditional patterns, resisting efforts to impose dominant styles, negotiating accommodations with dominant groups, and constructing alternative styles.

But this literature also points to a persisting historiographical issue. Some of the research on non-dominant groups – non-dominant in historians' but not necessarily historical terms – frames members of ethnic, religious and racial groups as minorities and even as subordinated people. Given the central questions about the making of modern sport – how and why this type came to be, how and why it became the dominant form, and what the social, economic and political consequences were – this framing is neither surprising nor entirely inaccurate. Still, some people became minorities only relatively late in their histories and only in the contexts of modern societies and modern sports. Certainly this is the case in many countries in South America, Africa and Asia where non-Caucasians were and remain numerical majorities; they also likely had rich histories of indigenous sports.[17] Consequently, such a framing may obfuscate much of a people's history and many of the negotiations that actually occurred prior to the points when modern versions of society and sport emerged. The possibilities for social hybridization, both of sports and of society, are not ones that many historians have considered. Nor have we sufficiently explored people's movements *away from* traditional styles of life and sport, which may be a critical process that occurred before or along with the more commonly cited instances of resistance, contestation, appropriation or adaptation.

Indeed, for many countries and groups of people at many points in time, the particulars of social production and reproduction and the processes by which societies did and did not change remain unclear. We have much to learn, for example, about how particular groups or individuals exerted their agency, what boundaries and constraints they faced and did or did not overcome, and why a particular set of relations and not others resulted. Some clues have emerged from analyses of local sports, clubs, movements and communities. Importantly, demographic research, which charts in space and time club formation and membership, has re-emerged, especially in the context of the nineteenth century. Such studies clarify who participants were and the social directions of a sport's 'development' and spread; in so doing, they speak to larger social processes of adoption, adaptation and hegemony, if not yet hybridization (for example, Gehrmann, 1989; Tranter, 1987, 1990b). Other research has focused on some of the mechanisms by which ordinary people gained access to facilities and opportunities (Hardy, 1982; Rosenzweig, 1983), the roles of institutions and agents of commerce in mediating and opposing sporting interests and experiences (invariably to the

benefit of one set of experiences) (Abrams, 1991; Cahn, 1994; Cashman, 1995; Lester, 1995), and the negotiations within clubs and among organizations, entrepreneurs and politicians (Holt, 1990; Jones, 1988; Kidd, 1996). A third set of studies has focused more broadly on local communities, both as geographic and shared-interest units, to examine how and why particular sports root in particular places and among particular people (for example, Holt, 1990; Kirsch, 1989; Lowerson, 1993; Vamplew and Stoddart, 1994). Attuned as they are to structural and ideological variables, these kinds of studies can accommodate important local sources of variance – conditions, interests, relations. They can thus account, for example, for why football dominated in industrial towns in nineteenth-century Germany (Gehrmann, 1989) but not in a town like Givors, France in the early twentieth century (Holt, 1989b), where cycling flourished.

Other clues about the processes of social production and reproduction lie in the environment, both physical and social, as some recent research on space suggests. Not too long ago, historians of ancient sports and societies were the primary investigators of the natural and the built environments. This is no longer the case, in part because historians of other eras have come to recognize the ways in which societies' physical realities shaped and mediated both the limits and possibilities of social forms, structures and relations. Across time, the actual forms of games, races and matches depended in part on the physical environment, on whether there were hills or lakes, unenclosed or fenced fields, tracks or courses. Historians of urban sport as well have argued that the physical environment of a city both shaped and was shaped by sporting facilities. Then, too, in both modern urban, industrial and older rural, agricultural societies, access to facilities such as parks and fields was a central political issue between various groups, and the control of these facilities affected local power relations and commercial opportunities (Cobley, 1994; Hardy, 1982; Metcalfe, 1990b; Riess, 1989). An important recent article by Henning Eichberg (1990) made a case for an even more dynamic view of space. In his study of nineteenth- and twentieth-century Berlin, Eichberg argued that not only did space and facilities express the interests of and help to account for a number of historically specific movements but they also belied a distinctive sport (or gymnastics or body) discipline that was central to the experiences of each movement's members. In all, Eichberg suggested, facilities served as both a base for and a window on a maze – a labyrinth, in his words – of social processes.

Indirectly at least, Eichberg's analysis implicates another dimension of social experience that has long been central to Western social history. This is the study of *mentalité*, or worldview and attendant values, beliefs and ideas. Today historians often use the word ideology rather than *mentalité*, but similar assumptions operate. As are physical spaces, ideologies are at once conditioners of and windows on social experience and the transformations, or lack of them, over time; they also suggest purposeful human action amidst structural boundaries.

Sport historians have long sought to understand the ideologies, or at least the values and ideas, expressed in and shaped by individuals, clubs, larger organizations and movements. Consequently, we are aware that particular world-views in part account for the differing styles of sport popular among the ancient Greeks versus the Romans (Auguet, 1994; Kyle, 1993), for the construction of the amateur code in English public schools (Mangan, 1981) and its adoption in American universities (Smith, 1988), for the ways in which the regular medical establishment constrained women's exercise options in the late nineteenth century (Vertinsky, 1990), and, as noted earlier, for the persistence of traditional sports among working-class men even when modern sports were available to them. Historical studies focusing on ideologies have also sharpened our understanding of the ways in which civil governments shape and control sporting movements to their advantage. On these matters, German historians have done some brilliant work, especially in the context of Nazism (Krüger, 1991), as have scholars of British imperial interests (Mangan, 1985). Much of the research on twentieth-century sporting movements, organizations and the emergence of mass sport and society has also addressed ideology-making and conflicts among competing ideologies and ideologues (for example, Dyreson, 1989; Mrozek, 1983).

Recently, sport historians have subsumed explorations of ideologies in more broadly framed studies. Implicitly if not explicitly, such research recognizes that ideologies operate and need to be understood within larger historical processes and experiences such as national identities (Van der Merwe, 1991), power-making (Metcalfe, 1991; Riordan, 1991a), the making of traditions (Korr, 1990; Holt et al., 1996; Roper, 1985), the significance of heroes and myths (Jarvie, 1991; Mangan, 1995), changes in sport policies (Baker, 1995), and diffusion (Brown, 1987). An important work in

this vein is Grant Jarvie and Graham Walker's *Scottish Sport in the Making of the Nation* (1994), which argued that sport was an integral ideological and experiential dimension of local and national identity. It also revealed the fact that sport, and particular sports, figured in various local, and sometimes conflicting, identities. In other words, sport was a part of what it meant to be Scottish, but local sporting preferences also translated into contests among Scots.

As Jeff Hill (1996) has recently suggested, these complex matters of identity and meaning – meaning in the sense of both meaningfulness and historical significance – may provide historians with a variety of questions and research directions. The questions he suggests, especially about multiple and occasionally conflicting meanings of a performance as text, about the power relations in which meanings are embedded, and about the mediation of messages, meanings and relations, may be particularly fruitful for historians and especially in the context of the construction of mass sport and society and its post-industrial aftermath. Some explorations of the ways in which sporting meanings and experiences are shaped and mediated in the social environment, especially via the sporting goods industry, the media and the state in the twentieth century, have already appeared. Stephen Hardy (1990), for example, produced a fine analysis of the ways in which the emergent sporting goods industry in the United States encouraged standard sporting behaviors and expectations and, in the process, augmented the social power of modern sport and of the urban middle classes. Two intriguing works on the media, both newspapers and television, have suggested that these organs created and controlled, respectively, the messages consumers gleaned from and about sports (Oriard, 1993; Whannel, 1992). Finally, as John E. Hargreaves (1986) and Bruce Kidd (1996) argued, the central governments of both Britain and Canada not only legitimated particular sport forms, messages, and organizations but also embraced them for political ends. A similar conclusion might be drawn about the United States, as well as other nations and national governments whose hegemony is bound up with dominant Western sports (Guttmann, 1994).

SOME FUTURE DIRECTIONS

Virtually every recent assessment of historians' scholarship has ended with recommendations for future research, and I commend these reviews and their proposals to readers. I shall not repeat them here; rather, I shall suggest four additional lines of enquiry that have the potential for enriching our social-historical understanding of sport and society.

One critical need lies in the un- and under-studied regions and peoples of the world. We certainly know very little about the content and course of ordinary life and society – and the forms and relations of sport therein – among people in Latin America, Africa, central and southern Europe (Germany excepted), and Asia. Even in Western, industrialized societies, the inhabitants of rural areas and small towns and villages have received little scholarly attention. This need extends as well to the multiple periods in people's history, rather than just their recent experiences. Only with such investigations can we really come to grips with the ways in which people created social forms and relations and with the dynamic processes of social production and reproduction. Indeed, these unknown experiences are the necessary testing grounds both for contemporary constructions of sport and for social theories.

Comparative, cross-cultural studies constitute a second potentially fruitful line of enquiry for similar reasons. These might focus on segments of a population in several countries – laborers in China, Britain and Mexico, for example – in a given period. Sport clubs and particular sports themselves could also be investigated in this fashion. In either case, historians might be able to refine our understandings of class and class relations, how local relations and traditions bear on experiences in a sport, and what the full range of structural constraints that bore on human agency were. Such studies might even enable us to see that given sports acquired different forms and meanings in different countries; hence *a* sport is really not the *same* sport worldwide. In turn, this finding would generate new questions about the impact of locales, traditions and popular meanings.

Another kind of comparative studies might also provoke new understandings and questions. These are ones that locate sport within an ensemble of social activity and are in the vein of studies of popular culture and work and leisure. As noted earlier, some research has already suggested the ways in which popular culture bore on sporting patterns, but we still know very little about the fit of many sports within a people's broader system of behaviors and meanings. Nor do we understand in much depth why people constructed sports; more simply, we have not adequately answered the question 'Why sports?' Why not other forms of social practice? Similarly, research that explores broader work and leisure patterns, rhythms and relations might provide additional, and ultimately more significant, clues about how people constructed the sports they did, as well as why sporting patterns varied at different points in time and among different groups of people. Such studies might also encourage us to revise our constructions of sport, of the experiences (or lack thereof) of particular groups, especially women, and even of the making of professional and amateur patterns and practices.

Finally, more research over the long *dureé* is warranted. British and German scholars especially have raised important questions about the role of traditions, the persistence of customary practices, and other behavioral, ideological and structural continuities in the making of sport and society over time. These need to be explored in other countries, if we are to understand fully the making of sports in and across time, as well as precisely what it is that a given generation or group generates anew or borrows and adapts from the past. Strategies for change may well be influenced by a people's collective memory, as, too, may be gender, class, and ethnic or race relations. Persisting expectations, relations and behaviors may also help to account for visible contemporary differences in sport forms, structures and meanings across nations and social blocs. We need, in other words, to begin to attend to continuities, as well as discontinuities, over time rather than focusing on what appears to be new in time. In so doing perhaps, we might understand better what, if anything, is ever new in the world of sport.

NOTES

1 I find myself in agreement with Jean Harvey's (1995) discussion of social history and his premises for the social history of sport. A recent book by Joyce Appleby, Lynn Hunt and Margaret Jacob (1994) has also influenced my thoughts.

2 I would like to thank a number of colleagues for their assistance in locating social historical materials from outside the US and Britain: Joe Arbena, Richard Cashman, Gertrud Pfister, Wray Vamplew and Kevin Wamsley.

3 Fortunately, several reviews assess some of the non-English language historical literature; see, for example, Krüger (1990) and Holt (1989b).

4 One has only to read various review essays to realize that no two historians define the term 'approach' in precisely the same way. In my mind, one approach is distinguished from another on the grounds of the questions one asks, the kinds of evidence one uses and what one assumes that evidence to be evidence of, and the assumptions one makes about things like agency, structure, causality and meanings.

5 Important exceptions to this approach did exist in Britain and Europe.

6 Some of the literature that I have drawn on in this and the next three paragraphs was the subject of critical assessments by North Americans in the 1980s: see, for instance, Adelman, 1983; Baker, 1983; Guttmann, 1983; Hardy and Ingham, 1983; Kyle, 1983; Morrow, 1983; Struna, 1985.

7 One of the most influential discussions of the historical bases for and characteristics of modern sport is Allen Guttmann's *From Ritual to Record: the Nature of Modern Sport* (1978).

8 Jeffrey Hill has developed this point more completely in his cogent review of recent British historiography (1996: 14). For a more complete review of changes in theoretical directions in sport history in the United States, see Struna, 1996b.

9 Stephen Hardy has published a massive and compelling examination of research in what he calls the 'urban paradigm'; see Hardy, 1997.

10 Other important recent examples of this genre include John E.B. Allen's *From Skisport to Skiing* (1993), George Kirsch's *The Creation of American Team Sports* (1989), Tony Mason's *Passion of the People? Football in South America* (1995), Kevin MacAleer's *Dueling: The Cult of Honor in Fin-de-Siècle Germany* (1994), Timothy Mitchell's *Blood Sport: A Social History of Spanish Bullfighting* (1991), and Keith Sandiford's *Cricket and the Victorians* (1994).

11 Unlike most of the other works cited in this chapter, Reeves's book aims at a popular audience and should be read accordingly.

12 Horst Ueberhorst (1990) has explored the larger matter of continuity *versus* change as a significant historical and political issue in German historiography. See also Krüger, 1987.

13 Steven Riess (1994) has reviewed much of the work coming out of the Anglo-American sphere on sport and class; his is a fine essay that addresses the research

and its themes in far more detail than space permits here.

14 For a fairly complete review of the literature on gender and sport, see Patricia Vertinsky's article in the *Journal of Sport History* (1994a).

15 Roberta Park (1994) has recently examined what is a large body of historical literature on health, fitness and exercise.

16 In what was the last of a series of literature reviews in the *Journal of Sport History* in 1994–5, Jeffrey Sammons examined the research and other writings on race and sport, primarily in the context of the United States. He also raises and discusses at greater length the limits of a universal construct of race.

17 Latin America may prove to be particularly fertile ground for important examinations of traditional, indigenous practices and of the social processes of adaptation, resistance and negotiation. Some research has begun to address dimensions of continuity and change there, especially in the twentieth century. See, for instance, Arbena, 1988; Carvallo et al., 1984; Pettavino and Pye, 1994.

REFERENCES

Abrams, L. (1991) *Workers' Culture in Imperial Germany: Leisure and Recreation in the Rhineland and Westphalia.* New York: HarperCollins Academic.

Adelman, M.L. (1983) 'Academicians and American athletics: a decade of progress', *Journal of Sport History*, 10 (1): 80–106.

Adelman, M.L. (1986) *A Sporting Time: New York City and the Rise of Modern Athletics, 1820–1870.* Urbana, IL: University of Illinois Press.

Allen, E. John, B. (1993) *From Skisport to Skiing: One Hundred Years of an American Sport, 1840–1940.* Amherst, MA: University of Massachusetts Press.

Appleby, J., Hunt, L. and Jacob, M. (1994) *Telling the Truth about History.* New York: W.W. Norton.

Arbena, J.L. (ed.) (1988) *Sport and Society in Latin America: Diffusion, Dependency, and the Rise of Mass Culture.* Westport, CT: Greenwood Press.

Auguet, R. (1994) *Cruelty and Civilization: the Roman Games.* London: Routledge & Kegan Paul.

Bailey, P. (1978) *Leisure and Class in Victorian England.* London: Routledge & Kegan Paul.

Baker, N. (1995) 'The amateur ideal in a society of equality. Change and continuity in post-Second World War British sport, 1945–48', *International Journal of the History of Sport*, 12 (1): 99–126.

Baker, W.J. (1983) 'The state of British sport history', *Journal of Sport History*, 10 (1): 53–66.

Baker, W.J. and Mangan, J.A. (eds) (1987) *Sport in Africa: Essays in Social History*. New York: Africana.

Beckles, H.M. and Stoddart, B. (eds) (1995) *Liberation Cricket: West Indies Cricket Culture*. Manchester: Manchester University Press.

Beezley, W.H. (1987) *Judas at the Jockey Club and Other Episodes of Porfirian Mexico*. Lincoln, NB: University of Nebraska Press.

Bose, M. (1994) *Sporting Colours: Sport and Politics in South Africa*. London: Robson Books.

Brailsford, D. (1969) *Sport and Society: Elizabeth to Anne*. London: Routledge & Kegan Paul.

Brailsford, D. (1991) *Sport, Time, and Society: The British at Play*. London: Routledge & Kegan Paul.

Brailsford, D. (1992) *British Sport: A Social History*. Cambridge: Lutterworth Press.

Brown, D.W. (1987) 'Muscular Christianity in the Antipodes: some observations on the diffusion and the emergence of a Victorian ideal in Australian social theory', *Sporting Traditions*, 3 (2): 173–87.

Burton, R.D.E. (1985) 'Cricket, carnival and street culture in the Caribbean', *British Journal of Sports History*, 2: 179–97.

Cahn, S.K. (1994) *Coming on Strong: Gender and Sexuality in Twentieth-century Women's Sport*. New York: Free Press.

Captain, G. (1991) 'Enter ladies and gentlemen of color: gender, sport and the ideal of African American manhood and womanhood during the late nineteenth and early twentieth centuries', *Journal of Sport History*, 18 (1): 81–102.

Carter, J.M. (1984) *Sports and Pastimes of the Middle Ages*. Columbus, GA: Brentwood University Press.

Carter, J.M. (1992) *Medieval Games: Sports and Recreations in Feudal Society*. Westport, CT: Greenwood Press.

Carvallo, J.D., Stein, S. and Stokes, S.C. (1984) 'Soccer and social change in early twentieth century Peru', *Studies in Latin American Popular Culture*, 3: 17–27.

Cashman, R. (1995) *Paradise of Sport: The Rise of Organized Sport in Australia*. Melbourne: Oxford University Press.

Cashman, R. and Weaver, A. (1991) *Wicket Women: Cricket and Women in Australia*. Sydney: New South Wales University Press.

Chandler, J. (1988) *Television and National Sport: The United States and Britain*. Urbana, IL: University of Illinois Press.

Coates, J.R. (1991) 'Recreation and sport in the African-American community of Baltimore'. Unpublished PhD dissertation, University of Maryland.

Cobley, A.G. (1994) 'A political history of playing fields: the provision of sporting facilities for Africans in the Johannesburg area to 1948', *International Journal of the History of Sport*, 11 (2): 212–31.

Crowther, N. (1996) 'Athlete and state: qualifying for the Olympic games in ancient Greece', *Journal of Sport History*, 23 (1): 34–43.

Cunningham, H. (1980) *Leisure in the Industrial Revolution c.1780–c.1880*. London: Croom Helm.

Daly, J. (1994) '"Civilising" the Aborigines: cricket at Poonindie, 1850–1890', *Sporting Traditions*, 10 (2): 59–67.

Davies, A. and Fielding, S. (eds) (1992) *Workers' Worlds: Cultures and Communities in Manchester and Salford, 1880–1939*. Manchester: Manchester University Press.

Decker, W. (1992) *Sports and Games of Ancient Egypt*. (trans. A. Guttmann). New Haven, CT: Yale University Press.

Dyreson, M. (1989) 'The emergence of consumer culture and the transformation of physical culture: American sport in the 1920s', *Journal of Sport History*, 16 (3): 261–81.

Edelman, R. (1993) *Serious Fun: a History of Spectator Sports in the USSR*. New York: Oxford University Press.

Eichberg, H. (1990) 'Race-track and labyrinth: the space of physical culture in Berlin', *Journal of Sport History*, 17 (2): 245–60.

Eisen, G. and Wiggins, D.K. (eds) (1994) *Ethnicity and Sport in North American History and Culture*. Westport, CT: Greenwood Press.

Finn, J.P.T. (1991) 'Racism, religion, and social prejudice: Irish Catholic clubs, soccer and Scottish society', *International Journal of the History of Sport*, 8 (1): 73–95.

Fletcher, S. (1984) *Women First: The Female Tradition in English Physical Education, 1880–1990*. London: Louds.

Gehrmann, S. (1989) 'Football in an industrial region: the example of Schalke 04 football club', *International Journal of the History of Sport*, 6 (1): 335–55.

Gerlach, L.R. (1994) 'Not quite ready for prime time: baseball history, 1983–1993', *Journal of Sport History*, 21 (2): 103–37.

Gissendanner, C. (1993) 'African-American women and competitive sport, 1920–1960', in S. Birrell and C. Cole (eds), *Women, Sport and Culture*. Champaign, IL: Human Kinetics. pp. 81–92.

Goldstein, W. (1989) *Playing for Keeps: A History of Early Baseball*. Ithaca, NY: Cornell University Press.

Gorn, E.J. (1986) *The Manly Art: Bare-knuckle Prize Fighting in America*. Ithaca, NY: Cornell University Press.

Guttmann, A. (1978) *From Ritual to Record: The Nature of Modern Sport*. New York: Columbia University Press.

Guttmann, A. (1983) 'Recent work in European sport history', *Journal of Sport History*, 10 (1): 35–52.

Guttmann, A. (1994) *Games and Empires: Modern Sports and Cultural Imperialism*. New York: Columbia University Press.

Hall, M.A. (1993) 'Gender and sport in the 1990s: feminism, culture, and politics', *Sport Science Review*, 2 (1): 48–68.

Hall, M.A. (1996) *Feminism and Sporting Bodies: Essays on Theory and Practice*. Champaign, IL: Human Kinetics.

Hardy, S. (1982) *How Boston Played: Sport, Recreation, and Community, 1865–1915*. Boston, MA: Northeastern University Press.

Hardy, S. (1990) '"Adopted by all the leading clubs": sporting goods and the shaping of leisure, 1800–1900', in R. Butsch (ed.), *For Fun and Profit: The Transformation of Leisure into Consumption*. Philadelphia: Temple University Press. pp. 71–101.

Hardy, S. (1997) 'Sport in urbanizing America: an historical review', *Journal of Urban History*, 23 (1): 675–708.

Hardy, S. and Ingham, A. (1983) 'Games, structures and agency: historians on the American play movement', *Journal of Social History*, 17 (3): 285–301.

Hargreaves, J.A. (1986) 'Where's the virtue? Where's the grace? A discussion of the social production of gender relations in and through sport', *Theory, Culture and Society*, 3 (1): 109–21.

Hargreaves, J.A. (1994) *Sporting Females: Critical Issues in the History and Sociology of Women's Sports*. London: Routledge & Kegan Paul.

Hargreaves, J.E. (1986) *Sport, Power and Culture: A Social and Historical Analysis of Popular Sports in Britain*. Cambridge: Polity Press.

Harvey, J. (1995) 'Historical sociology and social history: même combat', in K. Wamsley (ed.), *Method and Methodology in Sport and Cultural History*. Dubuque, IA: Brown & Benchmark. pp. 2–15.

Henricks, T.S. (1991) *Disputed Pleasures: Sport and Society in Preindustrial England*. Westport, CT: Greenwood Press.

Hill, J. (1996) 'British sports history: a post-modern future?', *Journal of Sport History*, 23 (1): 1–19.

Hobsbawm, E. (1974) 'From social history to the history of society', in T.C. Smout and M.L. Flinn (eds), *Essays in Social History*. Oxford: Clarendon Press.

Holt, R. (1989a) *Sport and the British: a Modern History*. Oxford: Oxford University Press.

Holt, R. (1989b) 'Ideology and sociability: a review of new French research into the history of sport under the early third republic, 1870–1914', *International Journal of the History of Sport*, 6 (3): 368–77.

Holt, R. (ed.) (1990) *Sport and the Working Class in Modern Britain*. Manchester: Manchester University Press.

Holt, R., Mangan, J.A. and Lanfranchi P. (eds) (1996) 'European heroes: myth, identity, sport', *International Journal of the History of Sport*, 13 (1).

Hong, F. and Mangan, J.A. (1995) '"Enlightenment" aspirations in an Oriental setting: female emancipation and exercise in early twentieth-century China', *International Journal of the History of Sport*, 12 (3): 80–104.

Hult, J.S. and Trekell, M. (eds) (1991) *A Century of Women's Basketball: From Frailty to Final Four*. Reston, VA: National Association for Girls and Women in Sport.

James, C.L.R. (1963) *Beyond a Boundary*. London: Stanley Paul.

Jarvie, G. (1991) *Highland Games: The Making of a Myth*. Edinburgh: Edinburgh University Press.

Jarvie, G. (1992) 'Sport, power and dependency in southern Africa', in E. Dunning and C. Rojek (eds), *Sport and Leisure in the Civilising Process*. London: Macmillan. pp. 183–200.

Jarvie, G. and Walker, G. (eds) (1994) *Scottish Sport in the Making of the Nation*. Leicester: Leicester University Press.

Jones, S.G. (1986) *Workers at Play: A Social and Economic History of Leisure 1918–1939*. London: Routledge & Kegan Paul.

Jones, S.G. (1988) *Sport, Politics and the Working Class: Organised Labour and Sport in Inter-war Britain*. Manchester: Manchester University Press.

Kidd, B. (1996) *The Struggle for Canadian Sport*. Toronto: University of Toronto Press.

Kirsch, G. (1989) *The Creation of American Team Sports: S Baseball and Cricket, 1838–72*. Urbana, IL: University of Illinois Press.

Korr, C. (1990) 'A different kind of success: West Ham United and the creation of tradition and community', in R. Holt (ed.), *Sport and the Working Class in Modern Britain*. Manchester: Manchester University Press. pp. 142–58.

Krüger, A. (1987) '"Sieg Heil" to the most glorious sports era of German sports: continuity and change in the modern German sports movement', *International Journal of the History of Sport*, 4 (1): 5–20.

Krüger, A. (1990) 'Puzzle solving: German sport historiography of the eighties', *Journal of Sport History*, 17 (2): 261–77.

Krüger, A. (1991) 'There goes this art of manliness: naturism and racial hygiene in Germany', *Journal of Sport History*, 18 (1): 135–58.

Krüger, A. and Riordan, J. (eds) (1996) *The Story of Worker Sport*. Champaign, IL: Human Kinetics.

Kyle, D.G. (1983) 'Directions in ancient sport history', *Journal of Sport History*, 10 (1): 7–34.

Kyle, D.G. (1993) *Athletics in Ancient Athens*, 2nd edn. Leiden: E.J. Brill.

Kyle, D. (1995) 'Philostratus, *repêchage*, running and wrestling: the Greek pentathlon again', *Journal of Sport History*, 22 (1): 60–5.

Laine, L. (ed.) (1991) *Sport and Cultural Minorities: Working Papers*. Helsinki: The Finnish Society for Research in Sport and Physical Education.

Laine, L. (ed.) (1993) *On the Fringes of Sport*. Sankt Augustin: Academia Verlag.

LeCompte, M.L. (1993) *Cowgirls of the Rodeo: Pioneer Professional Athletes.* Urbana, IL: University of Illinois Press.

Lenskjy, H. (1986) *Out of Bounds: Women, Sport and Sexuality.* Toronto: Women's Press.

Lester, R. (1995) *Stagg's University: The Rise, Decline, and Fall of Big-time Football at Chicago.* Urbana, IL: University of Illinois Press.

Levine, P. (1992) *Ellis Island to Ebbet's Field: Sport and the American-Jewish Experience.* New York: Oxford University Press.

Lowerson, J. (1993) *Sport and the English Middle Classes, 1870–1914.* Manchester: Manchester University Press.

MacAleer, K. (1994) *Dueling: The Cult of Honor in Fin-de-siècle Germany.* Princeton, NJ: Princeton University Press.

Maguire, J. (1986) 'Images of manliness and competing ways of living in late Victorian and Edwardian Britain', *British Journal of Sports History,* 3 (3): 265–87.

Malcolmson, R. (1973) *Popular Recreations in English Society, 1700–1850.* Cambridge: Cambridge University Press.

Mangan, J.A. (1981) *Athleticism in the Victorian and Edwardian Public Schools.* Cambridge: Cambridge University Press.

Mangan, J.A. (1985) *The Games Ethic and Imperialism: Aspects of the Diffusion of an Ideal.* Harmondsworth: Viking.

Mangan, J.A. (ed.) (1995) 'Tribal identities: nationalism, Europe, and sport', *International Journal of the History of Sport,* 12 (2).

Mangan, J.A. and Walvin, J. (eds) (1987) *Manliness and Morality: Middle-class Masculinity in Britain and America, 1800–1940.* New York: St Martin's Press.

Manley, M. (1988) *A History of West Indies Cricket,* rev. edn. London: Pan.

Martin, P. (1995) *Leisure and Society in Colonial Brazzaville.* Cambridge: Cambridge University Press.

Mason, T. (1980) *Association Football and English Society, 1863–1915.* Brighton: Harvester.

Mason, T. (ed.) (1989) *Sport in Britain: a Social History.* Cambridge: Cambridge University Press.

Mason, Tony (1995) *Passion of the People? Football in South America.* London: Verso.

McCrone, K.E. (1988) *Playing the Game: Sport and the Physical Emancipation of English Women, 1870–1914.* Lexington: University Press of Kentucky.

McElroy, M. and Cartwright, K. (1986) 'Public fencing contests on the Elizabethan stage', *Journal of Sport History,* 13 (3): 193–211.

McKendrick, N., Brewer, J. and Plumb, J.H. (1982) *The Birth of a Consumer Society: The Commercialization of Eighteenth-century England.* Bloomington, IN: Indiana University Press.

Metcalfe, A. (1982) 'Organized sport in the mining communities of south Northumberland, 1800–1889, *Victorian Studies,* 25: 469–95.

Metcalfe, A. (1987) *Canada Learns to Play: the Emergence of Organized Sport, 1807–1914.* Toronto: McClelland and Stewart.

Metcalfe, A. (1988) 'Football in the mining communities of east Northumberland, 1882–1914', *International Journal of the History of Sport,* 5 (3): 269–91.

Metcalfe, A. (1990a) '"Potshare bowling" in the mining communities of east Northumberland, 1800–1914', in R. Holt (ed.), *Sport and the Working Class in Modern Britain.* Manchester: Manchester University Press. pp. 29–44.

Metcalfe, A. (1990b) 'Sport and space: a case-study of the growth of recreational facilities in east Northumberland, 1850–1914', *International Journal of the History of Sport,* 7 (3): 348–64.

Metcalfe, A. (1991) 'The anatomy of power in amateur sport in Ontario, 1918–1936', *Canadian Journal of the History of Sport,* 22 (2): 47–67.

Miller, S.G. (1991) *Arete: Greek Sports from Ancient Sources.* Berkeley, CA: University of California Press.

Mitchell, T. (1991) *Blood Sport: A Social History of Spanish Bullfighting.* Philadelphia: University of Pennsylvania Press.

Möller, J. (1984) 'Sports and old village games in Denmark', *Canadian Journal of the History of Sport,* 15 (2): 19–29.

Morrow, D. (1983) 'Canadian sport history: a critical essay', *Journal of Sport History,* 10 (1): 67–79.

Mrozek, D.J. (1983) *Sport and American Mentality, 1880–1910.* Knoxville: University of Tennessee Press.

Nauright, J. and Broomhall, J. (1994) 'A woman's game: the development of netball and a female sporting culture in New Zealand 1906–70', *International Journal of the History of Sport,* 11 (3): 387–407.

O'Farrell, P. (1987) *The Irish in Australia.* Sydney: New South Wales University Press.

O'Hara, J. (ed.) (1994) *Ethnicity and Soccer in Australia.* Cambelltown, NSW: Australian Society for Sport History.

Oriard, M. (1993) *Reading Football: How the Popular Press Created an American Spectacle.* Chapel Hill, NC: University of North Carolina Press.

Paraschak, V. (1990) 'Organized sport for native females on the Six Nations reserve, Ontario, from 1968 to 1980: a comparison of dominant and emergent sport systems', *Canadian Journal of the History of Sport,* 21 (2): 70–80.

Paraschak, V. (1992) 'Aborigines and sport in Australia', *Australian Society for Sport History Bulletin,* 17: 15–19.

Paraschak, V. (1995) 'The native sport and recreation program, 1972–1981: patterns of resistance, patterns of reproduction', *Canadian Journal of the History of Sport,* 26: 1–18.

Park, R.J. (1985) 'Sport, gender and society in a transatlantic Victorian perspective', *British Journal of Sports History,* 2 (1): 5–28.

Park, R.J. (1987) 'Biological thought, athletics and the formation of a "man of character", 1830–1900', in J.A. Mangan and J. Walvin (eds), *Manliness and Morality: Middle-class Masculinity in Britain and America 1800–1940*. New York: St Martin's Press. pp. 7–34.

Park, R.J. (1991) 'Physiology and anatomy are destiny!? Brains, bodies, and exercise in nineteenth century American thought', *Journal of Sport History*, 18 (1): 31–63.

Park, R.J. (1994) 'A decade of the body: researching and writing about the history of health, fitness, exercise and sport, 1983–1993', *Journal of Sport History*, 21 (1): 59–82.

Parratt, C.M. (1994) 'With little means or time: working-class women and leisure in late Victorian and Edwardian England'. Unpublished PhD dissertation, Ohio State University.

Perkin, H. (1973) 'Social history', in F. Stern (ed.), *The Varieties of History: From Voltaire to the Present*, 2nd edn. New York: Vintage Books.

Pettavino, P.J. and Pye, G. (1994) *Sport in Cuba: the Diamond in the Rough*. Pittsburgh: University of Pittsburgh Press.

Pfister, G. (1990) 'The medical discourse on female physical culture in Germany in the 19th and early 20th centuries', *Journal of Sport History*, 17 (2): 183–99.

Plass, P. (1995) *The Game of Death in Ancient Rome: Arena Sport and Political Suicide*. Madison, WI: University of Wisconsin Press.

Poliakoff, M.B. (1987) *Combat Sports in the Ancient World: Competition, Violence, and Culture*. New Haven, CT: Yale University Press.

Reeves, C. (1995) *Pleasures and Pastimes in Medieval England*. Phoenix Mill, Gloucestershire: Alan Sutton.

Riess, S.A. (1989) *City Games: The Evolution of American Urban Society and the Rise of Sports*. Urbana, IL: University of Illinois Press.

Riess, S.A. (1991) 'Sport and the redefinition of American middle-class masculinity', *International Journal of the History of Sport*, 8 (1): 5–27.

Riess, S.A. (1994) 'From pitch to putt: sport and class in Anglo-American sport', *Journal of Sport History*, 21: 138–84.

Riordan, J. (1991a) *Sport, Politics, and Communism*. Manchester: Manchester University Press.

Riordan, J. (1991b) 'The rise, fall and rebirth of sporting women in Russia and the USSR', *Journal of Sport History*, 18 (1): 183–99.

Roberts, R. (1983) *Papa Jack: Jack Johnson and the Era of White Hopes*. New York: Free Press.

Roper, M. (1985) 'Inventing traditions in colonial society: Bendigo's Easter fair, 1871–1885', *Journal of Australian Studies*, 17: 31–40.

Rosenzweig, R. (1983) *Eight Hours for What We Will: Workers and Leisure in an Industrial City, 1870–1920*. Cambridge: Cambridge University Press.

Ruck, R. (1987) *Sandlot Seasons: Sport in Black Pittsburgh*. Urbana, IL: University of Illinois Press.

Ruhl, J.K. (1990) 'German tournament regulations of the 15th century', *Journal of Sport History*, 17 (2): 163–83.

Salter, M. (1995) 'Baggataway to lacrosse: a case study in acculturation', *Canadian Journal of History of Sport*, 26: 49–64.

Sammons, J.T. (1988) *Beyond the Ring: The Role of Boxing in American Society*. Urbana, IL: University of Illinois Press.

Sammons, J.T. (1994) '"Race" and sport: a critical, historical examination', *Journal of Sport History*, 21 (3): 203–78.

Sandiford, K.A.P. (1994) *Cricket and the Victorians*. Brookfield, VT: Ashgate Press.

Smith, R.A. (1988) *Sports and Freedom: The Rise of Big-time College Athletics*. New York: Oxford University Press.

Sports and Games in Ancient China (1986). Beijing: New World Press.

Stell, M.K. (1991) *Half the Race: A History of Australian Women in Sport*. North Ryde, NSW: Angus & Robertson.

Stoddart, B. (1987) 'Cricket, social formation and cultural continuity in Barbados: a preliminary ethnohistory', *Journal of Sport History*, 14 (3): 317–40.

Struna, N.L. (1985) 'In "glorious disarray": The literature of American sport history', *Research Quarterly for Exercise and Sport*, 56 (3): 151–60.

Struna, N.L. (1996a) *People of Prowess: Sport, Leisure, and Labor in Early Anglo-America*. Urbana, IL: University of Illinois Press.

Struna, N.L. (1996b) 'Sport history', in J. Massengale and R. Swanson (eds), *History of Exercise and Sport Science*. Champaign, IL: Human Kinetics.

Taz, C. (1995) *Obstacle Race: Aborigines in Sport*. Sydney: University of New South Wales Press.

Theberge, N. (1987) 'Sport and women's empowerment', *Women's Studies International Forum*, 10 (4): 387–93.

Theberge, N. (1994) 'Toward a feminist alternative to sport as a male preserve', in S. Birrell and C. Cole (eds), *Women, Sport, and Culture*. Champaign, IL: Human Kinetics. pp. 181–92.

Thompson, E.P. (1972) 'Anthropology and the discipline of context', *Midland History*, 3: 41–55.

Tranter, N.L. (1987) 'The social and occupational structure of organized sport in central Scotland during the nineteenth century', *International Journal of the History of Sport*, 4 (3): 301–14.

Tranter, N.L. (1990a) 'Organized sport and the working classes of central Scotland, 1820–1900: the neglected sport of quoiting', in R. Holt (ed.), *Sport and the Working Class in Modern Britain*. Manchester: Manchester University Press.

Tranter, N.L. (1990b) 'Rates of participation in club sport in the central lowlands of Scotland,

1820–1900', *Canadian Journal of History of Sport*, 21 (2): 1–19.

Tygiel, J. (1983) *Baseball's Great Experiment: Jackie Robinson and his Legacy*. New York: Oxford University Press.

Ueberhorst, H. (1990) 'The importance of the historians' quarrel and the problem of continuity for the German sport history', *Journal of Sport History*, 17 (2): 232–44.

Vamplew, W. (1988) *Pay Up and Play the Game: Professional Sport in Britain, 1875–1914*. Cambridge: Cambridge University Press.

Vamplew, W. and Stoddart, B. (eds) (1994) *Sport in Australia: a Social History*. Cambridge: Cambridge University Press.

Van der Merwe, F.J.G. (1991) 'Afrikaner nationalism in sport', *Canadian Journal of the History of Sport*, 22 (2): 34–46.

Verbrugge, M. (1988) *Able-bodied Womanhood: Personal Health and Social Change in Nineteenth-century Boston*. New York: Oxford University Press.

Vertinsky, P. (1990) *The Eternally Wounded Woman: Women, Exercise and Doctors in the Late Nineteenth Century*. Manchester: Manchester University Press.

Vertinsky, P. (1994a) 'Gender relations, women's history and sport history: a decade of changing enquiry, 1983–1993', *Journal of Sport History*, 21 (1): 1–58.

Vertinsky, P. (1994b) 'The social construction of the gendered body: exercise and the exercise of power', *International Journal of the History of Sport*, 11 (2): 147–71.

Walvin, J. (1975) *The People's Game: a Social History of British Football*. Bristol: Allen Lane.

Waterhouse, R. (1995) *Private Pleasures, Public Leisure: a History of Australian Popular Culture Since 1788*. South Melbourne: Longman.

Wetherell, D.G. and Kmet, I. (1990) *Useful Pleasures: The Shaping of Leisure in Alberta, 1896–1945*. Regina: Canadian Plains Research Center.

Whannel, G. (1992) *Fields in Vision: Television Sport and Cultural Transformation*. London: Routledge & Kegan Paul.

Whimpress, B. (1992) 'Few and far between: prejudice and discrimination among Aborigines in Australian first class cricket 1869–1988', *Journal of the Anthropological Society of South Australia*, 30 (1–2): 57–70.

Wiedemann, T. (1992) *Emperors and Gladiators*. London: Routledge & Kegan Paul.

Wiggins, D.K. (1977) 'Good times on the old plantation', *Journal of Sport History*, 4 (3): 260–84.

Wiggins, D.K. (1979) 'Isaac Murphy: black hero in nineteenth century American sport', *Canadian Journal of the History of Sport and Physical Education*, 10 (1): 15–33.

Wiggins, D.K. (1983) 'Wendell Smith, the *Pittsburgh Courier Journal* and the campaign to include blacks in organized baseball', *Journal of Sport History*, 10 (2): 5–29.

Wiggins, D.K. (1986) 'From plantation to playing field', *Research Quarterly for Exercise and Sport*, 57 (2): 101–16.

Xihuan, Z. (1991) 'China sports activities of the ancient and modern times', *Canadian Journal of the History of Sport*, 22 (2): 68–82.

Young, A. (1987) *Tudor and Jacobean Tournaments*. New York: Sheridan House.

Young, D.C. (1985) *The Olympic Myth of Greek Amateur Athletics*. Chicago: Ares.

Ziegler, E.F. (1993) 'Chivalry's influence on sport and physical training in medieval Europe', *Canadian Journal of History of Sport*, 24 (1): 1–28.

12

THE PHILOSOPHY OF SPORT: A HISTORICAL AND CONCEPTUAL OVERVIEW AND A CONJECTURE REGARDING ITS FUTURE

William J. Morgan

HISTORICAL BACKGROUND

The philosophy of sport is, like its counterparts, the history and sociology of sport, a relatively recent invention, having appeared on the intellectual scene in North America, its birthplace, only in the middle to late 1960s. These, of course, were heady times for North American colleges and universities, times of economic expansion and physical growth, of political unrest and revolt, and of intellectual experimentation and development. One important consequence of this political and intellectual agitation on college campuses was that old and revered academic disciplines found themselves under constant attack by a swelling student body of baby boomers distrustful of anything old and revered – indeed, distrustful of anybody, as the popular saying went, over the age of 35, and eager for change and alternative academic experiences. It is hardly surprising, therefore, that new academic fields like the philosophy of sport got their start during this period.[1]

However, two developments in particular were crucial to the academic debut of sport philosophy. The first was the emergence of sports studies out of the old and staid field of physical education. Whereas the traditional field of physical education was based exclusively on the medical and pedagogical study of physical activity and sport, the new, upstart field of sports studies championed a more ambitious intellectual agenda, one that retained the medical and pedagogical study of sport but ranged them alongside the philosophical, historical and sociological study of sport. This displacement of science and pedagogy as the mainstays of the curriculum made possible, then, a more abiding study of the cultural and historical contexts of sports. In this regard, the publication of Eleanor Metheny's *Movement and Meaning* (1968) and Howard Slusher's *Man, Sport, and Existence* (1967) solidified the place of the philosophy of sport in these burgeoning sports studies programs.

The second development was the long overdue consideration of sport by philosophy proper. The neglect of sport by philosophy is, alas, a long-standing one. Although there was a well-established tradition within philosophy of interrogating forms of life vital to societies and peoples (to wit, the philosophy of religion, art, science and education), sport, despite its influence on cultures as diverse as ancient Greece and modern-day America, managed somehow to avoid serious philosophic scrutiny. There were, of course, exceptions. For instance, Plato and Aristotle wrote approvingly, even at times enthusiastically, of play and sport, and modern philosophers such as Nietzsche and Heidegger used play as a metaphor to define their own distinctive world-views, and contemporary philosophers such as Sartre and Wittgenstein employed notions of sport and game to explicate their influential conceptions of human existence and language respectively. In the main, however, most philosophers simply ignored sport, convinced that it was too marginal an undertaking to warrant philosophic attention.

This dismissive regard for sport, and by implication anything having to do with the body, however, was not just a byproduct of philosophy's past, of its close association with religion and its contemplation of matters eternal. It was also a byproduct of philosophy's present, in particular, of fairly recent changes in its main paradigms that hindered the development of new philosophical subdisciplines like the philosophy of sport. I am speaking in this instance of the emergence and dominance of analytic philosophy in the Anglophone world, which supplanted the early twentieth-century pragmatic conception of philosophy (one that stressed the critical application of intelligence to social problems) with a scientific conception of philosophy (one that stressed rigor and precision, and so, the study of technical questions that admit of such rigor and precision).[2] The idea that philosophy should model itself after the sciences rather than, say, the arts is what united the two different strands of analytic philosophy that developed in England and America. In its first, positivistic strand, analytic philosophers focused on the logical analysis of concepts and propositions that were thought to unlock the complex structures of reality itself. These positivistic philosophers not only aspired to scientific rigor in their logical analyses but viewed philosophy as essentially continuous with science, that is, as answering problems that arise directly out of the practice of science. In its second, post-positivistic strand, the preoccupation with, some would say fetishization of, science fell out of favor as analytic philosophers concentrated their attention instead on the concepts used by ordinary speakers, concepts that were supposed to be the keys to resolving long-standing philosophical disputes. Even in this second strand, however, analytic philosophers continued to define philosophy as a narrow technical subject that demanded a rigor approaching that of science.

What was problematic about this triumph of analytic philosophy in the Anglophone intellectual world, especially to aspiring subjects like sport philosophy, is that it narrowed the purview of philosophy and insulated its practice. This was apparent in a number of respects. To begin with, because analytic philosophers were caught up in the effort to develop an autonomous disciplinary matrix for philosophy, they not only withdrew from the rest of the Academy but from the larger public as well – content to converse with one another in a technical jargon largely unintelligible to non-specialists.[3] Secondly, in their effort to purify philosophic enquiry, to make it suitably rigorous, they successfully marginalized alternative forms of philosophic enquiry like Continental philosophy, which kept in closer touch with public social problems and stressed interpretation over verification. Finally, analytic philosophers were sufficiently strong in number and influence to establish new forms of graduate study, fully in place by the 1960s, which made the study of logic the centerpiece of the curriculum, de-emphasized the history of philosophy, and eliminated most requirements for the study of foreign languages (on the brash and plainly chauvinistic presumption that the only philosophical work worth reading was that authored by English-speaking philosophers on both sides of the Atlantic).[4]

In spite of these significant impediments, however, the tide slowly began to change and philosophers finally started to take notice of sport, play and game. Though this shift occurred ever so gradually, and, alas, with modest effect to date, it is no surprise that philosophy journals sympathetic to Continental philosophy (*Philosophy Today* and *Man and World* come immediately to mind), and that Paul Weiss, a major philosopher with ties to the American pragmatic movement who wrote the influential book *Sport: a Philosophic Inquiry* (1969), led the way. Weiss's book was arguably the more important influence here given his high acclaim in the philosophic community. Indeed, that a philosopher of Weiss's international reputation considered sport a topic worthy of his time and talents was not lost on his colleagues, even his analytically inclined colleagues.

It was not until the early 1970s, however, that the philosophy of sport got its sea legs. The crucial year here is 1972 , for that is the year in which scholars from both sports studies and philosophy banded together to form the Philosophic Society for the Study of Sport (PSSS), an international scholarly organization devoted to the philosophical analysis of sport. Paul Weiss was installed as its first president in the same year. In 1974 the Society began publishing the *Journal of the Philosophy of Sport*, which remains to this day the most important scholarly vehicle for the serious philosophic study of sport.

CONCEPTUAL OVERVIEW

While historical sketches are useful for charting the intellectual development of subjects like the philosophy of sport, they shed little light on the intellectual issues that preoccupy them and that distinguish them from one another. So we need to address straightaway just what are the central questions and abiding issues that concern philosophers of sport. I should say that trying to answer this question by coming up with a tight and convincing definition of the philosophy of sport will not prove helpful for the same reason it has not proved helpful to those who have sought a similar definition of philosophy. The reason is, as is apparent even from our brief historical overview, that philosophers tend to fret more about the nature, scope and aim of their intellectual craft, about what precisely it is that they do, than other intellectual workers in the vineyard, which means that their resultant conceptions of philosophy usually end up being contested rather than accepted. But, fortunately, this dissensus regarding the definition of philosophy need not concern us here, for while there is little accord over the definition of philosophy there is almost complete accord over the sorts of questions that philosophers pose and try to answer. This suggests that the best way to convey what the philosophy of sport is all about is to first attend to these central philosophical questions and, then, to consider their implications for cultural practices like sport.

The major questions that philosophers address are three in number and correspond to the three major branches of philosophic enquiry. The first question is 'What is reality?', and goes by the formal name of metaphysics. Metaphysical enquiry can assume any one of three forms depending on what is meant by 'reality' in the above question. Reality might refer to nature, in which case it is called cosmology; it might refer to a spiritual substratum of the material world, in which case it is called theology; finally, it might refer to some set of features of being-human, of the human condition, in which case it is called ontology. However, since the study of nature has for all intents and purposes been appropriated by the natural sciences, and theology and philosophy have gone their separate ways for roughly a century, the study of reality in philosophy today is largely an ontological matter, that is, a study of (human) being *qua* being.

The second major question that philosophers grapple with is 'What is knowledge?', which goes by the formal name of epistemology. As in the first question, this question can also be broken down into yet more particular questions. Thus, epistemologists might ask what constitutes valid knowledge and how can

it be distinguished from mere beliefs. Additionally, they might investigate how different knowledge-claims can be squared with one another and arranged in some logically coherent manner (for example, appeals to religious beliefs, scientific evidence, reasoned arguments, basic intuitions). And finally, they might enquire as to the means by which we obtain knowledge of things, whether, for example, knowledge is rooted in sense experiences and/or in abstract concepts that tell us what the world is really like and what other people who share that world with us are really like.

The third, and last, major question that philosophers probe is 'What is value?', which goes by the formal name of axiology. This question can be put in two more particular ways. In the first way, we understand value to mean judgments of goodness and badness, of right and wrong conduct. This way of framing the question is known as ethics, and the point of ethical enquiry is to enquire as to how people *ought* to treat one another, and in more collective terms, how people ought to comport themselves with regard to the common good (social and political ethics). So defined, ethics is a prescriptive rather than a descriptive form of enquiry, that is, it is concerned with how people *ought* to treat and relate to one another (with prescribing norms of conduct), rather than with how in *fact* they are treating and relating to one another (with describing prevailing norms of conduct). However, by value we also might mean judgments that have to do with matters of aesthetic worth and significance, with, for example, what qualifies a particular artifact or performance as a work of art as opposed to something else. Questions of this type involve the study of what is formally known as aesthetics.

Now if my supposition that the question 'What is the philosophy of sport?' can best be answered by considering what these three questions come to when asked of sport, then we should be able to make clear just what the abiding and controversial issues and concerns of this philosophical sub-field are with greater precision and effect. To begin at the beginning, then, with the metaphysics of sport, the principal question here is what makes a given physical activity a sporting activity as opposed to some other related human movement activity (play, game, dance)? In other words, what are the basic features that mark off sports from other forms of physical enterprise that ascribe value and significance to particular forms of human movement? This question gives rise to two other central questions: 'What differences and distinctions can be drawn between sport and other related human movement phenomena?' and, lastly, 'What similarities and commonalities can be drawn between sport and other related human movement phenomena?'

The main controversies that attend metaphysical investigations of sport fall into three areas. The first area has to do with the kind of conceptual analysis metaphysicians employ in their efforts to define sport. Critics like MacAloon (1991), for example, have attacked the kind of clarity and precision such philosophers seek in their definitional enquiries, a precision, he argues, that glosses over the messy but subtle historical shifts that mark our cultural conceptions of sport and that signal important changes in their meanings. This quest for certainty and contempt for imprecision explains, then, according to MacAloon, why philosophical definitions of sport are virtually useless, why it is that the lifeless abstractions that pass for definitions in such metaphysically freighted discourse fail to penetrate the historically embedded meanings of sport. Defenders of philosophical definitions of sport (Morgan and Meier, 1995: 3) counter such attacks as caricatures of the kind of clarity conceptual analyses of sport aspire to. They argue that while it is true that definitional enquiry does aim to cut through the messiness and imprecision of our historical conceptions of sport, the point of doing so is to explicate and sharpen those historical meanings not to bypass or to distort them. After all, much of what is said about sport in our cultural conversations, and this is especially true of forms of popular culture, is said in confused and politically charged ways that often conceal more than they reveal. So efforts to uncover such confusions and obfuscations are best understood, when, of course, properly undertaken, as ways of getting clear about what such historical shifts in our cultural notions of sport mean and signify rather than as attempts to seek after an impossible precision.

The second area of controversy regarding conceptual analyses of sport concerns whether cultural practices like sport are best defined in formalist terms (Suits, 1973), or contextualist terms (D'Agostino, 1981; Lehman 1981). Proponents of formalist definitions of sport maintain that the purpose, meaning and significance of sport practices can be read off of their formal rules. So what counts as playing a sport, as an action in a sport, as an instance of sport, and as winning in a sport are all determined, on this view, by citing the formal rules of that sport. Proponents of contextualist accounts of sport, contrarily, maintain that sport is defined by both its rules and its ethos. The ethos of sport has to do with those social conventions that govern how the rules of a sport are to be interpreted and applied in particular instances. Contextualists argue that we need to account for these social conventions in our definitions of sport because it is these conventions, and not the rules, that determine what counts in the final analysis as a legitimate instance of sport.

The third, and last, area of controversy dealing with conceptual analyses of sport has to do with a specific feature of definitional accounts of sport, with, that is, the particular relation between sports and games. In his seminal essay 'The Elements of Sport', Bernard Suits (1973) argued that the basic elements of games are essentially, but not totally, the same as the basic elements of sports, which he summed up in the claim that all sports are games but not all games are sports. However, in later papers (1988, 1989) Suits amended his earlier view of this relation, which in the meantime had become the received view, by arguing that only some sports are games. In particular, he argued that sports come in two varieties rather than, as he earlier argued, one: what he called 'athletic performances' (gymnastics, diving, free-style skiing) and 'athletic games' (soccer, basketball, baseball). He defined athletic performances as practices that are constituted by ideals of performance rather than means-limiting rules. It is because performances lack such rules that explains, according to Suits, why they are not games, and further why they do not require referees to ensure rule compliance but judges to assess the artistry of the performance – how closely it comes to its constitutive ideals. By contrast, athletic games are rule-governed practices in just the sense specified in Suits's earlier essay: they rule out certain useful ways of reaching their goals (it is useful, but forbidden to hand-carry the ball to the cup in golf). It is because these sports have such rules that explains, according to Suits, why they are games, and further why they require referees to check for rule observance as opposed to judges to check for excellence achieved. It was this reworking of his account of games and sports, then, that sparked a spirited debate between Suits and critics such as Kretchmar (1989) and Meier (1988, 1989), who argued that Suits had got it right the first time, that indeed all sports are games because all sports possess the requisite kind of means-limiting rules.

Turning to the epistemological study of sport, the central question here, or so the literature suggests, has to do with how one gains knowledge of human movement forms like sport. In short, must one have an actual, lived experience of sport to claim knowledge of it, or is it the case that one can gain such knowledge by other abstract, intellectual means, by reflection, for instance, on others' first-hand experiences of sport? A related question concerns the organization of knowledge appropriate to sport. The issue here is not the psychological one of when is someone (psychologically) ready to learn sporting skills or strategies, but the logical one of how different forms of knowledge of sport can be fitted together into some sort of coherent pattern (for example, a coherent curriculum).

It is difficult to say much more about this realm of sport philosophy since its literature is not well established – one important mark of which is that there are no controversies currently raging within it that might better define and enliven its study. This dearth of literature is not easy to explain, if only because epistemology is a dominant, some would say the dominant, topic in contemporary philosophy. Two explanations, however, might account for its underdeveloped status. The first is that questions regarding the logical organization and integrity of knowledge have been largely ceded to the philosophy of education and to what remains of the field of the philosophy of physical education, a field which, unlike the philosophy of sport, has always considered itself a subsidiary of the philosophy of education. In short, questions regarding the logical basis of curriculum theory have long ceased to be, if indeed they ever were, important concerns for philosophers of sport. The second reason why epistemological investigations of sport, especially those dealing with what kinds of knowledge are crucial to participation in sports, have not fared as well as other kinds of philosophical investigations of sport is that many potential enquirers may well have been persuaded by Paul Ziff's (1974) forceful thesis that sport poses no special or significant epistemological problems. Whatever the reason, however, it is regrettable that we do not have more studies like Steel's (1977) and Kretchmar's (1982), studies which have penetratingly analysed the kinds of 'tacit' knowledge and abstract thinking that go on in sport, and that have shown the striking parallels that obtain between these kinds of athletic knowing and, for example, those kinds of knowing particular to scientific practices.

The ethical study of sport, which, it will be remembered, is one offshoot of axiological (value) enquiry, pivots on two pressing and highly controversial questions. The first question asks how athletes should treat one another (and in the case of animal sports, how they should treat sentient beings) in a sport setting. The second question asks how athletes should comport themselves, individually and collectively, in their pursuit of athletic excellence; more specifically, it asks what forms of conduct and aids to performance are compatible with good (in the moral sense previously specified) athletic practice. The first question raises a host of issues that deal with sportsmanship, competition, cheating, gender issues, and finally, issues regarding the use of animals in sports. The second question raises a more limited set of issues that focus on the use of performance-enhancing drugs in sport and on the moral problems such usage poses.

The moral literature in sport, in stark contrast to its epistemological counterpart, is voluminous, and growing by leaps and bounds. This literature naturally divides into a number of clusters that correspond to the two questions just mentioned. The first cluster, which includes the work of Keating (1964), Arnold (1983), Feezell (1986) and Dixon (1992), deals with the issue of sportsmanship. In particular, it asks what sort of virtues and qualities it instantiates, and what specific forms of conduct it prescribes. The second cluster, which includes the work of Pearson (1973), Delattre (1975), Leaman (1981), Fraleigh (1982) and Hyland (1984), focuses on the competitive character and complexion of sport and the pervasive problem of cheating. More specifically, it asks what would constitute a morally defensible notion of competition; what would make for a morally corrupt form of competition; what counts as cheating; and what ought to be our moral posture toward cheating?

The third cluster examines gender issues in sport. This body of work, which includes the essays of English (1978), Belliotti (1979), Young (1979), Messner (1988), Francis (1993–4), Simon (1993–4) and Duncan (1994), takes up two main themes. The first has to do with how women's identities, their sense of themselves as individuated and socialized bodily beings, are constructed and deconstructed in practices like sport and exercise. The second has to do with the equally vexing issue of women's equity in sport. That is, how are women going to achieve equal opportunity in the world of sport when the very sports that dominate that world appear to privilege males (calling as they do on the typically male physical features of strength, power and speed) and to purvey distinctly masculine features of physical conduct (aggression and violence)?

The fourth cluster of essays, which includes such authors as Singer (1973), Regan (1983), King (1991) and Scherer (1991), explores the moral standing of animals (whether they have specific rights or particular properties that command our respect and regard) in order to assess the moral standing of sports that feature them as objects of athletic exploit. Three categories of animal sports come under scrutiny in this regard:

1 sports in which humans use animals in their athletic pursuits (equestrian events, horse racing, polo);
2 sports that pit humans against animals in tests of athletic mettle (hunting, fishing, bull fighting);
3 sports in which animals are pitted against other animals either in contests of deadly combat or in contests to assess superior animal athletic prowess (cock fighting, dog racing).

The fifth, and last, cluster of essays targets the use of drugs by athletes to boost their performance. This body of work, which includes the essays of Thompson (1982), Perry (1983), Brown (1984), Simon (1984), Lavin (1987) and Gardner (1989), examines three moral issues that are raised by such drug use in sports. The first issue concerns the hidden and not so hidden technical imperatives and values of high-performance sport that impel athletes to take drugs in spite of the obvious threats to physical, psychological and social well-being they involve. The second issue centers on the moral permissibility of using drugs to improve performance and of efforts to outlaw or, short of that, to carefully regulate such use. And the third and last issue looks into the moral justification of mandatory drug testing programs designed to detect, mainly for punitive purposes, the presence of both performance-enhancing and recreational drugs.

Studies of the aesthetic features of sport, which comprise the other major part of axiological enquiry, and which feature the works of Kupfer (1983), Cordner (1984, 1988), Roberts (1986) and Best (1995), focus on two main questions. The first concerns whether sports require an aesthetic reception, that is, a qualitative view of their forms of movement, grace and style, in order to understand adequately and appreciate fully what they are about. The second question asks whether certain sports might not only require an aesthetic regard but might themselves qualify as bona fide works of art. The issue here is not so much whether sports must be viewed mindful of their aesthetic properties, but rather whether sports are intentionally conceived and crafted for aesthetic effect, and whether they are, both structurally and contextually speaking, suited for such a purpose. For

even though there are many objects in the universe that summon our aesthetic attention (mountains, sunsets), only a select sub-set of those objects (namely, those created precisely to elicit such an aesthetic response) qualify as works of art. The question, then, is whether it makes more sense to lump sport in with this latter, more narrowly defined, category of artifacts or with the former, much larger, category of objects and artifacts.

A CONJECTURE REGARDING THE FUTURE OF PHILOSOPHY AND THE PHILOSOPHY OF SPORT

I want to close my historical and conceptual survey of the philosophy of sport with an upbeat prognosis of its future. My interest in doing so is not born of wishful thinking, of a desire to put this subject in a flattering light that belies the facts, but of contemporary developments within philosophy proper and the philosophy of sport that augur well, or so I argue, for their entwined future. Oddly enough, the first of the two developments I have in mind here actually takes a page out of philosophy's past, to be exact, out of its pragmatic American past, and insists, as it did earlier in this century, that cultures and their signature social practices have priority over philosophy, and that, therefore, the main job of philosophy is, in Dewey's words, to apply critical intelligence to the resolution of social problems. The second development concerns the recent upsurge of moral studies of sport, a trend apparent in our above review of its literature, which suggests further that the chief point of applying critical intelligence to the problems of social life is to get a better moral fix on these problems.

What do I mean by the priority of culture and its practices, and in what sense does it enjoin that philosophy be reconceived as a tool of social reform and renovation? Mainly this: that philosophy does not possess its own special stock of suprahistorical categories, categories which, while they belong to no particular culture or tradition or historical period, somehow hold the key to understanding every culture or tradition or historical period known to us. That means that in order to get a handle on these culturally laden, historically embedded categories and the language-games that enframe them, the philosopher has to get a handle on the forms of life that give them their meaning. This is what Wittgenstein (1953: 174) meant when he said that 'understanding a language-game is sharing a form of life', and that concepts are best thought of as 'patterns which recur, with different variations, in the weave of our life'.

If the concepts philosophers use to do their work derive from the forms of life they study, then it follows that the task of philosophy is the chastened one Dewey suggested above of solving social problems by critically interrogating those forms of life. For while philosophy has no special concepts, methodology, or vantage point of its own, it can respond critically to developments in society by comparing, contrasting and pointing up the internal strengths and weaknesses of the reasons, beliefs and values that inform society at any given time. All of this is anticipated in Rorty's (1995: 199) remark that 'philosophy is always parasitic on, always a reaction to, developments elsewhere in culture and society'. What the moral emphasis that characterizes much of the present work that is going on in sport philosophy contributes to this pragmatic turn in philosophy is two things: first, just as there are no super concepts there are no super practices. That means that the cultural developments philosophy responds to cannot and should not be confined to one sphere of culture (for conservatives, religion; for liberals, politics; and for dyed-in-the-wool analytic philosophers, science). Second, that the problems philosophy is and ought to be responsive to are not technical ones but moral ones, problems that call into question our divergent and even conflicting conceptions of social justice and of the 'good' life.

However, if philosophy is to play this forceful moral role, then issues regarding its disciplinary autonomy and professional standing will have to cease to be issues. They will have to cease to be issues because in order to fulfill its task as an instrument of social reform, philosophy will have to blur the boundaries that are said to separate it off from the likes of cultural and social criticism. What goes for philosophy proper here goes as well, of course, for the philosophy of sport. For if it is to make its larger mark in society then it, too, will be obliged to go historical and sociological with its moral concerns and not worry about whether in doing so it has transgressed its disciplinary boundaries. As I see it, the only real worry that should concern philosophers of sport as they go about their critical and moral work, and the same can be said of historians and sociologists of sport insofar as we are still able to make these distinctions, is whether or not they have sufficiently tapped the full range of cultural resources that the study of sport

makes available to them. In this, I concur with Gorn and Oriard's contention that 'the study of sport can take us to the very heart of critical issues in the study of culture and society', but add as a caveat: only if we let that study take us there.[5]

A final worry. In championing the recent pragmatic turn in philosophy and the moral emphasis that turn has taken in recent work in the philosophy of sport, it might be asked if I am, wittingly or not, championing a chauvinistic agenda for future work in both of these areas. After all, pragmatism is an American movement and thus reflects a distinctly American, and so a distinctly limited, vision of what philosophic work in sport ought to look like in the future. But I think this worry is unfounded and that it need not dampen our optimism about the future of the philosophy of sport. My reasons for thinking so are three – two of which I have lifted directly from Rorty. First, whereas it is true that pragmatism is an American phenomenon closely linked to the American experiment in liberal democracy, there is no reason to think, as Rorty (1982: 70) nicely puts it, 'that the promise of American democracy [and the pragmatic spirit that nourished it] will find its final fulfillment in America, any more than Roman law reached its fulfillment in the Roman Empire or literary culture its fulfillment in Alexandria'. Secondly, although pragmatism is largely an American invention, I think Rorty (1995: 203) is pretty much right when he says that philosophy is not well suited to nationalist expression, to narratives of national exploit (unlike philosophy, however, sport is an especially powerful form of nationalist expression).[6] Thirdly, and lastly, the pragmatic emphasis on cultural and social reform is already close in spirit to the public commitments that define much of continental European philosophy (it is, for example, common practice for philosophers and intellectuals on the continent to write for local newspapers and political opinion journals), and, in fact, has ignited a renewed interest in continental European philosophy. Appearances to the contrary, then, these three reasons all seem to indicate that this new pragmatic spirit of philosophy will flourish wherever it takes root, and so should boost our optimism and enthusiasm for the future of philosophy and the philosophy of sport.

NOTES

1   As we shall soon see, however, not everything about these times was propitious for

the emergence of the philosophy of sport as an academic subject.

2 This sketch of American philosophy is heavily indebted to Richard Rorty's discussion in *Consequences of Pragmatism* (1982), and to the section on analytic philosophy in the *Cambridge Dictionary of Philosophy* (Audi, 1995).

3 Gruneau has written perceptively and forcefully of the similar debilitating effects of the professionalization of sociology, effects of which, ironically, are manifest in the proliferation of academic subdisciplines like the sociology and philosophy of sport. See the introduction of his *Class, Sports, and Social Development* (1983). I will come back to this point when I consider the future directions of sport philosophy.

4 I can personally vouch for these changes in the graduate programs of philosophy departments. For when I was a Masters student in the late 1960s and early 1970s, and a doctoral student in the mid-1970s, courses in formal and informal logic dominated, and even when coursework was offered in ethics it consisted largely of conceptual analyses of concepts like the 'good'. In particular, I can vividly recall a meeting I had as a doctoral student with the chair of a philosophy department at a major university. When I informed him I wished to do a dissertation on Heidegger's theory of time, he began to squirm noticeably in his seat. And when I added that I planned to use Heidegger's notion of time to investigate certain features of sport, he almost fell out of his seat. Needless to say, it was not a productive meeting, and I never again mentioned my interests either in Heidegger or sport to him or to any of my other philosophy professors.

5 This is one, among other reasons, why we have decided at my home institution, the University of Tennessee, to move our sports studies concentration into a cultural studies unit.

6 This is, for example, one of my current major research interests.

REFERENCES AND FURTHER READING

Arnold, P. (1983) 'Three approaches toward an understanding of sportsmanship', *Journal of the Philosophy of Sport*, X: 61–70.

Audi, R. (1995) *Cambridge Dictionary of Philosophy*. Cambridge: Cambridge University Press.

Belliotti, R. (1979) 'Women, sex, and sports', *Journal of the Philosophy of Sport*, VI: 67–72.

Best, D. (1995) 'The aesthetic in sport', in W.J. Morgan and K.V. Meier (eds), *Philosophical Inquiry in Sport*. Champaign, IL: Human Kinetics. pp. 377–89.

Brown, M. (1984) 'Paternalism, drugs, and the nature of sports', *Journal of the Philosophy of Sports*, XI: 14–22.

Cordner, C. (1984) 'Grace and functionality', *British Journal of Aesthetics*, 24: 301–13.

Cordner, C. (1988) 'Differences between sport and art', *Journal of the Philosophy of Sport*, XV: 31–47.

D'Agostino, F. (1981) 'The ethos of games', *Journal of the Philosophy of Sport*, VIII: 7–18.

Delattre, E. (1975) 'Some reflections on success and failure in competitive athletics', *Journal of the Philosophy of Sports*, II: 133–9.

Dixon, N. (1992) 'On sportsmanship and "running up the score"', *Journal of the Philosophy of Sport*, XIX: 1–13.

Duncan, M. (1994) 'The politics of women's body images and practices: Foucault, the Panopticon, and *Shape* magazine', *Journal of Sports and Social Issues*, 18: 48–65.

English, J. (1978) 'Sex equality in sports', *Philosophy and Public Affairs*, 7: 269–77.

Feezell, R. (1986) 'Sportsmanship', *Journal of the Philosophy of Sports*, VIII: 1–13.

Fraleigh, W. (1982) 'Why the good foul is not good', *Journal of Physical Education, Recreation, and Dance*. pp. 41–2.

Francis, L. (1993–4) 'Title IX: Equality for Women's Sports?', *Journal of the Philosophy of Sports*, XX–XXI: 32–47.

Gardner, R. (1989) 'On performance-enhancing substances and the unfair advantage argument', *Journal of the Philosophy of Sports*, XVI: 59–73.

Gorn, E. and Oriard, M. (1995) 'Taking sports seriously (Point of View)', *Chronicle of Higher Education*. p. 52a.

Gruneau, R. (1983) *Class, Sports, and Social Development*. Amherst, MA: University of Massachusetts Press.

Hoberman, J. (1995) 'Sport and the technological image of man', in W.J. Morgan and K.V. Meier (eds), *Philosophical Inquiry in Sport*. Champaign, IL: Human Kinetics. pp. 202–8.

Hyland, D. (1984) 'Opponents, contestants, and competitors: the dialectic of sport', *Journal of the Philosophy of Sport*, XI: 63–70.

Hyland, D. (1990) *Philosophy of Sport*. New York: Paragon House.

Keating, J. (1964) 'Sportsmanship as a moral category', *Ethics*, LXXV: 25–35.

King, R. (1991) 'Environmental ethics and the case against hunting', *Environmental Ethics*, 13: 59–85.

Kretchmar, S. (1982) 'Distancing: an essay on abstract thinking in sport performances', *Journal of the Philosophy of Sport*, IX: 6–18.

Kretchmar, S. (1989) 'On beautiful games', *Journal of the Philosophy of Sport*, XVI: 34–43.

Kretchmar, S. (1994) *Practical Philosophy of Sport*. Champagne, IL: Human Kinetics.

Kupfer, J. (1983) *Experience as Art: Aesthetics in Everyday Life*. Albany, NY: State University of New York Press.

Lavin, M. (1987) 'Sports and drugs: are the current bans justified?', *Journal of the Philosophy of Sport*, XIV: 34–43.

Leaman, O. (1981) 'Cheating and fair play in sport', in W.J. Morgan (ed.), *Sport and the Humanities: a Collection of Original Essays*. Bureau of Educational Research and Service, University of Tennessee. pp. 25–30.

Lehman, C. (1981) 'Can cheaters play the game?', *Journal of the Philosophy of Sport*, VIII: 41–6.

MacAloon, J. (1991) 'Are Olympic athletes professionals? Cultural categories and social control in US sport', in P. Staudohar and J. Mangan (eds), *The Business of Professional Sports*. Urbana and Chicago: University of Illinois Press. pp. 264–97.

Meier, K.V. (1988) 'Triad trickery: playing with sports and games', *Journal of the Philosophy of Sport*, XV: 11–30.

Meier, K.V. (1989) 'Performance prestidigitation', *Journal of the Philosophy of Sport*, XVI: 13–33.

Messner, M. (1988) 'Sports and male domination: the female athlete as contested ideological terrain', *Sociology of Sport Journal*, 5: 197–211.

Metheny, E. (1968) *Movement and Meaning*. New York: McGraw-Hill.

Morgan, W.J. and Meier, K.V. (1995) *Philosophic Inquiry in Sport*. Champaign, IL: Human Kinetics.

Osterhoudt, R. (1991) *The Philosophy of Sport: an Overview*. Champaign, IL: Stipes.

Pearson, K. (1973) 'Deception, sportsmanship, and ethics', *Quest*, XIX: 115–18.

Perry, C. (1983) 'Blood doping and athletic competition', *The International Journal of Applied Philosophy*, 1: 39–45.

Regan, T. (1983) 'Why hunting and trapping are wrong', in T. Regan, *The Case for Animal Rights*. Berkeley, CA: University of California Press.

Roberts, T. (1986) 'Sport, art, and particularity: the best equivocation', *Journal of the Philosophy of Sport*, XIII: 49–63.

Rorty, R. (1982) *Consequences of Pragmatism*. Minneapolis: University of Minnesota Press.

Rorty, R. (1995) 'Philosophy and the future', in H.J. Saatkamp (ed.), *Rorty and Pragmatism: the Philosopher Responds to His Critics*. Nashville, TN: Vanderbilt University Press. pp. 197–205.

Scherer, D. (1991) 'Existence, breeding, and rights: the use of animals in sports', *Between the Species*, Summer: 132–7.

Simon, R. (1984) 'Good competition and drug-enhanced performance', *Journal of the Philosophy of Sport*, XI: 6–13.

Simon, R. (1993–4) 'Gender equity and inequity in athletics', *Journal of the Philosophy of Sport*, XX–XXI: 6–22.

Singer, P. (1973) 'Animal liberation', *The New York Review of Books*, 5 April.

Slusher, H. (1967) *Man, Sport, and Existence: a Critical Analysis*. Philadelphia: Lea & Febiger.

Steel, M. (1977) 'What we know when we know a game', *Journal of the Philosophy of Sport*, IV: 96–103.

Suits, B. (1973) 'The elements of sport', in R. Osterhoudt (ed.), *The Philosophy of Sport: a Collection of Original Essays*. Springfield, IL: Charles C. Thomas. pp. 48–64.

Suits, B. (1988) 'Tricky triad: games, play, and sport', *Journal of the Philosophy of Sport*, XV: 1–9.

Suits, B. (1989) 'The trick of the disappearing goal', *Journal of the Philosophy of Sport*, XVI: 1–12.

Thompson, P. (1982) 'Privacy and the urinalysis testing of athletes', *Journal of the Philosophy of Sport*, IX: 60–5.

Weiss, P. (1969) *Sport: a Philosophic Inquiry*. Carbondale: Southern Illinois Press.

Wittgenstein, L. (1953) *Philosophical Investigations*. Oxford: Basil Blackwell.

Young, I. (1979) 'The exclusion of women from sport: conceptual and existential dimensions', *Philosophy in Context*, 9: 44–53.

Ziff, P. (1974) 'A fine forehand', *Journal of the Philosophy of Sport*, I: 92–109.

13

POLITICS AND SPORT

Barrie Houlihan

In 1968, at the height of the protest against racial inequality in the United States, John Carlos and Tommy Smith gave the 'black power' salute while on the Olympic victory podium at the Mexico City Games. The protest outraged Avery Brundage, President of the International Olympic Committee, who had them expelled from the Games, but generated overwhelming support among the African American population. Twelve years later, the occasion of the Olympic Games was again used by Americans as a platform for protest. However, this time the protest was led by Jimmy Carter, President of the United States, and the eventual boycott was directed at the actions of the Soviet Union in invading Afghanistan in 1979. More recently, in 1994, six Catholics were killed by Unionist terrorist gunmen while they watched the Republic of Ireland play Italy in a soccer World Cup match at a local bar in Loughinisland, Northern Ireland.

There are many more examples that could be added to these three where politics and sport have intersected. Yet it is far from clear what criteria have to be fulfilled for a particular decision or set of actions to be classified as the intertwining of politics and sport. The above episodes include examples of individual protest, organized terrorism and government policy where sport has been used in part as a resource and in part as an arena for political action. The lack of uniformity in the three examples highlights the problem of providing a precise and inclusive definition of politics. For many, politics is defined in terms of the actions of government: the authoritative use of power to make rules and laws that have precedence over rules from other sources in society

(Moodie, 1984: 23). The focus for study would then be the process of governmental decision-making and policy implementation and involve, for example, an examination of the decision by the Argentine military government to spend 10 per cent of the country's national budget on preparations for hosting the 1978 soccer World Cup (Mason, 1995: 71) or the decision, in 1949, by Walter Ulbricht, State Council Chairman, to 'create an exemplary performance oriented sport culture' in the German Democratic Republic (Hoberman, 1984: 202). This view tends to confine politics to specific institutions or arenas such as parliaments, courts, cabinets, central committees and political parties.

In contrast, there are those who reject this focus on governmental processes as overly narrow and based upon an artificial, and largely unsustainable, distinction between the public and private spheres. For Renwick and Swinburn politics 'takes place wherever conflict exists about goals and the method of achieving those goals' (1987: 14). This is a view supported by Ponton and Gill, who argue that politics is about the arrangements for ordering social affairs and consequently 'the student of politics cannot in principle exclude the possibility of political activity in any sphere of human life at any level, from the smallest of groups, such as the nuclear family, to the activities of international organizations' (1993: 8). Such a broad definition has the virtue of allowing an examination of the use of power within a range of non-governmental sports organizations ranging from the IOC (International Olympic Committee) and the major international federations (IFs) through the domestic governing body to the local sports club.

A final complexity in any attempt to discuss the relationship between politics and sport is the need to acknowledge that the definition adopted is itself an ideological product. It is not surprising that in liberal democracies the primary unit of political analysis is usually the individual, as reflected in Lasswell's often-quoted definition of politics as concerning 'who gets what, when and how' (1958), or society, as indicated by Crick's definition which sees politics as a way of 'ruling divided societies' (1964: 14). Marxists, however, would reject both these conceptualizations in favour of one that viewed politics as a reflection of class power and a phenomenon particular to capitalist societies (Callinicos, 1984).

There is little to be gained by attempting to engineer a consensus from these competing conceptualizations of politics. Rather, it is important to acknowledge the variety of definitions and the tensions that exist between them. For present purposes a distinction will be made between politics *and* sport and politics *in* sport. The study of politics *and* sport directs our attention to the use made by governments of sport and the process by which public policy is made and implemented. In democratic states our attention is focused on the interplay of political parties, representative bodies and interest groups in shaping policy outcomes. In authoritarian regimes our attention may be drawn, for example, to the interaction between the state bureaucracy and the ruling elite. For all regimes, whether democratic or not, we would also be concerned to identify the policy objectives that the government hoped to achieve through intervention in sport. The study of politics *and* sport is therefore concerned largely with an examination of the relationship of politics to sport in the public domain defined by recognized institutions of state.

A focus on the politics *in* sport is predicated upon a view of politics which does not recognize the demarcation between the public and the private and which treats politics as a ubiquitous aspect of all social institutions, including schools, sports clubs and governing bodies. Within this conceptualization, the power to act politically is derived from a variety of resources, including expertise, money and legitimacy, which are distributed across a wide range of social institutions. A focus on politics *in* sport leads to a consideration of issues concerned with the way in which organizations use power to pursue their own sectional interests at the expense of other social groups. Issues of gender equity, racial discrimination

and class advantage would all be legitimate foci for examination.

While consideration of government policy and the politics of the Olympic movement, for example, will be found in most recent social scientific studies of sport, the explicit examination of the relationship between politics and sport is comparatively recent. However, this omission is not due to a wilful myopia by political scientists as few of the social sciences can boast a significant literature dealing with sport before the 1970s. For students of politics the stimulus for interest in sport was a product of two major issues in international politics, namely the Cold War and the campaign against apartheid in South Africa. The return of the Soviet Union to Olympic competition in the early 1950s and its subsequent domination of the Summer Games during the 1960s, and the use of sport by 'East Germany' for purposes of nation-building and the promotion of its claim to recognition as the German Democratic Republic, created an awareness of the value of sport as a political resource. The use of sport by the communist bloc also acted as a stimulus to the development of public policy towards sport in Western Europe and the major democracies. The development of the international campaign against apartheid in sport reinforced the perception of sport as a valuable political resource. Both the Cold War and the anti-apartheid campaign raised the profile of the International Olympic Committee and the major international federations as potential, if not actual, actors in international politics.

Paralleling the rise in the profile of sport in international politics, but also stimulated by it, was a growing concern with equity issues in sport. The initial emphasis was on racial equality in sport and was most powerfully expressed by Edwards (1970; but see also Davis, 1966) in a study that contextualized the Carlos and Smith protest at the 1968 Olympic Games. By the late 1970s the focus on racial equality was complemented by similar concerns related to gender (see, for example, Mitchell, 1977), class (see, for example, Brohm, 1978; Hoch, 1972; James, 1963) and space (see, for example, Bale, 1989, 1994; Dulles, 1965; Hardy, 1981). Although the broadening of the focus on politics and sport may be seen as a dilution of the analysis of public policy and the role of the state, it may also be argued that the wider focus enables a more sophisticated examination of the inter-penetration of sporting and non-sporting organizations and the public and private spheres of social activity.

POLITICS AND SPORT: THE ROLE OF THE STATE

Attempting to make generalizations about the role of the state in sport should be a daunting prospect. Variations in political systems, wealth, sports traditions, educational systems and the extent of non-state institutional complexity should produce patterns of public policy characterized by their diversity rather than similarity. Yet it is surprising how similar public policy outputs are irrespective of whether the state is authoritarian or democratic, affluent or poor, or politically stable or volatile. For some, the similarity of state intervention in sport, particularly in capitalist economies, is explained as the product of class conflict and the state's strategic concern to protect bourgeois class interests and to 'rigorously [regulate] the use made of free time through the state repressive apparatus' (J.A. Hargreaves, 1985: 220; see also Brohm, 1978 for a similar analysis). A contrary view is that of Travis, who sees the accumulation of sport policy outputs as an incremental process that 'should not be seen as a normative planning and management process', but rather as 'a scatter of isolated legislation' (1979: 1 and 2). Between the Marxist explanation of policy similarity as the product of the structural tensions inherent in capitalist systems and an explanation that views policy choice as more haphazard, it is important to note the likely impact of diffusion in explaining policy similarity. For the vast majority of countries public policy relating to sport is a postwar concern, when the opportunities to borrow policy solutions were comparatively easy.

One of the earliest modern forms of policy intervention in sport was in order to control or outlaw particular sports. In Britain and the United States legislation has been used to outlaw blood sports (Gorn and Goldstein, 1993; Holt, 1989), while professional boxing is illegal in Sweden. Generally, explicit legislative intervention by governments to prohibit or promote particular sports is rare. However, governments are coming under increasing pressure, both domestically and from international sports bodies and some international governmental organizations, to regulate aspects of sport such as drug abuse, the freedom of movement of sportsmen and women between teams, the behaviour of monopolistic leagues, and the treatment of young athletes (Wilson, 1994). The success of the IOC's anti-doping campaign requires close cooperation with governments while the recommendations

of the Council of Europe on ethics in sport rely on government support for effective implementation.

A second motive for government involvement which pre-dates the postwar enthusiasm for more systematic state intervention was the improvement of military preparedness. The poor quality of conscripts during the First World War and the conventional assumption that the next major war would be similarly labour-intensive led many countries to introduce legislation aimed at improving the quality of volunteer recruits and conscripts. Canada, Britain and France all used legislation in the 1930s or early 1940s to create opportunities for physical training and fitness. Although the military rationale for government involvement in sport declined in prominence in the 1950s, it remained significant in those countries where territorial security was perceived to be still under threat. In the Soviet Union, for example, the GTO (Ready for Labour and Defence) scheme, which provided a framework for sports development for most of the Soviet period, contained shooting as one of the set range of sports up until the decline of the GTO in the late 1980s.

A third domestic motive for state involvement in sport (and one of the most common) is the belief that participation in sport facilitates social integration. Social integration is a loose term which can cover a diverse range of policy objectives including combating juvenile delinquency, establishing a sense of community during periods of rapid urbanization and the integration of diverse ethnic groups. For some, social integration is extended beyond simple social stability and is defined as integration into the work routines of a capitalist/industrial economy through an acceptance of the codification, rationalization and authority structures (governing bodies) of modern sport (Brohm, 1978; Gruneau, 1983; J.A. Hargreaves, 1982; J.E. Hargreaves, 1986; Hoberman, 1984; Mandell, 1984). In Britain, successive governments have invested in sports facilities and programmes as a solution to urban unrest (Coghlan, 1990; Henry, 1993; Houlihan, 1991) and in Northern Ireland there was an extensive programme of investment in public sport and recreational facilities aimed at bridging the gap between the Catholic/nationalist and Protestant/unionist communities (Sugden and Bairner, 1993). In France sport was seen as making a contribution to 'social discipline and a means of regenerating French youth' (Holt, 1981: 58). A similar motivation for government involvement may be found in an analysis of

Chinese (PRC) public policy where sport cultivates 'a sense of collective honour and the virtues of unity and mutual effort' (Xie, 1990: 30) and also in the development of policy in Brazil (Lever, 1983; Levine, 1980), and in Argentina (Humphrey, 1994; Krotee, 1979; Mason, 1995). However, while there are some who argue strongly for the integrative effect of sport (Lever, 1983), it must be acknowledged that sport has also provided an opportunity for political opposition, especially in repressive regimes. The support given by Muscovites to Spartak Moscow, the soccer team that was not sponsored by either the security services (as Dynamo Moscow was) or the army (as CSKA Moscow was), carried with it an implicit gesture of opposition to the communist establishment. In a similarly repressive South Africa, the visits by foreign teams provided black South Africans with the opportunity to voice their opposition to the white government by cheering for the visitors, whoever they happened to be. Finally, support for the Barcelona soccer team during the period of Franco's dictatorship, particularly when playing Real Madrid, symbolized not only Catalonian opposition to rule from Madrid, but also opposition to the absence of democracy.

A closely associated domestic motive concerns the attempt to use sport to build a sense of national identity. Irish history probably provides the first example of sport being used as a political resource in a nationalist and anticolonial movement. The role of the Gaelic Athletic Association in the late nineteenth and early twentieth centuries in promoting traditional ethnic sports and challenging English cultural hegemony, and the use of sport from 1922 by the newly established independent Irish state to reinforce its identity is well documented (Mandle, 1977, 1987). More recently an increasingly wide range of states have sought to promote nation-building and to overcome the centrifugal forces of strengthening ethnic identity. The Soviet Union attempted to use sport to submerge a broad range of ethnic communities within a Soviet identity (Riordan, 1978, 1988). During the period from 1968 to the late 1980s the Canadian federal government invested heavily in sport in order, in part, to develop symbols of national identity to which both the francophone and anglophone communities could subscribe (Macintosh et al., 1987).

Using sport as a source of unifying symbolism has also proved attractive to a very broad range of ex-colonies who often face the problem of having to cope with arbitrarily imposed territorial boundaries and ethnic diversity. Cultural reference points derived from military history or religion are often sources of division, thus making the malleability, low cost and high media visibility of sport especially attractive to poorer states. However, the use of sport for nation-building purposes tends to skew public investment away from facilitating mass participation and towards a narrow focus on a very limited range of elite sports. For example, Peru spent 80 per cent of its national sports budget on women's volleyball (Anthony, 1991: 332; see also Morton, 1982, and Peppard and Riordan, 1993 for similar conclusions relating to the Soviet Union). There is also considerable ambiguity regarding the effectiveness of sports symbolism in nation-building with the need to set the success of Irish sportive nationalism against the clear failure of attempts to use sport for nation-building in the former East Germany, the former Soviet Union, the former Yugoslavia and Canada. Finally, the ease with which subnational groups can exploit the symbolism of sport to further their separatist claims is amply demonstrated in Northern Ireland, Catalonia and Quebec (Broom, 1986; Hargreaves, 1996; Sugden and Bairner, 1993) and tends to suggest that it is easier to reinforce a bottom-up ethnic identity through sport than to support top-down state management of identity through sport.

Closely related to the use of sport for nation-building was the use of international sport to project a positive image of the nation abroad. If governments were solely concerned with reinforcing national distinctiveness and unity then they would be more inclined to foster the idiosyncratic and unique features of the ethnic culture. However, modern states want not only national unity and distinctiveness but also an international stage on which to project that identity. Hence the paradox of states utilizing an increasingly common array of cultural symbols (flags, currencies, anthems, stamps, armed forces, military uniforms and Olympic sports) to demonstrate their individuality. Success in sports events, and particularly the hosting of sports events, provides a benign and uncritical backdrop for the parade of national achievement. As Mandell noted 'the Soviets learned … that socialist citizens cannot cheer industrial Stakhanovites in stadiums and that there are no international festivals for steel workers' (1976: 262, quoted in Cantelon, 1982). The intensive investment in recent years by Britain, Canada and Australia in elite programmes and specialist academies confirms the continuing allure of international sporting success.

A more recent motive for government involvement is to support economic development. At a national strategic level Mexico, Japan and South Korea used the hosting of the Olympic Games as opportunities to project images of modern technological and organizationally sophisticated societies and economies. Other states have selectively developed those sports that helped to promote tourism. In Ireland, for example, the government has invested heavily in the provision of opportunities for golf, fishing and long-distance walking routes following tourist board surveys which found that one-third of all tourists participated in sport when on holiday and that the availability of sports opportunities influenced their holiday choice. However, it is more common for bids to host major sports events to be part of a regional or metropolitan economic strategy. The link between 'civic boosterism' and sport in the United States and Canada is well documented (Baade and Dye, 1988; Johnson, 1985, 1986, 1993; Riess, 1989; Scully, 1995) and is also evident in Japan (Horne and Jary, 1994; McCormack, 1991) and many Western European countries.

As should be clear from the above discussion, it is not always possible to isolate the domestic from the foreign policy motives for state intervention in sport. The rapid internationalization of sports competition in the past 50 years and the advances in media technology of the past 30 years have combined to make sport an increasingly attractive diplomatic resource. Its primary attraction to governments lies in its combination of high visibility and low cost. However, while some argue that sport provides a versatile and effective resource (Houlihan, 1994; Macintosh and Hawes, 1994) others would agree with Kanin (1980) that sport is peripheral to international relations and provides, at best, weak symbolism. Nevertheless, sports diplomacy retains its attraction to governments, partly because international sport adds to the repertoire of tools available for the pursuit of foreign policy goals but also because of the subtlety and malleability of sports diplomacy.

One of the most significant uses of sports diplomacy is as a device for building closer relationships between enemies. The most celebrated example of this use of sport occurred in the early 1970s when, as part of the gradual thawing of relations between the People's Republic of China and the United States, the latter sent a table tennis team to the PRC, followed a year later by a basketball team. The sports were carefully chosen for their diplomatic value. The USA was not a highly ranked table tennis nation, whereas the PRC had consistently produced some of the world's finest players. As the USA was not expected to win, its defeat would not result in any loss of prestige. Similarly, basketball is a minority sport in China and no loss of dignity would be attached to a Chinese defeat (Kropke, 1974). These sporting exchanges were an acceptable means for building contacts between the two countries, a process which led, in 1972, to the visit by President Nixon (Nafziger, 1978). Sport was used in a similar fashion during a period of great tension between the United States and the Soviet Union. In the late 1950s US troops were in the Lebanon and British forces were in Jordan ostensibly to forestall Soviet expansion, and Khrustchev talked of the world being on the brink of catastrophe. At the same time the USA and the USSR initiated an annual track and field competition which, while at times reflecting the tensions of the Cold War, generally provided opportunities for diplomatic bridge-building (Peppard and Riordan, 1993).

Sport is more commonly used as a means of maintaining good relations with allies or neighbours. The importance of the Commonwealth Games has increased as the significance of the Commonwealth in global politics has declined (Houlihan 1994). The quadrennial francophone games provide France with an important opportunity to renew its past colonial links and also to promote its claims to a global role. Rather than organizing specific sports events, the Soviet Union undertook an elaborate programme of bilateral sporting contacts with its non-communist neighbouring states and Warsaw Pact allies as part of a strategy of sports diplomacy (Peppard and Riordan, 1993). Similarly, but on a much smaller scale, the United States pursued sporting links with states in Central and South America as well as with Japan in the period leading up to the Second World War (Crepeau, 1980). President Harding hoped that continued sporting contact through baseball between Japan and the United States would help to improve relations (Sinclair, 1985). Unfortunately the power of baseball was not as great as Harding had hoped.

A more common use of sport is as a means of registering disapproval of a state's actions, either through attempts to isolate a state from international sporting competition or by the boycott of particular sports events. In 1995 Nigeria was the most recent state to be subject to sports sanctions because of its continued and serious abuse of human rights. But using sport as a sanction has a long history and includes the decision not to invite the major defeated states to the Olympic Games that followed the two world wars, and the Soviet Union's withdrawal from the 1974 World Cup rather than play against Chile so soon after the military overthrow of the democratically elected communist government of Salvador Allende.

A major illustration of the use of sports sanctions followed the invasion, in 1979, of Afghanistan by the Soviet Union. The invasion prompted a chorus of international criticism mainly because Afghanistan was considered to be outside the Soviet Union's traditional sphere of influence. The dilemma facing the USA was how to demonstrate its disapproval while not disrupting, too seriously, the delicate relationship between the two superpowers. According to Kanin 'Sport, that most peripheral and most publicised form of international relations, provided the perfect answer' (1980: 6). President Carter decided that boycotting the forthcoming Olympic Games to be hosted by the Soviet Union would be an appropriate diplomatic response. Despite the logic of a sport boycott being almost as unclear as the USA's diplomatic objectives, Carter eventually secured a boycott by 62 states, including Japan, PRC, West Germany and Canada.

The boycott of the 1980 Moscow Games is only one of a number of occasions when sport has been used to show diplomatic displeasure. Both South Africa and Israel have been faced with concerted attempts to exclude them from world sport. The attempt to isolate South Africa because of its policy of apartheid is well documented (Booth, 1998; Guelke, 1986, 1993; Kidd, 1988; Krotee, 1988; Lapchick, 1979). The South African case is important for a number of reasons, particularly because it provides an opportunity to consider the value of international sport as a resource in diplomacy and the interaction of domestic sport policy with the actions of international political actors. Much has been made of the powerful symbolism of sport to white South Africans, but an undermining of the opportunity to experience that symbolism through the application of a boycott was, in itself, an irritation rather than a major threat to apartheid. More important was the way in which the groups opposed to apartheid used international sport as an activity, and international sports organizations as fora, to promote the issue of apartheid. In essence the anti-apartheid organizations, especially the South African Non-Racial

Olympic Committee (SAN-ROC), successfully orchestrated a highly public debate on sports apartheid to establish the immorality of the regime and used the more easily accessed international sports bodies, such as the IOC, the Commonwealth Games Federation and the IAAF, as stepping-stones to more powerful organizations such as the Commonwealth Heads of Government Meetings and the United Nations. Sport's value was therefore primarily in providing a point of access to the agendas of major global political actors.

Israel has much in common with South Africa: both have been faced with hostile neighbours, both are relatively powerful in their region (and, in Israel's case, has powerful allies), and both have had to contend with sustained campaigns to exclude them from international sport. In the early years of Israel's existence it sent athletes and teams to a number of international sports competitions, including the regional Asian Games which take place under the auspices of the IOC (Simri, 1983). In 1962, however, the Games were awarded to the predominantly Muslim country of Indonesia which, despite expressions of goodwill, failed to allow Israeli athletes to participate. Israel attended the next two Asian Games (both in Bangkok) but the earlier problems recurred when the Games were awarded to Iran in 1974. Although Israeli athletes did attend they were faced with some boycotts by individual athletes. More worrying for Israel was the emergence of a concerted attempt to exclude them from future competitions. Between 1974 and 1976 Israel was excluded from the Asian Football Confederation (soccer) and from participation in future Asian Games. Israel's experience highlights the particular role of international sports organizations, such as the IOC and FIFA. Both these organizations expressed their opposition to Israel's exclusion but backed away from expelling the countries supporting the boycott, thus avoiding a direct confrontation with Asian, and particularly Islamic, sports organizations.

The politics of the Israeli sports boycott is still inadequately researched and the definitive analysis of the attempt to isolate South Africa from world sport has yet to be written. Both would provide valuable insights into the utility (and limitations) of sport as a diplomatic resource. Even a brief review of the US boycott of the Moscow Olympic Games makes apparent the variation in the interweaving of sporting and foreign policy objectives in different states. The response to Carter's call for a boycott provides an interesting insight into the motives for the decisions made by the targeted states and the extent to which sport is a cipher for the underlying pattern of relations between states. In Europe, for example, France, traditionally suspicious of US motives, opposed the boycott, as did traditionally neutral Ireland; Finland, probably due to its close proximity to the Soviet Union and its delicate relationship with the superpower, also opposed the boycott; Greece, hoping to become the permanent host of the Games was also opposed; the British government strongly supported the Americans, but could not convince its athletes who, with some exceptions, decided to attend. Outside Europe, in South America for example, the boycott call was also interpreted with regard to foreign policy priorities. For most South American states it was the superpower to the north rather than the Soviet Union that was the cause of greatest concern. Consequently, apart from Chile, all other countries accepted the Soviet invitation to Moscow, some, no doubt, desiring to demonstrate their independence from the USA and others with an eye on their standing in the non-aligned movement.

Just as sport can be used as a vehicle for registering disapproval of a state, it can also be an effective vehicle for signalling the re-admission of a state to the 'international community'. The hosting of the 1964 Olympic Games by Tokyo marked the state's return to diplomatic respectability. The location of the 1972 Games in Munich, a centre of National Socialism, not only indicated West Germany's status as a trusted member of the 'West', but also helped lay the ghost of Nazism. More recently, the visit by the South African cricket team to India in November 1991 and the attendance of a South African team at the Barcelona Olympic Games in 1992 confirmed the emergence of a new non-racial South Africa.

Reviewing the use of sport in diplomatic relations one is tempted to agree with Kanin and those who see sport as part of the ephemera of international relations. According to this view, sport may be dismissed as a low-cost, low-threat resource to be used casually by governments. The assessment of Peppard and Riordan differs insofar as they see positive sports diplomacy as being valuable, but not necessarily successful. 'Negative sport diplomacy, on the other hand, is virtually guaranteed to fail, because the breaking off of sporting relations or the announcement of a boycott can serve only as an expression of righteous indignation, which cannot change

the conduct of the country against which it is directed' (1993: 81). These views are overly pessimistic. By concentrating on the capacity of sports boycotts to change the behaviour of the target state they underplay the range of other functions that the diplomatic activity surrounding the boycott can fulfil. Taking the Moscow boycott as an example, it was important in providing an opportunity for a large number of states to send diplomatic signals to each other on a very public stage. States used the episode to demonstrate independence and/or solidarity, to build stronger links with particular states or groups of states or to loosen ties with particular power blocs, and to demonstrate commitment to causes. The call for a Moscow boycott provided a major arena for the exchange of diplomatic information within a low-risk context. In other words, one could argue that the lead-up to the 1980 Olympic Games enabled states to try out developments in foreign policy when the stakes were relatively low. It should also be borne in mind that while the Moscow boycott may confirm the sceptical view of negative sports diplomacy held by Peppard and Riordan, it is less easy to dismiss the contribution of sports sanctions to the ending of apartheid in South Africa.

A different motive for the utilization of sports diplomacy is for the promotion of individual state interests. Clearly the response to the various boycott campaigns was mediated by self-interest: but for many states they were reacting to the initiatives of others. Sport also provides a number of opportunities for the pursuit of a range of foreign policy objectives. Mention has already been made of the perceived value of hosting major sports events, particularly the soccer World Cup and the Olympic Games. Some states, such as Cuba (Sugden et al., 1990), have also used sport to assert the superiority of their ideology, while others, such as the PRC, have used sport to support their claim to global or regional diplomatic leadership (Pauker, 1964; Sie, 1978). Others, who have more limited diplomatic resources and more limited diplomatic aspirations, will use sport as a cheap and easily deployed resource. Very often the objective of sports diplomacy is simply to seek acknowledgement of their existence within the international system. Many of the sub-Saharan states found in apartheid an issue which brought with it the advantages of regional unity and a voice at the Commonwealth Heads of Government meetings and the United Nations that they otherwise would not have had. The two clearest examples of states using sport to further their foreign policy objectives concern East Germany and the PRC. The GDR, with powerful support from the USSR and the other Warsaw Pact states, used its 'diplomats in track suits' to pursue its claims to formal diplomatic recognition very successfully (Strenk, 1978 and 1980). In a similar fashion, both the PRC and Taiwan used sport as an element in their struggle for recognition of their claims to each other's territory (Chan, 1985; Guttman, 1984).

POLITICS IN SPORT

The discussion so far has made clear the variety of domestic and foreign policy motives that lead governments to use sport as a resource. As should also be clear, governments frequently seek to achieve their policy objectives through the cooperation (whether willing or otherwise) of sports organizations. At the domestic level the attempts by many governments to solve, in part, social or economic problems of urban decay through sport requires liaison with sports-governing bodies and local clubs whose cooperation is often achieved through the manipulation of tax arrangements or grant conditions. Similarly, international organizations, such as the IOC, FIFA and the IAAF, are subject to intense political pressure by governments and interest groups. However, to conceptualize the relationship as one where branches of the state politicize sports organizations by drawing them into a process of political bargaining and competition for power over decisions would be to misunderstand and romanticize the objectives and operation of sports organizations. Some sports bodies, such as the IOC and the Commonwealth Games Federation, have either explicit political goals as part of their charter, as has the IOC, or have an explicit political rationale in their origin, as with the CGF. Other sports bodies are an integral part of the state bureaucracy either because of the authoritarian nature of the regime or, more commonly, because of the problems of establishing an independent organizational structure for sport without state financial support. But even those organizations that eschew formal references to political objectives or are financially independent of the state are none the less immersed in a range of political issues that arise within sport itself.

If Lasswell's definition of politics, that it is concerned with the study of 'Who gets what when and how', is accepted, then it is impossible to ignore the significance of sports organizations in affecting access to, and the nature of, sports opportunities for individual sportsmen and women or of groups which may be defined, for example, geographically, or by sport or gender: they are in effect part of what Wilson aptly refers to as the private government of sport. Among the issues which currently dominate the character of politics in sport are commercialization, gender, and race and ethnicity. None of these issues is discrete; each overlaps and intertwines with the other, and each has both a domestic and a global political aspect. As most of these issues are discussed elsewhere it will be sufficient to identify the main contours of the debates.

Commercialization involves examining sport as both a source of profit and also as a vehicle for the transmission of capitalist values. For a growing number of multinational corporations (such as Kodak, American Express and British Airways) sport sponsorship is part of a global marketing strategy for non-sports goods and services. Other corporations, particularly the major television companies, have a closer interest in sports programmes as products, but they also see sport as a means of selling advertising. Thirdly, there is a set of corporations, such as Adidas, Nike and Puma, that produce sports goods and have a clear interest in the growth in interest in the particular sports they manufacture for. Fourthly, all capitalist enterprises have an interest in the capacity of sport to contribute to the assimilation of capitalist values in general and consumerist values in particular. Finally, there are the sports organizations, ranging from individual clubs and leagues to the IOC and the major national and international federations, who operate in an increasingly competitive environment and are concerned to secure a growing market share for their particular club, sport or group of sports.

The impact of the growth in for-profit clubs and leagues, the increase in sponsorship, the purchase of television rights and the expanding world market for sports goods on the development of sport has been considerable and includes changes to the rules of sports to suit sponsors (Goldlust, 1988; Whannel, 1992), the marginalizing of non-Western and especially non-Olympic sports (Glassford, 1981; Paraschak, 1991), and the undermining of the ethical basis of sport in the interest of more dramatic (aggressive) and more sensational sport (Coakley, 1998; Lawrence, 1986)). At a broader level, the increased commercialization of sport raises the prospect of continued asset-stripping of poorer countries and their reduction to a market for imported sports. Increasingly, Africa and South America are becoming sources of sporting talent for the rich countries. Most top-class Brazilian soccer players play abroad (five of the national squad in the mid-1990s played their soccer in the Japanese league) (Mason, 1995); nearly all the successful Cameroon side in the 1990 World Cup played their professional soccer outside their home country, and the Dominican Republic has long been a source of elite players for the North American baseball league (Klein, 1991). Whether the sporting relations between business and rich and poor countries are best defined as cultural imperialism or some less clearly articulated form of cultural globalization, it is clear that power is being deployed in a way that promotes the interests of some organizations, especially the MNCs, at the expense of others. Apart from the vulnerability of economically weak countries, the other potential victims of increasing commercialization are the domestic and international governing bodies whose control over sport is undermined by their need to attract sponsors, the increasing pressure from athletes for a greater share of commercial income and a greater say in decision-making, and from the growth in profit-orientated clubs and leagues. The future direction and impact of commercialism, the consequences of greater commercial sponsorship for state patronage and the long-term consequences for governing bodies are all issues that require further investigation.

A second major issue within sport is the question of equality of access, and especially the relationship between gender and race, and sporting opportunity. Much has already been written about the discrimination against women's sport and women in sport, the slow pace of change and the degree of inequality that remains (J.A. Hargreaves, 1994; Hult, 1989). There is a similarly large literature on race and ethnicity and sport (Eitzen, 1989; Hoberman, 1997; Lapchick, 1988; Schneider and Eitzen, 1989). Both these aspects of sport are covered in detail in this volume, and it is sufficient here to emphasize the extent to which both these dimensions of inequality are intensely political insofar as they can have a profound impact on individual choice and career opportunity. For both ethnic minorities and women there has been a general, if slow, improvement in opportunities to compete both in domestic leagues and at the highest international level. However, significant progress remains to be made in terms of access to

coaching, administration and management in sport. The most significant gap, though, is the level of representation in those organizations that exercise increasing influence over the future shape and direction of sport, namely the television companies, corporate marketing units and sports goods manufacturing companies.

That there are still important debates about the practice of 'stacking' (the location of black athletes in particular team positions due to stereotypical assumptions about temperament and ability), and the particular sports deemed suitable for women is a reflection of the continuing salience of these issues to the achievement of greater equality of opportunity in sport. However, what is worthy of note is the extent to which these issues have remained the subject of domestic, rather than international, politics. Few international federations or organizing bodies have given prominence to racism and sexism on their policy agendas beyond ritual condemnation. There are three possible reasons for this omission. The first is that the issue of equality has a low priority in the IOC and the major international federations as illustrated by the general reluctance of the international sports bodies to adopt a clear policy on apartheid and South African involvement in international sport. The second is that the high profile of the apartheid issue enabled most sports bodies to claim the moral high ground on an issue tightly focused on one particular state. In other words, opposition to apartheid was seen as obviating the need for more elaborate policy statements on similar forms of discrimination. Finally, action to ensure equality of access to sports competition for women has been inhibited by the unwillingness to risk offending Islamic states and losing their considerable financial contributions to Asian sport.

FUTURE THEMES

The likely future themes in the study of politics and sport can be divided into two categories: first, continuing and emerging political issues within sport; and secondly, developments in the political environment of sport. As regards the first category, the issue of equality of access in sport, particularly at international level, is likely to emerge as increasingly significant. The theme will be expressed in a number of different ways, including challenges to the continuing Eurocentrism of many international sports bodies, particularly the IOC, the relative under-representation of athletes from poorer countries at elite levels, and the limitation on the opportunities for women to participate in sport and its organization.

The second issue concerns anti-doping policy. By contrast to the issue of equality of access, the major international sports bodies have made significant efforts, in conjunction with a number of governments, to construct a policy aimed at eliminating drug abuse by athletes. In recent years the introduction of out-of-season testing and the development of international testing teams have greatly strengthened the anti-doping policy. The major problem lies in the implementation of the policy and especially whether the IOC and the major federations have both the resources and the will to support the policy. Resources are necessary to ensure that testing procedures keep pace with the increasing sophistication of drug abusers. More importantly, the major sports organizations will need sufficient resources to ensure compliance and coopera-tion by individual governments. Finally, the IOC and the IAAF in particular will need to continue to demonstrate that they have the will to implement the policy rigorously. There remain serious doubts regarding each of these aspects of policy implementation. There is little indication that either the IOC, the major feder-ations or individual governments are commit-ting sufficient resources to research to ensure that the newer, hormone-based drugs, can be detected accurately. There are also growing doubts that the scale of penalties agreed by international sports bodies can be applied uni-formly in member states. The attempt to impose four-year bans on German athletes foundered on the decision of the German courts. Finally, it is questionable whether the IOC and the federations are prepared to move beyond a cosmetic response to the problem. Much of the evidence given to the Dubin Enquiry (1990) following Ben Johnson's failure of a drug test at the 1988 Seoul Olympics and the account given by Voy (1991) suggest that there is, at the very least, a lack of firm commitment to eradicating drug abuse. The World Anti-Doping Agency, established in 1999 and to be jointly funded by the IOC, the international federations and governments may mark a watershed in anti-doping policy, but the level of disagreement and acrimony between partners that accompanied its forma-tion indicated the depth of mutual suspicion and hostility that persists among key policy actors.

Moving away from specific policy issues to the context within which they are shaped, there are three developments of interest. The first concerns the future role of government. The late 1980s saw the disappearance of two major motivations for government involvement in international sport, namely the ending of the Cold War and the collapse of apartheid. It is plausible to suggest that the loss of the stimu-lus of ideological confrontation and apartheid would result in a reduction in government investment in sport, reflecting the decline in the value of sport as a diplomatic resource. However, this seems far from being the case, particularly among developed states, where government investment has generally increased. That sport should remain a valued resource for governments in domestic politics is not surprising, while its continued utility in international politics is a reflection of the strength of the resurgence of nationalism and the politics of identity at the turn of the twentieth century (Cable, 1994; Parekh, 1994).

A second area of interest concerns the future role of the major international sports bodies. The control that they have exercised over the development of sport is coming under increas-ingly severe challenge, not only from individ-ual governments (which they are well used to coping with) and from commercial, particu-larly television, interests, but more recently from players' unions and agents, and interna-tional governmental organizations such as the European Union, the Council of Europe and, to a lesser extent, UNESCO. The capacity of the IOC and the major international federations to plot the course of sports development has always involved a compromise with other interests, but the entry of international govern-mental organizations (IGOs) and the increas-ing assertiveness of international athletes will weaken further that capacity, possibly in important areas such as sports aid to poorer countries and anti-doping policy.

The third significant development in the political context of sport is the increasing prominence of commercial interests. Sport has always been dependent on patronage, whether of employers, governments, churches, or the media and sports businesses. The increasing significance of corporate sponsorship and sports broadcasting is not necessarily a malign influence, particularly where governing bodies are relatively powerful or where the state acts as a counterbalance. However, the less popular sports and sport in poorer countries are both vulnerable to pressure from commer-cial interests and may be unable to prevent the distortion of sports development strategies to provide elite competition and performers. The evolution of the relationship between governing bodies and their international federations, governments and commercial interests is likely to remain a major concern for the foreseeable future.

POLITICS AND SPORT LITERATURE

Although the literature on politics and sport is extensive and growing rapidly it is important to note that the overlap of interests between political scientists and sociologists in particular, but also geographers, philosophers and historians is extensive and that there is much of interest for the study of politics and sport to be found in a broad range of social science literature. This is especially true regarding theoretical perspectives on domestic sports policy-making. Brohm (1978), J.E. Hargreaves (1986), Hoch (1972), and Cantelon and Gruneau (1982), provide analyses from a conflict/Marxist standpoint; a critical analysis is provided by Sage (1990) and by Henry (1993) who also provides an interesting overview of competing approaches; and Houlihan (1991) proposes a pluralist analysis. Galtung (1971, 1984, 1991) is one of the most stimulating analysts of the international politics of sport. Taylor (1986, 1988) examines the role of sport from a functionalist perspective on international relations. Finally, Houlihan (1994) provides a review of the capacity of the major perspectives in international relations to shed light on the role and significance of sport.

Canada (Kidd, 1996; Macintosh et al., 1987; Macintosh and Whitson, 1990), the United States (Coakley, 1998; Sage, 1990; Wilson, 1994) and Britain (Coghlan, 1990; Henry, 1993; Houlihan, 1991) all have a considerable literature devoted to an examination of domestic sport policy. For other countries the literature available in English is less abundant but the following provide some insight into domestic sports politics: Australia (Cashman, 1995; Lawrence and Rowe, 1986); China (Hoberman, 1987; Knuttgen et al., 1990; Kolach, 1972; Riordan and Jones, 1999); Europe (Bramham et al., 1989, 1993); Asia and Africa (Wagner, 1989); the former Soviet Union (Riordan 1977, 1978); Caribbean (Beckles and Stoddart, 1995); South America (Arbena, 1988; Lever, 1983). Wilson (1988) is also stimulating and there are useful contributions in the works edited by Wilcox (1994), Allison (1993) and Landry et al.

(1991). Finally, Houlihan (1997) examines the politics and policy of sport in five countries, Australia, Canada, Ireland, the United Kingdom and the United States.

There is a limited, but growing, number of single-country studies of sports foreign policy including Canada (Macintosh and Hawes, 1994), USA (Hulme, 1990; Kanin, 1980), and the former Soviet Union (Peppard and Riordan, 1993). There is also a growing literature on specific sports policy issues and themes. Those with the most extensive literature include drug abuse (Black Report, 1990; Donohoe and Johnson, 1986; Dubin, 1990; Goldman and Klatz, 1992; Houlihan, 1999; Voy, 1991), the Olympic Games (Espy, 1979; Guttman, 1984, 1992; Hill, 1992, 1996; Hoberman, 1986; Segrave and Chu, 1988), and South Africa and apartheid (Black, 1999; Booth, 1998; Bose, 1994; Guelke, 1986, 1993; Hoberman, 1991; Keech and Houlihan, 1999; Kidd, 1988; Krotee, 1988; Lapchick, 1976, 1979; Ramsamy, 1991).

Finally, there are a number of edited collections that are valuable sources, including Allison (1986, 1993), Arnaud and Riordan (1998), Landry et al. (1991), Lowe et al. (1976), Redmond (1986), Riordan and Krüger (1999), and Wilcox (1994).

REFERENCES

Allison, L. (ed.) (1986) *The Politics of Sport.* Manchester: Manchester University Press.

Allison, L. (ed.) (1993) *The Changing Politics of Sport.* Manchester: Manchester University Press.

Anthony, D. (1991) 'The north–south and east–west axes of development in sport: can the gaps be bridged?', in F. Landry et al. (eds), *Sport ... the Third Millennium.* Sainte-Foy: Les Presses de l'Université de Laval.

Arbena, J. (ed.) (1988) *Sport and Society in Latin America: Diffusion, Dependency and the Rise of Mass Culture.* Westport, CT: Greenwood Press.

Arnaud, P. and Riordan, J. (1998) *Sport and International Politics: the Impact of Fascism and Communism on Sport.* London: E&FN Spon.

Baade, R. and Dye, R. (1988) 'Sports stadiums and area development: a critical review', *Economic Development Quarterly*, 2 (August): 265–75.

Bale, J. (1989) *Sports Geography.* London: E&FN Spon.

Bale, J. (1994) *Landscapes of Modern Sport*, Leicester: Leicester University Press.

Beckles, H. McD. and Stoddart, B. (eds) (1995) *Liberation Cricket: West Indies Cricket Culture.* Manchester: Manchester University Press.

Black, D. (1999) 'Not cricket: the effects and effectiveness of the sport boycott against South Africa,' in N.C Crawford and A. Klotz (eds), *How Sanctions Work: Lessons from South Africa.* New York: St Martin's Press.

Black Report (1990) *Drugs in Sport: Second Report of the Senate Standing Committee on Environment, Recreation and Arts.* Canberra: Government Publishing Service.

Booth, D. (1998) *The Race Game: Sport and Politics in South Africa.* London: Frank Cass.

Bose, M. (1994) *Sporting Colours: South Africa's Return to International Sport.* London: Robson Books.

Bramham, P., Henry, I., Mommas, H. and van der Poel, H. (1989) *Leisure and Urban Processes: Critical Studies of Leisure Policy in Western European Cities.* London: Routledge.

Bramham, P., Henry, I., Mommas, H. and van der Poel, H. (1993) *Leisure Policy in Europe.* Oxford: CAB International.

Brohm, J-M. (1978) *Sport: a Prison of Measured Time.* London: Ink Links.

Broom, E.F. (1986) 'The role of Canadian provincial governments in sport', in G. Redmond (ed.), *Sport and Politics.* Champaign, IL: Human Kinetics.

Cable, V. (1994) *The World's New Fissures: Identities in Crisis.* London: Demos.

Callinicos, A. (1984) 'Marxism and politics', in A. Leftwich (ed.), *What is Politics? The Activity and Its Study.* Oxford: Basil Blackwell.

Cantelon, H. (1982) 'The rationality and logic of Soviet sport', in H. Cantelon and R. Gruneau (eds), *Sport, Culture and the Modern State.* Toronto: Toronto University Press.

Cantelon, H. and Gruneau, R. (eds) (1982) *Sport, Culture and the Modern State.* Toronto: Toronto University Press.

Cashman, R. (1995) *Paradise of Sport: the Rise of Organised Sport in Australia.* Melbourne: Oxford University Press.

Chan, G. (1985) 'The "two Chinas" problem and the Olympic formula', *Pacific Affairs,* 58 (3): 473–90.

Coakley, J.J. (1998) *Sport in Society: Issues and Controversies,* 6th edn. New York: McGraw Hill.

Coghlan, J.F. (1990) *Sport and British Politics since 1960.* Brighton: Falmer Press.

Crepeau, R.C. (1980) *Baseball: America's Diamond Mind, 1919–1941.* Orlando, FL: University of Central Florida Press.

Crick, B. (1964) *In Defence of Politics.* Harmondsworth: Penguin.

Davis, J.P. (1966) 'The Negro in American sport', in J.P. Davis (ed.), *The American Negro Reference Books,* Volume 2. Englewood Cliffs, NJ: Prentice-Hall. pp. 747–95.

Donohoe, T. and Johnson, N. (1986) *Foul Play? Drug Abuse in Sport.* Oxford: Basil Blackwell.

Dubin, L. (1990) *Commission of Enquiry into the Use of Drugs and Banned Practices Intended to Increase Athletic Performance.* Ottawa: Ministry of Supply and Services.

Dulles, F.R. (1965) *A History of Recreation: America Learns to Play.* Englewood Cliffs, NJ: Prentice-Hall.

Edwards, H. (1970) *The Revolt of the Black Athlete.* New York: Free Press.

Eitzen, D.S. (1989) 'Black participation in American sport since World War II', in D.S. Eitzen (ed.), *Sport in Contemporary Society: an Anthology,* 3rd edn. New York: St Martin's Press.

Espy, R. (1979) *The Politics of the Olympic Games.* Berkeley, CA: University of California Press.

Galtung, J. (1971) 'A structural theory of imperialism', *Journal of Peace Research,* 13 (2): 81–94.

Galtung, J. (1984) 'Sport and international understanding: sport as a carrier of deep culture and structure', in M. Ilmarineu (ed.) *Sport and International Understanding.* Berlin: Springer-Verlag.

Galtung, J. (1991) 'The sports system as a metaphor for the world system', in F. Landry et al. (eds), *Sport ... the Third Millennium.* Sainte-Foy: Les Presses de l'Université de Laval.

Glassford, G.R. (1981) 'Life and games of the traditional Canadian Eskimo', in G.R.F. Lüschen and G.H. Sage, (eds), *Handbook of Social Sciences of Sport.* Champaign, IL: Stipes. pp. 78–92.

Goldlust, J. (1988) *Playing for Keeps: Sport, the Media and Society.* Melbourne: Longman Cheshire.

Goldman, B. and Klatz, R. (1992) *Death in the Locker Room II.* Chicago: Elite Sports Medicine Publications.

Gorn, E.J. and Goldstein, W. (1993) *A Brief History of American Sports.* New York: Hill and Wang.

Gruneau, R. (1983) *Class, Sports and Social Development.* Amherst, MA: University of Massachusetts Press.

Guelke, A. (1986) 'The politicisation of South African sport', in L. Allison (ed.), *The Politics of Sport.* Manchester: Manchester University Press.

Guelke, A. (1993) 'Sport and the end of apartheid', in L. Allison (ed.), *The Changing Politics of Sport.* Manchester: Manchester University Press.

Guttmann, A. (1984) *The Games Must Go On: Avery Brundage and the Olympic Movement.* New York: Columbia University Press.

Guttmann, A. (1992) *The Olympics: a History of the Modern Games.* Urbana, IL: University of Illinois Press.

Hardy, S. (1981) 'The city and the rise of American sport: 1820–1920', *Exercise and Sports Science Review,* 9: 183–219.

Hargreaves, J.A. (ed.) (1982) *Sport, Culture and Ideology.* London: Routledge & Kegan Paul.

Hargreaves, J.A. (1985) 'From social democracy to authoritarian populism: state intervention in sport and physical recreation in contemporary Britain', *Leisure Studies,* 4.

Hargreaves, J.A. (1994) *Sporting Females: Critical Issues in the History and Sociology of Women's Sport.* London: Routledge.

Hargreaves, J.E. (1986) *Sport, Power and Culture.* London: Polity Press.

Hargreaves, J.E. (1996) 'The Catalanization of the Barcelona Olympic Games: a case study of nationalism in contemporary Spain', in A. Smith and C. Mar-Molinero (eds), *Nationalism and the Nation in the Iberian Peninsula.* Oxford: Berg.

Henry, I. (1993) *The Politics of Leisure Policy.* London: Macmillan.

Hill, C. (1992) *Olympic Politics.* Manchester: Manchester University Press.

Hill, C. (1996) *Olympic Politics: Athens to Atlanta, 1896–1996,* 2nd edn. Manchester: Manchester University Press.

Hoberman, J. (1984) *Sport and Political Ideology.* Austin, TX: University of Texas Press.

Hoberman, J. (1986) *The Olympic Crisis: Sport, Politics and the Moral Order.* New Rochelle, NY: Aristide D. Caratzas.

Hoberman, J. (1987) 'Sport and social change: sport, politics and the moral order', *Sociology of Sport Journal,* 4: 156–70.

Hoberman, J. (1991) 'Olympic universalism and the apartheid issue', in F. Landry et al. (eds), *Sport … the Third Millennium.* Sainte-Foy: Les Presses de l'Université de Laval.

Hoberman, J. (1997) *Darwin's Athletes: How Sport has Damaged Black America and Preserved the Myth of Race.* New York: Mariner Books.

Hoch, P. (1972) *Rip Off the Big Game.* New York: Anchor.

Holt, R. (1981) *Sport and Society in Modern France.* Hamden, CT: Archon Press.

Holt, R. (1989) *Sport and the British: a Modern History.* Oxford: Oxford University Press.

Horne, J. and Jary, D. (1994) 'Japan and the World Cup: Asia's first World Cup Final hosts', in J. Sugden and A. Tomlinson (eds), *Hosts and Champions. Soccer Cultures, National Identities and the USA World Cup.* Aldershot: Arena. pp. 65–75.

Houlihan, B. (1991) *The Government and Politics of Sport.* London: Routledge.

Houlihan, B. (1994) *Sport and International Politics.* London: Harvester-Wheatsheaf.

Houlihan, B. (1997) *Sport, Policy and Politics: a Comparative Analysis.* London: Routledge.

Houlihan, B. (1999) *Dying to Win: Doping in Sport and the Development of Antidoping Policy.* Strasbourg: Council of Europe Publishing.

Hulme, D.L. Jr (1990) *The Political Olympics: Moscow, Afghanistan, and the 1980 US Boycott.* New York: Praeger.

Hult, J. (1989) 'Women's struggle for governance in US amateur athletics', *International Review for the Sociology of Sport,* 24 (3): 249–64.

Humphrey, J. (1994) 'Triumph and despair: Brazil in the World Cup', in J. Sugden and A. Tomlinson (eds), *Hosts and Champions. Soccer Cultures, National Identities and the USA World Cup.* Aldershot: Arena. pp. 65–75.

James, C.L.R. (1963) *Beyond a Boundary.* London: Stanley Paul.

Johnson, A.T. (1985) 'The sports franchise relocation issue and public policy responses', in A.T. Johnson and J.H. Frey (eds), *Government and Sport: the Public Policy Issues.* Totowa, NJ: Rowman and Allenheld.

Johnson, A.T. (1986) 'Economic and policy implications of hosting sports franchises: lessons from Baltimore', *Urban Affairs Quarterly,* 21 (March): 411–34.

Johnson, A.T. (1993) *Minor League Baseball and Local Economic Development.* Chicago: University of Illinois Press.

Kanin, D.B. (1980) 'The Olympic boycott in diplomatic context', *Journal of Sport and Social Issues,* 4 (1): 1–24.

Keech, M. and Houlihan, B. (1999) 'Sport and the end of apartheid', *The Round Table: Commonwealth of International Affairs,* No. 349 (January).

Kidd, B. (1988) 'The campaign against sport in South Africa', *International Journal,* 43 (4): 643–64.

Kidd, B. (1996) *The Struggle for Canadian Sport.* Toronto: University of Toronto Press.

Klein, A. (1991) *Sugarball: the American Games, the Dominican Dream.* New Haven, CT: Yale University Press.

Knuttgen, H.G., Ma, Q. and Wu, Z. (eds) (1990) *Sport in China.* Champaign, IL: Human Kinetics.

Kolach, J. (1972) *Sport, Politics and Ideology in China.* New York: Jonathan David.

Kropke, R. (1974) 'International sport and the social sciences', *Quest,* 22 (June): 25–32.

Krotee, M.L. (1979) 'The rise and demise of sport: a reflection of Uruguayan society', *Annals of American Academy of Political and Social Science,* 445 (September).

Krotee, M.L. (1988) 'Apartheid and sport: South Africa revisited', *Sociology of Sport Journal,* 5: 125–35.

Landry, F., Landry, M. and Yerles, M. (1991) *Sport … the Third Millennium.* Sainte-Foy: Les Presses de l'Université de Laval.

Lapchick, R.E. (1976) *The Politics of Race and International Sport.* Westport, CT.: Greenwood Press.

Lapchick, R.E. (1979) 'South Africa: sport and apartheid politics', *Annals of the American Academy of Political and Social Science,* 445 (September): 155–65.

Lapchick, R.E. (1988) 'Discovering fool's gold on the golden horizon', *The World and I,* 3: 603–11.

Lasswell, H. (1958) *Politics, Who Gets What, When and How?* New York: Meridian.

Lawrence, G. (1986) 'It's just not cricket!', in G. Lawrence and D. Rowe (eds), *Power Play: Essays in the Sociology of Australian Sport*. Sydney: Hale and Iremonger. pp. 204–14.

Lawrence, G. and Rowe, D. (1986) *Power Play: Essays in the Sociology of Australian Sport*. Sydney: Hale and Iremonger.

Lever, J. (1983) *Soccer Madness*. Chicago: Chicago University Press.

Levine, R.M. (1980) 'Sport and society: the case of Brazilian futebol', *Luso-Brazilian Review*, 17 (2): 233–51.

Lowe, B., Kanin, D.B. and Strenk, A. (eds) (1976) *Sport and International Relations*. Champaign, IL: Stipes.

McCormack, G. (1991) 'The price of affluence: the political economy of Japanese leisure', *New Left Review*, 188: 121–34.

Macintosh, D., Bedecki, T. and Franks, N. (1987) *Sport and Politics in Canada: Federal Government Involvement since 1961*. Montreal: McGill-Queen's University Press.

Macintosh, D. and Hawes, M. (1994) *Sport and Canadian Diplomacy*. Montreal: McGill-Queen's University Press.

Macintosh, D. and Whitson, D. (1990) *The Game Planners: Transforming Canada's Sport System*. Montreal: McGill-Queen's University Press.

Mandell, R. (1976) 'The invention of the Soviet sports record', *Stadion*, 2.2: 250–64.

Mandell, R. (1984) *Sport, a Cultural History*. New York: Columbia University Press.

Mandle, W.F. (1977) 'The Irish Republican Brotherhood and the beginnings of the Gaelic Athletic Association', *Irish Historical Studies*, XX (80): 418–38.

Mandle, W.F. (1987) *The Gaelic Athletic Association and Irish Nationalist Politics, 1884–1924*. London: Christopher Helm.

Mason, T. (1995) *Passion of the People? Football in South America*. London: Verso.

Mitchell, S. (1977) 'Women's participation in the Olympic Games, 1900–1926', *Journal of Sport History*, 4: 208–28.

Moodie, G.C. (1984) 'Politics is about government', in A. Leftwich (ed), *What is Politics? The Activity and its Study*. Oxford: Basil Blackwell.

Morton, H.W. (1982) 'Soviet sport reassessed', in H. Cantelon and R. Gruneau (eds), *Sport, Culture and the Modern State*. Toronto: Toronto University Press.

Nafziger, J.A.R. (1978) 'The regulation of transnational sports competition: down from Mount Olympus', in B. Lowe, D.B. Kanin and A. Strenk (eds), *Sport and International Relations*. Champaign, IL: Stipes.

Paraschak, V. (1991) 'Sports festivals and race relations in the Northwest Territories of Canada', in G. Jarvie (ed.), *Sport, Racialism and Ethnicity*. London: Falmer Press.

Parekh, B. (1994) 'Discourses on national identity', *Political Studies*, 42 (3).

Pauker, E.T. (1964) *GANEFO: Sports and Politics in Djakarta*. Santa Monica, CA.: Rand Corporation.

Peppard, V. and Riordan, J. (1993) *Playing Politics: Soviet Sport Diplomacy to 1992*. Greenwich, CT: JAI Press.

Ponton, G. and Gill, P. (1993) *Introduction to Politics*. Oxford: Basil Blackwell.

Ramsamy, S. (1991) 'Apartheid and Olympism: on the abolishment of institutionalised discrimination in international sport', in F. Landry et al. (eds), *Sport … the Third Millennium*. Sainte-Foy: Les Presses de l'Université de Laval.

Redmond, G. (ed.) (1986) *Sport and Politics*. Champaign, IL: Human Kinetics.

Renwick, A. and Swinburn, I. (1987) *Basic Political Concepts*, 2nd edn. London: Stanley Thornes.

Riess, S.A. (1989) *City Games: the Evolution of American Urban Society and the Rise of Sports*. Urbana, IL: University of Illinois Press.

Riordan, J. (1977) *Sport in Soviet Society*. Cambridge: Cambridge University Press.

Riordan, J. (1978) 'Soviet sport and Soviet foreign policy', in B. Lowe, D.B. Kanin and A. Strenk (eds), *Sport and International Relations*. Champaign, IL: Stipes.

Riordan, J. (1988) 'The role of sport in Soviet foreign policy', *International Journal*, XLIII (Autumn): 569–95.

Riordan, J. and Jones, R. (1999) *Sport and PE in China*. London: E&FN Spon.

Riordan, J. and Krüger, A. (1999) *The International Politics of Sport in the Twentieth Century*. London: E&FN Spon.

Sage, G. (1990) *Power and Ideology in American Sport: a Critical Perspective*. Champaign, IL: Human Kinetics.

Schneider, J.J. and Eitzen, D.S. (1989) 'The perpetuation of racial segregation by playing position in professional football', in D.S. Eitzen (ed.), *Sport in Contemporary Society: an Anthology*, 3rd edn. New York: St Martin's Press.

Scully, G.W. (1995) *The Market Structure of Sports*. Chicago: University of Chicago Press.

Segrave, J.O. and Chu, D. (eds) (1988) *The Olympic Games in Transition*. Champaign, IL: Human Kinetics.

Sie, S. (1978) 'Sport and politics: the case of the Asian Games and the GANEFO', in B. Lowe et al. (eds), *Sport and International Relations*. Champaign, IL: Stipes. 279–95.

Simri, U. (1983) *Israel and the Asian Games*. Proceedings of an International Seminar, 26th ICHPER World Congress 1983, Natanya, Israel: Wingate Institute.

Sinclair, R.J. (1985) 'Baseball's rising sun: American interwar baseball diplomacy and Japan', *Canadian Journal of the History of the Sport*, XVI (2): 44–53.

Strenk, A. (1978) 'Diplomats in tracksuits: linkages between sports and foreign policy in the German Democratic Republic', in B. Lowe et al. (eds), *Sport and International Relations*. Champaign, IL: Stipes.

Strenk, A. (1980) 'Diplomats in tracksuits: the role of sports in the German Democratic Republic', *Journal of Sport and Social Issues*, 4 (1): 34–45.

Sugden, J. and Bairner, A. (eds) (1993) *Sport, Sectarianism and Society in a Divided Ireland*. Leicester: Leicester University Press.

Sugden, J., Tomlinson, J. and McCarten, E. (1990) 'The making of white lightning in Cuba: politics, sport and physical education 30 years after the revolution', *Arena Review*, 14 (1): 341–52.

Taylor, T. (1986) 'Sport and international relations: a case of mutual neglect', in L. Allison (ed.), *The Politics of Sport*. Manchester: Manchester University Press.

Taylor, T. (1988) 'Sport and world politics: functionalism and the state system', *International Journal*, XLIII (Autumn): 531–3.

Travis, A.S. (1979) *The State and Leisure Provision*. London: The Sports Council/Social Science Research Council.

Voy, R. (1991) *Drugs, Sport and Politics*. Champaign, IL: Human Kinetics.

Wagner, E.A. (ed.) (1989) *Sport in Asia and Africa: a Comparative Handbook*. Westport, CT.: Greenwood Press.

Whannel, G. (1992) *Fields in Vision: Television Sport and Cultural Transformation*. London: Routledge.

Wilcox, R.C. (ed.) (1994) *Sport in the Global Village*. Morgantown, WV: Fitness Information Technology.

Wilson, J. (1988) *Politics and Leisure*. London: Unwin Hyman.

Wilson, J. (1994) *Playing by the Rules: Sport, Society and the State*. Detroit: Wayne State University Press.

Xie, Q. (1990) 'Physical culture in the new China', in H.G. Knuttgen, Q. Ma and Z. Wu (eds), *Sport in China*. Champaign, IL: Human Kinetics. pp. 25–40.

14

PSYCHOLOGY AND THE STUDY OF SPORT

Diane L. Gill

ORIENTATION TO A PSYCHOLOGY PERSPECTIVE

Sport psychology, as discussed in this chapter, is a branch of exercise and sport science that focuses on individual behavior in sport and exercise. Before expanding on this definition, let us consider the psychology perspective on sport and society. Like the other cross-disciplinary perspectives in this section, psychology overlaps and has much in common with the sociological perspectives of most sport and society scholars.

First, many specific topics typically included within sport psychology are issues for sport and society. For example, most sport psychology texts and courses include information on aggression, gender and diversity, social influence and group dynamics. As well as sharing some topics, psychology and sociology share some traditions and current issues. In North America both the psychology of sport and the sociology of sport emerged as academic areas in the late 1960s as traditional physical education developed more specialized scholarly sub-areas. In the historical review of sport psychology in this chapter, you will notice scholars that we identify as sociologists.

As sport psychology and sociology developed their respective disciplines, they also experienced similar tensions associated with specialization and fragmentation. As sport psychology has continued to expand, it has developed subspecialties with accompanying divergent views and professional debates. Also, as sport psychology has gained recognition, we have attracted scholars and students from the 'parent' psychology discipline. This development had led to further divergence

and tensions between sport psychologists who identify as sport science scholars and those who identify as psychologists. The sociology of sport has experienced parallel growing strains. Although most of the other cross-disciplines are younger and less expansive, readers may well find that some of the issues and trends in this psychology chapter parallel those of other related perspectives.

Although we share some topics and professional issues, psychology is not sociology, and psychology offers a different perspective on sport and society. The classic difference, as recited in most sport psychology texts and courses, is that psychology focuses on the individual, whereas sociology focuses on society. Like most dichotomies, especially those recited at the beginning of texts and courses, this one is false. As noted in the preceding section, psychology and sociology overlap in content and issues. My own perspective on psychology clearly is social, and psychologists who attempt to understand individual behavior without recognizing the critical influence of society cannot truly understand behavior. Similarly, sociologists who forget that society consists of individuals and considerable individual variation, miss a great deal. This chapter may remind readers of the individual variation, and contribute to the understanding of sport and society.

As well as the focus on the individual, sport psychology has some other features that differ from other perspectives. Of the cross-disciplinary areas included in this section, psychology is the most developed and also the closest to the 'hard' sciences. Although some sport psychology scholars take more social approaches, others take particularly 'hard' line approaches and emphasize controlled research, physiological mechanisms and traditional scientific methods.

Finally, one of the key features of sport psychology today is the emphasis on application. As described in later sections of this chapter, North American sport psychology has shifted from its social psychology, research-oriented origins to an emphasis on direct application. That shift is evident in the number of sport psychologists and students interested in consulting with athletes, in the public recognition of applied sport psychology, and even in the research and scholarship. It should be noted that European sport psychology was much more applied and focused on competitive athletics before North Americans made the shift. In fact, as discussed in later sections, European sport psychology has now shifted from the overly applied focus to more diverse sport and exercise research issues with diverse participants, so that most international sport psychology now shares a similar research-application balance.

THE DISCIPLINE OF SPORT PSYCHOLOGY

As a branch of exercise and sport science, sport psychology is part of a multidisciplinary field that draws upon varied disciplines, and in my view, exercise and sport science is an *applied* field. That is, we try to integrate information from the varied sciences to understand sport and exercise from a biopsychosocial perspective.

The sub-areas within exercise and sport science incorporate information from related disciplines (for example, physics, sociology), but they draw from the disciplines *selectively*. Not all information in physiology and anatomy is equally applicable to exercise. And, not all aspects of psychology are equally applicable to sport. Exercise and sport scientists apply selected theories, concepts and methods from the basic disciplines to sport and exercise.

Borrowing theories and information does not constitute a scholarly field of study. As a multidisciplinary field, we integrate information and develop our own theories, concepts and methods to create unique knowledge. Many sport psychology scholars advocate sport-specific theoretical models and methods to address the unique aspects of sport and exercise. Rainer Martens's work on competitive

anxiety (to be discussed later) illustrated the value of sport-specific approaches, and other sport psychologists have developed other sport-specific constructs and measures that provide insights about sport behavior that cannot be gleaned from more general psychology research. Sport psychology, then, borrows selected, relevant information from its associated discipline of psychology, and also develops theoretical models and approaches that are unique to sport and exercise.

Although the term sport psychology implies that the field includes all aspects of psychology, that is not the case. The North American Society for the Psychology of Sport and Physical Activity (NASPSPA), one of the main professional organizations for sport psychology, includes three areas:

1 Motor learning/motor control, which focuses on cognitive and perceptual processes involved in learning and performing motor skills.
2 Motor development, which focuses on developmental psychology issues related to sport and motor performance.
3 Sport psychology. Sport psychology, as commonly interpreted and as used in this chapter, emphasizes certain sub-areas of psychology, particularly personality and social psychology. Like social psychology, sport psychology focuses on meaningful social behavior rather than portions of behavior. Psychophysiology, cognition and psychology areas that focus on portions of behavior contribute to our understanding of sport and exercise, but these issues are typically addressed within motor behavior.

The three areas within NASPSPA reflect the typical division in North America; we separate sport psychology from the related psychological areas within exercise and sport science. Notably, European sport psychology, and most sport psychology around the world, includes cognition, perception and other motor behavior topics within sport psychology, and psychological work on these topics at the international level is more applied and directly related to sport than in North America. However, Biddle (1995), citing data from the *Directory of European Sport Psychologists* (1993, FEPSAC), reported that motor behavior topics are relatively infrequent, and major research topics (for example, anxiety/stress, exercise and health, motivation, mental training) are similar to those of North America.

Sport and Exercise Psychology: A Definition

In a book published in 1986, I defined sport psychology as the scientific study of human behavior in sport and exercise (Gill, 1986). Today, that definition seems limited in several ways. First, most current sources refer to the field as sport *and exercise* psychology to ensure that the exercise component is not overlooked, and to counter the perception that sport = athletics. Many sport and exercise psychologists focus on health-oriented exercise, with individuals devoting research programs to such topics as psychophysiological aspects of exercise and stress or exercise motivation.

Secondly, 'scientific study' seems to exclude many applied and professional concerns that most sport and exercise psychologists consider part of the field. Applied sport psychology has mushroomed into the most visible aspect of the field and researchers are expanding the applied knowledge base. Thus, the definition of the field should be altered to include both the science and *practice* of sport and exercise psychology. Moreover, science is interpreted broadly to include alternative methods and sources of knowledge.

Finally, although I consider sport and exercise psychology a branch of exercise and sport science, that is not the only perspective today. A large number of sport psychologists have psychology backgrounds, consider sport psychology a branch of psychology, have no background in exercise science or physical education, and do not relate to the overall field of exercise and sport science.

These extensions and qualifications in defining sport psychology are not unique to me or to North America. Recently, the European Federation of Sport Psychology (FEPSAC) published a position statement, 'Definition of Sport Psychology' (1996). FEPSAC specifically noted a focus on human behavior, including affective, cognitive, motivational and sensorimotor dimensions of psychology, and defined sport as physical activity in competitive, educational, recreational, preventive and rehabilitative settings, including health-oriented exercise. The statement continued by noting that sport psychology draws upon: (a) sport practice, (b) psychology and (c) other sport sciences, and that sport psychologists have three interrelated tasks: research, education and application.

So, for this chapter, sport and exercise psychology is defined as:

> Sport and exercise psychology is that branch of exercise and sport science that involves the scientific study of human behavior in sport and exercise, and the practical application of that knowledge in sport and exercise settings.

The Complexity of Sport and Exercise Behavior

In sport and exercise psychology we try to understand meaningful behavior, rather than portions of behavior, and take a 'holistic' approach. We want to understand sport and exercise behavior as it occurs in the real world and apply that knowledge in sport and exercise practice. This is no easy task. Human behavior in sport and exercise, like human behavior everywhere, is complex. We cannot find one clear source or 'cause' of behavior. And, even when we think we understand a behavior (for example, why an athlete 'choked' in the big game, or how to help a student learn a skill), we may find that our explanation does not hold up a week later.

In trying to understand sport and exercise behavior, sport psychologists typically keep in mind one theme: both individual characteristics and the social situation affect behavior. This premise reflects a basic tenet of social psychology set forth in a formal but simple way by Kurt Lewin (1935) as:

$$B = f(P, E)$$

That is, behavior is a function of the person and the environment. As Lewin stated in his early work, individual and environmental factors do not operate independently; they interact. Personal characteristics influence behavior in some situations and not others; situational factors (for example, spectators, teachers' comments) affect different people in different ways; and the person affects the situation just as the situation affects the person. Thus, relationships among person (P), environment (E) and behavior (B) are dynamic and change over time. For example, a 10-year-old baseball player makes a costly error. If the child is anxious about competition (P) and then hears critical comments from the coach (E), the child likely will become even more anxious and make more errors, changing the situation for everyone. If the child is confident, receives constructive suggestions from the coach and encouragement from team mates, that child may be more alert the next time, and develop skills and confidence to carry into future games. We could list possible scenarios indefinitely. Any particular behavior takes place within the context of many interacting personal and environmental factors, and all those factors and relationships change over time. The dynamic complexity of sport and exercise behavior makes precise prediction nearly impossible. But, with greater understanding of individual and social processes and their relationships with behavior, we can make informed choices and enhance the sport experience for all participants.

HISTORICAL REVIEW OF SPORT PSYCHOLOGY

Interest in sport psychology is not new. Participants, the public and the occasional scholar have been intrigued by the mental side of physical activities for some time. Still, the 'disciplined' study of sport and exercise psychology did not emerge in North America until the late 1960s, when, like the scholars in the other subdisciplines, sport psychologists turned away from the traditional practice-oriented physical education, and looked to scientific psychology as a model. Although the specific historical events, trends and emphases differ, European sport psychology developed its disciplinary organization over a similar time frame. Within 20 years, academic sport psychologists built a knowledge base and developed an identifiable subdiscipline with professional organizations, journals and specialized graduate programs.

Since the mid-1980s North American sport psychologists have regained their interest in practice, and applied sport psychology has captured the interest of many sport psychologists and the general public. Moreover, in North America, Europe and around the world, both the art and science have moved beyond competitive sport to include the psychological parameters of health-oriented exercise and recreational sport activities.

In 1984, Wiggins noted, 'It is apparent that the growth of sport psychology in both Canada and the United States has been the result of sustained efforts by physical educators' (p. 10). Today, his statement is questionable. Several of today's sport psychologists were trained in general psychology, and lack specific training in either sport and exercise psychology or physical education. For years, most sport psychologists were trained and located in physical education or exercise and sport science departments. They borrowed theories and methods from general psychology while psychologists ignored sport. Now, many psychologists and psychology students look to sport as a setting for both research and practice.

Today, most sport and exercise psychology scholars identify with the larger discipline of exercise and sport science and share an understanding of the field. With more people entering the field from psychology, counseling or other backgrounds, and with increasing specialization within sport and exercise psychology (for example, psychophysiological, social, applied), the common ground is elusive. These pressures present challenges and opportunities as today's sport and exercise psychologists continue to advance the study of the art and science of human behavior in sport and exercise.

Early North American Foundations

Although sport and exercise psychology as a discipline is relatively young, scholarly interest in sport psychology extends further into the past. As long as sport and exercise activities have been around, psychology has played a role. Throughout the history of psychology as a science, a few psychologists have applied their theories to sport and exercise, and, as long as scholars have studied physical activity or exercise and sport science, some of those efforts have involved psychological issues.

The most recognized early psychology research with implications for sport psychology is Norman Triplett's (1898) lab study of social influence and performance, widely cited as the first social psychology experiment. Triplett's study is a benchmark for sport and exercise psychology because he used a physical task (winding fishing-reels), and even more because he was inspired by observations of sport. Specifically, Triplett, a cycling enthusiast, observed that social influence (pacing machine, competition) seemed to motivate cyclists to better performance, and designed his experiment to test those observations.

Other researchers from both psychology and physical education (often aligned with physical training and medical schools) espoused psychological benefits of physical education and conducted isolated studies of sport psychology issues. George W. Fitz (1895) of Harvard, operating from what may be the first physical education research lab in North America, conducted experiments on the speed and accuracy of motor responses. Wiggins (1984) also cites turn-of-the-century work by William G. Anderson on mental practice, Walter Wells Davis's studies of transfer of training, Robert A. Cummins's investigation of the effects of basketball practice on motor reaction, attention and suggestibility, and

E.W. Scripture's study of character development and sport.

Coleman Griffith

Clearly, the first person to conduct systematic sport psychology research and practice was Coleman R. Griffith. As a doctoral student at the University of Illinois, Griffith studied psychological factors in basketball and football, and caught the attention of George Huff, Director of Physical Welfare for Men at Illinois. Huff developed plans for an Athletics Research Lab, which was established in 1925 with Griffith as Director. Griffith was a prolific researcher who focused on psychomotor skills, learning and personality. Griffith taught sport psychology classes and published numerous research articles, as well as two classic texts, *Psychology of Coaching* (1926) and *Psychology and Athletics* (1928). As many current sport psychologists advocate, Griffith ventured into the field to make observations and interview athletes. For example, he used an interview with Red Grange after the 1924 Michigan–Illinois football game, in which Grange noted that he could not recall a single detail of his remarkable performance, to illustrate that top athletes perform skills automatically without thinking about them. Griffith also corresponded with Knute Rockne on the psychology of coaching and motivation. One quote from that correspondence, taken from a Rockne reply to Griffith of 13 December 1924, illustrates strategies of a successful coach and counters some popular images:

> I do not make any effort to key them up, except on rare, exceptional occasions. I keyed them up for the Nebraska game this year, which was a mistake, as we had a reaction the following Saturday against Northwestern. I try to make our boys take the game less seriously than, I presume, some others do, and we try to make the spirit of the game one of exhilaration and we never allow hatred to enter into it, no matter against whom we are playing. (From the Coleman Griffith Collection, University Archives, University of Illinois at Urbana-Champaign)

When the Athletics Research Lab closed in 1932, Griffith continued as a professor of educational psychology, but did not totally abandon sport psychology. In 1938 he was hired by Philip Wrigley as team sport psychologist for the Chicago Cubs.

Griffith's prolific research, publications and thoughtful insights place him among the most significant figures in the history of sport

psychology, and he is widely described as the 'Father of sport psychology in North America'. However, as Kroll and Lewis (1970) note, Griffith was a prophet without disciples, and 'father' is really a misnomer. Sport psychology research and practice did not continue in North America after Griffith's pioneering work. Parallel efforts in Germany by R.W. Schulte, and in Russia by Peter Roudik and A.C. Puni, continued there, but did not influence North America.

As Ryan (1981) noted, from Griffith's time through the late 1960s most physical education texts had sections on psychological aspects, and many physical education objectives were psychological, but research was sporadic. C.H. McCloy (1930) of Iowa examined character building through physical education, and Walter Miles (1928, 1931) of Stanford conducted studies of reaction time, but other work waited until the post-Second World War extension of psychological research on learning and performance, when several scholars such as Arthur Slater-Hammel at Indiana, Alfred (Fritz) Hubbard at Illinois, John Lawther at Penn State, and Franklin Henry at Berkeley, developed research programs in motor behavior that incorporated some current sport psychology topics.

In the 1960s more texts with psychology issues and information began to appear, including Bryant Cratty's (1967) *Psychology and Physical Activity*, and Robert Singer's (1968) *Motor Learning and Human Performance*.

Organization of the Sport Psychology Discipline

Sport psychologists began to organize in the late 1960s when a number of individuals developed research programs, graduate courses and, eventually, specialized organizations and publications.

NASPSPA As individuals developed research and graduate programs, they began to organize, at first meeting in conjunction with the American Association of Health, Physical Education and Recreation (AAHPER) (now American Alliance for Health, Physical Education, Recreation and Dance; AAHPERD). Soon, they developed plans for a sport psychology organization, and the North American Society for the Psychology of Sport and Physical Activity (NASPSPA) was officially incorporated in 1967. John Loy, an early member of NASPSPA as well as a sociology of sport scholar, described the history of NASPSPA prior to its first independent meeting in 1973, and his account is published in those proceedings (Loy, 1974).

At the 1972 meeting, NASPSPA members decided to hold the annual meeting separately from other organizations, and Rainer Martens and colleagues at the University of Illinois hosted the first independent meeting of NASPSPA at Allerton Park, IL, in May 1973. The Allerton meeting set the format that NASPSPA still follows. The meetings extended over several days, included major invited addresses as well as submitted research papers, and the special setting encouraged discussion before, during and after sessions. NASPSPA continued to be the major organizational force in sport psychology through the 1970s and 1980s; most active researchers and their graduate students joined, the conference drew high-quality submissions and the proceedings included some of the best work in the field.

The NASPSPA organization reflected the overlapping of sport psychology and motor behavior of the 1960s and 1970s. Many of the early sport psychology specialists branched out from motor learning, and NASPSPA included sub-areas of motor learning, motor development and social psychology of physical activity (now the sport psychology area). Those three sub-areas remain in NASPSPA, although each has changed and grown more specialized since NASPSPA's foundation.

International Organization Although NASPSPA clearly was the first and most prominent organization in the development of sport and exercise psychology in North America, international sport psychology also organized and influenced North American scholars.

In 1965 the International Congress of Sport Psychology in Rome marked the beginning of the International Society of Sport Psychology (ISSP). Miroslav Vanek (1993), a key figure in international sport psychology, noted that the use of psychology in sport was stimulated in the 1950s by the sovietization of top-level sport. Thus, international sport psychology traditionally has aligned more with performance enhancement of elite athletes and has a clearer applied psychology foundation than the more sport and exercise science-oriented discipline in North America.

Several sport psychologists from Europe and the Soviet Union were instrumental in forming an international society, including Paul Kunath (East Germany), Peter Roudik (Russia), Miroslav Vanek (Czechoslovakia), Morgan Olsen (Norway) and John Kane (England).

However, Ferruccio Antonelli (Italy), founding President of ISSP and organizer of the first International Congress in Rome in 1965, was the primary organizing force. The second international Congress was held in Washington, DC, in 1968, co-sponsored by NASPSPA and AAHPER. The 878-page proceedings of that congress (Kenyon and Grogg, 1970) includes papers by most of the sport psychology scholars mentioned in this section, and provides a nice overview of the emerging subdiscipline at that time. The international congress has continued to expand and meet every four years since then.

ISSP not only played a key role in the development of NASPSPA, but also inspired sport psychology organizations in Europe and Canada. The European sport psychology organization, FEPSAC, formed in 1968, continues as an active international force. Although NASPSPA has had a strong Canadian presence from its initial foundation, a separate Canadian organization formed in 1969 and developed in parallel with NASPSPA.

Publications Before organization of the discipline, specialized publications were not needed. Isolated psychology studies related to sports appeared in psychology journals, but were not really considered sport psychology research at that time. The major research journal for the sport psychology work of North American physical education scholars was the *Research Quarterly* (*RQ*), later renamed *Research Quarterly for Exercise and Sport* (*RQES*).

The *International Journal of Sport Psychology*, which began publishing in 1970, never served as the primary source or outlet for North American sport psychology scholars. The *Journal of Motor Behavior* (*JMB*) began publishing in 1969 and included some sport psychology research related to social psychology, such as research on social influence and motor performance. However, as sport psychology diverged from motor behavior into a separate subdiscipline with differing issues, perspectives and approaches, scholars sought specialized publications.

The most important publication outlet for sport psychology research during the early years was the NASPSPA proceedings, which included the most current research by leading scholars as well as invited addresses on important topics. Full proceedings of the 1973 (Wade and Martens, 1974) and 1975 (Landers et al., 1975) conferences were published, and from 1976 to 1980 the proceedings included only papers evaluated favorably by reviewers and editors. Thus, from 1976 to 1980, *Psychology of Motor Behavior and Sport* was the primary refereed sport psychology publication in North America.

In 1980 NASPSPA stopped publishing full papers, largely because of the 1979 appearance of the *Journal of Sport Psychology (JSP)*. JSP emerged from NASPSPA, particularly through the work of Rainer Martens and Dan Landers, and quickly became the primary outlet for the sport psychology research. *JSP (Journal of Sport and Exercise Psychology, JSEP,* since 1988) has served that purpose well. Through Dan Landers's 7-year term, and the subsequent editorial terms of Diane Gill (1985–90), Jack Rejeski (1991–4), Thelma Horn (1995–7) and current editor Bob Brustad, *JSEP* has been recognized as the leading publication outlet for sport and exercise psychology research.

Recent Development: The Science and Art of Sport and Exercise Psychology

The early organization of sport psychology paralleled the development of NASPSPA. In the late 1960s sport psychology scholars began to develop their own research base separate from motor behavior, established graduate programs, held annual conferences to share information, developed a research journal and gradually became the largest and most diverse of the three areas within NASPSPA. Some sociology of sport scholars, such as Gerald Kenyon and John Loy, contributed to the early social psychology emphasis, but during the first ten years sport psychologists closely aligned with motor behavior and looked to experimental psychology theories and research models for guidance.

Rainer Martens's (1975) text *Social Psychology and Physical Activity* reflects the content and orientation of those years. Major psychological theories (for example, inverted-U hypothesis, Zajonc's social facilitation theory, Atkinson's achievement-motivation theory) framed the content; most supporting research was from psychology; and the sport psychology research seldom involved *sport*, but typically involved experimental tests of psychological theory with laboratory motor tasks such as the rotary pursuit and stabilometer.

By the mid-1980s sport psychology had not only grown tremendously, but also changed direction. While motor behavior scholars continued to emphasize psychological theories and experimental research, sport psychologists moved to more applied issues and approaches. Martens was a leading advocate for change, and his 1979 article in the second issue of *JSP*, 'About smocks and jocks', prompted many sport psychologists to turn to more applied research and practical concerns. Martens observed that ten years of sport psychology research, while often theory-based and methodologically sound, told us little about sport behavior. Indeed, most of the research did not involve sport at all, but laboratory tasks that were too far removed from sport to help teachers, coaches and participants. Martens called for more research in the field, on relevant issues, and with attention to the development of *sport-specific* conceptual models and measures.

Martens's own work on competitive anxiety (Martens, 1977) illustrated that approach. Martens developed a conceptual framework, combining psychology models of anxiety with his own competition model; defined sport-specific constructs; developed psychometrically sound, sport-specific measures; and conducted systematic research in varied field settings. Martens's competitive anxiety work served as a model for subsequent sport-specific research and measures such as Gill's competitive orientation work (Gill, 1993; Gill and Deeter, 1988), Carron, Widmeyer and Brawley's (1985) group cohesion work, and Martens's continuing work on competitive anxiety (Martens et al., 1990).

Although some continued to emphasize theory-driven, controlled experimental research, many sport psychology scholars pursued applied issues with sport participants. One notable example of this approach is the youth sport coaching work by Ron Smith and Frank Smoll of the University of Washington. Smith and Smoll began their work in the late 1970s, took a practical issue (effective coaching in youth sports), conducted systematic observations and field research, developed sport-specific measures and approaches, and eventually developed coach education programs to put their research into practice (for example, Smith et al., 1979; Smoll and Smith, 1984, 1993).

Through the 1980s field research and applied issues moved to the forefront of sport psychology. Applied issues also captured the attention of students and the public, and brought more people into the field. Most sport psychology researchers made some moves in more applied directions, and a few took bigger steps to move away from research and focus on work with athletes. This applied focus caught the attention of some psychologists who began to see sport as a setting for clinical and counseling work.

With more diverse students and psychologists participating in sport psychology,

NASPSPA no longer fitted all interests. In particular, many sport psychologists wanted more discussion of applied issues, such as anxiety management techniques or certification of sport psychologists, as well as research information. NASPSPA did not respond to those interests, prompting the development of separate organizations and publications to accommodate applied interests and activities. John Silva was instrumental in organizing a 1985 meeting, which marked the beginning of the Association for the Advancement of Applied Sport Psychology (AAASP). As summarized in the first issue of the *AAASP Newsletter* (Winter, 1986), the purpose of AAASP is to promote the development of psychological theory, research and intervention strategies in sport psychology. John Silva became AAASP's first President, and AAASP held its first conference at Jekyll Island, GA, in October 1986. That first conference got AAASP off to a strong start and AAASP continues to hold an annual conference and maintains the basic structure set in 1985 with three inter-related sections: intervention/performance enhancement, social psychology and health psychology.

Martens's address at the first AAASP conference, like his earlier 'smocks and jocks' paper, advocated major changes in sport psychology research and practice and presented a challenge that many sport psychologists have accepted. Martens criticized sport psychology's reliance on orthodox science, and encouraged more diverse approaches to science and knowledge, such as idiographic and introspective methods.

Many sport psychology scholars took up Martens's challenge, and a series of articles by Tara Scanlan and her colleagues (for example, Scanlan, Ravizza and Stein, 1989; Scanlan, Stein and Ravizza, 1989) on their in-depth studies of enjoyment and stress in figure skaters, provided a model of sound research for other sport psychologists wishing to use alternative methodologies. Martens's (1987b) widely cited paper was published in the inaugural issue of *The Sport Psychologist (TSP)*, which was developed to focus on the emerging applied sport psychology literature and to be complementary to the successful *JSEP*. In his publisher's statement in the first issue, Martens noted that *TSP* was both an applied research and interpretive journal, and specifically called for applied research using less traditional methods, offering a publication outlet for the alternative approaches he called for in his paper. *TSP* was endorsed by ISSP, with Dan Gould and Glyn Roberts serving as founding co-editors.

With *TSP* focusing on applied research and professional issues, *JSP* focused on strong sport psychology research. In 1988, *JSP* added 'Exercise' to the title (becoming *JSEP*) and more explicitly sought research on health-oriented exercise as well as sport. *JSEP* and *TSP* continue to serve as strong complementary journals. Each makes important contributions to the knowledge base, and most sport and exercise psychologists value both sources of information.

AAASP also started its own journal, the *Journal of Applied Sport Psychology (JASP)* in 1989 with John Silva as Editor. *JASP* serves many of the same purposes as *TSP*, and gives applied researchers another outlet. *JASP* also provides AAASP information, publishes major addresses from the conference and has developed informative theme issues to add to the literature.

The rapid rise to prominence of AAASP and *TSP* is the most visible indicant of the growth of applied sport psychology in the 1980s, but some other organizations also added to this movement. In particular, several individuals trained in traditional psychology programs moved into sport psychology during this time, and psychology departments and organizations began to notice sport. Richard Suinn, a clinical psychologist and active member of the American Psychological Association (APA), did a great deal to bring sport psychology to public attention. Suinn and other psychologists, such as Steve Heyman, helped sport psychology scholar William Morgan organize a sport psychology presence within APA. After starting as an interest group, Division 47 – Exercise and Sport Psychology – became a formal division of APA in 1986.

NASPSPA, AAASP and Division 47 of APA are the primary North American sport and exercise psychology organizations, but sport psychology also has a presence in some other exercise and sport science organizations. AAHPERD, the original home of NASPSPA, includes a Sport Psychology Academy, and many sport psychology scholars, especially those with interests in applications to physical education teaching and coaching, participate in that organization. The American College of Sports Medicine (ACSM), a large organization dominated by exercise physiology and sports medicine, has expanded its sport psychology constituency and accommodated more sport and exercise psychology scholars and presentations in recent years.

Suinn's early work with skiers in the 1976 Olympics helped the US Olympic Committee (USOC) recognize the potential role of sport psychology. Several other sport psychologists began to work with teams, and in 1983 the USOC established an official sport psychology committee and a registry. Many sport psychologists have worked with athletes, coaches and training programs through the USOC since then, and in 1987, the USOC hired Shane Murphy as its first permanent full-time sport psychologist to work at the training center in Colorado Springs.

The highly visible sport psychology presence in the Olympics, and the individual efforts of several psychologists and sport psychology consultants who worked with elite athletes in universities, on professional teams and in private settings, raised new professional issues for sport and exercise psychology. Conversations at conferences and in graduate student offices abounded with questions such as: Who is a sport psychologist? What training do I need to become a sport psychologist? Must sport psychologists be licensed clinical psychologists? When does the role of the sport psychologist working with athletes cross with the role of the coach or the clinician? Such conversations, and often heated debates, were especially prominent at AAASP meetings, and AAASP expended considerable time and effort attempting to define and set standards for sport psychology practice. At the 1989 conference, AAASP approved the criteria for certification, and in 1991 began to confer the title, 'Certified Consultant, AAASP' on qualified candidates. AAASP's certified consultants are *not* licensed psychologists, and the consultant's role is defined as an educational role emphasizing psychological skill training. Although the AAASP certification criteria provide guidelines, the issues are by no means resolved. Diverse, and often divergent, views are expressed, and the debates continue.

The expansion of applied sport psychology courses and workshops created a market for more literature. Few sport psychology texts existed before the 1980s. Cratty's books were widely used, Martens's 1975 *Social Psychology and Physical Activity* served its purpose, and in the mid-1980s I wrote *Psychological Dynamics of Sport* (Gill, 1986) to fit the needs of undergraduate and graduate sport psychology courses. By the late 1980s, though, the market for sport psychology literature extended beyond physical education and graduate sport psychology programs, and many books appeared with an applied focus, such as Robert Nideffer's (1976) *The Inner Athlete*, Dorothy Harris and Bette Harris's (1984) *The Athlete's Guide to Sport Psychology*, Terry Orlick's (1980) *In Pursuit of Excellence* (now in 2nd edition, 1990), Rainer Martens's (1987a) *Coaches' Guide to Sport Psychology*, and Jean Williams's (1986) excellent volume *Applied Sport Psychology* (now in 3rd edition, 1998).

Sport and exercise psychology organizations and journals developed because the specialization flourished within exercise and sport science departments. Many of the scholars who organized the discipline in the 1960s and 1970s (such as Landers, Martens, Morgan, Singer) developed courses and began specialized graduate programs to train the next generation of sport and exercise psychologists. Sport and exercise psychology grew rapidly through the 1970s and 1980s to become one of the most popular graduate specializations. Today, most major PhD programs in exercise and sport science offer a sport and exercise psychology specialization. Undergraduate programs often include a 'hands-on' psychological skills course, as well as a core course based on sport and exercise psychology theory and research.

The general core or survey courses at both the graduate and undergraduate level continue to include the major topics that were introduced in the early courses, such as personality and individual differences, motivation, stress and anxiety, aggression and moral development, social influence and group dynamics. Specialized graduate programs have expanded greatly and diversified far beyond the survey courses of the early years. Scholars in graduate programs often offer advanced seminars on social, developmental, or psychophysiological sport and exercise psychology, as well as both research and practice-oriented applied courses and supervised experiences.

Interestingly, psychology departments have not incorporated sport and exercise psychology courses at either the undergraduate or graduate levels. Many psychologists have moved into sport and exercise settings for research and practice, but the development of the disciplinary knowledge base remains the task of the sport and exercise psychology specialists in exercise and sport science programs.

Summary: a Century of Sport Psychology History

The preceding sections reviewed 100 years of events and trends in the development of sport and exercise psychology. Formal organization was preceded by 70 years of isolated studies, which retrospectively can be labelled sport psychology. Although Coleman Griffith's sport psychology work, from 1925 to 1932, punctuated this period, sport and exercise psychology did not emerge as a discipline until the late 1960s, when several scholars with sport psychology interests initiated research meetings and formal organizations. During the next ten years graduate programs and research expanded, creating a knowledge base as well as specialized organizations and publications. During the 1980s sport psychology turned toward applied research and practice.

As the twenty-first century begins, sport and exercise psychology is very different from the discipline that emerged in the 1960s. The young discipline remained aligned with motor learning and performance, and relied heavily on experimental social psychology theories and research models in the early stages. Sport psychology made a strong move to sport-relevance about ten years later, as research moved to the field and scholars developed sport-specific models and measures to build a more relevant psychology of sport and exercise behavior. Shortly thereafter, with an influx of individuals from psychology and with more direct applied concerns, sport psychologists began to apply information more directly in education and consulting work.

SPORT AND EXERCISE PSYCHOLOGY TODAY – MOVING TO A GLOBAL FUTURE

As applied interests continue to expand, academic and research interests also are expanding and changing. Sport and exercise psychologists have responded to the public concern for health and fitness with increased research on health-oriented exercise. Healthy, active lifestyles, and preventive or rehabilitative exercise programs involve behaviors, and today's exercise instructors and health professionals recognize the value of the psychological component of exercise and sport science.

Although sport and exercise psychology is not an especially large subdiscipline (compared to exercise physiology, for example), it is incredibly diverse in both research and practice. Some researchers emphasize theory-based basic research with tight controls and search for underlying physiological mechanisms. Others shun traditional research, using interpretive approaches and searching for experiential knowledge. Some are not concerned with research at all, but seek information on strategies and techniques to educate, consult or clinically treat sport and exercise participants. The expansion of sport and exercise psychology

organizations and professional journals, each with its own orientation, reflects this diversity. Most likely both the research and practice sides of sport and exercise psychology will remain strong and continue to grow and change in the immediate future. The main question is whether these two sides of the field will grow together or apart. As Martens (1987b) suggested, scholars must conduct sound research, but that research must be relevant and aimed at answering questions about sport and exercise behavior. Sport and exercise psychology practitioners must have a grounding in the research and theory base, including knowledge of the science and the art, but must also incorporate their experiential knowledge as well as listen to participants to help develop and use the knowledge base. Researchers and practitioners, sport and exercise psychologists, physical educators and psychologists, sport psychologists and sport participants, must value the knowledge and skills of each other if, as Martens (1987b) advocated, we are once again to have one sport psychology.

As sport psychology moves into the new millennium, we are not only merging research and practice, but also moving toward a global sport psychology. With the electronic information revolution and increased international collaboration in conferences and projects, international communication and interaction have expanded exponentially, moving us toward shared research and professional identification as well as greater familiarity with cultural diversity.

First, sport psychology has expanded beyond its North American and European bases to become a truly international discipline. European sport psychology, particularly in the former soviet USSR and East Germany (GDR) was centrally controlled and focused on training elite athletes until recently. European sport psychology has continued to develop from its roots, but current issues and approaches encompass more diverse activities, especially health-oriented exercise, with more diverse participants. For example, Kunath (1995) a key organizer of European sport psychology and faculty member at the former GDR's German Academy of Physical Culture at Leipzig, described the historical emphasis on training coaches and elite athletes, and welcomed the current expansion of sport psychology to leisure sport, exercise for people with disabilities and health-oriented exercise.

Biddle made similar points in the introduction to his welcome contribution to international dialogue, an edited volume of diverse European perspectives on sport and exercise psychology (Biddle, 1995). Biddle noted the former emphasis on elite sport, but also confirmed the changes in former state-controlled sport psychology programs as well as in most of Western Europe. The volume includes several chapters on exercise and health topics as well as sport topics, with diverse contributions by authors from several European countries.

Moreover, sport and exercise psychology work is not confined to North America and Europe. Australia has many scholars and programs similar to those of Europe and North America, and the rise of sport and exercise psychology in Asian countries is particularly notable. Japan and Korea have developed strong sport and exercise psychology programs, as they have developed politically and economically. The 1989 ISSP conference was held in Singapore, and that meeting certainly enhanced mutual recognition of sport psychology research and approaches on the part of both Asian and Western countries. In 1994 I was fortunate to be invited to make a presentation at the International Conference of the Korean Alliance for Health, Physical Education, Recreation and Dance as well as at the Korean Society for Sport Psychology. I was able to meet and learn from many scholars from Korea and other countries, and also to visit several universities and the Korean Sport Science Institute. Korea has several university programs and sport psychology scholars who participate in international conferences and publish in top journals. Many Korean sport psychologists, like those of many countries, received their graduate training in North American universities. However, as with several other countries, the expanded number of programs and scholars should lead to more attention being paid to unique concerns and cultural variations.

The increased international presence at sport psychology conferences around the world, along with the long-overdue travels of some North American scholars to other parts of the world, should only add to the international dialogue. The AAASP recently implemented an international initiative under the direction of former president Tara Scanlan. The 1996 conference emphasized the international theme, with several invited speakers from around the world. As well as major speakers, a symposium entitled 'Sport and exercise psychology: a global perspective' included panelists from Australia, France, Korea, New Zealand, Norway, Russia, Spain and the United Kingdom (Gould, 1996). Although panelists noted specific features of sport psychology in their countries, common themes clearly emerge in both the research and professional

issues. For example, Chung (1996) noted that although research has typically been quantitative, some Koreans are taking more qualitative approaches to study motivation and peak performance; Fournier (1996) commented on attention to certification criteria and consulting ethics in France; and Stambulova (1996) noted the decline in the emphasis on elite sport with increased interest in exercise for health in Russia.

As well as exchanging information on professional issues and current topics, the increased international dialogue has enhanced sport and exercise psychology research. For example, the topic of anxiety has long been a major issue, and research has been conducted by scholars in several countries. Recently, that work has been shared more readily, international scholars cite each other's work, and some international collaborative efforts have taken place. Jones (1995), in a chapter reviewing competitive anxiety research, cites the Martens work on SCAT and more recent multidimensional models (Martens et al., 1990), his own and Lew Hardy's work (UK) on catastrophe models (for example, Jones and Hardy, 1990) and the work of Yuri Hanin (formerly of USSR, now Finland) on zone of optimal functioning (for example, Hanin, 1989). Dieter Hackfort of Germany is one of the most prominent sport psychology scholars doing anxiety research, and along with Spielberger of the United States, he co-edited an excellent volume on anxiety and sport that includes contributions from many of these and other international scholars (Hackfort and Spielberger, 1989).

International dialogue and participation in sport and exercise psychology likely will increase even more in the near future. Conferences are increasingly international, and with easy access to communication networks, information is increasingly shared even when travel is prohibitive. North America, Europe, Asia and Australia/New Zealand have internationally active sport psychology communities now, and other countries have some activity. For example, South America and Africa are less recognized internationally, but ISSP includes representatives from those areas, and several countries have developed organizations and increased their sport and exercise psychology activity. As sport and exercise psychology activity expands around the world, we will likely see continued recognition of common themes in both our research and practice. However, increased international dialogue should also decrease some of the North American/European dominance, and add greater insights into cultural variations and diversity. Overall, a more global sport and exercise psychology should enhance all our scholarship, and in turn enhance the sport and exercise experience for all participants.

REFERENCES

Biddle, S.J.H. (1995) *European Perspectives on Exercise and Sport Psychology*. Champaign, IL: Human Kinetics.

Carron, A.V., Widmeyer, W.N. and Brawley, L.R. (1985) 'The development of an instrument to assess cohesion in sport teams: the Group Environment Questionnaire', *Journal of Sport Psychology*, 7: 244–66.

Chung, C.H. (1996) 'Sport and exercise psychology in Korea', *Journal of Applied Sport Psychology: 1996 AAASP Abstracts*, 8: S4.

Cratty, B.J. (1967) *Psychology and Physical Activity*. Englewood Cliffs, NJ: Prentice-Hall.

FEPSAC (1996) 'Position statement of the European Federation of Sport Psychology (FEPSAC): I. Definition of sport psychology', *The Sport Psychologist*, 10: 221–3.

Fitz, G.W. (1895) 'A local reaction', *Psychological Review*, 2: 37–42.

Fournier, J.F. (1996) 'Sport and exercise psychology in France', *Journal of Applied Sport Psychology: 1996 AAASP Abstracts*, 8: S4.

Gill, D.L. (1986) *Psychological Dynamics of Sport*. Champaign, IL: Human Kinetics.

Gill, D.L. (1993) 'Competitiveness and competitive orientation in sport', in R.N. Singer, M. Murphey and L.K. Tennant (eds), *Handbook of Research on Sport Psychology*. New York: Macmillan. pp. 314–27.

Gill, D.L. and Deeter, T.E. (1988) 'Development of the Sport Orientation Questionnaire', *Research Quarterly for Exercise and Sport*, 59: 191–202.

Gould, D. (1996) 'Symposium: sport and exercise psychology: a global perspective', *Journal of Applied Sport Psychology: 1996 AAASP Abstracts*, 8: S3.

Griffith, C.R. (1926) *Psychology of Coaching*. New York: Scribners.

Griffith, C.R. (1928) *Psychology and Athletics*. New York: Scribners.

Hackfort, D. and Spielberger, C.D. (1989) *Anxiety in Sport: an International Perspective*. New York: Hemisphere.

Hanin, Y. (1989) 'Interpersonal and intragroup anxiety in sports', in D. Hackfort and C.D. Spielberger (eds), *Anxiety in Sport: an International Perspective*. New York: Hemisphere. pp. 19–28.

Harris, D.V. and Harris, B.L. (1984) *The Athlete's Guide to Sports Psychology: Mental Skills for Physical People*. New York: Leisure Press.

Jones, G. and Hardy, L. (1990) *Stress and Performance in Sport*. Chichester: Wiley.

Kenyon, G.S. and Grogg, T.M. (1970) *Contemporary Psychology of Sport*. Chicago: The Athletic Institute.

Kroll, W. and Lewis, G. (1970) 'America's first sport psychologist', *Quest*, 13: 1–4.

Kunath, P. (1995) 'Future directions in exercise and sport psychology', in S.J.H. Biddle (ed.), *European Perspectives on Exercise and Sport Psychology*. Champaign, IL: Human Kinetics. pp. 324–31.

Jones, G. (1995) 'Competitive anxiety in sport', in S.J.H. Biddle (ed.), *European Perspectives on Exercise and Sport Psychology*. Champaign, IL: Human Kinetics. pp. 128–53.

Landers, D.M., Harris, D.V. and Christina, R.W. (1975) *Psychology of Sport and Motor Behavior II*. University Park, PA: Pennsylvania State University Press.

Lewin, K. (1935) *A Dynamic Theory of Personality*. New York: McGraw-Hill.

Loy, J.W. (1974) 'A brief history of the North American Society for the Psychology of Sport and Physical Activity', in M.G. Wade and R. Martens (eds), *Psychology of Motor Behavior and Sport*. Urbana, IL: Human Kinetics. pp. 2–11.

Martens, R. (1975) *Social Psychology and Physical Activity*. New York: Harper & Row.

Martens, R. (1977) *Sport Competition Anxiety Test*. Champaign, IL: Human Kinetics.

Martens, R. (1979) 'About smocks and jocks', *Journal of Sport Psychology*, 1: 94–9.

Martens, R. (1987a) *Coaches' Guide to Sport Psychology*. Champaign, IL: Human Kinetics.

Martens, R. (1987b) 'Science, knowledge and sport psychology', *The Sport Psychologist*, 1: 29–55.

Martens, R., Vealey, R.S. and Burton, D. (1990) *Competitive Anxiety in Sport*. Champaign, IL: Human Kinetics.

McCloy, C.H. (1930) 'Character building through physical education', *Research Quarterly*, 1: 41–61.

Miles, W.R. (1928) 'Studies in physical exertion: I. A multiple chronograph for measuring groups of men', *American Physical Education Review*, 33: 379–87.

Miles, W.R. (1931) 'Studies in physical exertion: II. Individual and group reaction time in football charging', *Research Quarterly*, 2: 14–31.

Nideffer, R.M. (1976) *The Inner Athlete*. New York: Crowell.

Orlick, T. (1980) *In Pursuit of Excellence*. Champaign, IL: Human Kinetics. (2nd edn, 1990).

Ryan, E.D. (1981) 'The emergence of psychological research as related to performance in physical activity', in G. Brooks (ed.), *Perspectives on the Academic Discipline of Physical Education*. Champaign, IL: Human Kinetics. pp. 327–41.

Scanlan, T.K., Ravizza, K. and Stein, G.L. (1989) 'An in-depth study of former elite figure skaters: I. Introduction to the project', *Journal of Sport and Exercise Psychology*, 11: 54–64.

Scanlan, T.K., Stein, G.L. and Ravizza, K. (1989) 'An in-depth study of former elite figure skaters: II. Sources of enjoyment', *Journal of Sport and Exercise Psychology*, 11: 65–83.

Singer, R.N. (1968) *Motor Learning and Human Performance*. New York: Macmillan.

Smith, R.E., Smoll, F.L. and Curtis, B. (1979) 'Coach effectiveness training: a cognitive-behavioral approach to enhancing relationship skills in youth sport coaches', *Journal of Sport Psychology*, 1: 59–75.

Smoll, F.L. and Smith, R.E. (1984) 'Leadership research in youth sports', in J.M. Silva and R.S. Weinberg (eds), *Psychological Foundations of Sport*. Champaign, IL: Human Kinetics. pp. 371–86.

Smoll, F.L. and Smith, R.E. (1993) 'Educating youth sport coaches: an applied sport psychology perspective', in J. Williams (ed.), *Applied Sport Psychology*, 2nd edn. Mountain View, CA: Mayfield. pp. 36–57.

Stambulova, N. (1996) 'Sport and exercise psychology in Russia', *Journal of Applied Sport Psychology: 1996 AAASP Abstracts*, 8: S7.

Triplett, N. (1898) 'The dynamogenic factors in pacemaking and competition', *American Journal of Psychology*, 9: 507–53.

Vanek, M. (1993) 'On the inception, development and perspectives of ISSP's image and self-image', in S. Serpa, J. Alves, V. Ferreira and A. Paula-Brito (eds), *Proceedings VIII World Congress of Sport Psychology*. Lisbon: International Society of Sport Psychology. pp. 154–8.

Wade, M.G. and Martens, R. (1974) *Psychology of Motor Behavior and Sport*. Urbana, IL: Human Kinetics.

Wiggins, D.K. (1984) 'The history of sport psychology in North America', in J.M. Silva and R.S. Weinberg (eds), *Psychological Foundations of Sport*. Champaign, IL: Human Kinetics. pp. 9–22.

Williams, J.M. (1986) *Applied Sport Psychology*. Palo Alto, CA: Mayfield. (3rd edn, 1998).

PART THREE

KEY TOPICS

EDITORS' INTRODUCTION

The authors of the following 18 chapters were chosen because of their expertise related to the topic in question. We asked authors to write 'user-friendly, jargon-free, state-of-the-art' discussions of theory and research on their topics. We also asked them to include, where relevant, analyses of debates and controversies. Finally, we encouraged them to keep their discussions of general theoretical matters to a minimum because these matters would be discussed in the chapters on theoretical perspectives.

Subsequent conversations with authors emphasized that each chapter should provide readers with the following:

- An accessible introduction to important sociological issues related to the topic.
- An overview of the primary literature related to the topic combined with a bibliography useful to fellow experts and to those reading about the topic for the first time.
- References to theoretical debates and controversies that have informed research on the topic.
- A brief discussion of theorizing and research that, in the author's mind, needs to be done in the future.

Of course, the authors used these guidelines in their own ways. Therefore, each chapter is unique in that the content represents how the author has read the literature and incorporated it into his or her approach to the topic in question.

The following paragraphs provide brief sketches of each chapter. These sketches do not summarize the content of the chapters as much as they provide a general sense of their substantive and conceptual parameters.

CHAPTER OVERVIEWS

Part Three begins with Allen Guttmann's chapter on 'The Development of Modern Sports'. Guttmann identifies the origins of modern sports as he outlines the transformations that occurred in physical leisure activities in Western Europe from the Renaissance to the eighteenth and nineteenth centuries. His analysis is grounded primarily in a theoretical framework informed by the work of Max Weber. In line with this approach, he notes that modern sports were associated with and characterized by the following:

- An emphasis on *progress* as manifested through the measurement of performance and the recording of achievements and statistics for individuals and for events.
- Increasing *specialization* in the games played, the roles of game participants and the spaces in which games were played.
- *Rationalization* in the form of explicit rules, rule enforcement, and the standardization of the conditions of competition.

Although Guttmann notes that it may not be possible to identify precisely a single origin for modern sports, he points out that the diffusion and growth of these sport forms were aided by increasingly efficient modes of transportation and by other technology. This growth was accelerated through the twentieth century, especially in connection with processes of globalization and the capitalist promotion of global spectacles presented through terrestrial and satellite television. Guttmann sees both capitalism and modern sports as outgrowths of the seventeenth-century scientific revolution in Europe, and he concludes by noting that dominant global sport forms at the changeover to the third Christian millennium remain characterized by the instrumental rationality associated with that revolution.

In his chapter on 'Political Economy and Sport', George Sage clarifies the different meanings of political economy as they have been used in classical, neoclassical and radical theoretical approaches. Drawing on examples primarily from the United States, he discusses the political economy of mass sport, school sports, intercollegiate sports and professional sports. His discussions emphasize issues related to state intervention, access to sport participation and the connections between physical leisure activities, such as sport, and work. He highlights issues related to sports as business and athletes as worker–entertainers and discusses topics of monopoly (one-seller markets), monopsony (one-buyer markets) and alienated labour and sport. Sage concludes with a discussion of global political economy in which he examines the organization and consequences of sporting goods production, especially in Asian and Latin American countries.

The chapter on education by Roger Rees and Andrew Miracle deals with 'sport as education' as well as 'sport in education'. Rees and Miracle note that competitive sports are rarely included as a formal part of school programmes, but that many people around the world believe that sports serve educational functions for athletes at all levels of participation, especially during childhood and adolescence. After referring to data showing that educational functions are not automatically served by sport participation, they provide an historical overview of how and why sport became integrated into educational institutions in Britain and the United States. Rees and Miracle provide a general review of the literature related to sports as 'differentiating rituals' in schools and the role of sports in 'consensual rituals' designed to reaffirm social values in the schools. On the basis of studies done primarily in the United States, they conclude that there is little support for the notions that sport significantly enhances the academic lives of interscholastic athletes or that it serves as a positive force in school life. In closing, they provide a critique of research on sport and schooling. They highlight the need for research in countries other than the United States and the need for sports and sport participation to be taken more seriously by researchers in the sociology of education and in physical education. They suggest that sports in schools might, under certain circumstances, be sites for progressive social transformation.

Garry Whannel's chapter on 'Sport and the Media' outlines the theoretical and conceptual approaches that have informed past research, identifies the major topics and debates that have been discussed in much of the literature, and highlights research trends that characterize current work being done on the media. In

his introduction Whannel notes that work on sport and the media has been informed by sociological and semiological traditions. The former has focused on the three major aspects of the communicative chain: production, message, and audience reception. The latter has focused on the process of meaning production in terms of the organization and representational issues underlying media images and discourses. The major topics and debates identified by Whannel include the processes of commercialization and commodification that have accompanied the development of media sport. He focuses much of his attention on issues related to commercial television coverage and its impact on the production and consumption of sport around the world. Whannel also summarizes work done on media sport and the social construction of gender, race and national identities. He takes care to note the ways in which media representations are implicated in power relations in connection with each of these topics. In closing, Whannel explains that much of the current and future research on media sport has dealt and will continue to deal with the topic of globalization and the topic of sport and the body.

In the chapter 'Theorizing Sport, Social Class and Status', John Sugden and Alan Tomlinson review and raise questions about 'classical theories of social stratification as they relate to sport'. They begin with a review of how sport participation through history has reflected and constituted various forms of social differentiation and associated systems of power and privilege. Their point is that the emergence and growth of modern sports cannot be understood apart from the dynamics of social class. Sugden and Tomlinson then turn their attention to how analyses of sport, social class and status have been influenced by the stratification theories of Talcott Parsons, Karl Marx and Max Weber. Their review highlights analyses that have focused most directly on sport in society and provided the most useful models and concepts for understanding the multiple dimensions of power relations between social classes and other status groups. They give special attention to work informed by Gramsci's hegemony theory and by Weber's notion that power dynamics in society are grounded in political and social as well as economic factors. In connection with the latter body of work they highlight Bourdieu's analysis of sports and sport participation as related to a combination of economic and cultural capital. Bourdieu's version of the concept of *habitus* is introduced to aid understanding of the implications and expressions of social class under the conditions of complex and highly differentiated forms of capitalism. Sugden and Tomlinson emphasize that future analyses of power relations between classes and other status groups should extend the hegemony thesis and build on insights inspired by Bourdieu's work.

The chapter on 'Gender and Sport' highlights topics and issues that have elicited considerable attention since the publication in 1981 of the *Handbook of Social Science of Sport*.[1] Nancy Theberge notes that early forms of modern sports celebrated a version of masculinity constructed around competitiveness, toughness and physical dominance, and thereby served as sites for the construction of gender difference. Although athletic women have challenged hegemonic masculinity at various points since the late nineteenth century, women's sports participation has occurred usually in the face of numerous constraints and has been characterized by ambiguities and contradictions. Theberge discusses contemporary ideological struggles by using examples from women's ice hockey, professional golf and aerobics. Her examples illustrate, respectively, the issues of what counts as 'real' sport, constraints maintained by homophobia, and sexualized images of women's bodies. She also discusses men's sports as sites for the production of masculinity and relatively rare attempts within men's sports to challenge masculine hegemony. She emphasizes that race and class are implicated in the gender construction process that occurs in association with certain men's sports, and she closes with a review of issues related to the compulsory heterosexuality and homophobia that exist in women's and men's sports. Theberge notes in her conclusion that gender has become and continues to be a key topic in research on sport and society.

Grant Jarvie's chapter on 'Sport, Racism and Ethnicity' focuses primarily on race relations, black identity and black feminism as they are related to an understanding of sport in society. He discusses how popular arguments about sport, racism and ethnicity have contributed to general ideas about skin colour and physical abilities. This is followed by a discussion of how the concept of race, combined with racism, has been used as an explanatory principle in analyses of moral, cultural and social differences between people from different skin colour and ethnic backgrounds. He critiques neo-Marxist and post-Marxist research traditions, and highlights the work of C.L.R. James (*Beyond a Boundary*)[2] to show how sports in certain cultural settings have come full circle from being a symbol and tool of cultural imperialism to being a symbol of Creole nationalism. Jarvie then notes that the development of black feminist writings on sport would help challenge much of the existing work on sport and race. He also notes that there is a need for a new vocabulary that acknowledges the fluidity of identity, the social construction of race and ethnicity and the articulation of race and ethnicity with other categories such as class and gender. He concludes with a discussion of race relations as a form of established-outsider relations. Using work grounded in the ideas of Norbert Elias, Jarvie notes that race relations may be understood in terms of power relations among socially identified groups in a society, and that research should focus on how some groups come to impinge on and have power over other groups. Finally, he notes that future research and theorizing on race relations must avoid anti-historical and universalistic approaches.

The chapter by Lincoln Allison explores the complex connections between 'Sport and Nationalism'. Allison notes that as organized games became institutionalized, starting in Europe and North America, through the nineteenth and early twentieth centuries, there was a tendency for national identities to be associated with teams, contests and sports. However, despite the manner in which nationhood has been emphasized recently through the Olympics, television broadcasts of international sports and the commercial sponsorship of national sports teams, the connection between sport and national identity is neither automatic nor exclusive. The representational dynamics constructed around sports and sports teams may incorporate many identities other than those associated with national affiliation. For example, sports and teams may represent identities grounded in club affiliations, local and regional loyalties, ethnic and racial heritage, social class, religious affiliation and/or political ideology. As he explores issues related to nationalism and patriotism, Allison notes that there are no standard or universal relationships between national sport and political nationalism. Using figurational theory as a guide, he explains that the connection between sport, national identity and nationalism must be analysed on a case-by-case basis. Each analysis must take into account historical as well as unique social and cultural forces that are characteristic of the case in question. Allison closes with a discussion of national responses to globalization. He notes that the connections between issues of national identity and nationalism on the one hand, and the globalization of sports, sport organizations and sport events on the other hand, have not been studied long enough to identify distinct patterns. He concludes with the observation that even though sports are sites for many different expressions of national sentiments, we may never fully know all we wish to know about the subtle and complex relationships between these two spheres of social life.

In the chapter on 'Sport and Globalization', Joseph Maguire highlights the challenges faced when trying to understand processes of global interconnectedness while recognizing that these processes are manifested differently in different locations. This challenge is met, he notes, when we avoid dichotomous thinking and monocausal explanations, and when we take into account both the intended and unintended actions of people and the gender dynamics underlying the power relations associated with those actions. Maguire develops critiques of modernization, Americanization and dependency theories, and then uses a figurational approach to make the case that globalization is best understood as a balance and blend of 'diminishing contrasts and increasing varieties'. This balance and blend emerges in connection with changing, regionally unique sets of power relations in which powerful transnational actors play an important role. Finally, using a framework that takes into account the process of state formation, functional democratization and the civilizing process, Maguire outlines five historical phases of 'sportization' during which various forms of achievement sport have spread increasingly around the globe. He concludes by noting that sportization, at all points in history, is a process in which power and identity are contested in the context of emerging social figurations.

In the chapter on 'Social Control and Sport' Stan Eitzen explains how processes of social control are implicated in any attempt to understand the foundations of social order, the normative context of individual behaviour and group life, or the expression and identification of deviance in social life. He notes that normative conformity in social life is grounded in a combination of ideological and direct social control. Ideological social control occurs primarily through socialization and operates at the level of individual consciousness. Direct social control involves various forms of intervention that impact on behaviour and relationships. Eitzen then identifies the ways in which sports may be involved in both these forms of social control. He gives special attention to

the relationships between sports and societal integration, the transmission of values and the reproduction of gender and gender relations. He then focuses on the issue of social control *in* sports. Special attention is given to the organizational control of athletes and conditions of sports participation. Eitzen explains that officials, coaches and participants play key roles in social control processes. He closes with a discussion of future research in which he notes that studies of social control will be informed increasingly by paradigms and epistemologies emphasizing interpretive methodologies, concepts related to processes of human agency, and decentred models of social realities.

The topic of violence has long captured the attention of social scientists studying sports. The 1981 *Handbook* contained a chapter by Gladys Engel Lang entitled 'Riotous Outbursts in Sport Events' in which she used collective behaviour theory to describe and explain spectator violence. Kevin Young's chapter on 'Sport and Violence' in this volume emphasizes that the concept of 'sports violence' is multidimensional and difficult to define. Young begins his chapter with an overview of the diverse manifestations and explanations of crowd violence and of player violence. He also includes a brief discussion of other intentionally abusive and injurious acts, such as off-the-field assaults perpetrated by athletes or coaches, that may be understood best in connection with dominant sport forms in the cultures in which they occur. Secondly, Young provides an overview of issues related to policing sports violence. He discusses the topics of deterrence, litigation and social control, and identifies the complex issues faced when attempts are made to sanction and control sports violence through state intervention and the use of criminal law. Finally, Young reviews the diverse body of research on sports violence and the media. He notes that media effects are difficult to identify, but that the discourses and images presented through the media constitute a significant aspect of popular sport experiences in many societies today. In his conclusion, Young summarizes the approaches that hold the most promise for explaining various aspects of sports violence, and he makes suggestions for future research.

'Sport and health' has usually been discussed in physiological terms. Ivan Waddington, however, provides a sociological discussion of this topic in his chapter. He begins with a critical assessment of pervasive twentieth-century beliefs about the health benefits of sports participation. He notes that these beliefs have been associated with the emergence of an ethos of the healthy body and an associated ideology of 'healthism' in many countries. This ideology has significant political implications in that it identifies health as a matter of personal responsibility to the point that external sources of health problems are often underplayed in public consciousness and policy. He also draws attention to the contradiction between public beliefs about the health benefits of sports and the widespread sponsorship of commercial sports by tobacco companies. The theme around which Waddington organizes much of his critical discussion is that it is necessary to distinguish between moderate, rhythmic forms of exercise done by individuals, and forms of competitive sports in which participation occurs in connection with other people. Further, it is necessary to distinguish between various types and levels of sport participation. In the case of high-performance sports there is a dubious connection between sport and health. Stress injuries, overuse injuries and the expectation that athletes play with pain and injury are common in such sports. The health risks of participation are greatest in heavy contact sports and in those sports where male participants use their bodies as weapons and define violence and aggression as expressions of masculinity. Waddington concludes by emphasizing that it is difficult to generalize about the relationship between sport and health. He notes that discussions of this topic should identify the type and level of sport participation, the extent to which individuals have control over their participation and the forms of exercise involved in the sport.

The chapter on 'Sport and Disability' covers a range of topics that are relatively new to discussions of sport and society. Howard Nixon begins the chapter with explanations of the terms 'impairment', 'disability' and 'handicap' and he makes conceptual distinctions between 'temporary disability' caused by acute sport injury and 'permanent disability' due to chronic impairment caused by factors outside sport. Being 'handicapped', he notes, is grounded in social processes through which a person is discredited and stigmatized. The main body of the chapter is divided into two parts. In the first part Nixon deals with issues related to disability and handicap in sport. He discusses the exclusion and the participation barriers faced by people with certain disabilities, and he describes the Special Olympics and the Paralympics as examples of sports designed to accommodate disabilities. He also outlines the complex and contentious issues surrounding the segregation and integration of people with disabilities in sports competitions. Secondly, Nixon deals with issues related to disablement through sport. This section of the chapter provides a useful complement to key points made in Waddington's chapter on 'health', Young's chapter on 'violence', and Lüschen's chapter on 'doping'. Nixon discusses pain and injury as they are related to gender, the culture of high-performance sports and the provision of medical care for athletes. He also discusses briefly the links between the use of performance-enhancing substances, chronic injuries and disability. He concludes with a discussion of injuries in youth sports and school sports in the United States. In this final section he notes the difficulties in gathering data on injuries and the need for more accurate tracking of sports injuries and their impact on the lives of young people.

In the chapter on 'Body Studies in the Sociology of Sport', Cheryl Cole provides a review of what she describes as 'broad, diverse, and theoretically incongruent investigations of the body and sport'. She divides her review into three sections: the modern sporting body, deviant and/or transgressive bodies and commodified bodies. In the first section she summarizes the literature on sport and the body. She focuses on how sport and the modern athletic body are involved in the constitution of individual, group and national identities; how science and technology are involved in the production of modern sporting bodies; and how modernist moral discourses frame different athletic bodies. In the second section, Cole discusses how athletic bodies come to be inscribed as deviant or serve to push and challenge dominant ideas about nature and the natural order when they are not compatible with a discourse that assumes universal humanity and an essential notion of bodily perfection. Finally, Cole discusses sporting bodies as they have been constituted and commodified in the sphere of industrial capitalism. In this section she synthesizes investigations into the political implications of bodily practices and celebrity bodies in sports. Through her entire review of the literature, Cole raises questions about when, why, how and to what ends the body is investigated in the sociology of sport.

The chapter 'Doping in Sport as Deviant Behavior and Its Social Control' deals with what Günther Lüschen defines as one of the key 'social problems' issues in sport at the beginning of the twenty-first century. Lüschen begins the chapter with a discussion of the social structure of doping in sport. He highlights the difficulties encountered by those who have attempted to define what constitutes doping by athletes, and he points out that definitions have changed over time and from one governing body to another. Lüschen explains that drug use among athletes has increased as there have been increases in access to substances and in the stakes associated with competitive outcomes; as usage has increased so have efforts to test for and control doping among athletes. Lüschen makes the case that doping in sport raises sociological issues related to deviance and social control. Using a classical sociological framework, he maintains that doping is clearly an example of deviant behaviour that not only jeopardizes the essential character of 'sport as contest' but that also raises questions about the moral legitimacy of sport and sports organizations. He then uses classical deviance theory to explain doping in sport and the rationalization of doping by athletes and sports authorities. Using social control theory he notes that the containment of doping in sport depends on a combination of external and internal controls. After identifying the forms that these controls might take, Lüschen outlines the issues and problems associated with putting an international social control system into place as well as the necessity of having such a system. In his final section, Lüschen reviews and critiques data on the magnitude of doping in sport. His conclusion emphasizes that doping in sport remains a problem that is most accurately and effectively conceptualized in sociological terms.

The chapter on 'Sport and Emotions' deals with what Mary Duquin describes as the multisensual epicentre of sport. Duquin makes the case that emotions must be considered in analyses of the cultural, social and personal impact of sport. Although the topic of emotions has been considered only recently in research on sport and society, past research on identity formation and expression provides useful information on emotions and sport. As Duquin notes, there is research on emotions and emotional displays used as markers of meaning, values and identity at the cultural level. Research on sport subcultures has described the control and expression of emotion as a key part of the dynamics of competition and teamwork. Research on the structuring and restructuring of self-identities in connection with sports highlights the facts that memories are grounded in emotions and that feelings make sport experiences and events significant in people's lives. Duquin

explains that emotions are related clearly to the formation and expression of sexual identities in and through sports. She reviews information on sports spectating and nostalgia and notes that sports serve as sites for emotional experiences and expressions as well as sites for the formation of emotional attachments to teams and athletes. She closes with a discussion of future research and the need for interpretive, biographical and phenomenological studies that focus specifically on emotions. Such studies are needed to increase our understanding of cultural and social variations in emotional expression, disciplinary technologies and the management of emotions, emotional socialization and the links between emotional expression and moral behaviour in sports.

The chapter on 'Management, Organizations and Theory in the Governance of Sport' identifies and evaluates applied work and theory related to the management of public, quasi-public and voluntary sporting organizations in countries with developed economies. Ian Henry and Eleni Theodoraki note that an understanding of sports organizations depends on a general understanding of the overall social and cultural context of the industrialized societies in which the organizations are most prevalent. The shift during the 1980s and 1990s from a cultural emphasis on social democracy and the provision of welfare services to an emphasis on liberal individualism and the privatization of public leisure services has changed the context in which many sports organizations exist. Henry and Theodoraki point out that few people have done applied research on sports management but that there have been studies of sports organizations in a few countries. After reviewing this work, they present an empirical analysis of the structural characteristics of all national governing bodies (NGBs) recognized by the British Sports Council (now Sport England). Although this analysis is limited to sporting organizations in Britain, the authors provide a model of organizational structures that is useful for constructing taxonomies of sports organizations in other countries. They note that the structures of sports organizations vary widely and that management dynamics in these organizations are highly dependent on how they are funded. Recent trends in these sports organizations include a more professionalized, market-oriented approach to management that reflects a shift from social sporting goals to the financial goals of economic efficiency and economic return. Henry and Theodoraki conclude by noting that future organizational research will focus on various manifestations of this shift to 'new managerialist' approaches in different local and national contexts.

In the chapter on 'Emerging Arriving Sports: Alternatives to Formal Sports', Robert Rinehart focuses attention on new sport forms that various commentators and social scientists have referred to as alternative, lifestyle, whiz, panic and extreme. He notes that these diverse physical activities raise challenging questions for those concerned with defining sport. Throughout the chapter Rinehart identifies numerous sport forms that might be considered 'alternative' because they 'have not gained widespread attention from mainstream audiences'. Generally, these sport forms consist of activities that have emerged and taken shape in connection with the lifestyles and experiences of those who do them. The fact that these activities exist outside traditional, institutionalized administrative structures is part of what makes them attractive to participants and interesting to social scientists. Many new sport forms are associated with youth culture and anti-mainstream impulses. Participants tend to emphasize the experience of participation rather than competitive outcomes or external rewards. Rinehart gives special attention to the X Games, created and presented as a global media event by US cable network ESPN. He notes that the media coverage of these extreme sport forms has led many to see them as typical of alternative sports. His analysis leads him to identify eight contentious issues that commonly exist in connection with new alternative sport forms. Among these issues are resisting incorporation into mainstream sports, maintaining authenticity and legitimacy, defining the status of participants, dealing with corporate sponsorships, controlling images and events and struggling over forms of exclusion grounded in sexism, racism and homophobia. In his conclusion Rinehart suggests that new sport forms offer opportunities for research into youth cultures where an emphasis on music, opposition, freedom and thrills informs action, relationships and lifestyles.

NOTES

1   G. Lüschen and G. Sage (eds), *Handbook of Social Science of Sport* (Champaign, IL: Stipes, 1981); see also discussion of this volume in the General Introduction.
2   C.L.R. James, *Beyond a Boundary* (London: Stanley Paul, 1963).

15

THE DEVELOPMENT OF MODERN SPORTS

Allen Guttmann

Although the descriptions and the paradigmatic explanations of the difference varied, the 'grand theorists' of sociology – Comte, Marx, Toennies, Durkheim, Weber, Parsons, and Elias – all shared the conviction that there is a fundamental difference between modern society and the earlier forms of social organization from which modern society evolved. Premodern and modern sports exemplify that difference more clearly than most institutions. Among the 'grand theorists', Elias is the only one to have written extensively on sports (Elias and Dunning, 1986). He – like Marx (Wohl, 1973) and Weber (Guttmann, 1978) – has inspired a number of historical analyses of the development of modern sports (Dunning, 1973; Dunning and Rojek, 1992; Dunning and Sheard, 1979; Eichberg, 1978; Guttmann, 1986; Stokvis, 1979).

Historians disagree about the origins of modern sports. Their assertions about time and place depend in large measure upon which of the formal-structural characteristics of modern sports they emphasize. Some, influenced by the 'figurational sociology' of Elias (1969), have stressed the relative absence, in modern sports, of interpersonal violence on and off the field of play (Dunning, 1973; Dunning and Sheard, 1979). A strong case can be made, from this perspective, for Renaissance Italy and France as the birthplace of modern sports (Krüger and McClelland, 1984). Other scholars, influenced by Weber's analysis of the 'disenchantment of the world' and the dominance of 'instrumental rationality' (1920, 1922), have stressed such formal-structural characteristics as secularism, equality, rationalization, specialization, bureaucratization, quantification, and the

quest for records (Guttmann 1978, 1988). Seen from this perspective, eighteenth-century England is the birthplace of modern sports (Kloeren, 1935; Krockow, 1972; Mandell, 1976, 1984; Schöffler, 1935). Both interpretations of the origins of modern sports deserve to be taken seriously, but a more persuasive case can be made for the second.

RENAISSANCE SPORTS

The transition from medieval to Renaissance sports is a textbook instance of 'the civilizing process' (Elias, 1969). Medieval sports tended to be quite violent; the sports of the Renaissance tended not to be. At the top of the social hierarchy as at the bottom, there was a shift in emphasis from 'force to finesse' (Mehl, 1993: 21). The twelfth-century tournament, which was the aristocracy's favorite sport, was a loosely organized and poorly regulated mêlée that took place in open fields and meadowland. It claimed an extraordinary toll in dead and wounded knights. Folk football, the medieval peasantry's holiday pastime, was similarly violent. It was described by Sir Thomas Elyot – from the perspective of a Renaissance gentleman – as 'beastly fury, and extreme violence' (Guttmann, 1986: 49). Twentieth-century students of Elias characterize the British version of folk football as 'savage brawls' engendering 'excitement akin to that aroused in battle' (Dunning and Sheard, 1979: 25). Like the medieval tournament, the peasant's sport usually took place in the countryside.

In the course of approximately three hundred years, these two sports were transformed into strictly regulated contests closer to theatrical performances than to pitched battles. In France, where the literary myths of Tudor England exerted a powerful influence on the tournament, the bloody combats of the medieval mêlée evolved into highly conventionalized dramatic reenactments of the adventures of King Arthur and the knights of the Round Table, with ingeniously designed pageant cars and with gorgeous stage sets for lords and ladies impersonating Lancelot and Tristram, Gawain and Percival, Guinevere and Morgan le Fay. By the late Renaissance, 'ring tournaments' were popular and the clash of sword against armor had become the tinkle of a lance as it speared a brass ring. The French were the leaders, but the English and the Germans soon followed (Ariès and Margolin, 1982; Fleckenstein, 1985). By the sixteenth century, the English tournament was 'a highlight of Elizabethan courtly life, but it was a spectacle and a pageant, not a ... realistic preparation for war' (Vale, 1977: 11).

In Italy, the peasant's rough version of football was reshaped into the Florentine gentleman's *calcio*, an urban game played in the Piazza di Sante Croce. A contemporary print depicts the church and its square, the surrounding buildings, the rectangular playing field and the stands, the low fence that surrounded the field, and the pikemen whose threatening presence indicated the limits of 'the civilizing process' (Heywood, 1904: facing p. 170).

In conducting the Renaissance tournament and the game of *calcio*, a great deal of attention was paid to the participants' social status and appearance. The Great Tournament Roll of Westminister commemorates a tournament staged by Henry VIII in 1511 to celebrate the birth of his son by Catherine of Aragon. Thirty of the Roll's 36 pictures illustrate the entry and exit processions of the splendidly colorful knights and their grandly caparisoned mounts; just three of the pictures are devoted to the jousts between Henry and his opponents (Anglo, 1968). Heraldic devices certified the aristocratic lineage of every participant. The proper presentation of a game of *calcio* required a similar awareness of social status and appearance. In his *Discorso sopra il Giuoco del Calcio Fiorentino* (1580), Giovanni de' Bardi specified that the contestants should be 'gentlemen, from eighteen years of age to forty-five, beautiful and vigorous, of gallant bearing and good report'. The gentlemen players should wear 'goodly raiment and seemly, well fitting and handsome' (Heywood, 1904: 166–7; Mommsen, 1941).

The fascination with geometrical space that one observes in the game of *calcio* was even more obvious in the Renaissance fencer's art. Treatises on the sport emphasized the aesthetic appeal of the fencer's elegant movements. Camillo Agrippa's *Trattato di Scientia d'Arme* (1533) and Girard Thibault's *L'Académie de l'espée* (1627) were, for instance, illustrated by numerous diagrams of the appropriate positions to take before, during and after a match (Eichberg, 1977, 1978). For his copperplate print *The Fencing Hall* (1608), Willem Swanenburgh arranged his fencers around a complicated geometrical pattern drawn in the middle of a tiled floor.

To be fully effective, demonstrations of proper appearance require spectators to appreciate them. The relationship between Renaissance contest and spectacle is nicely encapsulated in the era's most influential conduct book, Baldesar Castiglione's *Il Cortegiano* (1528). How should the courtier behave when at play? He should 'strive to be as elegant and handsome in the exercise of arms as he is adroit, and to feed his spectators' eyes with all those things that he thinks may give him added grace'. He should 'attract the eyes of the spectators even as the lodestone attracts iron' (Castiglione (trans. Singleton), 1959: 99–100).

Not all Renaissance sports were characterized by the shift from force to finesse, by the focus on appearance and decorum. French peasants continued for generations to struggle for possession of a football 'like dogs battling for a bone' (Bouet, 1968: 257) and the humbler citizens of Venice fought with their fists to seize or defend the bridges that spanned the city's canals and linked its neighborhoods (Davidsohn, 1927: vol. 4: 284–6; Gori, 1993; Körbs, 1938: 13-15). None the less, the sports of the aristocrat – if not those of the commoner – were submitted to the dictates of instrumental rationality. They were more carefully regulated, far more standardized, more frequently marked by technical innovation, and much more 'civilized' than medieval sports had been.

Whether or not the transition 'from force to finesse' allows us to conclude that modern sports began in the Renaissance (Krüger and McClelland, 1984) depends on one's conception of modern sports. If the crucial difference is pervasive quantification and the quest for records made possible by quantification, then the origins of modern sports can be traced back no farther than the early eighteenth century. There were, of course, instances of the quantification of results even in antiquity, in Roman chariot races if not at the Olympic

Games. Rühl has, moreoever, uncovered some long-forgotten evidence of quantification in medieval sports; the victors at tournaments were determined by the number of points accumulated over the course of a series of jousts (Rühl, 1986, 1993). *Calcio* players scored points and Renaissance archery matches, which were immensely popular among the nascent bourgeoisie, also required an element of quantification. None of these instances of quantification remotely resembles the modern passion for precise measurement and statistical permutations.

And none of these instances prompted the use of quantified results as a way to set a sports record, which can, in fact, be defined as the best recorded quantified achievement. (The use of the term in this sense dates from the late nineteenth century.) McClelland notes correctly that Renaissance humanists urged the emulation of antiquity, but the mere emulation of ancient athletic feats fails to warrant the claim that 'the quest for records [was] already present, unnoticed in its embryonal state' (Krüger and McClelland, 1984: 11). Without systematic quantification and the comparison of quantified results, there was simply no way to establish sports records. This fact must be emphasized. Like the Greeks whom they admired, Renaissance theorists tended to conceptualize the world in static geometric forms in accordance with 'a metaphysics of finiteness'; modern sports, on the contrary, 'are associated ... with the theory of progress' (Ullmann, 1971: 336). Beyond every sports record lies, potentially, another record.

THE EIGHTEENTH AND NINETEENTH CENTURIES

A great deal of the difference between Renaissance and modern sports is suggested by two German terms, 'Maß' and 'Messen', both translated by the English word 'measure'. The first term refers to a sense of balance or proportion; the second to numerical measurements. The two terms differ as geometry differs from arithmetic. 'Maß' was demonstrated by the fancy equestrian ballets popular during the late Renaissance, in which French or Italian horsemen guided their mounts through a series of pirouettes and other dance steps. In fact, the 'geometric character' of equestrian ballet was inspired by and derived from the movements of the pavane and other grave and stately dances (Eichberg, 1978: 33). (The Olympic sport of dressage is a relic of this kind

of exercise, but dressage has been modernized 'by the introduction of a point system'; Eichberg, 1980: 362). 'Messen', in contrast, was strikingly observable in the English passion for horse races, for which the stopwatch was used as early as 1731.

An older generation of German historians (Kloeren, 1935; Schöffler, 1935) emphasized the English origins of modern sports, but more recent German scholarship has called attention to the transition from 'Maß' to 'Messen' that occurred in German schools like the one established by C.G. Salzmann at Schnepfenthal in 1784 (Bernett, 1971; Eichberg, 1974a, 1974b). At these elite academies, boys were encouraged to run, leap, throw, swim and climb. Their achievements were carefully recorded. As Salzmann wrote of J.C.F. GutsMuths, who taught with him at Schnepfenthal, 'Herr GutsMuths keeps faithful records of these exercises and that allows him to judge to the fraction of an inch what each pupil's strength can achieve and how much it increases from week to week' (Bernett, 1971: 75). While there is no doubt that educators like Salzmann and GutsMuths were enchanted by the possibilities of measurement, they were humanistically inclined and not particularly interested in competition. Looking at ice-skaters, G.U.A. Vieth observed, 'Beginners are enticed by races on the ice, but competition is not a good thing; the effort to skate faster destroys all the beauty of the activity' (Eichberg, 1974b: 27). In the long run, men like Salzmann, GutsMuths and Vieth contributed little to the development of modern sports.

The next generation of German physical educators actually retarded that development. Friedrich Ludwig Jahn and the *Turnbewegung* ('gymnastics movement') that he inspired represented a romantic 'return to nature' that was quite hostile to the notion of quantified achievement (Jahn, 1884–5). Citing some of the symbols of modern sports, Harro Hagen, twentieth-century spokesman for the *Turnbewegung*, urged the renunciation of 'concrete stadium, cinder track, tape-measure, stopwatch, manicured lawn, and track shoes. ... In their place comes the simple meadow, free nature' (Eichberg, 1973: 120). Hagen's views were typical. 'It is no accident', wrote Edmund Neuendorff, national leader of the *Deutsche Turnerschaft* (German Gymnastics Association), that modern sports 'originated in England, a land without music or metaphysics' (Neuendorff, 1934: vol. 4: 474).

Neuendorff was right about the origins of modern sports (if not about the nullity of English music and metaphysics). Most of the formal-structural characteristics of modern sports (Dunning, 1973; Guttmann, 1978) can be identified in eighteenth-century England (where there was a striking concern for quantification and for records; Kloeren, 1935). Whether or not the English enthusiasm for sports was driven by a mania for gambling, which is what many foreign observers thought, is debatable.

The rationalization of sports took many forms. As the passion for sports spread throughout English society, rules were codified. James Broughton, the century's most famous pugilist, established the rules of his combat sport in 1743 and introduced the use of the glove (for gentlemen amateurs) in 1747 (Brailsford, 1988). The written rules for cricket also date from this period when, for instance, the dimensions of the bat and the pitch were specified and niceties like the leg-before-wicket dismissal were mentioned. The first complete set of cricket rules appeared in 1744, which was also the first year from which we have records of a fully scored match.

Rules are useless without a means to enforce them. Two of the most important organizations in the history of modern sports were the Jockey Club (1752) and the Marylebone Cricket Club (1787). Both organizations were initially dominated by members of the aristocracy whose ambitions were national rather than local. To bring order into the sport of thoroughbred racing, James Weatherby, who was the Jockey Club's secretary, treasurer, solicitor and stakeholder, began in 1769 to publish the *Racing Calendar* (Birley, 1993: 136). Neither organization was able to achieve complete control of its sport until well into the next century, but a start was made, which is more than can be said of boxing (Brailsford, 1988; Brookes, 1978; Vamplew, 1976).

Whatever the intentions of the Jockey Club, eighteenth-century transportation was inadequate to 'nationalize' horse races, most of which remained purely local affairs for farm animals ridden by their owners. In 1836, Lord George Bentinck introduced the horse-drawn van to carry thoroughbreds from venue to venue. Four years later, railroads began to transport them (as well as the tens of thousands of spectators eager to spend 'a day at the races') (Vamplew, 1979). William Clarke's cricket team, the All-England Eleven, took to the rails in 1846 (Brookes, 1978: 101; Sissons, 1988: 10–11). Steamboats did for international competition what the railroad did for national. Thanks to the introduction of regularly scheduled transatlantic steamers in 1841, teams of touring English cricketers were able to depart for North America in 1859 and Australia in 1862 (Brailsford, 1991).

The revolutions in transportation and communication that are a staple of every historical account of the nineteenth century accelerated the formation of national sports organizations. England's incipiently bureaucratic Football Association (1863) was among the first. It was quickly followed by the Rugby Football Union (1871) and by national organizations for swimming (1874), boxing (1880), track and field (1880), rowing (1882) and cycling (1884). In the United States, the 22-club National Association of Base Ball Players was formed in 1859, only 15 years after Alexander Cartwright established the rules of the game (Seymour, 1960; Goldstein, 1989). By 1876, the United States was technologically advanced enough for a group of businessmen to form an eight-team National League of Professional Base Ball Clubs. A coast-to-coast rail network made it a simple matter for teams as distant as the Chicago White Sox and the New York Highlanders to compete on a regular basis. The invention of the telegraph made it possible for news of the results to be flashed from city to city. Technological innovations like the linotype and photogravure enabled newspapers to publicize these results within hours of the end of the contest.

Technological advances also transformed the implements with which the game was played. Every modern sport, from skiing to rollerskating, experienced this transformation. Cycling is a perfect example of this process. The sport began in 1817, when Karl Freiherr von Drais, an eccentric German nobleman, invented a simple two-wheeled device propelled by alternate thrusts of the foot against the ground. By mid-century, propulsion came by means of pedals attached to the axel of a large front wheel. In 1880, the Tangent and Coventry Tricycle Company introduced the chain drive. A year later, Erneste Michaux built a factory to mass produce bicycles for a booming market. John Boyd Dunlop invented a pneumatic tire in 1888 and the brothers Michelin outdid him, in 1891, with one that was tubeless and easily detachable. By this time, the dangerously unstable 'high wheeler' was replaced by the 'safety bike', which had two wheels of equal size (McGurn, 1987; Vigarello, 1988: 15–18).

Rowing was similarly transformed by rapid nineteenth-century invention. The clumsy oaken boats in which London's eighteenth-century ferrymen competed for Thomas Doggett's Coat and Badge (1715) became the lightweight modern scull. 'A typical boat in 1820 ... was thirty-five feet long, weighed 700 pounds, and ... seated ten rowers. ... In contrast, a typical shell in 1865, made of paper-thin

Spanish cedar with a single plank to a side, was forty feet long, weighed only 35 pounds, and … seated one rower' (Johns, 1983: 25–6). The iron outrigger, invented by Henry Clasper in 1845, and the sliding seat were important innovations. They efficiently transformed the oarsman's muscular efforts into a forward motion unthinkable in Doggett's time (Halladay, 1991; Wigglesworth, 1992).

The difference between the ferryman's awkward boat and the oarsman's streamlined scull is symbolic of the specialization that is another fundamental characteristic of modern sports. Folk football included 'elements of what later became highly specialized games' such as soccer, rugby, field hockey and American football (Dunning, 1973). Within the American version of the game, there was further specialization in that the players were distributed among eleven offensive and eleven defensive positions (to which, in the twentieth century, were added still other playing positions occupied by members of the 'specials' teams). Other sports revealed other kinds of specialization. The rules of golf do not stipulate offensive and defensive players, but every golfer relies on a variety of specialized clubs designed for a variety of different situations and conditions.

Among the specialized roles of modern sports is that of the sports physiologist. As preparation for sports participation became increasingly scientific, physiologists began to study athletes' bodies in order to explain their superior performances. By the end of the century, they were able to use the results of their study to guide athletes to still better performances (Hoberman, 1992). Journalists began to refer to athletes as 'perfected machines' (upon which coaches and trainers were expected to work in the spirit of mechanical engineers). Discussions of strategy and tactics resembled the time and motion studies of Fredrick Winslow Taylor.

Time and space were measured with increasing precision and they were both reconceptualized. The duration of the game of folk football was determined, more often than not, by the time it took to establish a winner. While this remains true in many modern sports, like tennis and golf, modern team games typically last for a predetermined number of minutes. Nineteenth-century players could interrupt the flow of time with a 'time out', but there was an inexorable clock that stopped the game even if it was a scoreless tie. (Among team games, cricket, baseball, and volleyball are temporal exceptions; soccer, rugby, American and Australian rules football, basketball, field hockey, ice hockey, lacrosse and team handball

are the rule.) The spatial parallel to the set time within which a contest must come to a conclusion is the set distance which is to be traversed in the shortest possible time (which, by the end of the nineteenth century, was frequently measured to the hundredth of a second).

Many premodern sports occurred in a space of their own, which was often considered sacred. Antiquity's Olympic Games and the sacrificial ballgames of the Aztec and Mayan cultures are two examples of this. Other sports, like the footraces that took place on the occasion of a medieval fair, took place wherever a suitable ground was to be found. Modern sports are almost invariably played in a specially designated and designed space that is poorly adapted to any other activity. In some cases, the site is either a natural one, as in surfing, or one that has been constructed in imitation of nature, as in golf. In most cases, however, the modern 'field' of play is a geometrically designed artefact.

The Football Association determined that soccer be played on a rectangular ground. The vertical goalpost bar was added in 1875, the sidelines seven years later. During the late nineteenth century, the Scots architect Archibald Leitch constructed the familiar doubledecker grandstands at Ibrox, Hampden, Stamford Bridge, Villa Park, Old Trafford, and other sites. Terraces were in place before 1900. Executive boxes were a twentieth-century addition (Bale, 1993, 1994). Nineteenth-century baseball, which was a more complexly quantified game than the various codes of football, was less modern than soccer in that the 'parks' in which the game was played were an odd mix of premodern and modern ludic spaces. The four bases were symmetrically situated and the field of play was bounded to the right and left by a pair of symmetrical foul lines radiating from home plate, but there was no outer boundary and the 'outfield' of each ball park had its own unique configuration.

During the sixteenth and seventeenth centuries, hundreds of ball houses were constructed for the elaborate indoor raquet games that were the precursors of modern tennis, but most premodern sports were played outdoors. The nineteenth century saw a proliferation of buildings specifically designed for swimming, bowling, ice skating, roller skating and other sports (Eichberg, 1988). Indeed, basketball was invented by James Naismith in 1891 in order to provide members of the Springfield, Massachusetts, YMCA with an indoors game that could be played despite New England's inclement winter weather (Guttmann, 1988: 70–4; Peterson, 1990).

Abstraction is still another aspect of rationalization. Many objects underwent what Vigarello (1988) terms *'déréalisation'*. Mimetic archery targets that *looked* like animals were transformed into abstract fields formed by concentric circles. In track-and-field sports, hedges became hurdles, streams became shallow rectangular pools of water, the hammer became a ball and chain. The steed upon which the Renaissance acrobat performed equestrian stunts became the nineteenth-century gymnast's wooden 'horse'. Innovations of this sort allowed the standardization required for equality of opportunity.

Rationalization also altered the means by which champions were selected. While it is still the custom to declare a boxer 'champion of the world' on the basis of a challenge bout, it is typical of modern team sports to determine championships by a fixed number of contests that take place in the course of a 'knock-out' or 'round-robin' tournament or in the course of an entire season of play. In the early years of baseball, teams like the New York Mutuals challenged teams like the Brooklyn Atlantics to a friendly match. After a summer of play, a team might claim to be the best in the nation, but there was no satisfactory way to test the claim. The solution was to create a league in which every team plays every other team a set number of times each season. To arrange for each of eight baseball teams to play each of seven other teams twenty-two times a summer over an area as large as the entire northeast quarter of the United States required a considerable facility with numbers. Today, after the increase in the number of teams and the expansion of baseball, basketball, football and ice hockey leagues across the entire American continent, a computer is required to schedule the times and places of the contests.

The mathematics necessary simply to schedule a season or to arrange for the World Cup are of no interest to the average sports fan, but the statistics of the game have an unbreakable hold on the modern fan's imagination. Cricket, with the number of runs scored and the number of wickets taken, is a good example of this; baseball is a still better one. The spatial separation of the players on the field and the specialization of their roles facilitated the accumulation of accurate individual and team statistics. The numerical aspects of the game – three strikes, four balls, three outs, four bases, nine innings, 154 games – provided the opportunity for infinitely varied arithmetical calculations. Nineteenth-century newspapers responded eagerly to the passion for statistical data and quickly introduced 'box scores' of individual games and a won–lost matrix indicating the position of each team on any given day of the season (Seymour, 1960).

THE TWENTIETH CENTURY

Throughout the twentieth century, modern sports have experienced an acceleration of change without a fundamental shift in direction. The measurement of times and distances has become increasingly precise. Hand-held stopwatches have been replaced by digital clocks, and tape-measures by electronic scanners. At the Olympic Games celebrated in Munich (1972), swimmers were timed to the thousandth of a second in a pool where lanes differed in length by no more than half a centimeter. In team games, the quantification of achievement has progressed to the point where multifactor regression formulae can be used to calculate the 'productivity' of each player. The quantification of modern sports is an ideal basis for computer games based on statistical probabilities. At Microsoft's research center, computer programmers have developed an electronic baseball game that will have three hundred different statistical categories (Katz, 1995).

The rationalization of facilities and equipment has also continued. Nineteenth-century runners were content to race on cinder tracks, the first of which was constructed in London in 1867, but their descendants compete on scientifically designed artificial surfaces. The 'containerization' of ludic space has gone so far that baseball games, once played on summer's grassy fields, can now take place in late October in immense domed stadia constructed at the cost of hundreds of millions of dollars (Bale, 1993; Eichberg, 1988). Although the craft that won the first America's Cup, in 1851, was constructed to race rather than to carry commercial cargoes, it seems almost as archaic as a Greek trireme when it is compared to the computer-modelled boats that now compete for the trophy. It is, in fact, difficult to think of a modern sport whose equipment has not been changed by the introduction of new materials and new designs.

Technological innovation has continued to produce new sports. Bicycles were followed by automobiles and airplanes, which meant, inevitably, races to see which automobile was the fastest, which airplane was able to fly faster, higher or farther. Whether one looks at a phenomenon as complicated as the Indianapolis 500 or at an object as simple as the vaulter's fiberglass pole, the importance of technology is obvious.

Athletes are now 'engineered' as intensely as their facilities and equipment. The scientific study of the human body and its movements is rightly thought to be an essential part of the quest for the most efficient athletic performance (Hoberman, 1992). Trial and error have been replaced by systematic study. German scientists led the way in the scientific selection and training of potential champions. To gain admission to East Germany's *Sportschulen*, where elite athletes were produced *en masse*, children submitted to ten days of tests that determined, among other things, the ratio of red blood cells to white. (The higher the percentage of red cells, the greater the potential for aerobic sports.) Once accepted, the children were trained by a centralized sports bureaucracy determined to enhance their nation's prestige by winning international competitions, garnering Olympic medals and setting sports records. When scientific evidence proved that anabolic steroids improved performances in all sports requiring bursts of strength, the bureaucrats introduced a secret, compulsory, carefully monitored and highly successful program to administer anabolic steroids to East Germany's male and female athletes.

Germans were not the only ones to utilize modern science in the quest for athletic supremacy. To rationalize human movement, computer experts like Gideon Ariel, an Israeli-born American, pioneered the use of simulations to model the optimal way to hit a golf ball, to ski, to run the 400 meter hurdles (Moore, 1977). The US Olympic Committee, which officially condemned the use of banned drugs, allegedly tolerated and even encouraged their use (Voy, 1991).

As the plague of illicit drugs indicates, modern sports are a thoroughly international phenomenon. If the railroad, the telegraph and the daily newspaper symbolize the nineteenth-century nationalization of modern sports, the Boeing 747 and the SONY television set can be taken as technological (and economic) symbols of the globalization of sports in the twentieth century. To organize regular international competition (as opposed to occasional challenges), international sports bureaucracies were formed. As early as 1894, steamships, the Atlantic cable and a cosmopolitan spirit enabled Pierre de Coubertin to found the International Olympic Committee (IOC) and plan successfully for the first Olympic Games of the modern era. By then, international industrial-commercial fairs, like London's 1851

Crystal Palace Exhibition, were common (and two of the first three modern Olympics took place, to their detriment, as constituent parts of a world fair).

The IOC was hardly a modern bureaucratic organization. Coubertin named the first members and the committee has, ever since, elected its own members. For decades, the IOC was composed mainly of titled aristocrats whose accomplishments as horsemen and marksmen exceeded their competence as sports administrators. None the less, the principle of regularly occurring international competition was established.

In the course of the twentieth century, similar organizations were established for dozens of other modern sports. The most important of them were those created to govern Association football (soccer), swimming and diving, and track and field: the Fédération Internationale de Football Association (1904), the Fédération Internationale de Natation (1908) and the International Amateur Athletic Federation (1912). The French, who led the way in global acceptance of the metric system, were also leaders in the establishment of the International Olympic Committee and the various international sports federations. England's insular and arrogant Football Association rejected membership in FIFA when the soccer federation was founded and withdrew twice when FIFA took positions unpopular in Great Britain.

The prerequisite for FIFA and every other international sports federation was the nineteenth-century diffusion of modern sports from England to the entire world (Bottenburg, 1994; Guttmann, 1994). Wherever British military men, colonial adminstrators, missionaries, educators, settlers, or entrepreneurs went, they carried with them their enthusiasm for cricket, soccer, rugby and the entire gamut of modern sports. Where the British exercised political control, as they did in India and through most of Africa, they tended to impose their games upon the people whom they ruled. Where the British were merely a dominant economic presence, which was the case in South America, their sports tended to be spread by the process of emulation; the sons of the local elite wanted to play British games just as they wanted to wear British clothes and speak English with a proper British accent. In areas where the United States rather than the United Kingdom exercised hegemonic influence, baseball rather than soccer became the most common sport. In the late nineteenth century, this was the case in Japan, in Central America and in Cuba. After the Second World War,

American political and economic hegemony led to the rapid global diffusion of basketball even where British sports had been supreme. On the islands of Trinidad and Tobago, for instance, young men who once wanted to become a second Learie Constantine now imitate Michael Jordan and Shaquille O'Neal (Mandle and Mandle, 1988).

In fact, they may actually *become* the next stars of the National Basketball Association. Premodern sports are almost invariably characterized by stringent rules of inclusion and exclusion based on differences in age, gender, race, ethnicity and social class. Participation in antiquity's Olympic Games, for instance, was initially limited to free (rather than enslaved) ethnically Greek males. Entry into a medieval tournament required proof of noble status. Nineteenth-century sports were more egalitarian, but there were exclusionary rules or customs barring African Americans from Major League baseball, preventing manual workers from participating in a number of amateur sports, and 'protecting' girls and women from sports that were thought to endanger their reproductive organs or to jeopardize their femininity. It is impossible to say whether these barriers were dismantled as a result of the general democratization of society or as a consequence of the desire to field the best team and to determine the absolutely best performance, but the logic of modern sports dictates equality of opportunity as a guarantee that victories are achieved and not simply ascribed. On the basis of royal dogma, Amenophis II of Egypt was proclaimed the greatest athlete of all time (Decker, 1987); Jesse Owens won races and set records to prove *his* superiority.

Unlike the more or less unplanned spread of sports in the nineteenth century, the global diffusion of late-twentieth-century sports has frequently been driven by multinational corporations (Bale and Maguire, 1993; Guttmann, 1994; Maguire, 1991, 1993). Nineteenth-century entrepreneurs like Albert Goodwill Spaulding were keen to export sports equipment, and twentieth-century sporting goods manufacturers, like Rossignol and Nike, compete fiercely on the international market; but the most dramatic development has been the promotion of sports spectacles and the advertisement of sports equipment via satellite television.

In 1977, when the right to telecast cricket tests went to the Australian Broadcasting Corporation rather than to Kerry Packer's Channel 9, Packer, with financial support from Benson & Hedges, organized and successfully marketed an alternative: the one-day cricket matches of World Series Cricket (Cashman,

1984: 159–67). The imbrication of sports leagues, equipment manufacturers, television networks and marketing organizations is immensely complicated. 'TWI [Trans World Sport], the company involved in selling the NFL [National Football League] highlights package to European broadcasters, is, in fact, a sister company of the IMG [International Marketing Group], the NFL's marketing agent for Europe' (Maguire, 1991: 321). Trans World Sport has no monopoly. NFL games can also be seen on Scanset in Scandinavia, on Tele 5 in Germany and Austria, on Canal Plus in France and Belgium, and on other stations the length and breadth of the continent. Television rights to the Olympic Games, which are seen by billions of viewers (and potential customers), now cost hundreds of millions of dollars.

HOW DID MODERN SPORTS EMERGE?

Since it is obvious that the Olympic Games, the World Cup, and many other sports events have become highly commercialized, globally marketed spectacles, it is hardly surprising that Marxist historians and sociologists have attempted to explain modern sports as an inevitable consequence of capitalist development (Brohm, 1976; Rigauer, 1969; Rittner, 1976; Vinnai, 1970; Wohl, 1973). They point out, quite correctly, that England was the first nation to develop mature industrial capitalism and that England was also the birthplace of modern sports. Their functionalist argument posits a necessary relationship between these two facts. The first led inevitably to the second because industrial capitalism requires a labor force that is physically healthy, manually dexterous, submissive to the temporal and spatial requirements of assembly-line work, and politically docile. The muscular exertion and the skills associated with sports participation are alleged to contribute to the workers' health and manual dexterity; the need to accept the rules of the game socializes factory hands to routinized work; and the entertainment afforded by sports spectacles diverts the exploited workforce from political action. Modern sports are, therefore, an instrument to preserve the class structure of capitalist society.

One response to this rather simplistic functionalist argument is to ask if modern sports do what Marxist historians and sociologists say they do. While moderate non-competitive exercise does improve a person's health, the intense competitiveness of modern sports causes countless major and minor injuries. Boxers suffer brain damage, gymnasts injure their backs, runners ruin their knees, and ballgames take their toll in broken arms and legs. The argument about manual dexterity is even less persuasive. The sport most closely associated with the working class is soccer (Association football), a game which minimizes the use of the hand and maximizes pedal dexterity (which is not especially prized by factory owners). The argument that sports participation socializes athletes to accept rules and regulations is much more plausible, especially when the insights of Gramsci and Foucault are added to those of Marx (Gruneau, 1983; Hargreaves, 1986; Rail and Harvey, 1995), but one must also acknowledge that games can encourage tactical inventiveness and a spirit of aggressive independence as well as an awareness of the arbitrary nature of the rules and a desire cleverly to evade them. The belief that modern sports induce political apathy may be valid in many cases, but there is also a great deal of evidence for the association of modern sports and movements for national independence (Guttmann, 1994: 171–88).

In addition to these specific objections, there are hard questions to be asked of Marxists who assert a causal relationship between capitalism and the development of modern sports. If these sports are an instrument used by capitalists to exploit proletarians, how is it that dozens of empirical studies have demonstrated that sports participation is almost always positively correlated with income and education (that is, the alleged exploiters are more likely to participate in sports than those whom they are said to exploit; Guttmann, 1981)? If modern sports are the product of capitalist development, why did they attain their most paradigmatic form in the German Democratic Republic, an avowedly anticapitalist society? It is doubtful that there is a good answer to either question.

What, then, is the relationship between capitalism and modern sports? The clue to the relationship can be found when one looks to the formal-structural characteristics of sports rather than to their alleged social functions. The historical simultaneity of capitalist development and the emergence of modern sports may be explained by the role of Weberian instrumental rationality in both phenomena. Rather than seeing one as a function of the other, we can see both, in their shared formal-structural characteristics, as a consequence of what the philosopher Alfred North Whitehead identified as the scientific revolution of the seventeenth century (1925). That century's mathematical discoveries were popularized in the eighteenth century, at which time we can observe the beginnings of our modern obsession with quantification in sports. The emergence of modern sports represents the slow development of an empirical, experimental, mathematical *Weltanschauung*. England's early leadership has less to do with Adam Smith than with Sir Isaac Newton and the founders of the Royal Society for the Advancement of Science.

The philosopher Hans Lenk has suggested this interpretation of the origins of modern sports: 'Achievement sports, that is, sports whose achievements are extended beyond the here and now through measured comparisons, are closely connected to the scientific-experimental attitudes of the modern West' (1972: 144). The historian Henning Eichberg noted the same connection (1973: 135–7). The plausibility of this hypothesis about origins is heightened by the fact that Romanticism, with its pervasive anti-scientific bias, encouraged the survival of premodern sports like hunting and fishing and hindered the emergence of modern sports. The strongest twentieth-century opposition to modern sports came from Romantics like the men who led the German *Turnbewegung*, men who were hostile to modernity in all its many forms (Guttmann, 1994: 141–5). Today, modern sports are a global phenomenon, but they are weakest in the Islamic world, where religious fundamentalism and a suspicion of modern science are strongest.

DISAPPEARANCE?

Have we entered a 'postmodern' era whose sports are characterized less by instrumental rationality and more by spontaneity and playfulness? French theorists like Ehrenburg (1991) have suggested this and have coined terms like 'les sports californiens' to categorize skateboarding, windsurfing, hang-gliding, and similar vertiginous activities whose thrills are 'sometimes compared with the pleasure that is derived from orgasm or drugs' (Midol and Broyer, 1995: 209). Such sports are unquestionably a part of today's ludic landscape, but, as Jarvie and Maguire have indicated, the announcement of 'postmodernity' seems premature (1994). Modern sports have existed side by side with traditional sports like Spanish bullfighting and Japanese sumo wrestling. They now share the global sports arena with 'les sports californiens', but, as Bromberger has shown in his study of French and Italian soccer (1995), there is no sign as yet that modern sports have lost their almost magical ability to excite and enthrall.

REFERENCES AND FURTHER READING

Adelman, Melvin (1986) *A Sporting Time*. Urbana, IL: University of Illinois Press.

Anglo, S. (1968) *The Great Tournament Roll of Westminster*, 2 vols. Oxford: Clarendon Press.

Ariès, Philippe and Margolin, J.C. (eds) (1982) *Les Jeux à la Renaissance*. Paris: Vrin.

Baker, William J. (1982) *Sports in the Western World*. Totowa: Rowman & Littlefield.

Bale, John (1993) *Sport, Space and the City*. London: Routledge.

Bale, John (1994) *The Landscapes of Sport*. Leicester: University of Leicester Press.

Bale, John and Maguire, Joseph (eds) (1993) *The Global Sports Arena*. London: Frank Cass.

Bernett, Hajo (1971) *Die pädagogische Neugestaltung der bürgerlichen Leibesübungen durch die Philanthropen*. Schorndorf: Karl Hofmann.

Birley, Derek (1993) *Sport and the Making of Britain*. Manchester: University of Manchester Press.

Bottenburg, Maarten van (1994) *Verborgen Competitie*. Amsterdam: Bert Bakker.

Bouet, Michel (1968) *Signification du sport*. Paris: Éditions universitaires.

Brailsford, Dennis (1969) *Sport and Society*. London: Routledge & Kegan Paul.

Brailsford, Dennis (1988) *Bareknuckles*. Cambridge: Lutterworth.

Brailsford, Dennis (1991) *Sport, Time, and Society*. London: Routledge.

Brailsford, Dennis (1992) *British Sport*. Cambridge: Lutterworth.

Bredekamp, Horst (1993) *Florentiner Fußball*. New York: Campus Verlag.

Brohm, Jean-Marie (1976) *Sociologie politique du sport*. Paris: Jean-Pierre Delarge.

Bromberger, Christian (1995) *Le Match de football*. Paris: Éditions de la Maison de l'Homme.

Brookes, Christopher (1978) *English Cricket*. London: Weidenfeld & Nicolson.

Cashman, Richard (1984) *'Ave a Go Yer Mug!* Sydney: Collins.

Castiglione, Baldesar (trans. Charles Singleton) (1959) *The Book of the Courtier*. New York: Anchor Books.

Davidsohn, Robert (1922–27) *Geschichte von Florenz*, 4 vols. Berlin: E.S. Mittler & Sohn.

Davis, Robert C. (1994) *The War of the Fists*. New York: Oxford University Press.

Decker, Wolfgang (1987) *Sport und Spiel im alten Aegypten*. Munich: C.H. Beck.

Dunning, Eric (1973) 'The structural-functional properties of folk-games and modern sports', *Sportwissenschaft*, 3: 215–32.

Dunning, Eric (1999) *Sport Matters*. London: Routledge.

Dunning, Eric and Rojek, Chris (eds) (1992) *Sport and Leisure in the Civilizing Process*. London: Macmillan.

Dunning, Eric and Sheard, Kenneth (1979) *Barbarians, Gentlemen and Players*. Oxford: Martin Robertson.

Ehrenberg, Alain (1991) *Le Culte de la Performance*. Paris: Calmann-Lévy.

Eichberg, Henning (1973) *Der Weg des Sports in die industrielle Zivilisation*. Baden-Baden: Nomos.

Eichberg, Henning (1974a) '"Auf Zoll und Quintlein": Sport und Quantifizierungsprozeß', *Archiv für Kulturgeschichte*, 56: 141–76.

Eichberg, Henning (1974b) 'Der Beginn des modernen Leistens', *Sportwissenschaft*, 4: 21–48.

Eichberg, Henning (1977) 'Geometrie als Barocke Verhaltensnorm', *Zeitschrift für historische Forschung*, 4: 17–50.

Eichberg, Henning (1978) *Leistung-Spannung-Geschwindigkeit*. Stuttgart: Klett-Cotta.

Eichberg, Henning (1980) 'Sport im 19. Jahrhundert: Genese einer industriellen Verhaltensform', in H. Ueberhorst (ed.), *Geschichte der Leibesübungen*. Vol. III. Berlin: Bartels und Wernitz. pp. 350–412.

Eichberg, Henning (1983) 'Leistung zwischen Wänden', *Berliner Historische Studien*, 9: 119–39.

Eichberg, Henning (1988) *Leistungsräume: Sport als Umweltproblem*. Münster: LIT-Verlag.

Eisenberg, Christiane (1999) *'English Sports' und deutsche Bürger*. Paderborn: Ferdinand Schöningh.

Elias, Norbert (1969) *Über den Prozeß der Zivilisation*, 2 vols. Berne: Francke.

Elias, Norbert and Dunning, Eric (1986) *Quest for Excitement*. Oxford: Basil Blackwell.

Fleckenstein, Josef (ed.) (1985) *Das ritterliche Turnier im Mittelalter*. Göttingen: Vandenhoek & Ruprecht.

Goldstein, Warren (1989) *Playing for Keeps*. Ithaca, NY: Cornell University Press.

Gori, Gigliola (1993) 'The Gioco del Ponte in the Italian sporting tradition', in Roland Renson, Teresa Gonzalez Aja, Gilbert Andrieu, Manfred Lämmer and Roberta Park (eds), *Actas del Congreso Internacional ISPES 1991*. Madrid: Instituto Nacional de Educación Física. pp. 114–18.

Gruneau, Richard (1983) *Class, Sports, and Social Development*. Amherst, MA: University of Massachusetts Press.

Guttmann, Allen (1978) *From Ritual to Record*. New York: Columbia University Press.

Guttmann, Allen (1981) 'Introduction to Bero Rigauer', *Sport and Work*. New York: Columbia University Press.

Guttmann, Allen (1986) *Sports Spectators*. New York: Columbia University Press.

Guttmann, Allen (1988) *A Whole New Ball Game*. Chapel Hill, NC: University of North Carolina Press.

Guttmann, Allen (1994) *Games and Empires.* New York: Columbia University Press.

Halladay, Eric (1991) *Rowing in England.* Manchester: University of Manchester Press.

Hargreaves, John (1986) *Sport, Power and Culture.* Cambridge: Polity Press.

Henricks, Thomas (1991) *Disputed Pleasures.* Westport, CT: Greenwood Press.

Heywood, William (1904) *Pallio and Ponte.* London: Methuen.

Hoberman, John M. (1992) *Mortal Engines.* New York: Free Press.

Holt, Richard (1981) *Sport and Society in Modern France.* London: Macmillan.

Holt, Richard (1989) *Sport and the British.* Oxford: Clarendon Press.

Indorf, Hans (1938) *Fair Play und der englische Sportgeist.* Hamburg: Friederischen, de Gruyter.

Jahn, Friedrich Ludwig (1884–85) *Werke* (ed. Carl Euler), 2 vols. Hof: G.A. Grau.

Jarvie, Grant and Maguire, Joseph (1994) *Sport and Leisure in Social Thought.* London: Routledge.

Johns, Elizabeth (1983) *Thomas Eakins.* Princeton, NJ: Princeton University Press.

Katz, Donald (1995) 'Welcome to the electronic arena', *Sports Illustrated*, 83 (1): 58–77.

Kircher, Rudolf (1927) *Fair Play.* Frankfurt: Frankfurter Societätsdruckerei.

Kloeren, Marie (1935) *Sport und Rekord.* Cologne: Kölner Anglistische Arbeiten.

Körbs, Werner (1938) *Vom Sinn der Leibesübungen zur Zeit der italienischen Renaissance.* Berlin: Weidmann.

Krockow, Christian Graf von (1972) *Sport und Industriegesellschaft.* Munich: Piper.

Krüger, Arnd and McClelland, John (eds) (1984) *Die Anfänge des modernen Sports in der Renaissance.* London: Arena.

Lenk, Hans (1972) *Leistungssport.* Stuttgart: Kohlhammer.

Lowerson, John (1993) *Sport and the English Middle Classes, 1870–1914.* Manchester: University of Manchester Press.

McGurn, James (1987) *On Your Bicycle.* New York: Facts on File.

Maguire, Joseph (1991) 'The media–sport production complex', *European Journal of Communication*, 6: 315–36.

Maguire, Joseph (1993) 'Globalization, sport development, and the media', *Sport Science Review*, 2: 29–47.

Mandell, Richard D. (1976) 'The invention of the sports record', *Stadion*, 2: 250–64.

Mandell, Richard D. (1984) *Sport.* New York: Columbia University Press.

Mandle, Jay R. and Mandle, Joan D. (1988) *Grass Roots Commitment.* Parkersburg: Caribbean Books.

Mason, Tony (1988) *Sport in Britain.* London: Faber & Faber.

Mehl, Jean-Michel (ed.) (1993) *Jeux, sports et divertissements au moyen âge et à l'âge classique.* Paris: Éditions du Comité des Travaux Historiques et Scientifiques.

Midol, Nancy and Broyer, Gerard (1995) 'Toward an anthropological analysis of new sport cultures', *Sociology of Sport Journal*, 12: 204–12.

Mommsen, Theodor (1941) 'Football in Renaissance Florence', *Yale University Library Gazette*, 16: 14–19.

Moore, Kenny (1977) 'Gideon Ariel and his magic machine', *Sports Illustrated*, 67: 52–60.

Neuendorff, Edmund (1934) *Geschichte der neueren deutschen Leibesübung*, 4 vols. Dresden: Limpert.

Peterson, Robert W. (1990) *Cages to Jump Shots.* New York: Oxford University Press.

Rail, Genevieve (ed.) (1998) *Sport and Postmodern Times.* Albany, NY: State University of New York Press.

Rail, Genevieve and Harvey, Jean (1995) 'Body at work', *Sociology of Sport Journal*, 12: 164–79.

Rigauer, Bero (1969) *Sport und Arbeit.* Frankfurt: Suhrkamp.

Rinehart, Robert E. (1998) *Players All.* Bloomington, IN: Indiana University Press.

Rittner, Karin (1976) *Sport und Arbeitsteilung.* Frankfurt: Limpert.

Rühl, Joachim K. (1986) 'Wesen und Bedeutung vom Kampfaussagen und Trefferzählungen für die Geschichte des spätmittelalterlichen Tourniers', in Giselherr Spitzer and Dieter Schmidt (eds), *Sport zwischen Eigenständigkeit und Fremdbestimmung.* Bonn: Institut für Sportwissenschaft. pp. 82–112.

Rühl, Joachim K. (1993) 'Measurement of individual sport-performance in jousting combats', in Roland Renson, Teresa Gonzalez Aja, Gilbert Andrieu, Manfred Lämmer and Roberta Park (eds), *Actas del Congreso Internacional ISPES 1991.* Madrid: Instituto Nacional de Educación Física. pp. 226–37.

Schöffler, Herbert (1935) *England: Das Land des Sportes.* Leipzig: Bernhard Tauchnitz.

Seymour, Harold (1960) *Baseball.* New York: Oxford University Press.

Sissons, Ric (1988) *The Players.* London: Kingswood.

Stokvis, Ruud (1979) *Strijd over Sport.* Deventer: Van Loghum Slaterus.

Stokvis, Ruud (1989) *De Sportwereld.* Alphen aan den Rijn: Samsom.

Ullmann, Jacques (1971) *De la gymnastique aux sports modernes.* Paris: Vrin.

Vale, Marcia (1977) *The Gentleman's Recreations.* Totowa: Rowman & Littlefield.

Vamplew, Wray (1976) *The Turf.* London: Allen Lane.

Vamplew, Wray (1979) 'The sport of kings and commoners', in Richard Cashman and Michael McKernan (eds), *Sport in History.* St Lucia: University of Queensland Press. pp. 326–42.

Vigarello, Georges (1988) *Une Histoire culturelle du sport.* Paris: Robert Laffont.

Vinnai, Gerhard (1970) *Fußballsport als Ideologie.* Frankfurt: Europäische Verlagsanstalt.

Voy, Robert (with Kirk D. Deeter) (1991) *Drugs, Sports and Politics*. Champaign, IL: Human Kinetics.

Weber, Max (1920) *Gesammelte Aufsätze zur Religionssoziologie*, 3 vols. Tübingen: Mohr.

Weber, Max (1922) *Wirtschaft und Gesellschaft*, 2 vols. Tübingen: Mohr.

Whitehead, Alfred North (1925) *Science and the Modern World*. Cambridge, MA: Harvard University Press.

Wigglesworth, Neil (1992) *The History of English Rowing*. London: Frank Cass.

Wohl, Andrzej (1973) *Die gesellschaftlich-historischen Grundlagen des bürgerlichen Sports*. Cologne: Pahl-Rugenstein.

16

POLITICAL ECONOMY AND SPORT

George H. Sage

MEANINGS OF POLITICAL ECONOMY

The term political economy comes from two Greek words, *polis*, which means a city as a political unit, and *oikonomia*, denoting the management of a household. Use of the two words together began first during the feudal period in Western Europe and were used to describe the study of managing the revenues and expenditures of feudal monarchs. Since political affairs were in the hands of the monarchs and landed aristocracy, revenues and expenditures were obviously both political and economic matters (Clark, 1991; Staniland, 1985).

For the past 250 years, political economy has been used as a term to express the interdependence of political and economic phenomena. Gondwe (1992) explains that political economy is characterized by a 'study of people in the social process of producing and distributing the means of their own reproduction, in a given social environment or geographical domain, under rules promulgated and enforced by a political state' (p. 12). From a political economy perspective, economic and socio-political issues are too closely interrelated to be analyzed independently of one another, so an effort is made to accept the interrelatedness of politics and economics. Moreover, political economic analyses typically go beyond issues of efficiency to address basic moral issues of social justice, equity and the public good. Thus, the field of political economy has always been a much broader field than the conventional study of either economics or political science (Caporaso and Levine, 1992; Hibbs, 1987).

Three very broad paradigms have contended, and still contend, for prominence – classical political economy, neoclassical economics and radical political economy. That these very different perspectives have persisted over time illustrates the pervasive contested ideological motif underlying them.

Classical Political Economy

During the latter part of the eighteenth century Adam Smith, one of the writers on political economy during that era, wrote what became the foundation document for a school of thought called classical political economy. In his treatise *An Inquiry Into the Nature and Causes of the Wealth of Nations* ([1776] 1993), Smith proposed a new socio-economic system to replace what remained of feudalism. For Smith, a good society allowed everyone, at least in theory, the opportunity to pursue his or her self-interest. His vision of an ideal society was one in which competition in the marketplace prevailed, with a minimum amount of government direction or control. He postulated an 'invisible hand' of nature which made sure that as each individual was pursuing his or her own self-interest the interest of society was simultaneously being served. Smith's so-called 'laws of the market' played an important role in legitimating the principle of *laissez-faire* capitalism – the doctrine that government should not interfere with commerce (Spiegel, 1991).

Neoclassical Economics

Classical political economy waned during the nineteenth century, with the emergence of the new discipline of modern economics. For disciples of what became known as neoclassical economics, the term 'political' in political economy was no longer useful and therefore should be dropped in economic analyses.

Neoclassical economics was conceived of as a value-free scientific discipline, a natural science, like physics, using the same 'scientific' methodology. Neo-economists adopted the standardized technical vocabulary of the natural sciences and based their theories on positive propositions in the same manner as other positive sciences, eschewing value judgements, public advocacy and non-economic issues (Gondwe, 1992; Heilbroner, 1996; Jevons, [1871] 1970; Marshall, [1890] 1953).

Radical Political Economy

In parallel with classical political economy, another group of eighteenth- and nineteenth-century political economists agreed with the classical political economists' challenge to the power of the state in commerce, but they saw a conflict between the growing power of *laissez-faire* capitalism and the democratic aspirations embodied in the Enlightenment. This early radicalism was basically a reaction to the wretched social and economic conditions of the working class which grew out of the industrialization process of Western Europe (Sherman, 1987).

The most influential radical political economist of the latter nineteenth century was Karl Marx. He constructed an impressive theoretical critique of capitalism. Whereas classical political economists defended the autonomy of capital as necessary for protecting individual freedom from domination by government and aristocrats, 'Marx argued that the power of capital subverted the ability of citizens to shape their society in accordance with their democratically determined collective interests. In short, the freedom of capital meant a loss of freedom for people' (Clark, 1991: 58). For Marx, government should be constituted to serve the collective interests of citizens. And government is legitimate only when it is democratically established and based on widespread participation, and publicly accountable (Marx, 1970, 1975).

Ideology and Political Economy

Three ideologies dominate discussions about political economy – liberal, conservative and radical. These three ideologies are discussed below as competing models of social order. Ideology is a set of ideas, concepts and rationalizations that a group of people use to legitimate and justify their beliefs and behavior.

Liberal Ideology and Political Economy
Liberal ideology is associated with the ideas of the Enlightenment. Initially, it stood for individual freedom and rights against the arbitrary power of the state, the church and other people. According to this early, or classical, liberal view, the good society was one that permits individuals to freely pursue their private interests without institutional controls, and government was best when it governed the least. Classical political economy, then, stressed individualism, self-interest, free trade and the security of property.

Conservative Ideology and Political Economy Whereas classical political economy was formed as part of the liberal revolution of the Enlightenment, other political economists of the nineteenth century were skeptical of liberalism. They were alarmed by what they considered the erosion of the old social order that was sweeping Western Europe in the nineteenth century. The basis of feudal society had been stability, mutual expectations and duties, and a sense of belonging to a stable social unit. Liberal ideas emphasizing individual freedom, secularism and constitutional democracy were destroying the old structures of authority and emotional bonds that had united individuals and communities. So conservative voices mounted a defense of traditional society, using the stability of medieval society as their model. What was required, conservatives believed, was a strengthening of traditional values and institutions, grounding them in either divine wisdom or the authority of institutions such as the church, the patriarchal family and the local community (Clark, 1991).

Neoclassical economics, which had superseded classical political economy by the beginning of the twentieth century, increasingly tilted toward a compatibility with conservative tenets.

Radical Ideology and Political Economy
Although there were several radical thinkers who preceded Karl Marx, the origins of radicalism as a political economic ideology can be traced to Marx's writings. Radical ideology viewed capitalist society as fundamentally flawed and needing to be totally reconstructed. Where classical liberals and conservatives viewed capitalism as synonymous with freedom and individual initiative, radical ideology argued that this freedom is a fallacy where

workers are concerned. Radical thought contended that the capitalist economy is an arena of exploitation of the working class by a more powerful and wealthy capitalist class, and workers' freedom of choice between working for a capitalist and not doing so actually translated into the freedom to choose between living and starving (Sherman, 1987).

As for the government, radicals saw it as an arena in which the capitalist class also dominated. Karl Marx argued that capital rather than government is the real ruler of society (Marx, 1973, 1975). The radical ideological vision of a reconstructed society included a vigorous commitment to egalitarianism in the process of governing. Everyone should have an opportunity to participate in the institutions governing their lives and should share in the benefits and outputs of those institutions.

The State and Political Economy

In spite of the different visions of political economy, the state has been involved in every type of market economy for the past 200 years, and its role has continued to greatly expand (Peterson, 1991). In the literature of political economy, two contrasting views of the power of the state in capitalist democracies have been identified: pluralism and elitism. In the pluralist view, capitalist democracies are not dominated by a ruling class, but instead by many different interest groups. Power, pluralists argue, is not held by one group but by a diverse set of social institutions, organizations and interest groups embodying the beliefs, values and worldviews of the citizens. This model asserts that power is exerted by a multitude of interests whose countervailing centers of power check each other to prevent abusive power and agenda-setting by any one group. Thus, according to pluralism, although groups are not necessarily equal in terms of power, no particular groups are able to dominate the decision-making process (Dahl, 1961).

Furthermore, pluralists see the state as attaining consensus and preserving social order through a continuous sequence of bargaining processes. The state, then, is regarded as a benign and neutral set of agencies that have no direct involvement in either furthering or eradicating divisions and inequalities.

According to the elitist view, the state is controlled by a small number of persons whose backgrounds, characteristics and values are similar. These people are well educated, mostly white and Protestant, and they are part of the wealthy classes of society. Elites are a relatively homogenous group and their basic interest is the maintenance and advancement of the capitalist economic system (Mills, 1956). As they 'wield power and govern, they do so by balancing their own economic interests with the general welfare' (Peterson, 1991: 36; see also Domhoff, 1990; Mills, 1956; Parenti, 1995).

To elaborate on that last point, the state plays an indispensable role in ensuring the reproduction of capitalist social relations, and the powers of the state are used to sustain the general institutional framework of capitalist enterprise. This is not to say that the state merely acts at the command of corporate capitalism. Elites must give and take, negotiate and compromise; but their balance of power is never threatened.

THE POLITICAL ECONOMY OF MASS SPORTS

Sport has become one of the most popular forms of cultural practice in the modern world. In this section, the focus is on the political economy of mass sports, which has often involved public policy on behalf of providing for people's leisure needs. Existing scholarship on this topic emphasizes that one of the major contested issues has been on whether the state should intervene in sporting practices or whether such matters should be left to the private sector.

Prior to the Industrial Revolution, there was little in the way of organized sporting practices. This is not to say there were no informal sports, for there were and they stretched back into antiquity. Social conditions changed with industrial expansion, setting the stage for the rise of modern sport. Population shifted from rural to urban areas, work was transformed from home trades and individualized occupations to a large-scale industrial mode of production. Dramatic changes occurred in the daily life of the working classes as they accommodated to factory exigencies, the long work day and urban living. As larger numbers of people congregated in the cities with their wretched living conditions, there was neither space nor the opportunity to enjoy traditional forms of leisure. The working classes found not only the means of production confiscated by the capitalist class but the time and place for leisure as well (Clarke and Critcher, 1985;

Gruneau, 1999; Hargreaves, 1986; Thompson, 1968, 1974).

Concerns about the lack of healthy leisure opportunities were publicly expressed by the press, medical practitioners, educators, social reformers and even capitalists, who saw the detrimental effects of industrial working life on health, family life and job performance. However, except for a few sporadic religious and local community efforts, little was done to provide for the leisure needs of industrial laborers during the first half of the nineteenth century. *Laissez-faire* capitalism, based on classical political economy perspectives, saw no need for intervention by the state to provide for the leisure needs of people (Butsch, 1990).

It was not until the latter decades of the nineteenth century and the early twentieth century, when the rise of collectivism and shifts in the relationship of the state to civil society began to take hold, that access to public leisure facilities became a terrain of class struggle. Industrialization and urbanization created numerous social problems, and public-spirited citizens and social agencies began to seriously ponder remedies for the health and physical needs of citizens.

Gradually, governments begin to play a more active role in sport and leisure for the masses. Beginning in the mid-nineteenth century, many local governments, through legislative intervention, funding and administrative control, began setting aside large areas of land and building city parks and playgrounds for the use of their citizens. Most provided playgrounds for young children, bicycling courses, bridleways for horse riding and open fields for competitive sports for adults. A few even had swimming baths (Adelman, 1986; Hardy, 1982; Hargreaves, 1986; Riess, 1989). Speaking about the United States, Goodman (1979) asserted that 'by 1905 almost everyone concerned with social reform was concerned with play and almost every reform organization was involved in assisting the rise of organized play in one form or another' (p. 61).

The creation of a public park and playground system marked a significant chapter in the history of many cities. Moreover, it showed that beyond serving capitalist interests, the state could be an instrument of reform and change (Hardy, 1982; Hargreaves, 1986; Paxson, 1974; Riess, 1989). Neoclassical economists and capitalist interests were divided over this development. On the one hand, there was a belief that the market should provide for the sporting and leisure needs of people; on the other hand, there was a recognition that large masses of people could never be accommodated by a private sector sport and leisure industry, and physically active leisure did enhance health and common ideals, so some state intervention was supported by the capitalist class. Still, the economic ideology of the time was a principal constraint on more dynamic public policies on behalf of leisure needs.

In Great Britain, the United States and Canada, the prosperous years after the First World War and the depression of the 1930s were especially important periods in the political economy of sport. In the 1920s, shorter working hours and higher wages resulted in increased discretionary time and the financial wherewithal for an increasing proportion of the population to play sports and other leisure activities. Various reforms were won from the state through campaigns and struggles of community action groups and organized labor. Despite the political conservativism and the dominance of neoclassical economic views, public support of sporting activities for the masses continued at an unprecedented rate, especially at the local governmental levels (Betts, 1974; Jones, 1988; Morrow et al., 1989). In the United States the number of cities that established municipal recreation programs increased from 41 in 1906 to 350 in 1914 and to 945 in 1929. The economic ideology of *laissez-faire* and an individual ethic was gradually weakening. This was manifested through greater access to public parks and public sports venues (Betts, 1974).

The Great Depression of the 1930s, with its accompanying massive unemployment, humiliation and fear, left millions of people with little money for the basic necessities of life, let alone discretionary money for leisure pursuits. However, it was during this decade that the US government made its most dramatic intervention into sport. Franklin D. Roosevelt, elected in 1932 in the depths of the depression, immediately created several types of programs to relieve the massive unemployment. One of these programs was the Civilian Conservation Corps (CCC). The work of the CCC was mainly aimed at conservation and forest protection, but as part of this program the men improved national and state parks, built swimming pools and other sport facilities (Betts, 1974).

Another of Roosevelt's programs was carried out through several agencies, including the Works Progress Administration (WPA), begun in 1935 under the Emergency Relief Appropriation Act. WPA projects were of great variety but included sport stadiums, swimming pools, gymnasiums and tennis courts. In Kansas alone, 344 public buildings were erected, including auditoriums, swimming pools and gymnasiums (Betts, 1974).

Also part of the Emergency Relief Appropriation Act was the National Youth Administration (NYA), which provided part-time work to high school and college students and to former students between the ages of 18 and 25. NYA participants built and repaired sport stadiums, swimming pools, tennis courts and other recreational facilities. At the time the United States entered the Second World War, more than ten federal agencies sponsored recreation or sport-related programs and services.

Since the Second World War, governments throughout the world have taken an increasing role in sport and physical recreation of all kinds and at all levels, from local to international. Two examples in the United States are Title IX of the Educational Amendments Act of 1972, which requires gender equity in all sports and physical education programs in educational institutions receiving federal government money, and the Healthy People 2000 campaign sponsored by the US Department of Health and Human Services. In Canada, the 'Active Living Campaign' focuses on a healthier lifestyle for all Canadians and is aided by government funding.

THE POLITICAL ECONOMY OF SCHOOL SPORTS

Public support for education was a contentious issue in Western countries throughout most of the nineteenth century. Classical political economy advocates felt that public education was anti-republican and a violation of individual rights. In the United States, it was not until the 1874 Kalamazoo Decision by the Supreme Court of Michigan that decisive support for public high schools was secured. The Kalamazoo Decision set off a flurry of state legislation on behalf of public high schools; by the beginning of the twentieth century a public system of high school education was in place throughout the United States.

As formal education grew throughout the world, various extra-curricular activities, such as debate teams and student government, began to grow. One of the activities that quickly gained a commanding popularity among secondary school students was interschool sports. It was in the public schools of

Britain during the early nineteenth century where interschool sports began. Though the schools were called 'public schools', they were not state supported; they were private (Mangan, 1981; Mangan and Walvin, 1987).

By the late nineteenth century, secondary school students in several Western countries were playing interschool sports. In the Boston area, high schools were fielding football teams and had formed an Interscholastic Football Association. In New York City a public Schools League was started in 1903, and by 1910 other cities had developed similar leagues (Hardy, 1982; Jable, 1979). By the 1920s, high school sport was firmly under the control of school authorities, with teams supervised by coaches hired as full-time faculty.

In capitalist states by the early twentieth century political and economic interests came to accept the idea that public education could actually advance capitalist interests. It was believed that school sports in particular could develop in students the lessons of teamwork, self-sacrifice, discipline and values that were transferable from the playing field to a productive life in the new industrial order. This form of sport was praised as an important medium for instilling young participants with common ideals, common modes of thought, cooperation and social cohesion in the service of the instrumental culture of capitalism. School sports, thus, were seen as an educational medium for transmitting advanced capitalist ideology in the name of building character (Mangan, 1986; Mangan and Walvin, 1987; Miracle, 1985; O'Hanlon, 1980; Spring, 1974).

THE POLITICAL ECONOMY OF INTERCOLLEGIATE SPORTS

Although intercollegiate sports are played in many countries of the world, the focus in this section will be on the United States because the political and economic aspects of this form of sport are most salient there. But before turning directly to collegiate sport, a brief commentary about the political economy of higher education in the United States is necessary.

In America, an alliance has been formed between capitalist enterprise, the state and higher education. The federal government contributes to the capitalist system and to higher education in the form of research contracts and grants; it also funds federal programs to aid higher education. Higher education, then, is essentially socialized primarily because state and federal governments own, operate, or finance most of the resources: buildings, laboratories, libraries, computer centers and faculties.

In turn, public higher education increasingly serves government agencies and corporate capitalism by providing training, skills and knowledge which are vital to the capitalist system. New technology advances so quickly that capitalist enterprise requires a highly educated and specialized workforce, not only to assist planning and decision-making, but to carry out its operations. Higher education supplies the industrial system with technological know-how at nominal cost to capitalist enterprise (Peterson, 1991; Soley, 1994; Sommer, 1995).

Intercollegiate sports began in the United States during the mid-nineteenth century, a time of rapid industrialization as well as rapid growth in higher education. Collegiate sports were founded through student initiative, unassisted and unsupported by faculties, administration or alumni (Smith, 1988). The original form of governance was modeled after the well-established sports in the private secondary schools of England (Mangan, 1981). Control was in student hands until faculty and administrations gradually wrested it away from students near the beginning of the twentieth century (Sage, 1998).

During the first half of the twentieth century intercollegiate sport grew in popularity, especially football and basketball. Gradually, economic considerations became more important, as college football games began to draw thousands of spectators to newly built stadiums, and basketball was played in larger and larger arenas. Although commercialized collegiate sport was a growing industry during the first half of the twentieth century, political and economic forces changed the very character of college sport in the post-Second World War period (Sage, 1998; Smith, 1988).

Television rights contracts, aggressive marketing, expanded schedules, proliferation of tournaments and bowl games and nationwide scheduling of events have all combined to incorporate 'big-time' intercollegiate sports into one of the most popular components of the financially successful commodified sports industry. Hart-Nibbrig and Cottingham (1986) analyzed the political economic factors that have shaped the evolution of college sport, and they contend that 'college sports are now closely tied to the market system, they are an extension of and reflection of modern, late twentieth-century American capitalism' (p. 2).

Contemporary 'big-time' college sport is a business enterprise – a part of the entertainment industry. But the official ideology of universities and their controlling organization, the NCAA, is that college sport is amateur sport. Universities and the NCAA evoke the amateur ideology to justify not paying student-athletes a wage or salary for their labor as athlete-entertainers. Instead, student-athletes are awarded what is euphemistically called a 'scholarship'. Thus, the college sport establishment uses a highly valued source of human capital – a college education, which can actually be obtained at a public university at a moderate cost – as the sole compensation for athletes.

The amateur ideology employed by 'big-time' college sports is not based on any interest in amateurism *per se*. Valorization of amateurism is merely a stratagem to avoid paying the athletes a legitimate wage. In reality, the scholarship is fundamentally a work contract. Colleges are really hiring athletes as entertainers, for that is what the productive enterprise is – sport entertainment. The claim that educational purposes preclude salaried compensation for athletic performance is testimony to the extensive attempts of the collegiate sport establishment to avoid its financial responsibilities. Athletic scholarships are actually a form of economic exploitation, the establishment of a wage below the poverty level for student-athletes – entertainers who directly produce millions of dollars for athletic departments (Byers, 1995; Sage, 1998).

The benefits of this system of wage-fixing for the NCAA and the universities are quite evident: the lower the wages, the greater the profits. Paying the workforce as little as possible is what every business enterprise strives to do. The NCAA and major universities have mastered this principle (Sage, 1987, 1998). Moreover, state and federal governments have protected this system of worker exploitation.

THE POLITICAL ECONOMY OF PROFESSIONAL SPORTS

Little in the way of professional sport existed in the first two-thirds of the nineteenth century. Prize fights and horse races were staged by entrepreneurs who charged admission to the events and paid boxers, horse owners and jockeys for their performances. But these events were sporadic, attracted small crowds and gained little media attention. However, during the latter three decades of the nineteenth century a combination of expanding industrialization and urbanization, enhanced by the revolutionary transformation in communication, transportation and other technological advances, provided the social structural framework for the development of professional sport.

The prosperous years before the First World War and the tumultuous 1920s were especially important periods in the rise of professional sport. The growth of cities, shorter working hours and higher wages were important social forces that combined with numerous other conditions to promote the expansion of professional sport.

The depression years were particularly hard for professional sport, but the industry rebounded quickly after the Second World War, and it has been one of the most financially successful industries for the past 50 years, penetrating every sphere of social life and becoming one of the most popular cultural practices. Professional sport has been transformed into a huge, commodified industry that more and more dominates everyday life in advanced capitalist countries. Young (1986) captures the essence of this trend: 'The most significant structural change in modern sports is the gradual and continuing commodification of sports. This means that the social, psychological, physical, and cultural uses of sport are assimilated to the commercial needs of advanced monopoly capital' (p. 12).

Worldwide, the professional sport industry has multiplied into a variety of organizations and occupations. First, a significant portion of the sporting industry is organized as profit-maximizing enterprises. Here, capital investors own, organize and control a sports business with a goal toward capital accumulation. An example of this is the professional team sport industry, composed of franchise owners, athletes, coaches and ancillary workers (Furst, 1971; Gruneau and Whitson, 1993; Quirk and Fort, 1992).

A second form of professional sport is organized with all of the trappings of a commercial enterprise but does not function strictly for profit because the sports teams have non-profit status granted by the government. The objective of these organizations is to balance the books so as to seem to be breaking even. In order to maintain a non-profit status, these programs must give the appearance – in their accounting practices – of not making a profit. In reality, many of these organizations are profitable, but the profits are hidden in the accounting. Examples of this in the United States are high school and intercollegiate athletics programs and some elite amateur programs (Byers, 1995; Yaeger, 1991).

Thirdly, the professional sport industry creates a market for associated goods and services, so numerous businesses accumulate capital indirectly by providing those goods and services. Some examples of this are the sporting goods industry (mostly manufacturers and retailers), the sport component of the mass media (including television, newspapers and magazines), businesses that benefit from sport events (hotels, airlines, restaurants) and advertisers (those buying sport advertising or sponsoring events). A less clear example is gambling; although one's immediate response may be that gambling and sport are unrelated, this is not the case. Billions of dollars are legally and illegally wagered annually on sporting events.

As a capitalist enterprise, professional team ownership is privatized and is structured to maximize profit. Indeed, the premise of capital accumulation is the foundation on which this industry is built. As members of the capitalist class, team owners have consistently favored a minimum of government interference, while at the same time they have lobbied and received unique and favorable national and local government protection. Since its beginnings, professional team sport has benefited from actions of the state, sometimes by favorable legislation, other times by favorable court rulings. Johnson and Frey (1985) have observed that 'government policy as implemented through legislation, court decisions, and bureaucratic rules and regulations is [an] … important variable in defining the nature and dynamics of American sport' (p. ix).

In the United States, the major means by which the state has protected the investments of professional team owners and has advanced capital accumulation have been the courts and Congressional legislation. From its beginnings, the professional sport industry has benefited from favorable court decisions that have enabled owners to monopolize their industry, and in cases where their power has been threatened they have joined forces with the courts to crush opposition. Thus, between their own power of ownership, personal wealth, legislative and judicial support, the owners' monopoly of professional team sports allows them several means of capital accumulation (Beamish, 1988; Quirk and Fort, 1992; Sage, 1998; Zimbalist, 1992).

Cartelization and Monopoly

A persisting focus in studies of political economy is on economic structures, relations of production and political systems that protect economic formations. These political economic processes are evident in analyses of the professional team sports industry. Professional team sports leagues operate as cartels. A cartel is a group of firms that organize together to control production, sales and wages within an industry. In the case of professional team sports, the cartel members are the owners of the various team franchises. The actual consequences of cartelized industries are varied and complex, depending upon such factors as the commodity produced and sold and the amount of the market actually under the control of the cartel. But in most cases the negative consequences impact labor and consumers most heavily. With respect to labor, cartels are able to hold down wages, and with respect to consumers, cartels typically restrict production and control sales and thus can set prices as high as they wish. The major benefits accrue to owners of individual firms through the maximization of joint profits (Quirk and Fort, 1992; Sage, 1998; Wilson, 1994).

During the formative stages of the first American professional team sport, baseball, team owners and promoters competed with each other in an open market, vying for athletes and spectators. But it became evident to a few promoters and potential owners of professional baseball teams that such competition was counterproductive to the interests of controlling sport labor and capital accumulation. They realized that labor and consumer issues could be better stabilized and joint profits more consistently realized by a collective, or cartel. Schimmel, Ingham and Howell (1993) note that 'this economic concentration and cartelization scenario has been played out not only in baseball, but also in basketball, football, hockey and soccer' (p. 214). Commenting on the organization of professional team sports, Freedman (1987) noted they 'have in general operated apart from normal business considerations, and their rules of business conduct have not been subject to governmental scrutiny to the same extent as any ordinary business' (p. 31).

Although cartels violate the intent of antitrust laws and are illegal in most businesses, Congress and the courts have consistently protected professional sports from antitrust accusations and have upheld the main economic relationships that derive from the cartel structure, namely monopoly and monopsony. A monopoly is a one-seller market, and in pro team sports franchises are protected from competition because the number of franchises is controlled by the team owners in all of the leagues; new franchises are not allowed to locate in, or relocate to, a given territory without approval of the owners.

Advantages of Monopoly for Franchise Owners Several advantages result from the monopoly position which the owners hold. First, by controlling the number of franchises within a league, the owners make them scarce commodities, which means their worth tends to appreciate. Applications for new franchises must secure the permission of three-quarters of the existing owners in a particular league. The scarcity of existing franchises and the difficulty of securing permission for a new franchise drive up the cost of expansion franchises. Owners divide the expansion fees generated when new franchises are created by them. The only alternative for someone who wants to establish a professional sport franchise is to start a new league (Harris, 1987; Quirk and Fort, 1992; Shropshire, 1995; Zimbalist, 1992).

A second advantage professional team sports enjoy from their monopoly position is protection from competition, which eliminates price wars and frees owners to set ticket prices as high as they believe the market will bear, thus maximizing their profits. It also enables each league to negotiate television contracts for the entire league without violating antitrust laws; indeed, this is protected in the United States by Congressional action in the 1961 Sports Broadcast Act (P.L. 87-331) (Wilson, 1994).

Some elaboration on the relationships between professional team sports and the television industry is needed to clarify the advantages of the monopoly position to pro sports. Professional sport and television have become mutual beneficiaries in one of capitalism's most lucrative associations. Professional sport leagues sell television networks the rights to broadcast league games; the networks then sell advertising to corporations who are selling a product and wish to advertise it. Because so many people are interested in professional sports, it is a natural setting for advertising.

Television networks are willing to spend enormous sums of money to secure broadcasting rights because they know they can then sell advertising profitably to corporations who in turn use 'the drama and power of sports to generate [consumer] demand and to realize a profit for advanced monopoly capital' (Young,

1986: 20). League-wide negotiation affords tremendous financial advantages to leagues, enabling them to secure much larger TV pacts then would be possible if each team negotiated its own TV contract (Quirk and Fort, 1992; Wilson, 1994).

Permitting each league to limit the number of franchises provides a third advantage to the monopoly power of the leagues. It enables owners to extract various forms of public subsidy from cities and states. Monuments to socializing the costs and privatizing the profits in professional sport are the numerous sport stadiums and arenas that have been built at public expense for the use of professional teams. About 80 per cent or over 40 of these imposing facilities have been built or renovated at taxpayer expense in cities across the US and Canada during the past 30 years, generally through revenue bonds issued by state, county or city governments (Cagan and de Mause, 1998; Danielson, 1997; Noll and Zimbalist, 1997; Rosentraub, 1999).

The reason that few pro sports team owners own the facilities in which their teams play is that when the government owns them, the owners are relieved of the burden of property taxes, insurance and maintenance costs, not to mention construction. Owners pay rent on the facilities, of course, but this usually covers only a fraction of overall operating expenses. Local taxpayers actually wind up subsidizing professional team owners (Rosentraub, 1999; Shropshire, 1995).

Another reason for team owners not owning their facilities is that it makes it much easier for them to move franchises to other cities should they become unhappy with existing financial arrangements (one sports writer called this the 'strip-mining' of cities). In the 1980s, three NFL owners actually made such a move (Oakland Raiders to Los Angeles, the Baltimore Colts to Indianapolis, and the St Louis Cardinals to Phoenix), and the incidence of owner 'extortion' appears to be increasing. Indeed, in 1995–96 alone four NFL franchises were moved: Los Angeles Rams to St Louis, Los Angeles Raiders to Oakland, Cleveland Browns to Baltimore, and Houston Oilers to Nashville (Baim, 1994; Ingham and Hardy, 1984; Sage, 1993; Schimmel et al., 1993; Zimbalist, 1992).

Socializing the costs and privatizing the profits in sport are not limited to sport facilities. A fourth example of the advantages of monopoly is the tax subsidy both sport franchises and private, non-sport businesses receive through the purchase of game tickets

by corporations because they can be deducted from taxes as a business expense. A large proportion of the season tickets for professional sports are purchased by businesses. In effect, then, taxpayers are subsidizing the cost for corporate executives and their friends to see professional sport contests. When this deduction was threatened by the Internal Revenue Service, professional sports and businesses combined their lobbying efforts to retain the subsidy (Sage, 1998).

Capital accumulation also accrues to professional sports owners through other tax breaks. Owners of professional franchises are given a number of ways to minimize taxable profits. One example is the depreciation of players. Most of the assets of a professional sports team are its players, so most of the cost of a franchise is player contracts. Owners can depreciate players the way farmers depreciate cattle and corporations depreciate company cars; the professional athletes' status is that of property. No other business in the United States depreciates the value of human beings as part of its business costs. The obvious beneficiaries of such tax breaks are the wealthy team owners (Sage, 1998).

Advantages of Monopsony for Franchise Owners   A practice that economists call monopsony, which means a one-buyer market, was adopted when the founders of Major League baseball were establishing cartelized operations in professional baseball. All Major League baseball owners used a provision in every player's contract – the reserve clause – to enable the owners to control the player's job mobility. Once a player signed a contract with a club, that team had exclusive rights over him; he was no longer free to negotiate with other teams because his contract had a clause that 'reserved' his services to his original team for the succeeding year. The reserve clause specified that the owner had the exclusive right to renew the player's contract annually, and thus the player was bound perpetually to negotiate with only one club; he became its property and could even be sold to another club without his own consent. Monopsony, in this case, was designed to control the costs of players by restricting interteam bidding. Other professional team sports never enjoyed formal exemption from antitrust laws, but they used other policies restricting player movement. In each case, the player's freedom of movement was restricted by some type of reservation system (Freedman, 1987; Lowenfish, 1991; Zimbalist, 1992).

Resentment against the reserve clause was persistent from its beginnings, and twice challenges to its constitutionality reached the US Supreme Court. In 1922 the Court ruled in favor of the baseball owners, contending in essence that Major League baseball was a sport, not a business, and therefore was entitled to immunity from antitrust laws. Freedman (1987) has summarized the court's action in this way: 'Professional baseball ... was granted an exemption from the application of the federal antitrust laws upon the ground that this professional sport was not engaged in interstate commerce or trade, and furthermore baseball was in essence not a commercial activity' (p. 32). Again in 1972 when it was challenged, the court favored letting the 1922 decision stand. It was not until 1976 that the courts finally struck down the reserve clause, substituting in its place a limited player mobility plan (Lowenfish, 1991).

Alienated Labor

The social relations of capitalism are played out in professional sport just as they are in other industries where capitalism prevails. Those who own the means of production, the team owners, hire athletes who, in effect, sell their skilled labor power for a wage. The amount owners pay athletes is always less than what they expect to make in revenue. Underpaid human labor is the key ingredient to the capitalist mode of production. However, in the process of selling their labor, athletes lose control over the 'product' they create – the competitive contest – they become alienated from their own expenditure of energy. In characterizing social relations of pro athletes as employees, Beamish (1982) said:

> As a form of activity that is completely subsumed under capitalist relations, professional athletes ... work under a historically specific set of production relations. Athletes do not own or control the means of producing their athletic labor-power. They have no access to professional leagues other than through the sale of their labor-power to existing franchise owners. (pp. 177–8)

To mitigate working conditions under capitalism, workers join unions to deal collectively, rather than individually, with management. Such organization began in the mid-nineteenth century, originally to represent the interests of trade and industrial workers with regard to increased wages, shorter hours, safer and more humane working conditions and benefits such as health plans. Just like trade and labor workers, the response of professional athletes to monopsony, abridgement of individual rights and other job restrictions has been unionization, collective bargaining and strikes (Jennings, 1990; Lowenfish, 1991; Staudohar, 1986).

Player unions and collective bargaining have had some significant successes, but unionization has met with significant resistance from owners. They have used their considerable personal wealth and influence in Congress and the courts to minimize the effectiveness of the player unions; the unions have not possessed equivalent legal and legislative clout to secure many of their needs (Jennings, 1990).

GLOBAL POLITICAL ECONOMY AND SPORT

A significant transformation in the world order has been under way during the past half century which can be characterized as a growing political, economic and cultural interdependence among the word's nations. The word most popularly used to characterize the comprehensive features of this process is 'globalization,' which Robertson (1992) says 'refers both to the compression of the world and the intensification of consciousness of the world as a whole' (p. 8; see also Waters, 1995).

In economics, the embracement of a market-based economy by developed and many developing nations, as well as former centrally planned economies, and the opening of international markets around the world have created what is increasingly being called a global economy. Transnational corporations (TNCs) based in developed countries are the major forces contributing to this growing global economy. These gigantic companies integrate their administrative and production systems worldwide through rationalized economic activities, modern bureaucratic organization, advanced communications networks, and scientific data calculations (Dunning, 1992; Stubbs and Underhill, 1994; World Bank, 1995).

TNCs are tilting the national economies of their home country away from basic industries and transferring the labor-intensive phases of production to Third World nations (Barnet and Cavanagh, 1994; Berberoglu, 1992; Grunwald and Flamm, 1985; Lorraine and Potter, 1993; Staudohar and Brown, 1987). Foreign investment by transnational corporations has eliminated nearly 12 million manufacturing jobs in industrialized countries between 1977 and 1995. Between 1963 and 1995, the proportion of the world's manufacturing exports accounted for by Third World nations increased from 4.3 to 14 per cent. At present, over one-third of the earnings of the 200 largest US transnationals are from revenues of their off-shore subsidiaries (Barnet and Cavanagh, 1994; Sklar, 1994).

TNCs are closely linked to the political apparatus of the country in which they are incorporated as well as to the other nations of their production and distribution operations. Political-economic agreements between nations, such as the European Union, GATT, NAFTA and others, commit nations to integration and interdependence. Political leaders in developed countries tend to believe that national interests are favorably served by the foreign expansion of transnational corporations. Political leaders in underdeveloped countries negotiate for favorable investment and trade agreements with cohorts in developed countries in hopes of improving their own economies as well as consolidating their own political ambitions. Thus a complementarity of interests exists between transnational corporations and governments in both developed and undeveloped countries (Arrighi, 1994; Berberoglu, 1992; Sherman, 1987).

Several theories have been proposed to attempt to account for the emergence, expansion and functioning of the international political economy – dual economy theory, dependency theory, world systems theory, Marxist theory. The theories range from those regarding the modern world economy as a natural consequence of a universal movement of economic forces toward higher levels of economic efficiency and global interdependence to 'imperialist industrialization' approaches which concentrate directly on the relations of production under imperialism and focus on the class nature of imperialist exploitation (Berberoglu, 1992; Sherman, 1987).

One way in which the globalized economy expands is through cultural products, such as music, art, sport and the mass media, especially film and television, which flow around the world to enhance the integration and interdependence tendencies in the world order. Films and music are produced, marketed, sold and consumed throughout the world, and top movie stars and musicians are world-wide celebrities. Large international sporting events are often mentioned as evidence of a global culture. Worldwide television audiences watch the Olympic Games, (Football) World Cup and French Open Tennis Tournament, to name only a few of the most popular international events. Real and Mechikoff (1992) claim that 'the largest number of people ever in human history to engage in one activity at the same time are the viewers watching the Olympic Games and World Cup' (p. 324).

Several trends highlight the interconnections between sports development and the global economy. For example: the growth and spread of commodified sport during the past century, the founding of international sports organizations, a worldwide approval of rules governing specific sports, increasing competition between national teams, regional championship events, such as the European Championships, Commonwealth Games, Pan American Games, Asian Games, numerous world championships and, of course, the Olympic Games. All of these events exhibit the key elements of political economy: production, distribution and consumption. All employ athletes from throughout the world, draw spectators the world over, attract advertisers of products made throughout the world and shape global sport consumer behavior. These, and others, highlight the growth of globalization in sports. (See Joe Maguire's contribution to this volume – Chapter 23 – for a more complete discussion of these trends in sports.)

Sporting Goods Production in the Global Economy

One aspect of the global economy is an international capital system and division of labor known as 'export-oriented industrialization', which is organized and driven by transnational corporations and their subsidiaries. In this system, product research, development and design typically take place in developed countries while the labor-intensive, assembly-line phases of product manufacture are relegated to Third World nations. The finished product is then exported for distribution in developed countries of the world. This system was originally employed by American companies in response to growing competition for American markets. It has now been adopted by transnational firms headquartered in Western Europe, Japan and elsewhere where consumer goods are sold on the world market (Barnet and Cavanagh, 1994; Berberoglu, 1992; Browne and Sims, 1993; Ward, 1990).

Shifting production from developed to underdeveloped countries is a strategy used by transnational corporations for several reasons: wages are lower and worker benefits fewer; the workforce is not likely to be organized, and if it is organized, it is less likely to be assertive; management can exert clear control over the work process, with few or no restrictions on hiring, firing, or reassigning workers; workplace health and safety regulations are less stringent or poorly enforced; the cost of protecting the environment and community health and safety are lower due to weak or poorly enforced regulations (Herman, 1994; Tiano, 1990).

Consequences of Export-Oriented Industrialization for Workers in the Developed and Third World Nations Moving plants and operations to Third World countries is a way for corporations to boost profits, but for workers and their communities in developed countries the consequences are usually grim. Closed plants, unemployed workers, community disintegration and a variety of related afflictions that undermine a nation's social fabric are the results of globalizing manufacturing. Increased rates of suicide, homicide, heart disease, alcoholism, mental illness, domestic violence and family breakup have been linked to the stress of unemployment when plants are closed and productive operations moved offshore. Entire communities become economically depressed when corporations relocate in foreign countries (Browne and Sims, 1993; Kamel, 1990; Perrucci et al., 1988; Scheer, 1994; Sklar, 1994; Staudohar and Brown, 1987).

Export processing industrialization has transformed the political economy of Third World countries. Historically, Third World nations specialized in the export of raw materials and agricultural goods; now, countries involved in export-oriented industrialization specialize in export of manufactured goods. For example, manufactured goods presently account for 55 per cent of all Mexican exports, 75 per cent of all Brazilian exports, 92 per cent of all Taiwanese exports, and 96 per cent of all South Korean exports (Berberoglu, 1987, 1992; Dunning, 1992; Lorraine and Potter, 1993; 'Who owns ...', 1994).

For workers in the Third World, transnational investment in assembly production has carried with it some heavy burdens: wages so low workers cannot provide for their basic needs, unjust and inhuman working conditions, sexual exploitation, social disruption, distorted economic development. Moreover, attempts to organize labor unions are often violently suppressed by government soldiers. Workplace democracy and worker rights are non-existent. Health and safety in the

workplace are often unregulated, as are pollution and other environmental protections (Herman, 1993; Ogle, 1990; Slater, 1991; Timm and Collingsworth, 1995). Thus, the neocolonial system of unequal economic and political relationships among the First and Third World countries described by Wallerstein's (1974, 1979, 1984) world-system model of global development seems to have relevance.

Export-Oriented Industrialization and the Manufacture of Sporting Goods Equipment Sporting goods manufacturing is not dislocated from other forms of production. It is, instead, interwoven with the process of accelerated globalization; indeed, one of the aspects of globalization is the transnationalization of sports goods manufacturing. Economist Robert Reich (1991) illustrates this point: 'Precision ice hockey equipment is designed in Sweden, financed in Canada, and assembled in Cleveland and Denmark for distribution in North America and Europe, respectively out of alloys whose molecular structure was researched and patented in Delaware and fabricated in Japan' (p. 112).

Sporting goods and equipment corporations in developed countries have also turned to the Third World because an endless supply of cheap labor makes it profitable and because foreign and trade policies provide the corporations with financial incentives. In the sporting goods and equipment industry, manufacturers who produce all of their products domestically are now a minority in an industry that has become increasingly dominated by imports.

Space does not permit any comprehensive treatment of the globalization of the manufacturing of sporting goods, but I shall describe two examples: the manufacture of sports footwear and apparel and the manufacture of Major League baseballs. It is important for the reader to understand that there are hundreds of other sporting goods manufacturers operating in Third World countries.

Making Sports Footwear and Apparel in Asia Many sporting goods and equipment manufacturers have 'run away' to numerous low-wage export-processing and assembling zones across the world, but nowhere has this phenomenon been more tangible than in Asia. Nike and Reebok are the world's largest suppliers of sports footwear and apparel. Nike is the market leader in the United States, with a 32 per cent market share (King, 1994; Quinn and Hilmer, 1994). Most of Nike and Reebok footwear and apparel are now made in factories in various countries of Asia. In all of the Nike and Reebok factories in Asia, women under the age of 25 from rural areas make up two-thirds of the total number of employees in these factories. It is their low wages and long hours which make Nike and Reebok commercially successful. As production of consumer goods becomes increasingly globalized, exploitation of women becomes globalized as well (Ballinger, 1992; Brookes and Madden, 1995; Wolf, 1992; Wyss and Balakrishnan, 1993).

A typical worker in the Indonesian plants that make Reebok and Nike products works for 19 cents an hour; workers in their plants routinely put in ten-and-a-half-hour days, six days a week, with forced overtime two to three times per week. When compulsory overtime is thrown in, a worker's monthly income is about $50. By Indonesian standards, that monthly wage is about 30 per cent less than the 'minimum physical needs' for a married person with one child (Ballinger, 1992; Ingi Labor Working Group, 1991).

Low wages and long hours are the main ingredients of the Nike's and Reebok's success, but the contribution of another cost-saving measure cannot be underestimated: minimal investment in safe working conditions. The typical Reebok and Nike worker labors in poorly ventilated buildings in stifling heat. Laws requiring industrial safety are almost useless in practice because employers do not follow the rules and regulations set out in the laws. There is a lack of proper knowledge of work-induced health hazards, and there is a lack of trained professionals and proper equipment to prevent and to treat work-related injuries. Not surprisingly, the results of cutting costs on safety and workers' health have been dreadful (Brookes and Madden, 1995; Wolf, 1992).

The record on workers' rights is horrible as well. Independent unions are not permitted, and labor organizers are routinely attacked, beaten and fired from their jobs. Nike and Reebok worker protests have been met with on-the-sport dismissals and managerial indifference ('Government punishes', 1995; Timm and Collingsworth, 1995).

Making Major League Baseballs in the Caribbean and Central America Rawlings Sporting Goods Co., headquartered in St Louis, has manufactured the baseballs used in Major League baseball for over 40 years. Prior to 1953, all Rawlings baseballs were manufactured in a plant in St Louis with unionized labor. In that year, to reduce labor costs,

Rawlings shifted manufacturing to Licking, Missouri. At first the Licking plant was non-union, but in 1956 it was organized by the Amalgamated Clothing and Textile Workers Union. The union immediately began efforts to improve wages and working conditions, so Rawlings began looking around for an alternative manufacturing site ('Keep your eye', 1990).

In 1964 Rawlings moved its baseball manufacturing to an offshore location in Puerto Rico. But when the initial tax 'holidays' for foreign investors ran out and minimum wage laws were implemented in Puerto Rico, many companies – including Rawlings Sporting Goods – left to exploit even cheaper labor in other countries. In 1969 Rawlings closed its Puerto Rican baseball manufacturing plant and relocated in Haiti, the poorest country in the Western hemisphere and one of the 25 poorest in the world.

Haiti was the ideal setting for Rawlings offshore baseball assembly operation: there were generous tax holidays, a franchise granting tariff exemption, the only legal trade unions were those run by the government. Strikes were illegal, and the minimum wage was so low that a majority of Haitians could not derive anything that might reasonably be called a 'living' from the assembly plants. Haitians who made baseballs for Rawlings earned less that $3 per day; the weekly average wage was $18. DeWind and Kinley (1988) noted: 'Far from creating a way out of poverty, the industry's wages provide the basis for only an impoverished standard of living' (p. 118).

In November 1990 the Rawlings plant in Haiti was suddenly closed. All baseball manufacturing was moved to a Rawlings plant in Costa Rica. This move represented the fourth time baseball production had been relocated in the past 30 years. In a press release announcing its departure from Haiti, the company said the closing of the plant was due to Haiti's 'unstable political climate'.

Rawlings opened a newly constructed plant in Turrialba, Costa Rica in January 1990. About 600 people, most of them women, are formally employed in the Turrialba facilities. The majority of the workers are 'sewers' who must stitch 30–35 baseballs to earn $5–6 a day. The work week is 48 hours long. Approximately 300 Costa Rican women also sew baseballs in their homes, earning 15 cents per ball (Sage, 1994; Wirpsa, 1990).

Nike's, Reebok's and Rawlings's export processing operations have indeed achieved commercial success, but they have been built by following a model which places profits over worker needs, a labor policy that violates the human rights of workers and that results in pervasive and often cruel suppression of those workers. Thus, for workers in sporting goods and equipment manufacturing in the Third World, there is overwhelming evidence that transnational investment in assembly production carries with it some heavy burdens (Sage, 1999).

These are only a few of the many examples of sporting goods export-oriented industrialization. Although a handful of Third World countries have benefited from the globalization process, and have made significant progress in industrialization and trade, the overall gap between First World and Third World nations keeps widening (Arrighi, 1991; United Nations, 1992). According to The World Bank (1995),

> the ratio of income per capita in the richest to that in the poorest countries has increased from eleven in 1870, to thirty-eight in 1960, and to fifty-two in 1985. This divergent relationship between growth performance and the initial level of income per capita not only applies to those extreme cases but is empirically valid on average over a sample of 117 countries. (p. 53)

NOTE

Rawlings is no longer owned by Figgie International. It is now a publicly held company.

REFERENCES

Adelman, M. (1986) *A Sporting Time: New York City and the Rise of Modern Athletics*. Urbana, IL: University of Illinois Press.

Arrighi, G. (1991) 'World income inequalities and the future of socialism', *New Left Review*, 189: 39–65.

Arrighi, G. (1994) *The Long Twentieth Century: Money, Power, and the Origins of Our Times*. New York: Verso.

Baim, D.V. (1994) *The Sports Stadium as a Municipal Investment*. Westport, CT: Greenwood Press.

Ballinger, J. (1992) 'The new free-trade heel', *Harper's Magazine*, pp. 46–7.

Barnet, R.J. and Cavanagh, J. (1994) *Global Dreams: Imperial Corporations and the New World Order*. New York: Simon & Schuster.

Beamish, R. (1982) 'Sport and the logic of capitalism', in H. Cantelon and R. Gruneau (eds), *Sport, Culture, and the Modern State*. Toronto: University of Toronto Press. pp. 142–97.

Beamish, R. (1988) 'The political economy of professional sport', in J. Harvey and H. Cantelon (eds),

Not Just a Game: Essays in Canadian Sport Sociology. Ottawa: University of Ottawa Press. pp. 141–57.

Berberoglu, B. (1987) *The Internationalization of Capital: Imperialism and Capitalist Development on a World Scale*. New York: Praeger.

Berberoglu, B. (1992) *The Political Economy of Development*. Albany, NY: State University of New York Press.

Betts, J.R. (1974) *America's Sporting Heritage: 1850–1950*. Reading, MA: Addison-Wesley.

Brookes, B. and Madden, P. (1995) *The Globe-Trotting Sports Shoe*. London: Christian Aid.

Browne, H. and Sims, B. (1993) *Runaway America: US Jobs and Factories on the Move*. Albuquerque, NM: Resource Center Press.

Butsch, R. (1990) 'Introduction: leisure and hegemony in America', in R. Butsch (ed.), *For Fun and Profit: the Transformation of Leisure into Consumption*. Philadelphia: Temple University Press. pp. 3–27.

Byers, W. (1995) *Unsportsmanlike Conduct: Exploiting College Athletes*. Ann Arbor, MI: University of Michigan Press.

Cagan, J. and de Mause, N. (1998) *Field of Schemes: How the Great Stadium Swindle Turns Public Money Into Private Profit*. Monroe, ME: Common Courage Press.

Caporaso, J.A. and Levine, D.P. (1992) *Theories of Political Economy*. Cambridge: Cambridge University Press.

Clark, B. (1991) *Political Economy: a Comparative Approach*. New York: Praeger.

Clarke, J. and Critcher, C. (1985) *The Devil Makes Work: Leisure in Capitalist Britain*. Basingstoke: Macmillan.

Dahl, R.A. (1961) *Who Governs?* New Haven, CT: Yale University Press.

Danielson, M.N. (1997) *Home Team: Professional Sports and the American Metropolis*. Princeton: Princeton University Press.

DeWind, J. and Kinley III, D.H. (1988) *Aiding Migration: the Impact of International Development Assistance on Haiti*. Boulder, CO: Westview Press.

Domhoff, G.W. (1990) *The Power Elite and the State: How Policy is Made in America*. New York: Aldine De Gruyter.

Dunning, J.H. (1992) *Multinational Enterprises and the Global Economy*. Reading, MA: Addison-Wesley.

Freedman, W. (1987) *Professional Sports and Antitrust*. New York: Quorum Books.

Furst, R.T. (1971) 'Social change and the commercialization of professional sport', *International Review of Sport Sociology*, 6: 153–73.

Gondwe, D.K. (1992) *Political Economy, Ideology, and the Impact of Economics on the Third World*. New York: Praeger.

Goodman, C. (1979) *Choosing Sides: Playground and Street Life on the Lower East Side*. New York: Schocken Books.

'Government punishes union organizers in Indonesia', (1995) *Workers Rights News*, Issue 11: 15.

Gruneau, R.S. (1999) *Class, Sports, and Social Development*. Champaign, IL: Human Kinetics..

Gruneau, R.S. and Whitson, D. (1993) *Hockey Night in Canada: Sport, Identities and Cultural Politics*. Toronto: Garamond Press.

Grunwald, J. and Flamm, K. (1985) *The Global Factory: Foreign Assembly in International Trade*. Washington, DC: Brookings Institution.

Hardy, S. (1982) *How Boston Played: Sport, Recreation, and Community, 1865–1915*. Boston, MA: Northeastern University Press.

Hargreaves, J. (1986) *Sport, Power and Culture*. New York: St Martin's Press.

Harris, D. (1987) *The League: the Rise and Decline of the NFL*. New York: Bantam Books.

Hart-Nibbrig, N. and Cottingham, C. (1986) *The Political Economy of College Sports*. Lexington, MA: Lexington Books.

Heilbroner, R. (1996) *Teachings from the Worldly Philosophy*. New York: Norton.

Herman, E. (1993) 'The end of democracy?', *Z Magazine*, 6: 57–62.

Herman, E. (1994) 'Survival of the fattest', *Z Magazine*, 7: 15–18.

Hibbs, D.A., Jr (1987) *The Political Economy of Industrial Democracies*. Cambridge, MA: Harvard University Press.

Ingham, A., Howell, J. and Schilperoort, T. (1987) 'Professional sports and community: review and exegesis', in K.B. Pandolf (ed.), *Exercise and Sport Sciences Reviews*, Volume 15. New York: Macmillan. pp. 427–65.

Ingi Labor Working Group (1991) 'Unjust but doing it! Nike operations in Indonesia', *Inside Indonesia*, June, pp. 7–9.

Jable, J.T. (1979) 'The Public Schools Athletic League of New York City: organized athletics for city school children, 1903–1914', in W.M. Ladd and A. Lumpkin (eds), *Sport in American Education: History and Perspective*. Washington, DC: American Alliance for Health, Physical Education, Recreation, and Dance. pp. 1–18.

Jennings, K.M. (1990) *Balls and Strikes: the Money Game in Professional Baseball*. New York: Praeger.

Jevons, W.S. ([1871]1970) *The Theory of Political Economy*. Harmondsworth: Penguin.

Johnson, A.T. and Frey, J.H. (eds) (1985) *Government and Sport: the Public Policy Issues*. Totowa, NJ: Rowman & Allanheld.

Jones, S.G. (1988) *Sport, Politics and the Working Class: Organized Labor and Sports in Inter-war Britain*. Manchester: Manchester University Press.

Kamel, R. (1990) *The Global Factory: Analysis and Action for a New Economic Era*. Philadelphia: American Friends Service.

'Keep your eye on the ball' (1990) *Denver Catholic Register*, 11 July, p. 14.

King, H. (1994) 'Nike in accord to purchase hockey equipment maker', *The New York Times*, 15 December, p. D4.

Lorraine, E. and Potter, E.H. (eds) (1993) *Multinationals in the Global Political Economy*. New York: St Martin's Press.

Lowenfish, L. (1991) *Imperfect Diamond: a History of Baseball's Labor Wars*, rev. edn. New York: Da Capo Press.

Mangan, J.A. (1981) *Athleticism in the Victorian and Edwardian Public School*. London: Cambridge University Press.

Mangan, J.A. (1986) *The Games Ethic and Imperialism*. New York: Viking Penguin.

Mangan, J.A. and Walvin, J. (eds) (1987) *Manliness and Morality: Middle-class Masculinity in Britain and America, 1800–1940*. New York: St Martin's Press.

Marshall, A. ([1890]1953) *Principles of Economics*, 8th edn. New York: Macmillan.

Marx, K. (1970) *A Contribution to the Critique of Political Economy* (trans. by S.W. Ryazanskaya), New York: International Publishers.

Marx, K. (1973) *Grundrisse* (trans. by Martin Nicholaus). Baltimore, MD: Penguin.

Marx, K. (1975) *Collected Works*. New York: International Publishers.

Mills, C.W. (1956) *The Power Elite*. New York: Oxford University Press.

Miracle, A.W. (1985) 'Corporate economy, social ritual and the rise of high school sports'. Paper presented at the annual meeting of the North American Society for Sport Sociology, Boston, MA.

Morrow, D., Keyes, M., Cosentino, W. and Lappage, R. (1989) *A Concise History of Sport in Canada*. Toronto: Oxford University Press.

Noll, R.G. and Zimbalist, A. (eds) (1997) *Sports, Jobs, and Taxes: The Economic Impact of Sports Teams and Stadiums*. Washington, DC: Brookings Institute.

Ogle, G.E. (1990) *South Korea: Dissent Within the Economic Miracle*. Atlantic Highlands, NJ: Zed Books.

O'Hanlon, T. (1980) 'Interscholastic athletics, 1900–1940: shaping citizens for unequal roles in the modern industrial state', *Educational Theory*, 30: 89–103.

Parenti, M. (1995) *Democracy for the Few*, 6th edn. New York: St Martin's Press.

Paxson, F.L. (1974) 'The rise of sport', in G.H. Sage (ed.) *Sport and American Society*, 2nd edn. Reading, MA: Addison-Wesley. pp. 80–103.

Perrucci, C.C., Perrucci, R., Targ, D.B. and Targ, H.R. (1988) *Plant Closings: International Context and Social Costs*. New York: Aldine De Gruyter.

Peterson, R.D. (1991) *Political Economy and American Capitalism*. Boston, MA: Kluwer Academic Publishers.

Quinn, J.B. and Hilmer, F.G. (1994) 'Strategic outsourcing', *Sloan Management Review*, 35: 51.

Quirk, J.P. and Fort, R.D. (1992) *Pay Dirt: the Business of Professional Team Sports*. Princeton, NJ: Princeton University Press.

Real, M. and Mechikoff, R.A. (1992) 'Deep fan: mythic identification, technology, and advertising in spectator sports', *Sociology of Sport Journal*, 9: 323–39.

Reich, R.B. (1991) *The Work of Nations: Preparing Ourselves for 21st Century Capitalism*. New York: Knopf.

Riess, S.A. (1989) *City Games: the Evolution of American Urban Society and the Rise of Sports*. Urbana, IL: University of Illinois Press.

Robertson, R. (1992) *Globalization: Social Theory and Global Culture*. Newbury Park, CA: Sage.

Rosentraub, M.S. (1999) *Major League Losers: The Real Cost of Sports and Who's Paying for It*. New York: Basic Books.

Sage, G.H. (1987) 'Blaming the victim: NCAA responses to calls for reform in major college sports', *Arena Review*, 11: 1–11.

Sage, G.H. (1993) 'Stealing home: political, economic, and media power and a publicly-funded baseball stadium in Denver', *Journal of Sport and Social Issues*, 17: 110–24.

Sage, G.H. (1994) 'Deindustrialization and the American sporting goods industry', in R.C. Wilcox (ed.), *Sport in the Global Village*. Morgantown, WV: Fitness Information Technology, Inc. pp. 39–51.

Sage, G.H. (1998) *Power and Ideology in American Sport: a Critical Perspective*, 2nd edition. Champaign, IL: Human Kinetics.

Sage, G.H. (1999) 'Justice do it! The Nike transactional advocacy network: organization, collective actions, and outcomes', *Sociology of Sport Journal*, 16 (3): 206–35.

Scheer, R. (1994) 'Welfare or work?', *The Nation*, p. 545.

Schimmel, K.S., Ingham, A.G. and Howell, J.W. (1993) 'Professional team sport and the American city: urban politics and franchise relocations', in Alan G. Ingham and John W. Loy (eds), *Sport in Social Development: Traditions, Transitions, and Transformations*. Champaign, IL: Human Kinetics Publishers. pp. 211–44.

Sherman, H.J. (1987) *Foundations of Radical Political Economy*. Armonk, NY: M.E. Sharpe.

Shropshire, K.L. (1995) *The Sports Franchise Game: Cities in Pursuit of Sport Franchises, Events, Stadiums, and Arenas*. Philadelphia: University of Pennsylvania Press.

Sklar, H. (1994) 'Disposable workers', *Z Magazine*, 7: 36–41.

Slater, P. (1991) *A Dream Deferred*. Boston, MA: Beacon.

Smith, A. ([1776]1993) *An Inquiry into the Nature and Causes of the Wealth of Nations* (ed. Kathryn Sutherland). New York: Oxford University Press.

Smith, R.A. (1988) *Sports and Freedom: the Rise of Big-time College Athletics*. New York: Oxford University Press.

Soley, L.C. (1994) *Leasing the Ivory Tower: the Corporate Takeover of Academia*. Boston, MA: South End Press.

Sommer, J.W. (ed.) (1995) *The Academy in Crisis: the Political Economy of Higher Education*. New Brunswick, NJ: Transaction Publishers.

Spiegel, H. (1991) *The Growth of Economic Thought*, 3rd edn. Durham, NC: Duke University Press.

Spring, J.H. (1974) 'Mass culture and school sports', *History of Education Quarterly*, 14: 483–98.

Staniland, M. (1985) *What is Political Economy? A Study of Social Theory and Underdevelopment*. New Haven, CT: Yale University Press.

Staudohar, P.D. (1986) *The Sports Industry and Collective Bargaining*. Ithaca, NY: Industrial and Labor Relations Press.

Staudohar, P.D. and Brown, H.E. (1987) *Deindustrialization and Plant Closure*. Lexington, MA: DC Heath.

Stubbs, R. and Underhill, G.R.D. (1994) *Political Economy and the Changing Global Order*. New York: St Martin's Press.

Thompson, E.P. (1968) *The Making of the English Working Class*. Harmondsworth: Pelican Books.

Thompson, E.P. (1974) 'Patrician society, plebeian culture', *Journal of Social History*, 7: 382–405.

Tiano, S. (1990) 'Maquiladora women: a new category of workers?', in K. Ward (ed.), *Women Workers and Global Restructuring*. Ithaca, NY: Cornell University Press. pp. 193–223.

Timm, R.W. and Collingsworth, T. (1995) 'Inside Bangladesh', *Worker Rights News*, 11: 1, 14–15.

United Nations (1992) *Human Development Report*. New York: Oxford University Press.

Wallerstein, I. (1974) *The Modern World-System*. New York: Academic Press.

Wallerstein, I. (1979) *The Capitalist World-Economy*. New York: Cambridge University Press.

Wallerstein, I. (1984) *The Politics of the World-Economy*. New York: Cambridge University Press.

Ward, K. (1990) *Women Workers and Global Restructuring*. Ithaca, NY: Cornell University Press.

Waters, M. (1995) *Globalization*. New York: Routledge.

'Who owns the world's assets and trade?' (1994) *Labor Notes*, February: p. 12.

Wilson, J. (1994) *Playing by the Rules: Sport, Society, and the State*. Detroit: Wayne State University Press.

Wirpsa, L. (1990) 'Where every Rawlings baseball is a foul ball', *National Catholic Reporter*, 28 December, p. 1.

Wolf, D.L. (1992) *Factory Daughters: Gender, Household Dynamics and Rural Industrialization in Java*. Berkeley, CA: University of California Press.

World Bank (1995) *World Development Report 1995: Workers in an Integrating World*. New York: Oxford University Press.

Wyss, B. and Balakrishnan, R. (1993) 'Making connections: women in the international economy', in G. Epstein, J. Graham and J. Nembhard (eds), *Creating a New World Economy.* Philadelphia: Temple University Press. pp. 421–35.

Yaeger, D. (1991) *Undo Process: the NCAA's Injustice for All.* Champaign, IL: Sagamore.

Young, T.R. (1986) 'The sociology of sport: structural Marxist and cultural Marxist approaches', *Sociological Perspectives*, 29: 3–28.

Zimbalist, A. (1992) *Baseball and Billions: a Probing Look Inside the Big Business of Our National Pastime.* New York: Basic Books.

17

EDUCATION AND SPORTS

C. Roger Rees and Andrew W. Miracle

The development of modern sport as a global entity has been inextricably linked to the concept of education. Modern sport originated in educational institutions primarily in Britain during the mid-to-late nineteenth century, and was exported worldwide as an integral part of that educational system. Within these institutions, sport was originally seen as a device for building and demonstrating 'character', a rather vague term which is still used as justification for its inclusion as an important extracurricular activity in schools and colleges today. As this review will show, sport in schools has been credited with teaching values of sportsmanship and fair play to participants, increasing athletes' educational aspirations, developing a sense of community and group cohesion among students, helping to reduce dropout rates, and giving poor and minority youth access to higher education.

However the educational 'effect' of sport has not been confined to educational institutions. It has been used to justify participation at all levels of society from community youth leagues to professional clubs. To this day sport maintains a moral component and individual participation in it is seen as worthwhile, an uplifting experience. Even professional athletes carry the moral baggage of sport's genesis. They are supposed to be role models for youth, and their behavior is often judged against a standard of morality rarely applied to other representatives of the entertainment industry such as film stars or rock musicians.

In a symbolic sense sport has become part of what historian Eric Hobsbawm (1983a) has called the 'invented traditions' of culture. That is, it demonstrates to us that certain characteristics (or myths) are true, and can be generalized at a societal level. When a few gifted athletes from low socio-economic backgrounds use interscholastic sports to advance their education and/or become extremely wealthy as professionals, many people use this as testament to the belief that society is 'open', and that everyone has the opportunity to be successful if they follow 'society's' rules. In American high schools these rules are literally written on the locker room walls. For example, slogans such as 'there is no "I" in team', 'quitters never win and winners never quit', and, 'show me a good loser and I'll show you a loser', teach us that we should sink our individuality into the greater goal of team victory and never cease to strive for this success. After all, America is a nation of 'winners' and we should be satisfied with nothing less than 'Being No. 1'. The failures of English soccer football[1] and cricket teams in international competition in recent years has been interpreted as symbolic of a general air of pessimism in the nation, and a 'willful nostalgia' for what has been perceived as a more positive sporting era in the past (Maguire, 1994).

These introductory comments illustrate two problems with regard to the issues of education and sport, one substantive, the other organizational. First, although sport is a global concept, organized sport in educational settings is more evident in some countries than in others. For example, in Germany and some Scandinavian countries organized interscholastic athletics[2] is almost non-existent. Furthermore, the issue of sport in higher education is primarily applicable to the United States where the educational value of quasi-professional sports in colleges is hotly debated. This means that a lot of the research reviewed in this chapter applies to countries that imported and adapted the original British model wherein sport was afforded such an important role in character development. Secondly, the ubiquitous belief in the educational value of sport has implications for the focus of this chapter, specifically the issue of interpreting 'education' in its broadest sense of socialization and enculturation versus the narrower sense of schooling. Although we concentrate on sport in educational institutions, we do recognize that the 'education' issue is important in volunteer programs (Fine, 1987; Landers and Fine, 1996), especially since children often enter these programs before they become involved in sports at school.

Underlying all these observations is the theme that sport as education has a very 'modernist' ring to it, and is very much part of the modernist tradition of progress and emancipation. The following review is a record of attempts by social scientists to interpret this tradition using a number of theoretical and methodological perspectives. These include empirical approaches designed to test the usually anecdotal evidence given to support competitive sports programs in schools and colleges. This research tries to assess what changes (if any) occur as a result of participation in interscholastic athletics. Other approaches from a Marxist and a critical theory perspective have challenged the underlying assumptions of 'equality' in society and shown how sport can help to perpetuate social class, race and gender inequalities, and encourage practices such as dieting, drug taking and aggression which endanger physical and mental health. In particular, feminist research has revealed the way sport can reinforce patriarchy as the 'natural' order of social relationships between males and females.

In the final section of the chapter we discuss what we consider to be the 'isolated' nature of the research on sport and education from several perspectives, and suggest research agendas to reduce this isolation. We advance three points: first, that sport and education are global concepts yet the research has largely reflected an 'American' perspective; second, that sport is an integral part of schooling which has largely been overlooked by educational sociologists; third, that the sociological research on sport and education has been virtually ignored by practitioners in the field of physical education. This field comprises the formal mechanism through which the 'educational' message of sport is delivered. The 'message' for physical educators and coaches is that we can no longer accept that the

simplistic 'Marie Antoinette' approach by itself ('let them play sport') is successful in reducing social problems such as racism, sexism, delinquency and school dropout. Programs need to be developed which use sport as a medium through which to raise such social issues, and examples of such programs are briefly reviewed.

HISTORICAL BACKGROUND[3]

There is consensus among scholars (for example, Dunning, 1971; Guttmann, 1994; Mangan, 1981) that organized sport was first institutionalized in the private (euphemistically called 'public') schools in Britain in the nineteenth century.[4] In this context sports were seen as an integral part of the curriculum because of their 'character building' properties. Sports, especially team games like cricket and rugby, were intended to teach 'manly' characteristics such as group loyalty, physical toughness and self-reliance. This cult of athleticism became so popular that by the 1880s compulsory games, sometimes every day, but usually three times a week, became the norm (Mangan, 1981). Such training was an integral part of the spartan discipline of boarding-school life, encouraging boys to think of themselves as socially elite, and preparing them for leadership at home[5] and abroad. As Mangan (1981: 136) has noted, the athletic emphasis became the basis of the muscular Christianity movement – a fusion of Christianity and social Darwinism in which it was the duty (and the right) of English gentlemen to help civilize what they perceived to be the 'less fortunate' races which became part of the expanding British Empire. Muscular Christianity became popularized in the romantic novels of Charles Kingsley, and especially in *Tom Brown's Schooldays* by Thomas Hughes, which did much to establish as part of popular mythology the idea that 'sport builds character', at least for boys (see Anderson, 1985; Redmond, 1978).

There is also evidence that sport was part of education in girls' private schools, although these physical activities were constrained by the educational myths of the time concerning female maturation. Victorian medical theories held that females had a limited amount of energy, which, during puberty, went into the development of the reproductive organs. Subjecting adolescent girls to the rigors of intellectual and physical activity during this crucial period would endanger their physical maturation and subsequently their ability to have children (McCrone, 1987). Moderate exercise however, would help develop moral qualities in girls, and help girls become 'fit' mothers and produce physically healthy and morally sound children (Park, 1987).

British public schools provided the model for education in the British empire, and school sports became a way of life for the sons of the elites. This was the case for cricket in the West Indies (Sandiford and Stoddart, 1987) and India (Mangan, 1986), soccer football in Argentina (Guttmann, 1994: 58–9), and cricket, soccer and rugby football in Africa (Guttmann, 1994: 63–6).[6] In the United States exclusive private schools based on the British model were developed during the mid-to-late nineteenth century. In these schools sport was believed to perform the same function as in the British public schools, extending institutional control, allowing students contact with games masters who acted as surrogate parents, teaching 'manliness', developing leaders, and preparing athletes for elite colleges and universities (Armstrong, 1984; Bundgaard, 1985). At the same time there was also great value attached to winning (Bundgaard, 1985; Mirel, 1982). As in the British model, morality was associated with sport, but in America this morality was really demonstrated through victory, because only through victory, it was thought, could one demonstrate character and moral superiority over one's opponents (Mrozek, 1983: esp. ch. 2).[7] The tradition of Americans as winners was 'invented' in the emerging 'American' sports of baseball and football. Football in particular 'exemplifies all the best in American manhood', and became required activities in the schools attended by the future leaders of America (Park, 1987: 69).

As in Britain, school sports were perceived primarily as activities for males, although at least some American commentators did accept their importance in female moral and physical development. It was thought that mild physical activity could turn weak girls into fit mothers, and the emphasis on the role of mother-hood among middle-class women was particularly strong given the great influx of (usually working-class) immigrants from Europe at that time. Moreover, middle-class wives who did not have children were held responsible for 'race suicide' (Smith-Rosenberg and Rosenberg, 1973).

The impetus to broaden the idea that sport builds character, which eventually led to sport becoming such an important force in American education, stemmed from concern with how to socialize the children of immigrants. The playground movement (Cavallo, 1981) was developed as a way to counter the perception that urbanization and immigration were threatening 'American' values. The city environment in which most of the immigrants lived was seen as having a corrupting influence on youth which could be countered by adult-supervised and organized play in city playgrounds and gymnasiums. These activities would help reduce juvenile delinquency, give a sense of moral purpose to youth, and allow them to break away from their ethnic roots and become 'Americanized' (Cavallo, 1981). Organizations such as the Young Men's Christian Association (YMCA), and the Public School Athletic League (PSAL),[8] helped to bring these organized games and sports to the masses.

Cavallo (1981: 48) has suggested that by the 1920s Americans were convinced that team games were essential for promoting ethnic harmony, physical vigor, moral direction, psychological stability and social skills in urban youth. As the 1920s began, athletics had been institutionalized in virtually every school district in America. That participating in sport (or in America, winning in sport) 'built character' was the accepted tradition or 'myth' which is at the root of the link between sport and education. Many contemporary coaches and school athletic administrators would endorse the social and educational value of sport in schools as strongly as their predecessors did. The educational value of athletics may have stood the test of time among coaches and athletes, but for many contemporary sport sociologists it is a controversial issue. This research is reviewed in the next section.

SPORT IN EDUCATIONAL INSTITUTIONS[9]

The role of sport in schools has been increasingly scrutinized by sociologists since Coleman's landmark study of American high schools in the late 1950s (1961a). In this study Coleman acknowledged the value of sport as a source of identity and school spirit, particularly for non-motivated students. However, he also felt that, by placing too great an emphasis on sport, schools ran the risk of subverting intellectual goals (Coleman, 1961b). According to Basil Bernstein (1975) school life can be analysed from the perspective of two types of rituals: consensual rituals which sustain a sense of community, and differentiating rituals that mark off different groups within the school. Rees (1995) has applied this classification system to show how involvement in school sports effects the learning of knowledge via the subject matter of the curriculum and the learning of values. As Coleman's comments suggest, sport can influence both of these areas. The organization of this section (loosely) follows Bernstein's classification, dealing first with the research on the differentiating rituals and the relationship between sport and the academic life of the school, followed by the role of sport in the consensual rituals and the social values these rituals reinforce.

School Sport and Academic Life

Proponents of school sports suggest that athletics is a positive influence on the formal education of students. Their arguments claim that participation in sports develops skills that are useful in the workplace. Even if the dream of making a living using athletic ability in professional sport is unrealistic, the drive and determination, positive self-concept and self-confidence taught on playing fields and in gymnasiums are excellent preparation for the world of work. Sport increases high school students' academic aspirations and provides them opportunities to further their education at college. For less academically motivated students, sport provides the motivation to stay in school and therefore reduces the school dropout rate. These positive claims are discussed in the following sections in light of empirical research studies.

Academic Aspiration and Achievement In his study of ten Chicago area high schools in the late 1950s, Coleman (1961a) identified differences between adolescent peer culture and adult culture along three dimensions – career aspirations, popularity and friendship. He showed that boys preferred career choices as famous athletes or jet pilots to missionaries or atomic physicists, while girls chose famous actresses over schoolteachers. Also, male adolescents chose things like athletic prowess or being a member of the leading crowd as criteria for popularity with peers instead of academic achievement more valued by adults. Finally, adolescents and parents were at odds on the characteristics of an ideal friend or dating partner.

This view of youth puts adolescents in opposition to adults in general and parents in particular. But Brown points out (1990: 174) that there is much evidence for 'congruence' between parents and teenagers in political, religious and moral values, and that peers more often reinforce rather than contradict the values of their parents (see also Youniss et al., 1994). Coleman's methodology of forcing respondents to choose between different statuses such as athlete or scholar was easily reproduced in subsequent research which tended to replicate his original findings (Eitzen, 1976; Thirer and Wright, 1985).

However, there are some puzzling inconsistencies in the research on sport and adolescent groups. For example, the wish to be remembered as a star athlete instead of a scholar might be seen as indicative of a peer culture running counter to adult requirements according to Coleman. However, the results of longitudinal studies on nationally representative samples of high school students consistently show that involvement in high school athletics leads to an increase in educational aspirations and a greater identification with school culture (Fejgin, 1994; Marsh, 1993; Melnick et al., 1988; Rees et al., 1990). Although these findings have sometimes been mediated by combinations of race and gender (Sabo et al., 1993), and prior academic self-concept (Marsh, 1993), none of the results shows a negative effect of sport on athletes' involvement with school culture.

The results of participation in sports on academic aspirations must also be discussed in relation to actual academic attainment. Those who believe in the educational value of high school athletics would argue that athletes must study to attain the grade point average necessary to remain eligible for school sports. They would also argue that athletes have to practice efficient time-management skills because of the time constraints imposed by school athletics, and that the self-esteem supposedly gained from sports can transfer to academics. To support such claims they can point to studies showing that athletes have similar or higher grade point average (GPA) than non-athletes (Rehberg, 1969; Schafer and Armer, 1968), and to more recent longitudinal research showing that participation has a small positive effect on grades (Fejgin, 1994; Hanks, 1979). Skeptics might suggest that athletes could be graded more leniently than non-athletes, or could benefit from special tutoring, or might take easy courses so as to remain academically eligible. Different measures of academic achievement besides GPA need to be considered in this discussion (Miracle and Rees, 1994: 136–8). For example, Marsh (1993) noted that participation in sport favorably affected academic activities such as being in an academic track, school attendance, taking science courses and time spent on homework, but also noted that sports participation had little effect on changes in academic achievement over time.

Clearly the nature of the relationship between academic aspirations, academic achievement and school sports is unresolved. The longitudinal research has improved on the early cross-sectional research designs because it has been able to isolate athletic effects, instead of just comparing athlete and non-athlete groups. However, the results of these studies need to be considered in conjunction with research that describes the relative importance of athletics and education in the cultural milieu of school life, and which examines the 'lived experience' of students.

Dropout Rates Advocates of school sports might also interpret the research on school dropout (Finn, 1989; McNeal, 1995; Melnick et al., 1992) as supporting the positive role of athletics in education. Participation in extracurricular activities has been seen as an important factor in reducing school dropout (Finn, 1989). In a study of the effect of extracurricular activities on high school dropout, using longitudinal data from the 'High School and Beyond' study, McNeal (1995) showed that participation in athletics and fine arts significantly reduced dropout rates, while participation in academic or vocational clubs did not. This relationship held after controlling for race,[10] socio-economic status, gender and employment. When all extracurricular activities were examined simultaneously only athletic participation remained significantly related to dropout reduction. McNeal suggested that the importance of athletic status in peer culture, the frequency of peer interaction characterizing athletics, and the time commitment necessary for participation may all contribute to the effect, but warned against overemphasizing the power of sports as the principal antidote to school dropout. Although the effects of participation in fine arts activities were not as prominent as athletics, they 'instill a less competitive focus in participants and foster a more "cooperative" environment', which McNeal saw as more conducive to finishing school (McNeal, 1995: 75).

In previous research, DiMaggio (1982) had advocated fine arts activities as a mode of attaining cultural capital and gaining access to the more 'elite' group of students who would have better school attitudes.[11] However, McNeal's results imply that the development of physical capital is equally if not more important to potential school dropouts. The concept of physical capital will be discussed in more detail in a later section, but if the only reason students stay in school is to play sports how is this helping their academic education? In some ways McNeal's findings tend to confirm

Coleman's original concern that athletics in schools can subvert educational goals.

Interscholastic sports and higher education
The idea that male (and increasingly female) high school students can translate the physical capital developed in high school sports into the cultural capital of a college education is one of our greatest cultural myths (Miracle and Rees, 1994: ch. 6; Spady, 1971). Conventional wisdom has it that athletic scholarships give athletes (particularly black athletes of low socio-economic status) access to university that might otherwise be unattainable, and a 'free ride' for the four or five years it takes them to graduate. This idea combines two of our most sacred myths – the importance of education as a path to upward mobility and the essentially open nature of access to education within society. In this section the validity of these myths is examined in light of research that highlights athletes' reasons for attending college, traces their academic progress, analyses graduation rates for different sports in different schools, and reports the difficulties experienced by some athletes when trying to balance the demands of their academic and sport schedules.

For example, Sabo, Melnick and Vanfossen's (1993) analysis of the 'High School and Beyond' data set found that the effect of participation in high school athletics on post-secondary educational success and upward mobility depended upon the participants' race/ethnic status, gender and type of school (urban, suburban, rural). Their results reflected the larger societal patterns of racial and gender stratification. In another analysis of the 'High School and Beyond' data, Snyder and Spreitzer (1990) showed that high school athletics had a positive effect on college attendance. However, controlling for the effects of race, socio-economic status and cognitive development revealed that the effect was strongest for students who had the lowest cognitive development, that is, the ones least suited for higher education who would have the most difficulty in graduating with a college degree. A National Intercollegiate Athletic Association (NCAA) sponsored study of a sample of male undergraduate baseball players and female undergraduate softball players at Division 1 schools showed that academic concerns were not among the most important in their decision about which school to attend. Indicators of the colleges' scholastic attributes (specifically, 'academic program' and 'curriculum/major') were ranked seventh and ninth on a list of ten reasons by the baseball players and third and seventh by the softball players. 'Amount of scholarship' was first choice for the males and second choice for the females (Doyle and Gaeth, 1990).

The results of these two studies confirm the rather obvious fact that athletic scholarships are given for athletic ability first (and academic ability second) to student-athletes whose primary interest is the amount of money they are receiving. This does not mean that student-athletes are not interested in their education, but that academic achievement and graduation is not guaranteed and may be problematic for some. One study of male basketball and football players at one NCAA Division 1 school showed that, in one academic year, 19 per cent were 'passing easily', carrying an average of 15.3 credit hours per semester with a GPA of 3.22. Most of the student-athletes (55 per cent) were 'getting by' with a GPA slightly above the 2.0 required by the NCAA for athletic participation. The remaining 26 per cent were 'struggling along', passing an average of only 5.1 credit hours with a GPA of 1.79 in the Fall semester and an average of 10.1 credit hours with a GPA of 1.78 in the Spring semester. This fell far short of the NCAA requirement of a 2.00 average for 24 credit hours for the academic year (Brede and Camp, 1987).

Research from case studies confirms that academics may be a special problem for some male athletes in Division 1 universities. In one such study the authors lived for four years with male college basketball players at one school. The players were mostly from lower- and middle-class backgrounds; 70 per cent of them were black. The dual pressures of big-time athletics and the demands of college work became too much for most of the athletes. Over the four-year period their early idealistic view that they would be able to use athletics to get an education was replaced by what the authors termed 'pragmatic detachment' towards academics. Turned off by hard courses, being pressured to win by coaches, and isolated in a 'jock' dorm where there was little peer support for studying, they became preoccupied with maintaining eligibility and the unlikely chances of a professional career (Adler and Adler, 1985). However, in-depth interviews with senior female basketball and volleyball players at another Division 1 school showed that these student-athletes managed to maintain a balance between sport and studying. The author argued that lack of professional outlets and public recognition for women's sports, and the lack of a 'jock' mentality by female athletes, accounted for this commitment to education (Meyer, 1990).

The educational problem of college athletics has been a popular issue among sport sociologists in America. Scholars who adopt a critical theory perspective (for example, Sage, 1990: ch. 8) see intercollegiate athletics as a 'quasi-professional' system which makes money for the universities at the expense of the educational needs of the student-athletes. This view is opposite to the popular myth of sport as a way for low socio-economic students to achieve an education. In defense of the sceptics, there are plenty of anecdotes and case studies of the system failing. On the other hand, the focus of the criticism has been big-time college programs in Division 1 schools. It is of interest to examine the effects (if any) on athletes' academic performance of recent NCAA reforms designed to reduce professionalism. Will the recent television exposure given to women's collegiate basketball lead to an increase in academic problems? Also, we have almost no information on how male or female athletes in Division 2 or Division 3 schools handle academic pressures, or whether this is a problem.

The research reviewed in this section does show that we should be wary of accepting grandiose claims for sport enhancing the academic life of athletes. Participation in high school sports consistently raises educational aspirations, and may reduce student dropout rates, but its effect on general academic achievement in high school and in college is less clear-cut. The importance of sport in consensual school rituals, and the values reinforced by these rituals is the subject of the next section.

School Sports and Values

The evidence presented in the historical background section supports the idea that sports entered school life because of their perceived socialization value. Societies that adapted the original model from the British public schools continue to stress the importance of sport as consensual rituals which are supposed to teach 'positive' values, develop school spirit and provide a bond between the school and the community.[12] In the United States rituals like pep rallies and homecoming perform such a function. These events have been vividly described by Burnett (1969), and more recently by Bissinger (1990) and Foley (1990a, 1990b), although there is no consensus on what values these rituals actually teach. For example, scholars using a conflict theory perspective (for example, O'Hanlon, 1980, 1982; Spring, 1974) agree that the importance of sport in education increases as schools assume more responsibility for social values such as 'morality' and 'citizenship', but that the real lessons taught by athletics are to accept competition as the principal method by which the scarce societal resources could be allocated (O'Hanlon, 1980: 103). Or, in Doug Foley's words, students are 'learning capitalist culture' through school sports (Foley, 1990b).[13] Studies reviewed in the following sections deal with the consensual function of athletic rituals and what values (if any) are learned through these rituals.

Building Character[14] Social scientists have used a number of methodologies to move beyond the usual anecdotal evidence given in support of the belief that sport builds character. For example, Kleiber and Roberts (1981) introduced the 'Kick-Soccer World Series' to a random sample of boys and girls in two elementary schools. This event simulated the conditions of organized sports with scores kept of league standings, leading to one champion team which was rewarded with trophies. When the participants in the program were compared with a control group of their peers who were not involved, the boys' scores on altruism were lower in the experimental group. The authors speculated that the emphasis on winning in organized sport might lead children to become more confrontational in interactions with their peers. The effect of participation in sport on personality development has also been examined in longitudinal research. For example, Best (1985) concluded that male athletes had the same values as their non-athlete peers when compared on such characteristics as social skills, self-control, honesty and independence. Rees, Howell and Miracle (1990) report similar findings in their analysis of the 'Youth in Transition' data set. While participation in high school sports increased self-esteem and the value attached to academic achievement, it also increased aggression and irritability and reduced the belief in the importance of being honest, the importance of self-control and of independence. However, these differences were the exception rather than the rule, and the general conclusion was that school sports did little to benefit or harm the social development of participants. The results of similar longitudinal research by Marsh (1993) and Fejgin (1994) showed that participation in sport at high school had no negative effects, and several positive influences on athlete's academic and discipline behavior.

Further insights into the role of sports and character development have been provided by the work of Bredemeier and Shields and their associates. In their research they have compared the level of moral reasoning used by high school and college athletes in several sports with the level used by non-athletes (see Shields and Bredemeier, 1995, for a review). Among other things, they have found that involvement in collegiate basketball is associated with less mature moral reasoning than is usual in the general population. However, in the case of high school basketball there were no significant differences in moral reasoning between athletes and non-athletes (Bredemeier and Shields, 1984, 1986). In a study of elementary school students, the longer boys participated in high-contact sports and girls in medium-contact sports, the lower the level of moral reasoning (Bredemeier et al., 1987). This research has shown that people often see moral decisions in sport as different from moral decisions in daily life contexts such as school or work. In sport they employ 'game reasoning', which 'may, at times, be a form of moral rationalization that seemingly legitimizes behavior that would ordinarily result in self-censure' (Shields and Bredemeier, 1995: 190). This concept of game reasoning, the idea that sport is a special domain where the normal social rules that restrain aggressive social interaction do not apply, is part of what has been called 'positive deviance' (Hughes and Coakley, 1991).

Delinquency[15] 'Positive deviance' can help to explain inconsistencies in the research, which has examined the relationship between participation in school sports, and antisocial activities such as theft, drunkenness, drug abuse and violence generally labeled juvenile delinquency. To the extent that this behavior in males was caused by the need to assert masculinity, or as a reaction to frustration, or weak social controls, participation in school sports was suggested as providing a 'deterrent' effect to delinquency (Segrave and Chu, 1978). While some research has shown athletes' delinquency rates to be lower than non-athletes' (for example, Hastad et al., 1984), others have shown the opposite (Buhrmann and Bratton, 1978). Further research has shown support for a 'reform' effect of sport (Stark et al., 1987), particularly in non-conventional sports such as Outward Bound programs (Kelly and Baer, 1971), and the traditional martial arts (Trulson, 1986).

While deterrent and reform theories assume the positive effect of sport, the concept of positive deviance suggests that activities labeled 'deviant' in other social contexts may be part of the socialization process into sport, particularly for male athletes. It can help to explain why 'athletes do harmful things to themselves and perhaps others while motivated by a sense of duty and honor' (Hughes and Coakley, 1991: 311). For example, why would male high school football players copy a scene in a popular film and risk their lives by lying down in the middle of on-coming traffic (Bernard, 1993; Forrest, 1993)? Why would they initiate a competition to see who could have the largest number of sexual encounters (Didion, 1993; Smolowe, 1993)? Why was 'improving athletic performance' given as the number one response in a national survey designed to study steroid use in high school males (Buckley et al., 1988)? And why do college female athletes experience a higher level of eating disorders than non-athlete groups (Black and Burckes-Miller, 1988; Thornton, 1990)? Moreover, high levels of athletic ability have not deterred high school football players (Campbell, 1989) or college male swimmers (Snyder, 1994) from crime sprees. Incidents such as these and many more examples of date rape, theft and drunkenness have led sociologists to see deviance as part of the culture of sport, a culture which supports deviant behavior in the pursuit of victory and reinforces gender and racial stereotypes.

School Sports, Masculinity and Race The theme of biologically based male superiority over females is one of the sub-texts of sport (Bryson, 1987, 1990) that is played out in the consensual rituals of high school athletics. For example, Foley (1990a) provided several examples of this theme in the school he studied. Football players prided themselves on being able to give and take physical punishment, play with pain and live promiscuous lifestyles. The 'powder puff' football game, in which teams of the most popular senior and junior girls put on football gear and played against each other for the amusement of the male athletes, actually reproduced male power. Ostensibly a role-reversal ritual, the game allowed the males to dress like female cheerleaders, and belittle the females' attempt at serious 'male' sport in a ridiculous and demeaning manner. Other research by Curry (1991, 1998) has documented the routine sexist attitude of male college athletes in their locker room talk, and incidents of sexual aggression by male athletes.

Given that male athletes are usually at the top of the status hierarchy in school cliques (Caanan, 1987; Rees, 1995), their values and behavior are likely to be copied by non-athlete groups. For example, being able to accept physical abuse was perceived to be a high-status characteristic in the male adolescent groups that Foley studied. How a boy dealt with physical pain led to him being labeled either as a 'real man' or as a 'wimp' or a 'fag' (Foley, 1990a).

Foley's study also showed little evidence of high school sport reducing racial tensions or helping the process of racial assimilation. In fact racial tensions in the community were replicated in the ritual of high school football. The racial 'jokes' of the white and Hispanic football players reinforced racial stereotypes, and decisions over starting roles and homecoming celebrations were interpreted as having racial overtones. Foley characterized high school football as reproducing racial inequality.

Mark Grey (1992) reached a similar conclusion in his study of a southwestern Kansas high school. Many minorities were recent immigrants (Hispanic and Southeastern Asian) whose children had had little experience with American sports. Although some played soccer and volleyball, their failure to get involved in football was taken by some community members as evidence that they were resisting assimilation.[16]

In summary, this brief review of research on sport and the consensual rituals of school life calls into question the traditional view of sport as a positive force in school life. While the longitudinal research generally shows no negative (but often little positive) changes in the 'character' of participants, research that decodes sport's symbolic role shows it reinforcing existing inequalities of gender and race, and perpetuating the status quo. These opposite views of social reality when it comes to the role of sport and schooling, and the implications for research and practice, will be discussed as part of the final section.

A CRITIQUE OF THE RESEARCH ON SPORT AND SCHOOLING

During the opening ceremony of the 26th Olympic Games in Atlanta, Georgia, on 19 July 1996, Juan Antonio Samaranch, President of the International Olympic Committee, proclaimed to the world that 'sport is education'. The 'global' image of sport education that he had in mind was probably very similar to the image of sport in upper-class British boarding schools described in the early part of this chapter. It was this image that had inspired the originator of the modern Olympics, Baron Pierre de Coubertin, over a century ago (MacAloon, 1981). It is safe to assume that findings from the empirical and critical research on sport and education reviewed in this chapter were not part of his vision, or the vision of most of the thousands of people in attendance, or the millions more watching on television. The limitations of sociology of sport knowledge about education are briefly discussed in the final section of this chapter, where we consider the 'isolated' nature of the research we have reviewed from several perspectives.

Globalization

Samaranch's image of the global nature of sport education notwithstanding, globalization research on sport and education is almost non-existent. Almost all the research reviewed in this chapter has been conducted in the United States. For example, we are aware of no comparative research studies focusing on the importance of school sport in countries that share sporting and educational traditions (such as, Britain and America). Is the perpetuation of class, race and gender differences that Foley demonstrated in a southwestern Texas school generalizable to other societies were the community involvement in school sports is less intense? To what degree are adolescents' views about sport generalizable across cultures and subject to societal and/or regional differences? Such research might help to provide interesting data to test recent globalization theories (Maguire, 1994; Robertson, 1992).

Recent theoretical advances in conceptualizing the body as an important factor in modern life also may help to advance this research endeavor. For example, Shilling (1993: 4–5) places corporeal concerns at the center of the issue of identity, and describes the body as 'an island of security in a global system characterized by multiple and inescapable risks'. He has extended Bourdieu's concept of capital to the body and has shown how Bourdieu's theories can be used to explain gender inequalities in general (Shilling, 1991a) as well as in education (Shilling, 1991b, 1992). Preliminary results in a study comparing German and American adolescents using the concept of body capital show that young people from both countries share many similar attitudes about the importance of sport and the body. Data also indicate that in some cases gender differences function in a similar way in both societies, but also that racial differences in America exert an independent effect (Brettschneider et al., 1996; Rees and Brandl-Bredenbeck, 1995; Rees et al., 1998).

Sociology of Education

The field of sociology of education has largely neglected the importance of sport as an educational force in American schools. With the notable exception of Coleman's work (1961a), and more recently that of Doug Foley (1990b), which came from both a sociological and an anthropological perspective, books on school life have failed to describe this important influence.[17] Most of the research reviewed in this chapter has been published in sociology of sport journals, not in journals specializing in sociology of education. Much interesting information on the role of sport in the life of American schools has to be gained 'second hand' from recent journalistic accounts of high school football (Bissinger, 1990) and basketball (Frey, 1994; Joravsky, 1995). These accounts are extremely interesting and locate the importance of sport within the school and the local community. However, they are atheoretical and concentrate almost exclusively on the lives of the athletic stars. Consequently they often fail to examine the general importance of sport in education.

There is a great need for studies that place sport within the context of school life, studies that show how adolescents 'make sense' out of school rituals including sports rituals. This research could test the 'disembodied' empirical findings of longitudinal research reviewed above within the 'lived experience' of students at school. For example, how important is female sport in the social life of the school and the community, especially in communities such as Iowa where women's basketball is taken so seriously? Can the phenomenon of successful female sport teams break down existing gender stereotypes that occur in school and community? What is the effect of gender and race in the production of physical capital among school children, and the translation of this to cultural and economic capital (Shilling, 1992)?

Physical Education

Perhaps more disturbing, from a practical perspective, is the fact that physical education practitioners, those teachers and coaches in a position to apply the research findings on sport and schooling, have paid scant attention to this body of knowledge, particularly in the United States. Pedagogical practice in physical education appears unaffected by the rather modest results from longitudinal research on the positive effects of sport, and warnings from critical scholars about sport perpetuating existing inequalities. The myth that sport encourages positive educational outcomes is still used to justify school athletics and physical education programs (Rees, 1997). Programs that use sport as a medium to teach self-control and self-responsibility (for example, Hellison, 1993; Hellison and Templin, 1991; Williamson and Georgiadis, 1992) or specifically to encourage moral development (for example, Romance et al., 1986) have been the exception rather than the rule.[18]

Also of value is the sport education model developed by Siedentop, Mand and Taggart (1986) which uses physical education lessons to teach fair play in sports, and gives students the opportunity to practice sports-related roles such as coach, referee and manager. This program has been successfully tested and widely applied in Australia (Alexander et al., 1996) and in New Zealand (Grant, 1992).

If sport sociologists are really serious about the practical applications of this knowledge they need to study physical education curriculum process at work. Following Bernstein's (1990) idea of the curriculum as a 'pedagogical device' through which interested parties decide what will become 'the official pedagogical discourse', Evans and Penney (1995) showed how disputes over the National Curriculum for physical education in Britain affected how the body will eventually be schooled. Sociologists are usually absent from such struggles at the school level, and so knowledge from the sociology of sport is not often heard by practitioners. Sociologists need to work closely with sports practitioners in non-confrontational contexts (Rees et al., 1991) in order to improve the educational effects of sport.[19]

CONCLUSION

This chapter reviewed the sociological research on sport and schooling – research that has tended to call into question the globe-wide myths that participation in sport inevitably provides positive social experiences and 'builds character'. We suggest research approaches should be designed to increase our knowledge about how children make sense of sport in schools. This research may reveal the contradictory nature of modern sport, and show that positive and negative influences exist side by side. If this is the case, the issue of education should become an important topic for applied sociology of sport. Sociologists, coaches and physical education teachers could cooperate in the goal of using sport to counter the problems of school dropout, gender and ethnic stereotyping, and parochialism.

NOTES

1   Although sport is a global concept, sometimes the terminology used to describe it is not. Soccer football here refers to the game of Association football, known as soccer in the United States but generally termed football in the rest of the world.

2   The word 'athletics' is used here and throughout the chapter in the American sense to describe a number of different sports rather than in the British sense which is equivalent to the American term 'track and field'.

3   Since other chapters discuss the genesis of modern sport, this section will deal primarily with the institutionalization of sport in schools. It draws upon previous reviews by the authors, particularly Miracle and Rees, (1994: ch. 2).

4   *Athleticism in the Victorian and Edwardian Public School* by James A. Mangan (Cambridge: Cambridge University Press, 1981) is an authoritative source on the growth of athleticism in British boarding schools.

5   Eric Hobsbawm (1983a) has suggested that the growth of sport at this time helped to 'invent the traditions' of Britain which gave stability to society and legitimated existing power relations. Private education expanded to meet the needs of a growing middle class. Before 1868 about 24 schools could seriously claim the status of 'public schools', but by 1902 this number had grown to between 64 and 104 depending on the criteria used for classification (Hobsbawm, 1983b). The best criterion for acceptance into this community of elite schools was athletic competition. Schools that played sports together shared an identity.

6   These references come from Allen Guttman's *Games and Empires: Modern Sports and Cultural Imperialism* (1994).

7   This belief is still an accepted part of American sporting tradition. The team that comes from behind to win is often described as 'showing great character'.

8   Historian Thomas Jable described the PSAL as 'a progenitor and leader of public school athletics' (1984: 235). For more information on the precursors of sport in American schools see this article, and also Cavallo (1981), Rader (1983) and Miracle and Rees (1994: ch. 2).

9   This section draws on some of the material reviewed by the first author in 'Sports and schooling' in *Education and Sociology: an Encyclopedia* (Rees, in press).

10 Melnick, Sabo and Vanfossen (1992) in an separate analysis of the same data set found that the effect of athletic involvement on dropout reduction applied only to rural black males, suburban Hispanic males, and rural Hispanic females. Respondents' school location (urban, suburban, rural) was not a variable in McNeal's study.

11 A similar argument, that the high status of school sports gives low socio-economic status students access to the 'leading crowd' through which their academic aspirations are raised, was made by Coleman (1961a: ch. 5).

12 The first author has vivid recollections of playing, both as a student and as a former student, in several 'Old Boy' rugby matches in England. These annual events pitted the current school rugby (or soccer football) team against a team of former pupils in a solidarity ritual at which attendance by the whole school was usually mandatory. Such events in Britain are (or were in the 1960s when single-sex schools were the norm) often followed in the evening by a dinner organized by the schools' 'Old Boy' association.

13 School rituals such as pep rallies place so much emphasis on intergoup competition in sport that the importance of intragroup competition is often overlooked. In one of the few studies on intra-team competition, Rees and Segal (1984) demonstrated support for O'Hanlon's argument. Collegiate football players in two Division 1 universities rated team mates who played the same position as they did (and were therefore competing with them) higher in liking and respect than other team mates, but only if perceptions of equity in competition were upheld. Players in the same positions whose football ability was perceived to be less than that of the respondents received lower liking and respect ratings.

14 This section draws on some of the material presented by Miracle and Rees (1994), particularly in Chapters 3, 4 and 5.

15 Space constraints do not allow a thorough review of the deviance and sport research. More detailed reviews have been made by Miracle and Rees (1994: ch. 5), Segrave and Hastad (1984) and Snyder (1994).

16 Grey quotes other research on assimilation of Portuguese students in a New England high school (Becker, 1990), and Punjabi students in a Californian high school (Gibson, 1988) in which failure to get involved in sport was similarly criticized by the school teachers and administrators.

17 For example, sport is hardly mentioned in Cookson and Persell's (1985) otherwise excellent book on American elite boarding schools, in Nancy Lesko's (1988) study on girls in a Catholic school, or in Penelope Eckert's (1989) book on social categories in school life.

18 These and other approaches are reviewed by Shields and Bredemeier (1995).

19 For an excellent example of this process at work with volunteer adults in youth sport, see McPherson (1986).

REFERENCES

Adler, P. and Adler, P.A. (1985) 'From idealism to pragmatic detachment: the academic performance of college athletes', *Sociology of Education*, 58: 241–50.

Alexander, K., Taggart, A. and Thorpe, S. (1996) 'A spring in their steps? Possibilities for professional renewal through sport education in Australian schools', *Sport, Education and Society*, 1 (1): 23–46.

Anderson, E.R. (1985) 'The Barby Hill episode in "Tom Brown's School Days": sources and influences', *Arete*, 2 (2): 95–110.

Armstrong, C.F. (1984) 'The lessons of sport: class socialization in British and American boarding schools', *Sociology of Sport Journal*, 1: 314–31.

Becker, A. (1990) 'The role of the school in the maintenance of ethnic group affiliation', *Human Organizations*, 49: 48–55.

Bernard, J.K. (1993) 'Lethal risk: young copy cats', *Newsday*, 23 October, pp. 20, 23.

Bernstein, B. (1975) *Ritual in Education. Class, Codes and Control*, Volume 3. London: Routledge & Kegan Paul.

Bernstein, B. (1990) *The Structuring of Pedagogic Discourse*. London: Routledge.

Best, C. (1985) 'Differences in social values between athletes and non-athletes', *Research Quarterly for Exercise and Sport*, 56: 366–9.

Bissinger, H.G. (1990) *Friday Night Lights: a Town, a Team, and a Dream*. Reading, MA: Addison-Wesley.

Black, D.R. and Burckes-Miller, M.E. (1988) 'Male and female college athletes: use of anorexia nervosa and bulimia nervosa weight loss methods', *Research Quarterly for Exercise and Sport*, 59 (3): 252–6.

Brede, R.M. and Camp, H.J. (1987) 'The education of college student-athletes', *Sociology of Sport Journal*, 4: 245–57.

Bredemeier, B.J. and Shields, D. (1984) 'Divergence in moral reasoning about sport and everyday life', *Sociology of Sport Journal*, 1: 348–57.

Bredemeier, B.J. and Shields, D. (1986) 'Game reasoning and interactional morality', *Journal of Genetic Psychology*, 147: 257–75.

Bredemeier, B.J., Weiss, M.R., Shields, D. and Cooper, B. (1987) 'The relationship between children's legitimacy judgments and their moral reasoning, aggression tendencies, and sport involvement', *Sociology of Sport Journal*, 4: 48–60.

Brettschneider, W.D., Brandl-Bredenbeck, H.P. and Rees, C.R. (1996) 'Sportkultur von Jugendlichen in der Bundesrepublik Deutschland und in den USA – eine interkulturelle vergleichende Studie. *Sportwissenschaft*, 26 (3): 249–71.

Brown, B.B. (1990) 'Peer groups and peer culture', in S.S. Feldman and G.R. Elliot (eds), *At the Threshold: the Developing Adolescent*. Cambridge, MA: Harvard University Press. pp. 171–96.

Bryson, L. (1987) 'Sport and the maintenance of masculine hegemony', *Women's Studies International Forum*, 10: 349–60.

Bryson, L. (1990) 'Challenges to male hegemony in sport', in M.A. Messner and D.F. Sabo (eds), *Sport, Men, and the Gender Order*. Champaign, IL: Human Kinetics. pp. 173–84.

Buckley, W.E., Yesalis, C.E., Friedl, K.E., Anderson, W.E., Streit, A.L. and Wright, J.E. (1988) 'Estimated prevalence of anabolic steroid use among male high school seniors', *Journal of the American Medical Association*, 260 (23): 3441–5.

Buhrmann, H.G. and Bratton, R.D. (1978) 'Athletic participation and deviant behavior of high school girls in Alberta', *Review of Sport and Leisure*, 3 (2): 25–41.

Bundgaard, A. (1985) 'Tom Brown abroad: athletics in selected New England public schools, 1850–1910', *Research Quarterly for Exercise and Sport* (Centennial Issue), 56: 28–37.

Burnett, J.H. (1969) 'Ceremony, rites and economy in the student system of an American high school', *Human Organization*, 28: 1–10.

Caanan, J. (1987) 'A comparative analysis of American suburban middle class, middle school and high school teenage cliques', in G. Spindler and L. Spindler (eds), *Interpretive Ethnography and Education*. Hillsdale, NJ: Erlbaum Press. pp. 385–406.

Campbell, R. (1989) 'Prison life dims glory days', *Fort Worth Star-Telegram*, 24 December, Section 1, pp. 1, 10.

Cavallo, D. (1981) *Muscles and Morals: Organized Playgrounds and Urban Reform, 1880–1920*. Philadelphia: University of Pennsylvania Press.

Coleman, J.S. (1961a) *The Adolescent Society: the Social Life of the Teenager and Its Impact on Education*. New York: The Free Press.

Coleman, J.S. (1961b) 'Athletics in high school', *Annals of the American Academy of Political and Social Sciences*, 338: 33–43.

Cookson, P.W. and Persell, C.H. (1985) *Preparing for Power: America's Elite Boarding Schools*. New York: Basic Books.

Curry, T.J. (1991) 'Fraternal bonding in the locker room: a profeminist analysis of talk about competition and women', *Sociology of Sport Journal*, 8 (2): 119–35.

Curry, T.J. (1998) 'Beyond the locker room: campus bars and college athletes', *Sociology of Sport Journal*, 15 (3): 205–15.

Didion, J. (1993) 'Trouble in Lakewood', *The New Yorker*, pp. 46–50, 52–60, 62–5.

DiMaggio, P. (1982) 'Cultural capital and school success', *American Sociological Review*, 47: 189–201.

Doyle, C.A. and Gaeth, G.J. (1990) 'Assessing the institutional choice process of student-athletes', *Research Quarterly for Exercise and Sport*, 61 (1): 85–92.

Dunning, E. (1971) 'The development of modern football', in E. Dunning (ed.), *The Sociology of Sport*. London: Frank Cass. pp. 133–51.

Eckert, P. (1989) *Jocks and Burnouts: Social Categories and Identity in the High School*. New York: Teachers College Press.

Eitzen, D.S. (1976) 'Sport and social status in American public secondary education', *Review of Sport and Leisure*, 1 (1): 110–18.

Evans, J. and Penney, D. (1995) 'Physical education, restoration and the politics of sport', *Curriculum Studies*, 3 (2): 183–96.

Fejgin, N. (1994) 'Participation in high school competitive sports: a subversion of school mission or contribution to academic goals?', *Sociology of Sport Journal*, 11 (3): 211–30.

Fine, G.A. (1987) *With the Boys: Little League Baseball and Preadolescent Culture*. Chicago: University of Chicago Press.

Finn, J. (1989) 'Withdrawing from school', *Review of Educational Research*, 59: 117–42.

Foley, D.E. (1990a) 'The great American football ritual: reproducing race, class, and gender inequality', *Sociology of Sport Journal*, 7: 111–35.

Foley, D.E. (1990b) *Learning Capitalist Culture: Deep in the Heart of Tejas*. Philadelphia: University of Pennsylvania Press.

Forrest, S. (1993) 'Costly move: car hits Syosset teen who was imitating film scene', *Newsday*, 19 October, pp. 5, 29.

Frey, D. (1994) *The Last Shot: City Streets, Basketball Dreams*. Boston, MA: Houghton Mifflin.

Gibson, M.A. (1988) *Accommodation without Assimilation: Sikh Immigrants in an American High School*. Ithaca, NY: Cornell University Press.

Grant, B.C. (1992) 'Integrating sport into the physical education curriculum in New Zealand secondary schools', *Quest*, 44 (3): 304–16.

Grey, M.A. (1992) 'Sports and immigrant, minority and Anglo relations in Garden City (Kansas) High School', *Sociology of Sport Journal*, 9 (3): 255–70.

Guttmann, A. (1994) *Games and Empires: Modern Sports and Cultural Imperialism*. New York: Columbia University Press.

Hanks, M.P. (1979) 'Race, sexual status and athletics in the process of educational achievement', *Social Science Quarterly*, 60: 482–96.

Hastad, D.N., Segrave, J.O., Pangrazi, R. and Peterson, G. (1984) 'Youth participation and deviant behavior', *Sociology of Sport Journal*, 1 (4): 366–73.

Hellison, D. (1993) 'The coaching club: teaching responsibility to inner-city students', *Journal of Physical Education, Recreation and Dance*, 64: 66–71.

Hellison, D. and Templin, T. (1991) *A Reflexive Approach to Teaching Physical Education.* Champaign, IL: Human Kinetics.

Hobsbawm, E. (1983a) 'Introduction: inventing traditions', in E. Hobsbawm and T.O. Ranger (eds), *The Invention of Tradition.* Cambridge: Cambridge University Press. pp. 1–14.

Hobsbawm, E. (1983b) 'Mass-producing traditions: Europe 1870–1914', in E. Hobsbawm and T.O. Ranger (eds), *The Invention of Tradition.* Cambridge: Cambridge University Press. pp. 263–307.

Hughes, R. and Coakley, J.J. (1991) 'Positive deviance among athletes: the implications of overconformity to the sport ethic', *Sociology of Sport Journal*, 8 (4): 307–25.

Jable, J.T. (1984) 'The Public Schools Athletic League of New York City: organized athletics for city school children, 1903–1914', in S. Riess (ed.), *The American Sporting Experience: a Historical Anthology of Sport in America.* West Point, NY: Leisure Press. pp. 219–38.

Joravsky, D. (1995) *Hoop Dreams: a True Story of Leadership and Triumph.* Atlanta, GA: Turner Publishing Company.

Kelly, J. and Baer, J. (1971) 'Psychological challenge as a treatment for delinquency', *Crime and Delinquency*, 17: 437–45.

Kleiber, D.A. and Roberts, G.C. (1981) 'The effects of sport experience in the development of social character: an exploratory investigation', *Journal of Sport Psychology*, 3: 114–22.

Landers, M.A. and Fine, G.A. (1996) 'Learning life's lessons in Tee Ball: the reinforcement of gender and status in kindergarten sport', *Sociology of Sport Journal*, 13 (1): 87–93.

Lesko, N. (1988) *Symbolizing Society: Stories, Rites, and Structure in a Catholic High School.* New York: Falmer Press.

MacAloon, J.J. (1981) *This Great Symbol: Pierre de Coubertin and the Origins of the Modern Olympic Games.* Chicago: University of Chicago Press.

Maguire, J. (1994) 'Sport, identity politics, and globalization: diminishing contrasts and increasing varieties', *Sociology of Sport Journal*, 11 (4): 398–427.

Mangan, J.A. (1981) *Athleticism in the Victorian and Edwardian Public School.* Cambridge: Cambridge University Press.

Mangan, J.A. (ed.) (1986) *The Games Ethic and Imperialism.* New York: Viking Press.

Marsh, H.W. (1993) 'The effect of participation in sport during the last two years of high school', *Sociology of Sport Journal*, 10 (1): 18–43.

McCrone, K.E. (1987) 'Play Up! Play Up! And Play the Game! Sport at the late Victorian Girls' Public Schools', in J.A. Mangan and R.J. Park (eds), *From 'Fair Sex' to Feminism: Sport and the Socialization of Women in the Industrial and Post-industrial Eras.* London: Frank Cass. pp. 97–129.

McNeal, R.B., Jr (1995) 'Extracurricular activities and high school dropouts', *Sociology of Education*, 64: 62–81.

McPherson, B.D. (1986) 'Policy-oriented research in youth sport: an analysis of the process and product', in C.R. Rees and A.W. Miracle (eds), *Sport and Social Theory.* Champaign, IL: Human Kinetics. pp. 255–87.

Melnick, M.J., Sabo, D.F. and Vanfossen, B.E. (1992) 'Effects of interscholastic athletic participation on the social, educational, and career mobility of Hispanic girls', *International Review for the Sociology of Sport*, 21 (1): 57–75.

Melnick, M.J., Vanfossen, B.E. and Sabo, D.F. (1988) 'Developmental effects of athletic participation among high school girls', *Sociology of Sport Journal*, 5 (1): 22–36.

Meyer, B.B. (1990) 'From idealism to actualization: the academic performance of female collegiate athletes', *Sociology of Sport Journal*, 7 (1): 44–57.

Miracle, A.W. and Rees, C.R. (1994) *Lessons of the Locker Room: the Myth of School Sports.* Amherst, NY: Prometheus Books.

Mirel, J. (1982) 'From student control to institutional control of high school athletics: three Michigan cities, 1883–1905', *Journal of Social History*, 16: 83–100.

Mrozek, D.J. (1983) *Sport and American Mentality, 1880–1910.* Knoxville, TN: The University of Tennessee Press.

O'Hanlon, T. (1980) 'Interscholastic athletics, 1900–1940: shaping citizens for unequal roles in the modern industrial state', *Educational Theory*, 30 (2): 89–103.

O'Hanlon, T. (1982) 'School sports as social training: the case of athletics and the crisis of World War I', *Journal of Sport History*, 9 (1): 5–29.

Park, R.J. (1987) 'Sport, gender and society in a transatlantic Victorian perspective', in J.A. Mangan and R.J. Park (eds), *From 'Fair Sex' to Feminism: Sport and the Socialization of Women in the Industrial and Post-industrial Eras.* London: Frank Cass. pp. 58–93.

Rader, B.G. (1983) *American Sports: From the Age of Folk Games to the Age of Spectators.* Englewood Cliffs, NJ: Prentice-Hall.

Redmond, G. (1978) 'The first *Tom Brown's Schooldays*: origins and evolution of "Muscular Christianity" in children's literature', *Quest*, 30: 4–18.

Rees, C.R. (1995) 'What price victory? Myths, rituals, athletics, and the dilemma of schooling', in A.R. Sadovnik (ed.), *Knowledge and Pedagogy: the*

Sociology of Basil Bernstein. Norwood, NJ: Ablex. pp. 371–83.

Rees, C.R. (1997) 'Still building American character: sport and the physical education curriculum', *The Curriculum Journal*, 8 (2): 199–212.

Rees, C.R. (in press) 'Sports and schooling', in D. Levine, A.R. Sadovnik and P.W. Cookson, Jr (eds), *Education and Sociology: an Encyclopedia.* New York: Garland Press.

Rees, C.R. and Brandl-Bredenbeck, H.P. (1995) 'Body capital and the importance of sport: a comparison of American and German adolescents', *Journal of Comparative Physical Education and Sport*, 17 (2): 50–6.

Rees, C.R. and Segal, M.W. (1984) 'Intra-group competition, equity, and interpersonal attraction', *Social Psychology Quarterly*, 47 (4): 319–32.

Rees, C.R., Brettschneider, W.D. and Brandl-Bredenbeck, H.P. (1998) 'Globalization of sports activities and perceptions of sport among adolescents from Berlin and suburban New York', *Sociology of Sport Journal*, 15 (3): 216–30.

Rees, C.R., Feingold, R.S. and Barrette, G.T. (1991) 'Overcoming obstacles to collaboration and integration in physical education', *Quest*, 43 (3): 319–32.

Rees, C.R., Howell, F.M. and Miracle, A.W. (1990) 'Do high school sports build character? A quasi-experiment on a national sample', *The Social Science Journal*, 27 (3): 303–15.

Rehberg, R.A. (1969) 'Behavioral and attitudinal consequences of high school interscholastic sports: a speculative consideration', *Adolescence*, 4: 69–88.

Robertson, R. (1992) *Globalization: Social Theory and Global Culture.* London: Sage.

Romance, T., Weiss, M.R. and Bockoven, J. (1986) 'A program to promote moral development through elementary school physical education', *Journal of Teaching in Physical Education*, 5: 126–36.

Sabo, D.F., Melnick, M.J. and Vanfossen, B.E. (1993) 'High school athletic participation and post-secondary educational and occupational mobility. A focus on race and gender', *Sociology of Sport Journal*, 10 (1): 44–56.

Sage, G.H. (1990) *Power and Ideology in American Sport: a Critical Perspective.* Champaign, IL: Human Kinetics.

Sandiford, K.A.P. and Stoddart, B. (1987) 'The elite schools and cricket in Barbados', *International Journal of the History of Sport*, 4 (3): 333–50.

Schafer, W. and Armer, J.M. (1968) 'Athletes are not inferior students', *Transactions*, 5: 21–6, 61–2.

Segrave, J.O. and Chu, D. (1978) 'Athletics and juvenile delinquency', *Review of Sport and Leisure*, 3 (2): 1–24.

Segrave, J.O. and Hastad, D.N. (1984) 'Future directions in sport and juvenile delinquency research', *Quest*, 36 (1): 37–47.

Shields, D.L.L. and Bredemeier, B.J.L. (1995) *Character Development and Physical Activity.* Champaign, IL: Human Kinetics.

Shilling, C. (1991a) 'Educating the body: physical capital and the production of social inequalities', *Sociology*, 25 (4): 653–72.

Shilling, C. (1991b) 'Social space, gender inequalities and educational differentiation', *British Journal of Sociology of Education*, 12 (1): 23–44.

Shilling, C. (1992) 'Schooling and the production of physical capital', *Discourse*, 13: 1–19.

Shilling, C. (1993) *The Body and Social Theory.* London: Sage.

Siedentop, D., Mand, C. and Taggart, A. (1986) *Physical Education: Teaching and Curriculum Strategies for Grades 5–12.* Palo Alto, CA: Mayfield.

Smith-Rosenberg, C. and Rosenberg, C. (1973) 'The female animal: medical and biological views of women and their role in nineteenth-century America', *Journal of American History*, 60: 332–56.

Smolowe, J. (1993) 'Sex with a scorecard', *Time*, 5 April, p. 41.

Snyder, E.E. (1994) 'Interpretations and explanations of deviance among college athletes: a case study', *Sociology of Sport Journal*, 11 (3): 231–48.

Snyder, E.E. and Spreitzer, E.S. (1990) 'High school athletic participation as related to college attendance among black, Hispanic, and white males: a research note', *Youth and Society*, 21 (3): 390–8.

Spady, W.G. (1971) 'Status, achievement, and motivation in the American high school', *School Review*, 79: 379–403.

Spring, J. (1974) 'Mass culture and school sports', *History of Education Quarterly*, 14: 483–99.

Stark, R., Kent, L. and Finke, R. (1987) 'Sport and delinquency', in M.R. Gottfredson and T. Hirschi (eds), *Positive Criminology.* Newbury Park, CA: Sage. pp. 115–24.

Thirer, J. and Wright, S.D. (1985) 'Sport and social status for adolescent males and females', *Sociology of Sport Journal*, 2: 164–71.

Thornton, J.S. (1990) 'Feast or famine: Eating disorders in athletics', *The Physician and Sportsmedicine*, 18 (4): 116–22.

Trulson, M.E. (1986) 'Martial arts training: A novel "cure" for juvenile delinquency', *Human Relations*, 39: 1131–140.

Williamson, K.M. and Georgiadis, N. (1992) 'Teaching an inner-city after-school program', *Journal of Physical Education, Recreation and Dance*, 63 (8): 14–18.

Youniss, J., McLellan, J.A. and Strouse, D. (1994) 'We're popular but we're not snobs: Adolescents describe their crowds', in R. Montemayor, G.R. Adams and T.P. Gullotta (eds), *Personal Relationships During Adolescence.* Thousand Oaks, CA: Sage. pp. 101–22.

18

SPORT AND THE MEDIA

Garry Whannel

MAPPING THE FIELD

The growth of television as a significant cultural form during the 1960s put the relationship between sport and the media on the public agenda. In late 1969, the US magazine *Sports Illustrated* drew attention to the ways in which television was transforming sport (Johnson, 1969/70). In effect, sport in the television age was a 'whole new game' (Johnson, 1973). The growing economic and cultural significance of television for sport gradually became a pertinent issue in countries around the world (see for example, Andreff and Nys, 1987; Guiront, 1978; Ivent, 1979; Scholz, 1993; *Sportsworld*, 1974; Tatz, 1987; *Telecine*, 1978). Clearly sport and television had developed a degree of interdependence (Parente, 1977). They belonged together 'like ham and eggs' (Claeys and Van Pelt, 1986). In the view of some, television had 'made' sport (McChesney, 1989).

Newsweek expressed concern, in 1967, over the extent to which television was the powerful partner in the relationship. Debates developed from the 1970s as to whether the effects of television were beneficial or harmful (Glasser, 1985; McIntosh, 1974). Rader (1984) and Whannel (1992) both argued that television had transformed sport. By the 1980s, academic research had mapped out the field and proposed research agendas (Critcher, 1987, 1992; Wenner, 1989a) and book-length studies had appeared (Chandler, 1988; Goldlust, 1987; Rader, 1984). It is noteworthy that, to date, far more critical attention has been paid to television sport than to sport coverage in the print media.

The study of the media has been informed by sociological and semiological traditions.

I will outline work in these areas and then discuss some key themes and topics before concluding by outlining current research trajectories. Typically, media sociology distinguishes three main aspects of the communicative chain: production, message and reception.

Production

Sociological study of the first part of the communicative chain, the production of media messages, involves the study of the structures and finances of cultural institutions and the sets of economic relations and legal constraints that underpin them; the production practices that develop within them; the producers, and the professional ideologies that frame their practices.

Media organizations exist within legal frameworks that determine their scope. In the United Kingdom, the BBC is a public corporation, and the ITV system is overseen by a public body, the Independent Television Commission. Both are charged with a statutory responsibility to provide a broad range of material, which includes sport coverage (Whannel, 1992). The introduction of Channel 4 in 1982, with its statutory obligation to be alternative and innovative, had an impact on the range of sports covered (*Sport and Leisure*, 1986) In the USA free market forces are not subject to as much restriction, but there are still laws, rules and regulations that impact upon sport coverage (see Horowitz, 1974, 1977; Siegfried et al., 1977).

The press in both countries is subject to less restriction from government. Sport coverage in the British tabloid press is dominated by a very small range of sports, with football typically providing more than half of the content. While some sport events, such as the Olympic Games and the soccer World Cup, win huge audiences, the audience for much television sport is not, by television's standards, large. Part of the appeal of sport for television producers is its cheapness. It can fill hours of the schedule at relatively low cost. A substantial amount of television sport, lacking major audience appeal, is outside peak time television, in the afternoon, or late at night.

Media institutions enter into dealings with the institutions of sport, and television is typically the dominant partner in the relationship, providing revenue and dictating the terms of the exchange (Bellamy, 1989). Media institutions also have to compete with each other, which BBC did very effectively during the establishment of ITV in the 1950s, reinforcing its claim of 'BBC for Sport' by signing up key sports, producers and commentators on long-term contracts. During the 1960s and 1970s BBC sustained its service with coverage of major events and a wide range of sports (BBC, 1974; Dimmock, 1964). However, more aggressive competition from ITV during the 1970s became a greater challenge (Milne, 1977). Weathering this, the BBC preserved its dominance until the end of the 1980s, when the satellite channel Sky Sport, with a growing power to outbid anyone else for the rights to major events, began to emerge as a much more serious competitor to terrestrial television. From the 1980s, the rise of satellite and cable began to restructure the television audience, launching dedicated sports channels, and producing a shift from large, fairly heterogenous audiences, to smaller, more homogenous ones (Eastman and Meyer, 1989). Developments in video recording, slow-motion, satellite transmission and digital technology over the years have had a major impact on enhancing the ability of television sport to produce spectacular entertainment (Hersh, 1993; Ward, 1976).

Much early media research centred on political messages and on the measurement of attitude or voting intention. However, attempts to 'prove' this variant of the stimulus–response model, typically found that media messages were more likely to produce reinforcement than change in attitude (Klapper, 1960). While the media did not appear to have fabulous powers to determine what people thought, it did, however, appear to have a power to determine what people thought about. Consequently, research began to focus on the role of cultural producers as gatekeepers (Breed, 1955; White, 1964) and agenda-setters (Cohen, 1963). Chalip and Chalip (1992) examined the ways in which

information is controlled by press and public relations departments, and Theberge and Cronk (1986) investigated the ways in which production practices and professional ideologies can serve to marginalize press coverage of women's sport.

The production of media messages typically involves hierarchization, personalization, narrativizing (posing the question 'Who will win?') and framing; establishing key events, key stars and framing the event for an audience (Cantelon and Gruneau, 1988). Gruneau's 1989 case study of television skiing describes the need of producers to make the event look more dramatic and 'make the course look faster'. Whannel (1992) takes a historical approach in identifying the formative moments of the conventions of commentary, visual coverage and programme construction. The changing shape of conventions and practices of structuring sporting events for television can on occasion be traced through the writing of practitioners, and cricket is well served here (see Johnston, 1956, 1966, 1975).

Jeremy Tunstall's (1977) study of specialist journalists outlines the ways that they function both as competitors and colleagues. Sports reporters tend to have far more contact with their competitors on other papers than they do with their colleagues on the same journal. A group solidarity and shared interests conflict with loyalty to a particular paper. In an under-resourced medium such as radio, the media professional often occupies a more isolated position (Gilmore, 1993). Journalists are often well aware of the gap between 'reality' and the media rendition of it (Koppett, 1994). Accounts by media sport professionals provide useful evidence for the professional ideologies that frame production practices (see for examples Blofeld, 1990; Bough, 1980; Martin-Jenkins, 1990; Maskell, 1988; Robertson, 1987; and Cosell, 1973, 1974).

Production practices can become taken for granted by media practitioners, and are naturalized very readily; tracing such practices in their formative moments can be instructive, revealing the choices that were later to solidify as professional commonsense. The conventions of commentary at the BBC, involving personalization, building audience interest and heightening drama were laid out by de Lotbiniere (1949) in a highly influential document that became the bible of commentary during the 1950s. Camera positions and cutting styles were established by processes of trial and error (see Wolstenholme, 1958) and only later, in the 1960s, became conventionalized. Sports journalism as a profession was, in large measure, a product of the late nineteenth century, as sports magazines appeared in significant numbers, and newspapers began including dedicated sports sections (see Gillmeister, 1993; Kelly, 1988; Mason, 1993). Accounts of the careers of journalists and commentators reveal much about the attitudes underlying the formations of these professional practices. The focus on stars, the construction of dramatic interest and the relative marginalization of expertise, are all common features of media sport journalism (see, for example, Andrews, 1993; Barber, 1970; Dalby, 1961; Fountain, 1993; Gibson, 1976; Glendenning, 1953; Talbot, 1973, 1976; West, 1986; Williams, 1985; Wynne-Jones, 1951).

Content

The second part of the communicative chain concerns the content as opposed to its production. In 1977 the *Journal of Communication* devoted an issue to media sport, with papers analysing the strategies used in commentary to build audience interest and heighten drama (Bryant et al. 1977). Some suggested that the excitement generated in commentary can serve to mask the relative lack of excitement in the match itself (Comiskey et al. 1977). Visual styles also served to heighten the excitement and spectacle (Williams, 1977).

Birrell and Loy (1979) analysed television sport partly in McLuhan's terms, but the more influential part of the paper argues that television sport can be understood in terms of a set of manipulations of time and space; a framework later adopted by Whannel (1992) to analyse the ways in which sport was transformed by television (see also Hesling, 1986). This transformation, involving spectacle, drama, personalization and immediacy, was, as Clarke and Clarke (1982) have argued, also a form of ideological reproduction in which competitive individualism, local regional and national identities and male superiority were all made to appear natural, rather than the consequence of specific cultural selections and presentations. The world of sport was one in which any explicit politics of race, gender or national identity were evacuated, whilst the representations were none the less permeated with particular ideologies (see also Daney, 1978).

In the television age sport has been turned into mass spectacle, a process that arguably began at the start of the 1960s (Crawford, 1992) and is epitomized in major sport events like the Olympic Games (Brennan, 1995; McPhail

and Jackson, 1989), the World Cup (Geraghty et al., 1986; Nowell-Smith, 1978; Wren-Lewis and Clarke, 1983) and the Superbowl (Real, 1989). The English FA (Football Association) cup final has been analysed (in two Open University television programmes) as a site on which representations of tradition, ritual and royalty are joined to the tension and drama of 'the people's game' (see also Colley and Davies, 1982). There are now extensive case studies that investigate the media portrayal of sport. Berg and Trujillo (1989) examine the centrality of winning in American sporting ideology and the ways in which the Dallas Cowboys were represented as a symbol of success. Young (1986) examines media coverage of the Heysel Stadium disaster, charting the various ways in which blame was attributed.

Other media have received rather less attention. Rowe (1990) examines different styles of sports writing. Brewster (1993) and Shaw (1989) chart the growth of football fanzines, which have also been analysed as a case in which the dominant values of a sporting world have been contested (Jary et al. 1991). Press coverage of a celebrated drugs case was examined by Donohew et al. (1989). Sports photography has received inadequate attention, although there is an excellent collection of examples (Smith, 1987). Bergan (1982) has catalogued comprehensively films featuring sport, and Leni Riefenstahl's controversial film of the 1936 Olympics has been analysed by Downing (1992). Pendred (1987) has produced an extensive catalogue of British sporting art, and Goldman (1983) has charted the history of British sporting prints. To date, though, the study of European media sport coverage by Blain et al. (1993), which examines the construction of national identities, is the most elaborate consideration of the print media; and while there has been much discussion of individual films there is no scholarly overview of sport in the cinema.

Audience

The third part of the communicative chain concerns reception and the audience. Information about audience size and demographic profile can be garnered from industry sources and from periodic publications by organizations like the BBC (see BBC, 1976, 1977; Marles, 1984). Barnett (1990) has argued that the audience for television sport is a soft one – heavily affected by the weather, the choice of viewing, the presence and absence of star figures and other factors. Terrestrial television has generally depended on the assembly of large heterogenous audiences, and even though sport has more appeal to men, most sport audiences consist of around 40 per cent women viewers. The rise of dedicated sport channels on satellite and cable has begun to disrupt long established viewing patterns and the imminent introduction in Britain of pay-per-view football is likely to trigger a dramatic shift in viewing habits, and in television industry economics. The press has a rather different pattern of consumption, in that different parts of the paper attract very different types of reader, a fact reflected in the separation of sport coverage from the rest of the paper, and in the growth of multiple-segment papers. Historically, the readership of sports pages has been predominantly male, and the mode of address to readers makes fewer attempts than television to pull in marginal consumers.

To win and to hold audiences and readers, it is necessary to establish points of identification, and to speak or write in modes that connect with the audience. The audience has to be cajoled into viewing (McVicar, 1982), and the values underpinning the presentation have to be capable of connecting with the audience (see Bailey and Sage, 1988). Strategies for media production must have some relation to the range of gratifications that viewers seek (Wenner and Gantz, 1989).

A major theme in media sociology concerns the impact of media messages, and much debate has gone on within sport institutions around two questions – the impact of television sport coverage on attendances, and on participation. Evidence on the impact of television sport on attendances at sporting events is mixed and inconclusive. In certain circumstances live television of an event does seem to reduce the crowd, while at others it has little or no effect. The growing amount of live football on British television has parallelled a steady growth for ten years in match attendances. This is a complex area with many variables. Football crowds may be affected by the history and traditions of a club, its current league position, its style of play, the opposition, the weather, presence or absence of star players, the level of unemployment in the area, the time of year, and availability of other alternatives, of which television is just one. On participation, many sport governing bodies have nurtured the hopes of a television-inspired boom in participation, often citing the gymnastics boom in the wake of Olga Korbut's Olympic success. There is indeed circumstantial evidence of a growth in participation, in such diverse sports as gymnastics, snooker and American football (in the United Kingdom), with a link to television coverage. Yet such effects may often be, as was the case with American football, somewhat transitory (see Olympia Seminar Working Papers, 1975). Decades of research into the effects of the media has tended to suggest that the media are more likely to produce reinforcement than change of attitude, and evidence that constructive attitudinal change can be produced by media messages is as yet unconvincing (see Wenner, 1994).

According to some, far from producing positive effects, the media can, consciously or unconsciously serve to reproduce negative attitudes such as an attachment to violence (Bryant and Zillman, 1983). A controlled experiment found that ice hockey commentaries that stressed violence were regarded as providing more entertainment than commentaries that de-emphasized the violence (Comiskey et al. 1977). Bryant carried out research in which groups of people watched tapes of sport events, with commentaries that either emphasized or de-emphasized the violence. He found that commentaries significantly affected audiences' interpretation of events, and found that viewers' enjoyment of the tapes with violent commentary was enhanced (see Bryant, 1989). Commentary style appeared to significantly influence viewers' perceptions of the degree of aggressiveness, and men enjoyed the aggressive play more than did women (Sullivan, 1987). Other research suggested that commentary contributed most to the enjoyment of a televised sports event where opponents were presented as hated foes rather than as friends (see Comiskey et al., 1977).

This research raises broader questions to do with cultural portrayals of and attitudes towards violence. Messages about violence must be distinguished from actual violence. It cannot be assumed that because people find pleasure in viewing a regulated physical combativeness in sport their tolerance of violence in other contexts is diminished. While investigation has suggested that the strongest motivations for sport viewing were the desire to thrill in victory, and a desire to let loose (Gantz, 1981), we still need to understand more about the reasons people consume media sport (see Zillman et al., 1979). It has long been clear, for example, that sport viewing is heavily subjective, and it could be argued that there is no such thing as a pre-existing event that people merely observe – the event is always a product of the activity of the onlooker (see Hastorf and Cantril, 1954). Identification with one participant is an important element of the sport-viewing experience, and Sapolsky and

Zillman (1978) found that informal social controls exerted by fellow viewers influenced perception. In a USA *v.* Yugoslavia basketball game watched by groups of friends, the social control of the group ensured that Yugoslav baskets were not enjoyed, whereas in a larger group, with friends in the minority, Yugoslav baskets got more appreciation.

The pleasures involved in sport viewing are complex and not readily analysed (see Duncan and Brammett, 1989). The experience of viewing is often ritualized and communal, as compared to the more solitary and casualized manner in which much television is consumed (see Eastman and Riggs, 1994). The conditions of viewing themselves inevitably have an impact on the ways in which pleasures are experienced (Sapolsky and Zillman, 1978). The distinctiveness of sport as a cultural form lies partly in its uncertainty. In its live form, it is a process, not a product and part of the pleasure lies in that elusive moment of free expression before the modes of media presentation transform it into a product (see Whannel, 1994a).

Semiological Analysis

When study of the media began to emerge as a distinct academic subject it developed in an interdisciplinary fashion, drawing upon history, sociology, literary theory and semiology. Semiology, literally the science of signs, but more precisely the study of meaning production, examines the process whereby language, whether visual, verbal or a combination of the two, produces meanings (Barthes, 1967). Early semiological analysis focused upon the message, or text, as the product of the system of language that makes meaning possible. It was the underlying system of a language – its codes and conventions – that were seen as enabling and governing the production of meaning. However, as this system only exists in the form of utterances – speech acts, written language, visual representation – in short, texts, texts became the object of analysis. The main aim of analysis, however, was to uncover or reveal the underlying systems of language that made the production of meaning possible.

There were two significant developments from this base. First, the text was seen as involving a process of encoding. In order to be intelligible, a message has to be composed according to sets of codes or conventions that the audience can decode (for example, the ways in which hats – cloth cap/bowler/top hat – act as signifiers of social class). The text is part of the communicative chain linking the production and consumption of a message – production–text–consumption. This concept was the basis of the encoding–decoding model (Hall et al., 1980).

Secondly, developments of early semiology explored the ways in which language acts to position, or interpellate, the reader or audience. The text carries within it subject-positions that readers come to occupy. An example is the patriotic identification that commentaries upon international football construct, positioning us as, for example, patriotic subjects who want England to win. Within this tradition there are complex and competing areas of theorization that cannot be explored in this chapter. However, an understanding of the influence of semiology can provide a useful context for reading the analyses of media sport coverage that this present review outlines.

A key starting point for media analysis in this tradition was the notion that television and the other media do not simply reflect the world, but rather construct versions, or accounts, of it. Buscombe's (1975) football monograph analyses in detail the way in which camera positions, cutting patterns, modes of editing, commentary, title sequences and presentation material, all serve to construct a particular image of football. Similarly, Peters (1976) analyses the ways that television's visual and verbal conventions served to relay a particular picture of the 1976 Olympic Games. Birrell and Loy (1979) analyse the ways in which television rearranges time and space in order to produce sport in televisual form. Buscombe (1975) and Peters (1976) argued that while television sport claimed to be merely presenting reality, it was in fact constructing a version of it, viewed from the position of an imaginary 'ideal' spectator. Television sport, then, has to be understood as involving a process of construction, in which choices as to camera position and angle, lens type and cutting patterns all have their impact on the appearance of the event.

The contributors to the Buscombe collection attempted to analyse television sport as a form of realism. However, there are many different forms, styles, and aesthetic conventions for representing the real. The combination of direct and indirect address in television sport, the use of visual devices like slow-motion, and action replay, and the use of graphics, cannot simply be seen as a variant of the realist conventions of narrative fiction. To dissect the complex combination of title montages, presentation, contributors, clips, action replays and actuality, it is more useful to think in terms of conflicting tensions between attempts to achieve transparency, rendering television's own mediations invisible, and a desire to build in entertainment values.

Analysis in this tradition tried to establish the codes, conventions and modes of organizing discourse that characterized media representations of sport (Goldlust, 1987; Whannel, 1992). Such analyses focused on the visual and verbal strategies that personalized and narrativized sport, and the ways in which ideological elements, such as national identification, the work ethic and masculinity were linked together (see also Fiske, 1983; O'Donnell and Boyle, 1996). The construction of media texts was seen as involving a selective juxtaposition in which events were relayed in the form of stories (see Pearson, 1988; Whannel, 1982) and golden moments and magic memories were assembled and re-arranged for the viewer (Whannel, 1989).

Work in this tradition is also concerned with the ways in which discourses are organized and the audience positioned by them. Nowell-Smith (1978) examines 'Television', 'football' and 'world' as terms, analysing the distinctiveness of the 'world' as constructed by television football, and contrasting the dominance of the Olympics by the symbolic politics of East *v.* West, with the 'world' of football, which is structured around the difference between 'North European' and 'Latin'. Morse (1983) argues that the object of sport discourse is the male body, but cultural inhibitions about gazing at male bodies mean that sport transforms voyeurism into scientific enquiry, emphasizing technical performance over aesthetic beauty. Sport on television, especially in slow motion, portrays the fantasy of the body as perfect machine. Television sport primarily addresses men, with female viewers relatively marginalized (see O'Connor and Boyle, 1991).

TOPICS AND DEBATES

Commercialization

The commercialization and commodification of sport since the Second World War has been a central theme of the sociology of sport, and the development of media sport has played a key role. Charles Critcher (1979) argued that there has been a transformative trend that commenced in the 1950s, at least in football, in which the major factors were the growth of professionalization, spectacularization, internationalization and commercialization. Some writers have noted the tensions between the emancipatory potential of sport and its function as a commodity. Sewart (1987) derided the

consequent degradation of athletic activity, subsumed to the logic of the marketplace, and argued that sport was being standardized and commodified.

Goldlust (1987) argued that from the 1960s onwards, television increasingly colonized sporting cultures and undermined communal control of sporting institutions. Whannel (1986) argued that in the United Kingdom, the crucial moment came in the mid-1960s when the launch of BBC2 in 1964 and the banning of television tobacco advertising in 1965 served to trigger a sponsorship revolution. This forced sport governing bodies to regard television coverage as crucial to financial survival, partly because of rights payments from television but also because of the money to be gained from sponsorship. Barnett (1990) has drawn attention to the rising power of satellite television, and to the shift from broadcasting as a public service towards broadcasting as a commodity to be chosen and purchased.

Much of the impetus for the transformation of sport came not from the traditional governing bodies but from maverick entrepreneurs who established themselves as sports agents, and who constituted the crucial mediation point between sport organizations, sport stars, television, sponsors and advertisers (see Aris, 1990; Stoddart, 1990; Wilson, 1988). The process of commodification involved the construction of calculated commercial packages that endeavoured to maximize the various opportunities inherent in sponsorship, advertising and merchandising. Snooker capitalized on its television success of the 1980s with new tournaments, new sponsors and expansion into new markets (see Burn, 1986). Television was the shop window that allowed for the promotion of sporting spectacle to new markets (see Maguire, 1990). The global reach of television and the economic power of the United States combined to foster a marked Americanization of the form, content and styles of sport television around the world (McKay and Miller, 1991). However, the process of bringing together an audience for new, imported or Americanized sporting spectacle was a complex one. Long-established sporting cultures are embedded in lived experiences with their own histories, rooted in national cultures, and transplanted cultural experiences cannot always succeed in establishing themselves (see Maguire, 1988).

The central role of television lies partly in its economic power. The major American networks were prepared to spend huge sums out-bidding each other for rights to major events (see Klatell and Marcus, 1988). The willingness of governing bodies to respond to the needs of television was heightened by the activities of sport entrepreneurs from outside the traditionally rooted world of the governing bodies. Jack Kramer, Kerry Packer, Mark McCormack, Horst Dassler of Adidas and Rupert Murdoch of News Corporation have been key figures in this process. Packer had the economic power to challenge the previously cosy relationship between cricket and television, and his own World Series Cricket ushered in floodlit cricket, coloured clothing, hard-sell advertising, more cameras, more close-ups and more replays (see Bonney, 1980; Haigh, 1993). Lawrence and Rowe (1987) argued that television cricket promoted capitalist ideology by legitimizing the capitalist social relations of production; socializing viewers to accept the values of capitalism; limiting the acceptance of what is fair, normal and desirable; promoting the myth of upward mobility; and diverting people's attention from the problems of life under capitalism.

Sport organizations were sometimes slow to respond to the process of commercialization. In the United Kingdom, the Sports Council commissioned a report on sponsorship that expressed concern at the power of sports agents, whilst being somewhat cautious about the revenue potential for sport that sponsorship offered (Howell, 1983). A report set up by the Sports Council to examine the potential impact of cable and satellite showed British sport relatively unprepared for the revolution to come (Jones, 1985). Satellite sport in the United Kingdom grew slowly at first, hampered by slow dish sales and competition between two providers, BSB and Sky (see Chippendale and Franks, 1991). However, once Sky Television, into which BSB was 'merged', had the field to itself, the rapidly growing revenue from the pay-per-channel services began to give satellite television enhanced scope to obtain the rights to major events. The imminent spread of pay-per-view transmission of major football matches and other big events is about to provide a significant new impetus to the commodification of sport.

The spectacularization of top-level sport on television, enabled by the growing technological command of image production and distribution, is a key part of the commodification process (Morris and Nydahl, 1985). Major sporting events win and hold enormous audiences – and have become global events. They serve to condense complex symbolic systems – of politics, nationalism, gender, race and aspiration (see Real, 1975; Wenner, 1989b).

The ceremonies and rituals surrounding the Olympic Games are in themselves a rich and complex field, juggling the needs of television from a comprehensible spectacle, the desire of Olympics organizers to demonstrate their munificence, the pressure to advertise a national culture, and the need to draw on aspects of the history, heritage and traditions of the host country, not necessarily easily read by the TV audience. The production of spectacle on this scale is necessarily laden with ideology (see Gruneau, 1989b; Tomlinson, 1989; Wren-Lewis and Clarke, 1983). Television sporting spectacle is a significant component of the media imperialism in which the cultural products of the developed West, with their elaborate spectacle and high production values, reach global audiences, at the expense of indigenous cultures (Whannel, 1985).

As it is unquestionably *the* major global sporting event, the Olympic Games offers an invaluable case study of these processes. The costs of staging the Games are huge (Zarnowski, 1992). Television rights payments grew rapidly from the 1970s and have become massive (Alaszkiewicz and McPhail, 1986). Although the International Olympic Committee and the organizing committees are not set up to make profits, there are, connected with the Olympics, extensive opportunities for profit-making and sales promotion (Lawrence, 1987). Excessive commercialization has been identified as a problem both from within and without the movement (Min, 1987). Sponsorship of the Games has been seen as compromising the ideals of Olympism (Whannel, 1994b). There have been widely circulated allegations of corruption at the heart of the movement (Simson and Jennings, 1992). Relationships between the Olympic Games and the media are the subject of a collection of conference papers (McPhail and Jackson, 1989) and, more recently an elaborate international research project has published its survey of the Olympic Games and television (Moragas et al., 1996).

The development of television sport in the United States offers another example of the dramatic speed and scope of the processes of commercialization and commodification. In the less regulated and more competitive television environment of America, there was, from the early days of broadcasting, a need for television to bring together sport and sponsor (Powers, 1984). ABC Television made a significant breakthrough for television sport in the 1960s with an emphasis on personalization, dramatization and spectacularization, epitomized in its slogan 'The Thrill of Victory, the

Agony of Defeat' (Sugar, 1980). They launched the long-running Wide World of Sports (Leitner, 1975) and transformed American social habits with live Monday night football, taking sport into the heart of prime time (Neal-Lunsford, 1992). The focus was one of intense individualization – in their own terms, 'up close and personal' (Spence, 1988). Their success heightened competition between the networks and prompted a massive escalation in rights payments (O'Neil, 1989). Without doubt, in America the transformation of sport by television can be seen at its most dramatic (Rader, 1984).

Women and Media Sport

Sport as a social practice serves to demarcate gender distinctions. Extensive research demonstrates the different treatment of boys and girls, men and women and male and female athletes. Dunne (1982) found that while magazines aimed at pre-pubescent girls feature positive images of sport, by the teen years, in magazines, sport is something that boys do and girls have little interest in. Margaret Duncan (1990) argued that sport functions as one of the last male strongholds. The sports photographs examined in her research highlighted female difference, emphasizing women as in a position of relative weakness. She argues that such photographs emphasized the other-ness of women, enabling patriarchal ends, and concludes that it 'remains to be seen whether the potentiality for representations of strong women becomes an actuality' (see also Hilliard, 1984).

Shifflett and Revelle (1994) conducted a content analysis of NCAA news and found that 73 per cent of space was devoted to male athletes and only 27 per cent to female, and more than three times as much space was devoted to photos of male athletes. Malec (1994) disputed their conclusions, pointing out that as there were more male athletes than female, NCAA was merely reflecting this. He pointed out that, in terms of prominence, 9 per cent of the paragraphs about women were on the front page compared to 5 per cent of the paragraphs about men.

Typically, images of women in sport involve constant reworkings of the variants of dominant femininity. Leath and Lumpkin (1992) examined *Women's Sport and Fitness* and found that as the magazine switched emphasis towards fitness it featured more non-athletes overall and fewer athletes on the cover.

Females were more likely to be posed rather than performing, black women athletes were rarely pictured, aggressive sports were covered less than traditional female-appropriate sports, and female athletes were liable to be described in terms devaluing their sporting achievements. The portrayals of sport and fitness in magazines represented a re-working of femininity that tried to reconcile active women with femininity (see Bolla, 1990; Horne and Bentley, 1989).

These gender constructions are not simply a matter of the production of difference – the gender differences involved are structured by power relations: by the subordination of women within patriarchy (see Duncan and Hasbrook, 1988). Higgs and Weiler (1994) found that

> although women were given greater coverage in individual sports, that coverage was divided into shorter and more heavily edited segments. In addition, commentators relied on gender marking, biased and ambivalent reporting, and a focus on personalities as opposed to athletic abilities when covering women's sports.

Williams, Lawrence and Rowe (1987) argued that, despite any gains that women have made in the struggle to obtain equality in Olympic competition, their participation was limited and their image, as defined by the media, is structured according to prevailing gender stereotypes (see also Yeates, 1992).

Feminist scholarship is concerned not merely with charting and documenting the construction of gender difference, nor with demonstrating the power relations underpinning difference but also with exploring ways of changing and combating such image production. Halbert and Latimer (1994) have argued that, although women have made great strides in sport, their achievements will continue to be meaningless as long as sports broadcasters undermine, trivialize and minimize women's performances through biased commentaries.

MacNeil (1988) has argued that leisure is a site of contestation in which women's participation presents new ideas of physicality, but residual patriarchal notions that sport is for men are difficult to alter. She describes the commodification of the feminine style through aerobic classes, sports clothes and videos; and argues that patriarchy is reproduced in a newly negotiated form that attracts women to buy a range of narcissistic commodities. She concludes that this exploits women by creating 'needs' that are in reality only 'wants' – female sexuality and glamour help to sell physical activity to women; and that advertising is a major impetus in the acceptance of the aerobic ritual and its style as 'feminine'. Media representations of active women, in activities such as aerobics and bodybuilding, are aligned with dominant hegemonic relations. They reproduce male dominance by continuing to associate women more with appearance than performance, objects for the gaze rather than acting subjects.

Masculinities and Media Sport

Research into images of men in sport has identified a systematic pattern of difference (Messner et al., 1993). There are close links between the cultures of sport and dominant constructions of masculinity (Miller, 1989). Television sport offers men a distraction, a private world apart from the pressure and constraints of life (Rose and Friedman, 1994). It is a world of toughness, competence and heroism which celebrates traditional 'masculine' qualities (Sabo and Jansen, 1992).

Just as there is no single monolithic femininity, nor is there a single simple homogenous masculinity. There are a range of images of masculinities available within images of sport, but these are typically delimited by the parameters of 'masculinity'. The world of American football is viewed, critically, in the film *North Dallas Forty* as a tough, brutal world in which there is no room for doubt or uncertainty (Whannel, 1993). The terrace subcultures of English soccer celebrate a tough, aggressive, self-asserting localism (Williams and Taylor, 1994). The rise of men's style magazines in the late 1980s marks a distinct commodification of masculine appearance, in which sport iconography plays a significant role.

Yet while male vanities are nurtured in media representations of sport, these still characteristically offer a vision in which emotions are only readily expressed in specific contexts like sporting victory, and in which relationships, feelings and desires are frequently rendered marginal (see Chapter 30 by Mary Duquin). Neale (1982) analyses *Chariots of Fire* in terms of male gazes at each other, implying a sexuality the film cannot acknowledge. Scorsese's *Raging Bull*, an antidote to the rather more glorified version of violence in boxing in *Rocky*, is seen by Cook (1982) as portraying a masculinity in crisis – only able to express emotion through violence.

The rise of feminist scholarship, the growth of an interest in the study of masculinity, and a growing body of work on sexualities, has brought the body centre stage as an object of study. Workouts, weight-training, bodybuilding have foregrounded a new masculine muscularity (see Klein, 1990). Gymnasia have become the site of cultural contestation, as the rituals of gay, straight and female users struggle to establish subcultural space (Miller and Penz, 1991).

Sport stars are frequently written about as role models, although what precisely this means is rarely clearly specified (Hrycaiko et al., 1978). They certainly do function as stars, and top-level sport has developed an elaborate and marketable star system. Hill (1994) discusses the problems associated with understanding heroes, stars and what they represent (see also Nocker and Klein, 1980). While pundits constantly assert that sport stars can be moral exemplars or bad influences, the relation between these images, morality and the youth market is undoubtedly more complex (Whannel, 1995b). There is reason to hypothesize that young people are very well able to distinguish between Gazza the football genius, Gazza the fat clown and Paul Gascoigne the man who allegedly beats up his wife. Sport stars are somehow being asked to follow in the footsteps of the Victorian heroes of Empire (see Howarth, 1973), and yet we live in different times when heroes are frequently knocked from their pedestals and the very concept of male heroism is fragile (see Hall, 1996; Harris, 1994; Izod, 1996).

Race and Media Sport

There are two major issues in this area. First, do the media provide stereotypical images of black athletes; and secondly, do apparently positive images of black achievement reinforce the stereotype of black athleticism, and so limit the perceptions of teachers and coaches about other accomplishments.

Sabo et al. (1996), in a study of American televising of international sport, found that producers appeared to make efforts to provide fair treatment of athletes, but that the treatment of race and ethnicity varied across productions. There was little evidence of negative representations of black athletes, but representations of Asian athletes drew on cultural stereotypes, and representations of Latino-Hispanic athletes were mixed, with some stereotyping.

Wonsek (1992) found that the majority of black college athletes were exploited by their institutions. She argued that within a historical and contemporary racist culture, some black athletes are elevated to superstardom while other black athletes do not receive an adequate education. The image of black success in athletics tends to support the stereotypical view that black students' abilities lie with sport rather than academic work. She concluded that the media perpetuates the image of the young black male as athlete only, with advertisements playing a significant role in this process.

Wenner (1995) identified a good guy/bad guy frame of reference that served to mark differences between sporting stars like Michael Jordan and Mike Tyson. Crawford (1991) examined the limited range of stereotypes of black athleticism in American movies. Majors (1990) argued that the cool pose adopted by black athletes provided a means of countering social oppression and racism and of expressing creativity, but the emphasis on athletics and cool pose among black males was often self-defeating, and came at the expense of educational advancement. Perversely, the very success of black athletes, generating a fund of 'positive' images, at the same time reproduces a negative stereotype, because of the lack of positive images of black achievement in other areas.

National Identities

Media representations of sport inevitably involve the production of images of national identities. There has always been a shortage, in media analysis, of strong cross-cultural research, in part because of the obvious logistical problems involved in researching a range of different linguistic communities. Blain, Boyle and O'Donnell (1993), in their analysis of the 1990 Soccer World Cup, were able to work with over 3,000 press reports from ten countries. Their book contains a rich range of empirical material, examining images of sporting events in different countries, images of British-ness in the foreign media, and of Europe in the British media, taking as their key examples the 1990 World Cup staged in Italy, the Wimbledon tennis championship of 1991 and the Barcelona Olympics of 1992. In a brief example, to illustrate the narrative frame through which the European media interpret the relation of the 'small' sporting nations like Cameroon and Costa Rica to Europe, they string together quotes from eight sources to demonstrate a hyper-narrative in which the 'insolent, impudent upstarts' are 'put in their place', 'taught a lesson', and given 'a harsh lesson in realism' by the European powers. At stake here, of course, is not just national identities but the construction of a 'European' identity (see also Boyle, 1992; O'Donnell, 1994).

Chandler (1988) examines the question of national identities through an analysis of the relation between the sport of a nation and its television system, contrasting the deregulated environment of the USA and the public service traditions of the United Kingdom. Whannel (1995a) suggests that the symbols of national identity have a degree of autonomy from national cultures, in examining the hero status that Englishman Jack Charlton acquired as manager of the Republic of Ireland football team. In Ireland traditional Gaelic sports have benefited from the support of a media system geared to the construction of a national culture (see Boyle, 1992), whereas in Scotland, with a media system oriented towards urban Scotland and mainstream team games, traditional sports like shinty became progressively more marginal (Whitson, 1983). In many parts of the Third World, television audiences are more likely to see European football than their own indigenous league, and, again, traditional and local-based sports become marginalized (Whannel, 1985).

National cinemas play a significant part in the linking of sporting cultures with the symbols of national identity, with *Chariots of Fire* an obvious example (Johnston, 1985). *True Blue*, which tells the story of the 1987 Oxford–Cambridge Boat Race and the tensions and disagreements over training and selection that led to the American members of the Oxford crew refusing to row, offers a revealing picture of a clash of cultures, in which the English public school–Oxbridge traditions are triumphantly re-asserted. American cinema's images of baseball are frequently also implicit statements about American identity (Crawford, 1988). They often allude to the pastoral romanticism that characterizes baseball's mythology (McCarthy, 1990; Mosher, 1995).

RESEARCH TRENDS

The sociology of sport is an expanding field, and as far as media sport is concerned the areas of globalization and the body are currently the focus of much work.

Globalization

There has been extensive recent debate on globalization and sport, and although by no means all the discussion centres on the media, many of the contributors see it as central (see Maguire, 1993a). There is general agreement that globalizing processes are at work. Some regard this as a new phenomenon, transcending the established structures of nation-states, seen as of declining relevance. Others see the process as a continuation of established patterns of cultural imperialism. For many analysts, globalizing processes in sport are closely linked to Americanization (Maguire, 1990). Whannel (1985) regards international television sport as a form of Western cultural imperialism.

Jean Harvey and Francois Houle (1994) consider whether Americanization or globalization is the most useful term to apply to sport, and argue that globalization is an alternative to Americanization and imperialism, not a form of it. They argue that the nation-state has been rendered much less important. Maguire (1990) examines the spread of American football to England. but points out with reference to soccer, that cultural exchange is not always a one-way process. Equally, the struggle for hegemony in this field is not confined to the UK–US dominance has been challenged by Europe and Japan. He points out that the commercialization of English sport has helped American commercialized sport to flourish in the United Kingdom.

Kidd (1991), writing in a Canadian context, talks of American capitalist hegemony, whilst Wagner (1990) suggests that the process is mundialization not Americanization and Americanization is just part of the homogenization of sport. Guttmann (1991) says globalization is just part of modernization, whilst McKay and Miller (1991) and McKay et al. (1993) say that the globalization of capital is a key part of the process. Rowe et al. (1994) also remind us of the complexities of international cultural exchange:

> In order to comprehend the reach of international images and markets it is necessary to move beyond the simple logic of cultural domination and towards a more multi-directional concept of the flow of global traffic, in people, goods and services.

Maguire has shown how these factors interact in the case of American football and basketball, and Jarvie and Maguire (1994: 231–2 analyse the ways in which, through the globalized production and consumption of ice hockey, events, decisions and activities in one part of the world can come to have significant consequences for individuals and communities in distant parts of the globe. One aspect of the process involves the production of cultural diversities (Maguire, 1993b).

Bellamy (1993) argues that American television and American sports are seeking new TV markets in Europe. However, he sounds a note of caution, suggesting that in a period of rapid expansion in TV sport hours, audience demand for more sport is unknown; that it is not known whether European audiences will develop appetites for American sports; and that with rights payments for sports such as soccer growing rapidly, European broadcasters may not have the means to make high payments.

Sport and the Body

Over the past 20 years the images of sport have come to focus more on the body. The growth of aerobics, workouts and jogging promoted more active images of femininity, but images of Lycra-clad female bodies also produced a sexualization of the sporting female (Hargreaves, 1994). Nor was this process limited to women. The gym, weights and workout subcultures spawned a new male muscularity that promoted a narcissism that objectified the male body. Male bodies are now much more commonly on display for the gaze. White and Gillett (1994) argue that representation of the muscular body as natural and desirable is rooted in an ideology of gender difference, championing dominant meanings of masculinity through a literal embodiment of patriarchal power. The foregrounding of the muscular body as a cultural ideal offers conservative resistance to progressive change and alternative masculinities by valorizing a dominance-based notion of masculinity.

The sociological interest in the body is not, of course, new, and the work of Elias, Foucault, Turner and others has been influential. There is a growing field of research focusing on the body, as can be noted in the launch, in 1995, of the journal *Body and Society*, the staging of a conferences on *Bodily Matters* and *Bodily Fictions*, and the recent publishing of several book-length studies (Butler, 1995; Duncan, 1996; Dutton, 1995; Falk, 1994; Goldstein, 1994; Grosz and Probyn, 1995; Lowe, 1995; Synnott, 1993). Some sport-related studies of this topic have already appeared (see, for example, Blake, 1996; Brackenridge, 1993; Horne, 1994; Horrocks, 1995; Scott and Morgan, 1993), but given the ubiquitousness of images of sport in the media, and the prominent role images of the body have come to play, it will inevitably be a growth area of scholarship.

REFERENCES AND FURTHER READING

Alaszkiewicz, R. and McPhail, T. (1986) 'Olympic television rights', *International Review for the Sociology of Sport*, 21 (2/3): 211–28.

Andreff, Bourg and Nys (1987) *Le Sport et la télévision*. Paris: Dalloz.

Andrews, David (1993) 'Sport, cultural studies and post-modernism: some observations on Baudrillard', in *Working Papers in Sport and Society*, Volume 1. Warwick: Department of Physical Education, Warwick University.

Aris, Stephen (1990) *Sportsbiz: Inside the Sports Business*. London: Hutchinson.

Bailey, C.I. and Sage, G.H. (1988) 'Values communicated by a sports event: the case of the Superbowl', *Journal of Sport Behaviour*, 11 (3): 126–43.

Barber, Red (1970) *The Broadcasters*. New York: Dial Press.

Barnett, Steven (1990) *Games and Sets: the Changing Face of Sport on Television*. London: British Film Institute.

Barthes, Roland (1967) *Elements of Semiology*. London: Jonathan Cape.

BBC (1974) *The Coverage of Sport on BBC TV*. London: BBC.

BBC (1976) 'Public opinion about the television and radio coverage of the 1974 World Cup', in *Annual Review of Audience Research Findings*, No. 2. London: BBC.

BBC (1977) *The People's Activities*. London: BBC.

Bellamy, Robert V. (1989) 'Professional sports organisations: media strategies', in L. Wenner (ed.), *Media, Sports and Society*. London: Sage. pp. 120–33.

Bellamy, Robert V. (1993) 'Issues in the internationalisation of the US sports/media: the emerging European market-place', *Journal of Sport and Social Issues*, 17 (3): 168–80.

Berg, Leah R. Vande and Trujillo, Nick (1989) 'The rhetoric of winning and losing: the American dream and America's team', in L. Wenner (ed.), *Media Sports and Society*. London: Sage. pp. 204–24.

Bergan, Ronald (1982) *Sports in the Movies*. London: Proteus.

Birrell, S. and Loy, J. (1979) 'Media sport: hot and cool', *International Review of Sport Sociology*, 14 (1): 5–18.

Blain, Neil, Boyle, Raymond and O'Donnell, Hugh (1993) *Sport and National Identity in the European Media*. Leicester: Leicester University Press.

Blake, Andrew (1996) *The Body Language: the Meaning of Sport*. London: Lawrence and Wishart.

Blofeld, Henry (1990) *My Dear Old Thing – Talking Cricket*. London: Stanley Paul.

Bolla, Patricia A. (1990) 'Media images of women and leisure: an analysis of magazine ads 1964–87', *Leisure Studies*, 9 (3): 241–52.

Bonney, Bill (1980) *Packer and Televised Cricket*. Sydney: NSW Institute of Technology.

Bough, Frank (1980) *Cue Frank*. London: MacDonald Futura.

Boyle, Raymond (1992) 'From our Gaelic fields: radio, sport and nation in post-partition Ireland', *Media Culture and Society*, 14 (4): 623–36.

Brackenridge, Celia (1993) *Body Matters: Leisure Images and Lifestyles*. Eastbourne: Leisure Studies Association.

Breed, Warren (1955) 'Social control in the news room', *Social Forces*, 33: 326–35.

Brennan, Christine (1995) 'Lillehammer as seen by the media', *Citius, Altius, Fortius*, 3 (1): 32–3.

Brewster, Bill (1993) '"When Saturday Comes" and other football fanzines', *The Sports Historian* (Journal of the British Society of Sports History), No. 13 (May): 11–21.

Bryant, J. (1989) 'Viewers' enjoyment of televised sports violence', in L. Wenner (ed.), *Media, Sports and Society*. London: Sage. pp. 270–89.

Bryant, J. and Zillmann, D. (1983) 'Sports violence and the media', in J.H. Goldstein (ed.), *Sports Violence*. New York: Springer-Verlag. pp. 195–211.

Bryant, J., Comiskey, P. and Zillmann, D. (1977) 'Drama in sports commentary', *Journal of Communication*, 27 (3): 140–9.

Burn, Gordon (1986) *Pocket Money*. London: Heinemann.

Buscombe, Edward (ed.) (1975) *Football on Television*. London: British Film Institute.

Butler, Judith (1995) *Bodies that Matter: On the Discursive Limits of 'Sex'*. New York: Routledge.

Cantelon, Hart and Gruneau, Richard S. (1988) 'The production of sport for television', in J. Harvey and H. Cantelon (eds), *Not Just a Game*. Ottawa: University of Ottawa Press. pp. 177–94.

Chalip, Laurence and Chalip, Pamela (1992) 'Gatekeeper categories: meanings of government types in a Los Angeles Olympic press kit', *Olympika: the International Journal of Olympic Studies*, 1: 136–53.

Chandler, Joan (1988) *Television and National Sport*. Chicago: University of Illinois Press.

Chippendale, Peter and Franks, Suzanne (1991) *Dished: the Rise and Fall of British Satellite Broadcasting*. London: Simon and Schuster.

Claeys, U. and Van Pelt, H. (1986) 'Introduction: sport and the mass media, like bacon and eggs', *International Review for the Sociology of Sport*, 21 (2/3): 95–102.

Clarke, A. and Clarke, J. (1982) 'Highlights and action replays', in J. Hargreaves (ed.), *Sport Culture and Ideology*. London: Routledge & Kegan Paul.

Cohen, Bernard C. (1963) *The Press and Foreign Policy*. Princeton, NJ: Princeton University Press.

Colley, Ian and Davies, Gill (1982) 'Kissed by history: football as TV drama', in *Sporting Fictions*. London: CCCS.

Comiskey, Paul, Bryant, Jennings and Zillmann, Dolf (1977) 'Commentary as a substitute for action', *Journal of Communication,* 27 (3): 150–53.

Cook, Pam (1982) 'Masculinity in crisis', *Screen,* 23 (3/4): 39–46.

Cosell, Howard (1973) *Cosell.* New York: Playboy Press.

Cosell, Howard (1974) *Like It Is.* New York: Playboy Press.

Crawford, S. (1988) 'The sport film, its cultural significance: movies portray America as America wants to see itself', *Journal of Physical Education, Recreation and Dance,* 59 (6): 45–9.

Crawford, S. (1991) 'The black actor as athlete and mover: an historical analysis of stereotypes, distortions and bravura performances in American action films', *Canadian Journal of History of Sport,* 22 (2): 23–33.

Crawford, Scott A.G.M. (1992) 'Birth of the modern sport spectacular: the Real Madrid and Eintracht Frankfurt European Cup Final of 1960', *International Journal of the History of Sport,* 9 (3): 433–8.

Critcher, Charles (1979) 'Football since the war', in J. Clarke, C. Critcher and W. Johnson (eds), *Working Class Culture.* London: Hutchinson.

Critcher, Chas (1987) 'Media spectacles: sport and mass communication', in A. Cashdan and M. Jordin (eds), *Studies in Communication.* Oxford: Basil Blackwell.

Critcher, Chas (1992) 'Is there anything on the box? Leisure studies and media studies', *Leisure Studies,* 11 (2): 97–122.

Dalby, W. Barrington (1961) *Come in Barry.* London: Cassell.

Daney, Serge (1978) 'Le sport dans la télévision', *Cahiers du Cinéma,* No. 292: 39–40.

Dimmock, Peter (1964) *Sports in View.* London: BBC.

Donohew, Lewis, Helm, David and Haas, John (1989) 'Drugs and bias on the sports page', in L. Wenner (ed.), *Media Sports and Society.* London: Sage. pp. 225–40.

Downing, Taylor (1992) *Olympia.* London: BFI.

Duncan, M.C. (1990) 'Sports photographs and sexual difference: images of women and men in the 1984 and 1988 Olympic Games', *Sociology of Sport Journal,* 7: 22–43.

Duncan, Margaret Carlisle and Brammett, Barry (1989) 'Types and sources of spectating pleasure in televised sport', *Sociology of Sport,* 6 (3): 195–211.

Duncan, Margaret Carlisle and Hasbrook, Cynthia A. (1988) 'Denial of power in televised women's sports', *Sociology of Sport Journal,* 4 (1): 1–21.

Duncan, Nancy (ed.) (1996) *Body Space: Destabilising Geographies of Gender and Sexuality.* London: Routledge.

Dunne, Mary (1982) 'Introduction to some of the images of sport in girls' comics and magazines', in Charles Jenkins and Michael Green (eds), *Sporting*

Fictions. Birmingham: Birmingham University Department of Physical Education and CCCS.

Dutton, Kenneth R. (1995) *The Perfectible Body.* London: Cassell.

Eastman, Susan Tyler and Meyer, Timothy P. (1989) 'Sports programming: scheduling, costs and competition', in L. Wenner (ed.), *Media Sports and Society.* London: Sage. pp. 97–119.

Eastman, Susan and Riggs, Karen E. (1994) 'Televised sports and ritual: fan experiences', *Sociology of Sport Journal,* 11 (3): 249–74.

Falk, Pasi (1994) *The Consuming Body.* London: Sage.

Ferrante, Arlene (1988) 'The construction of gender in the all-American symbol of baseball'. Paper presented at the International Communication Association Annual Conference (USA).

Fiske, John (1983) 'Cricket/TV/culture', *Metro (Media and Education Magazine),* No. 62.

Fountain, Charles (1993) *Sportswriter: the Life and Times of Grantland Rice.* New York: Oxford University Press.

Gantz, W. (1981) 'An explanation of viewing motives and behaviours associated with television sports', *Journal of Broadcasting,* 25: 263–75.

Geraghty, Christine, Simpson, Philip and Whannel, Garry (1986) 'Tunnel vision: television's World Cup', in A. Tomlinson and G. Whannel (eds), *Off the Ball: the Football World Cup.* London: Pluto. pp. 20–35.

Gibson, Alan (1976) *A Mingled Yarn.* London: Collins.

Gillmeister, Heiner (1993) 'English editors of German sporting journals at the turn of the century', *The Sports Historian* (Journal of the British Society of Sports History), No. 13 (May): 38–65.

Gilmore, Peter (1993) 'Sport on local radio: a producer's view', *The Sports Historian* (Journal of the British Society of Sports History), No. 13 (May): 26–30.

Glasser, Brian (1985) 'Is TV good or bad for sports?', *Sport and Leisure,* May–June, p. 24.

Glendenning, Raymond (1953) *Just a Word In Your Ear.* London: Stanley Paul.

Goldlust, John (1987) *Playing for Keeps: Sport, the Media and Society.* Melbourne: Longman.

Goldman, Paul (1983) *Sporting Life* (anthology of British sporting prints). London: British Museum.

Goldstein, Laurence (ed.) (1994) *The Male Body: Features, Destines, Exposures.* Michigan: University of Michigan Press.

Grosz, Elizabeth and Probyn, Elspet (1995) *Sexy Bodies: the Strange Carnalities of Feminism.* London: Routledge.

Gruneau, Richard (1989a) 'Making spectacles: a case study in television sports production', in L. Wenner (eds), *Media Sports and Society.* Thousand Oaks, CA: Sage. pp. 134–54.

Gruneau, Richard (1989b) 'Television, the Olympics and the question of ideology', in R. Jackson and

T. McPhail (eds), *The Olympic Movement and the Mass Media*. Calgary: University of Calgary Press.

Guiront, Michael (1978) 'Pro football and the mass media', *Review of Sport and Leisure*, (3/2).

Guttmann, Allen (1991) 'Sport diffusion: a response to Maguire and the Americanisation commentaries', *Sociology of Sport Journal*, 8 (2): 185–90.

Haigh, Gideon (1993) *The Cricket Wars: the Inside Story of Kerry Packer's World Series Cricket*. Melbourne: Text Publishing Company.

Halbert, Christy and Latimer, Melissa (1994) 'Battling gendered language: an analysis of the language used by sports commentators in a televised co-ed tennis tournament', *Sociology of Sport Journal*, 11: 309–29.

Hall, Stuart (1996) 'Introduction: who dares, fails', in *Soundings*, No. 3. London: Lawrence and Wishart.

Hall, S., Hobson, D., Lowe, A. and Willis, P. (eds) (1980) *Culture Media Language*. London: Hutchinson.

Hargreaves, Jennifer (1994) *Sporting Females*. London: Routledge.

Harris, Adrienne (1985) 'Women, baseball and words', *Psychcritique*, 1 (1): 35–54.

Harris, Janet C. (1994) *Athletes and the American Hero Dilemma*. Leeds: Human Kinetics.

Harvey, Jean and Houle, François (1994) 'Sport, world economy, global culture and new social movements', *Sociology of Sport Journal*, 11 (4): 337–55.

Hastorf, Albert H. and Cantril, Hadley (1954) 'They saw a game: a case study', *Journal of Abnormal and Social Psychology*, 2: 129–34.

Hersh, Phil (1993) 'Media facilities at the 1992 Olympic Games', *Citius, Altius, Fortius*, 1 (3): 4–5.

Hesling, W. (1986) 'The pictorial representation of sport on television', *International Review for the Sociology of Sport*, 21 (2/3): 173–94.

Higgs, Catriona T. and Weiler, Karen H. (1994) 'Gender bias and the 1992 Summer Olympic Games: an analysis of television coverage', *Journal of Sport and Social Issues*, 18 (3): 234–46.

Hill, Jeffrey (1994) 'Reading the stars: a postmodernist approach to sports history', *The Sports Historian*, No. 14: 45–55.

Hilliard, D. (1984) 'Media images of male and female professional athletes: an interpretive analysis of magazine articles', *Sociology of Sport Journal*, 1 (3): 251–62.

Horne, John (1994) 'Aspects of postmodernism and body culture – a view from Britain', *Japan Journal of Sport Sociology*, 2: 1–17.

Horne, John and Bentley, Christine (1989) 'Women's magazines, fitness chic and the construction of lifestyles', in *Leisure Health and Wellbeing*. Leeds: LSA.

Horowitz, I. (1974) 'Sports broadcasting', in R. Noll (ed.), *Government and the Sports Business*. Washington, DC: Brookings Institute.

Horowitz, Ira (1977) 'Sports telecasts: rights and regulations', *Journal of Communication*, 27 (3): 160–8.

Horrocks, Roger (1995) *Male Myths and Icons*. London: Macmillan.

Howarth, Patrick (1973) *Play Up and Play the Game: the Heroes of Popular Fiction*. London: Eyre Methuen.

Howell, Denis (1983) *Howell Report on Sponsorship*. London: CCPR.

Hrycaiko, D., McCabe, A. and Moriarity, D. (1978) 'Sport physical activity and TV role models', in *CAHPER Sociology of Sport Monograph Series*, Vanier City, Ottawa, ON: Canadian Association for Health, Physical Education and Recreation.

Ivent, G. (1979) 'Football and television', in *Review of Sport and Leisure*.

Izod, John (1996) 'Television sport and the sacrificial hero', *Journal of Sport and Social Issues*, 20 (2): 173–93.

Jarvie, Grant and Maguire, Joseph (1994) *Sport and Leisure in Social Thought*. London: Routledge.

Jary, David, Horne, John and Bucke, Tom (1991) 'Football fanzines and football culture: a case of successful cultural contestation', *The Sociological Review*, 39 (3): 581–97.

Johnson, W. (1973) 'TV made it all a new game', in J.T. Talamini and C.H. Page (eds), *Sport and Society*. Boston, MA: Little Brown. pp. 454–72.

Johnson, William (1969/70) 'Television and sport (5 articles)', *Sports Illustrated*, 22 Dec. 1969–26 Jan. 1970.

Johnston, Brian (ed.) (1956) *Armchair Cricket*. London: BBC.

Johnston, Brian (ed.) (1966) *Armchair Cricket*. London: BBC.

Johnston, Brian (ed.) (1975) *Armchair Cricket*. London: BBC.

Johnston, Sheila (1985) 'Charioteers and ploughmen', in M. Auty and N. Roddick (eds), *British Cinema Now*. London: BFI.

Jones, Emlyn (1985) *Sport in Space: Effects of Cable and Satellite Television*. London: Sports Council.

Kelly, Stephen F. (1988) *Back Page Football*. London: Macdonald Queen Anne Press.

Kidd, Bruce (1991) 'How do we find our voice in the new world order? A commentary on Americanisation', *Sociology of Sport Journal*, 8: 178–84.

Klapper, Joseph (1960) *The Effects of Mass Communication*, Glencoe, IL: Free Press.

Klatell, David A. and Marcus, Norman (1988) *Sports For Sale: Television, Money and the Fans*. Oxford: Oxford University Press.

Klein, A.M. (1990) 'Little Big Man: hustling, gender, narcissism and bodybuilding sub-culture', in M. Messner and D. Sabo (eds), *Sport, Men and the Gender Order*. Champaign, IL: Human Kinetics. pp. 127–40.

Koppett, Leonard (1994) *Sports Illusion, Sports Reality: a Reporter's View of Sports Journalism and Society.* Urbana and Chicago, IL: University of Illinois Press.

Lawrence, Geoffrey (1986) 'In the race for profit: commercialism and the Los Angeles Olympics', in G. Lawrence and D. Rowe (eds), *Power Play.* Sydney: Hale and Iremonger.

Lawrence, Geoffrey and Rowe, David (1986) 'The corporate pitch: televised cricket under capitalism', in G. Lawrence and D. Rowe (eds), *Power Play.* Sydney: Hale and Iremonger. pp. 166–78.

Leath, Virginia M. and Lumpkin, Angela (1992) 'An analysis of sportswomen on the covers and in the feature articles of *Women's Sport and Fitness* magazine, 1975–89', *Journal of Sport and Social Issues,* 16 (2): 121–6.

Leitner, Irving A. (1975) *ABC's Wide World of Sports.* New York: Golden Press.

Lotbiniere, Seymour de (1949) 'Technique of the running commentary', *BBC Quarterly,* 4 (1): 49.

Lowe, Donald M. (1995) *The Body in Late Capitalist USA.* London: Duke University Press.

MacNeil, Margaret (1988) 'Active women, media representations and ideology', in J. Harvey and H. Cantelon (eds), *Not Just a Game.* Ottawa: University of Ottawa Press. pp. 195–213.

Maguire, Joseph (1988) 'The commercialisation of English elite basketball, 1972–1988', *International Review for the Sociology of Sport,* 23 (4): 305–24.

Maguire, Joseph (1990) 'More than a sporting touchdown: the making of American football in England, 1982–1990', in *Sociology of Sport Journal,* 7 (3): 213–37.

Maguire, Joseph (1991) 'The media sport production complex: the emergence of American sports in European culture', *European Journal of Communication,* 6: 315–16.

Maguire, Joseph (1993a) 'Globalisation, sport development and the media/sport production complex', *Sport Science Review,* 2 (1): 29–47.

Maguire, Joseph (1993b) 'Globalisation and sportisation: diminishing contrasts and increasing varieties'. Paper presented at North American Society for the Sociology of Sport conference, Ottawa, Canada.

Majors, R. (1990) 'The cool pose', in M. Messner and D. Sabo (eds), *Sport, Men and the Gender Order.* Champaign, IL: Human Kinetics. pp. 109–14.

Malec, Michael A. (1994) 'Gender (in)equality in the NCAA News', *Journal of Sport and Social Issues,* 18 (4): 376–8.

Marles, Vivien (1984) 'The public and sport', in *BBC Broadcast Research Findings.* London: BBC.

Martin-Jenkins, Christopher (1990) *Ball By Ball: the Story of Cricket Broadcasting.* London: Grafton Books.

Maskell, Dan (1988) *From Where I Sit.* London: Willow.

Mason, Tony (1993) 'All the winners and the half times', *The Sports Historian* (Journal of the British Society of Sports History), No. 13 (May): 3–12.

McCarthy, John (1990) 'Field of Dreams and Dreams of Fields: baseball simulations as reality', *Play and Culture,* 3 (1): 32–43.

McChesney, Robert W. (1989) 'Media made sport: a history of sports coverage in the USA', in L. Wenner (ed.), *Media Sports and Society.* London: Sage. pp. 49–69.

McIntosh, Peter (1974) 'Mass media: friends or foes in sport', *Quest,* June: 35–45.

McKay, J. and Miller, T. (1991) 'From old boys to men and women of the corporation: the Americanisation and commodification of Australian sport', *Sociology of Sport Journal,* 8: 86–94.

McKay, J., Lawrence, G., Miller, T. and Rowe, D. (1993) 'Globalisation and Australian sport', *Sport Science Review,* 2 (1): 10–28.

McPhail, Tom and Jackson, Roger (eds) (1989) *The Olympic Movement and the Mass Media.* Calgary, Alberta: Hurford Enterprises.

McVicar, John (1982) 'Playing the crowd', in *Edinburgh International Television Festival Magazine* (London).

Messner, M. et al. (1993) 'Separating the men from the girls; the gendered language of televised sports', *Gender and Society,* 7 (1): 121–37.

Miller, L. and Penz, O. (1991) 'Talking bodies: female body-builders colonise a male preserve', *Quest,* 43: 148–63.

Miller, Toby (1989) 'Sport media and masculinity', in G. Rowe and D. Lawrence (eds), *Sport and Leisure.* Sydney, Australia: Harcourt Brace Jovanovich. pp. 74–95.

Milne, Alasdair (1977) 'Competition in British television – BBC *v.* ITV', *Combroad* (Jan/Mar): 9–14.

Min, G. (1987) 'Over-commercialisation of the Olympics 1988', *International Review for the Sociology of Sport,* 22 (2): 137–42.

Moragas, Miquel de, Rivenburgh, Nancy K. and Larson, James F. (eds) (1996) *Television in the Olympics.* London: John Libbey.

Morris, Barbra S. and Nydahl, Joel (1985) 'Sports spectacle as drama: image, language and technology', *Journal of Popular Culture,* 18 (4): 101–10.

Morse, Margaret (1983) 'Sport on television: replay and display', in E. Ann Kaplan (ed.), *Regarding Television.* Los Angeles: American Film Institute.

Mosher, Stephen D. (1995) 'Whose dreams? Basketball and celluloid America', *Journal of Sport and Social Issues,* 19 (3): 318–22.

Neal-Lunsford, Jeff (1992) 'Sport in the land of television: the use of sport in network prime-time schedules', *Journal of Sport History,* 19 (1): 56–76.

Neale, Steve (1982) '*Chariots of Fire*: images of men', *Screen,* 23 (3/4): 47–53.

Newsweek (1967) 'TV Influences sport', *Newsweek.*

Nocker, G. and Klein, M. (1980) 'Top level athletes and idols', *International Review of Sport Sociology,* 15: 5–21.

Nowell-Smith, Geoffrey (1978) 'TV – football – the world', *Screen*, 19 (4): 45–59.

O'Connor, Barbara and Boyle, Raymond (1991) 'Dallas with balls: television sport, soap opera and male and female pleasures', Paper presented to 4th International Television Studies Conference, London.

O'Donnell, Hugh (1994) 'Mapping the mythical: a geopolitics of national sporting stereotypes', *Discourse and Society*, 5 (3): 345–80.

O'Donnell, Hugh and Boyle, Raymond (1996) 'A semiotics of violent actuality: encoding football fan behaviour during Euro 92', *Leisure Studies*, 15 (1): 31–48.

O'Neil, Terry (1989) *The Game Behind the Game: High Stakes, High Pressure in TV Sports*. New York: Harper and Row.

Olympia Seminar Working Papers (1975) *The Role of Television in Promoting the Practice of Sport*. London.

Parente, Donald (1974) 'A history of TV and sports'. Urbana, IL: PhD thesis, University of Illinois at Champaign-Urbana.

Parente, Donald (1977) 'The interdependence of sport and television', *Journal of Communication*, 27 (3): 128–32.

Pearson, Roberta E. (1988) 'Take me out to the ball-game: narrative structure of TV baseball'. Paper presented at the ITSC Conference (London).

Pendred, Gerald (1987) *An Inventory of British Sporting Art in United Kingdom Public Collections*. Suffolk: Boydell Press.

Peters, Roy (1976) *Television Coverage of Sport*. Birmingham: CCCS.

Powers, Ron (1984) *Supertube: the Rise of Television Sports*. New York: Coward McCann.

Rader, Benjamin G. (1984) *In Its Own Image: How TV has Transformed Sports*. New York: Free Press.

Real, Michael (1975) 'Superbowl: mythic spectacle', *Journal of Communication*, 25 (1): 31–43.

Real, Michael (1989) 'Superbowl versus World Cup soccer: a cultural–structural comparison', in L. Wenner (ed.), *Media Sports and Society*. London: Sage. pp. 180–203.

Robertson, Max (1987) *Stop Talking and Give the Score*. London: Kingswood.

Rose, Agva and Friedman, James (1994) 'Television sport as mas(s)culine cult of distraction', *Screen*, 31 (1): 22–35.

Rowe, David (1990) 'Modes of sports writing', in *Journalism and Popular Culture*. London: Sage.

Rowe, David (1995) *Popular Cultures: Rock Music, Sport and the Politics of Pleasure*. London: Sage.

Rowe, David, Lawrence, Geoffrey, Miller, Toby and McKay, Jim (1994) 'Global sport? Core concern and peripheral vision', *Media Culture and Society*, 16 (4): 661–76.

Sabo, Don and Curry Jansen, Sue (1992) 'Images of men in sports media: the social reproduction of gender order', in S. Craig (ed.), *Men, Masculinity and the Media*. London: Sage. pp. 169–84.

Sabo, Don, Curry Jansen, Sue, Tate, Danny, Duncan, Margaret Carlisle and Leggett, Susan (1996) 'Televising international sport: race, ethnicity and nationalistic bias', *Journal of Sport and Social Issues*, 20 (1): 7–21.

Sapolsky, B.S. and Zillman, D. (1978) 'Enjoyment of a televised sporting contest under different conditions of viewing', *Perceptual and Motor Skills*, 46: 29–30.

Scholz, Rolf (1993) *Konvergenz im TV-Sport*. Berlin: Vistas.

Scott, Sue and Morgan, David (eds) (1993) *Body Matters: Essays on the Sociology of the Body*. London: Falmer.

Sewart, J. (1987) 'The commodification of sport', *International Review for the Sociology of Sport*, 22 (3): 171–92.

Shaw, Phil (comp.) (1989) *Whose Game Is It Anyway?* London: Argus.

Shifflett, Bethany and Revelle, Rhonda (1994) 'Gender equity in sports media coverage: a review of the NCAA News', *Journal of Sport and Social Issues*, 18 (2): 144–50.

Siegfried, John J. and Hinshaw, C. Elton (1977) 'Professional football and the Anti-Blackout Law', *Journal of Communication*, 27 (3): 169–74.

Simson, Vyv and Jennings, Andrew (1992) *The Lords of the Rings: Power, Drugs and Money*. London: Simon and Schuster.

Smith, Chris (1987) *Sport in Focus*. London: Partridge.

Spence, Jim (1988) *Up Close and Personal*. New York: Atheneum.

Sport and Leisure (1986) 'Minority sports: Channel Four', *Sport and Leisure*, July–Aug.

Sportsworld (1974) 'TV and minority sport', *Sportsworld*, Jan.

Stoddart, Brian (1990) 'Wide world of golf', *Sociology of Sport Journal*, 7 (4): 378–88.

Sugar, Bert Randolph (1980) *The Thrill of Victory (Inside ABC Sports)*. New York: Hawthorn Books.

Sullivan, D.B. (1987) 'The effects of sports television commentary on viewer perception of overt player hostility'. Unpublished masters thesis, Hartford, CT: University of Hartford.

Synnott, Anthony (1993) *The Body Social: Symbolism, Self and Society*. London: Routledge.

Talbot, Godfrey (1973) *Ten Seconds From Now: a broadcaster's Story*. London: Hutchinson.

Talbot, Geoffrey (1976) *Permission to Speak*. London: Hutchinson.

Tatz, Colin (1987) 'The corruption of sport', in G. Lawrence and D. Rowe (eds), *Power Play: Essays in the Sociology of Australian Sport*. Sydney, Australia: Hale and Iremonger. pp. 46–63.

Telecine (1978) 'Sport et télévision', *Téléciné*, 229 (June): 6–19.

Theberge, N. and Cronk, A. (1986) 'Work routines in newspaper sports departments and the coverage of women's sports', *Sociology of Sport Journal*, 3 (3): 195–203.

Tomlinson, Alan (1989) 'Representation, ideology and the Olympic Games: a reading of the opening and closing ceremonies of the 1984 Olympics', in R. Jackson and T. McPhail (eds), *The Olympic Movement and the Mass Media*. Calgary, Alberta, Canada: Hurford. pp. 7.3–7.12.

Tunstall, Jeremy (1977) *Journalists at Work*. London: Constable.

Wagner, E. (1990) 'Sport in Asia and Africa: Americanisation or mundialisation?', *Sociology of Sport Journal*, 7: 300–402.

Ward, Bill (1976) 'From Alexandra Palace to Elstree via satellite from Tokyo', *Broadcast Special*, 22 September.

Wenner, Lawrence A. (1989a) 'Media sports and society: the research agenda', in L. Wenner (ed.), *Media Sports and Society*. London: Sage. pp. 13–48.

Wenner, Lawrence A. (1989b) 'The Superbowl pre-game show: cultural fantasies and political subtext', in L. Wenner (ed.), *Media Sports and Society*. London: Sage. pp. 157–79.

Wenner, Lawrence (1994) 'Loving the game to death: heroes, goals and spectator emotion', *Journal of Sport and Social Issues*, 18 (4): 299–302.

Wenner, Lawrence A. (1995) 'The good, the bad and the ugly: race, sport and the public eye', *Journal of Sport and Social Issues*, 19 (3): 227–31.

Wenner, Lawrence and Gantz, Walter (1989) 'The audience experience with sports on television', in L. Wenner (ed.), *Media Sports and Society*. London: Sage. pp. 241–69.

West, Peter (1986) *Flannelled Fools and Muddied Oafs*. London: WH Allen.

Whannel, Garry (1982) 'Narrative and television sport: the Coe and Ovett story', in C. Jenkins and M. Green (eds), *Sporting Fictions*. Birmingham, UK: CCCS. pp. 209–30.

Whannel, Garry (1983) 'Sit down with us : TV sport as armchair theatre', in S. Glyptis (ed.), *Leisure and the Media*. London: Leisure Studies Association (Conference Papers N16).

Whannel, Garry (1985) 'Television spectacle and the internationalisation of sport', *Journal of Communication Inquiry* (School of Journalism and Mass Communication, University of Iowa), 2 (2): 54–74.

Whannel, Garry (1986) 'The unholy alliance: notes on television and the re-making of British sport', *Leisure Studies*, 5: 129–45.

Whannel, Garry (1989) 'History is being made: television sport and the selective tradition', in R. Jackson and T. McPhail (eds), *The Olympic Movement and the Mass Media*. Calgary, Alberta, Canada: Hurford. pp. 7.13–7.12.

Whannel, Garry (1992) *Fields in Vision: Television Sport and Cultural Transformation*. London: Routledge.

Whannel, Garry (1993) 'No room for uncertainty: gridiron masculinity in North Dallas Forty', in Pat Kirkham and Janet Thumin (eds), *You Tarzan: Masculinity, Movies and Men*. London: Lawrence and Wishart.

Whannel, Garry (1994a) 'Sport and popular culture: the temporary triumph of process over product', *Innovations*, 6 (3): 341–50.

Whannel, Garry (1994b) 'Profiting by the presence of ideals: sponsorship and Olympism', in *International Olympic Academy: 32nd Session*. Olympia, Greece: International Olympic Academy.

Whannel, Garry (1995a) 'Sport, national identities and the case of Big Jack', *Critical Survey*, 7 (2): 158–64.

Whannel, Garry (1995b) 'Sport stars, youth and morality in the print media', in *Leisure Cultures: Values, Genders, Lifestyles*. Eastbourne: Leisure Studies Association.

White, D.M. (1964) 'The gatekeeper', in L.A. Dexter and D.M. White (eds), *People, Society and Mass Communications Research*. New York: New American Library.

White, P.G. and Gillett, J. (1994) 'Reading the muscular body: a critical decoding of advertisements, in *Flex* magazine', *Sociology of Sport Journal*, 11: 18–39.

Whitson, D. (1983) 'Pressures on regional games in a dominant metropolitan culture: shinty', *Leisure Studies* 2 (2): 138–53.

Williams, B. (1977) 'The structure of televised football', *Journal of Communication*, 27: 133–9.

Williams, Claire Louise, Lawrence, Geoffrey and Rowe, David (1987) 'Patriarchy, media and sport', in G. Lawrence and D. Rowe (eds), *Power Play*. Sydney: Hale and Iremonger.

Williams, Dorian (1985) *Travels of a Commentator*. London: Methuen.

Williams, J. and Taylor, R. (1994) 'Boys keep swinging: masculinity and football culture, in England', in T. Newburn and E. Stanko (eds), *Just Boys Doing Business: Men, Masculinities and Crime*. London: Routledge. pp. 214–33.

Wilson, Neil (1988) *The Sports Business*. London: Piatkus.

Wolstenholme, Ken (1958) *Sports Special*. London: Sportsmen's Book Club.

Wonsek, Pamela L. (1992) 'College basketball on television: a study of racism in the media', in *Media Culture and Society*. London: Sage.

Wren-Lewis, Justin and Clarke, Alan (1983) 'The World Cup – a political football?', *Theory, Culture and Society*, 1 (3): 123–32.

Wynne-Jones, G.V. (1951) *Sports Commentary*. London: Hutchinson.

Yeates, Helen (1992) ' Women, the media and football violence', *Social Alternatives*, 11 (1): 17–20.

Young, K. (1986) 'The killing field: themes in mass media responses to the Heysel Stadium riot', *International Review for the Sociology of Sport*, 21 (2/3): 253–66.

Zarnowski, Frank (1992) 'A look at Olympic costs', *Citius, Altius, Fortius*, 1 (1): 16–32.

Zillmann, D., Bryant, J. and Sapolsky, B.S. (1979) 'The enjoyment of watching sports contests', in J.H. Goldstein (ed.), *Sports, Games and Play: Social and Psychological Viewpoints*. Hillsdale, NJ: Lawrence Erlbaum. pp. 241–78.

19

THEORIZING SPORT, SOCIAL CLASS AND STATUS

John Sugden and Alan Tomlinson

It was the American novelist and popular historian James Michener (1976) who suggested that, for most of this century, a glance at the boxing rankings in the American sports press was a reasonably accurate gauge of which social groups were situated towards the bottom of that country's social order. When Jewish, Italian and Irish names began to appear less frequently, this could be taken as a clear indication that these groups had become socially mobile and that boxing was no longer considered to be an appropriate sport for those on a higher social plane. If this relationship between sport and social standing pertains for the lower orders, then it can be applied equally to social élites and gradations in between. For instance, in the context of British society, involvement in a polo match in the grounds of Windsor Castle, participation in Henley's boating regatta or a trip to the grouse moors of Scotland can be taken as clear signals of high social status. Similarly, playing golf at Royal St Andrews, attending Twickenham for a rugby international, having a season ticket for a Premier Division football club, turning out in the park for the local pub's football team, and keeping and racing pigeons, all convey messages about the social location of the participants.

In addition to such anecdotal evidence, there is strong empirical support for the view that sports preference, occupational status and social class are closely related (Central Statistical Office, 1993; Lüschen, 1969; Minten and Roberts, 1989; Renson, 1976). It is not our intention to summarize such sources or to add to this database. Neither do we aim to build towards a grand theory of sport and social class. Rather, in this chapter we outline and interrogate some of the classical theories of social stratification as they relate to sport. Through the following selective review, our objective is to provide the reader with a guide to thinking critically about the relationship between the sports people play, who those people are and what they stand for.

SPORT AND SOCIAL CLASS IN HISTORICAL CONTEXT

We should not be too startled by the fact that in the modern world sport participation can be read as a rough shorthand for social differentiation. Sport and social hierarchy have always been close relatives. The key linkage between the two rests in the martial roots of sport and the significance of military prowess as a signifier of social standing. War and the heroic deeds of warriors are dominant themes of the classic writings emanating from the ancient societies of the southern Mediterranean. McIntosh (1993) notes that such tales are punctuated by episodes of athleticism whereby representatives of social elites demonstrated their physical abilities in sporting contests. At a time when the threat of war was omnipresent, and when the essential vehicle of battle was the male body and what it could wield or propel, it is not surprising that sports closely resembled actual war and *vice versa*:

> Throwing javelins, throwing discoi, archery and boxing are several times referred to, while athletic similes are used to describe military combat. (McIntosh, 1993: 21)

Such sports were not open to all. McIntosh supports his argument by drawing on the work of Elias who believes that 'the sport of ancient Greece was based upon an ethos of warrior nobility' (1993: 27). Albeit in different ways, the city-states of Athens and Sparta both evidenced systems of social stratification which were rooted in militarism and which found further expression through participation in sport and games. Participation in athletic contests and equestrian events such as chariot racing, were restricted according to social rank, which to begin with was related to a military pecking order, but which, over time, also became associated with inherited status and the wealth which this was likely to bestow. McIntosh (1993: 24) argues that the fact that participants in the ancient Olympics were required to train for a minimum of ten months before the competition, suggests that these athletes must have been dilettantes, drawn largely from the upper echelons of ancient Greek societies.

By the time of the civilization's imperial decline, sport in Greece had developed a quasi-professional dimension. Warrior-athletes were patronized by an élite which accrued prestige through the spectacles that it created, and through the success of its champions, who likewise gained kudos through demonstrations of sporting prowess.

Initially, the Romans drew heavily upon an imagination of Greece for much of their own cultural development, including an approach towards sports (1993: 29). Once more, in a society heavily dependent upon military achievement, prowess in warlike sport was highly acclaimed. However, the more universally dominant as a military force Rome became, and the more removed Roman citizens became from the actual scene of battle, the emphasis in sport switched from direct participation to patronage and spectatorship.

The circus developed as a central feature of the Roman social order. The capacity to own schools of gladiators, to nurture stables of chariot racers and to stage lavish games, in arenas like the Hippodrome or the Coliseum, came to be viewed as tokens of political authority and high social standing. Likewise, the quality of access a person had to the arena – where he could sit or stand, and how far he was away from the imperial vantage point – was linked to his status in the wider Roman society. The fact that women were not allowed to attend these events is a clear indication of their lowly status in ancient Rome.

A certain amount of respect accrued to slaves who fought in these spectacles. The most successful of them enjoyed star-like status (like many of today's top sport performers), although their fame in the arena did not translate into social mobility outside of it.

While Rome declined as a military and political force, many of its institutional features, including some aspects of its approach to sports, lingered in the cultural memory of feudal Europe. In a Hollywood version of the legend of Robin Hood, in the mid-1990s, there is a dramatic episode of a young boy being hunted down in Sherwood Forest by the Sheriff of Nottingham's soldiers and their hounds. His crime was to have used his bow and arrow to bring down one of the 'king's deer', and if caught his likely punishment would have been death by hanging. As with all legends this fable is rooted in historical fact, inasmuch as across feudal Europe people were being imprisoned and, in some cases, put to death for hunting beyond their station. At this particular juncture, where one stood in any social hierarchy was encompassed by a series of rights and prohibitions. The public behaviour of members of the nobility was governed by a code of chivalry which, on the one hand, forbade them to engage in manual labour or common trade and, on the other, required them to train for combat and participate in related activities, such as hunting. 'Kings, princes and lords, each within the limits of his own authority, everywhere tended to monopolize the pursuit of game in certain reserved areas' (Bloch, 1961: 303). In effect, what one could hunt (deer, foxes, rabbits, rats and so forth), what weapon or animal one could hunt with (lance, arrow, hawk, dog and the like), and where this hunting could take place (king's forest, private fiefdom or common land), developed as important signifiers of a person's social standing. At the same time, the nobility monopolized those sporting activities which 'bore the imprint of a warlike temper' (1961: 303) such as swordsmanship and jousting. These were the centrepiece of the medieval tournaments which became the favoured pastime of the nobility in the Middle Ages.

In time a class of champions emerged, roaming the land and selling their martial services to other, usually more wealthy, knights. The latter's status could be enhanced by the capacity to sponsor tournaments, and even if by proxy, win contests which ranged from one-to-one combat to full-scale mock battles (Huizinga, 1955a: 94–5). Prowess in war, and those sports which resembled it, along with the ceremonial adornments of combat, were read as tokens of where a person stood in the medieval social hierarchy:

Every order and estate, every rank and profession, was distinguished by its costume. The great lords never moved about without a glorious display of arms and liveries, exciting fear and envy. (Huizinga, 1955b: 9)

For the labouring and merchant classes, these principles of distinction were reversed. In the Middle Ages, engagement in work, that is labour and/or commerce, irrespective of its content, was an indicator of low social standing. It is only relatively recently, and certainly not before the eighteenth century, that occupation and status have been linked in positive terms (Plumb, 1974). The vast majority of people worked in agricultural production. The recreations of the lower orders were influenced by their closeness to nature and by the time rhythms dictated by the seasons and the yield of the land (Holt, 1989: 12–17). What they could do with any free time was severely limited by their frugal command over scarce resources and had to take account of both the clearly defined preserves of the nobility, and their own servile position within the feudal estate or fiefdom. Just as, both literally and metaphorically, serfs, vassals and other gradations within the feudal lower orders fed off the crumbs from the master's table, their experiences of sport and leisure were similarly dependent on their presence at the margins of tournaments and festivals organized by aristocratic and religious élites for their own gratification (Bloch, 1962: 163–76).

With the waning of the Middle Ages, the rigid caste system characteristic of those times began to crumble, eventually to be replaced by a structure of social differentiation based on class. It is at this point that social standing becomes defined more in terms of what people do to make a living and how they might publicly display their new economic status, rather than simply through birthright, inherited rights and prescribed opportunities. In the societies referred to in this brief, historical introduction, social standing was not, in any simple sense, directly tied to the production and possession of wealth. The majority of people were born into fixed and fenced status groups or castes which governed life opportunities thereafter. This included people's role in the production and consumption of wealth and, as we have seen, their relationship with sport and other leisure activities.

By the middle of the nineteenth century wholesale changes in Britain's political and economic relations – the Industrial Revolution – precipitated concomitant adjustments in social relations and their cultural product, including

sports. We will consider these changes in some detail later. At this point it is sufficient to point out that, on both sides of the Atlantic, by the death of Queen Victoria social class is established as the main dynamic of stratification and it is this, more than anything else, which influences the shaping of sport during the nineteenth and twentieth centuries. As seminal social histories and developmental sociologies of Association football/soccer (Mason, 1980) and rugby football (Dunning and Sheard, 1979) have shown, modern sports forms represented distinctive sets of values and in so doing provided a vehicle for the expression of social difference and differentiated social status. Association football in its amateur form was championed by the middle and upper classes, and developed in its professional form by the working and lower-middle classes. The attitudes and beliefs embodied in the particular sporting ethos expressed class-based status and values. The middle classes, for instance, believed that the amateur code of the game 'was good for the physique, it helped to build character, it perhaps led to diminution in drinking, it brought the classes together' (Mason, 1980: 229). Rugby football's 'Great Schism' of 1895 saw the split between the Northern English mass spectator form of the game, and amateur, Southern English-based Rugby Football Union (Dunning and Sheard, 1979: 198–200). The Northern Union became the Rugby League in 1922. The commercializing of the game in the North had been 'viewed with deep misgivings among the southern-based RFU, whose committee shared the distrust of their class for big crowds, especially working class crowds, at a time of growing industrial unrest' (G. Williams, 1989: 313). Class patronage shaped many forms of sports provision, in the United States as well as in other advanced societies (Cross, 1993: 102–3). As Coakley has summarized the issue:

in the case of socioeconomic stratification. People with resources are able to organize their own games and physical activities in exclusive clubs or in settings inaccessible to others. When this happens, sport becomes a tool for élite groups to call attention to social and economic differences between people and to preserve their power and influence in the process. (Coakley, 1994: 230)

There is little dispute that the growth of modern sports was and in many senses remains interwoven with the class dynamics of the time. However, there is less agreement as to how, precisely, sport features in the class nexus of advanced industrial societies. It is to a discussion concerning the most influential theoretical models of social class and its relationship to sport that we now turn.

THEORIES OF SOCIAL STRATIFICATION AND SPORT

In the most general of senses, class is the social and cultural expression of an economic relationship. Classes are made up of people who are similarly placed in terms of the contribution they make to economic production, the command over resources this gives them and the lifestyles which this helps to generate. Thus, in modern societies, classes are generated by participation in the industrial and commercial process and the most significant measures of class distinction are wealth and occupation (Giddens, 1993: 215). While few would disagree with Giddens's broad notion of social class as an economically grounded concept, there is considerable disagreement when it comes to analysing and interpreting precisely how social classes are formed, where they fit in the context of broader patterns of social stratification, and how they contribute to social construction and social change.

The remainder of this chapter presents some of the main lines of argument in this debate and is centred around the work of three leading theorists of social stratification: Talcott Parsons (1902–79), Karl Marx (1818–83) and Max Weber (1864–1920). In each case we have selected a number of authors who have sought to use the work of these classic theorists in their own investigations into sport. The order in which we have chosen to consider them is neither chronological nor reflective of their relative importance to mainstream sociology. Rather it implies the sequence and impact which these thinkers have had on the sociology of sport on both sides of the Atlantic.

Parsons: Functionalism, Sport and the Social Order

Making sense of the high levels of social differentiation associated with advanced capitalism dominated the thinking of one of America's leading twentieth-century sociologists, Talcott Parsons. He was intrigued by Durkheim's views on the transition from rural–agricultural societies to those centred around urban–industrial activity, interested in particular in the question of the division of labour in industrial societies, and the effect which this had on forms of social solidarity (Durkheim, 1964). In certain

respects, following Durkheim, Parsons's view of social stratification is a mirror image to that of Marx. He accepts that classes are for the most part determined according to how people are grouped in relation to the process of industrial production and commercial distribution, but unlike Marx's emphasis on class conflict, Parsons stresses the functional interdependency between social classes and the role played by a hierarchy of classes in the maintenance and development of the whole social system:

> Such organization naturally involves centralization and differentiation of leadership and authority; so that those who take responsibility for co-ordinating the actions of many others must have a different status in important respects from those who are in the role of carrying out specifications laid down by others. From a sociological point of view, one of the fundamental problems in such a system is the way in which these basic underlying differentiations get structured into institutionalized status differentiations. (Parsons, 1964: 327)

In a seminal essay on this subject, Davis and Moore (1966), adopt a similar perspective, arguing that, 'as a functioning mechanism a society must somehow distribute its members in social positions and induce them to perform the duties of these positions' (1966: 47). The authors believe that this leads inevitably to the unequal distribution of rewards and opportunities. Like Parsons, Davis and Moore regard the principle of inequality as an absolute necessity:

> Social inequality is thus an unconsciously evolved device by which societies ensure that the most important positions are conscientiously filled by the most qualified persons. (1966: 48)

Thus, the principle of inequality ensures a system of incentives which, over time, generates a stratified ebb and flow of effort, ability and talent. In this way, structured around occupations, a class system evolves which, in turn, generates a differentiated cultural product.

In terms of sport, early literature generated by North American sport sociologists was, at least in part, dedicated to revealing the relationship between social standing, occupational status and sport (Loy et al., 1978: 332–78). While there was an emphasis on class, other variables of stratification, such as race, ethnicity, gender and age, were also stressed. This literature tended to focus on three interrelated areas: identifying links between certain categories of sports and class categories – for instance, boxing and blue-collar workers

(Stone, 1957, 1969); viewing sport as a microcosm of the whole social order and looking at the stratified distribution of positions within given sports – such as 'stacking' in gridiron football in the United States (McPherson, 1974) and Canada (Ball, 1973); and evaluating sport as a vehicle for social mobility within and between classes and occupational status groups (Loy, 1969; Lüschen, 1969).

In many respects, this type of scholarship considered how, through its relationship with social class, sport contributed to the smooth running of American society. The functionalist view of sport and social classes has been condemned for being uncritical, ahistorical, noncomparative, teleological and inherently conservative (Jarvie and Maguire, 1994: 20–5). It may have been helpful to paint a picture of some central aspects of the relationship between social class and sport, but this did little to address some of the more penetrating debates concerning how differentiated sport cultures were socially constructed and what role they played in the articulation of power within and between classes.

By the middle of the 1970s, inspired largely by the work of Rick Gruneau, a new generation of North American sociologists began to question the Parsonian model in relation to its applicability to sport:

> When taken in its extreme formulations, the assumption that societies are purposeful goal-oriented systems seeking the fulfillment of a set of necessary 'imperatives' seems to have profound ideological consequences … the idea that social stability and systematic efficiency requires a certain amount of institutionalized inequality is more realistically explained as a reflection of power in the upper strata. (Gruneau, 1975: 143)

By introducing notions of ideology and power into the discussion, Gruneau was drawing attention to models of stratifaction within which there was room for the consideration of sport as a contested cultural phenomenon. He was led to this conclusion through a consideration of work in the tradition of British cultural studies and critical sociology. Specifically, Gruneau argued that an adequate model for understanding the relationship between sport and social stratification had to be located in the context of the debate between the respective legacies of Marx and Weber (Gruneau, 1983).

Marx: Sport and Class Struggle

For Marx, class was the most important principle of social organization and the chief motor of social development. He argued, with Engels – in *The Communist Manifesto* of 1848 – that 'the history of all hitherto existing society is the history of class struggle' (Marx and Engels, 1971: 237). Marx drew on the materialist philosophy of Feuerbach, the transcendental idealism of Hegel and the economics of Adam Smith and David Ricardo, to devise a model of historical transformation with social class as its centrepiece. People have to produce to live, Marx argues, and how they produce and with whom they engage in the production process, determines the form of their broader social, political and cultural development. That is to say, how people relate to the production process governs how they relate to one another and how, once grouped in this way, these social classes relate to each other in any given social structure. In his historical analysis Marx observes that in previous societies (previous to capitalism in late nineteenth-century Europe) classes were generated through unequal experience of the production process, and that such inequality fostered resentment, encouraged class struggle and, ultimately, led to revolution. This, he argues, is how ancient, Asiatic and feudal societies experienced transformation, and it is the process that led to the emergence of capitalism.

Capitalism was the generic label used by Marx for societies that cohered around market-driven forms of economic development and corresponding labour relations (the capitalist mode of production). For Marx, while classes existed in previous epochs, it was under capitalism that they became most firmly established and clearly delineated. He accepted that stratification in this period had the appearance of being multi-staged, with vestiges of the aristocracy jostling for position, with industrial, commercial and professional status groups at one end of the scale, and agricultural workers (peasants), vagabonds, blue-collar workers and small traders (shopkeepers) occupying niches towards the other. This is best exemplified in Marx's own works in *The Eighteenth Brumaire*, in which he delineated, in subtle analytical detail, the variety of class fractions (Marx, 1968).

However, he believed that as capitalism developed, its rapacious and insatiable appetite would lead inevitably to cycles of economic crises, forcing these class-fractions to form two, relatively monolithic and mutually antagonistic classes: the bourgeoisie (those who owned and/or controlled and benefited most from economic production); and the proletariat (those whose livelihood depended upon their labour power and the wages they earned). Marx theorized that an advanced stage would be reached when the proletariat would become conscious of its exploited position *vis-à-vis* the social order determined by capitalism, and would rise up to overthrow its bourgeois oppressor, heralding the establishment of communism, the first classless society. In this regard, for Marx, class was more than a static descriptor of social standing. It was, rather, a dynamic agency of revolutionary change.

Marx himself had nothing to say about sport and its relationship with social class. Since his death, as capitalism has continued to advance and as sport has developed in significance, both culturally and as an economic entity, it has been left to others to apply Marxist categories to the study of the relationship between sport and social class. Such applications have also drawn upon neo-Marxist debate and theory. The chief question which Marxists asked as the twentieth century progressed was, why, given the internal contradictions of the system, has capitalism survived so long? In other words, what has happened to class struggle? At least part of the answer, they believed, was to be found in the manner through which the ruling class and its agents were able to influence the world-view of the working class, thereby undermining the fermenting of revolutionary class-consciousness (Althusser, 1971; Marcuse, 1964; Miliband, 1977).

This analysis placed hitherto disregarded, or merely 'superstructural', features of political economy on the Marxist agenda. In this regard, as one of the twentieth century's most popular forms of cultural expression and mass communication, sport was (for the first time) considered worthy of serious treatment by mainstream Marxist scholars. As Ralph Miliband put it, 'the elaboration of a Marxist sociology of sport may not be the most urgent of theoretical tasks, but it is not the most negligible of tasks either' (Miliband, 1977: 53). The most significant question asked by scholars in this area was, what was the relationship between sport and class struggle?

Surprisingly, given the lack of an embedded tradition of radical socialist scholarship in the United States, it was an American, Paul Hoch, who, through his impacting book *Rip Off the Big Game* (1972), produced the first sustained neo-Marxist interpretation of modern sport. Hoch went beyond the anti-establishment sociology of sport, pioneered by Jack Scott (1971) and Harry Edwards (1973), and argued that rather than being corrupting in a piecemeal way, the whole American system of sport was 'a microcosm of modern capitalist society'

(Jarvie and Maguire, 1994: 96). While he emphasized the labour-exploitative nature of both professional and intercollegiate athletics, Hoch was not exclusively interested in the political economy of American sports. He also argued that sport was an inherently conservative institution that not only diverted the attention of the masses from their systematic oppression, but also peddled values and ideals that supported the status quo and led blue-collar workers to conspire in their own exploitation. Drawing upon some of the ideas of Thorsten Veblen (whom we discuss later) as well as Marx, Hoch writes that:

> the anthropomorphic cults, betting, and the predatory sporting temperament are good ways of keeping everyone drugged with animism and preternaturalism, thus ensuring that they will be no threat to the existing social dictatorship. This is more or less a refinement of Marx's religion-is-the-opium-of-the-masses argument. (Hoch, 1972: 54–5)

In other words, sport undermined the development of a radical class consciousness, by generating playful diversion or reproducing the conditions of labour. The latter point was eloquently made by Aronowitz in his comments on the homologous temporal patterns of labour and leisure:

> The structure of unbounded time reflects the conditions of bounded time. People join clubs that are organized, as workplaces are organized, and participate in do-it-yourself projects that resemble labour. Many workers of the generation that grew up in America in the 1920s and 1930s lead their leisure-time lives as if on a busman's holiday because the patterns of their earlier lives did not permit an imaginary world that defied the dominant culture. (Aronowitz, 1974: 127)

As early as 1975, Hoch's thesis had been criticized by Gruneau for being too restrictive, in the sense that his argument could not account for human agency and resistance to the impositions of 'the dominant institutional structure' (Gruneau, 1975: 144). It was a French theorist, working in the tradition of Althusser, who developed most fully Hoch's arguments to their theoretical and logical extreme. In his book *Sport: a Prison of Measured Time* (1978), Jean-Marie Brohm locates sport within the rubric of structuralism. In terms that would not be out of place in the functionalist lexicon, Althusser (1969, 1971) had argued that the productive mechanisms of capitalism dictate the form and content of social relations through institutional processes and agencies which automatically – that is, structurally – promulgate the interests of the ruling class.

These ideological state apparatuses – the legal system, the family, the institution of education, the political system, the media, the trade unions and so forth – organize the production of ideas in such a manner as to negate the possibility of any proletarian and dialectical critique of capitalism. Brohm adopts Althusser's framework and posits that within capitalism, sport too should be analysed as an ideological state apparatus. The following is an accurate summary of Brohm's thesis:

> Sport and recreation practices were viewed as part of the process through which a structure in dominance was secured or reproduced. In this sense sport: provided a stabilizing factor for the existing social order; provided a basis for reinforcing the commodity spectacle; provided a basis for reproducing patriarchy; provided a basis for regimenting and militarizing youth and reproducing a set of hierarchical, elitist and authoritarian values. If competitive sport is condemned to the dustbin then forms of recreation fare no better since they were viewed as ideological ways of running away from reality. That is, leisure practices were viewed as false techniques of escapism. (Jarvie and Maguire, 1994: 96)

Social change requires out-of-structure space for the working up and communication of anti-establishment ideas. Once this space is removed, as it is in structuralist accounts of social construction, how can social change be explained? The main failing of Hoch's and Brohm's theses was that they both grossly over-simplified the nature of the interface between individuals and institutions in the construction of cultural meaning. In each case working-class engagement in sport is represented as drone-like and uncritical. Furthermore, and particularly in Brohm's case, by theorizing sport as a total (capitalist) institution, that is, one from which there is no physical or intellectual escape, they denied the possibility that sport is something that can be positively possessed and valued by the working class and used by that class for its own purposes (Gruneau, 1983).

In more subtle hands, a Marxist view of sport and social class is, at least partially, salvaged. Some of the best examples of this are in the area of British social history and cultural studies. In his weighty historical interpretation of the making of the English working class, and in several related articles, E.P. Thompson (1968) described how sport and leisure featured as sites for class struggle. His work demonstrated how those social forces that emerged to pioneer the development of capitalism also sought to shape the ideological

and cultural production of the new age. For a relatively brief interlude in the eighteenth century, he argued, even though the commercial and social basis had shifted from agriculture to commerce, and from the countryside to the town, social hierarchy continued to be largely defined by pageant and display. As Thompson observed, this was a betwixt and between time, when the ties of dependency of the old order had been loosened or cut altogether and the regime of social relations supportive of industrialism was yet to be fully developed. It was, in Thompson's words, a society of 'Patricians and Plebs', who participated in a very theatrical and public culture, within which social distance was proclaimed by conspicuously distinctive styles of leisure (Thompson, 1974: 394–5).

However, as Thompson noted in an earlier article, even as the Regency aristocracy displayed its standing, the ground was being cut from beneath by the establishment of capitalism and the inexorable rise of an industrial and commercial bourgeoisie. To flourish, capitalism needed a disciplined and reliable labour force. One of the more pressing tasks for the new ruling class was the reformation of the working rhythms of those whose experience of labour remained anchored in a bucolic past and cycles of seasonal imperatives. Necessarily, the non-work habits of the masses formed part of the equation of reform, for what people did in their spare time had implications for how they related to the process of production. Thompson showed how an emergent bourgeoisie in England used its influence, both in government and within the church, to carry out a legal and moral crusade against the recreational habits of the lower orders. He catalogued seven ways in which the 'new labour habits were formed, and a new time-discipline was imposed … by the division of labour; the supervision of labour; fines; bells and clocks; money incentives; preachings and schoolings; the suppression of fairs and sports' (Thompson, 1967: 90). The fledgling working class did not readily surrender time-honoured customs and leisure practices. Such reform as did succeed only did so within a context of dynamics of resistance, struggle and domination between classes and class fractions (Thompson, 1967). Delves's exemplary study of the decline of folk football in the English city of Derby is in the tradition of Thompson's approach (Delves, 1981), illustrating how new cross-class alliances – the emergence of newly dominant class fractions with common interests in change and reform – accounted for the demise of the traditional form of folk football, and its supersession by the regulated, enclosed, more civilized and profitable sport form of horse racing.

Drawing on Thompson, and on Raymond Williams (1958, 1965, 1977), scholars such as Clarke and Critcher (1985), Hargreaves (1986) and Tomlinson (1986) developed the cultural studies position on the relationship between sport and leisure and social class. They used recent and contemporary history to reveal how, in general, the space for the generation of culture and ideas is highly contested territory and how, in particular, sport has featured in the ongoing struggle for power between dominant and subordinate groups in capitalist societies. These works are underpinned by the writings of Antonio Gramsci (1985, 1971), for whom society was the product of a relationship between political institutions – the formal apparatus of the state – and cultural institutions – the less formally structured and controlled theatre of civil society. It is within the latter, civil society, that the legitimacy of the state resides, or, in times of crisis, is challenged.

Sport is part of civil society and as such is located within the terrain on which those responsible for the articulation and dissemination of ideas (in a variety of ways), attempt to attract the mass of the population and influence them towards certain values and aspirations. Although some of the functionaries of civil society are antagonistic to the dominant group and purvey oppositional attitudes to their public, in normal circumstances the majority act in such a way as to provide widespread acceptance, by the population, of the world-view expressed by those in positions of political power. The result is the cultural, ideological and moral authority of the ruling class, which Gramsci refers to as hegemony. At no time is this a static condition inasmuch as counter-hegemonic challenges continue to be made and the ruling élite is constantly obliged to renegotiate the conditions under which its ideologically embedded authority remains dominant (Sugden and Bairner, 1993).

According to Hargreaves, in contrast to over-determined, structuralist accounts of sport, the hegemony thesis allowed sport to be analysed 'more as an autonomous cultural form', and, also, in a 'more subtle analysis of class power and how it is related to other aspects of power relations – such as gender, ethnicity and the nation' (Hargreaves, 1992: 263). This formulation introduces the possibility that sport and related activities can carry a range of meanings for different classes, some of which may be imposed through hierarchical institutional processes, but others of which may be generated by relatively unfettered subcultures of resistance and adaptation.

This is a view shared by Gruneau in his major study of sport and social stratification. After an exhaustive review of alternative positions, he opts for the concept of hegemony, 'because it allows for the notion that the accomplishment of social interaction is always contested, sometimes in very subtle, other times, quite significant ways', though he argues for a shift in the application of the concept of hegemony to include power relations between elements of social stratification that are not the direct products of class relations (Gruneau, 1983). This is certainly the approach taken by George Sage, who adapts Hargreaves's model to the study of American sport and utilizes hegemony theory to consider relations of domination and subordination around the themes of race and gender as well as class (Sage, 1990).

Hargreaves, though, views it as a violation of the concept's essentially Marxist premises when hegemony is used to account for other layers of social differentiation, such as race, ethnicity and gender (Hargreaves, 1992). As Hargreaves himself admits, once economic determinism is questioned as the pre-eminent principle of social order, the door is opened for a more pluralistic and less class-dependent analysis of stratification – one which pays, 'far more detailed attention … to the specific autonomous features of sport(s) and to the interactive relationship they have with social contexts' (1992: 278). In order to reformulate a theory of social class and sport which accommodates both the determining power of economic relationships, and the plurality of social relations which cannot be explained in purely economistic terms, it is necessary to turn to the works of Max Weber and some of those who have followed him.

Weber: Class, Status and Sport

Like Marx, Weber acknowledges the importance of economic dynamics in the overall design of the social order. However, unlike Marx, Weber believed that power and the determining forces and social groupings which flowed from it were not anchored, once and for all, in economic relations. Consequently, while he believed social class to be a very important variable of stratification, he also believed that there were other, equally significant, factors that influenced the nature and hierarchy of division in any given society. The main conceptual tool which Weber uses to counter-balance his own emphasis on the significance of social class is that of status. Status groups differ from classes inasmuch as they are identifiable according to socially constructed gradations which articulate around the attribution of honour or the lack thereof. Weber believed that political power was not necessarily synonymous with economic power or wealth and neither was political power sought solely as an avenue to riches:

> 'economically conditioned' power is not, of course, identical with 'power' as such. On the contrary, the emergence of economic power may be the consequence of power existing on other grounds. Man does not strive for power only in order to enrich himself economically. Power, including economic power, may be valued for its own sake. (Weber, 1971: 250)

Within Weber's framework, the occupation of positions of honour and command over economic resources interact, to provide the social order with its distinctive pattern. Status groups not only share economic conditions but also participate in a common 'style of life' which, through routine social interaction, on the one hand binds them from within, and on the other hand offers tangible expressions of distinctiveness from other gradations. According to Weber, 'such honorific preferences may consist of the privilege of wearing special costumes, of eating special dishes, taboo to others, of carrying arms' (1971: 260). Certainly, this formulation helps us to better understand the relationship between sport and status in the Middle Ages as described in the introduction to this chapter. In terms of applying Weber's model to sport and social stratification in recent and contemporary history we now turn to the works of Thorsten Veblen and Pierre Bourdieu.

It is an irony of capitalism that those who occupy the apex of a system that depends absolutely on the success of industrial enterprise, choose to express their social standing by distancing themselves completely from those activities which in any way resemble work, while engaging in the conspicuous display of dilettante forms of leisure which are premised on an infrastructure of labour and capitalist production. This is the kernel of Veblen's *The Theory of the Leisure Class* (subtitled 'An Economic Study of Institutions'), his analysis of the social consequences of the workings of capitalism in late nineteenth-century United States of America, published in 1899.

Along with Weber, Veblen acknowledged a debt to Marx, agreeing that, in his day, the basic form of hierarchy was tied to capitalism and the uneven distribution of wealth which this entailed. However, he makes the astute observation that, once established through 'pecuniary emulation' (making money), the ruling class sets itself apart from lower gradations by recreating the imagined lifestyles of the élites of previous eras. An exemption from work is a key feature of this imagery:

> From the days of the Greek philosophers to the present, a degree of leisure and of exemption from contact with such industrial processes as serve the immediate everyday purpose to human life, has ever been recognized by thoughtful men as a prerequisite to a worthy or beautiful, or even a blameless human life. In itself and in its consequences the life of leisure is beautiful and ennobling in all civilized men's eyes. (Veblen, 1953: 42)

For Veblen, status was not passively linked to wealth. On the contrary, 'wealth or power must be put in evidence, for esteem is awarded only on evidence' (1953: 42), through the 'nonproductive consumption of time'. In short, in order to maintain their status, the ruling class had to be seen to be busy, spending both time and money, doing nothing. In this regard, 'a life of leisure is the most conclusive evidence of pecuniary strength, and therefore of superior force' (p. 42). Suitable 'evidence' for a life of leisure comes in rich variety and includes styles of dress, modes of travel and tourism, appreciation for and possession of art and literature, honorary titles and insignia, and all other attributes of exclusive and 'good taste' in a wide variety of cultural products.

In Veblen's hands class and caste merge in the ways through which ruling élites, once established through economic success, bond and can be identified through shared participation in categories of activities which are exclusive and generative of high status. It is in this context that Veblen pays special attention to sport which, after war, he views as an ideal medium through which the ruling class can: display its physical superiority; recreate the imagined conditions of a more barbarous and yet, simultaneously, more 'chivalrous' past; promote socialization and character development of its children; and, finally, evaluate *parvenus* who would seek to join its ranks by using sport as a proving ground:

> Hence, the facility with which any new accessions to the leisure class take to sports; and hence the rapid growth of sports and of the sporting sentiment in any industrial community where wealth has accumulated sufficiently to exempt a considerable part of the population from work. (1953: 176)

Moreover, given the prohibition on work, other than war, sport, argues Veblen, is the only legitimate terrain where the ruling class (males) can engage in public displays of physical prowess:

> From being an honourable employment handed down from the predatory culture as the highest form of everyday leisure, sports have come to be the only form of outdoor activity that has the full sanction of decorum. (p. 172).

Veblen saw sport in his day as one of the 'modern survivals of prowess' (p. 172). He believed that the warlike temperaments, actions and nomenclature associated both with field sports (hunting) and athletics, legitimated ruling-class participation in them. Veblen recognized that sports provided élite groups with the perfect opportunity to define their boundaries, both from within, and in the eyes of outsiders. But he was acerbic in his condemnation of the posing and posturing which accompanied many of these activities:

> It is noticeable, for instance, that even very mild mannered and matter-of-fact men who go out shooting are apt to carry an excess of arms and accoutrements in order to impress upon their own imagination the seriousness of their undertaking. These huntsmen are also prone to a histrionic, prancing gait and to an elaborate exaggeration of the motions, whether of stealth or of onslaught, involved in their deeds of exploit. Similarly in athletic sports there is almost invariably present a good share of rant and swagger and ostensible mystification – features which mark the histrionic nature of these employments ... The slang of athletics, by the way, is in great part made up of extremely sanguinary locutions borrowed from the terminology of warfare. (p. 171)

Veblen's thesis concentrates almost exclusively on the activities of society's uppermost strata. However, in his work there are hints that he understood that the overlap between class and status operated at all levels of a social hierarchy which, as capitalism developed, became increasingly differentiated and complex. For a fuller understanding of how this pertains in contemporary society we must now turn to the work of the French social theorist, Bourdieu.

Like ourselves, Bourdieu recognizes that at least in part the relationship between sport and class is rooted in history. As a starting point for his discussion, Bourdieu notes that the emergence of 'sports in the strict sense ... took place in the educational establishments reserved for the 'élites' of bourgeois society, the English public schools, where the sons of aristocratic or upper-bourgeois families took over a number of popular – that is, vulgar – games, simultaneously changing their function' (Bourdieu, 1978: 823). He connects the rationalization of games into modern sports forms with a class-based philosophy of amateurism: 'the modern definition of sport ... is an integral part of a "moral ideal", i.e. an ethos which is that of the dominant fractions of the dominant class' (1978: 825). To play tennis or golf, to ride or to sail, was, as Bourdieu argues, to bestow upon the participant 'gains in distinction' (1978: 828). Sports in which lower-middle-class or working-class adolescents participate develop 'in the form of spectacles produced for the people ... more clearly as a mass commodity' (1978: 828).

Sports, therefore, are not self-contained spheres of practice: 'class habitus defines the meaning conferred on sporting activity, the profits expected from it; and not the least of these profits is the social value accruing from the pursuit of certain sports by virtue of the distinctive rarity they derive from their class distribution' (Bourdieu, 1978: 835). From this perspective, then, sports participation is not a matter of personal choice, of individual preference. It depends upon the financial resources available to the potential participant, the social status of those prominent in that activity, and the cultural meaning of a sport and the individual's relationship to those meanings.

Far from sport being an open sphere of limitless possibilities, it is a social phenomenon and cultural space that can operate, in Weberian terms (Parkin, 1974) as a form of social closure, in which potential entrants are vetted and excluded as suits the incumbent gatekeepers, and the inner world of the sports culture is tightly monitored and controlled. The same processes may be at work in golf club membership committees, and in other sports institutions in which entry requirements – written or unwritten – operate as potential barriers to open participation.

The recruitment and induction processes into, say, golf and tennis clubs, bear testimony to this. Take the apparently open-minded and egalitarian basis of a newcomer playing him or herself in at a tennis club. In order to do this the potential member must: communicate competently with the gatekeepers of a club; read the social interactions and etiquette and conventions of a club; comply with the dress code; be equipped with relatively sophisticated technology (today the aspirant would be unlikely to get far with a wooden Dunlop Maxply); and be able to play at a level of acceptable competence. This apparently open choice is in reality a possibility or trajectory based upon what Bourdieu recognizes as the power of economic and cultural capital:

> Class variations in sporting activities are due as much to variations in perception and appreciation of the immediate or deferred profits they are supposed to bring, as to variations in the costs ... Everything takes place as if the probability of taking up the different sports depended, within the limits defined by economic (and cultural) capital and spare time, on perception and assessment of the intrinsic and extrinsic profits of each sport in terms of the dispositions of the habitus, and more precisely, in terms of the relation to the body, which is one aspect of this. (Bourdieu, 1986: 212)

The notion of the habitus is central to the Bourdieuian framework: 'different conditions of existence produce different habitus – systems of generative schemes applicable, by simple transfer, to the most varied areas of practice' (Bourdieu, 1986: 170). The habitus embodies both that which is structured and that which is structuring: 'As a system of practice-generating schemes' it 'expresses systematically the necessity and freedom inherent in its class position and the difference constituting that position' (1986: 172). Rojek provides a useful summary of the concept: 'Habitus refers to an imprinted generated schema. The term "generative" means a motivating or propelling force in social behaviour. The term "schema" means a distinctive pattern or system of social conduct. For Bourdieu, the socialization process imprints generative schemata onto the individual' (Rojek, 1995: 67).

As with the neo-Marxists, Bourdieu recognizes that sport and leisure activities feature in an ongoing struggle for cultural domination which itself is linked to broader political contexts. As Jarvie and Maguire observe, however, Bourdieu emphasizes that the appropriation of distinctive, class-related lifestyles – including sports – are, through habitus, 'the product of an unconscious assimilation of tastes' (Jarvie and Maguire, 1994: 202), and that this itself is a highly complex and transhistorical process. Furthermore, Bourdieu is sensitive to the fact that classes are not monolithic. He argues that there can be divisions within classes and these too can be reflected in sports. His main example here is that of gender:

> An analysis of the distribution at a given moment of sporting activities among the fractions of the dominant class would bring to light some of the most hidden principles of the opposition between these fractions, such as the deep-rooted, unconscious conception of the relationship between the sexual division of labour and the division of the work of domination. (Bourdieu, 1986: 218)

For Bourdieu, then, sport is variously implicated in any class analysis: it acts as a kind of badge of social exclusivity and cultural distinctiveness for the dominant classes; it operates as a means of control or containment of the working or popular classes; it is represented as a potential source of escape and mobility for talented working-class sports performers (an elusive eventuality which, like state and national lotteries, work to keep the lower orders cowed yet hopeful); it articulates the fractional status distinctions that exist within the ranks of larger class groupings; and it reveals the capacity of the body to express social principles and cultural meanings, for physical capital (Wacquant, 1995) to connect with forms of economic and cultural capital.

In his subtle way, Bourdieu weaves with the threads of Marx, Weber – he refers to his study *Distinction* as an 'endeavour to rethink Max Weber's opposition between class and *Stand*' (Bourdieu, 1986: xii) – and Durkheim, and with many others whose own work derives from interpretations of these classic theorists, to articulate not a grand theory of sport and social class, but a way of thinking about how, in a dynamic way, sports participation and sports preference are intrinsically bound up with the production and reproduction of social hierarchies. It is the central significance of sport as a signifier of status which allows Bourdieu to overcome some of the more restrictive interpretations of both functionalism and Marxism.

CONCLUSION

As some of the other chapters in this volume reveal, people form significant social groups in society for a wide range of reasons, not all of which are tied up with their position *vis-à-vis* the production process. Some may be bound at birth through the status which *accrues* to their race, gender or ethnicity. Others may be placed in categories through their religious beliefs, their sense of national identity or simply through their age. As Dahrendorf emphasizes in his neo-Weberian approach, 'life chances are a function of two elements, *options* and *ligatures*' (Dahrendorf, 1979: 30). In this formulation, options refer to possibilities of choice, and ligatures are allegiances, bonds or linkages. The social habitus (Elias, 1993: 32) can be conceived in this fashion, with the tribe or the community placing the individual in the particular context, and the development of individual strands, at the level of instincts and feelings, indicating options for the future. All social groups feature, in different ways, in the process through which the social order is constructed, maintained and reformed. In other words, there is more to social stratification than social class and, while it remains a vital component, there is more to the articulation of status and power than class struggle.

It should be clear that we believe sport to be both reflective and constitutive of the plurality of power relations between classes and other status groups. In trying to make sense of this, we are struck by the utility of the concept of hegemony. However, like Gruneau (1983) and Sage (1998), we (see Sugden and Bairner, 1993; Tomlinson, 1988), suggest that the explanatory power of the hegemony thesis can be enhanced once it is released from its traditional anchorage in class relations (see, too, Bennett, 1986: xvi–xvii). Then the contest between political and civil society to shape and control the social order can be revealed, in given historical contexts, as one featuring all of the significant components of that order. It is only then that we can begin to understand, with the subtlety of Bourdieu, that sports and what they stand for are intimately connected to the way societies are constructed and changed.

REFERENCES

Althusser, L. (1969) *For Marx*. Harmondsworth: Penguin.

Althusser, L. (1971) *Lenin and Philosophy and Other Essays*. London: New Left Books.

Aronowitz, S. (1974) *False Promises: the Shaping of American Working Class Consciousness*. New York: McGraw-Hill.

Ball, D. (1973) 'Ascription and position. A comparative analysis of stacking in professional baseball', *Canadian Review of Sociology and Anthropology*, 10 (May): 97–113.

Bennett, T. (1986) 'Introduction: popular culture and "the turn to Gramsci"', in T. Bennett, C. Mercer and J. Woollacott (eds), *Popular Culture and Social Relations*. Milton Keynes: Open University Press. pp. xi–xix.

Bloch, M. (1961) *Feudal Society*, Volume 1. London: Routledge & Kegan Paul.

Bloch, M. (1962) *Feudal Society*, Volume 2. London: Routledge & Kegan Paul.

Bourdieu, P. (1978) 'Sport and social class', *Social Science Information*, 17 (6): 819–40.

Bourdieu, P. (1986) *Distinction – a Social Critique of the Judgement of Taste*. London and New York: Routledge & Kegan Paul.

Brohm, J-M. (1978) *Sport: a Prison of Measured Time*. London: Ink Links.

Central Statistical Office (1993) *Social Trends*, No. 23. London: HMSO.

Clarke, J. and Critcher, C. (1985) *The Devil Makes Work – Leisure in Capitalist Britain*. London: Macmillan.

Coakley, J.J. (1994) *Sport in Society: Issues and Controversies*, 4th edn. New York: Times Mirror/Mosby College Publishing.

Cross, G. (1993) *Time and Money: the Making of Consumer Culture*. London and New York: Routledge.

Dahrendorf, R. (1979) *Life Chances – Approaches to Social and Political Theory*. Chicago: University of Chicago Press.

Davis, K. and Moore, W.E. (1966) 'Some principles of stratification', in R. Bendix and S.M. Lipset (eds), *Class, Status and Power – Social Stratification in Comparative Perspective*, 2nd edn. London: Routledge & Kegan Paul. pp. 47–53.

Delves, A. (1981) 'Popular recreation and social conflict in Derby, 1800–1850', in E. Yeo and S. Yeo (eds), *Popular Culture and Class Conflict, 1590–1914: Explorations in the History of Labour and Leisure*. Brighton: Harvester Press. pp. 89–127.

Dunning, E. and Sheard, K. (1979) *Barbarians, Gentlemen and Players: a Sociological Study of the Development of Rugby Football*. New York: New York University Press.

Durkheim, E. (1964) *The Division of Labour in Society*. New York: Free Press.

Edwards, H. (1973) *Sociology of Sport*. Homewood, IL: Dorsey Press.

Elias, N. (1993) *Time: an Essay*. Oxford: Basil Blackwell.

Giddens, A. (1993) *Sociology*. Cambridge: Polity Press.

Gramsci, A. (1971) *Selections from the Prison Notebooks*. London: Lawrence and Wishart.

Gramsci, A. (1985) *Selections from Cultural Writings*. London: Lawrence and Wishart.

Gruneau, R. (1975) 'Sport, social differentiation, and social inequality', in D. Ball and J. Loy (eds), *Sport and Social Order*. Reading, MA: Addison-Wesley. pp. 117–84.

Gruneau, R. (1983) *Class, Sports, and Social Development*. Amherst, MA: University of Massachusetts Press.

Hargreaves, J. (1986) *Sport, Power and Culture: a Social and Historical Analysis of Popular Sports in Britain*. Cambridge: Polity Press.

Hargreaves, J. (1992). 'The hegemony thesis revisited', in C. Knox and J. Sugden (eds), *Rolling Back the Welfare State: Leisure in the 1990s*. Eastbourne: Leisure Studies Association. pp. 263–80.

Hoch, P. (1972) *Rip Off the Big Game: the Exploitation of Sports by the Power Elite.* New York: Doubleday.

Holt, R. (1989) *Sport and the British – a Modern History.* Oxford: Oxford University Press.

Huizinga, J. (1955a) *Homo Ludens – a Study of the Play Element in Culture.* Boston, MA: Beacon Press.

Huizinga, J. (1955b) *The Waning of the Middle Ages.* Harmondsworth: Penguin.

Jarvie, G. and Maguire, J. (1994) *Sport and Leisure in Social Thought.* London and New York: Routledge.

Loy, J. (1969) 'The study of sport and social mobility', in G. Kenyon (ed.), *Aspects of Contemporary Sport Sociology.* Chicago: The Athletic Institute. pp. 101–19.

Loy, J., McPherson, B. and Kenyon, G. (1978) *Sport and Social Systems.* Reading, MA: Addison-Wesley.

Lüschen, G. (1969) 'Social stratification and social mobility among young sportsmen', in J. Loy and G. Kenyon (eds), *Sport, Culture and Society.* New York: Macmillan. pp. 258–76.

McIntosh, P. (1993) 'The sociology of sport in the ancient world', in E.C. Dunning, J.A. Maguire and R.E. Pearton (eds), *The Sports Process – a Comparative and Developmental Approach.* Champaign, IL: Human Kinetics. pp. 19–38.

McPherson, B. (1974) 'Minority group involvement in sport: the black athlete', in J. Wilmore (ed.), *Exercise and Sport Sciences Review,* Vol. 2. New York: Academic Press. pp. 71–101.

Marcuse, H. (1964) *One-Dimensional Man.* Boston, MA: Beacon Press.

Marx, K. (1968) 'The Eighteenth Brumaire of Louis Napoleon Bonaparte', in K. Marx and F. Engels, *Selected Works.* London: Lawrence and Wishart. pp. 97–168.

Marx, K. and Engels, F. (1971) 'Social class and class conflict', in K. Thompson and J. Turner (eds), *Sociological Perspectives.* Harmondsworth: Penguin. pp. 245–9.

Mason, T. (1980) *Association Football and English Society 1863–1915,* Sussex: Harvester Press.

Michener, J. (1976) *On Sport.* London: Secker and Warburg.

Miliband, R. (1977) *Marxism and Ethics.* Oxford: Oxford University Press.

Minten, J. and Roberts, K. (1989) 'Trends in sports in Great Britain', in T.J. Kamphorst and K. Roberts (eds), *Trends in Sport – a Multinational Perspective.* AJ Voorthuizen: Giordano Bruno Culemberg. pp. 306–29.

Parkin, F. (1974) 'Strategies of social closure in class formation', in F. Parkin (ed.), *The Social Analysis of Class Structure.* London: Tavistock. pp. 1–18.

Parsons, T. (1964) *Essays in Sociological Theory.* New York: Free Press.

Plumb, J.H. (1974) 'Public literature and the arts in the eighteenth century', in M. Marrus (ed.), *The Emergence of Leisure.* New York: Harper & Row. pp. 11–37.

Renson, R. (1976) 'Social status symbolism of sport stratification', *Hermes* (Leuven), 10: 433–43.

Rojek, C. (1995) *Decentring Leisure: Rethinking Leisure Theory.* London: Sage.

Sage, G. (1998) *Power and Ideology in American Sport – a Critical Perspective,* 2nd edn. Champaign IL: Human Kinetics.

Scott, J. (1971) *The Athletic Revolution.* New York: Free Press.

Stone, G. (1957) 'Some meanings of American sport', in *The Proceedings of the National College Physical Education Association for Men,* 60th annual meeting.

Stone, G. (1969) 'Some meanings of American sport: an extended view', in G. Kenyon (ed.), *Aspects of Contemporary Sport Sociology.* Chicago: The Athletic Institute. pp. 5–16.

Sugden, J. and Bairner, A. (1993) *Sport, Sectarianism and Society in a Divided Ireland.* Leicester: University of Leicester Press.

Thompson, E.P. (1967) 'Time, work discipline and industrial capitalism', *Past and Present,* 38 (December): 56–97.

Thompson, E.P. (1968) *The Making of the English Working Class.* Harmondsworth: Penguin.

Thompson, E.P. (1974) 'Patrician society, plebian culture', *Journal of Social History,* VII: 382–405.

Tomlinson, A. (1986) 'Playing away from home: leisure, access and exclusion', in P. Golding (ed.), *Poverty and Exclusion.* London: Child Poverty Action Group. pp. 43–54.

Tomlinson, A. (1988) 'Good times, bad times and the politics of leisure: working-class culture in the 1930s in a small Northern English working-class community', in H. Cantelon and R. Hollands (eds), *Leisure, Sport and Working-Class Cultures: Theory and History.* Toronto: Garamond Press. pp. 41–64.

Veblen, T. (1953) *The Theory of the Leisure Class: an Economic Study of Institutions.* Mentor: New York.

Wacquant, L. (1995) 'Pugs at work: bodily capital and bodily labour among professional boxers', *Body and Society,* 1 (1): 65–93.

Weber, M. (1971) 'Class, status and power', in K. Thompson and J. Tunstall (eds), *Sociological Perspectives.* Harmondsworth: Penguin. pp. 250–64.

Williams, G. (1989) 'Rugby Union', in T. Mason (ed.), *Sport in Britain – a Social History.* Cambridge: Cambridge University Press. pp. 308–43.

Williams, R. (1958) *Culture and Society.* Harmondsworth: Penguin.

Williams, R. (1965) *The Long Revolution.* Harmondsworth: Penguin.

Williams, R. (1977) *Marxism and Literature.* Oxford: Oxford University Press.

20

GENDER AND SPORT

Nancy Theberge

This chapter examines the contribution of sport to gender relations and ideologies, 'the set of ideas that serve the interests of dominant groups' (Theberge and Birrell, 1994: 327). These are, of course, connected. Historically, sport has been organized as a male preserve, in which the majority of opportunities and rewards go to men. This arrangement is both the basis of, and a powerful support for an ideology of gender that ascribes different natures, abilities and interests to men and women.

The chapter begins with a brief account of the historical roots of modern sport, which laid the foundation for ideologies and practices that persist today. This is followed by a consideration of physicality as a key element of the connection between sport and gender. The bulk of the chapter is devoted to a discussion of recent research on the contribution of sport to the construction of gender and an ideology of gender difference.

HISTORICAL ROOTS AND THE GENDERING OF MODERN SPORT

The roots of contemporary sport were laid in the late nineteenth and early twentieth centuries in Britain and North America. In Britain, the main locus for these developments was the boys' public schools, which was the setting for the institutionalization of organized games. These games were infused with a Victorian version of masculinity, which celebrated competitiveness, toughness and physical dominance. 'Games playing in the boys' public schools provided the dominant image of masculine identity in sports and a model for

their future development in Britain and throughout the world' (Hargreaves, 1994: 43).

Women's participation in physical activity in Victorian Britain was much less developed and the subject of intense debate about the type and amount of activity that was suited to their supposedly more 'delicate' nature (Hargreaves, 1994). Victorian ideals held that women were morally and spiritually strong but physically and intellectually weak. The 'myth of female frailty', a lasting legacy of this ideal, became a defining feature of ideas about women, gender and physical activity (Theberge, 1989).

The model of male athleticism developed in Britain was transported to North America, where it developed in the context of social transformations of the late nineteenth and early twentieth centuries. With the rise of wage labor and economic concentration under industrial capitalism, many men were no longer secure in their role as breadwinner. As well, the separation of home and work caused men to spend more time away from their families. Along with the rise of universal schooling, this meant that young boys were spending more time with women, their mothers and teachers, and little time with men. 'With no frontier to conquer, with physical strength becoming less relevant to work, and with urban males being raised by women, it was feared that males were becoming "soft", that society was becoming feminized' (Messner, 1992: 14).

Turn-of-the-century gender relations were also transformed by changes in women's condition. Feminist political activism and women's movement into the paid labor force and higher education were a direct challenge to the ideology of separate, and gendered, spheres (Cahn, 1994: 7). Women's growing interest in sport posed a further threat to traditional ideologies. Within this context, debate raged about the challenge posed by the 'New Woman' (Smith-Rosenberg, 1985) and the implications of changing gender roles for men and masculinity (Cahn, 1994; Messner, 1992).

One response to the 'crisis of masculinity' (Kimmel, 1990: 58) of the period was the establishment of organizations that would provide opportunities for boys to reclaim their masculinity. These included the YMCA, the Boy Scouts and sport. A number of authors, writing of the rise in popularity of specific sports in this period, have traced these developments in part to an effort to establish a homosocial setting in which masculinity could be reasserted. In addition to Kimmel's (1990) and Howell's (1996) discussions of baseball, these include Gruneau and Whitson's (1993) analysis of the making of modern professional hockey, and Gorn's (1986) examination of bare knuckle boxing.

The early years of the twentieth century were crucial for the development of sport and the construction of gender ideologies. While most of the development was in men's sport, there was also significant expansion in women's athletics. One important setting for this was colleges and universities in Britain (Hargreaves, 1994) and North America (Theberge, 1989). Although access to higher education was still restricted mainly to the middle and upper classes, additional sporting opportunities for working-class women were present in the United States in industrial leagues (Theberge, 1989).

As in Victorian England, women's increased involvement in sport and physical activity in North America in the early years of the twentieth century was the subject of heated debate among physical educators and physicians. While some argued that mild forms of physical activity were beneficial, others saw physical exercise as incompatible with women's fragile nature and dangerous to their health. This debate was largely resolved by the adoption of a modified form of sport that was less strenuous and competitive than the 'real' sport played by men. Examples of the model are shortened race distances in running and swimming and six-player basketball, in which the game is slowed and movement restricted. This version of the game was developed specifically for women, to provide an appropriate alternative to men's basketball. The adoption of the modified model left intact the association between masculinity and sport that was embodied in the ideal established in Victorian public schools and entrenched in the burgeoning sporting culture of turn-of-the-century North America. This model confirmed the 'myth of female frailty' and offered apparent confirmation of the essential differences between the sexes (Theberge, 1989).

GENDER, SPORT AND PHYSICALITY: IDEOLOGICAL CONSTRUCTIONS

Susan Cahn (1994: 208) has suggested that the challenges to conventional ideologies posed by women's athletic participation early in this century led to a 'resulting sense of gender disorder'. She comments further that lurking beneath the surface of the debate about women's athleticism was the 'nagging question of power'. Contemporary interest in gender and sport explores in detail the question of power that Cahn identified in an earlier era.

A central theme in this work is the connection between physicality, sport and the construction of gender. Jennifer Hargreaves (1994: 146) describes the association: 'The acquisition of strength, muscularity and athletic skill has always been empowering for men, whereas for women it is valued far less and in some cases is denigrated'. The construction of gender difference was a key feature of the promotion of manly sports in nineteenth-century British public schools and turn-of-the-century North America and the basis for the adoption of the restricted model of female athleticism early in this century.

This association continues today. Connell (1987: 85) writes that 'images of ideal masculinity are constructed and promoted most systematically through competitive sport', where 'the combination of skill and force' in athletic competition becomes a defining feature of masculine identity. This point has been elaborated by Connell (1983, 1990, 1995) and others (Messner, 1990, 1992; Whitson, 1994).

It is important to recognize that the sense of empowerment through sport is not a universal experience for males. Indeed, for many boys and men, the experience of sport is one of frustration and disappointment (Klein, 1993; Messner, 1992). What is critical about the contribution of sport to the construction of gender is that sport provides an image of idealized, or 'culturally exalted' (Connell, 1995: 77) masculinity. Because this is the dominant or most powerful image it is *hegemonic*, a term taken from the Italian sociologist Antonio Gramsci's analysis of class relations. When applied to the analysis of gender, we may speak of particular forms of masculinity as hegemonic.

A key feature of hegemony is that it is historically constructed, within the context of particular social relations and institutional forms. For this reason, it is constantly challenged and open to reconstitution. Connell (1995: 77) describes this feature:

> I stress that hegemonic masculinity embodies a 'currently accepted' strategy. When conditions for the defence of patriarchy change, the bases for the dominance of a particular masculinity are eroded. New groups may challenge old solutions and construct a new hegemony. The dominance of *any* group of men may be challenged by women. Hegemony, then, is a historically mobile relation.

The analysis of gender and sport is concerned with the 'mobility' of relations and the manner in which sport reproduces or challenges hegemonic masculinity. The following sections of the chapter consider some of the main sites in which cultural struggles over the meaning of gender and sport are being waged most dramatically.

WOMEN'S SPORT AND THE CONTEMPORARY IDEOLOGICAL STRUGGLE

The condition of women in sport has changed tremendously since the early decades of the twentieth century. Much of this change has occurred in the past 25 years, and is the outcome of several developments. These include the feminist movement that presents an ongoing challenge to traditional gender roles and ideologies, legal and political initiatives that have yielded increased opportunities for women in sport, and the health and fitness movement which has raised awareness of the importance of physical activity. Unlike organized sport, the fitness movement has been promoted among both men and women and been an important influence on rising rates of participation in physical activity among women (Theberge and Birrell, 1994).

The progress that has occurred includes increases in the numbers of women participating in sport and in the variety of activities in which they are involved. These developments are an important challenge to the historical organization of sport as a male preserve. For many women this participation provides enjoyment and a sense of personal empowerment (MacKinnon, 1987; Theberge, 1987). At the same time, the contemporary era is marked by ambiguities and contradictions in the cultural meanings and implications of women's athleticism.

The 'contested terrain' (Messner, 1988) of women's sport is the subject of a growing body of research in a variety of settings. A theme common to these analyses is that while women are carving out a place in sport, their efforts to do so are constrained by broader forces. The particular dynamics of the struggles vary, owing to historical and institutional factors. Following is an account of recent research in three sporting sites with different histories of women's involvement but striking similarity in the persistence of cultural struggle. The activities considered are ice hockey, golf and aerobics.

Although women have been playing ice hockey for over a century, and for just about as long as men, recent years have seen impressive increases in the numbers of women in the sport (Etue and Williams, 1996). A particularly notable event is the admission of women's ice hockey to the Olympics, where it was included for the first time in the 1998 Winter Games in Nagano, Japan. Historically, ice hockey has been one of the most powerful signifiers of a conception of masculinity grounded in force and physical toughness (Gruneau and Whitson, 1993). The increased participation and visibility of women thus offers an important challenge to hockey's historical status as a 'flag carrier of masculinity', a term Lois Bryson (1990: 174) uses to refer to sports that 'quintessentially promote hegemonic masculinity and are sports to which a majority of people are regularly exposed'.

The challenge to hegemonic masculinity posed by women's ice hockey occurs in additional ways. The historical exclusion of women from sport has been most powerful in the case of team sports. The major exception is field hockey, which has been organized in schools and at the international level since the 1930s. In the Olympics, women's volleyball was added to the program for the 1964 Games, basketball in 1976 and field hockey, despite being well organized internationally for most of the century, was added only in 1980 (Theberge, 1989). As noted, ice hockey, the first team sport for women in the Winter Games, was contested for the first time in 1998.

Resistance to their participation in team sports has denied women one of the important forms of community and association that male athletes have long enjoyed (Theberge, 1987). The bonding that occurs in a team setting provides not only enjoyment but an important basis for the construction and confirmation of athletic identities. In my research in women's ice hockey, this process is documented in an examination of the construction of community on an elite level team. The analysis shows that in a broader cultural milieu marked by ambivalence toward women's hockey and women's sport generally, the team provides a context wherein women athletes 'collectively affirm their skills, commitment and passion for their sport' (Theberge, 1995: 401). In this respect, the development of hockey and other team sports is an important part of the ongoing challenge to the masculine preserve of sport.

Yet another challenge to masculine hegemony concerns the practice of women's hockey. The rules of men's and women's hockey are essentially the same, with the exception that women's hockey prohibits intentional body checking, that is intentional efforts to hit, or 'take out', an opponent. There is none the less extensive physical contact, as players constantly try to outmuscle and outmanoeuvre one another in an effort to control the puck and the play in a game (Theberge, 2000).

The prohibition against body checking is generally thought to result in a game in which speed, strategy and playing skills are featured more prominently than in a full contact game, which emphasizes power and force. Some believe that the absence of body checking results in lower rates of injury. Promoters of the prohibition cite the more limited contact game as a better version of the sport, and often comment that women's hockey need not be like men's. The legitimacy of this position, and the implied critique of the excessive violence and rates of injury in men's hockey are, however, overshadowed by a dominant view that men's hockey is the 'real' game. In interviews I conducted with players and coaches at an elite level, supporters of the inclusion of body checking describe this feature as 'part of the game', 'the way it should be', and 'part of the fun'. In the end, the effort to promote women's hockey as an attractive version of the sport is effectively neutralized by the hegemonic position of men's hockey, which is constructed as the 'real' game (Theberge, 2000).

The history of women's participation in golf provides some contrasts with hockey. Golf was introduced to North America in the late nineteenth century as a sport for middle- and upper-class men and their families. It has long welcomed women, though on very different terms than men (Crosset, 1995). In his study of women on the Ladies Professional Golf Association (LPGA) Tour, Crosset (1995) characterizes the position of women in golf as 'outsiders within', a reference to the variety of forms of gender segregation that historically maintained distinctions between men and women. These included restricted playing times for women, segregated clubhouses and separate tee boxes (that is, starting points, which shortened course distances) and club rules that prohibited women from wearing trousers or shorts in order to highlight differences between male and female members.

The gendering of women's golf is particularly influenced by the sport's commercial basis. Professional women's golf was organized in the 1940s, and despite its periodically shaky financial foundation, the sport has persisted as one of the few that offers women the possibility to pursue a career as professionals. The 'image problem' facing all women athletes has particular consequences in sports attempting to secure public acceptance and corporate sponsorship. These consequences are highlighted in the contradiction between what Crosset (1995) calls the 'prowess ethic', wherein players judge themselves by their performance on the course, and public and media preoccupation with their appearance and sexuality.

Tour members are annoyed by this preoccupation and corresponding inattention to their athletic skills. At the same time, they believe that pressures to obtain corporate and media support require the Tour to present an acceptable image, which is one of emphasized heterosexuality. In order to conform to this image, players devote considerable attention to their appearance, particularly their style of dress. Appearance is also an overriding preoccupation with LPGA staff and publicists, who 'relentlessly promote the image of femininity, motherhood and sexuality in an attempt to counter the "image problem"' (Crosset, 1995: 180).

The tension over image and its embodiment in emphasized heterosexuality surfaced dramatically in the spring of 1995. In a newspaper interview conducted at a major LPGA tournament, long-time CBS television golf commentator Ben Wright made a number of sexist and homophobic remarks about Tour players. These included statements that female golfers 'are handicapped by having boobs' and one of the tour's leading players 'was built like a tank' (Reese, 1996). The effort to discredit women athletes by disparaging their appearance and reconstructing them as unnatural women has been one of the main weapons employed in the effort to maintain sport as a masculine preserve (Birrell and Theberge, 1994).

Wright extended his assault by attacking the LPGA for what he – and many others – see as its lesbian image. He told the interviewer, 'Let's face facts here. Lesbians in the sport hurt women's golf. When it gets to the corporate level, that's not going to fly' (Reese, 1996: 24).

By voicing the unspoken concerns of many observers of women in sport, Wright fuelled the sense of disorder that underlies popular sentiment about women athletes and identified the particular costs of this unease for the commercial success of women's sport.

The most interesting and important aspects of Ben Wright's comments were not their substance. It is hardly news to hear women athletes disparaged as manly. Nor is the statement that there are lesbians in golf (as throughout society) inaccurate. What is significant about the incident is the response to Wright's comments by CBS and the LPGA. On publication of the remarks, Wright initially denied them and received the full support of CBS. When subsequent investigations provided convincing evidence that Wright had been quoted accurately, CBS reversed its position and suspended Wright. CBS and the LPGA then issued statements in which they tried to distance themselves from the incident, which each in its statement referred to as a distraction. With a substantial financial investment in televising golf, CBS has a major interest in upholding the wholesome image of the sport. By first supporting Wright in his denial, and then suspending him when further support would have been embarrassing, CBS throughout demonstrated its concern with avoiding controversy and jeopardizing its investment (Reese, 1996).

For its part, the LPGA has avoided the issue of homophobia by repeatedly denying that sponsors cite lesbianism as a basis for denying support. This position was the cornerstone of the Tour's response to the controversy generated by Wright's comments (Reese, 1996). In dealing with the episode, both CBS and the LPGA acted primarily to protect their investments, which they assumed would be jeopardized by public discussion of homophobia. The greatest tragedy of the Ben Wright incident was not his sexist and homophobic remarks but the lost opportunity to expose and attack homophobia and sexism in golf and all of sport.

The ideological struggle presented by aerobics is on initial examination quite different from that in hockey and golf. Unlike these, and virtually all competitive sports, from its inception as part of the 'fitness boom' of the 1970s aerobics has been organized primarily for women. For some women, aerobics has provided a safe space in which to pursue physical activity in an all-female setting, free of the competitive pressures of organized sport (Hargreaves, 1994). In this respect, aerobics has been part of the legitimation of physical activity for women and an important vehicle for the

empowerment through physical activity of individual women (Whitson, 1994).

Perhaps because it has been so heavily implicated in the changing scene of women's physical activity in recent decades, aerobics has been the subject of extensive analysis and critique. Much of this attention focuses on the contradictions embodied by aerobics as, on the one hand, a means of empowerment for some women and, on the other hand, a vehicle for reproducing some of the worst features of institutionalized sport, including excessive commercialism, competitiveness and the sexualization of women's physical activity. The commercialization of aerobics is evident in its incorporation into the leisure lifestyle industry, whose most prominent features include location in private fitness clubs and the marketing of leisure apparel. National and international organizations and competitions and a campaign to gain entry into the Olympics mark the arrival of aerobics into the world of competitive sport (Hargreaves, 1994).

A particular focus of critiques of aerobics has been sexualization. One of the most enlightening of these critiques is MacNeill's (1988) analysis of the production of '20 Minute Workout', a popular televised aerobics program of the late 1980s and early 1990s. MacNeill shows how through the use of audio (commentary and music) and visual (facial expressions of participants, camera angles and lighting) techniques, the show reconstructs women's physical activity as something closer to soft pornography. MacNeill concludes that while aerobics initially contained possibilities for reworking traditional ideologies of gender and physicality, it has been incorporated into dominant ideologies by feminizing and sexualizing women's physical activity.

More recent work on aerobics has explored women's experiences of the apparent contradictions of this activity that embodies both empowerment and domination through sexualization. Pirkko Markula's research with women 'aerobicizers' shows that while many women wanted to meet cultural ideals of the beautiful body, they were far from passive in their submission to the ideal. Rather, they maintained a scepticism, for example by questioning the cultural preoccupation with slimness and their own complicity in its pursuit. Markula (1995: 450) indicates that 'this questioning leaves many women puzzled: they want to conform to the ideal, but they also find the whole process ridiculous'.

Markula's research also shows that the skepticism that women expressed toward idealized images of women's bodies was particularly pronounced in their assessments of media presentations of exercising women. As well, the real life classes Markula studied were different from the video classes, in that the instructors were not picture-perfect, the participants did not wear skimpy clothing and many classes placed a higher emphasis on enhancing fitness, as opposed to appearance (Markula, 1995: 450). While the critical analysis of media presentations has provided important insight into cultural constructions of women's physical activity, the finding that women actively resist incorporation into these images – albeit not completely successfully – is significant.

Markula's (1995) research demonstrates the variety of reasons that women participate in aerobics, in addition to improving their bodies. These include enjoyment, because it provides a safe environment for being physically active, to meet and socialize with other women, to spend time on themselves, and for the energy it provides. The evidence accumulating from Markula's and others' work (for example, Haravon, 1995) provides support for Hargreaves's (1994: 247) observation that there is a clear contradiction between the popular image of aerobics, which emphasizes fashion and sexuality, and many women's personal experience.

The above discussion of three activities with different histories and conditions of women's involvement shows the variety of struggles around women's athleticism. In some respects, ice hockey, golf and aerobics all constitute significant challenges to masculine hegemony and the male preserve of sport. The team context and the intense physicality of women's ice hockey challenge some of the most important bases of the association of sport and masculinity. Women's long-time participation in golf and the professional opportunities available for nearly half a century have placed golf in the forefront of the struggle to improve the condition of women in sport. Aerobics has provided a safe space for women to be physically active and a means for the empowerment of individual women.

At the same time, each activity shows how women's efforts to make a place and to be empowered are constrained by dominant ideologies of gender, sport and physicality. In ice hockey, these result in a devaluation of the women's game as an alternative to the 'real' game played by men. In golf and aerobics, the athleticism of the activities is compromised by a relentless emphasis on emphasized heterosexuality. In golf, these pressures are directly tied to the sport's commercial basis and need to sell itself to the media and sponsors. Commercial pressures also operate in aerobics

through its incorporation into the leisure lifestyle industry and heavy reliance on the marketing of appearance and sexuality. These three activities are but a sample of possible illustrations of Jennifer Hargreaves's (1994: 3) observation that 'female sports have been riddled with complexities and contradictions throughout their history'.

SPORT AND THE PRODUCTION OF MASCULINITY

A developing body of research also examines men's experiences of sport and the processes whereby gender is produced. By exploring the complexities of the relationship between masculinity and sport, this work provides a needed corrective to the view that the two are 'naturally' associated.

Several themes are emphasized in this research. One is the manner in which men work at attaining physical prowess. The 'skill and force' that Connell (1987: 85) speaks of in his discussion of men's empowerment is not simply conferred upon them; it is something they struggle to obtain. This struggle is both emotional and physical. In his interview study with retired male athletes, Messner shows how respondents' views of athletic accomplishment emphasized bodily control. 'Rather than being a surprised spectator of one's own body, the successful athlete must learn to block or ignore fears, anxieties, or any other inconvenient emotions, while mentally controlling his body to perform prescribed tasks' (Messner, 1992: 64).

The struggle to gain control over the body is also explored in Connell's life history of an Australian 'Iron Man', who competes professionally in events involving swimming, running and surf-craft riding. Connell's subject 'lives an exemplary version of hegemonic masculinity' (1990: 93). This version relies fundamentally on his athletic prowess, which in turn is dependent on a training regime that demands intense discipline and motivation. The 'job' of the Iron Man is to master his body.

Research among male athletes also shows how the subculture of boys' and men's sport emphasizes gender difference, and within this, the celebration of masculine prowess and denigration of women and gay men. One of the best portrayals of this is Gary Alan Fine's study of Little League Baseball, *With the Boys*. Fine (1987) suggests that sports teams provide a context in which boys try out versions of behavior they perceive to be manly. In a discussion of the 'themes of preadolescent boys', he shows in rich detail how the culture of the teams is dominated by sexual and aggressive references that emphasize differences between the boys and anyone who is weaker, including women, gay men and younger children.

A similar point is made in Tim Curry's (1991) investigation of fraternal bonding in the locker room of a men's US university team. Curry's analysis shows how locker room culture celebrates masculinity and men's physical prowess. Essential elements of this process are the degradation of women and gay men and the association of sport with hypermasculinity. While noting the absence of definitive studies on the effects of participating in locker room culture, Curry (1991: 133) indicates that in his view 'sexist locker room culture is likely to have a cumulative negative effect on young men because it reinforces the notions of masculine privilege and hegemony, making that world view seem normal and typical'.

The aforementioned studies, and related work (for example, Gruneau and Whitson, 1993), elaborate the processes whereby masculinity is produced through social interaction in particular institutional contexts (Connell, 1995: 35). These contexts are historically specific. Like the earlier years of this century, the contemporary period is witnessing social changes with important implications for gender ideologies and their connections to sport. These include growing recognition of the problem of violence against women and children, the willingness of the legal system to intervene in domestic violence and regulate sexual harassment in the workplace, increasing automation and the growth of the service sector of the economy and the declining importance of physical work. 'All of these contribute to the erosion of a world in which a powerful male body could translate into social power' (Whitson, 1994: 359). These developments are the backdrop for the continued celebration in sport of a version of masculinity that is grounded in physical toughness and emphasizes gender difference and the denigration of women and gay men.

CHALLENGES TO MASCULINE HEGEMONY FROM WITHIN MEN'S SPORT

One of the most important contributions from the emerging work on men in sport is the analysis of challenges to hegemonic masculinity. Douglas Foley's (1990) study of a football season in small-town Texas shows how class, ethnic and gender relations are reproduced

and challenged by the rituals and practices associated with football. In a community that was 80 per cent Mexican American, the football team was a focus for working-class and Chicano resistance to middle-class and Anglo dominance. A Mexican coach provided a particularly powerful challenge to hierarchical relations by holding a position of authority on the team. This challenge, however, was short-lived. Following a pressure-packed season marked by a series of issues with racial undertones, the coach resigned, as Foley reports, 'sick of the strife and the pressure on my family' (Foley, 1990: 122).

Hegemonic masculinity, or the 'culturally exalted' version was challenged by some male Mexicanos who flaunted an 'anti-sport' lifestyle at football games and by football players who publicly endorsed the clean living image of the varsity athlete, while secretly breaking training regulations and team rules. At the same time, the traditional hierarchy of gender relations was confirmed by the role of female students as cheerleaders, the elevated status of football players and rituals like an annual 'powder puff' game[1] that ridiculed female students, dramatized gender differences and served as an 'expression of male dominance and privilege' (Foley, 1990: 119). While acknowledging the significance of challenges to dominant relations that occurred around football, Foley (1990: 133) concludes that 'such challenges have done little to transform the everyday culture that this major community ritual enacts'.

RACE AND THE CONSTRUCTION OF MASCULINITY

In his recent book *Masculinities*, R.W. Connell suggests that race relations are an integral part of the dynamic between hegemonic and other forms of masculinities and points to sport as an instance of this relationship. 'In a white supremacist context, black masculinities play symbolic roles for white gender construction. For instance, black sporting stars become exemplars of masculine toughness' (Connell, 1995: 80).

The celebration of black athleticism as an exemplary form of masculinity has a long history. Boxing, which perhaps more than any other sport embodies masculine imagery of physicality, has provided a particularly fertile setting for the construction of racialized versions of masculinity. In his biography of heavyweight champion Joe Louis, the first African

American athlete to gain heroic status among white Americans, Chris Mead (1985) shows how media accounts faithfully represented Louis as the successful embodiment of his race. Consistent with the 'race logic' (Coakley, 1998: 258) of the time that attributed intellectual superiority to white people and animal-like savagery to people of color, Louis's magnificent skills were attributed to his African heritage which, it was thought, located him somewhere closer to the animal kingdom than the human race. A 1935 account of a fight began with the statement, 'Something sly and sinister and perhaps not quite human came out of the African jungle last night to strike down and utterly demolish the huge hulk that had been Primo Carnera, the giant' (cited in Mead, 1985: 62). Later the same year a similar depiction appeared: 'Louis, the magnificent animal. He lives like an animal, untouched by externals. He eats. He sleeps. He fights. He is as tawny as an animal and he has an animal's concentration on his prey' (cited in Mead, 1985: 68).

Boxing remains a prime setting for the construction of black masculinity. One of the clearest contemporary examples is heavyweight Mike Tyson. Following a troubled background that included time spent in a youth detention centre and an abusive marriage to actress Robin Givens, Tyson was convicted in 1992 of raping an 18-year-old beauty pageant contestant and served nearly three years in an Indiana prison. In a disturbing commentary on the strategy employed by the defense team at Tyson's trial, Steptoe (1992) shows that the imagery celebrated in portrayals of Joe Louis is not a historical artifact. Playing to racial stereotypes, Tyson's attorney told the jury that Tyson 'is not a high school graduate. He's never been trained in public speaking. He's never been trained in the skills of projecting himself … He's been trained to do one thing, to defend himself in a ring and to go to battle in a ring' (quoted in Steptoe, 1992: 92). Invoking stereotypes of black men as hypersexual, the lawyer elicited testimony that Tyson's activities were part of a 'sex crazed rampage' he engaged in during a pageant rehearsal. Steptoe indicates that 'In effect [Tyson's lawyer] was saying to the jury: Tyson is your worst nightmare – a vulgar, socially inept, sex obsessed black athlete'. He was a black man guilty of 'the crudity of his sexual demands' (Steptoe, 1992: 92).

The racist constructions of Louis and Tyson are perhaps most notable for their transparency. Additional work examines more subtle and likely more powerful instances of the construction of black masculinity in sport. One of the more sophisticated analyses is

David Andrews's reading of the construction of US basketball star Michael Jordan as popular hero. Andrews argues that, contrary to his promoters' efforts to present Jordan as having 'no color' (1996: 125), Jordan's racial identity as an African American and the politics of race in America have been central to the construction and reconstruction of Jordan throughout his career. During Jordan's meteoric rise to stardom in the National Basketball Association (NBA) he was promoted as the exemplar of the natural athlete, a basketball player 'born to dunk'. Subsequently, and in accordance with the prevailing racial politics of 'Reagan's America' (Grossberg, 1992, cited in Andrews, 1996), which emphasized inclusiveness and conveniently ignored continuing racial and class divisions and tensions, Jordan's promoters reconstructed him in specifically non-racial terms. Thus, there was a move away from Nike's Air Jordan campaign that depicted his amazing physical skills to an advertising formula that emphasized Jordan's humility, inner drive and personal responsibility, human qualities that presumably transcend race (Andrews, 1996).

After several years of reigning as a public icon, Jordan's celebrated status was challenged by events in the spring and summer of 1993. In May, the *New York Times* reported on a late night visit to a gambling casino that Jordan made during a crucial championship series. This event prompted extensive media discussion of Jordan's well-known fondness for gambling, sometimes for large sums of money. A few months later, Jordan's father was murdered, while sleeping in his car at a roadside stop. The murder renewed interest in Jordan's gambling, as the media speculated that the crime was somehow related to this presumed underside of Jordan's character. Shortly after his father's murder, Jordan retired from basketball, a move widely assumed to be in part related to the stress of dealing with his father's death and media preoccupation with the murder. Andrews (1996) shows that in accounts of these later events, Jordan was reconstructed not as the hero who transcends race but as yet another example of an African American male whose character is ultimately flawed.

Jordan's career came full circle when he returned to the NBA in the spring of 1995. At the time the league was encountering increasing criticism over the behavior and image of a number of its star players (many of these African American), who were described by one writer as 'spoilsports and malcontents' (Leland, 1995, cited in Andrews, 1996). On his return, Jordan was hailed as a role model who would reclaim for the league some of the lustre it had lost in the public eye.

In a much more complex analysis than the brief summary here can suggest, Andrews (1996) shows that the meaning of Michael Jordan is about a multiplicity of images, not only of Jordan, but of black male athletes and whites. This is an excellent illustration of Connell's (1995) point that black masculinities play symbolic roles for white gender construction. Throughout the shifting imagery of Michael Jordan, hegemonic masculinity – white, heterosexual and cerebral as opposed to the presumed natural but undisciplined athleticism of African Americans – has provided the standard against which Jordan was constructed, first as hero, then as fallen icon, followed by renewed heroism. The repositioning of Michael Jordan provides powerful ideological support for a broader politics of racial relations centred around difference and white superiority.

COMPULSORY HETEROSEXUALITY, HOMOPHOBIA, GENDER AND SPORT

The analysis of compulsory heterosexuality and homophobia is critical to an understanding of gender and sport. Some discussion of this issue in the context of women's sport is offered in the above accounts of emphasized heterosexuality in golf and aerobics, and the Ben Wright incident on the LPGA. The preoccupation with femininity in sport is one of the most powerful manifestations of homophobia. Lenskyj (1991: 49) explains the association: 'Since the stereotype of "female-athlete" and "lesbian" share so-called masculine traits such as aggression and independence, the association between sport and lesbianism has frequently been made'. In a comment similar to Cahn's (1994: 208) remarks about the nagging question of power underlying the debate about women in sport, Lenskyj notes elsewhere that the popular association between sport and lesbianism is fundamentally an issue of male power:

> regardless of sexual preference, women who reject the traditional feminine role in their careers as athletes, coaches, or sport administrators, as in any other non-traditional pursuit, pose a threat to existing power relations between the sexes. For this reason, these women are the frequent targets of labels intended to devalue or dismiss their successes by calling their sexuality into question. (Lenskyj, 1986: 383)

The condition of gay men and sport also offers important insight. The exemplary masculinity celebrated in sport is determinedly heterosexual. Some indication of the processes whereby this is accomplished is included in above accounts of the subcultures of Little League baseball and the locker room of a US university team. One of the major themes in both settings is denigration of gays and emphasis on the difference between gays and 'real men' (and boys) who do sport.

While work in the sociology of sport has in recent years identified the problem of homophobia, there is less information on the experiences of gays and lesbians and the relations between heterosexuals and homosexuals in sport. The limited literature includes Laurie Schulze's (1990) examination of lesbians' readings of women's bodybuilding, which shows the contradictory meanings that lesbians assign to this activity. My research on an elite women's hockey team shows a degree of inclusiveness that unites lesbian and heterosexual players (Theberge, 1995, 2000). Additional insight is offered in Mike Messner's (1994) interview with decathlete and gay activist Tom Waddell, who describes the isolation he felt as a closeted gay man in sport and his vision for a break from the homophobic world of sport through the Gay Games.

Perhaps the most extensive analysis of homosexuals in sport is Brian Pronger's (1990) phenomenological interpretation of the experiences of gay men. Pronger suggests that the emphasized heterosexuality of sport separates gay men from this culture and provides then with a distinctive viewpoint. This viewpoint is the basis of a strategy Pronger calls 'ironic', meaning that while many gay men find the male locker room and athletic competition to be sexually charged, the relentless heterosexism of male sport forces them to act as and take the viewpoint of an outsider. Pronger suggests that in this response gay men reinterpret the athletic experience in ways that offer the potential to transform the heterosexist culture of sport (see Messner, 1992: 101).

GENDER, SPORT AND CHALLENGES TO HEGEMONIC MASCULINITY

The preceding discussion has offered an overview of the main themes in the literature on gender and sport, illustrated by discussions of representative research. This work focuses heavily on the contribution of sport to gender relations and the construction of gender ideologies. The key issues discussed are the manner in which sport reproduces or challenges hegemonic masculinity and the social conditions that underlie and enable these processes.

The discussion has stressed that the gendering of sport occurs within particular historical contexts and institutional conditions. The organization of sport in the latter part of the nineteenth century as a male preserve in which Victorian ideals of masculinity were celebrated remains the basis for its constitution today. Despite considerable advances in the conditions of women's participation over the past hundred years, sport remains a powerful vehicle for the construction of an ideology of gender difference. This ideology is grounded in the association of gender and physicality. While the accomplishments of women athletes should put to rest any vestiges of the myth of female frailty, contradictions and ambiguities about the meaning of women's athleticism continue. Challenges to masculine hegemony are countered by the continued marginalization and heterosexualization of women athletes and women's sport.

A particularly important development in recent scholarship on gender and sport is the analysis of men and the production of masculinity. This work elaborates the complexity of the processes whereby masculinity is constructed and achieved. It also explores the challenges to hegemonic masculinity posed by subordinated and marginalized men and alternative forms of masculinity. These challenges, along with those arising from women's sport, make clear the historical basis and mobility of gender relations.

The gendering of sport is inseparable from the dynamics of race and class. Although in need of development, work on minority men in sport is more advanced than that on minority women. Smith (1992) and Birrell (1990) have both noted the need for greater attention to the sporting experiences of women of color. This work is essential to the production of a more complete analysis of the dynamics of race, class and gender relations.

There is also a need for more research on the experiences of gays and lesbians in sport. While the significance of homophobia and heterosexism in sport has been identified as a political issue, we know much less about the dynamics of their operation in the everyday world of sport.

One of the most widely used textbooks in the sociology of sport identifies gender as the most popular topic in the field in the 1990s (Coakley, 1998). As the author, Jay Coakley,

notes in the sixth edition of *Sport in Society* (1998: 211), this is because authors have come to realize the importance of understanding the significance of gender issues in sport and the political implications of these issues. This chapter has attempted to indicate the basis for Coakley's assessment of the significance of the topic. The study of gender and sport is one of the most dynamic and important areas within the sociology of sport.

NOTE

1 'Powder Puff football' games traditionally have been played on many high school and college campuses in the United States. The participants are women students who want to play full contact football or some variation of it. In some cases the women wear standard protective equipment, but it is difficult for them to gain access to equipment that fits them properly. Therefore, most games are played in sweatsuits or shorts and shirts. While most of the women participants take the game seriously, the majority of the men who watch them tend to mock the abilities and actions of the women on the field. Some men may even cross-dress as cheerleaders to further trivialize what occurs on the playing field.

REFERENCES

Andrews, D. (1996) 'The fact(s) of Michael Jordan's blackness: excavating a floating racial signifier', *Sociology of Sport Journal*, 13: 125–58.

Birrell, S. (1990) 'Women of color, critical autobiography, and sport', in M. Messner and D. Sabo (eds), *Sport, Men, and the Gender Order: Critical Feminist Perspectives*. Champaign, IL: Human Kinetics. pp. 185–99.

Birrell, S. and Theberge, N. (1994) 'Ideological control of women in sport', in D.M. Costa and S.R. Guthrie (eds), *Women and Sport: Interdisciplinary Perspectives*. Champaign, IL: Human Kinetics. pp. 341–59.

Bryson, L. (1990) 'Challenges to male hegemony in sport', in M. Messner and D. Sabo (eds), *Sport, Men, and the Gender Order: Critical Feminist Perspectives*. Champaign, IL: Human Kinetics. pp. 173–84.

Cahn, S. (1994) *Coming on Strong: Gender and Sexuality in Twentieth Century Women's Sport*. New York: Free Press.

Coakley, J. (1998) *Sport in Society: Issues and Controversies*, 6th edn. New York: McGraw-Hill.

Connell, R. (1983) *Which Way is Up: Essays on Sex, Class, and Culture*. Boston, MA: Allen and Unwin.

Connell, R. (1987) *Gender and Power*. Stanford, CA: Stanford University Press.

Connell, R. (1990) 'An Iron Man: the body and some contradictions of hegemonic masculinity', in M. Messner and D. Sabo (eds), *Sport, Men, and the Gender Order: Critical Feminist Perspectives*. Champaign, IL: Human Kinetics. pp. 83–95.

Connell, R. (1995) *Masculinities*. Berkeley and Los Angeles: University of California Press.

Crosset, T. (1995) *Outsiders in the Clubhouse: the World of Women's Professional Golf*. Albany, NY: State University of New York Press.

Curry, T. (1991) 'Fraternal bonding in the locker room: a profeminist analysis of talk about competition and women', *Sociology of Sport Journal*, 8: 119–35.

Etue, E. and Williams, M. (1996) *On the Edge: Women Making Hockey History*. Toronto: Second Story Press.

Fine, G.A. (1987) *With the Boys: Little League Baseball and Preadolescent Culture*. Chicago: University of Chicago Press.

Foley, D. (1990) 'The great American football ritual: reproducing race, class, and gender inequality', *Sociology of Sport Journal*, 7: 111–35.

Gorn, E. (1986) *The Manly Art: Bare Knuckle Prize Fighting in America*. Ithaca, NY: Cornell University Press.

Grossberg, L. (1992) *We Gotta Get Out of this Place: Popular Conservatism and Postmodern Culture*. London: Routledge.

Gruneau, R. and Whitson, D. (1993) *Hockey Night in Canada: Sport, Identities and Cultural Politics*. Toronto: Garamond.

Haravon, L. (1995) 'Exercises in empowerment: toward a feminist aerobic pedagogy', *Women in Sport and Physical Activity Journal*, 4 (2): 23–44.

Hargreaves, J.A. (1994) *Sporting Females: Critical Issues in the History and Sociology of Women's Sports*. London and New York: Routledge.

Howell, C. (1996) 'A manly sport: baseball and the social construction of masculinity', in J. Parr and M. Rosenfeld (eds), *Gender and History in Canada*. Toronto: Copp Clark. pp. 187–210.

Kimmel, M. (1990) 'Baseball and the reconstitution of American masculinity, 1880–1920', in M. Messner and D. Sabo (eds), *Sport, Men, and the Gender Order: Critical Feminist Perspectives*. Champaign, IL: Human Kinetics. pp. 55–65.

Klein, A. (1993) *Little Big Men: Bodybuilding Subculture and Gender Construction*. Albany, NY: State University of New York Press.

Leland, J. (1995) 'Hoop dreams', *Newsweek*, 20 March, pp. 48–55.

Lenskyj, H. (1986) 'Female sexuality and women's sport', *Women's Studies International Forum*, 10: 381–6.

Lenskyj, H. (1991) *Women's Sport and Physical Activity: Research and Bibliography*, 2nd edn. Ottawa: Ministry of Supply and Services.

MacKinnon, C. (1987) 'Women, self–possession, and sport', in *Feminism Unmodified: Discourses on Life and Law*. Cambridge, MA: Harvard University Press. pp. 117–24.

MacNeill, M. (1988) 'Active women, media representations, and ideology', in J. Harvey and H. Cantelon (eds), *Not Just a Game: Essays in Canadian Sport Sociology*. Ottawa: University of Ottawa Press. pp. 195–211.

Markula, P. (1995) 'Firm but shapely, fit but sexy, strong but thin: the postmodern aerobicizing female bodies', *Sociology of Sport Journal*, 12: 424–53.

Mead, C. (1985) *Champion: Joe Louis, Black Hero in White America*. New York: Viking Penguin.

Messner, M. (1988) 'Sports and male domination: the female athlete as contested ideological terrain', *Sociology of Sport Journal*, 5: 197–211.

Messner, M. (1990) 'When bodies are weapons: masculinity and violence in sport', *International Review for the Sociology of Sport*, 25: 203–20.

Messner, M. (1992) *Power at Play: Sports and the Problem of Masculinity*. Boston, MA: Beacon Press.

Messner, M. (1994) 'Gay athletes and the gay games: an interview with Tom Waddell', in M. Messner and D. Sabo (eds), *Sex, Violence and Power in Sports: Rethinking Masculinity*. Freedom, CA: Crossing Press. pp. 113–19.

Pronger, B. (1990) *The Arena of Masculinity*. New York: St Martin's Press.

Reese, G. (1996) 'Unsportsmanlike conduct', *The Advocate*, 20 February, pp. 24–6.

Schulze, L. (1990) 'On the muscle', in J. Gaines and C. Herzog (eds), *Fabrications: Costume and the Female Body*. New York: Routledge. pp. 59–78.

Smith, Y. (1992) 'Women of color in society and sport', *Quest*, 44: 228–50.

Smith-Rosenberg, C. (1985) *Disorderly Conduct: Visions of Gender in Victorian America*. New York: Oxford University Press.

Steptoe, S. (1992) 'A damnable defense', *Sports Illustrated*, 24 February, p. 92.

Theberge, N. (1987) 'Sport and women's empowerment', *Women's Studies International Forum*, 10: 387–93.

Theberge, N. (1989) 'Women's athletics and the myth of female frailty', in J. Freeman (ed.), *Women: a Feminist Perspective*, 4th edn. Mountain View, CA: Mayfield. pp. 507–22.

Theberge, N. (1995) 'Gender, sport, and the construction of community: a case study from women's ice hockey', *Sociology of Sport Journal*, 12: 389–402.

Theberge, N. (2000) *Higher Goals: Women's Ice Hockey and the Politics of Gender*. Albany, NY: State University of New York Press.

Theberge, N. and Birrell, N. (1994) 'The sociological study of women and sport', in D.M. Costa and S.R. Guthrie (eds), *Women and Sport: Interdisciplinary Perspectives*. Champaign, IL: Human Kinetics. pp. 323–30.

Whitson, D. (1994) 'The embodiment of gender: discipline, domination, and empowerment', in S. Birrell and C. Cole (eds), *Women, Sport, and Culture*. Champaign, IL: Human Kinetics. pp. 353–73.

21

SPORT, RACISM AND ETHNICITY

Grant Jarvie

This chapter provides a review of some of the main currents of sociological thought which have informed a body of research in the area of sport, racism and ethnicity. It considers some of the main popular arguments about sport in discussions of race relations, black identity and black feminism and argues against the notion of any one body of thought being viewed as universally valid. The examples that people use may change but the underlying processes and social and political problems reflect not just traditions of social thought but also many voices of anger and frustration in a world that is left wanting on so many fronts. This chapter is critical of some European intellectual constructions of racism which have often been applied in a devastating manner in the field of sport studies.

POPULAR OPINIONS AND SOCIOLOGICAL ARGUMENTS

If popular arguments about sport, racism and ethnicity have contributed to a number of racist beliefs about different peoples' sporting abilities, so too have a number of popular arguments contributed to particular explanations of race relations within the sociology of sport. Popular arguments have often suggested that sport itself:

1 is inherently conservative and helps to consolidate patriotism, nationalism and racism;
2 has some inherent property that makes it a possible instrument of integration and harmonious race relations;

3 as a form of cultural politics has been central to the processes of colonialism and imperialism in different parts of the world;
4 has contributed to unique political struggles which have involved black and ethnic political mobilization and the struggle for equality of and for black peoples and other ethnic minority groups;
5 has produced stereotypes, prejudices and myths about ethnic minority groups which have contributed both to discrimination against and an under-representation of ethnic minority peoples within certain sports; and
6 is a vehicle for displays of black prowess, masculinity and forms of identity.

While such arguments are crucial facets of peoples' experiences of sport, racism and ethnicity, none of the above-mentioned arguments can be singled out as identifying an underlying 'cause'. In many ways, each of these individual arguments places too much emphasis on factor a, b, c or d without really analysing the relationships or interconnecting strands which make up the complex social structures and processes that facilitate racism, not only in Europe and America, but in all corners of the globe. Indeed, this holds regarding all social formations where differences in the logics and levels of hatred, inferiorization, contempt, persecution, prejudice and mythology contribute to unique and particular expressions of racism and ethnicity.

To such popular arguments might be added a number of sociological arguments which have been rooted within particular traditions of social thought. Such explanations have contributed to a broader understanding of sport, racism and ethnicity in at least four ways. They have:

1 researched racism and the politics of exclusion from sport;
2 highlighted how institutional racism occurs through sport;
3 deconstructed the theory and practice of many mythical equal opportunity policies which have operated for and against many sporting men and women of 'colour'; and
4 suggested that in particular sets of situations it is possible to identify a 'unity of racism' within and between sports (Wieviorka, 1995).

The sociology of sport has not been unlike other areas of sociology, black studies, or other arenas of social thought which have sought to explain both the complexity and the unity of racism and ethnicity within premodern, modern and postmodern societies. Yet even here certain traditions of social thought have both over- and under-emphasized particular facets of explanation. It might be argued that an over-determination of the degree of importance accorded to a particular or exclusive line of argument has meant that a reality-congruent body of knowledge on sport, racism and ethnicity has been slow to be forthcoming.

What follows is a short review of some of the ways in which racism and ethnicity have been approached in the sociology of sport arena. Yet it is necessary in the first instance to provide a short definitional discussion around the categories and experiences of race, racism and ethnicity.

RACE, RACISM AND ETHNICITY AS EXPLANATORY PRINCIPLES

It has to be said from the outset that the social sciences, and consequently certain elements within the sociology of sport and sports studies literature have contributed a great deal to the invention of racism. Although a body of work specifically within the social sciences was much later in coming, the idea of superior and inferior races, and particularly the idea that race shapes performance and athleticism, can be traced back to the Greeks of the Hellenic period if not at least to the Middle Ages. In Britain, Francis Galton, a cousin of Charles Darwin, drew on the notion of racial differences to promote debates within the Sociological Society of London (Galton, 1904). In Germany, Otto Ammon developed a body of ideas about racial chaos and the growing

influence of Jews in commerce, law, literature and politics. The climate of ideas in the nineteenth century was still far from the ideology of Nazism, but 'knowledge' of race was supposed to provide a key to moral, cultural and social differences within an evolutionary explanation of humanity. It was an intellectual climate that was to culminate in Nazism which drew upon not just sociology but medicine, biology, chemistry, genetics, anthropology, ethnology, psychiatry, jurisprudence and demography in the classification of populations and the treatment of Jews, Gypsies and mental patients, who were also racialized (Wieviorka, 1995: 5).

Theorists such as Alexis de Tocqueville and Max Weber did not always take up radical positions regarding race. Tocqueville did not really firmly decide one way or the other between slavery and American democracy. On the other hand, he did decidedly reject the false doctrines of racism which sought to legitimize the enslavement of 'blacks' on the grounds of their nature and behaviour. Tocqueville (1968: 443) offered an analysis of American anti-black racism, seeing it as rooted in a particular context, time and ideology. His reasoning only appears in outline in quotes such as the following:

> the white northerners shun negroes with all the greater care the more legislation has abolished any legal distinction between them ... in the North the white man afraid of mingling with the black is frightened by an imaginary danger. In the South, where the danger would be real, I do not think the fear would be less. (Tocqueville, 1968: 443).

For Max Weber (1978: 331), there was race only if there was a race consciousness anchored in a community identity which could lead to action, such as segregation or prejudice. These were not necessarily attributable to hereditary differences but to habitus. As Dunning (1996) points out, Weber used the term 'caste' to describe a racially divided society in which the caste relations are the 'normal form in which ethnic communities live side by side in a societalized manner'. The crucial point being made is that the experiences of caste, race and colour cannot be simply explained in terms of physical difference; rather, they represent a social structural figuration of some significance. The dynamics of such a process of racial stratification are but one source of social tension capable of producing forms of structural change.

Both Weber and Tocqueville used the term 'race' but it would seem that in terms of community identity or indeed communal identity, other types of community deserve to be mentioned. One of these is 'ethnicity' which, as a term, is often used in association with the term 'race' or 'racism'. The notion of ethnicity is often problematic in the sense that it is not often clear how, for example, it might be distinguished from the concept of nationality. Ethnicity, racism and race are so closely intermingled for many specialists that the terms are often found together, as for example in the titles of various books, the name of an important journal and the title of one of the research committees of the International Sociological Association (Jarvie, 1991). Because of the lack of clarity of the concept of ethnicity and its closeness to nationality, contributions to the sociology of sport have tended to refer to civic and ethnic forms of nationalism where the latter is closely related to racial group definitions (Bairner, 1998).

It is possible to identify at least three different ways in which the notion of ethnicity is referred to or used in the literature on race and racism. In the first case, the term ethnicity is closely associated with the concept of nationhood: an example is provided in the work of Anthony Smith (1996). Here the term ethnic nationalism refers to those groups and the related doctrines which, since the end of the eighteenth century, have claimed the status of nation and the right to self-determination and an independent state for every ethnic group. Secondly, as in the work of Stephen Steinberg, the objective is to enquire into the social relations that are concealed, either mythically or ideologically, by recourse to the notion of ethnicity (Steinberg, 1989). In the third case biological aspects have taken precedence over the social and the cultural. Even in the most recent writings of respected scholars of ethnicity such as Pierre Van den Berghe a form of bio-social theory of ethnic populations is proposed which ultimately explains more in terms of genetics than any other discipline (Van den Berghe, 1981).

The last point has a particular resonance within some of the sports literature and is worth commenting upon if only to critique the argument. Much of the early reasoning for black excellence in athletics and other sports has been misleadingly explained as if natural ability and genetics are key causal factors which explain black athletic excellence. The much-quoted work of Martin Kane (1971) provides an example in which the writer suggests that certain physical characteristics – for example, longer legs than whites, narrower hips – are some of the key physical features that have determined why blacks as a 'race' have excelled in sport. Kane concluded that

blacks are innately different from whites and that such differences, being genetic in origin, can be passed from one generation to the next. As Cashmore (1996: 105) points out, Kane's arguments border on being racist and at least absurd given that anthropologists have long since dismissed the concept of race as having any analytical value. There is no natural reason why blacks should not excel in all sports and yet the danger of the proposal contained in the work of Kane is that such beliefs are not only believed, by some, but are used to systematically deny access to certain sports. For instance, despite the fact that men and women of colour have held world swimming records, the myth of the poor black swimmer has been often used against various 'coloured' communities. On the other hand, the natural ability argument is often promoted either to marginalize certain racial groups within the ghetto of sports at the expense of other sectors of society, or to be selective about the sports that ethnic minority and black groups participate in or have access to. Since at least the 1970s sport has been a route to fame and fortune for numerous black sportsmen and women and yet for thousands of others it continues to conceal deep inequalities, racist beliefs, and to be a path to failure and disappointment.

Concepts such as 'nation', 'race', 'ethnic' or 'religious' group are not the only concepts that can provide key interdependent reference points for the analysis of racial figurations. Many others, such as the 'sect', 'tribe', 'clan', 'town' or 'region' could be mentioned, too. But the key point is that, in many complex and different ways, such figurations, and others, form a kind of terrain in which the growth of racism is an observable facet of contemporary life for those groups who both promote and suffer from racist behaviour. While it is impossible in this chapter to provide an in-depth analysis and critique of all of the key sociological explanations of the relationship between sport, racism and ethnicity which have been proposed so far, it is possible to provide an insight and general overview of some of the central perspectives and traditions of social thought in this regard. The sporting examples that are used in each case are merely illustrative of deeper concerns and sociological issues.

SPORT IN AN EMERGING SOCIOLOGY OF RACE RELATIONS

As a field of social scientific enquiry and research, much of the early sociology of race relations originated in the work of American social theorists. Between 1920 and 1960, American studies of race concentrated upon the analysis of the social and economic inequalities suffered by a generic figuration invariably referred to as 'negroes' (as opposed to various 'peoples of colour' who may or may not have viewed their primary identity as being, for example, Spanish, Mexican, Italian or black Americans), their cultural and psychological make-up, family relations and political isolation. Following the work of Park, the dominant assumption seemed to be that race relations were types of social relations between different peoples (Park, 1950). In this early classical tradition one of the main features of such relations was a consciousness of racial difference. Functionalist theories assumed that an eventual assimilation of racially defined minorities into the majority host society would occur over time. Any conflict that might have emerged from insider and outsider relations was viewed as but a latent function that would lead ultimately to social equilibrium. Racial prejudice and discrimination were seen as temporary phenomena during a period of mutual adjustment. Ethnic minority groups were encouraged to abandon their own culture and way of life for that of the host culture. In the work of Park this cycle of assimilation consisted of four stages, namely contact, conflict, accommodation and assimilation.

In 1950s Britain, the emerging field of what was called at the time race studies was dominated by two main themes. First, was the issue of coloured immigrants and the racist reaction to them by white Britons. Most studies of this period concentrated on the interaction between specific groups of coloured immigrants and whites in local situations (Solomos, 1989). A second theme was the role played by colonial history and imperialism in determining popular conceptions of colour and race. By 1948, early Marxist theories of race had proposed that racism was but a ruling class ideology which developed under capitalism in order to divide – and hence control – black and white workers who shared a common and fundamental class identity (Cox, 1948). By 1948 apartheid in South Africa had also emerged. In much the same way, early Marxist accounts of South African race relations tended to argue that concepts such as race and class had a greater salience *vis-à-vis* other structural principles such as gender and religion. In the South African context race was viewed as class and class as race. Such arguments were criticized as being historically inaccurate, generalist, deterministic and irredeemably functionalist.

In South African race relations, the main critique of early Marxist writings was embodied in pluralism and in particular the work of Van den Berghe (Van den Berghe, 1969). A dominant theme within this work was that social class in the Marxian sense of determination by the relationship to the means of production was not a meaningful reality under apartheid since colour rather than ownership of land or capital was the most important criterion of status. Under apartheid, white academic pluralist analyses of South Africa were essentially polarized around several broad themes. As a society South Africa was seen as:

1 a 'plural society': apartheid was seen to be best explained in terms of segmentation into corporate groups often with different cultures;
2 having a social structure compartmentalized into analogous, parallel, non-complementary and distinguishable sets of institutions;
3 having a motor of development which was seen to be a form of ethnological determinism in which institutions were autonomous in relation to one another and functioned according to their own 'inner logic'; and
4 having a unique social formation which polarized into two components: a capitalist economic system which was harmonious, just and functional, and a system of racial domination, which was conducive to conflict, unjust and dysfunctional.

When sport was viewed within this pluralist approach it was seen in itself to be functionally supportive and integral to a multiracial South African society in which a plurality of groups competed within the framework of apartheid. A core part of the pluralist thesis on sport under apartheid was that South Africa experienced more domestic and international pressure than any other nation at the time because its case was deemed not simply to be unjust and racist, but also ideological. The political ideology of apartheid mediated sporting participation and provision in South Africa (Jarvie, 1985). The argument, put simply, was that sport, while having a degree of relative autonomy, was best explained in terms of racial segregation and racial discrimination. For pluralist writers on South African sport, sporting freedom and the dismantling of apartheid would be brought about through external pressures being brought to bear on South Africa. Such pressures themselves were viewed as being functional.

Other attempts were made during the 1960s and 1970s to develop a generalized sociological framework for the analysis of race, racism and race relations (Cashmore, 1996). A more sophisticated approach, built upon Weberian premises, was most clearly illustrated in the work of John Rex (Rex, 1983). What Rex called race relations situations involving a particular type of intergroup conflict resulted in racially categorized groups being distinctively located within an overall system of social stratification. In Britain, Rex used this framework to analyse differences in black and white life-chances and concluded that race and racial discrimination resulted in blacks being located at the bottom of and outside the main white class structure. Insofar as this created a distinctive form of consciousness and political action then the process of forging a black underclass was seen to be in the making.

NEO-MARXIST AND POST-MARXIST TRADITIONS

A considerable number of neo-Marxist and post-Marxist approaches have subsequently been developed. Some have looked to provide a less deterministic account of the relationship between race, class and capitalism (Robinson, 1981). At least three concerns are flushed out in the work of such writers as William Dubois, C.L.R. James, Richard Wright, Angela Davis and many other black radical writers:

1   that the whole basis of Marxism as a Western construction is a conceptualization of human affairs and human development which has been drawn from the experiences of European peoples and as such it loses much of its explanatory power when faced with non-Western evidence;
2   even allowing for Marxist–Leninist terms such as imperialism and colonialism or even a view of world development based upon a materialist understanding of history, Marxism failed to consider or question the existence of modern slavery or specific forms of exploitation born out of, for example, black poverty in America or black reserve armies of labour in numerous social formations (it has also been suggested that classical Marxism itself paid insufficient attention to slavery as a key phase in the materialist analysis of history;
3   that Marxism paid little attention to the way in which racism mediated the organization of labour, or itself, as an expression of alienation, made a specific contribution to revolutionary or reformist change born out of the struggle of, for example, African peoples (Jarvie and Maguire, 1994).

American writers such as Harry Edwards (1970, 1973) have written extensively on the events surrounding the political events witnessed at the 1968 Olympic Games in Mexico City. The 'Black Power' demonstrations by American athletes Tommy Smith and John Carlos were explained in the following terms (Jarvie and Maguire, 1994: 101):

> For years we have participated in the Olympic Games carrying the USA on our backs with our victories and race relations are worse than ever. We are not trying to lose the Olympics for America, what happens is immaterial. But it is time for the black people of the world to stand up as men and women and refuse to be utilised as performance animals in return for a little extra dog food.

As a Marxist-informed analysis of racism and race relations in American sport the work of Edwards (1970) was sympathetic to many of the central themes that would be included in the political economy of sport. Certainly some or all of the following questions were central to developing a political economy of black sport: How has wealth been produced from the exploitation of the black athlete? How have black sporting struggles affected the emancipation of black people? Why in the 'land of the free' (the USA) was it not until 1932 that Tydie Pickett and Louise Stokes became the first African American women to participate in the Olympic Games? Who profits from the play and display of black athletic talent? How are black people represented within positions of power and influence in the world of sport or leisure? To what extent are terms such as alienation, racial capitalism, imperialism and colonialism useful in explaining the development of black sporting experiences?

Of the black Marxist/black radical writers who have commented upon sport, pride of place belongs to C.L.R. James. *Beyond a Boundary* remains a classic statement on the relationship between cricket and Caribbean society during the 1950s and early 1960s (James, 1963). In it, James recognized that an almost fanatical obsession with organized games was not merely an innocent social activity but also a potential signifier of oppression and liberation. He provided a statement about not only an expanded conception of humanity but also the necessity to break out from the colonial legacy which had affected the development of the West Indies. In placing cricket centre stage, James attempted to transcend the division between high and popular art. The cricketer in the 1960s was seen as a modern expression of an individual personality pushing against the limits imposed upon his or her full development by society (class/colonial/ nation/periphery). Non-white cricket came first to challenge then overthrow the domination of West Indian cricket by members of the white plantocracy. By the 1980s some writers had argued that the transformation of West Indian cricket had come full circle from being a symbol of cultural imperialism to being a symbol of Creole nationalism (Burton, 1991).

BLACK FEMINISM, IDENTITY POLITICS AND SPORT

Sojourner Truth's famous question 'Ain't I a woman?' was asked in the middle of the nineteenth century, and yet it remains a pertinent question that might be asked of many feminist writings on sport and leisure – although the forthcoming intervention by Professor Jennifer Hargreaves will alter this position. There is simply no black feminist intervention in sport or leisure equivalent to that made by C.L.R. James in *Beyond a Boundary* and yet black feminist thought has yielded a radical critique of both the sociology of sport and white European feminism (Mathewson, 1996; Plowden, 1995). The existence of athletes such as Anna Quirot, Esther Kiplagat, Lydia Cheromei, Derartu Tulu, Merlynne Ottey, Phyllis Watt, Jennifer Stoute and Hassiba Boulmerka could help to open up the history and experiences of black women athletes in Cuba, Kenya, Ethiopia, Jamaica, Great Britain and Algeria. Such case studies would be capable of not only opening up a broader understanding of identity politics but also of the role of sport in black communities.

For example, the case of Hassiba Boulmerka may be illustrative of a much-loved Arab African sporting woman forced at a particular moment in her athletic career to leave Algeria for France in order to escape a backlash from Muslim zealots (*The Independent*, 12 August 1991). Winner of the women's 1500 metres final at the World athletic championships in 1991, Boulmerka became the first Algerian, the first Arab and the first African woman to win a gold medal at any World athletic championships. On her return to Algeria, the then President Chadli Benjedid greeted her as a national heroine. But Muslim zealots denounced her from the pulpit for baring her most intimate parts (her legs) before millions of television viewers. Furthermore, President Benjedid was himself publicly denounced for embracing a woman in public. The row underscored the clash between modernity and Islamic traditionalism, the fastest growing social and political force in Algeria. It was a clash which

was all the more surprising given Algeria's position in the Arab world as the torchbearer of modernism, socialism and successful struggle for independence from colonial rule.

Women were emancipated early in Algeria's national struggle. They were obliged to carry out many tasks their husbands were unable to fulfil because they were dead, imprisoned or fighting against France. Since then, however, the progress made by Algerian women has been under threat. At the time there had been only two women ministers in the government, and parliament refused to pass a law to end the traditional practice of men voting by proxy for their womenfolk. Women in the mid-1990s made up less than a fifth of the paid workforce; 800,000 in a population of 25 million. Hassiba Boulmerka moved to France and the Islamicists lost an opportunity to promote national unity in Algeria. For if ever there was a modern popular figure in Algeria – one who had taken on the world and won – it was Hassiba Boulmerka.

All subjugated knowledges, such as black women's sporting history and biography, develop in cultural contexts. Dominant groups often aim to replace subjugated knowledge with their own specialized thought because they realize that gaining control over this dimension of the lives of members of subordinate groups simplifies control (Hill-Collins, 1990). While efforts to influence this dimension of oppressed groups' experiences can be partially successful, this level is more difficult to control than dominant groups would have us believe. For example, adhering to externally derived standards of beauty leads many African American women to dislike their skin colour or hair texture. Similarly, internalizing Eurocentric gender ideology leads some black men to abuse black women. These may be seen as a successful infusion of a dominant group's specialized thought into the everyday cultural context of African Americans. But the longstanding existence of a black women's blues tradition, and the voices of contemporary African American women writers all attest to the difficulty of eliminating the cultural contexts as fundamental sites of resistance.

Certainly the development of a tradition of black feminist writing on sport would help to challenge Eurocentric, masculinist and feminist thought which has at times pervaded the sociology of sport. Empowerment in sport has often meant black women rejecting existing personal, cultural and institutional structures that have historically supported racism. The practice of black feminist thinkers during the late 1980s and early 1990s necessitated an understanding of the relations between personal sporting biography and the history of sporting relations in various countries. Many of the personal troubles that black sportswomen in Britain, America and Africa experienced were in fact related to broader structural dynamics and meanings such as those that have been articulated through racism. Angela Davis wrote more forcefully on this issue when she argued that there is something in the nature of racism's role in society that permits those who have come through the ranks of struggles against it to have a clearer comprehension of the totality of oppression (Davis, 1989), the analogy being that white women must learn to acknowledge this as a potential starting point for not only understanding black women's experiences of sport but also oppression in general.

ESTABLISHED-OUTSIDER RELATIONS

One of the most sophisticated approaches to the study of race relations is to be found in work emanating from the sociology of Norbert Elias (Elias and Scotson, 1965/1994). At least two key principles dominated the sociological thought of Norbert Elias. First, he was concerned to understand the process of civilization which he defined as a process in which the balance between external restraints on behaviour and internal moral regulation changes in favour of the latter. Secondly, he criticized functionalism and structuralism for their tendency to reify social processes, and argued instead for a figurational or processual approach to sociology, that is, a conceptualization and testing of the constant and endless processual flux of all social relationships. With specific reference to the field of race relations it is the notion of established-outsider relations which is most pertinent to the discussion at hand (Elias and Scotson, 1965/1994). Drawing on Elias, Mennell raises the issue of the very terms race or ethnic relations perhaps being symptomatic of an action in ideological avoidance (Mennell, 1992). Their use serves to single out for attention peripheral aspects of these specific relations such as differences of skin colour and fails to recognize that which is central to an adequate understanding of race relations, namely differences of power – that is, race relations are simply established-outsider relations of a particular type and, as such, are characterized by differential power chances and the exclusion of less powerful groups from positions with a higher power potential.

Four particular features of the established-outsider figuration located in the work of Elias and Scotson (1965/1994) are worth special mention:

1 the tendency of members of established groups to perceive outsiders as law breakers and status violators or, as Dunning (1996: 13) points out 'in Elias's terms as anomic';
2 the tendency for the established to judge outsiders in terms of the minority of the worst, that is, in terms of the minority of outsiders who actually do break the law and violate standards;
3 the tendency for outsiders to accept the established group's stigmatization of them, that is to internalize the group charisma of the dominant group and their own group disgrace;
4 the tendency for the established to view outsiders as in some way unclean.

Under specific circumstances race relations may take on some or all of the above characteristics and as such it follows that such features may be part of certain sporting relations that involve established-outsider relations. Some of these relations may involve some or all of the above features. One of the many strengths of Eliasian research into sport, racism and race relations is that it rejects universal, law-like relationships as forming the key to explaining the balance of power between social groups.

Racial, gender and class bonds of interdependence may in fact be relatively determining, yet the degree of determination is flexible and specific to any particular form of development. The complex interaction of race and class dynamics in South Africa has often concealed other multifaceted forms of bonding, not least of which have been religious and national lines of interdependence between different groups. To apply the notion of established-outsider theory to race relations shows how the relations between different racial groups can be studied in the same way as relations between many other groups with unequal power chances. Thus, the main weight of any explanation of racial inequality, like any other social inequality, must rest on how groups come to impinge upon and have power over each other. Elias's theory of established-outsider relations has, for example, recently been utilized in laying the foundation of a figurational/process sociological understanding of the part played by sport in the development of race relations in the United States of America (Dunning, 1999). Such an analysis has involved, first, the conceptualization of race relations as involving fundamentally a question of power, and secondly, an exploration of the social conditions under which sporting prowess can become an embodied power resource, part of a habitus that has been used to offset disadvantages of racial inequality.

A NEW POLITICS OF RACE AND RACISM: A BLACK CRITIQUE

Mention must also be made of what came to be termed in the early 1990s 'the new politics of race and racism'. Underlying this new politics is a deep ambivalence amongst certain groups of social and political activists about the traditional categories that have been used to defend racist practices and policy. These identifications, it has been suggested, have been grounded in notions of the superiority of whites, Eurocentric discourses and the politics of 'otherness' (Gilroy, 1995; Giroux and McLaren, 1994). Within this genre of writing, the relationship between identity and being 'black' is seen as neither fixed nor secure in the sense that people take on different, changing identities and points of reference. It is an approach which challenges 'whiteness' as the universal norm. At stake here is an attempt to create a different kind of vocabulary for representing racism, race and border relations, that is, relationships that cross national boundaries. Central to this approach is the recognition that central concepts such as 'race', 'ethnicity' and 'black' should always appear historically in articulation with other categories and divisions such as class and gender.

Dyson has suggested that while the physical prowess of the black body has in the 1990s been acknowledged and exploited as a fertile zone of profit within mainstream American athletic society, the symbolic dangers of black sporting excellence also need to be highlighted (Dyson, 1994). Because of its marginalized status within the overall sphere of American sports, black athletic activity, argues Dyson, has often acquired a social significance that transcends the internal dimensions of the game, sport and skill. Black sport becomes an arena for testing the limits of physical endurance and forms of athletic excellence – while at the same time repudiating or symbolizing the American ideals (often mythical) of justice, goodness, truth and beauty. It also becomes a way of ritualizing racial achievement against socially or economically imposed barriers to sporting performance

(Dyson, 1994). That is to say that American athletes might have all been equal on the starting line but the social, economic, political and emotional struggles that any given athlete has to overcome to reach the starting line are far from equal.

Black sportspersons in America have often acquired the celebrity status of a heroine or hero, as viewed in the careers of people such as Joe Louis, Jackie Robinson, Althea Gibson, Wilma Rudolph, Mohammed Ali, Arthur Ashe, Carl Lewis, Michael Jordan, Valerie Brisco-Hooks, Evelyn Ashford, Florence Griffith-Joyner and, more recently, Tiger Woods. Such black sporting heroes and heroines have transcended the narrow boundaries of specific sports activities and have gained importance as icons of cultural excellence. Such people became symbolic figures who embodied the celebrity possibilities of success that were often denied other people of colour. They also captured and catalysed a black cultural fetishism for sport as a means of expressing a particular form of black cultural style and identity (Dyson, 1994). Sport was viewed as a vehicle for valorizing black power, sporting skills as a means of marking racial self-expression and sporting profit as a means of pursuing social and economic mobility.

The danger of valorizing a black sports industry or black culture industry is clearly spelled out in works by Cashmore (1997) and Hoberman (1997). More specifically, the question that is posed is can there be such a thing as authentic black culture when the industry, including the sports industry, that produces it is controlled by white-owned corporations? In developing a history of black culture in the West from the post-emancipation period to the present, Cashmore (1997: 172–81) argues that inflating the value of a commodified black culture may actually work against the interests of racial justice. Cashmore asserts that black entrepreneurs, when they have reached the top of the industry, have tended to act in much the same manner as their white counterparts in similar circumstances. They failed to destabilize the racial hierarchy and yet remained part of an African American elite.

CONCLUDING REMARKS

Any theoretical discussion within the postmodernist era is likely to end up in a discursive quagmire, a kind of epistemological equivalent of quicksand or a Scottish bog. Attempts to cling to theoretical or substantive realism or the interdependence between the two in the eclectic world of the twenty-first century remains difficult and yet, in conclusion, three observations can be made. First, that while anti-historical or non-developmental forms of explanation may supply useful insights into certain social experiences, including those that manifest themselves within racist and anti-pacifist contexts, they are a perilous guide to action. The practice of racism in sport is no modern phenomenon that has just emerged but has in fact resulted from a number of intended and unintended processes all of which have had a much longer development than many modern writers on the subject would seem to allow. Indeed not all social or historical problems may be sociological problems, but sociology and history certainly have something to say about sport, racism, ethnicity, anti-racist movements, black power, black feminism, racial prejudice, anti- semitism and a black perspective (Sammons, 1994; Wiggins, 1995).

Secondly, the danger of universalism is a very real one. This is not to deny different theories of race relations their travel but to caution against their universality as a way of explaining different situations throughout the globe. Perhaps a strong distinction needs to be made between the claims of any one explanation of racial tension, racism, or sport and its travelling authority as a blank generic imprimatur. Edward Said (1994) is worth listening to when he asks: 'Why is it that Islam and postmodernism or ethnicity and postmodernism are either mutually exclusive or irrelevant?' Why should such constituencies update themselves in the name of a postmodern epistemology or condition? If the historical and substantive irrelevance of the subject matter to the constituencies of postmodernism is demonstrable, why should, for example, Islamic fundamentalists find room for such a theory within their internal structures? Why should any anti-racist or black power movement hitch their interests to an alien body of knowledge and risk solidarity among themselves?

Finally, it might be suggested that racism is not merely an expression of particularism, or the way in which different racial and ethnic groups reject and accept modernity at different rates. Many postmodernists have argued for the unity of racism in the sense that it combines the two basic logics of inferiorization and differentiation and also the disjunction between universalist and particularist values. Such an argument is rejected in this chapter on the grounds that the specific, substantive and developmental analysis of sport, racism and ethnicity will take us much further forward

than broad generalizations, which have been the main focus of the specific overview provided here.

Acknowledgements

I am grateful for the comments and advice provided by Professor Dunning and Professor Coakley on an earlier draft of this chapter.

REFERENCES

Bairner, A. (1998) 'Civic and ethnic forms of nationalism in Northern Ireland', in G. Jarvie (ed.) *Sport in the Making of Celtic Cultures*. London: Cassells. pp. 10–28.

Burton, R. (1991) 'Cricket, carnival and street culture in the Caribbean', in G. Jarvie (ed.) *Sport, Racism and Ethnicity*. Sussex: Falmer Press. pp. 7–29.

Cashmore, E. (1996) *Making Sense of Sport*. London: Routledge.

Cashmore, E. (1997) *The Black Culture Industry*. London: Routledge.

Collins, P. Hill (1990) *Black Feminist Thought*. London: Unwin Hyman.

Cox, O. (1948) *Caste, Class and Race*. New York: Monthly Review Press.

Davis, A. (1989) 'Complexity, activism, optimism', *Feminist Review*, 37 (1).

Dunning, E. (1999) *Sport Matters: Sociological Studies of Sport, Violence and Civilization*. London: Routledge.

Dyson, M. (1994) 'Be like Mike? Michael Jordan and the pedagogy of desire', in H. Giroux and P. McLaren (eds), *Between Borders: Pedagogy and the Politics of Cultural Studies*. New York: Routledge. pp. 119–27.

Edwards, H. (1970) *The Revolt of the Black Athlete*. New York: Free Press.

Edwards, H. (1973) *Sociology of Sport*. Homewood, IL: Dorsey Press.

Elias, N. and Scotson, J. (1965/1994) *The Established and the Outsider: a Sociological Enquiry into Community Problems*. London: Frank Cass.

Galton, F. (1904) 'The study of engenics', *American Journal of Sociology*, 10 (1): 1–25.

Gilroy, P. (1995) *The Black Atlantic*. London: Routledge.

Giroux, H. and McLaren, P. (1994) *Between Borders: Pedagogy and the Politics of Cultural Studies*. New York: Routledge.

Hoberman, J. (1997) *Darwin's Athletes*. New York. Free Press.

James, C.L.R. (1963) *Beyond a Boundary*. London: Stanley Paul.

Jarvie, G. (1985) *Class, Race and Sport in South Africa's Political Economy*. London: Routledge.

Jarvie, G. (1991) *Sport, Racism and Ethnicity*. Sussex: Falmer Press.

Jarvie, G. and Maguire, J. (1994) *Sport and Leisure in Social Thought*. London: Routledge.

Kane, M. (1971) 'An assessment of Black is Best', *Sports Illustrated*, 18 January.

Mathewson, A. (1996) 'Nobody knows her name: the Black American sportswoman'. Unpublished paper presented at the North American Society for the Sociology of Sport Annual Conference, Birmingham, Alabama, November.

Mennell, S. (1992) *Norbert Elias: an Introduction*. Oxford: Basil Blackwell.

Park, R. (1950) *Race and Culture*. New York: Free Press.

Plowden, M. (1995) *Olympic Black Women*. Gretna: Pelican Publishing.

Rex, J. (1983) *Race Relations in Sociological Theory*. London: Routledge.

Robinson, C. (1981) *Black Marxism*. London: Zed Press.

Said, E. (1994) *Culture and Imperialism*. London: Vintage.

Sammons, J. (1994) 'Race and sport: a critical, historical explanation', *Journal of Sport History*, No. 1 (Spring): 203–77.

Smith, A. (1996) *Theories of Nationalism*. London: Macmillan.

Solomos, J. (1989) *Race and Racism in Contemporary Britain*. London: Macmillan.

Steinberg, S. (1989) *The Ethnic Myth: Race, Ethnicity and Class in America*. Boston, MA: Beacon Press.

Tocqueville, A. (1968) *Democracy in America*, Volume 1 (trans. George Lawrence). London: Collins–Fontana.

Van den Berghe, P. (1969) *Race and Racism*. New York: John Wiley.

Van den Berghe, P. (1981) *The Ethnic Phenomenon*. New York: Elsevier.

Weber, M. (1978) *Economy and Society*, Volume 1 (trans. Ephraim Fischoff). Berkeley–Los Angeles, CA: University of California Press.

Wieviorka, M. (1995) *The Arena of Racism*. London: Sage Publications.

Wiggins, D. (1995) *Sport in America: From Wicked Amusement to National Obsession*. Champaign, IL: Human Kinetics.

22

SPORT AND NATIONALISM

Lincoln Allison

NATIONAL IDENTITY IN SPORT

Do we have to go into this every year? In the United States it is more important that the Red Sox beat the Yankees or the 49ers beat the Bears than the fact that some kid who was born in California is the best in the world at returning serve … Yes, there is a modicum of pride that Agassi and Sampras were born in the land of the free and the home of Divine Brown. But in America we're less interested in where you're from than how you play … What we don't miss is people rooting for athletes because of their nationality rather than their skill. (Spander, 1995)

Thus Art Spander, the American sports columnist, reacting to being asked at the 1995 Wimbledon Tennis Championships how Americans would feel if Pete Sampras lost to the Japanese player Shuzo Matsuoka, given the economic tensions between the two countries. He might have turned his scorn on the Wimbledon crowd for the fanatical enthusiasm with which they greeted the performances of Greg Rusedski, a Canadian of partly English, partly Polish descent who had declared himself to be British from the point of view of international tennis.

The obvious hypothesis here might be the familiar invocation of American exceptionalism. The United States is in no sense an ethnic nation and international team games are only a tiny part of its sporting scene. They *do* sing their national anthem at sporting events, but not in the same sort of way that a Welsh rugby crowd sings '*Mae hen wlad fy nhadau*' (Land of my Fathers) or a Scottish crowd 'Flower of Scotland', both being tales of blood and sacrifice; thus in Britain children will pick up concepts of nationality entwined with their

ideas about sport. Even their notion of colour may start with blue for Scotland, red for Wales, green for Ireland and white for England.

On a second look, though, the American exceptionalism may be rather less exceptional than it appears as presented by Art Spander. Experienced non-American commentators on the Los Angeles Olympic Games in 1984 were generally agreed that the crowds and the presentation were the most nationalistic they had experienced. Commentators from five continents (including neighbours Canada) reacted even more strongly against American media presentation of the Atlanta Games in 1996, accusing it of 'chauvinism' and 'xenophobia'. When an American representative team finds itself in a real battle with non-American teams as, for example, the 1976 'college' Olympics basketball team did against the USSR or as successive US teams have in Ryder Cup golf since 1983, they arouse audience responses little different from those in nationalistic Europe. Indeed, most European press coverage following the 1999 Ryder Cup stressed what was described as the 'excessive' and 'distasteful' nationalism of the American crowd though it should be said that these comments were based on European golfing standards rather than European sporting standards defined more broadly. And that may be only a very superficial part of the national dimension in American sport, which can be said to be national at a far deeper level. American sport is dominated by games which are manifestly, proudly, even aggressively American. As with many other sports, in many other parts of the world, the expression of nationality lies more in the choice of sport than in the support for a team. Like much nationalism, the development of American sport did not take place entirely by accident, and absorbs a quantity of mythology. It is not merely myth, but official myth, for example, that baseball is an American game invented by Abner Doubleday at Cooperstown in 1839. Baseball is as demonstrably English as apple pie (and as cricket). It was well known by that name and as 'rounders' in the eighteenth century. In more recent years Senator Jack Kemp, a former professional (American) footballer and 1996 vice-presidential candidate has favourably compared his sport with the 'collectivist' and 'socialist' milieu of European soccer.

But whether we are talking about nationalism or patriotism or the development and expression of national identity – the matter of distinction will have to be suspended for the moment – it is clear that a national dimension is an important part of sport. This dimension starts with the immense added meaning that a sense of shared national identity gives to watching a team and (sometimes) an individual perform. This is put simply by Alan Sharpe, describing the experience of watching Scotland play football: 'For a time before, throughout and after [the match] I have the feeling that my personal worth is bound up with Scotland's success or failure' (Archer, 1976: 76). It is this intense feeling of identification which is the kernel of the relationship between sport and nationality.

There are, of course, other forms of identification, but none is so intense and demanding as a national identification, particularly in those many nations which are perceived by their members as being ancient and with a history of oppression, engendering a sense of loyalty that can be more like that to a tribe than to a modern institution. Thus there can be a collective sense of national humiliation when a national team is defeated; the event is taken to reflect on the state of the nation as a whole, quite apart from sport, and potentially on the standing of governments and politicians. In England, this is particularly apparent in the press treatment of defeats for the England cricket and football teams, as Joseph Maguire has documented (Maguire, 1995). But I have also been impressed by the intense collective sporting ambition and frustration experienced by the military-industrial elite in Thailand. This became apparent when I spoke to a conference in Bangkok in February 1995 at which the Thai Minister of Sport and most of the leading sports officials were present. It was clear that the central question of 'the politics of sport' concerned how national success might be organized and financed. Success in this case meant a high position in the medals table of the

Asian Games or any Olympic gold medal. The significance of such success to the elite became evident a year later when Somluck Khamsing became the first Thai to win an Olympic gold medal (for boxing). A grateful government awarded him $1.5 million in cash, a BMW car and a PhD (in Physical Education). This was by far the most substantial award made by a government to an Olympic champion.

The organization of modern sport has readily absorbed a national dimension. As organized games became institutionalized in the British Isles between 1860 and 1890, it was absolutely natural to add 'England v. Scotland' and 'England v. Wales' to an imaginative list of fixtures which included 'Oxford v. Cambridge' 'Gentlemen v. Players' and (often) 'Married Men v. Bachelors'. England played Scotland at football from 1872, barring world wars, until disorders and other commitments intervened in 1990. The two nations have competed at rugby union since 1871. Since the Scottish, the Welsh and the Irish barely played cricket, the attractions of an international dimension were more difficult for an England cricket team, but the problem was solved in 1882 when an Australian team defeated England in England for the first time and the *Sporting Times* referred to the death and cremation of English cricket: competition for the 'Ashes' has remained one of cricket's premier events ever since. In all three of these major sports, the code needed the stimulus of competition between nations and such competition was a natural expression of the national identities which people felt. 'British' teams have only come into existence because of organizations that insist on a nation-state identity, such as the Olympic Games. It is a paradox that Britain has been the origin of modern international sport which has blossomed, in the case of all three of the major English sports, into World Cups (in football from 1930, in cricket from 1975 and in rugby union from 1987), yet the existence of four national teams in football within the United Kingdom has often been seen as odd by outsiders. In some respects it is odd: that the Soviet Union, with its fifteen republics and 'hundred nationalities' and Yugoslavia, with its six republics and proverbial ethnic complexity, each fielded only one international football team while the British Isles had no fewer than five *is* odd. But the fates of the Soviet Union and Yugoslavia are illuminating in this respect.

If modern sport embraced international competition without question when it developed in the British Isles, the same assumptions were also made by the Olympic movement. The

Olympics have always thrived on international competition, their symbolic internationalism coexisting with, and being parasitic upon, the national symbols of flags and anthems and the publication of medals tables. The competition was predominantly Anglo-American in the early years, and for 40 years was bound up with the Cold War. De Coubertin recognized the potency of national aspirations in the popularity of the games and successive presidents of the IOC (and major participants such as the Soviet Union) have been resolute against the banning of nationality motifs in the games, as against the inclusion of stateless persons (Hill, 1993; Hoberman, 1986).

The power of the meaning of national identity in sport is something that has always been recognized by the supposedly amateur and non-commercial Olympic movement. But the commercial aspect of this power and its consequences for overtly professional sport are enormous. Television inevitably changes the status of a national team: in the pre-television era, we must watch our local team; the national team may play hundreds or (in Australia) even thousands of miles away, but television allows us all to support a national team. National identity is the most marketable product in sport. An English audience for football which normally had a ceiling of around ten million could leap to 32 million for the England–Brazil World Cup match in 1970. Women compose a small (though increasing) minority of football fans, around 7–12 per cent, but they were 44 per cent of the audience for England's games in the 1990 World Cup.

Both cricket and rugby have responded strongly to the commercial dominance of international games; in both cases the international level of the game was dominant even before the arrival of television. In neither game, for example, was it ever thought normal or proper for a player to turn down an opportunity to play for his country in order to play for his club. In both games the live televising of international matches was established at the outset of television's history. In both cases, world cups were invented with the global television market in mind. In cricket, the emphasis on televised international cricket was increased by the affair of the 'Packer Circus' in 1977: the Australian entrepreneur and media magnate Kerry Packer, protesting the exclusion of his network from rights to televise the Australian team, contracted four international squads to play in a 'World Series' to be televised by his Channel 9. The affair ended in compromise, but it accelerated the process whereby top cricketers play many more international matches than they did and many fewer matches of any other kind.

In Association football, the balance was always very different. In most countries the game has been about passionate club affiliation and, except on great occasions like the World Cup, the international form of the game has been less important than the club form. I have elsewhere illustrated the significance of a week in May 1988 when a minor club game at Wembley Stadium in London (Burnley *v.* Wolverhampton Wanderers) was watched by more than three times as many people as watched two of the world's top international sides (England *v.* Colombia) (Allison, 1988). In football, it has often been more important and more prestigious to play for Manchester United or Liverpool than for England or Wales. The authorities of the game in many European countries have been dominated by club interests which have been resistant to television and to any expansion of the international level of the game. One legendary English football club chairman, Bob Lord of Burnley, even threatened to burn any cameras that were brought into his stadium (Lord, 1963). In England, even recorded football was not regularly televised until 1964, more than a decade after live cricket and rugby were established and regular live football only came on television because of the competition from and influence of Rupert Murdoch's global satellite network in the 1990s. It is this which has undermined the traditional dominance of the live supporter, created a new breed of superstars and ensured that international forms of the game (including, in this case, international club competitions) will dominate both money and status in the game.

Perhaps the best-known example of an expression of identification with a national team came from the late Bjoerge Lillelien when Norway beat England 2–1 at football in 1981. Lillelien, who was doing the television commentary, went into a kind of nationalist rant-reverie. Some of the most famous words in his monologue were, 'William Shakespeare … Winston Churchill … Maggie Thatcher … we gave your boys a hell of a beating'. He spoke, it should be noted, to a Norwegian audience in English, as if he wanted his domestic listeners to know that the message was to be received by a wider world (which it duly was: English radio and television have repeated the monologue, lasting just over a minute, at regular intervals since). Here is a fairly pure example of identification; Norway is not entirely homogenous ethnically, having two languages and a Lapp minority, but it is about as homogenous ethnically as anywhere on earth, with even 94 per cent subscribing to the official (Lutheran) Norwegian established church. Thus a commentator like Lillelien can say 'we' in a way that almost seems like family and speak for his audience as he does so; he is in quite a different position from a middle-aged white commentator describing the feats of a predominantly black basketball or sprint relay team in the United States (or, for that matter, in Britain or France).

It is important to note that this fairly pure and straightforward identification of an overwhelming majority of a population with a team or with any other sporting institution is very much the exception rather than the rule: most cases are more complex and the idea of nationality which is represented by any given expression of sporting nationhood is usually divisive in some way. There are, first, the multinational states, including those like the Soviet Union and Yugoslavia when they existed, but also Spain and the United Kingdom. On the whole, sports associations and the relevant state agencies have been in favour of a single 'national' team per state and this has been encouraged by international federations. The United Kingdom is an exception in this respect; separate teams for England, Scotland, Wales and Ireland or Northern Ireland existed originally because they represented the only possibility of international competition, but they have persisted because of a fundamental British separation of the ideas of state and nation and because of their commercial viability. The anomalies seem less now that both the Soviet Union and Yugoslavia have collapsed and their constituent nationalities are represented in international sport.

Georgians have admitted to me that they did feel pride when they saw an athlete from the 'Soviet Motherland', usually a Russian, mount the rostrum to receive a gold medal at the Olympics or other major championships, even though they always thought of themselves as Georgians and have now come to reject the Soviet Union and want nothing to do with Russia. There were, so to speak, two separate and compatible levels of nationality. In Western multinational countries sporting sentiments have usually gone with the nation, even for those who accept or support the state. Catalans are notoriously poor supporters of the Spanish national football team and the Scots in particular tend to resent any 'British' team as being an English conception of 'England with extras'. The English cricket team is a complex institution in this respect: Wales and Scotland do not have teams that play at the highest ('Test') level of the game, so Welshmen and Scotsmen capable of playing at this level are treated as English. Even so, or perhaps for this reason, the late John Rafferty, one of Scotland's best-known sports journalists, used to exhort his readers to support all-comers against England on principle.

Conversely, there are several cases of nations denied national sports representation vesting their passion in a club. I have written elsewhere of how F.C. Barcelona has always been associated with the Catalan language and Catalan nationalism and how this representative role intensified during the Franco period between 1939 and 1975 (Allison, 1986: 1–3). In the Soviet Union Dinamo Kiev and Dinamo Tbilisi were focuses of national enthusiasm for Ukrainians and Georgians respectively. In the post-Soviet absence of this function as a national institution these clubs have struggled to maintain interest. In 1995 I watched Dinamo Tbilisi play Durugi in front of two hundred spectators in a stadium designed to seat 80,000. The Croatian clubs Dinamo Zagreb and Hadjuk Split were also examples of an international dimension within a supposedly national league when they played in the Yugoslav competition. (In Britain fans often unconsciously mimic this situation when the Welsh teams in the lower divisions of English professional competition – Cardiff, Swansea and Wrexham – play their usual English opponents.) An interesting set of stories about football and identification is to be found in Simon Kuper's book *Football Against the Enemy* (Kuper, 1994).

It is often legitimate to question which nation a national team represents where there are different conceptions of national identity. The clearest case and one of the best researched is that of Ireland. Association football in Ireland follows state boundaries, with separate teams for Northern Ireland and the Republic. Rugby Union, on the other hand, has an all-Ireland team which includes both Southern catholics and Northern protestants (rarely Southern protestants, very rarely Northern catholics). There are, in any case, the Gaelic games devised and organised by the Gaelic Athletic Association since 1884; these are principally Gaelic football and hurling and there is little possibility of international competition in these sports, except that hurling is broadly similar to the Scottish Highland game called shinty and there have been compromised code games between Gaelic and Australian Rules football representative teams, despite their playing with different-shaped balls (Sugden and Bairner, 1986, 1993a, 1993b).

All of these sports represent a different island. Gaelic sports have had an image deriving most of their history of being deeply 'fenian' or nationalist, Celtic, anti-British and 'taig' (peasant). These aspects of their existence were most controversially expressed by the ban on participants in 'British' sports, which was lifted in 1971; there remains a ban on participants who have ever served in the British armed forces. At the other end of the spectrum, the Northern Ireland football team represents 'hard line' protestant Unionism; very few catholics attend games and the crowd tend to be hostile to catholic players selected for their own team, especially if they play or have played for traditionally catholic clubs such as Glasgow Celtic. By contrast, the Irish rugby team has relatively aloof and 'West British' supporters who think of the violent commitments of Irish politics as being anachronistic and rather embarrassing; Irish rugby tends to be supported by the middle classes who also play golf and go game fishing, two other sports organized on an all-Ireland basis.

This leaves the Republic of Ireland's football team; of the four elements in this sporting scene, it is the most recent to come to prominence, having had fairly successful campaigns in the European Nations Championships of 1988 and the World Cups of 1990 and 1994, without previously making much impact on world football. All of this has been achieved under an English management team with no Irish connections (Jack Charlton and Maurice Setters) and a majority of English-born players of Irish extraction. The sense of identity which this team and its support suggests is a different kind of Irishness: cosmopolitan, urban, modern, flippant and with a strong affinity for English and American popular culture, though not for the English Establishment. Supporters strongly identify with a broad Irish diaspora rather than with catholic rural Ireland. There was a closely fought referendum on divorce in the Republic in November 1995; during the campaign there was much reference to a deep division between an 'old' and a 'new' Ireland. If the Gaelic Athletic Association is about the 'old' Ireland, the football team is strongly associated with the images of the 'new' Ireland (Doyle, 1993).

Ireland may be an extreme contrast to Norway in the fissiparity of its identity, but there are many countries that share some of its complexities. The Scottish football team, for example, also expresses significant vestiges of the religious and political wars which rent the British Isles in the seventeenth century. It may unite the politically opposed forces of Unionism and Nationalism, but it does still represent a *protestant* Scotland. In one survey, 52 per cent of (catholic) Celtic fans said they would support the Republic of Ireland against Scotland and some catholic fans even attend international matches to cheer for the opposition (Bradley, 1995). For example, a letter of complaint in the *Daily Record* after the Scotland versus Poland game in May 1990 alleged that, 'Some fans were even willing Jacki Dziekanowski to score for Poland' (*Daily Record*, 21 May) (Dziekanowski was one of two Poles playing for Celtic at the time). By contrast, the identity sought and approved by Scottish rugby fans seems to have changed dramatically. Until the 1960s they were thought of as representing a form of conservative, middle-class unionism; certainly, they sang 'God Save the Queen' loudly and loyally. By the 1990s the approved anthem had become the nationalist (and anti-English) 'Flower of Scotland'.

South African rugby and cricket teams in the period between the Nationalist Party's victory and institution of *apartheid* and the onset of the sport boycotts, that is between 1948 and 1970, clearly represented ethnic minorities. The rugby team was identified with the Afrikaners and the cricket team with the English, though some Afrikaners played for the cricket team and some anglophones for the rugby team. The overwhelming non-white majority, if they took any interest at all, supported any opponent against the representatives of their oppressors. However, the 'new' South Africa, following the election of President Nelson Mandela in 1994, appears to have shown a broadening of identification with national teams that are still overwhelmingly white. The 1995 Rugby World Cup continued a process which seemed to begin with the 1992 Cricket World Cup of people classified as black, coloured and Indian under *apartheid* coming to support the rugby and cricket teams: this change was most clearly symbolized by President Mandela wearing a Springbok shirt at the 1995 Rugby World Cup Final. No symbol of South Africa had been more purely the property of the Afrikaners than the springbok and the African National Congress had originally been committed to its abolition.

The Afrikaner affinity for rugby exemplifies a further complexity of the relationship between sport and national identity: particular sports can come to be seen to exemplify the spirit of a nation. I have already remarked on a form of this relation in the case of American exceptionalism in sport, but there are many important cases of borrowed traditions. Association football is not easily portrayed as anyone's 'national' sport; even in Brazil and Italy where its place in the culture is huge, it is recognized as a global institution. But there are several important cases of borrowed traditions. Indians are wont to remark that 'Cricket is an Indian game accidentally invented by the English', arguing that the tactical subtlety of the game and its timescale are more suitable to Indian culture than to English. Rugby is also seen as the 'national' pastime of Afrikaners, Welshmen and New Zealanders. In the Welsh case, nationalists originally opposed Welshmen playing rugby as yet another form of English acculturalization, much in the spirit of those Irish nationalists who established the Gaelic Athletic Association in 1884. It is also true that many of the great 'Welsh' rugby players were actually English; the Welsh Rugby Union defined players as Welsh if they played for a Welsh club, and in the greatest of all Welsh victories, the unofficial 'world championship' win over New Zealand in 1905, the Welsh captain, the pack leader and the full-back were all Englishmen. Yet it was already being argued that 'Rugby is ... the game of the Welshman'. As Dai Smith comments, 'Rugby had become "Welsh" ... because ... the social function had merged with sporting success to become a focus for nationality' (Smith, 1984: 35). The combination of club life and communal support, of the wholehearted physical and emotional commitment which the game requires, of the singing and music of the crowd which can inspire it, had come to seem more Welsh than English. It served to assimilate and make Welsh that quarter of the population of industrial South Wales who had flocked over the border from England to share in the coal and steel boom of late Victorian Wales. These people were excluded by the core criterion of Welshness, the language. Rugby played an important part in creating a new Welsh identity, so much so that some twentieth-century nationalists have conceded that the *only* thing that unites all Welshmen is support for 15 men in scarlet jerseys. It has not been necessary for the creation of this identity that players all 'represented' the national community in the simple sense of being drawn from it. During the 1990s an increasing number of able rugby players from the Southern hemisphere redefined themselves as Europeans in order to make the breakthrough into international rugby. Shane Haworth, a New Zealander who claimed to have a Welsh grandmother, represented Wales at full-back in the 1999 World Cup; he let it be known that he had had a

Welsh fleur-de-lys tattooed on one of his buttocks to complement the New Zealand fern which appeared indelibly on the other.

NATIONS, NATIONALISM, PATRIOTISM

So far, I have discussed the importance of national identity in sport (and to sport), ignoring two huge questions: What is a nation? and What is the significance of nationalism (as opposed to national identity) in sport and of sport for nationalism?

'Nation' and the concepts derived from it are among the most shifting and elusive in the entire study of society, not least because they arouse so much emotion. The root idea behind the word is that of birth, as in nativity; that is to say, we should expect a nation to be something you are born into, national identity being defined at birth. This was an implication of the Latin *nationem* from which our modern word developed, but it meant something more like 'clan', 'tribe', 'ilk' or even 'family' rather than the huge, perhaps multi-ethnic, agglomerations we call nations today. Eighteenth-century English conceived of 'nations' in this way and it was normal to refer to the 'nation of Smiths', the nations of Gypsies and 'Hebrews', or even the 'royal nation'. Thus to some extent the way we talk about nations today comprises a modern concept. We refer to nations defined by religion (Israel, Pakistan, Belgium), by language (Germany, Italy) and by ideology (the United States of America), though in all cases the common characteristic is attached to a defined territory. Perhaps the most coherent concept is that developed by such German writers as J.G. Fichte in arguing for German unification in the nineteenth century. According to this version, a nation possesses a common language and shares a common territory; it has a common 'spirit', the *Volkgeist*. The language relates to the territory through its names, its history and its story-telling, so that a common consciousness consists in the relation of language, history and territory. Unfortunately, this coherent theory applies to relatively few cases: it suggests that bi-lingual and multi-lingual nations are not really nations at all. Perhaps this thesis can be sustained in relation to Canada and South Africa, even about Belgium, but it seems to miss the point about Switzerland, Ireland and Wales. Nor can it explain the two dozen or so countries where Spanish is the principal language, and roughly the same number speak English. Many of these seem at least well on the way to developing a separate nationality, if they have not already got there.

The thesis that 'nation' is really a modern concept, in an extreme version, sees the apparent history of nationality in terms of the 'myths' and the 'invented' and 'selected' traditions that define nationality. Nations, according to this account, are principally the products of the national ideology promulgated by states and by movements seeking to form states. The state seeks, in Eugene Weber's famous phrase, to turn 'peasants into Frenchmen'; to do so it must emphasize the common language and history of France and eradicate the sense French citizens have that they are Basques, Catalans, Burgundians, Bretons, Corsicans, Flemings and so on (Weber, 1979). The national identity is mainly and usually a modern creation, which re-writes its own pre-modern history. If Ruritania contains a province called Mythologia, the Ruritanian government, through its propaganda and educational system, emphasizes the cases where Ruritanians and Mythologians have fought or worked together and forgets or puts in a bad light those Mythologians who argued and fought against incorporation into Ruritania. And if the Mythologians achieve independence, or a powerful movement for independence, they do the opposite; the crucial factor, to paraphrase John Stuart Mill, is that a person who regards himself or herself as Ruritanian finds obeying the orders of a fellow Ruritanian person or institution more acceptable than are orders from a foreigner. Thus the legitimacy of the 'nation-state' and some possible sources of its collapse (Gellner, 1983)

The alternative account of nationality is that the ethnic origins of nations are real and that no amount of the 'invention' or 'selection' of tradition can take away from this reality. This, naturally, is the account given or merely assumed by most nationalists: Gwynfor Evans takes it for granted that the Welsh who fought with King Arthur were Welsh in just the same way that he was (Evans, 1973, 1975), just as Zviad Gamsakhurdia takes it for granted that the Georgians whom St Nino converted to Christianity in the fourth century and even those encountered by Jason and the Argonauts more than 3,000 years ago were ancestors of modern Georgians (Gamsakhurdia, 1991). Both of these writers are on dubious ground in these particular claims, but there is scholarly support for the thesis that many modern national identities developed from an ancient *ethnie* (Smith, 1986). The extreme modernist thesis is, in any case, difficult for an English person to accept who knows their Shakespeare. In many

instances Shakespeare seems to express a form of nationalism which is more fully formed than it ought to be. His words can still be used to stir a modern English team, especially Henry V's speech before Agincourt:

> And gentlemen in England now a-bed
> Shall think themselves accursed they were not here
> And hold their manhoods cheap

On the other hand, Shakespeare can be seen as the voice of a peculiarly advanced nation-state, mythologizing the dynastic struggles of an earlier period into the language of English nationalism.

The extreme theses of 'modernism' and 'ethnicism' about nationality have little appeal. It seems reasonable to say that there are real ethnic histories and even shared national genetic traits, but that much of what makes a modern national consciousness or determines the identity of a given individual is the product of the invention and selection of tradition which has occurred in a modern and organized way. What makes an Allison a proud Englishman, a McInally an Irish nationalist and a McAllister a patriotic Scot (and any of them an American or Australian), must occur in modernity, since these are all national forms of the same tribal name and the tribe once ranged over much of the British Isles. Nevertheless, nationality must be treated as *real* whatever our theory of the role of mythology in its formation. Anybody who does not understand, in the cases of the Boers in South Africa or the Quebecois in Canada, that their combination of language, shared history and lore and sense of belonging to their territory have reinforced each other and created a nation, in the way that, say, the *pieds noirs* European settlers in Algeria never became a nation, is not going to understand them at all.

What, then, is nationalism? It is certainly not mere national identity, nor even the love of one's nation, which is logically separate and goes normally by the name of patriotism. The addition of an 'ism' implies one of two things: a nationalist must either have a tendency to concern himself (or herself) with his nation, to orient his actions and judgements towards it, or he must believe in the nation as a morally demanding form of collective existence. (A 'racist' may, similarly, have a tendency to discriminate and make judgements racially without having a coherent theory of race or he may be a 'racist' in a doctrinal sense, separately or as well, because he thinks race is an important concept.) In general, nationalists, as opposed to patriots, must have a political project for the nation, whether for independence, cultural preservation or aggrandizement.

SPORT AND NATIONALISM

The message of Murrayfield this weekend was bigger than scrummaging techniques and line-out skills ... Murrayfield was a message of Scottish identity and nationhood. (*Guardian,* 1991; Jarvie, 1993: 58)

Murrayfield is the Scottish national rugby stadium and the comment quoted above was made by a *Guardian* reporter on the atmosphere at the England–Scotland World Cup semi-final played there in 1991. It reminds us that the setting of international sport – flags, anthems, national colours and emblems, large crowds – are as easy and appropriate a setting for collective expressions of national identity as one could devise. It would seem a natural and easy movement from 'a message of Scottish identity and nationhood' to an expression of national*ism*. The enormous fervour of the occasion, which some commentators found both shocking and a little frightening, could not but affect people in many ways and therefore would amount to a kind of 'sporting nationalism'. The words of 'Flower of Scotland', sung with such fervour on that occasion, do, after all, refer to old battles and crow about the English being sent back across the border 'tae think again'. They also claim,

> But we can still rise now
> And be a nation again (Brand, 1978: 125)

Academic accounts of nationalism have tended to pay very little attention to sport. I have often attacked the assumption behind this lack of attention as a 'myth of autonomy' about sport which simply assumes that the activity is somehow inert in relation to other social and political phenomena (Allison, 1986: 1–26). On the other hand, figurational sociology offers us the basis of an argument that sport might be inert because it is a 'mimetic' activity, a product of the 'civilizing process'. It exists in a contained, parallel milieu to our normal interests and politics, its emotions, though not trivial or false, being within boundaries and not necessarily having any consequences beyond those boundaries: we watch the match, we care about nothing else as we do so, but we go home and give our 'serious' attention to something else (Dunning, 1992).

In the 1970s Phil Bennett, captain of a world-beating Welsh rugby team, is said to have addressed a tense and expectant changing-room something like as follows: 'For 1500 years the English have polluted our land ... exploited our resources ... raped our women ... Gentlemen, this afternoon we are playing the English'. For all that intensity of national and apparently anti-English feeling Wales voted by over four to one in that period (in May 1979) to reject devolution and to leave the political union with England unchanged. It was precisely the industrial valleys of South Wales where the support for the Welsh rugby team was massive which were overwhelmingly against political change. This suggests at least the possibility that the 'mimetic' emotions of sport can act as a 'safety valve' in politics, that they would express and deflate nationalist sentiment rather than enhance it. It may have been the same when Eastern European countries vanquished the USSR at sport in its heyday, as in the victories of the (then) Czechoslovakia over the (then) Soviet Union at ice hockey in the 1970s.

There is no reason to suppose a normal, let alone universal relation between national sport and political nationalism. Each case is different and context is all-important. It may be, as I have suggested, a negative, defusing relation on occasions. It may be purely inert: many of the five million English people with Irish family connections support the Irish rugby team or the Republic of Ireland football team. But this does not necessarily imply support for Irish unification or any other project which might be construed as Irish nationalism. Support for a national team may be a purely cultural link, like support for a club team.

But it is equally apparent that sport can act in an important catalytic way with respect to nationalism: after all, it was a soccer match which started the war between Honduras and El Salvador in 1969 which killed 6,000 people and left 24,000 wounded (Kapuscinki, 1990). There are many cases in which it would be more reasonable to infer that national sport had helped a nationalist cause than that it has hindered or made no difference.

A set of test cases for the efficacy of sporting nationalism is provided by states that have attempted to use sport to inculcate a larger national sentiment which would over-ride smaller nationalisms or tribalisms. Perhaps the greatest of these is the Soviet Union. Stalin's doctrine concerning the 'Problem of the Nationalities' prescribed a federal constitution and the maintenance of independent cultural institutions in the context of a strong centralized party which was to be the basis of real power (Stalin, 1947). When the Soviet Union seriously developed a sports policy after the

Second World War one might have expected it to be used as a kind of gesture to the nationalities as it did with much of the arts and folk culture. But in fact the immense efforts were directed to success (primarily in the Olympics) for the 'Soviet Motherland' which could be fed back to the population as a source of pride. Individual nationalities were portrayed only as willing contributors to the vast diversity of the great motherland itself.

Canada had a similar policy of fostering national sporting success to encourage national unity. The 'Proposed Sports Policy for Canadians' presented to the Canadian Amateur Sports Federation in 1970 set out to develop elite athletes for this purpose: its early successes were such that Canada was nicknamed 'the East Germany of the Commonwealth' after its victories in the 1978 Commonwealth Games in Edmonton (Olafson and Brown-John, 1986).

On balance, both of these policies seem to have been failures. They undoubtedly did have a positive effect in encouraging identification with the larger territorial unit as Georgians have admitted to me, but it was not enough to counteract opposite tendencies and it collapsed as other reasons for identification were weakened. The Canadian policy rather blew up when its greatest success, the victory of Ben Johnson in the 100 metres sprint in the 1988 Olympics, was destroyed by a drugs scandal; the Soviet Union's sports policy was increasingly exposed and derided as the state itself fell apart during *perestroika* after 1985. In both cases it can be said that the policy failed to produce real popular heroes who would seal the identification in popular culture. In both cases also there were sporting alternatives which could foster the smaller nationalism: the Quebecois had their ice hockey club teams, the Georgians and Ukrainians their club football teams. Ultimately, we can say the policies failed: the former Soviet republics now have their own sports teams and it would barely surprise anybody if that were not also to become true of Quebec within one or two decades.

African states may have had more success in using sport to weld diverse and even hostile tribes into national consciousness and support for the whole (Monnington, 1986). Support for the Nigerian or Camerounian football teams or for a what is now a tradition of Kenyan distance runners may have been important; but in these cases, as compared with Canada and the USSR, the basic forces of urbanization and modernization favour nation-building. It would be impossible even to suggest a qualitative assessment of how important sport is as a factor. The problem is the familiar one in social science of the unopenable box: a huge number of diverse influences affect millions of people who then perform complex actions, so that we can never say how important any factor was in a process.

Perhaps some of the greatest examples of sport to a nation-builder are more accidental, not without will, but certainly without a conscious strategy by state officials. Brazil is a vast and diverse land which has been successfully symbolized by a sporting institution, the football team(s) which won the World Cup in 1958, 1962 and 1970. Names like Pele, Vava, Didi, Jair, Garrincha created a huge pride in being Brazilian. The enormous admiration which these players inspired abroad helped a nation divided by class, race and distance identify itself and with itself. The victories of 1978 and 1986 by Argentina pale into comparison in terms of their effect on the global image of the country, but were a powerful force within Argentina. Finally, Australia offers an instructive comparison with Canada; the wide range and historical consistency of Australian sporting successes have played a large part in moulding the country's image and helping people to identify with it. Here, as in Brazil, there have been the superstars which Canada failed to produce, most notably cricketers of the calibre of Don Bradman and Ray Lindwall. Not only has Australia succeeded in absorbing millions of immigrants, but we must remember what a difficult proposition a successful federation of the whole country had seemed in the 1890s. Indeed, a political union between the eastern states and New Zealand seemed at one time more likely than the Australian state which came into existence and has persisted for over a century.

The British Isles present a situation which is quite different from the rest of the world. Here modern sport came into existence in the mid-nineteenth century, its genesis having everything to do with 'civil society' and nothing to do with the state. At this level it was always assumed that the sporting nation was different from the state and that (unlike almost everywhere else) national sporting representation did not have to be aligned with state boundaries. Only in exceptional cases where nation-state representation was required by international organizations (the Olympic Games) or by the necessity of producing a competitive team (the British Lions rugby team – now under threat from the pressures of other professional rugby competitions) was there international representation at the 'British' level. The question that arises concerns the effect that these uniquely stateless international teams have had on the maintenance of identity and the rise of nationalism. I have already reflected on the Welsh case, but the Scottish case seems quite different: in his study of Scottish nationalism Jack Brand sees sport (and especially the football team) as one of the institutions which has been important in maintaining identity and reviving nationalism. The mood and practices of sporting crowds have reflected rather than led political sentiment, but 'the fact was that football kept the feeling of Scottishness alive' (Brand, 1978: 138).

NATIONAL RESPONSES TO GLOBALIZATION

The British Isles may be an extreme case in another important sense, in that there is potentially a high level of political conflict between the forces of globalization and national sporting culture. It is important to note that globalization is an extremely complex and disputed concept (Falk, 1997; Ohmae, 1990, 1995) and that it is not within the scope of this chapter to examine it. But we cannot ignore the observation that the global governance of sport is relatively advanced, far more so, for example, than the governance of environmental regulation which is, in turn, more developed than the regulation of 'human rights'.

In sport, global governance is conducted by a combination of institutions which might be described as hyper-typical of global governance generally. There are international organizations of immense importance, with leaders whose route to authority is so complex that they are virtually unaccountable: the International Olympic Committee (under the presidency of Juan Samaranch since 1980) and FIFA (where Jaou Havelange was president from 1974 to 1998 are the most prominent examples. To these must be added transnational corporations, particularly in the media and most notably the global empire of Rupert Murdoch, but also those (often in sports goods) that sponsor sport. Then there is also the growth of an effective international system of law, especially at the global-regional level: for example, the decision of the European Court of Justice on 15 December 1995 about the case of Jean-Marc Bosman, which effectively outlawed some important aspects of football's 'transfer' system, may have a profound effect on the game.

There have been, during the 1990s, huge changes affecting British sports fans in all the major sports, all of which emanate from outside of Britain. Rugby League has changed in many ways, not least that it is played in the summer, as a result of its dependence on money from television, where the important corporate rivalries are Australian. Rugby Union has experienced an organizational earthquake as a result of the decision by the International Rugby Board in August 1995 to legitimize professionalism, a decision led by countries from the Southern hemisphere. Generally, sports fans have lost a wide variety of major events available on 'terrestrial' television as a kind of free public good. If cricket, specifically, has changed least, that is because it compromised earlier with the forces of television-driven global commercialism, during the 'Packer affair' of the 1970s.

Thus the forces which are deciding the future of British sport are predominantly international, while those which defined the shape it has had for the past hundred years were entirely national. One might expect a response of cultural nationalism, an attempt to protect 'our sports', which could appeal to the power of the democratic state to counter that of the global market, much as the French insisted on exceptions for the 'cultural' products of film and television during the 'Uruguay Round' of negotiations which led to the establishment of the World Trade Organization in 1992. Indeed, there have been some protests: Tony Banks, when a Labour Opposition MP, called for government intervention in the question of the loss of sport to terrestrial television, as has Sir Paul Fox, the former television executive. Banks was Minister of Sport from 1997 to 1999 and was involved in the institution of a European-approved but fairly weak system of 'listing' sporting events of national or cultural importance which were supposed to remain on free-to-air television. But perhaps the most significant defence of a sporting institution from global commercial forces was the intervention of the Monopolies and Mergers Commission in 1999 to prevent British Sky Broadcasting, part of the Murdoch empire, from taking over Manchester United, the richest football club in the world. A former Conservative Cabinet minister, David Mellor, hosts a radio programme in which correspondents frequently complain about the interventions of the international football authorities, FIFA and UEFA, in the British game. Leaders of the two major parties have been involved in lobbying FIFA in support of England's bid to stage the World Cup in 2006.

But it will prove very difficult to turn the simple emotional nationalism which is present when England play Germany at football into a sophisticated cultural nationalism which seeks to protect English (or British) sport from global governance. International sporting institutions have it in their favour that sport is naturally 'global': the interest in the 'world' championship and the 'world' record outstrip all else. Cultural and national boundaries are not real constraints on the movement of labour or media images in sport. Nor is censorship: even in Myanmar, where the government protects its citizens from most Western images, they watch the BBC's football programme *Match of the Day*. In any case, the issues do not come on to the agenda in the shape of 'national democracy versus global governance': they are more likely to be between international forces and, in any case, there are many people who gain from or believe in internationalization. Thus there are important underlying issues between sporting nationalism and globalization, but they seem at the time of writing unlikely to be mobilized effectively.

In conclusion, the admission must be repeated that, like much else in the understanding of society, we can only suspect and suggest many of the connections between sport and nationalism: we can never really *know*. But certainly sport sometimes channels, sometimes releases, sometimes even creates complex and powerful nationalist sentiments. *Pace* Art Spander, there is nothing odd or unusual about seeing sport as a vehicle for the expression of national sentiment; indeed, for many people, from Brazil to Scotland, it has probably been the greatest vehicle for the expression of such sentiment.

REFERENCES AND FURTHER READING

Allison, Lincoln (ed.) (1986) *The Politics of Sport*. Manchester: Manchester University Press.

Allison, Lincoln (1988) 'Sport and communities', *The World & I*, 3 (10).

Archer, Ian (ed.) (1976) *We'll Support You Ever More*. London: Hutchinson.

Bradley, Joseph (1995) *Ethnic and Religious Identity in Modern Scotland, Culture, Politics and Football*. Aldershot: Avebury.

Brand, Jack (1978) *The National Movement in Scotland*. Routledge & Kegan Paul.

Doyle, Roddy (1993) 'Republic is a beautiful word: Republic of Ireland 1990', in Nick Hornby (ed.), *My Favourite Year, A Collection of New Football Writing*. London: Witherby.

Dunning, Eric (1992) 'Figurational sociology and the sociology of sport', in Eric Dunning and Chris

Rojek (eds), *Sport and Leisure in the Civilizing Process: Critique and Counter-critique*. Toronto: University of Toronto Press. pp. 221–84.

Ellis, P. Berresford (1968) *Wales, A Nation Again*. London: Tandem.

Evans, Gwynfor (1973) *Wales Can Win*. Llandybie: Christopher Davies.

Evans, Gwynfor (1975) *A National Future for Wales*. Swansea: John Penry.

Falk, Richard (1997) 'Will globalisation win out?', *International Affairs*, 73 (1): 123–36.

Gamsakhurdia, Zviad (1991) *The Spritual Mission of Georgia*. Tbilisi: Ganatlebal.

Gellner, Ernest (1983) *Nations and Nationalism*. Oxford: Basil Blackwell.

Guardian (1991) 'Flowers sprouting over the border', 28 October.

Hill, Christopher (1992) *Olympic Politics*. Manchester: Manchester University Press.

Hill, Christopher (1993) 'The politics of the Olympic Movement', in Lincoln Allison (ed.), *The Changing Politics of Sport*. Manchester: Manchester University Press. pp. 84–104.

Hoberman, John (1986) *The Olympic Crisis*. New York: Cavatyas.

Jarvie, Grant (1991) *Sport, Racism and Ethnicity*. London: Falmer.

Jarvie, Grant (1993) 'Sport, nationalism and cultural identity', in Lincoln Allison (ed.), *The Changing Politics of Sport*. Manchester: Manchester University Press. pp. 58–63.

Kapuscinki, R. (1990) *Soccer War*. London: Granta.

Kuper, Simon (1994) *Football Against the Enemy*. London: Phoenix.

Lord, Bob (1963) *My Fight for Football*. London: Stanley Paul.

Maguire, Joseph (1995) 'Patriot games? English identity, nostalgia and media coverage of sporting disasters', *Working Papers in Sport and Society*, Volume 3, 1994–95. University of Warwick.

Monnington, Terry (1986) 'The politics of Black African sport', in Lincoln Allison (ed.), *The Politics of Sport*. Manchester: Manchester University Press. pp. 149–73.

Ohmae, Kenichi (1990) *The Borderless World*. London: Fontana.

Ohmae, Kenichi (1995) *The End of the Nation State: the Rise of Regional Economies*. New York: Free Press.

Olafson, G.A. and Lloyd Brown-John, C. (1986) 'Canadian international sport policy: a public policy analysis', in Gerald Redmond (ed.), *Sport and Politics*, 1984 Olympic Scientific Congress Proceedings, Volume 71: 69–76.

Riordan, Jim (1991) *Sport, Politics and Communism*. Manchester: Manchester University Press.

Smith, Anthony D. (1983) *Theories of Nationalism*. New York: Holmes & Meier.

Smith, Anthony D. (1986) *The Ethnic Origins of Nations*. Oxford: Basil Blackwell.

Smith, Dai (1984) *Wales! Wales?* London: Allen & Unwin.

Spander, Art (1995) 'Just enjoy the spectacle and stay off the tabloids', *Daily Telegraph*, 6 July.

Stalin, Joseph (1947) *Marxism and the National and Colonial Question.* Moscow Publishing House (original Russian edition, 1913).

Sugden, John (1995) 'Sport and nationalism in the modern world', *Working Papers in Sport and Society,* Volume 3, 1994–5. University of Warwick.

Sugden, John and Bairner, Alan (1986) 'Northern Ireland: sport in a divided society', in Lincoln Allison (ed.), *The Politics of Sport.* Manchester: Manchester University Press.

Sugden, John and Bairner, Alan (1993a) 'National identity, community relations and the sporting life in Northern Ireland', in Lincoln Allison (ed.), *The Changing Politics of Sport.* Manchester: Manchester University Press. pp. 171–206.

Sugden, John and Bairner, Alan (1993b) *Sport, Sectarianism and Society in a Divided Ireland.* Leicester: Leicester University Press.

Weber, Eugene (1979) *Peasants into Frenchmen: the Modernisation of Rural France, 1870–1914.* London: Chatto and Windus.

23

SPORT AND GLOBALIZATION

Joseph Maguire

Scaling the highest mountains, traversing the most difficult terrain, exploring the depths of the sea and skimming across the oceans, soaring through the skies and descending into deep valley gorges, tunnelling far into the interior of the earth and shaping its exterior with both 'natural' and 'artificial' surfaces and structures, sportsmen and sportswomen straddle the globe, and the 'sportization' of the planet seemingly knows no bounds. How is this globalization of modern sport to be understood? To begin to answer this question some of the main issues that underpin the debates regarding the connections between sport and globalization will be outlined. In addition, a review of the research of exponents of various traditions that have sought to understand these connections will be undertaken. On this basis, an alternative perspective on globalization and the diffusion of modern sport will be outlined. Finally, the role that sport plays in global processes will be examined.

STUDYING GLOBAL SPORT: ISSUES, QUESTIONS AND DIMENSIONS

What do we know about globalization? If a review of globalization research is undertaken, several areas of agreement can be identified. Analyses deal with processes that transcend the boundaries of nation-states. These processes are not of recent origin. These processes – involving what writers term increasing intensification of global interconnectedness – are very long-term in nature. While they have not occurred evenly across all areas of the globe, the more recent history of these processes would suggest that the rate of

change is gathering momentum. Despite the 'unevenness' of these processes, it is more difficult to understand local or national experiences without reference to these global flows. The flow of leisure styles, customs and practices from one part of the world to another, 'long-haul' tourism and global events, such as music festivals and the Olympic Games, are examples of these processes at work. In addition, people's living conditions, beliefs, knowledge and actions are intertwined, to varying degrees, with unfolding globalization processes.

These processes include the emergence of a global economy, a transnational cosmopolitan culture and a range of international social movements. Studies also identify that a multitude of transnational or global economic and technological exchanges, communication networks and migratory patterns characterize this interconnected world pattern. People, and nation-states, are woven together in a tighter and deeper interdependency network. These globalization processes also appear to be leading to a form of time–space compression. That is, people are experiencing spatial and temporal dimensions differently. There is a speeding up of time and a 'shrinking' of space. Modern technologies enable people, images, ideas and money to criss-cross the globe with great rapidity. Finally, while these processes lead, as noted, to a greater degree of interdependence, and also to an increased awareness of a sense of the world as a whole, we also see a concomitant resurgence of the local/national. These elements are two sides of the same coin. People become more attuned to the notion that their local lives, and national 'place' of living, are part of a single social space – the globe.

There are, however, a number of difficult conceptual issues that need to be grasped in understanding global processes. Advocates of competing traditions, including the modernization perspective, theories of imperialism, dependency theory, world systems theory, figurational/process sociology and globalization research, have sought to compare and contrast the development of different societies. More recently, these traditions have found expression in the study of sport. Competing claims have been made regarding the adequacy of these traditions. In section two an evaluation of how these traditions – or specific pieces of work within them – have variously advanced our collective fund of relatively adequate social scientific knowledge regarding the emergence, diffusion and globalization of sport cultures will be undertaken.

In understanding global sport processes several conceptual snares evident in the debates that have been generated by the antagonistic claims of the traditions referred to need to be avoided. These cul-de-sacs arguably centre on four main areas. First, the recourse to dichotomous thinking; secondly, the use of monocausal logic and explanation; thirdly, the tendency to view these processes as governed by *either* the intended *or* the unintended actions of groups of people; and fourth, the lack of an adequate account of gender power as it is represented and expressed in global processes. Janet Wolfe (1991), for example, has cogently argued that the omission of gender issues is a serious failing in globalization research.

If the recent literature in the sociology of sport is examined, several binary oppositions can be identified that structure debates about global sport developments. These include universalism versus particularism; homogenization versus differentiation; integration versus fragmentation; centralization versus decentralization; juxtaposition versus syncretization. Further, the monocausal logic that has been evident centres variously on either the technological, the economic or the political. These tendencies are vividly evident in the recent debates published in publications such as the *Sociology of Sport Journal*, the *Journal of Sport and Social Issues* and *Media, Culture and Society*.[1] An either/or resolution of this complex structured process will not do. Put simply, a balance or blend between intended ideological practices and unplanned sets of interdependencies structure globalization processes. The precise pattern must be studied empirically.

There is one further conceptual snare that must be avoided. The use of the globalization concept has prompted accusations from some quarters that those analyses that use the term are automatically and/or implicitly

emphasizing a homogenization thesis. Such analyses are then alleged to suggest that a global culture will emerge – or has already emerged – that will suspend or end conflict. But to associate the term globalization exclusively with such a modernization thesis, confirming the triumph of the West in some simple sense, does serious violence to a range of perspectives examining global development. Further, to suggest that such an approach assumes that all parties contribute equally in this global process is itself a parody of a set of complex arguments.

What then can we say so far with some certainty regarding the connections between globalization and modern sport? Globalization processes have no zero starting point. It is clear that they gathered momentum between the fifteenth and eighteenth centuries and continued apace throughout the twentieth century. Several of the more recent features of these processes can be identified. These include: an increase in the number of international agencies; the growth of increasing global forms of communication; the development of global competitions and prizes; and the development of standard notions of 'rights' and citizenship that have become increasingly standardized internationally. The emergence and diffusion of sport is clearly interwoven with this overall process. The development of national and international sports organizations, the growth of competition between national teams, the world-wide acceptance of rules governing specific, that is 'Western', 'sport' forms, and the establishment of global competitions such as the Olympic Games and soccer's World Cup tournament are all indicative of the occurrence of globalization in the sportsworld.

Neither the broader globalization processes, nor those identified here which relate to sport, are the direct outcome of inter-state processes. Rather, these processes need to be accounted for in relation to how they operate relatively independently of conventionally designated societal and socio-cultural processes. It is perhaps a point which those researchers who have examined the development of sport have yet to appreciate fully. While the globalization of sport is connected to the intended ideological practices of specific groups of people from particular countries, its pattern and development cannot be reduced solely to these ideological practices. Out of the plans and intentions of these groups something that was neither planned nor intended emerged.

The speed, scale and volume of sports development is interwoven with the broader global flow of people, technology, finance, images and ideologies (Appadurai, 1990). Global migration of both professional and college sports personnel was a pronounced feature of sports development in the 1980s. The flow from country to country of sports goods, equipment and 'landscapes' (for example, golf courses, artificial playing surfaces) has grown by such a scale and volume that it is currently a multi-billion dollar business. At the level of economics stands the fact that the flow of finance in the global sports arena has come to centre not only on the international trade in sports personnel, prize money and endorsements, but on the marketing of sport along specific, for example, American, lines. Crucial in all these regards, of course, has been the development of a 'media–sport production complex' which projects images to large global audiences (Maguire, 1993a). It can also be observed that global sports festivals such as the Olympics, the Asian Games and the Pan-American Games have come to serve as vehicles for the expression of ideologies that are not only national in character (the Berlin, Moscow and Los Angeles Olympics) but are also transnational in their consequences.

Both the intended and unintended aspects of global sport development require attention. The intended acts of representatives of transnational agencies or the transnational capitalist class are potentially more significant in the *short term*. Over the *longer term*, however, the unintended, relatively autonomous transnational practices predominate. These practices 'structure' the subsequent plans and actions of transnational agencies and the transnational capitalist class. Globalization processes involve a blend between intended and unintended practices. While people *have* to cope with the problems of interdependency which globalization engenders, the fact that these processes are relatively autonomous ensures that people can intervene. Global practices still lie within the province of human actions.

Although elite sports migrants, officials and consumers are no less caught up in this unfolding globalization process, they do have the capacity to reinterpret cultural products and experiences into something distinct. Furthermore, the receptivity of national popular cultures to non-indigenous cultural wares can be both active and heterogenous. That is not to overlook, however, that there is a political economy at work in the production and consumption of global sport products. Globalization is best understood as a balance and blend between diminishing contrasts and increasing varieties, a commingling of cultures and attempts by more established groups to

control and regulate access to global flows (Maguire, 1994a, 1994b, 1999). Global sport development can be understood in the same terms: that is, at the turn of this new century we are witnessing the globalization of sports and of the increasing diversity of sports cultures. What has so far been argued is a summary of available knowledge. Let me now turn to reviewing in more detail how exponents of different traditions have sought to explain these developments.

SPORT IN THE GLOBAL PROCESS: COMPETING TRADITIONS

It is perhaps interesting to note that scholars accept the basic premise that 'England became the cradle and focus of modern sporting life' (Dunning and Sheard, 1979; Gruneau, 1988; Guttmann, 1991). Here, however, the consensus breaks down. Different interpretations exist with regard to the dynamics underpinning the emergence and subsequent diffusion of modern sport (Dunning and Sheard, 1979; Gorn and Goldstein, 1993; J.A. Hargreaves, 1994; J.E. Hargreaves, 1986; Mandell, 1984). Similar themes, issues and questions that characterize the broader debate regarding global cultural flows, also surface in discussing modern sport. Not surprisingly, similar fault lines regarding homogeneity/heterogeneity; monocausal/multicausal; unidimensional/multidimensional; unity/fragmentation; universalism/particularism, are also evident. In the following section, key research is outlined and such work is positioned along the fault lines identified.

The clearest exposition of the modernization thesis as it applies to sport can be found in the work of Eric Wagner. Reviewing a diverse set of trends that are said to characterize global sport, Wagner correctly observes that 'Americanization is part of these trends but it is only one part of much broader processes; it is not by itself the key process' (Wagner, 1990: 400). This much is not incompatible with the argument presented in this chapter. Yet, Wagner mistakenly then assigns central status to what he terms, 'international modernization' (Wagner, 1990: 402). While he acknowledges important caveats, such as 'sport culture flowing in all directions', and a 'blending of many sport traditions', Wagner does appear to downplay the conflictual nature of these processes, over-emphasize the ability of people to pick and choose as they wish from global sport cultures, and see such development as a sign of progress. His concluding comments echo many of the features, and weaknesses, of the modernization perspective outlined earlier in this chapter. This is what he had to say:

> I think we make too much of cultural dependency in sports when in fact it is people themselves who generally determine what they do and do not want, and it is the people who modify and adapt the cultural imports, the sports, to fit their own needs and values. Bringing sports into a new cultural context probably serves more as examples available for people to pick up or trade if they wish, rather than any imposed or forced cultural change … The long term trend has to be, I think, towards greater homogenization, and I don't think there is anything bad or imperialistic about this; rather, these sports trends ultimately must reflect the will of the people. (Wagner, 1990: 402)

Though modernization was one of the first approaches within the field, ideas of this kind still surface in the literature on sport. Consider Baker and Mangan's (1987) collection of papers on sport in Africa (Wagner, 1989 on Africa), Cashman's exploration of the phenomenon of Indian cricket (1988), Arbena's evaluation of literature relating to Latin America and papers published in comparative sport studies edited by Wilcox (1995). In his early writing on this subject, Allen Guttmann supported this position, arguing that Wagner was 'correct to insist that we are witnessing a homogenization of world sports rather than an Americanization', and that 'the concept of modernization is preferable because it also implies something about the nature of the global transformation' (Guttmann, 1991: 187–8). Though he acknowledges that terms like 'Gemeinschaft and Gesellschaft, the traditional and the modern, the particularistic and the universalistic' employ an 'admittedly simplified dichotomy', Guttmann still works within a modernization time frame, and overlooks what Robertson describes as the 'universalization of particularism' and not just the 'particularization of universalism' (Robertson, 1992). This is odd. In other work by Guttmann, important lines of enquiry are opened up when he refers to the diffusion of game forms in the ancient world and to the influence of the Orient on the West (Guttmann, 1993). Guttmann's solution, as we shall see later, has been to adopt a cultural hegemony position and to concentrate on more recent events.

While advocates of a cultural imperialist and dependency theory approach would reject several, if not all, of the premises outlined by Wagner and Guttmann, these perspectives do share a common assumption that we are witnessing the homogenization of world sports. Within sport history research, informed by a cultural imperialist perspective, several insightful case studies of the connection between the diffusion of sport and imperialism have been provided (Mangan, 1986; Stoddart, 1988, 1989). The diffusion of sport, out of its European heartland, moved along the formal and the informal lines of Empire – particularly, though not exclusively, the British. But it was not just the diffusion of specific sports, such as cricket, that reflected this broader process (James, 1963). From a cultural imperialist perspective, what was also at stake was the diffusion of a cultural/sporting ideology and a form of Western cosmology. This argument can be highlighted with reference to the work of Henning Eichberg, John Bale and Johan Galtung.

Eichberg's study probes several of the issues identified. He suggests that Olympism is a 'social pattern' that reflects the 'everyday culture of the western (and east European) industrial society' (Eichberg, 1984: 97). He highlights several negative consequences of Olympism, including drugs, violence and the scientification of sport. Eichberg maintains that these excesses are not accidental or marginal, but logically related to the configuration of Western Olympic sport, with its emphasis on 'quicker, higher, stronger'. Olympism is seen to reflect the colonial dominance of the West and its spread across the globe has been remarkably successful. While it is possible to agree with Eichberg on this, Wilson overstates this case when he suggests that, 'the major impetus for the globalization of sport was the Olympic movement' (Wilson, 1994: 356). The dynamics underpinning the globalization of sport are more multifaceted than this. Indeed, as Eichberg argues, Western domination is increasingly subject to resistance. Alternatives to Olympism are emerging. These alternatives include, a resurgence of national cultural games, open air movements, expressive activities and meditative exercises. He concludes that 'the age of Western colonial dominance is coming to an end – and with it the predominance of Olympic sports', and that, 'new physical cultures will arise … from the different cultural traditions of the world' (Eichberg, 1984: 102). Not all, as we shall see, share Eichberg's optimism.

Tackling these issues within the subdiscipline of sports geography, John Bale paints a more conflict-ridden and destructive picture of the impact of the diffusion of sport along the lines of Empire. As Bale records, 'Western sports did not simply take root in virgin soil; they were firmly implanted – sometimes ruthlessly – by imperialists' (Bale, 1994: 8). For Bale, such 'sports colonization' marginalized, or destroyed, indigenous movement cultures and, 'as cultural imperialism swept the globe, sports played their part in Westernizing the landscapes of the colonies' (Bale, 1994: 8). There is much in this latter argument and Bale's pioneering study raises our understanding of sport landscapes to a new level. There are, however, grounds for suggesting that the homogenization process is not as complete as these observations appear to indicate. This reservation is not, however, shared by Galtung. In similar vein, to Bale and Eichberg, Galtung sets up his analysis with the following question:

> What happens when there is massive export of sports, radiating from Western centres, following old colonial trade and control lines, into the last little corner of the world, leaving cricket bats, soccer fields, racing tracks, courts of all sorts and what not behind? (Galtung, 1991: 150)

For Galtung, the answer is clear. Sports carry the socio-cultural code of the senders, and those from the West, 'serve as fully fledged carriers of the combination typical for expansionist occidental cosmology' (Galtung, 1991: 150). Unlike Eichberg, however, Galtung detects no hopeful alternatives. Whatever the merits of his overall argument, Galtung rightly points to the role of the body in these processes, and insightfully observes that, as people learn these body cultures at an early stage in their lives, they leave 'imprints that may well be indelible' (Galtung, 1991: 150).

Although the research highlighted above emphasizes a cultural imperialist perspective, variants of dependency theory have been used extensively in the study of sport. Several studies have also examined Latin and South America (Arbena, 1988, 1993; Mandle and Mandle, 1988). Alan Klein's study of Dominican baseball is an example of dependency research at its best (Klein, 1989, 1991). Grounded in a careful and sophisticated anthropological approach, he probes the contradictory status and role of baseball in relations between the Dominican Republic and the United States of America. Klein skilfully observes:

> Because baseball is the only area in which Dominicans come up against Americans and demonstrate superiority, it fosters national pride and keeps foreign influence at bay. But the resistance is incomplete. At an organizational level American baseball interests have gained power and are now unwittingly dismantling Dominican

> baseball. Therefore, just when the Dominicans are in a position to resist the influence of foreigners, the core of their resistance is slipping away into the hands of the foreigners themselves. (Klein, 1991: 3)

Despite noting, in similar fashion to Eichberg's interpretation of the Olympic movement, that 'Caribbean baseball is rooted in colonialism', Klein does not convey the sense of uniformity, or of total domination, that Galtung does. On the contrary, while pointing to the unequal nature of power relations, Klein remarks, 'having struggled in obscurity to refine the game Dominicans have made it their own, a game marked by their cadence and colour' (Klein, 1991: 156). Local responses to broader processes are acknowledged. Klein goes further, and argues that, 'the Dominicans are a beleaguered people who may someday rebel; to predict when the flash point will occur, look first to the firefights being waged in a game that has inspired their confidence. Look first at Sugarball' (Klein, 1991: 156).

Other scholars working within this broad cultural imperialist/dependency theory tradition downplay the role of Americanization, and instead, highlight the role of global capitalism. Bruce Kidd's study of sport in Canada, located within a broader analysis of the development of Canadian national culture, demonstrates several of the qualities of this approach (Kidd, 1981, 1991). Noting the potential importance of sport in the strengthening and enunciation of national identity, Kidd observes that the commodification of Canadian sport has served to undermine this potential. Focusing on the National Hockey League (NHL) as a 'critical case' in this regard, he highlights how both the ideological marketing strategy of the NHL and the general process of commodification between the two world wars served to 'accelerate the disintegration of beliefs and practices that had once supported and nurtured autonomous Canadian institutions' (Kidd, 1981: 713). For him, an explanation of these processes lies not in Americanization *per se* but in a critique of capitalism. Kidd observes:

> Explanation lies neither in US expansion nor national betrayal, but in the dynamics of capital. Once sport became a sphere of commodity production ... then it was almost inevitable that the best Canadian hockey would be controlled by the richest and most powerful aggregates of capital and sold in the richer and more populous markets of the US. The disappearance of community control over Canadian hockey strengthened a much larger process – the centralization of all popular forms of culture. (Kidd, 1981: 714)

Whereas Kidd deals with issues between 'core' economies, George Sage (1995) draws on the work of Wallerstein and adopts a more 'world-system model' to explain the global sporting goods industry. Surveying the social and environmental costs associated with the relocation strategies of multinational corporations, such as Nike, Sage concludes that such companies have been 'following a model which places exports over domestic needs, profits over worker rights, growth over the environment', and that, a 'neo-colonial system of unequal economic and political relationships among the First and Third World countries envisioned by Wallerstein's world-system model of global development becomes abundantly evident to even a casual observer' (Sage, 1995: 48). The important insights provided by Sage on the global sports goods industry need further exploration.

While noting the obvious American influences on Australian popular culture, McKay and Miller (1991) adopt a similar stance to Sage. They view the concept of Americanization to be of limited help in explaining the form and content of Australian sport. For them, the political economy of Australian sport can best be analysed by concepts such as post-Fordism, the globalization of consumerism and the cultural logic of late capitalism. Though McKay and Miller (1991), and McKay, Lawrence, Miller and Rowe (1993), prefer the term 'corporate sport', Donnelly has argued that the 'notion of corporate sport may easily be extended to indicate the Americanization of sport, since most of the conditions of corporate sport are either American in origin, or have been more fully developed in America' (Donnelly, 1996: 246). It would seem, however, that neither Sage, nor McKay and his fellow researchers, would accept this interpretation. As McKay and Miller remark, 'in the discourse of the daily report from the stock exchange, the Americans are not the only players in the cultural game' (McKay and Miller, 1991: 93). The dynamics of this 'cultural game', with its links with both a colonial past, but also with a recognition of Australia's geographical position in relation to its South-east Asia neighbours, can be fruitfully developed in the context of a discussion of global sport, nationhood and local identities.

Although McKay and Miller de-emphasize the pervasiveness of American control, and concentrate on the dynamics of global capitalism *per se*, the work by David Andrews would, at first sight, appear to be more in keeping with the position adopted by Donnelly. Andrews, for example, highlights the 'global structure

and local influence of the National Basketball League (NBA) as a transnational corporation, whose global ubiquity inevitably contributes to the hyperreal remaking of local identities' (Andrews, 1997: 72). Andrews goes on to argue that the NBA has been turned 'into one of the popular commodity-signs which had usurped the material economic commodity as the dynamic force and structuring principle of everyday American existence' (Andrews, 1997: 74). In language sometimes akin to that used by Adorno, and his fellow contributors to the Frankfurt School, Andrews argues that during the 1980s, 'the NBA became a hyperreal circus whose simulated, and hence self-perpetuating, popularity seduced the American masses' (Andrews, 1997: 74). This 'success' is not confined to the USA. Though it may be unwise to overestimate the knowledge of the powerful and underestimate the ability of 'locals' to reshape, resist, or simply ignore, the marketing strategies of multinationals, Andrews is correct to observe that the NBA does 'have a vivid global presence' (Andrews, 1997: 77). The source of debate, however as he himself acknowledges, is 'the extent to which the circulation of universal American commodity-signs has resulted in the convergence of global markets, lifestyles and identities' (Andrews, 1997: 77). Despite the manner in which he formulates the early part of his argument, Andrews highlights the, 'built-in particularity (or heterogeneity) in terms of the ways that products and images are consumed', and that, products, images and services from other societies 'to some extent … inalienably become indigenized' (Andrews, 1997: 77). As with the broader globalization literature, sociology of sport research is divided over the precise form and blend of homogeneity and heterogeneity characteristic of the global sports process.

What kind of assessment can be made regarding the state of play of the sociological study of global sport? Several writers have attempted some overall review (Donnelly, 1996; Harvey and Houle, 1994; Houlihan, 1994). While there are clear fault lines along which the literature lies, reflecting the more general globalization debate, there is also some overlap. Research from both a modernization and a cultural imperialism perspective concludes that a homogenization process is occurring. This common ground can be seen in Guttmann's work. While his early work endorsed a modernization perspective, his more recent contribution has swung in favour of a form of cultural imperialism (Guttmann, 1991, 1993, 1994). While issues of cultural struggle and contestation are much more to the fore in this latter work, the common denominator is still an continued emphasis on homogenization.

Within the broad 'Marxist' tradition (cultural imperialism, dependency theory, world-systems theory and hegemony theory), common emphasis is placed on power, exploitation and the role that multinationals play in local markets. While the relative role of Americanization and/or global capitalism is disputed, what is agreed upon is that modern sport is structured by a political economy in which multinationals play a decisive part. In some instances, as we have seen, a particularly unidirectional and monocausal focus is used to explain these processes. More recently, work by Andrews and Klein highlights, to a greater extent, issues of local resistance, reinterpretation and indigenization. In this, they are in keeping with a trend in the more general globalization literature, that emphasizes heterogeneity (Nederveen Pieterse, 1995). Harvey and Houle summarize aspects of this debate that have surfaced in the sociology of sport when they conclude:

> Thus, linking sport to globalization leads to an analysis of sport as part of an emergent global culture, as contributing to the definition of new identities, and to the development of a world economy. Therefore, the debate between globalization and Americanization is more than a question of vocabulary. Indeed, it is a question of paradigmatic choice, which leads to completely different interpretations of a series of phenomena. (Harvey and Houle, 1994: 346)

While the observations made here would endorse these writers when they argue that different interpretations of globalization more broadly, and global sport processes in particular, are 'a question of paradigmatic choice', there is room to doubt whether such interpretations are as polarized as they suggest. So what is the alternative?

TOWARDS AN ALTERNATIVE PERSPECTIVE ON GLOBAL SPORT PROCESSES

From a process/figurational perspective it is evident that in world terms 'Western' societies over time became the equivalent of the established groups within particular European nations. The spread of 'civilized', that is, Western, patterns of conduct occurred through the settlement of occidentals or through their assimilation by the upper strata of other nations. Crucially, the same 'double-bind'

tendencies that marked the upper classes' colonization of outsiders within the 'West' was and remains evident in the 'West's' dealings with 'outsider' (non-Western) nations and peoples. With this spread came a particular, contested view of civilization, of humanity as a whole. The members of 'Western' societies were acting as a form of established group on a world level (Elias, 1939/1982: 255). Their tastes and conduct, including their sports, formed part of this, and these practices had similar effects to those of elite cultural activities within 'Western' societies themselves. They acted as signs of distinction, prestige and power. Yet, just as the established groups within 'Western' societies found that their distinguishing conduct flowed, intentionally or unintentionally, across social strata, so the occidentals of the colonies also discovered that a similar process occurred in their dealings with their colonial social inferiors. Indeed, in the context of this cultural interchange, non-Western codes and customs began to permeate into 'Western' societies.

It is important to note, however, that the rise of the 'West' was contested and its 'triumph' was not inevitable. Furthermore, 'Western' culture had long been permeated by non-Western cultural forms, people, technologies and knowledge. In a word, these cultural interchanges stretch back to long before the 'West' became more dominant in cultural interchange. In addition, 'Western' culture was not itself exactly homogenous and all of a piece. Considerable variations existed within it. These cross-cultural processes were characterized by a combination of intentional and unintentional features. The manner and form of the commingling involved were dependent on several factors including the form of colonization, the position of the area in the large network of political, economic and military interdependencies, and the particular region's history and structure. Processes of commingling were (and are) characterized by unequal power relations. One means by which the established 'Western' elites maintained their status and distinction was through the *exercise* of specific forms of conduct. An example of this was their recourse to specific, status-enhancing sporting practices. This reinforced their distinctive culture, habitus and identity.

Determining the pattern or course of this commingling is an empirical question. The precise patterns experienced in specific countries or regions, and indeed in the broader global process, depend on the balance or blends of diminishing contrasts and increasing varieties, that is, of homogenizing and differentiating tendencies. At different stages the relative balance may incline in favour of one end of the continuum or another. In a specific phase, in a particular region, the dominant feature may favour a decrease in contrasts. This may be particularly the case where a form of colonization is taking place. Clearly the dynamics of these processes are closely connected to the prevailing balance of power between established and outsider groups.

Tracing this process over the long term it is clear that the social barriers built between established Westerners and the native outsiders have proved semi-permeable. The contrast between 'Western' and non-Western societies has indeed begun to diminish and we may already be living in a period that could be characterized as the waning of the 'West'. The form and extent to which 'Western' values have spread through specific regions however, reflect the history and structure of the areas in question. This also applies in the diffusion of non-Western conduct back to specific 'Western' nations. Established and outsider groups were and are active in the interpretation of 'Western' and non-Western conduct and cultural forms. *Pace* Robertson (1992), this recognition points to the possibility that existing varieties of 'civilized' conduct could survive and new ones emerge.

The figurational approach rejects the idea that the spread or diffusion of styles of behaviour depends solely on the activities of established groups. A two-way process of cultural interaction crosses the semi-permeable barriers that established groups – both within Western societies, and between them and non-Western societies – deployed to maintain their distinctiveness, power and prestige. The more they became interconnected with outsider groups, the more they depended on them for social tasks. In so doing, the contrasts between established and outsiders diminished. The power ratio between these groups moved in an equalizing direction. Concomitantly, new styles of conduct emerged (Elias, 1939/1982: 256). As 'civilized' forms of conduct spread across both the rising lower classes of 'Western' society and the different classes of the colonies, an amalgamation of the 'Western' and the indigenous patterns occurred. Each time this happened upper-class conduct and that of the rising groups interpenetrated. People placed within this situation attempted to reconcile and fuse the pattern of 'occidentally civilized societies with the habits and traditions of their own society' and in this they achieved a 'higher or lesser degree(s) of success' (Elias, 1939/1982: 309–14). Featherstone, in discussing a range of

these global flows, draws on the general work of Elias and observes:

> As Elias indicates in his synopsis to *The Civilising Process* the creation of larger nation-states and blocs and the nature of the power balances, interdependencies and linkages between and across them will influence the types of identity formation and personality structure which develop in various parts of the world. It is only relatively recently and in response to the current phase of intensified global competition and interdependencies that we have started to think that there might be a sociological problem here: how to develop a series of concepts which are adequate to understand this process. (Featherstone, 1995: 135–6)

Concepts such as diminishing contrasts, increasing varieties, established and outsiders, I/we, they/them balances and interdependent commingling, can arguably assist in this task.

What implications are there for the sociological study of world sport? Elias and Dunning did not deploy all of these concepts to assist their analyses of sport. This was unfortunate. Nevertheless, they were aware, unlike some advocates of other approaches, of the global reach of sports. Examining the growing seriousness of sport, Eric Dunning observed that three interrelated processes appear particularly significant. These are state-formation, functional democratization and the spread of sport through the widening network of international interdependencies (Dunning, 1986: 213). Dunning went on to conclude that 'it remains necessary to spell out precisely what the connections were between, on the one hand, the growing seriousness of sports participation and, on the other, state-formation, functional democratization and the civilizing process. It also remains to show how this trend was connected with the international spread of sport' (Dunning, 1986: 214). This is the task in which I am presently engaged.

Commenting on the diffusion of English pastimes to continental Europe and beyond, Elias addressed this connection between sportization and civilizing processes. Noting the reigning in of violence, the development of tighter, standardizing sets of rules, the development of governing bodies and the shift in body habitus, Elias observed that 'the sportization of pastimes, if I may use this expression as shorthand for their transformation in English society into sports and the export of some of them on an almost global scale, is another example of a civilizing spurt' (Elias, 1986: 21–2).

This sportization process did not merely involve the multi-layered flow of sports, personnel, technologies and landscapes – important though it is to explore the interconnected patterns these flows form (Maguire, 1994a). Studies of these sportization processes can also be understood 'as contributions to knowledge of changes in the social habitus of people and of the societies they form with each other' (Elias, 1986: 23). More important than simply the global movement of cultural wares, this shift towards the competitive, regularized, rationalized and gendered bodily exertions of achievement sport, involved changes at the level of personality, body deportment and social interaction. A more rationalized male body habitus came into evidence which was going to affect people and groups in different societies across the globe in fairly fundamental ways.

Though Elias did not fully develop his analysis of the export of this sportization of pastimes, he did point to the significance of the relative autonomy of these sport forms for their adoption outside of England. Referring to organizational developments occurring in the nineteenth century, Elias noted:

> Every variety of sport … has a relative autonomy in relation not only to the individuals who play at a given time, but also to the society where it developed. That is the reason why some sports which first developed in England could be transferred to and adopted by other societies as their own. The recognition of this fact opens up a wide field for further investigation. Why, for instance, were some initially English varieties of sport such as Association Football and tennis taken up by many different societies all over the world while the spread of cricket was mainly confined to an exclusive circle of Commonwealth countries? Why did the rugby variety of football not spread as widely as the Association variety? Why did the USA, without abandoning the English varieties completely, develop its own variety of football? (Elias, 1986: 39–40)

Questions of this type lie at the heart of an analysis of the links between sportization and globalization. Note that it is male achievement sport, emerging out of England, that is the dominant player. Though European rivals existed, in particular in the form of German and Swedish gymnastics and also the Czech Sokol movement, and although some older folk pastimes also survived, it was male achievement sport that was to affect people's body habitus on a global scale. That is not to suggest that there occurred no resistance to, reinterpretation or indeed recycling of, this body culture. Here, too, evidence of the interweaving of the local and the global is evident.

The spread of high-status 'English' sport forms to continental Europe during the nineteenth century prompted various reactions. In Nordic countries, English sport appears to have been readily embraced but also restylized in the light of local body culture and tradition. In Germany, sections of that society resisted this diffusion. National culture and identity were seen to be threatened by English sport forms. The body culture of the Turner Movement was viewed as superior by German patriots and, as such, English sport forms were labelled as socially inferior. The Germans were not alone. Great Britain's other main European rival, France, also had citizens who advocated resistance. For example, Pascal Grousset, who founded the Ligue Nationale de l'Education Physique in the late 1880s, condemned the importation of English games and values and argued that the French people would do better to seek their models in antiquity rather then from across La Manche (cited in Weber, 1991). Ancient games of 'football' were promoted and medieval competitive pageants revived but to no avail. Those like Baron de Coubertin, who were advocates of English games and public school values, but also Greek antiquity, won the day. By 1892, de Coubertin felt able to declare:

> Let us export our oarsmen, our fencers, our runners into other lands. That is the true free trade of the future; and the day it is introduced into Europe the cause of Peace will have received a new and strong ally. (Pierre de Coubertin, 1892)

Closely connected to the late nineteenth-century reinvention of tradition and the intensification of inter-state tensions, achievement sports came 'to serve as symbolic representations of competition between states' and 'as a status symbol of nations' (Elias, 1986: 23). Considering achievement sport development during the twentieth century, Elias went on to argue that:

> The achievement sport culminating today in the Olympic Games provides telling examples. There the struggle for world records has given the development of sport a different direction. In the form of achievement sport the playful mimetic tensions of leisure sport become dominated and patterned by global tensions and rivalries between different states. (Elias, 1986: 43–4)

What Elias did not fully appreciate and acknowledge however, is that while male achievement sport culture developed in and diffused out of an English context, aspects of it were more fully developed in a later phase of sportization in the context of North America and, in particular, the USA. In England, achievement sport was shackled by an amateur ethos which emphasized 'fair play' and downplayed seriousness. Yet, during the third sportization phase, along with the achievement sport body cultures, the notion of 'le fair play' did diffuse to continental Europe and to both the formal and informal British Empire (Maguire, 1993a). While such a notion might have been viewed as a sign of distinction and a cultural marker of English gentlemen, sport advocates in other societies chose to practise their sports differently and more seriously. By the fourth sportization phase, it was an American version of the achievement sport ethos that had gained relative ascendancy.

The third sportization phase then entailed the differential diffusion of 'English' sport forms. The remarks made by one historian, Ensor, highlight the British perception of this diffusion. In commenting on 'the development of organized games' Ensor observed that 'on any reckoning [this] may rank among England's leading contributions to world culture' (1936: 164). Whatever the merits of this evaluation, this diffusion was closely connected to two interrelated processes: the emergence of intense forms of nationalism, and a spurt in globalization processes. During this period we see the intensification of 'national' sentiment, the emergence of ethnic nation-states and the invention of traditions. This was to be the seedbed of what Elias noted was a feature of twentieth-century sport, namely the 'self escalating pressure of inter-state competition in sport and its role as a status symbol of nations' (Elias, 1986: 23).

From the 1920s through to the late 1960s then, the 'West' regulated the field of play, sport organizations, the surplus value associated with sporting festivals and the ideological meanings associated with such events. 'Western' and non-Western people actively – as opposed to passively – embraced some aspects of the sports that diffused out of the Anglo/Euro-American core. Galtung is right to assert that sport was and is a 'carrier of deep culture and structure' (1982: 136) and in the fourth phase this culture was 'Western' in orientation. Indeed, sport can be said to have become a 'global idiom' in this phase. Globalizing sport entailed a specific type of 'Western' masculine culture as embodied in and through achievement sport.

Yet we have to be careful here in our intra-civilizational analysis. While Galtung has correctly argued that sport is 'one of the most powerful transfer mechanisms for culture and structure ever known to humankind', in

suggesting this he overstates the extent to which 'Western' domination of global 'sport' cultures was and is complete (1991: 150). As Said noted 'it was the case nearly everywhere in the non-European world that the coming of the white man brought forth some sort of resistance' (1993: xii). On occasions, as already noted, non-Western people not only resisted and reinterpreted 'Western' masculine sport personnel, forms, models and marketing, they also maintained, fostered and promoted, on a global scale, their indigenous recreational pursuits.

While Galtung may be correct to suggest that competitive sports carry a 'message of western social cosmology' (1982: 137), this does not mean that people from non-occidental or indeed occidental cultures accepted them uncritically between the 1920s and the late 1960s. Studies of Trobriand cricket (Cashman, 1988), baseball in Japan (Snyder and Spreitzer, 1984), the diffusion of sport to Papua New Guinea (Seward, 1986), and the early twentieth-century development of 'Finnish baseball' (Meinander, 1992) all highlight the dynamic interchange between the local, national and the global. Despite what some 'soundbite sociologists' suggest, there is nothing sanguine about reaching this conclusion. What one is attempting to do is to describe and analyse how complex social processes really are. For example, while 'sport', or variants of this term, diffused across the globe, in its northern European heartland this form of body culture was reinterpreted and labelled by indigenous people in the light of local history and social structures. In Norway the term *Idrett* is used, which while referring to sport also incorporates broader traditional body culture. In contrast, in Finland, different terms are used that serve to distinguish between sport (*Urheilu*) and movement (*Liikunta*).

It is also important to note that representatives of indigenous cultures have proved adept at embracing a sport form, reinventing it and then recycling it back to the country of origin. The history of nordic skiing is an example of these processes at work. In turn, the core country also embraces cultural flows from outsider states and the 'reinvented' sport form diffuses further around the core. The diffusion of Canadian ice-hockey illustrates the processes involved (Maguire, 1996). It should also be observed that this phase of sportization/globalization witnessed the slow decline of modern sport's founding nation. In the emerging global sport figuration, English*men* were being beaten – in the early stages of this fourth phase, by fellow occidentals – at games at which they felt they had, by birthright, a 'god given' right to be winners.

Whereas the fourth phase of sportization clearly involved an elaborate political economy in which hegemonic control of sport lay with the 'West', control was never complete. Resistance took a variety of forms, such as the Cold War rivalry that was also played out in the sports world. There also occurred the slow assertion of women's rights and the challenge to hegemonic masculinity. The latter stages of this fourth phase were also characterized by the rise of non-Western nations to sporting prominence, and, sometimes, pre-eminence. Non-Western nations began to beat their former colonial masters, especially the English. This process has intensified in the fifth phase of sportization beginning in the late 1960s, and is apparent in a range of sports including badminton, cricket, soccer, table tennis and track and field. Here, African, Asian and South American nations were and are increasingly to the fore. In a sense, however, they still do so on 'Western' terms, for they do so through 'Western' sports.

This fifth phase of global sportization exemplifies both a decrease in contrasts but also an increase in varieties. It also highlights the need for detailed empirical case studies. The creolization of sports cultures may be under way but the precise matrix being formed remains to be charted. An increase in the varieties of structures, forms and identities can tentatively be identified. In this connection, Houlihan is correct to point to the need to develop criteria by which to judge the 'reach' and 'response' of global flows on local cultures. He is also correct to observe that it is important to assess whether these processes affect what he terms the 'core' or the 'ephemeral' aspects of that culture (Houlihan, 1994). Similar observations were made, as noted with regard to assessing the impact of Americanization processes in the case studies examining basketball and American football and the media–sport complex (Maguire, 1990: 216; 1993a). Equally, while he is correct to point to the need to 'distinguish between the globalization of particular sports and the globalization of the organizational processes and values of modern sport' (Houlihan, 1994: 367), it is important not to lose sight of the interconnections between the achievement sport ethos and how it is played out in different kinds of sports. Not all modern sports are the same. Further, while I would concur with Houlihan that it is foolish to claim that victory on the playing field can, in itself, be seen as having a dramatic effect on relations between nations, I would also agree with him

that 'profound differences will nonetheless still divide states and that these differences might be reflected in the sports they play' (Houlihan, 1994: 364). Perhaps one can go further and argue that only when new 'sports' gain cultural ascendancy, and along with these new sports, new global rivals are created, will sport assist in the development of new identities and the jettisoning of older 'invented traditions' (Maguire, 1993a). These issues, among others, arguably lie at the heart of the glocal (global/local) sports nexus.

CONCLUSION

The approach outlined here shares with Arnason the assumption that 'among the identities that are thus reinforced and reoriented by the global context, civilizational complexes and traditions are not the least important' (Arnason, 1990: 224). The concepts of diminishing contrasts and increasing varieties, overlooked in Robertson's work on globalization, help in more adequately conceptualizing such an analysis. These concepts also assist in making sense of the global diffusion, patterning and differential popularization of cultural wares, including sports. Diminishing contrasts and increasing varieties have not, however, been given due prominence in previous figurational accounts of sport. This may explain, in part, some of the misunderstandings and misinterpretations that have arisen over the past three decades. In this context it is particularly important to link the concepts of diminishing contrasts and increasing varieties to a broader intra-civilizational analysis. On this basis the implications for the study of sportization processes can be teased out. In the recent work of Featherstone (1995) and Featherstone and Lash (1995) extensive reference is made to figurational concepts and emphasis is given to the need to think processually and relationally. The need to examine the power dynamics of cross-cultural interdependency chains is also highlighted. Here too, however, as with Robertson, the twin concepts of diminishing contrasts and increasing varieties – as well as sport – are overlooked. Yet, to be fair, both Featherstone and Robertson are rightly pointing to the need for intra-civilizational analyses.

On the basis of what has been argued so far, several key points of departure can be identified which can assist in more adequately orientating analyses of the global sports process. First, adoption of a very long-term perspective can yield many benefits. Though it is legitimate to examine the making of modern sports, intra-civilizational analysis of the European ancient world and of other civilizations is also necessary. The longer-term links of these ancient civilizations with the making of modern sport should not be overlooked. Equally, the interdependency chains that tie more recent developments within the West to non-occidental cultures require consideration. In doing so it is important to distinguish between concepts of development and evolution and to avoid an ethnocentric approach. It is also necessary to grasp that the 'local' was and is never hermetically sealed from the 'other'. There is no sporting *Gemeinschaft* waiting to be discovered. The local was always semi-permeable and contoured by centrifugal and centripetal forces. In this connection, it needs also to be understood that this balance of forces was marked by a series of power struggles, elimination combat and a mutual contest of sameness, difference and commingling. The gendered, ethnic and class-based nature of these processes need careful unravelling. In doing so, the analysis must avoid the pursuit of monocausal explanations, the use of dichotomous thinking and the tendency to view these processes as governed by either the intended or the unintended actions of established or outsider groups of people. Analyses that emphasize the multifaceted, multidirectional and complex sets of power balances will be better placed to probe and trace the global sportization process.

Sport then plays a contradictory role in globalization processes and national identity formation. Sport development has been and continues to be contoured by the interlocking processes of diminishing contrasts and increasing varieties. The emergence of modern sport out of its European, and particularly British heartland, was, as noted, closely tied to globalization processes. Its standardization, organizational development and global diffusion both reflected and reinforced the global processes that were then being powered by the West. During the twentieth century sport was to become a 'global idiom'. Its laws were, as Ali Mazrui (1976: 411), noted, the first to be voluntarily embraced across the globe.

In certain respects sports also act as 'anchors of meaning' at a time when national cultures and identities are experiencing the effects of global time–space compression. Victory over Australia provides the English with a secure status point. The association of sport with a specific place and season also provides a sense of *Heimat*, a sense of invented 'permanence'. Think of Wimbledon, Super Bowl Sunday, the US Masters at Augusta and, for the English, test cricket from Australia during a European winter. These sport occasions are counterpoints to change. As was noted earlier, the formation of sport was closely connected to the invention of traditions that attempt to bind the past and present together. Yet, paradoxically, the media–sport production complex also erodes this sense of stability. Through satellite broadcasting the consumer can cross spaces and be at any sport venue across the globe. It also brings new varieties of sport subcultures to national cultures. New identities can be forged. Some British/ English males now identify with, and want to be famous American sports stars, such as the golfer Tiger Woods or ex-basketball player Michael Jordan.

Though sport has reinforced and reflected a diminishing of contrasts between nations, the close association of sport with national cultures and identities also means that moves towards integration of regions at a political level are undermined by the role of sport. Sport, being inherently competitive and based on a hierarchical valuing of worth, binds people to the dominant invented traditions associated with the nation. Yet, there may be also the first signs of countervailing trends. The tentative emergence of a European sports identity is a case in point. The incipient stages of this are evident in the formation of 'European' teams to play the United States of America in the men's Ryder Cup and women's Solheim Cup golf competitions. The athletics World Cup competition also has teams representing six 'geographical' areas, of which Europe is one. The degree to which the athletes involved feel any strong sense of identification with these areas is debatable but, as yet, is also unexplored. EU officials have also raised the idea of a common European team for the Olympics and also endorse a Formula One grand prix of Europe. As with European integration more generally, however, the sports process occupies contested terrain in which the defensive response of *strengthened* ethnic identities may yet win out over broader *pluralizing* global flows.

NOTE

1 For further reading see special issues *Sociology of Sport Journal*, 11 (4), 1994; the *Journal of Sport and Social Issues*, 20 (3), 1996; and *Media, Culture and Society*, 18 (4), 1996.

REFERENCES AND FURTHER READING

Andrews, D. (1997) 'The [Trans]National Basketball Association: American commodity-sign culture and global–local conjuncturalism', in A. Cvetkovich and D. Kellner (eds), *Articulating the Global and the Local: Globalization and Cultural Studies*. Boulder, CO: Westview Press.

Appadurai, A. (1990) 'Disjuncture and difference in the global cultural economy', *Theory, Culture and Society*, 7: 207–36.

Arbena, J.L. (ed.) (1988) *Sport and Society in Latin America: Diffusion, Dependency and the Rise of Mass Culture*. Westport, CT: Greenwood Press.

Arbena, J. (1993) 'Sport and nationalism in Latin America, 1880–1970: the paradox of promoting and performing "European" sports', *History of European Ideas*, 16: 837–44.

Arnason, J. (1990) 'Nationalism, globalization and modernity', *Theory, Culture and Society*, 7: 207–36.

Baker, W. (1982) *Sports in the Western World*. Totowa, NJ: Rowman & Littlefield.

Baker, W. and Mangan, J.A. (eds) (1987) *Sport in Africa: Essays in Social History*. New York: Africana.

Bale, J. (1994) *Landscapes of Modern Sport*. Leicester: Leicester University Press.

Cashman, R. (1988) 'Cricket and colonialism: colonial hegemony and indigenous subversion?', in J.A. Mangan (ed.), *Pleasure, Profit and Proselytism: British Culture and Sport at Home and Abroad, 1700–1914*. London: Frank Cass. pp. 258–72.

De Coubertin, P. (1892) Paper Presented at the Union des Sports Athletiques, Sorbonne, 25 November.

Donnelly, P. (1996) 'The local and the global: globalization in the sociology of sport', *Journal of Sport and Social Issues*, 20: 239–57.

Dunning, E. (1986) 'The dynamics of modern sport: notes on achievement – striving and the social significance of sport', in N. Elias and E. Dunning, *Quest for Excitement: Sport and Leisure in the Civilizing Process*. Oxford: Basil Blackwell. pp. 205–23.

Dunning, E. and Sheard, K. (1979) *Barbarians, Gentlemen and Players: a Sociological Study of the Developmental of Rugby Football*. Oxford: Martin Robertson.

Eichberg, H. (1984) 'Olympic sport: neocolonialism and alternatives', *International Review for the Sociology of Sport*, 19: 97–105.

Elias, N. (1939/1982) *The Civilizing Process: State Formation and Civilization*. Oxford: Basil Blackwell.

Elias, N. (1986) 'Introduction', in N. Elias and E. Dunning, *Quest for Excitement: Sport and Leisure in the Civilizing Process*. Oxford: Basil Blackwell. pp. 19–62.

Ensor, R.C.K. (1936) *England 1870–1914: the Oxford History of England*. Oxford: Clarendon Press.

Featherstone, M. (1995) *Undoing Culture: Globalization, Postmodernism and Identity*. London: Sage.

Featherstone, M. and Lash, S. (1995) 'Globalization, modernity and the spatialization of social theory: an introduction', in M. Featherstone, S. Lash and R. Roberston (eds), *Global Modernities*. London: Sage. pp. 1–24.

Galtung, J. (1982) 'Sport as carrier of deep culture and structure', *Current Research on Peace and Violence*, 5: 133–43.

Galtung, J. (1991) 'The sport system as a metaphor for the world system', in F. Landry, M. Landry and M. Yerles (eds), *Sport ... the Third Millennium*. Quebec: University of Laval Press. pp. 147–56.

Gorn, E.J. and Goldstein, W. (1993) *A Brief History of American Sports*. New York: Hill & Wang.

Gruneau, R. (1988) 'Modernization or hegemony: two views on sport and social development', in J. Harvey and H. Cantelon (eds), *Not Just a Game: Essays in Canadian Sport Sociology*. Ottawa: University of Ottawa Press. pp. 9–32.

Gruneau, R. and Whitson, D. (1993) *Hockey Night in Canada: Sport, Identities and Cultural Politics*. Toronto: Garamond Press.

Guttmann, A. (1991) 'Sports diffusion: a response to Maguire and the Americanization commentaries', *Sociology of Sport Journal*, 8: 185–90.

Guttmann, A. (1993) 'The diffusion of sports and the problem of cultural imperialism', in E.G. Dunning, J.A. Maguire and R. Pearton (eds), *The Sports Process: a Comparative and Developmental Approach*. Champaign, IL: Human Kinetics. pp. 125–38.

Guttmann, A. (1994) *Games and Empires: Modern Sports and Cultural Imperialism*. New York: Columbia University Press.

Hargreaves, J.A. (1994) *Sporting Females: Critical Issues in the History and Sociology of Women's Sports*. London: Routledge.

Hargreaves, J.E. (1986) *Sport, Power and Culture*. Cambridge: Polity Press.

Harvey, J. and Houle, F. (1994) 'Sport, world economy, global culture and new social movements', *Sociology of Sport Journal*, 11: 337–55.

Houlihan, B. (1994) 'Homogenization, Americanization, and Creolization of sport: varieties of globalization', *Sociology of Sport Journal*, 11: 356–75.

James, C.L.R. (1963) *Beyond a Boundary*. London: Stanley Paul.

Kidd, B. (1981) 'Sport, dependency and the Canadian state', in M. Hart and S. Birrell (eds), *Sport in the Sociocultural Process*. Dubuque, IA: William C. Brown. pp. 707–21.

Kidd, B. (1991) 'How do we find our own voices in the "new world order"? A commentary on Americanization', *Sociology of Sport Journal*, 8: 178–84.

Klein, A. (1989) 'Baseball in the Dominican Republic', *Sociology of Sport Journal*, 6: 95–112.

Klein, A. (1991) *Sugarball: the American Game, the Dominican Dream*. New Haven, CT: Yale University Press.

Maguire, J. (1990) 'More than a sporting "touchdown": the making of American football in Britain, 1982–1989', *Sociology of Sport Journal,* 7: 213–37.

Maguire, J. (1993a) 'Globalization, sport and national identities: the empires strike back?', *Society and Leisure,* 16: 293–322.

Maguire, J. (1993b) 'Globalization, sport development, and the media/sport production complex', *Sports Sciences Review,* 2: 29–47.

Maguire, J. (1994a) 'Preliminary observations on globalisation and the migration of sport labour', *The Sociological Review,* 3: 452–80.

Maguire, J. (1994b) 'Sport, identity politics and globalization: diminishing contrasts and increasing varieties', *Sociology of Sport Journal,* 11: 398–427.

Maguire, J. (1996) 'Blade runners: Canadian migrants and global ice-hockey trails', *Journal of Sport and Social Issues,* 20: 335–60.

Maguire, J. (1999) *Global Sport: Identities, Societies, Civilizations.* Oxford: Polity Press.

Mandell, R. (1984) *Sport: a Cultural History.* New York: Columbia University Press.

Mandle, J. and Mandle, J. (1988) *Grass Roots Commitment: Basketball and Society in Trinidad and Tobago.* Parkesburg, IA: Caribbean Books.

Mangan, J.A. (1986) *The Games Ethic and Imperialism.* London: Viking Press.

Mazrui, A. (1976) *A World Federation of Cultures: an African Perspective.* New York: Free Press.

McKay, J. and Miller, T. (1991) 'From old boys to men and women of the corporation: the Americanization and commodification of Australian sport', *Sociology of Sport Journal,* 8: 86–94.

McKay, J., Lawrence, G., Miller, T. and Rowe, D. (1993) 'Globalisation and Australian sport', *Sport Science Review,* 2: 10–28.

Meinander, H. (1992) 'Language, identity and sport: social patterns and expectations among Swedish sportsmen in Helsinki during the inter-war period', in *Sport and Cultural Minorities.* ISHPES Conference Proceedings, Turku, Finland. pp. 426–58.

Nederveen Pieterse, J. (1995) 'Globalization as hybridization', in M. Featherstone, S. Lash and R. Roberston (eds), *Global Modernities.* London: Sage. pp. 45–68.

Robertson, R. (1992) *Globalization: Social Theory and Global Culture.* London: Sage.

Sage, G. (1995) 'Deindustrialization and the American sporting goods industry', in R.C. Wilcox (ed.), *Sport in the Global Village.* Morgantown, WV: Fitness Information Technology. pp. 39–51.

Said, E. (1993) *Culture and Imperialism.* London: Chatto and Windus.

Seward, A.K. (1986) 'An attempt to perpetuate a cultural identity through traditional games in the face of the influence of Western sports in Papua New Guinea', in J.A. Mangan and R.B. Small (eds), *Sport, Culture and Society.* London: E&FN Spon. pp. 33–8.

Snyder, E. and Spreitzer, E. (1984) 'Baseball in Japan', in S. Eitzen (ed.), *Sports in Contemporary Society.* New York: St Martin's Press. pp. 46–50.

Stoddart, B. (1988) 'Cricket and colonialism in the English-speaking Caribbean to 1914: towards a cultural analysis', in T. Mangan (ed.), *Pleasure, Profit and Proselytism. British Culture and Sport at Home and Abroad, 1700–1914.* London: Cass. pp. 231–57.

Stoddart, B. (1989) 'Sport in the social construct of the lesser developed world: a commentary', *Sociology of Sport Journal,* 6: 125–35.

Wagner, E. (ed.) (1989) *Sport in Asia and Africa: a Comparative Handbook.* Westport, CT: Greenwood Press.

Wagner, E. (1990) 'Sport in Africa and Asia: Americanization or mundialization?', *Sociology of Sport Journal,* 7: 399–402.

Wilcox, R.C. (ed.) (1995) *Sport in the Global Village.* Morgantown, WV: Fitness Information Technology.

Wilson, J. (1994) *Playing by the Rules: Sport, Society, and the State.* Detroit: Wayne University Press.

Wolfe, J. (1991) 'The global and the specific: reconciling conflicting theories of culture', in A.D. King (ed.), *Culture, Globalization and the World-System.* London: Macmillan. pp. 161–73.

24

SOCIAL CONTROL AND SPORT

D. Stanley Eitzen

THE SOCIOLOGICAL UNDERSTANDING OF SOCIAL CONTROL

The Concept of Social Control

A perennial question for many sociologists is: How is social order possible? For some sociologists (for example, Durkheim, 1949; Parsons, 1951) the answer to this question is that the vast members of a social organization share a consensus on the norms, laws and values. In pre-modern societies social order occurs because the norms are shared and legitimated by deeply held religious authority. In modern complex societies social order is maintained as citizens accept the legal order and the state, which are believed to serve the common good. Other social theorists such as Marx (1909) reject the assumption of normative consensus, arguing rather that social order is the result of economic dominants using the law (Quinney, 1970) or the media (Parenti, 1986), or other institutions to hold power over the relatively powerless. Postmodern theorists reject both of these grand narratives, arguing rather that unity within contemporary societies is a myth. The old views depicted society with a single powerful political and economic center, predictable and moving in a straight, progressive line. The postmodern view sees society as decentered, with multiculturalism and multiple realities depending on one's class, racial, or gender standpoint. The social world is neither predictable nor moving inexorably toward a better state. Instead of normative consensus there are cultural wars and subgroup identities/loyalties that divide rather than unify society (see Lemert, 1993; Rosenau,

1992). Thus, postmodern theories reflect a fragmented and fragile society. If this view is correct, then social order rather than a given as the classic social theories postulated, is problematic. So, too, is social control, for it is the essence of social order.

Social control is a central concept in sociology (see, Berger, 1963; Horowitz, 1990; Janowitz, 1991; Liska, 1992; Wolff, 1964). Indeed, for some it is *the* central organizing concept of sociology (Gibbs, 1981, 1985). As Cuzzort has asserted:

> A sociocultural system cannot rely on random individual responses to create the structure and the cohesiveness required for organized effort. A society cannot, in other words, rely on people simply 'doing *their* thing'. A society must, in effect, generate ways that ensure that what gets done is 'society's thing'. (Cuzzort, 1989: 179)

Social control is fundamental because it focuses attention on three other essential concepts: social order, norms and deviance. Each social system (group, family, factory, team, school, hospital, prison, church, community and society) attempts to achieve conformity to the norms (the standards of right and wrong) of that social unit. If a social organization succeeds in controlling its members, then deviant behavior is minimized and social order is sustained. The irony is that attempts to achieve conformity in groups often meet with non-compliance, resistance or outright rebellion (Walton, 1990: 343–61). In short, social control is never perfect.

The Mechanisms of Social Control

All social groups have mechanisms to ensure conformity – mechanisms of social control.

Peter Berger (1963: 68–78) has identified eight sources of social control: (a) *force*, the use of violence or threats of violence; (b) *economic rewards or punishments*, the promise or denial of economic rewards; (c) *ridicule and gossip*, fear of being belittled for acting outside group expectations; (d) *ostracism*, the threat or actual removal from the group; (e) *fraud and deception*, actions to manipulate (trick) others to conform; (f) *belief systems*, the use of ideology to induce individuals to conform; (g) *the sphere of intimates*, pressures from close friends, peers, relatives to conform; and (h) *the contract*, actions controlled by the stipulations of a formal agreement.

The mechanisms of social control can be divided into two broad types by the means to achieve it: ideological control and direct intervention. The former aims at control through manipulation of ideas and perceptions; the latter controls the actual behavior of individuals (Eitzen and Baca Zinn, 1995: 170–90).

Ideological social control manipulates the consciousness of individuals so that they accept the ruling ideology and refuse to be moved by competing ideologies. Other goals are to persuade the members to follow the rules and to accept without question the existing distribution of power and rewards. These goals are accomplished in at least three ways. First, ideological social control is accomplished through the socialization of new members. This socialization process could be referred to as cultural control because the individual is given authoritative definitions of what should and should not be done, which make it appear as if there is no choice. Secondly, ideological conformity occurs by frontal attacks on competing ideologies by persons in authority. Finally, there are propaganda efforts by authorities to persuade the members what actions are moral, who the enemies are, and why certain courses of action are required.

Ideological social control is more effective than overt social control measures because individuals impose controls upon themselves (Collins, 1992: 63–85). Through the socialization process we learn not only the rules of a social organization but also the supporting ideology. The norms are internalized in this process. To the degree that this process works, individuals are not forced to conform, they *want* to conform. As Berger has observed: 'Most of the time we ourselves desire just that which society expects of us. We *want* to obey the rules' (Berger, 1963: 93).

Direct social control refers to attempts to reward those who conform and to punish or neutralize (render powerless) individuals

who deviate from the norms of the social organization. All but 'belief systems' from Berger's list of social control mechanisms are efforts at direct social control.

SOCIAL CONTROL THROUGH SPORT

Social Control in Society: Sport and Societal Integration

Sport helps to maintain societal integration in several ways (Eitzen and Sage, 1997). First, there is the strong relationship between sport and nationalism.

Sport and Nationalism Success in international sports competition tends to trigger pride among that nation's citizens. The Olympics and other international games tend to promote an 'us' versus 'them' feeling among athletes, coaches, politicians, the press, fans and even among those normally not very interested in sport. Goodhart and Chataway (1968) have argued, for example, that one type of sport is 'representative' in that it pits the representatives of political units against each other. Thus, international contests are viewed as political contests, where nations win or lose in a symbolic world war. Because this interpretation is commonly held, citizens of each nation involved unite behind their flag and their athletes (Ball, 1972; Hargreaves, 1992; Heinila, 1985).

The integral interrelationship of sport and nationalism is easily seen in the blatantly militaristic pageantry that surrounds sports contests. The playing of the national anthem, the presentation of the colors, the jet flyovers and bands forming a flag are all political acts supportive of the existing political system.

Sport as an Instrument of National Policy to Unify More explicitly, sports can be used as a propaganda vehicle, as a mechanism by which a society's ruling elite unites its citizens and attempts to impress the citizens of other countries (Frey, 1988; Strenk, 1977). A classic example of this was Adolf Hitler's use of the 1936 Olympic Games to strengthen his control over the German people and to legitimize Nazi culture. According to Mandell (1971), the festival planned for those games was a shrewdly propagandistic and brilliantly conceived charade that reinforced and mobilized the hysterical patriotism of the German masses.

Before the break-up of the Eastern bloc countries, the reunification of the two Germanies, and the demise of the Soviet Union, the

Communist nations used sport for promoting their common cause. Their domination of the Olympics, the Communists argued, provided convincing proof of the superiority of the Communist politico-economic system (Rosellini, 1992). This heritage continues for one of the few remaining Communist nations – Cuba. Cuba spends about 3 per cent of its budget on sport. In the Pan American Games, Cuba generally wins about 15 times more medals than the United States on a per capita basis, allowing its premier, Fidel Castro, to proclaim that this is proof of the superiority of the Cuban people and the Cuban social system. Clearly, these victories by Cuban athletes are a source of collective pride and national unity.

National efforts to use sport for political purposes are not limited to Communist countries. International sports victories are just as important to nations such as Canada and the United States. Canada has a federal agency, Sport Canada, and similar organizations at the provincial level that work to promote sports excellence. There is a federal Athlete Assistance Program, which gives living and training grants to outstanding athletes. There is a network of national training centers, with professional coaching, and a calendar of events. These efforts are made to enhance Canadian nationalism and the Canadian state's legitimacy (Kidd, 1991; see also, Macintosh et al., 1987; and Macintosh and Whitson, 1990).

Since 1972, the United States has organized sport to encourage athletic excellence in international arenas. Athletes have been subsidized by government and corporations, funds appropriated for the establishment of permanent training sites and eligibility rules modified to permit athletes to retain their 'amateur' standing while receiving money for appearances, performances and endorsements. Also, commissions have been formed to investigate the 'problem' of inferior international performances by US athletes. The clear assumption behind these efforts was that if the United States made the appropriate commitment to its athletes, they would prevail in international sports – proving the superiority of its politico-economic system. Not incidentally, such athletic superiority would have the added benefit of societal unity.

Sport is also an instrument of national policy among the developing nations. A study of the 133 members of the United Nations in 1973 showed that although 26 per cent of all nations had a cabinet-level post related to sport, 87 per cent of those classified as 'developing' had such a position (Goodhue, 1974). The probable reason for such keen interest is that sport provides a relatively inexpensive tool to accomplish national objectives of prestige abroad and unity at home.

As a final example of political elites using sport to unify its citizens, consider the racially divided nation of South Africa (Eitzen, 1995). Sport has been used to break down this division, at least in part. After the formal fall of apartheid and the election of Nelson Mandela, the sports world lifted its ban on South African participation in international competition. In 1995 the World Cup in rugby was held in South Africa and Mandela used this opportunity to achieve greater national unity. Even though the nation's team, the Springboks, symbolized white South Africa with a white sport and with white players, Mandela did what he could to get blacks to think of this team as *their* team. Speaking to a black audience, and wearing a Springbok's cap, Mandela said: 'This Springbok cap does honor to our boys. I ask you to stand by them because they are our kind.' To which *Sports Illustrated* editorialized: '*Our kind*. Not black. Not white. South African. The rugby team became a symbol for the country as a whole' (Swift, 1995: 33).

Sport as an Opiate of the Masses   Sport, as we have seen, can unite a nation's citizens because the people are manipulated by propaganda and the use of symbols, because they unite in pulling together to defeat 'them', and because of a shared pride in their country's athletic accomplishments. This unity stifles challenges to ruling elites and in so doing sport serves as an 'opiate of the masses'. For example, Janet Lever (1983) has shown how a fanatical interest in a sport (soccer) by Brazilians, enables the poor to forget partially the harshness of their lives and thus inhibits efforts to change the social conditions that oppress them. Similarly, in 1994, when Haiti was on the verge of a severe crisis, the embattled military ruler, Raoul Cedras, paid for the broadcasting rights to the World Cup soccer matches. The spirits of the Haitians were lifted as their adopted team, Brazil, was successful. Rather than massing in the streets to demonstrate against a political regime that oppressed them, the masses danced in the streets as their favorite team won. Moreover, as the games were broadcast on the government-owned station, the rulers used halftime to inflame anti-American feelings by showing footage of the US invasion of Panama in 1989, focusing on the bombing of residential areas (Squitieri, 1994). Thus, sport serves as both a temporary escape from the problems of world politics and as a safety valve for releasing tensions that might otherwise be directed toward disrupting and changing the existing power relationships in society (see Brohm, 1978; Hoch, 1972).

Sport also acts as an opiate by perpetuating the belief that persons from the lowest social classes can be upwardly mobile through success in sports. Although the chances of this occurring are exceedingly rare, most believe that sport is a mobility escalator. Again, poor youth who might otherwise invest their energies and talents in changing the system work instead on honing their athletic skills. The potential for change is thus impeded by sport.

Sport as an Agent of Ideological Social Control

Sport, as a social institution, is conservative. Sport promotes traditional values and societal arrangements. To illustrate this assumption, this section examines how social control mechanisms in sport are employed to foster the status quo in three representative areas: the transmission of societal values, traditional gender roles, and compulsory heterosexuality.

Sport and the Transmission of Values Sport serves to control persons ideologically by reinforcing society's values among the participants. In the United States sport transmits the values of success in competition, hard work, perseverance, discipline, teamwork and obedience to authority to participants and observers. This is the explicit reason given for the existence of children's sports programs such as Little League baseball and the tremendous emphasis on sports in US schools. Coaches commonly believe that they should not only teach sport skills but that they should also promote values. Thus, there is the common practice by coaches of placing signs in locker rooms to inspire traits in their athletes such as hard work, never giving up and teamwork. Some examples of the messages on these signs include: 'The will to win is the will to work'; 'By failing to prepare yourself you are preparing to fail'; 'Winners never quit and quitters never win'; 'United we stand, divided we fall' (Snyder, 1972).

Whether sport actually transmits these values or not is an empirical question. As sport is organized, it clearly makes the effort. According to Matza: 'The substance of athletics contains within itself – in its rules, procedures, training, and sentiments – a paradigm of adult expectations for youth' (1964: 207).

Sport and Traditional Gender Roles Sport in its organization, procedures and operation serves to promote traditional gender roles.

Most especially, sport advances male hegemony in practice and ideology by legitimating a certain dominant version of social reality. Bryson (1987) has argued that sport reproduces patriarchal relations through four minimalizing processes: definition, direct control, ignoring and trivialization. By definition, 'dominant forms of sport in most cultures are played and organized in ways that work to the advantage of most men and to the disadvantage of women' (Coakley, 1998: 232–3). Male standards are applied to female performance, ensuring female inferiority and even deviance. As Willis has argued: '[The ideal description of sport] is a *male* description concerning males. Where women become at all visible, then the terms of reference change. There is a very important thread in popular consciousness which sees the very presence of women in sport as bizarre' (1982: 120).

Sports participation is expected for men. Sport is strongly associated with male identity and popularity. For women, though, the situation is entirely different. As Willis has stated: 'Instead of confirming her identity, [sports] success can threaten her with a foreign male identity. … The female athlete lives through a severe contradiction. To succeed as an athlete can be to fail as a woman, because she has, in certain profound symbolic ways, become a man' (1982: 123). Superior women athletes are suspect because strength and athletic skill are accepted as 'masculine' traits. Thus, since 1968 the International Olympic Committee has a mandatory sex test for women participants (Cahn, 1994: 263).

Women's sport is minimized when it is controlled by men. This is the case in the gender composition of leadership positions in the International Olympic Committee, various international and national sports bodies, the National Collegiate Athletic Association, and the administrative and coaching roles in schools (Acosta and Carpenter, 1994).

Women in sport are minimized (and men maximized) when women's activities are ignored. The mass media in the United States have either overlooked women's sports or, when they are reported, the stories, photographs and commentary tend to reinforce gender role stereotypes (Eitzen and Sage, 1997, Chs 11 and 14). Regarding the former, studies of television coverage indicate that men's sports receive about 92 per cent of air time. Moreover, 97 per cent of the athletic figures employed in television commercials were males (Turner et al., 1995).

Women's sports are also ignored when cities and schools disproportionately spend enormous amounts on men's sports. As Nelson has argued:

> We live in a country in which the manly sports culture is so pervasive we may fail to recognize the symbolic messages we all receive about men, women, love, sex, and power. We need to take sports seriously – not the scores or the statistics, but the process. Not to focus on who wins, but on who's losing. Who loses when a community spends millions of dollars in tax revenue to construct a new stadium and only men get to play in it, and only men get to work there? Who loses when football and baseball so dominate the public discourse that they eclipse all mention of female volleyball players, gymnasts, basketball players, and swimmers? (Nelson, 1994: 8)

Women are also minimized when they are trivialized in sport. As noted above, the media framing of the female athlete reinforces gender stereotypes. Considering photographs of women and men athletes, Duncan (1990) found that these images emphasized gender differences:

1 female athletes who are sexy and glamorous are most common;
2 female athletes are often photographed in sexual poses;
3 in the framing of photos, male athletes are more likely to be photographed in dominant positions and female athletes in submissive positions;
4 camera angles typically focus up to male athletes and focus down on female athletes;
5 female athletes are more likely to be shown displaying emotions.

As Messner has argued: 'The choices, the filtering, the entire mediation of the sporting event, is based upon invisible, taken-for-granted assumptions and values of dominant social groups, as such the presentation of the event tends to support corporate, white, and male-dominant ideologies' (1988: 204–5).

Another example of the trivialization of women's sports activities is the naming of their teams. A study comparing the unifying symbols of women's and men's teams found that more than half of colleges and universities in the United States employ names, mascots and/or logos that demean and derogate women's teams (Eitzen and Baca Zinn, 1989). Thus, the naming of women's teams tends to define women athletes and women's athletic programs as second class and trivial.

In short, the secondary treatment of women in sport culturally defines and perceives them as inferior not only in sport but also, by inference, as less capable than men in many areas of life. As Bryson has posited:

> The dialectical element of the ideological processes underpinning contemporary sport is of crucial importance. These processes construct a form of dominant masculinity and in doing so define what is not approved. Each cultural message about sport is a dual one, celebrating the dominant at the same time as inferiorizing the 'other'. This dominant form of masculinity has been usefully called hegemonic masculinity, and the message it conveys renders inferior not only femininity in all its forms but also non hegemonic forms of masculinity. (Bryson, 1990: 173)

It is important to note that while this dominant ideology is perpetuated in many ways, it is also challenged and contested with some success in all institutional areas, including sport (Messner, 1988).

Sport and Sexuality   Sport has been socially constructed as a masculine activity. Young boys are inducted into a fiercely heterosexual world of male toughness and competitiveness that embodies a fear of effeminate and subordinates gay men (Hargreaves, 1994; see also Foley, 1990; Messner and Sabo, 1990; Pronger, 1990). In the United States boys learn to play (gridiron) football, where they develop both a social and a personal identity that is consistent with the hegemonic conception of masculinity (Sabo, 1987). This is the common pattern in other societies as well. In Australia, for example, virtually all boys are introduced to cricket, football (soccer) and rugby, which contributes to 'the construction of hegemonic masculinity' (Bryson, 1990: 175). Boys who do not participate in these manly sports are socially marginalized by peers as 'sissies'. Older boys and young men who do not fit the dominant behavior patterns of masculinity often face serious questions about their sexual orientation, with labels such as 'fag', 'gay' and 'queer' used to describe them (Coakley, 1998: 236). A common motivational ploy by some coaches is to question a male athlete's heterosexuality (calling him a 'pussy' or a 'fag' or placing tampons in his locker) if he does not play as aggressively as the coach demands. Curry's (1991) research on the male bonding in athletic locker rooms found that the talk there focused on the affirmation of traditional masculinity, homophobia, and misogynistic slurs against women. Curry reasons that athletes do not want to be singled out as unmasculine in any way. Thus, the 'expression of dislike for femaleness or homosexuality demonstrates to oneself and others that one is separate from it and therefore must be masculine' (Curry, 1991: 128). Needless to say, gay males are not welcome in the masculine sports world.

Female athletes, just as other women who enter traditional male domains, especially those in sports that require strength, endurance and aggression, face the social control mechanism of slander.

> Slander against female athletes usually takes the form of describing them as mannish, butch, musclebound, unpretty, unnatural, and otherwise unfeminine. It contains two related messages: one, that to be a female athlete is to be a lesbian (or at least in danger of becoming one), and two, that to be a lesbian is wrong. (Whitaker, 1982: 83)

Women in sport, more than men, endure intense scrutiny about their sexual identities. Many in society fear that women in sport transgress gender lines and that this disrupts the social order. 'The lesbian label is used to define the boundaries of acceptable female behavior in a patriarchal culture. When a woman is called a lesbian, she knows she is out of bounds' (Griffin, 1992: 252).

Lesbians are punished in sport. They are considered deviants. They are stereotyped by the media (Burroughs et al., 1995). Women (whether lesbian or not) sometimes face discrimination as they compete against men for coaching or sports administration jobs because of the assumption of homosexuality. Some coaches openly prohibit lesbian athletes from participation. Highly successful athletes (for example, Martina Navratilova) have lost millions of dollars in endorsement money after acknowledging their homosexuality. The Ladies Professional Golf Association has faced allegations, epithets and innuendo that its athletes were disproportionately lesbian in sexual orientation, which has damaged women's professional golf through losses of sponsorships, television coverage and fan support.

The result is that many lesbian athletes and coaches stay closeted. Others develop a lesbian identity (Palzkill, 1990). Others resist and work with heterosexuals to overcome homophobia, heterosexism, and sexism in sport (Griffin, 1992). The larger consequence of homophobia in sport is that compulsory heterosexuality remains the norm. And, as with gender roles, the mechanisms of social control in sport have sustained 'compulsory heterosexuality [as] part of a system of domination that perpetuates patriarchal relations and the wielding of power over other sexualities' (Hargreaves, 1994: 261).

SOCIAL CONTROL IN SPORT

Athletes engaged in sport beyond the informal play stage are subject to the authority of sports organizations. This section examines the organizational control of athletes and the roles within sport that control the participants.

Organizational Control of Athletes

Social order in sport is obtained through the establishment of sports organizations with the authority to establish and enforce rules for the play itself as well as the determination of participant eligibility. The key to social order is the term authority, which implies legitimate power. That is, the authorities are vested with power and this power is accepted by those affected, either because of tradition, the law, or charisma (Weber, 1947).

In the sports world there is a hierarchy of authority over athletes and individual sports (Harmer, 1991). Assuming that the athlete is in an 'amateur' team sport, the nearest governing organization is the club or school, followed, in ascending order, by league, district association, state association, national body and international body (for an analysis of international sports organizations, see Houlihan, 1994: 55–81). Another line of authority may involve specific events such as the Asian Games or the Olympic Games. Here, typically, political decisions have barred the athletes from various nations from participation (for example, the 1964–91 Olympic ban of the Union of South Africa). Professional sports have their own organizations (for example, the National Football League is divided into 30 teams, two leagues with subdivisions, and a commissioner, who is elected by the team owners). Political entities such as states or provinces and the nation-state constitute the final level of authority over sport. Legal authorities shape sports in many ways. They subsidize through the building of sports arenas and furnishing infrastructure such as roads and mass transit. They regulate (through licenses), restrict (through taxation) and insist (through legislation such as Title IX). They regulate television, provide anti-trust exemptions to professional sports leagues, and define criminal codes (Wilson, 1994). National leaders may also decide to prohibit their athletes from participating in an international event (for example, 34 Islamic nations prohibited their women from competing in the 1996 Olympics because participating violated Muslim rules for appropriate women's dress).

Sports organizations serve several controlling functions. First, they provide the essential function of determining and enforcing the rules of a sport. Secondly, they decide who shall be allowed to compete: 'From Little League to interscholastic athletic teams to the Olympic Games, entry into ever more competitive arenas is not predicated on an individual's desire [or ability] to compete. Instead, it rests on the sanctioning of athletes by an appropriate sports authority body' (Harmer, 1991: 24). The sports authority bodies establish the rules of eligibility. They do so to ensure fairness and equalize competition (weight classes in boxing, gender and age proscriptions, and minimal performance criteria). This gatekeeping function, while necessary, has been used, historically, to exclude or limit the participation of athletes from certain social categories. The notion of 'amateur' was used, for example, by the affluent to exclude members of the working class from their athletic activities (Guttmann, 1978). 'Amateur' has also been used as an exploitative ideology (Eitzen, 1989) whereby colleges and universities use 'amateur' athletes to generate considerable income for the schools and the sponsoring organization (Byers, 1995). African Americans were excluded from participation in mainstream US college and professional leagues, with rare exceptions, from the First World War until after the Second World War. This exclusion was a consequence of tradition, Jim Crow laws, institutional racism and even explicit rules in the bylaws of certain sports (for example, professional baseball, golf and bowling) (Chalk, 1975). Girls were excluded from participation on teams in Little League baseball until the 'boys only' clause was dropped as a result of a court case in the 1970s. Women were kept from competing in Olympic track and field events until 1928 by the men running the International Olympic Committee. Slowly, and reluctantly, women's events have been added to the Olympics, with women finally allowed to run a marathon in the 1984 Olympics.

A third function of sports organizations is to control the athletes' behavior on the field. While these bodies vary in their rules and enforcement zeal, they attempt to control excessive violence (Eitzen, 1985), the use of banned substances to enhance performance (see Wadler and Hainline, 1989, and Figone, 1988, for the case in the United States; see Johansson, 1987, for the situation in Sweden; and Pilz, 1988, for Germany), and point shaving (the unethical efforts by a player, coach, or referee to keep the points scored within the point spread used by gamblers when they bet on a game or match). They also sanction negatively, again with considerable variation, off-the-field behaviors by athletes, such as criminal acts, use of recreational drugs and, most especially, gambling on sports.

The sanctions used by sports organizations on deviant athletes, coaches and teams include reprimands, monetary fines (for professional athletes), suspensions and expulsions (Lumer, 1995). While necessary, the imposition of these sanctions by governing organizations is not always fair (Yaeger, 1991).

Controlling Roles

Within each sport social organization there are positions whose occupants exert control over others. This section focuses on three: officials, coaches and participants.

Officials A sports contest is governed by the official rules of the sport. Officials (rule enforcers) are assigned by leagues or associations to ensure that the rules of the sport are enforced during each contest. These officials (referees, umpires), interpret the formal rules of the game, assign penalties for infractions, and keep the game under control.

Research on officials has focused on their psychological traits (Fratzke, 1975) and profiled aspects of their subculture (Mitchell et al., 1982). Other studies reveal that there is a variation of rule enforcement within the fluid social context of a game (Askins et al., 1981; Snyder and Purdy, 1987).

Coaches Coaches have the formal tasks of teaching and training athletes to maximize their athletic performance and devising game strategies that maximize the chances of winning. Most important, the coach/player relationship is an asymmetrical power relationship. Coaches decide who makes the team, who plays and when. They divine the procedures for determining and enforcing team rules. Coaches determine training schedules. They sanction player behaviors that they deem detrimental to team goals.

There is a wide variation in coach-centered power over athletes (Pratt and Eitzen, 1989). A few coaches are open and democratic, allowing their athletes to make and enforce rules, and involving them in strategy decisions. At the opposite extreme, some coaches are tyrants, demanding total obedience to their authority. Except for the most democratic coaches, most are either paternalistic (Shogan, 1991) or authoritarian in their methods. With few exceptions, coaches impose their will over athletes. The result is that often the privacy rights of athletes are violated, their individual rights denied, and in extreme cases, athletes are subject to oppression, brutality and terror (Eitzen, 1992).

Why are so many coaches autocratic? Some have suggested that the coaching profession attracts those with inflexible and manipulative personalities but empirical research does not support this contention (the following relies on Coakley, 1994: 191–8). The key to understanding the tendency toward autocratic coaching behavior lies in the role of coach and the unique demands they face. First, the limits on coaching behaviors are set by communities and societies. Within the United States, for example, there is wide approval for demanding, autocratic coaches. Most players accept their subordination to higher authority (Hughes and Coakley, 1991). Ironically, a democratic society permits, even demands, undemocratic coaches (Eitzen, 1992).

A second and crucial basis for authoritarian coaches is the uniqueness of the coaching role. Coaches face distinctive pressures not found in other occupations. They are held totally accountable for game outcomes. The games are unpredictable, highly visible and the outcomes are objectively measured. Coaches react to their pressured situations in three characteristic ways. They seek public support by demanding that their athletes behave according to community norms (in dress, demeanor, patriotism and religiosity). Moreover, they generate community support by showing an absolute confidence in their methods and strategies. The other tactic is to control as much as possible. Thus, most coaches control on- and off-the-field behaviors, determine game strategy, and make all decisions during games.

Coaches are subject to social control also. Coaches are employed by clubs, schools and professional teams. When their behaviors go too far, they are subject to sanctions by those with authority over them. These outrageous behaviors include physical abuse of players, gambling, point shaving, drug abuse/alcoholism and insubordination. On rare occasions, coaches have been sanctioned because of the initiatives of aggrieved players who complained to authorities, threatened boycotts and brought grievances to the civil courts.

Participants Social control is not just the result of actions from the powerful who supervise and manage those below them in a social organization. Most significantly, social control emerges from interactions among peers within the informal social order. Sociological research

from such diverse settings as work (Roethlisberger and Dickson, 1939) and urban street corners (Whyte, 1943) have found that social norms, sanctions and roles emerge in informal interaction, resulting in social order. This social phenomenon has also been observed in sport settings where regulars participate as individuals with others they see during the activity but with whom they exchange few words. Nixon (1986) found, for example, that the regular participants in swimming constructed and maintained social order in that setting. This order involved an informal code of behavior, enforcement of rules, and role differentiation. The social control mechanisms by the participants included nonverbal cues, polite verbal prods and even aggressive retaliation.

Wacquant's (1992) ethnographic study of a boxing club/gym located in a Chicago ghetto is instructive concerning the informal but elaborate social order maintained by the participants. These implicit norms of the club 'are visible only in the conduct and demeanor of the regulars who have progressively internalized them, and they are brought to explicit attention only when violated' (Wacquant, 1992: 236).

Children at play also exert control over each other. Peers may mock behaviors that go beyond their norms such as boys not being aggressive or girls who are tomboys. Thus, behaviors are channeled in approved ways and gender is socially constructed (Kunesh et al., 1992; Thorne, 1993).

Male locker rooms are a sports setting where the informal norms promote homophobia and sexism. Peer group dynamics encourage such talk since to avoid such behaviors calls into question their masculinity (Curry, 1991).

Ethnographic studies of sport subcultures (for example, among bodybuilders, surfers, climbers, gymnasts) reveal that new members engage in the deliberate act of identity construction; that is, they adopt the attitudes, style of dress, speech patterns and behaviors of the established members of the subculture (Donnelly and Young, 1988). In short, the behavior of these neophyte members is controlled even *before* they become full members in the subculture through a process called 'anticipatory socialization'.

FUTURE DIRECTIONS FOR RESEARCH

As a central feature of social organization, social control has been studied and analysed by sociologists since the beginning of the discipline. Future research on social control will continue to be grounded in the fundamental social properties and processes of norms, values, socialization, deviance, social inequality, power, hegemony and bureaucracy.

Future research, while based on the connections between social control and traditional sociological concepts, will be inspired by new paradigms and epistemologies that will lead in new directions and toward greater insights and understandings. Research inspired by interactionist, critical theory and cultural studies frameworks is leading us beyond descriptive and correlational studies to interpretive studies. More attention in the future will be given to how decisions are made, the process of emerging norms and how socialization is related to control and power relations. New and renewed attention to human agency will lead away from a 'top-down' determinism toward a 'bottom-up' understanding of social life (Wolfe, 1991). This 'bottom-up' understanding requires that we do fieldwork, immersing ourselves in the social worlds we observe, engaged with people (Molotch, 1994). Moreover, it requires a new voice for the oppressed. The centered model of social reality that has dominated sociology will give way to the complexities of a decentered model of multiple realities. Complex realities require complex understandings, with contested terrains and different standpoints from which to understand social life.

Some examples of research questions involving social control in sport settings include:

1 Under what social conditions is norm/value transmission maximized in team sports?
2 How is social control experienced from different standpoints?
3 How do interlocking systems of inequality oppress women in sport?
4 How is oppression experienced by those who encounter double, and sometimes triple marginalization (Collins, 1990; Messner, 1992).
5 How do the relatively powerless in sport cope, adapt, resist, challenge and change oppressive social arrangements?
6 Under what conditions can the hegemony of the powerful be reduced or neutralized in sport?
7 As society becomes more decentered and traditional patterns of dominance change, what are the consequences for social control in sport?
8 What are the specific historical, social and material conditions that combine to socially construct the inequalities in power and privilege for women in sport?

REFERENCES

Acosta, R. Vivian and Carpenter, Linda J. (1994) 'Women in intercollegiate sport: a longitudinal study – seventeen years update, 1977–1994'. Department of Physical Education, Brooklyn College, New York.

Askins, R., Carter, T. and Wood, M. (1981) 'Rule enforcement in a public setting: the case of basketball officiating', *Qualitative Sociology*, 4: 87–101.

Ball, Donald W. (1972) 'Olympic Games competition: structural correlates of national success', *International Journal of Comparative Sociology*, 13 (September/December): 186–99.

Berger, Peter L. (1963) *Invitation to Sociology: a Humanistic Perspective.* Garden City, NY: Doubleday Anchor Books.

Brohm, Jean-Marie (1978) *Sport: a Prison of Measured Time.* (trans. Ian Fraser). London: Ink Links.

Bryson, Lois (1987) 'Sport and the maintenance of masculine hegemony', *Women's Studies International Forum*, 10: 349–60.

Bryson, Lois (1990) 'Challenges to male hegemony in sport', in Michael A. Messner and Donald F. Sabo (eds), *Sport, Men, and the Gender Order: Critical Feminist Perspectives.* Champaign, IL: Human Kinetics. pp. 173–84.

Burroughs, Angela, Ashburn, Liz and Seebohm, Leonie (1995) '"Add sex and stir": homophobic coverage of women's cricket in Australia', *Journal of Sport and Social Issues*, 19 (August): 266–84.

Byers, Walter, with Charles Hammer (1995) *Unsportsmanlike Conduct: Exploiting College Athletes.* Ann Arbor, MI: University of Michigan Press.

Cahn, Susan K. (1994) *Coming on Strong: Gender and Sexuality in Twentieth-Century Women's Sport.* New York: Free Press.

Chalk, Ocania (1975) *Pioneers of Black Sport.* New York: Dodd, Mead.

Coakley, Jay J. (1994) *Sport in Society: Issues and Controversies.* 5th edn. St Louis: C.V. Mosby.

Coakley, Jay J. (1998) *Sport in Society: Issues and Controversies*, 6th edn. New York: McGraw-Hill.

Collins, Patricia Hill (1990) *Black Feminist Thought: Knowledge, Consciousness, and the Politics of Empowerment.* Boston, MA: Unwin Hyman.

Collins, Randall (1992) *Sociological Insight: an Introduction to Non-Obvious Sociology*, 2nd edn. New York: Oxford University Press.

Curry, Timothy Jon (1991) 'Fraternal bonding in the locker room: a profeminist analysis of talk about competition and women', *Sociology of Sport Journal*, 8 (June): 119–35.

Cuzzort, R.P. (1989) *Using Social Thought: the Nuclear Issue and Other Concerns*. Mountain View, CA: Mayfield Publishing.

Donnelly, Peter and Young, Kevin (1988) 'The construction and confirmation of identity in sport subcultures', *Sociology of Sport Journal*, 5 (3): 223–40.

Duncan, Margaret Carlisle (1990) 'Sports photographs and sexual difference: images of women and men in the 1984 and 1988 Olympic Games', *Sociology of Sport Journal*, 7 (1): 22–43.

Durkheim, Emile (1949) *The Division of Labor in Society*. New York: Free Press.

Eitzen, D. Stanley (1985) 'Violence in professional sports and public policy', in Arthur T. Johnson and James H. Frey (eds), *Government and Sport: the Public Policy Issues*. Totowa, NJ: Rowman & Allanheld. pp. 99–114.

Eitzen, D. Stanley (1989) 'The sociology of amateur sport: an overview', *International Review for the Sociology of Sport*, 24 (2): 95–105.

Eitzen, D. Stanley (1992) 'Sports and ideological contradictions: learning from the cultural framing of Soviet values', *Journal of Sport and Social Issues*, 16 (December): 144–9.

Eitzen, D. Stanley (1995) 'Sport unites, sport divides: sport in a multicultural world'. Speech presented at North Central College, Naperville, Illinois (17 October).

Eitzen, D. Stanley and Baca Zinn, Maxine (1989) 'The de-athleticization of women: the naming and gender marking of collegiate sport teams', *Sociology of Sport Journal*, 6 (4): 362–70.

Eitzen, D. Stanley and Baca Zinn, Maxine (1995) *In Conflict and Order: Understanding Society*, 7th edn. Boston, MA: Allyn and Bacon.

Eitzen, D. Stanley and Sage, George H. (1997) *Sociology of North American Sport*, 6th edn. Dubuque, IA: William C. Brown and Benchmark.

Figone, Albert J. (1988) 'Drugs in professional sport: external control of individual behavior', *Arena Review*, 12 (May): 25–33.

Foley, Douglas E. (1990) 'The great American football ritual: reproducing race, class, and gender inequality', *Sociology of Sport Journal*, 7 (2): 111–35.

Fratzke, M. (1975) 'Personality and biographical traits of superior and average college basketball officials', *Research Quarterly*, 46: 484–8.

Frey, James H. (1988) 'The internal and external role of sport in national development', *Journal of National Development*, 1: 65–82.

Gibbs, Jack P. (1981) *Norms, Deviance, and Social Control*. New York: Elsevier.

Gibbs, Jack P. (1985) 'Social control', in Adam Kuper and Jessica Kuper (eds), *The Social Science Encyclopedia*. London: Routledge & Kegan Paul. pp. 765–8

Goodhart, Phillip and Chataway, Christopher (1968) *War Without Weapons*. London: Allen.

Goodhue, Robert M. (1974) 'The politics of sport: an institutional focus', in *Proceedings of the North American Society for Sport History*. pp. 34–5.

Griffin, Pat (1992) 'Changing the game: homophobia, sexism, and lesbians in sport', *Quest*, 44 (2): 251–65.

Guttmann, Allen (1978) *From Ritual to Record: the Nature of Modern Sports*. New York: Columbia University Press.

Hargreaves, J.A. (1994) *Sporting Females: Critical Issues in the History and Sociology of Women's Sports*. London: Routledge.

Hargreaves, J.E. (1992) 'Olympism and nationalism: some preliminary considerations', *International Review for the Sociology of Sport*, 27 (2): 119–37.

Harmer, Peter A. (1991) 'Athletes, excellence, and injury: authority in moral jeopardy', *Journal of the Philosophy of Sport*, 18: 24–38.

Heinila, Kalevi (1985) 'Sport and international understanding – a contradiction in terms?', *Sociology of Sport Journal*, 2 (3): 240–8.

Hoch, Paul (1972) *Rip Off the Big Game*. New York: Doubleday.

Horowitz, Allan V. (1990) *The Logic of Social Control*. New York: Plenum Press.

Houlihan, Barrie (1994) *Sport and International Politics*. Hemel Hempstead, Hertfordshire, UK: Harvester Wheatsheaf.

Hughes, Robert and Coakley, Jay (1991) 'Positive deviance among athletes: the implications of over-conformity to the sport ethic', *Sociology of Sport Journal*, 8 (4): pp. 307–25.

Janowitz, Morris (1991) *On Social Organization and Social Control* (ed. James Burk). Chicago: University of Chicago Press.

Johansson, Martin (1987) 'Doping as a threat against sport and society: the case of Sweden', *International Review for Sociology of Sport*, 22 (2): 83–97.

Kidd, Bruce (1991) 'How do we find our own voices in the "New World Order"? A commentary on Americanization', *Sociology of Sport Journal*, 8 (2): 178–84.

Kunesh, Monica A., Hasbrook, Cynthia A. and Lewthwaite, Rebecca (1992) 'Physical activity socialization: peer interactions and affective responses among a sample of sixth grade girls', *Sociology of Sport Journal*, 9 (4): 385–96.

Lemert, Charles (1993) 'After modernity, since 1979', in Charles Lemert (ed.), *Social Theory: the Multicultural and Classic Readings*. Boulder, CO: Westview Press. pp. 489–503.

Lever, Janet (1983) *Soccer Madness*. Chicago: University of Chicago Press.

Liska, Allen E. (1992) 'Introduction to the study of social control', in Allen E. Liska (ed.), *Social Threat and Social Control*. Albany: State University of New York Press. pp. 1–29.

Lumer, Christoph (1995) 'Rules and moral norms in sports', *International Review for the Sociology of Sport*, 30 (3/4): 263–81.

Macintosh, Donald and Whitson, Don (1990) *The Game Planners: Transforming Canada's Sport System.* Kingston: McGill–Queens University Press.

Macintosh, Donald, Bedecki, Tom and Franks, C.E.S. (1987) *Sport and Politics in Canada: Federal Government Involvement since 1981.* Kingston: McGill–Queens University Press.

Mandell, Richard D. (1971) *The Nazi Olympics.* New York: Macmillan.

Marx, Karl (1909) *Capital*, 3 volumes. Chicago: Charles H. Kerr.

Matza, David (1964) 'Position and behavior patterns of youth', in Robert E.L. Faris (ed.), *Handbook of Modern Sociology.* Chicago: Rand McNally.

Messner, Michael A. (1988) 'Sports and male domination: the female athlete as contested ideological terrain', *Sociology of Sport Journal*, 5 (3): 197–211.

Messner, Michael A. (1992) 'White men misbehaving: feminism, Afrocentrism, and the promise of a critical standpoint', *Journal of Sport and Social Issues*, 16 (December): 136–44.

Messner, Michael A. and Sabo, Donald F. (eds) (1990) *Sport, Men, and the Gender Order: Critical Feminist Perspectives.* Champaign, IL: Human Kinetics.

Mitchell, J., Leonard, Wilbert M. and Schmitt, Raymond L. (1982) 'Sport officials' perceptions of fans, players, and their occupations: a comparative study of baseball and hockey', *Journal of Sport Behavior*, 8: 54–65.

Molotch, Harvey (1994) 'Going out', *Sociological Forum*, 9 (June): 221–39.

Nelson, Mariah Burton (1994) *The Stronger Women Get, the More Men Love Football: Sexism and the American Culture of Sports.* New York: Harcourt Brace.

Nixon, Howard L. II. (1986) 'Social order in a leisure setting: the case of recreational swimmers in a pool', *Sociology of Sport Journal*, 3 (4): 320–32.

Palzkill, Birgit (1990) 'Between gymshoes and high-heels: the development of a lesbian identity and existence in top class sport', *International Review for the Sociology of Sport*, 25 (3): 221–34.

Parenti, Michael (1986) *Inventing Reality: the Politics of the Mass Media.* New York: St Martin's Press.

Parsons, Talcott (1951) *The Social System.* New York: Free Press.

Pilz, Gunter A. (1988) 'Fairness in sport – Eine fiktive oder reale Handlungsmoral?', in Elk Franke (ed.), *Ethische Aspekte des Leistungssports.* Clausthal-Zellerfeld, Germany: Deutsche Vereinigung fur Sportwissenschaft. pp. 23–34.

Pratt, Stephen R. and Eitzen, D. Stanley (1989) 'Contrasting leadership styles and organizational effectiveness: the case of athletic teams', *Social Science Quarterly*, 70 (June): 311–22.

Pronger, Brian (1990) *The Arena of Masculinity: Sports, Homosexuality, and the Meaning of Sex.* London: GMP Publishers.

Quinney, Richard (1970) *The Social Reality of Crime.* Boston, MA: Little, Brown.

Roethlisberger, F.J. and Dickson, W.J. (1939) *Management and the Worker.* Cambridge, MA: Harvard University Press.

Rosellini, Lynn (1992) 'The sports factories', *US News and World Report*, 17 February, pp. 48–59.

Rosenau, Pauline Marie (1992) *Post-Modernism and the Social Sciences: Insights, Inroads, and Intrusions.* Princeton, NJ: Princeton University Press.

Sabo, Donald F. (1987) 'The football coach as officiant in patriarchal society: conformity and resistance in the social reproduction of masculinity'. Paper at the annual meeting of the North American Society for the Sociology of Sport, Edmonton, Alberta, November 1987.

Shogan, Debra (1991) 'Trusting paternalism? Trust as a condition for paternalistic decisions', *Journal of the Philosophy of Sport*, 18: 49–58.

Snyder, Eldon E. (1972) 'Athletic dressing room slogans and folklore', *International Review of Sport Sociology*, 7: 89–102.

Snyder, Eldon E. and Purdy, Dean A. (1987) 'Social control in sport: an analysis of basketball officiating', *Sociology of Sport Journal*, 4 (4): 394–402.

Squitieri, Tom (1994) 'Soccer eases crisis, lifts spirits', *USA Today* (international edition), 28 June, p. 6A.

Strenk, Andrew (1977) 'Sport as an international political and diplomatic tool', *Arena Newsletter*, 1: 3–10.

Swift, E.M. (1995) 'Bok to the Future', *Sports Illustrated*, 3 July, pp. 32–3.

Thorne, Barrie (1993) *Gender Play: Girls and Boys in School.* New Brunswick, NJ: Rutgers University Press.

Turner, Edward, Bounds, James, Houser, Dan, Motsinger, Steve, Ozmore, David and Smith, Joe (1995) 'Television consumer advertising and the sports figure', *Sport Marketing Quarterly*, 4 (March): 27–33.

Wacquant, Loic J.D. (1992) 'The logic of boxing in black Chicago: toward a sociology of pugilism', *Sociology of Sport Journal*, 9 (3): 221–54.

Wadler, Gary I. and Hainline, Brian (1989) *Drugs and the Athlete.* Philadelphia: F.A. Davis.

Walton, John (1990) *Sociology and Critical Inquiry: the Work, Tradition, and Purpose*, 2nd edn. Belmont, CA: Wadsworth Publishing.

Weber, Max (1947) *The Theory of Social and Economic Organization* (trans. A.M. Henderson and Talcott Parsons). Glencoe, IL: Free Press.

Whitaker, Gail (1982) 'Social control mechanisms: ties that bind – and chafe', *Perspectives*, pp. 83–4.

Whyte, William F. (1943) *Street Corner Society.* Chicago: University of Chicago Press.

Willis, Paul (1982) 'Women in sport in ideology', in Jennifer Hargreaves (ed.), *Sport, Culture and Ideology.* London: Routledge & Kegan Paul. pp. 117–35.

Wilson, John (1994) *Playing by the Rules: Sport, Society, and the State*. Detroit, MI: Wayne State University Press.

Wolfe, Alan (1991) 'Introduction: change from the bottom up', in Alan Wolfe (ed.), *America at Century's End*. Berkeley, CA: University of California Press. pp. 1–13.

Wolff, Kurt H. (1964) 'Social control', in Julius Gould and William L. Kolb (eds), *A Dictionary of the Social Sciences*. New York: Free Press. pp. 651–2.

Yaeger, Don (1991) *Undue Process: the NCAA's Injustice for All*. Champaign, IL: Sagamore Publishing.

25

SPORT AND VIOLENCE

Kevin Young

The concept of 'sports violence' is elusive. Like other aspects of the social process, such as culture, the family, or crime, everyone thinks they know what it is until challenged to define it, or faced with having to do something about it. This is true not only for ordinary members of the public, but also for sports organizations themselves and those responsible for policing sport, including the courts.

Most people usually conceive of sports violence as falling into two areas – crowd violence (which often involves both crimes against persons and property) and player violence. In fact, if the conventional parameters of sports violence are broadened to include violent, abusive or otherwise injurious acts *related to sport*, it becomes clear that the subject may be far more heterogeneous than commonly assumed. Other forms of violence related to sport that go beyond crowd and player violence in the traditional sense are introduced below.

This chapter has three objectives: first, to descriptively and interpretively outline the principal manifestations of sports violence both on and off the field; secondly, to highlight the ways in which various aspects of sports violence have been policed by the authorities; and thirdly, to examine the relationship between sports violence and the mass media. The chapter concludes by summarizing the approaches which show the most promise in explaining the different aspects of sports-related violence, and by proposing some directions for future research.

SPORTS VIOLENCE: MANIFESTATIONS AND EXPLANATIONS

Crowd Violence

Sports crowd disorder is considered to have become a critical social problem in many countries. Fans of British and European sport, particularly soccer, have gained notoriety for their violent proclivities inside and outside stadia. However, violent crowd disturbances have also occurred with some frequency in many other parts of the world, including Australia and New Zealand, Central and South America, Africa, Asia and North America. In fact, disorderly incidents at sports have occurred in almost all societies containing rich sports cultures and consistent spectator followings.

A wide range of sports have been affected, some perhaps more surprising than others. These include baseball (Dewar, 1979), golf (Wade, 1978), cricket (Crofts, 1984; Gammon, 1981; Lynch, 1992), Australian Rules football (Main, 1985), wrestling (Kingsmore, 1968), ice hockey (Smith, 1979, 1983), boxing (Crothers, 1996; Lang, 1981), horse racing (Vamplew, 1980), basketball (Greer, 1983), motorcycle racing (Cunneen and Lynch, 1988; Veno and Veno, 1992), blood sports (Atyeo, 1979), lacrosse (Dunstan, 1973; Metcalfe, 1978), American and Canadian football (Young, 1988), rugby (Thompson, 1977) and, of course, soccer (Dunning et al., 1988; Williams et al., 1984).

It is equally clear that sports crowd disorder is not isolated to the present, as numerous historical accounts attest (Cameron, 1976;

Cashman, 1992; Dunning and Sheard, 1979; Guttmann, 1981, 1986). Whether it is rival groups of spectators fighting at Australian cricket games in the mid-nineteenth century or English soccer games in the last quarter of the nineteenth century, crowd problems at American baseball or football games during the inter-war years, or rioting fans at Canadian ice-hockey games in the 1950s and 1960s, the violent sports crowd is anything but new.

North American Approaches Given the cultural significance of sport in North American life, and historical evidence of crowd problems associated with North American sport, remarkably little sociological work has actually been written on the phenomenon. For the most part, much of the work that does exist is weakly theorized, ahistorical, or outdated. However, at least three general thematic orientations may be identified.

Social and psychological conflicts taking place in society Under this general heading, a number of attempts have been made to explain crowd disorder in terms of tensions that have emerged in the second half of the twentieth century between the fan, the athlete and society. Fimrite (1976), for example, argued that work and family pressures in American society cause widespread social frustration which becomes vented by crowd members at sports events. Similarly, Fontana (1978) proposed that violent conduct in a sports crowd could be explained in terms of a loss of individuality in an increasingly competitive, fractured and impersonal society. From this vantage point, disorder is seen as an attempt to reassert individualism and personal distinctness in a culturally meaningful setting.

Based on these and similar assumptions, a so-called 're-integration' thesis emerged in the 1960s and 1970s focusing on spectators' needs to re-establish forms of group identification (Beisser, 1967; Petryszak, 1977). In the words of Irving Goldaber, founder of the now defunct Centre for the Study of Crowd and Spectator Behavior in Miami:

> ... more people aren't making it. You work hard, you exist, but you haven't got much to show for it. There are increasing numbers of people who are deeply frustrated because they feel they have very little power over their lives. They come to sporting events to experience, vicariously, a sense of power. (cited in Gilbert and Twyman, 1983)

Also under the aegis of social conflicts taking place in society fall approaches that

account for sports crowd disorder by looking at social demographics such as religion, race and ethnicity. For example, numerous race-related riots at US high school and college football and basketball games in the 1960s and 1970s support Edwards's (1973) claim that sports crowd disorder may develop out of racial tensions. In Canada, Levitt and Shaffir (1987) have shown how the Christie Pits softball riots in Toronto in 1933 resulted from a series of anti-semitic acts perpetrated by English Canadians. What remains one of the largest single crowd riots in the history of North American sport – the Montreal 'Rocket Richard' riots of March 1955 – has also been interpreted in terms of ethnic hostilities between anglophone and francophone Canadians (Duperreault, 1981; Katz, 1955).

The celebratory nature of sport A second set of explanations for collective violence in North American sport has been based on the notion that the organization and structure of sport encourages expressive and often aggressive behavior by players and fans alike, normally under carnival-like conditions. Because many sports spectators have an informed knowledge of their game, they can immediately identify the significance of an event either in terms of seasonal goals (making the playoffs, winning championships) or in terms of the relations and rivalries that have developed historically between the contestants or, in some cases, the fans. Unlike crowds in other social contexts, the result is that sports crowds show a vested interest – a fanaticism – in the outcome of the event at hand. Combined with factors caused by aggregation (physical closeness, milling, tension, noise), sporting contests are thus characterized by emotionally charged behavior on the part of participants and spectators alike where proceedings can, under the appropriate conditions, 'get out of hand'.

Adopting this approach, Listiak (1981) and Manning (1983) demonstrate how sport is a setting for organized revelry. Listiak, for example, uses the context of Grey Cup celebrations in Canada to show how widespread public revelry and in some cases disorder are often rationalized by authorities, as well as local business people such as bar owners. In a study of the macro and micro aspects of North American sports crowd disorder, Young (1988) showed that stadium vandalism and the now infamous post-event riot (see Table 25.1) are consistently manifested forms of such excess. While the former has included the

Table 25.1   *Post-event riots in North America: select cases*

Date	Location	Event	Damage	Source
June 1994	Vancouver	Canucks lose in Stanley Cup Final	Police react to thousands of disgruntled fans using tear gas, chemical spray and a fatal rubber bullet. 1 dead, 200 injured (including 8 police), 50 arrests, and approx. $500,000 (Cdn.) in damage	*Macleans*, 27 June 1994
June 1993	Chicago	Bulls win third NBA title	2 dead, 682 arrests, shops looted, cars burned, $150,000 in damage	*Sports Illustrated*, July 1993
June 1993	Montreal	Canadiens win Stanley Cup	168 injured (including 49 police officers), over 110 arrests, stores smashed, $5 million (Cdn.) in damage	*Macleans*, 21 June 1993
February 1993	Dallas	Cowboys win Super Bowl	Fighting, vandalism, and looting results in 26 injured, 25 arrests, $150,000 property damage	Dallas Police Dept. (personal communication)
June 1992	Chicago	Bulls win second NBA title	1,016 arrests, 2 police officers shot and 90 others suffer injuries, 14 fires set, 2 celebrants seriously burned	*Calgary Herald*, 16 June 1992
June 1990	Detroit	Pistons win NBA title	8 dead, hundreds injured by fighting, stabbing and gunfire, over 100 arrests	*Calgary Herald*, 16 June 1990
November 1986	Hamilton, Ontario	Tiger-Cats win Grey Cup	Fires and vandalism resulting in $55,000 (Cdn.) in damages, 13 arrests, 1 police officer hospitalized	*Hamilton Spectator*, 1 Dec. 1986
May 1986	Montreal	Canadiens win Stanley Cup	Several thousand fans gathered in downtown Montreal, 20 stores looted, 6 arrested, 76 charges of mischief & breaking and entering laid, $1 million (Cdn.) in damage	*Globe & Mail*, 26, 27 May 1986
October 1984	Detroit	Tigers win World Series	1 dead, 80 injured, 41 arrested, cars overturned and burned, mass looting, $100,000 in property damage	*Time*, 29 Oct. 1984
November 1983	Toronto	Argonauts win Grey Cup	$100,000 (Cdn.) tab for thefts and vandalism, 22 fans charged	*Toronto Daily Star*, 29 Nov. 1983
October 1971	Pittsburgh	Pirates win World Series	Over 100 arrests, over 100 injured, 30 shops looted, 2 sexual assaults, 8 armed robberies, 4 vehicles overturned	*Time*, 29 Oct. 1984
October 1968	Detroit	Tigers win World Series	Looting, fires, cars overturned, one rape, over 200 fans arrested	*Time*, 29 Oct. 1984

destruction of stadium property such as goal-posts and the playing field, post-event revelry has involved widespread inebriation both inside and outside the stadium, brawling, looting, assault and even homicide (Johnson, 1993).

Precipitating factors at sports events   A third theme in North American work identifies aspects of the sports event itself as precipitants to crowd disturbances. Smith's (1976) early work, for example, examined crowd violence at a number of soccer games using Smelser's (1962) 'value-added' theory of collective behavior. Focusing on Smelser's notion of

structural conduciveness, Smith found one of the most common causes of crowd hostility to be player violence and unpopular decisions by officials. These findings led Smith to conclude that 'Sport probably often exacerbates the very strains that initially give rise to collective hostility' (1976: 205). Following Edwards and Rackages (1977), C. White (1970) and Lewis (1982), Smith (1983) went on to validate the 'violence-precipitates-violence' hypothesis using examples of crowd disturbances from hockey, baseball and basketball.

Although some research into North American crowd violence has attempted to couch the phenomenon in social, historical, and cultural antecedents, this body of work has tended to view disorder as a response to aspects of the sports event itself. Dewar's (1979) attempt to link spectator fights at baseball with such factors as the day of the week, starting time, seat location, inning of the game and temperature, and Green and O'Neal's (1976) account of how crowd size affects fan violence are classic examples. Consequently, other than some isolated examples, surprisingly little is known about the social causes of sports crowd disorder or about the demographics, lifestyles and values of disorderly fans in North America. This is a problem that British research into soccer hooliganism has attempted to overcome.

British Approaches   There seems little doubt that the greatest volume of research into sports crowd disorder has examined forms and causes of British soccer hooliganism. The debates between sociologists on this issue have become prolonged, complex and occasionally fractious (cf. Dunning, 1994: 128–9; Williams, 1991: 177) which, as a result, has made the identification of certain strands within this research rather complicated. While the recognizable 'Oxford School', 'Marxist', 'Leicester School' and 'Cultural Studies' camps continue to represent identifiable sets of ideas on the hooligan question, it is also possible to identify more recent, perhaps less well known, but still valuable approaches in this area. The different components of this body of work should not be thought of as mutually exclusive. No one approach is exhaustive; each has its own strengths and weaknesses.

The Oxford School 'ritual of soccer violence' thesis   Following observational work at Oxford United Football Club in the 1970s, Peter Marsh and his colleagues became the principal exponents of the so-called 'ritual of soccer violence' thesis (Marsh, 1975, 1982; Marsh et al., 1978; Marsh and Campbell, 1982). Building on Tiger's (1969) study of the aggressive behavior of *Men in Groups*, Marsh conceptualized aggression as a constructive means of controlling the social world in the process of achieving certain goals. He argued that it is the specific culture of groups that determines how aggression is expressed. With the focus on Britain, soccer crowd disorder was thus viewed as a unique cultural adaptation to the lower working-class environment, which manifests itself in terms of aggressive but largely symbolic and harmless rituals in soccer stadia, and thus facilitates the release of aggressive

impulses for young working-class adolescents. Writing in 1978, Marsh and his colleagues in fact cautioned British authorities that the catharsis offered through soccer-related aggression contained social value, and that if they 'take away the opportunities for boys and young men to engage in structured aggro, then we might very well be faced with a set of problems that are far more serious and much more difficult to control' (p. 134). Ironically, then, from this point of view, authorities have been faced with having to tolerate ritualized aggression at sports events such as soccer matches in order to avert more 'serious' violence elsewhere in society.

The approach of the Oxford School, and particularly its contention that hooliganism is largely a ritualistic 'fantasy' of violence, has met with strong criticism. What its advocates failed to recognize was the regularity with which serious, and sometimes fatal, injury has been caused by violent soccer fans. In particular, Marsh paid little attention to the pre- or post-match context, where hooliganism has been particularly injurious for a very long time. Rather, the main focus of the Oxford work was on hand-to-hand combat between fans during games. This completely overlooks several significant aspects of hooligan transaction, not the least of which are highly organized clashes between rival fighting groups outside the stadium, and aerial confrontations through the use of missiles, both of which became well-established characteristics of hooligan action during the 1980s. Moreover, theories focusing on the ritual of soccer 'aggro' entirely omit any notion of structural differentiation within the class background of violent fans, so fundamental to adequately explaining the phenomenon sociologically.

There is no denying some ritualistic dimension to the soccer crowd and soccer violence – many of the songs, chants, profanities and even aspects of inter-group fighting show elements of ritual. But to argue that hooliganism is largely ritualistic, and that actual violence plays no more than a peripheral role, raises serious doubts as to the potential of this approach, particularly in the wake of (at this point) almost three decades of widely reported, routinely injurious and, once again, occasionally fatal hooligan encounters.

Social deprivation theses and the Marxist perspective of Ian Taylor   Sports crowd disorder has been explained in some North American research in terms of the effects of social deprivation and disenfranchisement. With respect to disorder that has occurred at British soccer games, several sociologists

(Corrigan, 1979; Taylor, 1969, 1971, 1982a, 1982b) have posed similar hypotheses. The work of Ian Taylor, which essentially interprets hooliganism according to two different historical periods, is foremost in this category.

First, Taylor argues that contemporary modifications to the English game combined to bring about changes in the behavior of traditional fans. Central to Taylor's analysis are the concepts of *soccer subculture* and *soccer consciousness*. For him, the subculture of soccer in working-class communities is comprised of groups of working men culturally bound together in a general concern – a consciousness – for the game and for the local team in particular. According to Taylor, the rank-and-file supporter at the turn of the century viewed himself as a member of a 'collective and democratically structured enterprise' (1971: 145) in which players, managers, owners, and fans were all engaged in a kind of working-class 'participatory democracy'.

However, Taylor notes that certain post-war changes to the British game (its commercialization specifically) threatened this comfortable state of affairs. For the members of the working-class soccer subculture, Taylor argues, these changes had a traumatic effect. Their relatively deprived socio-economic status was, according to the argument, exacerbated by a feeling of alienation from the clubs that traditionally provided their cultural *raison d'être*. Taylor suggests that these groups constitute a 'subcultural-rump', and argues that it is principally they who engage in rowdy conduct at soccer. Hence, practices such as the invasion of the playing field and the destruction of property in and around stadia are interpreted as attempts by the remnants of a working-class subculture to reclaim a game which has become increasingly removed from their control. From this perspective and, as Edgell and Jary have written, disorder represents 'a highly specific protest against football's loss of class exclusivity' (1973: 227).

In the 1980s, Taylor (1982a, 1982b, 1987, 1989) revised portions of his earlier thesis in accordance with his Marxist approach to argue that contemporary manifestations of soccer hooliganism can better be understood if placed against ongoing crises of the British state. Such crises included industrial and residential dislocations in working-class experience producing differentiation within the working-class itself. For instance, Taylor (1987) argues that an increased upper working-class jingoism – a 'Little Englanderism' as he called it – crystallizing during the period of Margaret Thatcher's Conservative rule exacerbated Britain's hooligan problem. Thus, Taylor's most recent

contributions to the hooliganism debate locate many of the participants themselves in an altogether different segment of the working class than his earlier work. It is precisely this point of re-interpretation that has drawn criticism in other research, particularly that of the Leicester School.

By situating soccer hooliganism in the context of changes that have occurred recently in the structure and form of the British game, and in the effects of conservative politics on working-class experience as a whole, Taylor succeeds in demonstrating that 'no sensible discussion' (1987: 179) of this phenomenon can proceed unless developed against a social, economic and political backdrop. His incisive responses (1987, 1989) to the Bradford, Brussels and Sheffield tragedies[1] represent attempts to contextualize concrete events in this fashion. Nevertheless, Taylor's work has several limitations.

First, Taylor nowhere provides convincing evidence to support the notion of a 'participatory democracy' earlier this century. In fact, as Carroll (1980) has noted, it is extremely doubtful whether current soccer hooligans are cognizant of any 'illusion of control', as Taylor puts it, or are concerned with regaining it. Taylor's image of a 'golden age' of British soccer when all connected to the game shared homogeneous backgrounds and experiences is in this sense more likely a romanticized image of British sports history than one grounded in fact. Second, if, as Taylor suggests, fans have only recently turned to hooliganism through feelings of estrangement from the participatory democracy of the club–fan relationship, how do we account for the soccer crowd disturbances of the late nineteenth century and early twentieth century when this relationship allegedly reached a peak? Although he mentions pre-1960 forms of violence sporadically in his work, Taylor rejects the possibility of *extended* phases of crowd disorder at soccer before the 1960s (which seems to have been persuasively demonstrated in the empirical work of the Leicester School). His failure to acknowledge the span of the phenomenon results in an overall lack of historical clarity in his argument. Finally, since they are not based on any systematic empirical work, many of Taylor's insights regarding soccer hooliganism must remain speculative and impressionistic.

Theories of working-class subcultures In the 1970s, several researchers linked to the Centre for Contemporary Cultural Studies at Birmingham University, England (J. Clarke, 1973, 1978; Critcher, 1979; Hall, 1978) also attempted to locate soccer hooliganism in terms of class and cultural experiences. As J. Clarke wrote: 'Hooliganism comes out of the way in which the traditional forms of football watching encounter the professionalization and spectacularization of the game. It is one of the consequences of the changing relationship of the audience to the game' (1978: 49–50). In this way, soccer hooliganism was again interpreted as a reaction by mostly working-class males to commercializing processes developing in what has traditionally been seen as 'the people's game' (Walvin, 1975).

However, Clarke and others added to Taylor's thesis slightly by introducing a new focus on adolescent subcultures (such as skinheads) emerging out of post-Second World War changes in British working-class culture. Clarke argued that, among other things, the changing relationship between the generations in working-class communities had created greater independence for youths, and resulted in fewer constraints placed upon them in the public sphere, such as at sports events. Thus, traditional forms of crowd behavior at soccer such as profanity, pushing and other 'controlled' forms of aggression now became seen as escalating into more aggressive styles of spectatorship at the hands of young working-class men. As Critcher (1979: 171) remarked, 'Into the hiatus between the traditional supporter and the modern consumer stepped the football hooligan'.

There seems little doubt that the structurally sensitive approaches of Taylor, Clarke and others offer considerably more explanatory insight into a complex social problem than the ethological and microsociological ventures of Marsh and his colleagues. However, as with Taylor's early work, Clarke, Critcher and others produce little empirical evidence to support the argument that hooliganism, at least in its 1970s and 1980s manifestations, has been a response to destabilized working-class traditions and values. Stability of working-class social relations in the pre-1960 era is a view that both camps tend to assume rather too uncritically and, since both assume that soccer hooliganism began on a widespread basis for the first time during the early 1960s, is a view they are unlikely to relinquish.

The Leicester School and the 'social roots of soccer violence' thesis A number of sociologists at the Universities of Leicester (Eric Dunning, Patrick Murphy and John Williams) and Loughborough (Joseph Maguire), England, have situated the 'sociogenesis' of British soccer hooliganism in historical and class perspectives. Unlike other approaches discussed so far, their work is grounded in extensive and empirically tested comparisons of this phenomenon in its past and present configurations. Theoretically, the group's now extensive body of work (cf. Dunning, 1979, 1990, 1994; Dunning et al., 1981, 1982a, 1982b, 1984a, 1984b, 1988; Maguire, 1986, 1988/89; Williams, 1980, 1985, 1989, 1991; Williams et al., 1984, 1986, 1988) has been influenced most fundamentally by the 'figurational' or 'process sociology' of Norbert Elias (1978), and specifically Elias's notion of the 'civilizing process'.[2] Supplementary impetus has also been provided by Suttles's (1968) socio-anthropological work on the social order of American slums, and by several social histories of British sport (for example, Dunning and Sheard, 1979; Hopcraft, 1968; Hutchinson, 1975; Marples, 1954; Mason, 1980; Vamplew, 1980; Walvin, 1975).

A key theme in the work of the Leicester School, and one which represents a direct conflict with Taylor's 'Little England' thesis, is that hooligan groups are largely comprised of individuals from the poorest sections of the working class. Dunning et al. argue that the hooligan's deprived social condition is instrumental in the production and reproduction of normative codes of behavior such as strong emphases on ties of kinship and territory, loyalty to peers and family, conjugal role separation, male dominance, and aggressive expressions of masculinity. Their emphasis is as much on the relational as on the material aspects of the position of these groups, and Dunning and his colleagues also stress the reciprocity of 'causation' in the (con)-figurations concerned; that is, that the codes, bonding patterns and behavior of these groups, including their hooliganism in soccer contexts, contribute towards keeping them at the bottom of the social scale.

It is the reproduction of these social conditions that is presumed to lead to the development of a specific violent masculine style manifested regularly at soccer games. The context is soccer because, as Dunning argues, 'The match on the field of play itself is a match as they [the hooligans] see it on behalf of their community, not just the wider city but in particular the working-class sections of their city' (*Hooligan*, 1985). This is the thrust of the Leicester School's 'social roots' explanation of soccer hooliganism as it applies to Britain. In order to explain violence by English hooligan fans at international soccer matches, we are introduced to what Harrison had previously called the 'Bedouin Syndrome' (1974: 604).

Simply stated, this suggests that in the same way that rival neighborhood groups coalesce to defend their 'home territory' against visiting fans, so too is community solidarity of this type manifested on a regional scale (for example, northern fans fighting against southern fans) and a national scale (for example, English fans fighting against Dutch fans). *Hooligans Abroad* (Williams et al., 1984), the first of three book-length studies produced by the Leicester group, was, in fact, an attempt to substantiate such a scenario empirically in the context of the 1982 World Cup in Spain.

Much of the British research (for example, Critcher, 1979; Marsh et al., 1978; Taylor, 1971, 1982b) has postulated that hooliganism began on a broad scale in the 1960s and is thus, historically speaking, quite recent. By contrast, historical work leads the Leicester School to the conclusion that some patterns of soccer crowd disorder can be traced as far back as the last quarter of the nineteenth century. In fact, Dunning et al. argue that 'every phase of the Association game in Britain ... has been accompanied by episodes of spectator disorder' (1981: 342), although the pre-First World War and post-1960 periods are seen as most prolific in this regard. For example, the *Hooligan* documentary shows that the English Football Association was so concerned with increasing crowd disorder prior to the Second World War that military personnel were frequently allowed into matches free of charge to help informally police the unruly crowds.

The work of the Leicester School has become extremely well known both in Britain and internationally. It provides, arguably, the most theoretically ambitious and, without doubt, the most empirically tested approach to what is clearly a complex social phenomenon. Despite criticisms of having inflated the 'problem' of soccer hooliganism in earlier historical periods (Curtis, 1986), Dunning and his colleagues have gone far in mapping the sociogenesis of the phenomenon and linking it to the broader culture in which it emerges. A key strength of the Leicester School is that, quite unlike other approaches, this perspective is grounded in comprehensive and longitudinal empirical research (using methods as diverse as content and archival analysis, participant observation, interviewing), not only of soccer hooligan action, but also of the lifestyles, behaviors and attitudes of young men normally involved in hooliganism. This combination of empirical and theoretical work has placed the Leicester School in a position to suggest recommendations for conflict resolution and policy in this area (Sir Norman Chester Centre for Football Research, 1988; Williams et al., 1984). This is a compelling aspect of their work which others have been reluctant and/or unable to emulate.

Other research on British hooliganism[3] Scholarly approaches to British soccer hooliganism are diverse and go far beyond the parameters of these four models. Other studies which have contributed to the hooligan debate in Britain include: Murray's (1984) social history of the religious sectarianism that has exacerbated hostilities between two Scottish clubs and their supporters; Buford's (1992) ethnography of life *Among the Thugs*; Hornby's (1992) account of the dangerously obsessive appeal of soccer; Wagg's (1984) Marxist-critical appraisal of the cultural transformations taking place in the soccer world which have left 'spaces' filled by the destructive activities of young working-class supporters; Redhead and McLaughlin's (1985) and Robins's (1984) accounts of the intersections between soccer violence and the popular cultural and stylistic interests of young British men; Clarke and Madden's (1986, 1987) socio-economic analyses of soccer's fiscal problems; Redhead's (1986) examination of the cultural meaning of soccer for officials, players and followers; O'Brien's (1988/89) descriptive account of how soccer affects the lives of committed fans; studies of hooliganism and social identity in Scotland (Coalter, 1985; Finn, 1994; Giulianotti, 1994); studies comparing hooligan rates and practices in England and Scotland (Moorhouse, 1984, 1987); examinations of soccer, masculinity and hooliganism in Northen Ireland (Bairner, 1995); and, finally, Giulianotti's (1995) account of the methodological and hermeneutic complexities in studying hooliganism.

Research from other international contexts Many countries where organized sport is played, irrespective of the cultural or political background, have recorded problems of crowd disturbances at one time or another. Regretfully, however, despite a growing international body of work on sports crowd disorder, this literature remains limited, particularly that portion of it written in or translated into English. There are no obvious international schools of theory.

Perhaps best known of the work on sports crowd disorder outside North America and the United Kingdom is Lever's (1972, 1983) research on soccer in Brazil. Implementing a structural-functionalist approach, Lever shows how in South America, sport paradoxically demonstrates both unifying and divisive elements; unifying in the sense that it enhances inter- and intra-community relations, but divisive because it underlines that in Brazil only empowered groups such as elite athletes may be socially mobile. Lever raises two important issues. First, she shows how the way the Brazilian government organizes and markets soccer is consistent with the crude Marxist 'opiate of the masses' argument. For example, she writes that informal Brazilian policy 'seems to include the notion that soccer can be used to distract workers from their serious grievances' (1983: 61). Secondly, and again paradoxically, this unofficial attempt to mask social deprivation apparently fails as often as it succeeds, since soccer games both consistently attract huge paying audiences and represent venues for the expression of class conflict. The latter includes the throwing of urine bags by working-class fans into sections of middle-class fans. Lever's structural-functionalist approach cannot easily account for these lived contradictions and her work is now outdated, but her research constitutes a rich sociological appraisal of the cultural meanings of sport in South America. More critical and updated accounts of sports crowd disorder in South America may be found in Archetti and Romero (1994) and Mason (1995); the latter shows evidence that a number of South American countries including Argentina have 'been plagued by crowd violence in their stadiums' (1995: 137).

By now, most students of sports violence recognize the spurious nature of the claim that soccer hooliganism is a 'British disease'. While wanting to underplay neither the statistical normalcy nor the injurious outcomes of British hooliganism, it should be emphasized that this image is far from accurate. In content analyses of English newspapers, Williams et al. (1984) unearthed over 70 reports of spectator disorder at soccer matches in 30 different countries in which English fans were not involved between 1904 and 1983. Additionally, research by Williams and Goldberg (1989: 7) has identified numerous cases of hooliganism where English fans were the 'victims of foreign hooliganism' rather than the assailants.

Notwithstanding significant cultural variance in the nature and extent of hooliganism, evidence indicates that the phenomenon grew in a number of European countries throughout the 1980s (Williams and Goldberg, 1989). Prompted by domestic troubles of their own, European scholars have increasingly turned the spotlight on themselves, as may be witnessed by an expanding international literature on hooliganism. Countries known to have

experienced soccer hooliganism include: Greece, where fans behaved violently with some consistency throughout the 1980s (Panayiotopoulos, 1989); France, where fans of clubs such as Paris St Germain have been known to attack police with tear gas, flares, and other missiles, and where hooliganism has led to the closing of certain stadium sections and the playing of games behind closed doors (Young, 1991a: 563); Spain, where violent incidents grew steadily during the 1980s (Gonzales, 1992); Belgium, where hooligan fans have been known to meet each other to fight on neutral territory (Van Limbergen, 1989); Austria, where scholars have actually identified the existence of a 'Viennese disease' (Horak, 1991: 532); Sweden, where clubs have also been ordered to play games away from home because of violent fan behavior (*Calgary Herald*, 6 September, 1995: D2); and the Netherlands (Meijs and Van Der Brug, 1989; Van Der Brug, 1994), Germany (Pilz, 1996), and Italy (Dal Lago and De Biasi, 1994; Roversi, 1991) where soccer hooliganism has for several years intersected with far right politics and a burgeoning neo-Nazi movement.

Despite common references to a 'British disease', in terms of total numbers of fatalities, some of the most serious cases of soccer crowd disorder and stadium crushes[4] in the history of the sport have not involved British supporters at all. It is now well known, for example, that in May 1964 over 300 fans were killed in a riot that broke out at the National Stadium in Lima, Peru (*New York Times*, 25 May 1964), and in another notorious case of soccer-related violence, a one-week 'soccer war' was waged between Honduras and El Salvador in the summer of 1969 following a game played between the two countries on neutral ground in Mexico. In order to end the conflict, the Organization of American States had to intervene (*Newsweek*, 28 July 1969: 54). More recently, 83 people were killed and over 150 others injured in a stampede linked to the distribution of forged tickets at a World Cup qualifier held in Guatemala City in October 1996 (*Sports Illustrated*, 28 October 1996: 22).

Contrary to the popular myth that soccer hooliganism is unique to the United Kingdom, then, soccer-related violence appears to have occurred wherever the game is played (see Table 25.2). Young (1988) provides a long list of examples from settings as diverse as Uruguay, Chile, the United Arab Emirates, China, Libya, Turkey, the former Soviet Union and Bangladesh. A list published by the Office of International Criminal Justice at the University of Illinois (1994) reports similar cases from

Table 25.2 *International sports crowd disorder: select cases*

Date	Location	Sport	Event	Source
1985	Saudi Arabia	Soccer	Saudi spectators assault the referee during a game played against the United Arab Emirates in Riyadh	*Liverpool Echo,* 7 June 1985
1985	China	Soccer	More than 10,000 Chinese soccer fans riot following a loss to Hong Kong in a World Cup qualifier	*Globe & Mail,* 10 May 1985: 1
1989	Bangladesh	Soccer	100 people hurt, including 12 police officers, and 129 arrests made when fans of rival teams fight in port city of Chittagong	*Calgary Herald,* 26 Sept. 1989: A12
1989	Australia	Cricket	24 fans arrested, over 100 others evicted following drunken celebrations during a cricket game in Sydney	Lynch, 1992: 37
1990–93	Greece	Basketball	Numerous cases of fighting between rival supporters; missiles thrown and cause injury; teams ordered to play games behind closed doors	*The European,* 8–14 April 1994: 12
1991	Chile	Soccer	10 Chilean fans killed, 128 injured, 188 arrests as fans 'celebrated' after Liberator's Cup	*Calgary Herald,* 7 June 1991: E4
1993	Ghana	Soccer	36 Ghanians injured after fighting breaks out at a game between Ghana and the Ivory Coast	*Calgary Herald,* 11 Nov. 1993: E3
1993	Zambia	Soccer	30 fans injured in riot at World Cup qualifying game against Madagascar	*Calgary Herald,* 1 March 1993: D3
1996	Guatemala	Soccer	83 fans dead, over 150 others injured in a crush resulting from over-ticketing in a World Cup qualifying game in Guatemala City	*Sports Illustrated,* 28 Oct. 1996: 22

Albania, Peru, Egypt, the Ivory Coast and Sudan. Semyonov and Farbstein's (1989) work on the ecology of soccer riots in Israel is also worthy of note.

Finally, despite clear evidence that world soccer has more problems with violence off the field than other sports, it should not be understood as the only sport around which regular forms of collective violence have developed. The few studies indicating the existence of violent crowds at other sports have unfortunately been theoretically unsophisticated and empirically limited but include Adedeji's (1982) study of violence in Nigerian school sports, Main's (1985) brief commentary on Australian Rules

football fans, Crofts's (1984) and Lynch's (1992) reports of crowd violence at cricket games in Australia, and Gammon's (1981) account of 'unseemly behavior, on the pitch and off' (p. 37) in West Indies cricket.

Player Violence

If crowd violence has prompted official and public concern, until recently this has been less true of player violence, which has traditionally been condoned in many settings as 'just part of the game'. At the very least, this can be seen in the way that aggressive and injurious practices are encouraged to occur as routine components of games that would be socially and legally intolerable were they to transpire in other areas of life. In fact, only a cursory glance at the nature and organization of sport is necessary to demonstrate that many of our most popular sports, both at the recreational and elite level, are immersed in cultures of aggression and violence.

Several conceptual approaches have been offered for making sense of participant violence (Coakley, 1989; Goldstein, 1989). Emphasizing the heterogeneous origins of the phenomenon, Coakley (1989: 88) cautions that 'There is no single cause of violence in sport'. According to him, the commercialization of sport with its emphasis on heroic values and winning, the social organization of sports teams where 'violence becomes a means through which athletes cope with the social psychological deprivations they experience as team members' (p. 97), and the socialization of the athlete where violence learning takes place, are among the most likely causes of player violence.

Perhaps the most widely adopted typology of player violence was developed by the Canadian sociologist Michael Smith.[5] In his 1983 book *Violence and Sport*, and while aware of the reductionist tendencies of typologies, Smith classified player violence into four basic categories; the first two being relatively legitimate and the last two relatively illegitimate in the eyes of both sports organizations and the law:

1 *Brutal body contact* includes what Smith called the 'meat and potatoes' of our most popular sports such as tackles, blocks, body checks, collisions, hits and jabs. Depending on the sport under consideration, these are all acts that can be found within the official rules and to which most would agree that consent is given or at the very least implied.
2 *Borderline violence* involves acts prohibited by the official rules of a given sport but which occur routinely and are more or less accepted by most people concerned. Examples include the fist-fight in ice hockey, the wandering elbow in basketball, soccer, or road racing, or the 'knock-down' pitch in baseball or the 'bouncer' in cricket. Importantly, all of these practices carry potential for prompting further violence – the bench-clearing brawl in hockey, or retaliatory fighting in any of these other sports. Traditionally, sanctions imposed by sports leagues and administrators for borderline violence have been notoriously light, and fines have sometimes been covered by the clubs themselves.

3 *Quasi-criminal violence* violates the formal rules of the given sport, the law of the land and, to a significant degree, the informal norms of players. This type of violence usually results in injury and, as a result, considerable official and public attention. Quasi-criminal violence in hockey includes so-called 'cheap shots' or 'sucker punches', and has often been responded to by in-house suspensions or fines.
4 *Criminal violence* includes cases so seriously and obviously outside the margins of acceptability that they are handled as criminal from the outset. The broadly cited case used by Smith is that of Toronto hockey player Paul Smithers who, as a teenager in 1973, assaulted and killed an opponent in a parking lot following a local game.

Although Smith's socio-legal approach remains useful, it has two limitations. First, as discussed below, there has of late been some collapsing of his player violence categories prompted by shifting scales of public and legal tolerance. For example, incidents considered ten years ago as 'quasi-criminal violence', 'borderline violence', or merely 'brutal body contact' are being more closely scrutinized today by the authorities and, where litigated, may be dealt with under criminal rather than civil law. Secondly, Smith's typology overlooks the manner in which aspects of player violence may grow out of the gender process.

From antiquity to the present, masculinist spectator sport has traditionally been profoundly violent (Guttmann, 1986). As a burgeoning literature (see Waddington, Chapter 26 in this volume) shows, male athletes especially appear to be hyper-susceptible to injury and disablement.[6] Although parallels may be drawn here between the occupational hazards of professional athletes and those of other groups (especially blue-collar workers in the heavy industries such as construction workers, meat packers, offshore oil workers, miners and production line workers), most other types of workplace violence are neither normatively perpetrated by co-workers nor seen in such a positive fashion. Regarding professional athletes' use of force, injuries and their meanings, perhaps the closest parallel may be found between athletes and military personnel, who also follow strongly institutionalized regulatory structures – that is, they become injured, maimed, or sometimes killed, and go on to receive commendations such as awards, medals, special honors, and tributes for their dedication and sacrifice. Official recognition of this nature serves not just to honor the individual involved but to rationalize any doubts one might have as to the merit of the act, and ultimately consolidates it in dominant ideology as admirable and manly.

Feminist work on sport and gender (Bryson, 1987; Messner and Sabo, 1990; Theberge, 1997; Young et al., 1994; White and Young, 1997) urges us to understand male tolerance of risk and injury linked to sports violence not only as a passive social process but as a constituting one through which violence, injury and disablement become reframed as masculinizing. Thus, the cultural meanings of sports violence and living with injury for many men is linked to ideological issues of gender legitimacy and power, and rather than being understood as mere rituals associated with sport, now reflect wider forms of gender ordering.

As students of contrived sports identities (cf. Coakely, 1989; Donnelly and Young, 1988; King, 1996) have suggested, many sports are replete with players who have deliberately carved out gladiatorial, Rambo-like images for themselves in accordance with the assumed cultural expectations of their peer groups and hegemonic notions of manliness more broadly. Although players of certain positions (linemen in football, central defenders in soccer, forwards in rugby) are typically singled out for purposes of illustration, this masculinizing practice may actually be far more institutional than individual. The views of an NFL player on the 'adrenaline surge' he gets from 'decleating' opponents are far from unorthodox:

> I don't mind that I'm going to break blood vessels in my forehead when I hit somebody ... I enjoy hearing guys wheeze and seeing the snot run down their faces. I like the rush of numbness that goes through my body. ('The Poet', 1991: 64)

Messner (1990) documents similar cases of the violent appetites of many male athletes. For hockey 'enforcers', football 'warriors', rugby 'barbarians', soccer 'hard men' and the like, the costs of violence and injury become mediated by the contributions they are assumed to make to male peer group solidarity at and away from the arena.

At the professional level at least, such masculinizing features of male sport also function as occupational imperatives with very practical consequences. For example, many athletes feel an economic in addition to cultural pressure to work through body crises such as injury in order to sustain what for most is an inevitably brief career anyway. In the words of another NFL player whose leg was broken in the 1988 Super Bowl, 'My career is in my legs. My position is in jeopardy. You know what

they do to racehorses' (Leiber, 1989: 16). In a way, male sports 'workers' become locked into an occupational trap. Despite acknowledging that playing with injuries can lead to permanent physical damage, most are aware of their commodification by an industry largely intolerant to injury. Under further pressure from cultural requirements to display a particular brand of tough and unemotive masculinity, the professional athlete falls prey both to legally binding contractual obligations ('play or don't get paid') and to the revered values of his own work culture ('play hurt and show that you can take the pain like a man'). As we have seen, this is particularly true of heavy contact sports such as ice hockey and football where discourse is often telling. For example, the phrase 'you play unless the bone sticks through the meat' has long been used to rationalize injury in North American football. Emphasizing the gendered and often gynephobic trappings of forceful sports models, Messner has noted, 'To get the most out of athletes, coaches tend to ... threaten the athlete's masculinity and call him a "sissy" or a "woman" if he doesn't play while he's hurt' (1992: 101). Similar evidence of institutional complicity in player violence and injury is provided by Vaz (1982), Colburn (1985) and Smith (1983) with regard to macho participant roles and values in ice hockey.

In sum, while the causes of player violence are diverse, it is important to note, as Coakley (1989: 97) reminds us, that they are inevitably 'grounded in the social processes involved in the sport experience and in the socio-structural context in which sport exists'.

Other Forms of Violence Related to Sport

Following the definitional argument made in the introduction, incidents of sports-related violence in the past few years have included not only the aggressive practices of soccer fans, and the usual spate of on-field assaults and catastrophic injuries done by and to athletes, but also, for example:

- A pipe bomb explosion at the Centennial Olympic Games that killed 2 people and injured over 100 (*Sports Illustrated*, 5 August 1996: 22–31).
- The stabbing of a female professional tennis player – the Monica Seles case (*Sports Illustrated*, 17 July 1995: 18–26).
- The involvement of a world-class female figure skater in the off-ice assault of an opponent – the Tonya Harding/Nancy Kerrigan case (*Time*, 24 January 1994: 34–8).

- The rape conviction and jail term of a world boxing champion (Mike Tyson) who is known to have made the claim 'I like to hurt women when I make love to them' (*Sports Illustrated*, 31 July 1995: 62–74).
- The murder trial of an American football 'hero' – O.J. Simpson (*Newsweek*, 11 July 1994: 20–7)
- The depressingly common involvement of male athletes in sexual assault against women (cf. Benedict and Klein, 1997).
- The disclosure of the involvement of many male athletes in what *Sports Illustrated* aptly called 'sport's dirty little secret' (31 July 1995: 62), that is, partner abuse.
- Widespread cases of harassment, stalking and threat throughout the world of sport that have spawned a thriving muscle-for-hire security industry for both male and female athletes (*USA Today*, 14 July 1995: 3C).[7]
- Scandals throughout most levels of Canadian hockey regarding the sexual abuse of young boys, some of whom, now as adults, are beginning to 'go public' with their histories of victimization.[8]

As far as we can tell, cases such as these may represent only the tip of the proverbial iceberg. They are not normally thought of as 'sports violence', but they are all clearly intentionally abusive or injurious acts that cannot easily be separated from the sports process and that only begin to make sense when the socially, culturally and historically embedded character of sport is closely scrutinized. The domestic violence cases particularly underscore the fact that, far from operating as a world apart, the problem of violence related to sport interfaces with problems of violence elsewhere in society.

At the time of writing, and possibly due to the methodological complexities of tapping these kinds of sports-related acts by comparison with crowd or player violence, little empirically validated work has been done and even less is actually known about any one of these 'other' forms of sports-related violence. Research that is available includes examinations of the intersections between sex, violence and power in sport (Lenskyj, 1990; Messner and Sabo, 1994), studies of male athletes and sexual assault (Benedict and Klein, 1997; Crosset et al., 1995; Melnick, 1992), and accounts of fraternal bonding and rape culture in sport (Curry, 1991). Importantly, in addition to raising critical questions regarding the cultural significance of sport that leaves (especially elite) athletes relatively immune to charges of abuse and assault, all of this

research emphasizes the heavily gendered underpinnings of athlete–athlete and fan–athlete victimization.

POLICING SPORTS VIOLENCE: DETERRENCE, LITIGATION AND SOCIAL CONTROL

Crowd Violence

Concern with sports crowd disorder has prompted solicitous responses around the world. Proposed and implemented measures emanate from a number of groups representing diverse interests, although in most countries they have been initiated almost exclusively by legal authorities, politicians and sports officials. With the notable exception of the British context, scholarly assessments of social control measures introduced to curb crowd violence are actually quite rare.

So many recommendations for resolving hooliganism have been offered in the United Kingdom that there is space here to summarize only a select few. During the 1980s, the Conservative government of Margaret Thatcher perceived hooliganism as a national social problem requiring remedial action. A so-called 'War Cabinet' was implemented and aimed, especially in the immediate post-Heysel (1985) era, at resolving the hooligan issue. In practice, however, a number of what have been called hit-and-miss and present-centered policies were introduced that increased criminal charges and harsh sentencing procedures but ultimately did little to resolve the problem of hooliganism *per se*. For example, the 1984–1985 soccer season in England witnessed the first life jail term imposed on a violent fan (although it was subsequently rescinded by the courts).

In fact, the British government has sponsored investigations into hooliganism since the late 1960s.[9] For the most part, documents resulting from these inquiries have met with criticism from sociologists concerned with the long-term effectiveness of law-and-order responses. Typical here was the *Report of Committee of Inquiry into Crowd Safety and Control at Soccer Grounds* supervised by Mr Justice Popplewell following the 1985 Bradford fire and Heysel Stadium riot. Taylor's (1987) description of the report's content is broadly applicable to most other official reports written to date:

> The Report is ... notable for the general support it gives to the theory, held to so fruitlessly by authority in Britain since the mid-1960s, that there is

some kind of solution to the problem of soccer hooliganism in the extension of police powers of search and arrest and in the general revision of the criminal law. (p. 174)

Similar criticisms have been made of measures taken by British soccer clubs themselves, some of which can only be described as desperate. Such was the case with Chelsea Football Club in 1985 when the club chairman suggested installing an electrified fence around the playing field until the Greater London Council pressured him and his club into rejecting the idea.[10] Most other measures taken or considered by sports officials have been more thoughtful, if no more successful. Possibly the most widely publicized suggestion in this regard was the idea of introducing a national identity card scheme aimed at removing the protection of anonymous membership in the soccer crowd normally enjoyed by hooligan fans. From its inception, the long-term effectiveness of the scheme was questionable. Critics raised concerns about the feasibility of implementing an expensive identity card program at a time of fiscal retrenchment, especially when many of the larger clubs in Britain enjoy huge cumulative regular *and* occasional spectator followings. Additional concerns surrounded the wisdom and practicality of introducing a widespread identity card program when those with hooligan proclivities represent a relatively small percentage of the total fan population.

Assuming that violence inside stadia is caused or exacerbated by the traditional arrangement of standing to watch soccer games, most British clubs have in recent years reconfigured their stadia to include all-seat arrangements. Since a significant amount of hooligan violence still occurs outside the stadium itself, and since hooligan groups have been known to vandalize newly installed seating, and have been captured on film using seats as missiles in aerial confrontations with police, the long-term effectiveness of curbing hooliganism by changing the stadium environment once again remains uncertain.

In contrast to measures of this type, scholars have generally been critical of looking solely to game-centered solutions for soccer hooliganism, and the implementation of short-term punitive measures. Events over the past two decades in the United Kingdom show that the incidence of hooliganism does not decrease as more draconian policies are imposed. Despite their theoretical differences, both Taylor and Dunning would agree that since hooliganism is symptomatic of broader social crises, only

thoughtful social change is likely to seriously challenge the hooligan problem. Recognizing the unlikelihood of such social change in the immediate or long term, the Sir Norman Chester Centre for Football Research (1988) has made or supported several practical recommendations for tackling hooliganism domestically and abroad. These include more efficient and careful ticket distribution, comprehensive travel schedules enabling specially appointed stewards to supervise groups of travelling fans, fan membership schemes, adequate segregation by host clubs, the establishment of stronger community links with soccer fans, and even treatment programs for hooligan offenders. However, it remains the case that there is little agreement between scholars, soccer officials and the authorities with respect to appropriate responses to hooliganism, and that harsh criminal sanctions tend to resurface in the wake of highly publicized hooligan encounters.

While it is often assumed in North America that sports crowd disorder is minimal and unworthy of scholarly attention, there is evidence to suggest that a large number of clubs are also sufficiently concerned with a perceived crowd disorder problem to have attempted corrective measures of late (Young, 1988). Generally, these changes have taken the form of revisions in security procedures and in the sale of alcohol, and efforts to decrease the abusive, destructive and violent behavior of fans. Other specific examples include stiff increases in fines for trespassing on the field of play, increases in numbers of security personnel at games and reductions in the level of police tolerance regarding profane, abusive and/or violent fan conduct, the construction of special family enclosures and protective tunnels for players to enter and exit from the playing area safely, the closing of stadium sections known to contain consistently disorderly fans, and increases in frisking at stadium entrances.

While North American clubs have also expressed concern with alcohol-related offences, and while recommendations are regularly made by officials and police to restrict the sale of alcohol, the vast majority of North American stadia continue to sell alcohol. Although many stadia have reduced the strength and volume of the alcohol they sell and frequently terminate sales prior to the end of the game, these attempts may be understood in part as public relations efforts by clubs to mollify frustrated orderly fans and other concerned parties. Young's (1988) data suggest that clubs experiencing security problems with inebriated fans have at times underplayed the seriousness and number of offences taking place. This may be explained by the fact that many North American clubs are actually sponsored or owned by breweries.

As Williams (1985) indicates, a similarly delicate scenario exists for British soccer clubs. The Control of Alcohol Bill, introduced in 1985, has banned the possession or consumption of alcohol inside all soccer stadia; this again rests uneasily with the fact that many clubs are sponsored by breweries. One might note here that suggestions to reduce or ban the sale of alcohol at sports events, a popular position with politicians, may in fact not be as effective as is often assumed. For example, in the United Kingdom anti-alcohol policies have had only limited results since fans who choose to do so are quick to discover new and innovative ways of drinking.

Player Violence

As essentially self-regulating organizations, much like those of doctors and lawyers, sports leagues have traditionally preferred to practice their own versions of common law in dealing with player misconduct. This has included punitive responses such as warnings, fines, suspensions and other forms of deterrence. In North America, until the 1970s, such a process of self-regulation and in-house accountability met more or less with legal approval (Barnes, 1988: 97) and, where litigated, sports violence cases typically troubled judicial experts. Although much of the player violence occurring in Canada and the US satisfies the requirements of assault set out in their respective criminal codes, it is equally clear that assault in sport is, in principle at least, distinguished by a degree of immunity from criminal liability. Evidence for the inconsistent interpretation of legal jurisdiction over sports violence may be found in the now hundreds of investigations across the continent reviewed in socio-legal research (Barnes, 1988; Horrow, 1980, 1982; Reasons, 1992; Smith, 1983; Young, 1993; Young and Wamsley, 1996). Many other examples remain scattered and untapped in case law annals.

To my knowledge, no one has conducted a systematic analysis of all sports assault cases over the twentieth century in any one setting, although Grayson's (1988) review of British law and Barnes's (1988) meticulous survey of Canadian law remain the most comprehensive exegeses in this regard. Of the few quantitative studies that do exist, Watson and MacLellan (1986) found 66 cases of player–player assault

charges related to Canadian ice hockey (including 6 civil suits and 60 criminal charges) between 1905 and 1982. As Young (1993) has noted, the routine litigation of sports assault cases in Canada is, however, a post-war and relatively recent phenomenon. For example, approximately 75 per cent of Watson and MacLellan's cases occurred between 1972 and 1982. Similarly, an extensive review of the case law leads Reasons (1992) to identify what he calls 'the emergence of a "hockey crime wave"' (p. 9) in the 1970s.

An examination of sports law on both sides of the Atlantic since the 1970s suggests that at both amateur and professional levels athletes are increasingly concerned with their legal and civil rights. While the masculinist culture of sport still generally condones the violent premise of sports such as football, rugby and ice hockey, and while many players still expect to get hit, hurt and injured (Messner, 1990; Nixon, 1993; Young et al., 1994), part of this revelation is that excessively forceful conduct may be unacceptable and redressed legally. This reasoning has prompted a recent increase in the numbers of players willing to move beyond traditional codes of in-house policing and initiate charges against other players, as well as against coaches and owners, for various 'assaults' on their bodies.

In a review of litigated sports violence cases from the 1970s involving charges of assault, Horrow (1982) described some of the common defenses that jeopardize judicial resolution in favor of the plaintiff: the 'Battery and the Problem of Establishing Intent Defense'; the 'Assumption of Risk Defense'; the 'Consent Defense'; the 'Provocation Defense'; the 'Involuntary Reflex Defense'; and the 'Self Defense'. Still applicable to Canadian law in the 1990s, this list is by no means exhaustive of all defenses available or those used, but it underlines the difficulty litigators have had separating illegal from aggressive but nevertheless *acceptable* play. Underlying notions of voluntary assumption of risk (or, what in legal jargon, is known as *volenti non fit injuria*) have become associated with most of them (Young, 1993).

Such is true in National Hockey League (NHL) case law (Reasons, 1992). A precedent-setting example, the 1969 *R.* v. *Green* case, showed evidence that Ted Green of the Boston Bruins came off the boards and swiped his opponent Wayne Maki with the back of his glove. Maki retaliated by chopping Green on the head with his stick. In Horrow's (1980: 19) account, 'Green sustained a serious concussion and massive haemorrhaging. After two brain operations, he regained only partial sensation and has never recovered 100 per cent.' While charges were brought against both players, Green, having used a 'self-defense' argument, was acquitted with the following judicial assessment:

> No hockey player enters onto the ice of the National Hockey League without consenting to and without knowledge of the possibility that he is going to be hit in one of many ways once he is on the ice ... we can come to the conclusion that this is an ordinary happening in a hockey game and the players really think nothing of it. If you go behind the net of a defenceman, particularly one who is trying to defend his zone, and you are struck in the face by that player's glove, a penalty might be called against him, but you do not really think anything of it; it is one of the types of risks one assumes. (Horrow, 1980: 186)

Perhaps more than any other single act of player violence, fist-fighting in ice hockey has been comprehensively researched (Bloom and Smith, 1996; Goranson, 1982; Gruneau and Whitson, 1993; Smith, 1975, 1979, 1983; Weinstein et al., 1995; Young and Smith, 1988/89; Young and Wamsley, 1996). It has been a common court response to fight-related injuries to acquit defendants on similar grounds of consent. This has been true at both professional and amateur levels in Canada. Horrow (1980: 186) cites the Ontario case of *R. v. Starratt*, where the court argued that fist-fighting was so frequent in the NHL as to be viewed 'normal' as long as the force of the fight 'does not exceed that level authorized by the other players'. More recent Canadian cases are detailed in Young and Wamsley (1996).

In brief, players have traditionally been understood to either express or imply consent to certain levels of force used against them, *except* in cases of extraordinarily savage and injurious attacks. As tolerated as sports violence cases have been historically, their presence in tort and criminal law, coupled with what appears to be a decreasing social tolerance towards aspects of violence generally, has led litigators to more stringently re-evaluate certain sports offences as excessive and unjustifiable (D. White, 1986). Contrary to its legal conventions, *volenti* does not imply absolute consent, but consent only as a matter of degree. Needless to say, absolute notions of *volenti* are further diluted by acts of violence occurring outside the rules of games, or after the play has stopped, neither of which are given direct or implied consent by players.

While, again, there has been no systematic tally of litigated sports violence cases involving grievances initiated by players against other players, a review of the case law suggests that their numbers are growing. As D. White (1986: 1030–4) has argued:

> There is a clear trend that the criminal justice systems in Canada and the United States are becoming more and more willing to control illegal violence in sports ... Canadian prosecutors have used the criminal law ... frequently against athletes accused of violently injuring fellow players. There have been more than one hundred criminal convictions for offences involving player–player violence in the last fifteen years.

To date, case law indicates that charges and convictions for assault causing bodily harm are most widespread, although criminal charges of common assault, and even manslaughter and homicide are being heard (Reasons, 1992: 25).

Along with boxing, hockey appears most frequently in criminal reports, especially in Canada. Indeed, as Reasons notes, 'it may be said that Canada leads the common law world in criminally prosecuting its athletes for criminal violence' (1992: 8). A number of highly publicized cases from other international contexts suggest a wider trend toward the criminalization of sports violence. In the past decade, such cases include assault charges brought against a Canadian NHL player, manslaughter charges against another Canadian playing in the Italian Ice Hockey League, a Scottish soccer player jailed for three months for head-butting an opponent, and a French soccer star playing in England sentenced to two weeks in jail for kicking a spectator (see Table 25.3). Drawn from professional or top-level amateur sport, these are all examples of player violence entering the jurisdiction of either civil or criminal law. Over the same ten-year period, dozens of similar incidents at the amateur and recreational level, including college and high school, have resulted in charges, litigation, and/or prosecution across North America.

However, it would be a mistake to assume that legal intervention into sports violence has been uncontested or unilinear; this is not the case. In general, player violence is still defined ambiguously at best, and there remains little agreement among sports administrators and legal authorites as to the acceptable limits of aggressive, injurious, or otherwise risky sports conduct. Also, while civil and criminal charges against athletes may be on the increase, prosecutions remain rare and sentences light. For example, in the first of the cases cited above, hockey player Dino Ciccarelli's conviction on an assault charge was followed by a sentence

Table 25.3   *Recent 'sports crimes': select cases*

Year	Location	Sport	Charges and Legal Ruling	Source
1994	Italy	Ice hockey	Canadian ice-hockey player Jimmy Boni charged with intentional homicide in on-ice death of opponent. Boni eventually pleads guilty to the reduced charge of manslaughter and is fined $1800 (Cdn.)	*Macleans*, 28 Feb. 1994: 11 *Sports Illustrated*, 6 Dec. 1993: 66–79
1994	Wales	Rugby	Welsh rugby player Howard Collins sentenced to up to 6 months in jail for stomping on an opponent's head	*Calgary Herald*, 22 Dec. 1994: D2
1995	England	Soccer	Manchester United star Eric Cantona charged with common assault and sentenced to 2 weeks in jail for kicking a fan	*Calgary Herald*, 24 March 1995: D3
1995	England	Rugby	Rugby player Simon Devereux found guilty on charges of grievous bodily harm and jailed for 9 months by English court for punching an opponent	*The Sun*, 23 Feb. 1996: 16
1995	England	Soccer	Scottish soccer player with 3 previous convictions for assault sentenced to 3 months in jail for head-butting opponent	*Toronto Star*, 26 May 1995: C10
1995	Australia	Cricket	18-year-old Alexander Natera is charged with unlawful killing after he clashed heads with an opponent in a rugby game.	*Toronto Star*, 17 May 1995: B7
1996	Canada	Ice hockey	Criminal charges, including assault, laid against Canadian university players who swarm referee, punch and spear him with sticks following controversial goal in play-off game.	*Globe & Mail*, 28 Feb. 1996: 12

of one day in a Toronto jail of which he spent less than two hours in a cell signing autographs (*Sports Illustrated*, 5 September 1988: 34). At the same time, massive variability within and across societies in the implementation of the law in sports continues to undermine the integrity of legal intervention. And complicating this legal quagmire further still, there remains no compelling evidence that criminalizing player violence actually works.

SPORTS VIOLENCE AND THE MASS MEDIA

Because the various manifestations of sports violence reach most people indirectly through the mass media, it seems reasonable to argue that the media must take some responsibility for our perceptions and misperceptions of the forms and meanings the phenomena assume.

One of the most common sociological approaches to understanding the relationship between sports violence and the media – the so-called 'legitimation' perspective – focuses not so much on violence as such, but on the messages that accompany violence; messages often serving to condone or legitimize the behavior of violence-doers. Nowhere do these messages seem to be more blatant and pervasive than in media presentations of sports. Precisely how much sports violence is given a positive slant is not known, but unquestionably the media frequently convey the idea that violence is accepted, even desirable, behavior and that violence-doers are to be admired. This is done in a myriad of ways, some crude, some artful, some probably a reflection of the acceptance of pro-violence values and norms by media personnel. Examples may be found in an expansive literature (Adams, 1978; Gillett et al., 1996; Hall, 1978; Murphy et al., 1988; Smith, 1983; Walvin, 1986; Whannel, 1979; Young, 1986, 1990, 1991b, 1993; Young and Smith, 1988/89).

Notwithstanding qualitative differences in the conventions and approaches of media outlets (Young, 1990), Hall's (1978: 26) early description of the treatment of soccer hooliganism in the British popular press since the 1960s is in a sense indicative of the manner in which soccer-related disorder and other aspects of sports violence have been reported in the press more generally in a number of countries:

> graphic headlines, bold type-faces, warlike imagery and epithets, vivid photographs cropped to the edges to create a strong impression of physical menace, and ... stories [that] have been decorated with black lines and exclamation marks.

Hall speaks of 'editing for impact,' a process in which hooligan action comes to be marketed by a newspaper industry concerned largely with profit maximization. A cluster of issues including lurid news values, dramatic and distorting reporting techniques, and conservative world views combine to 'excite' the phenomena, argues Hall, an effect that can be witnessed in the heightening of public and official sensitization to the problem (public overestimation of threat, increases in policing procedures, etc.).

Also in relation to British soccer hooliganism, Walvin (1986: 88) argued that 'television violence may be less significant in stimulating acts of violence than it is in encouraging a stiffening of the law-and-order lobby'. In a similar but perhaps more historically and politically sensitive study of the relationship between hooliganism and the press, Murphy et al. (1988) illustrated the importance of long-term social processes and trends. For example, they showed how at various phases of British history official responses to and press coverage of hooliganism have played both amplifying and de-amplifying roles in what appear to be contrived ways. In the years immediately following the 1985 Brussels riot, for instance, and despite continuing disturbances at soccer games, media treatment of hooliganism was, if anything, underplayed. Clearly, the Leicester group understands political backdrop as a key determinant of the nature and extent of hooliganism news coverage. In this specific case, in the post-Heysel era when English soccer clubs were banned from European competition by the sport's ruling bodies and eager to return to it, British authorities and the media made frequent claims that soccer's problems were under control. Such claims, so the argument runs, seemed to disseminate the less-than-accurate impression that stringent law-and-order measures undertaken in Britain had been successful. Of course, what they also underlined was the complicity of the media in political matters.

That the media may have played an active rather than a passive role in aspects of collective violence at European soccer is also a view advanced in other research on the British context (Keen, 1986; Taylor, 1982b, 1987;

Vulliamy, 1985; Whannel, 1979; Young, 1986) and the continental European context (Pietersen and Holm Kristensen, 1988; Stollenwerk and Sagurski, 1989; Van Limbergen and Walgrave, 1988; Williams and Goldberg, 1989; Williams et al., 1988).

Numerous studies of media coverage have explored ways in which the North American electronic and print media also exploit aspects of sports crowd and player violence (Bryant and Zillmann, 1983; Coakley, 1988/89; Gillett et al., 1996; Morse, 1983; Smith, 1983; Theberge, 1989; Young, 1990, 1991b, 1993; Young and Smith, 1988/89). For example, emphasizing common trends in sports commentary found especially in the daily and tabloid newspapers (such as the use of melodramatic and eye-catching headlines, commendations of violent athletes and their bellicose styles of play, and a reliance on graphically violent photographs), Smith (1983) and Young and Smith (1988/89) concentrate on the messages that accompany acts of sports violence in the Canadian press. The result of these common coverage techniques, they contend, is at least to condone violent play and at worst to reproduce it. Morse (1983) and Gillett et al. (1996) have also shown how television coverage manipulates sport by stressing its rougher and often injurious elements, and P. White et al. (1995: 159) indicate how 'potentially health-compromising norms [are] reinforced by many well-known and respected sports figures who promote and defend violent play as a relatively harmless feature of sport'. Finally, the active role played by the North American media in their treatment of violence has also been shown to include the dissemination of myths, such as the notion that fist-fighting in ice hockey is non-injurious (Young, 1990), and that soccer hooliganism is an indigenously 'British disease' (Young, 1988).

The question of the *effects* of mass media portrayals of violence on 'spill-over' violence in society has also produced a substantial body of research (Comisky et al., 1977; Duperrault, 1981; Goranson, 1982; Gordon and Ibson, 1977; Hall, 1978; Moriarty and McCabe, 1977; Russell, 1979; Singer and Gordon, 1977; Smith, 1978, 1983; Whannel, 1979, 1986). While this outpouring of energy has not resulted in the conclusive establishment of a direct cause-and-effect relationship between media and real-life violence, the bulk of the evidence, especially that pertaining to television, points strongly in this direction. Assuming that media presentations of aggressive sports disproportionately privilege violent aspects of play, to what extent do viewers, including presumably impressionable young athletes, consume and become affected by such material?

Several early laboratory and field experiments (cf. Baron, 1977; Geen and Berkowitz, 1969) showed that subjects exposed to filmed or televised models displaying aggression tend to exhibit similar behavior when subsequently given the opportunity. Most of this work, however, took place in the laboratory, raising inevitable questions about generalizing from artificial environments to the real world. Also, most experimental work has been concerned with immediate effects, subjects usually being tested within minutes of viewing the aggressive model. In real life, of course, opportunities to aggress do not usually present themselves quite so readily. For example, the young hockey player who views a professional game on television does not have an opportunity to engage in imitative aggression immediately afterward. What about the longer-term and cumulative effects of exposure to an aggressive model?

A handful of Canadian studies of sports violence (Goranson, 1982; Moriarty and McCabe, 1977; Russell, 1979; Smith, 1974, 1983) have gone some way in answering this question, but Smith's (1979) study of Toronto hockey players seems to have approached the modelling hypothesis in the most direct way. Smith's respondents were asked: 'Have you ever learned how to hit another player illegally in any way from watching professional hockey?' Fifty-six per cent of the 604 respondents replied affirmatively, with only slight variations by age and level of competition. These players were then asked to describe what they had learned. A selection of their responses (for example, 'I learned how to trip properly') may be found in Smith (1983). Learning, however, is not necessarily *doing*. The above players were then asked: 'How many times during this season have you actually hit another player in this way?' Two hundred and twenty-two said 'at least once or twice,' and 90 of these, mostly elite amateurs, said 'five times or more'. Official game records verified these verbal responses; players who said they performed such acts received significantly more penalties than those who indicated they did not. Viewing aggressive media models in hockey, and perhaps sport in general, does appear to have a systematic long-term impact on the behavior of amateur players of different ages.

In brief, theoretical attempts to ascertain the effects of media portrayals of sports violence fall into several different theoretical camps.

From a learning point of view, modelling studies suggest that young athletes learn how to perform assaultive acts by watching big-league models on television and subsequently enact what they have learned, especially in sports leagues where such conduct is rewarded. This effect seems to be cumulative and long-term. Legitimation studies, focusing more on the messages that accompany violence than on violent acts themselves, suggest that the media approve of sports violence and violence-doers in a myriad of subtle and not-so-subtle ways, including selling products on the basis of their violence appeal. One suspects that such messages add up to one more way in which people learn that violence is acceptable sports behavior. But this has not been demonstrated unambiguously. More research on the effects of this kind of media content on violence in amateur sport is needed. Finally, the arousal–aggressive cues theory of aggression found in early work in media effects (cf. Arms et al., 1979, 1980; Geen and Berkowitz, 1969) is less than convincing. This approach, which suggests that the media imbue persons and objects in sports contexts with the capacity to 'pull' aggressive reactions from frustrated or angry players, has been widely criticized on methodological grounds.

Studies by Coakley (1988/89), Young and Smith (1988/89) and others have cautioned that a direct cause-and-effect relationship between media coverage of sports violence and imitative violence is yet to be validated empirically. Moreover, because audience readings of images and discourses in the sports media are probably heterogeneously linked to factors such as social class, gender, culture, regionality and ethnicity (Fiske, 1987: 17), caution should also be exercised in assuming that media coverage affects all sports audiences in the same way or indeed at all.

Nevertheless, Taylor (1982a), Keen (1986), Young (1988), Young and Smith (1988/89) and others have all shown that certain styles of sports violence coverage are associated with discourse effects and perhaps some limited behavioral effects. At the very least, the weight of the evidence suggests that media presentations of sports violence, particularly at the professional level, contribute to a social climate in sport conducive to violent behavior. Once again, it is a fact that most people are exposed to sports violence both on and off the field not directly but indirectly through the media. For this reason alone the mass media are of considerable importance in any comprehensive attempt to understand violence in sport.

CONCLUSION

Violence in sport is clearly a multi-dimensional and complex topic that has generated a huge volume of research and writing. The portion of it reviewed here underlines the importance of approaching the topic in the following three ways: *sociologically*, because far from existing in a vacuum, violent aspects of sport grow out of and exist relationally with other parts of the social process – witness the deeply gendered character of violence both on and off the field (cf. Dunning, 1986; Messner, 1990; Taylor, 1987; Theberge, 1989, 1997; Young, 1993); *culturally* and *cross-culturally*, because the often heterogeneous manifestations and meanings of sports violence are forged in the workshops of distinct cultures – witness the manner in which spectators from European countries differentially articulate their allegiance to the game of soccer (cf. Williams and Goldberg, 1989); and *historically*, because these manifestations and meanings are often far more grounded than new, and often as fluid as they are fixed – witness the multilinear developments and shifts in English soccer hooliganism across the last century highlighted by the figurational branch of the Leicester School (cf. Dunning et al., 1988).

Despite the colossal volume of work that has been produced on violence in sport, I would caution against complacency and contend that we still know relatively little about the phenomenon. This depends on the specific aspect of violence in question. For example, symbolized by the differential weighting of the sections in the early part of this chapter, there seems little doubt that the most substantial and rigorously theorized body of work in this area has examined forms and causes of British soccer hooliganism. By comparison, relatively little is known about sports crowd disorder in other parts of the world. This is also true of the phenomenon in North America where, with some exceptions, much of what we know comes from descriptive journalistic accounts.[11]

Inevitably, the literature on violence in sport is limited in other ways. From a burgeoning literature on both sides of the Atlantic, we know something about the relationship between sport, violence, injury and pain, but more information is needed. After a hiatus in the 1980s, socio-legal work on the relationship between sport and the law, and on what I have called elsewhere 'sports crimes' (Young, 1993, 1997a), is only just beginning to be revitalized. Because the bulk of the research on sports violence has privileged the experiences of men,

studies of risk-taking, physicality and violence among girls and women are required, especially in light of evidence from a number of countries that females are increasingly participating in aggressive, traditionally maledefined sports such as rugby, ice hockey and soccer. After years of research on the sports violence/media nexus, an impressive body of material has been amassed on coverage styles, but the question of 'media effects' remains prickly, and how audiences deconstruct and are impacted by mediated sports violence remains uncertain. And finally, next to nothing is known about what I have called here 'other forms of violence related to sport' – the involvement of sports personnel, as victims or offenders, in practices such as stalking, harassment, threat and abuse.

Of course, in drawing attention to these lacunae, my intent is not to discredit the important work that has been done in each of these areas, but simply to paint a 'what's been done, and what needs to be done?' type of picture. Assuming that readers agree with my assessment, perhaps we can begin the task of attending to some of these omissions in future sports violence research.

NOTES

1 In the history of English soccer, 1985 is considered a 'crisis year'. On 11 May 1985, as Bradford City played at home against Lincoln City, a fire broke out in a woodenframed stadium structure built in 1908. The section of the stadium burned to the ground in less than 10 minutes, and 57 people were burned to death trying to escape the fire. Then, 18 days later, on 29 May 1985, the European Champions Cup was due to be played between Liverpool of England and Juventus of Turin, Italy. Approximately one hour prior to kick-off, and following a period of mutual taunting between rival fan groups, a charge by the Liverpool fans into the Juventus 'end' resulted in the collapse of a retainer wall, injuring hundreds of fans. Thirty-nine mostly Italian fans died in the ensuing crush (Taylor, 1987; Young, 1986).

On 15 April 1989, Liverpool fans were again involved in a tragic incident prior to a cup game against Nottingham Forrest played at Hillsborough Stadium, Sheffield, although this time the tragedy was not hooligan-related. After the police opened a gate to accommodate latecomers, as many as 4000 Liverpool fans were channelled into the stadium, unaware that hundreds of fans inside the stadium were being crushed against a control fence. At least 94 fans were killed, over 200 injured (Scraton et al., 1995; Taylor, 1989).

2   Although he continues to work at the Sir Norman Chester Centre for Football Research, in the early 1990s John Williams splintered off from the Leicester School, expressing concerns, much as Ian Taylor has done, that the figurational approach of his colleagues has, among other things, led to a miscalculation of the 'scale and seriousness' of early outbreaks of English hooliganism (1991: 177). Three years later, Eric Dunning (1994) published a comprehensive rebuttal to Williams's self-titled 'rethinking'.

3   Although the generic term 'British hooliganism' is used in this chapter, research into the phenomenon in Britain has highlighted, in Williams's words, 'important national and cultural differences in patterns and forms of hooliganism' (1991: 177). There seems little doubt that among the countries of the United Kingdom, the most consistently bellicose and violent episodes at home and abroad have involved fans of the national English team.

4   Although they may co-exist, there is normally an important difference between crowd injuries being caused by violent fans and by crushes and stampedes brought on by such things as over-ticketing, negligent security procedures, or stadium collapses or fires. My intent is not to conflate these processes, but to indicate that their outcomes may nevertheless be similar.

5   Mike Smith, a pioneer in North American research on sports violence and an internationally respected scholar, died in June 1994. He is greatly missed by his colleagues and friends.

6   Preliminary work on women, sport and physicality (Theberge, 1997; White and Young, 1997; Young, 1997b; Young and White, 1995) suggests that many elite female athletes adopt similar play-through-pain attitudes as their male counterparts and also risk injury and disablement in their athletic pursuits.

7   Among a long list of male and female athletes from a range of sports who report being stalked, harassed or threatened is figure skater Katarina Witt. In 1992, an obsessed fan was charged on seven counts of sending obscene and threatening mail, and was sentenced to 3 years in a US psychiatric centre. In the case it was revealed that Harry Veltman II had, among other things, followed Witt around the world attempting to distract her as she skated in competition (*USA Today*, 14 July 1995: 3C).

8   In early 1997, the world of Canadian ice hockey was stunned by claims made by a current NHL player that his junior coach had sexually abused him on over 300 occasions. After a short trial, in which the complicity of others, including some high-profile names within the hockey community, was revealed or implied, hockey coach Graham James was sentenced to 3 years in jail. In February 1997 another man laid sexual abuse charges against two employees of Maple Leaf Gardens (home of the NHL's Toronto Maple Leafs). In the inquiry that followed, it was acknowledged that the Maple Leaf Gardens had earlier reached an out-of-court settlement of $60,000 with the man in return for not bringing criminal charges against them. At the time of writing, police have received a flood of calls from male hockey players across the country alleging similar types of abuse; the inquiry is ongoing.

9   These Government-sponsored reports include the Harrington Report (1968), the Lang Report (1969), the Wheatley Report (1972), the Report of a Joint Sports Council/Social Science Research Council Panel (1978), as well as the Popplewell Report (1985).

10   The use of penning, perimeter fencing, and segregation as crowd control procedures in British soccer has proved to be highly controversial. After perimeter fencing was installed at most grounds in the 1970s and 1980s, it was subsequently discovered that such fencing may in fact endanger not enhance crowd safety. Among other incidents, the Bradford fire and the Hillsborough Stadium tragedy in which many fans lost their lives trying to scale walls and fences designed originally to protect them, brought this fact into sharp relief. Numerous English clubs have actually removed perimeter fencing; from both a crowd control and crowd safety perspective, the change seems to have been successful so far (Sir Norman Chester Centre for Football Research, 1989: 19).

11   A thoughtful attempt to theorize North American sports crowd disorder may be found in Chapter 7 of Dunning (1999).

REFERENCES

Adams, R. (1978) 'Soccer hooliganism and the mass media: fictions and reality', *Youth and Society*, 30: 13–16.

Adedeji, J.A. (1982) 'Sport, violence and collective behavior in Nigerian post-primary and secondary school games'. Paper presented at the Tenth World Congress of Sociology, Mexico City.

Archetti, E.P. and Romero, A.C. (1994) 'Death and violence in Argentinian football', in R. Giulianotti, N. Bonney and M. Hepworth (eds), *Football, Violence and Social Identity*. London: Routledge. pp. 37–73.

Arms, R.L., Russell, G.W. and Sandilands, M.L. (1979) 'Effects on the hostility of spectators of viewing aggressive sports', *Review of Sport and Leisure*, 4: 115–27.

Arms, R.L., Russell, G.W. and Sandilands, M.L. (1980) 'Effects of viewing aggressive sports on the hostility of spectators', in R.M. Suinn (ed.), *Psychology in Sports: Methods and Applications*. Minneapolis, MN: Burgess. pp. 133–42.

Atyeo, D. (1979) *Violence in Sports*. Toronto: Van Nostrand Reinhold.

Bairner, A. (1995) 'Soccer, masculinity, and violence in Northern Ireland'. Paper presented at North American Society for the Sociology of Sport, Sacramento, California, November 1–4.

Barnes, J. (1988) *Sports and the Law in Canada*. Toronto: Butterworths.

Baron, R.A. (1977) *Human Aggression*. New York: Plenum.

Beisser, A.R. (1967) *The Madness in Sports*. New York: Appleton Century Crofts.

Benedict, J. and Klein, A. (1997) 'Arrest and conviction rates for athletes accused of sexual assault', *Sociology of Sport Journal*, 14: 86–95.

Bloom, G.A. and Smith, M.D. (1996) 'Hockey violence: a test of the cultural spillover theory', *Sociology of Sport Journal*, 13: 65–78.

Bryant, J. and Zillmann, D. (1983) 'Sports violence and the media', in J.H. Goldstein (ed.), *Sports Violence*. New York: Springer-Verlag. pp. 195–208.

Bryson, L. (1987) 'Sport and the maintenance of masculine hegemony', *Women's Studies International Forum*, 10: 349–60.

Buford, B. (1992) *Among the Thugs*. London: Mandarin.

Cameron, A. (1976) *Circus Factions: Blues and Greens at Tome and Byzantium*. Oxford: Clarendon Press.

Carroll, R. (1980) 'Football hooliganism in England', *International Review of Sport Sociology*, 15: 77–92.

Cashman, R. (1992) 'Violence in sport in Sydney before 1850', *ASSH Studies in Sports History*, 7: 1–10.

Clarke, A. and Madden, L. (1986) 'Professional football: the limits of economic analysis', *Leisure Management*, October, pp. 36–8.

Clarke, A. and Madden, L. (1987) 'Sportacular: the club, the community and the common cause', *Leisure Management*, February, pp. 16–17.

Clarke, J. (1973) 'Football hooliganism and the skinheads'. Occasional Paper, University of Birmingham.

Clarke, J. (1978) 'Football and working-class fans: tradition and change', in R. Ingham (ed.), *Football Hooliganism: the Wider Context*. London: Inter-Action Inprint.

Coakley, J. (1988–89) 'Media coverage of sports and violent behavior: an elusive connection', *Current Psychology: Research and Reviews*, 7: 322–30.

Coakley, J. (1989) 'Sport in society: an inspiration or an opiate?', in D.S. Eitzen (ed.), *Sport in Contemporary Society: an Anthology*. New York: St Martin's Press. pp. 88–101.

Coalter, F. (1985) 'Crowd behavior at football matches: a study in Scotland', *Leisure Studies*, 4: 111–17.

Colburn, K. (1985) 'Honor, ritual and violence in ice hockey', *Canadian Journal of Sociology*, 10: 153–70.

Comisky, P., Bryant, J. and Zillmann, D. (1977) 'Commentary as a substitute for action', *Journal of Communication*, 27: 150–2.

Corrigan, P. (1979) *Schooling the Smash Street Kids*. London: Macmillan.

Critcher, C. (1979) 'Football since the war', in J. Clarke (ed.), *Working Class Culture*. London: Hutchinson. pp. 161–84.

Crofts, M. (1984) 'Crowd behavior: Bay 13 at the World Series one day internationals', *Pelops*, 5: 17–21.

Crosset, T., Benedict, J. and MacDonald, M. (1995) 'Male student-athletes reported for sexual assault: survey of campus police departments and judicial affairs', *Journal of Sport and Social Issues*, 19: 126–40.

Crothers, T. (1996) 'Down and dirty', *Sports Illustrated*, 19 August, pp. 58–63.

Cunneen, C. and Lynch, R. (1988) 'The social meanings of conflict in riots at the Australian grand prix motorcycle races', *Leisure Studies*, 7: 1–18.

Curry, T. (1991) 'Fraternal bonding in the locker room: a feminist analysis of talk about competition and women', *Sociology of Sport Journal*, 8: 119–35.

Curtis, J. (1986) 'Isn't it difficult to support some of the notions of "The Civilizing Process"?: a response to Dunning', in C.R. Rees and A.W. Miracle (eds), *Sport and Social Theory*. Champaign, IL: Human Kinetics. pp. 57–65.

Dal Lago, A. and De Biasi, R. (1994) 'Italian football fans: culture and organization', in R. Giulianotti, N. Bonney and M. Hepworth (eds), *Football, Violence and Social Identity*. London: Routledge. pp. 73–90.

Dewar, C.K. (1979) 'Spectator fights at professional baseball games', *Review of Sport and Leisure*, 4: 12–26.

Donnelly, P. and Young, K. (1988) 'The construction and confirmation of identity in sport subcultures', *Sociology of Sport Journal*, 5: 223–40.

Dunning, E. (1979) *Soccer: the Social Origins of the Sport and its Development as a Spectacle and a Profession*. Leicester: University of Leicester Press.

Dunning, E. (1986) 'Sport as a male preserve: notes on the social sources of masculine identity and its transformations', in N. Elias and E. Dunning (eds), *Quest for Excitement: Sport and Leisure in the Civilizing Process*. Oxford: Basil Blackwell. pp. 267–84.

Dunning, E. (1990) 'Sociological reflections on sport and civilization', *International Review for the Sociology of Sport*, 25: 65–81.

Dunning, E. (1994) 'The social roots of football hooliganism: a reply to the critics of the "Leicester School"' in R. Giulianotti, N. Bonney and M. Hepworth (eds), *Football, Violence and Social Identity*. London: Routledge. pp. 128–58.

Dunning, E. (1999) *Sport Matters: Sociological Studies of Sport, Violence and Civilization*. London: Routledge.

Dunning, E., Maguire, J., Murphy, P. and Williams, J.J. (1981) 'If you think you're hard enough', *New Society*, 27 August, pp. 342–4.

Dunning, E., Maguire, J., Murphy, P. and Williams, J. (1982a) 'The social roots of football violence', *Leisure Studies*, 1: 139–56.

Dunning, E., Murphy, P. and Williams, J. (1982b) *Working Class Social Bonding and the Sociogenesis of Football Hooliganism: A Report to the Social Science Council*. Leicester: University of Leicester.

Dunning, E., Maguire, J., Murphy, P. and Williams, J. (1984a) 'Football hooliganism in Britain before the first World War', *International Review for the Sociology of Sport*, 19: 215–39.

Dunning, E., Murphy, P. and Williams, J. (1984b) 'Football hooliganism', *Research Council Newsletter*, 51: 19–21.

Dunning, E., Murphy, P. and Williams, J. (1988) *The Roots of Football Hooliganism: an Historical and Sociological Study*. London: Routledge & Kegan Paul.

Dunning, E. and Sheard, K. (1979) *Barbarians, Gentlemen and Players: a Sociological Study of the Development of Rugby Football*. New York: New York University Press.

Dunstan, K. (1973) *Sports*. Melbourne: Cassell.

Duperrault, J.R. (1981) 'L'Affaire Richard: a situational analysis of the Montreal hockey riot', *Canadian Journal of History of Sport*, XII: 66–83.

Edgell, S. and Jary, D. (1973) 'Football: a sociological eulogy', in M.A. Smith, S. Parker, and C.S. Smith (eds), *Leisure and Society in Britain*. London: Allen Lane. pp. 214–29.

Edwards, H. (1973) *The Sociology of Sport*. Homewood, IL: Dorsey Press.

Edwards, H. and Rackages, V. (1977) 'The dynamics of violence in sport', *Journal of Sport and Social Issues*, 1: 3–31.

Elias, N. (1978). *The Civilizing Process*. London: Basil Blackwell.

Fimrite, R. (1976) 'Take me out to the brawl game', in A. Yiannakis (ed.), *Sport Sociology: Contemporary Themes*. Dubuque, IA: Kendall/Hunt. pp. 200–3.

Finn, G.P.T. (1994) 'Football violence: a societal psychological perspective', in R. Giulianotti, N. Bonney and M. Hepworth (eds), *Football, Violence and Social Identity*. London: Routledge. pp. 90–128.

Fiske, J. (1987) *Television Culture*. New York: Methuen.

Fontana, A. (1978) 'Over the edge: a return to primitive sensation in play and games', *Urban Life*, 7: 213–29.

Gammon, C. (1981) 'This isn't cricket … but it is', *Sports Illustrated*, 6 April, pp. 37–42.

Geen, R.G. and Berkowitz, L. (1969) 'Some conditions facilitating the occurrence of aggression after observation of violence', in L. Berkowitz (ed.), *Roots of Aggression: A Re-examination of the Frustration–Aggression Hypothesis*. New York: Atherton.

Gilbert, B. and Twyman, L. (1983) 'Violence: out of hand in the stands', *Sports Illustrated*, 31 January, pp. 62–74.

Gillett, J., White, P. and Young, K. (1996) 'The Prime Minister of Saturday night: Don Cherry, the CBC, and the cultural production of intolerance', in H. Holmes and D. Taras (eds), *Seeing Ourselves in Canada: Media Power and Policy*. Toronto: Harcourt Brace. pp. 59–72.

Giulianotti, R. (1994) 'Taking liberties: Hibs casuals and Scottish law', in R. Giulianotti, N. Bonney and M. Hepworth (eds), *Football, Violence and Social Identity*. London: Routledge. pp. 229–62.

Giulianotti, R. (1995) 'Participant observation and research into, football hooliganism: reflections on the problems of entree and everyday risks', *Sociology of Sport Journal*, 12: 1–20.

Goldstein, J.H. (1989) 'Sports violence', in D.S. Eitzen (ed.), *Sport in Contemporary Society: an Anthology*. New York: St Martin's Press. pp. 81–8.

Gonzales, J.D. (1992) 'Hooliganism in Spanish football, 1981–1990: a sociological analysis'. Paper presented at Olympic Scientific Congress, Malaga, Spain, 15–20 July.

Goranson, R.E. (1982) *The Impact of Television Hockey Violence. La Marsh Research Program Reports on Violence and Conflict Resolution*. Toronto: York University Press.

Gordon, D.R. and Ibson, L. (1977) 'Content analysis of the news media: Radio'. *Report of the Royal Commission on Violence in the Communication Industry*. Toronto: Ontario Government Bookstore.

Grayson, E. (1988) *Sport and the Law*. London: Butterworths.

Green, R.G. and O'Neal, E.C. (1976) *Perspectives on Aggression*. New York: Academic Press.

Greer, D.L. (1983) 'Spectator booing and the home advantage: a study of influence in the basketball arena', *Social Psychology Quarterly*, 46: 252–61.

Gruneau, R. and Whitson, D. (1993) *Hockey Night in Canada: Sport, Identities, and Cultural Politics*. Toronto: Garamond.

Guttmann, A. (1981) 'Sports spectators from antiquity to renaissance', *Journal of Sport History*, 8: 5–27.

Guttmann, A. (1986) *Sports Spectators*. New York: Columbia University Press.

Hall, S. (1978) 'The treatment of football hooliganism in the press', in R. Ingham (ed.), *Football Hooliganism: the Wider Context*. London: Inter-Action Inprint. pp. 15–37.

Harrison, P. (1974) 'Soccer's tribal wars', *New Society*, 5 September, pp. 602–4.

Hooligan (1985) Thames Television, produced by Ian Stuttard.

Hopcraft, A. (1968) *The Football Man*. London: Penguin.

Horak, R. (1991) 'Things change: Austrian football hooliganism from 1977–1990', *Sociological Review*, 39: 531–48.

Hornby, N. (1992) *Fever Pitch: A Fan's Life*: London: Victor Gollancz.

Horrow, R. (1980) *Sports Violence: The Interaction between Private Law Making and the Criminal Law*. Arlington, VA: Carrollton Press.

Horrow, R. (1982). 'Violence in professional sports: is it part of the game?', *Journal of Legislation*, 9: 1–15.

Hutchinson, J. (1975) 'Some aspects of football crowds before 1914'. Proceedings from Conference for the Study of Labour History, University of Sussex, Paper 13.

Johnson, W.O. (1993) 'The agony of victory', *Sports Illustrated*, 5 July, pp. 30–7.

Katz, S. (1955) 'Strange forces behind the Richard hockey riot', *Macleans*, 17: 11–110.

Keen, D. (1986) 'Exterminate them', *New Statesman*, 31 January, p. 16.

King, A. (1996) 'The fining of Vinnie Jones', *International Review for the Sociology of Sport*, 31: 119–35.

Kingsmore, J. (1968) 'The effect of professional wrestling and professional basketball contests upon the aggressive tendencies of male spectators', PhD dissertation, University of Maryland.

Lang, G.E. (1981) 'Riotous outbursts at sports events', in G.R. Luscher and G.H. Sage (eds), *Handbook of Social Sciences of Sport*. Champaign, IL: Stipes. pp. 415–39.

Leiber, J. (1989) 'Broken but unbowed', *Sports Illustrated*, 20 March, p. 16.

Lenskyj, H. (1990) 'Power and play: gender and sexuality issues in sport and physical activity', *International Review for the Sociology of Sport*, 25: 235–46.

Lever, J. (1972) 'Soccer as a Brazilian way of life', in G.P. Stone (ed.), *Games, Sport and Power*. New Brunswick, NJ: Transaction Inc. pp. 138–59.

Lever, J. (1983) *Soccer Madness*. Chicago: University of Chicago Press.

Levitt, C. and Shaffir, W. (1987) *The Riot at Christie Pits*. Toronto: Lester and Orpen Dennys.

Lewis, J.M. (1982) 'Fan violence: an American social problem', *Research in Social Problems and Public Policy*, 12: 175–206.

Listiak, A. (1981) '"Legitimate deviance" and social class: bar behavior during Grey Cup week', in M. Hart and S. Birrell (eds), *Sport in the Sociocultural Process*. Dubuque, IA: Wm. C. Brown. pp. 532–63.

Lynch, R. (1992) 'A symbolic patch of grass: crowd disorder and regulation on the Sydney Cricket Ground Hill', *ASSH Studies in Sports History*, 7: 10–49.

Maguire, J. (1986) 'The emergence of football spectating as a social problem 1880–1985: a figurational and developmental perspective', *Sociology of Sport Journal*, 3: 217–44.

Maguire, J. (1988/9) 'Violence of soccer matches in Victorian England: issues in the study of sports violence, popular culture and deviance', *Current Psychology: Research and Reviews*, 7: 285–97.

Main, J. (1985) 'Sport cops a bloody nose', *Your Sport: Australia's Monthly Sport Magazine*, 1: 8–11.

Manning, F. (1983) *The Celebration of Society*. Bowling Green, OH: Bowling Green State University Press.

Marples, M. (1954) *A History of Football*. London: Secker & Warburg.

Marsh, P. (1975) 'Understanding aggro', *New Society*, 3 April, pp. 7–9.

Marsh, P. (1982) *Aggro: the Illusion of Violence*. Oxford: Basil Blackwell.

Marsh, P. and Campbell, A. (eds) (1982) *Aggression and Violence*. Oxford: Basil Blackwell.

Marsh, P., Rosser, E. and Harré, R. (1978) *The Rules of Disorder*. London: Routledge & Kegan Paul.

Mason, A. (1980) *Association Football and English Society, 1863–1915*. Brighton: Harvester.

Mason, A. (1995) *Passion of the People: Football in South America*. London: Verso.

Meijs, J. and Van Der Brug, H. (1989) 'Dutch supporters at the European Championships in Germany'. Paper presented at the European Congress on Violence Control in the World of Sports, Athens, Greece, 17–19 February.

Melnick, M. (1992) 'Male athletes and sexual assault', *Journal of Physical Education, Recreation and Dance*, May–June, pp. 32–5.

Messner, M. (1990) 'When bodies are weapons: masculinity and violence in sport', *International Review for the Sociology of Sport*, 25: 203–21.

Messner, M. (1992) 'Pro balls', *Details*, pp. 100–1.

Messner, M. and Sabo, D. (eds) (1990) *Sport, Men, and the Gender Order: Critical Feminist Perspectives'*. Champaign, IL: Human Kinetics.

Messner, M. and Sabo, D. (1994) *Sex, Violence, and Power in Sports: Rethinking Masculinity.* Freedom, CA: The Crossing Press.

Metcalfe, A. (1978) 'Working class physical recreation in Montreal, 1860–1895', in H. Cantelon and R. Gruneau (eds), *Working Papers in the Sociological Study of Sport and Leisure* (Monograph 1). Kingston, ON: Queen's University Press.

Moorhouse, H.F. (1984) 'Professional football and working class culture: English theories and Scottish evidence', *Sociological Review*, 32: 285–316.

Moorhouse, H.F. (1987) 'Scotland against England: football and popular culture', *British Journal of Sports History*, 4: 189–202.

Moriarty, R. and McCabe, A. (1977) *Studies of Television and Youth Sports.* Report of the Royal Commission on Violence in the Communication Industry. Toronto: Ontario Government Bookstore.

Morse, M. (1983) 'Sport on television: replay and display', in E. Kaplan (ed.), *Regarding Television: Critical Approaches – an Anthology.* Los Angeles: University Publication of America. pp. 44–66.

Murphy, P., Dunning, E. and Williams, J. (1988) 'Soccer crowd disorder and the press: processes of amplification and de-amplification in historical perspective', *Theory, Culture and Society*, 5: 645–93.

Murray, B. (1984) *The Old Firm: Sectarianism, Sport and Society in Scotland.* Edinburgh: John Donald.

Nixon, H. (1993) 'Accepting the risks of pain and injury in sport: mediated cultural influences on playing hurt', *Sociology of Sport Journal*, 11: 78–87.

O'Brien, T. (1988/9) 'The fans' beliefs', *Current Psychology: Research and Reviews*, 7: 347–59.

Office of International Criminal Justice, University of Illinois (1994) Sports Violence: Issues for Law Enforcement (conference brochure).

Panayiotopoulos, D. (1989) 'Violence as a crime in the athletic field and Greek law'. Paper presented at the European Congress on Violence Control in the World of Sports, Athens, Greece, 17–19 February.

Petryszak, N. (1977) 'The bio-sociology of joy in violence', *Review of Sport and Leisure*, 2: 1–16.

Pietersen, B. and Kristensen, B.H. (1988) 'An empirical survey of the Danish roligans during the European Championships '88'. Paper prepared for the Danish State Institute of Physical Education.

Pilz, G. (1996) 'Social factors influencing sport and violence: On the "problem" of football violence in Germany', *International Review for the Sociology of Sport*, 31: 49–65.

The Poet (1991) *Sports Illustrated*, 2 September, pp. 62–84.

Reasons, C. (1992) 'The criminal law and sports violence: hockey crimes'. Unpublished paper, University of British Columbia, Vancouver, BC.

Redhead, S. (1986) *Sing When You're Winning.* London: Pluto.

Redhead, S. and McLaughlin, E. (1985) 'Soccer's style wars', *New Society*, 16 August, 225–8.

Report of Committee of Inquiry into Crowd Safety and Control at Soccer Grounds (The Popplewell Report) (1985). London: HMSO.

Report on Football Hooliganism to the Minister of Sport (The Harrington Report) (1968). Unpublished.

Report of the Inquiry into Crowd Safety at Sports Grounds (The Wheatley Report) (1972). London: HMSO.

Report of a Joint Sports Council/Social Science Research Council Panel (1978) *Public Disorder and Sporting Events.* London: Social Sciences Research Council.

Report of the Working Party on Crowd Behaviour at Football Matches (The Lang Report) (1969). London: HMSO.

Robins, D. (1984) *We Hate Humans.* Markham, ON: Penguin.

Roversi, A. (1991) 'Football violence in Italy', *International Review for the Sociology of Sport*, 26: 311–32.

Russell, G.W. (1979) 'Hero selection by Canadian ice hockey players: skill or aggression?' *Canadian Journal of Applied Sports Sciences*, 4: 309–13.

Scraton, P., Jemphrey, A. and Coleman, S. (1995) *No Last Rights: The Denial of Justice and the Promotion of Myth in the Aftermath of the Hillsborough Disaster.* Oxford: The Alden Press.

Semyonov, M. and Farbstein, M. (1989) 'Ecology of sports violence: the case of Israeli soccer', *Sociology of Sport Journal*, 6: 50–9.

Singer, B. and Gordon, D. (1977) *Content Analysis of the News Media: Newspapers and Television.* Report of the Royal Commission on Violence in the Communications Industry. Toronto: Ontario Government Bookstore.

Sir Norman Chester Centre for Football Research (1988) *An Investigation of the Measures for Improving Spectator Behaviour Currently in Use at Seven English Football Clubs: Summary of Preliminary Research Findings and Recommendations.* Leicester: University of Leicester Press.

Sir Normal Chester Centre for Football Research (1989) *Football and Football Spectators after Hillsborough: a National Survey of Members of the Football Supporters Association.* Leicester: University of Leicester Press.

Smelser, N.J. (1962) *The Theory of Collective Behavior.* New York: Free Press.

Smith, M.D. (1974) 'Significant others' influence on the assaultive behaviour of young hockey players', *International Review of Sport Sociology*, 3: 45–56.

Smith, M.D. (1975) 'Sport and collective violence', in D.W. Ball and J.W. Loy (eds), *Sport and Social Order: Contributions to the Sociology of Sport.* Reading, MA: Addison-Wesley, pp. 277–333.

Smith, M.D. (1976) 'Hostile outbursts in sport', in A. Yiannakis (ed.), *Sport Sociology: Contemporary Themes*. Dubuque, IA: Kendal/Hunt. pp. 203–5.

Smith, M.D. (1978) 'Precipitants of crowd violence', *Sociological Inquiry*, 48: 121–31.

Smith, M.D. (1979) 'Hockey violence: a test of the violent subculture hypothesis', *Social Problems*, 27: 234–47.

Smith, M.D. (1983) *Violence and Sport*. Toronto: Butterworths.

Smith, M.D. (1987) *Violence in Canadian Amateur Sport: A Review of Literature*. Report of the Commission for Fair Play, Government of Canada.

Stollenwerk, H. and Sagurski, R. (1989) 'Spectator conduct during the 1988 European Football Championships with special consideration of pertinent news coverage in the printed media'. Paper prepared for the Council of Europe.

Suttles, G. (1968) *The Social Order of the Slum*. Chicago: Chicago University Press.

Taylor, I. (1969) 'Hooligans: soccer's resistance movement', *New Society*, 7 August.

Taylor, I. (1971) 'Soccer consciousness and soccer hooliganism', in S. Cohen (ed.), *Images of Deviance*. New York: Penguin. pp. 134–65.

Taylor, I. (1982a) 'On the sports violence question: soccer hooliganism revisited', in J. Hargreaves (ed.), *Sport, Culture and Ideology*. Boston, MA: Routledge & Kegan Paul. pp. 152–97.

Taylor, I. (1982b) 'Class, violence and sport: the case of soccer hooliganism in Britain', in H. Cantelon and R. Gruneau (eds), *Sport, Culture and the Modern State*. Toronto: University of Toronto Press. pp. 39–97.

Taylor, I. (1987) 'Putting the boot into a working-class sport: British soccer after Bradford and Brussels', *Sociology of Sport Journal*, 4: 171–91.

Taylor, I. (1989) 'Hillsborough, 15 April 1989: some personal contemplations'. Unpublished paper.

Theberge, N. (1989) 'A feminist analysis of responses to sports violence: media coverage of the 1987 World Junior Hockey Championship', *Sociology of Sport Journal*, 6: 247–56.

Theberge, N. (1997) '"It's part of the game": physicality and the production of gender in women's hockey', *Gender and Society*, 11: 69–87.

Thompson, R. (1977) 'Sport and deviance: a subcultural analysis'. PhD dissertation, University of Alberta.

Tiger, L. (1969) *Men in Groups*. London: Thomas Nelson and Son.

Vamplew, W. (1980) 'Sports crowd disorder in Britain, 1870–1914: causes and controls', *Journal of Sport History*, 7: 5–21.

Van Der Brug, H. (1994) 'Football hooliganism in the Netherlands', in R. Giulianotti, N. Bonney and M. Hepworth (eds), *Football, Violence and Social Identity*. London: Routledge. pp. 174–96.

Van Limbergen, K. (1989) 'The societal backgrounds of hooliganism in Belgium'. Paper presented at the European Congress on Violence Control in the World of Sports, Athens, Greece, 17–19 February.

Van Limbergen, K. and Walgrave, L. (1988) *'Euro '88': Fans and Hooligans*. Youth Criminology Research Group Report to the Minister of the Interior.

Vaz, E. (1982) *The Professionalization of Young Hockey Players*. Lincoln, NB: University of Nebraska Press.

Veno, A. and Veno, E. (1992). 'Managing public order at the Australian Motorcycle Grand Prix', *ASSH Studies in Sports History*, 7: 49–79.

Vulliamy, E. (1985) 'Live by aggro, die by aggro', *New Statesman*, 7 June, pp. 8–10.

Wade, D. (1978) 'Are golf's galleries getting out of hand?', *Golf Digest*, November, pp. 60–1.

Wagg, S. (1984) *The Football World: a Contemporary Social History*. Brighton: Harvester.

Walvin, J. (1975) *The People's Game: the Social History of British Football*. Harmondsworth: Allen Lane.

Walvin, J. (1986) *Football and the Decline of Britain*. Basingstoke: Macmillan.

Watson, R.C. and MacLellan, J.C. (1986) 'Smitting to spitting: 80 years of ice hockey in Canadian courts', *Canadian Journal of History of Sport*, 17: 10–27.

Weinstein, M.D., Smith, M.D. and Wiesenthal, D.L. (1995) 'Masculinity and hockey violence', *Sex Roles*, 33: 831–47.

Whannel, G. (1979) 'Football crowd behavior and the press', *Media, Culture and Society*, 1: 327–42.

Whannel, G. (1986) 'The unholy alliance: notes on television and the remaking of British sport', *Leisure Studies*, 5.

White, C. (1970) 'Analysis of hostile outbursts in spectator sports', *Dissertation Abstracts International*, 31: 6390A.

White, D. (1986) 'Sports violence as criminal assault: development of the doctrine by Canadian criminal courts', *Duke Law Journal*, 1030–4.

White, P. and Young, K. (1997) 'Masculinity, sport, and the injury process: a review of Canadian and international evidence', *Avante*, 3: 1–30.

White, P., Young, K. and Gillett, J. (1995) 'Bodywork as a moral imperative: some critical notes on health and fitness', *Loisir et Société*, 18: 159–82.

Williams, J. (1980) 'Football hooliganism: offences, arrests and violence – a critical note', *British Journal of Law and Society*, 7: 104–11.

Williams, J. (1985) 'In search of the hooligan solution', *Social Studies Review*, 1: 3–5.

Williams, J. (1989) '"C,mon, la! We'll get in!"', *New Statesman and Society*, 21 April, 14–15.

Williams, J. (1991) 'Having an away day: English football spectators and the hooligan debate', in J. Williams and S. Wagg (eds), *British Football and Social Change: Getting into Europe*. Leicester: Leicester University Press.

Williams, J. and Goldberg, A. (1989) *Spectator Behaviour, Media Coverage and Crowd Control at the 1988 European Football Championships: a Review of* data from Belgium, Denmark, the Federal Republic of Germany, Netherlands and the United Kingdom. Strasbourg: Council of Europe.

Williams, J., Dunning, E. and Murphy, P. (1984) *Hooligans Abroad: the Behaviour and Control of English Fans in Continental Europe.* London: Routledge & Kegan Paul.

Williams, J., Dunning, E. and Murphy, P. (1986) 'The rise of the English soccer hooligan', *Youth and Society,* 17: 362–80.

Williams, J., Dunning, E. and Murphy, P. (1988) *Hooliganism after Heysel: Crowd Behaviour in England and Europe, 1985–1988.* Leicester: University of Leicester Press.

Young, K.M. (1986) 'The killing field: themes in mass media responses to the Heysel stadium riot', *International Review for the Sociology of Sport,* 21: 253–64.

Young, K.M. (1988) 'Sports crowd disorder, mass media and ideology', PhD dissertation, McMaster University, Ontario.

Young, K.M. (1990) 'Treatment of sports violence by the Canadian mass media'. Report to Sport Canada's Applied Sport Research Program, Government of Canada, Ottawa.

Young, K.M. (1991a) 'Sport and collective violence', *Exercise and Sport Science Reviews,* 19: 539–87.

Young, K.M. (1991b) 'Writers, rimmers, and slotters: privileging violence in the construction of the sports page'. Paper presented at the North

American Society for the Sociology of Sport, Milwaukee, WI, 6–9 November.

Young, K.M. (1993) 'Violence, risk, and liability in male sports culture', *Sociology of Sport Journal,* 10: 373–96.

Young, K.M. (1997a) 'From sports violence to sports crime: aspects of violence, law, and gender in the sports process'. Paper presented at National Conference on Sport, Youth, Violence, and the Media, University of Southern California, Los Angeles, CA, 2–4 April.

Young, K.M. (1997b) 'Women, sport, and physicality: preliminary findings from a Canadian study', *International Review for the Sociology of Sport,* 32: 297–305.

Young, K.M. and Smith, M.D. (1988/1989) 'Mass media treatment of violence in sports and its effects', *Current Psychology: Research and Reviews,* 7: 298–312.

Young, K. and White, P. (1995) 'Sport, physical danger and injury: the experiences of elite women athletes', *Journal of Sport and Social Issues,* 19: 45–62.

Young, K.M. and Wamsley, K. (1996) 'State complicity in sports assault and the gender order in twentieth century Canada: preliminary observations', *Avante,* 2: 51–69.

Young, K.M., White, P. and McTeer, W. (1994) 'Body talk: male athletes reflect on sport, injury, and pain', *Sociology of Sport Journal,* 11: 175–95.

26

SPORT AND HEALTH: A SOCIOLOGICAL PERSPECTIVE

Ivan Waddington

There is a large and expanding literature on the relationships between physical activity and health. Almost all of this literature has been written from a physiological perspective and has typically been concerned with issues such as the relationship between physical activity and cardiovascular functioning, or the way in which exercise can help to control obesity. However, very little has been written about the relationship between exercise, sport and health from a *sociological* perspective. The central objective of this paper is to try to develop a distinctively sociological approach to understanding some of the key issues in the relationship between exercise, sport and health. More specifically, the objectives of this paper are threefold: to outline and critically to examine the widely accepted idea that sport and exercise have beneficial consequences for health; to examine the different patterns of *social relations* associated with sport and exercise; and to examine some of the *physiological* consequences of these social differences, in terms of the rather different impacts that sport and exercise can have on health.

SPORT, EXERCISE AND THE HEALTHY BODY ETHOS

There are probably few ideas which are as widely and uncritically accepted as that linking sport and exercise with good health. What is particularly striking about this ideology is its near universal acceptance across a range of societies, for, in developing and developed societies, in capitalist and communist societies and in democratic and totalitarian societies, there is a broad consensus that 'sport is good for you'.

The ideology linking sport and health has a long history. In nineteenth-century Britain, the birthplace of many modern sports, an ideology of athleticism that linked sport with health, both physical and 'moral', was developed in the Victorian public schools (Mangan, 1981), while the promotion and maintenance of the health of schoolchildren has long been an area of concern to physical educators. Colquhoun and Kirk (1987: 100), for example, note that when physical education was introduced as a subject in the elementary school curriculum in the early twentieth century, it 'had the express purpose of improving the medical, physical and hygiene provision for children in schools'. Throughout the inter-war period, *The Health of the School Child*, the annual report of the Chief Medical Officer of the Board of Education, regularly made reference to the importance of physical education for the health of schoolchildren, and the idea that sport and exercise are associated with health is widely known and accepted by British schoolchildren today; a study for the Sports Council (1995: 128) noted that 'the health and fitness message seems to be well known by children. Virtually all of them, 92 per cent agreed that it was important to keep fit … In addition, most children, 82 per cent, agreed that they felt fit and healthy when they did sport and exercise.' Not surprisingly, the idea that sport is health-promoting and even life-enhancing is one which is frequently stressed by those involved in sport;

to quote the former Olympic gold medalist Sebastian Coe: 'Sport is an integral part of a healthy lifestyle in today's society' (foreword to Mottram, 1988).

Such views have been endorsed in a variety of official and semi-official health publications. In 1988, *The Nation's Health*, a report from an independent team (Smith and Jacobson, 1988), noted that regular and moderate exercise has a number of health benefits while *The Allied Dunbar National Fitness Survey* (Sports Council and Health Education Authority, 1992) and the Department of Health in its *Health of the Nation* (1993) similarly noted a number of health benefits associated with regular physical activity.

Such statements are not confined to Britain. In 1993 an authoritative report from the American College of Sports Medicine and the Center for Disease Control recommended that adults should take 30 minutes of moderate activity on most days of the week (Wimbush, 1994). Nor are such views limited to capitalist societies, or to countries in the developed world. Riordan, for example, has pointed out that governments in developing societies frequently place considerable stress on the development of sport, not only for the consequences which sport can have for nation-building and national integration but also for the effects it can have on hygiene and health; indeed, Riordan (1986: 291) argues that 'of all the functions of state-run sport in modernising societies, that to promote and maintain health must take first place', and he goes on to point out that 'in many such states sport comes under the aegis of the health ministry'. Elsewhere, Riordan (1981: 18) has pointed out that, following the Bolshevik Revolution in October 1917, the new Soviet government saw regular participation in physical exercise as 'one – relatively inexpensive but effective – means of improving health standards rapidly and a channel by which to educate people in hygiene, nutrition and exercise'. Similarly, following the victory of the communists in China in 1949, emphasis was placed 'on the need to promote national sports, expand public health and medical work, and safe-guard the health of mothers, infants and children'. This policy, which dates from 1950, was endorsed by Mao in June 1952 when he called upon the Chinese people to 'promote physical culture and sport, and build up the people's health' (Clumpner and Pendleton, 1981: 111).

However, it might be noted that although the ideology linking sport and health is very widespread, the view that sport is good for health has only relatively recently come to be applied to women as well as men for, during much of the nineteenth century, women were actively discouraged from taking part in vigorous exercise, which was often seen as *damaging* to their health. Patricia Vertinsky (1990: 39), in describing the situation in late nineteenth-century Britain, writes:

> The widespread notion that women were chronically weak and had only finite mental and physical energy because of menstruation had a strong effect upon the medical profession's and consequently the public's attitude towards female exercise and sport.

She argues that:

> Not infrequently, medically defined notions of optimal female health … have justified the practice of viewing female physiological functions as requiring prescribed and/or delimited levels of physical activity and restricted sporting opportunities. (Vertinsky, 1990: 39, 1)

Sheila Fletcher (1987: 145) has similarly noted that women's growing participation in cycling, swimming, golf and hockey in the late nineteenth century was met with resistance from eugenists such as Dr Arabella Kenealy who, in 1899, argued that women were in danger of neutering themselves by over-indulgence in athletics. The resistance to women's full participation in sport has similarly been documented for nineteenth-century New Zealand (Crawford, 1987), Canada (Lenskyj, 1987) and America (Vertinsky, 1987).

THE IDEOLOGY OF HEALTHISM AND VICTIM BLAMING

It is perhaps not surprising that those involved in what is sometimes called the 'fitness industry' have generally supported the idea that sport and exercise are health-promoting, though it might be noted that such people have frequently conflated the concepts of fitness, health and beauty as a means of more effectively marketing their services. Perhaps of rather greater importance, however, since they directly affect every schoolchild in many countries in the developed world, have been recent developments in school physical education which have promoted the role of regular physical activity in achieving and maintaining health. In this context, Colquhoun (1991: 5) has written of an 'explosion' of interest from the physical education profession in teaching health-related issues, an explosion which, he suggests, is indicated by the burgeoning number of professional articles and curriculum guides in several countries, especially Britain, Australia, Canada and the USA.

This is of course not a new role for physical education which, as we saw earlier, has had an association with health and medicine reaching back to the introduction of physical education in the primary school curriculum in Britain. However, Kirk and Colquhoun have suggested that:

> the recent re-emergence of health matters to occupy a place of central importance in school physical education marks a new moment in both the production of physical educators' views of their professional mission and in the production of a new health consciousness in society at large. (1989: 417)

Colquhoun and Kirk (1987) have identified several processes which, they suggest, have influenced this re-orientation of physical education towards health-related issues, including a growing societal interest in health matters, the prevalence of heart disease and the spiralling costs of medical care; to these might be added the fact that many physical education teachers, perhaps conscious of the relatively low status of their subject *vis-à-vis* what are often considered more 'academic' subjects, have been more than happy to draw upon the prestige associated with medicine and science to provide what they hope will be a more secure and 'intellectual' basis for their subject.

However, Colquhoun (1991) has suggested that this emerging ideology of health-based physical education (HBPE) is not unproblematic, for it presents a very partial and distorted view of the causes of health and illness. Drawing upon Crawford's (1980) concept of 'healthism', Colquhoun argues that health-based physical education is premised upon and helps to disseminate the idea that our health is largely under our own control. More specifically, he argues that:

> by focusing on individual lifestyle as the major determinant of an individual's health, health based physical education (HBPE) conforms to the practices of conventional health education and has therefore been severely restricted in its potential for emancipation, social justice, equality and social change. Indeed, the political issues which accompany HBPE have not yet been fully exposed. (Colquhoun, 1991: 6)

The ideology of healthism, it is argued, serves to focus attention on individual responsibility for our own health and, simultaneously, to divert attention away from wider social processes – for example, poverty, unemployment, industrial pollution, or the poor quality or lack of accessibility of health services – which may be associated with high levels of illness; by thus shifting responsibility for health away from manufacturers, governments and other powerful groups, the ideology of healthism diverts attention away from the key issues in the politics of health. As Crawford (1980: 368) has noted, it perpetuates the misleading – or, at best, greatly oversimplified – idea that we can, *as individuals*, control our own existence. Moreover, our assumed ability individually to control our lives gradually becomes transformed into a moral imperative to do so, for, suggests Crawford (1984), we live in an era of a new health consciousness where to be unhealthy has come to signify individual moral laxity. Thus slimness signifies not only good health but also self-discipline and moral responsibility whereas fatness, in contrast, signifies idleness, emotional weakness and moral turpitude. In this sense our bodies, whether slim or obese, signify not merely our health status for they also become, quite literally, the embodiment of moral propriety or laxity. Within this context, those who fall ill are increasingly likely to be seen not as unfortunate and innocent victims of processes beyond their control but, rather, as people who, through their moral laxity and lack of self-discipline, have 'brought it on themselves'. The Victorian differentiation between the 'deserving' and the 'undeserving' poor is, in some respects, in the process of being replicated in the differentiation between the 'deserving' and 'undeserving' sick.

SPORT AND HEALTH: COMMERCIAL LINKS

One area that casts doubt on the assumed close relationship between sport and the promotion of healthy lifestyles is that of sports sponsorship and, in particular, the widespread sponsorship of sport by the manufacturers of two of the most widely used drugs in the Western world: alcohol and tobacco. In relation to the former, concern has been expressed about sponsorship of sport by breweries. Dealy (1990), for example, has drawn attention to the health problems associated with alcohol abuse and with the widespread practice of under-age drinking in the United States and has expressed concern at the close relationship between the NCAA and the breweries. It is, however, the relationship between sport and the tobacco industry which has been the cause of greatest concern. Taylor (1985) has pointed out that since the 1970s, business sponsorship of sport has grown rapidly in Britain with the tobacco companies being by far the biggest spenders. Sports sponsorship is, he notes, a relatively cheap and highly cost-effective means of advertising for the tobacco companies, not least because in Britain it enables them to circumvent the 1965 ban on the advertising of cigarettes on television, for cigarette manufacturers have continued to reach large television audiences *via* the televised coverage of such popular sporting events as the Embassy Snooker World Championships, Benson and Hedges Cricket and the Silk Cut Rugby League Challenge Cup. Sponsorship of sporting events by tobacco companies is now very widespread; sports that have been sponsored by tobacco companies in Britain include motor racing, power boat racing, cricket, speedway, snooker, darts, bowls, horse racing, tennis, rugby union, rugby league, basketball, badminton, show jumping, motor cycling and table tennis.

Sponsorship of sporting events by tobacco companies is, of course, not confined to Britain. In 1982 Dr Thomas Dadour introduced into the Western Australian parliament a Bill to ban all forms of cigarette advertising and promotion. Had the Bill been passed, one of the first casualties would have been the advertising at the Australia vs England Test Match, which was sponsored by Benson and Hedges who had been the Australian Cricket Board's main sponsor for more than ten years. The Bill was narrowly defeated. The following year, the state government of Western Australia introduced another Bill similar to Dr Dadour's. This Bill was also defeated following intensive lobbying by, amongst others, those associated with the cigarette-sponsored sports under threat (Taylor, 1985: 48–9). In a more recent and perhaps even more revealing incident in 1995, the highly successful Swedish yacht *Nicorette*, which is sponsored by a company that manufactures products designed to help people give up smoking, was banned from the Cape to Rio Race, which is sponsored by the tobacco giant Rothmans. The captain of the *Nicorette* protested against the decision (which was reversed some two weeks later) by saying that 'Rothmans is scared of [the] boat and the healthy lifestyle it seeks to promote.' Given the close relationship which is often claimed between sport and healthy lifestyles, many people may find it more than a little incongruous that the organizers of a sporting event should not only accept sponsorship from a cigarette manufacturer but that they should also ban an entry sponsored by a

manufacturer of products which are explicitly designed to help people give up smoking (*The Times*, 14 September 1995; *Guardian*, 27 September 1995).

The widespread sponsorship of sporting events by tobacco companies would not, at least in the context of the present argument, be of any significance were it not for the fact that, by the early 1980s, cigarette smoking was estimated to be responsible for more than 300,000 premature deaths a year in the United States, and nearly half a million deaths a year in Europe. In a 1982 report, the US Surgeon-General described cigarette smoking as 'the chief, single, avoidable cause of death in our society, and the most important public health issue of our time', whilst in Britain the Royal College of Physicians, in their report *Smoking and Health Now*, referred to the annual death rate caused by cigarette smoking as 'the present holocaust' (Taylor, 1985: xiv, xvii). Without labouring the point, one might reasonably suggest that the ideology which associates sports with healthy lifestyles sits uneasily with the widespread acceptance of sports sponsorship by breweries and, even more so, by tobacco companies.

EXERCISE AND HEALTH

There is now a substantial body of data from both epidemiological and clinical studies which indicates that moderate, rhythmic and regular exercise has a significant and beneficial impact on health. In Britain, the Coronary Prevention Group (1987) has listed the following range of beneficial effects on health:

- Improved cardiovascular function, which is associated with reduced cardiac morbidity and mortality.
- Increased metabolic rate with advantages from a nutritional viewpoint.
- Better control of obesity.
- An increase in the HDL/LDL ratio (HDL – high-density lipoprotein – is the 'good' type of cholesterol; LDL – low-density lipoprotein – is the 'bad' type of cholesterol).
- Decreased blood pressure.
- Delayed onset of post-menopausal osteoporosis.
- Improved glucose tolerance in diabetes.
- Antidepressant, and possible anti-anxiety effects, which may be associated with an increase in the brain of levels of endorphins – substances whose effects are broadly those of an intrinsic heroin-like substance.

The Royal College of Physicians of London (1991: 28) has echoed these views, arguing that:

> There is substantial evidence that regular aerobic exercise such as walking, jogging, dancing or swimming is beneficial to general physical and psychological health. Regular exercise appears to be particularly effective in prevention of coronary disease and osteoporosis and of some value in the management of obesity and diabetes.

Studies in North America point to similar conclusions, and suggest that regular exercise is associated with reduced mortality from all causes, from cardiovascular disease and from cancer of combined sites (Paffenbarger et al., 1986; Blair et al., 1989) while a review of four population surveys (two carried out in Canada and two in the United States), suggests a positive association between physical activity and lower levels of anxiety and depression (Stephens, 1988).

It should be noted that some of these health benefits are very substantial. The British Medical Association (BMA), for example, has noted that insurance statistics indicate that men with only moderately high blood pressure can expect to live about 15 years less than men with low blood pressure, and it noted that regular exercise 'is potentially a major non-pharmacological method of lowering blood pressure' (BMA, 1992: 18). Similarly, one of the studies in the United States (Paffenbarger et al., 1986) indicates that death rates among men whose work or leisure involves regular exercise are between one-third and one-half lower than those among men whose lives are more sedentary. There are, moreover, three items of good news for those who would seek to improve their health via regular exercise. First, the evidence indicates that the protective effect of exercise persists at all ages, and after other risk factors such as smoking and weight are taken into account; secondly, these benefits can be produced relatively quickly – in just a three-month period – in both men and women of all ages, though it should be noted that they are maintained only while the activity is maintained; and thirdly, the beneficial effects are more striking in those who are least active (that is, elderly people or those with chronic disease) (Smith and Jacobson, 1988: 126–8).

At first glance, studies like those cited above might seem to indicate that the health-based arguments in favour of sport are overwhelming. There are, however, important provisos to be borne in mind when considering studies on the relationship between exercise and health. The first of these is that these studies do not suggest that *all* exercise is beneficial; rather, they indicate that exercise *of a particular kind, amount and intensity* has a beneficial impact on health. *The Nation's Health* (Smith and Jacobson, 1988: 126) for example, refers quite specifically to the beneficial effects of what it calls 'moderate, rhythmic and regular exercise', which it goes on to define as exercise such as that involved in brisk walking, running or swimming for 20–30 minutes about three times each week. The British Medical Association (1992: 14) similarly suggested that the 'recommended amount of exercise from a health perspective is about twenty to thirty minutes of moderate exercise three times a week'. It noted that the exercise that is most frequently suggested is brisk walking, and added that the level of activity which produces significant health benefits 'is related to the initial level of fitness: for the middle-aged sedentary individual, this may correspond to walking, cycling slowly or gentle swimming' (1992: 14). The precise activity which is considered to constitute 'adequate' exercise varies from one study to another, but activities mentioned in this context include 'energetic getting about' and manual work around the house and garden (Morris et al., 1980), dancing (BMA, 1992) and regular climbing of stairs (Paffenbarger et al., 1986). It is important to emphasize therefore, that what these studies have documented is a beneficial effect on health of 'moderate', or even gentle, forms of exercise; as Morris et al. noted, the activities which were defined in their study as constituting adequate exercise were 'by no means extreme', and they added, of the 17,944 men who took part in their study, that 'our men are no athletes' (1980: 1210). The British Medical Association similarly noted that several studies, and 'particularly those from North America, have suggested that only rather low levels of activity are necessary to confer some degree of protection against heart disease both in terms of the intensity of effort and of the total amount of exercise taken' (BMA, 1992: 19).

This is an important point to note for, quite clearly, one cannot assume that the health benefits associated with moderate exercise will simply be duplicated – still less can one assume that they will be increased – by exercise which is more frequent, of longer duration and of greater intensity, for exercise of this kind, as we shall see later, may generate substantial health 'costs' in terms of additional stresses or injuries, for example those associated with 'overuse'. In short, to suggest that a 30-minute gentle swim three times a week is good for one's health does not mean that running

70 miles a week as a means of preparing for running marathons is good for one's health in an equally simple or unproblematic way. Indeed, it might be noted that one of the American studies, which found that death rates generally went down as levels of physical activity increased, also found a reversed trend at the highest levels of physical activity. The authors note that this result may have been associated with methodological difficulties in the study, though they also recognize that it may reflect 'actual increased hazards associated with vigorous activities' (Paffenbarger et al., 1986: 606). It might also be noted that one study in New Zealand (Sullivan et al., 1994) – significantly it was a study of competitive athletes, many of whom were ranked in the top 10 per cent nationally in their age group and might therefore be expected to have engaged in relatively intensive training – found a strong positive association between exercise and a large number of symptoms, including anxiety related to competition, stitches, lightheadedness, muscle cramps, wheezing, chest pressure, 'spots in front of the eyes', retching and incontinence of urine and stool, while it was negatively associated with only a few symptoms, including headaches, abdominal bloating, sneezing and depression.

The second proviso concerning the studies cited above is that most relate primarily to exercise or activity levels rather than specifically to sport. Although sport and exercise are overlapping categories, there are nevertheless important differences between them, and these differences have important implications for their health consequences. It is to these issues that we now turn.

EXERCISE AND SPORT

Most sociological definitions of sport include the element of physical exertion as an essential component (Edwards, 1973; Guttmann, 1978; MacPherson et al., 1989). However, if all sport necessarily involves physical exercise, it is not the case that all physical exercise involves sport, for what is usually considered a further necessary component of sport – the competitive element – is frequently more or less absent from many forms of physical exercise. Moreover, since sport is inherently competitive, it must involve more than one person, for while one can exercise alone, one cannot play sport alone, since one needs an opponent. This relatively obvious difference between sport and exercise has important

implications for their potentially very different health consequences.

As we have seen, most of the studies cited earlier were concerned with the health consequences of 'moderate, rhythmic and regular' exercise. One important difference between sport and exercise is that non-competitive exercise involves a rather different pattern of social relations than does sport and, associated with this, the former is much more likely than is the latter to involve physical movements of a rhythmic nature and, of critical importance, the intensity of the exercise is likely to be, to a much higher degree than in the case of sport, under the control of the individual participant. Consider, for example, the situation of a person who regularly takes a brisk walk, or goes jogging or swimming, as a means of 'keeping fit', or perhaps as a means of weight control. When such activities are undertaken alone, as they frequently are, the precise nature of the physical movement – that is the action of walking, jogging or swimming – as well as both the duration and the intensity of the exercise, are to a high degree under the control of the individual involved in the exercise. Thus, for example, a person jogging or swimming alone can determine for how long to continue the exercise, and at what pace. Where exercise of this kind is undertaken in a small group of perhaps two or three friends, as is also common, the duration and intensity of the exercise are likely to involve a level of activity agreed upon by all participants and with which all participants are reasonably comfortable. It is important to note that this is not the situation in the case of sport.

As we noted earlier, sport cannot be played alone for it must involve two or more opposing players. This, together with the fact that sport involves not only cooperation but also, and in a highly institutionalized form, competition, means that sport, and particularly team sport, is usually a considerably more complex social activity than is non-competitive exercise. Consider, for example, a game of soccer or rugby or American football. The game involves a complex interweaving of the actions of a substantial number of players, together with the relationships between players and match officials, club coaches and many others including, at the elite level, large numbers of fans. Even if we considerably oversimplify the situation by confining our analysis simply to the interactions between the players, it is clear that we are dealing here with a social phenomenon of some complexity. Elias and Dunning (1986: 193) drew upon the example of Association football (soccer) to illustrate what they called the 'dynamics of sport groups'. They wrote:

From the starting position evolves a fluid figuration formed by both teams. Within it, all individuals are, and remain throughout, more or less interdependent; they move and regroup themselves in response to each other. This may help to explain why we refer to this type of game as a specific form of group dynamics. For this moving and regrouping of interdependent players in response to each other *is* the game.

It may not be immediately clear that by using the term 'group dynamics' in this context we do not refer to the changing figurations of the two groups of players as if they could be considered in separation, as if each had dynamics of its own. That is not the case. In a game of football, the figuration of players on the one side and that of players on the other side, are interdependent and inseparable. They form in fact a single figuration. If one speaks of a sport-game as a specific form of group dynamics, one refers to the overall change in the figuration of the players of both sides together.

One aspect of the complex structure of sports such as football is that each match tends to develop what is often called a 'game pattern'. Though there is sometimes a tendency to speak of this game pattern as though it were something separate from the players, it is important to remind ourselves that it is in fact nothing other than the complex interweaving of the actions of a large number of players. However, it is also important to note that, as the game pattern becomes more complex – for example as we move from a two-person game such as tennis to a multi-person game such as soccer – it becomes increasingly beyond the ability of any single player to control this game pattern and, indeed, from the perspective of any single player, this game pattern may appear to have a life of its own.

An associated aspect of the complex structure of many sports is that, in comparison with non-competitive exercise, any individual player is much less able to control his/her own movements and the pace and intensity at which he or she is required to play. Thus while the lone jogger and walker can determine their own movements with minimal reference to others, the movements of, for example, a soccer or rugby or ice-hockey player can only be understood in relation to the movements of other players on their own and the opposition side. Moreover, as a means of beating opposing players, players frequently initiate moves, or respond to the moves of others, involving rapid changes of pace and direction. In most sports, this gives rise to a pattern of movement which is the very opposite of rhythmic, for it

often involves sharp and intensive bursts of anaerobic activity, interspersed with short periods in which individual players may be able to take a 'breather'. It is important to emphasize, first, that the frequency and intensity of these bursts of anaerobic activity are, at least in complex games, largely beyond the ability of any single player to control; secondly, that players are almost inevitably constrained by the moves of their opponents to engage in activities which are anything but rhythmic; and thirdly, that many of these movements, such as those involved in rapid acceleration and deceleration, or the twisting or turning movements involved in rapid changes of direction, impose considerably greater stresses on the body than do the much more rhythmic movements involved in non-competitive walking, jogging or swimming. These considerations, however, do not exhaust the health-related differences between sport and exercise. The competitive character of sport, in particular, requires further elaboration.

SPORT AND COMPETITION

Dunning (1986a) has pointed out that the growing competitiveness of modern sport is a long-term trend which may be traced back over two or more centuries. This process has, however, been particularly marked in the post-1945 period, and has been associated with, amongst other processes, the increasing politicization and commercialization of sport, both of which have had the effect of greatly increasing the importance of, and the rewards associated with, winning while downgrading the traditional value associated with taking part (Waddington and Murphy, 1992). This trend towards the growing competitiveness of sport has not, however, been without health 'costs' for athletes, most particularly in the form of more stress injuries and overuse injuries, and increased constraints to continue competing while injured.

A common sight in many sports is that of the trainer or physiotherapist running on to the field of play to treat an injured player, often by the application of an aerosol spray to a painful area, thereby enabling the player to continue. However, as Donohoe and Johnson (1986: 94) have pointed out, one of the functions of pain is to '"warn" us that we need to rest the damaged area', and they suggest that most athletes and coaches 'fail to recognize the damage that can be caused by suppressing pain'. This issue is part of the more general concern about overuse and recurrent injuries, a growing problem which is clearly associated with the increasing constraints on sportsmen and women to compete and more particularly to win with, one suspects, often scant concern for the potential longer-term health risks. Donohoe and Johnson (1986: 93) have noted that 'To succeed in modern sport, athletes are forced to train longer, harder, and earlier in life. They may be rewarded by faster times, better performances and increased fitness, but there is a price to pay for such intense training'. Part of the price of such intense training and of the readiness – often encouraged by coaches and medical advisers – to continue training and competing despite injury, is unquestionably paid in the form of overuse and recurrent injuries, which now constitute a serious problem in sport, and not just at the adult elite level. As Donohoe and Johnson (1986: 93) have noted, the 'long-term effects of overuse injuries are not known, but some concerned doctors have asked whether today's gold medallists could be crippled by arthritis by the age of 30' and they cite world-class competitors who have, in their words, 'been plagued by a succession of overuse injuries'.

Examples of athletes who have continued to compete with painful and potentially serious injuries are almost innumerable. In her autobiography, Olga Korbut, the former Olympic gold-medal-winning gymnast, described how, following the 1972 Munich Olympics, the successful Soviet gymnastics team was taken on a tour of what was then West Germany. She wrote:

During that tour of Germany, the lumbago in my back began to hurt more and more. The novocaine injections took away the pain for a while, but I needed time to rest and heal. By the end of the tour, I walked as though I had a stake in my spine …

She added that 'My strongest memories of that entire period are fatigue, pain, and the empty feeling of being a fly whose blood has been sucked out by a predatory spider' (Korbut, 1992: 81–2).

It would be very wrong to imagine that such incidents only occurred under the now defunct communist systems of Eastern Europe, for examples of athletes playing on despite painful and potentially serious injuries are commonplace and there is considerable evidence to suggest that, particularly at the elite level, there are considerable constraints on players to play through pain and injury 'for the good of the team'. Consider, for example, the following extract from a pre-match team talk to the

Wigan Rugby League team by their coach, John Monie:

There's just one more thing I want to enforce. It doesn't matter what's wrong with you when you're injured, I want you on your feet and in the defensive line … I don't care if the physio's out there and he wants to examine you and all that stuff. That's not important. What's important is … you've got twelve team-mates tackling their guts out, defending like anything inside the 22 and we've got the physio telling a guy to see if he can straighten his knee out.

I don't care what's wrong with you … if the opposition's got the ball, I want you on your feet and in the defensive line …

There are no exceptions to that rule. So from now on, the only reason you stay down hurt and get attention from the sideline is because there's a break in play or you're unconscious – no other reasons will be accepted. (Hanson, 1991: 77)

Monie's team talk may perhaps be regarded as the English equivalent of the American view that 'you play unless the bone sticks through the meat' which, as Young (1993: 382) has noted, has long been used to rationalize injury in the NFL. Although it may not always be expressed in such blunt terms, it is clear that, particularly at the elite level, there is a common expectation – which is shared by many players – that whenever possible, players should continue to play through injury 'for the good of the team', even if this means playing with painkilling injections. Hanson reported, for example, that Wigan Rugby League players frequently played after having been given painkilling injections; before the Rugby League Cup Final at Wembley in 1990, so many players had painkilling injections that the club doctor, Dr Zaman, came into the dressing room 'clutching a collection of used syringes and needles' and asked of a Wembley official, 'Do you have a box for sharps?' (Hanson, 1991: 193). Don Strock, former quarterback with the Miami Dolphins, has described how players would group around 'injured teammates during a game to screen from spectators the use of painkilling injections, then hide the needles under the carpet-like synthetic "turf"'(cited in Young, 1993: 376). The Russian international soccer player Andrei Kanchelskis, who until recently was playing in England, was reported to have played in an international match for Russia after having no fewer than eight painkilling injections for a stomach strain (*Guardian*, 3 April 1995), while the former England soccer captain Gary Lineker, who retired after a long struggle with a chronic foot injury, indicated that he had been concerned about continually using painkilling drugs. He was reported as saying of his retirement: 'It is as if a huge weight has been lifted from me. I no longer have to worry whether I'll be fit enough to get through a match and I will no longer have to suffer the dizzy spells and stomach complaints that come with a dependency on anti-inflammatory drugs' (*Daily Mirror*, 21 November 1994).

It is clear that experiences of this kind are commonplace among elite players; in England a survey of 725 professional soccer players carried out by the magazine *Four Four Two* (October 1995) revealed that 70 per cent of players had been asked to play when not fully fit. As Young et al. (1994: 190) have noted:

> Overt and covert pressures are brought to bear on injured athletes to coerce them to return to action. These may include certain 'degradation cere-monies' ... such as segregated meal areas, constant questioning from coaches, being ostracized at team functions, or other special treatment that clearly identifies the injured athlete as separate.

An example of this kind of ostracism con-cerns the former Liverpool Football Club man-ager, Bill Shankly, regarded by many as one of the greatest-ever soccer club managers; Shankly refused to speak to any player who was unavailable to play because of injury (*On the Line*, BBC Radio Five Live, 12 March 1996). Young et al. (1994: 190) have argued that:

> Pressure placed on the player to return to action before full recovery is in one sense intended to enhance the team's ability to win, but in the process, the long-term health of the athlete is often given little consideration.

Although such pressures on players to toler-ate and to play through pain may in some respects be associated with particular concep-tions of masculinity – to be examined later – it is also clear that there are broadly similar con-straints on women athletes to continue com-peting despite pain and injury and that many women athletes respond in a broadly similar way to their male counterparts. For example, in comparing their research in Canada on female athletes' experience of pain and injury with their earlier research on the experience of male athletes, Young and White (1995: 51) write that 'If there is a difference between the way male and female athletes in our projects appear to understand pain and injury, it is only a matter of degree ... it is clear that both men and women adopt similar techniques to help to displace the centrality of pain in their sports lives'. An example of the way in which pain is

denied is provided by the example of 'D', one of the elite women athletes interviewed by Young and White (1995: 51):

> The first time my injury occurred, I ignored it assuming it would go away, as did my previous aches and pains. Bruising, swelling, and muscle pain are integral aspects of basketball. Once the pain persisted, it became annoying. It never occurred to me at the age of 14 that my body was breaking down and needed a rest. I simply pushed harder because my injury was causing me to fall behind in my progress.

Young and White (1995: 52) add that:

> Years of denial and persistence have seriously weakened D's knees and ankles, and surgery to repair cartilage tears has left her legs badly scarred. At the time of writing, D remains in pain, is unable to play her sport, and uses painkillers almost daily.

D's reference to injuries during her teenage years suggests that the problem of overuse and recurrent injuries is not confined to adults. In relation to children's sport, Donnelly (1993: 96) has noted that:

> As children encounter opportunities for increas-ingly lucrative careers as professional athletes, parents are tempted to encourage their children to become heavily involved in professional sports at early ages. As evidenced by increasing demands for international success in sport as a justification for government and corporate spending on elite participation, and by a variety of attempts to establish schemes for the early identification of athletic talent, there is an obvious trend toward earlier and more intensive athletic involvement for younger and younger children.

Donnelly notes that injuries characteristic of overtraining among young athletes have been widely reported in the literature (for example, Rowley, 1986), and that such injuries were also reported by a majority of the 45 recently retired high-level athletes who were interviewed in Donnelly's study and who spoke about their own experiences as young athletes.

Given the highly competitive characteristic of much modern sport, it should come as no surprise to learn that overuse and recurrent injuries are very common. Thus Lynch and Carcasona (1994) have noted that a study of 123 male players in a Danish soccer club found that 37 per cent of all injuries were overuse injuries, while a Swedish study of 180 senior male soc-cer players found that 31 per cent of injuries were due to overuse. FIFA's report on soccer's 1994 World Cup, held in the United States, indicated that 12 per cent of all treatments of players were for chronic injuries or ailments which predated the World Cup Finals (Nepfer, 1994: 190). It would, however, be quite wrong to think that such injuries only occur at the elite level, for there is little doubt that in most Western countries sport at *all* levels has become increasingly competitive and this has given rise to large numbers of recurrent injuries at the non-elite, as well as the elite level. A large-scale survey carried out in England and Wales for the Sports Council found that one-third of all injuries resulting from participation in sport or exercise were recurrent injuries. On the basis of this study, the Sports Council estimated that in England and Wales there are 10.4 million incidents a year resulting in recurrent injuries (Sports Council, 1991: 25). Quite clearly, we are not dealing with a phenomenon that is confined to elite sport, but one that is extremely widespread.

SPORT, VIOLENCE AND AGGRESSIVE MASCULINITY

Many sports, unlike most forms of non-sporting exercise, involve physical contact and are, in effect, mock battles. This is perhaps most evident in the case of combat sports, in some of which – for example, boxing – a central object is to inflict physical damage on one's opponent. Clearly, however, the use of violence is not confined to combat sports, for though the level of physical violence permitted in sport has, in general, shown a long-term decline as sports have become more 'civilized' (Dunning, 1990; Dunning and Sheard, 1979), the use of physical violence to a greater or lesser degree remains a central characteristic of modern sport. In this regard, Dunning (1986b: 270) has noted that:

> All sports are inherently competitive and hence conducive to the arousal of aggression. Under specific conditions, such aggression can spill over into forms of open violence that are contrary to the rules. In some sports, however – rugby, soccer, hockey and boxing are examples – violence in the form of a 'play-fight' or 'mock battle' between two individuals or groups is a central and legitimate ingredient.

Many sports have, in present-day societies, become enclaves for the expression of physical violence, not in the form of unlicensed or uncontrolled violence, but in the form of socially sanctioned violence as expressed in violently aggressive 'body contact'; indeed, in the relatively highly pacified societies of the modern West, sport is probably the main – for many people the only – activity in which they are regularly involved in aggressive physical contact with others.

The link between sport, aggression and violence provides an important key to understanding why sport is a major context for the inculcation and expression of gender differences and identities, for sport constitutes perhaps the most widely available arena for the legitimate expression of masculine aggression and for the display of traditional and dominant notions of masculinity involving physical strength and courage. Thus, Young et al. (1994: 176), drawing upon their interview data with Canadian adult male athletes, have noted that the use of force and violence and the tolerance of risks, pain and injury are valued by many male athletes as masculinizing, while the sporting performances of women, gay men and men pursuing alternative versions of manliness are, by contrast, trivialized. In similar fashion, Sheard and Dunning (1973), in their essay on the rugby club as a type of 'male preserve', have noted that many of the songs traditionally sung in rugby clubs stress and reinforce masculinity by mocking not only women, but also gay men.

Young et al. (1994) have pointed out that these traditional and dominant concepts of masculinity involve, as a central proposition, the idea that 'real' men play sport in an intensely confrontational manner. In the more violent contact sports, this may mean that bodies are used as weapons for, as Messner (1990: 203) has noted:

> In many of our most popular sports, the achievement of goals (scoring and winning) is predicated on the successful utilization of violence – that is, these are activities in which the human body is routinely turned into a weapon to be used against other bodies, resulting in pain, serious injury, and even death.

In such a context, players are expected to give and to take hard knocks, to injure and to be injured and, when injured, to 'take it like a man'. A prime example is provided by American football which, though considerably less violent than it was in the late nineteenth century, remains, by comparison with most sports, relatively violent; it is significant that proponents of American football list among what they see as the positive features of the game its bellicosity and its similarities to actual warfare and the pain and self-sacrifice which it requires, whilst injury becomes what Guttmann (1978: 121) has called 'a certificate of virility, a badge of courage'. For many players and fans alike, relatively violent sports such as American football and rugby are, precisely because of their violent character, arenas *par excellence* for young men to demonstrate their masculinity. Not surprisingly, injury rates associated with such sports are considerably higher than those associated with most other sports and very much in excess of those associated with non-competitive exercise. In relation to American football, for example, Guttmann (1988: 161–2) has pointed out that:

> The percentage of players incurring injuries severe enough to cause them to miss at least one game a season is over 100 percent; this means not that every NFL player is injured at least once each season, but that those who are not injured are more than offset by those who are injured several times. The average length of a playing career has dropped to 3.2 years, which is not long enough to qualify a player for inclusion in the league's pension plan.

Studies from England (Sports Council, 1991) and New Zealand (Hume and Marshall, 1994) similarly indicate that injury rates in rugby are substantially above those in any other sport.

THE EPIDEMIOLOGY OF SPORTS INJURIES

Sports injuries are extremely common and, quite clearly, the risk of injury has to be taken into account in any attempt to assess the health 'costs' and 'benefits' of sport and exercise. In this context, a large-scale study carried out for the Sports Council in England and Wales (1991) provides a great deal of relevant information and is worth examining in some detail.

A postal questionnaire, which asked about participation in sports and exercise and injury experiences in the previous four weeks, was sent to a sample of 28,857 people, selected at random from the lists of family (primary care) physicians. The response rate was 68 per cent. Of the 17,564 usable responses, 7,829 respondents (45 per cent) had taken part in vigorous exercise or sport; 1,429 had been injured, and they reported a total of 1,803 injuries (1991: 2).

The number of injury incidents was weighted and multiplied to provide estimates of the annual incidence of sports injuries in England and Wales. On this basis, it was estimated that there were 19.3 million incidents resulting in new injuries and a further 10.4 million incidents resulting in recurrent injuries, making a total of no fewer than 29.7 million injuries a year. The direct treatment costs of

new and recurrent injuries were estimated at £422 million, with costs of lost production (due to days off work) estimated at £575 million, giving a total annual cost of sporting injuries of £997million (1991: 25, 31). In the light of these data, one can understand why one text on sports injuries (Vinger and Hoerner, 1982) is subtitled 'The Unthwarted Epidemic'.

As was noted earlier, injury risks vary markedly from one sport to another with, not surprisingly, the highest risks being associated with contact sports. The Sports Council study (1991: 33) found, for example, that rugby was by far the most dangerous sport, in terms of risk of injury, with an injury rate of 59.3 per 100 participants per four weeks. The second most dangerous sport was soccer (39.3) followed by martial arts (36.3), hockey (24.8) and cricket (20.2). A study in New Zealand (Hume and Marshall, 1994) similarly found that rugby union had the highest injury rate, while other high-risk sports included horse riding, soccer, cricket, netball, rugby league, basketball and snow skiing. That there is a close association between physical contact and injury risk is clear; Lynch and Carcasona (1994: 170-1) cite a study of youth outdoor and indoor soccer in the United States which found that 66 per cent of injuries in the outdoor league and 70 per cent of injuries in the indoor league resulted from physical contact.

Not surprisingly, the Sports Council study in England and Wales found that the activities with the lowest risks of injury were the non-contact and rhythmic (and largely non-competitive) activities involved in 'keep fit' (6.5 incidents per 100 participants per 4 weeks) and swimming and diving (2.9). However, even relatively rhythmic and non-contact activities may be associated with substantial injury risks; Heil (1993: 5) notes that it has been estimated that in the United States a third of the nation's 15 million joggers sustain a musculoskeletal injury each year and nearly a half of habitual runners experience lower extremity injury, while there are also one thousand spinal injuries each year as a result of swimmers diving into water.

Although the majority of sporting injuries are relatively minor, a substantial number are more serious. The Sports Council study (1991: 18–19) found that 25 per cent of new injuries and 31 per cent of recurrent injuries required treatment by a family doctor, hospital or other health professional, while 37 per cent of new injuries and 43 per cent of recurrent injuries involved some restriction on activities. This restriction was usually on the injured taking part in sports or exercise, though 7 per cent of all injuries resulted in the participants taking time off work; in all 11.5 million working days a year are lost in England and Wales as a result of sports injuries. A study in New Zealand (Hume and Marshall, 1994) found that 15 per cent of consultations at the Dunedin Hospital Emergency Department were for sports injuries, which also accounted for 9 per cent of all injury hospitalizations in New Zealand, and 17 per cent of all injuries compensated by the Accident Compensation Corporation. Both the risk of injury, and also the risk of serious injury, increase in more violent contact sports. Thus Young (1993: 377), writing of American football, has argued that:

> No workplace matches football for either the regularity or severity of injury … football injuries may include arthritis, concussion, fractures, and, most catastrophically, blindness, paralysis and even death … a review of heat stresses such as cramp, exhaustion and stroke related to amateur and professional football … reported 29 player deaths between 1968 and 1978 … the 1990 season represented the first in over 60 years without a player death.

CONCLUSION

What conclusions, then, can we draw about the relationships between exercise, sport and health? Three points would seem to emerge from the data reviewed in this chapter. The first is that no simple generalization can adequately encapsulate the complexity of these relationships. The second, related, point is that it is clearly necessary to differentiate between exercise and sport for they involve, as we have seen, rather different patterns of social relationships and, associated with this, they are likely to have rather different consequences for health. The third point is that we also need to differentiate between types and levels of sport, with the distinctions between contact and non-contact sport and between elite and mass sport being particularly important.

If we make these distinctions, it may be possible to reconcile what, at first sight, may appear to be radically incompatible findings. Thus, on the one hand, there does seem to be overwhelming evidence indicating that regular, rhythmic and moderate exercise has a significant and beneficial impact on health. On the other hand, Young (1993: 373) may also be correct in his claim, which appears to relate primarily to North America, that:

> By any measure, professional sport is a violent and hazardous workplace, replete with its own unique

forms of 'industrial disease'. No other single milieu, including the risky and labor-intensive settings of miners, oil drillers, or construction site workers, can compare with the routine injuries of team sports such as football, ice-hockey, soccer, rugby and the like.

In general, it is probably reasonable to suggest that in the case of rhythmic, non-competitive exercise where body movements are, to a relatively high degree, under the control of the individual participant, the health benefits substantially outweigh the health costs. However, as we move from non-competitive exercise to competitive sport, and as we move from non-contact to contact sport, so the health costs, in the form of injuries, begin to mount. Similarly, as we move from mass sport to elite sport, the constraints to train longer and more intensively and to continue competing through pain and injury also increase, with a concomitant increase in the health risks. The health-related arguments in favour of regular and moderate exercise may be overwhelming, but such arguments are rather less persuasive in relation to sport in general, and very much less persuasive in relation to elite, or professional, sport.

REFERENCES

Blair, S.N., Paffenbarger, R.S., Clark, D.G., Cooper, K.H. and Gibbons, L.W. (1989) 'Physical fitness and all-cause mortality', *Journal of the American Medical Association*, 262 (17): 2395–401.

British Medical Association (1992) *Cycling: Towards Safety and Health*. Oxford and New York: Oxford University Press.

Clumpner, R.A. and Pendleton, B.B. (1981) 'The People's Republic of China', in J. Riordan (ed.), *Sport Under Communism*. London: C. Hurst. pp. 103–40.

Colquhoun, D. (1991) 'Health based physical education, the ideology of healthism and victim blaming', *Physical Education Review*, 14 (1): 5–13.

Colquhoun, D. and Kirk, D. (1987) 'Investigating the problematic relationship between health and physical education: an Australian study', *Physical Education Review*, 10 (2): 100–9.

Coronary Prevention Group (1987) *Exercise, Heart, Health*. London: Coronary Prevention Group.

Crawford, R. (1980) 'Healthism and the medicalization of everyday life', *International Journal of Health Services*, 10 (3): 365–89.

Crawford, R. (1984) 'A cultural account of "health": control, release, and the social body', in J.B. McKinley (ed.), *Issues in the Political Economy of*

Health Care. New York and London: Tavistock, pp. 60–103.

Crawford, S.A.G.M. (1987) 'Pioneering women: recreational and sporting opportunities in a remote colonial setting', in J.A. Mangan and R.J. Park (eds), *From 'Fair Sex' to Feminism*. London: Frank Cass. pp. 161–81.

Dealy, F.X., Jr (1990) *Win at Any Cost: the Sell Out of College Athletics*. New York: Carol Publishing Group.

Department of Health (1993) *The Health of the Nation: a Strategy for Health in England*. London: HMSO.

Donnelly, P. (1993), 'Problems associated with youth involvement in high-performance sport', in B.R. Cahill and A.J. Pearl (eds), *Intensive Participation in Children's Sports*. Champaign, IL: Human Kinetics. pp. 95–126.

Donohoe, T. and Johnson, N. (1986) *Foul Play: Drug Abuse in Sports*. Oxford: Basil Blackwell.

Dunning, E. (1986a) 'The dynamics of modern sport: notes on achievement-striving and the social significance of sport', in N. Elias and E. Dunning, *Quest for Excitement*. Oxford: Basil Blackwell. pp. 205–23.

Dunning, E. (1986b). 'Sport as a male preserve: notes on the social sources of masculine identity and its transformation', in N. Elias and E. Dunning, *Quest for Excitement*. Oxford: Basil Blackwell. pp. 267–83.

Dunning, E. (1990) 'Sociological reflections on sport, violence and civilization', *International Review for the Sociology of Sport*, 25 (1): 65–82.

Dunning, E. and Sheard, K. (1979) *Barbarians, Gentlemen and Players*. Oxford: Martin Robertson.

Edwards, H. (1973) *Sociology of Sport*. Homewood, IL: Dorsey Press.

Elias, N. and Dunning, E. (1986) *Quest for Excitement*. Oxford: Basil Blackwell.

Fletcher, S. (1987) 'The making and breaking of a female tradition: women's physical education in England, 1880–1980', in J.A. Mangan and R.J. Park (eds), *From 'Fair Sex' to Feminism*. London: Frank Cass. pp. 145–57.

Guttmann, A. (1978) *From Ritual to Record*. New York: Columbia University Press.

Guttmann, A. (1988) *A Whole New Ball Game*. Chapel Hill and London: University of North Carolina Press.

Hanson, N. (1991) *Blood, Mud and Glory*. London: Pelham.

Heil, J. (1993) 'Sport psychology, the athlete at risk and the sports medicine team', in J. Heil, *Psychology of Sport Injury*. Champaign, IL: Human Kinetics.

Hume, P.A. and Marshall, S.W. (1994) 'Sports injuries in New Zealand: exploratory analyses', *New Zealand Journal of Sports Medicine*, 22: 18–22.

Kirk, D. and Colquhoun, D. (1989) 'Healthism and physical education', *British Journal of Sociology of Education*, 10 (4): 417–34.

Korbut, O. (1992) *My Story*. London: Century.

Lenskyj, H. (1987) 'Canadian women and physical activity, 1890–1930: media views', in J.A. Mangan and R.J. Park (eds), *From 'Fair Sex' to Feminism*. London: Frank Cass.

Lynch, J.M. and Carcasona, C.B. (1994), 'The team physician', in B. Ekblom (ed.), *Handbook of Sports Medicine and Science: Football (Soccer)*. Oxford: Blackwell Scientific. pp. 166–74.

Mangan, J.A. (1981) *Athleticism in the Victorian and Edwardian Public School*. Cambridge: Cambridge University Press.

MacPherson, B.D., Curtis, J.E. and Loy, J.W. (1989) *The Social Significance of Sport*. Champaign, IL: Human Kinetics.

Messner, M. (1990) 'When bodies are weapons: masculinity and violence in sport', *International Review for the Sociology of Sport*, 25 (3): 203–18.

Morris, J.N., Everitt, M.G., Pollard, R. and Chave, S.P.W. (1980) 'Vigorous exercise in leisure-time: protection against coronary heart disease', *The Lancet*, 6 December: 1207–10.

Mottram, D.R. (ed.) (1988) *Drugs in Sport*. London: E&FN Spon.

Nepfer, J. (ed.) (1994) FIFA World Cup Report. Zurich: FIFA.

Paffenbarger, R.S., Hyde, R.T., Wing, A.L. and Hsieh, C-C. (1986) 'Physical activity, all-cause mortality, and longevity of college alumni', *New England Journal of Medicine*, 314 (10): 605–13.

Riordan, J. (1981) 'The USSR', in J. Riordan (ed.), *Sport Under Communism*. London: C. Hurst. pp. 13–53.

Riordan, J. (1986) 'State and sport in developing societies', *International Review for the Sociology of Sport*, 21 (4): 287–303.

Rowley, S. (1986) *The Effect of Intensive Training on Young Athletes: a Review of the Research Literature*. London: The Sports Council.

Royal College of Physicians of London (1991) *Medical Aspects of Exercise*. London: Royal College of Physicians.

Sheard, K. and Dunning, E. (1973) 'The rugby football club as a type of "male preserve": some sociological notes', *International Review of Sport Sociology*, 3–4 (8): 5–24.

Smith, A. and Jacobson, B. (eds) (1988) *The Nation's Health*. London: King Edward's Hospital Fund for London.

Sports Council (1991) *Injuries in Sport and Exercise*. London: The Sports Council.

Sports Council (1995) *Young People and Sport in England, 1994*. London: The Sports Council.

Sports Council and Health Education Authority (1992) *Allied Dunbar National Fitness Survey*. London: Sports Council and HEA.

Stephens, T. (1988) 'Physical activity and mental health in the United States and Canada: evidence from four population surveys', *Preventive Medicine*, 17: 35–47.

Sullivan, S.N., Wong, C. and Heidenheim, P. (1994) 'Exercise related symptoms', *New Zealand Journal of Sports Medicine*, 22: 23–5.

Taylor, P. (1985) *The Smoke Ring*. London: Sphere Books.

Vertinsky, P. (1987) 'Body shapes: the role of the medical establishment in informing female exercise and physical education in nineteenth-century North America', in J.A. Mangan and R.J. Park (eds), *From 'Fair Sex' to Feminism*. London: Frank Cass. pp. 256–81.

Vertinsky, P. (1990) *The Eternally Wounded Woman*. Manchester and New York: Manchester University Press.

Vinger, P.F. and Hoerner, E.F. (eds) (1982) *Sports Injuries: the Unthwarted Epidemic*. Littleton, MA: PSG.

Waddington, I. and Murphy, P. (1992) 'Drugs, sport and ideologies', in E. Dunning and C. Rojek (eds), *Sport and Leisure in the Civilizing Process*. Basingstoke: Macmillan. pp. 36–64.

Wimbush, E. (1994) 'A moderate approach to promoting physical activity: the evidence and implications', *Health Education Journal*, 53: 322–36.

Young, K. (1993) 'Violence, risk and liability in male sports culture', *Sociology of Sport Journal*, 10 (4): 373–96.

Young, K. and White, P. (1995) 'Sport, physical danger, and injury: the experience of elite women athletes', *Journal of Sport and Social Issues*, 19 (1): 45–61.

Young, K., White, P. and McTeer, W. (1994) 'Body talk: male athletes reflect on sport, injury, and pain', *Sociology of Sport Journal*, 11 (2): 175–94.

27

SPORT AND DISABILITY

Howard L. Nixon II

DISABILITY AND HANDICAP IN SOCIETY

Definitions: Impairment, Disability and Handicap

The term 'disability' often has a different connotation in sport than in the larger society. To be disabled in sport typically means that an athlete is out of action for a while and is named on the 'disabled list'. Thus, the reference is to a temporary restriction of an athlete's opportunity to participate. Disability can mean something entirely different in relation to sport, however. The term can refer to persons with permanent disabilities that restrict the use of certain physical or mental capacities and participation in certain kinds of activities but do not necessarily prevent involvement in sport. For example, a person who is paralyzed and relies on a wheelchair for mobility is permanently physically disabled but also can be a serious wheelchair road racer, competing regularly in races across the United States. In this case, disability does not necessarily imply being out of action as an athlete. Thus, a person can be disabled in society, but not be disabled in certain kinds of sports or sports roles.

We can see from the preceding paragraph that some definitions are needed to clarify the basic terminology for discussion of disability and sport. Impairment, disability and handicap should be distinguished first (see Nixon, 1991: 2–15). An impairment is a biomedical condition – that is, an organic or functional disorder that underlies a disability or handicap. Its existence implies that something is missing or deviant in a person's physical, physiological,

or mental make-up. Impairment can result from disease, an accident, or a defective gene. Impairments generally are distinguished in terms of physical, organic, emotional, sensory, mental, learning and speech conditions.

People with impairments that have persisted for several months or more are considered disabled when their impairment hinders their ability to use certain skills, carry out certain tasks, or participate in certain activities or roles. Impairments are the basis for disabilities, but people who are impaired are not necessarily disabled. The extent to which impaired persons are disabled depends on the nature of the task, role, or activity demands of the situation and how they relate to impaired persons' capabilities. Thus, disability is situational, and the amount a person is disabled depends on how much a situation demands skills that a person has or does not have.

Being handicapped is a social phenomenon. A disabled or impaired person is handicapped when he or she is cast into an inferior status merely on the basis of being impaired or disabled. The relationship of a person's impairment and disability to his or her personality and to the resources and social attitudes in a particular situation affects role performance. When environments or relationships do not accommodate or adapt to impairments or disabilities, handicapping may result. Thus, handicaps are like disabilities in that they are the result of how people construct environments, relationships, or roles; they are not inevitable results of impairments. Handicaps more than disabilities, however, incorporate negative value judgments of the social or moral worth of impaired persons. These discrediting judgments constitute stigmatization, with the discredited impairment or disability – which is the stigma – serving as the defining quality of a person's identity.

An example from sport should help clarify the distinctions among the terms just presented. Joan was born with an eye disease that produced a retinal deficiency and is visually impaired. As a result of the retinal deficiency, Joan cannot play baseball or softball because she cannot see the movement of the ball in the field or at bat. Thus, in baseball or softball played by conventional rules, she is visually disabled. When peers poke fun at Joan or treat her as inferior because she cannot see or play softball with them during recess or in physical education classes at school, she is handicapped. Joan is not disabled or handicapped in these cases merely because she cannot see very clearly; she is disabled because the rules of the game structure it to require the ability to follow a silent ball in motion. Joan is handicapped because her peers believe she is inferior to them because she cannot see or play ball with them. If a beeper were placed inside the ball and another player or coach called out the path of the ball as it headed toward her, she would be able to participate in the game – called 'beep baseball' – and would no longer be severely disabled in relation to it. If peers viewed her with respect for her effort instead of with scorn because she happened not to be able to see, she no longer would be handicapped.

People with impairments and disabilities have been accustomed to being handicapped and treated as members of a deviant minority group (Stroman, 1982; Nixon, 1984a). Deviant status has meant that disabled persons have been relegated to a position outside the mainstream. Minority status has meant that disabled persons as a stereotyped and stigmatized category or group have been accorded degraded status, little power, and few opportunities for economic advancement or success.

In mainstream sports, injuries are very common and tend to be expected as a normal part of the sports experience (Nixon, 1993a). A number of injuries are serious enough to prevent athletes from competing. Thus, temporary disability is relatively common in sport, especially at the highest and most serious levels of competition. Despite its relative prevalence, disabled status in sport has shared some of the stigma of disability in the larger society. The labeling and segregating process that has accorded disabled persons deviant or minority status is illustrated by an injured football player who must appear at practice wearing a highly visible red cross or other stigmatizing symbol of inactivity or disability. Thus, in sport and in society, people with disabilities frequently experience degrading, demeaning, inferior and generally unsympathetic treatment merely because they are disabled. While high-status members of sports teams and society may at least initially have enough social credit to offset tendencies toward handicapism for a while, they ultimately may feel the sting of the handicapism embedded in society.

This handicapism involves patterns of prejudice and discrimination built into the attitudes, rules, regulations and laws by which organizations, communities and society normally operate. When coaches accord encouragement and respect only to active players, subtly or explicitly tell players that 'real men' play hurt, and relegate injured players to visibly stigmatized status on the sidelines, they are intentionally or unintentionally displaying negative attitudes toward disabled players and undermining their status. The fact that athletes became injured as a result of physical sacrifices for the good of the team typically has little impact on how they are treated when they are disabled because the culture and structure of sport are oriented toward keeping players in action. The unwillingness of coaches to consider candidates with permanent disabilities and rules that prohibit athletes with certain disabilities from trying out for teams also illustrate handicapism in sport.

In this chapter, we will explore what is currently known about disability and handicap in sport and how sport disables athletes. In considering these topics, the definitions and conceptual distinctions previously presented should be kept in mind. Bear in mind that relatively little sociological research has focused on permanently disabled persons and sport and that despite their prevalence in sport, injuries, pain and disability only began to attract attention among sport sociologists during the 1990s.

DISABILITY AND HANDICAP IN SPORT

Disability and Sports Performance

The essence of sport is organized physical competition in which opponents use their natural physical endowment and the physical skills they have developed through training and experience to perform physical tasks more proficiently than their competitors in an effort to win. In some cases, such as boxing, football, rugby, hockey, and wrestling, physical contact is an expected part of the competition. In others, such as basketball, baseball, soccer and road races, physical contact occurs, but is often outside the rules. In sports such as tennis, physical contact is not part of the competition even though competitors directly interact with one another, while in sports such as crew and events such as high jumping, competitors do not directly interact and compete in parallel fashion or against a standard such as a clock or a height. Since sports competitions are varied and can have complex formal and informal structures, the adaptations needed to accommodate persons with certain kinds of impairments within a sport and across different sports may be varied and complex.

When a sports role emphasizes or requires certain physical or mental capacities and no adaptation or accommodation is made to compensate for impairments related to those capacities, persons with such impairments will be disabled in that sports role. For example, blind persons are disabled in sports or sports roles requiring vision, such as ball sports or sports such as boxing or wrestling in which a competitor has to fend off an attacking opponent. People who cannot use their arms or legs are disabled in sports requiring the use of those impaired limbs. Although disabilities have an objective dimension and imply some restriction of activity or performance, people with disabilities can play sports that do not require the impaired abilities or parts of the body or are adapted to minimize the significance of particular impairments. For example, in the former case, many popular individual and team sports, from tennis to football, can be played without restriction by people who cannot hear. In the latter case, blind people can wrestle as long as the competitors maintain physical contact throughout the match. It is also possible that a person disabled for one type of role in a sport may be able to play another role in the same sport. It is not unusual for baseball players in the twilight of their careers who no longer have the arm strength or mobility to play center field or shortstop to perform competently at first base, which does not emphasize either of those qualities. The designated hitter role has also extended the careers of many baseball players who could not play the field any more, but still were able to hit. While sports and sports roles currently exist that allow people with impairments, disabilities, or declining skills to participate in sport, many sports and sports roles continue to present substantial barriers to participation for such people.

Barriers to Participation and the Exclusion of Disabled Persons from Sport

Many sports are structured in ways that prevent persons with certain kinds of disabilities from participating. In fact, the highest levels of competition in sport, such as intercollegiate, Olympic, or professional sports, may require types of physical endowment and degrees of proficiency that only an elite few can attain. Yet even at the non-elite and recreational levels of sport, people with various disabilities find barriers to participation.

Sports often require modifications of their structure, equipment, or facilities for people with impairments to be able to surmount the barriers to participation that disable them in those sports. The types and amount of adaptation or accommodation required to make a sport accessible to people with disabilities may depend on whether the competition is integrated or segregated. Resistance to adaptation of a sport is an important factor in preventing disabled persons from participating. For example, if wrestling did not have a special rule to accommodate blind competitors, it would be very difficult for them to compete fairly against sighted opponents. Few mainstream sports make accommodations to permit accessibility for persons with disabilities. Thus, physically talented athletes with disabilities typically have to display their athletic talents in segregated competitions against other disabled competitors. Indeed, in some cases such as the Special Olympics, competition has been 'controlled' (Coakley, 1994: 84–7) so that fellowship and pride in the display of physical skills are valued more than competitive outcomes. In other settings, highly competitive athletes with disabilities compete alongside non-disabled athletes in parallel competitions, such as wheelchair racers in marathon road races.

Controlled Competition: the Case of the Special Olympics

The Special Olympics Sport Program was established in 1968 by the Kennedy Foundation, with the help of the Chicago Park District, and quickly grew to become the world's largest sports program of training and competition for mentally retarded individuals (Songster, 1986). The First International Special Olympic Games took place in Chicago, where over 1,000 mentally retarded athletes from across the United States and Canada competed in track and field and swimming. By the 1980s, the program involved more than one million athletes and thousands of coaches and volunteers from the United States and 60 other countries in summer and winter events, and included over 20 officially approved and demonstration sports, ranging from aquatics to weight lifting. The Special Olympics remains the world's largest program of physical fitness, sports training and sports competition for people with mental retardation. The Developmental Sports Skills program was created to expose severely and profoundly mentally retarded people to physical fitness and sports activities. Nearly one million people take part in the Special Olympics in every state of the United States and in over 140 other countries (Gran-Net Communications, 1995).

The Special Olympics philosophy emphasizes the values of physical fitness, courage, joy, sharing, maximum effort, fairness in competition, friendship and family togetherness (Songster, 1986). Its motto is 'Let me win but if I cannot win, let me be brave in the attempt'. Underlying this philosophy is the assumption that controlled sports competition can make everyone feel like a winner, which is assumed to build self-confidence, self-esteem and a sense of achievement. Furthermore, Special Olympians who display such qualities are assumed to destigmatize their mental retardation by getting other people to focus more on their abilities than their disabilities. Awards such as ribbons or medals are given to every competitor to convey their actual level of performance and to enhance their pride of achievement. Special Olympians, who are eight years old or older and generally have an IQ of 70 or less, compete against others of roughly equal ability, based on age, gender and prior sports experience. A major goal of the Special Olympics is for participants to move on to regular sports programs. Participants in regular interscholastic or intramural sports cannot compete in the Special Olympics.

Although Special Olympics officials and organizers have seen this program as a vehicle for participants to enter the mainstream of society free of the stigma of their disability (Songster, 1986; Whitman, 1995), others have questioned its potential for achieving this goal (Orelove and Moon, 1984; Orelove et al., 1982). For example, after identifying several benefits of the Special Olympics, Orelove and Moon (1984) argued that this program hurt the mainstreaming of mentally retarded people by promoting handicapism and segregation. They recognized that the Special Olympics could enable mentally retarded participants to experience success, increase their social contacts in a supportive environment, and improve their physical skills. They also saw the benefits of parental involvement with their child and widespread community involvement in the Special Olympics. At the same time, they contended that organizing the Special Olympics as a segregated program focused public attention on the disability rather than ability, which was contrary to the professed goals of the organizers. That is, the notion of equal physical or sports ability was only applied in relation to other mentally retarded people. As long as mentally retarded children, youths and adults are only compared with each other, they will not be given other, less restrictive recreational opportunities. That is, they will be handicapped by a philosophy of segregation, which may be intended to protect them in controlled competition. To the extent that such restriction of opportunity occurs, the attainment of another professed goal of the Special Olympics, to propel participants into regular sports programs, will be thwarted. Orelove and Moon also observed that fund-raising practices that induce pity, sympathy, or the need for charity encourage a protective attitude that can handicap people who are mentally retarded and seek more independence and respect. Furthermore, they argued, segregated activities give mentally retarded people little practice in routine mainstream interactions and little motivation to seek such experiences.

From the Special Olympics to the Paralympics

With limited research, we cannot draw any clear conclusions at this point about the direct effects of the Special Olympics on the 'mainstreaming' or integration of people with mental retardation. Some evidence has been cited, however, indicating that participation in the Special Olympics elevates levels of social competence, self-esteem and physical fitness (Shriver, 1995/1996).[1] It is evident, too, that advocacy activities, legislative initiatives, court decisions and 'normalization' and deinstitutionalization movements on behalf of people with mental retardation and other impairments have increased the legal rights, visibility and participation of these people in the mainstream of society in the United States and other nations (Labanowich, 1988; Nagler, 1993; Stroman, 1989; West, 1994). We have even seen athletes with disabilities on Wheaties cereal boxes, a site where some of the most prominent American sports heroes have been displayed (Nixon and Frey, 1996: 222–3).

Opportunities for outstanding athletes with physical and sensory impairments to compete at a high level and achieve some visibility have been provided by the Paralympics, which have developed into a counterpart of the Olympic Games. The Paralympics grew out of the International Wheelchair Games organized at Stoke Mandeville Hospital in England in 1948 by Dr Ludwig Guttmann, who organized his Games to coincide with the 1948 London Olympics (Dukes et al., 1995a). Although these sports competitions have been segregated, unlike marathons in which wheelchair racers compete, they have little resemblance to the Special Olympics. Athletes are intensely competitive and highly serious about their sport, and the competitions are advertised for *elite* athletes with physical or visual impairments. Athletes must meet strict qualifying criteria to be selected for their national teams and be allowed to compete in the Paralympics. The guiding philosophy of the Paralympic movement is to provide these elite athletes with athletic opportunities and experiences equivalent to those of their elite able-bodied counterparts in sport (Dukes et al., 1995b).

Held first in 1960 in Rome shortly after the Rome Olympic Games and limited only to wheelchair athletes, the Paralympic Games have evolved into an event sponsored by four different international federations: the Cerebral Palsy International Sports and Recreation Association (CP-ISRA); the International Blind Sports Association (IBSA); the International Stoke Mandeville Wheelchair Sports Federation (ISMWSF); and the International Sports Organization for the Disabled (ISOD). The latter organization has control over sports for amputee athletes as well as athletes with a variety of other impairments, including dwarf athletes (Dukes et al., 1995a). The four member federations are joined together under the auspices of the International Coordinating Committee of World Sports Organizations for the Disabled (ICC).

The tenth Paralympics in 1996, held in the host city – Atlanta – of the 1996 Summer Olympics, involved approximately 100 nations, 17 sports (including 14 Olympic sports) and 2 demonstration sports over a ten-day period. The 1996 Paralympic Games were about one-third the size of the Olympic Games, with approximately 4,000 athletes, 1,000 coaches and team staff members, 1,500 officials and technical personnel and 15,000 volunteers. These Games are officially recognized by the International Olympic Committee (IOC) and are governed by the International Paralympic Committee (IPC) (Labanowich, 1988; Dukes et al., 1995b).

Paralympic sports may include minor modifications of the rules to accommodate the disabilities of competitors. Athletes are classified into competitive units by a three-step process: medical classification with certifiable disabling conditions; functional classifications according to levels of functional ability such as balance, coordination, movement, and motor skills; and functional classification by sport to determine functional ability within particular sports. Combining the four basic categories defined by the four international federations with the different functional classifications results in approximately 700 Paralympic sporting events, compared to the approximately 330 events in the Olympic Games (Dukes et al., 1995c).

Cook (1995) sought to dispel misconceptions about the Paralympics and their participants by challenging ten popular myths about the Paralympics. Her analysis clarifies the nature of these competitions and important facts about the athletes as people with disabilities. For example, she pointed out the distinction between the types of participants in the Special Olympics and the Paralympics, the elite nature of Paralympic athletes, and the separate identities of the Olympic Games and the Paralympics. In fact, the increasing involvement of people with varied types and degrees of disabilities in many different sports below the elite international and national levels (Hamel, 1992; Sherrill, 1986) has very likely contributed to changing attitudes about the capabilities of these people and added to the interest in sport and physical recreation among people with disabilities.

Issues of Competition and Integration

At the elite level, the growth of the Paralympic movement alongside the increasing visibility of wheelchair sports has increased interest in integrated sports among elite athletes and their advocates (Brasile, 1990; Labanowich, 1988; Lindstrom, 1992; Paciorek et al., 1991). Labanowich (1988), for example, has criticized the Paralympics because it has been segregated from the mainstream and because it has segregated athletes with different types of impairments from each other. He argued that disabled people in general challenged these types of restrictions of their opportunities. He also argued that elite disabled athletes aspired to participate alongside and against able-bodied athletes at the highest levels of their sports, including the medal sports of the Olympics.[2] He saw wheelchair sports, with their mix of competitors with different categories of physical impairment, such as spinal paralyzed, amputees and cerebral palsied, as a model for integration.

The general approach to integration has been to include disabled athletes in competitions for able-bodied athletes. The participation of wheelchair racers in marathon road races, such as the Boston Marathon and the New York City Marathon, is an example of this approach. Although George Murray, Craig Blanchette, Doug Heir, and a number of other wheelchair racers have achieved international prominence in such competitions, they also have faced some resistance from race organizers, based mainly on questions about safety, spectacle and authenticity (Brandmeyer and McBee, 1986). Organizers have claimed that wheelchairs create dangerous risks for runners, and that serious accidents could occur on wet and uneven pavements at high speeds. Some also have been concerned that participants in wheelchairs might be more concerned about conveying a political message about the capabilities and rights of disabled persons than about competing in a race, which could turn their races into spectacles (Nixon and Frey, 1996: 223). The serious attitudes and high levels of accomplishment of wheelchair racers as athletes have silenced many of these types of criticisms, but the issue of integration remains salient both in the mainstream and in disabled sports realms.

Efforts by the Sport for the Disabled movement to integrate medal events of the Olympic Games have met resistance (Brasile, 1990; Labanowich, 1988; Lindstrom, 1992). Results from Brasile's (1989) survey of disabled and non-disabled basketball and track and field participants showed that more disabled participants expressed higher overall participation incentive levels. His survey also showed that among quadriplegic respondents, more severely disabled respondents had higher mean scores than less disabled respondents on social affective and social integration incentive measures. Brasile (1990) suggested that these latter results might mean that sports participation may be especially valued for its possible social reintegration benefits by athletic participants who are most severely disabled. Perhaps less disabled athletes feel less stigmatized and are more content to participate in competitions with other disabled athletes, especially if the competition is intense and at a relatively high level.

Lindstrom (1992) pointed to a paradox that emerged with the development of elite sports programs for disabled athletes. On the one hand, eligibility for sport for athletes in various disability categories was conceived with the idea that being disabled created a disadvantage in competition with able-bodied participants, which was rectified by sports involving only disabled athletes. Yet some athletes in these categorical or segregated sports have become so proficient that they are capable of competing on relatively equal footing against able-bodied athletes in certain sports. At the same time, the disability eligibility criterion in certain sports for disabled athletes is set at a low enough level to permit minimally disabled persons to participate. Thus, Lindstrom (1992) identified three types of integration situations for policy consideration:

1 athletes who are not significantly disadvantaged by their disabilities in competitions with able-bodied athletes, as in the case of former Major League pitcher Jim Abbott, who has one hand;
2 athletes with minimal disabilities who are not generally seen as disabled persons but who qualify for certain disabled sports, such as people with circulation defects in a lower limb or with a cruciate ligament injury who are eligible for sitting volleyball in the Paralympics or World Championships;
3 able-bodied athletes in sports adapted for athletes with disabilities.

The first situation also includes disabled athletes who are able to compete against able-bodied athletes with minimal adaptations of the sport, as in the case of blind wrestlers. This situation and the case of disabled athletes who compete in mainstream sports without any accommodations are likely to involve talented disabled athletes who represent a very small proportion of the athletes in their sport and generally create little controversy. They are more likely to inspire admiration or awe, but probably have little effect on general attitudes and behavior toward people with disabilities because they are seen as exceptional cases.

Over the past two decades, newspapers, popular books and magazines, and academic publications, have given attention to disabled athletes in competitions with able-bodied athletes (Nixon, 1989, 1994a). For example, many sports fans are familiar with the stories of one-armed Major League outfielder Pete Gray and one-armed Major League pitcher Jim Abbott. Stories have also been written about athletes with a variety of other disabilities competing in high-level integrated sports, including deaf college basketball players (Keteyian, 1985) and professional boxers (Cook, 1987) and amputee triathletes and marathoners competing against able-bodied opponents (Iole, 1988; Young, 1989). In addition, blind and visually impaired athletes have successfully competed with and against outstanding sighted athletes in triathalons, wrestling, judo, karate, swimming, crew, track and field, marathons, powerlifting, gymnastics, tandem cycling, sailing, basketball, soccer and football (Becker, 1988; Buell, 1986; Cordellos, 1981; Ludovise, 1988; Sullivan and Gill, 1975; Whiteside, 1992; Young, 1989). The stories of these athletes reflect their strong desire to compete at high levels of sport and achieve recognition as athletes rather than as athletes with disabilities.

Strong motivation to compete often is necessary to overcome a variety of personal and social barriers to participation in mainstream sports. For example, the resistance of many mainstream sports to mixing disabled and able-bodied athletes, as with wheelchair racers and runners, and especially, the resistance to adapting mainstream sports to open them up to athletes with various disabilities has limited the number of opportunities for disabled athletes in mainstream sports. The Disabled Sports movement itself has also at least implicitly resisted such forms of integration. Organizations such as the IPC have sought to preserve the identity and status of the Paralympics as sport for disabled athletes, which for them has meant reinforcing a segregated sports model (Lindstrom, 1992).

Brasile (1990) proposed that having able-bodied athletes compete in wheelchairs against disabled athletes in wheelchairs was a novel approach to integration, which made the disabled athletes and their sports the agents of integration. However, critics of this notion (for example, Lindstrom, 1992) have argued that having athletes with minimal disabilities and able-bodied athletes compete in sports for disabled athletes places substantially disabled athletes at a competitive disadvantage and may result in minimally disabled and non-disabled athletes squeezing them out of opportunities to compete at high levels. Lindstrom (1992) proposed that trying to integrate majority-group able-bodied athletes into sports developed and adapted for minority-group disabled athletes amounted to reverse integration that effectively undercut the original rationale for creating the sports for disabled competitors. Concern about relegation of disabled athletes to second-class or minority status within sports constructed for them or their exclusion from competition altogether raises a question about when and how athletes with disabilities generally can be effectively integrated into mainstream sports without being disadvantaged by their impairments or disabilities.

In an analysis of the mainstream sports integration of people with disabilities, Nixon (1989, 1994a) showed how integration efforts can be complicated by a mismatching of structural aspects of sports and the abilities of participants with disabilities. This analysis also demonstrated conditions under which persons with disabilities can succeed in sport and achieve broader social integration through sport. Genuine integration is not simply having disabled and able-bodied athletes participate in the same sport or event (see Labanowich, 1979; Nixon, 1984b; Sherrill, 1986). By 'genuine integration' of disabled and able-bodied athletes is meant here that: (a) interaction is not affected by stigma, prejudice, or discrimination; (b) disabled competitors do not feel deviant, inferior, or specially favored because they are disabled; and (c) disabled athletes' impairments and disabilities are recognized and accepted but do not disable these athletes in competition or handicap them in interaction with their able-bodied counterparts. In general, genuine integration occurs when interaction between disabled and able-bodied athletes does not involve stigma or handicapping or avoidable disability.

Genuine sports integration occurs when there is *appropriate* integration (Nixon, 1984b). Appropriate integration refers to conditions when the personal sports-related attributes, abilities and backgrounds of participants with disabilities match the structural parameters of the sports situation. Included among the parameters of sports structure that could affect competitions involving disabled and able-bodied athletes are: (a) the type of sport; (b) the amount of adaptation or accommodation to disability; and (c) the degree or intensity of competition. An important aspect of efforts to match disabled athletes to particular sports is to determine the degree of actual limitation or disability of disabled athletes in specific roles and situations in the sport. Structuring sports to provide appropriate integration can be especially difficult when an impairment, such as hearing or seeing, is invisible or hard to measure (Nixon, 1989, 1994a). The basic principle for genuine and appropriate integration of disabled athletes in mainstream sports is the matching of the *abilities* of these athletes to the demands of the various situations likely to be encountered in their role in a sport. When disabled athletes are able to meet the demands of their sport, they can compete on an equal basis with able-bodied athletes and increase the likelihood of avoiding or minimizing impairment or disability-related stigmatization and handicapping.

The principle of *ability-role matching* applies to sports participants who are not normally considered disabled as well as to disabled participants. *Any person* could be inappropriately integrated in a sport when he or she is grossly deficient – or unable or disabled – in the performance of his or her role in that sport and in the social skills needed to interact effectively in the sport. People who are not competent to meet the demands of their sports and related social roles risk disapproval, blows to their self-esteem and, if they are otherwise disabled, a reinforcement of stigma and their sense of being handicapped. Under such conditions, interaction beyond sport is also likely to be adversely affected. Competition always carries certain social and emotional risks associated with losing. The risks are compounded for disabled competitors in more intensely competitive environments, which could amplify unacknowledged performance disabilities or amplify unaccommodated performance disabilities for which there are no accommodations in equipment, rules or the physical demands of the sport itself. Thus, inappropriate integration could result from a poor fit between an individual's competitive motivation, abilities and skills, and the motivation, abilities and skills required by a particular sports role. Inappropriate integration in sport could lessen chances of genuine integration of disabled and able-bodied people outside sport by reinforcing negative or demeaning conceptions of disabled people that stigmatize and handicap them. On the other hand, appropriate integration could facilitate genuine integration by generating respect for the abilities and skills of disabled people and 'normalizing' them.

A basic premise underlying this reasoning is that disabled and able-bodied people interact comfortably and with mutual respect in and out of sport when both are able to handle the performance and interaction demands of their respective roles. Nixon (1989, 1994a) offered case study evidence to provide a provisional empirical justification for this reasoning. Some (for example, Hahn, 1984) have questioned whether disabled people benefit from integration when it involves emulating or adjusting to able-bodied achievement values that generally have not accommodated the special needs of people with impairments and disabilities. Yet, disabled athletes themselves have shown that they want opportunities to compete in elite mainstream sports, and some have distinguished themselves with outstanding performances. The Sports for the Disabled movement, leading up to the Paralympic Games, has met the goals and needs of many other disabled athletes, and its categorical and segregated structure has been staunchly defended by the leaders of this movement. The Special Olympics and other less competitive models of sport have met the needs of other disabled people. The notion of appropriate integration implies that people with disabilities ought to have opportunities for sports participation that match their motivation, abilities and skills, just as able-bodied people have. Thus, an opportunity structure that best meets the sports needs and interests of disabled people includes a continuum of options in different sports, ranging from relatively uncompetitive recreational sports where 'everyone is a winner' to highly competitive elite sports where only a very talented few are selected or earn the right to compete. Battles over which sports model is most appropriate for disabled people reflect disagreements in the mainstream of society over the amount and types of emphasis to place on competition and achievement values and over whether disabled people benefit more from trying to adjust to institutionalized roles in the mainstream, having mainstream society accommodate to their special needs, or staying within segregated realms where roles have been developed especially for them and their sense of difference is minimized.

DISABLEMENT THROUGH SPORT

We have been considering how persons with permanent disabilities participate in sport. The idea that people who are disabled can participate in sport, especially at elite levels, contradicts the idea that an athlete who is disabled must be placed on a disabled list and held out of action. We have observed that disabilities are defined in terms of specific role and situational demands, which means that a person who is viewed as disabled in society due to physical, sensory, or mental impairments, still may be able to meet the demands of a role in a particular sport. In some cases, the sport may be adapted to accommodate for a disability, as in the case of wrestling for blind people; in others, the disabilities of athletes are essentially irrelevant to the demands of the sport, as in the case of deaf basketball players.

While disabled people may be able to compete successfully in sport at very high levels, sport also may disable people through serious injuries that make it difficult or impossible to continue to perform in that sport or even meet the demands of other kinds of roles in society. Sport as a cause of disablement through chronic pain and injuries is a troubling social issue that will be the focus of the remainder of this chapter.

The idea that sport disables participants is contrary to a popular belief that sport promotes health and fitness (Edwards, 1973; 119–20, 325–8). The reality is that for high-level athletes, sports participation can be a source of chronic pain (Brody, 1992; Kotarba, 1983), and for professional athletes in sports such as football, it may even reduce longevity (Breo, 1992; Huizenga, 1994; Munson, 1991). Although the reality of physical risks, pain and injuries is understood to be part of the experience of athletes at all levels, sports cultures and socialization often minimize, normalize, or glorify this reality (Curry, 1991; Curry and Strauss, 1994; Frager, 1995; Huizenga, 1994; Kotarba, 1983; Messner, 1990; Nixon, 1993a, 1993b; Sabo, 1986; Stebbins, 1987). In fact, a 'sport ethic' that emphasizes the need for serious athletes to accept risks and play through pain appears to be an important cultural influence on athletes (Hughes and Coakley, 1991).

'Positive deviance' describes cases where conformity to this kind of ethic is so intense, extensive, or extreme that the behavior exceeds conventional expectations for effort or commitment (Ewald and Jiobu, 1985). Athletes who engage in positive deviance are not deviant in the sense that they are violating the rules of sport; their deviance is instead a case of being overzealous in conforming to the norms or 'ethic' of the sports culture. Hughes and Coakley (1991) hypothesized that athletes are especially vulnerable to pressures to overconform to norms of the sport ethic such as accepting risks and playing with pain when they have low self-esteem, have identities tied to sport and rely heavily on sport for social mobility and status.

Athletes are socialized to accept pain and injuries as a normal part of sport because pain and injuries happen so frequently in sport. For example, in one study of nearly 200 male and female varsity athletes at a medium-sized NCAA Division I institution (Nixon, 1993b, 1994b, 1996a, 1996b),[3] 80 per cent said that they had been seriously hurt in sport, and over 66 per cent said they had been disabled by sports injuries for two weeks or more on at least one occasion. The amount of pressure to play with pain and injuries is indicated by the findings that 94 per cent of the athletes who had been seriously injured said they had 'played hurt', about half of these athletes said they felt some influence from significant others to play hurt, and over 90 per cent agreed with the statement that 'being an athlete means that you have to be willing to accept risks'. A high percentage of these athletes also agreed with statements about the difficulty athletes have in quitting, even after serious injuries; the need for athletes to push themselves to their physical limits; and the expectation that athletes have to play with an injury or pain sometime. In addition, many agreed with the popular slogan 'no pain, no gain'. Overall, a majority of the surveyed athletes agreed strongly or with reservations with 20 of 31 statements indicating a willingness to play hurt. When these results are coupled with the finding that over 45 per cent of the previously injured athletes reported lingering effects of their injuries, we can see that athletes are highly vulnerable to chronic pain and lingering or permanent disability as a result of their sports involvement.

Sports Status and Gender Effects on Pain and Injury-related Attitudes and Behavior

Being a lineup regular increased the likelihood of having lingering effects of sports injuries and of having more injuries. Males and holders of an athletic scholarship had more surgeries for athletic injuries, and males were more likely than females to be significantly disabled by sports injuries for periods of weeks or months. Athletes were most likely to talk to athletic trainers and doctors about their pain and injuries when they seemed sympathetic and caring. They also were more likely to seek medical attention when their coaches seemed sympathetic and caring, but they tended to avoid or conceal their injuries from authorities, such as coaches, trainers and doctors, when these people were seen as likely to push them to play hurt.

Although males were more inclined to express tough attitudes about risk, pain and injury and to feel pressure from coaches and fans to play hurt, no gender differences were found in help-seeking or avoidance behavior regarding injuries (Nixon, 1996b). In fact, male and female athletes in this study did not significantly differ on most measures of pain and injury attitudes and behavior. Males may experience more injuries and more serious disabilities because the intensity of contact or violence in male sports is greater. Males may differ in certain attitudes, such as toughness, and feel more pressed to play hurt because they are generally more intense about their sports involvement and feel a greater need to affirm their gender identity through physical risk-taking. Thus, the gender differences in pain and injury attitudes and behaviors found in this research may reflect residual effects of traditional stereotypical Western or North American socialization into manhood through sport.

Another study, based on in-depth interviews with a small sample of Canadian adult male athletes, revealed that serious injury typically was seen as a masculinizing experience (Young et al., 1994). These men tended to accept physical risk in sport and not to question their past injuries and the continuing pain and injury they caused. Although the men saw it as masculinizing, elite female athletes in Western Canada were also found to be willing risk-takers who were relatively unreflective about the implications of playing with injuries (Young and White, 1995). These two studies suggest that the few but noteworthy gender differences in pain- and injury-related attitudes and behavior found among Division I college athletes in the United States may disappear or narrow substantially at higher levels of sport. That is, both male and female athletes may feel the effects of a culture of sport that tells them to take physical risks and play hurt. Unless coaches, trainers, or doctors appear sympathetic and caring when they are hurt, these athletes may risk a series of disabling injuries that could lead to chronic pain or lifetime disability.

The notion that physicality and injuries in sport are associated with masculinity is belied by increasing evidence to the contrary from women's sports. Another study revealing the inaccuracy of this notion was conducted by Theberge (1993). Her research showed that for members of an elite Canadian women's ice-hockey team playing at the highest AA level in their country, pain and especially injury were taken for granted as part of their sport. The women did not fight on the ice because penalties were too severe, but the manner of play was still highly aggressive. Despite rules against intentional body checking, players frequently unintentionally and intentionally used their bodies and body contact, colliding with opponents and crashing against the boards, to maneuver for position. The intense and aggressive style of play resulted in numerous injuries affecting virtually all the main parts of the body. Among these women, as it is among men studied in elite amateur and professional sports, players measured their ability partially in terms of their capacity to stay in the game

and even play well in spite of pain and injuries. Thus, the physicality that leads to pain and injuries was defined by these female hockey players as an important dimension of their sport, indicating the lack of gendering of these qualities in sport at high levels of competition. Not surprisingly, the trainer was routinely present in the locker room of the team that Theberge studied.

Pain and Injury from the Student Trainer's Perspective

An interview study of 22 male and female undergraduate and graduate students enrolled in an athletic training internship program at a large NCAA Division I university showed the kinds of social relations involving trainers, coaches and athletes in regard to the handling of pain and injuries (Walk, 1994). Athletes demeaned the student trainers and tried to avoid their services, but they also used the student trainers to help them fake injuries, avoid highly demanding workout sessions, and misuse athletic training and medical services in other ways. At times, student trainers formed alliances with athletes to circumvent the wishes of sports authorities. At other times, the student trainers formed alliances with staff trainers to deal with the resistance of athletes and coaches to their provision of medical services. These alliances reflect the complicated tensions surrounding medical treatment in sports networks on college campuses – and elsewhere in sport (see Nixon, 1992).

A universally held belief among the trainers was that serious injuries were an inevitable part of sport. While the acute injuries in sports such as football and hockey did not surprise the student trainers due to their intensity of violent contact, the number of seemingly avoidable chronic overuse injuries, such as stress fractures and bursitis, in these and other sports surprised them. The student trainers observed that the athletes were aware of the risks of chronic or later-life disabilities from their sports participation, but they seemed willing to accept these risks. As in the case of athletes, acceptance of the inevitability of injuries as 'part of the game' was necessary for trainers to justify their involvement in sport.

One means for trainers to deal with the injury issue was to encourage the use of protective equipment as a preventive measure, which conveyed the message that anyone could get hurt. They realized, however, that they had little power to force athletes to use such equipment or to take other preventive actions. To the extent that athletes downplay their own chances of being seriously hurt (see Breo, 1992), they are unlikely to engage in such preventive or precautionary behavior. Student trainers also noted the general unwillingness of athletes with chronic injuries to quit sport despite the risk of arthritis and other disabling conditions. In a number of cases, injured athletes pushed themselves too hard during rehabilitation and recovery, and contributed to the chronic nature of their injuries and re-injuries. Few seemed to question the costs of recurrent and serious sports injuries. Most of the trainers believed that the reason athletes stayed in sport despite pain and the risk of permanent disability was 'love of sport'. Another reason that athletes may have stayed in sport was that trainers were reluctant to advise them to discontinue participation. Indeed, the general orientation of medical personnel affiliated with sports organizations tends to be to return athletes to action.

RETIREMENT, INJURIES, DISABILITY AND THE ROLE OF MEDICAL PERSONNEL

Chronic pain and injuries are a major reason for the end of athletic careers, and athletes in more combative and violent sports are likely to be more damaged by their sports involvement (Huizenga, 1994; Nixon and Frey, 1996: 201–3). College athletes whose careers are ended by injury may also suffer emotional or psychological damage from their injury. Research by Kleiber and Brock (1992) showed that five to ten years after the end of their athletic careers, college athletes who aspired to play professional sport and suffered a career-ending injury had lower self-esteem and life satisfaction than their counterparts with professional orientations who did not have their careers ended by injury. Their research also showed that there was no difference in self-esteem or life satisfaction between former college athletes whose careers were ended by injury and those whose careers did not end by injury when the athletes were not seriously oriented toward a professional sports career. These former athletes who had a low professional orientation had levels of self-esteem and life satisfaction approximately equal to the level of athletes with a high professional orientation who did not suffer a career-ending injury. A study conducted for the National Football League Players Association (NFLPA) and reported in a five-part series in the *Chicago Sun Times* (Hewitt, 1993a, 1993b, 1993c, 1993d, 1993e) focused on the post-career consequences of sports injuries for athletes who reached the professional level. This study considered whether former NFL players thought their careers were worth the pain and injuries they suffered. It surveyed 645 players whose careers covered the period from the early 1940s to 1986.

Although every NFL player is injured every year, many players end their careers with an injury, and the NFL replaces its 1,650 players every four years, only approximately one-third of the players carried the optional NFLPA-negotiated career-ending injury coverage. According to Miki Yaras, director of benefits for the NFLPA, her efforts to sell the insurance to players were complicated by players' perceptions that they will escape serious injury. She observed that the players tended to be macho young men who thought of themselves as invincible. She further noted that the players often made the mistake of assuming that the NFL would take care of them if they experienced a career-ending injury (Breo, 1992). The realization of their mistake often comes when players retire and face a lifetime of costly disability.

More than one-third of the former players in the NFLPA survey indicated that they had retired as a result of a disabling injury, and almost two-thirds indicated that they had a permanent injury from football. Despite public statements by many of the players that they would play again despite their injuries and disabilities, the responses to the survey showed that most recently retired players have expressed increasing doubts about the value of the physical damage from football. This pattern of increasing doubts may reflect the fact that professional football became more violent and disabling between the early years and the 1970s. The percentage of retired players who said they had a permanent injury from football rose from 38 per cent for those retiring before 1959 to 60 per cent for those retiring in the 1960s and then to a peak of 66 per cent for those retiring in the 1970s. The figure for the late 1980s was 65 per cent, and based on an update of the survey, the preliminary figure for 1993 was 61.1 per cent. The update also revealed that the percentage of players who said the main reason they retired was a disabling injury increased from 37 per cent in 1990 to 41.4 per cent in 1993. The disabling injury rate in the NFL in the 1990s was over three times the injury rate for workers in the high-risk construction industry. Furthermore, the average length of life of NFL players is 62 years, which is 10 years shorter than the average lifespan of American males. According to Hewitt (1993a), the NFL challenged these statistics, but whether or not they are precise indicators of changes in injury rates, the pattern they indicate is clear. Injuries have become more severe and costly over the history of the NFL.

Although professional athletes today (for example, Stebbins, 1987) may be more inclined than elite amateur athletes (for example, Young and White, 1995; Young et al., 1994) to question the value of physical sacrifice for their sport, there still is evidence that professional football players continue to take serious risks with their bodies and health (Huizenga, 1994). Perhaps in the late stages of their career and in retirement, the costs of chronic pain and disabling injuries become more apparent. In recent years, a number of former professional athletes have sued for multimillion awards to compensate for the disabling effects of sports injuries. The largest award in suits against team doctors in North America by 1995 was $5.5 million, which former professional hockey player Glen Seabrooke won in a suit against the former orthopedic physician for his team, the Philadelphia Flyers (Nocera, 1995). Due to an excessively demanding and painful rehabilitation program without proper medical monitoring following surgery, he developed a condition called 'reflex sympathetic dystrophy'. This condition left him without use of his left arm and shoulder and with chronic pain that offered no prospect of relief.

The tendency of team medical personnel to downplay or ignore chronic or acute pain and other indicators of potentially debilitating conditions often stems from the difficult role strain that team doctors and trainers typically face (Huizenga, 1994; Smith, 1994). These medical personnel are torn between responding to the demands of their employer to keep players on the field and to their ethical commitment in medicine to attend to the long-term health needs of players as patients. A former NFL team physician, Robert Huizenga, commented that the tendency to feel like a member of the team often subtly affects one's decisions as a doctor (Nocera, 1995: 82). Doctors often succumb to pressure from owners and management to rush players back into action, despite medical doubts about their readiness to play. The clearest case of conflict of interest in this regard involved Dr Arthur Pappas, an orthopedic surgeon and part-owner of the Major League baseball team

Boston Red Sox, who lost a $1.7 million judgment to a Red Sox player, Marty Barrett. Barrett's lawyers argued that Pappas's medical judgment was clouded by his financial interest in the club and its drive to earn a place in the American League Championship Series (Nocera, 1995). When the power of owners, management and coaches dictate the conditions of medical treatment of athletes, the athletes become very vulnerable to unintentional or intentional medical malpractice. Thus, athletes can be disabled by the physical strains, pressures and contact of the contest on the field or by the inadequate, inattentive or incompetent medical treatment of the pain and injuries produced on the field of play. When their disability forces retirement, they often must wait 35 or more years to begin receiving their sports pension.

HEALTH, DRUGS AND SPORT

The prevalence of drug use of various kinds in high-level amateur and professional sport has been highly publicized over the past decade, with stories ranging from the steroid use of sprinter Ben Johnson, which cost him an Olympic gold medal, to the deadly cocaine experimentation of basketball star Len Bias, the ultimately deadly lifelong alcohol abuse of baseball legend Mickey Mantle, and the doping of Soviet bloc Olympic athletes (Nixon and Frey, 1996: 116–20). The NFLPA survey revealed that former players used a variety of drugs, including novocaine, cortisone, anti-inflammatories, amphetamines, caffeine tablets, alcohol, steroids, marijuana and cocaine, to cope with injuries or to enhance performance. Nearly 10 per cent of the players said they did not know what drugs they were taking. The sources of prescription drugs for more than half of the players were the team doctor and trainer (Hewitt, 1993b). Former NFL team physician Robert Huizenga speculated about the linking of the use of steroids and other performance-enhancing drugs to chronic injuries and disability on the basis of his first-hand observations inside the locker room (Huizenga, 1994; Smith, 1994). The dilemma for athletes in responding to team or peer pressure to use drugs is that they lack the medical expertise to question a doctor's judgment, they are discouraged from seeking medical opinions not authorized by the team physician, and their judgment is often colored by the intense desire or perceived need to get back on the field (Huizenga, 1994).

CHILDREN, YOUTHS, INJURIES AND DISABILITY

Serious injuries and disabilities are not confined to athletes at the university, elite amateur and professional levels of sport. For example, it has been estimated that approximately 25 per cent of the 8 million participants in secondary and high school sports programs in the US experience some kind of injury (National Institutes of Health, 1992: 3). Government support for efforts to reduce the incidence and severity of injuries in scholastic sports programs has been motivated by both the physical and financial costs of these injuries. The costs of personal injury and product liability insurance, for example, have escalated with the increasing incidence of injuries, especially severe injuries. Thus, injuries have become a major factor in athletic budgets in American schools and colleges, and we can assume that this portion of budgets has grown as participation in interscholastic and intercollegiate athletics has grown with the increased number of female participants since legislation prohibiting gender discrimination in school programs was passed in 1972 (Nixon and Frey, 1996: 260). Furthermore, growing interest in sports such as soccer and the attraction of larger and more aggressive athletes to such sports have contributed to increased numbers of injuries. According to the US Consumer Product Safety Commission, in 1994, 1.3 per cent of the 162,115 soccer players treated in hospital emergency rooms had to be admitted to the hospital, and 1.3 per cent of the 425,000 football players given emergency room care had to be hospitalized. The National Electronic Injury Surveillance System of the US Consumer Product Commission also estimated that the number of soccer injuries in the United States increased from nearly 140,000 in 1990 to over 162,000 in 1994, which is nearly a 16 per cent rise. A major cause of soccer injuries, up to 25 per cent, has been field conditions (Birch, 1995). Many knee injuries in indoor soccer have been attributed to the hard artificial turf.

The high injury rates in male contact sports are easy to understand. Perhaps surprisingly, though, a girls' non-contact sport, cross-country running, was found to produce the highest injury rates in a 13-year study (from 1979 to 1992) of 18 high school sports and 60,000 participants in the Seattle area (reported in Bloom, 1993). Approximately one of every three female cross-country runners was injured, with tendinitis of the knee, shin splints, ankle sprains and stress fractures of the

leg the most frequent injuries. Injured runners averaged two injuries per season, and the incidence rate was 61.4 injuries per 100 runners. Boys' cross-country running ranked fifth in injury rates, with a rate approximately two-thirds of the girls' rate. The second-, third- and fourth-ranked sports for injuries were football, wrestling and girls' soccer. Among the factors thought to contribute to the high injury rates for female cross-country runners are the lack of fitness for this sport, which is staged during the later months of the year, after a summer layoff and the pressure to train harder to earn the increased recognition and opportunities for college athletic scholarships that have become available for female athletes. Anatomical and physiological factors also seem to contribute to females' greater susceptibility to certain kinds of injuries, such as stress fractures.

Other studies (for example, Murray, 1992) have shown generally comparable patterns of injuries across sports, with the incidence of injuries for females less than for males due to the smaller number of female participants but with the rates of injury about the same for females and males in high school sports. The main injury 'agent' has been contact with another person, in about half the cases; and the proportion of injuries in practices and contests has been found to be about the same (Murray, 1992). Relative injury rates in practices and contests vary according to the degree to which practices simulate contests. For example, in wrestling and basketball, practices often closely approximate actual matches or games, while in football, players usually tackle dummies and have limited and less intense physical contact with teammates in practice (Powell, 1992).

It has been estimated by a sports medicine researcher (Requa, 1992) that, on average, approximately one of three high school athletes, or about 2 million athletes, will have at least one time-loss injury during a season. About one-quarter of these injuries is likely to result in a visit to a physician. An estimated 2–3 per cent of these injuries result in hospital visits and 1–2 per cent in hospitalizations. Since injury rates decrease with age, the junior high school rate is likely to be less than the high school rate. Injury rates in youth sports programs outside the school are very difficult to estimate, but one survey of nearly 1,000 adult San Francisco Bay area exercisers involved in more than 100 competitive sports and recreational activities (Alvarado, 1992) indicated that the highest injury rate was sustained by in-line skaters, at 20 per 1,000 hours of activity (20/1,000). The injury rate per 1,000 hours for competitive sports was 16, which was twice the average rate of injuries, with basketball 18, racquetball 14, volleyball 9 and tennis 8. Individual activities, including walking, exercise equipment and bicycling, had fewer total injuries than group activities and sports, 10 per 1,000, but running was an exception, with an injury rate of 16. People with prior injuries were more likely to sustain injuries again than other people were to sustain a first injury, indicating that even in recreational sports, there may be a tendency to downplay the significance of past injuries. Furthermore, although we expect more and more serious injuries to occur at more competitive and intense levels of highly organized sports, a large number of injuries are likely to occur in unsupervised and relatively unorganized physical recreation and sports activities because of the large number of casual participants (Requa, 1992).

US government officials have sought better injury data collection to improve the surveillance system for injuries and facilitate the implementation of measures to reduce injuries. One of the obstacles to establishing effective surveillance systems is the liability issue. Some experts have suggested that better injury data could invite more lawsuits and that data supplied by insurance companies may be unreliable as it could be contaminated by the financial interests of these companies, which is to reduce the amount they must pay for injury claims (National Institutes of Health, 1992: 4). Obtaining accurate injury data has been made problematic in part because of the social factors in sport that make the treatment of injuries difficult, that is, factors such as athletes who hide injuries so that they can continue to play, coaches who encourage athletes to overlook pain and injuries so they continue competing and athletes who exaggerate pain and injuries to avoid workouts.

In developing useful surveillance systems for assessing the rates and effects of sports, it is important to focus on long-term effects. Most studies have concentrated on short-term effects and have overlooked re-injury and long-term effects (Requa, 1992). One study of ankle sprains in 84 young athletes (Smith and Reischl, 1986) revealed that 70 per cent had sustained an ankle sprain, and 80 per cent of those who had been injured had sprains on more than one occasion. At the time of the study, 50 per cent still showed residual symptoms and 17 per cent said they were participating even though their actions were still affected by their injury. It is evident from these results that playing hurt begins with young

athletes and that the foundation for chronic and potentially disabling conditions can begin very early in an athlete's career. Understanding the factors contributing to playing with pain and injuries in childhood and youth should help ameliorate the long-term disabling consequences of sports injuries. Sociologically, an athletic environment that offers encouragement of athletes to talk realistically about their pain and injuries, to seek medical attention when it is needed, and to take an appropriate amount of time for healing and rehabilitation seems especially relevant to the reduction of unnecessary chronic pain and disability from sport. In addition, athletes seem less likely to risk injury when they avoid overtraining, which sport psychologist William Morgan called 'the disease of excellence' (quoted in Phinney, 1988). Perhaps surprisingly, Morgan proposed that recreational bicyclists may be more prone to overtraining than elite riders because recreational cyclists may have more difficulty fitting their rides into their daily schedules and may ride too many miles when they are able to get on their bicycle.

CONCLUSION

The risks of pain and injury cannot be eliminated from sport, especially at the higher levels of sport that are implicitly structured to produce pain and injury through highly intense and often combative competition. Yet unless the authority of sports medicine practitioners is independent of coaches, owners and other sports management personnel, the welfare of athletes will be unnecessarily at risk. Furthermore, unless the rules of sport are constructed and enforced to eliminate excessively violent or risky actions, athletes will risk severe and chronic pain, injury and disability every time they step on the field of play. When athletes are driven by the Sport Ethic, sports authorities, or their personal motives to overtrain or play hurt, they will put themselves at risk of serious and continuing pain, injury and disability. Sports officials who fail to address the physical safety and well-being of athletes or who put athletes at risk by irresponsibility or incompetence are likely to find themselves in court as targets of lawsuits, especially in the United States. Thus, future research should focus not only on collecting better medical data about pain, injury and disability in sport. It also should examine the cultural and social conditions of sport that contribute to high rates of pain, injury and disability production; the reactions of athletes to the consequences of acute and chronic pain, injury and disability; the attentiveness of sports officials to pain, injury and disability in sport; and the role of legislators, public officials and the courts in making sport safer.

For athletes considered able-bodied, chronic disability typically portends or represents the end of their athletic career. For other athletes with permanent disabilities, who are labeled disabled persons, sports careers are pursued despite the disability or in competitions where disability is minimized or adaptations are made for it. The contrasting meanings of disability in conventional sport and in disabled sport reflect the different ways that physical abilities are seen and interpreted in relation to sports performance in different sports settings. Two of the most striking developments in sport since the mid-1970s have been the increasing involvement and levels of performance of people with permanent disabilities. A major issue today regarding the involvement of disabled people in sport is how or whether they should be integrated (Hoffer, 1995). A variety of models of segregated and integrated sports involvement for disabled athletes exist today, reflecting to some extent the different abilities and goals of these athletes. The effectiveness of these different sports models in meeting the needs of disabled athletes with different abilities and goals should be a focus of future research. This research should also explore the conditions under which rules, practices and facilities can make different sports more accessible to people with disabilities and more compatible for integrated competition involving both disabled and able-bodied athletes. Although the Special Olympics model has positive benefits for participants, we must be mindful of the desire of many highly skilled and ambitious disabled athletes to achieve the attention, respect and money that able-bodied athletes often risk their bodies to earn (Hoffer, 1995).

NOTES

1 Sargent Shriver cited this research (conducted at Yale and Texas Tech Universities) in his capacity as Chairman and CEO of the Special Olympics International of Washington, DC. His wife, Eunice Kennedy Shriver, founded the Special Olympics.
2 The International Olympic Committee has permitted the participation of disabled athletes in demonstration and exhibition sports, including downhill skiing by amputee skiers in 1984 and 1988, two wheelchair races in 1984, and a modified giant slalom for amputee skiers and a cross-country race for blind skiers in 1988 (Labanowich, 1988: 269).
3 Results from this research have been summarized in Nixon and Frey (1996: 104–6).

REFERENCES

Alvarado, D. (1992) 'Skating means injuries, survey says', *The Charlotte Observer*, 8 June, p. 3E.

Becker, D. (1988) 'Disabled college center plays beyond blindness', *USA Today*, 17 February, p. 2c.

Birch, D. (1995) 'Soccer's growing pains', *The Baltimore Sun*, 10 October, pp. 1D, 7D.

Bloom, M. (1993) 'Girls' cross-country taking a heavy toll, study shows', *New York Times*, 4 December, pp. 1, 34.

Brandmeyer, G.A. and McBee, G.F. (1986) 'Social status and athletic competition for the disabled athlete: the case of wheelchair road-racing', in C. Sherrill (ed.), *Sport and Disabled Athletes*. Champaign, IL: Human Kinetics. pp. 181–7.

Brasile, F.M. (1989) 'Participation motivation among wheelchair athletes', *Dissertation Abstracts International*, 49: 2806A (University Microfilms No. 8823084).

Brasile, F.M. (1990) 'Wheelchair sports: a new perspective on integration', *Adapted Physical Activity Quarterly*, 7: 3–11.

Breo, D. (1992) 'The sure Super Bowl bet – injured players are penalized for life', *JAILMA*, 267: 706–7.

Brody, R. (1992) 'The price of playing', *Sport*, July, pp. 66–70.

Buell, C. (1986) 'Blind athletes successfully compete against able-bodied opponents', in C. Sherrill (ed.), *Sport and Disabled Athletes*. Champaign, IL: Human Kinetics. pp. 217–23.

Coakley, Jay J. (1994) *Sport in Society: Issues and Controversies*. St Louis: Mosby.

Cook, K. (1987) 'A fighter who will be heard from', *Sports Illustrated*, 16 November, pp. 95–7.

Cook, T.L. (1995) 'Top ten myths of the Paralympics [on-line]', *The Atlanta Journal-Constitution*. http://www.ajc.com/oly/gzzto p 10.htm

Cordellos, H. (1981) *Breaking Through: the Autobiography of the World's Greatest Blind Athlete*. Mountain View, CA: Anderson World.

Curry, T.J. (1991) 'A little pain never hurt anybody: "Positive deviance" and the meaning of sport injury'. Paper presented at the North American Society for the Sociology of Sport annual meeting, November, Milwaukee, WI.

Curry, T.J. and Strauss, R.H. (1994) 'A little pain never hurt anybody: a photo-essay on the normalization of sport injuries', *Sociology of Sport Journal*, 11: 195–208.

Dukes, J.T., Dunson, B., Harper, R., Heffron, T.M., Milly, J., Turner, R. and Usher, J. (1995a) 'The history of the Paralympics [on-line]', Grady College of Journalism of the University of Georgia. http://www.grady.uga.edu/megalabinc/paralympics/history.html

Dukes, J.T., Dunson, B., Harper, R., Heffron, T.M., Milly, J., Turner, R. and Usher, J. (1995b) 'Paralympic fact sheet [on-line]', Grady College of Journalism of the University of Georgia. http://www.grady.uga.edu/Paralympics/Fact Sheet.html

Dukes, J.T., Dunson, B., Harper, R., Heffron, T.M., Milly, J., Turner, R. and Usher, J. (1995c) 'The classification of athletes [on-line]', Grady College of Journalism of the University of Georgia. http://www.grady.uga.edu/megalabinc/paralympics/home.html

Edwards, H. (1973) *Sociology of Sport.* Homewood, IL: Dorsey.

Ewald, K. and Jiobu, R.M. (1985) 'Explaining positive deviance: Becker's model and the case of runners and bodybuilders', *Sociology of Sport Journal*, 2 (2): 144–56.

Frager, R. (1995) 'The "overrated" dangers of injuries playing football', *The Baltimore Sun*, 12 November, p. 8D.

Gran-Net Communications. (1995) 'Special Olympics Massachusetts [on-line]', http://www.gran-net.com/olympics/mso_home.htm

Hahn, H. (1984) 'Sports and the political movement of disabled persons: examining nondisabled social values', *Arena Review*, 8 (1): 1–15.

Hamel, R. (1992) 'Getting into the game: new opportunities for athletes with disabilities', *The Physician and Sportsmedicine*, 20: 121ff.

Hewitt, B. (1993a) 'A game of pain', *Chicago Sun Times*, 19 September, pp. 17B–20B.

Hewitt, B. (1993b) 'Playing at any cost', *Chicago Sun Times*, 20 September, pp. 92–3.

Hewitt, B. (1993c) 'Through the tears', *Chicago Sun Times*, 21 September, pp. 83–5.

Hewitt, B. (1993d) 'Opposing views', *Chicago Sun Times*, 22 September, pp. 98–9.

Hewitt, B. (1993e) 'Pension benefits good, but they could be better', *Chicago Sun Times*, 23 September, pp. 97, 99.

Hoffer, R. (1995) 'Ready, willing and able', *Sports Illustrated*, 14 August, pp. 64–76.

Hughes, R. and Coakley, J. (1991) 'Positive deviance among athletes: the implications of overconformity to the Sport Ethic', *Sociology of Sport Journal*, 8 (4): 307–25.

Huizenga, R. (1994) *You're okay, it's just a bruise'.* New York: St Martin's Griffin.

Iole, K. (1988) 'Life after death has 25-year-old on the run', *Burlington (VT) Free Press*, 7 July, pp. 1A, Back Page.

Keteyian, A. (1985) 'Spotlight: when Willie Brown is on the court, action speaks louder than words', *Sports Illustrated*, 4 March, n.p.

Kleiber, D.A. and Brock, S.C. (1992) 'The effect of career-ending injuries on the subsequent well-being of elite college athletes', *Sociology of Sport Journal*, 9 (1): 70–5.

Kotarba, J.A. (1983) *Chronic Pain: Its Social Dimensions.* Beverly Hills, CA: Sage.

Labanowich, S. (1979) 'The psychology of wheelchair sports', *Therapeutic Recreation*, 12: 11–17.

Labanowich, S. (1988) 'A case for the integration of the disabled into the Olympic Games', *Adapted Physical Activity Quarterly*, 5: 264–72.

Lindstrom, H. (1992) 'Integration of sports for athletes with disabilities into sport programmes for able-bodied athletes', *Palaestra*, 8: 28–32, 58–9.

Ludovise, B. (1988) 'She's finding her way', *Los Angeles Times*, 15 February, p. 4.

Messner, M.A. (1990) 'When bodies are weapons: masculinity and violence in sport', *International Review for the Sociology of Sport*, 25: 203–20.

Munson, L. (1991) 'Main event: the scrap heap', *The National Daily*, 1–3 March, pp. 30–4.

Murray, D.G. (1992) 'High school injury surveillance systems', in National Institutes of Health (ed.), *Conference on Sports Injuries in Youth: Surveillance Strategies Proceedings.* Bethesda, MD: National Institutes of Health. NIH Publication N. 93–3444. pp. 39–47.

Nagler, Mark (1993) *Perspectives on Disability*, 2nd edn. Palo Alto, CA: Health Markets Research.

National Institutes of Health (1992) *Conference on Sports Injuries in Youth: Surveillance Strategies: Executive Summary.* Bethesda, MD: NIH Publication No. 93–3444.

Nixon, H.L. II (1984a) 'Handicapism and sport: new directions for sport sociology research', in N. Theberge and P. Donnelly (eds), *Sport and the Sociological Imagination.* Fort Worth, TX: Texas Christian University Press. pp. 162–76.

Nixon, H.L. II (1984b) 'The creation of appropriate integration opportunities in sport for disabled people: a guide for research and action', *Sociology of Sport Journal*, 1 (2): 184–92.

Nixon, H.L. II (1989) 'Integration of disabled people in mainstream sports: case study of a partially sighted child', *Adapted Physical Activity Quarterly*, 6: 17–31.

Nixon, H.L. II (1991) *Mainstreaming and the American Dream: Sociological Perspectives on Parental Coping with Blind and Visually Impaired Children.* New York: American Foundation for the Blind.

Nixon, H.L. II (1992) 'A social network analysis of influences on athletes to play with pain and injuries', *Journal of Sport and Social Issues*, 16: 127–35.

Nixon, H.L. II (1993a) 'Accepting the risks of pain and injury in sport: mediated cultural influences on playing hurt', *Sociology of Sport Journal*, 10 (2): 183–96.

Nixon, H.L. II (1993b) 'Cultural beliefs, status factors, and vulnerability to pain and injuries in sport'. Paper presented at the American Sociological Association annual meeting, Miami, FL.

Nixon, H.L. II (1994a) 'Mainstream sports integration of people with disabilities: a case study of the effects of visual impairment', in M.Sc. Sociology of Sport and Sports Management (by distance learning). Module 3, Unit 5, Part 13. University of Leicester, UK: Centre for Research into Sport and Society. pp. 109–32.

Nixon, H.L. II (1994b) 'Social pressure, social support, and help seeking for pain and injuries in college sports networks', *Journal of Sport and Social Issues*, 18: 340–55.

Nixon, H.L. II (1996a) 'The relationship of friendship networks, sports experiences, and gender to expressed pain thresholds', *Sociology of Sport Journal*, 13 (1): 78–86.

Nixon, H.L. II (1996b) 'Explaining pain and injury attitudes and experiences in sport in terms of gender, race, and sports status factors', *Journal of Sport and Social Issues*, 20 (in press).

Nixon, H.L. II and Frey, J.H. (1996) *A Sociology of Sport*. Belmont, CA: Wadsworth.

Nocera, J. (1995) 'Bitter medicine', *Sports Illustrated*, 6 November, pp. 74–88.

Orelove, F.P. and Moon, M.S. (1984) 'The Special Olympics program: effects on retarded persons and society', *Arena Review*, 8 (1): 41–5.

Orelove, F.P., Wehman, P. and Wood, J. (1982) 'An evaluative review of Special Olympics: implications for community integration', *Education and Training of the Mentally Retarded*, 17: 325–9.

Paciorek, M.J., Tetreault, P. and Jones, J. (1991) 'The integration of athletes with disabilities into amateur athletics: the 1991 US Olympic Festival', *Palaestra*, 8: 30–3.

Phinney, C.C. (1988) 'Overtraining: the disease of excellence', *Bicycling*, 54 (August): 57–8.

Powell, J.W. (1992) 'National Athletic Trainers' Association high school study', in National Institutes of Health (ed.), *Conference on Sports Injuries in Youth: Surveillance Strategies Proceedings*. Bethesda, MD: National Institutes of Health. NIH Publication N. 93-3444. pp. 49–57.

Requa, R.K. (1992) 'The scope of the problem: the impact of sports-related injuries', in National Institutes of Health (ed.), *Conference on Sports Injuries in Youth: Surveillance Strategies Proceedings*. Bethesda, MD: National Institutes of Health. NIH Publication N. 93-3444. pp. 19–24.

Sabo, D.F. (1986) 'Pigskin, patriarchy, and pain', *Changing Men: Issues in Gender, Sex, and Politics*, 16: 24–5.

Sherrill, C. (ed.) (1986) *Sport and Disabled Athletes*. Champaign, IL: Human Kinetics.

Shriver, S. (1995/1996) 'Guide to giving', *US News & World Report*, 25 December/1 January, Letters section.

Smith, R.W. and Reischl, S.F. (1986) 'Treatment of ankle sprains in young athletes', *American Journal of Sports Medicine*, 14: 465–71.

Smith, S. (1994) 'High cost of glory', *Sports Illustrated*, 14 November, pp. 156–61.

Songster, T.B. (1986) 'The Special Olympics Sport Program: an international sport program for mentally retarded athletes', in C. Sherrill (ed.), *Sport and Disabled Athletes*. Champaign, IL: Human Kinetics. pp. 73–9.

Stebbins, R.A. (1987) *Canadian Football: the View from the Helmet*. London, ON: Centre for the Social and Humanistic Studies of the University of Western Ontario.

Stroman, D.F. (1982) *The Awakening Minorities: the Physically Handicapped*. Washington, DC: University Press of America.

Stroman, D.F. (1989) *Mental Retardation in Social Context*. Washington, DC: University Press of America.

Sullivan, T. and Gill, D. (1975) *If You Could See What I Hear*. New York: Signet.

Theberge, N. (1993) 'Injury, pain and "playing rough" in women's hockey'. Paper presented at the North American Society for the Sociology of Sport annual meeting, November, Ottawa, Ontario, Canada.

Walk, S. (1994) 'Peers in pain: the experiences of student athletic trainers'. Paper presented at the North American Society for the Sociology of Sport annual meeting, November, Savannah, GA.

West, J. (1994) *Federal Implementation of the Americans with Disabilities Act, 1991–1994*. New York: Milbank Memorial Fund.

Whiteside, K. (1992) 'A lock on success', *Sports Illustrated*, 24 February, pp. 6–7.

Whitman, J. (1995) 'History of Special Olympics [online]', http://aces211.acenet.auburn.edu/so/history.htm

Young, K. (1989) 'Seeing and believing', *Sports Illustrated*, 6 March, p. 82.

Young, K. and White, P. (1995) 'Sport, physical danger, and injury: the experiences of elite women athletes', *Journal of Sport and Social Issues*, 19: 45–61.

Young, K., White, P. and McTeer, W. (1994) 'Body talk: male athletes reflect on sport, injury, and pain', *Sociology of Sport Journal*, 11 (2): 175–94.

28

BODY STUDIES IN THE SOCIOLOGY OF SPORT: A REVIEW OF THE FIELD

Cheryl L. Cole

The conversations accompanying the current surge of work in body studies tend to cast the historical relationship of the body and sociology in terms of absence or neglect. Efforts to explain that exclusion have turned to themes variously related to the mind–body dualism and its manifestation in academic divisions of labor (cf. Franklin, 1996; Hargreaves, 1987; Turner, 1984; Waldby, 1997). The well rehearsed and commonly accepted diagnosis – summarized by Loy, Andrews and Rinehart (1993) as the 'non-body bias of sociology in general and sport sociology in particular' – leads, somewhat predictably, to calls for 'embodying' or bringing the body back into sociology and the sociology of sport. Although 'body studies' and a distinctive sub-area called 'sociology of the body' are recent developments, the coordinates of exclusion ('absence' and 'imperative embodiment'), at least by my view, misconstrue the historical appearance of the body in sociology, including the sociology of sport. Indeed, Loy et al. hint at the ambiguity and confusion embedded in the 'non-body bias' claim by identifying the 're-discovery of the early writings of Norbert Elias' and the 're-reading of essays by Erving Goffman' as indispensable to the development of the contemporary intellectual body enterprise (1993: 71).

These prominent narratives of neglect present two interdependent problems: they effectively locate scholars as agents of intervention and thereby encourage the displacement of the historical affinities between the body and sociological themes. My purpose in drawing attention to the limitations of this past–present logic is not to advocate a 'presentist' reading of classical sociological texts. Instead, I mean to draw attention to the historical specificity of *perception* – which is to say that, where, when and how bodies appear and how they are perceived are intimately bound to historically specific dynamics and pressures. To some (perhaps, even a great) extent, contemporary concern with the body has been shaped by medical and health crises, particularly AIDS, new reproductive technologies, epidemics of addiction and genetic engineering, in a context marked by the general privatization of health and citizenship. These historical and culturally specific events foster anxieties and contribute to wide-ranging political contests organizing and organized around various bodies. Moreover, these dynamics and events challenge apparently clear-cut distinctions between self and other, give rise to disputes around traditional forms of authority and knowledge, and destabilize modern foundations.

Emily Martin (1992) articulates and affirms the thesis of the historical specificity of bodily appearance when she proposes that contemporary interest in the body is inextricably bound to economic and technological transformations. Martin, like the scholars I review below in the 'modern bodies and modern sport' section, views one of 'Fordism's' primary effects to be the organization of the collective nature of bodies.[1] That is, factory-based production and corporate capitalism, which created new demands for a new kind of worker, enabled and were enabled by new forms of discipline permeating sexuality, reproduction, family life, leisure and consumption. Recalling Lévi-Strauss's (1967) proclamation that phenomena become the object of acute analysis precisely when they are ending, Martin argues that the newly invigorated academic body industry is an expression and effect of the transformation from Fordism to post-Fordism. Drawing on David Harvey's (1989) characterization of post-Fordism, she describes contemporary conditions in terms of just-in-time production, constant innovation, accelerated labor processes, requisite deskilling and reskilling, time–space compression, and the continual flow of capitalism across borders. These late-twentieth-century characteristics of production and consumption, by Martin's view, reconfigure and produce a contradictory bodily formation rooted in 'the ability to respond to constant change in the environment and the nature and kind of work one does in a context of widespread fear of mortal loss of employment, status, housing, and health' (1992: 129).

Moreover, theoretical resources are like technologies delineating the body's appearance. Works inspired by feminism, Foucault, Bourdieu, de Certeau and Deleuze exemplify mutually reinforcing ways of thinking and lines of inquiry shaping contemporary body studies. Feminism, perhaps more than other theoretical developments, has stimulated far-ranging debates as it has shaped sociology's and sport studies' self-consciousness about the body. While early feminist work tends to cast body issues in familiar terms of repressive power, a self-authorial-self contained within the body (that is, the liberal individual), and liberation aimed at throwing off repression in the name of self-sufficiency and will, more recent feminist criticism builds on Foucauldian interventions in traditional ways of thinking about power. Indeed Foucault's conceptualizations of the normalization of power and the power of normalization have been central to advancing arguments about the body. (Andrews, 1993, Rail and Harvey, 1995, and Theberge, 1991 provide strong overviews of Foucault's application to sport-body studies. Defrance, 1995, Laberge, 1995, and Shilling, 1993 provide provocative analyses of Bourdieu's theoretical influence on body–sport studies.) Despite prominent theoretical directives to examine everyday operations of power and the body, to investigate relationships among power, bodily practices, gestures, motions, habits, styles and location, and the body politic, what it means to study the body and sport, to subject the body–sport relationship to the analytic gaze, remains far from settled.

In this chapter, I discuss the broad, diverse and theoretically incongruent investigations of the body and sport. Given the rapid growth of body studies, the review I offer is neither definitive nor comprehensive; instead, my aim is to introduce some of the most productive trends in body studies. My approach to this literature is generally thematic and is organized around three (despite the wide continuum of possibilities) primary, but interdependent, corporeal manifestations: the modern sporting body; deviant/transgressive bodies; and commodified bodies. Because the body–sport coupling is deeply enmeshed in modern beliefs and dynamics (see Andrews, Chapter 7 of this volume), I begin by reviewing literature that contemplates the relations among bodies, sport and modernity. In the second section, I examine research on deviant and transgressive bodies, emphasizing those investigations that challenge commonsensical or more familiar formulations of deviance and violence. I conclude by surveying the research on commodified, spectacular fit and athletic bodies, the sort of desires and practices such bodies incite, and their extension into the political realm. The final section directs attention to the potent force of mass produced and commodified bodily images.

SPORTING BODIES AND MODERN PROCESSES

Scholarship whose fundamental concern is modern processes and practices, sport and the body tends to address a wide range of questions related to the stabilization of modern state formation, industrialization, urbanization, colonialization and normalization. It draws attention to the place of sport and the modern athletic body in securing 'our' sense of 'selves' as particular kinds of individuals, people and nations; it investigates the implication of science and technology in the production of modern sporting bodies – including multiple expressions of the normal and abnormal; and, it examines how modern moral discourses and corporeal norms are implicated in producing responses of fascination and horror to various athletic bodies. The overview of the historical sociological examinations of sport, bodies and the modern state and contemporary investigations of modern science and sporting bodies provides a useful background, as well as multiple possibilities, for making sense of various corporeal expressions discussed throughout this chapter.

Modern Bodies and Modern Sport

The role of sport in the modern project of producing desirable and normalized bodies is examined by Dunning (1993), Dunning and Sheard (1979), Gruneau (1993), Gruneau and Whitson (1993), Hargreaves (1986, 1987), Harvey and Sparks (1991), Kimmel (1990) and Messner (1992). In general, they investigate the various ways in which sporting practices, within a context defined by the values and dynamics of modernity, are indissolubly connected to what might be called the 'somatization of social stratification'. That is, they seek to understand how sport, as a physical activity, is related to observable bodily movements and postures embedded in the social order and bodily competencies associated with the needs defined by capitalism.

In an exceptionally suggestive essay, Harvey and Sparks (1991) contend that adequate accounts of modern sport and the body must address 'fundamental questions about the political status of the body and the processes of politicization of the body … the political ends the body serves and the political means used to secure those ends' (p. 164). To this end, and following Defrance (1987), Holt (1981, 1982) and Rosanvallon (1990), Harvey and Sparks examine the development of nineteenth-century French gymnastics. By locating gymnastics in this context, they show how bodily practices, like gymnastics, were shaped by concrete and practical struggles to unify the nation, secure state authority and force, and manage a society of individuals. Initially, gymnastics was banned as a practice that potentially undermined the state's struggle for authority and its active production of citizens; that is, gymnastics was banned because it potentially endowed bodies, particularly working-class bodies, with capacities at odds with the state, while providing a space to promote republican ideology. But, Harvey and Sparks show how the state's position on gymnastics changed when external threats made clear the state's needs for physically fit and obedient military bodies. Inspired by gymnastics' capacity to enhance national goals, the state sanctioned and expanded military gymnastics to schools and public fairs. Gymnastics, according to Harvey and Sparks, became part of a disciplinary regime – a pedagogical instrument – for encoding and enacting a sense of individual and collective duty and responsibility.

A collective body of sociological literature examines athleticism in English public schools and bodily production. Hargreaves (1987) considers sport as a technology of the gentleman's body; Dunning and Sheard (1979) examine the civilized body; and Gruneau (1993) and Hargreaves (1987) discuss the effects of sport and the worker's body. As Hargreaves, among others, notes, athletics were a means of expanding the authoritative gaze of non-school work activities to the 'soul' of the students; they were bodily and emotional practices constitutive of the gentleman's body. These practices, Hargreaves explains, were never 'simply' about the cultivation of proper values, gait and posture. Instead, the cultivation of the bourgeois sporting body was a means of marking bodily differences which delineated and rationalized hierarchies of privilege. Moreover, by Hargreaves's view, these bodily activities were vital to the cultivation of an English self and all that entailed: the bodies produced were positioned as naturally superior to internal subordinate groups such as the working class and women as well as to Continental foreigners and the external colonialized in the context of empire.

Gruneau (1993) and Hargreaves (1987) describe the political effects of asymmetrical bodily resources and bodily practices by examining the distinction between team sport (an instrument for confirming class superiority) and physical exercise and rationalized sport (deployed as technologies to produce new and respectable workers' bodies). While Gruneau and Hargreaves both identify military and national efficiency as central concerns shaping disciplinary bodily practices, Gruneau privileges the concrete struggle around sport's early association with spectacle, vice and moral depravity. He discusses how the ideologies of civilizing amateurism and health were used to inflect sport with moral and economic utility; that is, he examines how ways of thinking about sporting practices were reshaped through modern metanarratives, particularly those directed at the body. As Gruneau states clearly, 'The objective in all this was not just the pursuit of better sporting performances, it was to participate in a certain kind of culture and live life in a certain way' (p. 90). The division between rationalized physical activity, a positive force invested in social improvement and the production of bodies capable of performing the tasks required in industrial societies (Gruneau, 1993; Hargreaves, 1987; Kimmell, 1990) and other sport forms associated with unruly practices, 'valueless diversionary spectacle', and hedonistic distractions like idleness, gambling, drink and violence (Gruneau, 1993: 86; Hargreaves, 1986, 1987), established moral parameters which fragmented the working class. For Gruneau, it is telling that even sport defined through civilizing amateurism, muscular Christianity and healthy bodies was easily subject to commercialization.

While Kimmel (1990) builds on premises similar to those discussed above, he pursues the making of white middle-class masculine bodies in and through modern sport. Most specifically, he stresses the relationship between the crisis of masculinity in late nineteenth-century America, sport as a bodily practice, and the characteristics of modernity. For Kimmel, the changes associated with modernism, the erosion of traditional foundations, women's gains, the increasing number of immigrants in urban–industrial areas, fear of effeminacy associated with urban areas (its visible homo-sexual subculture) and loss of economic and workplace autonomy, played a large part in the crisis of masculinity. Modern sport, particularly baseball, was a practice used to contain and relieve anxieties associated with white middle-class masculine insecurities. Kimmel is quick to note that sport did not simply relieve anxieties nor simply bolster white middle-class identities, but functioned as a disciplinary apparatus that instilled submission to authority, bodily ideals and the values of the work-place.

In fairness, I need to say that although the above research acknowledges antagonisms and resistances generated through the bodily practices associated with modern sport, I have stressed the prominent dynamics (in order to clarify them) discussed by these scholars. Yet, it is curious that while all recognize sport as a disciplinary domain, and recognize the relation between sporting practices, bodily posture and deportment, and social hierarchy, none systematically interrogates the *interdependency* of corporeal identities.[2] This notion of inter-dependency is key to much of the work (particularly post-structuralist) on the body. Moreover, while the research reviewed implies the position of modern science in sport (through categories such as hygiene, social improvement and allusions to the coupling of the machine and the body), modern science is not a central concern. Science, the production of corporeal identities and their interdependency are more explicit objects of analysis in the next section and throughout the chapter.

Modern Sport, Science and the Body

Although a rapidly developing area of body studies, science studies is 'just' beginning to influence the body–sport literature. In this section, I discuss the literature related to

science studies that is useful for understanding the body–sport relationship. I divide this work into two categories based on the larger problems that direct their research: those studies concerned with the negative effects of scientific interventions into natural human bodies and those that presume that scientific productions of the natural body are expressions and effects of modern power. It is the second project that offers the most potential for guiding studies of the body–sport relation.

John Hoberman is author of two of the few book-length studies (*Mortal Engines and Darwin's Athletes*) which interrogate scientized athletic bodies. Here, I focus on *Mortal Engines* (1992) because in it Hoberman traces what he calls the unknown story of scientific sport. In his routing of history, he divides the science–sport relation into two moments distinguished by the science–body relation: the age of scientific truth-seeking, which sought to reveal and record; and the Age of Calibration (marked by preoccupation with measurement and transgression of natural limits), which emphasized science's capacity to enhance performance. Hoberman characterizes the early science–sport relation as dominated by a mode of perception and optical techniques aimed at revealing and clarifying natural laws of the body. This 'pre-modern science', Hoberman suggests, includes the anthropology of racial biologies which questioned the relationships between intelligence and physical attributes, civilized and savaged bodies; the work of Brown-Sequard (the forerunner of modern endocrinology) which considered the biological and regenerative significance of testicular abstracts; physiologist and inventor Etienne-Jules Marey's photography which rendered movement visible in ways not accessible to the human eye; Galton's eugenics; and Taylor's fatigue research. Hoberman's concern is with those sciences that most enthusiastically interrogated sport performances. Most specifically, Hoberman is interested in the manifestation of scientized corporeal violences of the self: the mutant identities developed through high-performance sport. 'Human identity' (which is Hoberman's self-defined concern) is breached when the source of performance is other than the original self or the exercise of that self, as it would be with the hidden hand of science and prosthetics. By Hoberman's view, scientized sport is dangerous and pathological to the extent that it calls into question or violates human identity.

Whereas Hoberman (1992) presumes neutral and universal categories of the human and self that are then pressed upon by science, much of the social study of science and sport examines the implication of modern science in the production of bodies, boundaries and truths which it claims to simply reveal. Cecile Lindsay (1996) concretizes the historical development of seemingly ahistorical categories by drawing attention to scientific attempts to order bodies at the turn of the century. She argues that the display, and popularity of such displays, of unnameable and anomalous bodies (for example, freak shows) were a response to scientific observation, classification and ranking of bodies. She explains the fascination with extraordinarily strong and muscled bodies:

> Although a number of important studies have demonstrated the establishment of restrictive cultural norms (particularly gender roles and appearance) at about this time, it also seems clear that the era of the freak show was in some ways more receptive to the transgression of such classificatory categories than twentieth-century culture has become. For although Gould and Pyle [authors of *Anomalies and Curiosities of Medicine*] considered Eugen Sandow's muscular development to be anomalous enough to merit photographic plates in their work, they also praise his beauty and grace. ... At a time when the conventional distinctions and categories by which we have come to order existence were crystallizing, a measure of 'play' still existed within and between classes of beings. (p. 360)

Rony (1992) examines the documentation of bodily movement of ethnographic subjects through the chronophotographe, a device invented by physiologist Etienne Jules-Marey to record serial movement (a device crucial to time–motion studies and the development of capitalist workers). Her investigation of the visualization of bodily movement and its implication in the taxonomic ranking of peoples clarifies the broader political implications of posture and movement which legitimated modern sport practices, discussed by Dunning and Sheard (1979), Gruneau (1993), and Hargreaves (1987). Most specifically, Rony examines the films made of West African bodies by French physician Felix-Louis Regnault (who believed that film was the ideal scientific medium to study race because film would capture 'the raced body' as it was revealed through movement). Her work suggests more than scientific bias; it suggests that science is inseparable from narratives of evolution governing in the films. As Rony points out, the representation of the savage through movement was simultaneously a means of identifying Westerners as the civilized and normal and of teaching Westerners how to read bodies and bodily movement for signs of the primitive and savage.

The role of science in the production of the natural body in sport and through exercise has been discussed by Cole (1998), Cole and Orlie (1995), Derrida (1993), Franklin (1996), Hausmann (1995), Sedgwick (1992) and Urla and Swedland (1995). In outlining the paradoxical dimensions of modern sport, Franklin (1996) focuses on the contradictions made apparent through appeals to the natural. She compares, for example, the contradictory logic of 'the natural' guiding the deployment of steroids and sport and new reproductive technologies. In the discourse of new reproductive technologies, the natural body is preserved through the use of steroids, while in sport-drug discourses, prohibitions of steroids are implemented in the name of preserving the natural body. Along similar lines, Derrida (1993) and Sedgwick (1992) address the problematic modern logic of absolutes that distinguish sport/exercise (the embodiment of free will) from drugs/addiction (the embodiment of insufficient free will). Derrida does so by foregrounding the discourse of 'drugs' and the concept's historical and cultural inscriptions and its moral-ethico valuation. Derrida argues that the scientific policing of chemical prosthetics in sport denies and persistently elides the body's technological condition; he complicates the practice of drug-tracking by challenging which substances are – and are not – labelled drugs; and, finally, he argues that sport is a drug – intoxicating and depoliticizing. Sedgwick considers the invention of the exercise addict, which she views as the limit-case of addiction because the object of addiction is replaced by the self (the self addicted to the self), as an expression of the crisis of modern logic – its outmoded absolutes of the organic body, free will and the natural. For Sedgwick, steroid-man (the cyborg), not the organic body, is a sign of our contemporary cultural condition. For both, scientific attempts to visualize interior spaces of purity and authentic performances, exemplified in sport domains, are efforts to conserve conceptual oppositions that no longer hold in late modernity.

Susan Birrell and I (1990) examine the case of male-to-female transsexual Renee Richards to investigate fissures and disruptions in the sex/gender system. Our analysis acknowledges how such fissures and disruptions are incorporated under the sign of the 'natural' through the scientific category of gender dysphoria and technologies of gender; yet, our focus remains on the media's negotiation of the problems posed by Renee Richards. In short, we suggest the media obscure the historical relationship between women and sport by staging the debate through essentialist and liberal terms. We conclude that these at time correspondent and at times contradictory liberal and essentialist claims represent women through their appearance as suitable objects of masculine pleasure. In *Changing Sex*, an investigation of the historical development of scientific and medical technologies that sustain the medico-legal regulation of transsexuals, Bernice Hausmann (1995) turns to academic analyses of Renee Richards to demonstrate dominant research patterns which emphasize the reproduction of gender to the exclusion of technologies. She draws attention to the Barr body test in order to demonstrate how scientific technologies ascribe values to 'chromosomes as the supposedly undeniable signifiers of sex' (p. 12). In so doing, Hausmann makes the crucial point that 'technology impinges on the constitution of "women" as well as transsexuals' (p. 12). Hausmann's theoretically and empirically rigorous study is an exemplar of post-Foucault (1980a) and post-Laqueur (1990) scholarship: her historical insights into the centrality of scientific technology in the constitution of sex will no doubt help shape body studies as it advances through science studies of sport.[3]

Most obviously, Hausmann's argument is related to academic investigations of sex-testing technologies in high-performance sport. Although these examinations have provoked much public debate and remain an ongoing source of controversy, the Barr body and other 'gender verification' tests have received only limited attention by academics. Jennifer Hargreaves (1994) situates her examination of gender verification within a larger narration of the historical discrimination faced by women since the beginning of the modern Olympic Games. By her view, sex testing is yet another symptom of the more general backlash directed at women in the Olympics. Although she offers numerous criticisms of the procedures, her criticisms coalesce in what she identifies as the public and private indignities suffered by the women subjected to the various technical practices.

Hood-Williams (1995) approaches gender verification by considering the limits of the analytical construct of gender deployed in feminist work on gender verification. By his view, the feminist distinction between sex and gender conceals the discursive construction of

sex. Ultimately he endorses an ahistorical constructionist position which erases the materiality, the historical, cultural and structural formation of sex, and limits our understanding of the relations among sex and other identities. M. Ann Hall's (1996) comments regarding sex testing demonstrate how universal constructs erase historical understanding of the body and categories grounded in nature. While trying to avoid the power relations implicated in one category (woman), Hall argues for a continuum of sex, suggesting that the two-sex system itself is a defiance of nature. This argument, appealing as it seems, positions the body outside of history, and actively participates in the elision of power relations by invoking the liberal notion of personhood. Much important criticism has been directed at the notion of personhood as it has been invoked to replace women (for example, Brown, 1996; Gatens, 1996; Pateman, 1988) and as it has been produced by science.

My own work on gender verification (Cole, 1995) is based on the assumption that universal categories like sex accrue meanings in particular contexts. Therefore, I argue that to understand the political significance of 'sex tests' we need to radically contextualize our object of study. For example, my research examines 'sex tests' in the context of Cold War America: it attempts to unravel the mass media's presentation of Soviet athletes, particularly in terms of how they differ from American athletes. In this case, I show how the bodies of Soviet athletes were *made* to appear different and deviant and, specifically, how they were made to represent the anti-democratic body and 'creations of a filthy workshop'. The deviant female Soviet athlete was one of these creations. Such makings (through photography and narrative) show how the Soviet body served as a phantasmatic space on which anxieties, speculations and fantasies were projected in order to imagine the American body, the operation of power in America, and the body's implication in democracy. In the context of the Cold War, scientific probes for sex in high-profile sport, I argue, cannot be separated from popular constructions of democratic and communist bodies. Sex testing brings together numerous dynamics woven throughout this section. It is deployed to render visible suspected deviance in ways that establish the normal and desirable: it is implicated in the production of national identity, a sense of self, and even who counts as human. Indeed, much of the research on normalization of feminine bodies bridges work on science, sport and bodies in the realm of the popular.[4] The deviant body, the necessary other of the normal, is interrogated in the next section.

EMBODIED DEVIANCE AND SPORT

The modern dynamics of identity (normal/abnormal) discussed previously help us make sense of what otherwise might be the puzzling regular appearance of non-normative bodies in a domain ostensibly dedicated to universal humanity and bodily perfection. Indeed, in the sporting realm, images of immoral and/or evil bodies are not atypical but are routinely conjured up through a proliferation of categories and images related to the aberrant, abject, anomalous, corrupt, criminal, cyborg, grotesque, hybrid, monstrous, queer, subversive, unruly and violent (Halberstam, 1995). Such bodies appear controversial and threatening; they are represented as social problems which, in particular moments and cases, unsettle familiar models of humanness and modern categories of existence. Not surprisingly, science is typically called upon to render visible and treat such bodies. Our understanding of scientific visualizations and inscriptions of embodied normative violations and the possibilities created through these inscriptions is indebted to science studies (for example, Terry and Urla, 1995; Treichler et al., 1998). Scholarship in this area does not in any simple way seek to prove science is sexist nor racist; instead, it attempts to illuminate the levels of mediation that participate in the presentation of 'the Objective' and 'Nature'. The exponential increase in investigations of deviant and exoticized bodies is not just attributable to science studies, but is a response to contemporary conditions, complex shifts in representation and the fascination, as well as the discomfort, such bodies mobilize.

Bodies, Violence and Sport

The diverse and far-ranging literature related to bodies, violence and sport has been shaped by seemingly incompatible psycho-physiological theories (Dunning, 1993). 'Catharsis theory' depicts as integral to the development of modern sport its sanctioned status for channelling otherwise instinctual aggressive, unproductive and criminal drives and desires. The pervasiveness (as well as the implication) of this way of thinking about sport and bodies is demonstrated in contemporary theories of criminal biology, research and public policies. For example, Wilson and Herrnstein (1985) provide evidence of the decidedly racist motives advanced through the articulation of violence, character and bodily appearance. In their words,

> An impulsive person can be taught greater self-control, a low-IQ individual can engage in satisfying learning experiences, and extroverted mesomorphs with slow autonomic nervous system response rates can earn honest money in the National Football League instead of dishonest money robbing banks. (quoted in Dumm, 1993: 103)

Thomas Dumm (1993) clarifies the implications of such ways of thinking in his analysis of the Los Angeles Police Department's abuse of Rodney King.[5] As Dumm explains, such a theory assumes that King was predisposed to violence and responsible for the choice he made: in this case, King's crime was his 'decision' not to play professional football. Wilson and Herrnstein's declaration is an expression of what I identify in my research as a central dynamic governing the national imagination in 1980s America – the sport/gang dyad (Cole, 1996).

In the context of 1980s America, sport, posited as a bodily activity vital to crime control, simultaneously produces and legitimates racial representations of bodily deviance and dangers. These monstrous representations, which signify crime out-of-control, justify increased investment in the police/control industry. Accruing momentum during Reagan's war on drugs, national discourse linked racially coded, bodily sporting practices to social order and utopic possibilities and non-sporting alternatives (appearing most vividly in the figure of the gang), with breakdown of law and order. A crucial effect of this discourse is the sort of violences, particularly those associated with transnational capitalism and its economic reorganization like those noted by Martin earlier, that it obscures (Cole, 1996). Jay Coakley (1997) and Toby Miller (1997) offer insightful discussions of the need to rethink our common-sense image of violence as simply acts performed by particular bodies. Coakley and Miller both call for attending to violences that are not so easily imagined. We begin to understand why it is difficult to think about and see violence in other ways – in less embodied forms – when we consider the dynamics of modern logic and the categories of act/identity (what/who) governing the national imagination.

Related to the representation of dystopic and violent bodies is the belief, as described by

Dunning, 'that we are living today in one of the most violent periods in history. A not insignificant part of this belief consists in the widespread feeling that violence is currently increasing in, and in conjunction with, sports' (1993: 39). The violences associated with sport, particularly those associated with masculine display, have been investigated by Messner (1992) and Gruneau and Whitson (1993). Such research documents not only the bodily violence directed at others but the sorts of violence enacted on one's own body (Connell, 2000; Kimmell, 1990; Messner, 1992). Gruneau and Whitson (1993) also discuss the aggressive masculine physicality of hockey as a requisite practice for deflecting aggressive behaviors of others. Moreover, they suggest that economic class is intertwined with and shapes ideal masculine physiques, notions of appropriate strength and expressions of force. The complex relationship among social location, bodily ideals, expressions of strength and force, is elaborated in work influenced by Bourdieu (see, for example, Bourdieu, 1986) and, most prominently by Loic Wacquant's ethnographic studies of boxing.

By examining 'the pugilistic point of view,' Wacquant (1995, 1998a) strives to disrupt tropes of violence that reduce boxing to an excessively brutal and uncivilized activity and its practitioners as naturally predisposed to violence. Multiple and inter-related dimensions shape the pugilistic point of view. Boxers view their practice as a highly skilled bodily craft distinct from street violence; as a skill compelling sophisticated technical and tactical know-how; and as a career which enables earning a living. Physical excellence in the ring is understood to be a display of character; evidence of hard work and discipline; a sign of overall moral excellence and commitment; and a means to otherwise elusive symbolic capital. In this sense, boxing, for its practitioners, is a vehicle for ontological transcendence – a practice and form through which fighters can fashion themselves into new beings who transcend social determinations. Wacquant neatly summarizes his point:

> to outsiders it stands as the penultimate form of dispossession and dependency, a vicious and debasing form of submission to external constraints and material necessity. For fighters, boxing represents the possibility of carving out a margin of autonomy from their oppressive circumstances and for expressing their ability to seize their own fate and remake it in accordance with their inner wishes'. (1995: 501)

In short, then, a pugilist is not simply a 'doer' but the 'doing' ('doing' refers to the acts associated with corporeal acquisitions) affectively manifest in 'self'. Wacquant (1998a, 1998b) summarizes the moral conduct proper to professional boxers through the category of 'sacrifice'. Sacrifice is defined in terms of a series of relations: a relation in which one gives over body and soul to the sport and the reorganization of series of relationships of self and others and self to self.

In his research on the intense practices fighters engage in (that is, labor on the body) to convert bodily into pugilistic capital, Wacquant draws attention to the numerous knowledges and skills accrued by fighters. Among those skills is the capacity to 'read' bodies – the ability to instantaneously assess opponents' bodies, to locate vulnerabilities, in order to determine strategies that should be deployed. Questions related to 'reading' and 'recognizing' bodies (as mentioned explicitly by Rony [discussed previously] and implied in many of the investigations reviewed herein) continually surface in body studies and constitute crucial dimensions of the investigations of bodybuilding, particularly female bodybuilders which I discuss below.

Bodybuilding and the Un/Making of the Natural Order

Abject bodies, those which unsettle conventional couplings and distinctions related to sex, raise compelling questions.[6] In so doing, they create occasions to examine typically concealed operations of power as they render visible the contests that maintain proper boundaries. Scholarship on abject and abnormal bodies builds on theories that undermine the illusory autonomy of bodies and identities as bodily property (the self-contained self) and investigate the dynamics that enact, encode and enable these illusions (dynamics associated with classificatory systems, threat, containment, resistance, moral codes, self/other identities, and social order). Although this scholarship shares a critique of universal and absolute categories foundational to modern ontological claims, critical interpretations of such disruptions and claims about their subversive implications depend upon the theoretical perspectives (particularly the conceptualization of power) underlying the analysis.

Although recognizably normal bodies are bound up in bodybuilding practices (Feher, 1987), my focus in this section is on scholarship concerned with public competitive bodybuilding culture, a culture that explicitly seeks to produce and display physiques wilfully transformed in terms of size, shape, definition and tone (Linder, 1995). Given the immense amount of research concerned with the relationship between sport and representations of women's bodies as foundationally weak or defeminized and masculinized, it is no coincidence that the hypermuscular female bodybuilder, a vivid illustration of disturbances or boundary breaches, has been taken up as an object of study across disciplines. Numerous investigations trace the range of practices and techniques of production of the female bodybuilder as well as the possibilities that she holds for destabilizing the heteronormative equation of body, sex, gender and sexuality:[7] lines of inquiry have been dispersed around a wide-ranging set of issues related to consumption and capitalism; transformation, resistance and empowerment; recuperation or normalization of the threats posed by the muscular female; complex stigmatizing processes; identification and desire; and the performativity of gender.[8]

Bolin (1992a, 1992b) and Mansfield and McGinn (1993) investigate the tensions generated through bodybuilding's promise of agency and empowerment. They contend that bodily transformations among women bodybuilders are powerfully enabled and constrained by beauty culture. By Bolin's view, a racially regulated beauty culture mediates and governs women's bodybuilding experiences as it complicates (and produces inconsistent) judging and shapes the ideal that practitioners seek to approximate. Bodybuilding culture, again by Bolin's view, is gendered in ways which contain deviations associated with masculinizing effects in order to maintain the female body as an object of male desire. Mansfield and McGinn (1993) similarly conclude that beauty conventions 'make safe' bodybuilding for social, cultural and economic consumption; but they draw attention to the maintenance of the feminine through a masquerade akin to the hyperbolic feminine codes adopted in drag.

Drag, performance and shock are central themes organizing the analyses of women and bodybuilding. Kuhn (1988) and Schulze (1990) call attention to the performative dimensions of gender arguing that, in women's bodybuilding, it is muscle (rather than hyperbolic feminine codes) which functions as drag: 'while muscles can be assumed, like clothing, women's assumption of muscles implies a transgression of the proper boundaries of sexual difference' (p. 17). Patton (2001) points to the irony of dressing up women bodybuilders in order to erotize them and make

them appear like the girl next door. 'The girl next door with muscles,' Patton writes, 'looks so much like the presumably male models who populate ads for transsexual phone lines in both heterosexual male and gay male sex magazines that one wonders how heterosexuality can survive its own gender construction' (p. 12) Haber (1996) examines the recuperation of the bodies of female bodybuilders, particularly those who remain proximate to consumer culture. She maintains that the bodies of women bodybuilders hold more subversive potential than the other female athletic bodies because of bodybuilders' elevated ability to disturb phallocratic ways of seeing. By Haber's view, subversion is an effect of 'shock' produced by a radically altered aesthetic code that makes spectators aware of the artificiality of sexuality, sex and gender.

Because the *Pumping Iron* films encapsulate the contradictions and questions animated by bodybuilding, they are key objects of social criticism.[9] In *Pumping Iron II: The Women,* the visible struggle over the line demarcating the normal and deviant woman bodybuilder is represented by a contest between the feminine Rachel McLish and muscular, mannish Bev Francis (Balsamo, 1996). Robson and Zalcock (1995) examine 'radical elements of reading gender' by focusing on Francis's unruly and deviant female body. By their view, the film's emphasis on 'gender trespass' demands that the audience reconsider what it is to be a woman.

Holmlund (1989) compares and contrasts the narrative structures of the two *Pumping Iron* films. She contends that, although apparently parallel, the narratives are driven by asymmetrical questions: *Pumping Iron* is primarily concerned with who will win, while *Pumping Iron II* is fundamentally concerned with visualizing sexual difference. Indeed, Robson and Zalcock argue that the questions of 'Who will win?' and 'Who should win?' are indissolubly paired through the filmic narrative and simultaneously undermine any sense of a dispassionate selection of the winner. That is, by their view, the typically concealed mechanisms that fix heteronormative femininity are rendered visible by the film. Viewing the film, according to Robson and Zalcock, requires witnessing the reconstruction of the female body in ways that erase its reproductive signs. Given this, they conclude that the abject bodybuilder violates not only the biological but the social program.

In their analyses of *Pumping Iron II*, Kuhn (1988) and Balsamo (1996) consider the interceding position of Carla Dunlap, the only African American competitor and winner of the contest. Kuhn contends that Dunlap's position as mediator signifies the film's failure to resolve the conundrum of the female bodybuilder. Balsamo, however, suggests that Dunlap's position clarifies the interarticulation of racial and sexual difference. As sexual difference is less easily seen, Balsamo argues, attention is directed to seeing racial difference. Questions of visible sexual difference are fundamental to those investigations informed by psychoanalysis. In these studies, the emphasis clearly shifts from the effects of the sport on the female body to masculine desire, the politics of looking at masculine and feminine bodies, and the psychic dynamics produced by the masculine, muscular female.

Patton (2001) suggests that the partial erasure of differences between men's and women's bodybuilding (comparable contest procedures and musculature) is reinscribed through judging 'metastandards'. These metastandards draw on conventions of sport and spectacle to govern pleasure and looking at bodies. The pleasure associated with sport is governed by objective ideals through which bodily performances are judged (through knowledges reducing the body to an effect of judging) and identification with particular players; the pleasure associated with the spectacular is achieved through the simple act of viewing the body. Based on this distinction, Patton offers an explanation for the inconsistent judging noted by other researchers. The vacillation between sport and spectacle in women's bodybuilding is an effect of the recognition of the sexual dimension of judging – a dimension repressed in male bodybuilding. Similarly, Pelligrini (1997) contends that in male bodybuilding same-sex identification is foregrounded while same-sex desire is pushed to the background. As Patton (2001) explains, 'the erotic pleasure derived from viewing women athletes makes visible the possibility of the male viewer's pleasure (homosexual desire) in viewing male athletes'; thus, the vacillation between spectacle and sport functions to contain and relieve male spectatorial crisis. Schulze (1990) agrees that 'the danger to male heterosexuality lurks in the implication that any male sexual interests in the muscular female body is not heterosexual at all, but homosexual: not only is *she* 'unnatural,' but the female body builder has the power to invert *male* sexuality' (p. 40).

Questions of desire and deviant bodies, of course, exceed competitive body bodybuilding and sexuality. For instance, in his article 'The desire to punish,' William Connolly (1995) asks about the multiple codes of desires circulating through us: specifically, Connolly is concerned with the conditions of the desire to punish, the ways in which desire is embedded in revenge, and the desire for particular identifications and bodies. Questions of desire – desire's multiple and far-reaching forms – are central to the investigations of celebrity bodies which follow.

Celebrity, Bodies and Deviance

Reeves and Campbell (1994) suggest that sport, like Hollywood, functions as a 'chronotope' (a term borrowed from Bakhtin (1981) to explain the narrative relevance of setting). Sport, like Hollywood, evokes magical transformations, individual triumphs, boundless opportunity and exhilarating freedom. These utopic themes are visualized through the bodies of the Hollywood or sport star. Given this, disruption to ideal embodiment – the result of a star's participation in some event or act which challenges the ideal – results in scandal. In this section, I review research that examines the bodies of sport celebrities and scandal, drawing attention to ways in which these studies consider the political dimension of representations of corporeal deviance.

Several studies have examined how Leonard Bias (an African American basketball player who died from cocaine-related causes within 48 hours after being drafted to play for the Boston Celtics) was made into a central figure in Reagan's war on drugs. Indeed, Reeves and Campbell (1994) claim that Bias was positioned as 'the chief transgressor of the cocaine narrative' and functioned to elevate fear of black males and to justify enactment of repressive policies (1994: 67, see also Baum, 1996). They examine the media's coverage of Bias's death through the sequential stages of 'social drama' (breach, crisis, address and separation). In addition to demonstrating the symbolic capital of the racially coded athletic body, they show how each stage of social drama necessitated and produced visible embodiments. By their view, these visualizations worked to locate and contain deviance in the bodies of others, to identify threat and justify interventions at bodily levels.

Research on Magic Johnson's public announcement that he tested positive for HIV antibodies, like that by Reeves and Campbell, underscores the media's active production of corporeal deviance. Rowe (1994) defines the Magic Johnson crisis in terms of a 'robust sporting body acquiring the virus' and investigates how contradictory meanings and the potential unmaking of celebrity were managed. King (1993) considers how popular conjectures about 'mode of transmission' (associated with moral depravity and perversion) challenged the specific meanings that a sports hero's body must carry to maintain commercial value. By Rowe's account, Johnson's appeal and marketability were jeopardized because the virus potentially reinstated the requisite displacement of hierarchies of difference (racial difference and the burden of racist stereotypes of bodily sexual excess). Studies of the Johnson-AIDS media coverage demonstrate how 'the family' performed a double function by temporizing Johnson's deviance and making the bodies of women (groupies) bearers of infection of both athletes and family (Cole and Denny, 1994; Crimp, 1993; King, 1993; Rowe, 1994). Cole and Denny (1994) show how the prominent narrative around Johnson worked through a logic of containment to visualize threat, infection and criminality on the bodies of African American professional athletes and the more general African American community.

Samantha King (2000) builds on and contributes to these insights, particularly those concerned with the deviant body and the body politic, in her detailed examination of *Skate the Dream*, a Canadian AIDS fundraiser held in 1992 to pay tribute to Canadian skater Brian McCall. As King points out, while McCall's AIDS-related death would appear to raise anxieties about stigmatized sexualities (given the continual maintenance of the non-normative masculinity crucial to figure skating's high national profile and commercial success, see Adams, 1993), *Skate the Dream* is, most explicitly, a public display of compassion and kindness. King's project considers how the encoding and enactment of heteronormative codes (and corresponding performances of compassion and kindness) function to secure Canadian identity and citizenry. She shows how identification with heteronormative figures makes this illusion possible by erasing Canada's internal struggles and historical responses to AIDS. The analysis also raises questions about the political implications of the representations of the body of the child-citizen (a primary means of representing McCall) and the dead body.

Mechanisms for visualizing deviance in and through the body, a central feature of modern power, are made evident in analyses on media coverage of O.J. Simpson. Several scholars have discussed the ways in which 'the unimaginable' was made 'imaginable'. Of particular interest is the 27 July 1994 cover of *Time* 'featuring a

"photo-illustration" of O.J. Simpson's mug shot that darkened his skin, blurred his features, and thickened the stubble on his chin' (Gubar, 1997: 169). Gubar intimates the encoding and enactment of two tragedies: domestic violence, allegedly culminating in the murders of Nicole Brown Simpson and Ronald Goldman; and the historical racial violence against black men. In the latter case, Gubar directs attention to the interplay of 'blackface' and character assassination. 'Blacken the man, *Time* magazine implies, and you simultaneously drain him of his moral discernment while accentuating his physicality, thus intensifying brawn even as you criminalize it' (p. 169). The bodily – racial and athletic – performances which fostered Simpson's popularity and profitability are discussed in various ways in Morrison and Lacour's (1997) *Birth of a Nation'Hood*. Popularity, profitability and the modern dynamics of corporeal subjectivity are foregrounded in the remainder of the chapter.

SPORTING BODIES AND CONSUMER CULTURE

As suggested above, the imperatives of industrial capitalism, including the development of science, shaped the relations among modern power, sport and body. In this section, I review research that concentrates on and seeks to provide insight into another dimension of industrial capitalism – the growth of consumer culture. Most specifically, I review those studies that advance our understanding of the dynamics that govern desire, ways of seeing bodies, and those that, in general, direct the relations among sport, bodies and consumer culture. The questions raised and addressed by the research reviewed in this section bring together the multiple dynamics and issues previously raised throughout this chapter (particularly those concerned with the somatization of social stratification and our sense of self as it is made over and against those marked as deviant).

Modern Bodies, Sport and Consumption

Boscagli (1996), Featherstone (1982), Gruneau (1993), Hargreaves (1987), Lears (1989) and Mrozek (1989) describe and problematize the privileged position of the early modern sporting body in advertising. Each argues, in different ways, that the durability and cultural strength of the bodily aesthetic generated at the intersection of sport and consumer culture cannot be understood in purely economic terms. Rather than reducing the commercialized sporting body to a means of consumer expansion, each explores various dimensions of the social and political in order to more fully explain the capacity of the sporting body in securing consumers. Gruneau (1993) profiles the sporting body as a sign of happiness, success, health and youthful masculine vitality in advertising, the narrowing boundaries of the healthy body and the stress on social improvement in the context of early industrial capitalism. As Gruneau shows, the values associated with and displayed in 'civilized sport' are not sealed off from advertising. Instead, the values are appropriated by advertising in ways that have facilitated the anxieties and aspirations mobilized through the bodily codifications associated with civilized sport and have constituted larger markets based around emergent forms of social distinction. In general, Gruneau's project can be characterized as a study of the pedagogic function of the sporting figure in advertising and its relation to a new way of being in the modern world.

Lears (1989), like Gruneau, acknowledges the relationship between the sporting body in advertising and the elevated preoccupation with health, self-improvement and cleanliness which accompanied early modern industrialization. However, Lears is more interested in the connection between the iconography of the athletic body in advertising and wide-ranging racial relations. He underscores the ways in which racial ideals embedded in colonial relations were expressed through the body and associated products. Moreover, he shows how the multiple meanings engendered by the ideal body are deeply embedded in comparative categories like nature/culture and civilization/barbarism. Lears also draws attention to the connections among athletic ideals, advertising, fears of immigrants, threats to bodily boundaries and beliefs in scientific progress. In sum, he shows how capitalism and colonial knowledges intersect to shape bodily practices and consumer behavior.

John Hargreaves (1987) provides the most explicit discussion of modern strategies of power in the context of sporting advertisements. Building on Foucault, he invokes discipline as a meta-concept to explain the general dynamic which informs the relations sport, consumer culture, the mobilization of desire, and consumption. In short, he argues that the desires generated through such advertisements stimulate 'individuals' to enthusiastically discipline themselves in ways that endorse 'the modern, "normal" individual' (p. 141). That is, he conceptualizes commercialized among sport and fitness and the consumption of products as normalizing practices of the self. At the same time he invokes discipline as a meta-concept, Hargreaves underscores the importance of context in understanding how particular values and identities are mobilized through commercialized fitness industries.

Boscagli (1996) considers Eugen Sandow, the most famous of Edwardian bodybuilders, to examine the reformulation of masculine physiques, ways of thinking about bodybuilding and modern consumer culture. On one level, she explains this developmental phase of bodybuilding in terms of the zoo's invention. The zoo, a space in which wildness and nature are strategically displayed, was a product (a space for looking and consumption) of the 'rationalization of urban space and modern culture of consumption' (1996: 102). Just as mechanization reduced the use value of animals, mechanization along with Taylorism decreased the use value of the body and the cultural authority of masculinity: bodybuilding, then, served as a monumentalization of the masculine body. Boscagli adds another dimension to her explanation by building on the Nietzchean notion of 'beast of prey'. She uses Nietzche's concept to imagine 'kitsch spectacles of eroticized masculinity' and the forms of consumption they incite. (Kitsch, in this case, is a category of representation that refers to an imitation in excess, aligned with ornamentation.) Finally, she points to the use of photography by Sandow to incite consumer participation in commercialized fitness practices and to promote the sales of other products (for example, cigarettes and beer). The profitability of Sandow's athletic clubs, the popularity of the training tools he devised, his best-selling handbooks, and his position as a physical trainer of kings and queens, serve as evidence of the marketability of knowledge and expertise of the body. Along related lines, Mrozek (1989) examines Barnarr McFadden's and Charles Atlas's promotion of commercial physical culture. Mrozek argues that the shift from conversion ('the banishment of the physical sin of muscular weakness') through moral reflection or spiritual conviction to conversion through work on the body is crucial to understanding the profitability of their ventures. This theme is paralleled by Lears' history of sport, self and consumer culture.

Featherstone (1982) extends Boscagli's (1996) recognition of the role of communication technology in the commercialization of bodily practices. While Boscagli emphasized the use of photography by Sandow, the use of photography in the development of sports-cards and the emerging cult of the sports celebrity, Featherstone illuminates the pivotal position of the new media, particularly Hollywood cinema, in the normalization and commodification of the body. He addresses the relevance of higher wages and the reorganization of space and display in the commodification of the body; yet, he continually returns to the media's pedagogic role, its reshaping of consciousness in terms of emotional vulnerability, and the self-scrutinizing encouraged by media representations of the ideal (the fit and sporting) body. Featherstone also highlights the heightened importance of the celebrity in media representations of the ideal and the contemporary politics of fitness. The theme of celebrity bodies and the present-day fitness industry is discussed in the next section.

Celebrity Bodies and the Fitness Industry

The contemporary crisis of health care and its corresponding images of public health have been mediated through the category of 'lifestyle'. Ingham (1985) characterizes the contemporary politics of lifestyle as a manifestation of the post-Fordist crisis of the welfare state. The category of 'lifestyle', as Ingham explains, is a contemporary arrangement in which individuals are increasingly held accountable for their bodily conditions. By his view, the rhetorical conflation of individuals, unhealthy bodies and blame displaces broader social and political issues. Indeed, various scholars have identified this period as one governed by rhetoric of risk, independence and self-sufficiency. Kroker and Kroker (1987) call it 'Body McCarthyism'; Singer (1989) discusses it as 'the new sobriety'; and Wagner (1997) calls it the New Temperance. While Ingham (1985) focuses on these dynamics in the context of the US, Peterson (1997) examines these shifts in the Australia context. Research by Bunton (1997), Nettleton (1997) and Stacey (1997) consider the relations between popular knowledges and national and individual preoccupations with healthy bodies and lifestyle in the UK. Most specifically, Bunton and Nettleton highlight the interplay between the categories of risk and individual responsibility (for managing that risk) which shape

knowledges and governance of the self. Glassner (1989, 2001) sees the increasing emphasis on fitness activities in the US as a tactic to manage the increasing contingency and instability which characterize the postmodern era. For Ingham (1985), the escalating concern with 'the fit body' as a sign of a healthy and productive citizenry is indissolubly tied to the ways in which social problems and dependency are translated into individual and characterological deficiencies.

According to Susan Jeffords (1994), 'America's' concern with reinvigorating its economy during the 1980s is prominently expressed in hard, muscular male bodies, particularly film-celebrity bodies like Sylvester Stallone. Ewen (1988), Howell (1990, 1991), Jeffords (1994) and Willis (1991) concentrate on the mass circulation of images of fit, hard bodies in ways that echo Jeffords's general argument. Ehrenreich (1990) and Sedgwick (1992) highlight the hard body's inverse by interrogating expressions of dependency and the logic of addiction during the 1980s. The interdependence of fitness and addiction is discussed in terms of free will and discipline and insufficient free will and threat by Sedgwick (1992), Wagner (1997) and Cole (1998). All of the above work on hypermuscular celebrity bodies shows how such bodies are more than simple heuristic tools to imagine the healthy body politic: hypermuscular celebrity bodies are representations implicated in everyday associations of order and disorder. That is, these studies concentrate on the hypermuscular celebrity body as a sign of individual and national well-being, embedded in values which shape what and who count as other and a threat to the nation: embodiments of characterological failure defined through addiction, dependency and economic poverty.

Ewen (1988), Feuer (1995) and Howell (1990, 1991) explore 'trickledown' versions of the ideal, hard, masculine body which fueled the fitness industry by examining the links among consumer culture, individualism, yuppie lifestyle and the fit body. Advertisements which showed images of fit and hard bodies as well as fitness clubs, according to Ewen, were fundamental to 'the middle-class bodily rhetoric of the 1980s. Such advertisements, taken together, represent a culture in which self-absorbed careerism, conspicuous consumption and a conception of self as an object of competitive display have fused to become the preponderant symbols of achievement' (1988: 194). Willis (1991) draws a similar conclusion in her work on the spatial governance of contemporary women's fitness practices. By her view, the workout, which she identifies as perhaps 'the most highly evolved commodity form yet to appear in late twentieth-century consumer capitalism,' promotes bodily rivalry and depoliticizes and isolates women (1991: 69).

The constitution of the new (1980s) yuppie fitness consumer is most explicitly elaborated by Howell (1990, 1991) in his examination of Nike. Howell shows how Nike built on and contributed to discourses which targeted Baby Boomers. Most specifically, he highlights the link between 1960s artifacts, bodily aesthetics, possessive individualism and consumer fitness in the discourses associated with Nike. By Howell's view, the working-out yuppie is a symptom of a 'consumerist definition of the quality of life' that 'encompasses a self-preservationist conception of the body' (1991: 266, 267). Moreover, Howell explains the interplay between the fit body, political claims and related notions of character, morality and responsibility:

> Individuals are encouraged to adopt instrumental strategies to biologically better themselves so as to avoid deterioration. ... Such strategies are politically encouraged and applauded by state bureaucracies who seek to reduce health costs by educating the public against bodily neglect ... The 'lean-machine' lifestyle of self-betterment gives the individual a sense of pleasure, freedom, success, mobility, and self-esteem. (p. 267)

Although cinema celebrities like Douglas Fairbanks and Mary Pickford have been potent forces in the commodification of fitness (Featherstone, 1982), scholars argue that the celebrity body is elevated to new levels in 1980s and 1990s workout cultures. Indeed, multiple analyses of the articulation of self, agency and body facilitated through contemporary fitness culture (including popular feminism) have evaluated the pivotal position of celebrity (Bordo, 1991; Cole and Hribar, 1995; Radner, 1995; Urla and Swedlund, 1995). Indeed, Radner argues that *Jane Fonda's Workout Book* represents 'an exemplary moment in which exercise ... becomes a central discourse of feminine culture' (1995: 145). Radner argues that 'doing Jane' (an abbreviation meant to capture the relation among the celebrity sign Fonda, fitness practices, consumerism and nationalism) is a symptom of a reconfigured American femininity which offers women a model of agency and self-mastery directed at bodily appearance. Her reference to Fonda as 'Citizen Jane' offers much potential for new contributions to this literature; however, she offers a notion of contemporary feminine citizenship which

depends upon a somewhat problematic assumption about the declining importance of reproduction in defining women's bodies.

Hribar (1995, 1996) builds on and contributes to the analysis of celebrity, the marketing of transformations and self-mastery, and fitness culture. For example, she examines the discursive effects of the representations of Susan Powters's transformations as they are promoted under her signature 'Stop the Insanity' (through seminars, infomercials and books). In order to do so, Hribar contextualizes Powters's celebrity in a contemporary therapeutic culture dominated by self-help and New Age movements. Building on Wicke's thesis that '[t]he celebrity zone is the public sphere where feminism is ... now in most active cultural play' (1994: 757), Cole and Hribar (1995) highlight the relationship between Nike's celebrity status and women's fitness. Most specifically, they are concerned with the ways of thinking that relationship encourages. Most recently, Hribar (1997) has considered the elaborate discourse of corporeal transformation 'substantiated' by talk show host Oprah Winfrey and its relationship to the constitution of ethical subjects. By drawing attention to work on the self in terms of the ethical subject, Hribar is attempting to use Foucault's later writings (which remain relatively unexplored in sport studies) which redirect questions about subjectivity and power.[10]

Late Capitalism's Transcendent Celebrity Bodies

Just as the previously discussed work on celebrity scandal and celebrities and fitness illustrates how celebrity bodies are implicated in historically specific fields of gender, class and race relations, investigations of the ideal sports celebrity seek to show the ways in which representations of celebrity, including the celebrity body, are socially and politically motivated. Because ideal sport celebrities are habitually represented through bodily performances which defy historical forces and location, much of the work on ideal celebrities seeks to provide a 'thick description' of the historical and political conditions of possibility which 'make' celebrity and celebrity bodies. Here, I review research which considers the historical and political meanings and values associated with 'Michael Jordan', perhaps the most recognizable celebrity body-image in the world. These investigations consider the complex and multidimensional forces behind the

African American male body, contemporary capitalism and Jordan.

Michael Dyson (1993) argues that understanding 'the use to which Jordan's body is put as seminal cultural text and ambiguous symbol of fantasy' requires investigating the wide range of influences shaping Jordan's bodily aesthetic's commercial viability and exploitability. Most specifically, he draws attention to the long history of sport in establishing community; the complicated relationship between racialized masculinity, physical prowess and black culture; and the processes of commodification in late capitalism. By Dyson's view, exploring the tension between the ahistorical version of personhood advanced through Jordan and the ubiquitous influence of black culture embodied by Jordan is a productive means of advancing theoretical and empirical understandings of the Jordan phenomenon. Indeed, Dyson foregrounds the encoding and enactment of a black aesthetic as the key distinguishing motif in Jordan's style of play. By black aesthetic, Dyson refers to three elements in Jordan's play: *the will to spontaneity* (improvization); *stylization of the performed self*; and *edifying deception* (Jordan's hang-time which seemingly disrupts the time/space continuum).[11] On one level, Dyson explains the economic and symbolic migrations of the black bodily aesthetic and black cultural creativity – Jordan's commodification – through 'white desires to domesticate and dilute [the black male body's] more ominous and subversive uses' (p. 70). On another level, he addresses the complexity of desires mobilized through Jordan by discussing late capitalism's exploitation of black youth's preoccupation with style and the possibilities of resistance (however minimal) Jordan's visibility might provide to black youth.

Mary McDonald (1996) addresses the uneasy tension between the historical profile of African American men and Jordan's ability to mobilize consumer desire without arousing dread. McDonald's investigation, then, is aligned with Dyson's argument about white desires to domesticate the black male. Key to understanding Jordan, for McDonald, is the notion of the black male body as an 'already read text' and Jordan's ability to comfort consumers. By McDonald's view, consumer comfort is achieved as Jordan is made into an expression of the new right's pro-family agenda. While Jordan appears in the 'already read text' in terms of natural physicality, McDonald shows how his athleticism is given supernatural status through various camera angles and slow-motion replays which

exaggerate (even scientize) Jordan's physical feats. At the same time, she illuminates the multiple practices are deployed to locate Jordan in the new right's normalizing discourse of family values. This discourse has two effects: it distances Jordan from threatening images of a racially coded hypersexuality and it reinforces the notion of the 'failed black family' which is presupposed in the pro-family agenda. (The failed black family is a central element in the discourse which translates inner city poverty and crime into threatening images of black masculinity.) These tensions between Jordan's celebrity and images of threatening African American masculinity is the primary concern of the final two studies I discuss.

In 'American Jordan' (1996), I examine how Jordan's body functions to reproduce an image of 'America' as a compassionate and caring nation in a moment defined by defunding of social welfare programs and punitive resentment directed at urban black youth. It examines why Michael Jordan is such a profitable sign for Nike and prolific image for America by considering what Nike calls its 'P.L.A.Y.' (Participate in the Lives of America's Youth) campaign. P.L.A.Y., which features Michael Jordan as America's hero, is represented as a practical challenge to recent developments that deny 'kids' access to sport activities. Through P.L.A.Y. advertisements, Americans are invited to look at Michael Jordan to see the American mission, way of life, ideals and fantasies of childhood. America's investment in Jordan is made evident when consumers are asked to imagine (through the sport/gang dyad) the dire consequences of an America without Michael Jordan. As Nike and Michael Jordan come to signify the themes of self-made success and 'made in America,' both are made into prominent signs of nation and national interests even as they are invested in and by transnational capital. This study shows how the sport/gang dyad and Jordan are used to advance understandings of urban America's problems that render visible easily recognizable forms of violence and criminality. 'American Jordan' is used as evidence of the transcendent success promised by America while rendering invisible and unrepresentable the violences of the material conditions (inseparable from transnational capital and the erosion of the welfare state) that shape lived experience of already economically vulnerable populations.

Andrews (1995) traces the evolution of Jordan's celebrity in relation to a genealogy of modern racism and its changing tactics (from early modern scientific bases to a cultural racism advanced by moral panics and social science). Jordan's celebrity image, Andrews contends, is not stable or consistent but is bound up in how 'race' is articulated in particular historical moments. Thus, Jordan, like race, is a 'conjuncturally informed, and materially manifest, discursive construct' (1995: 126). Using Jordan as a means to discuss the practices associated with contemporary racism, Andrews identifies four distinct and overlapping stages of Jordan's racial signification. His work suggests that the shift from Jordan's position as an up-and-coming star to his status as an All-American icon was accompanied by a shift in representations. At the representational level, Jordan's physical achievements shifted from evidence of innate skill to evidence of exemplary character. This conflation of (achievement/character) works in tandem with discourses that deny the historical effects of racism. As accusations of gambling addiction surfaced and Jordan's father was murdered, Jordan was cast as another black NBA player whose lifestyle slowed his productivity and who was – in general – suspect. However, in the final stage chronicled by Andrews, we see a series of exchanges of bodily deviance initiated by the arrest of two youths accused of murdering Jordan's father: from Jordan to Daniel Green, alleged killer of James Jordan; Jordan, as the physically absent, but revitalized NBA superstar, taken up as a normalizing figure to demonize the new rank-and-file NBA players; the scrutiny of NBA bodies in search of (deviance/transcendence) the next Jordan. As Andrews summarizes his project, it 'identif[ies] the discursive epidemics that delineate Jordan's evolution as a promotional icon and that act as a marker of American cultural racism which oscillates between patronizing and demonizing representations of African American Otherness' (1995: 153).

In sum, Andrews and the others who have written on Jordan show, albeit in various ways, how the claim of transcendence – the illusory body untouched by historical and political contexts (of which Jordan is the representative *par excellence*) – is itself an element of racial difference and a formative and formidable aspect of Jordan's celebrity. It is in a context where everyday global pressures and forces are so difficult to see that Michael Dyson offers a description of the consumer who 'symbolically reduces Jordan's body to dead meat (McDonald's McJordan hamburger), which can be consumed and expelled as waste' (1993: 70). The depiction, meant to evoke images of bodies that discomfort, asks consumers to think about what is being socially and psychically consumed in a context dominated by transnational trade in bodies.

THE HORIZON OF THE BODY

As I stated in the introduction, I have reviewed only a limited sample of the scholarship on the body which represents a productive direction for sport–body studies. The flood of work that has investigated bodies would seemingly address the concern articulated by Loy, Andrews and Rinehart which I discussed in the opening pages of this chapter. Yet, charges of neglect and criticisms about the absence of the body in scholarly work continue. Pamela Moore (1997) uses the introduction to her recently published collection *Building Bodies* to offer the latest variation of the theme of neglect and imperative embodiment. By Moore's view:

> Despite all this flurry of corporeal fascination, bodies – in the more traditional sense of muscles, nerves, genes, and blood – are strangely absent in contemporary academic discussions. This strain of body studies has reached an impasse. In doing away with biology, it has also done away with the ability to think of corporeality, rather than inscription or construction, in other than essentialist ways. It joins a contemporary abhorrence for aberrant flesh, whether fat bodies or the leaking corpus of AIDS. Abstract thought, social structures, or power are privileged over mundane flesh and blood. Uncomplicated, not an issue for those interested in politics, history, or language, bodies remain as they ever were – natural. Scholars are happier with cyborgs, which exist in the head, than with uncontrollable, resisting, fleshy bodies. Only the steely-eyed ones with their bodies firmly encased in plastic will do. (1997: 1)

How are we to make sense of Moore's observation and prescription?

Moore contends that the genre of body studies is complicit with the historical neglect of the body. By Moore's view, body studies facilitates an exchange of sorts: the body is exchanged and displaced as it is used as a means to think about some other end. In this chapter, the body has been linked to matters ranging from modern power, masculinity, femininity, desire, consumption, national identity, embodied deviance, celebrity and transnational trade in bodies. As Moore would have it, the body should be both means and end: using the body to address other matters, like subjectivity or technology, displaces, yet again, what she takes to be bodily matter – mundane flesh and blood. For Moore, a more advantageous perspective is achieved by focusing on the biological because it maintains the properly bounded object.

I agree with Moore's contention that the study of the biological is crucial. Indeed, the biological is and will continue to be a crucial dimension of body studies. But, its importance is not attributable to its privileged status as or proximity to the real body (which seems to be implied in Moore's quip about the scholarly fashionable cyborg). The biological body to which Moore directs attention is no more stable, bound, objective (in terms of clearly defined), nor grounded than the bodies investigated in the research discussed within this chapter. Whether we focus on the biological, individual bodies, or the body politic (all of which are related), the body is always already invested in a complex network of power which works, in part, by rendering itself invisible. Still, Moore's comments are symptomatic of and raise questions about visualizing bodies and their continual elusiveness. While such anxieties and questions are symptoms of our historical condition, such anxieties and questions will inform and direct body studies for the foreseeable future.

Acknowledgement

I would like to thank Jay Coakley for his generous sharing of ideas and thought-provoking exchanges regarding the body, sport and power.

NOTES

1   I use the term Fordism as it is typically used in sociological literature, to designate a series of organizational and economic strategies associated with mass production and consumption. For an overview of Fordism, see Harvey (1989).

2   By 'interdependency' I mean to draw attention to the way that the modern regime organized itself through a division between the normal and pathological – producing a deviance and threat located in the body (corporeal subjectivity). Interdependency points to the relational dimensions of identity and presumes that identity relies on the periphery to establish its center. Therefore it cannot posit any self-identical ideal upon which it is founded. Foucault names those self–other relations 'dividing practices'. His work recognizes mutual dependence and emphasizes the production of the self's border as a social process of producing and policing the other. For example, the category of free will (partially constitutive of the liberal subject) is dependent upon what it excludes, the compulsive, abnormal and deviant. Later in this chapter I use the term 'dyad' to advance Foucault's notion by weaving together insights from Foucault and Derrida. See Andrews (this volume, Chapter 7) for an outline of Derrida's concerns.

3   While Foucault historicizes the truth of sexuality, Laqueur builds on Foucault's work to historicize what appears to be a natural two-sex system.

4   Urla and Swedland (1995) provide an excellent example of the complex construction of the normative feminine body. Indeed, much of the work on the normalized feminine body could contribute to and benefit from science studies. See, for example, Bartky, 1988; Bolin, 1992b; Bordo, 1988, 1991, 1993; Daniels, 1992; MacNeill, 1994; Markula, 1992, 1995; Whitson, 1994.

5   On 31 March 1991 the brutal beating of an African American man named Rodney King by four members of the Los Angeles Police Department was captured by George Holliday on home video. The 81-second video was shown repeatedly on CNN and NBC and appeared to provide unquestionable evidence of the LAPD's violent assault on King. Despite the evidence, the four officers were acquitted: their acquittal ignited rebellions across Los Angeles. For discussions on how it was possible that the video was interpreted by jurors in ways that made King the aggressor, see Gooding-Williams (1993).

6   Elizabeth Grosz (1992) defines the abject as 'borderline states in which there is confusion and lack of distinction between subject and object' (p. 198). See Kristeva (1982) for the discussion of the abject that has been most influential in contemporary feminist scholarship. Jackie Stacey (1997) also provides a highly accessible discussion of abjection in *Teratologies: A Cultural Study of Cancer* (London and New York: Routledge).

7   The term heteronormative refers to normalizing practices which produce systems and sex and sexuality that appear to be linked and natural. See note 8 and Butler (1990, 1993) for a more in-depth discussion of heteronormativity.

8   Performativity is a term popularized in gender studies by Judith Butler's (1990) *Gender Trouble*. The notion of performativity, as she

clarifies it in *Bodies that Matter* (1993), refers to '"imitation" … at the heart of the heterosexual project and its gender binarisms'. As Butler explains, 'hegemonic heterosexuality is itself a constant and repeated effort to imitate its own idealizations … heterosexual performativity is beset by an anxiety that it can never fully overcome … its efforts to become its own idealizations can never be finally or fully achieved, and … it is consistently haunted by that domain of sexual possibility that must be excluded for heterosexualized gender to produce itself' (p. 125).

9 Although the *Pumping Iron* films were made in the United States, the criticism represented here is not restricted to US scholars.

10 In Foucault's *The Use of Pleasure* he shifts the direction of the questions asked in his middle works (*Discipline and Punish* and *The History of Sexuality*, *Volume I*) regarding knowledge, power and the self. In his last works, he accounts more fully for the self as a relay of power – a self constituted in and productive of power. For helpful discussions of Foucault's later work, see Dumm (1996), Orlie (1997), Ransom (1997) and Simons (1995).

11 Boyd (1997) discusses this bodily aesthetic associated with an altered, nuanced and faster-paced game in terms of improvization, and equates it to 'jazz in its prime' (p. 112). This bodily aesthetic and playing style have been taken up to formulate and visualize popular distinctions between playground and textbook basketball (Boyd) and criminality and intellect.

REFERENCES AND FURTHER READING

Adams, M.L. (1993) 'To be an ordinary hero: male figure skaters and the ideology of gender', in T. Haddock (ed.), *Men and Masculinities: A Critical Anthology*. Toronto: Canadian Scholar's Press. pp. 163–81.

Andrews, D.L. (1993) 'Desperately seeking Michel: Foucault's genealogy, the body, and critical sport sociology', *Sociology of Sport Journal*, 10: 148–67.

Andrews, D.L. (1995) 'The fact(s) of Michael Jordan's blackness: excavating a floating racial signifier', *Sociology of Sports Journal*, 16: 125–58.

Andrews, D.L. (1996) 'Deconstructing Michael Jordan: reconstructing postindustrial America', *Sociology of Sport Journal*, 13: 315–18.

Aycock, A. (1992) 'The confession of the flesh: disciplinary gaze in casual bodybuilding', *Play and Culture*, 5: 338–57.

Bakhtin, M. (1981) *The Dialogic Imagination: Four Essays* (trans. M. Holquist). Austin, TX: University of Texas Press.

Balsamo, A. (1996) *Technologies of the Gendered Body: Reading Cyborg Women*. Durham, NC: Duke University Press.

Bartky, S. (1988) 'Foucault, femininity and the modernization of patriarchal power', in I. Diamond and L. Quinby (eds), *Feminism and Foucault: Reflections on Resistance*. Boston, MA: Northeastern University Press. pp. 61–86.

Baum, D. (1996) *Smoke and Mirrors: the War on Drugs and the Politics of Failure*. Boston, MA: Back Bay Books.

Birrell, S. and Cole, C.L. (1990) 'Double fault: Renee Richards and the construction and naturalization of difference', *Sociology of Sport Journal*, 7: 1–21.

Bolin, A. (1992a) 'Vandalized vanity: feminine physiques betrayed and portrayed', in F.E. Mascia-Lees and P. Sharpe (eds), *Tattoo, Torture, Mutilation, and Adornment*. Albany, NY: State University of New York Press. pp. 79–99.

Bolin, A. (1992b) 'Flex appeal, food, and fat: competitive bodybuilding, gender, and diet', *Play and Culture*, 5: 378–400.

Bordo, S. (1988) 'Anorexia nervosa: psychopathology as the crystallization of culture', in I. Diamond and L. Quinby (eds), *Feminism and Foucault: Reflections on Resistance*. Boston, MA: Northeastern University Press. pp. 87–117.

Bordo, S. (1991) 'Material girl: the effacements of postmodern culture', in L. Goldstein (ed.), *The Female Body: Figures, Styles, Speculations*. Ann Arbor, MI: University of Michigan Press. pp. 106–30.

Bordo, S. (1993) *Unbearable Weight: Feminism, Western Culture and the Body*. Berkeley and Los Angeles: University of California Press.

Boscagli, M. (1996) *Eye on the Flesh: Fashions of Masculinity in the Early Twentieth Century*. Boulder, CO: Westview Press.

Bourdieu, P. (1986) *Distinction: a Social Critique of the Judgement of Taste*. London: Routledge.

Boyd, T. (1997) *Am I Black Enough for You? Popular Culture from the 'Hood and Beyond*. Bloomington and Indianapolis: Indiana University Press.

Brown, W. (1996) *States of Injury: Power and Freedom in Late Modernity*. Princeton, NJ: Princeton University Press.

Brownell, S. (1995) *Training the Body for China: Sports in the Moral Order of the People's Republic*. Chicago: University of Chicago Press.

Bunton, R. (1997) 'Popular health, advanced liberalism, and *Good Housekeeping* magazine', in A. Peterson and R. Bunton (eds), *Foucault: Health and Medicine*. London: Routledge. pp. 223–49.

Butler, J. (1990) *Gender Trouble: Feminism and the Subversion of Identity*. New York: Routledge.

Butler, J. (1993) *Bodies that Matter: On the Discursive Limits of 'Sex'*. New York: Routledge.

Coakley, J. (1994) *Sport and Society: Issues and Controversies*. St Louis: Mosby.

Coakley, J. (1997) 'Controlling deviance and violence through sports: Let's be cautious', Paper presented at a national conference on Sport, Youth, Violence, and the Media, Los Angeles, 3–4 April.

Coakley, J. and Hughes, R. (1991) 'Positive deviance among athletes: the implications of overconformity to the sport ethic', *Sociology of Sport Journal*, 8: 307–27.

Cole, C.L. (1995) 'Imagined communities: sexing the body, sport, and national identity in Cold War America'. Paper presented at the Pacific Sociological Association meetings, San Francisco.

Cole, C.L. (1996) 'American Jordan: P.L.A.Y., consensus, and punishment', *Sociology of Sport Journal*, 13: 366–97.

Cole, C.L. (1998) 'Addiction, exercise, and cyborgs: technologies of deviant bodies', in G. Rail (ed.), *Sport in Postmodern Times*. Albany, NY: State University of New York Press. pp. 261–76.

Cole, C.L. and Andrews, D.L. (1996) 'Look, it's NBA ShowTime!: Visions of race in the popular imaginary', *Cultural Studies: a Research Annual*, 1: 141–81.

Cole, C.L. and Denny, H. (1994) 'Visualizing deviance in (post)Reagan America: Magic Johnson, AIDS, and the promiscuous world of professional sport', *Critical Sociology*, 20: 123–47.

Cole, C.L. and Hribar, A. (1995) 'Celebrity feminism: Nike style (post-Fordism, transcendence, and consumer power)', *Sociology of Sport Journal*, 12: 347–60.

Cole, C.L. and Orlie, M. (1995) 'Hybrid athletes, monstrous addicts, and cyborg natures', *Journal of Sport History*, 22 (2): 228–39.

Connell, R.W. (1987) *Gender and Power*. Stanford, CA: Stanford University Press.

Connell, R.W. (2000) 'I threw it like a girl: some difficulties with male bodies', in C.L. Cole, J.W. Loy and M.A. Messner (eds), *Exercising Power: the Making and Re-making of the Body*. Albany, NY: State University of New York Press.

Connolly, W. (1995) *The Ethos of Pluralization*. Minneapolis: University of Minnesota Press.

Crimp, D. (1993) 'Accommodating Magic', in M. Garber, J. Matlock and R.L. Walkowitz (eds), *Media Spectacles*. New York: Routledge. pp. 255–66.

Daniels, D.B. (1992) 'Gender (body) verification (building)', *Play and Culture*, 5: 370–7.

Davis, L. (1990) 'The articulation of difference: white preoccupation with the question of racially linked genetic differences among athletes', *Sociology of Sport Journal*, 7: 179–87.

Defrance, J. (1987) *L'Excellence corporelle: la formation des activités physiques et sportives modernes 1770–1914*. Rennes, France: Presse Universitaire Rennes.

Defrance, J. (1995) 'The anthropological sociology of Pierre Bourdieu: genesis, concepts, relevance', *Sociology of Sport Journal*, 12: 121–31.

Derrida, J. with Autrement (1993) 'The rhetoric of drugs: an interview', *Differences*, 5: 1–25.

Dumm, T. (1993) 'The new enclosures: racism in the normalized community', in R. Gooding-Williams (ed.), *Reading Rodney King, Reading Urban Uprising*. New York: Routledge. pp. 178–95.

Dumm, T.L. (1996) *Michel Foucault and the Politics of Freedom*. Thousand Oaks, CA: Sage.

Dunning, E. (1993) 'Sport in the civilizing process: aspects of the development of modern sport', in E.G. Dunning, J.A. Maguire and R.E. Pearton (eds), *The Sports Process: a Comparative and Developmental Approach*. Champaign, IL: Human Kinetics. pp. 39–70.

Dunning, E. and Sheard, K. (1979) *Barbarians, Gentlemen and Players: a Sociological Study of the Development of Rugby Football*. Oxford: Martin Robertson.

Dyson, E.M. (1993) *Reflecting Black*. Minneapolis: University of Minnesota Press.

Ehrenreich, B. (1990) *Fear of Falling: the Inner Life of the Middle Class*. New York: Pantheon.

Elias, N. (1978) *The Civilising Process. Volume I: The History of Manners*. Oxford: Basil Blackwell. (Originally published in 1939).

Elias, N. and Dunning, E. (1986) *Quest for Excitement: Sport and Leisure in the Civilizing Process*. Oxford: Basil Blackwell.

Ewen, S. (1988) *All Consuming Images: the Politics of Style in Contemporary Culture*. New York: Basic Books.

Featherstone, M. (1982) 'The body in consumer culture', *Theory, Culture, and Society*, 1: 18–33.

Feher, M. (1987) 'Of bodies and technologies', in H. Foster and DIA Art Foundation (eds), *Discussions in Contemporary Culture*. Seattle, WA: Bay. pp. 159–65.

Feuer, J. (1995) *Seeing Through the Eighties: Television and Reaganism*. Durham, NC: Duke University Press.

Foucault, M. (1979) *Discipline and Punish: the Birth of a Prison* (trans. A. Sheridan). New York: Vintage Books.

Foucault, M. (1980a) *The History of Sexuality, Volume 1* (trans. R. Hurley). New York: Vintage Books.

Foucault, M. (1980b) 'Truth and power', in C. Gordan (ed.), *Power/Knowledge: Selected Interviews and Other Writings, 1972–1977*. New York: Pantheon. pp. 109–33.

Foucault, M. (1980c) 'Two lectures', in C. Gordan (ed.), *Power/Knowledge: Selected Interviews and Other Writings, 1972–1977*. New York: Pantheon. pp. 78–108.

Foucault, M. (1989) 'What calls for punishment?', in S. Lotringer (ed.), *Foucault Live*. New York: Semiotext(e). pp. 280–92.

Franklin, S. (1996) 'Postmodern body techniques: some anthropological considerations on natural and postnatural bodies', *Journal of Sport and Exercise Psychology*, 18: 95–106.

Gatens, M. (1996) *Imaginary Bodies: Ethics, Power and Corporeality*. New York: Routledge.

Gillett, J. and White, P. (1992) 'Male bodybuilding and the reassertion of hegemonic masculinity: a critical feminist perspective', *Play and Culture*, 5: 358–69.

Glassner, B. (1989) 'Fitness and the postmodern self', *Journal of Health and Social Behavior*, 30: 180–91.

Glassner, B. (2001) 'Fitness as postmodern action', in C.L. Cole, J.W. Loy and M.A. Messner (eds), *Exercising Power: the Making and Remaking of the Body*. Albany, NY: State University of New York Press.

Gooding-Williams, R. (ed.) (1993) *Reading Rodney King/Reading Urban Uprising*. New York: Routledge.

Gould, G. and Pyle, W. (1896). *Anomalies and Curiosities of Medicine*. New York: Bell.

Grosz, E. (1992) 'Julia Kristeva', in E. Wright (ed.), *Feminism and Psychoanalysis: a Critical Dictionary*. Oxford: Basil Blackwell. pp. 194–200.

Gruneau, R. (1993) 'The critique of sport in modernity: theorizing power, culture, and the politics of the body' in E.G. Dunning, J.A., Maguire and R.E. Pearton (eds), *The Sports Process: a Comparative and Developmental Approach*. Champaign, IL: Human Kinetics. pp. 85–110.

Gruneau, R. and Whitson, D. (1993) *Hockey Night in Canada: Sport, Identities and Cultural Politics*. Toronto: Garamond Press.

Gubar, S. (1997) *Racechanges: White Skin, Black Face in American Culture*. New York: Oxford University Press.

Haber, H. (1996) 'Foucault pumped: body politics and the muscled woman', in S. Hekman (ed.), *Feminist Interpretations of Michel Foucault*. University Park: Pennsylvania State University Press. pp. 137–58.

Halberstam, J. (1995) *Skin Shows: Gothic Horror and the Technology of Monsters*. Durham, NC: Duke University Press.

Halberstam, J. and Livingstone, I. (eds) (1995) *Posthuman Bodies*. Bloomington, IN: University of Indiana Press.

Hall, M.A. (1996) *Feminism and Sporting Bodies: Essays on Theory and Practice*. Champaign, IL: Human Kinetics.

Haraway, D. (1991) 'A cyborg manifesto: science, technology, and socialist-feminism in the late twentieth-century', in *Simians, Cyborgs, and Women: the Reinvention of Nature*. New York: Routledge.

Hargreaves, J.A. (1994) *Sporting Females: Critical Issues in the History and Sociology of Women's Sports*. London: Routledge.

Hargreaves, J.E. (1986) *Sport, Power and Culture*. New York: St Martin's Press.

Hargreaves, J.E. (1987) 'The body, sport and power relations', in J. Horne, D. Jary and A. Tomlinson (eds), *Sport, Leisure and Social Relations*. London: Routledge & Kegan Paul. pp. 139–59.

Harvey, D. (1989) *The Condition of Postmodernity*. Cambridge, MA and Oxford: Basil Blackwell.

Harvey, J. and Sparks, R. (1991) 'The politics of the body in the context of modernity', *Quest*, 43: 164–89.

Hausmann, B.L. (1995) *Changing Sex: Transsexualism, Technology, and the Idea of Gender*. Durham, NC: Duke University Press.

Hoberman, J. (1992) *Mortal Engines: the Science of Performance and the Dehumanization of Sport*. New York: The Free Press.

Hoberman, J. (1997) *Darwin's Athletes: How Sport has Damaged Black America and Preserved the Myth of Race*. Boston, MA: Houghton Mifflin.

Holmlund, C. (1989) 'Visual difference and flex appeal: the body, sex, sexuality, and race in the Pumping Iron films', *Cinema Journal*, 28: 38–51.

Holt, R. (1981) *Sport and Society in Modern France*. London: Macmillan.

Holt, R. (1982) 'Change and continuity in late 19th century French sport', in *Social History of Nineteenth Century Sport* (Proceedings of the Inaugural Conference of the British Society for Sports History). pp. 1–25.

Hood-Williams, J. (1995) 'Sexing the athletes', *Sociology of Sport Journal*, 12: 290–305.

Howell, J. (1990) 'Meanings go mobile: fitness, health and the quality of life debate in contemporary America'. Unpublished doctoral dissertation, University of Illinois at Urbana-Champaign.

Howell, J. (1991) 'A revolution in motion: advertising, and the politics of nostalgia', *Sociology of Sport Journal*, 8: 258–71.

Hribar, A.S. (1995) 'Scientific movements: bodily knowledges and info-queen Susan Powter'. Paper presented at the annual meetings of the North American Society for the Sociology of Sport (NASSS), Sacramento, November.

Hribar, A.S. (1996) 'Susan Powter: economies of celebrity and fitness'. Paper presented at the annual meetings of the North American Society for the Sociology of Sport (NASSS), Birmingham, November.

Hribar, A.S. (1997) 'Oprah, exercise, and public culture'. Paper presented at the annual meetings of the North American Society for the Sociology of Sport (NASSS), Toronto, November.

Ingham, A. (1985) 'From public issue to personal trouble: well-being and the crisis of the fiscal state', *Sociology of Sport Journal*, 2: 43–55.

Jarvie, G. and Maguire, J. (1994) *Sport and Leisure in Social Thought*. London: Routledge.

Jeffords, S. (1994) *Hard Bodies: Hollywood Masculinity in the Reagan Era*. New Brunswick, NJ: Rutgers University Press.

Kimmel, M. (1990) 'Baseball and the reconstitution of American masculinity, 1880–1920', in M. Messner and D. Sabo (eds), *Sport, Men, and the Gender Order: Critical Feminist Perspectives*. Champaign, IL: Human Kinetics. pp. 55–66.

King, S. (1993) 'The politics of the body and the body politic: Magic Johnson and the ideology of AIDS', *Sociology of Sport Journal*, 10: 270–85.

King, S. (2000) 'Border crossings: AIDS, figure skating, and Canadian identity', *Journal of Sport and Social Issues,* 24: 148–75.

Klein, A. (1992) 'Man makes himself: alienation and self-objectification in bodybuilding', *Play and Culture,* 5: 326–37.

Kristeva, J. (1982) *Powers of Horror: an Essay on Abjection* (trans. L. Roudiez). New York: Columbia University Press.

Kroker, A. and Kroker, M. (1987) 'Panic sex in America', in A. Kroker and M. Kroker (eds), *Body Invaders: Panic Sex in America.* New York: St Martins Press. pp. 10–19.

Kuhn, A. (1988) 'The body and cinema: some problems for feminism', in S. Sheridan (ed.), *Grafts.* New York: Verso. pp. 11–24.

Laberge, S. (1995) 'Toward an integration of gender into Bourdieu's concept of cultural capital', *Sociology of Sport Journal,* 12: 132–46.

Laberge, S. and Sankoff, D. (1988) 'Physical activities, body habitus, and lifestyles', in J. Harvey and H. Cantelon (eds), *Not Just a Game: Essays in Canadian Sport Sociology.* Ottawa, ON: University of Ottawa Press. pp. 267–86.

Laqueur, T. (1990) *Making Sex: Body and Gender from the Greeks to Freud.* Cambridge, MA: Harvard University Press.

Lalvani, S. (1996) *Photography, Vision, and the Production of Modern Bodies.* Albany, NY: State University of New York.

Lears, T.J.K. (1989) 'American advertising and the reconstruction of the body, 1880–1930', in K. Grover (ed.), *Fitness in American Culture.* Amherst, MA: University of Massachusetts Press, and the Margaret Woodbury Strong Museum, Rochester, NY. pp. 47–66.

Lévi-Strauss, C. (1967) *Tristes Tropiques: an Anthropological Study of Primitive Societies in Brazil* (trans. J. Russell). New York: Atheneum.

Linder, G. (1995) 'An ethnography of discipline: elite bodybuilding in Los Angeles'. Unpublished doctoral dissertation, the University of North Carolina at Chapel Hill.

Lindsay, C. (1996) 'Bodybuilding: a postmodern freak show', in R. Thomson (ed.), *Freakery: Cultural Spectacles of the Extraordinary Body.* New York: New York University Press. pp. 356–67.

Loy, J., Andrews, D.A. and Rinehart, R. (1993) 'The body in culture and sport: toward an embodied sociology of sport', *Sport Science Review,* 2: 69–91.

MacAloon, J. (1990) 'Steroids and the state: Dubin, melodrama and the accomplishment of innocence', *Public Culture,* 2: 41–64.

McDonald, M. (1996) 'Michael Jordan's family values: marketing, meaning, and post-Reagan America', *Sociology of Sport Journal,* 13: 344–65.

McKay, J. (1990) 'The "moral panic" of drugs'. Paper presented at the Australian Sociology Association Conference, Queensland, December.

MacNeill, M. (1994) 'Active women, media representations, and ideology', in S. Birrell and C.L. Cole (eds), *Women, Sport, and Culture.* Champaign, IL: Human Kinetics. pp. 273–88.

Maguire, J. (1991) 'Bodies, sportscultures and societies: a critical review of some theories in the sociology of the body', *International Review for the Sociology of Sport,* 18: 33–51.

Mansfield, A. and McGinn, B. (1993) 'Pumping irony: the muscular and the feminine', in S. Scott and D. Morgan (eds), *Body Matters.* London: Falmer Press. pp. 49–68.

Markula, P. (1992) 'Total-body-tone-up: paradox and women's realities in aerobics'. Unpublished doctoral dissertation, University of Illinois at Urbana-Champaign.

Markula, P. (1995) 'Firm but shapely, fit, but sexy, strong but thin: the postmodern aerobicizing female bodies', *Sociology of Sport Journal,* 12: 424–53.

Marshall, D. (1997) *Celebrity and Power.* Minneapolis: University of Minnesota Press.

Martin, E. (1992) 'The end of the body?', *American Ethnologist,* 19: 121–40.

Mauss, M. (1992) 'Techniques of the body', in J. Crary and S. Kwinter (eds), *Incorporations.* New York: Zone Books. pp. 454–576. (Originally published in 1934).

Messner, M. (1992) *Power at Play: Sport and the Problem of Masculinity.* Boston, MA: Beacon Press.

Miller, T. (1997) 'Sport and violence: glue, seed, state, or psyche?', *Journal of Sport and Social Issues,* 21: 235–8.

Moore, P. (ed.) (1997) *Building Bodies.* New Brunswick, NJ: Rutgers University Press.

Morgan, T. (1994) 'Pages of whiteness: race, physique magazines, and the emergence of gay public culture, 1950–1960', *Found Object,* 4: 108–26.

Morrison, T. and Lacour, C. (eds) (1997) *Birth of a Nation'Hood: Gaze, Script, and Spectacle in the O.J. Simpson Case.* New York: Pantheon Books.

Mrozek, D. (1989) 'Sport in American life: from national health to personal fulfillment', in K. Grover (ed.), *Fitness in American Culture: Images of Heath, Sport, and the Body, 1830–1940.* Amherst, MA: University of Massachusetts Press, and the Margaret Woodbury Strong Museum, Rochester, NY. pp. 18–46.

Nettleton, S. (1997) 'Governing the risky self: how to become healthy, wealthy, and wise', in A. Peterson and R. Bunton (eds), *Foucault: Health and Medicine.* London: Routledge. pp. 207–22.

Orlie, M. (1997) *Living Ethically, Acting Politically.* Ithaca, NY: Cornell University Press.

Orlie, M. and Cole, C.L. (1997) 'Living ethically Nike style: or how to transcend history immanently'. Paper presented at the annual meetings of the North American Society for the Sociology of Sport (NASSS), Toronto, November.

Pateman, C. (1988) *The Sexual Contract.* Cambridge: Polity Press.

Patton, C. (2000) 'Rock hard', in C.L. Cole, J.W. Loy and M.A. Messner (eds), *Exercising Power: the Making and Re-making of the Body*. Albany, NY: State University of New York Press.

Pelligrini, A. (1997) *Performance Anxieties: Staging Psychoanalysis, Staging Race*. New York: Routledge.

Peterson, A. (1997) 'Risk, governance and the new public health', in A. Peterson and R. Bunton (eds), *Foucault: Health and Medicine*. London: Routledge. pp. 189–206.

Radner, H. (1995) 'Speaking the body: Jane Fonda's workout', in *Shopping Around: Feminine Culture and the Pursuit of Pleasure*. New York: Routledge. pp. 141–74.

Rail, G. and Harvey, J. (1995) 'Body at work: Michel Foucault and the sociology of sport', *Sociology of Sport Journal*, 12: 164–79.

Ransom, J.S. (1997) *Foucault's Discipline: the Politics of Subjectivity*. Durham, NC: Duke University Press.

Reeves, J. and Campbell, R. (1994) *Cracked Coverage: Television News, the Anti-cocaine Narrative, and the Reagan Legacy*. Durham, NC: Duke University Press.

Robson, T. and Zalcock, B. (1995) 'Looking at Pumping Iron II: the women', in T. Wilton (ed.), *Immortal, Invisible Lesbians and the Moving Image*. London and New York: Routledge. pp. 182–92.

Rony, F.T. (1992) 'Those who squat and those who sit. The iconography of race in the 1985 films of Felix-Louis Regnault', *Camera Obscura*, 28: 263–89.

Rosanvallon, P. (1990) *L'etat en France: de 1789 à nos jours*. Paris: Seuil.

Rowe, D. (1994) 'Accommodating bodies: celebrity, sexuality, and "Tragic Magic"'. *Journal of Sport and Social Issues*, 18: 6–25.

Schulze, L. (1990) 'On the muscle', in J. Gaines and C. Herzog (eds), *Fabrications: Costume and the Female Body*. New York: Routledge. pp. 59–78.

Scott, L.M. (1993) 'Fresh lipstick – rethinking images of women in advertising', *Media Studies*, 7: 141–5.

Sedgwick, E. (1992) 'Epidemics of the will', in J. Crarry and S. Kwinter (eds), *Incorporations*. New York: Zone Books. pp. 582–95.

Shilling, C. (1993) *The Body and Social Theory*. Thousand Oaks, CA: Sage.

Simons, J. (1995) *Foucault and the Political*. New York: Routledge.

Singer, L. (1989) 'Bodies–pleasures–power', *Differences*, 1: 45–65.

Sparks, R. (1990) 'Social practice, the bodily professions and the state', *Sociology of Sport Journal*, 7: 72–82.

Stacey, J. (1997) *Teratologies: A Cultural Study of Cancer*. London and New York: Routledge.

Terry, J. (1990) 'Lesbians under the medical gaze: scientists search for remarkable sex differences', *Journal of Sex Research*, 27: 317–39.

Terry, J. and Urla, J. (eds) (1995) *Deviant Bodies*. Bloomington, IN: Indiana University Press.

Theberge, N. (1991) 'Reflections on the body in the sociology of sport', *Quest*, 43: 123–34.

Treichler, P., Cartwright, L. and Penley, C. (1998) *The Visible Woman*. New York: New York University Press.

Turner, B. (1984) *The Body and Society*. Oxford: Basil Blackwell.

Urla, J. and Swedland, A. (1995) 'The anthropometry of Barbie: unsettling ideals of the feminine body in popular culture', in J. Terry and J. Urla (eds), *Deviant Bodies*. Bloomington, IN: Indiana University Press. pp. 277–313.

Vigerello, G. (1995) 'The life of the body in *Discipline and Punish*', *Sociology of Sport Journal*, 12: 158–63.

Wacquant, L. (1992) 'The social logic of boxing in black Chicago: toward a sociology of pugilism', *Sociology of Sport Journal*, 9: 221–54.

Wacquant, L. (1995) 'The pugilist point of view: how boxers think and feel about their trade', *Theory and Society*, 24: 489–535.

Wacquant, L. (1998a) 'A fleshpeddler at work: power, pain and profit in the prizefighting economy', *Theory and Society*, 27: 1–42.

Wacquant, L. (1998b) 'Sacrifice', in G. Early (ed.), *Body Language: Writers on Sport (Greywolf Forum Two)*. Saint Paul, MN: Graywolf Press. pp. 47–60.

Wagner, D. (1997) *The New Temperance: the American Obsession with Sin and Vice*. Boulder, CO: Westview Press.

Waldby, C. (1997) *Aids and the Body Politic: Biomedicine and Sexual Difference*. New York: Routledge.

Whitson, D. (1994) 'The embodiment of gender: discipline, domination, and empowerment', in S. Birrell and C.L. Cole, *Women, Sport, and Culture*. Champaign, IL: Human Kinetics. pp. 353–72.

Wicke, J. (1994) 'Celebrity material: materialist feminism and the culture of celebrity', *South Atlantic Quarterly*, 94: 751–78.

Willis, S. (1991) *Work(ing) Out. A Primer for Everyday Life*. New York: Routledge.

Wilson, J.Q. and Herrnstein, R. (1985) *Crime and Human Nature*. New York: Simon & Schuster.

29

DOPING IN SPORT AS DEVIANT BEHAVIOR AND ITS SOCIAL CONTROL

Günther Lüschen

Doping is the use of artificial substances or methods 'foreign to the body' to enhance physical performance. This is a definition that in variant forms is found in announcements of the International and United States Olympic Committees (IOC and USOC), and a number of other national sport organizations and sport federations. It is built on a causal model that defines a stimulus (artificial substance) and an effect (enhancement of performance).

THE SOCIAL STRUCTURE OF DOPING

A List of Doping Substances, References to Methods and Underlying Models

The range of doping substances is quite wide and includes stimulants as well as muscle-building steroids. In more systematic detail the most common doping substances and their uses are as follows (Hollmann, 1996; Wadler and Hainline, 1989).

- *Anabolic steroids* were originally developed at the Medical School of the University of Rochester in order to strengthen muscle tissue in old age, and were widely used in the Second World War. They are now being used to enhance muscle build and power. As testosterone, steroids are naturally found in the human body, and in its many forms they have muscle-building and masculinizing effects. They also enhance aggressiveness, well-being and sexual prowess. Side-effects are considered

problematic, although the full range of side-effects is not yet known.
- Human growth hormones are used with the widespread belief that they are beneficial for building certain muscle groups; in a recently occurring form like IGF_1 (Insulin Growth Factor 1) they can also not be detected by biomedical tests. However, effects are not clear and research is inconclusive. What was found were discrepant side-effects in body build among children.
- *Amphetamines* in sport help endurance and assist in overcoming fatigue, while their clinical use is increasingly narrow. They were used widely in the Second World War as part of the so-called 'pilot's chocolate'. As they have to be administered at competitions for immediate effects their detection is easy, and with increased biomedical testing at sport events their use has strongly declined. Moreover, side-effects are widely known and even after prolonged use can result in dizziness, tremor, hallucination, etc. allowing their detection by outsiders as well.
- *Cocaine,* a doping substance with a long history, supposedly enhances muscle strength for up to three hours, as a well-known test by Freud demonstrated in 1884. It was widely used among NFL football players in the 1980s and among tennis players to combat fatigue, although research about its effects is inconclusive. In terms of side-effects cocaine is dangerous and, with consequences like cardiac arrest, even life-threatening.
- *Ephedrine, phenyle and associate substances* are often used in sports, yet their effects on performance are ambiguous. Their side-effects

are many, among them nervousness, agitation, confusion and stroke.

- *Caffeine* has some low-level effects on short-range endurance activities and somewhat stronger ones on long-range activities. Among its side-effects are hypertension, delirium, increased cholesterol and even coma and death.
- *Barbiturates and benzodiazepines* have some positive effects among athletes for tremor control and for euphoric feelings, yet they have also negative effects on reaction time, cognitive functions and visual skills.

This is an incomplete list and there are a number of other substances that have some popularity in special sports, such as *beta-blockers* in shooting sports.

These substances supposedly have a direct effect on performance. They are internationally typically classified as doping substances. In the United States, the term 'doping' is not widely used and such performance-enhancing substances and their uses are subsumed with other euphoric substances under the general term of *drug abuse*. Doping substances are thus lumped together with alcohol, nicotine and other substances that have no apparent effect on sport performance. Given their general negative image and levels of heavy abuse, alcohol and nicotine received more attention in the US Congress Hearings of the 1980s (1985, 1988) than doping substances that really had an impact on performance. In so doing, these Hearings, in their efforts to control the whole range of drugs and enlightening substances, defeated the intent to regulate the fairness of competitive sport and root out performance-enhancing substances, let alone address the various specific methods. The 1989 Hearings of the US Senate Judiciary Committee, however, rectified that situation stressing explicitly the use of steroids in American amateur and professional sport (1990).

As concerns substances that have a known effect on performance, these effects, except for steroids, are often lower than anticipated, with many results not proved through proper research. Moreover, side-effects are many and the doping substances mentioned above are life-threatening in quite a few cases. While many sources assume only limited effects of doping for performance enhancement, for example, some American authors estimate performance advantages for steroids to be no higher than 3–5 per cent (Wadler and Hainline, 1989), newer results and systematic observations from former East Germany put the advantage in the case of anabolic steroids for specific disciplines much

higher, with performance increases of up to 10 per cent (Berendonk, 1992: 131–93).

As far as the access to substances is concerned, many of them are readily available as ordinary pharmaceutical products and at a low price, while a few such products, like human growth hormones, are more difficult to obtain and thus fetch fairly high prices. There is often debate – and inconclusive evidence in many cases – on the potential effects of the substances, with the listing of products in a generic list. Because of the common usage of some of these products in ordinary medication, an increasingly problematic area is also the issue of wilful versus innocent violation of the doping code; this includes the administration of substances unknown to the athlete and the usage of doping substances as a component of medication to fight an illness or impairment (Young, 1996).

A separate issue is the area of negative doping – that is, administration of substances that impair performance – which was widely known in equestrian sports (Scott, 1968). At times it comes to the attention of the public, when individual athletes state that they are closely guarding their food intake for fear of being secretly administered performance-decreasing substances. No attention is being paid to this phenomenon in official rulings and the extent of such violations is unknown.

As not only pharmaceutical substances were being used to enhance performance but also such methods as blood doping, that is, the withdrawal and later retransfusion of the athlete's own blood, a reference to methods or procedures was introduced in definitions of doping. There was also debate over the inclusion of psychological methods such as hypnosis in the list of illegal practices, adding to the difficulties of definition and enforcement. Here and for psychology in particular the fine line between good coaching and illegal procedure is demonstrated most aptly by Stemme and Reinhardt (1988), in what they call psychological 'Super-Training'. For all practical purposes, it uses common insights and knowledge from psychology in athletic coaching.

When reference to methods was introduced into the definition of doping, the strictly causal model as part of the definition was called into question. When the typical time-lag in the inclusion of specific substances into respective lists was debated and the use of generic or groups of generic products rather than brand names was suggested, the way was already prepared for reference to a new model of scientific reasoning. Also, illegal procedures and concern over psychological means and methods such as hypnosis suggested an enlargement of the definition; thus, statements like 'intent to enhance performance' appeared. For quite a while in the 1980s this led to a definitional debate in the United States and elswhere resulting in formulations that mentioned 'sole intent' and a normative formulation such as 'unfair manner' (USOC, 1989). Not only did this open up the definition of doping beyond material substances, it also meant moving over into a model of teleology in scientific terms. Yet, it made testing and conviction of offenders also more difficult. Thus, after a 'revisionist interim' there has been for mainly practical purposes of biomedical control a move back to a predominantly causal model. Thus, the list of forbidden substances that the IOC Commission regularly publishes is again the sole basis for regulation and control, as the *USOC Guide to Prohibited Substances and Methods* (March 1996) shows. Of course, the list was and is never up to date and was revised from time to time since its first publication in 1967, when new products were appearing or new evidence was forthcoming. Thus, steroids were only listed from 1975 onwards, the natural steroid-component testosterone was not listed before 1982 and blood doping was added as late as 1984. Of course, the debate around and the inclusion of intent with an implicit teleological model had also suggested that an exclusive reliance on a causal model was not enough, regardless of the fact that it was needed for matters of prosecution and proof.

The Emergence of Doping in Sport

Use of doping substances is not new. The Greek physician Galenos (130–200 CE), an important forerunner of modern medicine and a sports' physician, mentioned the use of substances to enhance performance and there are reports of doping animals since the eighteenth century. In recent times there are numerous reports about incidents where athletes suffered after the use of doping substances; this ranges from the collapse of the American marathon runner Thomas Hicks in the 1904 St Louis Olympics, the death of the Danish cyclist Jensen in the 1960 Rome Olympics to the death of the British cyclist Simpson in the 1967 Tour de France.

In the 1950s Dianabol, a steroid component, was widely used among American and Soviet athletes. The 1960 Rome Olympics were thus quite irregular in results, as not all teams were 'in the know'. When knowledge, information and supply of steroids changed quite drastically

and fast, the subsequent Olympic Games up to the late 1980s were probably as much influenced by illegal use of doping substances as any before and thereafter. Methods of detection were not yet well developed early in this period and thus allowed a fairly wide use.

What is also of genuine interest is the fact that up to a 1974 IOC Commission meeting in Innsbruck, the use of steroid substances was not considered problematic. Even in the late 1970s, the German Sports Medicine Association was still not unanimous in forbidding steroids (Berendonk, 1992: 44–7), taking a clear position only thereafter. Thus, the spectacular convictions and disqualifications of athletes have only occurred since the 1980s, when 19 athletes at the PanAmerican Games in Caracas in 1983 were found in violation of the doping code. This development culminated in the disqualification of the Canadian Ben Johnson at the 1988 Seoul Olympics and of the German Katrin Krabbe before the 1992 Barcelona Games.

In the meantime quite a number of biomedical control centers have been established, and it is now possible to monitor top athletes for doping in many countries all year round, in and out of competition. With regard to testing machinery, a whole industry has emerged selling the most modern instruments and, as of 1996, at costs in excess of half a million dollars. However, there seems to be a situation where the controllers and their methods continually lag behind the newest inventions and products. Thus, Russian officials at the 1996 Atlanta Games were claiming not to have known the effects of the steroid-component Bromanton, although its effect was well documented in Russian scholarly publications. Moreover, pointing to the fact that this product was not on the IOC list of forbidden substances, the International Court of Arbitration accepted that formal argument and re-established four Russians and one Lithuanian as medal winners at the expense of, among others, a Briton and a North Korean who had supposedly competed fairly.

The reasons behind the more recent high involvement and public concern with doping, including methods of its control, are many:

- Performance enhancement through doping procedures has become widely known and acknowledged among athletes and their supporting cast.
- At a time of ever smaller differences in performance outcome even a small enhancement through illegal means may result in a win and thus justify the use of and rationalize doping.

- The material profits from sport contests have risen exponentially for individual athletes, in particular after professionals were allowed to enter the Olympic Games and when the latter were increasingly commercialized.
- Pharmaceutical products have become available on a much broader scale, and it appears that the pharmaceutical industry or respective labs are capable of developing ever more refined products.
- Opinion expressed in the media and common public opinion have taken note of the illegality of doping procedures, thus suggesting and demanding increased and more efficient controls.
- Methods of control by biomedical tests and respective machinery have become more sophisticated and effective, thus allowing more convictions.

A major influence in raising awareness about doping and its subsequent control has occurred through the European Community (EC) since 1963 and the moves of the French government, which introduced a law against doping in 1965 (Alaphilippe, 1977; Hallouin and Jeannot-Pagès, 1990). Of course, these moves were preceded by the spectacular and widely reported death of Jensen, and internally in sport by the widespread use of Dianabol in international competition since the late 1950s. The expansion of doping, paralleled by public concern, occurred at an ever-higher level into the 1980s, when more effective controls emerged. One should also observe that medical experts gradually changed their position on steroids and eventually, from 1980, came out more forcefully against doping and anabolic steroids in particular.

The controls and convictions at the 1983 PanAmerican Games in Caracas did mark a turning point (Lüschen, 1984); not to the degree, of course, that there was no more use of doping substances and methods, but rather, the high amount of uncontrolled usage was no longer possible. Of course, control from now on had a double meaning. Control meant, on the one hand, the possibility of detection through biomedical tests; but control on the side of doping athletes and their cast also meant discontinuing doping before an upcoming meet so a substance could no longer be detected. It is only recently that testing methods have been refined that allow the detection of illegal substances long after their administration. Even so, substances are consistently being generated that at any given moment cannot be detected.

Considering the problems of definition, the fact that biomedical doping control must be incomplete, and the existence of a wide-ranging culture of experts and athletes with factions for and against doping, there are major sociological problems to be addressed concerning doping.

1 The implied model in the definition of doping is a problem for sociology of knowledge.
2 Sociology identifies doping as deviant behavior with a broader sense of control that is based on a teleological model, in sociology proper referred to as social control.
3 As an important basis and tool for doping policy, sociology through proper research has to address the problem of the magnitude and social organization of doping.

Of these three major issues, there is empirical information available only for the last one, pertaining to the magnitude and some incidental structural information on doping. The two former sociological issues can, so far, be discussed on theoretical grounds only.

Some Further Observations on Definitions and the Structure of Doping

Roger Caillois in his classic 'Structure and classification of games' (1955) identifies four classes of games in which *agon, alea, mimicry* and *ilinx (vertigo)* predominate. As far as sport is concerned, it is normally understood to be agonistic, but it has elements of mimicry and vertigo as well, while alea is out, after the toss of a coin at the beginning of a match has occurred. But the experience of sport is not only that of agon. Sport is to a high degree a game of mimicry and pretence in dress codes as well as in the employment of pretence in strategy and tactic. Such quality condones the administration of doping. For the problem of doping, vertigo is, however, of major importance. Csikszentmihalyi (1975) has observed the feeling of 'flow' as part of specific sport disciplines, and in mountaineering in particular. One might also suggest that the doping experience, where an athlete extends his/her means beyond the initial physical or mental control and capability, contains such an element of flow or vertigo. Caillois himself referred to the use of alcohol as a corrupt or paidiatic form of vertigo. The feeling of getting 'high' corresponds to *flow*, and the use of doping substances and of amphetamines or cocaine in particular means a similar experience. Such correspondent structures denote the kinship between games, sports and doping.

While the biomedical nature of doping has so far been emphasized, the epistemological concerns about the definition as well as the structure of the doping culture at large imply that doping indeed is a sociological problem (Bette and Schimank, 1995). The material substance and its consequence are predominantly biomedical issues, but the structure of its uses is predominantly a question that sociologists have to address.

Bette and Schimank (1995) in an analysis drawing on the systems theory of Luhmann have first and foremost identified the structure of elite sport as the condition under which doping prevails; they make reference to the limitless victory code as well as to political and commercial influences, and society at large. They identify the precarious structures of doping before they advance their analysis to a social critique of doping control. They see the role of sociology essentially in terms of proper diagnosis and enlightenment with, in their opinion, not altogether optimistic prospects. The analysis presented here, in identifying doping as deviant, has its roots in a belief in sociological knowledge and wisdom that allows policy advice for direct social intervention. As part and parcel of society itself, this type of sociology implies a more optimistic prediction for doping in sport than Bette and Schimank are willing to offer.

DOPING, DEVIANCE AND SOCIAL CONTROL

Problems of Deviance, Deviant Behavior, Law and Control

Calling doping deviant is a major point of debate. Doping, according to the basic idea of sport based on equality of chance in competition, has to be understood as being illegal and deviant. Doping is officially defined as illegal and deviant after sport organizations have so identified the practice at variant times since the late 1960s. Its appearance as a wrongful action in codes or court decisions of civil law also identify doping as deviant. But at this point there also appear restrictions.

Doping is not a criminal offence, and thus not part of penal law. Even its inclusion in codes of civil law does not go unchallenged. An athlete can do things to his/her body as he/she likes it; only if there is an effect for somebody else, is there a legal implication. Of course, the latter is a legal area widely uncontested. It came to bear when an American runner sued the IAAF for compensation. It can also be envisioned that fellow competitors that were cheated out of a win could seek compensation through the courts. An indication of concern for the issue is an increased number of legal discussions and analyses pertaining to doping since the early 1960s (Alaphilippe, 1977; Hallouin and Jeannot-Pagès, 1990; Jacobs and Samuels, 1995; Karaquillo, 1994; Schild, 1986; Vieweg, 1991, 1996).

There are no clear indications at this time to what degree the control of doping might indeed become a matter for the legal system. After the French went all out to prosecute violating athletes, they revised their law in 1989 and the most recent developments stress conciliation and arbitration instead of penalizing the athlete (Braillat, 1994; Karaquillo, 1994; Sfeir, 1996). In Germany the civil law case of Krabbe eventually reached the Supreme Federal Court (*Bundesgerichtshof*). There is still legal activity in the United States, but the number of spectacular court cases seems to have declined, in particular after a higher court struck down the ruling of a local court for $20 million compensation against the IAAF.

The issue of deviant behavior and the definition of doping as deviant is at times being challenged on the grounds that more or less everybody does it, that society is lenient towards doping anyway (Vargas, 1994) or that anti-doping positions refer to an antiquated view of sport ethics (König, 1995). Actually, such arguments are based on little empirical evidence and spring from common sense plus a distortion of the theoretical argument. The fact that deviance goes on in society is no reason to call such acts normal and acceptable. Neither law in general is built on such premises nor does the system of sport have to abide by such understanding of violations of rules and principle. Arguments like these do pose a challenge, however, to outline the degree and type of deviance plus its socio-cultural determinants.

The socio-cultural dimension as well as the socio-historical one both suggest a number of structural determinants of doping as deviant behavior. Moreover, sport organizations have taken a clear stance after their earlier reluctance to address the problem; after all, the use of doping substances severely alters a fair outcome of sport competitions. Thus, the German Track Association (DLV) declared a number of records invalid; and more or less all national and international sport federations and disciplines are now addressing the problem and establishing rules for doping control. At the same time, it is obvious that the present situation in doping control offers a far from sufficient degree of standardization (Jacobs and Samuels, 1995). Reasons for the inconsistencies are many, ranging from the early development of doping controls to the variety of legal interpretations within countries. Moreover, there is a wide variety of intercultural acceptance or rejection as far as the use of euphoric substances is concerned. Consequently, the IOC Doping Commission finds itself cast into the role of legal originator and major arbitrator.

At least for consistency it can be stated so far: The rules of the IOC Commission clearly establish doping as deviant behavior (de Merode, 1996), and there are no known cases of sport federations that accept doping as proper and within the range of normality. Bodybuilding may be the exception, identifying itself in this regard as an activity outside of the institution of sport. It is widely known that there are variances in enforcement and engagement in doping among individual sport disciplines; still, the higher number of violations in disciplines such as cycling or weightlifting does not make doping practices in these sports legal and normal either.

Deviance Theory and the Structure of Doping Subcultures

There are essentially two theoretical arguments that explain the emergence of doping on a broad scale in modern society and sport. Durkheim's theory of anomie (1893) would explain it as a reflection of discrepant norms in society. Merton's theory (1968) would rather explain it as a result of the high demands, motivations and rewards in top athletics that would test the limits of performance and thus suggest the use of illegal means. Merton's theory appears to be the more powerful explanation for what happens in modern sport and society. It addresses on a more abstract level the systems analysis of Bette and Schimank (1995), who incorporate a variety of structural conditions in society and within elite sport itself in their analysis of the emergence of doping.

In a more specific approach to deviance, Merton, in his article on 'Social structure and anomie' (1968), distinguishes generalized goals and institutionalized means of action. In a systematic distribution of acceptance and/or rejection of these dual patterns he generates four patterns that he labels *conformity, ritualism, innovation, retreatism*. Of these, *innovation* is

the pattern that is found in doping. It means the acceptance of the generalized goal of high performance in sport while at the same time it rejects the institutionalized means by replacing them with illegal doping. The term 'innovation' carries no sense of morality at this point and refers to the illegal behavior of the criminal as well as to the doping of athletes.

From observations of criminal behavior, Sutherland and Cressey (1974) proposed a theory of *differential association* to explain criminal and deviant behavior. This theory assumes that deviant behavior is and cannot be performed in solitude for a number of reasons. There is the fact of mutual support and (in the case of doping) of supply; moreover, as criminal and deviant behavior require a certain competence and knowledge, there is a need of social learning. Both suggest that doping is an act that is performed as part of a deviant subculture, or by a group of persons that show features of secret societies. Also common experiences show that it is more than the individual athlete who is involved (Berendonk, 1992): there is mutual support and encouragement by a subculture of athletes. It is typical that coaches and physicians are involved; and so is a whole range of suppliers of illegal doping substances or practices. The theory is mainly descriptive, but it certainly suggests quite a number of research questions and interpretive suggestions.

Finally, there are two variants of social control theory. Reckless (1961) distinguishes a theory of *inner* and *outer containment*. Inner containment is the process of socialization of the human personality, where an individual via self control or *inner containment* is aware of what is right or wrong. *Outer containment* is the set of normative, group, organizational and societal controls, including those of the law. Containment, or its absence, is quite relevant for doping in sport and, in the case of external control by sports organizations, their weakness in this respect may explain part of the present situation.

Social control theory according to Albert K. Cohen (1955) is essentially a matter of subcultures, and in the case of deviance their delinquent norms and morale. Cohen finds in his observation of delinquent boys that there is also an apparent connection with the social class system. Actually, with reference to Robert Merton's general deviance theory, the stakes and material interests are higher the lower an individual's position by social class or status. Consequently, the payoff in the case of doping is higher as well; it would explain why members of lower social classes would consequently be more easily enticed to seek success through illegal means. The affiliation of individual sport disciplines to levels of the social stratification system and the related higher occurrence of doping in disciplines like cycling and weightlifting suggest the validity of Cohen's observations.

Problems of Quasi-legitimacy and Rationalization

The occurrence of doping and weak social controls is not happening without a certain level of legitimacy and condonement. If one disregards the variance in cross-cultural mores and practices, which, with regard to euphoric substances, can be substantial, then in modern societies as a source of quasi-legitimacy for doping in sport the high incidence of medical treatment and medical manipulation in society overall come to mind. Moreover, the culture of medicine that emerged since the nineteenth century parallel to modern sport has generated a whole subculture of sport medicine itself.

Ivan Illich in his publication *Medical Nemesis* (1976) has referred to this process in modern society as 'medicalization'. It refers not only to the emergence of the medical profession but to a process and orientation, where modern man seeks out medical treatment and intervention by drugs for a whole variety of real and supposed ailments. One has to see this also on the background of a lesser trust in God and religion with the emergent belief that mankind through science can interfere in human and societal affairs to a high degree. Among others, death through the merits of modern medicine can supposedly be escaped for longer than ever before. An indication of such expectation and implied reorientation toward medically manipulated health are the enormous costs that modern societies bear without much regret from the general population. With rates of 14 per cent of the GDP in the United States for health expenditures, medical efforts and interventions carry with them a high level of acceptance and legitimacy; and the annual debates concerning high health costs originate rather among politicians and the interests they represent than among the general population Against this background, the use of pharmaceutical products is basically condoned and has a supposed legitimacy, and thus – to an albeit lesser degree – so do doping substances as well.

Medicalization can also be found in sport itself, contributing to the aura of legitimacy of doping practices. Since the early involvements of medicine in sport affairs from Clemens Tissot, Per-Henryk Ling to Emil Du Bois-Reymond and Rudolf von Virchow in the nineteenth century, there has been an increasing interest and engagement of medical practitioners and of medical science in sport and in elite sport in particular. It obviously served both sport and medicine alike. In modern times and at major sports events a major part of the typical supporting cast of a sports team consists of a variety of medical personnel. In terms of treatment and rehabilitation, sports medicine has become a specialty by itself.

Modern highly trained athletes consistently and frequently suffer from a variety of ailments that need a variety of medical interventions. On the one hand, this means that the fine line between medical treatment of an injury, the preparation of proper diets and the administration of an illegal performance-enhancing drug is often difficult to draw. On the other hand, medicalization of the sport system suggests that any means of propping up the human body may be legitimate as well. Analysis of these developments may lead to athletes' being identified as 'Mortal Engines' (Hoberman, 1992).

Of course, at this point, either externally or internally, the issue is not so much legitimization but rationalization. After all, the rules are spelled out quite clearly, there is a list of forbidden substances put out by the IOC plus the open invitation for an athlete to consult with a medical specialist in many countries. Rationalization also occurs, of course, in other ways. Quite typical is the argument or thought that a win is not for oneself but for some other unit – for a club, for a nation to which an athlete belongs. It is an open question to what degree such rationalization is also suggested to an athlete by his or her deviant doping subculture or by the club and team to which he/she belongs. Anyway, psychological displacement appears to be easy and strongly suggests itself when there is an inner conflict via containment or a set of norms and values an athlete was brought up with.

A Descriptive Outline of Social Control

When discussing the issue of doping control, it is first of all the enormous machinery of biomedical controls that comes to mind; it is the system of natural science that is modeled on the principle of causality. Social control actually goes beyond such a model and implies a notion of teleology and intent without excluding the causal model. It is further reaching and recognizes that causal-model controls will all the time be incomplete. In its most general meaning it means 'the capacity of a society to regulate itself according to desired principles and values' (Janowitz, 1975). For the problem of doping in sport, it refers not only to external control by society, it means the capacity of organizations and groups as well as their members to regulate their own affairs according to their specific principles and values. With regard to the latter and to the situation of the sporting contest, such control has to refer to the specific rules that govern the event as well as to the basic principles and the morality under which a contest occurs. Thus, it extends on the one hand to the level of society and on the other to the role that an individual is committed to. In a way, social control recognizes the athlete as an autonomous person as well.

A descriptive overview can identify such control on three levels as *external macro-level, external meso-level* and *internal micro-level* controls. To a degree they reflect the theory of inner and outer containment.

External Controls on the Macro Level
Beyond the societal context with its system of normative controls that extends into problems of morality there is first and foremost the law that must be considered as an external control of the macro level. It is an interesting question to what degree the law should be involved in the control of doping.

It is not at all certain that a matter like doping, with relatively low concern for society at large, should be a special concern for penal or criminal law. Of course, one might envision that doping violations would hurt moral concerns to such a degree that the law would have to move in to rectify such a situation. Actually, that does not seem to be the case; and the level of supposed legitimacy in a period of medicalization in society makes it unlikely that doping in sport will become a major legal concern of society. On the contrary, should cases of doping in sport clog up courts in the civil law, society might well react by disregarding the issue altogether.

Of course, doping is not only a matter of morality and the law, it may concern the political system beyond the sphere and institution of sport itself. Such is the case in countries like Germany, where the parliament and its respective sport committee have become involved in an anti-doping campaign and the demand for doping control. More recently, public prosecutors have investigated former East German officials and sport executives, claiming that they did physical harm to former athletes of the GDR. Such a move was of course legally prompted, but there was no question that such a pursuit was also politically motivated. In this case the difficulty will not only be to prove that doping occurred without an athlete's consent, it will also have to show without reasonable doubt that specific doping substances were harmful in their side-effects, or more precisely, were prescribed in a harmful way. As the cases of a number of athletes in Western nations show, they often overloaded themselves when taking doping substances. Such action was seemingly based on the layman's suggestion that more would produce higher performance.

Unlike German legal officials, representatives of the law in the United States would be much more reluctant to move into the prosecution of athletes or officials. Politial institutions and the federal government since the Nixon Administration have developed a hands-off attitude as far as matters of sport are concerned (Chalip, 1991, 1996). Thus, the campaign seen in the Federal Republic of Germany is less likely to occur in the United States. While France, with its centralized governmental structure, could be expected to show a political involvement in doping affairs as well, it has not shown the same engagement as have German political circles, despite its early involvement in the introduction of anti-doping laws (Hallouin and Jeannot-Pagès, 1990).

External Meso-level Controls Meso-level controls can be understood as the quasi-legal controls and anti-doping rules of sport organizations and federations from the IOC down to national level and local sport organizations. This includes the whole system of biomedical testing centers that have developed in major sporting nations around the world. The IOC and its special Doping Commission have been involved in the problem of doping for more than 30 years. Despite difficulty of enforcement and periodic inefficiency, the IOC has reclaimed a sense of authority in recent history. In part, the central position of the IOC Commission is the result of a need for clear and consistent rules as well as identification of illegal substances and methods, internationally and among all sport federations.

There is no question, however, and ample evidence exists (Vrijman, 1996), that internationally the variety and inconsistency of doping control is high. So far there is no clear set of rules that is consistent throughout national and international sport federations. Moreover, only recently has a common movement emerged among sport organizations that doping must be controlled by sport itself lest it lose its moral authority and autonomy. In line with the theory of differential association (Sutherland and Cressey, 1974), there is no doubt that sport organizations themselves for long periods of time condoned illegal doping practices. Among others, the Dubin Report has shown this to be true for the Canadian Track Association (1990). Several national sport organizations suggested the same in their lax attitude or even wilfull neglect. The problem of rationalization, discussed in terms of the athlete above, can be equally observed in relation to sport organizations. Doping practices in the American NFL appear to be rampant because of commercial interests, and there is no question that former East German athletes and physicians rationalized their behavior with overriding national interests (Berendonk, 1992).

The most recent past shows a common and rising concern among sport organizations and federations on the international as well as national level to control and root out doping. While there are exceptions to this development, the major problem at this time is rather achieving universal consistency in rules as well as practices. It is not uncommon that federations have explicit rules and yet do not follow them.

On the international scene it should have been a priority to establish first an organization or commission to secure the standardization of doping controls; instead, controlled by legal experts, the International Court of Arbitration in Lausanne was founded before there was any serious attempt at standardizing rules and procedures that would withstand the challenge of legal authorities. Thus, this court will find itself in a position of having to rule specific cases and convictions invalid because regulations are not standard or controls cannot keep up with the most progressive developments in the doping scene. And presently non-observance of rules or inconsistencies among sport organizations and their control commissions are often to be found. Only in 1999, in response to strong public pressure, did the IOC establish a new control commission.

The issue of meso-level controls through sport organizations addresses, in the end, the question of autonomy of sport in controlling its own affairs, and that of doping in particular (Vieweg, 1991). The need to stress and build on such autonomy appears to be strong for a number of reasons. First, and because of the minor concern with doping as an offence in criminal law, there is a need to address doping from within the system; the observation of basic principles in sporting contests, such as equality of chance and fairness, requires sport

organizations to react accordingly. Secondly, there is a need for control from within to stop any future major case-loads of doping violations in civil law. It would not be in the best interests of sport and its moral integrity for athletes and sport organizations to routinely settle their grievances over major payments and doping violations in public courts. What is suggested here is not the establishment of quasi-legal suits within sport and its own courts, so much as the prevention of doping violations as a matter of principle to make civil lawsuits obsolete. Conciliation as introduced first in France (Karaquillo, 1994) may be one way to strengthen the autonomy of sport and in turn the moral fiber of the system.

Developments in the near future will show whether the autonomy of sport and the proper enactment of quasi-legal rulings in its own courts and commissions can be established. Commercial interests and those of individual athletes with their supporting cast may well interfere with such institutionalization. Should they succeed, it may well be the beginning of a new era of sport, where elite sport with mainly entertainment functions is clearly separated from the participant sport that could be re-established in such a process, such as the amateur rule or something similar.

Indications are that the inconsistency in meso-level controls is in a period of transition. The rapid advances in medical technology as a basis for the increase of doping practices found the sport scene and its organizations unprepared for control for many years. Instead, the doping subculture corrupted major segments of national and international sport organizations, and that included the Olympic Games up until very recently. External macro-level controls, as well as those in line with the rules of sport as a game and contest, will encourage and should facilitate the development of meso-controls within sport organizations. After all, at the macro level the institution of sport and the sporting contest are models of trust and morality; and the sporting contest itself cannot continue if principles of reciprocity, equality of chance and fairness are not observed. This brings us to discussion of controls at the micro level.

Internal Micro-level Social Controls As internal micro-level controls one can identify all those structures and processes that occur at the interpersonal or individual level. The latter may be a matter of an individual's personality and learning experiences – the inner containment dimension. Foremost among micro-level controls are those established during sports contests and in interpersonal or intergroup relations. They pertain to an athlete's relationship to his or her own team or sport subculture. They also include the relationship to an opponent or an opposing team in a contest.

The moral implications at this level of structure and analysis are overwhelming and it is not only a matter of following the rules of the game or the sport organization. Paramount at this level is what normally will be referred to as *fairness*. It is a misunderstanding to relate this to altruism and voluntarily giving up part of one's own gains and rewards. It is a pattern of behavior that is entirely related to the maintenance of the contest, its integrity and the preservation of the opponent, whose destruction would itself destroy the contest and any future encounter. It is a pattern identified within the context of the sporting contest distinguished from cooperation (Lüschen, 1970); it is a form of behavior that Kant observed also for parties at war and that Simmel had in mind when he talked about '*Vereinheitlichung' des 'Kampfspiels'*(this refers to the unifying potential of the contest) (1923: 200), qualifying, however, that in its pure form there are no outside interests.

There is every indication that in elite athletics the individual athlete has and will pursue his or her selfish interests, but only to the degree that the opponent, who is also the future opponent on another occasion, will not be hurt and betrayed. Application of this fine distinction to what happens in the case of doping and the abstention from such and similar behavior, is one of the most powerful reasons why sport and the athlete are cast in a role of important moral agent. There are violations of this principle, there is a high potential for cheating in sport (Lüschen, 1976), but the challenge to the principles of association and fairness posed by such behavior are still a far cry from a situation in sport where fairness has become nonexistent. Durkheim (1887/1993) reminds the social science observer at this point that the existence of rules and norms is actualized through their violation and deviant behavior. It is thus an error to conclude from doping code violations, and those of prominent athletes in particular, that violations are common and widespread.

Social Control, Morale and Periodic Changes

Models of change are typically unidirectional and their authors often proclaim a period of moral and cultural demise. With the obvious onslaught of doping in the 1970s and 1980s this seemed also to be the case for doping and its magnitude. Similarly, there is a widespread feeling about a general moral decay in society, assuming for doping that it is actually proof of a general demise of culture and society. Such models of change as that of Spengler are simple and popular, yet often unwarranted. They indicate a limited understanding of the interdependence of social structure and the character of structural change.

Others have pointed to the fact that there are rather eras of periodic change, and that, for example, an emphasis on formality and society may be followed by periods of informality and community again. The same might be advanced for doping in sport. After a period of heightened consciousness about this phenomenon and increased concern from meso- and macro-level controls, there will be a period of observance of the doping code and of principles of fairness again.

That it is doping which brings issues of morality, fairness and justice to the foreground has to do with the fact that it ultimately corrupts and destroys the core of sport as it is found in the sporting contest. This is no small concern for sport, nor is it for society at large. Hence the emergence of a variety of social controls and public concerns. The issue and sociological study of doping in sport also reveals the degree to which sociology is actually a moral science (Durkheim, 1887/1993).

The Special Case of Legal Control

Legal or quasi-legal control within sport itself can be understood as special forms of external social control. It is an interesting problem by itself that at least since the introduction of special doping laws in France, with a number of other members of the EU with the notable exception of Germany following suit, doping has become a focus of legal discussions all over the world. Within a sporting context only labor disputes in American professional sport have so far received similar attention from the law. This development warrants an analysis all by itself; it may be explained as a consequence of the extension and increased specialization of the legal system as much as it is the result of the increased prevalence of and material damage done through doping in sport. That is to say, in terms of civil law, with increased amounts of money to be earned, both sports organizations and athletes deprived of their renumerations have an interest in rectifying the situation and suing for damages.

The situation is less clear with regard to criminal or penal law. The consequences for society and other parties as well as for the athletes themselves do not suggest the law should follow suit. It is this point of view that made the French retract part of their earlier law of 1965 which criminalized the violating athlete. Indeed, there is a tendency in France now to protect rather than punish an athlete found in violation of the doping code (Alaphilippe, 1988; Breillat, 1994; Sfeir, 1996). In the United States, there is a widespread belief that individual autonomy, so dear in the US Constitution, means that everyone can do to his/her body as he/she likes. Thus, there need not be any legal prohibition on the use of doping substances, and the damage done to others, to a given sport organization or matters of due process – a frequent challenge of athletes against sport authorities – can be handled by civil law.

Court rulings in terms of the privacy principle have been somewhat two-edged. On one hand, the argument has been that nobody under such provision should be exposed to a urine or other tests that violate his/her privacy rights (High Court of Colorado). On the other hand, courts, such as the High Court of California, have ruled that participation in sport is entirely voluntary and that privacy principles are not a concern, such as in open exposure in the locker room; thus, privacy concerns connected to drug testing were declared void. It is such rulings, let alone inconsistencies in legal matters in certain countries, that demonstrate the difficulty in achieving a legally based doping control model around the world. German courts would be less likely to protect individual and privacy rights; courts in dictatorial systems will be even more lenient in approving tests of a supposedly doping athlete.

From Legal Concerns to Stressing the Autonomy of Sport

As legal systems are society-bound, their variance in structure emphasizes the need to place the doping controls within the system of international sport itself. It will, however, be a formidable task to develop such an international quasi-legal system. Moreover, it will not only be a formidable task to set up the rules and norms for the anti-doping code, enforcement of the code will require an even greater effort. This is yet another reason to focus as much on normative and moral controls as on the controls built around a tight model of causality and biomedical testing. Moreover, the general expectation is that through an increased concern for the autonomy of sport internal social controls will also be encouraged that, eventually, will result in a decline of doping.

A much further-reaching proposal to stress the autonomy of sport and of the individual athlete has been developed by Bird and Wagner, with their proposal of a drug-diary (1996). The open listing of substances used will allow inspection, it will severely punish undisclosed doping and it expects, through such a procedure, by stressing the autonomy and self-responsibility of the athlete, a reduced incidence of doping. It is a rational, economically inclined calculation; it tries to avoid disadvantages of the 'negative list' and expects, through collegial control among athletes themselves, the development of specific norms and, through such a form of social control, a lesser likelihood of doping overall.

THE EXTENT OF DOPING IN SPORT AND THE STATE OF RESEARCH

How much doping is going on in sport at this time nobody knows for sure; neither an exact incidence nor a serious estimate can be provided. That it is happening, and that it has almost all sporting nations and a number of famous athletes involved has been sufficiently documented (Berendonk, 1992: 30–3).

As with all forms of deviant and criminal behavior, this is a familiar situation most succinctly demonstrated by an early research project on criminal behavior in the United States which, according to Wallerstein and Wyle (1947), found 86 per cent of adults admitting that they committed an act of larceny (theft) at least once in their lifetime. What can be concluded for criminal behavior, that less than the total amount of committed crime gets detected, of those detected a considerably lower number go to court, and only a minority of those engaging in such crime are finally convicted, can also as a general tendency be expected for doping in sport. There is now modern technology that allows detection of the use of steroids months after their actual application. Testing throughout the year and unannounced testing is being performed, and all winners are being tested as a routine at major sport events. Thus, observation is probably more stringent now in sport than typically occurs in law enforcement for criminal behavior, yet there is a strong suspicion that the most sophisticated dopers still get away with it and enjoy an illegal advantage over those that have not doped.

Although there is a high level of reliability for the claim that the use of stimulants such as amphetamines has rapidly declined, since these products have to be consumed at a sport event itself to have any effect and consequently are easily detectable, the situation is different with steroids, which may have been used at a much earlier time and at the time of testing are no longer detectable. There are also substances like creatine which are found naturally in meat products and, thus, as long as they are not used in higher doses, it cannot be confirmed that their occurrence in the body is due to an artificial substance illegally administered. Furthermore, there are a few known substances like IGF$_1$ (Insulin Growth Factor 1) that cannot be detected at all.

With these provisos in mind, the following results can only be considered rough estimates and, by definition, reflect an incidence of deviant behavior lower than is actually true. Of course, one should also observe that certain statements by anti-doping advocates are commonly overstatements: one of the more infamous statements of a former British team physician prior to the Atlanta Olympic Games put the rate of expected dopers at 75 per cent of all athletes. Statements like these receive wide attention in the mass media, even if their truth value is low. One need only consider the fact that in certain sport disciplines doping would not result in performance enhancement to reach the conclusion that a rate of three out of four Atlanta participants doping could not possibly be true, even if in disciplines that are more prone to doping behavior every athlete had indeed doped.

Distortions in public discussions also occur because an element of inner-group versus outer-group or ethnocentricity is at work and assumes other teams to have notoriously higher drug users. Such was the case before the Atlanta Games in public statements made in the United States regarding Chinese athletes and by Europeans regarding American athletes. These observations on the non-reliability of doping rates support the general contention that better research is needed than is available so far and that presently available results should only be used after considerable scrutiny.

Some of the best results are those so far provided by biomedical test institutes and from routine testing at sports events. For the more recent past these results refer mainly to steroid abuse for reasons mentioned above. Stimulants are easy to detect and thus have gone out of fashion. Regardless of the number of convictions, the number of tests performed is also a good indication of the magnitude and costs of biomedical testing.

German Control in Cologne for 1995 reported a total of 8,939 tests of which 125, equalling 1.4 per cent, were found to be positive. Of those found to be positive, relatively more were non-German samples (3.5 per cent). Of course, this does not allow the conclusion that Germans dope less. One could equally conclude that non-Germans were less sophisticated in hiding the use of doping substances. Overall, and given the general publicity the practice of doping in sport receives, the rate appears to be rather low. Yet, it is quite typical that in the recent past other studies have come up with similar figures. G.H. Pope et al. (1988) found a steroid use among male college athletes of 1.7 per cent.

Curry and Wagman (1999) reports for American power-weightlifters that two out of three of them used steroids at least once in their lifetime. High rates of steroid users were also found by Delbeke et al. in Flanders among bodybuilders (1995). Yet, the subculture of bodybuilding has for long been known for its doping prowess and as a supply line for athletes in other activities. Ljundqvist at the World Congress on Doping in Rome reported a detection rate of 1.3 to 2.6 per cent at athletic events, although he cautions that detection rates for steroids at athletic events were at that time almost useless as detectability and respective secure periods for the use of substances were well known among athletes and their supporting cast. Scarpino et al. (1990) report that in a quota sample 6 per cent of Italian athletes acknowledged themselves to be drug users, while 7 per cent stated that access to doping substances was easy. Vogels et al. (1996), in a study of regular gym attendants, found that 6 per cent of them had used some type of performance-enhancing substance at least once. These rates contrast with earlier reports (EC, 1964), when in the early 1960s at the Italian Championship 50 per cent of amateur cyclists tested positive, while the rate for soccer players in the same year was only 1.1 per cent.

In the United States there have been two areas that have received wide attention with regard to doping and drug abuse: professional athletes and adolescents. The former enjoy more or less permanent attention in the mass media. Shortly after the Atlanta Olympic Games a number of the main television and radio stations had athletes or insiders appear and disclose anonymously their use of drugs and pain-killers. Hearings in the US Congress in the 1980s confirmed a wide use of drugs, but because of definitional problems the attention focused mainly on alcoholism among elite athletes. What was noteworthy was the fact that athletes, team owners and union representatives alike were of the opinion that they would and could control their own affairs. That, by all indications, seems not to be the case, since economic and commercial considerations alone appear to be the overpowering principles. Thus, in one confidential statement the players of one team disclosed that all of their regulars were routinely doped with substances called Emperor 1,2,3 to enhance aggressiveness, muscle build and to kill pain endured at and after a game. Their quarterback star player, however, was not doped as the side-effects of the doping substances were not known and might have destroyed the player as a high-prized commodity, leading to a considerable loss for the team owners. Also, a later hearing before the US Senate Judiciary Committee (1990) that focused exclusively on steroids confirmed their wide use, and among professional athletes in particular. However, as Vieweg maintained from German experiences, a higher rate among professionals should not necessarily be assumed as at that level challenges and controls by fellow athletes will also be stronger (1996). Yet, considering the theory of differential association, in team games and commercial sport organizations, when doping is uniformly engaged in by everyone, the control by fellow athletes is not sufficient.

The use of doping substances among adolescents has been fairly well surveyed in the United States due to the relatively high usage and its consistent appearance as an issue in electoral politics. One of the theoretically and analytically most interesting studies by Martha Stuck (1990) confirms a rather high usage of drugs among adolescents and, in line with the above interpretation of legitimization of drug usage in a medicalized society, finds the adolescent drug subculture to be conformist rather than deviant. For sport, however, she finds that athletes take to drugs comparatively less than ordinary students.

With regard to the use of steroids among high school students, Johnston et al. (1995) found in a panel study on drug use that there was no increase in the consumption of substances like steroids and that over a 5-year period the rate for at least one-time use of steroids was fairly stable at 1.6–2.4 per cent. There is no indication, however, to what degree this usage relates to sport or to an attempt to build one's body and

its muscles for appearance. All indications from studies like these suggest, of course, that the rate of usage of doping substances among adolescents is lower than is generally suggested by statements of politicians and commentators.

One of the few quantitative surveys directly concerned with the use of doping was conducted by Ferrando among former and present Spanish Olympic athletes (1995). Data about attitudes, self-reported behavior and the potential for meso-level control by sport organizations show the rate of those having ever knowingly used doping substances is at a low level of 1 per cent. Five per cent say they are not sure, while 21 per cent fully or 'a little' agree that doping is necessary in high-level competition. Seventy-six per cent would never take drugs, even if they knew it was to their advantage. Yet, only 27 per cent have trust that doping will be stopped in the near future, while 53 per cent have doubts and 18 per cent do not expect sport organizations to have the capability to do it. Regardless of the limited reliability of such data, they do indicate a low conscious usage; more important, they indicate that normative and moral controls were very much on the minds of the respondent Spanish elite athletes.

Picou and Gill (1990) identify the historical stages of doping since the Second World War and note there has been a steady increase in attention and usage among basketball players. At the same time, an analysis of testing procedures and convictions in France shows a steady increase in the number of athletes tested, while at the same time the rate of convictions has declined (Irlinger et al., 1994). There is also some evidence that indeed, as Donike claimed, there are differences in the periods 'before and after Caracas' (Lüschen, 1984), when a number of athletes were convicted of doping at the Pan-American Games or did not even attend the games when they learned they would be tested by more powerful testing means.

The period of high and increased usage among athletes in the Olympic Games, so typical of the period from 1972 to 1988, appears to be over. Whether the Atlanta Games of 1996, supposed to be 'the cleanest ever', were indeed so clean, remains an open question. Biomedical testing was certainly at an all-time high and yet produced only few positive tests. Suspicion abounds, however, whether individual athletes were able to conceal their involvement with drugs or got away with it for reasons that have to do with the inconsistency, reliability, and validity of testing methods and procedures.

CONCLUSION

One conclusion is to state that doping in sport will be with us for the foreseeable future as it has been with high-performance sport since antiquity (Hollmann, 1996). Although this is probably true with reference to the past, we should draw a more sociologically inclined conclusion with reference to the future and with reference to potentially effective controls. When Bette and Schimank (1995) see doping as related to the differentiation of elite sport in modern society, and Hoberman (1992) expects it to be even more pronounced in future society, they imply at least some variability. Using Durkheim's theory we may go even further and view doping and doping control in sport as related to problems of morality within sport and in interdependence with morality in society at large. As far as the latter is concerned, sport reflects the morality and social structure of the society of which it is a part. However, it may well provide a special function for moral consciousness and reinforcement within society. There is no question that in the eyes of the public around the world at this time, national and international sport is anything but a model of morality. This perception is tied to the recent reality concerning doping in sport, even if all indications are that doping, even in modern elite sport, is anything but normal. In line with Durkheim's theory, sport has the potential, if there is more conscious control of doping in particular, to provide the moral impetus that is needed for the survival of the instution of sport as well as society in the future.

Therefore, the control of doping is not only a matter of biomedical testing because such testing will never bring effective control. Doping must be controlled socially and through the moral fibre of society and from the morality of sport within the society.

REFERENCES AND FURTHER READING

Alaphilippe, François (1977) 'Sanction disciplinaire et sanction penale du dopage', in J.P. Lafarge and P. Dumas (eds), *Dopage des sportifs*. Paris: Ed. Cujas. pp. 21–34.

Alaphilippe, François (1988) 'A propos de la lutte contre le dopage', *Revue Juridique et Economique du Sport*, 6: 46–50.

Bailette, F. (1991) 'Anatomie de la destructive sportive', *Quel corps* 41: 169–92.

Berendonk, Brigitte (1992) *Doping. Von der Forschung zum Betrug*. Reinbek: Rowohlt.

Bette, Karl-Heinrich (ed.) (1994) *Doping im Leistungssport*. Stuttgart: Naglschmidt.

Bette, Karl-Heinrich and Schimank, Uwe (1995) *Doping im Hochleistungssport*. Frankfurt: Suhrkamp.

Bird, Edward J. and Wagner, Gert (1996) 'Economic and social methods for reducing the dilemmas of drug regulation in high-performance sport'. Paper presented at an International Symposium 'Doping in Sport and Its Legal and Social Control'. University of Alabama at Birmingham.

Breillat, Jean-Christophe (1994) 'La conciliation, un regard neuf sur la contenieux sportif', *Revue Juridique et Economique du Sport*, 31: 73–85.

Breivik, Gunnar (1992) 'Doping games. A game theoretical exploration of doping', *International Review for the Sociology of Sport*, 27: 235–56.

Caillois, Roger (1955) 'Structure and classification of games', *Diogenes*, 12: 62–75.

Caillois, Roger (1961) *Men, Play and Games*. Glencoe, IL: Free Press.

Catlin, Don H. and Murray, Thomas H. (1996) 'Performance-enhancing drugs, fair competition and Olympic sport', *Journal of the American Medical Association*, 276 (3): 231–7.

Chalip, Lawrence L. (1991) 'Sport and the state', in F. and M. Landry and M. Yerles (eds), *Sport in the Third Millennium*. Sainte-Foy: University of Laval Press. pp. 243–50.

Chalip, Lawrence L. (1996) 'Interpretative und kritische Analyse der Sportpolitik', in G. Lüschen and A. Rütten (eds), *Sportpolitik*. Stuttgart: Naglschmidt. pp. 25–52.

Clasing, D. (1992) *Doping. Verbotene Arzneimittel im Sport*. Stuttgart: Fischer.

Cohen, Albert K. (1955) *Delinquent Boys*. Glencoe, IL: Free Press.

Council of Europe (1964) *Doping of Athletes*. Strasbourg: EC (mimeo).

Csikszentmihalyi, Michael (1975) *Beyond Boredom and Anxiety*. San Francisco: Jossey–Bass.

Curry, L.A. and Wagman, D.E. (1999) 'Qualitative description of the prevalence and use of anabolic androgenic steroids by United States powerlifters', *Perceptual and Motor Skills*, 88 (1): 224–33.

Delbeke, F.T., Landuyt, J. and Debackere, M. (1995) 'The abuse of doping agents in competing bodybuilders in Flanders', *International Journal of Sports Medicine*, 16: 66–70.

Digel, Helmut (1994) 'Doping als Verbandsproblem', in Karl-Heinriche Bette (ed.), *Doping in Leistungssport*. Stuttgart: Naglschmidt. pp. 131–52.

Donike, Manfred and Kaiser, G. (1980) *Dopingkontrollen*. Köln: Bundesinstitut für Sportwissenschaft.

Dubin, Charles S. (1990) Commission of Inquiry into the Use of Drugs and Banned Practices Intended to Increase Athletic Performance. Ottawa: Minister of Supply and Services.

Durant, R.H., Rickert, V.I., Ashworth, C.S., Newman, C. and Slavens, G. (1993) 'Use of multiple drugs among adolescents who use anabolic steroids', *New England Journal of Medicine*, 328: 922–6.

Durkheim, Emile (1893) *De la division du travail et social*. Paris: Félix Alcan.

Durkheim, Emile (1993) *Ethics and the Sociology of Morals*. Buffalo: Prometheus (orig. 1887).

European Community (1964) *Doping in Sport.* Strasbourg: EC, Out-of-School-Education Document (mimeo).

Faber, A. (1974) *Doping als unlauterer Wettbewerb und Spielbetrug*. Zürich: Schulthess.

Ferrando, Manuel G. (1995) *Los deportistas olimpicos españolas. Un perfil sociológico*. Madrid: Consejo Superior de Deportes.

Findlay, Hilary A. (1996) 'Penalties and due process mechanisms in Canada's anti-doping program'. Paper presented at an International Symposium 'Doping in Sport and Its Legal and Social Control', University of Alabama at Birmingham.

Franke, Elk (1994) 'Dopingdiskurse: Eine Herausforderung für die Sportwissenschaft', in Karl-Heinrich Bette (ed.), *Doping im Leistungssport*. Stuttgart: Naglschmidt. pp. 67–99.

Hallouin, J.C. and Jeannot-Pagès, G. (1990) *La repression du dopage dans le sport. Actualité Législative Dalloz*, 9–10.

Heikkala, J. (1993) 'Modernity, morality and the logic of competing', *Interational Review of Sociology of Sport*, 28 (4): 355–71.

Heinilä, Kalevi (1983) 'The totalization process in international sport', *Sportwissenschaft*, 12 (2): 235–54.

Hoberman, John (1992) *Mortal Engines: the Science of Performance and the Dehumanisation of Sport*. New York: Free Press.

Hollmann, Wildor (1996) 'On the history and present evidence of doping', Paper presented at an International Symposium 'Doping in Sport and Its Legal and Social Control', University of Alabama at Birmingham.

Illich, Ivan (1976) *Medical Nemesis*. New York: Parthenon.

Irlinger, Paul, Augustini, M., Duret, P. and Louveau, C. (1994) 'Dopingbekämpfung in Frankreich', in Karl-Heinrich Bette (ed.), *Doping im Leistungssport*. Stuttgart: Naglschmidt. pp. 177–89.

Jacobs, James B. and Samuels, Bruce (1995) 'The drug testing project in international sports: dilemmas in an expanding regulatory regime', *Hastings International and Comparative Law Review*, 18 (3): 557–89.

Janowitz, Morris (1975) 'Sociological theory and social control', *American Journal of Sociology*, 81: 82–7, 101–8.

Jennings, Andrew (1996) *Das Olympia-Kartell*. Reinbek: Rowohlt.

Johansson, Martin (1987) 'Doping as threat against sport and society. The case of Sweden', *International Review of Sociology of Sport*, 22: 83–96.

Johnston, Lloyd D., O'Malley, James and Bachman, Jerald (1995) *National Survey Results on Drug Use from the Monitoring the Future Study*. Rockville, MD: US Department of Health and Human Services.

Karaquillo, Jean-Pierre (1994) 'La procédure de conciliation: Quand? Comment', *Revue Juridique et Economique du Sport*, 31: 87–92.

Katz, David L. and Pope, Harrison G. (1990) 'Psychiatric effects of anabolic steroids', in US Senate Hearings 4-3 and 5-9-1989, The Steroid Abuse Problem in America. Washington, DC: US Government Printing Office.

Keck, Otto and Wagner, Gert (1990) 'Asymmetrische Information als Ursache von Doping im Hochleistungssport', *Zeitschrift für Soziologie*, 19 (2): 108–16.

König, Eugen (1995) 'Criticsm of doping: the nihilistic side of technological sport and the antiquated view of sport ethics', *International Review of Sociology of Sport*, 30: 3–4.

Ljundquist, Arne (1988) 'Misuses of hormones in sports', in P. Bellotti et al. (eds), *World Symposium on Doping in Sport*. Rome: FIDAL. pp. 107–10.

Lüschen, Günther (1970) 'Association, cooperation and contest', *Journal of Conflict Resolution*, 14 (1): 20–34.

Lüschen, Günther (1976) 'Cheating in sport', in D. Landers (ed.), *Social Problems in Athletics*. Urbana, IL: University of Illinois Press. pp. 67–77.

Lüschen, Günther (1984) 'Before and after Caracas. Drug abuse and doping as deviant behavior in sport', in K. Olin (ed.), *Contribution of Sociology to the Study of Sport*. University of Jyväskylä. pp. 54–67.

Lüschen, Günther (1993) 'Doping in sport. The social structure of a deviant subculture', *Sport Science Review*, 2 (1): 92–106.

Lüschen, Günther (1994) 'Doping als abweichendes Verhalten. Methodologische und inhaltliche Aspekte', in Karl-Heinrich Bette (ed.), *Doping im Leistungssport*. Stuttgart: Naglschmidt. pp. 7–27.

Lüschen, Günther (1996) 'Doping in sport as deviant behavior and social control. A rising problem in sport and society?', Paper presented at an International Symposium 'Doping in Sport and Its Legal and Social Control', University of Alabama at Birmingham.

Lüschen, Günther und Sfeir Lüschen, Leila (1998) 'Die Struktur des Dopings im Sport, seine rechtliche und sociale Kontrolle – eine vergleichende Untersuchung über Frankreich und die USA', in K. Vieweg (ed.) *Doping: Realität und Recht*. Berlin: Duncker und Humblot.

de Merode, Alexandre (1996) 'Aspirations and ideals in the Olympic Games', *Journal of the American Medical Association*, 276 (3): 247.

Merton, Robert E. (1968) 'Social structure and anomie', in *Social Theory and Social Structure*. Glencoe, IL: Free Press.

Payne, S.D.W. (1990) *Medicine, Sports and the Law.* Oxford: Blackwell.

Picou, J. Steven and Gill, Duane A. (1990) 'Drug use among basketball players: an historical analysis of use situations', *Applied Research in Coaching of Athletics,* pp. 67–79.

Pommerehne, Werner and Hartmann, Hans (1979) 'Ein ökonomischer Ansatz zu Dopingkontrolle', *Jahrbuch für Sozialwissenschaften,* pp. 102–43.

Pope, Harrison G., Katz, D.L. and Champoux, R. (1988) 'Anabolic-androgenic steroid use among 1,010 college men', *Physican Sports Medicine,* 16: 75–84.

Reckless, W.C. (1961) 'A new theory of delinquency and crime', *Federal Probation* 25: 42–6.

Revue Juridique et Economique du Sport (1994) 'La justice sportive (arbitrage et conciliation)', Special Issue, 31: 1–142.

Salva, Paul and Bacon, George E. (1991) 'Anabolic steroids: interest among parents and athletes', *Southern Medical Journal,* 84: 552–6.

Scarpino, Vilma, Arrigo, A., Benzi, G., Gavattini, S., laVecchia, C., et al. (1990) 'Evaluation of prevalance of doping among Italian athletes', *Lancet,* 336: 1048–50.

Schild, W. (1986) *Rechtliche Fragen des Doping.* Heidelberg: Müller.

Scott, Marvin B. (1968) *The Racing Game.* Chicago: Aldine.

Sfeir Lüschen, Leila (1996) 'The legal control of doping in competitive sport in France', Paper presented at an International Symposium 'Doping in Sport and Its Legal and Social Control', University of Alabama at Birmingham.

Simmel, Georg (1923) *Soziologie.* Berlin: Duncker & Humblot.

Stemme, Fritz and Reinhardt (1988) *Super-Training.* Dusseldorf: Econ.

Stuck, Martha F. (1990) *Adolescent Worlds. Drug Use and Athletic Activity.* New York: Praeger.

Sutherland, E.H. and Cressey, Donald (1974) *Criminology.* Philadelphia: Lippincott.

United States Congress (1985) Sports and drug abuse. Hearing 9-25-84. Washington, DC: US Government Printing Office.

United States Congress (1989) Sports and drug abuse prevention. Hearing 9-10-87. Washington, DC: US Government Printing Office.

United States Olympic Committee (1988) *Drug Free.* Colorado Springs, CO: USOC.

United States Senate, Committee of the Judiciary (1990) The steroid abuse problem in America.

Focusing on the use of steroids in college and professional football today. Hearings 4-3 and 5-9-1989. Washington, DC: US Government Printing Office.

Van Galen, W. and Diederijks, Jos (1990) *Sportblessures.* Haarlem: De Vrieseborch.

Vargas, Yves (1994) 'Sport, crime et châtiment: la pureté de l'epure', *Education physique et sport* (Paris), 45: 11–12.

Vieweg, Klaus (1991) 'Doping und Verbandsrecht', *Neue Juristische Wochenschrift,* 24: 1511–16.

Vieweg, Klaus (1996) 'A legal analysis of the German situation', Paper presented at an International Symposium 'Doping in Sport and Its Legal and Social Control', University of Alabama at Birmingham.

Vieweg, Klaus (ed.) (1998) *Doping: Realität und Recht.* Berlin: Duncker und Humblot.

Vogels, T. et al. (1996) 'Correlates of the use of performance-enhancing drugs among young patrons of gymnasiums in the Netherlands', *Drugs: Education, Prevention and Policy,* 3 (1): 39–48.

Voy, Robert O. (1991) *Drugs, Sport, and Politics.* Champaign, IL: Human Kinetics.

Vrijman, Emile N. (1996) 'A comparison of anti-doping regulations of international sports governing bodies and the issue of harmonisation', Paper presented at an International Symposium 'Doping in Sport and Its Legal and Social Control', University of Alabama at Birmingham.

Waddington, Ivan (1996) 'The development of sports medicine', *Sociology of Sport Journal,* 13 (2): 176–96.

Waddington, Ivan and Murphey, Patrick (1992) 'Drugs, sport and ideologies', in E. Dunning and C. Rojek (eds), *Sport and Leisure in the Civilizing Process.* Basingstoke: Macmillan. pp. 36–64.

Wadler, Gary I. and Hainline, Brian (1989) *Drugs and the Athlete.* Philadelphia: Davis.

Wagner, Gert (1994) 'Wie können die Doping-Zwickmühlen überwunden werden?', in Karl-Heinrich Bette (ed.), *Doping im Leistungssport.* Stuttgart: Naglschmidt. pp. 101–30.

Wallerstein, I. and Wyle, F. (1947) 'Our law-abiding law-breakers', *Probation* 25 (April): 107–12.

Young, Richard R. (1996) 'Problems with the definition of doping: does lack of fault or the absence of performance enhancing matter?', Paper presented at an International Symposium 'Doping in Sport and Its Legal and Social Control', University of Alabama at Birmingham.

30

SPORT AND EMOTIONS

Mary E. Duquin

Sport is movement, belief and desire, bound together in a multisensual event whose epicenter is emotion. From ecstasy to agony, whether participating or spectating, emotions underlie our motives for play, our most vivid and memorable experiences, and often our reasons for leaving the arena. Sport is a teacher and shaper of value in emotional life. Sport experiences can enrich emotional development by cultivating capacities for care, self-worth, strength of will, good judgement, compassion, understanding, love and friendship. Sport experiences can also undermine interpersonal relations and self-worth by contributing to feelings of fear, resentment, envy, malice, self-pity, despair, insensitivity and alienation. These examples illustrate the importance of emotions in understanding the impact of sport and leisure on individuals and social relations. Yet, emotion is a relatively new area of research in sociology, and few sport scholars have focused specifically or primarily on emotions (Elias and Dunning, 1986; Ferguson, 1981; Maguire, 1991; Rail, 1990, 1992; Snyder, 1990). Research on identity formation, social expression and self-realization have, however, yielded rich sources of insight into emotions in sport and leisure.

Emotions are significant in the construction of athletic identities, as well as in the formation of culture, class, gender, race, sexual and moral identities. Sport often plays a key role in how we learn to experience our physical and emotional selves, how we come to define pleasure, and what emotions we learn to express (Rojek, 1985). Much of modern sport involves learning to control emotions, of disciplining the self and managing emotional lives. The extensive research on the normalization of pain and

injury in sport reflects this emphasis on repressing and managing emotions. Emotions also figure prominently in our inventions of new sport forms, in our resistance to dominant sport forms, in our reasons for leaving sport and in our changing identities as a result of our withdrawal.

Research on sport spectating is primarily about the pleasures of being a fan, expression of community, social bonding and nostalgia. The emotional experiences of sport spectating are sometimes compared to the sacred emotions of religious rituals that give meaning to personal and cultural life. Media and communication studies of sport spectating have investigated the personal pleasures of looking: voyeurism and narcissism. These studies have probed the effects of mass mediated sport on the emotional experience of spectating. The study of emotions in culture-making institutions like sport and leisure raises a host of interesting questions about how individuals learn to define emotion, experience emotion, feel emotion and share emotion in contemporary life (Denzin, 1990).

EMOTIONS: EXPRESSION AND IDENTITY FORMATION

A significant number of studies on emotions in sport have focused on identity formation: on the emotional socialization experienced in sport, the emotional work required in constructing athletic identities, and the effects of sport on reproducing social identities of culture, gender, class, race, sexuality and subculture. Research in this area poses some of the following questions. How do emotions, expressed in sport and leisure, contribute to individual and group identity formation and the expression and presentation of the self? How does the socialization of emotions in sport contribute to the reproduction of structures of stratification and hierarchy in culture? How do sport and leisure contribute to the production, experience and meaning of cultural emotional forms?

Culture

The study of emotion is central to the figurational sociology of Elias (1978, 1987) and his followers (Dunning et al., 1988; Dunning and Rojek, 1992; Dunning and Sheard, 1979; Maguire, 1993). According to Elias, since the Middle Ages there has been a long-term trend toward control over affect and the restraint of emotion in society. With the pacification of everyday life, mimetic forms of behavior, where intense emotions are expressed in controlled ways, have come to characterize modern forms of sport and leisure. Figurationalists contend that the pleasurable controlled decontrolling of emotions, the quest for battle excitement, or the quest for exciting significance, underlies much of sport and leisure practice. While the figurational perspective has provided insight into the emergence of modern sport and the relationship of sport to emotion, Maguire (1991) notes that research has tended to focus on sports that confirm the theory's model of sport, 'That is, sports where a high degree of "battle excitement" is recurrently generated and where the emphasis of identity formation is on intense forms of manliness' (p. 29). Maguire (1991) suggests that the figurational research agenda be expanded to explore in more detail the identity formation qualities of sport, to investigate the self-expressive and emotional self-management aspects of sport and to address contemporary concerns with techniques of bodily discipline. Hargreaves (1994), too, suggests that the figurational perspective needs to address gender relations in greater detail and to consider the links between violence encouraged in male sport and violence against women. Studies focused on the relationship between violence in sport and contemporary power relations may further illuminate the concept of the civilizing process. On a theoretical level, differences exist between researchers, like Hargreaves, whose work is motivated by a 'passionate objectivity' and those figurationalists who strive for emotional 'detachment' in the production of theory and research (Dunning and Rojek, 1992: 162–6).

For nations and cultures, emotions and emotional displays are used as expressive markers of meaning, values and identity (Nauright and Chandler, 1996; Tomlinson, 1992; Werbner, 1996). On a cultural level, emotions in sport can be used to generate national fervor or to express political ideology (Hoberman, 1988). For example, in Soviet muscular socialism sport came 'closest to religious ritual in serving to provide … cohesion, solidarity, integration, discipline, and emotional euphoria' (Riordan, 1987: 376). Emotions also reflect different cultural values, as in Curry and Weiss's study (1989) of Austrian and US athletes. In this study, competition, as an emotional motivator for sport involvement, was more likely to characterize US athletes than Austrian athletes. Labeling emotional displays can be a significant process in constructing a culture's identity. Giulianotti's (1995) study of conflicting state, media and fan interpretations of the expressive behaviors of Scottish fans at football matches is a good example of how the meaning of a group's emotional display can be contested, thus affecting control over a group's identity formation.

Subculture

Emotions play a key role in constructing sport subculture identities (Gallmeier, 1987; Stevenson, 1991). Different sports evoke and idealize identifying forms of emotional expression. Sport subcultures offer different emotional experiences in terms of building community, establishing individual identity and demonstrating emotional control. For example, feelings of social bonding may be incidental or essential to group identity. Donnelly and Young (1988) found camaraderie, friendship and generosity to be important emotions for display among rugby players, while Klein (1986) found bodybuilders to be emotional loners, who abandon social bonding and rarely emote freely. Displaying appropriate emotional characteristics communicates important meanings not only to the larger culture but to members within the subculture itself. In describing the rescue of a novice rock climber who froze on a climb, Donnelly and Young report:

> The individual burst into tears upon reaching safety, but neither Donnelly nor the third member of the team could bring themselves to comfort him. By freezing, losing composure, he had jeopardized the safety of the party, and in the harsh

and somewhat unfeeling social world of climbers he could not be forgiven. The incident was never discussed, the individual never climbed again, and the resulting awkward interaction led him to drop out of the circle of friends. (1988: 228–9)

This description of rock climbers may be contrasted with the subculture of women's ice hockey. In most team sports, a significant part of subcultural identity formation is the emotional bonding that develops among athletes. In her study of ice hockey players Theberge (1995) noted the importance of shared emotion in the process of building a community. She observed that, 'Following games that were particularly physical or ... exciting, the dressing room was a loud and raucous place where players shared stories ... about their on-ice challenges and accomplishments ... these occasions are defining moments in the construction of community ... Team membership ... offers a context in which women hockey players collectively affirm their skills, commitment, and passion for their sport' (1995: 400–1).

Rail's (1990, 1992) classic phenomenological study of physical contact in women's basketball aptly demonstrates the myriad emotions athletes experience in establishing their identities in sport subcultures. Rail describes physical contacts as embodied emotions that may be orientated toward either communication or alienation. In the following passage she discusses the emotional difference between playful and violent contacts in basketball.

Feelings of control, as well as feelings of desire, hope, daring, physicality, toughness, powerfulness, strongness, cleverness, skillfulness, effectiveness, superiority, pride, bravery, and assertiveness are central to the organization of playful contacts ... In violent contact ... the self attempts to regain what has been lost or threatened, the emotional feelings of loss, shame, frustration, helplessness, anxiety, fear, anger, rage, hostility and hatred are central to the organization of violent contact ... the player's emotions may flood over her, overwhelming her in a 'blind rage' or she may act 'cold-bloodedly'. In either case, the player is drawn into the violent contact and becomes part of it. Violence radiates through the bodies of both the player and her victim. (1990: 276–7)

This insightful study is one of the few ethnographic projects that has examined women's emotional experience and understanding of physical aggression in sport. Additional research is needed to investigate how violent emotional experiences in sport might affect the ongoing construction of self and social identity.

The ability of athletes to manage their emotions is crucial in adopting sport identities. In an interesting study of the gymnastic subculture, Snyder (1990) found that athletes were expected to regulate feelings of nervousness, control fears of injury and pain, and manage feelings of frustration and disappointment. He noted that, while 'subcultural norms do not preclude individual variations in the display of emotions, ... some gymnasts "flood out" and lose control of their emotions and composure ... other gymnasts, perhaps the most competent, maintain their composure and emotional control ... These "ice maidens" are generally admired for their poise, composure, and dignity in a tense situation' (p. 266). The artful (and gendered) expectation in women's gymnastics is to make power, strength and speed look graceful, smooth and elegant. Emotion management plays a crucial role in affecting an 'appropriately feminine' presentation of the self to judges and audience.

The suppression of emotions related to pain and injury is a common expectation in most athletic subcultures (Curry, 1986; Nixon, 1994b). Whether giving or taking pain, athletes learn to desensitize themselves to the pain or violence of their sport. When learning to inflict pain on others is part of the sport socialization process, is rewarded and is connected to identity formation, some athletes eventually learn to take pleasure in pain-giving. One effect of the normalization of sado-ascetic sport practices and the suppression of empathetic emotions related to pain, is that athletes may become emotionally callused and thus morally compromised. While aggression and suppression of feelings are traditionally related to hegemonic masculinity, emotional management of feelings of pain, fear and injury is often as characteristic of women's sports today as men's sports (Nixon, 1994a, 1996a, 1996b; Young, 1991, 1993; Young et al., 1994). Modern sport practices and ideology exploit athletes' feelings of loyalty, need-achievement and self-identity. Overconformity to a sport ethic that requires self-sacrifice, risk-taking, rejecting limits, ignoring pain and playing hurt results in normalizing injuries in sport and valorizing a self-destructive athlete model (Curry and Strauss, 1994; Duquin, 1994; Hughes and Coakley, 1991). Research into the relationship between sport practice and the emotions of care, empathy and sensitivity shows that overconformity to the sport ethic and unreflective, automatic obedience to authority is detrimental to the physical, emotional and moral well-being of athletes (Duquin, 1984, 1993; Duquin and Schroeder-Braun, 1996).

Althletes may resist dominant cultural ideologies or highlight alternate values by defining or redefining the relationships between physical activity, emotion and meaning (Birrell and Richter, 1987; Gotfrit, 1991; Midol and Broyer, 1995). In her compelling ethnography of a skateboarding subculture, Beal (1995) found that skateboarders actively resisted high-pressured, competitive, controlled and inflexible sport environments. These athletes valued cooperation, friendship, self-esteem, flexibility, creativity and freedom of expression. Skateboarding was primarily about finding fun places to skate. Similarly, alternate sports and alternate sport groups may arise in response to marginalized or countercultural values. Midol (1993) described how the French, in the 1970s, developed the fun movement around the concept of the whiz,

> ... that is, speed, fluidity, entertainment, freedom linked to the imaginary notion of 'kick' which stands for new sensations, a sense of harmony, of risk, a taste for the extreme ... whether it be on snow, water, concrete or in the air, fun space is a 'sport' – by which is meant a space situated midway between myth and reality ... (p. 23)

Alternate sports may thus be a search for the expression of emotions not permitted or too rarely experienced in traditional sport and leisure forms.

Structuring and Restructuring Self-identities

Memory work (Haug, 1987; Messner, 1996; Sironen, 1994; Viejola, 1994), life-mode biography (Ottesen, 1994) and deep hermeneutic procedures (Nagbol, 1994) are particularly powerful methods for investigating the importance of emotions in forming self-identity and for examining the relationship between agency and social structure. In a particularly poignant example of memory work, Tiihonen (1994) relates how being asthmatic and an athlete affected the construction of his multiple and changing self-identities. His illness created an anxious corporeality while various social contexts, home, school, community, sport teams and the army, shaped his experiences and emotional responses that affected his self-images. He relates how the emotional experiences he had in sport contributed to his learning about class, power, authority, social bonding, gender relations and sexuality.

> Changing from a boy into a man is not the easiest task in Finnish culture. Suicides, the dangers of life, fear of the unknown, the pressure to succeed,

and the fear of failure are all too well known ... The club I belonged to was a bourgeois club. Later, when I joined the town's working-class club, I noticed the difference ... the boys did not act superior towards each other; they were straight forward and cold when they felt like it ... I learned that you should not be feminine, sentimental, over-friendly ... I cannot remember that masculinity was defined at all, other than through denial – through what a man should not be. By rules, hidden fears and the insolent language of the gang – 'homo', 'wanker' – we became men. (pp. 54–5) ... Because of asthma, I had to consider the relationship to myself and my identity ... The prolonged coughing attacks and constricted breathing made me depressed and caused me to question the meaning and sense of sport. A good game, a successful performance, and the feeling of belonging prompted me to try again ... the team spirit, the things done together and the appreciation of others ... attracted me. (p. 56) ... The disciplined body is the basis for the use of power, and especially so in the army. This ... body finds it difficult to express and receive emotion, which is continually repressed by hazing ... I could not take the military exercises, the only aim of which seemed to be to humiliate ... Such exercises were carried out in a way that my asthma could not bear; we went at full pace with no pause for breath. (p. 58) ... For the most part I have enjoyed those situations ... when I have done something for someone with my body, as in a football game, or by being united with other players and in front of the spectators ... Imagine the feeling when, as an object under ... thousands of pairs of eyes, you manage a good ball trick, a tackle, a pass, a goal. Even more important is the support you get from your own team, which, following a goal, exhibits strong physical emotions. Isn't that something in a culture which shies away from touching? (p. 58)

Memory is tied to emotion; feelings make events significant. In memory work, replaying past emotions reveals the forces and everyday events that helped to shape self-identity. In yet another moving piece of memory work, Viejola (1994) describes developing her self-identity through a series of face rituals played both in and out of sport. She recalls learning female codes of behavior and remembers the different emotional patterns of females and males in learning about friendship, dispute, love and team play.

> You extended yourself to win, and to outstrip, I extended myself to tie, and to get closer. Your wills were directed against each other; ours adjoined ... Your relationships mostly began from the moment you hit the same sport, where there was something to play ... Your friendships happened. Mine

existed, very close, all the time, even when the other was absent … The form of energy in my social space is empathy, sympathy, feeling of close-ness; or as their opposite hate, bitterness, and exclusion. The energy of your social space is force, counterforce and collision. (pp. 32–9)

She goes on to describe the mixed team play of a floorball game where emotions were felt and expressed differently.

When I fail in something during the game, I get embarrassed and feel sorry for my team. You let off steam by hitting the walls or the floor with your stick, or you play foul if the ball is otherwise robbed from you. You and your friends don't espe-cially mind breaking the rules, hitting ankles, pushing … but I get mad because in my mind these tricks violate the equality of the players … The game moves our emotions … Your emotions are as 'true' as mine, as 'real' in the situation they are felt in. But we interpret situations differently, and, consequently, feel different feelings. We put our souls into the game with equal passion, but we only project ourselves into our own emotions. We are not able to enter into each other's projections, each other's emotions. (pp. 36–8)

Memory work reveals how emotions are socialized in sport and how individuals can become active agents in constructing their emotional lives. One major advantage of such methodology is that personal memory work exposes the complex interaction of various social statuses (for example, class, gender, sexuality) in the emotional patterning of indi-vidual lives.

For many athletes self-identities must be restructured after leaving sport. The circum-stances under which one leaves sport affects one's emotional responses to withdrawal. Career-ending injuries or sudden, unexpected reasons for discontinuing sport involvement can result in depression, a sense of loss and an anxious search for a new self-identity (Astle, 1986). Kleiber and Brock (1992) call this event a disruption in one's life narrative that can affect life satisfaction for many years. Emotions sur-rounding leaving sport voluntarily after a suc-cessful experience can lead to feelings of rebirth as well as feelings of excitement in being able to explore other options now that one's sport career is over (Curtis and Ennis, 1988; Johns et al., 1990). However, leaving sport as a result of burnout can be an emo-tionally draining process. Modern training procedures are often overcontrolled and dehu-manizing, resulting in athletes feeling trapped, stifled and out of control. The continual pres-sure for higher performance standards leads to

severe chronic physical and emotional stress (Hoberman, 1992; Koukouris, 1994; Swain, 1991). For dedicated athletes who have little time to develop themselves in areas outside of sport, self-identity can be very narrowly and precariously defined. As Coakley (1992) explains, for these athletes

… sport involvement became analogous to being on a tightrope … they knew they couldn't shift their focus to anything else without losing their balance … and they knew there would be no net to catch them … they started to feel insecure. Their insecurity affected their performance. And their inability to meet performance standards led them to withdraw socially and emotionally from those around them … they had little to fall back on … no viable alternative identities for interacting with other people in meaningful ways. (p. 276)

Those who choose to leave sport have often been pejoratively characterized in sport research as 'drop outs'. However, in the case of high-pressured, sometimes abusive sport prac-tices, athletes who decide to leave sport may be seeking a healthier emotional environment than is available in their present sport setting (Duquin, 1995).

Gender and Sexuality

Research on women's experience of emotion in sport has centered on two somewhat contra-dictory realities in relation to gender identity. While sport and exercise often empower women, recent research has demonstrated how the sport/fitness movement has re-territorialized women's bodies, instilling feel-ings of shame, constant self-surveillance and anxiety about meeting new standards of femi-ninity (Bolin, 1992; Bordo, 1989; Featherstone, 1991). The fitness industry focuses women's energy on disciplinary practices in an attempt to achieve 'the look' of a fit and desirable woman. Duncan (1994) observes that, 'For many women, the experience of shame that comes from not living up to beauty disguised as health encourages confession in a way that reinforces the authority of the panoptic gaze … the equa-tion between feeling good and looking good works in reverse. Look becomes a sign of feel, so if you look good you must therefore feel good … ' (p. 57). This toned, tightened, no-fat feminine ideal distorts women's body image, causing anxiety, a fear of fat and in many cases a self-loathing that leads to serious eating disor-ders. Markula's (1995) revealing study of aero-bicizing women notes that, 'the very part of our bodies that identify us as females: the rounded bellies, the larger hips, the thighs, the softer underarms … are also the ones we hate the most and fight the hardest to diminish. Logically then, we hate looking like women' (p. 435).

At the same time, women's participation in sport has challenged the idealized passivity and weakness of hegemonic femininity. Sport and physical activities have long been powerfully sensual and emotional experiences for women. Hargreaves (1994: 92) documents this historic reality in her reference to a nineteenth-century woman's euphoric description of the pleasures of cycling:

> Hers is all the joy of motion, not to be underestimated, and the long days in the open air; all the joy of adventure and change. Hers is the delightful sense of independence and power … And, above all, cycling day after day, and all day long will speedily reduce or elevate her to that perfect state of physical well-being, to that healthy animal condition, which in itself is one of the greatest pleasures in life. (Greville, 1894: 264)

Research shows that women are likely to have emotional experiences in sport that not only strengthen their bonds with other women, but increase their feelings of self-worth, power and control (Birrell and Cole, 1994; Blinde et al., 1994; McDermott, 1996; Theberge, 1987). These positive experiences provide a basis for reshaping gender identity and expression both in individual women and in the culture at large.

Sexual identity and homophobia are critical areas in the study of emotional experience in sport (Blinde, 1990; Burroughs et al., 1995; Griffin, 1993; Lenskyj, 1991). Harassment and discrimination are part of the emotional reality of many athletes' lives in traditional sport. Lesbians in sport may experience fear, isolation, alienation, persecution and stigmatization as a result of heterosexist assumptions and homophobic sport environments. Likewise, those who reproduce homophobic fears and prejudice in sport are diminished in their ethical capacities for care, understanding, compassion, courage, tolerance, love and self-worth (Oakley, 1992).

Women have long derived pleasure from the homosocial and sensual interaction that sport affords (Hargreaves, 1994; Patzkill, 1990). The physical nature of sport lends itself to expanding erotic and hedonistic sensibilities. For lesbian athletes sport can be a site for emotional support and emotional grounding. Kaskisaari (1994) describes sport as a place to express lesbian identity:

> if you have a team which not only accepts relationships between women but takes them

for granted. You then have a woman-activated women's team … in the sense that women become active in women's company, by the touch of a woman, and by making love with a woman; woman-activated in the sense that a woman is actively drawn to relationships with women. (1994: 18)

However, she goes on to discuss the negative emotional impact sport can also have on lesbian athletes.

> Although sport was felt to be a secure place to which one could escape the demands of femininity, it later proved to be a very heterosexist area controlled by male interests. Sport required that the women sacrifice their gender and sexuality. Feelings associated with femininity – emotional support, the need for warmth and gentleness, feelings of powerlessness and weakness – were denied. (1994: 19)

For lesbian athletes, confirming and positive emotional experiences in sport depend a great deal on the degree to which the sport experience is women-identified, free of homophobia and heterosexist assumptions, and openly welcoming of sexual diversity.

Within the past ten years a wealth of critical scholarship has shown how sport contributes to the construction of male identities and the reproduction of a gender hierarchy (Connell, 1990; Corrigan, 1991; Laitinen and Tiihonen, 1990; McLaren, 1991; Messner, 1992; Trujillo, 1995). The emotional consequences of sport participation on male identity and male bonding are complex. Messner (1992) describes many of the emotional benefits of sport for males.

> … Vast numbers of boys and men … have found sport to be a major context in which they experience fun, where they relax and build friendships with others, where they can push their bodies toward excellence, where they may learn to co-operate toward a shared goal, and where they may get a sense of identification and community in an otherwise privatized and alienating society. (1992: 171)

At the same time, feminist and critical scholars have documented the emotional and physical costs of male sport involvement that often reproduces a hegemonic form of masculine identity characterized by violence, male dominance, ritualized aggression, homophobia, misogyny and emotional callousness (Curry, 1991; Messner and Sabo, 1990; Sabo and Panepinto, 1990; Whitson, 1990). While many sport practices continue to reproduce dominating forms of masculinity, recent scholarship has emphasized the importance of identifying other masculinities in sport as well as noting the importance of culture, race, ethnicity, class and sexuality as they affect the range and quality of emotional and expressive experiences that males may have in sport (Bissinger, 1990; Coakley and White, 1992; Foley, 1990; Maguire, 1986; Tomlinson, 1992). For example, Klein's (1995) study of Mexican and Anglo baseball players revealed a continuum of masculinity with Mexican players more capable than their North American team mates of exhibiting tender emotions, showing vulnerability and hurt, and displaying physical affection. Majors's (1990) description of the strong, proud, 'cool pose' expressive of black athletes, Connell's (1990) study of the emotional discipline of an Iron Man champion and Wacquant's (1992) study of the social construction of an emotionally protected and secure space for boxers in a Chicago gym all testify to the complex interaction of masculine identity formation and emotional experience in sport.

The open expression of sexual identity in traditionally heterosexist male sport is rare for gay men. To avoid suffering many gay men pass as straight, and in their position as outsider and observer, they develop what Pronger (1990) calls an ironic sensibility. Yet, the physical nature and social bonding aspects of sport can be a source of erotic pleasure for gay athletes. Pronger (1990) expresses the emotional experience of participating in the Gay Games when he writes:

> In gay athletic culture, the athlete is someone with whom one shares an erotic world and a way of being in it. At the Gay Games, immersed in that shared world for a week, most of us couldn't stop smiling. The erotic desirability of that truly gay pleasure is an integral part of the gay sports experience. (1990: 270)

Messner (1996) has also discussed the important role sport plays in shaping sexual identity and erotic desire. He concluded that systems of oppression and domination are intrinsically connected with the ways we come to shape our sexual desires and pleasures. He posed the following important questions regarding erotic desire:

> How do institutional power relationships shape, mediate, repress, sublimate, and desublimate desire? How do individuals and groups respond in ways that reproduce, subtly change, or overtly challenge oppressive conventions? How do people (for instance, athletes and spectators) actively take up the construction of their own sexual identities and communities? And how do these sexual identities, relations, and practices intersect with other kinds of differences and inequalities within a socially structured matrix of domination? (1996: 230)

These questions point to the importance of sport in directing homo-social desire. The highly physical nature of sport makes it a likely site for the expression of erotic energy. While traditional sport may officially promote heterosexism, opportunities for alternate forms of erotic pleasure are often realized in sport.

Sport Spectating and Nostalgia

Sport fans experience a broad spectrum of emotions, both personal and communal, when watching sport. Researchers studying emotions in sport spectating have been primarily interested in describing the motives of sport fans, the pleasures of spectating, and the effects of sport fandom and sport nostalgia. According to Real and Mechikoff (1992), 'The nature of the interpretive community in which the sport fan places himself or herself and the degree of psychological identification with the athletes contributes to dimensions of both breadth and depth in fan mythic identification' (p. 324). For many fans, spectating is enjoyable because of the excitement, suspense, aggression and drama involved in sporting contests (Bryant et al., 1994; DeNeui and Sachau, 1996). When fans identify closely with teams they tend to feel deep emotions both positive and negative. Fans experience anxiety, frustration, anger, hostility, sadness and depression when their team does poorly and elation, ecstasy, enjoyment, self-fulfillment, self-esteem and social prestige when their team does well (Wenner, 1990; Zhang et al., 1996). As Trujillo and Krizek (1994) explain, 'Despite ... problems with sport, true fans seem to have an emotional attachment ... powerful senses of identity, community, continuity, narrativity, therapy, spirituality, and self-discovery' (p. 321).

The enjoyment of spectating and the pleasures of looking have also been studied in reference to mass-mediated sport (Gantz and Wenner, 1995; Trujillo, 1995). Using media theory, Duncan and Brummett (1989) demonstrated how three sources of spectating pleasure – fetishism, voyeurism and narcissism – characterized the televised sport spectacle of the 1988 Winter Olympic Games. Through the discourses, technologies and practices of television, athletes were made into fetish objects and viewers offered the pleasures of voyeurism, and narcissistic identification with athletes. The power of mass-mediated sport to affect emotions and cultural meanings is supported by Real and Mechikoff when they write that, 'mass mediated sport today is capable of providing for the deep fan crucial expressive, liminal, cathartic, ideational mechanisms and experiences for the representation, celebration and interpretation of contemporary social life ... ' (1992: 337). These representations are not, however, always the preferred or dominant readings of the sport spectacle (Lalvani, 1994). For example, in a media study of NFL football, Duncan and Brummett (1993) found that some women spectators made 'subversive attacks upon the televised football spectacle for the oppositional powers and pleasures associated with it ... By remarking on the awkwardness, arrogance, and stupidity of the football players, the women symbolically reduced the game to an absurd, comical spectacle, an event unworthy of great seriousness' (pp. 68–9). By their 'ironic detachment' from the game these women refused a patriarchal reading of the text and instead derived pleasure by comically undercutting the football spectacle. The refusal to respond with 'appropriate' emotional affect to the practices of culture-making institutions is a form of radical empowerment.

Research in the sociology of nostalgia (a remembrance of the past) focuses on both private and public sport nostalgia (Howell, 1991; Mosher, 1991). Emotional themes related to private sport nostalgia include remembering affiliative bonds, heroic efforts, overcoming obstacles, self-discovery, pain and failure (Healey, 1991). People derive pleasure from recounting sport narratives that have helped them define who they are and the values they hold. According to Snyder (1991):

> Nostalgia is defined in terms of the remembrance of the past that is imbued with positive feelings such as pleasure, joy, satisfaction, and goodness. (p. 228) ... Private sport nostalgia is linked to the benchmarks of people's sport involvement and identity at different times in their life cycle; these emotions are generally positive reflections on the past, yet there is also the feeling of pathos and yearning for the past ... collective sport nostalgia extends the concepts of the 'sacred' and 'collective representations' ... and seems to be related to social conditions of change and unrest. (p. 237)

Public sport nostalgia, as represented for example in sports Halls of Fame, is conservative in that these museums preserve and affirm dominant or official values of a culture while indirectly rejecting alternative values (Snyder, 1991). Slowikowski (1991), in discussing the emotional and symbolic effects of the Olympic flame ceremony, suggested that,

'In the postmodern era people feel unmoored, uncentered, in a world viewed as spiraling blindly toward oblivion ... Perhaps, postmodern practices such as the flame tradition are efforts to keep reviving, through reference to old situations, that which is deadened by technology and instrumentalization' (p. 247). The undermining of a sense of community and solidarity in the modern era, the greater visibility of diversity in values, and the challenge by minorities and women to traditional patterns of authority may all be reasons for the growth in sport nostalgia.

FUTURE RESEARCH

Given the relatively new status of emotions as a research topic in the sociology of sport and leisure, scholars have raised and begun to answer a number of interesting questions. Our understanding of the importance of emotions in sport and leisure, however, could benefit from a research agenda focused specifically on emotions.

Memory work and life-mode biographies provide a rich and evocative source for understanding how agency and social structure interact in sport and leisure to affect emotional life and identity formation. Denzin (1990) envisions the study of emotions as primarily interpretive, biographical and phenomenological.

> I envision our project as being one that interrogates human experience from the inside ... We must inquire into what kind of gendered emotional being this late postmodern period is creating. We should be doing work on the structures of emotional experience, on the forms of emotional feeling and intersubjectivity, on the violent emotions, on temporality and emotionality, on moments of epiphany and shattering emotionality, ... on the cultural constraints on emotionality, on the diseases of emotionality that our late postmodern period valorizes, defines, treats, and cures. (1990: 108–9)

Research should also continue in the area of historical change in emotional life as a result of modernity. However, new research needs to explore changes in emotional expression in many different cultures and political systems over time. In some cultures emotions are primarily viewed as self-expressions, while in other cultures emotions are better understood as public performances that convey information about social situations or relations (Gordon, 1990; Harré, 1986). Research should take into account different groups with varying power and status positions in society. How do emotional experiences and expectations for emotional control or expression in sport and leisure differ within social hierarchies such as race, gender, class, sexuality, age and ability (Hochschild, 1990; Kunesh et al., 1992)? Researchers also need to demonstrate how long-term trends toward pacification, commercialization, privatization and individualization affect emotional expression in contemporary sport, leisure and cultural relations (Maguire, 1991; McDonald, 1996; Rojek, 1985).

More research is needed on the emotional effects of the disciplinary technologies of the body that are part of sport and fitness practices today. How is shame manipulated to increase discipline and self-surveillance (Scheff, 1990)? How do disciplinary practices empower us, increasing our feelings of freedom, achievement and self-development? What, also, are the dangers of emotional repression, obedience and discipline in modern sport? As Heikkala (1993) observes:

> Achievement and progress through discipline are the certainties of our everyday lives and discourses and, as such, are difficult to question. In the context of sport, the deep ethical question is the value of the unquestionable subjection to the rationale of competing. Self-discipline in sport is a prerequisite for achievement ... But this should not obscure the possibility that practices blindly followed and not fully reflected on are the beginnings of fascism. Not historical fascism, but fascism that 'causes us to love power, to desire the very thing that dominates and exploits us' (Foucault, 1985: xiii) giving the feeling of power through obedience. (1993: 411)

How do disciplinary technologies teach athletes to manage their emotions in sport? How do sport and leisure dampen and heighten emotional response? Which emotions are likely to be dampened, which heightened? What emotional experiences in sport and leisure are likely to elicit deviant behaviors, resistance behaviors, or obedient/passive behaviors (Alder and Alder, 1988; Bloom and Smith, 1996; Thoits, 1990). How has resistance to modern technologies of the body altered the structure, practice and emotional experience of sport and leisure including the development of new sport and leisure forms (Rinehart, 1996)?

Finally, we need more research on the emotional socialization that takes place in sport and the effects this socialization has on constructing moral identities (Duquin, 1984; Duquin and Schroeder-Braun, 1996; Shields and Bredemeier, 1996; Shields et al., 1995).

Sport structures and ideologies influence the moral climate of sport, the quality of the coach–athlete relationship and the moral consciousness of athletes (Bykhovskaya, 1991; Cruz et al., 1995; Lee and Cockman, 1995; Pilz, 1995). We need research on the links between emotional expression in sport and moral behavior. How do sport and leisure ideologically represent emotions like empathy, compassion and care? How do athletes come to define the moral requirements of a sport? How can the ethic of care be incorporated into sport practice? Are there long-term emotional and moral effects of sport participation? Some important research has been done on the relationship of sport to violence prevention and conflict resolution (Branta et al., 1996; Hellison et al., 1996; Taylor, 1996). Yet, more research is needed on how emotions experienced in sport and leisure contribute to the moral identities of self and community.

How we approach our research on emotions in sport and leisure is also important. Trujillo and Krizek (1994) believe that

> ... all researchers ... should pay closer attention to the emotions of the people we study as well as to the emotions we experience as researchers ... Our feelings and emotions as people influence how we approach our subjects and how we interpret our data. By failing to pay attention to feelings and emotions we lose an opportunity to understand our subjects and ourselves in richer ways. (p. 322)

Dispassionate research does not necessarily privilege the rational or scientific but rather privileges our right to obscure our own motivations, emotions and values that characterize our life and work.

REFERENCES AND FURTHER READING

Alder, P. and Alder, P. (1988) 'Intense loyalty in organizations: a case study of college athletics', *Administrative Science Quarterly*, 33 (4): 401–17.

Astle, S. (1986) 'The experience of loss in athletes', *Journal of Sports Medicine*, 26 (3): 279–84.

Beal, B. (1995) 'Disqualifying the official: an exploration of social resistance through the subculture of skateboarding', *Sociology of Sport Journal*, 12 (3): 252–67.

Birrell, S. and Cole, C. (1994) *Women, Sport and Culture*. Champaign, IL: Human Kinetics.

Birrell, S. and Richter, D. (1987) 'Is a diamond forever?: feminist transformations of sport', *Women's International Forum*, 10 (4): 395–409.

Bissinger, H. (1990) *Friday Night Lights: a Town, a Team, a Dream*. Reading, MA: Addison-Wesley.

Blinde, E. (1990) 'Pressure and stress in women's college sports: views from athletes'. Paper presented at the annual meeting of the American Alliance for Health, Physical Education, Recreations and Dance, New Orleans.

Blinde, E., Taub, D. and Han, L. (1994) 'Sport as a site for women's group and societal empowerment: perspectives from the college athlete', *Sociology of Sport Journal*, 11 (1): 51–9.

Bloom, G. and Smith, M. (1996) 'Hockey violence: a test of cultural spillover theory', *Sociology of Sport Journal*, 13 (1): 65–77.

Bolin, A. (1992) 'Flex appeal, food, and fat: competitive bodybuilding, gender and diet', *Play and Culture*, 5: 378–400.

Bordo, S. (1989) 'The body and the reproduction of femininity: a feminist appropriation of Foucault', in A.M. Jaggar and S.R. Bordo (eds), *Gender/Body/Knowledge: Feminist Reconstructions of Being and Knowing*. New Brunswick, NJ: Rutgers University Press. pp. 13–33.

Branta, C., Lerner, J. and Taylor, C. (1996) 'Facilitating social skills in urban school children through physical education', *Peace and Conflict: Journal of Peace Psychology*, 2 (4): 305–20.

Bryant, J., Rockwell, S. and Owens, J. (1994) '"Buzzers beaters" and "barn burners" the effects of enjoyment of watching the game go "down to the wire"', *Journal of Sport and Social Issues*, 18 (4): 326–40.

Burroughs, A., Ashburn, L. and Seebohm, L. (1995) '"Add sex and stir": homophobic coverage of women's cricket in Australia', *Journal of Sport and Social Issues*, 19 (3): 266–84.

Bykhovskaya, I. (1991) 'Sports, new way of thinking and human values', *International Review for Sociology of Sport*, 26 (3): 193–200.

Coakley, J. (1992) 'Burnout among adolescent athletes: a person failure or social problem?', *Sociology of Sport Journal*, 9 (1): 271–85.

Coakley, J. and White, A. (1992) 'Making decisions: gender and sport participation among British adolescents', *Sociology of Sport Journal*, 9 (1): 20–35.

Connell, R.W. (1990) 'An iron man: the body and some contradictions of hegemonic masculinity', in M. Messner and D. Sabo (eds), *Sport, Men and the Gender Order: Critical Feminist Perspectives*. Champaign, IL: Human Kinetics. pp. 83–97.

Corrigan, P. (1991) 'The making of the boy: meditations on what grammar school did with,to and for my body', in H. Giroux (ed.), *Postmodernism, Feminism and Cultural Politics*. Albany, NY: State of New York Press. pp. 174–95.

Cruz, J., Boixados, M., Valiente, L. and Capdevila, L. (1995) 'Prevalent values in young Spanish soccer players', *International Review for Sociology of Sport*, 30 (3 + 4): 353–70.

Curry, T. (1986) 'A visual method of studying sports: the photo-elicitation interview', *Sociology of Sport Journal*, 3 (3): 204–16.

Curry, T. (1991) 'Fraternal bonding in the locker room: a profeminist analysis of talk about competition and women', *Sociology of Sport Journal*, 8 (2): 119–35.

Curry, T. and Strauss, R. (1994) 'A little pain never hurt anybody: a photo-essay on the normalization of sport injuries', *Sociology of Sport Journal*, 11 (2): 195–208.

Curry, T. and Weiss, O. (1989) 'Sport identity and motivation for sport participation: a comparison between American college athletes and Austrian student sport club members', *Sociology of Sport Journal*, 6 (3): 257–68.

Curtis, J. and Ennis, R. (1988) 'Negative consequences of leaving competitive sport? Comparative finding for former elite-level hockey players', *Sociology of Sport Journal*, 5 (2): 87–106.

DeNeui, D. and Sachau, D. (1996) 'Spectator enjoyment of aggression in intercollegiate hockey games', *Journal of Sport and Social Issues*, 20 (1): 69–77.

Denzin, N. (1990) 'On understanding emotion: the interpretive-cultural agenda', in T. Kemper (ed.), *Research Agendas in the Sociology of Emotions*. Albany, NY: State University of New York Press. pp. 85–116.

Donnelly, P. and Young, K. (1988) 'The construction and confirmation of identity in sport subcultures', *Sociology of Sport Journal*, 5 (3): 223–40.

Duncan, M. (1994) 'The politics of women's body images and practices: Foucault, the panopticon, and *Shape* magazine', *Journal of Sport and Social Issues*, 18 (1): 48–65.

Duncan, M.C. and Brummett, B. (1989) 'Types and sources of spectating pleasure in television sports', *Sociology of Sport Journal*, 6: 195–211.

Duncan, M.C. and Brummett (1993) 'Liberal and radical sources of female empowerment in sport media', *Sociology of Sport Journal*, 10 (1): 57–72.

Dunning, E. and Rojek, C. (1992) *Sport and Leisure in the Civilizing Process*. Toronto: University of Toronto Press.

Dunning, E. and Sheard, K. (1979) *Barbarians, Gentlemen and Players*. New York: New York University Press.

Dunning, E., Murphy, P. and Williams, J. (1988) *The Roots of Football Hooliganism*. London: Routledge & Kegan Paul.

Duquin, M. (1984) 'Power and authority: moral consensus and conformity in sport', *International Review for Sociology of Sport*, 19: 295–304.

Duquin, M. (1993) 'One future for sport: moving toward an ethic of care', in G. Cohen (ed.), *Women and Sport: Issues and Controversies*. Newbury Park, CA: Sage.

Duquin, M. (1994) 'The Body Snatchers and Dr Frankenstein revisited: the social construction and deconstruction of bodies and sport', *Journal of Sport and Social Issues*, 18 (3): 268–81.

Duquin, M. (1995) 'Athletic persistence: the importance of social structure', in K. Henschen and W. Straub (eds), *Sport Psychology: an Analysis of Athlete Behavior*. Longmeadow, MA: Mouvement Publications. pp. 57–62.

Duquin, M. and Schroeder-Braun, K. (1996) 'Power, empathy and moral conflict in sport', *Peace and Conflict: Journal of Peace Psychology*, 2 (4): 351–68.

Elias, N. (1978) *The Civilising Process*. Oxford: Blackwell.

Elias, N. (1987) 'On human beings and their emotions: a process-sociological essay', *Theory, Culture and Society*, 4: 339–61.

Elias, N. and Dunning, E. (1986) *Quest for Excitement: Sport and Leisure in the Civilising Process*. Oxford: Basil Blackwell.

Featherstone, M. (1991) 'The body in consumer culture', in M. Featherstone, M. Hepworth and B.S. Turner (eds), *The Body: Social Process and Cultural Theory*. London: Sage. pp. 170–96.

Ferguson, J. (1981) 'Emotions in sport sociology', *International Review of Sport Sociology*, 16: 15–23.

Foley, D. (1990) 'The great American football ritual: reproducing race, class and gender inequality', *Sociology of Sport Journal*, 7 (2): 111–35.

Foucault, M. (1985) 'Preface', in G. Deleuze and F. Guattari (eds), *Anti-Oedipus: Capitalism and Schizophrenia*. London: The Athlone Press. pp. xi–xiv.

Gallmeier, C. (1987) 'Putting on the game face: the staging of emotions in professional hockey', *Sociology of Sport Journal*, 4: 347–62.

Gantz, W. and Wenner, L. (1995) 'Fanship and the television sports viewing experience', *Sociology of Sport Journal*, 12 (1): 56–74.

Giulianotti, R. (1995) 'Football and the politics of carnival: an ethnographic study of Scottish fans in Sweden', *International Review for Sociology of Sport*, 30 (2): 191–217.

Gordon, S. (1990) 'Social structural effects on emotions', in T. Kemper (ed.), *Research Agendas in the Sociology of Emotions*. Albany, NY: State University of New York Press. pp. 145–79.

Gotfrit, L. (1991) 'Women dancing back: disruption and the politics of pleasure', in H. Giroux (ed.), *Postmodernism, Feminism and Cultural Politics*. Albany, NY: State of New York Press. pp. 174–95.

Greville, Lady (ed.) (1894) *Ladies in the Field: Sketches of Sport*. London: Ward & Downey.

Griffin, P. (1993) 'Homophobia in women's sports: the fear that divides us', in G. Cohen (ed.), *Women in Sport: Issues and Controversies*. Newbury Park, CA: Sage. pp. 193–203.

Hargreaves, J.A. (1994) *Sporting Females: Critical Issues in the History and Sociology of Women's Sport*. New York: Routledge.

Harré, R. (1986) *The Social Construction of Emotions*. Oxford: Blackwell.

Haug, F. (1987) *Female Sexualization: a Collective Work of Memory*. London: Verso.

Healey, J. (1991) 'An exploration of the relationships between memory and sport', *Sociology of Sport Journal*, 8 (3): 213–27.

Heikkala, J. (1993) 'Discipline and excel: techniques of the self and body and the logic of competing', *Sociology of Sport Journal*, 10 (4): 397–412.

Hellison, D., Martineck, T. and Cutforth, N. (1996) 'Beyond violence prevention in inner city physical activity programs', *Peace and Conflict: Journal of Peace Psychology*, 2 (4): 321–38.

Hoberman, J. (1988) 'Sport and the technological image of man', in W. Morgan and K. Meier (eds), *Philosophic Inquiry in Sport*. Champaign, IL: Human Kinetics.

Hoberman, J. (1992) *Mortal Engines: the Science of Performance and the Dehumanization of Sport*. New York: Free Press.

Hochschild, A. (1990) 'Ideology and emotion management: a perspective and path for future research', in T. Kemper (ed.), *Research Agendas in the Sociology of Emotions*. Albany, NY: State University of New York Press. pp. 117–42.

Howell, J. (1991) '"A revolution in motion": advertising and the politics of nostalgia', *Sociology of Sport Journal*, 8 (3): 258–71.

Hughes, R. and Coakley, J. (1991) 'Positive deviance among athletes: the implications of overconformity to the sport ethic', *Sociology of Sport Journal*, 8 (4): 307–25.

Johns, D., Lindner, K. and Wolko, K. (1990) 'Understanding attrition in female competitive gymnastics: applying social exchange theory', *Sociology of Sport Journal*, 7 (2): 154–71.

Kaskisaari, M. (1994) 'The rhythmbody', *International Review for Sociology of Sport*, 29 (1): 15–21.

Kleiber, D. and Brock, S. (1992) 'The effect of career-ending injuries on the subsequent well-being of elite college athletes', *Sociology of Sport Journal*, 9 (1): 70–5.

Klein, A. (1986) 'Pumping irony: crisis and contradiction in bodybuilding', *Sociology of Sport Journal*, 3 (2): 112–33.

Klein, A. (1995) 'Tender machos: masculine contrasts in the Mexican baseball league', *Sociology of Sport*, 12 (4): 370–88.

Koukouris, K. (1994) 'Constructed case studies: athletes' perspectives on disengaging from organized competitive sport', *Sociology of Sport Journal*, 11 (2): 175–94.

Kunesh, M., Hasbrook, C. and Lewthwaite, R. (1992) 'Physical activity socialization: peer interactions and affective responses among a sample of sixth grade girls', *Sociology of Sport Journal*, 9 (4): 385–96.

Laitinen, A. and Tiihonen, A. (1990) 'Narratives of men's experiences in sport', *International Review for the Sociology of Sport*, 25 (3): 185–200.

Lalvani, S. (1994) 'Carrying the ideological ball: text, discourse and pleasure', *Sociology of Sport Journal*, 11 (2): 155–74.

Lee, N. and Cockman, M. (1995) 'Values in children's sport: spontaneously expressed values among young athletes', *International Review for the Sociology of Sport*, 30 (3 + 4): 337–49.

Lenskyi, H. (1991) 'Combating homophobia in sport and physical education', *Sociology of Sport Journal*, 8 (1): 61–9.

Maguire, J. (1986) 'Images of manliness and competing ways of living in Late Victorian and Edwardian Britain', *British Journal of Sport History*, 3: 265–87.

Maguire, J. (1991) 'Towards a sociological theory of sport and the emotions: a figurational perspective', *International Review for the Sociology of Sport*, 26: 25–35.

Maguire, J. (1993) 'Bodies, sports cultures and societies: a critical review of some theories in the sociology of the body', *International Review for the Sociology of Sport*, 28 (1): 33–50.

Majors, R. (1990) 'Cool pose: black masculinity and sports', in M. Messner and D. Sabo (eds), *Sport, Men and the Gender Order*. Champaign, IL: Human Kinetics. pp. 109–14.

Markula, P. (1995) 'Firm but shapely, fit but sexy, strong but thin: the postmodern aerobicizing female bodies', *Sociology of Sport Journal*, 12 (4): 424–53.

McDermott, L. (1996) 'Toward a feminist understanding of physicality within the context of women's physically active and sporting lives', *Sociology of Sport Journal*, 13 (1): 12–30.

McDonald, M. (1996) 'Michael Jordan's family values: marketing, meaning and post–Reagan America', *Sociology of Sport Journal*, 13 (4): 344–65.

McLaren, P. (1991) 'Schooling the postmodern body: critical pedagogy and the politics of enfleshment', in H. Giroux (ed.), *Postmodernism, Feminism and Cultural Politics*. Albany, NY: State of New York Press. pp. 174–95.

Messner, M. (1992) *Power at Play: Sports and the Problem of Masculinity*. Boston, MA: Beacon Press.

Messner, M. (1996) 'Studying up on sex', *Sociology of Sport Journal*, 13 (3): 221–37.

Messner, M. and Sabo, D. (eds) (1990) *Sport, Men and the Gender Order*. Champaign, IL: Human Kinetics.

Midol, N. (1993) 'Cultural dissents and technical innovations in the "whiz" sports', *International Review for the Sociology of Sport*, 28 (1): 23–9.

Midol, N. and Broyer, G. (1995) 'Toward an anthropological analysis of new sport cultures: the case of whiz sports in France', *Sociology of Sport Journal*, 12 (2): 204–12.

Mosher, S. (1991) 'Fielding our dreams: rounding third in Dyersville', *Sociology of Sport Journal*, 8 (3): 272–80.

Nagbol, S. (1994) 'Helgoland on Amager', *International Review for the Sociology of Sport*, 29 (1): 85–96.

Nauright, J. and Chandler, T. (eds) (1996) *Making Men: Rugby and Masculine Identity*. London: Frank Cass.

Nixon, H. (1994a) 'Social pressure, social support, and help seeking for pain and injuries in college sports networks', *Journal of Sport and Social Issues*, 18 (4): 340–55.

Nixon, H. (1994b) 'Coaches' views of risk, pain and injury in sport, with special reference to gender differences', *Sociology of Sport Journal*, 11 (1): 79–87.

Nixon, H. (1996a) 'The relationship of friendship networks, sports experiences, and gender to expressed pain thresholds', *Sociology of Sport Journal*, 13 (1): 78–86.

Nixon, H. (1996b) 'Explaining pain and injury attitudes and experiences in sport in terms of gender, race, and sports status factors', *Journal of Sport and Social Issues*, 20 (1): 33–44.

Oakley, J. (1992) *Morality and the Emotions*. New York: Routledge.

Ottesen, L. (1994) 'Sport in different types of lifemode biographies. An alternative analysis of sports habits', *International Review for the Sociology of Sport*, 29 (1): 63–82.

Patzkill, B. (1990) 'Between gym shoes and high-heels. The development of a lesbian identity and existence in top class sport', *International Review for the Sociology of Sport*, 25 (3): 221–32.

Pilz, G. (1995) 'Performance sport: education in fair play? (Some empirical and theoretical remarks)', *International Review for the Sociology of Sport*, 30 (3/4): 391–403.

Pronger, B. (1990) *The Arena of Masculinity: Sports, Homosexuality, and the Meaning of Sex*. New York: St Martin's Press.

Rail, G. (1990) 'Physical contact in women's basketball: a first interpretation', *International Review for the Sociology of Sport*, 25 (4): 269–84.

Rail, G. (1992) 'Physical contact in women's basketball: a phenomenological construction and contextualization', *International Review for the Sociology of Sport*, 27 (1): 1–22.

Real, M. and Mechikoff, R. (1992) 'Deep fan: mythic identification, technology, and advertising in spectator sports', *Sociology of Sport Journal*, 9 (4): 323–39.

Rinehart, R. (1996) 'Dropping hierarchies: toward the study of a contemporary sporting avant-garde', *Sociology of Sport Journal*, 15 (2): 159–75.

Riordan, J. (1987) 'Soviet muscular socialism: a Durkheimian analysis', *Sociology of Sport Journal*, 4 (4): 376–93.

Rojek, C. (1985) *Capitalism and Leisure Theory*. London: Tavistock.

Sabo, D. and Panepinto, J. (1990) 'Football ritual and the social reproduction of masculinity', in M. Messner and D. Sabo (eds), *Sport, Men, and the Gender Order*. Champaign, IL: Human Kinetics. pp. 115–26.

Scheff, T. (1990) 'Socialization of emotions: pride and shame as causal agents', in T. Kemper (ed.), *Research Agendas in the Sociology of Emotions*. Albany, NY: State University of New York Press. pp. 281–304.

Shields, D. and Bredemeier, B. (1996) 'Sport, militarism, and peace', *Peace and Conflict: Journal of Peace Psychology*, 2 (4): 369–84.

Shields, D., Bredemeier, B., Gardner, D. and Bostrom, A. (1995) 'Leadership, cohesion and team norms regarding cheating and aggression', *Sociology of Sport Journal*, 12 (3): 324–36.

Sironen, E. (1994) 'On memory-work in the theory of body culture', *International Review for the Sociology of Sport*, 29 (1): 5–11.

Slowikowski, S. (1991) 'Burning desire: nostalgia, ritual and the sport-festival flame ceremony', *Sociology of Sport Journal*, 8 (3): 239–57.

Snyder, E. (1990) 'Emotion and sport: a case study of collegiate women gymnasts', *Sociology of Sport Journal*, 7 (3): 254–70.

Snyder, E. (1991) 'Sociology of nostalgia: Sport Halls of Fame and museums in America', *Sociology of Sport Journal*, 8 (3): 228–38.

Stevenson, C. (1991) 'The Christian athlete: an interactionist-developmental analysis', *Sociology of Sport Journal*, 8 (4): 362–79.

Swain, D. (1991) 'Withdrawal from sport and Schlossberg's model of transitions', *Sociology of Sport Journal*, 8 (2): 152–60.

Taylor, C. (1996) 'Sports and recreation: community anchor and counterweight to conflict', *Peace and Conflict: Journal of Peace Psychology*, 2 (4): 339–50.

Theberge, N. (1987) 'Sport and women's empowerment', *Women's Studies International*, 10: 387–93.

Theberge, N. (1995) 'Gender, sport, and the construction of community: a case study from women's ice hockey', *Sociology of Sport Journal*, 12 (4): 389–403.

Thoits, P. (1990) 'Emotional deviance: research agendas', in T. Kemper (ed.), *Research Agendas in the Sociology of Emotions*. Albany, NY: State University of New York Press. pp. 180–206.

Tiihonen, A. (1994) 'Asthma – the construction of the masculine body', *International Review for the Sociology of Sport*, 29 (1): 51–61.

Tomlinson, A. (1992) 'Shifting patterns of working-class leisure: the case of knur-and-spell', *Sociology of Sport Journal*, 9 (2): 192–206.

Trujillo, N. (1995) 'Machines, missiles, and men: images of the male body on ABC's Monday Night Football', *Sociology of Sport Journal*, 12 (4): 403–23.

Trujillo, N. and Krizek, B. (1994) 'Emotionality in the stands and in the field: expressing self through baseball', *Journal of Sport and Social Issues*, 18 (4): 303–25.

Viejola, S. (1994) 'Metaphors of mixed team play', *International Review for the Sociology of Sport*, 29 (1): 31–47.

Wacquant, L. (1992) 'The social logic of boxing in black Chicago: toward a sociology of pugilism', *Sociology of Sport Journal*, 9 (3): 221–54.

Wenner, L.A. (1990) 'Therapeutic engagement in mediated sports', in G. Gumpert and S.L. Fish (eds), *Talking to Strangers: Mediated Therapeutic Communications*. Norword, NJ: Ablex. pp. 223–44.

Werbner, P. (1996) 'Fun spaces: on identity and social empowerment among British Pakistanis', *Theory, Culture and Society*, 13 (4): 53–80.

Whitson, D. (1990) 'Sport in the social construction of masculinity', in M. Messner and D. Sabo (eds), *Sport, Men and the Gender Order: Critical Feminist Perspectives*. Champaign, IL: Human Kinetics. pp. 19–30.

Young, K. (1991) 'Violence in the workplace of professional sport from victimological and cultural studies perspectives', *International Review for the Sociology of Sport*, 26 (1): 3–12.

Young, K. (1993) 'Violence, risk and liability in male sports culture', *Sociology of Sport Journal*, 10 (4): 373–96.

Young, K., White, P. and McTeer, W. (1994) 'Body talk: male athletes reflect on sport, injury, and pain', *Sociology of Sport Journal*, 11 (2): 175–94.

Zhang, J., Pease, D. and Hui, S. (1996) 'Value dimensions of profession sport as viewed by spectators', *Journal of Sport and Social Issues*, 20 (1): 78–94.

31

MANAGEMENT, ORGANIZATIONS AND THEORY IN THE GOVERNANCE OF SPORT

Ian Henry and Eleni Theodoraki

The aim of this chapter is to identify and evaluate key developments in the management of sporting organizations and the theorizing of the management of sporting organizations in the contemporary context. The focus of this account will be principally on public sector, quasi-public sector[1] and voluntary sector sporting bodies, rather than on commercial sporting organizations. This is not to imply that commercial sporting organizations do not have a significant role to play in the political economy of sport; clearly this is not the case. However, the nature of organizational behaviour in the commercial sector is substantially different from that of those organizations, traditionally important in the sporting world, which are constrained and guided by their memberships or by governmental influences, such that treatment of both categories of organization within a single framework is less than helpful.

Two further preliminary points are worth stressing at the outset. The first is that much of the commentary which follows relates to the governance of sport in the developed economies of liberal democracies, and draws principally upon English-language sources. Such limitations are worth acknowledging at the outset in an international handbook of this type. The second point to emphasize derives from the distinction between organization theory and theories of organizations. The former refers to predominantly prescriptive accounts, guiding the organizational behaviour of managers and other stakeholders. The latter is rather more directly concerned with understanding organizational behaviour rather than spelling out prescriptions. Both types of

analysis will form part of the commentary which follows. Of course, analysis will have implications for practice and vice versa, and the divisions between these two approaches should not be watertight, but it is nevertheless worth emphasizing that the concerns of this chapter go beyond management prescription.

The structure of the chapter falls into four substantive sections. The first identifies changes in the context within which the governance of sport takes place. The second reviews the major approaches to theorizing management and organization theory developments in the sporting domain. The third deals in detail with one attempt to evaluate how sports organizations' structures and strategies are being adapted to changes in the wider context, while the final section identifies the impact of new managerialism on public, quasi-public and voluntary sector sporting bodies.

THE CHANGING CONTEXT OF THE GOVERNANCE OF SPORT IN THE DEVELOPED ECONOMIES

The past few decades have seen major change in political, economic, social, cultural and organizational terms in the major industrialized societies. Attempts in the social sciences to conceptualize this change have resulted in the proliferation of terminology using the prefix 'post-': terms such as the 'post-welfare society', 'postmodern' and 'post-Fordist' reflect attempts to encapsulate the dimensions of such change. It is important, if we are to contextualize the nature of the governance and management of sport in contemporary societies, that we outline the nature of change in these fields. Thus what follows below, is a discussion of the changing environments of the governance of sport along these five dimensions.

The major shift in political terms since the early 1970s or so has been from the post-war consensus politics of social democracy to the liberal individualism of the 1980s and early 1990s. The politics of the welfare state is said to have given way to a post-welfare condition in which the role of the state as a provider of welfare services is diminished, while its role in facilitating the operation of a free market is magnified (Pierson, 1991). Even non-Conservative governments in the 1980s and early 1990s, such as those of Spain under Felipe González, France under Mitterrand, Greece under Papandreou, were said to be promoting neo-liberal policy approaches. However, the embracing of post-welfarism is perhaps most closely associated with the politics of Thatcherism (Henry, 1993).

The implications for sports policy of political change are spelt out most clearly in the British case with a shift from the policy line advocated in the 1975 government White Paper *Sport and Recreation*, in which sport and recreation was said to be 'one of the community's everyday needs', and 'part of the general fabric of social services' (Department of the Environment, 1975), towards that advocated in the 1980s and early 1990s in which privatization of many public leisure services and the 'marketization' of those services retained in the public sector, were features reflecting the dominance of neo-liberal thinking.

Sports does not disappear from the political agenda in the neo-liberal era, but sports policy is no longer an aspect of welfare policy (Coalter et al., 1988). In particular, as the role of the nation-state itself begins to be questioned, its prominence threatened by the growing importance of transnational political and economic phenomena (such as the European Union, or the transnational corporation), so sport gains major significance to governments in the process of nation-building and the reproduction of national identities (Maguire, 1993). In the case of Britain this is very evident in the rationale for sports investment given in the 1995 White Paper *Sport: Raising the Game* (see especially John Major's preface to the document: Department of National Heritage, 1995) while similar rationales are rehearsed by the socialist governments of Spain (Gonzalez and Urkiola, 1993), and Greece (Nassis, 1994). Support for sport in the neo-liberal era is

provided not so much directly from the public purse, but increasingly from sources such as national lotteries, football pools and other sports-related gambling income (as in the funding systems in Greece, France and the United Kingdom).

The developed economies of the Western world have undergone profound restructuring over the period since the beginning of the 1970s. The globalization of production systems has, it is argued, featured the transfer of jobs from developed to low-wage economies, particularly in South East Asia, with the Western economies retaining only those forms of production that either require high levels of technological input, or are automated. In addition, the developed economies have experienced considerable growth in service sector employment (Allen, 1988). Since growth in service sector jobs has not compensated for loss of jobs in the manufacturing sector, high levels of unemployment and underemployment have been generated (with specific gendered implications) (McDowell, 1989). Such shifts have been explained by regulation theorists (Aglietta, 1979; Boyer, 1986; Lipietz, 1987) as a move from a Fordist economic system in which there is full employment, based predominantly on mass production manufacturing, with high monetary wages and a high social wage (in the form of welfare benefits and services), to a post-Fordist system in which production is managed in such economies at low cost through reduced financial and social wages. The financial wage is reduced by employing fewer people (though, in the case of 'core' workers with key skills, paying them more) with a pool of workers (the 'peripheral' workforce) who are in seasonal, part-time or insecure, low-paid jobs or who are unemployed. The social wage is reduced by doing away with or reducing the universally available benefits of the welfare state and replacing them with safety-net low-level welfare provision for the most desperate cases. Thus consumer rights for some (those in full employment) replace welfare rights (health care, education, housing, and even leisure and sport for all) which had been virtually universally available. The regulation theorists' account may represent perhaps something of a caricature of the shifts that have actually occurred, since neither all low-tech jobs nor all universal welfare rights have been lost (Allen, 1992), but it nevertheless serves to highlight significant underlying trends which have clear implications for sport and leisure (Bramham et al., 1993).

Economic changes that imply, in developed economies, a cleavage between a core and a peripheral workforce, are reflected in the development of what has been termed the two-tier social structure, with the gap between rich and poor in Western European societies growing from the period since the middle 1970s (Lash and Urry, 1994) This phenomenon has important consequences for all areas of policy and for sports policy and sports organizations specifically, since, as the economic distance between the new poor and the new rich develops, so the cultural distance between these groups grows, reflecting in effect different sporting markets or client groups.

The cultural correlate of post-Fordism is postmodernism. Postmodernists promote the claim that cultural distinctions between high and low culture are dissolving and that new cultural constellations of lifestyle groupings are emerging as new social groups (particularly the 'new service class') seek to establish some cultural distance between themselves and others (Featherstone, 1990). People no longer identify themselves as they did in the premodern period by reference to place, or as in the modern by reference to their affiliation to a nation state or to a social class. New identities are fluid, in part globalized, but interpreted at local level, promoting notions of hybridity, with cultural selection of multiple identities from a range of available cultural resources (Hall, 1992). Thus national cultures and class cultures are said to give way to more fluid lifestyle groupings in the 'postmodern era'. Sport forms, it is claimed, are subject to change with 'individualized', 'commercialized', and 'mediatized' sport forms emerging in developed economies (DeFrance and Pociello, 1993; Rojek, 1994).

Invariably the major shifts in political, economic, social and cultural terms are reflected in changes in the dominant organization forms evident in developed industrial societies. The dominant form of organizational structure of the modern era was bureaucracy, and, particularly in the 1960s and early 1970s, the dominant organizational strategy was that of corporate management with its defining feature of vertical and horizontal integration to gain economies of scale and synergies in production and distribution with long chains of organizational command in large-scale organizations, operating in stable economic, political and cultural environments. The dominant form in the contemporary era is one of a smaller, flatter organizational unit, capable of responding quickly to changes in economically, politically and culturally volatile environments (see, for example, Peters and Waterman, 1982; Piore and Sabel, 1984).

Whether or not such changes constitute *structural* shifts to a new set of economic, political and cultural realities is a matter of debate in the literature (Featherstone, 1995), but what seems to be undeniable is that significant change has occurred along each of the dimensions highlighted in this section and that such changes will have had a significant impact on the behaviour and management of sporting organizations. We are thus led on to the question of how the theorizing of organizational behaviour has changed over the past two decades and to the manner in which such theorizing has impacted upon the analysis of the activities of sports organizations.

SPORTS ORGANIZATIONS AND THE ORGANIZATIONAL THEORY LITERATURE

The organizational theory literature in the field of sports organizations is relatively undeveloped. With the exception of a burgeoning group of studies in the Canadian literature, there is an absence of systematic analysis of the sports field in the English-language literature. This may be in part a reflection of historical circumstances, the growth of interest in sport as a legitimate area of 'serious' social analysis coinciding with the intellectual crisis of organizational theory represented in postmodernism. It may also simply be a reflection of the academic interest of those involved in the study of sport and sports organizations.

To review the literature relating to organizational analysis and sports organizations it will be useful to build on the account of the development of organization theory provided by Reed and Hughes (1992), who suggest that since the early 1960s or so organization theory can be characterized as having developed through three major stages, with the dominant emphasis of organization theory in the 1960s on organizational survival and adaptation to new environments, giving way in the 1970s to a concern with the political and ideological dimensions of power in organizations, and subsequently in the 1980s and early 1990s to a focus on discourse analysis and the reproduction of organizational realities. Dividing work into this simplified, tripartite chronological framework, allows us to categorize that work on sporting organizations which has been undertaken, while highlighting also gaps in the application of theory in the sports context.

Thus we can distinguish the following:

- Work derived from the rationalist, positivist approach developed from Weber's analysis of bureaucracy, which seeks to capture organizational reality by identifying structural features of organizations and their environments and to evaluate the relationship between them, often by reference to statistical association. (We will use the term Weberian to refer to this tradition in this chapter, though Weber's own work was in part aimed at clarifying the limitations of such a rationalist/positivist approach.) Seminal work in this tradition would include the contingency approaches of the Aston School (Pugh and Hickson, 1976) and of Burns and Stalker (1961).
- Analysis of power and organizational politics, which in part reflects a radical critique of the unidimensional nature of Weberian analysis; this represents a perspective (or set of perspectives) in which the organization is conceived, not as a set of structural properties, but as an arena in which agencies compete for valued resources in shifting contexts. Organizational reality is determined by the outcomes of ongoing struggles which characterize any organization. Typical proponents are Clegg and Dunkerley (1980) and Mintzberg (1983).
- Analysis of organizations as constituted by symbolic processes, generating social realities by the construction of varying types of discourse. This tradition is influenced by the critique of modernist notions of organizational theory. Modernist organization analysis implies a search for rational scientific theories of a distinctive object which will allow us to facilitate the development of stability and control in organizations. The postmodern critique focuses on, not a single, distinctive theoretical object, the organization, but on the fragmented cultural realities in an organization, in which theories of management or of organization are used as legitimating tools for promoting one notion of reality over another. The result of this critique may be the displacement of the notion of a universal truth as the goal of organizational theory, but it need not mean the displacement of objectivity and reason. Theories of organization, like all social theory, may be culturally contingent, but that is not to say that they are arbitrary. Cooper and Burrell (1988) and Gergen (1992) provide examples of this type of approach to understanding organization. In prescriptive management theory this approach is linked to the contemporary concern with the construction of organizational cultures, the hegemony of one set of cultural values, one organizational reality, over others.

In the field of analysis of sports organizations, the main focus has been on the first of these three types of approach. Little has been attempted in terms of analysis of power in sports organizations, with the exception of some material inspired by feminist analysis, such as White and Brackenridge (1985), Hall, Cullen and Slack (1989) and Hult (1989), and occasional case studies, such as that of Ashton (1992), an account of the construction of a new governing body for squash in Britain out of its predecessor women's and men's organizations. Work of the third type outlined above, even in its more applied form of analysis of emerging organizational cultures, has not been evident in the work on sports organizations, though one may find advocacy of the application of such approaches in the sports and leisure field (Frisby, 1995).

In the British context also there has been little work in the Weberian tradition relating specifically to sports organizations or national governing bodies (NGBs). This tradition has, however, been very evident in the Canadian work, and research relating to bureaucratization and related phenomena has reflected the major research efforts in this field in Canada. Four types of 'Weberian' work in this field may be identified:

1 that which seeks to clarify the significance of conceptual frameworks relating to organizational structural and environmental variables (Frisby, 1982; Slack and Hinings, 1987);
2 that which seeks to operationalize theoretical constructs, suggesting ways which in principle would allow measurement of the structural and environmental dimensions of national governing bodies (Frisby, 1985);
3 that which seeks to establish empirically (by using the operational measures) the extent to which the national governing bodies exhibit bureaucratization, and related phenomena, such as standardization, specialization, and professionalization (Chelladurai and Haggerty, 1991; Kikulis et al., 1989; Slack, 1985; Thibault et al., 1991); and finally
4 that which seeks to clarify the relationship between structural features and efficiency of NGBs (Chelladurai et al., 1987; Frisby, 1986).

We may conclude, then, that the application of organization theory in the sport domain has not in effect kept pace with that in the mainstream field of organizational analysis.

However, we may also wish to consider whether or not organizational forms themselves in the sport sector have evolved in response to changes in the organizational environment. The following section seeks to provide a partial response to this question in focusing on an empirical study which deals with one type of such sporting organization (national governing bodies of sport) in one national context (that of Britain), but which also serves to illustrate the dominant form of organizational analysis in the sports field.

A REVIEW OF ORGANIZATIONAL TYPES IN THE NATIONAL GOVERNING BODIES OF BRITAIN

The aim of the study summarized in this section (which is reported in full in Theodoraki and Henry, 1994) was to establish the types and range of organizational structures of organizations in the national governing body (NGB) sector in the United Kingdom. Focusing as it does on the structural characteristics of the organizations, it constitutes a form of analysis that relates most clearly to the third of the forms of traditional 'Weberian' analysis identified above. It adopts a methodology similar to that of Kikulis et al. (1989) in that it seeks to derive a taxonomy of British sport NGBs by reference to structural features of those organizations. It differs, however, in a number of respects. In particular, operational measures employed differ, reflecting in part the different context of the British and Canadian sports systems, and their histories, and the availability of data.

The nature of this study was influenced by Mintzberg's (1979) classic analysis of organizational structures, and sought to establish whether the analysis of NGBs, would provide support for the existence of Mintzberg's five ideal-typical structural configurations of organizations. The NGBs incorporated as subjects in this study were selected in the following manner. All governing bodies for England recognized by the Sports Council were approached to obtain permission to view any of their files held centrally by the Sports Council.[2] For those that replied positively annual reports and accounts were reviewed, and each of the organizations was subsequently sent a questionnaire, and where necessary contacted in person or by telephone, to elicit further information over an 18-month period (1992–4). A response rate of 48.5 per cent was achieved and 45 sports NGBs

filled in and returned the questionnaire. Although the sample incorporates a wide spectrum of different sports, some types of sports organization are excluded. In particular, acknowledgement should be made of the fact that large and affluent NGBs with a high media profile, such as the Football Association or the Rugby League, were thus excluded from the analysis.

The statistical analysis of the data generated by the survey involved two principal stages. The first is a review of the strength and direction of the relationship between the variables employed in the study (a table of correlations is presented in Table 31.1). The second involves conducting cluster analysis on the data to establish whether homogeneous groups of cases could be identified.[3] The number of clusters identified was six.

The cluster analysis had two principal objectives. The first was simply to establish what types of structure existed in the NGB sector. This would allow, for example, a review of whether growing professionalization in this sector would be reflected in organizational structures. The second objective was to consider whether organizations for different types of sport, particularly the newer, individualistic forms of sporting activity, would differ from those representing more established, traditional sports.

The variables employed for clustering purposes were adapted from those developed in the classical Aston Studies programme (Pugh and Hickson, 1976), falling into two categories: contextual variables (complexity of organizational environment, task and technology, organizational size, age and resources) and structural variables (specialization, standardization and centralization).

This tabular data displays some conforming to, and some deviation from, the relationships anticipated by contingency theorists such as Burns and Stalker or by Mintzberg. It was anticipated that the size of organizations, for example, would be positively associated with standardization of tasks and the formalization of objectives, specialization, age of organization and professionalization of staff. Similarly, complexity of organizational environment was expected to be negatively associated with centralization and standardization, but positively associated with specialization. Older organizations would also be expected to exhibit greater professionalization of staff, and greater standardization of tasks. The reasoning underlying these anticipated relationships is as follows. The larger organizations become, the more likely they are to require subdivision of

Table 31.1　Correlation between variables for the sample of national governing bodies of sport

	1	2	3	4	5	6	7	8	9	10	11	12	13	14	15	16
Context																
Size (no. of employees)	1.0000	0.1236	0.2528	-0.1983	0.1452	0.1368	0.0518	0.0168	0.4237**	0.0327	0.1077	0.1030	0.0607	-0.1022	-0.0198	0.1083
Size (no. of volunteers)	0.1236	1.0000	-0.2166	-0.1584	-0.3415*	-0.1151	-0.1849	0.0979	0.1017	0.1216	0.0200	0.0118	-0.0818	0.0604	-0.0460	0.2517
Age (number of years the organization has existed)	0.2528	-0.2166	1.0000	-0.3248*	0.1008	0.1871	0.0058	-0.0663	0.2594	-0.1568	0.0727	0.0463	0.1596	-0.0337	0.1672	-0.0211
Professionalization	-0.1983	-0.1584	-0.3248*	1.0000	-0.0631	-0.1022	-0.0910	0.1118	-0.0712	-0.0251	0.1000	0.1330	-0.0856	0.1663	-0.1279	-0.0073
Percentage of women managers	0.1452	-0.3415*	0.1008	-0.0631	1.0000	-0.1447	0.1052	-0.0558	-0.0601	-0.1051	-0.0457	-0.0861	-0.1382	-0.2069	0.1025	0.0120
Percentage of women employees	0.1368	-0.1151	0.1871	-0.1022	-0.1447	1.0000	-0.0691	0.1179	0.1250	-0.1058	-0.1177	-0.1400	-0.2199	0.0617	-0.1310	-0.0078
Percentage of ethnic minority managers	0.0518	-0.1849	0.0058	-0.0910	0.1052	-0.0691	1.0000	-0.7484**	-0.3098*	-0.1937	0.0852	-0.3826**	0.1819	-0.1171	0.0284	-0.1861
Percentage of employees from ethnic minorities	0.0168	0.0979	-0.0663	0.1118	-0.0558	0.1179	-0.7484**	1.0000	0.5002**	0.0768	-0.0354	0.2927	-0.1116	0.0594	0.0935	0.2424
Complexity of environment	0.4237**	0.1017	0.2594	-0.0712	-0.0601	0.1250	-0.3098*	0.5002**	1.0000	0.1480	-0.0053	0.3108*	0.2286	-0.1758	-0.0490	0.0897
Task complexity (major events)	0.0327	0.1216	-0.1568	-0.0251	-0.1051	-0.1058	-0.1937	0.0768	0.1480	1.0000	-0.3147*	0.1057	0.0114	-0.3480*	0.0571	0.2097
Task complexity (sport development)	0.1077	0.0200	0.0727	0.1000	-0.0457	-0.1177	0.0852	-0.0354	-0.0053	-0.3147*	1.0000	-0.1710	0.0039	0.2672	0.6332**	-0.2721
Structural variables																
Specialization	0.1030	0.0118	0.0463	0.1330	-0.0861	-0.1400	-0.3826**	0.2927	0.3108*	0.1057	-0.1710	1.0000	-0.0029	-0.1415	-0.2327	0.0312
Standardization	0.0607	-0.0818	0.1596	-0.0856	-0.1382	-0.2199	0.1819	-0.1116	0.2286	0.0114	0.0039	-0.0029	1.0000	-0.0918	0.0255	0.0000
Formalization of objectives	-0.1022	0.0604	-0.0337	0.1663	-0.2069	0.0617	-0.1171	0.0594	-0.1758	-0.3480*	0.2672	-0.1415	-0.0918	1.0000	0.2290	0.0382
Centralization	-0.0198	-0.0460	0.1672	-0.1279	0.1025	-0.1310	0.0284	0.0935	-0.0490	0.0571	0.6332**	-0.2327	0.0255	0.2290	1.0000	-0.0227
Political control of executives	0.1083	0.2517	-0.0211	-0.0073	0.0120	-0.0078	-0.1861	0.2424	0.0897	0.2097	-0.2721	0.0312	0.0000	0.0382	-0.0227	1.0000

*Significant at the 0.05 level.
**Significant at the 0.01 level.

1. Size (no. of employees); 2. Size (no. of volunteers); 3. Age (number of years the organization has existed); 4. Professionalization; 5. Percentage of women managers; 6. Percentage of women employees; 7. Percentage of ethnic minority managers; 8. Percentage of employees from ethnic minorities; 9. Specialization; 10. Complexity of environment; 11. Task (complexity of organization); 12. Task (sport development); 13. Standardization; 14. Formalization of objectives; 15. Centralization; 16. Political control of executives.

duties and responsibilities to remain effective. Thus, because of problems of control, larger organizations would be expected to be more standardized in the way they operate, have more formalized objectives, and greater specialization. They are also more likely to seek to ensure that standards are maintained by appointing professionally qualified staff, as the resources of the organization increase with size. Age and size might also be assumed to be related as new organizations will tend to be small until they are able to establish themselves. This rationale is specified more fully in Mintzberg's (1979) derivation of a series of hypotheses relating to expected relationships.

Within the sample of NGBs, size was significantly positively related to specialization (r = 0.42), though no other statistically significant correlations were evident in respect of size. The complexity of organizational environment was also negatively associated with the formalization of objectives as anticipated (r = -0.35), and specialization was positively associated with one measure of complexity of task (that of sports development) (r = 0.31), though not with the other measure employed (organization of national and international events) (r = -0.31). These relationships at least might be said to be consistent with the hypotheses promoted by Mintzberg, though in general correlations were weak.

However, some relationships were less consistent with the anticipated findings. For example, younger organizations tended to be more, rather than less, professionalized than their older counterparts (r = -0.32), suggesting perhaps that newer NGBs were *less* likely to appoint unqualified staff to management positions. Organizations with a high level of involvement in the organization of national and international events also tended to be more centralized (r = 0.63) and to operate in less complex organizational environments (r = -0.31).

The proportion of women in management positions was significantly related only to the size of the volunteer population working in the organization (r = -0.34), suggesting perhaps that women were less likely to be employed in managerial positions when larger volunteer populations are incorporated within NGBs. Participation in voluntary organizations more generally is disproportionately male (Central Statistical Office, 1991). Organizations employing managers of Afro-Caribbean or Asian extraction tended to employ fewer people from these ethnic groups (r = -0.75) and to exhibit less specialization (r = -0.31) and to be less involved in sports development (-0.38). By contrast, employees from these ethnic groups were more likely to be found in organizations with a greater degree of specialization (r = 0.50).

The presentation of the table of correlation coefficients, however, may mask underlying relationships between particular subgroups of organizations. For this reason, cluster analysis was undertaken, identifying organizational groups with homogeneous characteristics.

A breakdown of the key characteristics of the clusters is provided in Table 31.2. All variables are standardized for the population of organizations as a whole. Thus the means and standard deviations for each of the clusters may be easily compared with those of the population as a whole.

- **Cluster 1** contains the following 16 NGBs: National Cricket Association, Tennis and Racquets Association, Petanque Association, RAC Motor Sports Association, British Sub Aqua Club, National Federation of Anglers, Eton Fives Association, Cyclists Touring Club, National Caving Association, English Women's Bowling Association, the Croquet Association, British Association of Paragliding Clubs, Amateur Fencing Association, Martial Arts Commission, British Cycling Federation, English Bobsleigh Association. This cluster exhibits the structural configuration that conforms most closely to Mintzberg's *machine bureaucracy*. The complexity of the organizational environment in this cluster was fairly low, and there was a relatively high degree of standardization. Organizations tended to be large, with some exceptions (these were Petanque, Eton Fives, Bobsleigh and Martial Arts), and specialization and centralization were limited. The proportion of women in management positions in these organizations was also relatively low compared to the figures for other clusters and the size of the volunteer force was significant (though for both of these variables there was a greater variability than for the population as a whole, with standard deviations of 1.38 and 1.53 respectively). Thus this cluster seems to exhibit some of the classic features of traditionalist NGBs, with standardized work routines, relatively simple organizational environments, predominantly large volunteer work forces and with traditional gender roles in management.
- **Cluster 2** contains seven NGBs: the Hockey Association, Amateur Rowing Association, British Water Ski Federation, British Korfball Association, British Mountaineering Council, Squash Rackets Association and British Ski Federation. This was the cluster

Table 31.2 Characteristics of clusters – British national governing bodies of sport

Variables	Machine bureaucracy N = 16		Professional bureaucracy N = 7		Decentralized simple structure N = 7		Simple structure N = 8		Bureaucratized simple structure N = 5		Specialized simple structure N = 2	
	Mean	SD	Mean	SD	Mean	SD	Mean	SD	Mean	SD	Mean	SD
Size	0.21	1.36	0.63	0.97	−0.40	0.51	−0.53	0.23	−0.06	0.60	−0.20	0.22
Volunteers	0.39	1.53	0.01	0.70	−0.27	0.19	−0.32	0.24	−0.24	0.44	−0.30	0.23
Age	−0.03	1.01	0.18	0.96	−0.63	0.52	0.27	1.10	0.20	1.50	0.24	0.19
Professionalization	−0.01	1.06	0.28	0.32	0.38	0.88	−0.02	1.43	−0.73	0.46	−0.32	0.56
Percentage of women in management	−0.29	1.38	−0.08	1.01	0.19	0.55	0.13	0.70	0.64	0.00	−0.17	0.46
No. of women employees	−0.10	1.02	0.14	0.31	0.00	0.71	0.29	1.39	−0.87	0.80	1.32	0.77
Percentage of ethnic minority mangers	0.17	0.07	−0.95	2.29	0.17	0.07	0.17	0.07	0.19	0.00	0.19	0.00
No. of employees from ethnic minorities	−0.21	0.15	1.28	2.03	−0.24	0.11	−0.24	0.10	−0.28	0.00	−0.28	0.00
Specialization	−0.07	0.47	1.85	0.33	−0.64	0.50	−0.71	0.68	−0.62	0.28	0.73	0.93
Complexity of environment	−0.69	0.93	0.60	1.52	−0.34	0.81	−0.18	0.75	0.10	0.98	0.01	0.86
No. of international and national events	0.07	0.77	0.00	0.80	−0.81	1.39	0.75	0.38	0.40	0.50	−1.71	1.00
Sports development	−0.04	0.76	0.72	1.61	0.14	1.23	−0.46	0.31	−0.40	0.60	0.13	1.12
Standardization	0.67	0.78	−0.02	0.64	−0.96	0.00	−1.12	0.47	0.89	0.72	0.36	0.00
Formality of objectives	0.16	1.23	−0.09	0.45	−0.37	0.43	0.53	1.21	−0.24	0.65	−1.23	0.00
Centralization	−0.19	0.34	0.20	0.62	−1.42	0.00	1.11	0.00	1.11	0.00	−1.42	0.00

which most closely resembled Mintzberg's *professional bureaucracy*. The cluster is dominated by established Olympic sports and outdoor pursuits (with korfball as a notable exception). This cluster contained predominantly larger organizations with higher levels of professionalization together with higher levels of specialization, and lower levels of standardization and centralization, which are consistent with greater professional autonomy. Although these organizations focused more on sports development than the population of organizations as a whole, and operated in relatively complex environments, there was a high degree of variability in respect of these variables.

• **Cluster 3** contains seven NGBs: the English Ski Council, English Basketball Association, Aircraft Owners and Pilots Association, BMX Association, British Federation of Sand and Land Yacht Clubs and the National Rounders Association. These tended to be small, young, professionalized organizations operating with a low level of voluntary involvement and a comparatively low emphasis on organization of major events. They operated in simple environments, they were relatively unbureaucratized, exhibiting little standardization, specialization and with formalized objectives. However, unlike Mintzberg's ideal-type simple structure, centralization was low. Thus, this cluster reflected what was in effect a *professionalized and decentralized simple structure*.

• **Cluster 4** contains eight organizations: the English Ladies Golf Association, British Surfing Association, British Crown Green Bowling Association, English Folk Song and Dance Society, the Cricket Council, Bicycle Polo Association and the Road Time Trials Association. These organizations were very small in terms of professional staff, though two of them, Ladies Golf and Crown Green Bowls, had very large organizational memberships. The organizations were similar to those of Cluster 3, being small, with few volunteers, low specialization and low standardization. However, by contrast they tended to be events oriented (rather than sports development oriented) in their activities, and to be less professionalized. More significantly, they exhibited a higher degree of centralization, conforming to the configuration which Mintzberg terms the simple structure but which we will refer to as the *typical simple structure* in order to differentiate it from the other simple structure clusters.

• **Cluster 5** contained five organizations: the English Indoor Bowling Association, British Gliding Association, British Microlight Aircraft Association, the Amateur Boxing Association, and the Hurlingham Polo Association. These organizations exhibited low levels of professionalization or specialization, with high levels of centralization of decision-making and standardization of role. The focus of these organizations in terms of task was on organization of events rather than on sports development. In addition, though women were evident in management positions, these organizations employed fewer women and workers from ethnic minorities, and operated with a low level of volunteers. Unlike Mintzberg's ideal-type simple structure, there was a high degree of standardization in such organizations, and they are perhaps, therefore, best described as *bureaucratized simple structures*.

• **Cluster 6** contained two organizations: the Women's League of Health and Beauty and the English Table Tennis Association. These organizations, though relatively small in terms of professional staff, and using few volunteers, exhibited some bureaucratic features such as standardization, specialization and centralization. They employed a higher proportion of women than any other cluster, but a smaller proportion of these occupied managerial positions. Perhaps the defining feature of this cluster, which was clearly also an example of simple structure, is the level of specialization, which sets it apart from the bureaucratized simple structure. Thus we have termed this cluster the *specialized simple structure*.

What then are the lessons we can learn from these sorts of empirical findings? Perhaps the most striking feature to emerge from the clustering procedures was the preponderance of variations on the simple structure. This, however, is not surprising, in the sense that sports administration in a predominantly amateur set of sports has traditionally implied amateur management. Such management, in relatively small organizations, may implicitly rely on the flexibility which simple structures permit.

Although four of the clusters represented variations of the simple structure form, it was not possible to identify any of the clusters as necessarily moving towards more developed organizational forms. Some had plans to formalize their operations in response to interaction with the Sports Council as a major grant-aiding body (and this tendency is likely to have been reinforced by the increasing reliance on funding from the National Lottery with its insistence on the development of business plans). In this sense they may be described as 'nascent professional bureaucracies'. Other organizations gave little indication of impending change. Indeed the average ages of the 'typical', the 'specialized' and the 'professionalized' simple structures were greater than those of the other clusters, indicating perhaps that they were not simply new organizations in transition.

The six organizational clusters identified in the data operated in a variety of environments. Environmental complexity was operationalized in this study by reference to the number of organizations with which interaction took place and the rate of intensity of such interaction. The organizational cluster operating in the most complex environment was that of the professional bureaucracy. Machine bureaucracies operated with the lowest level of environmental complexity, while the different types of simple structure fluctuated about the mean. Mintzberg (1979) argues that the more complex the environment in which an organization operates the more likely it is that the structure will be an organic one. It is argued that in a stable environment, an organization is better able to predict future conditions and so, all other things being equal, can more readily insulate its operating core and standardize its activities, establish rules, formalize work and plan actions or standardize its skills. But this relationship also extends beyond the operating core. In a highly stable environment the whole organization may take on the form of a protected, or undisturbed system, which can standardize its procedures from top to bottom.

One of the claims advanced earlier in this chapter is that sporting organizations in 'advanced' industrial societies such as Britain are operating in an increasingly volatile social, economic and political environment. However, it is clear that complexity of environment does vary considerably between organizations and the dynamic nature of the environment in which some operate is by no means universal. In relation to the physical environments in which NGBs operated major differences were found in relation to facilities, resources and opportunities. The National Federation of Anglers for example, had had to allocate considerable amounts of money to research into water pollution, and the Royal Automobile Club and the British Gliding Association had had to lobby politicians in an attempt to create favourable opinions regarding recreational use of land for motor sport and of aviation air space

respectively. On the other hand the English Ladies Golf Association had recently benefited from the building of a considerable number of new golf courses, reflecting the availability of grants for conversion of farm land.

Among the key issues to be addressed in the study were: whether any distinction could be made between the organizational structures for what might be described as traditional, collectivist sport, and for new individualistic sports; whether there was any evidence of a move away from traditional bureaucratic organizational forms; and whether there was any evidence of the emergence of new, more flexible, entrepreneurial organizational forms as the economic base of NGBs experienced instability with the threatened (and in many instances actual) reduction of public funding. A clear point to emerge from examining the clusters identified, is that NGBs for both 'traditional' sport forms and for the new, more 'individualistic' sport forms, are incorporated in virtually all clusters. There is no differentiation in the data between organizational, structural configurations for 'traditional' and 'new' or 'individualized' sports. These terms are crudely defined but it is evident that whether NGBs are for sports which are low cost, 'new' sports (for example, Petanque Association), 'high-tech', high-cost sports (for example, Aircraft Owners and Pilots Association), or for exotic high-cost pursuits (for example, English Bobsleigh Association, Hurlingham Polo Association), no distinctive configurations are evident.

It may be the case that it is not the nature of the sport forms nor the age of the NGB which will be key in influencing organizational response so much as the health of the organization in terms of size of membership base and economic position, and as a consequence, resource dependence of the organization. It may be that the need to seek new forms of financial support may result in pressures to restructure. Thus, for example, at the time of the research the Amateur Boxing Association was considering forming itself into a limited company, while officials of the NGB for Crown Green Bowling argued strongly for the need to streamline its committee structure to make their organization more flexible and responsive to the environment. How such organizations respond to environmental change and/or reshape their own environment can only be adequately explained if the nature of historical, contemporary contextual and contemporary internal figurations are subject to detailed investigation, underlying the need for complementary forms of analysis.

What this study serves to illustrate then is the complexity of the nature of organizational forms in the NGB sector in one national context. Similarly patterns with an emphasis on variants of simple structures are also identified in Canadian (Kikulis et al., 1989) and Dutch (Onderwater and Richards, 1994) studies which seek to construct taxonomies of organizational structures for national or provincial governing bodies of sport. Nevertheless, despite this pattern of complexity, there are some discernible commonalities across nation-state boundaries, in particular the widespread advocacy of 'new managerialism'.

NEW MANAGERIALISM AND SPORTS ORGANIZATIONS

If one of the major foci of the development of sports organizations has been sports organizations' structures and their response to changing contexts, another has been the development of new managerial styles or philosophies. We have traced elsewhere the emergence and evolution of professionalization in the public sector delivery of sport and leisure services in Britain (Henry, 1993), arguing that there has been a shift from an initial concern with the provision of physical infrastructure in the early 1970s to a concern with maximizing sports participation and providing access for disadvantaged groups in the later 1970s and early 1980s, to a concern with economic efficiency and economic return from public sector facilities in the later 1980s and early 1990s.

In the British context, the development of a leisure semi-profession in the 1970s and early 1980s took the classic form of other welfare semi-professions (Esland, 1980). However, this strategy for the development of a profession was founded in the supportive context of the welfare system. As neo-liberal approaches to macro-economic planning have developed, so too welfare strategies have been replaced by, for example, the privatization of services and/ or the introduction of market competitiveness into the public sector. Thus there is a far greater emphasis on market principles in management both in the private sector expanded by privatization and within the newly 'market oriented' public sector. This has major implications for the management skills and approaches and the management style of sport and recreation management, and reflects a more generic turn in public sector management to what has been termed 'new managerialism',

not simply in the British case but more broadly in the international context.

Lane (1995) highlights how such changes have become evident across the spectrum of welfare services in developed economies, while Farnham and Horton (1993) provide detailed analysis relating to specific services in the British context, and Leach et al. (1994) provide an account of the impact on British local government structures and approaches of the new managerialism.

In terms of the management of sports facilities specifically, the introduction of increasing revenue targets for management has fostered the primacy of financial rather than social sporting goals. The submission of management of these types of facility to competitive bidding processes, has led in a number of European countries (for example, France, Britain, Spain and the Netherlands) to the growing involvement of the commercial sector in the management and operation of public sports facilities. Even where public sector management of such facilities has been retained, a more commercial-like approach may well be evident in the way that public sector managers carry out their role. Financial efficiency concerns may militate against social effectiveness in the running of such facilities.

Some cities, such as Sheffield (UK), have in effect relinquished direct control of the workforce in sport and recreation services. An independent body, Sheffield International Venues Ltd, was set up in the early 1990s by the local authority as a trust employing the personnel involved in running the city's newest sports facilities built for the World Student Games in 1991. Policy in relation to the use of the facilities was, in effect, ceded to the management of this Trust, with the local authority simply stipulating the required financial performance for the facilities. Management of the older, traditional facilities in the city, however, remained under the direct control of the city council and its own workforce. This arrangement mirrors the notion of a two-tier society, with a two-tier system of consumer rights of access to sports facilities for those who can afford it, and safety net 'welfare' provision of poorer-quality facilities at non-market prices for those who cannot (see Henry and Paramio-Salcines, 1996 for a detailed account of such changes).

CONCLUSION

In this review of the management of sports organizations and facilities in the public, quasi-public and voluntary sectors, we have sought to outline the changing context of sports management and the responses to such changing contexts of sports organizations. In addition, the chapter has highlighted the implications for theorizing behaviour of sports organizations. It is certainly the case that the growing prominence of sport in contemporary developed economies has fostered a more 'professional' approach to management. However, this professionalization has not led to adoption of a single set of organizational structures or strategies, even within a given national context, as the discussion above of emerging organizational structures in the British context serves to illustrate.

Nevertheless, there are general and generic tendencies among public sector organizations to adopt 'new managerialist' approaches incorporating limits to the size of the public sector, privatization, decentralization and the introduction of new types of market mechanism into arenas previously dominated by bureaucratic organizational forms (OECD, 1993). These general tendencies have specific implications for particular areas of public sector work such as sports management, which raise issues, for example, of resource dependence on declining public sector budgets (and its replacement by resource dependence on lottery and gambling income); of the supplanting of social (sports development) criteria of organizational effectiveness by goals of economic efficiency; of the debureaucratization and flexibilization of organizational structures; and of the generating of new priorities in terms of managerial skills required in sports management contexts. Having cited such tendencies one should be cautious in claims about their manifestation, since they will be more or less significant, and will take different forms, in different sports sectors and in different local and national contexts. Nevertheless, it will remain a significant concern for the analysis of sports organizations to chart and explain variation in the manifestation of these phenomena.

NOTES

1 Quasi-public sector bodies in this context are voluntary bodies that rely solely or substantially on public sector budgets for financial support.
2 The British Sports Council was renamed 'Sport England' in early 2000.
3 The method employed for the cluster analysis was Ward's method of hierarchical

agglomerative clustering with squared Euclidean measures. The variables employed in the analysis were converted to Z-scores, since different scales had been used in the generating of raw scores. The number of clusters employed was decided by inspection of the dendrogram produced by the SPSSX package. A full description of the methodology, the operationalization of concepts and the construction of variables is provided in Theodoraki and Henry (1994).

REFERENCES

Aglietta, M. (1979) *The Theory of Capitalist Regulation: the US Experience*. London: Verso.

Allen, J. (1988) 'Towards a post-industrial economy', in J. Allen and D. Massey (eds), *The Economy in Question*. London: Sage.

Allen, J. (1992) 'Post-industrialism and post-Fordism', in S. Hall, D. Held and T. McGrew (eds), *Modernity and Its Futures*. Cambridge: Polity/Open University Press.

Ashton, J. (1992) 'Women's representation in governing bodies of sport: a case study in squash'. Unpublished MSc project, Loughborough University, Loughborough, UK.

Boyer, R. (1986) *La Théorie de la régulation: un analyse critique*. Paris: Editions de la Decouverte.

Bramham, P., Henry, I., Mommaas, H. and van der Poel, H. (1993) 'Conclusion', in P. Bramham, I. Henry, H. Mommaas and H. van der Poel (eds), *Leisure Policies in Europe*. Wallingford, UK: CAB International.

Burns, T. and Stalker, D. (1961) *The Management of Innovation*. London: Tavistock.

Central Statistical Office (1991) *Social Trends*. London: HMSO.

Chelladurai, P. and Haggerty, T. (1991) 'Measures of organisational effectiveness of Canadian national sport organisations', *Canadian Journal of Sport Science*, 16 (2): 126–33.

Chelladurai, P., Szyszlo, M. and Haggerty, P. (1987) 'Systems based dimensions of effectiveness: the case of national sport organisations', *Canadian Journal of Sport Science*, 12 (1): 111–19.

Clegg, S. and Dunkerley, D. (1980) *Organization, Class and Control*. London: Routledge.

Coalter, F.W., Duffield, B. and Long, J. (1988) *Recreational Welfare: the Rationale for Public Leisure Policy*. Aldershot: Avebury.

Cooper, R. and Burrell, G. (1988) 'Modernism, post-modernism, and organizational analysis: an introduction', *Organization Studies*, 9 (1): 91–112.

DeFrance, J. and Pociello, C. (1993) 'Structure and evolution of the field of sports in France (1960–1990): a "functional", historical, and prospective analytical essay', *International Review for the Sociology of Sport*, 28 (1).

Department of National Heritage (1995) *Sport: Raising the Game*. London: HMSO.

Department of the Environment (1975) *Sport and Recreation*. London: HMSO.

Esland, G. (1980) 'Professions and professionalism', in G. Esland and G. Salaman (eds), *The Politics of Work and Occupations*. Milton Keynes: Open University Press.

Farnham, D. and Horton, S. (1993) 'The new public service managerialism: an assessment', in D.F.S. Horton (ed.), *Managing the New Public Services*. London: Macmillan.

Featherstone, M. (1990) *Global Culture: Nationalism, Globalization and Modernity*. London: Sage.

Featherstone, M. (1995) *Undoing Culture: Globalization, Postmodernism and Identity*. London: Sage.

Frisby, W. (1982) 'Weber's theory of bureaucracy and the study of voluntary sport organisations'. Paper presented at the North American Society for the Sociology of Sport Conference.

Frisby, W. (1985) 'A conceptual framework for measuring the organisational context of voluntary leisure service organizations', *Loisir et Société/ Society and Leisure*, 8 (2): 605–13.

Frisby, W. (1986) 'Measuring the organisational effectiveness of national sport governing bodies', *Canadian Journal of Applied Sports Science*, 11 (1): 94–9.

Frisby, W. (1995) 'Broadening perspectives on leisure service management and research: what does organisation theory offer?', *Journal of Park and Recreation Administration*, 13 (1): 58–72.

Gergen, K. (1992) 'Organization theory in the post-modern era', in M. Reed and M. Hughes (eds), *Rethinking Organisation: New Directions in Organization Theory and Analysis*. London: Sage.

Gonzalez, J. and Urkiola, A. (1993) 'Leisure policy in Spain', in P. Bramham, I. Henry, H. Mommaas and H. van der Poel (eds), *Leisure Policies in Europe*. Wallingford, UK: CAB International.

Hall, M.A., Cullen, D. and Slack, T. (1989) 'Organizational elites recreating themselves: the gender structure of national sport organizations', *Quest*, 41 (1): 28–45.

Hall, S. (1992) 'The question of cultural identity', in S. Hall, D. Held and T. McGrew (eds), *Modernity and Its Futures*. Cambridge: Polity/Open University Press.

Henry, I. (1993) *The Politics of Leisure Policy*. London: Macmillan.

Henry, I.P. and Paramio-Salcines, J.-L. (1996) 'Sport, urban regeneration and urban regimes: the case of Sheffield' (vol. *Sport in the City*). University of Memphis: unpublished proceeding.

Hult, J. (1989) 'Women's struggle for governance in US amateur athletics', *International Review for the Sociology of Sport*, 24 (3): 249–63.

Kikulis, L., Slack, T., Hinings, B. and Zimmerman, A. (1989) 'A structural taxonomy of amateur sports organizations', *Journal of Sport Management*, 3 (2): 129–50.

Lane, J.-E. (1995) *The Public Sector: Concepts, Models and Approaches*. London: Sage.

Lash, S. and Urry, J. (1994) *Economies of Signs and Space*. London: Sage.

Leach, S., Stewart, J. and Walsh, K. (1994) *The Changing Organisation and Management of Local Government*. London: Macmillan.

Lipietz, A. (1987) *Miracles and Mirages: the Crisis of Global Fordism*. London: Verso.

Maguire, J. (1993) 'Globalisation: sport and national identities: "The empire strikes back"?', *Loisir et Société*, 16 (2): 293–322.

McDowell, L. (1989) 'Labour and life', in M. Ball, F. Gray and L. McDowell (eds), *The Transformation of Britain: Contemporary Social and Economic Change*. London: Fontana.

Mintzberg, H. (1979) *The Structuring of Organisations*. London: Prentice-Hall.

Mintzberg, H. (1983) *Power in and around Organizations*. London: Prentice-Hall.

Nassis, P. (1994) 'Strategic relations theory and the development of sports policy in Greece 1980–93. Unpublished PhD Thesis, Loughborough University, Loughborough.

OECD (1993) *Management Developments Survey 1993*. Paris: OECD.

Onderwater, L. and Richards, G. (1994) 'Sports-management' (unpublished research report). Tilburg: Katholieke Universiteit Brabant.

Peters, T. and Waterman, R. (1982) *In Search of Excellence*. London: Harper & Row.

Pierson, C. (1991) *Beyond the Welfare State?: the New Political Economy of Welfare*. Cambridge: Polity Press.

Piore, M. and Sabel, C. (1984) *The Second Industrial Divide*. New York: Basic Books.

Pugh, D. and Hickson, D. (1976) *Organizational Structure in its Context: the Aston Programme*. London: Saxon House.

Reed, M. and Hughes, M. (1992) *Rethinking Organisation: New Directions to Organisation Theory and Analysis*. London: Sage.

Rojek, C. (1994) *Decentring Leisure: Rethinking Leisure Theory*. London: Sage.

Slack, T. (1985) 'The bureaucratisation of a voluntary sport organisation', *International Review for the Sociology of Sport*, 20 (2): 145–66.

Slack, T. and Hinings, B. (1987) 'Planning and organisational change: a conceptual framework for the analysis of amateur sport organisations', *Canadian Journal of Sport Sciences*, 12 (2): 185–93.

Theodoraki, E. and Henry, I. (1994) 'Organisational structures and contexts in British national governing bodies of sport', *International Review for the Sociology of Sport*, 29 (3): 243–67.

Thibault, L., Slack, T. and Hinings, B. (1991) 'Professionalism, structure and systems: the impact of professional staff on voluntary organisations', *International Review for the Sociology of Sport*, 26 (1): 83–99.

White, A. and Brackenridge, C. (1985) 'Who rules sport? Gender divisions in the power structure of British sports organisations from 1960', *International Review for the Sociology of Sport*, 20 (1/2): 95–107.

32

~~EMERGING~~ ARRIVING SPORT: ALTERNATIVES TO FORMAL SPORTS

Robert E. Rinehart

New Year's resolutions: 'Not to watch any sport described as extreme, ultra or radical. As soon as they break out a ramp or a board of any kind, I'm outta there'. Steve Hummer, *Atlanta Journal-Constitution*; cited in Mal Florence, 'Morning Briefing', 1998.

USER-FRIENDLY SPORT: AN INTRODUCTION

At the turn of the century, a variety of factors influence sport – both participatory and spectatorial sport. Shifting attitudes toward leisure and sport, a market-driven global economy, the participation of multinational corporations in sport (whose loci are largely centered in 'first world' countries), and increased access to venues have all heightened participation and spectatorship for many sport forms. In fact, much discourse surrounds the growing sense that sport is not sport unless and until it becomes televised – that the very act of being televised validates and authenticates its claim to being sport. Of course, this approach begs the question of how we will describe and label those physical activities that children are doing in their neighborhoods.

Of course, the question of sport/non-sport has a long history in discussion of sport in society.[1] Most recently this question has been related to funding issues, modernist concerns of high versus low sport, and, more broadly, the power relationships among the various players of contemporary sport. In point of fact, the deliberate sense that sport and television are linked may be a first-world, westernized ethnocentrism – but clearly, there are distinct

differences between alternative and extreme sport and folk sport, and the impact of television might be one of the significant differences (though, of course, in some cases these distinctions elide: e.g., the Highland Games). But the survival of contemporary sport forms is dependent, to a large degree, upon the existence of critical mass. A critical mass of participants surely is important, but a critical mass of spectators at this point in history is also vital. Thus, a relationship between mass media and sport participants has led to the arrangement of a new kind of marriage in which sport is wed to television. As columnist Dave Perkins writes about mountain biking in the 1996 Olympics, the new sports are 'primarily ... made for TV. [They] certainly [are] not made for spectating in person' (1996: D1). While I might debate these inferences about in-person spectating, it is true that the newer sports typically move through space in a different way from arena-bound sports like soccer and football and baseball. They lend themselves to tighter camera angles, quick shots and close-ups of the action – reminiscent of recent Hollywood productions – a hyper-MTV, a more virtual style of presentation.

Many of these newer sports themselves are self-conscious, seemingly aware of the fact of being seen, and, though they are still fundamentally practices of the body in space and time, they are also about presentation to others. They are about performance. They are, even at the grass-roots levels away from television cameras, about sharing the experience and about community. Sports like American football had their roots in this type of community – where college students and young professors (male) got together to test their abilities. Rules were implicit; and the affiliative sense one got of belonging to a football group was larger than any other sense of self. In the early days, playing football was an end in itself, not a means to a professional career. But that has changed, and now the so-called 'alternatives' to the mainstream sports of American football, soccer, rugby, baseball, basketball, volleyball and so on,[2] are cutting-edge opportunities for alternative sports enthusiasts. These opportunities are sought actively by boarders of all varieties – surf, skate, snow, wake, skysurf – as well as in-line skaters, to name just a few, in their quest to become or remain active without the interference of undue authority. In the eyes of many alternative sports practitioners, 'authority' is represented by coaches, managers, organizing committees, corporate sponsors, media, rules enforcers, among many others. However, as will be discussed below, the 'anti-mainstream' impulse among some participants in many of these sports (cf. snowboarding) has gradually eroded.

ALTERNATIVE, EXTREME OR GLOBAL FAD?

New sports include what French scholar Nancy Midol might call 'whiz' sports (though her take on them is from a more participatory angle). These are sports in which time is compressed and action is rampant. New sports might include what Arthur and Marilouise Kroker (1989) term 'panic sport', what some athletes and analysts term 'alternative' sport, and what US cable network ESPN and many others term 'extreme' sport. One writer explained it this way:

> The 'extreme' moniker simply refers to a growing number of physically and mentally intense activities that have not been formally recognized as legitimate sports by most media and/or society. ... But the need for legitimacy has been realized. (Rees, 1997: 32–3)

The terms used to identify these new sport forms are fundamentally important, because some terms have exclusive connotations, or emphasize only one facet of the attraction of the sports. Thus, for example, 'whiz' sport might exclude something like the teamwork-oriented, endurance-rewarding Eco-Challenge (or ESPN's Extreme Adventure Race) or endurance running and ultra marathons from the mix.

'Extreme' sport might similarly exclude those activities that are not seen on television.

Whatever we choose to name these new sport forms at this point in time, 'they' have arrived. Advertisers clearly are pleased that the tough-to-reach 12–34-year-old male market is the fundamental market associated with these sports and the related media coverage. In 1996, the inaugural year of the newly named 'X Games' (and the second year of the event), live attendance was calculated at 201,350; in 1997 it moved to San Diego and the attendance was 219,900, and in 1998 it was 242,850. In 1997, ESPN, ESPN2, ESPN International and ABC's Wide World of Sports put out 37 hours of coverage; additionally, ESPN reached 71 million households, ESPN2 reached 48 million and ESPN International was broadcast in 198 countries in 21 languages (ESPN Sportszone, 1997). ESPN and ESPN2, respectively, have garnered (in 1998) 0.7 and 0.5 ratings for the X Games televised to US households. ABC pulled in a 2.3 rating in 1997 and a 1.6 rating in 1998 (Brockinton, 1998).

The 'alternative sports' phenomenon is worldwide, and this has not gone unnoticed by people in the media. For example, London-based writer Simon Barnes claims that his 'favourite is an event called street luge racing – I hope they won't take the heat off the event by stopping the traffic first' (1995: 42). 'X Games celebrate alternatives' reads the headline in *The Moscow* [Russia] *Tribune* (1996), direct from the AP wire service. 'Extreme Sports: Why Americans are risking life and limb for the big rush' blares the front cover of the *US News & World Report* (Koerner, 1997). In New Zealand, where extreme sports like bungy jumping proliferate, the focus is on tourist cash and economic benefits (Henderson, 1998; Neems, 1998).

Interest among athletes is a key dimension of the alternative sport phenomenon. At the 1997 X Games, there were nearly five hundred competitors from over 20 different countries, including Russia, Italy, Brazil, Mexico, Japan, Israel, Korea, Australia, New Zealand, France, South Africa, Kazahkstan and Canada. *Daily Bread*, an in-line magazine started by skaters, has had spreads on local in-liners from Asia (titled 'Futuretrip'), the UK, Spain, Italy, Switzerland (with the Lausanne and Zurich competitions highlighted), Finland, Germany – plus a more recent photo spread of locals from 5 August to 30 September 1998 in 20 cities throughout the world, including Tokyo, Munich, Düsseldorf and Flensburg in Germany; Brussels, Edinburgh, Melbourne, Barcelona, Stockholm, Amsterdam, Dublin, Lausanne,

Vienna, Belfast, Copenhagen, London, Ljubljana in Slovenia, and Sarnia and Toronto, Canada.

And the corporations are leading the way. Interest among corporations, from small, sport-based sponsors to large, multinational corporations, has also been key to the growth of these newer, alternative sports. A small sampling of businesses who have aligned with alternative sports includes the Italian multinationals Benetton and Roces, and corporations such as Salomon, Bauer, Senate and Tribe Distribution. There are also web-based companies/distributors like rollerwarehouse.com, skate-utopia.com, airbornesk8.com along with more typical corporate sponsors of the X Games, like AT&T, Coors, Nike, Taco Bell, Mountain Dew, Chevrolet, Pontiac, Pringles, Rollerblade, Slim Jim, VISA and Snickers. Clearly, these companies have found a niche market.

The point is that, while the more conservative sports guardians have marginalized these alternative sports, there is a large demand for and response to extreme and alternative sports. The sports themselves do not always matter to the companies (much as, it is claimed, sports don't really matter to Rupert Murdoch).[3] Some companies do profess empathy with the sports. Nike's social reconstruction campaigns are perhaps the most famous. Notable as well are Benetton's Colors campaigns, and Roces's slogan 'team unity – brotherhood – conviction – respect' smacks of similar 'social design' strategies. The authenticity of the makers clearly matters to many of these sports' enthusiasts. Thus, snowboarders will buy Jake Burton products because they are aware of his involvement in and commitment to the sport. Of course many professionals in in-line skating have wheels named after themselves, which is clearly an attempt to capitalize on this authenticity/athlete-identification phenomenon. The wary buyer is faced with the challenge of sorting out which wheels work best for him or her.

Since many of these 'alternative' activities are promoted as 'made-for-television sports', it seems logical that television is key to these sports' ultimate proliferation. As television increased its sensory appeal for viewers in technological advances meant for mainstream sports, the technologies soon became appropriated and combined with a quick-shot, hand-held camera, MTV-style of production. Sportscaster Jim Lampley once described the immediacy of viewer involvement as the 'you-are-there audio' (Home Box Office, 1991). But many of the appropriated-for-television sports have gone steps farther in attempting to 'virtualize' the experience of elite participation while retaining recognition of the ideology associated with mass participation (often ecological in nature). Added to slo-motion replay, the zoom, the heightened audio and so on, are the street luge's 'luge-cams, mounted directly on the sled, to enhance the viewer's perspective by traveling at 60 mph just inches off the ground' (Brooker, 1998: 251), the skysurfers' helmet cam; a variety of robotic, crane-robotic and pole cams; the high-resolution video camera used by camera-operators for the Winter X Games' Skier X (six skiers at once) and the snowboarders' slopestyle events; and the 'rope cam, a miniature RF [radio frequency] camera located on the handle of the rope to get close ups of the competitors' (Brooker, 1998: 253). The quality of production is incredibly good, and any 'roughness' of shots is purposeful, seemingly adding to the virtual rush the at-home viewer is meant to feel when watching these events.

NAMING SOME NAMES: AMALGAMS OF SKILLS AND THRILLS

What are alternative sports? They are activities that either ideologically or practically provide alternatives to mainstream sports and to mainstream sport values. Raymond Williams's (1977) categorizations of 'dominant, residual, and emergent' can be helpful in providing a framework for determining what sports fall into mainstream or emergent categories. Of course, there is overlap between and among the Williams's categories, by sport and by level of sport. Thus, a pick-up football game can be both mainstream, because of the intersections with professional and collegiate football, and residual, because it is an 'effective element of the present' (p. 122) mainstream football nexus.

Alternative sports may have elements of the mainstream or residual in them. However, their obvious difference from the mainstream 'is that they have not gained widespread acceptance from mainstream audiences' (Rinehart, 1998a: 403). Other differences are highlighted by a range of debates. For example, there are debates surrounding team versus individual sports (though media moguls have tried to extend individual extreme sports into more of a team orientation). There are debates about the importance of professionalism in the sports, about incorporation of grass-roots oppositional sport forms into the mainstream, and about professional/amateur statuses. Finally, there are debates surrounding the lifestyle, aesthetics and competitive characters of the sports.

There is, of course, overlap between mainstream and these alternative-to-the-mainstream sports. ESPN certainly does not control exclusively the coverage of these sports, though the point could be made that the omnipresence of ESPN, and the very dominance of the electronic media, provides a cultural dominance over the mere presentation of extreme, alternative sports in the electronic sportscape (see Rinehart, forthcoming). Thus, until other media companies come on to the scene, ESPN will maintain dominant market share and will play a major role in shaping for the [virtual] world what extreme sports will consist of, constitute, and become.

Forms of what might be considered alternative sports that are proliferating around the globe could be variously categorized as extreme, alternative, whiz, lifestyle, or panic in their fundamental expression though it may not be appropriate to view them always as 'extreme'. Alternative sports at this point in history include, but are certainly not limited to, sport forms such as the following:[4] hang gliding, high wire, ski flying, soaring, caving, land and ice yachting (ice sailing), mountainboarding, showshoeing, speed biking, speed skiing, steep skiing, air chair, jetskiing, open water swimming, powerboat racing, snorkeling, speed sailing and trifoiling (all mentioned, among others, in Tomlinson, 1996). There are skateboarding (cf. Beal, 1995; Beal and Weidman, forthcoming), whitewater kayaking (see, for example, Mounet and Chifflet, 1996, forthcoming; Watters, forthcoming), korfball (cf. Crum, 1988), professional beach volleyball (cf. Silverstein, 1995), surfing (see, for example, Pearson, 1981; Booth, forthcoming), and windsurfing (cf. Wheaton, 1997, forthcoming; Wheaton and Tomlinson, 1998). There are ultimate fighting (amalgam of styles, probably deriving from the martial arts), 'extreme' skiing (the films of Warren Miller may have driven the desire for this activity; see, for example, Kremer, forthcoming; and Kay and Laberge, forthcoming), deep water diving (fixed weight, variable weight and absolute diving), paragliding, sandboarding (du Lac, 1995), and the Miner's Olympics. There are barefoot snow skiing, parachute skiing, mono skiing, para bungee (bungee from a hot-air balloon), bungee from a helicopter, underwater hockey, canoe polo, bicycle polo, jai alai (which, similar to pelota, is a 'new world' form with slightly different cultural significance, rule structure and context), SCUBA (self-contained underwater breathing apparatus) diving, BASE (buildings, antenna tower, span, earth) jumping, indoor climbing (artificial climbing wall), ultra marathoning (Grenfell, 1998), netball and bicycle stunt and freestyle (cf. Kubiak, 1997). Various countries and cultural regions also have emerging forms of alternative sports. From Australia there are trugo (a mallet game with rubber ring) and sphairee (miniaturized tennis) (*The Sports Factor*, 25 September 1998). In Switzerland there is ski-horsing (skiers drawn downhill by horses). There is pelota, a demonstration sport in the Barcelona Olympics; belote, a similar game, from Belgium; and pole sitting and pole jumping from Holland, where, respectively, people sit in the middle of lakes on poles for time and people jump irrigation channels in contests for distance (personal communication, Morris Levy, 1999).

Additionally, according to Donnelly, 'there is also real risk – in solo climbing, deep sea diving, ocean yacht racing, hot air balloon epics, Himalayan and other high altitude mountaineering ...' (Sportsoc discussion, 3 February 1997). Seemingly calmer alternatives to mainstream sports (though participants might dispute this) include dance sport, one of the newer entries into Olympic sports, which makes its Olympic appearance in 2000 at the Sydney Games (cf. *The Times*, 1995; B. Thomas, 1998).

High risk is generally considered a factor in extreme sports, but not necessarily in alternative sports. Individuality is privileged over a team orientation, and perhaps that is one reason why purists are initially skeptical when ESPN has gone to doubles and triples performing simultaneously (as in skateboarding or in-line).

There are also a variety of international competitions involving alternative sports. These include but are not limited to international windsurfing competitions like the one held in Essaouira, Morocco, 'known as Wind City Afrika ... [where] international windsurf competitions are held ... each spring' (Keeble, 1995: 163). There are the Hi-Tec Adventure Racing Series (Thomas, 1998b) and a variety of adventure races around the world (see, for example, Bell, forthcoming; Cotter, forthcoming) (for example, the Eco Challenge, the Raid Gauloises and the Morocco Adventure Race). There are triathlons, probably the most famous of which is the Ironman, held in Hawaii annually. There are street basketball tournaments like the Gus Macker 3-on-3 (Brewington, 1993) and the Hoop-It-Up World Championship (Forest, 1993). There are the Vans Triple Crown of Skateboarding (cf. Howe, 1998), the Highland

Games (cf. Jarvie, 1991), the World Masters Games, the Youth Games, the Corporate Games, Goodwill Games, Gay Games, World Transplant Games and the Maccabbee Games. All are alternative to mainstream sports in one way or another. Additionally, because they are somewhat marginalized, despite being appropriated by the International Olympic Committee, some might include the Paralympics in this list. Both the Paralympics and the Special Olympics are examples of what were once alternatives to mainstream sports but which, due to institutionalization, have become increasingly mainstream themselves. Of course, this liminal area – whether sport is mainstream or emerging, solidified in the public consciousness or merely arriving – appears to be a realm in which many 'successful' contemporary sports have dwelled at some point in their histories.

THE X GAMES: MEDIATED ALTERNATIVE SPORT

Among some people, especially many young people around the world, the X Games, originally the Extreme Games, have somehow come to signify radical alternative sports. What are 'extreme' sports? In the first incarnation of the X Games (the eXtreme Games), in an attempt to link the site of Fort Adams, Rhode Island with extreme sport, co-host Suzi Kolber intoned,

> This is an attitude toward life; passion that comes from the soul. From its beginnings, Rhode Island has been distinguished by its support for freedom, its rebellious, authority-defying nature. Fort Adams, built to defend, looms large this week as a new generation makes its stand. It's an opportunity to redefine the way we look at sports. (ESPN, broadcast 1 July 1995)

Yet some practitioners – and writers – have disputed the very term 'extreme' as merely a blatant and cynical attempt to capitalize on a wave of oppositional sport forms and, by doing so, for corporations such as ESPN to appropriate trendy oppositional forms.

ESPN, the cable network based in the United States and owned since 1995 by the Disney Corporation (along with ABC-TV), in 1995 started The eXtreme Games, which attempted to capitalize on the word 'extreme'. The company realized that the word 'extreme' was problematic: ESPN quickly distanced itself from the word 'extreme', 'as it became passé and the network decided it carried a negative connotation' (Rother, 1997: B-2). Amy Cacciola, then-Assistant Director of Marketing and Communications for the X Games, said that

'the word "extreme" is completely overused. There's extreme skiing, and everything you see nowadays has the word "extreme" on it' (personal communication, 4 October 1996).

The Games was a summer made-for-television sport event which, in 1995, displayed non-mainstream sports (mainly for male participants). These included:

- skateboarding (see, for example, Beal and Weidman, forthcoming);
- in-line skating (a.k.a., Rollerblading) (see, for example, Rinehart, forthcoming);
- sky surfing (see, for example, Koyn, forthcoming; Sydnor, forthcoming);
- street luge;
- Eco Challenge;
- BMX dirt bike jumping (see, for example, Downs, forthcoming; Kusz, forthcoming);
- barefoot (ski) jumping;
- bungee jumping;
- sport climbing (see, for example, Donnelly, forthcoming; Dornian, forthcoming);
- mountain biking (see, for example, Eassom, forthcoming; Bridgers, forthcoming).

No one knew whether or how well the televised event would be received. Chris Fowler, who co-hosted the eXtreme Games in 1995, has since written that:

> The X Games might never amount to a true revolution, maybe just a welcome diversion on the crowded sports calendar. But if you arrive with an open mind, you'll get sucked in. The energy is contagious. Even if we're *still* not certain exactly what to expect. (1998: 250, emphasis in original)

It is worth noting that, by undercutting potential criticism, Fowler has anticipated and thus appropriated objections that a more 'pure' sports audience might make. Yet there remains an element of truth to the uncertainty he identifies, despite his inevitable and concerted effort at selling the Games through his words.

Over the years since 1995 the events of the ESPN Summer X Games (name changed in January of 1996) have evolved and become known to include the following major event categories. There are:

- skateboarding (street and both single and doubles vert; and, as exhibitions, downhill, women's halfpipe and off-road skateboarding);
- in-line skating (aggressive, street, vert and vert triples, and downhill);
- sky surfing;
- street luge (dual and 'Super Mass Street' events);

- Extreme Adventure Race;
- bicycle stunt (flatland, dirt jumping, street, and single and doubles vert);
- barefoot waterski jumping;
- wakeboarding;
- sportclimbing (difficulty and speed);
- snowboarding big air.

All events are open to both males and females, though television time follows the pattern of mainstream sport coverage in that it focuses on men and generally ignores the women (see, for example, Dennis-Vano, 1995).

In late January of 1997, ESPN aired a Winter X Games, which included such extreme sports as:

- snowboarding (which was incorporated into the Olympic venue at the Nagano Games in 1998 – is it still 'alternative'?) (see, for example, Burton, forthcoming; Humphreys, forthcoming);
- super-modified shovel racing;
- ice climbing;
- snow mountain bike racing;
- crossover slopestyle snowboarding.

In 1999, the Winter X Games, broadcast from Crested Butte, Colorado (16–22 January, just two weeks prior to the Super Bowl), included:

- snocross (snomobiles racing);
- free skiing (Skier-X, with six skiers racing simultaneously);
- snowboarding (Boarder-X, again with multiple snowboarders);
- snow mountain bike racing downhill;
- speed, speed and difficulty ice climbing;
- slopestyle skiboarding;
- slopestyle, big air and halfpipe snowboarding (ESPN2, 1999).

MEDIA LOGICS: CAPITALISTIC INNOVATION

Though the previous references to alternative sports may seem exhaustive, the alternative sportscape is certainly not limited to just what I've listed. It is difficult and would be very tedious to list all the variants that ESPN and Fox Sports Network have presented to viewers with the hope of attracting a large audience. But three of the more notable ones include the following. First, ESPN's H2O Winter Classic, which combines professional snowboarders with professional surfers, each doing one day of the activities in Mammoth Mountain and Huntington Beach, California, for a total score. Second, The World's Strongest Man competitions, whose events have included towing an

airplane, lifting logs and barrel walking. Third, the Boardercross (Boarder-X) competitions, 'in which six riders simultaneously race down a giant slalom course filled with gulches, corkscrews and other obstacles' (Benc, 1998: C-7). The list continues to grow, as amalgams of previously known sports are given new twists, or existing sports are combined with other existing sports. Meanwhile the marketing departments of ESPN, Fox and other media companies around the world are constantly thinking up new combinations and ways of selling them to viewers. In such a context, change is inherent.

Perhaps the rate and ever presence of change is one of the key differences between established, mainstream sports and these newer, constantly evolving, alternative sports. Not only do most alternative sports enthusiasts welcome change, but they often provide the impetus to it. Of course, nostalgia is present, but with new and different challenges ever being sought, the nostalgia for a seemingly tamer past is short-lived. By creating new sport forms, many of the athletes in alternative sports hope to be the next entrepreneur who works at her/his play, and who incidentally makes it big. Some of the models for this pattern are snowboarder Jake Burton, in-line skaters Anjie Walton and Arlo Eisenberg, and skateboarder Tony Hawk. The dynamics associated with this quest and the creativity that permeates alternative sports tend to produce change that is often radical, so that sports are mutated rapidly into mildly unrecognizable forms. In mainstream sport, on the other hand, most of the changes are superficial, often constrained by the fear of undermining an established product and, of course, the nostalgia that reaffirms many people's connections with the sport.

TROUBLES IN PARADISE: GROWING PAINS, GREED, OR GOOD WILL?

With any new sport form (or, in this case, phenomenon), there will be problems, conflicts, debates. In each of the sports previously listed, there are adamant practitioners who want to make their visions known. The athletes' views do not always coincide with the views of profit-oriented companies, nor do they coincide with the nostalgic ideas of a sports-savvy public. But much of the conflict and controversy that is associated with these sports arises because participants are highly committed and possess different ideas about process and goals.

Alternative sports emerge in contexts where dynamics revolve around a range of contentious issues. These include:

- the incorporation of grass-roots practitioners into the mainstream;
- outsider/insider status of athletes;
- professional/amateur standings of athletes;
- purity, authenticity and genuineness of the sports;
- multinational corporate sponsorship and globalization/Americanization arguments;
- the philosophies behind the sports: lifestyle, aesthetics, competition;
- self-regulation versus governance by others;
- sexism, racism and homophobia.

I can only touch briefly on these issues, and they tend to overlap, but an insightful reader will perhaps look particularly at other chapters in this volume and seek out conceptual frameworks that might be useful for analyzing alternative as well as mainstream sports.

The Incorporation of Grass-roots Practitioners into the Mainstream

Elsewhere, I have pointed out that corporate strategies for producing mass acceptance among in-line skaters and skateboarders involve fan identification with the sport's personalities, modeling behavior of younger participants, corporate sponsorship and embracing of certain sports and individuals over others, and an uneasy, contested dynamic between performers' (who represent actual practitioners) artistic impulses and the (inferred) competitive impulses of mainstream audiences (Rinehart, 1998a: 402–3).

Such strategies are deliberate. They are meant to create mass acceptance and audience. If they are successful, they will serve also to undercut the very oppositional nature of these particular alternative sports. Of course, Ron Semiao, the so-called 'innovator' of the X Games for ESPN, says that he is 'always on the lookout for "what's emerging and what's stale" so the X Games can stay on the cutting edge' (cited in Rother, 1997: B-2).

So, grass-roots participants are urged to get more involved, while non-participants are urged to get involved (at least as spectators) in the sports. This multi-pronged attack on the viewing/participating public thus creates a larger fan base, so that 'alternative' gradually melds into 'mainstream', at least in terms of the sports' acceptance.

Outsider/Insider Status of Athletes

Surfing culture is illustrative of the overt problem outsiders have in some of the more insular alternative sports. For example, surfers from California to Hawaii to Australia have continually resisted efforts by 'style' companies (that is, clothing or equipment manufacturers) who have not demonstrated a long-term commitment to the sport. Tommy Hilfiger's apparel line fairly recently attempted to penetrate the admittedly tough surfing apparel market, when its 'core men's casual clothing line slow[ed]' (Earnest, 1998: D5). Its attempt was made easier by the fact that a long-time, well-known surfing family in southern California was acting as consultants for Hilfiger, thus effectively acting on behalf of the company. The authenticity of the family helped it to better penetrate the surfing apparel market. Clearly, Hilfiger, Nike and others have realized the importance of the insider status, as some of their sport apparel lines have failed.

The insider–outsider lines can become confused, however, by a savvy company. When ESPN first broadcast the eXtreme Games in 1995, there was really no such thing as a short downhill race for in-liners. ESPN suggested to the 10K skaters that such a downhill race would make for good television. Many of the skaters scoffed, claiming that a short, straight, packed downhill on in-line skates was too dangerous. But ESPN persevered, increased the prize money and what one writer characterized as a 'carnival act for a TV event' (Seltsam, 1996: 15) became something that by 1999 younger skaters have come to accept and define as exciting. Marvin Percival (affiliated with Sk8Deal, an on-line speed skating firm based in Andover, Massachusetts), a father of in-line speed skaters, revealed to me that one of his sons is eager to participate in the 'extremely dangerous' but exciting short downhill course. He explains that his son's background in the more legitimate speed skating gives him a 'tremendous amount of credibility' in the new sport (personal communication, 18 December 1998).

Pretenders in the extreme sports are soon revealed. Wheaton (forthcoming) has demonstrated that committed, 'core' members of windsurfing clubs are more concerned with what windsurfers do than with how they pose. And the posing or the authenticity – revealed in style, self-identification, insider argot and knowledge issues – quickly becomes clear to insiders. Put another way, a skater wrote to the editor of *Daily Bread*: 'Who fucking cares what people wear when they skate? Get a life! Any real skater should know that it's not the look it's the attitude [*sic*]' (Cook, 1995: no page).

Professional/Amateur Standings of Athletes

Many extreme or alternative sport enthusiasts participate without any chance of financial gain. They do the activity for the pure love, the excitement and differentness of the sport. In fact, many of these participants either don't consider their activity a 'sport', or don't care. It is something they do, on weekends or whenever they can find the time. In a traditional sense, these people are considered amateurs, though their aptitude, dedication and commitment to the sports may be very high.

But with the advent of ESPN's X Games and similar programming, those athletes who benefit financially from the sports and in the process become role models have challenged people to think about the meanings of professional and amateur in new ways. For example, Katie Brown, a difficulty route climber, began climbing in 1993 at age 13, won the 1996 X Games in Difficulty, and, as a 16-year-old, left 'her Georgia home to follow the professional climbing circuit …' (Brooker, 1998: 214). Joining a professional circuit – which of course typically includes the X Games – is only one of the many routes that alternative sports enthusiasts may take. Street luger Michael 'Biker' Sherlock owns a skateboard company. In-line pioneer Arlo Eisenberg has starred in films, made commercials, been an editor/writer for skating magazines, toured the world professionally, and his family owns a skatepark in Plano, Texas.

It seems that the traditional binaries of professional and amateur are not applicable to many extreme sportists. Many of the core members of these groups are fairly young and, like surfers who follow the waves or skiers who work at ski resorts in order to ski daily, they have creatively generated space for themselves so that they may continue to live the lifestyle of extremist.

Purity, Authenticity and Legitimacy of – and in – Alternative Sports

There are several ways in which the credibility of extreme sports may be interrogated. First, there is the very authenticity of the sport itself. Extreme sports have been routinely criticized by mainstream purists who tend to deride the particularly 'invented' character of the participants

and the sports.[5] Secondly, the legitimacy of the sports is questioned. The 'non-competitive', made-for-television nature of the sports can make them seem illegitimate to mainstream sports enthusiasts. Thirdly, there are questions about the authenticity of the participants themselves. Such questions frame the credibility of the sport in terms related to the insider–outsider statuses of the participants.

When issues of purity and authenticity are discussed it is helpful to note that the Super Bowl is considered by the vast majority of people in the United States to be an authentic event for American football. Yet it began only in 1967. And the Vince Lombardi Trophy that is steeped in nostalgia and remembrance (and historical authenticity) was given for the first time to the winners of Super Bowl V in 1972 (see Rinehart, 1998b: 73–5). Even though the Super Bowl was only 34 years old (in the year 2000) it has achieved a sense of authenticity and the appearance of credibility. Money and media attention have been powerful in speeding up history in this case.

Basketball is said to have been invented by Canadian James Naismith as he sought to develop a form of indoor recreation that could be done during the cold winter months in the Northeastern United States. He borrowed elements from a variety of sports at the time and as basketball evolved, rules and game-play were refined. As basketball enthusiasts brought the game to others, as it gained more and more exposure, it took on the patina of authenticity. It simultaneously achieved mainstream status and credibility.

The Skins Game, an event in which high-profile golfers have been known to make putts that earn them $200,000, began in Reagan's 1980s America as a made-for-television event. Today it is doing quite well in terms of television audience ratings. In 1996, 'nearly 6 million homes tuned in … making [it] the second-highest rated golf telecast of the year, behind the Masters' (Price, 1997: F-5).

So it is with extreme sports. Each of them derived from somewhere, from some person or persons who the participants usually hold up as founders of the sport. Each of the sports is said to have an origination myth and writer Kevin Brooker has established a time-line identifying important events in the sports highlighted on ESPN's 'Way Inside ESPN's X Games'. According to ESPN coverage, the sport of wakeboarding can be traced back to 1922 when Ralph Samuelson 'straps two pine boards … onto his feet and takes off behind a motorboat on Lake Pepin, MN'. Then in 1985, surfer Tony Flynn developed 'the Skurfer, a hybrid of a water ski and a surfboard', while 'Jimmy Redmon is working on his Redline brand board' in Texas. In 1990, 'Herb O'Brien's H.O. Sports introduces the first compression-molded board, the Hyperlite', and on the story goes. Another example is the Australian game of sphairee, a miniaturized game of tennis. Said to have been invented in the 1960s by Sydney resident and former linguistics professor Frederick Arthur George Beck, the rationale (there is usually a rationale as well as an origination story) was that he sought to play a tennis-like sport in a small space (Radio National, 1998).[6]

With new sport forms there are issues of legitimacy along with issues of authenticity. Among some of those who feel qualified to comment on sports there has developed a high–low sport ideology that is similar to a high–low culture ideology. Popular sport (that is, sport made specifically for television, rather than mainstream sport which has been appropriated by television), according to this ideology, is decried at the same time that the importance of its popularity is acknowledged. The thinking seems to be that if they are 'made for television', are they not in the same category as so-called 'trash sports' like roller derby, professional wrestling and the Billy Jean King–Bobby Riggs tennis match? This thinking, of course, assumes the paradoxical view that credibility and authenticity are defined in terms of elite sport, but everyone should be engaged in it (for a lengthy discussion of this point, see Rinehart, 1998b).

Often, the legitimacy issue is confused with what Benjamin Lowe termed 'expressive' and 'spectacle' sports (1977: 29). Thus, those sports in which judges are used to determine the quality of performance and the outcomes of competitive events are, oddly, seen as less than sport. In mainstream sports this would be the case for diving, gymnastics and synchronized swimming. In extreme sports it would be the case for nearly all the events. Apparently, some people see more objective measures of achievement and success as being more legitimate and view the inclusion of subjectivity as 'soft' sport and as being indicative of a lack of legitimacy.

Finally, those associated with the sports themselves raise authenticity questions. Core members of the sports appreciate skillfulness, but it is possible for a person to be an authentic member of an extreme sport group and not be the most skillful participant. The works of scholars such as Belinda Wheaton in windsurfing (forthcoming), Peter Donnelly in climbing (Donnelly and Young, 1988) and Becky Beal and Lisa Weidman in skateboarding (forthcoming), show clearly that a participant's authenticity is socially determined. Attitude, style, world-view and the meanings given to the participant's involvement are all used to determine membership in the subculture associated with the sport.

Multinational Corporate Sponsorship

Companies involved in the sports themselves sponsor individual athletes and events. Manufacturers such as Roces, Benetton, Salomon and others have aligned themselves with a variety of the sports, producing equipment and apparel for these so-called niche markets. In some cases, the athletes themselves have attempted to control, through a range of strategies (including the importance of insider status to consumers), the production end of their sports. For example, Jake Burton makes snowboards and Arlo Eisenberg manufactures and distributes in-line skate products.

But there appear to be at least two other aspects to the intersection between corporations, businesses and athletes. One is the sponsorship of events and individuals by multinational corporations whose primary function has little or nothing to do with sport. One might infer a sliding scale of extreme sport involvement when applied to sponsors so that, looking at sport sponsorship from the point of view of corporate involvement in the sport, a range of possibilities could be seen. For example, a company founded by an athlete would be seen as highly legitimate (individual insider status). Next in the order of legitimacy would be a company like Roces (a skate manufacturer), with a corporate face (corporate insider). Next would be a company that has taken over some original-insider, like Benetton who took over Rollerblade (corporate insider/outsider). Next would be a company like Nike, whose expertise is in sport, but not especially in extreme sports. Lastly, there would be a corporation like Mountain Dew, which has blatantly appropriated the 'extreme' tag and used it humorously. Different groups would perhaps debate the order of these characterizations as far as legitimacy (a 'pretender' like Nike, it could be argued, might create more backlash than Mountain Dew, whose stance was that it never pretended to be extreme), but these general descriptions of corporate legitimacy might be a good starting point for discussion.

Clearly, multinational corporations have seen that extreme sports (for both men and women) are a lucrative avenue for producing, recruiting and servicing consumers. However, the strategies used by corporations do not always coincide with the self-proclaimed ethos of alternative sport, such as individuality, actual participation and authenticity.

There is a great deal of conflict between alternative sports and mainstream sports. For example, alternative sports have deeply impacted viewership in the 12–34 age range, in some cases usurping the power that mainstream sports have held over young males for generations (Greenfeld, 1998). Furthermore, the debates around issues of globalization, Americanization and so on, intersect with alternative sport, especially since it is so deeply enmeshed with international media like Fox and Disney (see Sage, Chapter 16, and Maguire, Chapter 23). The story of who controls the presentation of these sports is the story of the conflicts and contestations over who owns, and who will control the economics, but also the soul of these sports.

Lifestyle, Aesthetics and Competition

There has been an interesting non-complaint associated with alternative and extreme sport, and that is that there are rarely reports of athletes suffering burnout. Until the advent of control by others such as agents, site coordinators, sponsors and ESPN, for example, this was a non-issue. Now, however, when fun has somehow been made into work for these athletes – and with competition added to the mix – there are more and more complaints.

In-line skater Arlo Eisenberg once said, 'Our sports – Rollerblading – have never really had grass-roots'. He claims that this, more than anything else, has made forms of in-line skating more vulnerable to outside influences: 'ESPN is great in terms of exposure but it's dangerous in how they present [in-line skating] – making it something that is wasn't meant to be ... based on competition. ... New kids don't want another "sport"' (personal communication, 31 October 1996).

The core members of in-line and of other extreme sports have claimed that they initiated their participation because it was something they could do by themselves, because it didn't require adult (coaches, officials, etc.) supervision, and because it was challenging. They formed a great support network for one another. Enthusiasts appreciated the excellent moves of other participants in ways that were inconsistent with a 'competitive ethic'. Two anecdotes, one from footbag and one from

professional skateboarding, can be used to explain the different ethos of some alternative sports participants.

In the first case, footbag (also known as Hacky-Sack) is played as part of Orangewood High School's (Redlands, CA) physical education curriculum. One of the students, who had been footbagging for three years (in 1996), Rick Bunting, said 'It brings the body and the mind together. ... I think it's almost a type of meditation in a sense' (cited in McCuin, 1996: H3).

In the second case, a writer describes a skateboarding event involving two top boarders:

> At the 1997 X Games, skateboarders Chris Senn and Andy Macdonald battled for the gold medal and $5,000 on the street course. Macdonald nailed his final 60-second run, including something called a back flip where he went up one ramp, turned, twisted and landed going down another ramp ... Two skateboarders later, Senn stepped to the top of the ramp. For 53 seconds, he was perfect, flying down ramps, sliding along rails and bringing the packed crowd to its feet. But with seven seconds remaining, Senn bit it on the black asphalt. Said Senn: 'I thought Andy won'. (Norcross, 1997: D-3)

But Senn won, and Macdonald and Senn were both incredibly gracious, explaining how the other's tricks were outstanding, and how much fun it was to watch the other perform. Later, Senn explained a bit of the ethos for skateboarding, and perhaps for other alternative sports: 'It's like painting or music. You can't judge anybody. It's an art form, not a sport' (1997: D-3). And yet, of course, it is both.

Of course, as more and more people begin to participate, and bring in more of a competitive ethos to the sports, the very nature of the sports will continue to change. And as corporations like ESPN see that competition sells on television, that head-to-head combat between six skiers, with the naturally occurring spills and tumbles, and crashes in the street luge, bring in audience, the mainstream values of American sport will continue to impact the original, non-competitive ethos of these sports.

Self-regulation versus Governance by Others

To some extent, previous issues like multinational corporate involvement, issues of authenticity and credibility and lifestyle issues intersect with the issue of self-regulation of the sports. To what degree, for instance, does corporate involvement promote the growth of the sport as opposed to serving exclusively the fiduciary interests of the corporation? When 'stars' in the 'cult of celebrity' become perceived as sell-outs, there immediately arises a problem of authenticity. And when participants have a world-view that doing the sport on a daily basis is fundamental to insider status, and a once-a-year televised X Games (what some might term good exposure for the sports, others might see as exploitation) only shows the winning contestants, there is a perception that the self-control of the sport is being wrested from its founders.

This then becomes an issue of self-determination versus governance by others. A case in point is the recent co-optation of snowboarding by the International Olympic Committee for the 1998 Winter Olympics.

Sean O'Brien of *Transworld Snowboarding Business Magazine* (cited in Thomas, 1998a) says, 'If it wasn't for snowboarding coming to the resorts, overall skier visitation numbers would be in the toilet' (1998a: C14). Clearly, snowboarding – and snowboarders – have changed the nature of recreational use for many recreationalists (estimated at about 4 million in the United States, but with up to '10 trips a year' per person, versus about two trips a year for skiers, according to Greg Ralph, Marketing Director at Bear Mountain, CA, cited in P. Thomas, 13 March 1998a: C14). Critical mass of participants – thus, educated spectators – was an important factor in the decision to 'Olympize' the sport.

Early on, the IOC's ski arm, the International Ski Federation (FIS), began a 'snowboard tour to rival the ISF [International Snowboard Federation] circuit' and then worked its way (according to many of the ISF riders) into the mainstream (Dufresne, 1998: C10). The ISF at this point in time, it should be noted, personifies self-governance for snowboarders.

Many snowboarders, however, not willing to be so readily appropriated by what they saw as the strong-arm tactics of the IOC, chose to boycott the 1998 Nagano Games. They were especially disappointed by the fact that their events were sponsored by equipment and clothing manufacturers whose apparel they could not wear. This scenario involved motivations similar to those in the 1992 USA Men's Basketball 'Dream Team''s Nike/Reebok conflict. But the Games still went on and, as US Olympic snowboarder Lisa Kosglow said,'some of the other [ISF] riders have a lot of resentment ... It's a whole sellout issue' (cited in Dufresne, 1998: C10).

Some alternative sports like skateboarding 'have been around [a long time and have]

created the model for all the sports after them. Time, experience, they have the most solid, definite identity', according to Arlo Eisenberg (personal communication, 31 October 1996). They are more solidly entrenched, and thus less likely to become overtly appropriated and changed by outsiders. But the newer, less-homogeneous sports are more ripe for multi-nationals to co-opt. Many of the athletes in these sports have chosen to ride the wave and, rightly or wrongly, have decided that they can be better agents for change within the corporate structure than by fighting it from the outside. Arlo Eisenberg puts it this way: 'Our goal to maintain purity and integrity is not anathema to ESPN's goal to make money. Long-term, make it something worth watching' (personal communication, 31 October 1996).

Sexism, Racism, and Homophobia

It is said that ESPN eXtreme Games founder Ron Semiao ' jumped off the couch, went to a bookstore and found there was no magazine that encompassed more than one non-mainstream sport such as skateboarding, sport climbing and snowboarding. Each had its own magazine and its own culture' (Rother, 1997: B-2). Indeed, it is true. Just as each of these sports has its 'own magazine and its own culture', it also has its own opportunity to welcome new members who are, in the beginning, different from the existing membership. However, many of these sports are expensive. As Thorstein Veblen observed at the end of the nineteenth century, the wealthy classes have ways of 'conspicuously consuming' that covertly lock others out of their leisurely pursuits (1979 [1899]). In the nineteenth century, it was sailing, polo, fox hunting and other expensive sports. Exclusivity remains a part of traditional or mainstream sports today, and it is also characteristic in a range of alternative sports. For example, here is a listing of costs to equip and train for skysurfing:

> Skysurfboard: $500–$750. Camera helmet: $500. Jumpsuit: $250. PC7 camera: $2,500. Of course, you first need to be certified to skydive, which can take several weeks: $1,500. For training at the pro level, figure 12 jumps a day, six days a week. At $16 a jump, that's $1,152 per week for the sky-surfer, another $1,152 if you want a camera flyer to record it all for posterity. Call Daddy. (Brooker, 1998: 66)

Expenses in many alternative sports can be quite high. For snowboarders, climbers, BASE jumpers, adventure challenge teams, and for anyone aspiring to become professional in their sport there is travel to and from sites. Travel costs are added to costs for equipment, support personnel, training, insurance and entry fees. Overall, these expenses can be quite daunting.

Alternative sports can be exclusionary in additional ways as well. More recent evidence from some of the magazines found by X Games developer Ron Semiao reveals a dearth of female athletes and a concomitant lack of press coverage for the women who do participate (see, for example, Dennis-Vano, 1995, 'Look out boys, here we come'). Because few, if any, alternative sports are found in or are sponsored by public schools, laws calling for gender equity, such as Title IX in the United States, cannot be used to force changes. Parity for girls and women is not yet enforced, and the organizational structures of these sports are in their early and formative stages of development. In other words, many alternative sports are still grass-roots, partly informal activities, and are not legally bound to create parity for girls and women. Rarely are young girls and women welcomed into some of the sports, though again the degree of acceptance for females is uneven, largely dependent upon the specific sports themselves.

Though studies have not looked at the prevalence of sexism, racism, and homophobia in extreme sports, segments from a few letters from some of the magazines indicate that they have not gone unnoticed:[7]

> How come ESPN only showed girls skating on ESPN2? That reeked cuz I don't get it and I've been dying to see girls skate since I've started skating. ESPN sucks! (McCoy, 1996: no page)

> ['humorous' reply from writer Chris Pontius to a letter to the editor] If you're such a tough man, what the hell are you ironing clothes for? That's woman's work! You also have been using a stapler ... Craig, are you a male secretary? It makes me excited to know that there's some mad, deranged male secretary running around St Louis beating up on the beginning skaters. (Pontius, 1997: no page)

> [in response to a letter that had stated 'I agree that chickz shouldn't skate'] You are an idiot. Simon's article was stupid, but I still like him because I figure, like alcohol and Christianity, sexism was just a phase. But people like you take it serious. I notice by your last name that you're an Italian, and I think almost every girl I've made love to has been an Italian. How does it feel to know that half-breeds and niggers are fucking your women? (Pontius, 1997: no page)

As one reads through the skateboarding magazine *Big Brother*, one can find many attempts to outrageously offend: there is an advertisement for 'Fuct' with a nearly naked Penthouse Pet of the Year, covered only by three 'Fuct' stickers. A part of the copy reads, 'For all your sexual, perverted, sexist, racist, purist, anarchist, separatist, blasphemous, nihilist needs'. It is an ad for skateboard 'street wear' (1997 (October): no page). Or there is the ad for Shorty's™ (a distributor): 'This ad is for Quickies™ ('removable shield speed bearings') which displays what appears to be a vagina and anus stuffed with Quickies products. The disclaimer states: 'Attention Parents: This is not a real human anus and vagina in this ad. [Below that:] Attention Readers: I hope you enjoy this issue. Despite what we just told your parents, it will probably be our last' (1995: no page).

The obvious attempts to shock, titillate and, ultimately, sell products to young skateboarders capitalizes on the 'outlaw' image of skateboarding. The content in many ads, letters to the editor and articles (such as the 'The Second Annual Bong Olympics') is anti-authority, in every possible theme, so that, as it shocks and offends, it creates a feeling of adolescent kinship. The message is: us against the Other, however the Other may be defined. As evidenced, homophobia, sexism and racism can be blatant, but they can also be subtle: Kusz (forthcoming) has provided a compelling case that, in BMX bike riding, 'the individuals who practice these activities and the representational strategies used to construct ["whiteness"]' have made this very whiteness 'a racially neutral category' (ms., p. 25). 'Whiteness', in Kusz's view, has become an assumed dominant category such that in much research on extreme sports, 'the issue of the racial identity of BMXers is almost always unnoticed or not of interest to viewers of the sporting activity' (ms., p. 17).

~~EMERGING~~ ARRIVING SPORT: SOME CONCLUSIONS

There are many issues and choices facing those involved with alternative and extreme sports. Practitioners, organizers, corporations, media and spectators are all concerned with the emergence, and successful arrival, of their favorite sports. The people involved in the sports obviously have a vested interest in issues that are both familiar (having seen the mainstream sports models) and singular. But another group – scholars, particularly sports and popular culture scholars – needs to voice its concerns for the future of these sports. Whereas many of the world's mainstream sports are established and solidified in their rules, organizational structures and informal practices (see Chapter 15 by Guttmann), alternative and extreme sports are simultaneously emerging and arriving, some of them as postmodern forms. When the various constituencies in particular sports are not in agreement, problems are common. Sometimes, the problems are not unlike those in mainstream sports. Where will they receive funding? How will they gain support while still retaining control over the conditions of participation? How will they attract the biggest and best audience? How is it possible to make entry into and power over the sports more egalitarian – open for all? But alternative sports also face issues and challenges that are rare in mainstream sports. How might they establish credibility and gain regional, national and worldwide acceptance? How might they retain their cutting-edge aspects while establishing mass appeal? How can they resist the hyper-competitive American model for sport when their sport is inherently tied to lifestyles at least partially characterized by resistance to dominant culture?

Additionally, a few researchers are looking at some of the issues that surround alternative sports, seeing in the sports opportunities to expand our understanding of why and how humans seek out ever-more sensational practices. Issues of authenticity, subcultural formation, body culture, popular cultural trends and practices – all these, and more, a few (usually) younger scholars are examining. But, oftentimes, the tools we use to apprehend new practices are more appropriate for older practices. Thus, it is important for scholars studying these new sport forms to immerse themselves in a vast new array of tool kits which may more aptly reflect the practices of the (usually) younger practitioners.

It is not enough for established scholars to look at youthful practices. While the points of view from anyone may be judged for proper fit, actual practitioners (or participant observers) are needed to tell about the nuances of the sports from insider points of views. Youthful scholars may also be better able to contextualize the new and ever-changing experience of youth so that more readers may understand music, opposition, freedom and thrill aspects of youth culture more empathically.

The situation seems highly fitting: a new set of issues for a new set of sport forms as we enter the new millennium.

NOTES

1 The question itself is a self-reflexive one. Though humans have reflected upon the condition and status of life and the human body/mind/spirit/soul since at least the philosophies of the Gnostics, Socrates, Plato, Aristotle, Lao Tze, and so on – the decidedly self-reflective nature of 'what is sport' (what is play, what is game) has been, in Western societies, one which typically is cited as running from at least Huizinga, through Caillois to Loy and then branching out in myriad ways. (Its very Westernness is an interesting phenomenon, as well.) However, as in contemporary society, the need to play and to engage in sporting practices is generally more satisfying when one is more 'other-aware' than 'self-aware'. Thus, to many sportspeople who *do* rather than *talk about*, 'What is sport' is a moot question.

2 Most of the mainstream sports are derived from English-speaking countries for many reasons, but also, according to Guttmann (1994) and others, because of the colonization (and thus spread) by British rule. Additionally, of course, missionaries, travelling teams, tourists and mass movement of people have added to the spread of cultural artifacts like sport. This is not unlike the spread of alternative sports. But, now, the magic of television adds to the spread, quick cultural understanding (and teaching) of a variety of sports and, of course, much of the technological power in television (and electronic media) is centered in the 'first world'.

3 Rupert Murdoch's attempt at acquiring Manchester United (£575 million, US$1.93 billion), following his purchase of the Los Angeles Dodgers, was first characterized this way: 'The media magnate … uses control of sports in his bid for global satellite television dominance …' (*The New Zealand Herald*, 7 September 1998: A1); five days later, the *New Zealand Weekend Herald* blared the following headline: 'Murdoch's motive is global TV coverage: Analysts believe media baron Rupert Murdoch wants domination of world sports and entertainment' (12–13 September 1998: C-8); previously, in Australia, ABC moderator Stan Correy characterized Murdoch as 'the only-in-it-for-the-pay TV subscribers' media mogul' (3 October 1996). Murdoch is continually characterized as a businessman who happens to be involved in sport media.

4 The limitations of one's standpoint are well documented. This list, although not exhaustive, has been constructed to provide colleagues around the globe with a vision of what they might consider 'alternative' sports. The observation that the list is biased is a valid one, and it raises the issue of whether we are witnessing the Americanization or globalization of sport forms (see Chapter 23 by Maguire), including these emergent sports, *vis-à-vis* corporate involvement and impetus for their very sustenance.

5 And yet, inevitably, there has been a backlash of sorts, particularly as newspaper writers have entered into the debate (debates are good for selling newspapers) of the legitimacy of these new sport forms. See some of the debates about ballroom dancing in the Olympics (cf. B. Thomas, 1998; *The Times*, 1995). Or see the comparison of extreme sport to art by modernist 'Critic-At-Large' Welton Jones (1997), in which Jones discusses sport, art, spectacle and contest/performance. A different take on these sports might be to see them as carrying elements of the postmodern, that the very fact of their amalgamated nature, their evolving forms, is perhaps a bit of mixing between some of the competitive natures of mainstream sports and some of the 1960s counter-culture ethos: for instance, Terry Orlick's (1978) New Games seem to be a valid predecessor to some of the activities, if not world-view, of these alternative sport forms and enthusiasts.

6 Apparently, tennis was originally termed 'Sphairistikon' by a Frenchman, and Sphairee is derivative of that original term (I am grateful to Eric Dunning for this insight). The games, similar in methodology but not scope, obviously follow the same pattern. Just as snowboarding has its origination myths, both etymologically and pragmatically deriving from surfing on long 'boards' in the sea to waves of snow, so too do most of these emergent sports have roots in other forms, or amalgams of other forms.

7 I'm not trying to say that these letters are necessarily representative of all of the athletes in the sports, but more that they are circulated meanings, available in the codified discourse which reinstills their meanings. That there is discussion of some of the issues of (overt) sexism and (covert) racism in extreme sports is no doubt a good thing; that it degenerates into name-calling and adolescent gestures is disquieting.

REFERENCES

Barnes, Simon (1995) 'Taking extreme measures in effort to save the earth', *The Times*, 18 April, p. 42.

Beal, Becky (1995) 'Disqualifying the official: an exploration of social resistance through the subculture of skateboarding', *Sociology of Sport Journal*, 12 (3): 252–67.

Beal, Becky and Weidman, Lisa (forthcoming) 'Authenticity in the skateboarding world', in Robert Rinehart and Synthia Sydnor (eds), *To the Extreme: Alternative Sports Inside and Out*. Albany, NY: State University of New York Press.

Bell, Martha (forthcoming) 'Eco-Challenge: adventure racing and expedition epics', in Robert Rinehart and Synthia Sydnor (eds), *To the Extreme: Alternative Sports Inside and Out*. Albany, NY: State University of New York Press.

Benc, Doug (1998) 'Snowboard title to US', *The Press-Enterprise* (Riverside, CA), 2 February, p. C-7.

Booth, Douglas (forthcoming) 'Expression sessions: surfing, style and prestige', in Robert Rinehart and Synthia Sydnor (eds), *To the Extreme: Alternative Sports Inside and Out*. Albany, NY: State University of New York Press.

Brewington, Peter (1993) '3-on-3 game grows from teen dream', *USA Today*, 6 July, pp. 1C, 2C.

Bridgers, Lee (forthcoming) 'Over the brink and through the endangered dirt with the pious bikesurfers of Moab, Utah', in Robert Rinehart and Synthia Sydnor (eds), *To the Extreme: Alternative Sports Inside and Out*. Albany, NY: State University of New York Press.

Brockinton, Langdon (1998) 'ESPN, ABC ready X Games ad packages', *Street & Smith's Sportsbusiness Journal*, 1 (29): 20.

Brooker, Kevin (1998) *Way Inside ESPN's X Games*. New York: Hyperion/ESPN Books.

Burton, Jake (forthcoming) 'Snowboarding: the essence is fun', in Robert Rinehart and Synthia Sydnor (eds), *To the Extreme: Alternative Sports Inside and Out*. Albany, NY: State University of New York Press.

Caillois, Roger (1961) *Man, Play, and Games*. New York: Free Press.

Cook, Jason (1995) 'Sk8 by shootings', *Daily Bread*, 10, no page.

Cotter, Jim (forthcoming) 'Eco (ego?) Challenge: British Columbia, 1996', in Robert Rinehart and Synthia Sydnor (eds), *To the Extreme: Alternative Sports Inside and Out*. Albany, NY: State University of New York Press.

Crum, Bart (1988) 'A critical analysis of korfball as a "non-sexist sport"', *International Review for the Sociology of Sport*, 23 (3): 233–41.

Dennis-Vano, Donna (1995) 'Look out boys, here we come', *InLine: the Skate Magazine*, 4 (8): 28–9.

Donnelly, Peter (1997) 'Re: Still more on x-games. Sociological aspects of sports discussion', SPORTSOC@VM.TEMPLE.EDU 3 February.

Donnelly, Peter (forthcoming) 'The great divide: sport climbing vs. adventure climbing', in Robert Rinehart and Synthia Sydnor (eds), *To the Extreme: Alternative Sports Inside and Out*. Albany, NY: State University of New York Press.

Donnelly, Peter and Young, Kevin (1988) 'The construction and confirmation of identity in sport subcultures', *Sociology of Sport Journal*, 5 (3): 223–40.

Dornian, David (forthcoming) 'Xtreem', in Robert Rinehart and Synthia Sydnor (eds), *To the Extreme: Alternative Sports Inside and Out*. Albany, NY: State University of New York Press.

Downs, Brett (forthcoming) 'Small bikes, big men', in Robert Rinehart and Synthia Sydnor (eds), *To the Extreme: Alternative Sports Inside and Out*. Albany, NY: State University of New York Press.

Dufresne, Chris (1998) 'Culture crash', *Los Angeles Times*, 30 January, pp. C1, C10.

du Lac, J.F. (1995) 'Going to extremes', *The Sacramento Bee*, 18 June, Travel, pp. 1, 4.

Earnest, Leslie (1998) 'Surf 'n' turf: Hilfiger wades into niche market with insiders' help', *Los Angeles Times*, 26 June, pp. D1, D5.

Eassom, Simon (forthcoming) 'Mountain biking madness', in Robert Rinehart and Synthia Sydnor (eds), *To the Extreme: Alternative Sports Inside and Out*. Albany, NY: State University of New York Press.

ESPN (1995) Broadcast of The eXtreme Games, 24 June–3 July. Bristol, CT.

ESPN2 (1998) Broadcast of Winter X Games, 16–20 January. Bristol, CT.

ESPN2 (1999) Broadcast of Winter X Games, 16–22 January. Bristol, CT.

ESPN Sportszone (1997) The X Games. http://espn.go.com/xgames/summerx97/index.html

Florence, Mal (1998) 'He's in no mood for any more radical moves', 'Morning Briefing', *Los Angeles Times*, 31 December, p. D2.

Forest, Stephanie Anderson (1993) 'Terry Murphy's wonderful wannabe road show', *Business Week*, 22 November, p. 88.

Fowler, Chris (1998) 'As inside as it gets', in *Way Inside ESPN's X Games*. New York: Hyperion/ESPN Books. pp. 249–50.

Greenfeld, Karl Taro (1998) 'A wider world of sports', *Time*, 9 November, pp. 80–1.

Grenfell, Chris (1998) 'Value constructs of ultra distance runners'. Paper presented at the North American Society for the Sociology of Sport annual meeting, Las Vegas, NV, 7 November.

Guttman, Allen (1994) *Games and Empires: Modern Sports and Cultural Imperialism*. New York: Columbia University Press.

Henderson, John (1998) 'Queenstown, the capital of action', *Los Angeles Times*, 8 November, p. L17.

Home Box Office, Inc. (HBO) (1991) 'Play by Play: A History of Sports Television (Part 2)'.

Howe, Jeff (1998) 'The outsiders', *Village Voice*, 25 August, p. 182.

Huizinga, Johann (1950 [1938]) *Homo Ludens*. Boston, MA: Beacon Press.

Humphreys, Duncan (forthcoming) 'Selling out snowboarding: the alternative response to commercial co-optation', in Robert Rinehart and Synthia Sydnor (eds), *To the Extreme: Alternative Sports Inside and Out*. Albany, NY: State University of New York Press.

Jarvie, Grant (1991) *Highland Games and the Making of Myth*. New York: Columbia University Press.

Jones, Welton (1997) 'There's an art to determining what's sporting', *San Diego Union-Tribune*, 29 June, p. E-3.

Keeble, James (1995) *Morocco (from Thomas Cook)*. Lincolnwood, IL: Passport Books.

Koerner, Brendan I. (1997) 'Extreeeme', *US News & World Report*, 30 June, 122 (25): 50–60.

Koyn, Tamara (forthcoming) 'Free dimensional sky-diving', in Robert Rinehart and Synthia Sydnor (eds), *To the Extreme: Alternative Sports Inside and Out*. Albany, NY: State University of New York Press.

Kremer, Kirsten (forthcoming) 'May 27, 1998', in Robert Rinehart and Synthia Sydnor (eds), *To the Extreme: Alternative Sports Inside and Out*. Albany, NY: State University of New York Press.

Kroker, A., Kroker, M. and Cook, D. (1989) 'Panic Olympics' in A. Kroker, M. Kroker and D. Cook (eds), *Panic Encyclopedia: the Definitive Guide to the Postmodern Scene*. New York: St Martin's Press.

Kubiak, Diane (1997) 'Stunt team spins through town', *Post-Tribune* (Valparaiso, IN), pp. B1, B2.

Kusz, Kyle (forthcoming) 'BMX, extreme sports, and the white male backlash', in Robert Rinehart and Synthia Sydnor (eds), *To the Extreme: Alternative Sports Inside and Out*. Albany, NY: State University of New York Press.

Lowe, Benjamin (1977) *The Beauty of Sport: A Cross-Disciplinary Inquiry*. Englewood Cliffs, NJ: Prentice-Hall.

Loy, John W. (1968) 'The nature of sport: a definitional effort', *Quest*, 10 (May): 1–15.

McCoy, Tasha (1996) In 'Call Box', *Box*, 10 (Fall): no page.

McCuin, Jill Walker (1996) 'Hackin with the "Sack" is big-time', *The San Bernardino Country Sun*, 4 January, p. H3.

Moscow Tribune (1996) 'X Games celebrate alternatives', 28 June, p. 21.

Mounet, Jean-Pierre and Chifflet, Pierre (1996) 'Commercial supply for river water sports', *International Review for Sociology of Sport*, 31 (3): 233–56.

Mounet, Jean-Pierre and Chifflet, Pierre (forthcoming) 'Whitewater sports: from extreme to standardization (trans. Genevieve Rail)', in Robert Rinehart and Synthia Sydnor (eds), *To the Extreme: Alternative Sports Inside and Out*. Albany, NY: State University of New York Press.

Neems, Jeff (1998) 'Extreme sports', Nexus (University of Waikato), 15 September, pp. 12–15.

Norcross, Don (1997) 'Skateboarders raise competition to an art form', *The San Diego Union-Tribune*, 24 June, p. D-3.

Orlick, Terry (1978) *The Cooperative Sports and Games Book: Challenge without Competition*. New York: Pantheon Books.

Pearson, Kent (1979) *Surfing Subcultures of Australia and New Zealand*. St Lucia, Queensland: University of Queensland Press.

Pearson, Kent (1981) 'Subcultures and sport', in John W. Loy, Gerald S. Kenyon and Barry D. McPherson (eds), *Sport, Culture and Society: a Reader on the Sociology of Sport*, 2nd edn. Philadelphia: Lea & Febiger. pp. 131–45.

Perkins, Dave (1996) 'Like it or not, this sport's legit', *The Toronto Star*, 31 July, p. D1.

Pontius, Chris (1997) 'Letters', *Big Brother*, 29 (October): no page.

Price, Lew (1997) 'Skins made-for-TV event?', *The Press-Enterprise* (Riverside, CA), 29 November, p. F-5.

Radio National (1996) 'Same game ... different attitude', Background Briefing, 10 March, Australian Broadcasting Corporation.

Radio National (1998) 'Australian Invented Sports', *The Sports Factor*, 25 September, Australian Broadcasting Corporation.

Rees, Johanna (1997) 'Catchin air at the X Games', *The San Diego Union-Tribune*, 19 June, 'Night & Day', pp. 32–3, 35.

Rinehart, Robert (1998a) 'Inside of the outside: pecking orders within alternative sport at ESPN's 1995 "The eXtreme Games"', *Journal of Sport and Social Issues*, 22 (4): 398–415.

Rinehart, Robert (1998b) *Players All: Performances in Contemporary Sport*. Bloomington, IN: Indiana University Press.

Rinehart, Robert (forthcoming) 'Dropping into sight: commodification and co-optation of in-line skating', in Robert Rinehart and Synthia Sydnor (eds), *To the Extreme: Alternative Sports Inside and Out*. Albany, NY: State University of New York Press.

Rother, Caitlin (1997) 'ESPN innovator's prime directive was to make sports fun to watch', *The San Diego Union-Tribune*, 21 June, p. B-2.

Seltsam, Pat (1996) 'The games formerly known as Extreme', *Speed Skating Times: International Inline & Ice Speed Skating News*, 15.

Silverstein, Sam (1995) 'Storming the beaches', *Pro Athlete Insider*, 4 (1): 22–5, 28–30.

Sydnor, Synthia (forthcoming) 'Soaring', in Robert Rinehart and Synthia Sydnor (eds), *To the Extreme: Alternative Sports Inside and Out*. Albany, NY: State University of New York Press.

The Times (1995) 'Strictly Olympian: ballroom dancers may soon be quickstepping for gold', 5 April, p. 15.

Thomas, Bob (1998) '"DanceSport" may join the Olympics', *Chicago Tribune*, 25 July, Sect. 1, p. 15.

Thomas, Pete (1998a) 'Boarders take care of business', *Los Angeles Times*, 13 March, p. C14.

Thomas, Pete (1998b) 'Gauntlet thrown for Castaic gantlet', *Los Angeles Times*, 23 October, p. D10.

Tomlinson, Joe (1996) *The Ultimate Encyclopedia of Extreme Sports*. Carlton Books Limited.

Veblen, Thorstein (1979 [1899]) *The Theory of the Leisure Class*. New York: Penguin Books.

Watters, Ron (forthcoming) 'The wrong side of the thin edge', in Robert Rinehart and Synthia Sydnor (eds), *To the Extreme: Alternative Sports Inside and Out*. Albany, NY: State University of New York Press.

Wheaton, Belinda (1997) 'Consumption, lifestyle and gendered identities in post-modern sports: the case of windsurfing'. Unpublished doctoral dissertation, University of Brighton.

Wheaton, Belinda (forthcoming) 'Windsurfing: a subculture of commitment', in Robert Rinehart and Synthia Sydnor (eds), *To the Extreme: Alternative Sports Inside and Out*. Albany, NY: State University of New York Press.

Wheaton, Belinda and Tomlinson, Alan (1998) 'The changing gender order in sport? The case of windsurfing', *Journal of Sport and Social Issues*, 22 (3): 252–74.

Williams, Raymond (1977) *Marxism and Literature*. Oxford: Oxford University Press.

PART FOUR

SPORT AND SOCIETY RESEARCH AROUND THE GLOBE

EDITORS' INTRODUCTION

Just as sport is a global phenomenon, so too is the study of sport and society. Although most authors of previous chapters were born and/or educated in England, Canada, or the United States, scholarship in the field certainly is not confined to those countries. In fact, doing research and theorizing about sport and society has been or has recently become widely recognized as important in many countries around the world.

The following chapters appear in alphabetical order of title; titles refer to continents, nation-states, regions or culture areas. The intent of each chapter is to highlight briefly the status of sport and society theory and research in a particular geographical area, with special attention given to the sociology of sport. The content of these chapters differs widely because the histories of the field and the overall cultural contexts in which it has emerged vary so much from one country or region to another. As many scholars have met and worked with their colleagues from other parts of the world, they have discovered that this diversity contributes to the growth and vitality of the field as a whole. These chapters are intended to facilitate and add to that growth and vitality. Hopefully, they will also contribute to a degree of methodological, conceptual and theoretical standardization without scarificing or doing injury to the diversity.

33

AFRICA

Denver J. Hendricks

Africa occupies one-fifth of the earth's surface and, as the third largest continent, could swallow the USA, the whole of Eastern and Western Europe, India, Japan, New Zealand, Paraguay and Uruguay with room to spare. It includes one-tenth of the world's population, and two-thirds of the entire Arab world (*Nuwe Afikaanse Kinder Ensiklopedie*, 1982). The continent comprises 60 countries and roughly 1,000 languages and dialects are spoken there. At face value, it may appear that to speak of a 'sociology of sport of, or for Africa' would represent a gross oversimplification.

Very little, if any, information is available on the sociology of sport in Africa. Contact and communication between scholars in the field has been rare. The African Association for Physical Education, Health Education, Recreation and Dance was formed as recently as 1994. It presented the first opportunity for scholars within the domains mentioned to exchange ideas about the subject area within its broader context (Amusa and Agbonjinmi, 1994). It also created the first opportunity for scholars from Africa in the field of sports sociology to share a platform on the continent.

DATA GATHERING

In order to ascertain what the status of the sociology of sport is in the different countries of Africa, 113 questionnaires were circulated to institutions in 39 countries across the continent, and also in Mauritius and Madagascar, since the latter two usually participate in international sport as part of the 'African zone'. Every institution of higher learning on the continent listed in the *The World of Learning* (1996)

which had a department of physical education or sociology, or a faculty or institute which was considered to be a possible host to the discipline, was surveyed.

Twenty-seven questionnaires were returned, representing a response rate of 24 per cent, which, given the numerous problems associated with postal and telecommunications services on the African continent, was considered to be satisfactory. Responses were received from the following countries: Burkina Faso (1), Ghana (1), Kenya (3), Mauritius (1), Morocco (1), Namibia (1), Nigeria (4), South Africa (13), Tanzania (1) and Tunisia (1).

THE SOCIOLOGY OF SPORT IN ACADEMIC INSTITUTIONS IN AFRICA

The sociology of sport was included as a discipline within the curricula of 51 per cent of the responding institutions at the undergraduate level, and 37 per cent at the graduate level. Respondents at 48 per cent of the institutions indicated that they were aware of individuals at their institutions who were engaged in research activity in the discipline. Sociology of Sport courses were generally included in the curricula of human movement studies, physical education, sports administration, and recreation departments, or, in isolated cases, in departments of psychology, sociology, and international studies. Students who enrolled for courses in the sociology of sport originated primarily from human movement studies, physical education, sports management and recreation departments, while again in isolated cases, they also derived from departments of sociology, education, international studies and business administration. Respondents reported having graduated approximately 3,029 students who took courses in sport sociology at the first degree level, 282 at the honours level (4th year), 167 at the Masters level and 53 at the Doctoral level over the five years ending in 1997.[1]

Scholars in the Sociology of Sport in Africa

From the data gathered from respondents, it would appear as if all the staff who were responsible for teaching sociology of sport courses held qualifications in physical education (or similar disciplines), while approximately 42 per cent also held qualifications in sociology. Approximately 33 per cent were trained in the sociology of sport specifically. It is significant also that 30 per cent of teachers of courses in the sociology of sport had obtained their qualifications in the United States, while the others had generally acquired them in their home countries.

Course Content

The most popular topic covered in undergraduate courses in the subject area in Africa were politics and sport, followed by gender issues in sport, social stratification and mobility in/through sport, and sport as a social phenomenon. Next in line was violence in sport and sport and culture (equally popular), while socialization into/through sport, sport and the media, and sport and the economy enjoyed similar status. Given the continent's colonial past and the apartheid question at its southernmost point, it is significant that race and sport was lower down on the popularity scale as a topic taught within the sociology of sport in Africa than might have been expected.

Research Topics

The research topics with which scholars busy themselves in the discipline seem to correlate a lot more closely with the generally prevailing problems of the African continent. Topics such as 'Sport and recreation in deprived communities', 'Poverty and violence: sport and recreation as possible solutions', 'Sport and development', 'Aspirations and achievements' and the like, correspond with the African stereotype of poverty, violence (under-)development and instability. However, topics such as 'Role models in sport', 'Sport and the religion of football' 'Female student perceptions of

competitive athletes', 'Gender and sport' and other such issues appear to be as popular. This is probably a reflection of the fact that many of the scholars involved in the Sociology of Sport in Africa have their academic roots in Western countries, and in the USA in particular, where these topics are, or were once, fashionable.

Popular Issues

It is peculiar that undergraduate course offerings and research activities seem to differ somewhat from the issues which respondents have identified as being currently the most topical in their societies. Respondents confirm that racism in sport, access to participation in sport, professionalism in sport, ethics in sport and sport and development, are as popular in debates within sporting circles in their countries as are politics in sport. So is gender equity, which also enjoys prominence in course content and research. Other topical sports issues which receive popular attention in sociology of sport courses in Africa include crowd management and violence, drug (ab)use, match fixing, sport for street children, facilities, the decline of amateurism, religious segregation and nation-building, to mention but a few.

Publication

With the limited number of responses received it was difficult to determine the extent of publication within the discipline but, on average, rates appeared to be particularly low, with most activity (apparently) taking place at institutions in Nigeria.

CONCLUSION

Despite the scepticism expressed at the beginning of this chapter about the concept of a sociology of sport in Africa, it would appear as if there is sufficient commonality within the foci in the discipline across countries on the continent to substantiate its authenticity. It would appear as if its character has been shaped by the fact that many scholars in the field in Africa obtained their qualifications in Western countries, particularly in the USA, and that they experienced a number of influences in that connection which they brought with them upon returning home. Finally, the evidence of a focus upon issues that plague the continent generally, such as poverty, violence, (under-) development, racism, access to sport and the like, seems to be characteristic of the emerging sociology of sport in Africa, and justifiably so. The emergence of the African Association for Physical Education, Health Education, Recreation and Dance is bound to provide a strong impetus for the development of the subject area on the continent.

NOTE

1   The majority of Masters and PhD students included in these figures graduated from the Institut Supérieur du Sport et de l'Education Physique in Tunisia.

REFERENCES

Amusa, L.O. and Agbonjinmi, A.P. (1994) *Who's Who in Physical Education, Health Education, Recreation and Dance Training Institutions in Africa*. Ibadan, Nigeria: LAP Publications Ltd.

Nuwe Afrikaanse Kinder Ensiklopedie (1982). Cape Town: Nasou.

The World of Learning (1996). London: Europa Publications Limited.

34

AUSTRALIA AND NEW ZEALAND[1]

Chris Collins

In spite of the 'supposed' predominance and at least 'lay' acceptance of the importance of sport in the cultures of both countries, serious academic study of sport in Australia and New Zealand has been limited, most particularly up until the mid-1980s. Despite sport having been pointed to as a significant site for 'quests for identity' (albeit male dominated and based on invented or selected traditions, symbols, myths and nostalgia), 'mainstream' historians and sociologists within the region have shown comparatively little interest in sport in society as a subject of serious academic enquiry.[2]

Theoretically, early studies tended to be dominated by forms of structural-functionalism – not surprisingly given its orthodoxy in mainstream sociology up until at least the 1960s and early 1970s. This dominance, suggest Lawrence and Rowe (1986a), was accentuated by the fact that studies were often undertaken by physical education graduates, most of whom had returned from having completed postgraduate study in the United States. Given these influences, the foci of enquiry were usually directed towards issues such as sport as a social institution and various types of functional analysis of sport-related phenomena.

A more critical theorizing began to emerge in the 1980s and was undoubtedly strongest in Australia. Sandercock and Turner's (1981) analysis of Australian Rules football and Pearson's (1982) work on surfing and masculinity provide such examples, as do the works of Tatz, Williams, Rowe, McKay and Lawrence which began to appear in journals such as *Arena*[3] during the 1980s. Lawrence and Rowe (1986b) present an updated selection of these essays on the sociology of Australian

sport in their edited book *Power Play*,[4] which was the first such publication in the region. Here sport was regarded as a social institution explicitly and implicitly linked to the social structure, with the focus of enquiry primarily on the 'symbiotic relationship' between sport and capitalism. Issues addressed ranged from commercialism, nationalism and patriarchy, to popular culture and the media.

The latter half of the 1980s and the early 1990s witnessed an increasing emergence of multidisciplinary critical social analyses of sport and leisure in society.[5] The range of theorizing now utilized represents a broadening of theoretical approaches, and has come to include analyses from standpoints such as political economy, structuralism, figurational sociology, postmodernism, post-structuralism, feminism and post-structuralist feminism. Perhaps of most significance is the strong work being undertaken in Australia, which might broadly be described as falling within the cultural studies tradition; studies drawing on feminist theorists have also been significant. A wide variety of areas related to the phenomena of sport in society are also now being addressed, such as power relations, media, gender, the body, identity formation, and to a lesser extent, ethnicity.

Nevertheless, while there has been an increase in critical social-cultural analyses of sport in the past five to ten years, it still does not figure significantly in 'mainstream' vehicles for sociological dialogue in New Zealand and Australia. For example, up until 1996, the *Australia and New Zealand Journal for Sociology* had only published six articles related to sport or leisure in the preceding decade. This does not reflect, however, a lack of work undertaken in the field. Rather it is more likely to point to a preference amongst academics pursuing this field of study for more specialist and international forums created by various sport and leisure journals and publications. It also reflects the fact that most academics studying sport in society do not emanate from 'mainstream' sociology departments, but from departments which include anything from tourism, parks and recreation, physical education and human movement to media studies, business management and education (or varying combinations of these). This latter point demonstrates the continuing limited interest in sport or leisure on the part of most 'traditional' departments of sociology, which are still more likely to view such areas as superficial and lacking significance.

Nevertheless, the emergence within the region of organizations focused on promoting the study of sport and leisure in society has facilitated increased intellectual exchange and research. Probably of greatest significance has been the Australian Society for Sports History and its publication *Sporting Traditions*, which has provided a valuable vehicle for historians and sociologists studying sport. More recent has been the formation in 1991 of the Australian and New Zealand Association for Leisure Studies (ANZALS), a body established to facilitate scholarly debate, the exchange of ideas and research and publications in the interdisciplinary field of leisure studies. Its annual *ANZALS Leisure Research Series* journal[6] shows signs of providing a valuable outlet for publication of research undertaken within the region. Such forums provide indications of increasing collective effort and organization amongst academics within this field of study, though with regard to *ANZALS*, the focus is more commonly on the broader phenomena of leisure than on sport.

This growth in academic enquiry within the region has been paralleled and linked to the dramatic increase in tertiary level undergraduate and postgraduate programmes of study in both countries. In New Zealand, for example, seven out of the eight universities now deliver programmes of study directed towards sport and leisure, compared with only one such university programme – at Otago University – 25 years ago. Most universities now deliver courses that include components orientated towards a critical analysis of sport or leisure in their social context, with three providing opportunities for a strong social science emphasis. The growth in non-university tertiary programmes in New Zealand (polytechnics) has been just as

dramatic, though the evidence would suggest that teachers of such programmes are primarily adopting technical and functionalist approaches to the study of sport.

A counter influence to this dramatic growth in tertiary level programmes in Australia and New Zealand has been the funding pressure that has come on the tertiary education environment in both countries during the 1990s. This has led to pressures within institutions to rationalize course offerings where possible, and has slowed the dramatic development of new programmes and courses that was occurring. However, despite this context, sport-related courses have fared relatively well, probably due to their success in attracting student numbers, which has become an increasingly important criterion for gaining resources.

While the dramatic growth in tertiary level programmes has increased the number of academics focusing on the study of sport and leisure in society, there has not been an equivalent rise in research output in the field. As Veal (1993) notes, in contrast to places such as the UK where a similar growth of undergraduate courses occurred, the development within this region has occurred primarily in advance of the establishment of a strong research infrastructure and research culture. In Australia, the dramatic growth in courses took place in the Colleges of Advanced Education and Institutes of Technology where funding structures did not reflect the notion of academics as researchers, and while amalgamation with universities occurred in 1992, Veal argues that the funding situation has not changed. The point of note is that academics in both countries have largely been preoccupied with course development, department building, legitimacy battles and so forth, and the establishment of strong research cultures and infrastructures has been slow.

Furthermore, research that has been undertaken has often been applied in nature, such as focusing on aspects of sport and leisure management and service delivery with available funding frequently linked to the knowledge- and task-requirements of public sport and leisure agencies. This has reinforced the tendency for departments to orientate themselves, in terms of both staffing and course design, towards the vocational and perceived functional needs of the 'industry', meaning that the output of more theoretically informed critical analysis of sport and leisure has been limited. Nevertheless, as departments have strengthened and begun to broaden, their postgraduate programmes have developed, with increasing numbers of students engaging in research, which is in turn strengthening the research cultures and infrastructures. This, combined with the growing need for external examiners and supervisors, means that intellectual exchange and organization between academics within the field is likely to continue to grow and develop. The dramatic advancement in information technologies (such as the Internet and e-mail) and their growing use by university academics in what is, seen from a North American or European standpoint, a remote region of the world, is also significant.

In summary, the period since the mid-1980s has witnessed an emergence in Australia and New Zealand of a more multidisciplinary critical analysis of sport. It was in 1981 that Pearson and McKay lamented the paucity and theoretical limitations of the state of the study of sport in this region. The past dominance of structural-functionalist approaches has given way to an ever-broadening range of critical theoretical paradigms representing an increasingly multidisciplinary focus. Probably most significant were the neo-Marxist approaches, with strong work coming out of Australia within the developing cultural studies tradition; also important was the contribution of various feminist analyses. During the 1990s the theorizing continued to broaden. The challenge for the new decade remains for those within this field of study to ensure that the social analysis of and theorizing about sport in Australia and New Zealand become more firmly embedded and developed from a basis of theoretically informed and rigorously conducted research.

NOTES

1 This overview was written in 1996.
2 Clearly there are exceptions to this. For example, in New Zealand see Richard Thompson's work on the relationships between race, sport and politics. Thompson, R. (1964) *Race and Sport*. London: Oxford University Press and Thompson, R. (1975) *Retreat from Apartheid: New Zealand's Sporting Contacts with South Africa*. Wellington: Oxford University Press.
3 A journal which adopted a Marxist orientation.
4 While this represented a move beyond the structural-functionalist type analyses more typical of the 1970s, subsequent reviewers of *Power Play* criticised it for demonstrating class reductionism in a neo-Marxist paradigm, for not developing any theoretical

complexity or effective praxis (Easton, 1992), for wearing 'its heart on its sleeve' (Vamplew, 1987, cited by Rowe and Lawrence, 1990a) and for overstretching its case given the lack of supporting empirical research (Cashman, 1989: cited by Rowe and Lawrence, 1990a).
5 For example: from Australia, Stoddart (1986 and 1988), Goldlust (1987), Tatz (1987 and 1995), Sissons (1988), Rowe and Lawrence (1990a), McKay (1991), Vamplew et al. (1992), Vamplew and Stoddart (1994), O'Hara (1994) and Cashman (1995); and from New Zealand, Phillips (1987), de Jong (1991), Perkins and Cushman (1993), Trenberth and Collins (1994) and Cameron (1996). Examples of studies related to Australia or New Zealand appearing in various academic journals/publications: Cunneen and Lynch (1988), Wearing (1992), McKay (1993), Veal and Weiler (1993), Kirk and Twigg (1995), de Jong (1986), Shannon (1987), Fougere (1989), Thompson (1988 and 1990), Hindson and Gidlow (1994), Nauright (1995), and Trevelyan and Jackson (1995).
6 For example, at the time of writing, four of the eight papers in the latest volume were focused specifically on sport, with papers addressing the marginalisation of women in sport, sport management education, domestic labour and the gendered conditions of participation in sport, and motivations in masters sport (1995, *ANZALS Leisure Research Series*, Vol. 2).

REFERENCES AND FURTHER READING

Cameron, J. (1996) *Trail blazers. Women who Manage New Zealand Sport*. Christchurch: Sports Inclined.

Cashman, R. (1995) *Paradise of Sport: the Rise of Organised Sport in Australia*. Melbourne: Oxford University Press.

Cunneen, C. and Lynch, R. (1988) 'The social-historical roots of conflict in riots at the Bathurst Bike Races', *Australian and New Zealand Journal of Sociology*, 24 (1): 5–31.

Cushman, G. (1995) 'The development of leisure studies in Aotearoa – New Zealand', *ANZALS Leisure Research Series*, 2: 44–60.

de Jong, P. (1986) 'Making sense of New Zealand rugby', *Sites*, 12 (Autumn): 29–42.

de Jong, P. (1991) *Saturday's Warriors*. Palmerston North: Massey University Sociology Department.

Easton, H. (1992) 'Review of "Sport, men and the gender order; critical feminist perspectives"',

Australia and New Zealand Journal of Sociology,
28 (1): 285–9.

Fougere, G. (1989) 'Sport, culture and identity:
the case of rugby football', in D. Novitz and
B. Willmott (eds), *Culture and Identity in
New Zealand.* Wellington: GP Books. pp. 110–22.

Goldlust, J. (1987) *Playing for Keeps: Sport, the Media
and Society.* Melbourne: Longman Cheshire.

Hindson, A. and Gidlow, B. (1994) 'The trickledown effect of top level sport: myth or reality?
A case study of the Olympics', *Leisure Options:
Australian Journal of Leisure and Recreation,* 4 (1):
16–24.

Kirk, D. and Twigg, K. (1995) 'Civilising Australian
bodies: the game ethic and sport in Victorian
Government Schools, 1904–1945', *Sporting Traditions,* 11 (2): 3–34.

Lawrence, G. and Rowe, D. (1986a) 'Towards a sociology of sport in Australia', in G. Lawrence and
D. Rowe (eds), *Power Play: the Commercialisation of
Australian Sport.* Sydney: Hale & Iremonger.
pp. 13–45.

Lawrence, G. and Rowe, D. (eds) (1986b) *Power Play:
the Commercialisation of Australian Sport.* Sydney:
Hale & Iremonger.

McKay, J. (1991) *No Pain, No Gain? Sport and
Australian Culture.* Sydney: Prentice-Hall.

McKay, J. (1993) *Why So Few? Women Executives in
Australian Sport.* Canberra: Australian Sports
Commission, National Sports Research Centre.

Nauright, J. (ed.) (1995) *Sport, Power and Society in
New Zealand: Historical and Contemporary Per-
spectives.* Australian Society for Sports History,
Studies in Sports History, 11.

O'Hara, J. (ed.) (1994) *Ethnicity and Soccer in
Australia.* Sydney: Australian Society for Sports
History.

Pearson, K. (1982) 'Conflict, stereotypes and masculinity in Australian and New Zealand surfing',
Australian and New Zealand Journal of Sociology,
18 (2): 117–35.

Pearson, K. and McKay, J. (1981) 'Sociology of
Australian and New Zealand sport: state of the
field overview', *Australian and New Zealand Journal
of Sociology,* 17 (2): 70–1.

Perkins, H. and Cushman, G. (eds) (1993) *Leisure
Recreation and Tourism.* Auckland: Longman Paul.

Perkins, H. and Gidlow, B. (1991) 'Leisure research in
New Zealand: patterns, problems and prospects',
Leisure Studies, 10: 93–104.

Phillips, J. (1987) *A Man's Country? The Image of the
Pakeha Male – a History.* Auckland: Penguin.

Rowe, G. and Lawrence, D. (eds) (1990a) *Sport and
Leisure, Trends in Australian Popular Culture.*
Sydney: Harcourt Brace Jovanovich.

Rowe, G. and Lawrence, D. (1990b) 'Introduction', in
G. Rowe and D. Lawrence (eds), *Sport and Leisure,
Trends in Australian Popular Culture.* Sydney:
Harcourt Brace Jovanovich. pp. 1–23.

Rowe, G. and Lawrence, D. (1995) 'Negotiations and
mediations: journalism, professional status and
the making of the sports text', *Media Information
Australia,* 75: 67–70.

Sandercock, L. and Turner, I. (1981) *Up Where,
Cazaly?* London: Granada.

Shannon, A. (1987) 'Studying youth sport and
physical education in New Zealand: a review and
sociological prescription', *Sites,* 14: 17–34.

Sissons, R. (1988) *The Players: a Social History of the
Professional Cricketer.* Sydney: Pluto.

Sparks, R. (1995) 'Leisure and sport management
education in New Zealand: a situation analysis
and a proposal', *ANZALS Leisure Research Series,*
2: 94–124.

Stoddart, B. (1986) *Saturday Afternoon Fever: Sport in
the Australian Culture.* Sydney: Angus and
Robertson.

Stoddart, B. (1988) 'The hidden influence of sport', in
V. Burgmann and J. Lee (eds), *Constructing a
Culture: a People's History of Australia since 1788.*
Fitzroy, Victoria: McPhee Gribble. pp. 124–35.

Tatz, C. (1987) *Aborigines in Sport.* Bedford Park,
South Australia: Australian Society for Sports
History, Flinders University.

Tatz, C. (1995) *Obstacle Race: Aborigines in Sport.*
Sydney: University of New South Wales Press.

Thompson, S. (1988) 'Challenging the hegemony:
New Zealand women's opposition to rugby and
the reproduction of a capitalist patriarchy',
International Review for the Sociology of Sport, 23 (2):
205–12.

Thompson, S. (1990) '"Thank the ladies for the
plates": the incorporation of women into sport',
Leisure Studies, 9: 135–43.

Thompson, S. (1989) 'Sport sociology in
New Zealand', *International Review for the Sociology
of Sport,* 24 (1): 37–41.

Thompson, S. (1995) 'Playing around the family:
domestic labour and the gendered conditions of
participation in sport', *ANZALS Leisure Research
Series,* 2: 125–36.

Trenberth, L. and Collins, C. (eds) (1994) *Sport
Management in New Zealand.* Palmerston North:
Dunmore Press.

Trevelyan, M. and Jackson, S. (1995) 'Clash of the
codes: a comparative analysis of media representation of violence in rugby union and rugby
league', *Sporting Traditions,* 11: 113–38.

Vamplew, W., Moore, K., O'Hara, J., Cashman R. and
Jobling, I.F. (eds) (1992) *The Oxford Companion to
Australian Sport* (2nd edn). Melbourne: Oxford
University Press.

Vamplew, W. and Stoddart, B. (eds) (1994) *Sport in
Australia: A Social History.* Melbourne: Cambridge
University Press.

Veal, A.J. (1993) 'Getting the act together: leisure
research in Australia', in A. Boag, C. Lamond and
E. Sun, *Proceedings, ANZALS Inaugural Conference.*

Queensland: ANZALS and Centre for Leisure Research, Griffith University. pp. 29–32.

Veal, A.J. and Weiler, B. (eds) (1993) *First Steps ... Leisure and Tourism Research in Australia and New Zealand.* Sydney: Australia and New Zealand Association for Leisure Studies.

Wearing, B. (1992) 'Leisure and women's identity in late adolescence: constraints and opportunities', *Loisir-et-société/Society and Leisure,* 15 (1): 323–42.

35

EASTERN EUROPE

Gyöngyi S. Földesi

In the years when sport sociology was evolving in Western societies, sociology was a forbidden science in all of Eastern Europe except Poland. Under communist regimes, sociology was considered a 'bourgeois pseudo-science'. Research centres and sociology departments were closed down, and lecturing and publishing in sociology was prohibited. During the 1960s when sociological studies were allowed again in the region, sport sociology was among the first branches of sociology to emerge. Its rise was promoted by the particular importance of sport at that point in time in the Eastern bloc, but its development was also constrained for the same reason. Moreover, because of the persistent hegemony of Marxism, advances in sport sociology were delayed by limited theoretical and methodological approaches in sociology and in the sport sciences. Historical materialistic perspectives were confused with sociological perspectives in the first studies of social issues in sport. This was even true in the work done by the pioneers who contributed much to the promotion of sport sociology in their country and/or the international arena (Ciupak, 1965; Erbach and Buggel, 1972; Novikov and Makimenko, 1972; Schiller, 1965; Wohl, 1961, 1965, 1968; Zöld, 1965).

Not until the 1970s did a new generation of scholars use a range of other sociological approaches. This did not occur in each 'socialist' state, but it occurred at least in Poland and Hungary (Baly and Takács, 1974; B. Krawczyk, 1966, 1974; Z. Krawczyk, 1977; Takács, 1972, 1974). Efforts to study serious social problems in sport failed in the other countries of the former Eastern bloc. Efforts to reveal the true social, economic and political components of the socialist sport model were sanctioned.

Even the publication of Polish and Hungarian research data on 'sensitive issues' such as drug use, the health of top athletes and the status and role of top sports, was prohibited or impeded.

In the early 1970s the sociology of sport in Poland entered a new stage of development in both quantitative and qualitative research. The need for new paradigms, improved research methods and an interdisciplinary approach was recognized and partly satisfied in the two decades following the identification of these problems (Krawczyk and Krawczyk, 1989).

The Hungarian case illustrates perfectly the contradictory character of the growth of sport sociology in Eastern Europe. Sport in Hungary had been the subject of social commentary since the turn of the century (Takács, 1969). Sport sociology became an autonomous discipline in the 1960s. At first, researchers did only empirical research and focused their attention on micro-level issues and formulated only ad hoc theories. This trend changed in the 1970s as new attempts were made to analyse sport-related social phenomena and processes at the macro level and to formulate middle-range theories. The research produced only modest results, but there was significant progress in other areas. Research centres were established, the quantity and quality of empirical surveys improved, the number of publications and doctoral theses increased and international cooperation widened. Initially, the policy of the International Committee for the Sociology of Sport (ICSS, now ISSA) helped greatly to establish professional relationships and facilitate participation in international projects. Later, Polish–Hungarian connections, and even the officially promoted cooperation in sport sciences among some socialist countries, contributed to the advance of cross-cultural studies.

There were two sets of attitudes that influenced the work of sport sociologists during the socialist regime. On the one hand, sociologists were critical and revealed serious social problems in Hungarian sport and about Hungarian society – all of which were denied by those holding power in the communist regime. These problems included the following:

- When comparing the 1950s with the 1970s, it was clear that the openness of Hungarian sport had diminished significantly (Földesi, 1984a, 1985).
- Sports at elite levels had become a form of work, and the top Hungarian amateur athletes were in fact professional (Bakonyi and Nádori, 1971; Földesi, 1984b, 1985; Laki and Nyerges, 1980).
- The lifestyle and time commitments of the Hungarian population made it impossible for all but a few people to participate regularly in sport (Magyar, 1983; Laki and Makszin, 1984; Takács, 1985; Földesi et al., 1991).
- There were huge inequalities in sport participation opportunities between social strata and groups, and the inequalities were greater in Hungary than in other 'socialist' countries or in France (Földesi et al., 1991).
- The physical education and sportclass[1] system was dysfunctional in that it contributed to inequalities in sport instead of promoting equal chances (Laki and Makszin, 1985; Makszin and Laki, 1984; Takács, 1991).

On the other hand, although Hungarian sport sociologists had more freedom to do research than was the case for their colleagues in other Communist countries (except again Poland), they could not examine more-or-less taboo topics. For example, they could not raise questions about the nature of the so-called socialist sport model, or the relationship between sport and politics, sport and religion, sport and mass media, or the social functions of football. In fact, even though the personal courage of sociologists influenced the choice of research topics, most research reflected the principle of the so-called 'Three T' policy (prohibition = *tiltás*, tolerance = *türès*, support = *tàmogatàs*) which played a powerful self-regulating role. The 'Three T' policy was a peculiarity of the soft dictatorship in Hungary. It served informally to direct and control all cultural and scientific life so that it conformed to temporary political interests and possibilities.

Generally speaking, sociology of sport research was tolerated, but it was not funded at a level that enabled scholars to do serious research.

The political changes that occurred in 1989–90 created a new situation in Eastern Europe. The shift to a new political system has had an impact on sport sociologists. There are no longer political restrictions on a scholar's freedom to choose research topics, and there are new opportunities and ways to obtain research funds. Nevertheless, little research has been undertaken, and only two sociological works have been published (Földesi, 1994a, 1994b). Sport sociology in Eastern Europe has had to face a new set of difficult problems. These include the following:

- Sport sociology in Eastern Europe, as is the case in other regions, is not a field of enquiry characterized by a high degree of 'intellectual action in the Goffmanian dramaturgical sense' (MacAloon, 1987: 116). A number of theoretically informed experts work in the field, but since the early 1990s the number of sport sociologists has diminished because the brightest intellectuals are emigrating and moving to the welfare states in Western Europe, and especially to the USA.
- Sport sociology is included in university curricula to a greater extent than it has been in the past, but it is impossible to educate new generations of sport sociologists because of limited material resources and the shameful financial situation in both research and education.
- No matter how little state money was granted for sociological research in sport prior to 1989, sociologists could count on it with certainty. Since the transition they have had to apply to different foundations for research funds, and they have encountered the biases built into the funding policies of the foundations. For example, regardless of the quality of their research, proposed projects on sport have not been defined as competitive with those in other fields of culture. This is because sport sciences have been underrated in academic circles and because sport sociology has not been defined as credible within sociology as a whole. Sociology has served a special political role in Eastern Europe in that it has emphasized critical analysis that promoted political struggle and social progress, and sociologists have not seen sport sociology as being committed to the same goals. The resulting reduction of state subsidies has led to a decrease in the quantity of investigations

and an associated decline of social-scientific publications on sport.

- The regularly organized cooperation in sport sociology among the former socialist countries ceased to exist. Although state subsidies from the socialist regime made it possible, at least for a few experts, to participate in international congresses and conferences, most sport sociologists today must cover all the costs if they want to join the international community of their profession. Very few can afford to do this. The danger of their relative isolation continues, now caused by an economic rather than a political 'iron curtain'. As sport sociologists have attempted to avoid isolation, Warsaw has been very helpful. For example, a scientific seminar on the transformation of sport in post-communist countries was organized there in 1995. The goal was to promote sport sociology in the countries that had weak research traditions. However, this and other efforts have faced major financial difficulties. A lack of resources continues to make it impossible for many sport sociologists to become a part of international scientific life or to keep abreast of issues through modern forms of communication, through the use of computers, or simply through continued subscriptions to current journals.
- Sociology in Eastern Europe was traditionally defined as a science of the opposition. At present, its traditional *self-definition* raises an important issue in the minds of some people: if sociology continues to focus attention on a critical analysis of social problems, it can 'be easily suspected of supporting a return to the previous authoritarian system' (Andorka, 1991: 468). A similar issue is raised even more strongly in connection with the sociology of sport. Because sport was in a privileged situation in the communist regime, and because it has suffered many problems since the collapse of the regime, it offers too many opportunities for critical analyses of issues that many people do not want to discuss.

Since the early 1990s sport sociologists have seldom been asked to contribute to solving the problems connected with the radical changes that have occurred in sport. However, because of the complexities and difficulties associated with the transformations related to sport, a few sport sociologists have been invited to utilize their research to discover better ways of making and managing change. At this point in time the question remains open as to whether sport sociologists will have enough wisdom and knowledge to respond effectively to this new challenge.

NOTE

1. 'Sportclass system' is part of the educational system. In certain public schools (elementary, junior high and high schools) there are classes with a special curriculum containing more sport classes than usual, with the aim of promoting the sports careers of children with a talent for sport.

REFERENCES

Andorka, R. (1991) 'Hungarian sociology in the face of the political, economic and social transition', *International Sociology*, 6 (4): 465–9.

Baly, I. and Takács, F. (1974) *Sportszociológia. Válogatás* (Sport Sociology. Selected Studies). Budapest: Közgazdasági és Jogi Könyvkiadó.

Bakonyi, L. and Nádori, L. (1971) 'A magyar NB-I-es labdarúgók, szociológiai és szociálpszichológiai vizsgálata' (Sociological and psychological study of Hungarian first division football players), *Testneveléstudomány*, Part 1 (1): 5–6.

Ciupak, Z. (1965) 'O sporcie jako zjawisku moralnym' (Sport as a moral phenomenon). *Kultura Fizyczna*, No. 6.

Erbach, G. and Buggel, E. (1972) 'Sociological problems in the presentation of development tendencies of socialist physical culture in the German Democratic Republic', *International Review of Sport Sociology*, 7: 103–10.

Földesi, S.G. (1983) *Az élsportolói státus Magyarországon* (The Social Status of Top Athletes in Hungary). Budapest: OTSH Testnevelési és Sporttudományos Tanács.

Földesi, S.G. (1984a) 'Az élsport két generáció értékrendjében' (Top sport in the value system of two generations), *Az ifjúságpolitika megalapozását szolgáló kutatások. MSZMP KB Társadalomtudományi Intézet*, 154–305.

Földesi, S.G. (1984b) *Magyar olimpikonok önmaguktól és a sportról* (Hungarian Olympians about Themselves and Sports). Budapest: Közgazdasági és Jogi Könyvkiadó.

Földesi, S.G. (ed.) (1985) *Sport a változó világban* (Sport in a Changing World). Budapest: Sport.

Földesi, S.G. (1994a) *Helyzetkép a lelátóról* (Report on Football Stadia). Budapest: Testnevelési Főiskola.

Földesi, S.G. (ed.) (1994b) *A magyar felsőoktatás testnevelése és sportja (1993–1994)* (Physical Education and Sport at Hungarian Universities). Budapest: Testnevelési Főiskola.

Földesi, S.G., Louveau, C. and Metoudi, M. (1991) 'A sportolásra fordított idô Franciaországban és

Magyarországon' (Time spent on sport in France and in Hungary), *Magyar Testnevelési Egyetem Közleményei*, 1 (Melléklet), pp. 1–111.

Krawczyk, B. (1966) *Plany zyciowe a preferencje zawodowe absolwentów AWF* (Plans for Life Professional Preferences of Graduates of the Academy of Physical Education). Warsaw: PWN.

Krawczyk, B. (1974) 'Use of sociology in competitive sport', *International Review of Sport Sociology*, vol. 1.

Krawczyk, B. and Krawczyk, Z. (1989) 'Sociology of sport in Poland', *International Review for the Sociology of Sport*, 24 (1): 19–33.

Krawzcyk, Z. (1977) 'Theory and empiricism in the social sciences regarding physical culture', *International Review of Sport Sociology*, vol. 1.

Laki, L. and Makszin, I. (1984) Életkörülmények – Életmód – Életszín – vonal (Conditions of life – way of life – standard of life), *Sporttudomány*, 4: 17–21.

Laki, L. and Makszin, I. (1985) 'Az iskolai testnevelés és sport néhány problémája Magyarországon' (Some problems of physical education and sport at schools in Hungary), in S.G. Földesi (ed.), *Sport a változó világban*. Budapest: Sport. pp. 25–67.

Laki, L. and Nyerges, M. (1980) 'Élsport és társadalom' (Top sport and society), *Tanárképzés, testnevelés, sport* (Budapest), pp. 173–86.

MacAloon, J. (1987) 'An observer's view of sport sociology', *Sociology of Sport Journal*, 4 (2): 103–15.

Magyar, B. (1983) *A testkultúra egy munkáskerület lakosságának értékrendjében. Testnevelésdoktori értekezés* (Physical Culture in the Value System of the Inhabitants in a Workers' District). Budapest: Testnevelési Főiskola.

Makara, P. (1984) 'A tömegsport a mai társadalomban' (Mass sport in the contemporary society). *Egészségnevelés*, 2 : 67–72.

Makszin, I. and Laki, L. (1984) 'Az iskolai testnevelés és sport, valamint a testnevelés tagozatos képzés szerepe és helyzete az élsport utánpótlásban' (The state and role of physical education, sport and special teaching in physical education in the recruitment of top sport), *Testnevelési Főiskola Közleményei* (Melléklet), 3: 3–61.

Novikov, A.D. and Makimenko, A. (1972) 'Influence of selected socio-economic factors on the level of sport achievements in the various countries', *International Review of Sport Sociology*, 7: 27–44.

Nyerges, M. (1982) 'Az élsport társadalmi funkciói és az élsportolók életmódjának néhány szociológiai összefüggése' (Relations between social functions of top sport and the way of life of top athletes). Doktori értekezés, ELTE (doctoral thesis, ELTE University) p. 152.

Schiller, J. (1965) 'A sportszociológiai kutatások problémái' (Some problems of sport sociological studies), *Magyar Testnevelési Főiskola Közleményei*, 2: 277–81.

Takács, F. (1969) 'Adalék a magyar Polgári "sportszociológia" bírálatához' (Contribution to the criticism of sport sociology in Hungary), *Magyar Testnevelési Főiskola Tudományos Közlemények*, 2: 145–72.

Takács, F. (1972) 'A testkultúra fogalma és néhány tudományelméleti problémája' (Concept of physical culture and related theoretical problems), *Testnevelési Főiskola Tudományos Közlemények*, 1: 95–100.

Takács, F. (1974) 'Bevezető, tanulmány', (Introductory study) in I. Baly and F. Takács (eds), *Sportszociológia. Válogatás*. Budapest: Közgazdasági és Jogi Könyvkiadó. pp. 9–57.

Takács, F. (1985) 'Testkultúra és életmód' (Physical culture and way of life), in S.G. Földesi (ed.), *Sport a változó világban*. Budapest: Sport. pp. 25–67.

Takács, F. (1991) 'Iskolai testnevelésünk a szociológia tükrében' (School physical education in the mirror of sociology) *A Magyar Testnevelési Egyetem Közlemények*, 2 (Melléklet): 3–50.

Wohl, A. (1961) *Spoleczno-historyczne podloze sportu* (The Socio-historical Foundation of Sport). Warsaw: SiT.

Wohl, A. (1965) 'O obiektywnym charakterze prw rozwoju kultury fizycznej' (The objective character of the laws governing the development of physical culture), in *Proceedings of a Scientific Conference Devoted to the Theory of Physical Culture*. Warsaw: SiT.

Wohl, A. (1968) *Spoleczne problemy kultury fizycznej* (Social Problems of Physical Culture). Warsaw: AWF.

Zöld, J. (1965) 'A sportszerűség vizsgálatának néhány elvi és gyakorlati kérdése' (Some theoretical and practical issues of the study of sportsmanship), *Magyar Testnevelési Főiskola Közleményei*, 2: 82–100.

36

FRANCE

Jacques DeFrance

There have been strong sociological traditions in France ever since the work of Durkheim and Le Play at the end of the nineteenth century, the very period when sports and gymnastic activities were starting in the country. It was in that period that the sociological study of education began, but physical education, sports and games were not yet legitimate enough as school subjects to become matters of sociological reflection. A different kind of research was conducted by the French anthropological school and, in the 1930s, Marcel Mauss outlined a programme for a sociology of bodily techniques but little work was carried out according to his plan.

As in some other European countries, the sociology of sport took off in France in the 1960s when sports became mass activities and when the state began to develop firm policies in the sports domain. The first wave of sociological work included empirical and psycho-social enquiries into sports practice (for example, Bouet, 1968) and the role of sport in mass leisure, which was increasing at that time (Dumazedier, 1962). Also involved was a critical sociology of sport. It was mostly inspired by neo-Marxism and political sociology, and described the institution of sport as an 'ideological state apparatus' and denounced the sports policy of the de Gaulle government, especially in the years around 1968 (Brohm, 1978).

During the 1970s, this early work was supplemented by three trends connected with developments in the French social sciences. An historical tradition gave rise to work on the history – including the social history – of sports and physical education (Arnaud and Camy, 1986). And the development of French

structuralism and post-structuralism led, through the work of Michael Foucault and Pierre Bourdieu, to two other sets of research.

Following Foucault, Vigarello elaborated an 'archaeology of knowledge' directed towards the body, and he provided the history of a norm of body-use which has held since the sixteenth century – the norm of rectitude: stand up straight! (Vigarello, 1978). Arguing along the lines of *Discipline and Punish*, he shows how a minutely detailed organization of schooling, military training, medical practice, etc. produced a usage of space and time in which the body becomes precisely settled. He shows how this norm emerged, took different forms in different areas, especially in physical education and orthopaedics, and how it has become more and more internalized since the 1930s and 1950s. This work opened up a field of research around the history of science and sports techniques, following a French tradition in the history of ideas (Bachelard, Canguilhem).

In connection with Bourdieu, sociological and historical analyses were conducted which took sports and physical activities, not as separate realities, but as a differentiated whole which is sociologically divided and symbolically structured and which raises two sets of sociological questions.

First, how do the techniques and games which are called 'sports' and 'gymnastics' come to constitute a 'sportsworld' with its own rules and values, limits and hierarchies, rhythms and history? Socio-historical research shows that the institutionalization of sports does not progress to its complex connection with social life from the impetus of individuals but, on the contrary, evolves from its undifferentiated status within education, military training or as folk games, to a specialized activity with a separate social organization. This process of 'autonomization' receives its impetus through group struggles, and is specific to different countries according to the particularities of their social and political structures (the case of France between 1775 and 1914 is analysed by DeFrance, 1987).

Second, following in the frame of Bourdieu's *Distinction*, it has been shown that the involvement of the sportsperson with his or her sport cannot be understood apart from two kinds of relationships: the relationship that links this sport with the system of all other sports; and the relationship of those who choose this sport with those who choose other kinds of sports. Simultaneous enquiries into several sports, coordinated by Christian Pociello, have shed light on the logic of sports choices in France at the end of the 1970s, a conflictful conjuncture at which sports practice acquired a new symbolic relevance in the lifestyles of different social classes (Pociello et al., 1981).

Other kinds of work on sport have recently appeared, for example, on football, national identity and international relations (*Actes de la Recherche en Sciences Sociales*, 1994; Wahl, 1986), the political science of sport (Ehrenberg, 1991), women and sport (Davisse and Louveau, 1991), the anthropology of sport (Bromberger, 1995; Bruant, 1992) and new sociological models of sport (Duret, 1993, inspired by Batanski and Thévenot).

REFERENCES AND FURTHER READING

Arnaud, P. and Camy, J. (eds) (1986) *La naissance du Mouvement Sportif Associatif en France. Sociabilités et formes de pratiques sportives.* Lyons: Presses Universitaires de Lyon.

Bouet, M. (ed.) (1968) *La Signification du sport.* Paris: Presses Universitaires de France.

Bourdieu, P. (1988) 'Program for a sociology of sport (1980)', *Sociology of Sport Journal*, 5 (2): 153–61.

Brohm, J.M. (1978) *Sport: a Prison of Measured Time.* London: Ink Links.

Bromberger, C. (with Hayot, A. and Mariottini, J.M.) (1995) *Le Match de Football: Ethnologie d'une passion partisane à Marseille, Naples et Turin.* Paris: Maison des Sciences de l'Homme.

Bruant, G. (1992) *Anthropologie du geste sportif. La construction sociale de la course à pied.* Paris: Presses Universitaires de France.

Davisse, A. and Louveau, C. (1991) *Sports, école, société: la part des femmes.* Joinville le Pont: Actio.

DeFrance, J. (1987) *L'Excellence corporelle. La formation des activités physiques et sportives modernes, 1770–1914.* Rennes/Paris: Presses Universitaires Rennes/STAPS.

Dumazedier, J. (1962) *Vers une civilisation des loisirs.* Paris: Seuil.

Duret, P. (1993) *L'héroïsme sportif.* Paris: Presses Universitaires de France.

Ehrenberg, A. (1991) *Le culte de la performance.* Paris: Calmann-Lévy.

Pociello, C. (dir.) et al. (1981) *Sports et société. Approche socio-culturelle des pratiques.* Paris: Vigot.

Pociello, C. (1983) *Le Rugby ou la guerre des styles.* Paris: A.M. Métailié.

Vigarello, G. (ed.) (1978) *Le Corps redressé. Histoire d'un pouvoir pédagogique.* Paris: Presses Universitaires de France.

Wahl, A. (1986) 'Le footballeur Français: de l'amateurisme au salariat (1890–1926)', *Le Mouvement social*, 135 (April–June): 7–31.

37

GERMANY[1]

Klaus Heinemann

Though noteworthy sociological work on sport had already been carried out before the late 1970s (Habermas, 1958; Linde and Heinemann, 1968; Plessner, 1954; Rigauer, 1969; Risse, 1922), it was not until then that sport sociology established itself in the Federal Republic of Germany (FRG) as a separate teaching and research area.

Sport sociology prior to the late 1970s was primarily studied by sociologists interested in problems of sport as well as other areas of sociological research (for example, Eichberg, Grieswelle, Hammerich, Heinemann, Neidhardt, von Krockow, Linde and Lüschen). Sport sociology during this phase did not exist as an independent, established and accepted research field; but rather sport was considered within the context of cultural sociology, leisure-time sociology or the theory of social conflict or social change.

During the late 1970s, though, an independent sociology of sport developed. Omnibus volumes of sport sociology were published (Hammerich and Heinemann, 1975; Lüschen and Weis, 1976) and followed by introductions to sport sociology (Grieswelle, 1978; Heinemann, 1998; Rigauer, 1982). University chairs for sport sociology became established, especially because sport sociology was increasingly becoming an element of physical education teacher training in keeping with the growing significance and institutionalization of sport science. Two different scientific societies of sport sociology were founded in Germany: the section of sport sociology affiliated with the German Association of Sociology of Sport, and the section of sport sociology affiliated with the German Society of Sport Sciences.

Since that time, sport sociology has become a well-established scientific discipline recognized in sociology as well as in sport sciences. Only a brief summary of the scientific profile and peculiarities of the field can be given here. For example, there is not enough space to evaluate and describe in detail the following outstanding investigations: Baur on movement socialization in relatives of the family, socialization in sport, on the socialization of body movements; Bette on the sociology of the body and sport and doping; Heinemann, Horch, and Schubert on sport organization and on the economy of sport; Winkler, and Heinemann and Schubert on voluntary work, Rittner on new developments in the landscape of sport; and Pilz on hooliganism and aggression in sport – just to mention a few of the important sport sociologists in Germany. For a more detailed overview on the sociology of sport in Germany, see Heinemann (1992a, 1992b).

One important discussion in Germany during the 1980s centred on the constitutional basis of sport sociology. Two alternatives were identified for defining sport sociology and outlining areas of research. One alternative emphasized the interpretation of sport as a social system, and the other emphasized a theoretical approach derived from a sociology of the body. The development and constitution of sport as a system cannot be described in detail here. However, it is necessary to mention Eichberg's (1973) works in which the emergence of sport, in particular the idea of achievement, is reconstructed in the context of social history. Also important is Cachay's (1988) study in which he applied Luhmann's functional-structural system theory as a basis for outlining the historic process by which sport developed into a system that was independent of other subsystems of society. In addition to works concerning the problem of what the sport system constitutes, it is necessary to recognize here studies examining the inner workings of the sport system. Of special importance is the observation that the traditional concept of sport is losing significance and that a variety of 'models of sport' have been created. This work, done by different authors who have selected and used many different models, identifies distinctions expressing various forms of sport. Their research presents a unique understanding of sport, unique sport ideologies, and particular forms of performing and organizing sport. Heinemann (1998), for example, presents a model in which he differentiates sports into expressive, competition-oriented, commercial and instrumental forms.

Sport sociology has also been defined by considering it part of a sociology of the body. Research based on this approach has focused on the development of sport in modern society as it is influenced by the evolution of a conception of the body that assumes that the social control and predictability of the body can be perfected through our awareness. Analyses have focused on how the body becomes an instrument that we can control and dominate and for which our mind is therefore responsible. Therefore, an approach based on a sociology of the body has for some time been the basis of sport sociology in Germany (compare, for example, the works in the book by Klein, 1985, and Bette, 1989).

Studies of the organization of sport in clubs are especially important in sport sociology because this type of organization is so pervasive in Germany, probably more so than in any other country in the world. Such studies also make important contributions to the sociology of voluntary organization.

The study of sports clubs as voluntary associations occurs on two levels. First, there are studies done on a microsociological level. These focus on the social structure of club members, their relationships with each other, and specific integration and motivation problems. They involve an analysis of goals, structures and culture but also of decision-making processes and bureaucratization. Secondly, there are studies done on a macrosociological level. These focus primarily on the relation of the club with its social environment.

Following smaller scale studies on sports clubs, the first large empirical study on sports clubs in Germany was conducted between 1973 and 1977 (Schlagenhauf, 1977; Timm, 1979). In addition to case studies, the Deutscher Sportbund (German Sport Federation, DSB) conducts regular financial and structural analyses of 80,000 sports clubs. These provide a comprehensive picture of equipment, sports offered, the extent of volunteer work, the type of financing and the membership of sports clubs, so that extensive general information on the club environment is available (Heinemann and Schubert, 1994).

Winkler and Karhausen (1985) have examined the DSB and selected member federations. Their study consists of documentary analyses of approximately 1,500 written questionnaires from volunteer and full-time paid management employees, and of interviews with experts from the different federations. Conclusions have been drawn regarding the structure of the DSB and its member organizations, their financial situation, their goals and tasks, their personnel structure, problems of volunteer and full-time paid employees, and political decision-making processes within sport organizations.

In recent years there has been a rapid emergence of many commercial sport enterprises (such as fitness centres). These provide new types of sport organization and participation opportunities, and they offer competition for sports clubs. Physical education teachers who cannot find employment in the school system have avoided unemployment and created new opportunities and income by founding such commercial sport enterprises. These enterprises have been the subject of an empirical investigation by Dietrich, Heinemann and Schubert (1990). Their research uses various forms of data analysis to identify the determinants of demand for sport offered in the private market sector of the economy, the number of commercial enterprises and the professionalization of opportunities for employees in this field.

A larger number of sport sociological studies can be summarized under the heading 'social figures in sport'. These represent a significant proportion of sport sociology studies in Germany. A complete overview of these studies cannot be given, but the most important have focused on the structural characteristics and motivation of the individual involved in sport, the characteristics of high-performance athletes, and the peculiarities of volunteer workers, fans, coaches and exercise supervisors, and physical education teachers.

In addition to research on social structures done through investigations of organizational structures of sport, there have also been important sociological studies on social processes, such as events and changes within given social structures. The processes of socialization (Becker, 1986) and aggressive or violent behavior (Pilz, 1982; Pilz and Wewer, 1988) have received much attention in particular.

In recent years three new themes in the sociology of sport in Germany have been observed. First, there have been investigations on the embededdness of sport in modern societies, and the extent to which the development of sport can be explained by modernization theories (Bette, 1993; Hinsching and Borkenhagen, 1995). Secondly, there have been studies of the adoption, after the unification of the sport in the former GDR to the sport of the FRG (Baur et al., 1995). And thirdly, there has been an emerging interest in socioeconomic problems associated with sport (Heinemann, 1995; Weber, 1995).

NOTE

1   This overview was written in 1996.

REFERENCES

Baur, J., Koch, U. and Telschow, S. (1995) *Sportvereine im Übergang: die Vereinslandschaft in Ostdeutschland.* Aachen.

Becker, P. (ed.) (1986) *Sozialisation und Sport.* Reinbek: Rowohlt.

Bette, K.-H. (1989) *Körperspuren. Zur Semantik und Paradoxie moderner Körperlichkeit.* Berlin: de Gruyter.

Bette, K.-H. (1993) 'Sport und Individualisierung', *Spectrum der Sportwissenschaft,* 5.

Cachay, K. (1988) *Sport und Gesellschaft.* Schorndorf: Hoffman.

Dietrich, K., Heinemann, K. and Schubert, M. (1990) *Kommerzielle Sportanbieter.* Schorndorf: Hoffmann.

Eichberg, H. (1973) *Der Weg des Sports in die industrielle Zivilisation.* Baden-Baden: Nomos.

Grieswelle, D. (1978) *Sportsoziologie.* Stuttgart: Kohlhammer.

Habermas, J. (1958) 'Soziologische Notizen zum Verhältnis von Arbeit und Freizeit', in G. Funke (ed.), *Konkrete Vernunft. Festschrift für E. Rothacker.* Bonn: Bovier.

Hammerich, K. and Heinemann, K. (eds) (1975) *Texte zur Soziologie des Sports.* Schorndorf: Hoffmann.

Heinemann, K. (1992a) 'Sport sociology: fundamental aspects', in H. Haag, O. Grupe and A. Kirsch (eds), *Sport Science in Germany.* Berlin and Heidelberg.

Heinemann, K. (1992b) 'Sport sociology: socio-economic aspects', in H. Haag, O. Grape and A. Kirsch (eds), *Sport Science in Germany.* Berlin and Heidelberg.

Heinemann, K. (1995) *Einführug in die Ökonomie des Sports.* Schorndorf: Hoffmann.

Heinemann, K. (1998) *Einführung in die Soziologie des Sports,* 4th edn. Schorndorf: Hoffmann.

Heinemann, K. and Schubert, M. (1994) *Der Sportverein – Ergebnisse einer repräsentativen Untersuchung.* Schorndorf: Hoffmann.

Hinsching, J. and Borkenhagen, F. (ed.) (1995) *Modernisierung und Sport.* St Augustin: Academia.

Klein, M. (ed.) (1985) *Sport und Körper.* Reinbek: Rowohlt.

Linde, H. and Heinemann, K. (1968) *Leistungsengagement und Sportinteresse. Eine empirische Studie zur Stellung des Sports im betrieblichen und schulischen Leistungsfeld.* Schorndorf: Hoffmann.

Lüschen, G. and Weis, K. (eds) (1976) *Die Soziologie des Sports.* Darmstadt: Luchterhand.

Pilz, G.A. (1982) *Sport und Gewalt.* Schorndorf: Hoffmann.

Pilz, G.A. and Wewer, W. (1988) *Erfolg oder Fair Play?* Munich: Compress.

Plessner, H. (1954) 'Soziologie des Sports', in *Jahrbuch der Studiengesellschaft für praktische Psychologie.* Göttingen: Dt Universitätszeitung.

Rigauer, B. (1969) *Sport und Arbeit.* Frankfurt: Suhrkamp.

Rigauer, B. (1982) *Sportsoziologie.* Reinbek: Rowohlt.

Risse, H. (1922) *Soziologie des Sports.* Münster: Atalas.

Schlagenhauf, K. (1977) *Spsortvereine in der Bundesrepublik Deutschland.* Schondorf: Hoffmann.

Timm, W. (1979) 'Sportvereine in der Bundesrepublik Deutschland', Teil 2. Schorndorf: Hoffmann.

Weber, P. (1995) *Die wirtschaftliche Bedeutung des Sports.* Schorndorf: Hoffmann.

Winkler, J. and Karhausen, R.R. (1985) *Verbände im Sport.* Schorndorf: Hoffmann.

38

INDIA

Ian McDonald

'In India', wrote S.K. Gupta in 1987, the 'sociology of sport has remained an unexplored area of research' (1987: 306). At the time of writing, ten years on, Indian society and its sports have undergone dramatic developments. Images of a land of unchanging tradition, and of a country wracked by poverty and disease, now owe more to tired clichés that persist in the popular Western imagination than to a serious analysis of the complex and dynamic nature of contemporary India. A revealing index of the scale and nature of the social changes which have been and are taking place is provided by cricket – the premier sport in the sub-continent. India has played host to the cricket World Cup twice: in 1987 (with Pakistan), and in 1996 (with co-hosts Pakistan and Sri Lanka). On the first occasion, the tournament was sponsored by Reliance, an Indian-based industrial firm, for £800,000. In 1996, sponsorship was provided by ITC, the multi-national Indian tobacco giant, for £8 million. Unlike 1987, the 1996 World Cup was a global television spectacle of unprecedented glamour and hype. Satellite television enabled the 1996 tournament to serve variously as: a marketing strategy to reach the hearts and pockets of an affluent, materialistic and cricket-mad South Asian middle class; a political strategy to facilitate sub-continental supremacy over England as the new epicentre of cricket as a global game; and as part of an economic strategy to entice multi-national interest and investment. In tune with the Indian government's policy of economic liberalization, it was a carnival of globalization and it generated a financial profit of £21 million (*Asian Age*, July 1996, p. 1). Evidence of increased tensions since 1987, in particular arising out of cricket nationalism,

were also apparent at the 1996 World Cup. Both India and Pakistan failed to reach the final in 1987, yet unlike 1996, defeats were not then widely interpreted within the media as national humiliations. Nor were they catalysts for outbreaks of ethnic and communal intolerance. With cricket in the vanguard, sport in India provides fertile terrain for its sociological study in the era of globalization.

However, despite the developments of the past decade there is still a paucity of sociological studies of sport. Here, at least, it seems, is an 'unchanging tradition'. Echoing Gupta's comments made seven years before, D.P. Vora noted that the 'sociology of leisure ... has been practically unexplored in our country' (1994: 111). An extensive search through bibliographies prepared by the Indian Council of Social Sciences Research, the *Indian Social Sciences Research Abstracts Quarterly*, and many other Indian and non-Indian sources, merely confirms that the sociological study of sport in India remains essentially virgin territory. The few studies that have been undertaken by Indian scholars are empirically narrow and theoretically functionalist (for example see Gupta, 1987; Manna, 1989; Reddy, 1988; Sohi, 1981; Vora, 1994). Even *Sport in Asia and Africa: a Comparative Handbook*, edited by Eric A. Wagner, admits that, of all the geographical areas covered, a 'notable exception is the Indian sub-continent' (1989: xii). Although now dated, the most authoritative and detailed sociological study of sport in India remains *Patrons, Players and the Crowd: the Phenomenon of Indian Cricket*, published in 1980 by the Australian social historian Richard Cashman.

The relationship between traditional/ modern sports and urban/rural society in India, is complex and contradictory. In an insightful account of the 1996 cricket World Cup, Marqusee (1996) makes graphically clear the unrivalled status of international level cricket for all classes throughout the sub-continent. In India, other modern sports such as field hockey and soccer, and traditional activities like wrestling, are more unevenly geographically and socio-economically distributed. A thriving, widely read sports press is testimony to the important space occupied by sport in Indian society. However, by way of contrast, India's barren quest for medals at the 1988 and 1992 Summer Olympic Games, and the single bronze medal from tennis player Leander Paes at the Atlanta Games, seem to confirm the observation of an Indian sports administrator, quoted in Bose (1986: 18) that, 'Sport is against our Indian ethos ... we are just not organized for sports'. Whilst this is the view of an administrator lamenting the narrow social base of organized participant sport which, he feels, has frustrated attempts to create a media-winning Olympic squad in a country with the second largest population in the world (about 866 million and rising), it does reflect governmental indifference towards the country's sporting infrastructure. However, attempts to characterize the sport–society relationship will always be more impressionistic than scientific in the absence of systematic sociological research.

Understanding the marginality of the sociology of sport can be approached by locating sociology as a discipline within the academic structures of independent India. The late eminent sociologist M.N. Srivinas noted how the independent Indian states' commitment to Nehruvian ideas of economic development, social welfare and higher education provided a setting in which the social sciences were able to advance (1987: 135–8). However, he argues, sociology achieved recognition rather slowly compared to economics, political science, international relations and history – as these disciplines appeared more relevant to the exigencies of building the new nation-state. When sociology did emerge, it also was preoccupied with the social development problematic.

R. Guha asserts that the later and subordinate emergence of sociology explains its domination by a Eurocentric, economistic view of development (1989: 339). This structural-functionalist sociology has been challenged in recent years by a more critical approach, and by the emergence of subaltern studies – a South Asian form of cultural studies – which is committed, amongst other things, to 'deconstructing colonial historiography (Lal, 1996). None of these approaches, however,

has yet demonstrated a systematic orientation to the study of sport. Perhaps the most likely source from which a sociology of sport may emerge is out of the broadening of the cultural studies paradigm which is currently occurring in India. Crucially for the study of sport, popular culture, alongside feminism, ecology and a radical critique of modernity, are key constitutive elements of cultural studies in South Asia. It is perhaps here more than elsewhere that the beginnings of a sociological analysis of sport may be seeded. After over 50 years of political independence in India, the development of a sociology of Indian sport presents a timely and exciting challenge.

REFERENCES AND FURTHER READING

Bose, M. (1986) *A Maiden View: the Magic of Indian Cricket*. London: George Allen & Unwin.

Cashman, R. (1980) *Patrons, Players and the Crowd: the Phenomenon of Indian Cricket*. New Delhi: Orient Longman.

Guha, R. (1989) 'Sociology in India: some elective affinities', *Contributions to Indian Sociology* (New Delhi), 23 (2): 339–46.

Gupta, S.K. (1987) 'Parents' and teachers' attitudes and reactions towards participation in sports by young athletes of a university in an Indian state', *International Review for Sport Sociology*, 22 (4): 305–16.

Kurien, C.T. (1994) *Global Capitalism and the Indian Economy*. New Delhi: Orient Longman.

Lal, V. (1996) *South Asian Cultural Studies: a Bibliography*. New Delhi: Manohar Publishers.

Manna, S. (1989) 'Patterns of recreation in an urban setting', *Man in India*, 68 (2): 179–94.

Marqusee, M. (1996) *War Minus the Shooting: a Journey through South Asia during Cricket's World Cup*. London: Heinemann.

Nandy, A. (1989) *The Tao of Cricket: On Games of Destiny and the Destiny of Games*. New Delhi: Viking and Penguin.

Patnaik, P. (1996) 'Of cricket, communalism and commerce', *Frontline*, 5 April, pp. 14–15.

Reddy, P.C. (1988) 'Social inequality, discrimination and sport in India', *Sport and Humanism: Proceedings of the International Workshop of Sport Sociology in Japan*. pp. 280–9.

Sohi, A.S. (1981) 'Social status of Indian elite sportsmen in perspective of social stratification and mobility', *International Review of Sport Sociology*, 165: 61–77.

Srivinas, M.N. (1987) 'Development of sociology in India: an overview', *Economic and Political Weekly* (Bombay), 27 (4): 135–8.

Vora, D.P. (1994) 'Leisure as understood by school-going children in an urban setting', *Indian Council of Social Science Research Abstracts Quarterly*, xxiii (1&2): 111–15.

Wagner, E.A. (ed.) (1989) *Sport in Asia and Africa: a Comparative Handbook*. London: Greenwood Press.

39

JAPAN

Koichi Kiku

SOCIAL CHANGES IN POST-WAR JAPAN AND TRENDS IN SOCIOLOGICAL STUDIES OF SPORT

The term 'sport sociology' was used in Japan as early as 1932, but genuine systematic study did not begin until the establishment of the Japanese Society of Physical Education (JSPE) in 1950.

Since 1950 there have been changes in the focus and content of research and writing related to the sociology of sport. In the 1950s, just after the Second World War, the main research focus was on group learning in small groups that participated in school-based physical education. Additional research focused on the recreational participation of workers, especially in the context of industrial physical education and workplace physical education. During the 1960s, researchers turned their attention to studies of community sports in cities and other areas of dense population, and to studies of agricultural and fishery regions and other areas of sparse population. In association with the Tokyo Olympics in 1964 there were studies of national physical strength training exercises and the examination of specific Olympic-related affairs. During the 1970s attention was given to a wider range of systematic studies of sports participation. Research investigated the relationship between individuals and sports by levels of consciousness, attitude and personality from the social psychological viewpoint. Other efforts were made in the realm of physical education to promote fitness throughout the life course, sports development, and sports and leisure among the elderly. In the 1980s and 1990s research on

each of these themes increased in scope as researchers used more complex methodologies and computer-aided statistical analyses, and larger studies were undertaken that involved multiple cooperation among scholars.

A review of sociological research on physical education/sports in Japan shows that the field emerged initially as a 'sociology of physical education' (the study of physical education phenomena in the education sector), and not as 'sport sociology' (the study of a much wider range of sports phenomena). This initial emphasis has caused the pattern of research to be dictated excessively by social changes and it has promoted themes that follow these changes as explained below. It has also delayed the introduction of a genuine theoretical sociological regimen and policy studies based on theoretical models.

INTERNAL/EXTERNAL FACTORS AFFECTING STUDY TRENDS

Physical education was a compulsory subject under the post-war Japanese 'New University System'. This resulted in the mass production of university graduates and scholars who were physical education majors. These graduates were employed to teach exercise and physical activities in the 'General Education Course'. Generally speaking, they had little or no interest in theoretical perspectives or theoretically informed research. Therefore they concentrated their studies on the educational aspects of sports.

Consequently, most research in the 1950s focused on small group learning of physical education, and then in the 1960s the focus expanded to problems related to the learning of physical education as it occurred in urban and rural areas. With the increased rate of economic growth in the 1970s attention turned to a focus on sports throughout the life course. Therefore, sport sociology in Japan can be said to have experienced shifts in direction through strong influences from political, economic and social change; additionally, research has been influenced by important educational goals, as identified by the education system.

CURRENT TRENDS

Since the mid-1970s there has been an emergence of studies based on established sociological theories. Initially these studies were based mainly on structural-functionalism (Talcott Parsons) and Marxism. Recent studies have expanded to include a variety of subjective or interpretive research approaches based on symbolic interactionism, phenomenological sociology, ethnomethodology and frame analysis (Erving Goffman).

These recent changes have occurred primarily because of the establishment of the Japan Society of Sport Sociology (JSSS) in 1991 and its influence on its members and on the research approaches used in sport sociology. There are two reasons for this. First, scholars who graduated in physical education since 1991 have emphasized higher quality, theory-based research. This was an outgrowth of the establishment of doctoral courses in physical education study and Japanese university reform that made physical education an elective subject instead of a compulsory 'General Education Course'. Secondly, these new physical education graduates were joined by graduates in mainstream sociology who shared research interests related to sports and physical activity. These recent developments have led to more sophisticated analyses of the historical and social phenomenon of sports. Current research, for example, is likely to be informed by cultural studies, figurational sociology and Bourdieu's sociology.

Research on the 'sociology of the body' has also begun to emerge. Additionally, an International Symposium on 'The Formation of the Modern Nation-State and Sport' was staged in 1997. The development of sport sociology in the future requires that scholars come in both physical education and sociology come together and use their subtle differences in methodology and approach to build on past research and take research forward in new directions.

THE SPORTS ENVIRONMENT AND SUSTAINABLE DEVELOPMENT IN JAPAN

Japan is an island state, with about 80 per cent of the land mass consisting of mountains and hills. During the post-war era this geographical situation led to a social consensus that Japan should develop the use of mountainous land and the sea to achieve economic growth. In other words, economic growth in Japan has involved industrial construction and has encouraged heavy chemical industry; mountainous terrain has been levelled and further land reclaimed mainly in the city areas, to improve sites for housing and industrial use. It is no overstatement that Japan has achieved its post-war high economic growth at the expense of its natural beauty.

However, after the first 'oil shock' in 1973, Japan's economy shifted from one based on high industrial growth to one characterized by post-industrial low growth, in the same manner as other advanced economic nations. Lifestyle in Japan has gradually been changing from one accentuating labour to one accentuating leisure, and so the national demand for leisure and sports has increased. Japan experienced economic growth in the GDP of more than 5 per cent annually between the late 1980s and early 1990s – a period known as the 'bubble' economy. These good business conditions and the high demand for sports and leisure pushed the Ministry of International Trade and Industry (MITI) to promote an 'Act for the Development of Resort Complex Construction' (The Resort Act) in 1987. The purpose of this law was for the government to aggressively encourage private business to develop and construct golf courses, ski areas, camping areas and facilities related to marine sports (marinas, for example).

Due to this activity, Japan was exposed to the environmental menace of a construction rush to build sports and leisure facilities. For example, in 1988, there were 1,619 golf courses in the entire country, but in the period after 1988 development plans were produced for a further 970, an increase of about 60 per cent in one step. The same trends can be seen in ski resorts, camping areas and marinas. In particular, golf course development caused serious environmental damage through destruction of the landscape. There was also damage to the health of residents in nearby areas because of the indiscriminate use of agricultural chemicals to maintain the greens and fairways of the golf courses. As a result, there were many studies and reports on environmental damage in the early 1990s. This overdevelopment of sports facilities created conditions similar to those that existed during earlier times when high economic growth forced 'pollution' on the general public living around factories.

However, after the collapse of the bubble economy in 1992, resort development throughout the country changed or was cancelled due to a decrease in private investment. The emphasis among those interested in sports and leisure is now on more familiar, cheap and environmentally friendly pursuits instead of expensive, environmentally damaging activities. There is increasing interest in Japan in the co-existence of sport and the environment. Even an Alpine course prepared for the Nagano Winter Olympics of 1998 was modified due to environmental concerns.

In 1990, in the midst of the bubble economy, the Japan Society of Sports Industry (JSSI) was established with support from MITI and industrial circles. The purpose of the JSSI is to develop the sports industry; however, they must consider sustainable development for both sports and the environment from many viewpoints. For example, as far as ski facilities are concerned, the interest is on building courses that combine with nature, rather than constructing competition courses as before.

The relationship between the sports environment and sustainable economic development, with particular reference to residents living around these facilities, is one of the most important subjects for the attention of sport sociology in Japan.

FURTHER READING

Inoue, S. (1989) 'Sports and social theory in Japan', *Sociological Journal of Physical Education and Sport,* 8: 211–23 (in Japanese).

Kiku, K. (1996) 'An understanding of the historical trends in sport sociology in Japan from the viewpoint of the sociology of knowledge', in *The '96 Seoul International Sport Science Congress Proceedings,* Volume 1, pp. 219–35.

Matsumura, K. (1993a) 'Sport and social change in the Japanese rural community', *International Review for the Sociology of Sport,* 28 (2/3): 135–44.

Matsumura, K. (1993b) *Sociology of Sport and the Japanese Rural Community.* Tokyo: Dowa-Shoin (in Japanese).

Sugawara, R. (1984) *A Basic Theory of Sport Sociology.* Tokyo: Fumaido-Syuppan (in Japanese).

Tatano, H. (1979) 'Methodological subjects on the sociology of physical education and sports in Japan', *Research Journal of Sport Sociology,* 9: 139–63 (in Japanese).

Yoka Kaihatsu Centre (1996) *Leisure's White Paper '96* (in Japanese).

40

KOREA (AND SOUTH EAST ASIA)

Burn-Jang Lim

Sport sociology in Korea has achieved note-worthy progress over the past several years, and yet, it is only fair to say that the current state of the discipline lags behind the international standard. The quantity of research in the field as well as the outcome is comparatively meagre. These shortcomings are primarily due to the short history of the discipline in Korea. Efforts to investigate sport phenomena from sociological perspectives have only begun to expand in recent years.

Sport sociology was first introduced to Korea in the early 1960s in the form of the introductory course at Seoul National University. Since then, the field has been rapidly developing as one of the major subdisciplines in sport science. In the mid-1970s, sport sociology was accepted as a subdiscipline of KAHPERD (Korean Alliance for Health, Physical Education, Recreation and Dance), and formed its own association under the name of the Korean Sport Sociology Society (KSSS) in 1990. The sociological investigation of sport phenomena was motivated at first by the social importance and utility of the research findings, rather than by deep disciplinary interest.

THE BIRTH AND DEVELOPMENT OF SPORT SOCIOLOGY

It is only since the 1960s that the sociological aspects of sport have drawn the attention of sport scientists in Korea. The term 'sport sociology' first appeared in 1963 in a book titled *Introduction to Physical Education* written by Jang Young-Whan. The book introduced the term and the scope of the field as one of the sub-areas of sport study. The first sport sociology book was '*che-yuk-sa-whoi-hak*' (sport sociology) published in 1973 by the Ministry of Education as an independent volume in '*che-yuk-kyo-yuk-ja-ryo-chong-seo* 11' (Collection of Materials on Physical Education, Volume 11).

The Seoul National University graduate school was, in 1963, the first to offer a Masters degree programme in sport sociology. A Doctoral programme was established in 1983. Since then, courses in sport sociology have been added to graduate programmes in other universities, and by the 1980s, almost all universities in Korea offered courses in sport sociology as part of their graduate programmes.

It was not until the 1980s that scholars in the field of sport sociology in Korea gave serious attention to the need for a more formalized and unified academic community. As the interests in the sociological aspects of sport grew and the number of scholars specializing in the area increased, there arose an awareness of the need to share and distribute information among those interested in sport sociology. Seoul National University had become, by then, the centre of sport sociology academics, holding regular seminars and meetings from 1984 under the name of the Sport Sociology Study Group (SSSG).

Looking back, formation of the SSSG marked the declaration of independence as an academic discipline for sport sociologists and the beginning of an era of search for a strong identity for the discipline. The search bore fruit in the early 1990s when, on 18 August 1990, the Korea Sport Sociology Association (the former name of KSSS) was formally established. The formation of KSSS opened networks of communication among sport sociologists in Korea and abroad. It also stimulated research, providing a medium, the *KSSS Journal*, through which such research could be published. Taken together, these developments accelerated the growth of sport sociology in Korea.

The KSSS, which is still in the process of growing and developing, is working vigorously to contribute to sport sociology in the international context. In 1991 a member of the KSSS was elected Vice President of the International Sociology of Sport Association (ISSA), and the *ISSA Bulletin* has been edited and published in Korea since that time.

Under the auspices of KSSS, many sport sociologists with international reputations have visited Korea for seminars and workshops. For example, Morigawa visited in 1991; Barry McPherson and Kari Fasting in 1992; John Loy and Günther Lüschen in 1993; R. Morford, Fujiwara, Peter Donnelly and Matsumura in 1994; Saeki and Lee Vander Valden in 1995; Gyöngi Földesi, Joseph Maguire and Kurt Weis in 1996; and Donald Sabo and George Sage in 1997. Several of these scholars revisited Korea twice or even three times. All participants – Korean scholars and students, and the visitors – were able to feel a special sense of satisfaction and pride at having contributed to the development of sport sociology in Korea. These efforts, fostering the growth of the discipline and international cooperation, will continue in the twenty-first century.

Having described its birth and development, we can say that according to the developmental stages described by Mullins (1973), sport sociology in Korea is in its network stage. The formation of KSSS marked the beginning of this stage, preceded by a rather long and slow normal stage. We foresee that sport sociology in Korea will enter the cluster stage in the fairly near future.

THE STATE OF SPORT SOCIOLOGY RESEARCH AND THE PROSPECTS FOR THE FUTURE

During the period from 1960 to 1993, there were 1,294 research papers, Masters theses and Doctoral dissertations published in Korea. Five hundred and thirty-one papers were published in the *KSSS Journal* and *KAPHERD Journal*, and 763 Masters theses and Doctoral dissertations were published (Son, 1993).

An analysis of issues of the *KSSS Journal* from 1992 through 1998 shows various research topics and methodologies associated with sociological studies of sport. Seventy-two per cent of the studies were quantitative, while 28 per cent were qualitative. In the quantitative studies,

researchers used the following techniques: 40 per cent used regression, 26 per cent used ANCOVA, 23 per cent used ANOVA, and others used *t*-tests, path analyses and chi-square analyses.

Recently, more researchers have used qualitative methods in their investigations of sport phenomena in a cultural context. Although the major topics of papers published in the *KSSS Journal* were socialization and organization (19 per cent and 17 per cent of the papers, respectively), gender, ageing, and sports and leisure involvement have become newly emerging issues. In fact, 43 per cent of the papers published in the *KSSS Journal* between 1995 and 1998 were devoted to these latter three topics. This trend reflects responses among sport sociologists to sport phenomena as they relate to social welfare amidst Korean society's rapid economic development.

There is every reason to believe that the future of sport sociology in Korea looks bright. First, Korea has already witnessed rapid growth in the prevalence and visibility of sport as a social phenomenon; more people are interested in a better quality of life, and consider sport as one of the leisure activities vital to achieve a higher quality lifestyle. Secondly, the quality of life that people pursue requires scientific investigation so as to interpret which aspects of prevailing lifestyles can be improved and how to do so. This kind of scientific verification can be more persuasive if it describes and also explains and interprets the phenomena at hand, as has been done in sport sociology. Thirdly, the pursuit of quality of life is being institutionalized in the form of various sport organizations within society; sport has truly become a social mechanism for its members to interact with and maintain their membership in society, and Koreans are beginning to be keenly aware of sport's social significance. Fourthly, there are many young Korean scholars who are well trained and dedicated to producing knowledge in the field and even more young graduate students who are willing to join in the search for sociological significance in the realm of sport. Finally, there is strong leadership among academics in the field, and this enables the emerging discipline to develop further and provides a healthy environment for such development to continue.

REFERENCES AND FURTHER READING

Ahn, W.H. and Lim, S.W. (1992) *Sociology of Sport*. Seoul: Hyoung Seol Publications.

Cho, M.R. (1976) *Sociology of Sport*. Seoul: Hyoung Seol Publications.

Cho, M.R. and Han, S.I. (1981) 'Sport sociology', in *Collection of Materials on Physical Education*, Volume 11. Ministry of Education. Seoul: Seoul Daily Newspaper Publishing Company.

Han, S.I. (1981) *Sociology of Sport*. Seoul: Dong Hwa Publishers.

Korean Society for the Sociology of Sport (1993–1999). *Journal of KSSS*, vols 1–12.

Lee, J.G. (1975) *Sociolgy of Physical Education and Sport*. Seoul: Kyoung Lim Publications.

Lee, J.Y. (1991) 'The tasks and perspective in sociology of sport in Korea', *KSSS Newsletter*, 1, 2–7.

Lee, J.Y. (1994) 'The perspective and tasks in sociology of sport in Korea', *Proceedings of '93 KSSS Annual Conference*, pp. 1–12.

Lim, B.J. (1994) *Sociology of Sport*. Seoul: Dong Wha Publishers.

Lim, S.W. (1991) 'A study on the academic system and perspective in sociology of Sport'. Doctoral dissertation, Dong Ah University.

Mullins, N.C. (1973) *Theories and Theory Groups in Contemporary American Sociology*. New York: Harper & Row.

Son, S.J. (1993) 'Current studies in sociology of sport in Korea', *The Korean Journal of Physical Education*, 33 (3): 97–105.

41

LATIN AMERICA

Joseph L. Arbena

Defined as everything in the Western hemisphere south of the United States, Latin America has produced little scholarly analysis of sport and society, though information and insights are found in other types of writings, such as journalistic accounts, club histories and popular biographies. What has been done focuses on soccer, normally treats only the author's own country, and is rarely available in English. Nowhere does a single author or academic group dominate (Arbena, 1989 and 1999).

Argentina has contributed several important works to this limited field. Mafud (1967) considers soccer an expression of a people's social character and fears that in modern Argentina the pressure to win is causing soccer to lose its ludic content and popular appeal. Sebreli (1981) finds soccer the product of industrialization and urbanization which create alienated workers who seek identity through sports and are easily manipulated by political leaders. Winning gives way to making money; the game becomes a productive activity, the player a mere factor of production.

Romero (1985) holds that soccer's crisis parallels patterns in the political and economic spheres and regrets the increase in violent fan clubs. Archetti (1985) labels soccer a masculine discourse, carried out in explicitly sexual terms, which moves from verbal to actual violence as insecure groups seek to define and maintain that male identity, and links that image of masculinity to the construction of a national identity (Archetti, 1994). Levinsky (1995) examines the business side of soccer to explain its alleged current crisis, and defends (Levinsky, 1996) the controversial behavior of soccer star Diego Maradona, both on and off

the field, seeing him as a 'rebel with a cause' who fights to correct injustice, and who has been abused and misrepresented for threatening the world's soccer power structure.

Levinsky is also founder of the Argentine Institute of Sport Sociology and director of a university sport sociology program, both too new to allow evaluation of their labors. Also, Alabarces, on the faculty of the University of Buenos Aires, and some colleagues have organized a working group on 'Sport and Society' within the Latin American Council on the Social Sciences (CLACSO) and are teaching courses and doing research in the sports studies field. In addition, Tulio Guterman has constructed a website for publication of a digital journal, *Lecturas: Educación Física y Deportes* (www.sirc.ca/revista/efdxtes.htm), dedicated to physical education and sports, mainly but not exclusively in Argentina. Most articles are in Spanish, but most are abstracted in English as well.

In brief, concerning soccer, in Argentina, as in Mexico (Fernández, 1994), Colombia (Araújo Vélez, 1995), and throughout Latin America, there is concern about violence in the stadiums, commercialization, the export of star players, inept or corrupt management, the impact of illicit drugs and falling attendance. Renowned Uruguayan historian Galeano (1995) laments the attempts of rational forces to rob soccer of its spontaneity and joy, while expressing his faith that the unexpected will prevail.

Other sports earning some attention are boxing – to praise its heroes or condemn its brutality – baseball and auto racing, though most writings focus on the sports' internal practices, not their social contexts. Extensive writings on bullfighting rarely leave the ring (Arbena, 1989).

Studies from other countries raise important questions. DaMatta is representative of Brazilians who link their country's soccer culture to the popular festival practices of carnival and samba (DaMatta et al., 1982). Cuba since 1959 offers numerous comments on sports, usually praising athletic heroes to prove that the socialist revolution serves the nation when compared to the exploitative sports system under pre-1959 capitalism (Pettavino and Pye, 1994). Sánchez León (1994) joins numerous Peruvians in asking why their country does not fare better in international competition.

Writers in English, except those treating cricket, have produced relatively little. Lever (1983) argues that soccer contributes to Brazil's national integration. Beezley (1988) links the rise of modern Mexican sports to the larger modernization process. Arbena (1993, 1995) suggests that sports reflect political and social struggles throughout Latin America's history and illustrates ways that governments use sports to promote national identity. Ruck (1991) and Klein (1991) demonstrate the relationship between baseball and society in the Dominican Republic and the impact of the United States on local identities and economics. Moss (1991) not an academic, offers a sympathetic and well-illustrated introduction to the late Argentine driver Juan Manuel Fangio, a respected national hero, and to a sport (Formula One racing) that has a huge following in Argentina and Brazil. Sands (1993) places part of Mexico's rich equestrian tradition in its long-term historical context and shows how it helps to reproduce contemporary values and gender relations. Mason (1995) finds soccer an English import adapted to the local cultures of southern South America. Burns (1996), less sympathetic than Levinsky, notes the political and social significance in Argentina of the drug-plagued Maradona, but holds him partially responsible for his own problems. Klein (1997) identifies the multiple meanings of baseball across the United States–Mexican border.

Because of its centrality in the Anglophone Caribbean, cricket has received substantial attention. Building on James's (1983) monumental essay, numerous authors have sought to understand cricket as a tool of British colonialism, a source of West Indies nationalism, an arena for racial identity and conflict, an expression of popular culture, and a possible vehicle for regional integration (Beckles and Stoddart, 1995; Manley, 1995).

REFERENCES

Alabarces, P. and Rodríguez, M.G. (1996) *Cuestión de pelotas: fútbol, deporte, sociedad, cultura*. Buenos Aires: Atuel.

Araújo Vélez, F. (1995) *Pena máxima: juicio al fútbol colombiano*. Bogotá: Planeta.

Arbena, J.L. (1989) *An Annotated Bibliography of Latin American Sport: Preconquest to the Present*. Westport, CT: Greenwood Press.

Arbena, J.L. (1993) 'Sport and social change in Latin America', in A.G. Ingham and J.W. Loy (eds), *Sport in Social Development: Traditions, Transitions and Transformations*. Champaign, IL: Human Kinetics. pp. 97–117.

Arbena, J.L. (1995) 'Nationalism and sport in Latin America, 1850–1990: the paradox of promoting and performing "European" sports', *The International Journal of the History of Sport*, 12 (2): 220–38.

Arbena, J.L. (1999) *Latin American Sport: An Annotated Bibliography, 1988–1998*. Westport, CT: Greenwood Press.

Archetti, E.P. (1985) 'Fútbol, violencia y afirmación masculina', *Debates en la Sociedad y la Cultura*, 2 (3): 38–44.

Archetti, E.P. (1994) 'Masculinity and football: the formation of national identity in Argentina', in R. Giulianotti and J. Williams (eds), *Game without Frontiers: Football, Identity and Modernity*. Aldershot: Arena. pp. 225–43.

Beckles, H.M. and Stoddart, B. (eds) (1995) *Liberation Cricket. West Indies Cricket Culture*. Manchester: Manchester University Press.

Beezley, W.H. (1988) *Judas at the Jockey Club and Other Episodes of Porfirian Mexico*. Lincoln: University of Nebraska.

Burns, J. (1996) *Hand of God*. London: Bloomsbury.

DaMatta, R., Guedes, S.L., Neves Flores, L.F.B. and Vogel, A. (1982) *Universo do futebol: esporte e sociedade brasileira*. Rio de Janeiro: Ediçoes Pinakotheke.

Fernández, J.R. (1994) *El fútbol mexicano: ¿un juego sucio?* México, DF: Editorial Grijalbo.

Galeano, E. (1995) *El fútbol a sol y sombra*. Madrid: Siglo Veintiuno Editores.

James, C.L.R. (1983) *Beyond a Boundary*. New York: Pantheon Books.

Klein, A.M. (1991) *Sugarball: the American Game, the Dominican Dream*. New Haven, CT: Yale University Press.

Klein, A.M. (1997) *Baseball on the Border: a Tale of Two Laredos*. Princeton, NJ: Princeton University Press.

Lever, J. (1983) *Soccer Madness*. Chicago: University of Chicago.

Levinsky, S. (1995) *El negocio del fútbol.* Buenos Aires: Ediciones Corregidor.

Levinsky, S. (1996) *Maradona: rebelde con causa.* Buenos Aires: Ediciones Corregidor.

Mafud, J. (1967) *Sociología del fútbol.* Buenos Aires: Editorial Américalee.

Manley, M. (1995) *A History of West Indies Cricket*, rev. edn. London: André Deutsch.

Mason, T. (1995) *Passion of the People? Football in South America.* London: Verso.

Moss, S. (1991) *Fangio: a Pirelli Album.* London: Pavilion Books.

Pettavino, P.J. and Pye, G. (1994) *Sport in Cuba: the Diamond in the Rough.* Pittsburgh: University of Pittsburgh Press.

Romero, A.G. (1985) *Deporte, violencia y política (crónica negra, 1958–1983).* Buenos Aires: Centro Editor de América Latina.

Ruck, R. (1991) *The Tropic of Baseball. Baseball in the Dominican Republic.* Westport, CT: Meckler.

Sánchez León, A. (1994) 'The history of Peruvian women's volleyball', *Studies in Latin American Popular Culture,* 13: 143–52.

Sands, K.M. (1993) *Charrería Mexicana: an Equestrian Folk Tradition.* Tucson: University of Arizona Press.

Sebreli, J.J. (1981) *Fútbol y masas.* Buenos Aires: Editorial Galerna.

42

NORDIC COUNTRIES

Kari Fasting and Mari-Kristin Sisjord

This chapter provides a brief overview of the sociology of sport in the Nordic countries of Denmark, Finland, Norway and Sweden. Sport sociology in these countries has been developed primarily by scholars affiliated with colleges and university departments of sport and physical education. The most prominent contributions in the field stem from people with backgrounds in education, history, philosophy and/or sociology.

Since the late 1970s, there has been a growing interest in many different topics related to sport in society. This interest is manifested in scientific research as well as curricula in sport studies. The number of sport scholars is rapidly increasing, which to a great extent is a result of the development of PhD programmes. A number of scholars have been and continue to be vital catalysts in the development of sport sociology in terms of scientific production and the recruitment of new scholars. These include Lars Magnus Engstrøm (Sweden), Kari Fasting (Norway), Kalevi Heinilä (Finland) and Henning Eichberg (Denmark).

The scientific work in the Nordic countries covers many topics; the most predominant are:

- Socialization and sport. This has been a major topic of interest in all four countries. Scholars have studied socialization questions in their own countries, and they have done comparative work. As in other countries, this research was most extensive during the 1970s and the 1980s.
- Sports organizations. Scholars have studied various aspects of sports organizations. In Finland, concerns have focused on questions connected to structure, policy and economy. In the other countries, research has been done on voluntary work,

professionalization, leadership and gender issues in organizations.
- The relationship between top-level sport and recreational sport. In connection with research on organizations, there has been frequent attention given to top-level sport in relation to its structure within society, and also to dimensions of top-level sport at the individual level, including such aspects as value orientation, lifestyle, patterns and development of sport careers, and social mobility. Research on gender issues is significant in the four countries. There have been studies comparing women's and men's sport participation, and studies of barriers to participation, the meaning of sport in girl's and women's culture and their daily lives, gender and sport organizations, gendered media coverage and sport presentations in magazines, sexual harassment in sport, homophobia in sport, and gender, body and physicality.
- Values and sport. This topic has been studied from various perspectives in each of the four countries. Research has been done on values and top-level sport, values in youth sport, values and doping, and values, lifestyle, rules and morality.

Research on sport in society in the Nordic countries has been influenced by international trends in the field. For example, much of the research on socialization and sport was inspired by the social role–social system model, which was the dominant paradigm in the 1970s. Parallel to this, other research areas have clearly been influenced by North American sport sociology. However, the influence of European heritage is also obvious. Danish scholars have been closer to the

German and French traditions, while the Anglo-American traditions have been more dominant in Finland, Norway and Sweden. In recent years, however, scholars across the Nordic countries have incorporated and used dominant theories in the field, such as those developed by Bourdieu, Giddens, Luhmann and Foucault. Research on gender and sport has been influenced by feminist theory, and Nordic feminist scholars have made major contributions to the understanding of gender and sport.

43

PORTUGAL

Salomé Marivoet and Claudia Pinheiro

In order to discuss the sociology of sport in Portugal, as well as to provide a better understanding of the realities on which we have focused our research, it is important to contextualize the development of this subject within the wider field of the sociology of knowledge. In that way, it will be easier to understand the difficulties we have faced in our investigations and which have helped to shape them.

In the Portuguese context, sociology-related areas made a late appearance. The existence of a dictatorial regime for nearly 40 years made the publication of any sociological knowledge impossible. Similarly, research that intended to analyse any area of Portuguese society from a sociological perspective was unwelcome.

The BA(Hons) Degree in Political and Social Science was the only route to the study of social reality. However, its content and purpose did not aim at critical and free social thought. On the contrary, it tended to reproduce and maintain the political status quo. Even an attempt by the Jesuits at the beginning of the 1960s, to start a BA(Hons) Degree in the Sociology of Work, was unsuccessful.

As a result of this conjuncture, students with an interest in this field of study had to pursue their studies in foreign universities. This fact meant that after the establishment of the democratic regime in 1974 such people were the only ones qualified to lecture in sociology and capable of undertaking sociological research on Portuguese society.

All these drawbacks have intensified the difficulty of developing the sociology of sport in Portugal, a country where, as in many others, general sociologists do not show much interest in the sociology of sport. It has been in the physical education context where the need for it has been recognized, especially after 1975 when it became a subject taught on university courses.

Some authors in physical education and sports have been making an effort to analyse sports with a critical eye, even though much of what they have written can be considered as ideological. Among such authors, one who deserves some mention is José Esteves, a pioneer whose book *O Desporto e as Estruturas Socias* (Sport and Social Structures) was first published in 1967, with its third and last edition in 1975.

With the introduction of the sociology of sport into the curriculum of the Lisbon and Oporto Institutes of Physical Education and Sport in 1975, the first academic work began to appear. Yet it did not receive much attention from the sociological community. This is understandable, especially if we take into account the fact that, even today, there is no specific degree requirement to teach the sociology of sport in any of Portugal's university faculties of physical education and sport. Nevertheless, among the studies done in this area, we have to draw attention to the research of Teixeira de Sousa on the activities of physical education professionals in 1984, and on associationism in sport in Portugal in 1986.

In the second half of the 1980s and due to the interest and intervention of some state institutions, the sociology of sport was given a new stimulus. Owing to Portugal's entry into the European Community, and with the heightening of relationships at the Committee for the Development of Sport (CDDS) level of the European Council, a need to carry out several studies of sports was felt in order to further the understanding of its social contexts as a means for improving sports policies. To fulfil such purposes, a group of sociologists – the Directorate General for Sports – was appointed at the Portuguese Ministry of Education. Among the studies done by this group we should mention the work of Salomé Marivoet on *Habitos Desportivos da População Portuguesa* (Sporting Habits of the Portuguese Population) and *Violência no Desporto* (Violence and Sport), published in 1989 and 1991 respectively.

The publication of these studies by a state institution has sensitized people in general and in sport in particular to the need to analyse the sports phenomenon sociologically. These studies were also communicated to the sociological community through conferences and scientific journals.

Another point that deserves mention is that the media regularly express an interest in a sociological perspective and this frequently promotes the discussion of sports issues.

As a result of these favourable trends, several academic articles written by sociology students have begun to appear, even though sociology of sport as a subject or sports-related modules have not yet been introduced into the undergraduate sociology curriculum.

The 1990s have been characterized by a new stimulus to the sociology of sport. As a result of the establishment of new BA(Hons) Degrees in Physical Education and Sport, the number of sociology of sport lecturers in Portugal has increased. At present there is a total of 14 lecturers, among whom two are Professors, two have PhDs and two have MAs. The latter were obtained in foreign universities. We have, however, to record our regret that some of the academic work that has been done by lecturers in the sociology of sport in Portugal does not use a sociological approach to the phenomenon of sport. Incursions into anthropology and psychology have been the most frequent, with the exception of the work done by Professor Teixeira de Sousa, by Salomé Marivoet for her Masters Degree in 1994 (Lisbon) on 'Envolvimentos Sociais em Carreiras Desportivas' (Social Involvement in Sporting Careers) and by Claudia Pinheiro for her Masters in 1993 (Leicester, England) on 'The Development of Women's Sport in England: 1860–1920'.

Despite the difficulties that the sociology of sport has encountered in Portuguese society, it has been possible to constitute a group of colleagues who are not only interested in moving the sociology of sport forward and making it better known among the sociology community more generally, but also in publishing the investigations they have made so far. The first sociology of sport meeting in Portugal took place in 1995. Another was held in 1996. In the same year, the aforesaid group established itself as a constituent of the Portuguese Sociological Association (Associação Portuguesa de Sociologia, SESD), which has responsibility for organizing these types of initiatives.

REFERENCES AND FURTHER READING

Costa, A. (1997) *Á Volta do Estádio: O Desporto, o Homem e a Sociedade*. Oporto: Campo das Letras.

Esteves, J. (1999) *O Desporto e as Estruturas Sociais, Um Ensaio de Interpretação do Fenómeno Desportivo*. Lisbon: Edições Universitarias Lusófaras (4th edition).

Marivoet, S. (1987) *Metodologia da Carta da Procura Desportiva e Recreativa*. Lisbon: Desporto e Sociedade-Sociologia Desportiva No. 2.

Marivoet, S. (1988) *Aspectos Sociológicos do Desporto*. Lisbon: Livros Horizonte.

Marivoet, S. (1989) *The Evolution of Violence Associated with Sports in Portugal (1978–1987)*. Lisbon: DGD.

Marivoet, S. (1993) 'Envolvimentos Sociais no Desporto, Abordagem Sociológica das Práticas Desportivas em Quadros Competitivos – um estudo de caso'. Lisbon: ISCTE.

Pinheiro, C. (1993) *The Development of Women's Sports in England: 1860–1920*. Leicester: University of Leicester.

Sousa, J. Teixeira de (1984) *Estudo do Campo As Actividades dos Profissionais da Educação Física*. Lisbon: UTL/ISEF.

Sousa, J. Teixeira de (1988) *Contributos para o Estudo do Associativismo Desportivo em Portugal*. Lisbon: UTL/ISEF.

Sousa, J. Teixeira de (1996) *Para Sociologia do Futebol Profissional Portugués*. Lisbon: FMH/UTL.

44

SPAIN

Núria Puig

The study themes which predominate in the sociology of sport in Spain today can be grouped in three main areas: the evolution and significance of sport; the organization of sport; and social attitudes to sport. The first is of a more global character and sets out to interpret the significance of sport in contemporary society. Work in this area has only recently begun. The other two belong more to the tradition of earlier days, are more developed from an empirical point of view and involve a greater number of people.

THE EVOLUTION AND SIGNIFICANCE OF SPORT

This theme encompasses research that situates sport in a general context (historical, economic, social, political and so on) and develops theories destined to explain the significance of sport in contemporary society.

It was in this way that Martínez del Castillo and his collaborators (1991a, 1992) studied the sports labour market and projected its development to the year 2000. In Spain today some 49,000 people are employed in the sectors of sports education, movement studies, management and training. Work situations are very heterogeneous (ranging from well-paid full-time employment to voluntary work with symbolic remuneration), as are the variety of professional profiles. Moreover, traditional differences persist according to sex, educational levels and age.

Very different is the work by Lagardera (1992, 1994), which the author himself defines as historical sociology – very much along the lines of the research by Elias and Dunning – which is not the same as social history. The

theme which Lagardera has been researching for some years now can be summarized in the following question:

> What do we need to know today about the history of sport that might offer us keys to interpet from the necessary historical perspective the evolution and genuine social significance of the phenomenon?' (Lagardera, 1994)

García Ferrando has contributed to reflection on the significance of sport in contemporary society by laying special emphasis on its cultural significance. To this end, he has had recourse to Bell's theories on postindustrial society and the autonomy of its 'backbone' elements (García Ferrando, 1995).

THE ORGANIZATION OF SPORT

The first studies in this field almost invariably took the form of analyses of sporting facilities. Initial efforts culminated in the preparation between 1986 and 1991 of the Censo Nacional de Instalaciones Deportivas (National Census of Sporting Facilities) (Martínez del Castillo et al., 1991b).

Another theme which began as a political debate and which has given rise to limited studies, is that of the role of public institutions; more precisely the relationships between sport, society and the Welfare State. Nevertheless, although attempts have been made to offer an overall perspective on the issue (Puig, 1993), a broad empirical study is still needed to encompass what for the moment are partial verifications or simple hypotheses.

For his part, Moreno (1993) has concerned himself with the weakness of the associative movement in sport and the difficulties encountered by clubs when it comes to surviving amidst public initiatives and the profound changes taking place in sport. However, the study of sports organizations in Spain is practically non-existent, apart from a few notable exceptions. Very little is known, for instance, about their financial structure, about the percentage of volunteers or professionals working in them, or about the types of organizations that might be established.

SOCIAL ATTITUDES TO SPORT

The first survey on participation in sport for the whole of Spain was carried out in 1968 (Instituto Nacional de Estadística, 1968). The second was made in 1974 (Instituto Nacional de Estadística, 1975) and the three most recent ones, directed by García Ferrando, were conducted in 1982, 1985 and 1990 (García Ferrando, 1982, 1986, 1991). This means that it is possible to observe the evolution at least over the past 15 years of Spanish people's attitudes to sport using comparable data.

Since 1968, the 12 per cent of the adult population then actively (two hours a week on average) involved in sport increased to 36 per cent in 1991. Such an increase, which, as mentioned earlier, might be due in part to the efforts made by government bodies since 1979, also reflects the diversification of the traditional model of sport observable in advanced societies (Heinemann, 1986; Heinemann and Dietrich, 1989; Puig and Heinemann, 1991). Thus, sport has developed in such a way as to incorporate diverse value systems thanks to which it is practised *en masse* on the one hand and by a wide spectrum of society's members on the other. The most relevant phenomena in this process are the continuing practice of sport among elderly people and the spectacular increase in the participation of women.

The participation of women in sport has been the object of several studies and seminars. These are becoming more complex and involve an attempt to build up a theoretical framework for shedding light on the specific characteristics of the socialization of Spanish women (Buñuel, 1991; Vázquez, 1992).

The study of social attitudes to sport has gradually evolved from descriptive and quantitative aspects to more complex ones which, in consequence, have required more suitable methods, essentially qualitative, and theoretical references, in this case more in keeping with phenomenology, symbolic interactionism and figurational sociology.

Studies on how sport contributes to the configuration of an individual or group identity include those by Medina (1992) on the role of pelota in the consolidation of Basque communities outside the Basque Country, Durán (1992, 1994a, 1994b) on hooliganism in Spanish football, and Puig (1996) on youth and sport.

Finally, the role of the Olympic Games in the configuration of collective identities and the diffusion of cultural values has been exhaustively treated by Moragas, Rivenburgh and Larson (1995). The analysis they have carried out on the way in which different television networks around the world retransmitted the opening ceremony of the Barcelona Olympics reveals on the one hand the importance of this event in the consolidation at home and the diffusion abroad of the cultural identity of the host city and country and, on the other (and this is the more suggestive contribution) the interaction between the global and the local and the clear dialectic existing between these two levels in all the countries where the ceremony was broadcast. Each television network *reconstructed* the ceremony in its own way or, to be more precise, filtered it through the cultural codes of their respective viewers. In this way they tempered the idea of globalization as a hegemonic and unidirectional process.

FINAL REMARKS

At present, the sociology of sport in Spain has its own profile, firmly anchored in the sport sciences more generally. Theoretical debate is now well under way, discussing the value of different methods, the choice (or lack of it) between quantitative and qualitative methods and so on. A corpus of genuinely scientific knowledge has been built up whose connection with the practice and management of sport is made through the complex mechanisms that link the world of science to that of political decisions. The Spanish sociology of sport, the genesis of which was closer to the political concerns of the time of the transition from dictatorship than to the academic world, has finally embraced the scientific and university tradition of contemporary sociology. As a discipline, it has entered a new phase, hopefully one of maturity.

Even so, a lot remains to be done, from themes that have been only very partially studied, like that of sports organizations, to others that have been practically ignored, such as the body. Regarding this subject, there are major translations available, but as yet no studies carried out in Spain. Now that the process is under way, there is no doubt that, little by little, the number of subjects covered and the degree of sophistication in their analysis will increase.

NOTE

This overview was written in 1996.

A broader version of this article can be found in Puig, Núria (1995) 'The sociology of sport in Spain', *International Review for the Sociology of Sport*, 30 (2): 123–40.

REFERENCES

Buñuel, A. (1991) 'The recreational physical activities of Spanish women: a sociological study of exercising for fitness', *International Review for the Sociology of Sport*, 26 (3): 203–16.

Durán, J. (1992) 'El vandalismo en el fútbol en España: un problema social y político a la espera de un tratamiento científico', *Sistema*, 110/111: 155–74.

Durán, J. (1994a) 'El vandalismo en el fútbol como problema sociológico. La configuración de un modelo teórico', in J.I. Barbero (ed.), *Ciencias Sociales y Deporte*. Pamplona, Asociación Española de Investigación Social Aplicada al Deporte (Investigación Social y Deporte, 1), pp. 137–42.

Durán, J. (1994b) 'La sociología figuracional de Norbert Elias como respuesta a los retos teóricos y metodológicos de la sociología del deporte: el caso del vandalismo en el fútbol'. Paper presented at the Congress 'Los Retos de las Ciencias Sociales Aplicadas al Deporte' (The Challenges of Social Sciences applied to Sport), Valladolid, Asociación Española de Investigación Social Aplicada al Deporte, 21–22 October.

García Ferrando, M. (1982) *Deporte y sociedad*. Madrid: Ministerio de Cultura.

García Ferrando, M. (1986) *Hábitos deportivos de los españoles (sociología del comportamiento deportivo)*. Madrid: Ministerio de Cultura, Instituto de Ciencias de la Educación Física y el Deporte.

García Ferrando, M. (1991) *Los españoles y el deporte (1980–1990). Un análisis sociológico*. Madrid: Ministerio de Educación y Ciencia, Instituto de Ciencias de la Educación Física y el Deporte.

García Ferrando, M. (1995) 'The development of contemporary sport and the theory of post-industrial society: the Spanish case'. Unpublished manuscript.

Heinemann, K. (1986) 'The future of sports: challenge for the science of sport', *International Review for the Sociology of Sport*, 21 (4): 278–85.

Heinemann, K. and Dietrich, K. (1989) *Der nicht-sportliche Sport. Beiträge zum Wandel im Sport*. Schorndorf: Verlag Hofmann.

Instituto Nacional de Estadística (1968) *Encuesta sobre actividades deportivas*. Madrid.

Instituto Nacional de Estadística (1975) *Encuesta sobre actividades deportivas*. Madrid.

Lagardera, F. (1992) 'De la aristócrata gimnástica al deporte de masas: un siglo de deporte en España', *Sistema*, 110/111: 9–36.

Lagardera, F. (1994) 'El sistema deportivo: dinámica y tendencias'. Paper presented at II Congrés Català de Sociologia, Girona (Spain), May.

Martínez del Castillo, J., Puig, N., Fraile, A. and Boixeda, A. (1991a) *La estructura ocupacional del deporte en España. Encuesta realizada sobre los sectores de entrenamiento, docencia, animación y dirección*. Madrid: Ministerio de Educación y Ciencia, Consejo Superior de Deportes.

Martínez del Castillo, J., Puig, N., Boix, R., Millet, Ll. and Paez, J.A. (1991b) *Las instalaciones deportivas en España*. Madrid: Ministerio de Educación y Ciencia, Consejo Superior de Deportes.

Martínez del Castillo, J., Navarro, C., Fraile, A., Puig, N., Jimenez, J., Martinez, J. and De Miguel, C. (1992) *Deporte, sociedad y empleo. Proyección del mercado deportivo laboral en la España de los noventa. En los sectores de entrenamiento, docencia, animación y dirección*. Madrid: Ministerio de Educación y Ciencia, Consejo Superior de Deportes.

Medina, F.X. (1992) 'El deporte como factor en la construcción sociocultural de la identidad', in J.I. Barbero (ed.), *Ciencias Sociales y Deporte*. Pamplona: Asociación Española de Investigación Social Aplicada al Deporte (Investigación Social y Deporte, 1), pp. 143–6.

Moragas, M., Rivenburgh, N. and Larson, J.F. (1995) *Television in the Olympics*. London: John Libbey.

Moreno, A. (1993) 'El asociacionismo deportivo en España', *Apunts. Educació Física i Esports*, 33: 58–63.

Puig, N. (1993) 'Revisión histórica de la política deportiva en España. Lecciones que se pueden extraer de cara el futoro', in *Actas de los 3os. Encuentros de Política Deportiva*, Barakaldo (Bilbao), pp. 93–105.

Puig, N. (1996) *Joves i esport*. Barcelona: Generalitat de Catalunya, Secretaria General de l'Esport.

Puig, N. and Heinemann, K. (1991) 'El deporte en la perspectiva del año 2000', *Papers*, 38: 123–41.

Vázquez, B. (1992) 'La presencia de la mujer en el deporte español', in *El ejercicio físico la práctica deportiva de las mujeres*. Madrid: Ministerio de Asuntos Sociales, Instituto de la Mujer. pp. 9–15.

INDEX